CASES AND MATERIALS

# INTELLECTUAL PROPERTY

## Trademark, Copyright and Patent Law

SECOND EDITION

*by*

ROCHELLE COOPER DREYFUSS
Pauline Newman Professor of Law
New York University School of Law


ROBERTA ROSENTHAL KWALL
Raymond P. Niro Professor of Intellectual Property Law
Director, DePaul University College of Law Center for Intellectual Property
Law and Information Technology

FOUNDATION PRESS
NEW YORK, NEW YORK
2004

THOMSON
─────────★─────────™
WEST

© 1996 FOUNDATION PRESS
© 2004 By FOUNDATION PRESS
        395 Hudson Street
        New York, NY 10014
        Phone Toll Free 1–877–888–1330
        Fax (212) 367–6799
        fdpress.com
Printed in the United States of America

**ISBN** 1–56662–812–1

 *TEXT IS PRINTED ON 10% POST CONSUMER RECYCLED PAPER*

WE WISH TO DEDICATE THIS BOOK WITH LOVE TO OUR
RESPECTIVE HUSBANDS:

ROBERT M. DREYFUSS

and

JEFFREY L. KWALL

*

# ACKNOWLEDGEMENTS

Many people have assisted in the preparation of both this and the prior edition. In connection with the second edition specifically, we would like to thank David O. Carson, General Counsel, U.S. Copyright Office, and Tanya M. Sandros, Attorney Advisor, U.S. Copyright Office, for their insight and assistance in connection with the Digital Millennium Copyright Act. For providing us with reprints of photographs and other inserts, we wish to add a special thanks to sculptor James Earl Reid, photographer Ron Portee, and Terry Abrahamson. We would like to give special thanks to Professors Shubha Ghosh and Paul Janicke for their particularly helpful comments on the previous edition. To Deans Ricky Revesz (N.Y.U.) and Glen Weissenberger (DePaul), we extend our gratitude for their ongoing support.

Many students also have played an important role in the preparation of this edition and we would like to thank all of them for their tireless efforts. From DePaul, Brenda Allison, Valerie Baxendale, Aaron Gole, Ellen Gutiontov, Christine Moran, Darla Nykamp, Angela Larimer, and Aaron Ryan, From New York University, Michelle B. Lee (LLM Class of 2003), who read much of the draft for comments and added immeasurably to our understanding of the negotiations on the Madrid Protocol. We would both like to thank Nicole Arzt for the extraordinary help that she provided in preparing this edition for publication. Professor Dreyfuss also would like to acknowledge financial support from the Filomen D'Agostino and Max E. Greenberg Research Fund.

Professor Kwall also would like to say a special thank you to her parents, Millie and Abe Rosenthal, for keeping those intellectual property articles coming, and to her three daughters, Shanna, Rachel, and Nisa, for helping her keep a sense of perspective throughout this project. For her part, Professor Dreyfuss thanks her mother, Dorothy Gartner, for showing her how to juggle a professional career and children. Special gratitude is also owed to the jugglees, Marc, and Nicole and David Seaman.

In the Acknowledgement Section of the prior edition, we also acknowledged one another though recognizing this practice as somewhat unorthodox. During the years between the publication of the first and second editions, we celebrated together the Bat Mitzvah of two of Professor Kwall's daughters and the wedding of Professor Dreyfuss' daughter. Our personal and professional relationship has grown even more satisfying and fun over the years, and it still combines intense scholarly discussion with many a good giggle!

Finally, we both would like to extend our ongoing appreciation to the person who inspired the problem method approach we have adopted in this casebook, Professor Edward H. Rabin of the University of California at Davis School of Law.

ROCHELLE COOPER DREYFUSS
ROBERTA ROSENTHAL KWALL

April, 2004

# SUMMARY OF CONTENTS

# TABLE OF CONTENTS

\*

# TABLE OF CASES

Principal cases are in bold type. Non-principal cases are in roman type. References are to Pages.

*

# INTELLECTUAL PROPERTY

## Trademark, Copyright and Patent Law

*

# INTRODUCTION TO INTELLECTUAL PROPERTY

Students deciding which upper level courses to pursue in law school are frequently puzzled by the term "intellectual property." The term seemingly conjures up images of the study of highly complex and esoteric but nonetheless mysterious subject matter. In some respects, this image is not all that far from the truth, since in all candor the study of intellectual property does include a large degree of sophisticated subject matter. We can, however, clarify the mysterious nature of the area at the outset. The "core" subjects of intellectual property are trademarks, copyrights and patents. Each of these areas is governed by a federal statute. In addition, intellectual property encompasses state law analogues such as trade secrets, the right of publicity, moral rights, as well as traditional unfair competition. The advent of the Internet has added a new set of laws on domain names.

Although some of these topics may seem quite unfamiliar at the outset, it is important to keep in mind that they all define the property rights of owners of intangible assets. Copyrights and patents protect ownership rights with respect to products created through intellectual efforts such as writings and inventions (although this definition of subject matter suffices for this Introduction, you will soon see that it is vastly oversimplified). Trademarks and (to some extent) domain names, which indicate the source of a particular product or service, protect the investment businesses make in goodwill and in marketing methods. Thus, the intangible nature of intellectual property contrasts with the more tangible nature of realty and personalty, the study of which will be familiar to those of you who have already taken a property course. As we will demonstrate below, the doctrines and theoretical underpinnings of all types of property law are similar. Therefore, before embarking on a specific study of the areas of intellectual property, it will be useful to consider generally both the theoretical similarities as well as the differences between property and intellectual property law.

Nearly all of the doctrines of intellectual property law as well as tangible property law reflect a fundamental tension between the desires of property owners versus the desires of other people or entities. Examples of this tension in real property law include a landowner's inability to exclude people from her property in certain circumstances;[1] the doctrines that define the respective rights of landlords and tenants; and zoning laws which attempt to balance a landowner's interests against those of the government.

Similarly, trademark law generally deals with balancing the rights of trademark owners and others who wish to use the same or a similar

---

[1] See, e.g., State v. Shack, 58 N.J. 297, 277 A.2d 369 (1971), in which the Supreme Court of New Jersey upheld the right of a legal aid attorney and a social worker to visit the living quarters of workers in a migrant labor camp over the objections of the landowner/farmer/employer.

1

trademark. Trademark law thus attempts to define not only the appropriate geographic area of trademark use but also the relevant product boundaries in which a particular trademark may be used. In addition, the heart of most trademark infringement litigation revolves around the question of the similarity of the trademarks at issue. Trademark owners are mainly granted the right to prevent other trademark uses that are likely to cause consumer confusion.

A similar tension inheres in copyright law, which seeks to resolve the appropriate balance between protecting creators' rights and insuring the optimal access to copyrighted works. Perhaps the most notable example of this balance is the fair use provision which is codified at 17 U.S.C. § 107. This provision sets forth a balancing test to be used in determining whether a particular unauthorized use of copyrighted property will be allowed. The 1976 Copyright Act is replete with other examples of qualifications of a copyright owner's rights under various circumstances.[2]

Patent law, like copyright law, tries to reward creators for enriching public welfare without unduly sacrificing the interest of the public in enjoying access to their creations. In addition, patent law recognizes that the storehouse of knowledge can grow only if every inventor is allowed to expand upon the insights of earlier creators. As Sir Isaac Newton purportedly stated, "If I have seen farther, it is by standing on the shoulders of giants."[3] Thus, patent law has traditionally been structured to leave principles and products of nature in the public domain. Protection is mainly available only for applications of these principles and refinements of these products. Even then, only truly significant advances over prior art will merit patents.

The legal concept of ownership also is quite similar for all types of property in that the owner's rights consist of her legal *interests* in the object in which the property is embodied. This conception of property contrasts markedly with the lay person's definition of property which focuses on physical ownership of the thing itself. For example, real property cases refer to these legal interests as a bundle of rights which include the right to exclude, the right to possess, the right to use, the right to dispose, and the right to manage and derive an economic benefit. Ownership of property in the legal sense is not synonymous with ownership of the land itself, but instead constitutes ownership of these legal interests in the land. Thus, although a landlord actually owns a particular piece of land and may have certain legal interests in that property, his tenant also has a legal interest in the property. The tenant's legal interest can be protected in court and thus also constitutes property in the legal sense.

Using copyright law as a relevant comparison, you will see that ownership of the object in which a copyrighted work is embodied is distinct from ownership of the copyright. See 17 U.S.C. § 202 of the 1976 Copyright

---

[2] See generally §§ 107–118 of the 1976 Copyright Act. See also Assignments 10 & 11.

[3] See Robert Merton, On the Shoulders of Giants: A Shandrean Postscript (Free Press, 1965).

Act. Moreover, § 106 of the Act secures for copyright owners the sole rights to reproduce and distribute the protected work; to publicly perform and display it, to publicly perform sound recordings digitally, as well as the right to prepare derivative works. The copyright owner's exclusive ability to exercise this bundle of rights enables her to safeguard, in large measure, the pecuniary value of the copyrighted work. These six rights thus represent the judicially protectable interests which render copyright ownership valuable.

Having explored some of the theoretical similarities between intellectual property and tangible property, it is also useful to identify the ways in which intellectual property law differs from tangible property law. Some of the more obvious differences are that tangible property law protection is common law in nature whereas trademark, copyright, and patent protection are statutory. Moreover, intellectual property rights are not perpetual. There is a specific duration for copyright and patent protection and trademark rights exist only as long as the owner actually uses the trademark.

The limitations on the duration of protection under copyright and patent law relate to the issue of balancing the optimal degree of public access to intellectual property and the proprietary rights of the owners of the protected material. Although a landowner does not possess an unqualified right to exclude others from his property, the issue of public access to realty generally is less compelling than it is for certain types of intellectual property. For example, part of the reason for the "right versus access" tension in the area of copyright law is that substantial protection for copyrighted works potentially conflicts with the First Amendment. A similar conflict between the need for public dissemination (and use) and the protection of proprietary interests also is manifested in other areas of intellectual property. For patents, keep in mind that Newton could not have seen so far had he been enjoined from standing on his predecessor's shoulders. With respect to trademarks, the law must distinguish between the use of a trademark as a vocabulary word (for example, to name unique goods or to discuss the trademark owner) and its use as a tool for marketing goods and services.

Moreover, from an economics standpoint, tangible property is considered a "private good" because, generally speaking, a possessory interest in tangible property cannot be used by more than one person without each person interfering with the other's enjoyment.[4] In contrast, patents and copyrights can be considered "public goods" in that their possession is nonrivalrous. That is, it is possible for many people to simultaneously enjoy

---

[4] An example: two people cannot simultaneously drink the same cup of coffee. At worst, they will consider it unsanitary. At best, each will drink too fast in order to acquire a fair share (although note that different people can occupy different *interests* in the same piece of realty, i.e., a landlord and tenant; and that two or more people actually can own concurrent interests in tangible property in certain instances, i.e., joint tenants). In contrast, two or more people can simultaneously enjoy a picture of a cup of coffee.

the benefits of an invention without interfering with one another.[5] Thus, whereas the consequence of private ownership of tangible property is to increase social wealth, private ownership of intangible property may decrease it by providing too little access to the protected property. The other side of this argument is that without these protections, people may not have the incentive to create works and inventions that will ultimately benefit society.

Finally, the goals of intellectual property and tangible property law are in some critical ways not at all alike. Since the supply of tangible property is essentially fixed, conservation is a vital concern in the law of property. Without property law, there would a tragedy of the commons. That is, property would be inefficiently utilized as no one would have the incentive to preserve it and protect it for future use. But the supply of ideas is not at all fixed and so there is no need to conserve them. To the contrary, if there is a tragedy, it is of the "anticommons:" intellectual property law is aimed at encouraging the development and dissemination of new ideas; the need for authorization can slow the flow of information and lead to negotiation standoffs.[6] In addition, people feel differently about their intellectual creations than they do about their land and personalty, and so reputational interests come into play in intellectual property law in a way that they do not in property law. For example, trademarks are protected from tarnishment and copyright protects the integrity of works of fine art.

Now for a few words about our specific approach to intellectual property. Substantively, our book is divided into the three major areas of copyright, trademark, and patent law. Our central insight is that these regimes can, and should, be viewed as a whole. But while each of these regimes faces the same types of problems, the solutions must be tailored specifically to the needs of the industries protected. Thus, we stress the commonalities of the regimes and the reasons underlying the differences.

Insofar as possible, the chapters in each subject area are organized in a parallel manner to reflect their similarities. Common concerns typically are discussed in detail in one of the regimes, and the pertinent discussions in the other regimes will further elaborate upon, and cross reference to, the relevant core discussions.

Furthermore, our approach does not sever state law from its federal counterparts. Our combined teaching experience has convinced us that the applicable doctrines of state law can best be examined in the appropriate chapters of the other three core areas. Essentially these state laws offer similar protections to less concrete types of subject matter. With the exception of the relatively recent moral rights provision of the copyright statute, the state law analogues involve no federal statutes and can easily be juxtaposed with the material covered in the corresponding core sections.

[5] An example: two people can use the same discovery of a new flavored coffee brewing technique to make her own cup of coffee without interfering with the other's enjoyment.

[6] See Michael A. Heller & Rebecca Eisenberg, Can Patents Deter Innovation? The Anticommons in Biomedical Research, 280 Sci. 698 (1998).

Treating state law in this manner complements our integrated approach by illustrating the doctrinal relationship between state law and the other core areas of intellectual property.

We believe that our integrated approach is not only doctrinally sound, but also mirrors the reality of law practice in intellectual property. In many, if not most, of the reported cases, the complaints contain counts grounded in more than one of the major substantive areas of intellectual property. Indeed, there are whole industries that now rely on multiple forms of protection.[7] Not surprisingly, theorists have also come to advocate a more unified approach to intellectual property.[8]

---

[7] See, e.g., Dennis S. Karjala, Distinguishing Patent and Copyright Subject Matter. 35 Conn. L. Rev. 439 (2003); Karl F. Jorda Software Protection: Copyrights, Patents, Trade Secrets and/or Sui Generis, 4 ILSA J. Int'l & Comp. L. 337 (1998); A. Samuel Oddi, An Uneasier Case for Copyright than for Patent Protection of Computer Programs, 72 Neb. L. Rev. 351 (1993). See also Carl Tobias, The White Comm'n and the Federal Circuit, 10 Cornell J.L. & Pub. Pol'y 45, 55 (2000)(discussing a proposal in an early draft of the 1998 Report on Structural Alternatives for the Federal Courts of Appeals to add copyright to the Federal Circuit's docket because technological changes had brought patent and copyright together).

[8] See, e.g., Gideon Parchomovsky and Peter Siegelman, Towards an Integrated Theory of Intellectual Property, 88 Va. L. Rev. 1455 (2002); Tyler T. Ochoa and Mark Rose, The Anti–Monopoly Origins of the Patent and Copyright Clause, 84 J. Pat. & Trademark Off. Soc'y 909 (2002); Maureen A. O'Rourke, Toward a Doctrine of Fair Use in Patent Law, 100 Colum. L. Rev. 1177 (2000); J.H. Reichman, Charting the Collapse of the Patent–Copyright Dichotomy: Premises for a Restructured International Intellectual Property System, 13 Cardozo Arts & Ent. L.J. 475 (1995); Margaret Chon, Postmodern "Progress": Reconsidering the Copyright and Patent Power, 43 DePaul L. Rev. 97 (1993); Toshiko Takenaka, Extending the New Patent Misuse Limitation to Copyright: Lasercomb America, Inc. v. Reynolds, 5 Software L.J. 739 (1992); Rochelle Cooper Dreyfuss, A Wiseguy's Approach to Information Products: Muscling the Copyright and Patent Into a Unitary Theory of Intellectual Property, 1992 S. Ct. Rev. 195; John Shepard Wiley, Copyright at the School of Patent, 58 U. Chi. L. Rev. 119 (1991).

ASSIGNMENT 1

# TRADEMARK PROTECTION: INTRODUCTION

The three federal intellectual property regimes with which this course deals have much in common, for they all create exclusive rights in informational products. Of the three, copyright and patent law are by far the most similar, both in terms of the needs of the people protected (authors and inventors), and in terms of the goals and substance of the law. Accordingly, these regimes will be considered successively, in Assignments 6–13 and 14–24. This Unit investigates trademark law, which deals with the somewhat different requirements of those who produce and sell goods and services.

In many ways, trademark law is the most curious of the three federal intellectual property regimes. First, of the three, it is the only one that lacks an explicit constitutional basis. That is, Article I, Section 8, Clause 8 of the United States Constitution grants Congress the power to "promote the progress of science and useful arts, by securing for limited times to authors and inventors the exclusive right to their respective writings and discoveries." This provision, commonly called the "Copyright Clause," is ample basis for both copyright and patent legislation. However, when Congress attempted, in 1870, to use the same authority to enact a registration system to protect marketing symbols, the Supreme Court balked. According to the *The Trademark Cases*:

> "Any attempt . . . to identify the essential characteristics of a trademark with inventions and discoveries in the arts and sciences, or with the writings of authors, will show that the effort is surrounded with insurmountable difficulties.

> "The ordinary trade-mark has no necessary relation to invention or discovery. The trade-mark recognized by the common law is generally the growth of a considerable period of use, rather than a sudden invention. It is often the result of accident rather than design, and when under the act of Congress it is sought to establish it by registration, neither originality, invention, discovery, science, nor art is in any way essential to the right conferred by that act. If we should endeavor to classify it under the head of writings of authors, the objections are equally strong. In this, as in regard to inventions, originality is required. And while the word *writings* may be liberally construed, as it has been, to include original designs for engravings, prints, & c., it is only such as are *original*, and are founded in the creative powers of the mind. The writings which are to be protected are *the fruits of intellec-*

**6**

*tual labor*, embodied in the form of books, prints, engravings, and the like. The trade-mark may be, and generally is, the adoption of something already in existence as the distinctive symbol of the party using it."[1]

Thus deprived of Copyright Clause authority, Congress shifted gears. When it enacted a new trademark law, it expressly did so under its Commerce Clause powers.[2] This solution has, however, proved to be somewhat problematic. Since this Clause speaks only of commerce "with foreign nations, and among the several states, and with the Indian tribes," it was not originally read to give Congress authority over purely intrastate activity. And although the Clause can be understood to encompass activities affecting interstate commerce,[3] federal trademark law is still used mainly by those who wish to market goods in more than one state.[4]

The second difficulty flows from the first: while it is easy to see why the framers of the Constitution would want to provide exclusive rights in writings and discoveries, it is somewhat harder to understand the justification for protecting trademarks. As *The Trademark Cases* noted, patents and copyrights protect works that are original. Producing original works is expensive; exclusive rights in these works provide a mechanism for recouping costs and generating the sort of profit that will encourage others to engage in similar creative efforts. But a trademark can be something as simple as a red triangle.[5] Indeed, trademarks are often symbols, designs, and words that are already a part of the "public domain"—the general storehouse of knowledge. Since the costs of using something already in existence are low, there is no need to devise a vehicle for recouping the costs of creation.

One traditional justification for creating exclusive rights in marks is that it prevents consumer confusion. Consumers are often unable to examine goods (or services)[6] to determine their quality or source. Instead, they must rely on the labels attached to the products offered for sale. The material on these labels is, therefore, a kind of language. Since language is

---

[1] 100 U.S. 82, 93–94 (1879)(emphasis in original).

[2] U.S. Const. art. I, § 8, cl. 3. Congress initially limited trademark registration to marks used in foreign commerce and commerce with the Indians, Act of March 3, 1881, 21 Stat. 502. It added registration for marks in interstate commerce in the Act of Feb. 20, 1905, ch. 592, 33 Stat. 724.

[3] See, e.g., Heart of Atlanta Motel v. United States, 379 U.S. 241 (1964). But see U.S. v. Lopez, 514 U.S. 549 (1995) and its progeny (restricting congressional power under the Commerce Clause).

[4] See also International Bancorp, LLC v. Societe des Bains de Mer, 329 F.3d 359 (4th Cir. 2003)(discussing Congress's prescriptive authority to protect marks in international commerce).

[5] See, e.g, Bass Ale: according to the label, its red triangle was the first registered trademark in England.

[6] Trademark law protects marketing symbols that are used on goods ("trade marks") and on services ("service marks"). It also protects the marks of collectives, such as the Ladies' Garment Workers Union ("collective marks"), as well as the marks of certification organizations, such as Good Housekeeping's Seal of Approval ("certification marks"), see Assignment 2. Unless otherwise noted, this Unit uses the term "trademark" in a generic sense, to encompass all symbols used for marketing purposes.

effective only if words have clear and unique meanings, the source of a particular product must have exclusive authority over the marketing symbols it uses. As an example, consider the consumer who wishes to purchase a yellow sponge cake surrounding a creamy filling. The cake is likely to come wrapped in plastic; there is no way to test it for freshness, to ascertain the presence of a filling, or to determine its taste. Instead, the consumer must utilize the information on the label. If there is only one producer that can label this cake "Twinkie," then the consumer can rely on the producer's reputation for freshness and the Twinkie's reputation for creamy deliciousness. If, however, other merchants can use the same designation, and other Twinkies are not fresh, or creamy, or delicious, then the consumer could easily wind up dissatisfied.

This justification for trademark law leads directly to the third problem: whom does the law protect? The consumer-confusion rationale suggests that the right of action should belong to the consumer who was confused by an ambiguously labeled product into making the wrong purchase. In actual fact, however, consumers generally do not have standing to sue under trademark law. Rather, trademark law gives to the producer who regularly uses a mark the right to prevent others from using the same mark, or a confusingly similar mark, on the same goods, or on related goods.

The reason for vesting the right in the producer rather than the confused consumer could be that the law is trying to reduce the number of lawsuits by concentrating all claims in one litigant (the producer) rather than spreading them out among many (the consumers). The problem with this explanation is that it assumes that the consumers' interests are aligned with the producers'. This is certainly true in the Twinkie example, but it is not universally true. For example, the $5 "Rolex" is a popular street corner purchase. It is not very likely that a person who pays $5 for a watch actually believes she is buying an exquisitely engineered Swiss chronometer. Rather, she probably wants to enjoy the look of a Rolex without sacrificing her bank account. Still, the owner of the Rolex mark ("Rolex") can use trademark law to prevent these vendors from using its mark on watches.

A more producer-centered explanation for trademark rights is therefore needed. Thus, the broad language in *The Trademark Cases* must be taken with a grain of salt. Trademark owners may not be making the same social contribution that authors and inventors make, but they are doing something that requires, and deserves, the protection of exclusivity. That contribution is the production of goodwill: the investment in quality, reputation, and service. That is, without the promise that others can be prevented from utilizing their marks, merchants will not invest their efforts in creating goodwill. Why, for example, would the owner of the Twinkie mark (Interstate Bakeries Corp.[7]) use the best ingredients and

[7] Interstate is the current owner, but this was not always the case. The stated manufacturer is Hostess, which at the time of the last edition, was owned by Continental Baking Co., which was owned by ITT. These changes in ownership are another reason why

hire good bakers when another manufacturer could use inferior products and workers, operate at lower costs, and sell Twinkies for less? Not only will Interstate Bakeries lose sales, the inferior products will destroy its reputation. For Rolex, exclusivity also gives its mark a certain cachet. The cachet is itself a selling point—and a kind of value—to a certain type of customer.

There are, however, significant downsides to trademark protection. For many people, the drive to own "name brand" products leads them to make purchases they cannot afford. Worse, there have been reports linking robbery and murder to trademarked goods, such as sneakers, that appeal to teenagers.[8] And even without the complication of crime, there is reason for concern. Developing strong marks seems to go hand-in-hand with annoying television commercials and pop-up ads, ugly roadway signs, and nonbiodegradable packaging. The expense of regulation and clean-up should be counted in the costs imposed by trademark law.

## 1.   FEDERAL TRADEMARK PROTECTION

The above description implies that the right to enjoin unauthorized uses is at the heart of trademark law. There is a sense in which this is true. Producers want an unambiguous avenue of communication with consumers and a legal right to exclusive use of their marks enables them to have one. Thus, trademark law has its origins in the common law of the states, where it was formulated to prevent a merchant from using a competitor's mark to "pass off" (or "palm off") her goods—that is, to misrepresent them as those of her competitor in order to deceive consumers into buying them by mistake. In most states, the law slowly expanded to prohibit other practices that lead to deterioration of marketing value, including dilution of the mark's value by overuse, its tarnishment through unsavory associations,[9] and—most recently—its unauthorized use as a domain name and on websites.

The development of substantive federal trademark law took a similar course. When Congress enacted the Lanham Act in 1946, 15 U.S.C.A. §§ 1051–1129,[10] it adopted the unfair competition themes of state law, to

trademarks are important to consumers, who need a reliable way to identify products, even through corporate mergers, spin-offs, and other business realignments.

[8] Kim Foltz, The Media Business: Addenda; New Nike Commercials Promote Good Conduct, N.Y. Times, July 5, 1990, Sec. D, p. 8, col. 2 (reporting on a $5,000,000 advertising campaign launched by Nike to promote good behavior).

[9] The American Law Institute has set out these laws in Restatement of the Law Third, Unfair Competition (1995). (Despite its name, this is the first time this law has been restated as a whole; portions of it were, however, included in the first (but not the second) Restatement of Torts.)

[10] Trademark legislation also embodies one more curiosity. Whereas the patent law is called the "Patent Act" and the copyright statute is called the "Copyright Act," the trademark law is almost always referred to as the "Lanham Act." Indeed, most practitioners refer to specific provisions of this Act by the numbering system of the bill that led to the final legislation. This casebook, however, uses the numbering system of 15 U.S.C.A. unless otherwise noted. In this Unit, all statutory references are, therefore, to 15 U.S.C.A., unless specifically stated otherwise.

the point that federal courts (and this casebook) often use state formulations of unfair competition principles to inform their understanding of federal trademark law. Over the years, the Lanham Act has also expanded, both through judicial and legislative action. Whether it now fully mirrors state law protections is an issue that will be dealt with later in this Unit.[11]

Since federal and state law cover essentially the same practices, what then is the need for federal legislation? The answer lies in recognizing that protecting investments in goodwill requires more than just the substantive right to prevent consumer confusion. To see this, ask how it is that multiple uses of the same trademark can occur. One possibility is that the second (junior) user really is trying to pass off. In such cases, the substantive right to prevent confusion is enough protection: the first (senior) user can obtain an injunction that will protect the integrity of his mark. However, it is also possible for two perfectly honest merchants to choose the same trademark. After all, entrepreneurs tend to start small and grow. Two merchants could adopt the same mark in different geographical areas and it could take many years for them to run into each other. When, however, their markets do meet, there will be a real problem. If they are both honest merchants, they will want to avoid consumer confusion. But to do so, one will have to abandon his old mark, adopt a new one, design new labels, and then inform customers of the change. This will entail considerable costs: who should bear them? In the passing-off situation, it was clear who acted in bad faith, but in this instance, neither party did. Accordingly, there is no criterion for deciding who keeps the mark and who pays the switching costs.

The bottom line is that in a world in which merchants expand from one trading region to another, trademark protection is greatly enhanced by a system of registration. First, merchants need a list that they can consult in order to avoid adopting marks that are already taken. Second, to solve the problem of multiple use, the system needs a priority rule—a way to determine who among multiple-users has the right to keep the mark, and who must pay to switch to a new mark. Of course, states could adopt such systems—and in fact, many of them have. However, since states can solve multiple-user problems only within their own borders, what is really needed is a national system, or, as international trade increases, an international system. Indeed, registration is so much a key to trademark law that early federal law, including the one at issue in *The Trademark Cases*, addressed that issue alone. And although the Lanham Act does contain substantive provisions, its principal significance lies in its Registers and in its priority rules. Both the Registers and the priority rules are described below, in Section 2. The Act also executes the United States' obligations under international trademark treaties. The avenue these create for protecting marks on a global basis is described below in Section 3.

(The Lanham Act enumeration is provided in the Statutory Supplement.)        [11] See Assignment 3.

## 2.   THE APPLICATION PROCESS

STATUTORY MATERIALS: §§ 1111, 1051–52, 1057–59, 1062–64, 1066–68, 1070–72, & 1091

The requirements for registration of a trademark—use of the mark as a marketing symbol in commerce, use of the mark interstate, and distinctiveness—will be covered in detail in Assignment 2. This section describes the application process for national trademark registration and the priority rules. A problem demonstrating the application of these rules is found in Assignment 4.

The Lanham Act creates three ways to establish an entitlement to registration: 1) use, 2) bona fide intent to use, and 3) trademark registration in a foreign country.[12] Domestic applicants (that is, those who begin to utilize their marks first in the United States) generally rely on one of the first two methods (use or intent to use), which are described in this Section and are governed by the Rules of Practice in Trademark Cases, 37 C.F.R. §§ 2.2–2.189. Foreign applicants (that is, those whose marks are utilized or registered abroad before they are used in the United States) usually rely on a foreign registration, which is described in Section 3. The "domestic" routes are, however, available even to foreign applicants, and many of them, in fact, use both routes.

Before 2003, registrations were made on standardized forms available from the Patent and Trademark Office. However, in a recent modernization move, registration has largely migrated to the Internet, where the PTO now offers several electronic filing methodologies.[13] No matter which is used, the same information is demanded.

*Use-based applications*

The application consists of three elements: the fee, the application form, and a drawing of the mark. The form asks for the name of the applicant, a detailed description of all of the goods or services for which she is using the mark,[14] and information about the mark, including a color specimen in an image file format acceptable to the PTO.[15] This information determines the scope of the rights the applicant will enjoy once the trademark is registered, for it delineates the words, goods, and services where the applicant wishes to prevent ambiguity.

In addition, the application seeks information that will facilitate the ability of others to search the Register. First, the applicant is asked to help keep the Register indexed by categorizing her goods or services according to

[12] §§ 1051(a), 1051(b), and 1126(d).

[13] http://www.uspto.gov/teas/eTEASpageA.htm.

[14] 37 C.F.R. §§ 2.21–2.47.

[15] 37 C.F.R. §§ 2.56–2.59. Formally, a specimen "showing the mark as used on or in connection with the goods" is required, with "specimen defined as a 'label, tag, or container,'" 37 C.F.R. §§ 256(a) and (b). The new on-line system does not, however, appear to accommodate the submission of an actual label.

an international classification scheme to which the PTO adheres.[16] Second, the applicant's rendition of the mark must conform to strict size and style requirements to maintain the readability of the Register.[17] The applicant must also state the date of first use and first use in commerce. These statements fulfill the Lanham Act's Commerce Clause limitation. They also establish the date from which the applicant is considered the owner of the mark. As among two applicants for the same or a similar mark for similar goods, it is the applicant with the earliest use who is entitled to the registration.[18] Further, once a mark is registered, the registered owner acquires the right to prevent others from adopting and using a confusingly similar mark for similar goods, as of the date the application was filed.[19]

The application ends with a declaration, a verified (i.e. sworn) statement (which can be signed with an electronic signature) that to the best of the applicant's knowledge, the mark does not so resemble a mark already in use in connection with similar goods that consumers could be confused.[20] This statement forces the applicant to do her part in assuring that the registration system performs its intended function of creating clear lines of communication between consumers and producers.

After the application is completed and the fee paid,[21] an examiner from the PTO determines whether the mark qualifies under the Lanham Act's general requirements for federal trademark protection.[22] If the application appears to satisfy these requirements, the PTO then publishes the mark in its *Official Gazette*. Those who believe they would be injured if the mark were registered have 30 days from the time of publication in which to oppose registration.[23] If no one opposes the mark, the PTO issues to the applicant a certificate of registration and registers the mark on the *Principal Register*. The owner can then notify others that the mark is registered by displaying it in conjunction with the words "Registered in U.S. Patent and Trademark Office" or, as is more common, with the symbol ®.[24]

*Intent-to-use applications*

In contrast to the traditional requirement that an applicant be using the mark in commerce before filing to register it, 1988 amendments to the Lanham Act permit an applicant to file for trademark protection as soon as she can demonstrate a bona fide intention to use the mark in commerce.[25]

---

[16] 37 C.F.R. § 2.32. See the upper right-hand corner of the application form.

[17] 37 C.F.R. §§ 2.51–2.53.

[18] §§ 1051–52. As we will see in Assignment 4, an earlier user of the mark may have some rights, even if she files later.

[19] See Assignment 3. When the registered owner may exercise the right to exclude will be examined in Assignment 4.

[20] § 1051(a)(1).

[21] This date will be considered the applicant's filing date for the purpose of international filings, see below. 37 C.F.R. § 2.21. As noted, electronic application—and electronic payment—are encouraged. A successful submission is followed by an email transmission that acknowledges receipt and summarizes the submission.

[22] 37 C.F.R. §§ 2.61–2.69.

[23] § 1063.

[24] § 1111.

[25] Trademark Law Revision Act of 1988, Pub.L. 100–667, 102 Stat. 3935.

The reasons for this change are discussed below in connection with international applications. An intent-to-use application substantially mirrors a use-based application in its components. For instance, the applicant must still submit the fee, drawing, and application. However, there are several differences between the two methods of registration. Because the mark has not yet been used, the applicant obviously need not state the first date of use or date of use in commerce. Instead, she verifies that she believes she is the owner of the mark and that she has a bona fide intention to use the mark in the future on a product in interstate commerce.[26] Moreover, she is not expected to submit the specimen of the mark required of a use-based applicant. Instead, she must still submit a drawing of the mark similar to that required of a use-based applicant. In this case, the drawing is more important than with the use-based application because the PTO will not have a specimen to determine what the mark looks like.

Once the PTO receives the application, it evaluates the proposed trademark, applying the same requirements as for a use-based application. If the mark conforms to the Lanham Act's general provisions, it will be published, as with the use-based application. If no one successfully opposes registration, the applicant receives a Notice of Allowance.[27] The Notice of Allowance does not, however, constitute federal registration of the mark. Within six months of the issuance of a Notice of Allowance, the applicant must file a verified written Statement of Use indicating that she has followed through on her bona fide intention to use the mark in commerce.[28] This written statement must include the date the mark was first used in commerce, the manner of use, the specimen of the mark as used, and a fee. Once the applicant has filed this Statement of Use, the PTO issues a certificate of registration and places the mark on the Principal Register.

If the applicant has not used the mark in commerce by the end of the six month period following the issuance of the Notice of Allowance, she may file for six-month extensions of time to show use of the mark.[29] The first request for an extension consists of a written statement asserting her continuing bona fide intention to use the mark and a fee. However, subsequent requests must be accompanied by a showing of good cause reasons for needing the extension.[30] "Good cause" statements must cite specific ongoing efforts to use the mark in commerce, such as continued market research about mark selection or promotional activities which will eventually lead to use in commerce. The applicant can further rely on good cause to extend the time for beginning use. However, the total time period from the issue of the notice of allowance to actual use cannot exceed 36 months.[31]

Note that although intent-to-use applications can have the effect of reserving a mark for up to three years, the applicant does not acquire the rights that attach to registration until use begins and the mark is regis-

[26] 37 C.F.R. § 2.33(b).
[27] 37 C.F.R. §§ 2.88–2.89.
[28] 37 C.F.R. § 2.88.
[29] 37 C.F.R. § 2.89.

[30] 37 C.F.R. § 2.89(d).
[31] 37 C.F.R. § 2.89(e)(1).

tered. That is, during the interim period between application and registration, the applicant cannot use federal registration as a basis for enjoining others from adopting the mark, nor can she prevent prior users from expanding their businesses. After the mark is registered, interim adoptions can be enjoined on the same bases as are available to any registered user. In essence, nationwide rights are acquired as of the filing date, but they are subject to a condition subsequent—that the applicant convert the Notice of Allowance into an actual registration.

*Registration problems*

The material above described an application that is ultimately approved. Problems can, however, crop up along the way. First, it is sometimes the case that more than one party applies to use similar marks on similar goods. If so, an interference may be declared.[32] Alternatively, when the mark is published, someone may claim registration will cause ambiguity, or dilute the communicative capacity of that party's mark, in which case, that party may file an opposition.[33] Oppositions and interferences are handled similarly: in an inter partes proceeding, complete with discovery, live-witness testimony, briefs and oral argument, the Trademark Trial and Appeal Board (TTAB), an agency court within the PTO, determines who has the right to the mark, whether the application should be approved, or (in the case of multiple users of similar marks) whether the Commissioner of Trademarks should register both marks with limitations on each of the concurrent uses.[34] Appeals from the Board are generally to the Court of Appeals for the Federal Circuit (CAFC). Alternatively, an action against the Commissioner of Trademarks can be instituted in federal district court.[35]

Of course, it is also possible that the examiner simply does not consider the mark registrable. She may, for example, think the mark is too similar to a mark that is already registered; or that the mark must remain in the public domain because it is generic, i.e., the only word for the goods on which it will be used; or that it is merely descriptive of the goods and therefore not distinctive enough to function as a trademark. In such cases, the examiner and applicant enter into correspondence, the applicant will explain why the mark should be registered or make changes to meet the examiner's objections. If the two agree on a registrable mark, the course described above will be followed.

If they cannot agree, there are two possibilities. First, the applicant could appeal the disallowance of registration to the TTAB,[36] and then through the federal judicial system in the manner noted above. However, when the problem is lack of distinctiveness, there is sometimes a second choice. If the mark is capable of becoming distinctive—that is, if people

[32] § 1066.

[33] § 1063.

[34] § 1067–68.

[35] § 1071. Dissatisfied parties can petition the Supreme Court for review of the regional circuit decision or the Federal Circuit decision, but such petitions are rarely granted.

[36] § 1070.

could become accustomed to thinking of it as source-indicative (if it is, in other words, capable of acquiring "secondary meaning"), the applicant can register it on the *Supplemental Register*.[37]

Marks on the Supplemental Register do not enjoy the benefits available to marks on the Principal Register. Registration on the Supplemental Register does not, for example, provide constructive notice to subsequent adopters that the mark is in use and so does not confer on the trademark owner the right to enjoin others from using the mark. In addition, this registration does not confer the advantage of certain types of relief, such as the right to stop others from importing infringing goods.[38] The Supplemental Register does, however, offer significant benefits. First, it is a mechanism of actual notice: those who want to avoid ambiguity can use the Supplemental Register as an additional resource for finding marks that have been previously adopted. Marks on the Supplemental Register can even be displayed with the ® that provides actual notice of federal registration.[39] Second, owners of marks on the Supplemental Register can use the federal courts to assert state-based rights and even certain federal rights. Third, marks listed on the Supplemental Register can usually be registered on the Principal Register after five years' use.[40] Finally, registration on the Supplemental Register meets some of the requirements needed to obtain the benefits of trademark treaties that the United States has entered with foreign countries.

*Maintenance*

Trademark protection and registration last for however long a mark is in use. However, affirmative steps must be taken to maintain registration. Certificates of registration remain in force for ten years and can be renewed for additional ten-year periods upon payment of fees. In addition, registrants must file periodic affidavits averring continuing use, or setting out special circumstances accounting for nonuse.[41]

These requirements are partly designed to preserve the Commerce Clause limitations of the Lanham Act because they insure that the marks that receive protection are in commerce and thus within Congress's prescriptive jurisdiction. More important, however, they keep the Register free of deadwood. That way, symbols that are particularly evocative can be utilized even after the original trademark owner has discarded them. The Act also has two other ways to clear the Register of marks that, for one reason or another, no longer meet Lanham Act requirements. In certain circumstances, a cancellation proceeding can be instituted in the PTO. These are handled much like oppositions.[42] In addition, certain types of invalidity can be asserted in infringement actions.[43] However, as the public

---

[37] § 1091. Electronic filing is also available for supplemental registrations.

[38] §§ 1094 & 1096.

[39] § 1111.

[40] § 1052(f).

[41] §§ 1058–59. This too can be accomplished on-line.

[42] § 1064.

[43] § 1115(b).

becomes accustomed to the mark, certain problematic aspects to protecting it are thought to become less important. Thus, after five years, the trademark owner can file an affidavit to have the mark considered "incontestable," which (in this context) means that some (but by no means all) challenges become unavailing.[44]

*Registration as a solution to the problem of multiple users*

This registration system helps to solve the problem of multiple users in a number of ways. First, the Principal and Supplemental Registers, along with the symbol ® next to registered marks, may provide newcomers with *actual notice* of what marks have already been taken, thereby allowing them to avoid adopting marks that are likely to confuse consumers.[45] More important, the Principal Register provides *constructive notice* that a mark is in use, thereby conferring on its owner the right to enjoin anyone who, after the application date, adopts the same or a similar mark for similar goods.[46]

Registration does not, however, constitute a complete solution to the multiple-user problem. First, the Registers do not list all marks that are in use. For example, marks protected only under state law do not appear on them. Accordingly, newcomers researching the availability of a particular mark must consult not only the federal Registers, but also state registers, trade journals, catalogues, newspapers, magazines, and the like. Since federal registration rights ultimately date from the date of application, it is also wise to check applications and Notices of Allowance.[47] Even then, some potential problems will be missed. For example, as the next section will demonstrate, the Registers may not show marks that are entitled to appear by virtue of international filings. Omissions are important because registration on the Principal Register does not necessarily create priority vis á vis these marks. That is, prior users are entitled to continue to use their marks in the geographic areas where they were used prior to the filing for registration. They are even entitled to a small zone of geographic expansion.

## 3.   THE INTERNATIONAL STAGE

STATUTORY MATERIALS: § 1126; Paris Convention, Arts. 2, 4, 6[bis], 9, & 10; TRIPS Agreement Arts. 15–24.[48]

Trademark *rights* are geographically bounded in that a mark can be enforced only in the jurisdiction in which it is recognized. U.S. marks, for

---

[44] § 1065. This issue will be discussed in Assignments 2 and 4.

[45] § 1111.

[46] § 1072. The issue of *when* the registered trademark holder can bring such an action will be examined in Assignment 4.

[47] The PTO has digitized much of this material and made it available at its website.

[48] The text and signatories of the principal international intellectual property instruments can be found at the website of the World Intellectual Property Organization, the UN organization which administers them, www.wipo.int. The TRIPS Agreement is administered by the World Trade Organization, which likewise posts information on its web-

example, are infringed only when there is a likelihood of consumer confusion in the United States.[49] Trademark *use* is not, however, territorially constrained. Many producers sell their products in global markets. Moreover, when consumers travel, they encounter foreign advertisements and use foreign goods and services. Even those who stay home learn about foreign products by talking to travelers, watching foreign television and films, surfing the Internet, and reading international publications. Consider, for example, the following marks:

SN 69,973. The Coca-Cola Company, Atlanta, Ga. Filed Mar. 19, 1959.

The trademark consists of the distinctively shaped contour, or conformation, and design of the bottle as shown.
Owner of Reg. Nos. 22,406, 415,755, and others.
For Carbonated Soft Drink.
First use July 8, 1916.

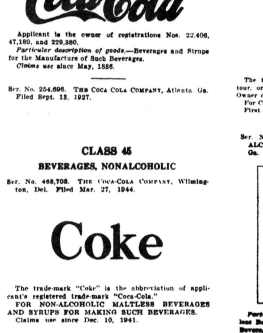

Ser. No. 254,695. THE COCA COLA COMPANY, Atlanta, Ga. Filed Sept. 13, 1927.

Applicant is the owner of registrations Nos. 22,406, 47,189, and 229,380.
*Particular description of goods.*—Beverages and Sirups for the Manufacture of Such Beverages.
*Claims use* since May, 1886.

Ser. No. 254,696. THE COCA COLA COMPANY, Atlanta. Ga. Filed Sept. 13, 1927.

## CLASS 45

### BEVERAGES, NONALCOHOLIC

Ser. No. 468,708. THE COCA-COLA COMPANY, Wilmington, Del. Filed Mar. 27, 1944.

# Coke

The trade-mark "Coke" is the abbreviation of applicant's registered trade-mark "Coca-Cola."
FOR NON-ALCOHOLIC MALTLESS BEVERAGES AND SYRUPS FOR MAKING SUCH BEVERAGES.
Claims use since Dec. 10, 1941.

Ser. No. 243,569.   (CLASS 45. BEVERAGES, NON ALCOHOLIC.)   THE COCA-COLA COMPANY, Atlanta. Ga. Filed Jan. 10, 1927.

*Particular description of goods.*—Nonalcoholic, Maltless Beverages and Sirups for the Manufacture of Such Beverages.
*Claims use* since Oct. 22, 1926.

No matter who purchases a beverage labeled with these marks, and no matter where they are purchased, a specific product, taste, and quality are expected. Because these expectations help to sell soda pop, and because its reputational interests are at stake whenever products labeled with these

site, www.wto.int. The latter also includes material on disputes resolved under the auspices of the WTO.

[49] See, e.g., American Rice, Inc. v. Arkansas Rice Growers Co-op. Ass'n, 701 F.2d 408 (5th Cir.1983).

marks are purchased, the owner of the U.S. trademarks would like to own them worldwide.

To achieve worldwide ownership, trademark owners must rely on the law of each nation in which they market their products. Treaties make this possible. There are several major international agreements that facilitate worldwide trademark protection. The principal multilateral treaty has, historically, been the International Convention for the Protection of Industrial Property.[50] Commonly called the Paris Convention, it pertains to both patents and trademarks. It was promulgated in 1883, adopted by the United States in 1887, and implemented through domestic legislation in 1903. The Paris Convention is recognized by well over 100 countries.

As it pertains to trademark law, the Convention has four important features. First, under Art. 2 of the Convention:

> "[n]ationals of any country of the Union shall . . . enjoy in all the other countries of the Union the advantages that their respective laws now grant, or may hereafter grant, to nationals."

This "national treatment" provision assures trademark holders in each Paris Convention nation that their applications to register marks in other Union countries will receive the same attention these countries accord to domestic applications. Moreover, national treatment means that rights acquired in each Union country will be equivalent to the rights enjoyed by that nation's own trademark holders. In short, Art. 2 insures that all producers operating within a Union country do so on a level playing field: no merchant can use domestic trademark law to acquire a competitive advantage.[51]

Second, Articles 9 and 10 provide manufacturers with a minimum level of substantive protection against products bearing unauthorized trademarks and false designations of source or origin.

Third, under Art. 6[bis], signatories agree to facilitate global marketing by reserving marks that become internationally known for the producers who made them famous. It requires signatories to:

> "refuse . . . the registration, and to prohibit the use, of a trademark which constitutes a reproduction, an imitation, or a translation, liable to create confusion, of a mark considered by the competent authority of the country of registration . . . to be so well known in that country as already the mark of a person entitled to the benefits of this Convention."

In other words, Art. 6[bis] allows companies like Coca Cola and Rolex to invest in goodwill with the confidence that their marks will be available to them as they expand internationally. They will not be forced to contend with locals who inadvertently adopt similar marks. Nor will they need to deal with opportunists, who register known marks with the hope of passing

---

[50] Other important international treaties that cover trademark rights include the General Agreement on Tariffs and Trade (the GATT Agreement) and the Trademark Law Treaty. Both set minimum standards of trademark protection that a member must apply to both its domestic marks and to the marks recognized by other member nations.

[51] See also Art. 6[quinquies].

off their goods as those of the major producer, or with "trademark pirates," who register well known marks for the sole purpose of soliciting payoffs from genuine producers.

The fourth major feature of the Paris Convention is a priority rule. Under Art. 4, an applicant who has filed in one Paris Convention country can claim the date of that application as the filing date in every other Union country—provided that the second filing occurs within six months of the first. For example, imagine that someone applies to register a mark in France on January 1, 1994 and then applies in the United States on May 1, 1994. Since both the U.S. and France are in the Paris Union, and since May is within six months of January, the filing date of the *U.S.* application will be considered to be January 1, 1994, and not May 1.[52]

Why does this matter? As we saw, it is sometimes the case that two parties apply to register similar marks for similar goods. For wholly domestic applications, the Commissioner will award the trademark to the party who used the mark first, or in the case of intent-to-use applications, who applied first and later met the use requirements. Applications that are filed under the Paris Convention, however, can claim the Paris Convention date for priority purposes. If that date precedes the date on which a domestic applicant first used the mark, the Paris Convention applicant will be awarded the trademark. To continue with the example begun above: if a domestic applicant had applied to register a similar mark for similar goods on February 10, 1994, and based its application on a first-use date of February 1, 1994, that applicant would be out of luck. Although the domestic applicant engaged in activity in the United States before the foreign applicant, the foreign applicant would enjoy the benefit of the Paris Convention date of January 1. Since January 1 precedes February 1, the foreign applicant would win the right to register the mark.

Note that the effect of Art. 4 is to create another way to acquire trademark rights in the United States, for it allows registration to be based upon a previous filing in a Paris Convention country rather than on use (or on intent-to-use, followed by use). The application method is similar to the one described above, making allowances for the differences in require-ments. But since many of the Paris Convention countries do not require applicants to have made any use of their mark prior to registration, this back door into the benefits of the Lanham Act has proved troublesome for Americans. After all, designing a mark, making up specimens, attaching the mark to goods, and offering the marked goods for sale can be expensive and time consuming. In a race between a domestic applicant who plans to base her application on this burdensome process and a Union applicant, who need do no more than file two applications, the domestic applicant will usually lose.[53]

Indeed, the 1988 Amendments to the Lanham Act were aimed, in part, at solving this problem. The intent-to-use provision was introduced to give

[52] This priority rule is enacted into do-mestic legislation in § 1126(d).

[53] See, e.g., SCM Corp. v. Langis Foods Ltd., 539 F.2d 196 (D.C.Cir.1976).

wholly domestic applicants an avenue for applying for trademark protection that did not involve the financial investment of the use provision. In addition, the Amendments increased the burden on Paris Union applicants by requiring, for the first time, that these applicants state a bona fide intention to use the mark in commerce.[54] Actual use may not, however, be required prior to the registration of Paris Union marks, the way that it is for intent-to-use marks. Thus, even after the Amendments, a Union applicant may still be in a better position than a domestic applicant.[55]

More recently, international norms of intellectual property protection have come to be set by the General Agreement on Tariffs and Trade (GATT). As initially enacted, GATT was designed to increase international commerce by reducing tariffs and other barriers to trade. When this Agreement went into force in 1948 with the United States as an original signatory, the parties to GATT focused on commerce in products like corn, chickens, lamps, and steel; it was only in 1986, during the so-called Uruguay Round of GATT trade negotiations, that intellectual property was introduced into the discussion. After a slow start in which the propriety of treating intellectual products as equivalent to grain, poultry, and manufactured goods was questioned, the Uruguay Round ended in 1994 with an agreement on Trade–Related Aspects of Intellectual Property Rights (TRIPS). Like the entire GATT, TRIPS is administered by a new body, the World Trade Organization (WTO).

Under TRIPS, members agreed to a set of basic principles. The first two mirror the Paris Convention: signatories to TRIPS agree to accord national treatment to foreign trademark applicants and to accord priority according to the applicant's national filing date.[56] The third extends the core principle of the GATT to intellectual property: it requires member countries to accord to other member nations most-favored-nation (MFN) treatment.[57] This means that any time one member of the GATT enters into an agreement related to intellectual property with any other member, the advantages of the agreement are generalized to apply to all other signatories.

The fourth significant feature of TRIPS is that it establishes a set of universal minimum standards—in addition to those of the Paris Convention—governing the use of intellectual products. Although U.S. law largely complied with these norms before TRIPS, the agreement did require some modifications to all three federal intellectual property regimes. The changes

---

[54] §§ 1126(c), (d)(2), (e).

[55] Another problem with Art. 4 is that the six-month grace period between the foreign and United States filings creates a blind spot in the registration system—a period when the mark is not in the federal system but is nonetheless entitled to federal registration.

[56] Final Act Embodying the Results of the Uruguay Round of Multilateral Trade Negotiations and Marrakesh Agreement Establishing the World Trade Organization, signed at Marrakesh (Morocco), April 15, 1994, Annex 1C, Agreement on Trade–Related Aspects of Intellectual Property Rights, Arts. 3(1) and 4A(1), reprinted in The Results of the Uruguay Round of Multilateral Trade Negotiations—The Legal Texts (GATT Secretariat ed. 1994)[hereinafter, the TRIPS Agreement].

[57] Id., Art. 4.

in trademark law that went into effect on January 1, 1996 were minor and will be discussed in the Assignments to which they pertain. The TRIPS Agreement also requires heightened protection for geographic indications, particularly with respect to wines and spirits. Whether the United States is fully compliant with these provisions will also be discussed in Assignment 2.

Because the Paris Convention and the TRIPS Agreement create opportunities to protect marks on a nearly worldwide basis, they represent important benefits to international businesses. They are not, however, a perfect solution to the problem of international protection because of the expense of filing applications in every country where the mark will be used. Substantive law and filing requirements are not identical and so local counsel must usually be hired and separate applications drawn up. Better would be a unitary system that allowed a producer to obtain worldwide protection with a single filing. The Madrid Agreement created exactly this sort of a unitary registration system. However, it was based on a view of trademark rights which is fundamentally different from that of the United States. To create a unitary system that the United States could join, a different instrument was required. The next section describes the Madrid Agreement, which most industrialized countries have been utilizing, the United States' problems with it, and then the new Protocol that the United States has recently agreed to enter.

*The Madrid Agreement*[58]

The Madrid Agreement for the International Registration of Trademarks was signed in 1891. As of this writing, there are seventy signatories. In order to obtain an international registration under the Madrid Agreement, an applicant must secure a basic registration in her home country. The applicant may then extend this protection to other Madrid member countries by instructing her home office to file an international application with the International Bureau of the World Intellectual Property Office, designating the other countries where protection is sought.

The International Bureau reviews the application to confirm that it meets certain formalities,[59] accepts the registration on the International Register, and notifies each national office where registration was requested.[60] The national office of each country has a year from the notification date to refuse registration of the mark.[61] If it does not refuse registration during that time, it may not object to the registration of the mark, and the mark will be deemed registered in that country.[62] If the national trademark office does refuse registration within the one-year period, the applicant has

---

[58] The authors would like to thank Michelle Lee, New York University Law School LLM Class of 2003, for the following discussion.

[59] The International Bureau reviews the international application to ensure that its contents are consistent with the home registration. It imposes no real substantive requirements and does not maintain an examination system.

[60] Madrid Agreement, art. 4, para. 3.

[61] Madrid Agreement, art. 5, paras. 1–2.

[62] Madrid Agreement, art. 5, para. 5. (providing that offices failing to refuse extension within one year lose the right to do so).

the opportunity to respond to the refusal and argue that the mark is registrable under the laws of the relevant country.[63] Once a mark is successfully registered in a particular country it is entitled to all the protections it would have received had an original filing been made in that country's national trademark office.[64]

An international registration remains in effect for twenty years.[65] However, during the first 5 years of registration it is dependent on the basic home-country registration and will lapse if that basic registration is successfully challenged.[66] Such a challenge is called a "central attack," because a successful attack on the basic registration will render all of the other national registrations based on that basic registration to also fail.

Under the Madrid Agreement all applications and all correspondence with the International Bureau must be in French. Applicants pay a single fee for the International registration, a nominal supplement for each additional International Class, beyond three, into which the goods or services applied for fall, and a "complementary fee" for any subsequently requested extensions of the application.[67] The fees are then divided equally and distributed among the member nations.[68] The individual countries are not allowed to charge any additional fees for trademarks that they examine pursuant to requests that a registration be extended into that country.

*U.S. Problems with the Madrid Agreement*

The United States' problems with the Madrid Agreement stem mainly from the fact that the Agreement makes worldwide rights contingent on a home-country registration. As we saw, many foreign countries do not impose a use requirement; the United States does. Some countries permit registrations for a broad array of goods and services; the United States limits registration to the narrowly drawn specifications of goods and services in which the mark is being used. Furthermore, some countries do not examine applications extensively; the United States does. As a result, if the United States were to join the Agreement, foreign trademark applicants would enjoy significant advantages over their American counterparts. Foreigners could bootstrap a non-use based registration into a quick and cheap U.S. registration. These marks would then be recognized for a broader array of goods or services than would be available to American registrants. Moreover, because there would be unused (foreign) marks that were nonetheless eligible for registration in the United States, it would be difficult to conduct searches to determine whether a particular symbol could be adopted as a U.S. trademark.

The "central attack" provisions of the Madrid Agreement are also considered detrimental to U.S. registrants. Because there are a number of

[63] Madrid Agreement, art. 5, paras. 3, 6.

[64] Madrid Agreement, art. 4, para. 1. ("[T]he protection of the mark in each of the contracting countries concerned shall be the same as if the mark had been filed therein direct.").

[65] Madrid Agreement, art. 6, para. 1.

[66] Madrid Agreement, art. 6, para. 3.

[67] Madrid Agreement, art. 8, para. 2.

[68] Madrid Agreement, art 8, paras. 4–5.

grounds for cancellation of a U.S. registration that are not available in other countries, any foreign trademark that is based on a U.S. registration is extremely vulnerable. Thus, U.S. trademark holders who want their foreign marks judged under more lenient foreign law criteria cannot rely on Madrid Agreement applications: even were the United States to join the Agreement, they would still need to file a separate application in each country where registration is sought to avoid the invocation of U.S. law through the Agreement's central attack provision.

The Madrid Agreement also poses administrative problems. Even where there is little or no objection to a trademark application in the United States, the examination period takes at least a year. The twelve-month period set by the Madrid Agreement to review extension requests would not be sufficiently long for the U.S. Patent and Trademark Office to review and act upon foreign registrations—and that does not even take into consideration the need to translate all the documents from French into English. In order to comply with the twelve-month requirement, and at the same time avoid having the U.S. trademark register flooded with marks that do not comply with U.S. standards, international applications would have to be given preference, thereby delaying the processing of domestic applications. To make matters worse, the nominal fees received from the international filings would not be sufficient to pay the costs associated with this increased workload. The result would be increased applications fees for domestic applicants, who would essentially be subsidizing the international trademark filings and, on top of that, would have their own applications further delayed as a result.

*The Madrid Protocol*

In 1989, the Madrid nations supplemented the Agreement with the "Madrid Protocol," which creates a new method for obtaining international trademark protection with a single application and also deals with a number of the issues that has prevented the United States from joining the Madrid Agreement. Most notable of these changes is the requirement that only a basic *application*, rather than a basic *registration*, is required as a prerequisite for an international application. The result of this change, together with the advent of the intent-to-use application, is that U.S. applicants no longer have to wait until the mark is in use before they can file an international application.

The Madrid Protocol also allows member nations up to eighteen months to refuse an application;[69] in countries that allow for opposition proceedings, this eighteen-month period may be extended further provided notice of an anticipated opposition is provided.[70] Together with the addition of English as an acceptable language for communication with the International Bureau and allowance of each individual trademark office to charge its own filing fees, this provision limits the need to give any preferential treatment to international applications, and avoids unnecessary delay of domestic U.S. applications. And while central attack is still available under

---

[69] Madrid Protocol, art. 5, para. 2 (b).        [70] Madrid Protocol, art. 5, para. 2 (c).

the Madrid Protocol, the instrument permits applicants to avoid its worst features: if a home-country mark is invalidated, the Protocol gives the applicant three months in which to convert her Madrid application into a series of national applications, each of which will retain the priority date of the original international application.[71]

Unfortunately, however, not all of the United States' problems with the Agreement are eliminated in the Protocol. An applicant who seeks to avoid challenges under U.S. law by transforming the Protocol application into national applications must pay (in addition to the Protocol's fees) the application fees associated with the filing of national applications.[72] Furthermore, U.S. trademark owners would still be limited by the narrowly drawn specifications in U.S. applications, even when they are applying for protection in countries where greater flexibility is permitted. Thus, they would essentially be paying the same amount as other applicants to obtain a registration limited to a fraction of the protection otherwise available.

*Accession to the Madrid Protocol*

Despite these remaining problems, the United States decided not to make further substantive objections to the Protocol. However, a procedural problem (involving the number of votes the EU could cast) remained a hurdle until 2002. In that year, an agreement with the EU was reached, at which point, the Senate advised and consented to it and Congress enacted implementing legislation, which President Bush signed on November 2, 2002. The effective date is November 2, 2003. It remains to be seen how accession will change U.S. practice, but the PTO's website indicates that it will be ready to accept Protocol-based applications.[73]

---

[71] Madrid Protocol, Art. 9quinquies.

[72] Id.

[73] The PTO has published its new regulations, which amend 37 C.F.R. Parts 2 and 7, at 68 Fed. Reg. 55748 (Sept. 26, 2003).

# REQUIREMENTS FOR TRADEMARK PROTECTION: PHYSICAL USE, COGNITIVE USE (DISTINCTIVENESS) AND REQUIREMENTS FOR FEDERAL REGISTRATION

Laypersons will talk of the "Twinkie trademark" or the "Rolex trademark." Trademark lawyers do not speak this way. They say, "Rolex as a trademark for watches" or "Twinkie for cakes." The difference here is more than rhetorical style; it captures the essence of trademark law. Owning a trademark is not a right to a *word*, rather it is a right to a *signal*—to a particular use of a word. It is control over a message that flows from producer to consumer, a message that is short, but nonetheless rich with information. The trademark for a product, for example, can signal much about the product's nature and source. Since the objective of trademark law is to make it possible to send these signals in an unambiguous way, a trademark is protected only when it is being used to designate a product's source or origin. Producers may desire to communicate other types of information to consumers (e.g., information about product quality), but unless the subject matter at issue is serving this denotative function, it cannot be protected as a trademark.

There are two different ways of protecting trademarks: registration on the Principal Register is the best option for those marks that meet the requirements for federal registration, whereas state law and § 43(a) of the Lanham Act (covered in Assignment 3) protect marks that have acquired trademark status absent federal registration. Appropriate trademark subject matter includes not only words, but also symbols, product packaging (trade dress), and even product configuration. All subject matter functioning as trademarks, regardless of whether such subject matter has been registered on the Principal Register, must satisfy certain key requirements. These include physical use and cognitive use. In addition, although some of the Lanham Act's requirements for federal registration parallel the more generalized rules for protection, the statute does contain certain specific rules regarding both initial registration and maintenance. All of these requirements for trademark protection are the subject of this Assignment.

Before proceeding, a few preliminary observations about the concept of "use" are in order. This Assignment demonstrates that "use" has both physical and cognitive components. The physical dimension of "use" has three components. First, use entails "actual use" of the trademark in commerce. "Actual use" means, in essence, that the word or symbol must have a spatial association with goods or services such that consumers perceive it as a signal conveying information about the trademark owner and its products. Second, use requires an element of display. Third, to be a *federal* trademark, the signal must come within the jurisdiction of the Lanham Act by being used in interstate commerce. On the cognitive side, the word or symbol must be "distinctive:" intrinsically capable of being understood as a signal rather than as a description of the goods. Marks that are descriptive (absent proof that the mark is functioning as a signal), generic or functional do not meet the requirement of distinctiveness.

## 1.   PRINCIPAL PROBLEM

Congratulations. This is your first day as a trademark examiner in the United States Patent and Trademark Office. The first matter to come across your desk involves Coach handbags. Coach has been designing and selling exclusive handbags for approximately fifty years. Its products are sold exclusively under its own label and are marketed nationally in about fifty stores across the country owned by Coach, in clearly marked Coach display cases in expensive stores, and through Coach mail order catalogues. Although the various styles of Coach bags do not resemble one another, they do share certain features. All are produced from full-grain black or brown cowhide, contain exterior binding at external seams, and incorporate brass hardware components. Over the years, Coach has attached to all of its handbags lozenge-shaped plastic tags in a light-sparkly grey color. These tags are embossed with the name "Coach Leatherware." The tags, suspended from beaded brass chains, have become valuable through Coach's promotional efforts and by virtue of its upscale reputation. The value of these grey tags is mirrored in Coach's advertising slogan: "It's Not a Coach Bag Without the Coach Tag." In fact, these tags alone often are stolen.

Three years ago, Coach opened a telephone order business for its handbags. It secured the "1–800" telephone number whose digits correspond on the telephone dial to the phrase "HANDBAG." Coach has used and heavily advertised this telephone number in magazines and newspapers for about two years. Coach also wants to launch a new line of microfiber handbags. The advantage of these products are that they are made of a sturdy material rather than the traditional cowhide, and therefore, are much lighter than Coach's other handbags. Coach desires to market these handbags by the designation "The SICILY SOPHISTICATE line." These handbags, like all Coach bags, will be made in the United States. Coach has not yet begun to manufacture the microfiber bags but Coach has referred to this line by the SICILY SOPHISTICATE designation in e-mail correspondence with its lawyers, store representatives, and potential customers.

Coach has applied to register the following items on the Principal Register: the mark COACH for its entire product line; three specific handbag designs; the gray shaped leather tags; the slogan "It's Not a Coach Bag Without the Coach Tag;" the "1–800" telephone number; and the trademark SICILY SOPHISTICATE. You have been hearing rumors that attorneys are complaining that your office is taking too long to render registration decisions, and that new examiners will be judged not only by their performance but also by their speed. So, you need to decide quickly what position you will be taking on these applications. Before deciding, consider the following materials.

## 2.   MATERIALS FOR SOLUTION OF PRINCIPAL PROBLEM

A.   STATUTORY MATERIALS: §§ 1051, 1052–54, 1056, 1064–65, 1091, & 1127

B.   CASES

# Microstrategy Incorporated v. Motorola, Incorporated

United States Court of Appeals, Fourth Circuit, 2001.
245 F.3d 335.

■ MOTZ, CIRCUIT JUDGE.

Motorola, a global communications and electronics company, produces electronic hardware. In June 2000, Motorola held a business summit of its marketing officers to determine how to market more effectively its services and products on a worldwide basis. The company decided to develop a new brand to establish a more cohesive corporate identity. In early July, Motorola contacted three advertising agencies, inviting each to compete in creating this new brand. One agency, Ogilvey & Mather, suggested the use of "Intelligence Everywhere" as a trademark and global brand for Motorola products. Ogilvey & Mather also represented that its attorneys had conducted a trademark search for "Intelligence Everywhere," which revealed no conflicting use of the phrase as a trademark.

Motorola selected Ogilvey & Mather as its agency and began its normal procedures for clearing "Intelligence Everywhere" as a trademark. In-house trademark counsel for Motorola performed and commissioned various trademark searches for "Intelligence Everywhere" and turned up no conflicting trademark uses of the phrase. On October 5, 2000, in-house counsel informed Motorola management that no conflicting marks had been found and that the phrase was available for use as a mark in the United States and throughout the world. However, in-house counsel also informed Motorola management that a Canadian company, Cel Corporation, had registered the domain name "intelligenceeverywhere.com" and further investigation revealed that Cel might be using the name as a trademark on some products. A month later, Motorola obtained Cel's rights to "Intelligence Everywhere."

On October 19, 2000, Motorola filed an intent-to-use application with the United States Patent and Trademark Office for the registration of the trademark "Intelligence Everywhere," indicating its intent to use this mark on a vast array of its products and services. On December 10, 2000, Motorola registered the domain name "intelligenceeverywhere.com" with Network Solutions, Inc. in Herndon, Virginia.

On January 8, 2001, MicroStrategy, a producer of communication software, notified Motorola that MicroStategy had been using "Intelligence Everywhere" as a trademark since "at least as early as 1998." A. 461. MicroStrategy further stated that the mark had obtained common law protection, and that Motorola's intended use of the mark would constitute unlawful infringement. Motorola responded by expressing its belief that its use of the mark would not violate state or federal law and its intent to continue using the mark. MicroStrategy then submitted its own application to the United States Patent and Trademark Office seeking to register the trademark, "Intelligence Everywhere."

On February 13, 2001, MicroStategy filed this action in the United States District Court for the Eastern District of Virginia, raising claims of trademark infringement, trademark dilution, and cybersquatting. Micro-Strategy moved the court for a preliminary injunction to prevent Motorola's intended use of the mark. Such an injunction would have prevented Motorola from launching its planned global advertising campaign around the "Intelligence Everywhere" mark, otherwise scheduled to begin the week of March 19, 2001. On February 23, 2001, the district court heard oral argument and denied the motion for a preliminary injunction.

After noting an interlocutory appeal on its trademark infringement claim, MicroStrategy then moved this court for expedited consideration of that appeal.

\* \* \*

[W]e turn to the question of whether MicroStrategy has demonstrated substantial likelihood of success on the merits in its trademark infringement claim. For a plaintiff to prevail on a claim of trademark infringement, the plaintiff must first and most fundamentally prove that it has a valid and protectable mark. See Petro Stopping Ctrs. v. James River Petroleum, 130 F.3d 88, 91 (4th Cir. 1997).

The district court held that MicroStrategy had failed to show a likelihood of success on this critical, initial burden. The court reasoned that although the record demonstrated that MicroStrategy had registered approximately 50 marks, it failed to register "Intelligence Everywhere" as a mark and, therefore, did not qualify for protection under 15 U.S.C. § 1114(1) (1994 & Supp. V 1999). With respect to MicroStrategy's claim under the common law of Virginia, the court concluded that "a careful review" of the record did "not reveal" that MicroStrategy used the term "Intelligence Everywhere" to "identify MicroStrategy as a source of goods or services." A. 51.

Of course, as MicroStrategy points out, a mark need not be registered to garner federal trademark protection. Rather, "it is common ground that § 43(a) [of the Lanham Act, 15 U.S.C. § 1125 (1994 & Supp. V 1999)] protects qualifying unregistered trademarks." *Two Pesos, Inc. v. Taco Cabana, Inc.*, 505 U.S. 763, 768, 120 L. Ed. 2d 615, 112 S. Ct. 2753 (1992). But § 43(a) of the Lanham Act, like Virginia common law,[a] does require that in order to obtain trademark protection "a designation must be proven to perform the job of identification: to identify one source and distinguish it from other sources." 1 J. Thomas McCarthy, McCarthy on Trademarks and Unfair Competition § 3:3 (4th ed. 2000). "Not every single word [or] phrase ... that appears on a label or in an advertisement qualifies as a protectable mark." See id. If a purported mark fails to identify its source, it is not protectable—under state or federal law. Id.; see also 15 U.S.C. § 1127 (1994) (" 'trademark' includes any word, name, symbol, or device, or any combination thereof ... used by a person ... to identify and distinguish his or her goods"). As the Sixth Circuit recently put it, "a plaintiff must show that it has actually used the designation at issue as a trademark"; thus the designation or phrase must be used to "perform[] the trademark function of identifying the source of the merchandise to the customers." *Rock & Roll Hall of Fame v. Gentile Prods.*, 134 F.3d 749, 753 (6th Cir. 1998).

After careful examination of the 252 pages of MicroStrategy documents that the company has submitted in support of its motion for preliminary injunction, we agree with the district court: MicroStrategy has failed to demonstrate that it has likely used "Intelligence Everywhere" to identify MicroStrategy as the source of its goods or services.

MicroStrategy has offered 24 documents (not including duplicates of press releases), dating from March 1999 through early 2001, in which it has used the term "Intelligence Everywhere." These include two annual reports, several press releases, brochures, sales presentations, a product manual, a business card, and newspaper articles. Although most of these documents contain several pages of densely printed material and some are quite lengthy, typically each refers only once to "Intelligence Everywhere," and that reference follows no particular design or sequence, i.e., sometimes its on the cover, sometimes not, most often "Intelligence Everywhere" appears in the midst of text. Use of a trademark to identify goods and services and distinguish them from those of others "does not contemplate that the public will be required or expected to browse through a group of words, or scan an entire page in order to decide that a particular word, separated from its context, may or may not be intended, or may or may not serve to identify the product." *In re Morganroth*, 208 U.S.P.Q. 284, 288 (T.T.A.B. 1980); *Ex parte Nat'l Geog. Soc.*, 83 U.S.P.Q. 260 (Comm'n Pat. 1949). Yet that is precisely the sort of examination one is forced to employ

---

[a] Section 43(a) of the Lanham Act "tracks classic principles of state law of unfair competition." 4 J. Thomas McCarthy, McCarthy on Trademarks and Unfair Competi- tion § 27:18 (4th ed. 2000); see also Lone Star Steakhouse & Saloon, Inc. v. Alpha of Virginia, Inc., 43 F.3d 922, 929 n.10 (4th Cir. 1995).

even to find the term "Intelligence Everywhere" in many of MicroStrategy's materials.

Moreover, MicroStrategy has not used any "constant pattern" or design to highlight "Intelligence Everywhere." Unlike certain MicroStrategy trademarks, e.g., "Intelligent E–Business," MicroStrategy has not consistently placed "Intelligence Everywhere" on a particular part of the page, or in a particular type, or labeled it with "TM,"[b] or consistently used a distinctive font, color, typeset or any other method that makes "its nature and function readily apparent and recognizable without extended analysis." Id. "[A] designation is not likely to be perceived as a mark of origin unless it is repetitively used, as opposed to only an occasional or isolated use." 1 McCarthy § 3.3.

On its business card and elsewhere, MicroStrategy characterizes "Intelligence Everywhere" as the company "mission," A. 313. Although in the proper context, a mission statement, like a slogan, can serve as a trademark, a company mission statement or slogan is certainly not by definition a trademark. Rather, mission statements, like "slogans often appear in such a context that they do not identify and distinguish the source of goods or services. In such cases, they are neither protectable nor registrable as trademarks." See 1 McCarthy § 7:20 (emphasis added). So it is here. MicroStrategy has not demonstrated that it has used the mission statement to identify and distinguish the source of its products or services. If anything, the phrase has been used to advertise MicroStrategy's goods, without identifying the source of those goods. Unless used in a context whereby they take on a dual function, advertisements are not trademarks.

Moreover, the record does not bear out MicroStrategy's claim that the company "for years has used the mark consistently in widely distributed sales brochures [and] product manuals sold with the software, and advertising for its Broadcaster software"; the mark "is commonly placed right next to the name, Broadcaster." Brief of Appellant at 32. The two items that MicroStrategy provides to support this proposition are a Broadcaster product brochure, copyrighted in 2000, and a Broadcaster administrator guide, which indicates it was published in September 1999. Nothing in the record indicates precisely how "widely" these items have been distributed. What is clear is that not even in these two documents did MicroStrategy use "Intelligence Everywhere" "consistently" as a trademark "right next to the name, Broadcaster." Moreover, on the last page of the brochure, when MicroStrategy lists its trademarks, including "MicroStrategy Broadcaster"

[b] Only infrequently has MicroStrategy designated "Intelligence Everywhere" with a TM (just five times in pre–2001 documents, see A. 109, A. 116, A. 324 (duplicated at A. 447), A. 327 (duplicated at A. 443 with TM and at A. 348 and A. 344 without TM); A. 354), while it has consistently designated other phrases with the "TM." Moreover, although on eight documents presented to us MicroStrategy has included lists of its trademarks, the company omits "Intelligence Everywhere" from its lists of trademarks about as often as it includes the phrase. Notably, although the company lists 18 trademarks in its handsomely printed 64–page 1999 annual report, it does not include "Intelligence Everywhere" among them. See A. 221.

and fourteen other marks, it does not list "Intelligence Everywhere." A. 99.[c]

What appears to have eluded MicroStrategy is that "even though a word, name, symbol, device, or a combination of words [a slogan] may be used in the sale or advertising of services or on or in connection with goods" it is not protectable as a trademark "unless it is used as a mark." *In re Morganroth*, 208 U.S.P.Q. at 287 "Intelligence Everywhere" could function as a trademark, but MicroStrategy has not clearly demonstrated that it has, in fact, used the phrase as a mark.

For these reasons, MicroStrategy has at this juncture utterly failed to provide a basis for a court to find the probability of its trademark usage, let alone trademark infringement by Motorola. Rather, MicroStrategy has presented a record of limited, sporadic, and inconsistent use of the phrase "Intelligence Everywhere." Obviously, this does not constitute "a clear and strong case" of likelihood of success on the merits. Of course, MicroStrategy may yet prevail on its infringement claim at trial. But the company has not demonstrated that this is likely, let alone that the district court abused its discretion in refusing to grant the requested preliminary injunction.[d] The judgment of the district court is therefore

AFFIRMED

■ NIEMEYER, CIRCUIT JUDGE, dissenting.

To deny MicroStrategy a preliminary injunction at this stage of the proceedings, when no trial has yet been held, ensures that any rights MicroStrategy may have in the mark "Intelligence Everywhere" will be seriously undermined, if not permanently destroyed, by Motorola's planned advertising campaign promoting its identical mark in a contiguous, complementary product market. Because the outcome on the nature and scope of MicroStrategy's alleged senior mark is not a foregone conclusion at this time, likelihood of success on the merits is not a determinative factor on the appropriateness of entering a preliminary injunction. But, because the balance of hardships so clearly favors MicroStrategy, the principles of equity suggest that we enter a preliminary injunction to prohibit Motorola's use of its junior mark "Intelligence Everywhere" until a trial can be held to determine whether MicroStrategy has a valid, senior interest in the mark.

But weighing most heavily in favor of MicroStrategy is the certainty that Motorola's widespread use of the identical mark in a complementary product market will effectively and permanently destroy MicroStrategy's mark if an injunction is not entered. Motorola's resources far exceed those of MicroStrategy's, and Motorola's proposed use of the mark will be nearly

---

[c] Examination of the excerpt of the administrator guide presented to us reveals a similar story.

[d] Given our resolution of this appeal, we need not, and do not, reach the district court's holding on the likelihood of confusion between MicroStrategy's and Motorola's use of the phrase "Intelligence Everywhere." We do note some skepticism, however, as to the district court's conclusion that "Intelligence Everywhere" is a descriptive mark.

universal. Thus, considering only the relative harms, I believe that the harm from delay of Motorola's introduction of "Intelligence Everywhere"—a delay that does not necessarily entail the loss of development expenses—is outweighed by the irreparable injury that will occur to MicroStrategy's mark, even if it is able to prevail on the merits.

Even on the merits, MicroStrategy's chances of prevailing at trial are quite good and certainly are nowhere as bleak as the majority suggests. Any doubt about MicroStrategy's eventual success, as the majority observes, would come from questions about how consistently MicroStrategy has been in using the "Intelligence Everywhere" slogan as a trademark. Yet, even as to this, the closest question on the merits, there is a good deal of evidence in the record in MicroStrategy's favor.

First, while MicroStrategy has not consistently used the mark in all of its corporate documents, the record certainly does reflect that MicroStrategy has used the mark consistently as a trademark with respect to its "Broadcaster" software.[a] On the cover of the software user's manual, which is distributed with the software, the mark is set out in prominent, highlighted text. Moreover, every MicroStrategy business card features the mark, set off with quotation marks, in initial capital letters, with the TM signal next to it. Either of these consistent uses alone could be enough to establish the adoption of "Intelligence Everywhere" as a mark, and together, they provide MicroStrategy with considerable evidence to present at trial on the first element of its infringement claim.

If it is able to establish this element, MicroStrategy is almost certain to prevail on the other elements of its infringement claim. Despite the district court's contrary conclusion, it cannot seriously be contended that MicroStrategy's use of "Intelligence Everywhere" is descriptive rather than suggestive. The phrase does not impart information about MicroStrategy or its products directly—the hallmark of a descriptive mark—but instead "requires some operation of the imagination to connect" the meaning of the phrase to MicroStrategy and its products, the very definition of a suggestive mark. A potential customer faced solely with the slogan would be unable to describe precisely what product or services were offered by MicroStrategy.

I would reverse its ruling and remand for entry of a preliminary injunction pending trial.

## G. Heileman Brewing Company, Inc. v. Anheuser–Busch, Inc.

United States Court of Appeals, Seventh Circuit, 1989.
873 F.2d 985.

■ CUDAHY, CIRCUIT JUDGE.

---

[a] The majority irrelevantly cites to non-use in contexts other than "Broadcaster," which says nothing about its adoption of the mark in connection with this specific product.

Defendant-appellant Anheuser–Busch, Incorporated ("Busch") appeals a judgment declaring that "LA" is not a protectible trademark for a low alcohol beer introduced by Busch in 1984. The district court found that the initials LA are merely descriptive of low alcohol beer and have not acquired secondary meaning. Accordingly, the district court concluded that the use of LA (or "L.A.") by G. Heileman Brewing Company ("Heileman") and Miller Brewing Company ("Miller") on their own low alcohol beer labels does not constitute trademark infringement or unfair competition. We affirm.

I

While traveling in Australia in 1981, August A. Busch III, the president and chief executive officer of Anheuser–Busch, studied the production and marketing of low alcohol beer, a product that has experienced immense popularity in that country since its introduction in 1979. In Australia, the name "LA" has gained widespread recognition as signifying low or light alcohol beer on labels such as Tooth LA, South Australian LA, Courage LA, and Carling LA. After returning to the United States, Mr. Busch directed his company to commence research and development of a low alcohol beer. Internal memoranda during this early planning phase reveal that Anheuser–Busch aspired to preempt the low alcohol beer market and emulate the success enjoyed previously by Miller in capturing the low calorie beer segment with its "LITE" beer. Anheuser–Busch envisaged a new low alcohol product that would appeal to current lifestyle trends, which emphasize physical fitness and moderate drinking habits.

In an effort to select a brand name that could become the "bar call of the 80's," Busch retained the Interbrand Corporation to develop and test potential names for its new low alcohol beer. After researching the subject, Interbrand advised Busch that using "LA" as a stand-alone brand name "would not, in all likelihood, be protectible since it clearly and obviously stands for low alcohol, and as such is clearly an abbreviation of the generic descriptor." Trial Exhibit 12. Interbrand also warned Busch that low alcohol or LA would probably be referred to as a category descriptor for all low alcohol beers, including those produced by other brewing companies, thereby presenting a significant potential for confusion. Id. Therefore, Interbrand recommended a corporate source approach employing the name "LA from Anheuser–Busch," which Busch ultimately adopted.

On January 20, 1984, Anheuser–Busch issued a press release announcing its new product and informing the industry and the public that "LA from Anheuser–Busch" was a "light alcohol product." Trial Exhibit 22. In its efforts to develop an effective marketing strategy, Busch proceeded warily in pursuit of its dual objectives: to use LA as an arbitrary or suggestive term in order to attain trademark protection and, concurrently, to describe the unique low alcohol quality of its new beer to consumers without violating regulations that proscribed the advertising of reduced alcohol content. Busch orchestrated a publicity campaign in which it tacitly encouraged public relations and advertising agencies, as well as media representatives, to describe LA to consumers as low, less or light in alcohol.[a] Heileman, 676 F.Supp. at 1459. The district court found that, although Anheuser–Busch personnel equated LA with low alcohol in communications within the company and in advertising and point-of-sale materials, Busch subsequently sought to disclaim the initialism in various ways. For example, it deleted the periods from the letters; it claimed that the letters had no meaning; it modified its advertising message from "low alcohol" to "half the alcohol" and promoted the phrase "reduced alcohol" as the category descriptor for the new beer. Id. at 1458.

Meanwhile, the concept of low alcohol beer had been fermenting elsewhere in the beer industry. On March 7, 1984, the Stroh Brewery Company obtained BATF approval for two beer labels: SCHAEFER LA and OLD MILWAUKEE LA. Despite objections from Busch, Stroh then issued a press release announcing its plans to market SCHAEFER LA. Likewise, Heileman had been developing its own version of low alcohol beer since early 1982. Apprised of Busch's new LA product, of Stroh's announced plans to market SCHAEFER LA and of the BATF approval of both brewers' beer labels, Heileman announced on March 29, 1984, its plans to market low alcohol beer under labels containing its own house marks with "L.A." as a category descriptor—for example, CARLING BLACK LABEL L.A. and BLATZ L.A. Heileman, 676 F.Supp. at 1452. Miller was also on the LA campaign trail. In March of 1984, Miller began developing a low alcohol beer and sent its brand manager to Australia to study the established low alcohol beer market there. After consulting its retained advertising agency, Miller ultimately adopted "SHARP'S LA" as its brand name.

On March 16, 1984, Anheuser–Busch became the first user of the LA label in commerce by sending shipments of low alcohol beer to its wholesalers. After learning of Heileman's plans to begin using the LA label, Anheuser–Busch sent a cease and desist letter to Heileman, dated April 2, 1984, claiming exclusive trademark rights in the initials LA. Heileman responded on April 18 by filing this action to protect its right to use "L.A." with a Heileman house mark on its own low alcohol beer. The following day, Heileman commenced use of the "L.A." mark in commerce.

In its complaint, Heileman seeks a declaratory judgment that LA is descriptive and generic and that, therefore, its use does not constitute trademark infringement or unfair competition. In addition, Heileman requests injunctive relief permanently enjoining Busch from interfering or threatening to interfere with Heileman's use of the term "LA" to denominate low alcohol beer. Miller's complaint requests similar relief.

II

[The court found the case justiciable.]

[a] By the time of trial, Anheuser–Busch had spent approximately $27,000,000 advertising its LA beer.

III

A

The principal argument raised on appeal by Busch is that the district court misapplied the law in holding that the initials LA are merely descriptive and unprotectible. As we delineated in Miller Brewing Co. v. G. Heileman Brewing Co., 561 F.2d 75, 79 (7th Cir.1977), cert. denied, 434 U.S. 1025, 98 S.Ct. 751, 54 L.Ed.2d 772 (1978), a term for which trademark protection is claimed generally fits somewhere in the spectrum of classifications ranging from (1) generic or common descriptive and (2) merely descriptive to (3) suggestive and (4) arbitrary or fanciful. A generic or common descriptive term is one which is commonly used as the name or description of a kind of goods. It cannot become a trademark under any circumstances [, e.g., "light beer," "decaffeinated coffee"].... A merely descriptive term specifically describes a characteristic or ingredient of an article. It can, by acquiring a secondary meaning, i.e., becoming "distinctive of the applicant's goods" (15 U.S.C.A. § 1052(f)), become a valid trademark [, e.g., "bubbly champagne," "Auto Page"]. A suggestive term suggests rather than describes an ingredient or characteristic of the goods and requires the observer or listener to use imagination and perception to determine the nature of the goods. Such a term can be protected without proof of a secondary meaning [, e.g., "Tide," "Coppertone"]. An arbitrary or fanciful term enjoys the same full protection as a suggestive term but is far enough removed from the merely descriptive not to be vulnerable to possible attack as being merely descriptive rather than suggestive [, e.g., "Kodak," "Black & White" scotch]. Id. (citations omitted). In Walt–West Enterprises v. Gannett Co., 695 F.2d 1050 (7th Cir.1982), we provided further clarification:

> Properly understood, the so-called trademark spectrum reflects levels of judicial skepticism concerning whether the term actually serves the source denoting function which a mark is supposed to perform. Terms which are arbitrary, fanciful, or suggestive as applied to a given product or service are naturally understood by the consuming public as designations of origin: it is unlikely that such terms would be understood as anything else.... Descriptive terms, on the other hand, are ill-suited to serve as designations of origin, for such terms are naturally understood by the consuming public in their ordinary descriptive sense.

Id. at 1057. Thus, if LA is deemed generic, as Heileman and Miller assert, it is not entitled to trademark protection. Contrariwise, if LA is suggestive, as Busch contends, it is protectible. Finally, if LA is merely descriptive, as the court below determined, it is protectible only upon proof of secondary meaning.

It is unarguable that the phrase "low alcohol" is descriptive and unamenable to trademark protection. But whether the initials for this descriptive phrase should also be deemed descriptive presents a separate, yet related, issue. The law in this circuit is ostensibly incongruous and thus requires some clarification.

Anheuser–Busch argues that the district court misapplied the legal standard in determining the protectibility of initials and that, therefore, we should review the district court's decision de novo. Specifically, Busch adverts to the district court's observation in footnote 48 to its opinion that "initials are merely short forms of the words for which they stand and should be accorded the same degree of protection as those words." Heileman, 676 F.Supp. at 1493 n. 48. This formulation was presumably based on the language in National Conference of Bar Examiners v. Multistate Legal Studies, Inc., 692 F.2d 478, 488 (7th Cir.1982), cert. denied, 464 U.S. 814, 104 S.Ct. 69, 78 L.Ed.2d 83 (1983), that "[a]bbreviations for generic or common descriptive phrases must be treated similarly." In National Conference, this court reversed the district court's decision according trademark protection to the phrase "Multistate Bar Examination" and its initials "MBE." We reasoned that [u]nder settled trademark law if the components of a trade name are common descriptive terms, a combination of such terms retains that quality. We note further that [the fact that] plaintiffs also use the initials "MBE" to designate their test is of no consequence. Abbreviations for generic or common descriptive phrases must be treated similarly. Id. at 488 (citing FS Services, Inc. v. Custom Farm Services, Inc., 471 F.2d 671, 674 (7th Cir.1972)).

Busch argues vigorously against the concept that the initials of descriptive words are inherently descriptive. Instead, Busch contends that the "accepted rule" for determining whether initials are to be treated similarly to the descriptive or generic words that they represent is whether the letters have become generally recognized as descriptive or generic by the general public. According to Busch, National Conference misstates the law in this circuit by misreading the principle of FS Services, Inc. v. Custom Farm Services, Inc., 471 F.2d 671 (7th Cir.1972). In FS Services, we indeed stated that "abbreviations for generic terms where they are generally recognized must be treated similarly." 471 F.2d at 674 (emphasis supplied). There we concluded that the letters "FS have come to signify 'farm service' ... [which] are descriptive or generic terms." Id. Busch cites FS Services and numerous other authorities as support for the principle that initials for descriptive phrases are not ipso facto descriptive; rather, only if initials are generally recognized as signifying the corresponding descriptive phrases are they to be treated similarly for purposes of trademark protection. See, e.g., Modern Optics v. Univis Lens Co., 234 F.2d 504 (C.C.P.A.1956)("CV," initials for "continuous vision," not ipso facto unregistrable; "as a general rule, initials cannot be considered descriptive unless they have become so generally understood as representing descriptive words as to be accepted as substantially synonymous therewith").

Of course, we are aware that Busch's point is valid in principle: the ultimate test of descriptiveness is recognition by the consuming public. But this does not mean that the statement of the district court in footnote 48 is incorrect in any fundamental way. It is possible, although not likely, that the public might become acquainted with initials used in connection with a product without ever being aware that the initials were derived from, and stood for, a descriptive phrase or a generic name. This is conceivable, though rather improbable, because the connection between the initials and the descriptive words is in normal course very likely to become known. The process of identifying initials with the set of descriptive words from which they are derived is, after all, usually fairly simple. Ordinarily, no flight of imagination or keen logical insight is required. There is a natural assumption that initials do generally stand for something. All that needs to be done is to convert the next-to-obvious to the obvious by answering the inevitable question: What do the initials stand for?

As a rule, no very extensive or complicated process of education or indoctrination is required to convey that initials stand for descriptive words. The relatively straightforward answer to an evident question identifies the initials with the descriptive phrase from which they are derived. By contrast, the process whereby the same initials might acquire a secondary meaning pointing to the source of the product is often lengthy and expensive. As a practical matter, there must be a presumption that initials mean, or will soon come to mean, to the public the descriptive phrase from which they are derived. Although the matter is certainly not foreclosed, there is a heavy burden on a trademark claimant seeking to show an independent meaning of initials apart from the descriptive words which are their source. The imposition of such a burden is consistent with the policy of the trademark laws to guard against unjustified appropriation from the public domain of terms needed to perform a descriptive function. Such a burden is also consonant with the general rule that the claimant of trademark law protection bears the burden of establishing by a preponderance of the evidence that an unregistered mark is entitled to trademark status.

Thus, the district court's statement in footnote 48 to the Heileman opinion certainly does not miss the mark so fundamentally as to constitute legal error per se. Rather, it reflects the court's common sense view that, as a practical matter, initials do not usually differ significantly in their trademark role from the descriptive words that they represent.

B

Nor do we think, as Busch suggests, that the court's observation in footnote 48 tainted the district court's factual analysis and ultimate determination that LA is merely descriptive. To the contrary, the court acknowledges throughout its exhaustive opinion that the true test is one of consumer perception—how is LA perceived by the average prospective consumer? Accordingly, the court made specific factual findings that consumers actually understood LA as standing for and descriptive of low alcohol. See Heileman, 676 F.Supp. at 1459, 1460, 1487–88. These factual findings were based upon elaborate consumer surveys as well as Busch's own promotional advertising campaign and extensive media publicity.

Notwithstanding the parties' numerous objections to the consumer survey evidence submitted to the district court, we think the district court carefully and thoroughly sifted through this barrage of statistics and properly ascribed greater weight to those surveys warranting it.

In particular, we agree that the marketing studies conducted by Dr. Yoram Wind, a Professor of Marketing at the Wharton School of the University of Pennsylvania, were not entitled to great weight. In order to determine whether the initialism LA connotes (or denotes) low alcohol when displayed on a can of beer, Dr. Wind isolated the responses of those consumers who had never seen, heard of or tried LA beer. Of this sampling, comprised of those wholly unfamiliar with LA beer, only 4.9% associated LA with light, low or less alcohol, while 76.5% recognized LA as a brand name. When those respondents who had some prior exposure to LA were also taken into account, approximately 80% of the total pool surveyed, after being shown a can of "LA from Anheuser–Busch," identified Anheuser–Busch as the source of the beer. Based on these results, Dr. Wind concluded that LA does not connote low alcohol beer to consumers; rather, consumers perceive LA as a brand name.

We are persuaded by the view of the district court that Dr. Wind's primary focus on a thoroughly uninformed consumer audience renders his conclusions highly suspect. Whether initials stand in the public mind for the descriptive words from which they are derived is a question to be answered by looking at the public as it is—not as it might be in a total and unnatural state of disinformation. Consumer perception should be assessed by examining the average potential consumer in the context of the existing marketplace and exposed to the information currently available in the marketplace. This approach is supported by both law and logic. The opinions of the totally uninformed in an abstract, hypothetical context are of dubious relevance because they do not accurately reflect the perceptions of potential beer purchasers. Typically, someone must first be informed of the existence and nature of a product before he chooses to purchase or consume it. It is the perception of this somewhat informed audience that massive advertising is intended to impact. See Application of Abcor Development Corp., 588 F.2d at 814. In addition, evidence of the context in which a mark is used on labels, packages or in advertising material is probative in assessing the likely reaction of prospective purchasers to the mark. See id. It is normal for the public to learn through advertising, casual exposure or word-of-mouth that the initials of descriptive phrases stand for those descriptive phrases. To disregard these factors and focus on a hypothetical, unenlightened public is illogical and may lead to illusory results.

Further, Dr. Wind's finding that a majority of the total consumer audience perceived LA as a brand name is not determinative of the issue presented. Even though a term is prominently displayed and perceived by poll respondents as a brand name on a beer label, the term may nonetheless be classified as merely descriptive for trademark purposes.

For these reasons, we believe that the district court properly discounted the statistical evidence proffered by Busch and accorded greater weight to the survey results submitted by Heileman and Miller. These results demonstrated that a majority of prospective consumers recognize that LA, as applied to beer, stands for and describes low alcohol. Heileman, 676

F.Supp. at 1487–88. These consumer survey results were buttressed by the evidence of Busch's initial massive advertising campaign and media publicity which were likely to create a public perception that LA means light or low alcohol. See Anheuser–Busch, Inc. v. Stroh Brewery Co., 750 F.2d 631, 649 (Bright, J., dissenting)("I think it crucial to consider the initials 'LA' in the context of the Anheuser–Busch advertising and the probable course of development in the low alcohol beer segment."). Busch has failed to sufficiently counter this evidence and, therefore, has not met the burden of proof entitling it to trademark protection.

[The court goes on to acknowledge that a different conclusion was reached in the Eighth Circuit, which classified LA as suggestive and entitled to protection, Anheuser–Busch, Inc. v. Stroh Brewery Co., 750 F.2d 631 (1984).]

C

Since we do not think that the district court clearly erred in its factual determination that LA is merely descriptive, we further conclude that the district court did not err in denying the requests by Heileman and Miller for a declaratory judgment that LA is generic, as well as for permanent injunctive relief. Heileman and Miller claim that, because LA is generic as a matter of law, they are entitled to an injunction permanently enjoining Busch from interfering with Heileman and Miller's use of the LA name. Presumably, the concern is that the "merely descriptive" designation may allow Busch to later claim secondary meaning and again seek trademark protection. Otherwise we do not understand why the plaintiffs would link a determination of genericness to their request for a permanent injunction. Heileman and Miller contend somewhat cryptically in their briefs that a permanent injunction and a "generic" declaration are necessarily intertwined. If so, our independent conclusion that the district court did not abuse its discretion in denying permanent injunctive relief obviates the need for us to decide the genericness question. In any event, we think LA is probably not generic.

As we recently explained in Henri's Food Products Co., Inc. v. Tasty Snacks, Inc., 817 F.2d 1303, 1305–06 (7th Cir.1987),

> an adjective can be a generic term when that word is a part of a common descriptive name of a kind of goods. In order to be generic, however (as the word implies), the word in question must serve to denominate a type, a kind, a genus or a subcategory of goods.

The dispositive question is whether "LA" was

> a commonly used and commonly understood term prior to its association with the product or products at issue. And the dictionary, with its continuing catalogue of words arriving in and departing from common speech, is an especially appropriate source of evidence about the meaning attached by a linguistic group to a particular [ ] symbol.

Gimix, Inc. v. JS & A Group, Inc., 699 F.2d 901, 905 (7th Cir.1983). With respect to this issue, the district court cited two historical facts which, in its view, precluded a finding of genericness: low alcohol beer was a new arrival on the beer market in this country and, prior to April 27, 1984, BATF regulations prohibited references to low alcohol content in the advertising or labeling of beer. Consequently, consumer surveys illustrated that many consumers evidently were unaware of low alcohol beer at all and, as the district court found, "it was not surprising that the poll takers found that these consumers, as well as those with only recent exposure to the product, had not formed a consensus that 'LA' or 'low alcohol' is the name of a distinctive type of beer." Heileman, 676 F.Supp. at 1490. In addition, the district court noted that there was no evidence that either "LA" or "low alcohol" is defined by any lexicon as a genus of beer. Id. at n. 45. Based upon these findings, it is certainly reasonable to conclude that LA is not generic. Cf. Miller Brewing Co. v. G. Heileman Brewing Co., 561 F.2d 75, 80 ("light" classified as generic where it had been widely used in the beer industry before Miller began using "LITE" and was defined in the dictionary as a characteristic of beer).

\* \* \* \* \*

In the present case, the initials LA were used descriptively (or possibly generically) in Australia for "low alcohol." They were removed from that context to be brought back by Mr. Busch for use in the United States. Although it is conceivable that they would not fulfill a descriptive function here as well, it is the more plausible assumption that they would.

It would be unusual trademark policy to accord exclusive rights and trademark protection to Anheuser–Busch, which appropriated the LA appellation from Australia and then used it in a descriptive manner to preempt the low alcohol beer market in this country. The trademark laws . . . are designed to protect names selected by a company and promoted with the intent of indicating the ownership and source of the goods. It is inconsistent with the objectives of the trademark laws to suggest that the protection of those laws should be extended to cases in which a company attempts to arrogate for business-promotional reasons a mark that is essentially descriptive. Anheuser–Busch, Inc. v. Stroh Brewery Co., 750 F.2d at 651 (Bright, J., dissenting). The determination by the district court that LA is merely descriptive and unprotectible is supported by the record and consistent with sound policy. Therefore, the decision of the district court is affirmed.

## Two Pesos, Inc. v. Taco Cabana, Inc.

Supreme Court of the United States, 1992.
505 U.S. 763, 112 S.Ct. 2753, 120 L.Ed.2d 615.

■ JUSTICE WHITE delivered the opinion of the Court.

The issue in this case is whether the trade dress of a restaurant may be protected under § 43(a) of the Trademark Act of 1946 (Lanham Act), 15 U.S.C. § 1125(a), based on a finding of inherent distinctiveness, without proof that the trade dress has secondary meaning.

I

In 1987, Taco Cabana sued Two Pesos in the United States District Court for the Southern District of Texas for trade dress infringement under § 43(a) of the Lanham Act, 15 U.S.C. § 1125(a)(1982 ed.). The case was tried to a jury, which was instructed to return its verdict in the form of answers to five questions propounded by the trial judge. The jury's answers were: Taco Cabana has a trade dress; taken as a whole, the trade dress is nonfunctional; the trade dress is inherently distinctive;[a] the trade dress has not acquired a secondary meaning[b] in the Texas market; and the alleged infringement creates a likelihood of confusion on the part of ordinary customers as to the source or association of the restaurant's goods or services. Because, as the jury was told, Taco Cabana's trade dress was protected if it either was inherently distinctive or had acquired a secondary meaning, judgment was entered awarding damages to Taco Cabana.

The Court of Appeals ruled that the instructions adequately stated the applicable law and that the evidence supported the jury's findings. In particular, the Court of Appeals rejected petitioner's argument that a finding of no secondary meaning contradicted a finding of inherent distinctiveness.

In so holding, the court below followed precedent in the Fifth Circuit. Chevron Chemical Co. v. Voluntary Purchasing Groups, Inc., 659 F.2d 695 (C.A.5 1981). We granted certiorari to resolve the conflict among the Courts of Appeals on the question whether trade dress which is inherently distinctive is protectable under § 43(a) without a showing that it has acquired secondary meaning. 502 U.S. ___ (1992). We find that it is, and we therefore affirm.

II

The Lanham Act[c] was intended to make "actionable the deceptive and misleading use of marks" and "to protect persons engaged in . . . commerce against unfair competition." § 45, § 15 U.S.C. 1127. Section 43(a) "prohibits a broader range of practices than does § 32," which applies to registered marks, Inwood Laboratories, Inc. v. Ives Laboratories, Inc., 456 U.S. 844, 858 (1982), but it is common ground that § 43(a) protects qualifying unregistered trademarks and that the general principles qualifying a mark for registration under § 2 of the Lanham Act are for the most part

---

[a] The instructions were that to be found inherently distinctive, the trade dress must not be descriptive.

[b] Secondary meaning is used generally to indicate that a mark or dress "has come through use to be uniquely associated with a specific source." Restatement (Third) of Unfair Competition § 13, Comment e (Tent. Draft No. 2, Mar. 23, 1990). "To establish secondary meaning, a manufacturer must show that, in the minds of the public, the primary significance of a product feature or term is to identify the source of the product rather than the product itself." Inwood Laboratories, Inc. v. Ives Laboratories, Inc., 456 U.S. 844, 851, n. 11 (1982).

[c] The Lanham Act, including the provisions at issue here, has been substantially amended since the present suit was brought. See Trademark Law Revision Act of 1988, 15 U.S.C.A. § 1121.

applicable in determining whether an unregistered mark is entitled to protection under § 43(a).

Marks which are merely descriptive of a product are not inherently distinctive. When used to describe a product, they do not inherently identify a particular source, and hence cannot be protected. However, descriptive marks may acquire the distinctiveness which will allow them to be protected under the Act. Section 2 of the Lanham Act provides that a descriptive mark that otherwise could not be registered under the Act may be registered if it "has become distinctive of the applicant's goods in commerce." §§ 2(e), (f), 15 U.S.C. §§ 1052(e), (f). This acquired distinctiveness is generally called "secondary meaning." The concept of secondary meaning has been applied to actions under § 43(a).

The general rule regarding distinctiveness is clear: an identifying mark is distinctive and capable of being protected if it either (1) is inherently distinctive or (2) has acquired distinctiveness through secondary meaning. Restatement (Third) of Unfair Competition, § 13, pp. 37–38, and Comment a (Tent. Draft No. 2, Mar. 23, 1990). It is also clear that eligibility for protection under § 43(a) depends on nonfunctionality. It is, of course, also undisputed that liability under § 43(a) requires proof of the likelihood of confusion.

Recognizing that a general requirement of secondary meaning imposes "an unfair prospect of theft [or] financial loss" on the developer of fanciful or arbitrary trade dress at the outset of its use, petitioner suggests that such trade dress should receive limited protection without proof of secondary meaning. Petitioner argues that such protection should be only temporary and subject to defeasance when over time the dress has failed to acquire a secondary meaning. This approach is vulnerable for the reasons given by the Court of Appeals. If temporary protection is available from the earliest use of the trade dress, it must be because it is neither functional nor descriptive but an inherently distinctive dress that is capable of identifying a particular source of the product. Such a trade dress, or mark, is not subject to copying by concerns that have an equal opportunity to choose their own inherently distinctive trade dress. To terminate protection for failure to gain secondary meaning over some unspecified time could not be based on the failure of the dress to retain its fanciful, arbitrary, or suggestive nature, but on the failure of the user of the dress to be successful enough in the marketplace. This is not a valid basis to find a dress or mark ineligible for protection. The user of such a trade dress should be able to maintain what competitive position it has and continue to seek wider identification among potential customers.

The Fifth Circuit was quite right in Chevron, and in this case, to inquire whether trade dress for which protection is claimed under § 43(a) is inherently distinctive. If it is, it is capable of identifying products or services as coming from a specific source and secondary meaning is not required. This is the rule generally applicable to trademark, and the protection of trademarks and trade dress under § 43(a) serves the same statutory purpose of preventing deception and unfair competition. There is no persuasive reason to apply different analysis to the two.

It would be a different matter if there were textual basis in § 43(a) for treating inherently distinctive verbal or symbolic trademarks differently from inherently distinctive trade dress. But there is none. The section does not mention trademarks or trade dress, whether they be called generic, descriptive, suggestive, arbitrary, fanciful, or functional. Nor does the concept of secondary meaning appear in the text of § 43(a). Where secondary meaning does appear in the statute, 15 U.S.C.A. § 1052 (1982 ed.), it is a requirement that applies only to merely descriptive marks and not to inherently distinctive ones. We see no basis for requiring secondary meaning for inherently distinctive trade dress protection under § 43(a) but not for other distinctive words, symbols, or devices capable of identifying a producer's product.

Engrafting onto § 43(a) a requirement of secondary meaning for inherently distinctive trade dress also would undermine the purposes of the Lanham Act. Protection of trade dress, no less than of trademarks, serves the Act's purpose to "secure to the owner of the mark the goodwill of his business and to protect the ability of consumers to distinguish among competing producers. National protection of trademarks is desirable, Congress concluded, because trademarks foster competition and the maintenance of quality by securing to the producer the benefits of good reputation." Park 'N Fly, 469 U.S. 189, 198 (1985), citing S. Rep. No. 1333, 79th Cong., 2d Sess., 3–5 (1946)(citations omitted). By making more difficult the identification of a producer with its product, a secondary meaning requirement for a nondescriptive trade dress would hinder improving or maintaining the producer's competitive position.

Suggestions that under the Fifth Circuit's law, the initial user of any shape or design would cut off competition from products of like design and shape are not persuasive. Only nonfunctional, distinctive trade dress is protected under § 43(a). The Fifth Circuit holds that a design is legally functional, and thus unprotectable, if it is one of a limited number of equally efficient options available to competitors and free competition would be unduly hindered by according the design trademark protection. This serves to assure that competition will not be stifled by the exhaustion of a limited number of trade dresses.

On the other hand, adding a secondary meaning requirement could have anticompetitive effects, creating particular burdens on the start-up of small companies. It would present special difficulties for a business, such as respondent, that seeks to start a new product in a limited area and then expand into new markets. Denying protection for inherently distinctive nonfunctional trade dress until after secondary meaning has been established would allow a competitor, which has not adopted a distinctive trade dress of its own, to appropriate the originator's dress in other markets and to deter the originator from expanding into and competing in these areas.

As noted above, petitioner concedes that protecting an inherently distinctive trade dress from its inception may be critical to new entrants to the market and that withholding protection until secondary meaning has been established would be contrary to the goals of the Lanham Act. Petitioner specifically suggests, however, that the solution is to dispense with the requirement of secondary meaning for a reasonable, but brief period at the outset of the use of a trade dress. If § 43(a) does not require secondary meaning at the outset of a business' adoption of trade dress, there is no basis in the statute to support the suggestion that such a requirement comes into being after some unspecified time.

## Qualitex Co. v. Jacobson Products Co., Inc.

Supreme Court of the United States, 1995.
514 U.S. 159, 115 S.Ct. 1300, 131 L.Ed.2d 248.

■ JUSTICE BREYER delivered the opinion of the Court.

The question in this case is whether the Lanham Trademark Act of 1946 permits the registration of a trademark that consists, purely and simply, of a color. We conclude that, sometimes, a color will meet ordinary legal trademark requirements. And, when it does so, no special legal rule prevents color alone from serving as a trademark.

I

The case before us grows out of petitioner Qualitex Company's use (since the 1950's) of a special shade of green-gold color on the pads that it makes and sells to dry cleaning firms for use on dry cleaning presses. In 1989 respondent Jacobson Products (a Qualitex rival) began to sell its own press pads to dry cleaning firms; and it colored those pads a similar green-gold. In 1991 Qualitex registered the special green-gold color on press pads with the Patent and Trademark Office as a trademark. Registration No. 1,633,711 (Feb. 5, 1991). Qualitex subsequently added a trademark infringement count, 15 U.S.C.A. § 1114(1), to an unfair competition claim, § 1125(a), in a lawsuit it had already filed challenging Jacobson's use of the green-gold color.

Qualitex won the lawsuit in the District Court. 21 U.S.P.Q. 2d (BNA) 1457 (C.D.Cal.1991). But, the Court of Appeals for the Ninth Circuit set aside the judgment in Qualitex's favor on the trademark infringement claim because, in that Circuit's view, the Lanham Act does not permit Qualitex, or anyone else, to register "color alone" as a trademark. 13 F.3d 1297, 1300, 1302 (1994).

The courts of appeals have differed as to whether or not the law recognizes the use of color alone as a trademark. Compare NutraSweet Co. v. Stadt Corp., 917 F.2d 1024, 1028 (C.A.7 1990)(absolute prohibition against protection of color alone), with In re Owens–Corning Fiberglas Corp., 774 F.2d 1116, 1128 (C.A.Fed.1985)(allowing registration of color pink for fiberglass insulation), and Master Distributors, Inc. v. Pako Corp., 986 F.2d 219, 224 (C.A.8 1993)(declining to establish per se prohibition against protecting color alone as a trademark). Therefore, this Court granted certiorari. 512 U.S. (1994). We now hold that there is no rule absolutely barring the use of color alone, and we reverse the judgment of the Ninth Circuit.

II

The Lanham Act gives a seller or producer the exclusive right to "register" a trademark, § 1052, and to prevent his or her competitors from using that trademark, § 1114(1). Both the language of the Act and the basic underlying principles of trademark law would seem to include color within the universe of things that can qualify as a trademark. The language of the Lanham Act describes that universe in the broadest of terms. It says that trademarks "include any word, name, symbol, or device, or any combination thereof." § 1127. Since human beings might use as a "symbol" or "device" almost anything at all that is capable of carrying meaning, this language, read literally, is not restrictive. The courts and the Patent and Trademark Office have authorized for use as a mark a particular shape (of a Coca–Cola bottle), a particular sound (of NBC's three chimes), and even a particular scent (of plumeria blossoms on sewing thread). In re Clarke, 17 U.S.P.Q.2d (BNA) 1238, 1240 (TTAB 1990). If a shape, a sound, and a fragrance can act as symbols why, one might ask, can a color not do the same?

A color is also capable of satisfying the more important part of the statutory definition of a trademark, which requires that a person "use" or "intend to use" the mark

> "to identify and distinguish his or her goods, including a unique product, from those manufactured or sold by others and to indicate the source of the goods, even if that source is unknown." § 1127.

True, a product's color is unlike "fanciful," "arbitrary," or "suggestive" words or designs, which almost automatically tell a customer that they refer to a brand. Abercrombie & Fitch Co. v. Hunting World, Inc., 537 F.2d 4, 9–10 (C.A.2 1976)(Friendly, J.). The imaginary word "Suntost," or the words "Suntost Marmalade," on a jar of orange jam immediately would signal a brand or a product "source"; the jam's orange color does not do so. But, over time, customers may come to treat a particular color on a product or its packaging (say, a color that in context seems unusual, such as pink on a firm's insulating material or red on the head of a large industrial bolt) as signifying a brand. And, if so, that color would have come to identify and distinguish the goods—i.e. to "indicate" their "source"—much in the way that descriptive words on a product (say, "Trim" on nail clippers or "Car-Freshner" on deodorizer) can come to indicate a product's origin. See, e.g., J. Wiss & Sons Co. v. W. E. Bassett Co., 462 F.2d 567, 569 (1972); Car-Freshner Corp. v. Turtle Wax, Inc., 268 F.Supp. 162, 164 (S.D.N.Y.1967). In this circumstance, trademark law says that the word (e.g., "Trim"), although not inherently distinctive, has developed "secondary meaning." See Inwood Laboratories, Inc. v. Ives Laboratories, Inc., 456 U.S. 844, 851, n.11 (1982)("secondary meaning" is acquired when "in the minds of the public, the primary significance of a product feature ... is to identify the source of the product rather than the product itself."). Again, one might ask, if trademark law permits a descriptive word with secondary meaning to act as a mark, why would it not permit a color, under similar circumstances, to do the same?

We cannot find in the basic objectives of trademark law any obvious theoretical objection to the use of color alone as a trademark, where that color has attained "secondary meaning" and therefore identifies and distinguishes a particular brand (and thus indicates its "source"). In principle, trademark law, by preventing others from copying a source-identifying mark, "reduces the customer's costs of shopping and making purchasing decisions," 1 J. McCarthy, McCarthy on Trademarks and Unfair Competition § 2.01[2], p. 2–3 (3d ed. 1994)(hereinafter McCarthy), for it quickly and easily assures a potential customer that this item—the item with this mark—is made by the same producer as other similarly marked items that he or she liked (or disliked) in the past. At the same time, the law helps assure a producer that it (and not an imitating competitor) will reap the financial, reputation-related rewards associated with a desirable product. The law thereby "encourages the production of quality products," *ibid.*, and simultaneously discourages those who hope to sell inferior products by capitalizing on a consumer's inability quickly to evaluate the quality of an item offered for sale. It is the source-distinguishing ability of a mark—not its ontological status as color, shape, fragrance, word, or sign—that permits it to serve these basic purposes. See Landes & Posner, Trademark Law: An Economic Perspective, 30 J. Law & Econ. 265, 290 (1987). And, for that reason, it is difficult to find, in basic trademark objectives, a reason to disqualify absolutely the use of a color as a mark.

Neither can we find a principled objection to the use of color as a mark in the important "functionality" doctrine of trademark law. The functionality doctrine prevents trademark law, which seeks to promote competition by protecting a firm's reputation, from instead inhibiting legitimate competition by allowing a producer to control a useful product feature. It is the province of patent law, not trademark law, to encourage invention by granting inventors a monopoly over new product designs or functions for a limited time, 35 U.S.C.A. §§ 154, 173, after which competitors are free to use the innovation. If a product's functional features could be used as trademarks, however, a monopoly over such features could be obtained without regard to whether they qualify as patents and could be extended forever (because trademarks may be renewed in perpetuity). See Kellogg Co. v. National Biscuit Co., 305 U.S. 111, 119–120 (1938)(Brandeis, J.); *Inwood Laboratories, Inc.*, at 863 (White, J., concurring in result)("A functional characteristic is 'an important ingredient in the commercial success of the product,' and, after expiration of a patent, it is no more the property of the originator than the product itself.")(citation omitted). Functionality doctrine therefore would require, to take an imaginary example, that even if customers have come to identify the special illumination-enhancing shape of a new patented light bulb with a particular manufacturer, the manufacturer may not use that shape as a trademark, for doing so, after the patent had expired, would impede competition—not by protecting the reputation of the original bulb maker, but by frustrating competitors' legitimate efforts to produce an equivalent illumination-enhancing bulb. See, e.g., *Kellogg Co.*, at 119–120 (trademark law cannot be used to extend monopoly over "pillow" shape of shredded wheat biscuit after the patent for that shape had expired). This Court consequently has explained that, "in general terms, a product feature is functional," and cannot serve as a trademark, "if it is essential to the use or purpose of the article or if it affects the cost or quality of the article," that is, if exclusive use of the feature would put competitors at a significant non-reputation-related disadvantage. *Inwood Laboratories, Inc.*, 456 U.S. at 850, n.10. Although sometimes color plays an important role (unrelated to source identification) in making a product more desirable, sometimes it does not. And, this latter fact—the fact that sometimes color is not essential to a product's use or purpose and does not affect cost or quality—indicates that the doctrine of "functionality" does not create an absolute bar to the use of color alone as a mark. See *Owens–Corning*, 774 F.2d at 1123 (pink color of insulation in wall "performs no non-trademark function").

It would seem, then, that color alone, at least sometimes, can meet the basic legal requirements for use as a trademark. It can act as a symbol that distinguishes a firm's goods and identifies their source, without serving any other significant function. See U.S. Dept. of Commerce, Patent and Trademark Office, Trademark Manual of Examining Procedure § 1202.04(e), p. 1202–13 (2d ed. May, 1993)(hereinafter PTO Manual) (approving trademark registration of color alone where it "has become distinctive of the applicant's goods in commerce," provided that "there is [no] competitive need for colors to remain available in the industry" and the color is not "functional"); see also 1 McCarthy §§ 3.01[1], 7.26 ("requirements for qualification of a word or symbol as a trademark" are that it be (1) a "symbol," (2) "used ... as a mark," (3) "to identify and distinguish the seller's goods from goods made or sold by others," but that it not be "functional"). Indeed, the District Court, in this case, entered findings (accepted by the Ninth Circuit) that show Qualitex's green-gold press pad color has met these requirements. The green-gold color acts as a symbol. Having developed secondary meaning (for customers identified the green-gold color as Qualitex's), it identifies the press pads' source. And, the green-gold color serves no other function. (Although it is important to use some color on press pads to avoid noticeable stains, the court found "no competitive need in the press pad industry for the green-gold color, since other colors are equally usable." 21 U.S.P.Q.2d (BNA) at 1460.) Accordingly, unless there is some special reason that convincingly militates against the use of color alone as a trademark, trademark law would protect Qualitex's use of the green-gold color on its press pads.

III

Respondent Jacobson Products says that there are four special reasons why the law should forbid the use of color alone as a trademark. We shall explain, in turn, why we, ultimately, find them unpersuasive.

First, Jacobson says that, if the law permits the use of color as a trademark, it will produce uncertainty and unresolvable court disputes about what shades of a color a competitor may lawfully use. Because lighting (morning sun, twilight mist) will affect perceptions of protected color, competitors and courts will suffer from "shade confusion" as they try to decide whether use of a similar color on a similar product does, or does not, confuse customers and thereby infringe a trademark. Jacobson adds that the "shade confusion" problem is "more difficult" and "far different from" the "determination of the similarity of words or symbols."

We do not believe, however, that color, in this respect, is special. Courts traditionally decide quite difficult questions about whether two words or phrases or symbols are sufficiently similar, in context, to confuse buyers. They have had to compare, for example, such words as "Bonamine" and "Dramamine" (motion-sickness remedies); "Huggies" and "Dougies" (diapers); "Cheracol" and "Syrocol" (cough syrup); "Cyclone" and "Tornado" (wire fences); and "Mattres" and "1–800–Mattres" (mattress franchisor telephone numbers). See, e.g., G. D. Searle & Co. v. Chas. Pfizer & Co., 265 F.2d 385, 389 (C.A.7 1959); Kimberly–Clark Corp. v. H. Douglas Enterprises, Ltd., 774 F.2d 1144, 1146–1147 (C.A.Fed.1985); Upjohn Co. v. Schwartz, 246 F.2d 254, 262 (C.A.2 1957); Hancock v. American Steel & Wire Co., 203 F.2d 737, 740–741 (Pat. 1953); Dial–A–Mattress Franchise Corp. v. Page, 880 F.2d 675, 678 (C.A.2 1989). Legal standards exist to guide courts in making such comparisons. See, e.g., 2 McCarthy § 15.08; 1 McCarthy §§ 11.24–11.25 ("Strong" marks, with greater secondary meaning, receive broader protection than "weak" marks). We do not see why courts could not apply those standards to a color, replicating, if necessary, lighting conditions under which a colored product is normally sold. See Ebert, Trademark Protection in Color: Do It By the Numbers!, 84 T. M. Rep. 379, 405 (1994). Indeed, courts already have done so in cases where a trademark consists of a color plus a design, i.e., a colored symbol such as a gold stripe (around a sewer pipe), a yellow strand of wire rope, or a "brilliant yellow" band (on ampules). See, e.g., Youngstown Sheet & Tube Co. v. Tallman Conduit Co., 149 U.S.P.Q. (BNA) 656, 657 (TTAB 1966); Amsted Industries, Inc. v. West Coast Wire Rope & Rigging Inc., 2 U.S.P.Q.2d (BNA) 1755, 1760 (TTAB 1987); In re Hodes–Lange Corp., 167 U.S.P.Q. (BNA) 255, 256 (TTAB 1970).

Second, Jacobson argues, as have others, that colors are in limited supply. See, e.g., *NutraSweet Co.*, 917 F.2d at 1028; Campbell Soup Co. v. Armour & Co., 175 F.2d 795, 798 (C.A.3 1949). Jacobson claims that, if one of many competitors can appropriate a particular color for use as a trademark, and each competitor then tries to do the same, the supply of colors will soon be depleted. Put in its strongest form, this argument would concede that "hundreds of color pigments are manufactured and thousands of colors can be obtained by mixing." L. Cheskin, Colors: What They Can Do For You 47 (1947). But, it would add that, in the context of a particular product, only some colors are usable. By the time one discards colors that, say, for reasons of customer appeal, are not usable, and adds the shades that competitors cannot use lest they risk infringing a similar, registered shade, then one is left with only a handful of possible colors. And, under these circumstances, to permit one, or a few, producers to use colors as trademarks will "deplete" the supply of usable colors to the point where a competitor's inability to find a suitable color will put that competitor at a significant disadvantage.

This argument is unpersuasive, however, largely because it relies on an occasional problem to justify a blanket prohibition. When a color serves as a mark, normally alternative colors will likely be available for similar use by others. See, e.g., *Owens–Corning*, 774 F.2d at 1121 (pink insulation). Moreover, if that is not so—if a "color depletion" or "color scarcity" problem does arise—the trademark doctrine of "functionality" normally would seem available to prevent the anticompetitive consequences that Jacobson's argument posits, thereby minimizing that argument's practical force. The functionality doctrine, as we have said, forbids the use of a product's feature as a trademark where doing so will put a competitor at a significant disadvantage because the feature is "essential to the use or purpose of the article" or "affects [its] cost or quality." *Inwood Laboratories, Inc.*, 456 U.S. at 850, n.10. The functionality doctrine thus protects competitors against a disadvantage (unrelated to recognition or reputation) that trademark protection might otherwise impose, namely their inability reasonably to replicate important non-reputation-related product features. For example, this Court has written that competitors might be free to copy the color of a medical pill where that color serves to identify the kind of medication (e.g., a type of blood medicine) in addition to its source. See *id.*, at 853, 858, n.20 ("Some patients commingle medications in a container and rely on color to differentiate one from another"); see also J. Ginsburg, D. Goldberg, & A. Greenbaum, Trademark and Unfair Competition Law 194–195 (1991)(noting that drug color cases "have more to do with public health policy" regarding generic drug substitution "than with trademark law"). And, the federal courts have demonstrated that they can apply this doctrine in a careful and reasoned manner, with sensitivity to the effect on competition. Although we need not comment on the merits of specific cases, we note that lower courts have permitted competitors to copy the green color of farm machinery (because customers wanted their farm equipment to match) and have barred the use of black as a trademark on outboard boat motors (because black has the special functional attributes of decreasing the apparent size of the motor and ensuring compatibility with many different boat colors). See Deere & Co. v. Farmhand, Inc., 560 F.Supp. 85, 98 (S.D.Iowa 1982), aff'd, 721 F.2d 253 (C.A.8 1983); Brunswick Corp. v. British Seagull Ltd., 35 F.3d 1527, 1532 (C.A.Fed.1994), cert. pending, No. 94–1075; see also Nor–Am Chemical v. O. M. Scott & Sons Co., 4 U.S.P.Q.2d (BNA) 1316, 1320 (E.D.Pa.1987)(blue color of fertilizer held functional because it indicated the presence of nitrogen). The Restatement (Third) of Unfair Competition adds that, if a design's "aesthetic value" lies in its ability to "confer a significant benefit that cannot practically be duplicated by the use of alternative designs," then the design is "functional." Restatement (Third) of Unfair Competition § 17, Comment c, p. 175–176 (1995). The "ultimate test of aesthetic functionality," it explains, "is whether the recognition of trademark rights would significantly hinder competition." *Id.*, at 176.

The upshot is that, where a color serves a significant nontrademark function—whether to distinguish a heart pill from a digestive medicine or to satisfy the "noble instinct for giving the right touch of beauty to common and necessary things," G. K. Chesterton, Simplicity and Tolstoy 61 (1912)—courts will examine whether its use as a mark would permit one competitor (or a group) to interfere with legitimate (nontrademark-related) competition through actual or potential exclusive use of an important product ingredient. That examination should not discourage firms from creating aesthetically pleasing mark designs, for it is open to their competitors to do the same. See, e.g., W. T. Rogers [Co. v. Keene, 778 F.2d 334 (C.A.7 1985)] (Posner, J.). But, ordinarily, it should prevent the anticompetitive consequences of Jacobson's hypothetical "color depletion" argument, when, and if, the circumstances of a particular case threaten "color depletion."

Third, Jacobson points to many older cases—including Supreme Court cases—in support of its position. In 1878, this Court described the common-law definition of trademark rather broadly to "consist of a name, symbol, figure, letter, form, or device, if adopted and used by a manufacturer or merchant in order to designate the goods he manufactures or sells to distinguish the same from those manufactured or sold by another." McLean v. Fleming, 96 U.S. 245, 254 (1877). Yet, in interpreting the Trademark Acts of 1881 and 1905, 21 Stat. 502, 33 Stat. 724, which retained that common-law definition, the Court questioned "whether mere color can constitute a valid trade-mark," A. Leschen & Sons Rope Co. v. Broderick & Bascom Rope Co., 201 U.S. 166, 171 (1906), and suggested that the "product including the coloring matter is free to all who make it." Coca–Cola Co. v. Koke Co. of America, 254 U.S. 143, 147 (1920). Even though these statements amounted to dicta, lower courts interpreted them as forbidding protection for color alone. See, e.g., *Campbell Soup Co.*, 175 F.2d at 798, and n.9; Life Savers Corp. v. Curtiss Candy Co., 182 F.2d 4, 9 (C.A.7 1950)(quoting *Campbell Soup*).

These Supreme Court cases, however, interpreted trademark law as it existed before 1946, when Congress enacted the Lanham Act. The Lanham Act significantly changed and liberalized the common law to "dispense with mere technical prohibitions," S. Rep. No. 1333, 79th Cong., 2d Sess., 3 (1946), most notably, by permitting trademark registration of descriptive words (say, "U–Build–It" model airplanes) where they had acquired "secondary meaning." See *Abercrombie & Fitch Co.*, 537 F.2d at 9 (Friendly, J.). The Lanham Act extended protection to descriptive marks by making clear that (with certain explicit exceptions not relevant here),

> "nothing . . . shall prevent the registration of a mark used by the applicant which has become distinctive of the applicant's goods in commerce." § 1052(f).

This language permits an ordinary word, normally used for a nontrademark purpose (e.g., description), to act as a trademark where it has gained "secondary meaning." Its logic would appear to apply to color as well. Indeed, in 1985, the Federal Circuit considered the significance of the Lanham Act's changes as they related to color and held that trademark protection for color was consistent with the

> "jurisprudence under the Lanham Act developed in accordance with the statutory principle that if a mark is capable of being or becoming distinctive of [the] applicant's goods in commerce, then it is capable of serving as a trademark." *Owens–Corning*, 774 F.2d at 1120 .

In 1988 Congress amended the Lanham Act, revising portions of the definitional language, but left unchanged the language here relevant. § 1127. It enacted these amendments against the following background: (1) the Federal Circuit had decided *Owens–Corning*; (2) the Patent and Trademark Office had adopted a clear policy (which it still maintains) permitting registration of color as a trademark, see PTO Manual § 1202.04(e)(at p. 1200–12 of the January 1986 edition and p. 1202–13 of the May 1993 edition); and (3) the Trademark Commission had written a report, which recommended that "the terms 'symbol, or device' ... not be deleted or narrowed to preclude registration of such things as a color, shape, smell, sound, or configuration which functions as a mark," The United States Trademark Association Trademark Review Commission Report and Recommendations to USTA President and Board of Directors, 77 T. M. Rep. 375, 421 (1987)(hereinafter Trademark Commission); see also 133 Cong. Rec. 32812 (1987)(statement of Sen. DeConcini)("The bill I am introducing today is based on the Commission's report and recommendations."). This background strongly suggests that the language, "any word, name, symbol, or device," § 1127, had come to include color. And, when it amended the statute, Congress retained these terms. Indeed, the Senate Report accompanying the Lanham Act revision explicitly referred to this background understanding, in saying that the "revised definition intentionally retains ... the words 'symbol or device' so as not to preclude the registration of colors, shapes, sounds or configurations where they function as trademarks." S. Rep. No. 100–515, at 44. (In addition, the statute retained language providing that "no trademark by which the goods of the applicant may be distinguished from the goods of others shall be refused registration ... on account of its nature") (except for certain specified reasons not relevant here). § 1052.

This history undercuts the authority of the precedent on which Jacobson relies. Much of the pre–1985 case law rested on statements in Supreme Court opinions that interpreted pre-Lanham Act trademark law and were not directly related to the holdings in those cases. Moreover, we believe the Federal Circuit was right in 1985 when it found that the 1946 Lanham Act embodied crucial legal changes that liberalized the law to permit the use of color alone as a trademark (under appropriate circumstances). At a minimum, the Lanham Act's changes left the courts free to reevaluate the preexisting legal precedent which had absolutely forbidden the use of color alone as a trademark. Finally, when Congress re-enacted the terms "word, name, symbol, or device" in 1988, it did so against a legal background in which those terms had come to include color, and its statutory revision embraced that understanding.

Fourth, Jacobson argues that there is no need to permit color alone to function as a trademark because a firm already may use color as part of a trademark, say, as a colored circle or colored letter or colored word, and may rely upon "trade dress" protection, under § 43(a) of the Lanham Act, if a competitor copies its color and thereby causes consumer confusion regarding the overall appearance of the competing products or their packaging, see § 1125(a). The first part of this argument begs the question. One can understand why a firm might find it difficult to place a usable symbol or word on a product (say, a large industrial bolt that customers normally see from a distance); and, in such instances, a firm might want to use color, pure and simple, instead of color as part of a design. Neither is the second portion of the argument convincing. Trademark law helps the holder of a mark in many ways that "trade dress" protection does not. See § 1124 (ability to prevent importation of confusingly similar goods); § 1072 (constructive notice of ownership); § 1065 (incontestible status); § 1057(b)(prima facie evidence of validity and ownership). Thus, one can easily find reasons why the law might provide trademark protection in addition to trade dress protection.

### IV

Having determined that a color may sometimes meet the basic legal requirements for use as a trademark and that respondent Jacobson's arguments do not justify a special legal rule preventing color alone from serving as a trademark (and, in light of the District Court's here undisputed findings that Qualitex's use of the green-gold color on its press pads meets the basic trademark requirements), we conclude that the Ninth Circuit erred in barring Qualitex's use of color as a trademark. For these reasons, the judgment of the Ninth Circuit is

Reversed.

## TrafFix Devices, Inc. v. Marketing Displays, Inc.

Supreme Court of the United States, 2001.
532 U.S. 23, 121 S.Ct. 1255, 149 L.Ed.2d 164.

■ KENNEDY, J. delivered the opinion of the Court.

Temporary road signs with warnings like "Road Work Ahead" or "Left Shoulder Closed" must withstand strong gusts of wind. An inventor named Robert Sarkisian obtained two utility patents for a mechanism built upon two springs (the dual-spring design) to keep these and other outdoor signs upright despite adverse wind conditions. The holder of the now-expired Sarkisian patents, respondent Marketing Displays, Inc. (MDI), established a successful business in the manufacture and sale of sign stands incorporating the patented feature. MDI's stands for road signs were recognizable to buyers and users (it says) because the dual-spring design was visible near the base of the sign.

This litigation followed after the patents expired and a competitor, TrafFix Devices, Inc., sold sign stands with a visible spring mechanism that looked like MDI's. MDI and TrafFix products looked alike because they were.

\* \* \*

II

It is well established that trade dress can be protected under federal law. The design or packaging of a product may acquire a distinctiveness which serves to identify the product with its manufacturer or source; and a design or package which acquires this secondary meaning, assuming other requisites are met, is a trade dress which may not be used in a manner likely to cause confusion as to the origin, sponsorship, or approval of the goods. In these respects protection for trade dress exists to promote competition. As we explained just last Term, see *Wal–Mart Stores, Inc. v. Samara Brothers, Inc.*, 529 U.S. 205, 120 S.Ct. 1339, 146 L.Ed.2d 182 (2000), various Courts of Appeals have allowed claims of trade dress infringement relying on the general provision of the Lanham Act which provides a cause of action to one who is injured when a person uses "any word, term name, symbol, or device, or any combination thereof . . . which is likely to cause confusion . . . as to the origin, sponsorship, or approval of his or her goods." 15 U.S.C. § 1125(a)(1)(A). Congress confirmed this statutory protection for trade dress by amending the Lanham Act to recognize the concept. Title 15 U.S.C. § 1125(a)(3) (1994 ed., Supp. V) provides: "In a civil action for trade dress infringement under this chapter for trade dress not registered on the principal register, the person who asserts trade dress protection has the burden of proving that the matter sought to be protected is not functional." This burden of proof gives force to the well-established rule that trade dress protection may not be claimed for product features that are functional. *Qualitex*, at 164–165, 115 S.Ct. 1300; *Two Pesos, Inc. v. Taco Cabana, Inc.*, 505 U.S. 763, 775, 112 S.Ct. 2753, 120 L.Ed.2d 615 (1992). And in *Wal–Mart*, we were careful to caution against misuse or over-extension of trade dress. We noted that "product design almost invariably serves purposes other than source identification." *Id.*, at 213, 120 S.Ct. 1339.

Trade dress protection must subsist with the recognition that in many instances there is no prohibition against copying goods and products. In general, unless an intellectual property right such as a patent or copyright protects an item, it will be subject to copying. As the Court has explained, copying is not always discouraged or disfavored by the laws which preserve our competitive economy. *Bonito Boats, Inc. v. Thunder Craft Boats, Inc.*, 489 U.S. 141, 160, 109 S.Ct. 971, 103 L.Ed.2d 118 (1989). Allowing competitors to copy will have salutary effects in many instances. "Reverse engineering of chemical and mechanical articles in the public domain often leads to significant advances in technology." *Ibid.*

The principal question in this case is the effect of an expired patent on a claim of trade dress infringement. A prior patent, we conclude, has vital significance in resolving the trade dress claim. A utility patent is strong evidence that the features therein claimed are functional. If trade dress protection is sought for those features the strong evidence of functionality based on the previous patent adds great weight to the statutory presumption that features are deemed functional until proved otherwise by the party seeking trade dress protection. Where the expired patent claimed the features in question, one who seeks to establish trade dress protection must carry the heavy burden of showing that the feature is not functional, for instance by showing that it is merely an ornamental, incidental, or arbitrary aspect of the device.

In the case before us, the central advance claimed in the expired utility patents (the Sarkisian patents) is the dual-spring design; and the dual-spring design is the essential feature of the trade dress MDI now seeks to establish and to protect. The rule we have explained bars the trade dress claim, for MDI did not, and cannot, carry the burden of overcoming the strong evidentiary inference of functionality based on the disclosure of the dual-spring design in the claims of the expired patents.

III

In finding for MDI on the trade dress issue the Court of Appeals gave insufficient recognition to the importance of the expired utility patents, and their evidentiary significance, in establishing the functionality of the device. The error likely was caused by its misinterpretation of trade dress principles in other respects. As we have noted, even if there has been no previous utility patent the party asserting trade dress has the burden to establish the nonfunctionality of alleged trade dress features. MDI could not meet this burden. Discussing trademarks, we have said " '[i]n general terms, a product feature is functional,' and cannot serve as a trademark, 'if it is essential to the use or purpose of the article or if it affects the cost or quality of the article.' " *Qualitex*, 514 U.S., at 165, 115 S.Ct. 1300 (quoting *Inwood Laboratories, Inc. v. Ives Laboratories, Inc.*, 456 U.S. 844, 850, n. 10, 102 S.Ct. 2182, 72 L.Ed.2d 606 (1982)). Expanding upon the meaning of this phrase, we have observed that a functional feature is one the "exclusive use of [which] would put competitors at a significant non-reputation-related disadvantage." 514 U.S., at 165, 115 S.Ct. 1300. The Court of Appeals in the instant case seemed to interpret this language to mean that a necessary test for functionality is "whether the particular product configuration is a competitive necessity." 200 F.3d, at 940. See also *Vornado*, 58 F.3d, at 1507 ("Functionality, by contrast, has been defined both by our circuit, and more recently by the Supreme Court, in terms of competitive need"). This was incorrect as a comprehensive definition. As explained in *Qualitex*, and *Inwood*, a feature is also functional when it is essential to the use or purpose of the device or when it affects the cost or quality of the device. The *Qualitex* decision did not purport to displace this traditional rule. Instead, it quoted the rule as *Inwood* had set it forth. It is proper to inquire into a "significant non-reputation-related disadvantage" in cases of aesthetic functionality, the question involved in *Qualitex*. Where the design is functional under the *Inwood* formulation there is no need to proceed further to consider if there is a competitive necessity for the feature. In *Qualitex*, by contrast, aesthetic functionality was the central question, there having been no indication that the green-gold color of the laundry press pad had any bearing on the use or purpose of the product or its cost or quality.

The Court has allowed trade dress protection to certain product features that are inherently distinctive. *Two Pesos*, 505 U.S., at 774, 112 S.Ct. 2753. In *Two Pesos*, however, the Court at the outset made the explicit analytic assumption that the trade dress features in question (decorations and other features to evoke a Mexican theme in a restaurant) were not functional. *Id.*, at 767, n. 6, 112 S.Ct. 2753. The trade dress in those cases did not bar competitors from copying functional product design features. In the instant case, beyond serving the purpose of informing consumers that the sign stands are made by MDI (assuming it does so), the dual-spring design provides a unique and useful mechanism to resist the force of the wind. Functionality having been established, whether MDI's dual-spring design has acquired secondary meaning need not be considered.

There is no need, furthermore, to engage, as did the Court of Appeals, in speculation about other design possibilities, such as using three or four springs which might serve the same purpose. Here, the functionality of the spring design means that competitors need not explore whether other spring juxtapositions might be used. The dual-spring design is not an arbitrary flourish in the configuration of MDI's product; it is the reason the device works. Other designs need not be attempted.

## In re Dial–A–Mattress Operating Corporation

United States Court of Appeals, Federal Circuit, 2001.
240 F.3d 1341.

■ MAYER, CHIEF JUDGE.

Dial–A–Mattress Operating Corporation (Dial–A–Mattress) appeals the judgment of the Trademark Trial and Appeal Board affirming an examiner's rejection of its intent-to-use application to register "1–888–M–A–T–R–E–S–S" as a service mark. Because the mark is descriptive of the relevant services, and has acquired prima facie distinctiveness as the legal equivalent of one of Dial–A–Mattress' previously-registered marks, we reverse.

### Background

Dial–A–Mattress sells mattresses and related bedding through retail stores and a telephone "shop-at-home" service. In 1996, it filed an intent-to-use application to register "1–888–M–A–T–R–E–S–S" as a service mark for "telephone shop-at-home retail services in the field of mattresses." It claimed that the proposed mark is inherently distinctive, or alternatively, that it acquired distinctiveness and was registerable pursuant to section 2(f) of the Trademark Act, 15 U.S.C. § 1052(f). In support of its application, Dial–A–Mattress cited a number of its previously-registered marks, including: "DM DIAL A MATRES" (and design) (Registration No. 1,554,-

222, obtained August 29, 1989); "(212) M–A–T–T–R–E–S" (Registration No. 1,589,453, obtained March 27, 1990) (the "(212)" portion of the mark is depicted with broken lines to indicate that "the area code will change"); "1–800–MATTRES, AND LEAVE OFF THE LAST S THAT'S THE S FOR SAVINGS" (Registration No. 1,728,356, obtained October 27, 1992); and "DIAL A MATTRESS," (Registration No. 1,339,658, obtained January 26, 1993).

Dial–A–Mattress also presented a declaration of its assistant general counsel, Robert Isler, in which he said that it nationally advertised the (212) M–A–T–T–R–E–S mark, and provided exemplars of that mark's use. He said that Dial–A–Mattress sought to register "1–800–MATRESS," "1–888–MATRESS" and "1–888–MATTRES" to further protect its existing marks, and because it received an "inordinate number" of customer calls on these lines (one million in sixteen months after July 1996). Isler inferred that people who called on these lines were attempting to reach Dial–A–Mattress, but were either unfamiliar with the correct spelling of "mattress" or misdialed.

After several office actions, the examiner rejected the "1–888–M–A–T–R–E–S–S" application because the mark is generic for the relevant services and therefore unregisterable. The examiner found that even if it is not generic, it is "merely descriptive" and Dial–A–Mattress presented insufficient evidence of acquired distinctiveness to permit registration of the mark under section 2(f) of the Trademark Act.

Dial–A–Mattress appealed the rejection to the Trademark Trial and Appeal Board, which affirmed. Because there was no dispute that the (888) toll-free area code designation is devoid of source-indicating significance, that "M–A–T–R–E–S–S" is the legal equivalent of the word "mattress," and that "mattress" is generic for the identified service, the board determined that the mnemonic "1–888–M–A–T–R–E–S–S" is generic.

The board also affirmed in the alternative, holding that the proposed mark is descriptive, and that Dial–A–Mattress presented insufficient evidence of acquired distinctiveness to permit registration. It determined that none of Dial–A–Mattress' previously-registered marks were the legal equivalents of its proposed mark; therefore they were not prima facie evidence of acquired distinctiveness. It also found the Isler declaration insufficient to demonstrate acquired distinctiveness because it did not show that customers who called the 1–888–M–A–T–R–E–S–S line understood it to be identified with Dial–A–Mattress. This appeal followed.

*Discussion*

We review the board's conclusions of law de novo and affirm its findings of fact if they are supported by substantial evidence. We first address whether the mark "1–888–M–A–T–R–E–S–S" is generic and therefore unregisterable as a trademark. Generic terms are common names that the relevant purchasing public understands primarily as describing the genus of goods or services being sold. They are by definition incapable of indicating a particular source of the goods or services, and cannot be registered as trademarks; doing so "would grant the owner of the mark a monopoly, since a competitor could not describe his goods as what they are." *In re Merrill Lynch, Pierce, Fenner & Smith, Inc.*, 828 F.2d at 159, 4 U.S.P.Q.2D (BNA) at 1142.

The determination of whether a mark is generic is made according to a two-part inquiry: "First, what is the genus of the goods or services at issue? Second, is the term sought to be registered ... understood by the relevant public primarily to refer to that genus of goods or services?" *H. Marvin Ginn Corp.*, 782 F.2d at 990, 228 U.S.P.Q. (BNA) at 530. Placement of a term on the fanciful-suggestive-descriptive-generic continuum is a question of fact. The Director of the United States Patent and Trademark Office (Director) bears the burden of proving a term generic. *In re The Am. Fertility Soc'y*, 188 F.3d 1341, 1345, 51 U.S.P.Q.2D (BNA) 1832, 1834 (Fed. Cir. 1999). Any competent source suffices to show the relevant purchasing public's understanding of a contested term, including purchaser testimony, consumer surveys, dictionary definitions, trade journals, newspapers and other publications.

Where a term is a "compound word" (such as "Screenwipe"), the Director may satisfy his burden of proving it generic by producing evidence that each of the constituent words is generic, and that "the separate words joined to form a compound have a meaning identical to the meaning common usage would ascribe to those words as a compound." *In re Gould Paper Corp.*, 834 F.2d 1017, 1018, 5 U.S.P.Q.2D (BNA) 1110, 1110 (Fed. Cir. 1987). However, where the proposed mark is a phrase (such as "Society for Reproductive Medicine"), the board "cannot simply cite definitions and generic uses of the constituent terms of a mark"; it must conduct an inquiry into "the meaning of the disputed phrase as a whole." *In re The Am. Fertility Soc'y*, 188 F.3d at 1347, 51 U.S.P.Q.2D (BNA) at 1836. The In re Gould test is applicable only to "compound terms formed by the union of words" where the public understands the individual terms to be generic for a genus of goods or services, and the joining of the individual terms into one compound word lends "no additional meaning to the term." Id. at 1348–49, 51 U.S.P.Q.2D (BNA) at 1837.

Here, there is no dispute that the genus is telephone shop-at-home services for retail mattresses. Nor does Dial–A–Mattress contest the following evidence and legal conclusions offered by the Director: (1) the area code designation (888) in the proposed mark by itself is devoid of source-indicating significance; (2) "matress" is the legal "equivalent" of the word "mattress"; and (3) the word "mattress" standing alone is generic for retail services in the field of mattresses.

Instead, Dial–A–Mattress contends that the board erred in holding this quantum of evidence sufficient to demonstrate that the term "1–888–MA–T–R–E–S–S" is generic. It specifically challenges the rule the board adopted in rendering its decision: "If the mark sought to be registered is comprised solely of the combination of a designation (such as a toll-free telephone area code) which is devoid of source-indicating significance, joined with material which, under the Ginn two-part test, is generic for the identified goods or services, then the mark as a whole is generic and unregisterable." *In re Dial A Mattress Operating Corp.*, 1999 TTAB LEXIS 623, *at *8*, 52 U.S.P.Q.2D (BNA) 1910 at 1913. Dial–A–Mattress argues that Ginn and In re The American Fertility Society, require evidence that the proposed mark as a whole is understood by the relevant public to refer to the relevant genus of goods or services. Because the Director offered no proof of the meaning the relevant purchasing public ascribes to the term in its entirety, Dial–A–Mattress contends the term is not generic.

The Director says the board's test is consistent with In re Gould arguing that the proposed mark is more akin to a compound word than to a phrase. He argues that because it is undisputed that both (888) and "MATRESS" are generic, joining the two together creates a term with no additional meaning than the individual meanings of each of its constituent parts. However, the Director provides no justification for this conclusion. Instead, he relies on the reasoning of *Dranoff–Perlstein Assocs. v. Sklar*, 967 F.2d 852, 859–60, 23 U.S.P.Q.2D (BNA) 1174, 1180 (3rd Cir. 1992), that trademark protection should not be granted to telephone numbers composed of a generic mnemonic word because it would preclude competitors from the use of this tool, and "achieve the kind of unfair competitive advantage the genericness doctrine is supposed to prevent."

We conclude that the board applied the wrong test in holding that the Director meets his burden of proving an alphanumeric telephone number generic merely by showing that it is composed of a non-source-indicating area code and a generic term. "The commercial impression of a trade-mark is derived from it as a whole, not from its elements separated and considered in detail. For this reason, it should be considered in its entirety. . . . " *Estate of P.D. Beckwith, Inc. v. Comm'r of Patents*, 252 U.S. 538, 545–46, 40 S. Ct. 414, 64 L. Ed. 705 (1920). The Director must produce evidence of the meaning the relevant purchasing public accords the proposed mnemonic mark "as a whole." *In re The Am. Fertility Soc'y*, 188 F.3d at 1348, 51 U.S.P.Q.2D (BNA) at 1836. In re Gould does not apply here because "1–888–M–A–T–R–E–S–S"—a mnemonic formed by the union of a series of numbers and a word—bears closer conceptual resemblance to a phrase than a compound word. See *In re The Am. Fertility Soc'y*, 188 F.3d at 1348–49, 51 U.S.P.Q.2D (BNA) at 1837 (explicitly limiting the holding of In re Gould to "compound terms formed by the union of words"). It is devoid of source-indicating significance, but "(888)" is not a word and is not itself a generic term for selling by telephone.

Analyzing the "1–888–M–A–T–R–E–S–S" mark as a whole, substantial evidence does not support the conclusion that the mark is generic. There is no record evidence that the relevant public refers to the class of shop-at-home telephone mattress retailers as "1–888–M–A–T–R–E–S–S." See *H. Marvin Ginn Corp.*, 782 F.2d at 991, 228 U.S.P.Q. (BNA) at 532. "Telephone shop-at-home mattresses" or "mattresses by phone" would be more apt generic descriptions. Like the title "Fire Chief" for a magazine in the field of fire fighting, a phone number is not literally a genus or class name, but is at most descriptive of the class. Id. Moreover, like the term "cash management account," "1–888–M–A–T–R–E–S–S" does not "immediately and unequivocally" describe the service at issue. See *In re Merrill Lynch, Pierce, Fenner & Smith, Inc.*, 828 F.2d at 1571, 4 U.S.P.Q.2D (BNA) at 1144.

Finally, given that telephone numbers consist of only seven numbers and typically can be used by only one entity at a time, a competitor of a business that has obtained a telephone number corresponding to a "mattress" mnemonic for all practical purposes is already precluded from using and promoting the number. A rule precluding registerability merely shifts the race from the Trademark Office to the telephone company. Dial–A–Mattress also observes that its competitors have not been precluded from using mnemonic telephone numbers as marketing tools and would of course remain free to use "mattress" to describe their goods and services in formats other than the promotion of mnemonic telephone numbers consisting of the term.

Conclusion

Accordingly, the judgment of the Trademark Trial and Appeal Board is reversed.

REVERSED

[In a subsequent part of the opinion, the court held that although the proposed mark was descriptive it had acquired distinctiveness as the legal equivalent of other marks already in use by the company.].

NOTES

**1.** *Categories of marks.* On a federal level, trademarks cannot be registered without an allegation of use. Trademarks cannot be maintained without filing affidavits of continuing use. Priority depends on use. There are four types of marks that the Lanham Act protects—trade marks, service marks, collective marks and certification marks. Section 1127 of the Lanham Act defines all four categories of marks in terms of their use, and all categories are made registrable by §§ 1052–1054. A trademark (when not used in its generic sense to refer to all kinds of marks protected by the Lanham Act), is a mark that is used with goods (e.g. games, chickens, perfumes). A service mark is used in connection with services (e.g. dry cleaners, travel agencies, investment advisors). A certification mark is a mark that one entity owns to signal something about goods or services produced or provided by others—for example, that the goods are especially well-made (e.g. the Good Housekeeping Seal of Approval), that they are produced with a particular material (e.g. the Woolmark), that they are made in a specific place (e.g. Champagne), or that they are manufactured by a certain organization (e.g. the Ladies' Garment Workers Union). A collective mark is a mark that members of an association use to identify their own goods or services (e.g. the twin pines of cooperative grocery stores or Sebastian for hair-care products sold through salons).

The requirements for trademarks set out in the Principal Cases apply equally to all these marks. There are, however, additional requirements for certification marks. A certification mark is intended to signal that the goods or services in connection with which it is used have met an objective standard. Accordingly, the owner of a certification mark must be neutral and cannot be using the mark for marketing purposes itself. Moreover, a certification mark can be cancelled if the owner fails to exercise control over its use or discriminatorily refuses to certify goods that meet the standard, § 1064(5). Because organizations sometimes try to evade the strict requirements for certification marks by registering their symbols as collective marks, there have been occasional attempts to abolish the collective mark category.[1]

In addition to defining protectable marks, § 1127 also defines a "trade name" and "commercial name" as terms that identify a business or vocation. Because they do not appear in conjunction with goods or services and do not send the appropriate sort of signal to consumers, they do not qualify for protection under the Lanham Act simply by virtue of being trade names. However, there is nothing in the Act that prevents a company from acquiring a trademark right in its trade name by using it on goods or services. For an example, look back at the registrations of Coca Cola for soda pop that were reproduced in the last assignment. The company that is listed as owning these marks is the Coca Cola Company.

**2.** *Use as a signal in commerce: the physical dimension.* As discussed in the Introduction to this Assignment, the physical dimension of use in commerce requires actual use in commerce. *Microstrategy, Inc.* shows that this element typically calls for the mark owner to use it in a sufficiently public way so that an appropriate segment of the public understands the mark as a source identifier of the products or services.[2] In determining whether such an association by the public is present, courts generally inquire into the activities undertaken by the adopter of the mark. Many courts take a flexible approach to this question that focuses on the "totality of the circumstances." In interpreting this aspect of the "use in commerce" requirement, courts do not limit the Lanham Act's application to activities that generate a profit.[3] In the Principal Problem, has Coach demonstrated actual use in commerce for all of its proposed marks?

[1] See, e.g., Frederick Breitenfeld, Collective Marks—Should They Be Abolished?, 47 Trademark Rep. 1 (1957). See also Note, The Collective Trademark: Invitation to Abuse, 68 Yale L.J. 528 (1959).

[2] For an interesting decision holding that an unregistered service mark used for casino services provided to U.S. citizens by a foreign casino operator constitutes use in foreign trade and thus satisfies the use "in commerce" requirement of the Lanham Act, see International Bancorp, LLC v. Societe des Bains de Mer etc., 329 F.3d 359 (4th Cir. 2003).

[3] Planetary Motion, Inc. v. Techsplosion, Inc., 261 F.3d 1188, 1194–95 (11th Cir. 2001)(noting that under the "totality of circumstances" approach, "use in commerce" can be established even in the absence of sales or profit-making activity); Allen Chance v. Pac–Tel Teletrac Inc., 242 F.3d 1151, 1158 (9th Cir. 2001)(noting that advertising, combined with other non-sales activity, can establish use in commerce).

The display component of use is defined in the definition of "use in commerce" in the Lanham Act[4], and it typically involves the physical requirement of affixation. Since marks receive trademark protection in order to facilitate communication between consumers and producers, the law requires that the marks be affixed in a way that makes it possible for consumers to make the connection. For most items, this is not a problem: the trademark goes on a label and the label is attached to the product. The only issues for most tangible goods are, therefore, whether symbols on shipping carton, store displays, and store packaging material are protectable. Usually, the answer is no. The mark must be seen prior to sale.[5] Shipping cartons and package inserts are not seen at the time of sale and packaging material that is thrown out by the store never is seen. Display material is usually considered mere advertising unless it is very closely associated with the product. Most of the problem cases arise when goods are sold through intermediaries, like pharmacists, where control over what consumers see is not in the hands of the producer, or when the choice among products in the product category is made by someone other than the ultimate consumer (as with medicine—chosen by doctors—and casebooks— chosen by law professors).[6] In such instances, it is not always clear who is communicating with whom. In *MicroStrategy*, does the majority opinion sufficiently emphasize the role that the mark plays for the buyers who see it, or is the concern more for competitors? What is the appropriate emphasis?

With respect to the issue of affixation, service marks always are somewhat problematic since there are no goods on which to affix them. The 1988 Amendments to the Lanham Act added a provision defining "use in commerce" for services when the mark "is used or displayed in the sale or advertising of services and the services are rendered in commerce."[7] Thus, in the context of service marks, advertising can take on a more crucial role since there are no products upon which to affix the mark. How should the affixation requirement be applied to products and services sold on the Internet?

**3.** *Use as a signal in commerce: the cognitive dimension.* As discussed in the Introduction, only distinctive marks are capable of being source indicators. Therefore, marks that are deemed generic, descriptive, or functional are excluded from protection. Word marks are generally categorized according to the categorization of meanings used in *Heileman*—generic, descrip-

[4] § 1127 (definition of "use in commerce").

[5] In re Bright of America, Inc., 205 U.S.P.Q. 63 (T.T.A.B. 1979).

[6] *See, e.g.,* In re Schiapparelli Searle, 26 U.S.P.Q.2d 1520 (1993)(examiner refused to register mark THE ACTIVE INGREDIENT IS QUALITY for pharmaceuticals where the specimens of record were brochures describing the goods). In *Searle*, the nexus between the consumer and producer was doubly tenu-

ous. The consumer did not chose the product (the doctor chose it), and the consumer did not pluck it off the shelf (the pharmacist selected it).

[7] 15 U.S.C. § 1127 (revised definition of "use in commerce"). *See also* Lloyd's Food Prods., Inc. v. Eli's, Inc., 987 F.2d 766, 768 (Fed. Cir. 1993)(noting that with respect to service marks, the use of the mark in "sales" or "advertising" materials of different description becomes "all the more important").

tive, suggestive, and arbitrary.[8] These categories compose a spectrum ranging from marks that never can function as trademarks (generic), to marks that can function as trademarks with additional investment by the mark owner (descriptive), to marks that qualify for trademark protection immediately (suggestive and arbitrary). Federal and state law generally protect words in similar fashion,[9] and thus the same spectrum of classification is utilized in analyzing both federal and state claims. Thus, the Seventh Circuit in *Heileman*, a case about state unfair competition law, used Lanham Act terminology. Conversely, *Heileman* is cited in cases brought under federal law. When trade dress or product configuration is at issue, often the cognitive use issue concerns the functionality of the mark. Functionality is considered below, after the four categories of meaning derived from *Heileman* are explored.

(a). *Arbitrary marks.* At first blush, one might think that producers always will adopt arbitrary marks. After all, once such a mark is coined, it functions immediately as a trademark (and can be placed on the Principal Register). No extra investment is required to make it intrinsically distinctive, and no arguments need be had with the examiner about whether it falls on the suggestive rather than descriptive side of the line. In fact, at common law, a coined mark had considerable advantages in litigation. The objective in early cases was usually to prevent passing off—that is, to stop the defendant from marketing his goods in a manner that diverted the plaintiff's consumers to himself. If the plaintiff's mark was at all descriptive of the goods, courts generally took the view that the defendant was using it in its descriptive capacity, and not in order to fool customers. Accordingly, the plaintiff needed to prove that the defendant actually intended to confuse consumers and that he succeeded.[10] If, however, the plaintiff's mark was arbitrary, the use of the very same arbitrary word on defendant's goods gave rise to a presumption that the defendant intended to pass off. Then, the plaintiff only needed to adduce proof that consumers were likely to be confused.

(b). *Descriptive marks.* Why, then, would producers ever adopt anything but a coined term? One reason is to save on the costs of consumer education. Choosing an arbitrary word such as APPLE for computers is cute, but convincing customers to pay thousands of dollars for something that sounds like fruit is not simple. Much better is to call yourself by a name that gives purchasers some sense of what it is that is being sold and some hook on which to hang an association between the mark and the product.

To a certain extent, the best hook is one that actually names the product—INTERNATIONAL BUSINESS MACHINES or PERSONAL

[8] These categories are generally credited to Abercrombie & Fitch Co. v. Hunting World, Inc., 537 F.2d 4 (2d Cir.1976).

[9] A specific illustration of this point is that just as *Heileman* was willing to permit the name of a category to function as a trademark when there was only one product in the category, so too § 1127 of the Lanham Act specifically permits the registration of the name of a "unique product."

[10] See, e.g., American Washboard Co. v. Saginaw Mfg. Co., 103 F. 281 (6th Cir.1900).

COMPUTER, for example. Unfortunately, words like these are so graphic, customers are likely to perceive them as product descriptions, and not as marks. Similarly, titles and slogans are considered inherently descriptive of the underlying work.[11] That is why generally descriptive words and phrases cannot be protected or registered without proof of secondary meaning. "Secondary meaning" means that consumers have come to see the mark as a signal, not as as a description.[12] Once a mark has developed secondary meaning, the primary meaning recedes, and so the mark becomes capable of distinguishing the products of the trademark owner from the goods of other producers. In some instances, phrases or slogans can be so highly descriptive that they are precluded from acquiring distinctiveness as a trademark.[13] Do you think this is a problem with the slogan in the Principal Problem?

(c). *Suggestive marks.* Given that descriptive marks are too informational and arbitrary marks are not informative enough, the obvious conclusion is that suggestive marks are just right. Terms like COPPERTONE provide hints about the product, but they are only clues: "[a] suggestive mark . . . requires imagination to make a connection between the mark and an attribute of the product."[14] Moreover, since these words are capable of distinguishing one producer's version of the product category from another's, they can be registered immediately. For this reason, companies attempt to argue quite strongly that their marks are suggestive rather than descriptive.[15] There is no need to establish secondary meaning because, like arbitrary marks, customers know from their very first encounter with these terms that they are trademarks.

(d). *Generic marks.* The previous discussion leaves us with the question of why Anheuser–Busch chose to ignore Interbrand's advice and adopt a mark as descriptive as LA for low alcohol beer. Some companies are attracted to descriptive marks because they hope that in an unconscious way, customers will come to think of their product as the only really genuine version of the goods—a strategy that worked for IBM for many

---

[11] See Heirs of the Estate of William F. Jenkins v. Paramount Pictures Corp., 90 F.Supp.2d 706, 711 (E.D. Va. 2000)(noting "that the title of a single expressive work may receive trademark protection only upon a showing that the title is not generic, and that it has acquired secondary meaning"). General laudatory phrases also are considered descriptive of the alleged merit, characteristics, or quality of the product or service. See, e.g., In re Nett Designs, Inc., 236 F.3d 1339 (Fed. Cir. 2001)("THE ULTIMATE BIKE RACK"); *In re Boston Beer Co. L.P.,* 198 F.3d 1370 (Fed. Cir. 1999)("THE BEST BEER IN AMERICA").

[12] In Zipee Corp. v. United States Postal Service, 140 F.Supp.2d 1084 (D.Or. 2000), the court held the phrase "postal service," stand-

ing alone, to be descriptive, but because it had acquired secondary meaning as a designation of source (the United States Postal Service),the term was deemed a protectable mark.

[13] In re Boston Beer Co. L.P., 198 F.3d 1370, 1373 (Fed. Cir. 1999); see footnote 10.

[14] Official Airline Guides, Inc. v. Goss, 6 F.3d 1385, 1391 (9th Cir.1993).

[15] See, e.g., J & J Snack Foods Corp. v. Nestle USA, Inc., 149 F.Supp.2d 136, 150–51 (D.N.J. 2001)(finding, on motion for preliminary injunction, that no significant mental leap or imagination was required to understand that the phrase "BREAK & BAKE," when used in connection with pre-made cookie dough, means no mixing required).

years. However, Anheuser–Busch may have been trying to do more. The court mentioned that "[i]nternal memoranda during this early planning phase reveal that Anheuser–Busch aspired to preempt the low alcohol beer market." In other words, the company was hoping to acquire trademark rights over the *only* way that customers knew to ask for low alcohol beer. That way, every time someone came into a bar and asked for a low alcohol beer, the bartender would be required to fill the order with Anheuser–Busch's product. Heileman, Miller, and other brewers would never make a sale, and so Anheuser–Busch would "preempt" the market.

Trademark law is intended to facilitate competition, not stifle it. Accordingly, trademark rights can never be granted in the only effective means of referring to a product category. This is true whether customers perceive the word as a description or whether they perceive it as a trademark. If a word is generic—if it is the way the public[16] has come to describe the category to which the goods belong—it can never be protected: it cannot be registered under federal law, nor will it be protected by the unfair competition law of any state. Such words must remain in the public domain for the use of every producer's customers.

Many courts have relied upon the "who-are-you/what-are-you" test in determining whether a term is generic: "A mark answers the buyer's questions 'Who are you?' 'Where do you come from?' 'Who vouches for you?' But the generic name of the product answers the question 'What are you?' "[17] However, because a mark may answer both questions simultaneously, Congress has adopted the "primary significance of the registered mark to the relevant public" test in determining when a registered mark is subject to cancellation on the ground that it has become generic.[18]

In the context of telephone numbers, particularly those containing a generic term, competitive advantage is a major concern. Do you agree with the ruling in *Dial–A–Mattress* the genericity of the alphanumeric telephone number should be determined in its entirety within the context of its use as a telephone number rather than by analyzing mechanically its component parts? The PTO issued an administrative guideline in 1994 requesting that examiners deny registration applications if the mark consists of "a merely descriptive or generic term with numerals in the form of a telephone

---

[16] Wide use of a term in a generic sense by third parties and competitors in a given industry is sufficient to find genericity. Stuhlbarg Int'l Sales Co. v. John D. Brush & Co., 240 F.3d 832, 840 (9th Cir. 2001).

[17] Golf Warehouse, L.L.C. v. Golfer's Warehouse, Inc., 142 F.Supp.2d 1307, 1310 (D.Kan. 2001)(*quoting* Official Airline Guides, Inc. v. Goss, 6 F.3d 1385, 1391 (9th Cir. 1993)).

[18] § 1064(3). In Microsoft Corp. v. Lindows.com Inc., 64 U.S.P.Q.2d 1397 (W.D. Wash. 2002)(order denying preliminary in-junction), the court questioned the applicability of the "what-are-you" test as failing to provide a "conclusive answer" to its inquiry into whether "Windows" is generic or descriptive. In that case, the court denied Microsoft's request for a preliminary injunction enjoining the defendant's use of Lindows or Lindows.com in connection with its software or other computer products or services. In so ruling, the court questioned whether "Windows" is a non-generic designation eligible for federal trademark protection.

number."[19] Although this administrative guideline is not binding on courts, it does provide some guidance as to how the PTO believes the Lanham Act should be interpreted. In the Principal Case, the Federal Circuit implicitly rejected the reasoning of this guideline. In an earlier decision, Dial–A–Mattress Franchise Corp. v. Page,[20] the Second Circuit upheld the plaintiff's right to enjoin a competitor from using "1–800–MATTRESS" in light of the plaintiff's prior use and promotion of a local telephone number "MATTRES." The court reasoned that "[t]elephone numbers may be protected as trademarks, and a competitor's use of a confusingly similar telephone number may be enjoined as both trademark infringement and unfair competition."[21] Moreover, the fact that the numbers in question spelled a generic term did not preclude the plaintiff from being protected against the defendant's use of a confusingly similar number and corresponding set of letters. In this case, as in the Principal Case, the court did not give effect to the anti-competition policy underlying the prohibition on the use of generic marks. How did the Federal Circuit justify this aspect of its decision? The issue raised in Dial–A–Mattress also is relevant to the status of domain names.

Should the Principal Problem be decided the same way as the Principal *Dial–a–Mattress* case?

(e). *Functional marks.* The doctrine of functionality is closely related to the ban on generic marks, as it too prevents producers from stifling competition by asserting trademark rights in an element that is needed to market properly goods within a product category. The best example of functionality comes from a case decided by Learned Hand under state unfair competition law, Crescent Tool Co. v. Kilborn & Bishop Co.[22] Claiming that the public had come to identify the crescent-shaped head of its wrenches as its trademark, the plaintiff argued that the defendant should be enjoined from producing a product of a similar shape. Judge Hand disagreed. He recognized that the plaintiff had a right to prevent passing off, and that it had established a protectable trademark in the name "Crescent Tool Company." However, he refused to enjoin the production of other crescent shape wrenches. In his view, only "nonessential" elements of a product can serve as a trademark. If the crescent shape is essential to the proper operation of a wrench in tight places, it cannot be protected by trademark law.

More recently, in America Online, Inc. v. AT & T Corp.,[23] the Fourth Circuit upheld the District Court's ruling that AOL could not enforce the phrase "You Have Mail" as a trademark. The Circuit Court emphasized that the functional manner in which AOL uses this mark is consistent with the public perception of the phrase as one that describes the fact to subscribers they have mail in their electronic mailboxes (as opposed to a

---

[19] Trademark Manual of Examining Procedure § 1209.03(*l* )(3rd ed. 2002).

[20] 880 F.2d 675 (2d Cir. 1989).

[21] *Id.* at 678.

[22] 247 Fed. 299 (2d Cir.1917).

[23] 243 F.3d 812 (4th Cir. 2001).

phrase that describes a service related to AOL).[24] In so holding, the court observed that "the repeated use of ordinary words functioning within the heartland of their ordinary meaning, and not distinctively, cannot give AOL a proprietary right over those words, even if an association develops between the words and AOL."[25] Further, the court observed that even functional features that have acquired secondary meaning cannot serve as legally protectable marks.[26] This case is interesting because it provides an illustration of the functionality doctrine applied in the context of a word mark, as opposed to trade dress or product configuration.

As discussed in Note 14, there are numerous bars to registration, including that the subject matter at issue is either functional (see Note 14f ) or generic. Moreover, federal registrations for marks that are deemed functional or generic may be cancelled at any time (see Note 10), and are unable to obtain "incontestable" status (see Note 11).[27] Thus, functionality and genericity are treated the same from the standpoint of both registration and cancellation. Again, just as state law refuses to enforce trademarks rights in words that are generic or functional, the Lanham Act also specifically prohibits protection for such subject matter. Many of the cases involving functionality are similar to *TrafFix Devices* in that the defendants are raising functionality as a defense to an infringement claim. Note 4 continues a discussion of functionality specifically in the context of trade dress.

**4.** *Trade dress and competition.* In recent years, trade dress has become a very important type of protection, perhaps because in the United States inadequate protection exists for design protection. Note that trade dress protection can extend beyond product packaging to the shapes of products themselves. In recent years, the Supreme Court has rendered several significant decisions on this topic. In reading this Note, think about how well the Court's decisions have confined Lanham Act claims to features that market participants do not need to compete effectively with the trade dress holder.

*Two Pesos* held that inherently distinctive trade dress is protectable under § 43(a) of the Lanham Act (providing federal protection for unregistered subject matter) without a showing of secondary meaning. By deferring to the district court's determination of inherent distinctiveness, *Two Pesos* applied to trade dress the same analysis used for trademarks. This analysis, which was utilized in *Heileman*, classifies marks into the categories discussed in Note 3. Arbitrary and suggestive trade dress are considered "inherently distinctive," whereas descriptive trade dress requires secondary meaning to be protected. Unfortunately, *Two Pesos* failed to acknowledge the extent to which trade dress protection could confer an

---

[24] *Id.* at 820.

[25] *Id.* at 822.

[26] *Id.*

[27] *See, e.g.,* § 1064(3)(providing for the cancellation of trademarks that become generic or are functional); § 1065(4)(preventing incontestable status in a generic term); and § 1115(b)(8)(stipulating functionality as a defense to incontestability).

essentially exclusive right to a particular—possibly non-inventive—marketing feature, which would last as long as the product was sold. Was *Two Pesos* right to see trade dress as little different from trademarks?[28] The *Two Pesos* Court was concerned with protecting the signals of start-up companies and small businesses, but the interests of competitors—and the public—are equally at issue when a design becomes popular. Besides, start-ups and small businesses have other ways to protect themselves: they can use labels and other symbols to distinguish their goods and, in some cases, they can protect their distinctive designs with copyrights or design patents.

Subsequently, *Qualitex* held that although a color may not be inherently distinctive and thus capable of trademark protection at the outset, colors that have acquired secondary meaning and thus are source indicative can be registered. *Qualitex* appears to settle the conflict among the circuits regarding the trademark status of color, but the opinion still leaves some important issues unanswered. How satisfactorily does the Court in *Qualitex* apply the functionality doctrine? Does the Court provide sufficient guidance for lower courts to make this determination? If impact on competition is the primary consideration in determining whether to register a particular color as a trademark, how and by whom shall this determination be made? Does the opinion decide whether color can ever be so inherently distinctive that it should be accorded trademark protection before developing secondary meaning? Do you think many colors are likely to qualify for color trademark protection in light of the standard articulated by the Court? In the context of the Principal Problem, would you categorize the sparking gray tags as functional? Further, does the *Qualitex* opinion indicate whether sounds and fragrances would also qualify as appropriate trademark subject matter? What about product configurations?

Are the problems raised by the protection of color marks significantly different from the problems surrounding the protection of the trade dress at issue in *Two Pesos*? Does *Qualitex*, in fact, overrule *Two Pesos* on the secondary meaning issue? In a later decision, Wal–Mart Stores, Inc. v. Samara Brothers, Inc.,[29] the Supreme Court held that product-design trade dress, unlike product-packaging trade dress, can never be inherently distinctive. Therefore, product-design trade dress is protectable only upon a showing of secondary meaning that the design has become source-indicative. After *Samara*, the holding in *Two Pesos* is apparently limited to product packaging. Thus, it is important to distinguish between product-design and product-packaging. Is it so easy to tell the difference between these concepts? What is the trade dress protecting in *Two Pesos*: the signal for the food sold at the restaurant (in which case, the dress is packaging) or the layout of the restaurant (in which case the dress is design)? Is the color of a press pad really part of its design or simply its packaging? Is there a difference between product design—which is the term the Supreme Court

---

[28] For an interesting critique of *Two Pesos*, see Glynn Lunney, Jr., The Trade Dress Emperor's New Clothes: Why Trade Dress Does Not Belong on the Principal Register, 51 Hastings L.J. 1131 (2000); Glynn Lynney, Jr., Trademark Monopolies, 48 Emory L.J. 367 (1999).

[29] 529 U.S. 205 (2000).

uses—and product *configuration*, the term more commonly seen in the scholarly literature? Would it make more sense to require secondary meaning in all trade dress cases? How does the product-design vs. product-packaging trade dress analysis affect the Principal Problem? See also Note 6 in Assignment 8 (discussing a congressional experiment with protection for vessel hulls, a form of product configurations).

How does *TrafFix* affect the analysis? It held functional a feature that was the subject of an expired patent and settled questions regarding the allocation of the burden of proof on functionality. (The burden now clearly falls on the trade dress holder). However, it does not create a firm test for applying the functionality doctrine. The Court notes that resolution of the functionality inquiry may involve questions of competitive need (in certain cases of aesthetic functionality), as well as whether the feature "is essential to the use or purpose of the device or when it affects the cost or quality of the device." Although the *TrafFix* Court cites prior Supreme Court precedent, as well as several lower court cases involving functionality, ultimately it is unclear which test for functionality should be applied. Instead, the Court decides that the design at issue must be functional because it was previously patented. Since not every case raising claims of functionality involves designs that were formerly patented, this solution to the functionality puzzle has limited application. Further, *TrafFix* also fails to make clear how patent cases should be handled. Patented products include many features; not all of them contribute to the inventiveness that merited the patent. For example, a screwdriver with a patented tip will also have a shaft, a handle, a color, and a grip made of a specific material. Can the (non-inventive) shaft, handle, color, or grip serve as a trademark, or does the patent awarded to the screwdriver as a whole bar a trademark on all its other features?

**5.** *Evidentiary issues.* Several of the key questions covered in this Assignment turn on factual inquiries about how words are used and what customers think. These questions also arise in connection with other issues, such as trademark cancellation and infringement. The three most popular methods for shedding light on these issues are: dictionary research, Lexis/Nexis searches, and consumer surveys. Sometimes, the testimony of real-life consumers is taken as evidence. A few litigants have even resorted to the testimony of expert linguists.[30]

The admissibility of surveys has been a very controversial issue. Surveys are attacked for problems such as polling the wrong universe of consumers,[31] asking the wrong questions,[32] utilizing the wrong environment,[33] displaying the goods or the mark badly,[34] and poor analytical

[30] See, e.g., Quality Inns Int'l. v. McDonald's Corp., 695 F.Supp. 198 (D.Md. 1988)(on the significance of "Mc").

[31] See, e.g. Zippo Mfg. Co. v. Rogers Imports, Inc., 216 F.Supp. 670 (S.D.N.Y.1963).

[32] See, e.g., Sears, Roebuck & Co. v. Allstate Driving School, Inc., 301 F.Supp. 4 (E.D.N.Y.1969).

[33] See, e.g., Scotch Whiskey Assoc. v. Consolidated Distilled Products, Inc., 210 U.S.P.Q. (BNA) 639 (N.D. Ill. 1981).

methodology.[35] Since surveys are, in essence, the comments of out-of-court declarants that are offered for the purpose of proving the truth of the statements declared, they can also be attacked as hearsay. Nonetheless, surveys are to a large extent the only evidence directly probative of what consumers are thinking at the time of the litigation, and so they are widely admitted under a doctrine of necessity.[36] See also Assignment 3.

**6.** *Benefits of federal registration.* Since the Lanham Act offers protection to unregistered subject matter (see § 43(a), discussed in Assignment 3), students often ask what additional benefits are offered through federal registration. In its web site,[37] the Patent and Trademark Office actually answers this question very succinctly, specifying the following five benefits of federal registration:

  1) Constructive notice nationwide of the trademark owner's claim;

  2) Evidence of ownership of the trademark;

  3) Jurisdiction of federal courts may be invoked

  4) Registration can be used as a basis for obtaining registration in foreign countries;

  5) Registration may be filed with United States Custom Service to prevent importation of infringing foreign goods.

As discussed in the previous Assignment, registration on the Supplemental (§ 1091) rather than the Principal Register satisfies some of these benefits (although not benefits 1 and 5). Registration on the Supplemental Register creates a record of use. After five years, the mark can be moved almost automatically to the Principal Register.

**7.** *Use versus intent to use.* As discussed in Assignment 1, in 1988 the Lanham Act was amended to allow for the filing of trademark registrations based on "a bona fide intention to use a trademark in commerce."[38] The filing of such an application establishes priority for the applicant as of the filing date, although the applicant must file a statement of actual use within six months (although extensions can be obtained for up to thirty-six months).[39] It is difficult to overstate how fundamentally this 1988 Amendment altered U.S. trademark law. Before this change, federal registration was mainly aimed at enabling producers to transfer the goodwill they had acquired in one location to other locations. It did that by creating a national register that constructively notified every producer in the United States to avoid using the same mark. Without use, there was no right to enter the federal registration system because there was no goodwill to

[34] See, e.g., Carter–Wallace, Inc. v. Procter & Gamble Co., 434 F.2d 794 (9th Cir. 1970).

[35] See, e.g., Sheller–Globe Corp. v. Scott Paper Co., 204 U.S.P.Q. (BNA) 329 (T.T.A.B. 1979).

[36] See, e.g., Zippo Mfg. Co. v. Rogers Imports, Inc., 216 F.Supp. 670 (S.D.N.Y. 1963).

[37] See www.uspto.gov/web/offices/tac/tmfaq.htm#Basic002 under trademarks and "frequently asked questions."

[38] § 1051(b)(1).

[39] § 1051 (d). See also www.uspto.gov, under 37 CFR sec. 2.89.

transfer. Or, before use, the producer had not accomplished the socially desirable goal of creating goodwill, and therefore had not paid the price for admission to the federal system. The intent-to-use provisions undermine the core of this rationale. The right to transfer goodwill across the nation is now based on something the PTO has done, not on the applicant's accomplishment of a socially desired activity. In the Principal Problem, why will the intent to use application be beneficial for Coach?

**8.** *Token uses.* Before the 1988 amendment to the Lanham Act, it often happened that a company invested heavily in bringing a symbol to the point where it could be used, only to find that it was unregistrable; that, for example, another entity fulfilled the requirements for registering the mark sooner. To reduce this risk, courts were inclined to consider some rather flimsy transactions as meeting the use requirement. Examples include single sales, sales internal to the company, soliciting orders from friends, and flying mock-ups cross country.[40] Although the intent-to-use amendment was largely aimed at other concerns, one side benefit is that it removes the need for this so-called "token use" doctrine. Accordingly, a portion of the Senate Report accompanying the amendment implies that it legislatively overrules the token use cases:

> Token use is a contrived and commercially transparent practice—nothing more than a legal fiction. At the same time, token use is essential under current law because it recognizes present day marketing costs and realities; it reduces some of the legal and economic risks associated with entering the marketplace; and it nominally achieves the threshold 'use' required to apply for federal registration and the creation of trademark rights in advance of commercial use.

> Unfortunately, token use is not available to all businesses and industries. For example, it is virtually impossible to make token use of a trademark on a large or expensive product such as an airplane. The same is true for service industries (that is, hotels, restaurants, and banks) prior to opening for business. Similarly, it is difficult for small business and individuals to avail themselves of token use because they frequently lack the resources or the knowledge to engage in the practice. Token use is also troublesome for another reason. It allows companies to obtain registration based on minimal use. Often these companies change their marketing plans and subsequently do not make commercial use. The result is that the trademark register is clogged with unused marks, making the clearance of new marks more difficult and discouraging others from adopting and using marks that should otherwise be available.

\* \* \*

[40] See, e.g., Wallace Computer Services, Inc. v. Sun Microsystems, Inc., 13 U.S.P.Q.2d (BNA) 1324 (N.D.Ill.1989); Bertolli USA Inc. v. Filippo Bertolli Fine Foods Ltd., 662 F.Supp. 203 (S.D.N.Y.1987); Beech Aircraft Corp. v. Lightning Aircraft Co., 1 U.S.P.Q.2d 1290 (T.T.A.B. 1986).

Since token use becomes unnecessary and inappropriate under the intent-to-use application system proposed by S.1883, the definition of "use in commerce" in § 1127 of the Act is strengthened to reflect this significant change in the law.[41]

The courts also have held that this amendment has eliminated "token use" as a means of registration.[42] As the last paragraph of the Senate Report excerpted above illustrates, Congress intended a quid pro quo. In return for creating a way to reserve a mark without use, it stiffened the requirements for use. Thus, intent-to-use applications will be closely examined. If the applicant's intentions seem to be realistic and the applicant has no track record of reserving marks it never uses, Notices of Allowance will be granted. At the same time, token or sham uses will not be taken as sufficient to establish actual use. Accordingly, the Statement of Use affidavit that accompanies a request to convert an Allowance into an actual registration will have to based on use "in the ordinary course of trade."

**9.** *Foreign words.* Under the "doctrine of foreign equivalents," the PTO generally translates foreign words into English in order to decide where on the meaning spectrum they fit. Weiss Noodle Co. v. Golden Cracknel and Specialty Co.[43] is an example. In that case, registration of "Ha–Lush–Ka" for egg noodles was refused on the ground that halushka means noodles in Hungarian. The reasons for this practice (which the PTO occasionally forgets to use) are first, goods with foreign names are often aimed initially at ethnic markets. In those markets, the name is as generic as the English translation is to English speakers. Second, when the larger society acquires a taste for foreign goods, it often acquires an interest in the culture as well. Since it will want to use the same word that members of the culture use for the category, the word also becomes generic to English speakers. For example, no one calls a tortilla a corn pancake. Thus, in *Heileman*, Anheuser–Busch should not have been surprised that America calls its Australian-inspired product by the name Australians attach to the category.

In Mohegan Tribe v. Mohegan Tribe and Nation,[44] the plaintiff sought to enjoin the defendants from using the names "Mohegan" and "Mohegan Tribe" under the Lanham Act.[45] The court concluded that the plaintiff did not possess a legally protectable interest in the names. The court found the words to be generic because the names denote a person or people of a particular heritage, ancestry or nationality: "[A] Mohegan tribe must be permitted to describe itself as such because that is what it is."[46] The plaintiff attempted to claim that the term "Mohegan" was arbitrary, and thereby entitled to automatic protection because it means "wolf," rather

---

[41] Sen. Rep. No. 100–515, at 4–6; 1988 U.S.C.C.A.N. at 5580–5582.

[42] *See, e.g.,* Allard Enterprises, Inc. v. Advanced Programming Resources, Inc., 146 F.3d 350, 357 (6th Cir. 1998)("the purpose of this revision 'was to eliminate "token use" as a basis for registration' ").

[43] 290 F.2d 845 (C.C.P.A.1961).

[44] 255 Conn. 358, 769 A.2d 34 (2001).

[45] Plaintiffs sued under § 43(a) of the Lanham Act (see Assignment 3) as well as state common law.

[46] 769 A.2d at 44.

than a Native American tribe, in the Algonquin family of languages. The court decided that the doctrine of foreign equivalents did not apply here because "an appreciable number of members of the general public are unlikely to be conversant in the language from which the word originates, and when the word has a commonly accepted meaning in the English language."[47]

**10.** *Cancellation*. Under § 1064, any party "who believes that he is or will be damaged" by a mark on the Principal Register can petition for its cancellation. Cancellation proceedings, which are akin to the interferences described in Assignment 1, can be used to air any of the defenses to infringement that are based on the mark's suitability for registration. A mark also can be cancelled if it has been abandoned, see Assignment 4, or if it has become generic or is functional. In addition, certification marks can be cancelled if they are used discriminatorily, or for purposes other than to certify. Grounds for cancellation must be divided into two categories: those that can be raised only before the mark becomes incontestable (see Note 11 ) and those that can be raised at any time.

Cancellation proceedings have several advantages over litigation. The administrative procedure is cheaper and usually quicker than adjudication. Moreover, in most cases, cancellation is the clearest way to put a mark back into the public domain. This procedure is not, however, an appropriate vehicle for a challenger to argue that it is using a registered mark in a manner that is not infringing.

**11.** *Incontestability*. Section 1065 provides that after five years of continuous use, certain registered marks become incontestable, and such marks can then no longer be cancelled upon specified grounds. The grounds upon which an incontestable mark cannot be challenged are: first, that the mark should not have been registered because it was confusingly similar to another mark that was already in use at the time of the application; and second, that the mark is not entitled to protection because it is not inherently distinctive and lacks secondary meaning. Thus, "incontestability" is something of a misnomer in that only these two major defenses are lost once a mark achieves that status. This leaves more than 20 defenses that are good at any time.[48] These defenses include the genericity or functionality of a mark;[49] the problems listed in § 1052(a)–(c); defenses based on the geographic limits of trademarks, see Assignment 4; and the statutory defenses listed in § 1115(b): fraud in procuring registration, abandonment, use of the mark to misrepresent source, fair use, pre-registration use by the defendant, prior registration by the defendant, use of the mark to violate the antitrust laws, and the equitable defenses of laches, estoppel, and acquiescence.[50]

---

[47] Id. at n.25.

[48] Thomas McCarthy puts the number at 21, 5 J. Thomas McCarthy, Trademarks and Unfair Competition § 32.147 (4th ed. 2002).

[49] § 1064(3).

[50] See also § 1064(5) (providing for cancellation at any time for certification marks in particular instances).

In Park 'N Fly, Inc. v. Dollar Park and Fly, Inc.,[51] the Supreme Court held that the owner of a registered mark can use the incontestable status of a mark to enjoin an infringing use, and the defendant in such an action may not allege that the trademark in question is not valid due to its descriptive nature. This case thus established that incontestability can be used both defensively against the cancellation of a mark, as well as offensively in an infringement action. In *Park 'N Fly*, the dissent objected on the ground that the mark PARK 'N FLY for airport parking services had been registered without any evidence of secondary meaning, and that the record still lacked evidence of secondary meaning for this descriptive mark.[52] From a policy standpoint, what objections can be raised with respect to the *Park 'N Fly* decision?

**12.** *Registration and consumer standing.* Who should have standing to oppose registration? There has been controversy over the question whether individuals (as opposed to competitors) have standing to oppose registration. On the one hand, § 1063 of the Act gives the right to "any person who believes that he would be damaged." On the other hand, federal law generally limits rights of action to those directly affected by the activity that is the focus of the claim.[53] In Ritchie v. Simpson,[54] the Federal Circuit articulated a "real interest" test. In that case, William B. Ritchie, a member of the public, opposed Orenthal James Simpson's application to register the marks O.J. SIMPSON, O.J., and THE JUICE for use with a broad range of goods, including figurines, trading cards, sportswear, medallions, coins, and prepaid telephone cards. The opposition claimed that the marks were either immoral or scandalous matter (*see 14a*) or primarily merely a surname (see Note 14h). The Trademark Trial and Appeal Board ("Board") dismissed, holding that Mr. Ritchie did not have standing. The Federal Circuit reversed. First, the court noted that standing before an administrative agency is broader than the standards adopted under Art. III of the Constitution for standing before federal courts. Second, the court observed that the issue of immorality and scandalousness are ones on which public input is especially important. Under its "real interest test," the opposer must "have a legitimate personal interest in the opposition" and he or she must reasonably believe in the claim of potential injury. Thus, Mr. Ritchie's allegations–that he would be damaged by the registration of the marks because the marks disparage his values—especially those values relating to his family–were enough to create standing. And this was true even though his fears about giving federal protection to marks arguably "synonymous with wife-beater and wife-murderer," might be widely shared. The court sent the case back to the PTO to determine whether, in fact, these marks violate the standards of the statute. The PTO website shows "The Juice" application has been abandoned.

**13.** *Disclaimers.* Disclaimer practice is governed by §§ 1056–57 of the Lanham Act. These provisions permit registration of marks that contain

---

[51] 469 U.S. 189 (1985).

[52] Id. at 211.

[53] See, e.g., Sierra Club v. Morton, 405 U.S. 727 (1972).

[54] 170 F.3d 1092 (Fed. Cir. 1999).

unregistrable elements, so long as the trademark owner makes clear that she is not acquiring an exclusive right in the unprotectable parts of her mark. Composite marks comprised of all non-registrable sub-parts are not allowed to be registered, even with a disclaimer. Some portion must be capable of registration.[55]. Why wasn't a disclaimer required by the court in *Dial–a–Mattress*? See also Note 10, Assignment 3.

**14.** *Registrable subject matter.* All of the exclusions and qualifications to federal registration appear in § 1052. As you read the following materials, think about what policies you believe underlie the treatment in § 1052 of the various categories of trademarks.

a.   *§ 1052(a): immoral, scandalous and disparaging matter; false connections.* This subsection precludes registration for immoral, deceptive, or scandalous subject matter. In *In re Old Glory Condom Corp.*,[56] the T.T.A.B. held that the mark, "OLD GLORY CONDOM CORP," with an accompanying design of a condom decorated in a manner suggestive of the American flag, was not scandalous. In that case, the court emphasized that the issuance of a registration does not mean the government is endorsing the goods to which the mark is applied. Does § 1052(a) "represent a permissible means toward achieving a valid government purpose"?[57] What is the justification for withholding the benefit of registration from such marks? Can any valid constitutional objections be made regarding the operation of this subsection? Is this subsection consistent with the operation of First Amendment doctrine regarding categorization of speech? In lieu of denying registration, is there a better way to deal with marks that are ostensibly vulgar or in poor taste?

Generally, a mark's offensiveness is judged in the context of the mark's entire use (in other words, by also considering the labels and designs accompanying the mark). Some of the marks that have been approved by the T.T.A.B. could be considered controversial. For example, it approved the representation depicted below of a urinating dog for commercial paper:[58]

[55] Pilates, Inc. v. Georgetown Bodyworks, Inc., 157 F.Supp.2d 75, 81 (D.D.C. 2001)(holding that PILATES STUDIO not registrable after owner disclaimed both words individually).

[56] 26 U.S.P.Q.2d 1216 (T.T.A.B. 1993).

[57] See Davis, Registration of Scandalous, Immoral, and Disparaging Matter Under Section 2(a) of the Lanham Act: Can One Man's Vulgarity be Another's Registered Trademark?, 54 Ohio St. L.J. 331, 338 (1993).

[58] *Id.* at 400.

If a judgment must be made with respect to the immoral or scandalous nature of a particular mark, how should a court go about making this determination? The legislative history of the provision apparently is scarce, and courts therefore have looked to the "ordinary and common meaning" of scandalous.[59] Do you agree? Whose sensibilities should be relevant—only the prospective users or the public at large? How can judges avoid determining the relevant sensibilities without placing undue reliance on their own subjective views?

In In re Mavety Media Group Ltd.,[60] the Federal Circuit held that the T.T.A.B. had erred in its determination that "Black Tail" for an adult entertainment magazine was scandalous. The court objected to the T.T.A.B.'s exclusive reliance on dictionary reference defining "tail" as sexual intercourse, thus ignoring the more fundamental question of whether a substantial composite of the general public would regard the term as a reference to African–American women as sexual objects. The dictionary references relied upon in *Mavety* included not only vulgar, but also non-vulgar definitions of "tail" that would apply in the context of an adult magazine (i.e., rear end). The court noted that "the record is devoid of factual inquiry by the Examiner or the Board concerning the substantial composite of the general public, the context of the relevant marketplace, or contemporary attitudes."[61] It concluded that the mark should be approved for publication and an opposition could perhaps be brought by a group that finds the mark to be scandalous (see Note 12).

What is the policy underlying § 1052(a)'s preclusion of registration for marks "which may disparage or falsely suggest a connection with persons, . . . institutions, beliefs, or national symbols, or bring them into contempt, or disrepute"? The following test is used to determine whether a particular mark is barred from registration based on the "false connection" aspect of § 1052(a): "The mark must be shown to be the same as or a close approximation of the person's previously used name or identity. It must be established that the mark (or part of it) would be recognized as such. It must be shown that the person in question is not connected with the goods or services of the applicant, and finally, the person's name or identity must

[59] In re McGinley, 660 F.2d 481, 485 (C.C.P.A.1981).

[60] 33 F.3d 1367 (Fed.Cir.1994).

[61] Id. at 1372.

be of sufficient fame that when it is used as part or all of the mark on applicant's goods, a connection with that person is likely to be made by someone considering purchasing the goods."[62]

How should "disparagement" be established? Should the test for disparagement differ from the test for whether a mark is scandalous? In a 45-page opinion citing social science and historical research, along with standard legal analysis, the T.T.A.B. cancelled six marks belonging to the Washington Redskins on the ground that materials utilizing the word "Redskins" (including a caricature) are disparaging to Native Americans.[63] The parties seeking cancellation also argued that the marks were scandalous, but the Board did not agree with this ground.[64] Ultimately, a district court reversed the T.T.A.B. on the ground that its disparagement ruling was unsupported by substantial evidence.[65] The cancellation did not, of course, directly affect the decision whether to continue to use the name "Redskins" for a football team.

b. *§ 1052(a): deceptive matter vs. § 1052(e): deceptively misdescriptive matter.* Under § 1052(f), marks that are deceptive never can be registered, whereas marks that are deceptively misdescriptive can be registered after they have acquired secondary meaning. Thus, it becomes necessary to distinguish between deceptive and deceptively misdescriptive marks. The following inquiries have been developed to aid this analysis. First, does the matter for which registration is desired misdescribe the goods? Second, are consumers likely to believe the misrepresentation? If the answer to both of these questions is yes, the mark is deceptively misdescriptive. If however, the misrepresentation would materially influence the purchasing decision, the mark is considered deceptive rather than merely deceptively misdescriptive.[66] In light of this test, how would you rule on the registrability of the mark SILKEASE for women's blouses and dresses made of polyester crepe de chine? What about CAMEO for jewelry (earrings, necklaces and bracelets) that do not contain cameos or cameo-like elements?

c. *§ 1052(b): flag or coat of arms.* This subsection prohibits the registration of a mark which "[c]onsists of or comprises the flag or coat of arms or other insignia of the United States, or of any State or municipality, or of any foreign nation, or any simulation thereof." Does this language preclude the registration of a mark which comprises the coat of arms of a foreign municipality? Do you think the depiction of the American flag in *Old Glory* discussed in Note 14a would be barred by this subsection?

---

[62] In re Sauer, 27 U.S.P.Q.2d (BNA) 1073, 1074 (T.T.A.B. 1993)(registration of design of a ball saying BO BALL denied on the ground that the mark falsely suggests a connection with athlete Bo Jackson).

[63] Harjo v. Profootball, Inc., 50 U.S.P.Q.2d (BNA) 1705, 1743 (T.T.A.B. 1999).

[64] Id. at 1748–49.

[65] Pro–Football, Inc. v. Harjo, 284 F.Supp.2d 96 (D.D.C. 2003).

[66] See In re Budge Manufacturing Co., 857 F.2d 773, 775 (Fed.Cir.1988). See also Hoover Co. Royal Appliance Mfg. Co., 238 F.3d 1357 (Fed. Cir. 2001)(affirming T.T.A.B's decision that "THE FIRST NAME IN FLOORCARE" is neither deceptive nor deceptively misdescriptive).

d.  *§ 1052(c): identifying matter of a living individual.* This subsection precludes registration of a mark which "consists of or comprises a name, portrait, or signature identifying a particular living individual except by his written consent." It also precludes registration of the same with respect to a deceased President during the life of his widow, except with the written consent of his widow. The key here is whether the use in question identifies the particular individual, and thus it applies not only to full names, but also to surnames, nicknames and shortened names. A name will "identify" a particular individual for purposes of this subsection only if the individual in question will be associated with the mark because "that person is so well known that the public would reasonably assume the connection, or because the individual is publicly connected with the business in which the mark is used."[67] What do you think is the purpose of this provision? Should anybody be able to bring an opposition based on this subsection, or must the opposer have some connection to the person identified by the mark?

e.  *§ 1052(d): matter which resembles another mark so as to be likely to cause confusion.* As will be discussed in Assignment 3, likelihood of consumer confusion is the bottom line determination in trademark infringement actions. Section 1052(d) incorporates this policy into the registration requirements, so that an applicant's mark cannot be registered if it is likely to cause confusion with a registered mark. According to McCarthy, this subsection is the most common basis for rejection of applications for registration.[68] Section 1052(d) does provide, however, that concurrent registrations may be issued in certain circumstances.

f.  *§ 1052(e): functional subject matter.* Section 1052(e) provides statutory recognition of the common law doctrine of functionality by precluding registration for any matter "that, as a whole, is functional." See Notes 3(e) and 4.

g.  *§ 1052(e): geographical designations.* Geographic marks that are not primarily geographically descriptive are registrable (one example is DUTCHBOY for paint). In contrast, terms which function primarily as indicators of geographical origin are not registrable on the Principal Register.[69] Until 1993, marks that were deemed geographically descriptive or geographically deceptively misdescriptive could only be registered after a showing of secondary meaning. Geographically deceptive marks are never registrable. The analysis for making these determinations parallels that for determining misdescriptiveness discussed in Note 14b. Specifically, with respect to geographic marks, two questions initially must be asked: First, is

---

[67] Ceccato v. Manifattura Lane Gaetano Marzotto & Figli S.p.A., 32 U.S.P.Q.2d (BNA) 1192, 1195 (T.T.A.B. 1994). See also In re Sauer, 27 U.S.P.Q.2d (BNA) 1073, 1074–75 (T.T.A.B. 1993)(registration of design of a ball saying BO BALL denied on the ground that the mark identifies Bo Jackson).

[68] J. Thomas McCarthy, 3 McCarthy on Trademarks and Unfair Competition § 19.75 (4th ed. 2002).

[69] An arbitrary name attached to a location is generally protectable until the surrounding public associates the name with the geographic place. See Tortoise Island Homeowners Ass'n. v. Tortoise Island Realty, Inc., 790 So.2d 525, 533 (Fla. Dist. Ct. App. 2001).

the term one which primarily conveys a geographic connotation, and would people believe that the goods come from that place (this is typically referred to as a goods/place association)? Second, do the goods in fact come from that place? If the answer to these questions is affirmative, the mark is geographically descriptive. If the answer to the first question is yes, and the answer to the second is no, the mark is geographically deceptively misdescriptive. In addition, if people would actually buy the goods in reliance on the fact that they come from a particular geographical location, the mark is deceptive.[70] In the Principal Problem, how would you categorize the mark "SICILY SOPHISTICATE" for the new handbag line?

In 1993, § 1052 was amended in light of the United States' adherence to the North American Free Trade Agreement, so that it now bars registration for terms which are geographically deceptively misdescriptive.[71] Thus, geographically deceptive marks are treated the same as geographically deceptively misdescriptive marks, obviating the need to consider whether consumers actually rely on the misdescription in their purchasing decision. This amendment is applicable to applications filed after December 8, 1993, but a grandfather provision allows registration for such marks which were in use and had become distinctive prior to this date.

Additionally, the TRIPS Agreement (see Assignment 1) requires protection for geographical indications. TRIPS Article 22 defines "geographical indications" as ones "which identify a good as originating in the territory of a Member, or a region or locality in that territory, where a given quality reputation or other characteristic of the good is essentially attributable to its geographic origin." Article 22 also states that "Members shall provide the legal means for interested parties to prevent: (a) the use of any means in the designation or presentation of a good that indicates or suggests that the good in question originates in a geographical area other than the true place of origin in a manner which misleads the public as to the geographical origin of the good." Congress, however, has never amended § 1052(e) to comport with this provision, and the meaning of the term "misleading" is the subject of some debate.[72] Does permitting registration of "SICILIY SOPHISTICATE" in the Principal Problem comport with the TRIPS Agreement?

Moreover, TRIPS Article 23 provides that Members should "prevent use of a geographical indication identifying wines for wines not originating in the place indicated by the geographical indication in question even where the true origin of the goods is indicated or the geographical indication is used in translation or accompanied by expressions such as 'kind', 'type' or the like." This standard is especially strict because it prevents the use of

---

[70] See In re California Innovations Inc., 329 F.3d 1334 (Fed. Cir. 2003); In re Save Venice New York, 259 F.3d 1346 (Fed. Cir. 2001); The Institut National Des Appellations D'Origine v. Vintners International Co., 958 F.2d 1574, 1580 (Fed.Cir.1992); In re Sharky's Drygoods Co., 23 U.S.P.Q.2d (BNA) 1061, 1062 (T.T.A.B. 1992).

[71] See § 1052(e)(3) & (f).

[72] See Peter Brody, "Protection of Geographical Indications in the Wake of TRIPs: Existing United States Laws and the Administration's Proposed Legislation," 84 TMR 520 (1994).

geographical indications even absent situations in which the public is misled. Section 1052(a) was amended to comport with Article 23 of TRIPS so that it now bars registration of all wine and spirit trademarks that contain a geographic term which is not representative of the product's origin, even if the designation is not misleading. Nevertheless, the European Union believes our legislation still is not sufficiently protective.[73]

h. *§ 1052(e): primarily merely surnames.* Section 1052(e)(4) precludes immediate registration for a mark that is "primarily merely a surname," but such marks can be registered after they have acquired secondary meaning. How do you think courts determine whether a mark is source indicative or "primarily merely a surname?" Should registration of "Sousa" as a trademark for fireworks and entertainment services be granted in light of the fame of composer John Philip Sousa?

i. *§ 1052(f): distinctiveness/dilution.* This subsection essentially states that only marks that are distinctive of an applicant's goods can be registered. As discussed in Note 3, descriptive marks can acquire distinctiveness through secondary meaning. The term "secondary meaning" actually is a misnomer. A term acquires secondary meaning when its *primary* meaning in consumers' minds is the trademark meaning. There are, in effect, two ways to demonstrate that a mark has passed from being descriptive and has come to the point where it distinguishes the goods of one particular producer. First, evidence can be used to show how consumers actually perceive the mark. Second, as this subsection provides, the applicant can establish a prima facie case of secondary meaning by proving that the mark has been in substantially exclusive and continuous use for a period of five years. If the PTO cannot rebut the case, then the mark can be placed on the Principal Register.

Pursuant to a 1999 amendment to this subsection, the registration of any mark that would cause dilution within the meaning of the Lanham Act is expressly precluded from being registered. Such marks also can be cancelled within five years from the date of the mark's registration (see Note 10).[74] Dilution is explored in Assignment 3.

**15.** *Subject matter: Lanham Act's intersection with patent and copyright law.* There was a time when it was thought that the intellectual property regimes were, in a sense, mutually exclusive; that once one scheme of protection was chosen, the right holder had made an election and was also barred from relying on another regime. This notion has waned over the years.[75] For example, early cases held that once a patent expired, its trademark became public.[76] However, the cases so holding have been

[73] See Stacy Goldberg, Who Will Raise the White Flag? The Battle Between the United States and The European Union Over the Protection of Geographical Indications, 22 U. Pa. J. Int'l Econ. L. 107 (2001).

[74] § 1064.

[75] See, e.g., Application of Yardley, 493 F.2d 1389 (Ct.Cust. & Pat.App.1974) (permitting copyright registration of a design formerly subject to a design patent).

[76] Kellogg Co. v. National Biscuit Co., 305 U.S. 111 (1938); Singer Mfg. Co. v. June Mfg. Co., 163 U.S. 169 (1896).

distinguished away, so that in more recent years, patentees have been able to hold onto a trademark after patent expiration.[77]

Sometimes protection for certain subject matter straddles both trademark and copyright law. For example, recent cases have involved musical compositions and signature performances. Although the law has recognized sounds as within the scope of trademark protection when they have become source-indicative of a particular good or service,[78] courts have refused to extend trademark protection to a musical composition when the song is serving as the trademark for itself. In EMI Catalogue Partnership v. Hill, Holliday, Connors, Cosmopulos Inc.,[79] the Second Circuit decided that a musical composition cannot be protected as its own trademark because "[t]he different, source-identifying function of trademarks requires that a trademark in a musical composition not be coextensive with the music itself."[80] The court reasoned that granting a musical composition trademark status "would stretch the definition" of a trademark and extend trademark law into an area already protected by copyright law.[81] Subsequently, in Oliveira v. Frito–Lay, Inc.,[82] the same court determined that although musical compositions can serve as trademarks even though they are also protected by copyright law, a performer cannot acquire "a trademark or service mark signifying herself in a recording of her own famous performance."[83] Noting that trademark protection for such subject matter would not be "unthinkable," the court nonetheless declined the opportunity to "recognize" this "previously unknown" right on the ground that it "would be profoundly disruptive to commerce."[84] Moreover, building designs, as embodied in any tangible medium of expression, are protected under copyright law (see Assignment 8 Note 5), but now buildings may also be trademarked. Recent litigation has involved the Rock and Roll Hall of Fame and Museum [85] and the New York Stock Exchange.[86] Should a

[77] See, e.g., Snap–On Tools Corp. v. Winkenweder & Ladd, Inc., 250 F.2d 154 (7th Cir.1957).

[78] See the example of the three NBC's chimes discussed in *Qualitex*.

[79] 228 F.3d 56 (2d Cir. 2000).

[80] *Id.* at 64.

[81] *Id. See also* Herbko International, Inc. v. Kappa Books, Inc., 308 F.3d 1156 (Fed. Cir. 2002)(holding that the title to a single book cannot be trademarked, in part because the limited times protection of copyright suggests that upon the expiration of the book's copyright, "others have the right to reproduce the literary work and to use the title to identify the work.").

[82] 251 F.3d 56 (2d Cir. 2001).

[83] *Id. at* 62.

[84] *Id.* at 63. Cf. Comedy III Productions, Inc. v. New Line Cinema, 200 F.3d 593, 595

(9th Cir. 2000)(rejecting the argument that a movie clip from a short film featuring The Three Stooges was protectable under the Lanham Act as a collection of trademarks based on the "name, the characters, the likeness, and the overall 'act' of The Three Stooges.").

[85] Rock and Roll Hall of Fame and Museum, Inc. v. Gentile Prods., 134 F.3d 749, 751 (6th Cir. 1998)(noting that Ohio approved the trademark/service mark registrations of the Museum's building design and that the Museum received federal registration in November of 1997); Rock and Roll Hall of Fame and Museum, Inc. v. Gentile Prods., 71 F.Supp.2d 755 (N.D. Ohio 1999)(holding that plaintiffs have not used the building design as a trademark).

[86] New York Stock Exchange, Inc. v. New York, New York Hotel LLC, 293 F.3d 550 (2d Cir. 2002). The topic of trademark protection for buildings is treated in the fol-

person's image or likeness be capable of achieving trademark status?[87]

**16.** *Other regulatory regimes.* The Lanham Act is not the only provision of law that regulates labels and trademarks. For example, trademark law intersects with the Federal Food, Drug and Cosmetics Act.[88] Also, the Olympic and Amateur Sports Act grants the United States Olympic Committee the exclusive right to use such words as "Olympic," "Olympiad," and "Pan–American."[89] The Federal Circuit has held that this provision requires the T.T.A.B. to consider an opposition by the U.S.O.C. to the application for the registration of the mark "PAN AMERICAN" for toy and model trucks.[90] Thus, trademark holders must thread their way through various state and federal laws, as well as the regulations adopted thereunder. Certain industries also have ethical codes that govern the choice of identifying marks.[91]

lowing student note: The Skyscraping Reach of the Lanham Act: How Far Should the Protection of Famous Building Design Trademarks be Extended? 94 Nw. L.Rev. 1509 (2000).

[87] See ETW Corporation v. Jireh Publishing, Inc., 332 F.3d 915 (6th Cir. 2003)(rejecting "a sweeping claim to trademark rights in every photograph and image of golfer Tiger Woods"). See also Assignment 13 treating the right of publicity.

[88] *See, e.g.,* In re Schiapparelli Searle, 26 U.S.P.Q.2d 1520 (T.T.A.B. 1993)(Board affirms decision to deny registration for the phrase THE ACTIVE INGREDIENT IS QUALITY for pharmaceuticals).

[89] 36 U.S.C.A. § 380(a). See also Assignment 4. Another such statute is The Indian Arts and Crafts Act, 25 U.S.C. § 305, which gives the Indian Arts and Crafts Board the power to create trademarks for individual Indians, Indian tribes or Indian Arts and Crafts organizations, and to assign the trademarks free of charge to the individual Indians, Indian tribes or Indian Arts and Crafts organizations. 25 U.S.C. 305a(g). In general, this statute was designed to promote the economic welfare of native Americans through the development of arts and crafts. The statute uses the term "Indian" in lieu of "Native American."

[90] United States Olympic Committee v. Toy Truck Lines, Inc., 237 F.3d 1331 (Fed. Cir. 2001).

[91] See, e.g., Model Code of Professional Responsibility EC 2–11 (1979); Model Rules of Professional Conduct Rule 7.5 (1980).

# ASSIGNMENT 3

# THE SCOPE OF THE TRADEMARK HOLDER'S RIGHTS: INFRINGEMENT AND CONTRIBUTORY INFRINGEMENT

The previous Assignment explored the requirements for trademark protection. This Assignment discusses the activities that are considered infringing. The public uses trademarks in a large variety of ways. Most obviously, trademarks are used in connection with the sale of goods and services—to distinguish them, to advertise them, and to search for them. But these are not the only usages. Some people like to adorn themselves in trademarked goods—to demonstrate their solidarity with a school or team, to transmit messages about the superior state of their finances, or to express their aesthetic sensibilities. Trademarks are also used as a vehicle for discussing the trademark owner and as a way to navigate the Internet. The core issue in this Assignment is to decide which of these activities causes the harm that trademark law is intended to prevent. To that end, we examine the rights of action recognized under state and federal law. Because the public uses trademarks in a variety of ways, there are quite a few such rights at issue.

First, consider federal law. The traditional target of trademark protection is passing off, which involves use of a trademark on a product (or for a service) in a manner that is likely to cause consumer confusion as to the source or origins of the product (or service). This activity is covered by § 1114, which provides a remedy for such infringement when the trademark is federally registered. The likelihood of consumer confusion is also actionable under § 1125(a), commonly referred to as § 43(a).[1] This provision is mainly aimed at offering federal protection to symbols that are not federally registered, but that are protected under state law. In addition, it protects all marks and trade dress from a set of "rather amorphous practices that are commonly arranged under the loose rubric of 'unfair competition.'"[2] Among other things, this provision covers false designations of origin and false descriptions and representations. In these cases, courts utilize the same standard of likelihood of confusion that is used in the § 1114 cases. As Lois Sportswear v. Levi Strauss, McDonald's Corp. v.

---

[1] Section 43 is the number of this section as it appeared in the bill that resulted in the Lanham Act. In this text, we will follow this general practice of using the § 43 designation for all parts of the section that we cover.

[2] ETW Corp. v. Jireh Publishing, Inc., 332 F.3d 915, 939 (6th Cir. 2003)(Clay, J., dissenting).

Druck and Gerner, and Two Pesos v. Taco Cabana, illustrate, the key questions for both rights of action are 1) how identical the *marks* must be to create a likelihood of confusion and 2) how identical the *products* must be to create a likelihood of confusion. As you will see, modern marketing practices, including especially the popularity of "lifestyle marketing" (that is, selling goods in a broad array of loosely related categories), puts pressure on courts to recognize even rather disparate usages as potentially confusing.

The value of a mark can also be undermined by uses that do not cause consumer confusion. Section 43(c) protects against the dilution of famous marks. The scope of dilution—indeed, even the existence of the harm of dilution—is extremely controversial. As Moseley v. V Secret Catalogue, demonstrates, the federal statute is certainly intended to deal with uses that undermine a mark's cachet and blur its distinctiveness. In addition, it may cover situations where the mark is tarnished by being used in unsavory contexts. Among the key issues in these cases are how to show harm and what counts as "famous."

The other rights recognized in § 43 include causes of action for false advertising, for false endorsements, and reverse passing off (instead of selling one's own goods as the trademark holder's, this is about selling the trademark holder's goods as one's own). These rights are described in Note 11(b), and in Dastar Corp. v. Twentieth Century Fox Film Corp., which is reproduced in Assignment 9.

The most recent addition to federal trademark law deals with harms caused by usage of trademarks on the Internet. To begin, consider the customer looking for trademarked goods on the Internet. Likely, he will do one of two things. Either he will type the trademark, followed by a top level domain name (such as .com) into the address box of his browser or he will type the trademark into a search engine. If the domain name that corresponds to the trademark is owned by someone other than the trademark holder, the first strategy will bring the customer directly to a site over which the trademark holder has no control; the second strategy will generate a list of search results, which will include this other person's site. Either way, the customer will wind up finding alternatives to the trademark holder's products, or viewing the trademark in unauthorized settings, or even reading complaints about the trademark holder at a "gripe site" (a so-called "sucks.com" site). To make matters worse, those who want to maintain such sites need not rely exclusively on snagging the domain name that corresponds to the trademark. It can be enough to include the trademark in the text of the site because search engines will usually list any domain name in the search result that mentions the trademark. Some search engines look at keywords (metatags); those who want to attract the trademark holder's potential customers can list the trademark as one of their metatags. Furthermore, the order in which search results are reported can be manipulated by paying for special listing privileges, by utilizing the trademark on the site repeatedly, or by establishing links to the site. Those who are really intent on disrupting the trademark holder's business can also register as domain names variants of the trademark or even misspelled versions that will attract bad spellers and poor typists.

Some of these problems can be dealt with under the trademark laws described above. For example, as Playboy Enterprises v. Welles, shows, unauthorized use of a trademark on an Internet site in a manner likely to cause confusion as to the source of the products sold at that site, will be actionable under §§ 1114 or 43(a). However, traditional law may not reach those Internet uses that do not involve the sale of goods or services. For example, it may not reach someone who claims a domain name corresponding to a trademark and then seeks ransom from the trademark holder to get it transferred. Section 43(d) was added to prevent cyberpiracy by giving trademark holders a right of action against bad faith registrations of domain names that are confusingly similar to distinctive marks and that are dilutive of famous marks.

In addition to rights of action aimed at those who directly utilize trademarks without authorization, federal law sometimes permits suit against those who make infringement possible. Section 1114(1)(b) creates a right of action against those who reproduce the mark on labels, packages and the like. As discussed in Note 13, one who abets infringement by intentionally inducing another to infringe may be liable for contributory infringement.

Aside from federal law, there are two other sources of infringement claims. First, there is state law. All the states recognize rights of action for passing off. The likelihood of consumer confusion is judged using the same sorts of factors that are used in federal law. Some states may, in addition, use unfair competition law to protect less distinctive aspects of a trademark holder's marketing scheme, such as advertising motifs and business methods. Furthermore, about half the states had antidilution statutes before dilution was recognized federally. These statutes may cover less famous marks and usages that undermine distinctiveness in ways that the federal legislation has not been interpreted as reaching. Some states recognize other causes of action, such as claims for misappropriation of intellectual material, which can include trademarks.[3] Misappropriation is examined in the context of copyright law in Assignment 13. Litigants with both state and federal claims will usually assert both; they can pursue all their rights in either state or federal court.[4]

A second source of protection is contractual. Acquisition of a domain name requires entry into a web of contractual relations with the organiza-

[3] See, e.g., Board of Trade of the City of Chicago v. Dow Jones & Co., Inc., 98 Ill.2d 109, 456 N.E.2d 84, 74 Ill.Dec. 582 (1983)(use of the stocks in the Dow Jones Industrial Average, an index of stock market value, to create an investment vehicle is misappropriation of the trade values and reputation of the publisher of the index).

[4] These actions are generally brought in federal courts, which have jurisdiction over both federal trademark claims and also any "claim of unfair competition when joined with a substantial and related claim under the ... trade-mark laws." 28 U.S.C. § 1338(a). Since federal jurisdiction in trademark cases is concurrent with that of the states, § 1338(a), these actions can be heard in state courts as well.

tions that maintain the Internet and that register the upper level domain names. These contracts may provide for alternative means for resolving disputes between domain name registrants and trademark holders. Walmart v. wallmartcanadasucks.com, involves dispute resolution under the Uniform Domain Name Resolution Policy (known as UDRP). UDRP was promulgated by the Internet Corporation for Assigned Names and Numbers (ICANN), which is largely in charge of administering the Internet. Under the UDRP, companies that are in the business of registering domain names ending in .com, .org., and .net (as well as certain managers of country code domains) have agreed to require all registrants to agree to be amenable to resolving disputes over the registration and use of domain names through a dispute resolution service provider approved by ICANN. Although domain name registrars have further agreed to abide by the outcome of these resolutions, losing parties (domain name holders and trademark holders) are permitted to pursue their rights in court. ICANN obviously offers a method of dispute resolution that is different from a court. However, the bases for an ICANN claim are similar to the bases available under § 43(d).

The cases in this Assignment discuss not only infringement, but also some of the common law defenses to infringement, such as claims that the use is privileged as a parody or a nominative use. These defenses, along with the statutory defenses of the Lanham Act, will be the examined further in Assignment 4.

## 1. PRINCIPAL PROBLEM

You have decided that being a trademark examiner is too much tension for too little money, so you've become a trademark attorney and now work for Grateway, Inc., a company that has been selling computers on the Internet for over a decade. Recently, it decided to offer a line of cases for carrying its portable products, such as laptops, MP3 players, and handheld personal digital assistants (PDAs). Grateway, which has long used cows on its packaging, has chosen to carry on with the bovine theme, and to make its cases of full-grain cowhide. The cases are extremely sturdy: they are cushioned on the inside to protect the computers from shock and they have rugged exterior bindings and seams on the outside that prevent the bags from being easily knocked over. The cases are all pearl grey, a color that exactly matches the plastic on Grateway's computer products. Each case has an oval, color-coordinated hangtag which is attached by a chain. These are embossed with the word "Grateway."

Grateway computers are sold on the Internet, and the cases are to be offered in the same way. This part of the site will open with the following header:

Come to Grateway and see why folks across America believe that our cases are twice as nice and last twice as long as designer brand handbags like Coach, Gucci, and Louis Vuitton.

Underneath, each case in the line will be pictured and described. As you probably can guess, the header is more than just a cute statement. It has a special role in cyberspace: folks who use text-based search engines to find Coach, Gucci, or Louis Vuitton will—indeed—come to Grateway. In fact, to assure that folks come to Grateway, the company also plans to list these terms as metatags. Further, Grateway discovered that no one has claimed the domain name "coachbaggage.com," so it has procured the site itself. Since it thinks that Coach is likely to eventually offer a line of computer bags, this site will give Grateway a place to explain to consumers the many advantages that Grateway cases have over Coach's offerings.

Before going on-line with this line, upper management has consulted you. Needless to say, they are specifically worried that Grateway will be sued by Coach—ironically, the very company whose trademarks you examined so long ago. As you remember, among other things, Coach was issued registrations for the mark, *COACH*, for its product line, and for its "light-sparkly" grey oval hangtags. Coach was denied protection for the designs of three bags, but it has since run ads that focus on the beauty of its bindings, and people have come to identify Coach with heavily stitched edgings. Please advise as to whether Coach could bring a successful action under § 1114 for infringement, or under § 43 for infringement, dilution, false advertising or cyberpiracy. Could Grateway be sued under the UDRP process?

## 2.   MATERIALS FOR SOLUTION OF PRINCIPAL PROBLEM

### A.   STATUTORY MATERIALS: §§ 1114, 1121, & 1125

For ICANN dispute resolution, see the following websites:

http://www.icann.org/udrp/

http://arbiter.wipo.int/domains/gtld/udrp/index.html

### B.   CASES:

### (1) Infringement under §§ 1114 and 43(a)

## Lois Sportswear v. Levi Strauss & Co.

United States Court of Appeals, Second Circuit, 1986.
799 F.2d 867.

■ TIMBERS, CIRCUIT JUDGE.

I

We summarize only those facts believed necessary to an understanding of the issues raised on appeal.

Appellee [Levi Strauss & Co.] is a world famous clothing manufacturer. One of its most popular products is a line of casual pants known as Levi Jeans. Appellee began manufacturing its denim jeans in the 1850s. Each pair of jeans contains numerous identifying features. One such feature is a distinct back pocket stitching pattern. This pattern consists of two intersecting arcs which roughly bisect both pockets of appellee's jeans. Appellee has an incontestable federal trademark in this stitching pattern. Appellee has used this pattern on all its jeans continuously since 1873. In many ways the back pocket stitching pattern has become the embodiment of Levi Jeans in the minds of jeans buyers. The record is replete with undisputed examples of the intimate association between the stitching pattern and appellee's products in the buying public's mind. Not only has appellee spent considerable sums on promoting the stitching pattern, but various competitors have run nation-wide advertisement campaigns touting the advantages of their jeans' back pockets over appellee's. In addition, one of the largest chains of jeans retailers, the Gap Stores, has run numerous advertisements featuring pictures of appellee's back pocket stitching pattern as the entire visual portion of the ad. The record also contains numerous examples of the public's phenomenal reaction to the stitching pattern and the jeans it epitomizes. These examples range from national magazine cover stories to high school yearbook dedications.

Appellant Lois Sportswear, U.S.A., Inc. ("Lois") imports into the United States jeans manufactured in Spain by [appellant] Textiles Y Confecciones Europeas, S.A. ("Textiles"). The instant litigation was commenced because appellants' jeans bear a back pocket stitching pattern substantially similar to appellee's trademark stitching pattern. On appeal appellants do not challenge the district court's conclusion that the two stitching patterns are substantially similar. Nor could they; the two patterns are virtually identical when viewed from any appreciable distance. In fact, the results from a survey based on showing consumers videotapes of the back pockets of various jeans, including appellants', indicate that 44% of those interviewed mistook appellants' jeans for appellee's jeans.[a] Appellants instead rely on their use of various labels, some permanent and some temporary, to distinguish their jeans and defeat appellee's trademark infringement and unfair competition claims.

The evidence is undisputed that appellants and appellee manufacture and sell a similar product. While stratifying the jeans market with various styles and grades seems to be the current rage, there can be no dispute that the parties before us compete to sell their jeans to the public. The record does indicate that appellants have attempted to target their "designer" jeans at a decidedly upscale market segment. There also was evidence, however, that appellants' jeans were selling at deep discount in cut-rate clothing outlets. Moreover, there was substantial evidence which indicated that appellee's jeans, although originally marketed as work pants, had achieved a certain elan among the fashion conscious. The evidence suggests

[a] The value of this survey as evidence of actual consumer confusion is disputed by the parties. The district court found that the survey suffered from some methodological shortcomings relating to its simulation of the post-sale environment. The court gave the survey results little weight in determining actual confusion. The survey, however, remains strikingly probative of the similarity of the two stitching patterns.

that appellee's jeans have achieved fad popularity in all sectors of the jeans market. Finally, appellee produced affidavits stating that it was planning to enter the designer jeans market.

[The district court granted appellee's motion for summary judgment, holding that while the labels may prevent confusion as to source at the time of the sale, they do not prevent confusion in the post-sale context.]

II

Appellants' arguments, for the most part, focus only on the likelihood that consumers will buy appellants' jeans thinking they are appellee's jeans due to the similar stitching patterns. Appellants point to their labeling as conclusive proof that no such confusion is likely. We agree with the district court, however, that the two principle [sic] areas of confusion raised by appellants' use of appellee's stitching pattern are: (1) the likelihood that jeans consumers will be confused as to the relationship between appellants and appellee; and (2) the likelihood that consumers will be confused as to the source of appellants' jeans when the jeans are observed in the post-sale context. We hold that the Lanham Act, 15 U.S.C.A. §§ 1051–1127 (1982), as interpreted by our Court, was meant to prevent such likely confusion.

Turning to the principal issues under the Lanham Act, in either a claim of trademark infringement under § 32 or a claim of unfair competition under § 43, a prima facie case is made out by showing the use of one's trademark by another in a way that is likely to confuse consumers as to the source of the product. Compare 15 U.S.C.A. § 1114(1)(a)("use . . . of a registered mark . . . [that] is likely to cause confusion") with 15 U.S.C.A. § 1125(a)("use in connection with any goods . . . [of] a false designation of origin"). See Thompson Medical Co., Inc. v. Pfizer Inc., 753 F.2d 08, 213 (2d Cir.1985)(quoting Mushroom Makers, Inc. v. R. G. Barry Corp., 580 F.2d 44, 47 (2d Cir.1978), cert. denied, 439 U.S. 1116 (1979)("The ultimate inquiry in most actions for false designation of origin, as with actions for trademark infringement, is whether there exists a 'likelihood that an appreciable number of ordinarily prudent purchasers [will] be misled, or indeed simply confused, as to the source of the goods in question' ")(footnote omitted)).

In deciding the issue of likelihood of confusion in the instant case, the district court relied on the multifactor balancing test set forth by Judge Friendly in Polaroid Corp. v. Polarad Electronics Corp., 287 F.2d 492, 495 (2d Cir.), cert. denied, 368 U.S. 820 (1961).

At the outset, it must be remembered just what the Polaroid factors are designed to test. The factors are designed to help grapple with the "vexing" problem of resolving the likelihood of confusion issue. Polaroid, 287 F.2d at 495. Therefore, each factor must be evaluated in the context of how it bears on the ultimate question of likelihood of confusion as to the source of the product. It also must be emphasized that the ultimate conclusion as to whether a likelihood of confusion exists is not to be determined in accordance with some rigid formula. The Polaroid factors serve as a useful guide through a difficult quagmire. Each case, however, presents its own peculiar circumstances. In the instant case it also is critical first to determine just what type of actionable confusion as to source is presented. Appellants place great reliance on their labeling as a means of preventing any confusion. While such labeling may prevent appellants' use of appellee's stitching pattern from confusing consumers at the point of sale into believing that appellee manufactured and marketed appellants' jeans, the labeling does nothing to alleviate other forms of likely confusion that are equally actionable.

Turning to an application of the Polaroid test, we must stress at the outset that the district court's detailed findings on each of the Polaroid factors are entitled to considerable deference.

The first factor—the strength of the mark—weighs heavily in appellee's favor. We have defined the strength of a mark as "its tendency to identify the goods sold under the mark as emanating from a particular source." McGregor–Doniger, Inc. v. Drizzle, Inc., 599 F.2d 1126, 1131 (2d Cir.1979). As discussed above, appellee's back pocket stitching pattern is a fanciful registered trademark with a very strong secondary meaning. Virtually all jeans consumers associate the stitching pattern with appellee's products. We agree with the district court that the evidence indicates as a matter of law that appellee's stitching pattern is a very strong mark. This factor is crucial to the likelihood of confusion analysis since appellee's intimate association with the trademark makes it much more likely that consumers will assume wrongly that appellee is somehow associated with appellants' jeans or has authorized the use of its mark, or, in the post-sale context, that appellee has manufactured the jeans.

The second factor—the degree of similarity of the marks—also weighs in favor of appellee. As the district court correctly observed, the two stitching patterns are "essentially identical." Both patterns consist of two intersecting arcs placed in the exact same position on the back pockets of the jeans. The only difference—the fact that appellants' arcs extend 3/4 inch further down the pocket at their intersection—is imperceptible at any significant distance. In light of the fact that the stitching pattern is in no way dictated by function and an infinite number of patterns are possible, the similarity of the two patterns is striking. When this striking similarity is factored into the likelihood of confusion analysis, its great importance becomes clear. In view of the trademark's strength, this nearly identical reproduction of the stitching pattern no doubt is likely to cause consumers to believe that appellee somehow is associated with appellants or at least has consented to the use of its trademark. In the post-sale context, this striking similarity no doubt will cause consumers to transfer the goodwill they feel for appellee to appellants, at least initially. This misuse of goodwill is at the heart of unfair competition. Appellants' reliance on the effect of their labeling with respect to this factor underscores their misguided focus on only the most obvious form of consumer confusion. Appellants' labeling in no way dispels the likelihood that consumers will conclude that appellants' jeans are somehow connected to appellee by virtue of the nearly identical stitching patterns.

The third factor—the proximity of the products—also weighs in favor of appellee. Both products are jeans. Although appellants argue that their jeans are designer jeans and are sold to a different market segment than appellee's jeans, there is significant evidence in the record of an overlap of market segments. Moreover, even if the two jeans are in different segments of the jeans market, such a finding would not switch this factor to appellants' side of the scale. We are trying to determine if it is likely that consumers mistakenly will assume either that appellants' jeans somehow are associated with appellee or are made by appellee. The fact that appellants' jeans arguably are in a different market segment makes this type of confusion more likely. Certainly a consumer observing appellee's striking stitching pattern on appellants' designer jeans might assume that appellee had chosen to enter that market segment using a subsidiary corporation, or that appellee had allowed appellants' designers to use appellee's trademark as a means of reaping some profits from the designer jeans fad without a full commitment to that market segment. Likewise, in the post-sale context a consumer seeing appellants' jeans on a passer-by might think that the jeans were appellee's long-awaited entry into the designer jeans market segment. Motivated by this mistaken notion—appellee's goodwill—the consumer might then buy appellants' jeans even after discovering his error. After all, the way the jeans look is a primary consideration to most designer jeans buyers.

The fourth factor—bridging the gap—is closely related to the proximity of the products and does not aid appellants' case. Under this factor, if the owner of a trademark can show that it intends to enter the market of the alleged infringer, that showing helps to establish a future likelihood of confusion as to source. We have held that the trademark laws are designed in part to protect "the senior user's interest in being able to enter a related field at some future time." Scarves By Vera, Inc. v. Todo Imports Ltd., 544 F.2d 1167, 1172 (2d Cir.1976). In the instant case, the district court rejected as irrelevant appellee's affidavits which stated that appellee was planning to enter the designer jeans market, since the affidavits did not assert that appellee's designer jeans entry would utilize the stitching pattern.[b] We do not believe, however, that the form appellee's entry into the market segment might take is especially relevant to the likelihood of confusion issue. Appellee's entry into the market, regardless of the form it might take, would increase the chances of consumer confusion as to the source of appellants' jeans because of likely consumer expectations that appellee's designer jeans would bear its famous stitching pattern. If one knew only that appellee had entered the designer jeans market and then saw appellants' jeans in a post-sale context, it is very likely that one could confuse them for appellee's entry. See McGregor–Doniger, 599 F.2d at 1136 ("Because consumer confusion is the key, the assumptions of the typical consumer, whether or not they match reality, must be taken into account."). Also, appellee has an interest in preserving its trademark should

[b] This omission no doubt was an oversight on appellee's part since every pair of jeans it has manufactured since 1873 has exhibited the stitching pattern.

it ever wish to produce designer jeans with the stitching pattern. The Lanham Act is meant to protect this interest.

The fifth factor—actual confusion—while not helping appellee, does not really hurt its case. Appellee's only evidence of actual confusion was a consumer survey which the district court discounted due to methodological defects in simulating the post-sale environment. Of course, it is black letter law that actual confusion need not be shown to prevail under the Lanham Act, since actual confusion is very difficult to prove and the Act requires only a likelihood of confusion as to source. While the complete absence of actual confusion evidence after a significant period of competition may weigh in a defendant's favor, such an inference is unjustified in the instant case in view of the survey evidence, even with its methodological defects. While these defects go to the weight of the survey, it is still somewhat probative of actual confusion in the post-sale context. In any event, the record indicates that sales of appellants' jeans have been minimal in the United States thus far and there has been little chance for actual confusion as yet. It would be unfair to penalize appellee for acting to protect its trademark rights before serious damage has occurred.

The sixth factor—the junior user's good faith in adopting the mark—weighs in favor of appellants. The evidence before the district court, when viewed in a light favorable to appellants, indicates that appellants happened on the stitching pattern serendipitously. It must be remembered, however, that intentional copying is not a requirement under the Lanham Act. Also, intent is largely irrelevant in determining if consumers likely will be confused as to source. The history of advertising suggests that consumer reactions usually are unrelated to manufacturer intentions.

The seventh factor—the quality of the respective goods—does add some weight to appellants' position. Appellee has conceded that appellants' jeans are not of an inferior quality, arguably reducing appellee's interest in protecting its reputation from debasement. It must be noted, however, that under the circumstances of this case the good quality of appellants' product actually may increase the likelihood of confusion as to source. Particularly in the post-sale context, consumers easily could assume that quality jeans bearing what is perceived as appellee's trademark stitching pattern to be a Levi's product. The fact that appellants have produced a quality copy suggests that the possibility of their profiting from appellee's goodwill is still likely.

The eighth and final factor—the sophistication of relevant buyers—does not, under the circumstances of this case, favor appellants. The district court found, and the parties do not dispute, that the typical buyer of "designer" jeans is sophisticated with respect to jeans buying. Appellants argue that this sophistication prevents these consumers from becoming confused by nearly identical back pocket stitching patterns. On the contrary, we believe that it is a sophisticated jeans consumer who is most likely to assume that the presence of appellee's trademark stitching pattern on appellants' jeans indicates some sort of association between the two manufacturers. Presumably it is these sophisticated jeans buyers who pay the most attention to back pocket stitching patterns and their "meanings." Likewise, in the post-sale context, the sophisticated buyer is more likely to be affected by the sight of appellee's stitching pattern on appellants' jeans and, consequently, to transfer goodwill. Finally, to the extent the sophisticated buyer is attracted to appellee's jeans because of the exclusiveness of its stitching pattern, appellee's sales will be affected adversely by these buyers' ultimate realization that the pattern is no longer exclusive.

Our review of the district court's application of the Polaroid factors convinces us that the court correctly concluded that consumers are likely to mistakenly associate appellants' jeans with appellee or will confuse the source of appellants' jeans when the jeans are observed in the post-sale context. This result is eminently reasonable in view of the undisputed evidence of the use by one jeans manufacturer of the trademark back pocket stitching pattern of another jeans manufacturer, coupled with the fact that the trademark stitching pattern is instantly associated with its owner and is important to consumers. There is simply too great a risk that appellants will profit from appellee's hard-earned goodwill to permit the use.

■ Miner, Circuit Judge, dissenting (omitted).

## McDonald's Corporation v. Druck and Gerner, DDS., P.C.

United States District Court, N.D. New York, 1993.
814 F.Supp. 1127.

■ Scullin, District Judge.

### BACKGROUND

Plaintiff McDonald's Corporation ("Plaintiff" or "McDonald's") is a Delaware corporation whose principal place of business is in Oak Brook, Illinois. McDonald's and its franchisees operate over 8,000 restaurants in the United States, over 400 of which are located in New York State. McDonald's maintains a regional office in Latham, New York (the "Latham office"), located approximately 150 miles from Plattsburgh, New York.

Defendant Druck and Gerner, D.D.S., P.C., d/b/a McDental ("McDental" or "Defendant") is a New York professional corporation located in Plattsburgh, New York that provides dental services under the name "McDental." Drs. Druck and Gerner named their corporation "McDental," and have operated under this name since the business opened on March 20, 1981 in the Pyramid Mall in Plattsburgh. At the time that they opened, Drs. Druck and Gerner placed an orange illuminated sign with the name "McDental" above the front of the office, and placed a fee schedule sign in the window. Shortly after opening in 1981, Defendant obtained a state service mark for the name "McDental" from the State of New York.

McDonald's alleges that it first learned of McDental in 1987, and that it quickly communicated its concern of Defendant's use of its name by way of protest letters sent to Defendant. The parties communicated via correspondence regarding the use of the name McDental, and engaged in settlement discussions, but were unable to reach an agreement.

Having been unsuccessful in its attempts to persuade Defendant to cease using the name "McDental," McDonald's initiated this lawsuit on August 30, 1990, alleging trademark infringement pursuant to 15 U.S.C.A. §§ 1114, 1121 and 1125, dilution of business pursuant to N.Y.Gen.Bus.Law § 368–d and unfair competition under New York common law. Plaintiff seeks a permanent injunction against all further use of "McDental," all costs associated with this action (including the cost of its consumer survey), and reasonable attorney's fees.

## DISCUSSION

### I. TRADEMARK INFRINGEMENT CLAIMS

The first step in resolving [the claims under §§ 1114 and 1125] is determining whether Plaintiff possesses a trademark entitled to protection; if this is established, the court must then determine the "likelihood of confusion" with Plaintiff's marks that will result from Defendant's use of its mark. See McDonald's Corporation v. McBagel's, Inc., 649 F.Supp. 1268, 1272 (S.D.N.Y.1986).

### A. FAMILY OF MARKS

McDonald's has used in commerce, and obtained federal registrations for, a number of marks distinguished by the "Mc" formative and is the exclusive owner of numerous registrations issued by the USPTO. These registrations encompass both food-related (e.g., "McDonuts") and non-food/generic ("generic")(e.g., "McD", an all-purpose cleaner) items. Underlying its trademark infringement claims is Plaintiff's contention that it possessed at the time of McDental's inception, and continues to possess, a family of "Mc" marks such that Defendant's use of "McDental" is likely to cause confusion among consumers. This contention has been addressed by other courts in litigation involving this plaintiff. See, e.g., J & J Snack Foods Corp. v. McDonald's Corporation, 932 F.2d 1460 (Fed.Cir.1991)(in affirming USPTO ruling that denied trademark registration to snacks food company, court held that McDonald's possesses a family of marks wherein the prefix "Mc" is used with generic food names); McDonald's Corp. v. McBagel's Inc., 649 F.Supp. 1268, 1272 (S.D.N.Y.1986)(court held that McDonald's owned a family of marks using "Mc" in combination with a generic food item).

The McBagel's court, which granted McDonald's request to enjoin the defendant's use of the name "McBagel's" for its restaurant, stated that, "[w]hile it does not hold a registered mark in 'Mc', plaintiff may claim protection for this prefix as a common component of a 'family of marks.'" Id. at 1272 (reference omitted). And, the McBagel's court noted that, "[t]he existence vel non of a family of marks is a question of fact based on the distinctiveness of the common formative component and other factors, including the extent of the family's use, advertising, promotion, and its inclusion in a number of registered and unregistered marks owned by a single party." Id. On an appeal from the USPTO, the Federal Circuit Court of Appeals defined a "family of marks" as a group of marks having a recognizable common characteristic, wherein the marks are composed and used in such a way that the public associates not only the individual marks, but the common characteristic of the family, with the trademark owner. Simply using a series of similar marks does not of itself establish the existence of a family. There must be a recognition among the purchasing public that the common characteristic is indicative of a common origin of the goods. J & J Snack Foods at 1462.

Evidence produced at trial and recent caselaw clearly establish that Plaintiff possesses a family of marks comprised of the prefix "Mc" combined with food items. However, in the present case, Plaintiff must show that it has a protectable family of marks using the "Mc" prefix such that the use of "McDental" would be confused with Plaintiff's family of marks. As the McBagel's court explained: Under the Lanham Act, Section 32(1)(a), 15 USC § 1114(1)(a); as well as Section 43(a), 15 USC § 1125(a), defendants are liable for infringement if their use of the name [McDental] is likely "to cause confusion, or to cause mistake or to deceive" typical consumers into believing some sponsorship, association, affiliation, connection or endorsement exists between McDonald's and defendants. McBagel's, 649 F.Supp. at 1273.

Whether the family of marks possessed by Plaintiff is entitled to protection from Defendant's use of "McDental" turns on "whether there exists a 'likelihood that an appreciable number of ordinarily prudent purchasers [will] be misled, or indeed simply confused, as to the source of the goods in question.' " Thompson Medical Co., Inc. v. Pfizer, Inc., 753 F.2d 208, 213 (2d Cir.1985)(citation omitted). The Second Circuit has held that "such an assessment properly turns on the examination of many factors," and that this list is not exhaustive—the court may consider others. Id. at 213–214 (citation omitted). The factors are: [The] strength of the mark, the degree of similarity between the marks, the proximity of the products, the likelihood that the prior owner will bridge the gap, actual confusion, and the reciprocal of defendant's good faith in adopting its own mark, the quality of defendant's product, and the sophistication of the buyers. Id. at 213 (citing Polaroid Corp. v. Polarad Elects. Corp., 287 F.2d 492, 495 (2d Cir.), cert. denied, 368 U.S. 820, 82 S.Ct. 36, 7 L.Ed.2d 25 (1961)).

Applying the Polaroid factors, the court finds that, as in Quality Inns [International, Inc. v. McDonald's Corp.], 695 F.Supp. 198 (D.Md. 1988)(enjoining use of the mark "McSleep Inn" for a chain of economy hotels), the following factors are of particular importance in assessing the likelihood of confusion in this case: the strength of the mark; the evidence of confusion; the similarity between the marks (including signage and advertising); the proximity of the markets for the products and services identified for the marks, and the likelihood that Plaintiff will bridge the gap; and the intent of Defendant in choosing its mark and its good faith in doing so. See Quality Inns, 695 F.Supp. at 217. The court will discuss each of these seriatim.

a.   Strength of the mark

Although the strength of Plaintiff's family of marks has already been discussed at some length, it should be noted that Plaintiff offered at trial numerous exhibits and testimony attesting to the widespread familiarity of the public with Plaintiff's use of the "Mc" language. Based on all of the evidence this court concludes, as others have, that Plaintiff's family of marks is a strong one. See, e.g., id. at 211–212; McBagel's, 649 F.Supp. at 1274–1275.

b.   Evidence of confusion

Plaintiff also presented survey evidence through its witness, Philip Johnson. Johnson conducted two surveys, in 1988 and 1991, both of which evidenced a likelihood of confusion resulting from Defendant's name. Among the conclusions drawn from the surveys was a finding that some 30% of the population surveyed associated Defendant's name with Plaintiff, the same percentage that another court found to be "substantial." Quality Inns at 218.

In addition to the survey evidence, Plaintiff introduced into evidence deposition testimony including that of former employees of Defendant. See Deps. of Kari Hathaway; William Miller; Holly Lamar. This testimony supports a finding that Defendant's name caused confusion among the public as to whether Defendant was somehow associated with Plaintiff. The court finds simply incredible Dr. Druck's testimony that he never heard anyone, even in a joking manner, associate McDental with McDonald's prior to the commencement of this lawsuit, nor did he himself ever associate the name with that of the Plaintiff.

c.   Similarity between the two marks

The Quality Inns court stated that, "it is not the logo or the word 'sleep' that causes the [infringement] problem; it is the use of the fancifully coined word 'McSleep'." Id. at 220. Likewise, the similarity between Defendant's name and Plaintiff's various "Mc" marks is obvious, and Defendant cannot hope to distinguish the two on the basis that it is the "Dental" and not the "Mc" that makes the name "instantly recognized." See id.

d.   Proximity of the products and the likelihood that Plaintiff will bridge the gap

This factor involves the likelihood "that customers mistakenly will assume either that [the defendant's goods] are somehow associated with [the plaintiff's] or are made by [the plaintiff]." Centaur Communications, Ltd. v. A/S/M Communications, Inc., 830 F.2d 1217, 1226 (2d Cir. 1987)(citation omitted). Initially, it would appear that dental services and fast food have nothing in common, except for the obvious connection between eating and dentistry, and that this factor should thus be weighed in Defendant's favor.

There was no showing at trial that the Plaintiff planned to enter the dental business per se. However, Dr. Cromie, who works with the Ronald McDonald charity houses, testified that since 1985, Plaintiff has included toothbrushes and other similar products in certain of its "Happy Meals" (a product for children). Dr. Cromie also testified that Plaintiff has sponsored dental cleaning via a mobile van that has travelled to different parts of the country, including parts of northern New York. Finally, Dr. Cromie added that the University of Mississippi, through a grant from Plaintiff, has been devising a dental machine for children. Although Dr. Cromie testified that Plaintiff provided the money for this machine, he could not say for certain whether the Plaintiff's name is on the machine.

The Quality Inns court found a connection between fast food and lodging, as one is logically associated with the other. See Quality Inns, 695 F.Supp. at 220–221. However, notwithstanding the fact that oral hygiene normally follows the ingestion of fast (or any other) food, this court is disinclined to find that Plaintiff, even if it begins providing dental floss with its french fries, is likely to "bridge the gap" in any appreciable manner in this case. The evidence presented by Plaintiff did not convince the court that the proximity of the products in this case, or the likelihood that Plaintiff will "bridge the gap," i.e., enter the field of dental service, weighs in Plaintiff's favor.

e.  Intent of Drs. Druck and Gerner and good faith in choosing the name "McDental"

When asked at trial why the name "McDental" was chosen for the business, Dr. Druck testified that the name was chosen because it had a "cute" sound to it, and a "quality of retentiveness." Dr. Druck disavowed any attempt to capitalize on the Plaintiff's well-recognized name and its association with family service and quality. He claimed, in essence, that the name was chosen because a friend of his and Dr. Gerner's, Mr. Josh Patrick, thought it was a name that they could remember—more so than other type names—that he never perceived any association with the two names, nor did he perceive anyone else having any association between the two, even in a social or humorous context.

The court need not deliberate long on the question of intent here. In short, the court finds that the explanations and statements of Drs. Druck and Gerner regarding the choice of the name "McDental" defy common sense and credibility; that they were fully cognizant of the name's similarity to McDonald's and chose to capitalize on Plaintiff's popularity. Consequently, the court easily finds that the good faith factor weighs in Plaintiff's favor.

Summarizing the relevant Polaroid factors, the court concludes that the strength of Plaintiff's mark, evidence of confusion, similarity of the marks and lack of good faith on the part of the individual defendants in choosing their name together support a finding of trademark infringement that warrants the issuance of an injunction in this case.

## Two Pesos, Inc. v. Taco Cabana, Inc.

Supreme Court of the United States, 1992.
505 U.S. 763, 112 S.Ct. 2753, 120 L.Ed.2d 615.

[The majority opinion, which appears in Assignment 2, held that inherently distinctive trade dress is protectable under § 43(a) without a showing of secondary meaning. The Court did not, however, address the more basic question of whether § 43(a) creates the kind of trade dress claim that Taco Cabana asserted. That issue was addressed in a concurring opinion:]

■ JUSTICE STEVENS, concurring in the judgment.

[T]he Court interprets [§ 43(a)] as having created a federal cause of action for infringement of an unregistered trademark or trade dress and concludes that such a mark or dress should receive essentially the same protection as those that are registered. Although I agree with the Court's conclusion, I think it is important to recognize that the meaning of the text has been transformed by the federal courts over the past few decades. I agree with this transformation, even though it marks a departure from the original text, because it is consistent with the purposes of the statute and has recently been endorsed by Congress.

I

It is appropriate to begin with the relevant text of § 43(a). Section 43(a) provides a federal remedy for using either "a false designation of origin" or a "false description or representation" in connection with any goods or services. The full text of the section makes it clear that the word "origin" refers to the geographic location in which the goods originated, and in fact, the phrase "false designation of origin" was understood to be limited to false advertising of geographic origin. For example, the "false designation of origin" language contained in the statute makes it unlawful to represent that California oranges came from Florida, or vice versa.[a]

For a number of years after the 1946 enactment of the Lanham Act, a "false description or representation," like "a false designation of origin," was construed narrowly. The phrase encompassed two kinds of wrongs: false advertising and the common-law tort of "passing off."[b] Neither "secondary meaning" nor "inherent distinctiveness" had anything to do with false advertising, but proof of secondary meaning was an element of the common-law passing-off cause of action.

[a] This is clear from the fact that the cause of action created by this section is available only to a person doing business in the locality falsely indicated as that of origin.

[b] The common-law tort of passing off has been described as "a tort consist[ing] of one passing off his goods as the goods of another." 1 J. Thomas McCarthy, Trademarks and Unfair Competition § 5.2, p. 133 (2d ed. 1984) (McCarthy).

II

Over time, the Circuits have expanded the categories of "false designation of origin" and "false description or representation." One treatise[c] identified the Court of Appeals for the Sixth Circuit as the first to broaden the meaning of "origin" to include "origin of source or manufacture" in addition to geographic origin.[d] Another early case, described as unique among the Circuit cases because it was so "forward-looking,"[e] interpreted the "false description or representation" language to mean more than mere "palming off." L'Aiglon Apparel, Inc. v. Lana Lobell, Inc., 214 F.2d 649 (C.A.3 1954). The court explained: "We find nothing in the legislative history of the Lanham Act to justify the view that [§ 43(a)] is merely declarative of existing law.... It seems to us that Congress has defined a statutory civil wrong of false representation of goods in commerce and has given a broad class of suitors injured or likely to be injured by such wrong the right to relief in the federal courts." Id., at 651. Judge Clark, writing a concurrence in 1956, presciently observed: "Indeed, there is indication here and elsewhere that the bar has not yet realized the potential impact of this statutory provision [§ 43(a)]." Maternally Yours, Inc. v. Your Maternity Shop, Inc., 234 F.2d 538, 546 (CA2). Although some have criticized the expansion as unwise,[f] it is now "a firmly embedded reality."[g] The United States Trade Association Trademark Review Commission noted this transformation with approval: "Section 43(a) is an enigma, but a very popular one. Narrowly drawn and intended to reach false designations or representations as to the geographical origin of products, the section has been widely interpreted to create, in essence, a federal law of unfair competition.... It has definitely eliminated a gap in unfair competition law, and its vitality is showing no signs of age."[h]

Today, [t]he federal courts are in agreement that § 43(a) creates a federal cause of action for trademark and trade dress infringement claims. 1 J. Gilson, Trademark Protection and Practice § 2.13, p. 2–178 (1991). They are also in agreement that the test for liability is likelihood of confusion. And the Circuits are in general agreement, with perhaps the exception of the Second Circuit,[i] that secondary meaning need not be

---

[c] 2 id., § 27:3, p. 345.

[d] Federal–Mogul–Bower Bearings, Inc. v. Azoff, 313 F.2d 405, 408 (C.A.6 1963).

[e] Walter J. Derenberg, 32 N.Y. U. L. Rev., at 1047, 1049.

[f] See, e.g., Kenneth B. Germain, Unfair Trade Practices Under § 43(a) of the Lanham Act: You've Come a Long Way Baby—Too Far, Maybe?, 64 Trademark Rep. 193, 194 (1974)("It is submitted that the cases have applied Section 43(a) to situations it was not intended to cover and have used it in ways that it was not designed to function").

[g] 2 McCarthy § 27:3, p. 345.

[h] The United States Trademark Association Trademark Review Commission Report and Recommendations to USTA President and Board of Directors, 77 Trademark Rep. 375, 426 (1987).

[i] Consistent with the common-law background of § 43(a), the Second Circuit has said that proof of secondary meaning is required to establish a claim that the defendant has traded on the plaintiff's good will by falsely representing that his goods are those of the plaintiff. See, e.g., Crescent Tool Co. v. Kilborn & Bishop Co., 247 F. 299 (1917). To my knowledge, however, the Second Circuit has not explained why "inherent distinctiveness" is not an appropriate substitute for

established once there is a finding of inherent distinctiveness in order to establish a trade dress violation under § 43(a).

## III

Even though the lower courts' expansion of the categories contained in § 43(a) is unsupported by the text of the Act, I am persuaded that it is consistent with the general purposes of the Act. For example, Congressman Lanham, the bill's sponsor, stated: "The purpose of [the Act] is to protect legitimate business and the consumers of the country." 92 Cong. Rec. 7524 (1946). One way of accomplishing these dual goals was by creating uniform legal rights and remedies that were appropriate for a national economy. Although the protection of trademarks had once been "entirely a State matter," the result of such a piecemeal approach was that there were almost "as many different varieties of common law as there are States" so that a person's right to a trademark "in one State may differ widely from the rights which [that person] enjoys in another." H. R. Rep. No. 944, 76th Cong., 1st Sess., 4 (1939). The House Committee on Trademarks and Patents, recognizing that "trade is no longer local, but ... national," saw the need for "national legislation along national lines [to] secure to the owners of trademarks in interstate commerce definite rights." Ibid.[j]

Congress has revisited this statute from time to time, and has accepted the "judicial legislation" that has created this federal cause of action. Recently, for example, in the Trademark Law Revision Act of 1988, Pub. L. 100–667, 102 Stat. 3935, Congress codified the judicial interpretation of § 43(a), giving its imprimatur to a growing body of case law from the Circuits that had expanded the section beyond its original language.

Although Congress has not specifically addressed the question whether secondary meaning is required under § 43(a), the steps it has taken in this subsequent legislation suggest that secondary meaning is not required if inherent distinctiveness has been established.[k] First, Congress broadened

proof of secondary meaning in a trade dress case. Most of the cases in which the Second Circuit has said that secondary meaning is required did not involve findings of inherent distinctiveness. For example, in Vibrant Sales, Inc. v. New Body Boutique, Inc., 652 F.2d 299 (1981), cert. denied, 455 U.S. 909 (1982), the product at issue—a velcro belt—was functional and lacked "any distinctive, unique or non-functional mark or feature." 652 F.2d, at 305. Similarly, in Stormy Clime Ltd. v. ProGroup, Inc., 809 F.2d 971, 977 (1987), the court described functionality as a continuum, and placed the contested rain-jacket closer to the functional end than to the distinctive end. Although the court described the lightweight bag in LeSportsac, Inc. v. K Mart Corp., 754 F.2d 71 (1985), as having a distinctive appearance and concluded that the District Court's finding of nonfunctionali-

ty was not clearly erroneous, id., at 74, it did not explain why secondary meaning was also required in such a case.

[j] Forty years later, the USTA Trademark Review Commission assessed the state of trademark law. The conclusion that it reached serves as a testimonial to the success of the Act in achieving its goal of uniformity: "The federal courts now decide, under federal law, all but a few trademark disputes. State trademark law and state courts are less influential than ever. Today the Lanham Act is the paramount source of trademark law in the United States, as interpreted almost exclusively by the federal courts." Trademark Review Commission, 77 Trademark Rep., at 377.

[k] "When several acts of Congress are passed touching the same subject-matter, subsequent legislation may be considered to

the language of § 43(a) to make explicit that the provision prohibits "any word, term, name, symbol, or device, or any combination thereof" that is "likely to cause confusion, or to cause mistake, or to deceive as to the affiliation, connection, or association of such person with another person, or as to the origin, sponsorship, or approval of his or her goods, services, or commercial activities by another person." 15 U.S.C.A. § 1125(a). That language makes clear that a confusingly similar trade dress is actionable under § 43(a), without necessary reference to "falsity." Second, Congress approved and confirmed the extensive judicial development under the provision, including its application to trade dress that the federal courts had come to apply.[1] Third, the legislative history of the 1988 amendments reaffirms Congress' goals of protecting both businesses and consumers with the Lanham Act. And fourth, Congress explicitly extended to any violation of § 43(a) the basic Lanham Act remedial provisions whose text previously covered only registered trademarks.[m] The aim of the amendments was to apply the same protections to unregistered marks as were already afforded to registered marks. See S. Rep. No. 100–515, p. 40 (1988). These steps buttress the conclusion that § 43(a) is properly understood to provide protection in accordance with the standards for registration in § 2. These aspects of the 1988 legislation bolster the claim that an inherently distinctive trade dress may be protected under § 43(a) without proof of secondary meaning.

## IV

In light of the general consensus among the Courts of Appeals that have actually addressed the question, and the steps on the part of Congress to codify that consensus, stare decisis concerns persuade me to join the Court's conclusion that secondary meaning is not required to establish a trade dress violation under § 43(a) once inherent distinctiveness has been established. Accordingly, I concur in the judgment, but not in the opinion of the Court.

---

assist in the interpretation of prior legislation upon the same subject." Tiger v. Western Investment Co., 221 U.S. 286, 309 (1911).

[1] As the Senate Report explained, revision of Section 43(a) is designed "to codify the interpretation it has been given by the courts. Because Section 43(a) of the Act fills an important gap in federal unfair competition law, the committee expects the courts to continue to interpret the section.

"As written, Section 43(a) appears to deal only with false descriptions or representations and false designations of geographic origin. Since its enactment in 1946, however, it has been widely interpreted as creating, in essence, a federal law of unfair competition. For example, it has been applied to cases involving the infringement of unregistered marks, violations of trade dress and certain nonfunctional configurations of goods and actionable false advertising claims." S. Rep. No. 100–515, p. 40 (1988).

[m] See 15 U.S.C.A. §§ 1114, 1116–1118.

## (2) Dilution under § 43(c)

# Moseley v. V Secret Catalogue, Inc.

Supreme Court of the United States, 2003.
537 U.S. 418, 123 S.Ct. 1115, 155 L.Ed.2d 1.

■ JUSTICE STEVENS delivered the opinion of the Court.[a]

In 1995 Congress amended § 43 of the Trademark Act of 1946, 15 U.S.C. § 1125, to provide a remedy for the "dilution of famous marks." That amendment, known as the Federal Trademark Dilution Act (FTDA), describes the factors that determine whether a mark is "distinctive and famous," and defines the term "dilution" as "the lessening of the capacity of a famous mark to identify and distinguish goods or services." The question we granted certiorari to decide is whether objective proof of actual injury to the economic value of a famous mark (as opposed to a presumption of harm arising from a subjective "likelihood of dilution" standard) is a requisite for relief under the FTDA.

I

Petitioners, Victor and Cathy Moseley, own and operate a retail store named "Victor's Little Secret" in a strip mall in Elizabethtown, Kentucky. They have no employees.

Respondents are affiliated corporations that own the VICTORIA'S SECRET trademark, and operate over 750 Victoria's Secret stores, two of which are in Louisville, Kentucky, a short drive from Elizabethtown. In 1998 they spent over $55 million advertising "the VICTORIA'S SECRET brand—one of moderately priced, high quality, attractively designed lingerie sold in a store setting designed to look like a wom[a]n's bedroom." They distribute 400 million copies of the Victoria's Secret catalog each year, including 39,000 in Elizabethtown. In 1998 their sales exceeded $1.5 billion.

In the February 12, 1998, edition of a weekly publication distributed to residents of the military installation at Fort Knox, Kentucky, petitioners advertised the "GRAND OPENING Just in time for Valentine's Day!" of their store "VICTOR'S SECRET" in nearby Elizabethtown. The ad featured "Intimate Lingerie *for every woman*"; "Romantic Lighting"; "Lycra Dresses"; "Pagers"; and "Adult Novelties/Gifts." An army colonel, who saw the ad and was offended by what he perceived to be an attempt to use a reputable company's trademark to promote the sale of "unwholesome, tawdry merchandise," sent a copy to respondents. Their counsel then wrote to petitioners stating that their choice of the name "Victor's Secret" for a store selling lingerie was likely to cause confusion with the well-known victoria's secret mark and, in addition, was likely to "dilute the distinctiveness" of the mark. They requested the immediate discontinuance of the use of the name "and any variations thereof." In response, petitioners changed

[a] Justice SCALIA joins all but Part III of this opinion.

the name of their store to "Victor's Little Secret." Because that change did not satisfy respondents, they promptly filed this action in Federal District Court.

The complaint contained four separate claims: (1) for trademark infringement alleging that petitioners' use of their trade name was "likely to cause confusion and/or mistake in violation of 15 U.S.C. § 1114(1)"; (2) for unfair competition alleging misrepresentation in violation of § 1125(a); (3) for "federal dilution" in violation of the FTDA; and (4) for trademark infringement and unfair competition in violation of the common law of Kentucky. In the dilution count, the complaint alleged that petitioners' conduct was "likely to blur and erode the distinctiveness" and "tarnish the reputation" of the VICTORIA'S SECRET trademark.

After discovery the parties filed cross-motions for summary judgment. The record contained uncontradicted affidavits and deposition testimony describing the vast size of respondents' business, the value of the VICTORIA'S SECRET name, and descriptions of the items sold in the respective parties' stores. Respondents sell a "complete line of lingerie" and related items, each of which bears a VICTORIA'S SECRET label or tag. Petitioners sell a wide variety of items, including adult videos, "adult novelties," and lingerie. Victor Moseley stated in an affidavit that women's lingerie represented only about five per cent of their sales. In support of their motion for summary judgment, respondents submitted an affidavit by an expert in marketing who explained "the enormous value" of respondents' mark. Neither he, nor any other witness, expressed any opinion concerning the impact, if any, of petitioners' use of the name "Victor's Little Secret" on that value.

Finding that the record contained no evidence of actual confusion between the parties' marks, the District Court concluded that "no likelihood of confusion exists as a matter of law" and entered summary judgment for petitioners on the infringement and unfair competition claims. With respect to the FTDA claim, however, the court ruled for respondents.

Noting that petitioners did not challenge Victoria Secret's claim that its mark is "famous," the only question it had to decide was whether petitioners' use of their mark diluted the quality of respondents' mark. Reasoning from the premise that dilution "corrodes" a trademark either by " 'blurring its product identification or by damaging positive associations that have attached to it,' " the court first found the two marks to be sufficiently similar to cause dilution, and then found "that Defendants' mark dilutes Plaintiffs' mark because of its tarnishing effect upon the Victoria's Secret mark." (quoting *Ameritech, Inc. v. American Info. Technologies Corp.*, 811 F.2d 960, 965 (C.A.6 1987)). It therefore enjoined petitioners "from using the mark 'Victor's Little Secret' on the basis that it causes dilution of the distinctive quality of the Victoria's Secret mark." The court did not, however, find that any "blurring" had occurred.

The Court of Appeals for the Sixth Circuit affirmed. In a case decided shortly after the entry of the District Court's judgment in this case, the

Sixth Circuit had adopted the standards for determining dilution under the FDTA that were enunciated by the Second Circuit in *Nabisco, Inc. v. PF Brands, Inc.*, 191 F.3d 208 (1999). See *Kellogg Co. v. Exxon Corp.*, 209 F.3d 562 (C.A.6 2000). In order to apply those standards, it was necessary to discuss two issues that the District Court had not specifically addressed— whether respondents' mark is "distinctive,"[b] and whether relief could be granted before dilution has actually occurred. With respect to the first issue, the court rejected the argument that Victoria's Secret could not be distinctive because "secret" is an ordinary word used by hundreds of lingerie concerns. The court concluded that the entire mark was "arbitrary and fanciful" and therefore deserving of a high level of trademark protection. On the second issue, the court relied on a distinction suggested by this sentence in the House Report: "Confusion leads to immediate injury, while dilution is an infection, which if allowed to spread, will inevitably destroy the advertising value of the mark." H.R.Rep. No. 104–374, p. 1030 (1995), U.S.Code Cong. & Admin.News 1995, pp. 1029, 1030. This statement, coupled with the difficulty of proving actual harm, lent support to the court's ultimate conclusion that the evidence in this case sufficiently established "dilution."

In reaching that conclusion the Court of Appeals expressly rejected the holding of the Fourth Circuit in *Ringling Bros.–Barnum & Bailey Combined Shows, Inc. v. Utah Div. of Travel Development*, 170 F.3d 449 (1999). In that case, which involved a claim that Utah's use on its license plates of the phrase "greatest *snow* on earth" was causing dilution of the "greatest *show* on earth," the court had concluded "that to establish dilution of a famous mark under the federal Act requires proof that (1) a defendant has made use of a junior mark sufficiently similar to the famous mark to evoke in a relevant universe of consumers a mental association of the two that (2) has caused (3) actual economic harm to the famous mark's economic value by lessening its former selling power as an advertising agent for its goods or services." Because other Circuits have also expressed differing views about the "actual harm" issue, we granted certiorari to resolve the conflict. 535 U.S. 985, 122 S.Ct. 1536, 152 L.Ed.2d 463 (2002).

II

Traditional trademark infringement law is a part of the broader law of unfair competition, see *Hanover Star Milling Co. v. Metcalf*, 240 U.S. 403, 413, 36 S.Ct. 357, 60 L.Ed. 713 (1916), that has its sources in English common law, and was largely codified in the Trademark Act of 1946 (Lanham Act). See B. Pattishall, D. Hilliard, & J. Welch, Trademarks and Unfair Competition 2 (4th ed. 2000) ("The United States took the [trademark and unfair competition] law of England as its own"). That law broadly prohibits uses of trademarks, trade names, and trade dress that are

---

[b] It is quite clear that the statute intends distinctiveness, in addition to fame, as an essential element. The operative language defining the tort requires that 'the [junior] person's … use … caus[e] dilution of the distinctive quality of the [senior] mark.' 15 U.S.C. § 1125(c)(1). There can be no dilution of a mark's distinctive quality unless the mark is distinctive." Nabisco, Inc. v. PF Brands, Inc., 191 F.3d 208, 216 (C.A.2 1999).

likely to cause confusion about the source of a product or service. See 15 U.S.C. §§ 1114, 1125(a)(1)(A). Infringement law protects consumers from being misled by the use of infringing marks and also protects producers from unfair practices by an "imitating competitor." *Qualitex Co. v. Jacobson Products Co.,* 514 U.S. 159, 163–164, 115 S.Ct. 1300, 131 L.Ed.2d 248 (1995).

Because respondents did not appeal the District Court's adverse judgement on counts 1, 2, and 4 of their complaint, we decide the case on the assumption that the Moseleys' use of the name "Victor's Little Secret" neither confused any consumers or potential consumers, nor was likely to do so. Moreover, the disposition of those counts also makes it appropriate to decide the case on the assumption that there was no significant competition between the adversaries in this case. Neither the absence of any likelihood of confusion nor the absence of competition, however, provides a defense to the statutory dilution claim alleged in count 3 of the complaint.

Unlike traditional infringement law, the prohibitions against trademark dilution are not the product of common-law development, and are not motivated by an interest in protecting consumers. The seminal discussion of dilution is found in Frank Schechter's 1927 law review article concluding "that the preservation of the uniqueness of a trademark should constitute the only rational basis for its protection." Rational Basis of Trademark Protection, 40 Harv. L.Rev. 813, 831. Schechter supported his conclusion by referring to a German case protecting the owner of the well-known trademark "Odol" for mouthwash from use on various noncompeting steel products. That case, and indeed the principal focus of the Schechter article, involved an established arbitrary mark that had been "added to rather than withdrawn from the human vocabulary" and an infringement that made use of the identical mark.

Some 20 years later Massachusetts enacted the first state statute protecting trademarks from dilution. It provided:

> "Likelihood of injury to business reputation or of dilution of the distinctive quality of a trade name or trade-mark shall be a ground for injunctive relief in cases of trade-mark infringement or unfair competition notwithstanding the absence of competition between the parties or of confusion as to the source of goods or services." 1947 Mass. Acts, p. 300, ch. 307.

Notably, that statute, unlike the "Odol" case, prohibited both the likelihood of "injury to business reputation" and "dilution." It thus expressly applied to both "tarnishment" and "blurring." At least 25 States passed similar laws in the decades before the FTDA was enacted in 1995. See Restatement (Third) of Unfair Competition '25, Statutory Note (1995).

III

In 1988, when Congress adopted amendments to the Lanham Act, it gave consideration to an antidilution provision. During the hearings on the 1988 amendments, objections to that provision based on a concern that it might have applied to expression protected by the First Amendment were voiced and the provision was deleted from the amendments. H.R.Rep. No. 100–1028 (1988). The bill, H.R. 1295, 104th Cong., 1st Sess., that was introduced in the House in 1995, and ultimately enacted as the FTDA, included two exceptions designed to avoid those concerns: a provision allowing "fair use" of a registered mark in comparative advertising or promotion, and the provision that noncommercial use of a mark shall not constitute dilution. See 15 U.S.C. § 1125(c)(4).

On July 19, 1995, the Subcommittee on Courts and Intellectual Property of the House Judiciary Committee held a 1–day hearing on H.R. 1295. No opposition to the bill was voiced at the hearing and, with one minor amendment that extended protection to unregistered as well as registered marks, the subcommittee endorsed the bill and it passed the House unanimously. The committee's report stated that the "purpose of H.R. 1295 is to protect famous trademarks from subsequent uses that blur the distinctiveness of the mark or tarnish or disparage it, even in the absence of a likelihood of confusion." H.R.Rep. No. 104–374, p. 2 (1995), U.S.Code Cong. & Admin.News 1995, pp. 1029, 1030. As examples of dilution, it stated that "the use of DUPONT shoes, BUICK aspirin, and KODAK pianos would be actionable under this legislation." *Id.,* at 3. In the Senate an identical bill, S. 1513, 104th Cong., 1st Sess., was introduced on December 29, 1995, and passed on the same day by voice vote without any hearings. In his explanation of the bill, Senator Hatch also stated that it was intended "to protect famous trademarks from subsequent uses that blur the distinctiveness of the mark or tarnish or disparage it," and referred to the Dupont Shoes, Buick aspirin, and Kodak piano examples, as well as to the Schechter law review article. 141 Cong. Rec. 38559–38561 (1995).

## IV

The Victoria's Secret mark is unquestionably valuable and petitioners have not challenged the conclusion that it qualifies as a "famous mark" within the meaning of the statute. Moreover, as we understand their submission, petitioners do not contend that the statutory protection is confined to identical uses of famous marks, or that the statute should be construed more narrowly in a case such as this. Even if the legislative history might lend some support to such a contention, it surely is not compelled by the statutory text.

The District Court's decision in this case rested on the conclusion that the name of petitioners' store "tarnished" the reputation of respondents' mark, and the Court of Appeals relied on both "tarnishment" and "blurring" to support its affirmance. Petitioners have not disputed the relevance of tarnishment, presumably because that concept was prominent in litigation brought under state antidilution statutes and because it was mentioned in the legislative history. Whether it is actually embraced by the statutory text, however, is another matter. Indeed, the contrast between the state statutes, which expressly refer to both "injury to business reputation" and to "dilution of the distinctive quality of a trade name or trademark," and the federal statute which refers only to the latter, arguably supports a narrower reading of the FTDA. See Klieger, Trademark Dilution: The Whittling Away of the Rational Basis for Trademark Protection, 58 U. Pitt. L.Rev. 789, 812–813, and n. 132 (1997).

The contrast between the state statutes and the federal statute, however, sheds light on the precise question that we must decide. For those state statutes, like several provisions in the federal Lanham Act, repeatedly refer to a "likelihood" of harm, rather than to a completed harm. The relevant text of the FTDA, provides that "the owner of a famous mark" is entitled to injunctive relief against another person's commercial use of a mark or trade name if that use "*causes dilution* of the distinctive quality" of the famous mark. 15 U.S.C. § 1125(c)(1) (emphasis added). This text unambiguously requires a showing of actual dilution, rather than a likelihood of dilution.

This conclusion is fortified by the definition of the term "dilution" itself. That definition provides:

> "The term 'dilution' means the lessening of the capacity of a famous mark to identify and distinguish goods or services, regardless of the presence or absence of—
>
> "(1) competition between the owner of the famous mark and other parties, or
>
> "(2) likelihood of confusion, mistake, or deception." § 1127.

The contrast between the initial reference to an actual "lessening of the capacity" of the mark, and the later reference to a "likelihood of confusion, mistake, or deception" in the second caveat confirms the conclusion that actual dilution must be established.

Of course, that does not mean that the consequences of dilution, such as an actual loss of sales or profits, must also be proved. To the extent that language in the Fourth Circuit's opinion in the *Ringling Bros.* case suggests otherwise, we disagree. We do agree, however, with that court's conclusion that, at least where the marks at issue are not identical, the mere fact that consumers mentally associate the junior user's mark with a famous mark is not sufficient to establish actionable dilution. As the facts of that case demonstrate, such mental association will not necessarily reduce the capacity of the famous mark to identify the goods of its owner, the statutory requirement for dilution under the FTDA. For even though Utah drivers may be reminded of the circus when they see a license plate referring to the "greatest *snow* on earth," it by no means follows that they will associate "the greatest show on earth" with skiing or snow sports, or associate it less strongly or exclusively with the circus. "Blurring" is not a necessary consequence of mental association. (Nor, for that matter, is "tarnishing.")

The record in this case establishes that an army officer who saw the advertisement of the opening of a store named "Victor's Secret" did make the mental association with "Victoria's Secret," but it also shows that he did not therefore form any different impression of the store that his wife and daughter had patronized. There is a complete absence of evidence of any lessening of the capacity of the Victoria's Secret mark to identify and distinguish goods or services sold in Victoria's Secret stores or advertised in its catalogs. The officer was offended by the ad, but it did not change his conception of Victoria's Secret. His offense was directed entirely at petitioners, not at respondents. Moreover, the expert retained by respondents had nothing to say about the impact of petitioners' name on the strength of respondents' mark.

Noting that consumer surveys and other means of demonstrating actual dilution are expensive and often unreliable, respondents and their *amici* argue that evidence of an actual "lessening of the capacity of a famous mark to identify and distinguish goods or services," § 1127, may be difficult to obtain. It may well be, however, that direct evidence of dilution such as consumer surveys will not be necessary if actual dilution can reliably be proven through circumstantial evidence—the obvious case is one where the junior and senior marks are identical. Whatever difficulties of proof may be entailed, they are not an acceptable reason for dispensing with proof of an essential element of a statutory violation. The evidence in the present record is not sufficient to support the summary judgment on the dilution count. The judgment is therefore reversed, and the case is remanded for further proceedings consistent with this opinion.

■ JUSTICE KENNEDY, concurring.

As of this date, few courts have reviewed the statute we are considering, the Federal Trademark Dilution Act, 15 U.S.C. § 1125(c), and I agree with the Court that the evidentiary showing required by the statute can be clarified on remand. The conclusion that the VICTORIA'S SECRET mark is a famous mark has not been challenged throughout the litigation, and seems not to be in question. The remaining issue is what factors are to be considered to establish dilution.

For this inquiry, considerable attention should be given, in my view, to the word "capacity" in the statutory phrase that defines dilution as "the lessening of the capacity of a famous mark to identify and distinguish goods or services." 15 U.S.C. § 1127. When a competing mark is first adopted, there will be circumstances when the case can turn on the probable consequences its commercial use will have for the famous mark. In this respect, the word "capacity" imports into the dilution inquiry both the present and the potential power of the famous mark to identify and distinguish goods, and in some cases the fact that this power will be diminished could suffice to show dilution. Capacity is defined as "the power or ability to hold, receive, or accommodate." Webster's Third New International Dictionary 330 (1961); see also Webster's New International Dictionary 396 (2d ed. 1949) ("Power of receiving, containing, or absorbing"); 2 Oxford English Dictionary 857 (2d ed. 1989) ("Ability to receive or contain; holding power"); American Heritage Dictionary 275 (4th ed. 2000) ("The ability to receive, hold, or absorb"). If a mark will erode or lessen the power of the famous mark to give customers the assurance of quality and the full satisfaction they have in knowing they have purchased goods bearing the famous mark, the elements of dilution may be established.

Diminishment of the famous mark's capacity can be shown by the probable consequences flowing from use or adoption of the competing mark. This analysis is confirmed by the statutory authorization to obtain injunctive relief. 15 U.S.C. § 1125(c)(2). The essential role of injunctive relief is to "prevent future wrong, although no right has yet been violated." *Swift & Co. v. United States,* 276 U.S. 311, 326, 48 S.Ct. 311, 72 L.Ed. 587 (1928). Equity principles encourage those who are injured to assert their rights promptly. A holder of a famous mark threatened with diminishment of the mark's capacity to serve its purpose should not be forced to wait until the damage is done and the distinctiveness of the mark has been eroded.

In this case, the District Court found that petitioners' trademark had tarnished the VICTORIA'S SECRET mark. The Court of Appeals affirmed this conclusion and also found dilution by blurring. The Court's opinion does not foreclose injunctive relief if respondents on remand present sufficient evidence of either blurring or tarnishment.

### (3) Infringement on the Internet: the UDRP and § 43(d)

## Wal–Mart Stores, Inc. v. Wallmartcanadasucks.com

Administrative Panel Decision (WIPO Arbitration And Mediation Center), 2000.
Case No. D2000–1104, http://arbiter.wipo.int/domains/decisions/html/2000/d2000–1104.html

Henry H. Perritt, Jr., Sole Panelist:

Introduction

This case involves [the] narrow[] question whether a domain name including the suffix "sucks" is confusingly similar to the text string to which "sucks" is appended, or, alternatively, whether a criticism or parody privilege extends to the use of the suffix "sucks." As sole panelist, I conclude that a domain name including the word "sucks" cannot be confusingly similar, and that a privilege for criticism and parody reinforces that conclusion.

Parties' Contentions

A.  Complainant

The complainant asserts that Respondent registered and is using the domain name "wallmartcanadasucks.com" in bad faith.

In the United States, Complainant owns, among other trademarks, United States Registration Number 1,783,039, registered July 20, 1993, for the mark Wal–Mart for use in retail department store services (U.S. 101). Among the marks Complainant owns and uses in Canada is Canada Registration Number TMA502,605, registered October 21, 1998, for the mark Wal–Mart for use in retail department store services.

Complainant's Wal–Mart mark is famous. The Wal–Mart mark is famous in part, because the mark has been in continuous use since at least 1962. The mark is also famous because Complainant is the world's number one retailer with stores in the United States, Canada, Puerto Rico, Mexico, Brazil, Argentina, China, United Kingdom, Korea, Indonesia and Germany.

Complainant argues that the domain name "wallmartcanadasucks.com" is identical or confusingly similar to Complainant's Wal–Mart trademark. The Complainant requests that the Administrative Panel appointed in this proceeding issue a decision that the contested domain name be transferred to the Complainant.

B. Respondent

The Respondent asserts that wallmartcanadasucks.com is run as a freedom of expression site. As with wallmartcanadasucks.com, the use of the sucks.com suffix attached to a company name has become a standard formula for Internet sites protesting the business practices of a company. For instance, the use of wallmartcanadasucks.com would, in no way, be confused as a site run by Wal–Mart. "Anyone with even the tiniest speck of intelligence would realize that Wal–Mart would never be running a site called: wallmartcanadasucks.com. In fact, the only reason Wal–Mart wishes to own the disputed domain name is to take it out of circulation. They do not wish to use it, but wish to keep it from individuals who wish to use it to post complaints against them."

Analysis

A. Introduction

The Respondent hardly appears with clean hands. He has been found in the past to be a Cybersquatter with respect to this complainant. His correspondence with the complainant could support an inference, as complainant suggests, of extortion—"pay me or I will continue to use the Web to disparage and embarrass you." In Panel Decision No.D2000–0477, the Respondent was found to have violated [ICANN's Uniform Domain Name Resolution Policy (UDRP)] on facts involving use of the suffix "sucks" in a domain name.

But distasteful conduct should not stampede UDRP decision makers into an unwarranted expansion of the domain name dispute process. The UDRP has a narrow scope. It is meant to protect against trademark infringement, not to provide a general remedy for all misconduct involving domain names. Posting defamatory material on a Web site would not justify revocation of a domain name under the UDRP. "Bad faith" under the UDRP is a term of art. It does not reach every use of a domain name that might constitute bad faith in the ordinary sense of term. Disciplined construction of the UDRP is appropriate for another reason. The Policy should not be used to shut down robust debate and criticism. Allowing trademark owners to shut down sites that obviously are aimed at criticism of the trademark holder does just that.

The remainder of this panel decision reviews the rules of decision to be applied to this dispute, and separately analyzes the likelihood of confusion, treatment of parody and criticism under the Lanham Act, explores the relationship between the legitimacy of Respondent interests and the content of the accused Web site, evaluates the evidence of solicitation of payment for the accused domain name, and presents factual findings and conclusions.

B.   Rules of decision

"A Panel shall decide a complaint on the basis of the statements and documents submitted and in accordance with the Policy, these Rules and any rules and principles of law that it deems applicable." Rules for Uniform Domain Name Dispute Resolution 15(a) (hereinafter "ICANN Rules")

Under the Policy, the complainant has the burden to prove each of the following three elements:

(i) the accused domain name is identical or confusingly similar to a trademark or service mark in which the complainant has rights; and

(ii) the Respondent has no rights or legitimate interests in respect of the domain name; and

(iii) the accused domain name has been registered and is being used in bad faith. Uniform Domain Name Dispute Resolution ("UDRP" ) & 4(a).

Bad faith may be shown by establishing:

(i) circumstances indicating that the Respondent has registered or has acquired the domain name primarily for the purpose of selling, renting, or otherwise transferring the domain name registration to the complainant who is the owner of the trademark or service mark or to a competitor of that complainant, for valuable consideration in excess of the Respondent's documented out-of-pocket costs directly related to the domain name; or

(ii) the Respondent has registered the domain name in order to prevent the owner of the trademark or service mark from reflecting the mark in a corresponding domain name, provided that the Respondent has engaged in a pattern of such conduct; or

(iii) the Respondent has registered the domain name primarily for the purpose of disrupting the business of a competitor; or

(iv) by using the domain name, the Respondent has intentionally attempted to attract, for commercial gain, Internet users to its web site or other on-line location, by creating a likelihood of confusion with the complainant's mark as to the source, sponsorship, affiliation, or endorsement of your web site or location or of a product or service on the Respondent's web site or location. UDRP & 4(b).

[The other source of law is] the U.S. Anti–Cybersquatting Consumer Protection Act ("ACPA"), 15 U.S.C. § 1125(d).

The ICANN Policy and the ACPA have similar elements. First, a complainant must show that the accused domain name is identical or confusingly similar to the complainant's trademark. Second, the accused domain name must be registered or used in bad faith. Both the ICANN Policy and the ACPA offer nonexclusive factors for determining bad faith. The ICANN Policy includes some factors not included in the ACPA. The ACPA includes some factors not included in the ICANN Policy. Both the ICANN Policy and the ACPA consider the degree to which the Respondent has legitimate interests in the accused domain name. Accordingly, cases applying the ACPA can be useful reference points for interpreting the ICANN Policy. In addition, trademark cases determining likelihood of confusion can be useful in interpreting the first element of the ICANN Policy.

In any event, the ICANN rules permit a panel to decide a complaint in accordance with "any rules and principles of law that it deems applicable." ICANN Rules & 15(a). U.S. ACPA and trademark infringement cases are natural sources of rules and principles of law to apply in resolving this dispute.

## C.   Likelihood of confusion

The ICANN Policy and the ACPA have a similar requirement that a complainant must show that the accused domain name is identical or confusingly similar to the complainant's trademark. Bad faith, no matter how egregious, cannot supply a likelihood of confusion where it does not otherwise exist.

Two lines of authority are pertinent to this dispute. The first involves application of factors for determining likelihood of confusion under the Lanham Act to a Web page using the word "sucks" to signify criticism. The second involves the treatment of parody and criticism under the ACPA and the Lanham Act more generally.

### 1.   [Likelihood of confusion under the Lanham Act]

[On this issue, the Panelist examined several of the factors listed in Bally Total Fitness Holding Corp v. Faber, 29 F.Supp.2d 1161 (C.D. Cal. 1998), which involved the use of the phrase "Bally sucks" on a web page. These included the similarity of the marks, evidence of actual confusion, marketing channels used, degree of care likely to be exercised, and the defendant's intent in selecting the mark:]

Applying the Bally analysis to the instant case, I conclude that wallmartcanadasucks.com is not identical or similar to Wal–Mart's marks. They serve fundamentally different purposes. Wal–Mart's domain names serve as commercial advertisements and indications of sources of products and services. wallmartcanadasucks.com is criticism. As in Bally, a reasonably prudent user would not mistake the wallmartcanadasucks.com site for any of Wal–Mart's official sites. As in Bally, the primary purpose of the accused site is criticism, not promotion of goods related to Wal–Mart goods. Thus the information disseminated through the sites of Respondent and complainant are not related. As in Bally, prohibiting the Respondent from using wallmartcanadasucks.com and variants on the name would effectively isolate him from Internet users he wishes to reach in connection with his criticism of Wal–Mart. As in Bally, the Respondent cannot exercise his right to publish critical commentary about Wal–Mart without making reference to Wal–Mart. As in Bally, there is little likelihood that Wal–Mart will extend its business to operate an official anti Wal–Mart site. The Bally analysis, therefore, is strong authority for finding no likelihood of confusion.

2.   Parody and criticism under the Lanham Act

A number of cases decided under the ACPA and, more generally, under the Lanham Act, have considered special treatment for accused domain names and marks that are used for parody or criticism.

> "In general, a reference to a copyrighted work or trademark may be permissible if the use is purely for parodic purposes. To the extent the original work must be referenced in order to accomplish the parody, that reference is acceptable." Lyons Partnership v. Giannoulas, 179 F.3d 384, 388 (5th Cir. 1999) (affirming summary judgment for defendant asserting parody defense, citing Campbell v. Acuff–Rose Music, 510 U.S. 569 (1994))

Trademark law more generally recognizes a privilege for use of marks for parodic or critical purposes. Often, such a purpose influences the likelihood of confusion analysis. The Restatement recognizes the special position that criticism occupies in trademark law:

> "One who uses a designation that resembles the trademark, trade name collective mark or certification mark of another, not in a manner that is likely to associate the other's mark with the goods, services, or business of the actor, but rather to comment on, criticize, ridicule, parody, or disparage the other or the other's goods, services business, or mark, is subject to liability without proof of the likelihood of confusion only if the actor's conduct meets the requirements of a cause of action for defamation, invasion of privacy, or injurious falsehood." Restatement (Third) of Unfair Competition § 25 cmt. i (1995).

In domain name disputes it is critical whether the accused domain name itself signifies parodic or critical purposes, as opposed to imitation of trademark.

People for the Ethical Treatment of Animals v. Doughney, 113 F.Supp.2d 915 (E.D. Va. 2000) involved an unsuccessful parody defense to a claim of trademark infringement, dilution and violation of the Anti–Cybersquatting Act. The defendant registered the domain name peta.org, and used it to encourage consumption of meat and animal products. "Only after arriving at the 'peta.org' web site could the web site browser determine that this was not a web site owned, controlled or sponsored by PETA ("People for the Ethical Treatment of Animals"). Therefore, the two images: (1) the famous PETA name and (2) the "People Eating Tasty Animals" web site was not a parody because not simultaneous." Thus there was considerable likelihood of confusion as to the sponsorship of the Web site, and only a weak link to freedom of expression.

Unlike peta.org, walmartcanadasucks.com clearly signifies the critical purpose of the accused domain, and leaves no doubt in the mind of reasonable consumers that the site is not sponsored by the complainant.

OBH, Inc. v. Spotlight Magazine, Inc., 86 F.Supp.2d 176 (W.D.N.Y. 2000) involved a successful suit for injunction against use of the domain name www.thebuffalonews.com. The defendant used the domain name for an apartment finder service that competed with the plaintiff's Buffalo News's apartment finding service. Among other things, the defendant criticized the Buffalo News service as inferior to his own. The district court determined that:

> "The Court is not persuaded that the message of defendants' web site constitutes a parody. A parody 'depends on a lack of confusion to make its point,' and 'must convey two simultaneous-and contradictory-messages: that it is the original, but also that it is not the original and is instead a parody.' " Defendants' web site does not clearly convey two simultaneous-and contradictory-messages: that it is The Buffalo News web site, but also that it is not The Buffalo News site. The Court finds defendants' web site confusing, at best. For example, the greeting "Welcome to www.thebuffalonews.com" at the top of web site does not immediately contradict an Internet user's assumption that he or she has accessed the plaintiffs' web site. Only when a user reads through the web site does he or she discover defendants' actual message. Because defendants' web site relies, at least to some extent, on confusion to make its point, defendants' argument that their use of the mark is a parody must fail.

Unlike the domain name thebuffalonews.com, walmartcanadasucks.com itself makes it clear that the Web site is not sponsored by the complainant.

\* \* \* \* \*

E.  Content of wallmartcanadasucks site and legitimacy of Respondent interests

The complainant must establish that the Respondent "has no rights or legitimate interests in respect of the domain name." Whether the complainant can establish this element depends on the legitimacy of the contents of Respondent's Web site accessible through wallmartcanadasucks.com and the use of that domain name as a means of accessing that Web site.

The accused Web site contains little criticism of Wal–Mart products or practices other than its efforts to control use of its name in Web domain names. This supports an inference that the Web site is closely related to earlier Cybersquatting cases involving this Respondent [in which the respondent's registration of confusing marks were decided in Wal–Mart's favor], rather than the kind of criticism of an enterprise that friends of the Internet might be comfortable in encouraging.

Do the cases allowing critical or parodic use of infringing marks or domain names extend to this kind of criticism? Can the Respondent be said to have a legitimate interest in a domain name used for purposes of criticizing prior domain name litigation? The U.S. Supreme Court has suggested that the quality of criticism is immaterial.

"The threshold question when fair use is raised in defense of parody is whether a parodic character may reasonably be perceived. Whether, going beyond that, parody is in good taste or bad does not and should not matter to fair use." Campbell v. Acuff–Rose Music, Inc., 510 U.S. 569, 582–83 (1994).

Thus whether wallmartcanadasucks is effective criticism of Wal–Mart, whether it is in good taste, whether it focuses on the right issues, all are immaterial; the only question is whether it is criticism or parody rather than free-riding on another's trade mark.

F.   Solicitation of Payment for Domain Name

One of the factors to be considered under the ICANN Policy in determining bad faith is whether the Respondent has solicited payment for transfer of the accused domain name. The record associated with the first two disputes between this complainant and this Respondent included a letter sent by the Respondent to the complainant asking for payment for consulting services relating to identification of domain names that Wal–Mart should register. Wal–Mart, and the sole panelist in Decision No. 2000–477 concluded that this request for payment satisfied the requirement of subparagraph 4 (b)(i).

I am unwilling to extend that inference from the earlier cases to this case. There has been no demand for payment for transfer of walmartcanadasucks.com. Nor has there been any request for payment for consulting services in connection with walmartcanadasucks.com. The inference of a demand for payment for transfer of the domain name was only weakly supported in the earlier cases, and there is no basis for it in this case. The letter regarding consulting services made no reference to transfer of domain names, and has not been renewed.

Conclusions

By using the domain name wallmartcanadasucks, the Respondent has not intentionally attempted to attract, for commercial gain, Internet users to its web site or other on-line location, by creating a likelihood of confusion with the complainant's mark as to the source, sponsorship, affiliation, or endorsement of the respondent's web site or location of a product or service on the Respondent's web site or location. There is no likelihood of confusion between wallmartcanadasucks and Wal–Mart's products and services. Accordingly, the complainant has not established the elements of a violation of the ICANN Policy.

## Playboy Enterprises, Inc. v. Welles

United States Court of Appeals, Ninth Circuit, 2002.
279 F.3d 796.

■ T.G. NELSON, CIRCUIT JUDGE.

Playboy Enterprises, Inc. (PEI), appeals the district court's grant of summary judgment as to its claims of trademark infringement, [and] unfair competition against Terri Welles; Terri Welles, Inc.; Pippi, Inc.; and Welles' current and former "webmasters," Steven Huntington and Michael Mihalko. We have jurisdiction pursuant to 28 U.S.C. § 1291, and we affirm in part and reverse in part.

## Background

Terri Welles was on the cover of Playboy in 1981 and was chosen to be the Playboy Playmate of the Year for 1981. Her use of the title "Playboy Playmate of the Year 1981," and her use of other trademarked terms on her website are at issue in this suit. During the relevant time period, Welles' website offered information about and free photos of Welles, advertised photos for sale, advertised memberships in her photo club, and promoted her services as a spokesperson. A biographical section described Welles' selection as Playmate of the Year in 1981 and her years modeling for PEI. After the lawsuit began, Welles included discussions of the suit and criticism of PEI on her website and included a note disclaiming any association with PEI.[a]

PEI complains of four different uses of its trademarked terms on Welles' website: (1) the terms "Playboy" and "Playmate" in the metatags of the website;[b] (2) the phrase "Playmate of the Year 1981" on the masthead of the website; (3) the phrases "Playboy Playmate of the Year 1981" and "Playmate of the Year 1981" on various banner ads, which may be transferred to other websites; and (4) the repeated use of the abbreviation "PMOY '81" as the watermark on the pages of the website.[c] PEI claimed that these uses of its marks constituted trademark infringement, dilution, false designation of origin, and unfair competition. The district court granted defendants' motion for summary judgment. PEI appeals the grant of summary judgment on its infringement and dilution claims. We affirm in part and reverse in part.

## Discussion

### A. Trademark Infringement

Except for the use of PEI's protected terms in the wallpaper of Welles' website, we conclude that Welles' uses of PEI's trademarks are permissible, nominative uses. They imply no current sponsorship or endorsement by PEI. Instead, they serve to identify Welles as a past PEI "Playmate of the Year."

[a] The disclaimer reads as follows:

"This site is neither endorsed, nor sponsored, nor affiliated with Playboy Enterprises, Inc. PLAYBOY(R) PLAYMATE OF THE YEAR(R) AND PLAYMATE OF THE MONTH(R) ARE REGISTERED trademarks of Playboy Enterprises, Inc."

[b] Metatags are hidden code used by some search engines to determine the content of websites in order to direct searchers to relevant sites.

[c] PEI claims that "PMOY" is an unregistered trademark of PEI, standing for "Playmate of the Year."

We articulated the test for a permissible, nominative use in *New Kids On The Block v. New America Publishing, Inc.*[d] The band, New Kids On The Block, claimed trademark infringement arising from the use of their trademarked name by several newspapers. The newspapers had conducted polls asking which member of the band New Kids On The Block was the best and most popular. The papers' use of the trademarked term did not fall within the traditional fair use doctrine [of § 1115(b)(4) of the Lanham Act]. Unlike a traditional fair use scenario, the defendant newspaper was using the trademarked term to describe not its own product, but the plaintiff's. Thus, the factors used to evaluate fair use were inapplicable. The use was nonetheless permissible, we concluded, based on its nominative nature.

We adopted the following test for nominative use:

First, the product or service in question must be one not readily identifiable without use of the trademark; second, only so much of the mark or marks may be used as is reasonably necessary to identify the product or service; and third, the user must do nothing that would, in conjunction with the mark, suggest sponsorship or endorsement by the trademark holder.

We noted in *New Kids* that a nominative use may also be a commercial one.

In cases in which the defendant raises a nominative use defense, the above three-factor test should be applied instead of the test for likelihood of confusion set forth in *Sleekcraft*.[e] The three-factor test better evaluates the likelihood of confusion in nominative use cases. When a defendant uses a trademark nominally, the trademark will be identical to the plaintiff's mark, at least in terms of the words in question. Thus, application of the *Sleekcraft* test, which focuses on the similarity of the mark used by the plaintiff and the defendant, would lead to the incorrect conclusion that virtually all nominative uses are confusing. The three-factor test—with its requirements that the defendant use marks only when no descriptive substitute exists, use no more of the mark than necessary, and do nothing to suggest sponsorship or endorsement by the mark holder—better addresses concerns regarding the likelihood of confusion in nominative use cases.

We group the uses of PEI's trademarked terms into three for the purpose of applying the test for nominative use. First, we analyze Welles' use of the terms in headlines and banner advertisements. We conclude that those uses are clearly nominative. Second, we analyze the use of the terms in the metatags for Welles' website, which we conclude are nominative as well. Finally, we analyze the terms as used in the wall-paper of the website. We conclude that this use is not nominative and remand for a determination of whether it infringes on a PEI trademark.

1.  Headlines and banner advertisements.

---

[d] 971 F.2d 302, 306 (9th Cir.1992) (describing a nominative use as one that "does not imply sponsorship or endorsement of the product because the mark is used only to describe the thing, rather than to identify its source").

[e] AMF Inc. v. Sleekcraft Boats, 599 F.2d 341, 348–49 (9th Cir. 1979)

To satisfy the first part of the test for nominative use, "the product or service in question must be one not readily identifiable without use of the trademark[.]" This situation arises "when a trademark also describes a person, a place or an attribute of a product" and there is no descriptive substitute for the trademark. In such a circumstance, allowing the trademark holder exclusive rights would allow the language to "be depleted in much the same way as if generic words were protectable." In *New Kids,* we gave the example of the trademarked term, "Chicago Bulls." We explained that "one might refer to the 'two-time world champions' or 'the professional basketball team from Chicago,' but it's far simpler (and more likely to be understood) to refer to the Chicago Bulls." Moreover, such a use of the trademark would "not imply sponsorship or endorsement of the product because the mark is used only to describe the thing, rather than to identify its source." Thus, we concluded, such uses must be excepted from trademark infringement law.

The district court properly identified Welles' situation as one which must also be excepted. No descriptive substitute exists for PEI's trademarks in this context. The court explained:

> [T]here is no other way that Ms. Welles can identify or describe herself and her services without venturing into absurd descriptive phrases. To describe herself as the "nude model selected by Mr. Hefner's magazine as its number-one prototypical woman for the year 1981" would be impractical as well as ineffectual in identifying Terri Welles to the public.

We agree. Just as the newspapers in *New Kids* could only identify the band clearly by using its trademarked name, so can Welles only identify herself clearly by using PEI's trademarked title.

The second part of the nominative use test requires that "only so much of the mark or marks may be used as is reasonably necessary to identify the product or service[.]" *New Kids* provided the following examples to explain this element: "[A] soft drink competitor would be entitled to compare its product to Coca–Cola or Coke, but would not be entitled to use Coca–Cola's distinctive lettering." Similarly, in a past case, an auto shop was allowed to use the trademarked term "Volkswagen" on a sign describing the cars it repaired, in part because the shop "did not use Volkswagen's distinctive lettering style or color scheme, nor did he display the encircled 'VW' emblem." Welles' banner advertisements and headlines satisfy this element because they use only the trademarked words, not the font or symbols associated with the trademarks.

The third element requires that the user do "nothing that would, in conjunction with the mark, suggest sponsorship or endorsement by the trademark holder." As to this element, we conclude that aside from the wallpaper, which we address separately, Welles does nothing in conjunction with her use of the marks to suggest sponsorship or endorsement by PEI. The marks are clearly used to describe the title she received from PEI in 1981, a title that helps describe who she is. It would be unreasonable to assume that the Chicago Bulls sponsored a website of Michael Jordan's simply because his name appeared with the appellation "former Chicago Bull." Similarly, in this case, it would be unreasonable to assume that PEI currently sponsors or endorses someone who describes herself as a "Playboy Playmate of the Year in 1981." The designation of the year, in our case, serves the same function as the "former" in our example. It shows that any sponsorship or endorsement occurred in the past.

In addition to doing nothing in conjunction with her use of the marks to suggest sponsorship or endorsement by PEI, Welles affirmatively disavows any sponsorship or endorsement. Her site contains a clear statement disclaiming any connection to PEI. Moreover, the text of the site describes her ongoing legal battles with the company.

For the foregoing reasons, we conclude that Welles' use of PEI's marks in her headlines and banner advertisements is a nominative use excepted from the law of trademark infringement.

2. Metatags.

Welles includes the terms "playboy" and "playmate" in her metatags. Metatags describe the contents of a website using keywords. Some search engines search metatags to identify websites relevant to a search.[f] Thus, when an internet searcher enters "playboy" or "playmate" into a search engine that uses metatags, the results will include Welles' site.[g] Because Welles' metatags do not repeat the terms extensively, her site will not be at the top of the list of search results. Applying the three-factor test for nominative use, we conclude that the use of the trademarked terms in Welles' metatags is nominative.

As we discussed above with regard to the headlines and banner advertisements, Welles has no practical way of describing herself without using trademarked terms. In the context of metatags, we conclude that she has no practical way of identifying the content of her website without referring to PEI's trademarks.

A large portion of Welles' website discusses her association with Playboy over the years. Thus, the trademarked terms accurately describe the contents of Welles' website, in addition to describing Welles. Forcing Welles and others to use absurd turns of phrase in their metatags, such as those necessary to identify Welles, would be particularly damaging in the internet search context. Searchers would have a much more difficult time locating relevant websites if they could do so only by correctly guessing the long phrases necessary to substitute for trademarks. We can hardly expect someone searching for Welles' site to imagine the same phrase proposed by the district court to describe Welles without referring to Playboy—"the nude model selected by Mr. Hefner's organization.... " Yet if someone could not remember her name, that is what they would have to do.

[f] See Brookfield Communications, Inc. v. West Coast Entertainment, 174 F.3d 1036, 1045 (9th Cir.1999).

[g] We note that search engines that use their own summaries of websites, or that search the entire text of sites, are also likely to identify Welles' site as relevant to a search for "playboy" or "playmate," given the content of the site.

Similarly, someone searching for critiques of Playboy on the internet would have a difficult time if internet sites could not list the object of their critique in their metatags.

There is simply no descriptive substitute for the trademarks used in Welles' metatags. Precluding their use would have the unwanted effect of hindering the free flow of information on the internet, something which is certainly not a goal of trademark law.[h] Accordingly, the use of trademarked terms in the metatags meets the first part of the test for nominative use.

We conclude that the metatags satisfy the second and third elements of the test as well. The metatags use only so much of the marks as reasonably necessary[i] and nothing is done in conjunction with them to suggest sponsorship or endorsement by the trademark holder. We note that our decision might differ if the metatags listed the trademarked term so repeatedly that Welles' site would regularly appear above PEI's in searches for one of the trademarked terms.

3.  Wallpaper/watermark.

The background, or wallpaper, of Welles' site consists of the repeated abbreviation "PMOY '81," which stands for "Playmate of the Year 1981." Welles' name or likeness does not appear before or after "PMOY '81." The pattern created by the repeated abbreviation appears as the background of the various pages of the website. Accepting, for the purposes of this appeal, that the abbreviation "PMOY" is indeed entitled to protection, we conclude that the repeated, stylized use of this abbreviation fails the nominative use test.

B.  Trademark Dilution

The district court granted summary judgment to Welles as to PEI's claim of trademark dilution. We affirm on the ground that all of Welles' uses of PEI's marks, with the exception of the use in the wallpaper which we address separately, are proper, nominative uses. We hold that nominative uses, by definition, do not dilute the trademarks.

Dilution works its harm not by causing confusion in consumers' minds regarding the source of a good or service, but by creating an association in consumers' minds between a mark and a different good or service.

Uses that do not create an improper association between a mark and a new product but merely identify the trademark holder's products should be excepted from the reach of the anti-dilution statute. Such uses cause no harm. The anti-dilution statute recognizes this principle and specifically excepts users of a trademark who compare their product in "commercial

---

[h] Admittedly, this hindrance would only occur as to search engines that use metatags to direct their searches.

[i] It is hard to imagine how a metatag could use more of a mark than the words contained in it, but we recently learned that some search engines are now using pictures. Searching for symbols, such as the Playboy bunny, cannot be far behind. That problem does not arise in this case, however, and we need not address it.

advertising or promotion to identify the competing goods or services of the owner of the famous mark."

For the same reason uses in comparative advertising are excepted from anti-dilution law, we conclude that nominative uses are also excepted. A nominative use, by definition, refers to the trademark holder's product. It does not create an improper association in consumers' minds between a new product and the trademark holder's mark.

When Welles refers to her title, she is in effect referring to a product of PEI's. She does not dilute the title by truthfully identifying herself as its one-time recipient any more than Michael Jordan would dilute the name "Chicago Bulls" by referring to himself as a former member of that team, or the two-time winner of an Academy Award would dilute the award by referring to him or herself as a "two-time Academy Award winner." Awards are not diminished or diluted by the fact that they have been awarded in the past. Similarly, they are not diminished or diluted when past recipients truthfully identify themselves as such. It is in the nature of honors and awards to be identified with the people who receive them. Of course, the conferrer of such honors and awards is free to limit the honoree's use of the title or references to the award by contract. So long as a use is nominative, however, trademark law is unavailing.

The one exception to the above analysis in this case is Welles' use of the abbreviation "PMOY" on her wallpaper. Because we determined that this use is not nominative, it is not excepted from the anti-dilution provisions. Thus, we reverse as to this issue and remand for further proceedings.

## Conclusion

For the foregoing reasons, we affirm the district court's grant of summary judgment as to PEI's claims for trademark infringement and trademark dilution, with the sole exception of the use of the abbreviation "PMOY." We reverse as to the abbreviation and remand for consideration of whether it merits protection under either an infringement or a dilution theory.

NOTES

**1.** *"The likelihood of confusion test": §§ 1114, 43(a).* The test for likelihood of confusion differs somewhat in its articulation in the various circuits, but essentially all of the tests focus on the same type of factors. The *Polaroid* test used in *Lois Sportswear* is representative, although some courts consider additional factors.[5] In addition to those factors mentioned in the cases, what other factors would you deem relevant to a consideration of likelihood of confusion?

---

[5] See, e.g., Payless Shoesource, Inc. v. Reebok International Ltd., 998 F.2d 985, 988 (Fed.Cir.1993); Ferrari v. Roberts, 944 F.2d 1235 (6th Cir.1991); Centaur Communications v. A/S/M Communications, 830 F.2d 1217, 1228 n. 2 (2d Cir.1987).

In terms of the test's operation, no single factor is determinative and courts typically perform a balancing test in weighing the various factors.[6] Should the balancing process differ depending upon whether the action is one for trademark infringement or trade dress infringement under § 43(a)? Keep in mind that registered trademarks are entitled to a prima facie presumption of validity.[7] Can you think of any circumstances in which the likelihood of confusion test should be reduced to a "possibility of confusion" standard?

There is disagreement among the circuits as to the standard of appellate review regarding likelihood of confusion. Although the majority of circuits treat this issue purely as a question of fact, subject to a clearly erroneous standard, a few circuits treat it as a mixed question of law and fact. These courts hold that although likelihood of confusion is a question of law subject to de novo review, the specific findings supporting this conclusion are questions of fact subject to the clearly erroneous standard.[8]

a. *Strength of the mark.* Courts often determine strength with reference to the generic-descriptive-suggestive-arbitrary spectrum utilized at the registration stage, see Assignment 2. The cases almost universally say that the stronger the mark, the more protection it should receive. Is the reason for this view that consumers are more likely to be confused when a strong mark is infringed, or is there some other theory at work here? Couldn't an argument be made that confusion is more likely to be mitigated with a strong mark?

In assessing the strength of a plaintiff's mark, a court must evaluate the impact of certain factual scenarios. For example, what should be the relevance of third parties owning registrations for similar marks that are used on similar goods? What about situations such as the one in *McDonald's*, where the plaintiff owns a family of marks? Should a mark's status as incontestable be taken into account?[9] On incontestability, see Assignment 2.

b. *Similarity of marks.* In evaluating this factor, should only the marks themselves be considered, or should courts also consider the text and graphics surrounding the marks? Should the answer to this question depend on whether a registered trademark is at issue as opposed to subject matter under § 43(a)?

c. *Similarity of goods/bridging the gap.* These two factors are somewhat related in that the more proximate the products, "the shorter the gap

---

[6] Id.

[7] See §§ 1057(b) & 1115(a).

[8] The Ninth Circuit, in contrast, treats the issue as a mixed question of law and fact, but accords the clearly erroneous standard of review to the entire issue. A student work exploring this topic generally is Patricia J. Kaeding, Clearly Erroneous Review of Mixed Questions of Law and Fact: The Likelihood of Confusion Determination in Trademark Law, 59 U. Chi. L. Rev. 1291 (1992).

[9] See Times Newspapers, Ltd. v. Times Publishing Co., 25 U.S.P.Q.2d (BNA) 1835, 1840 (M.D.Fla.1993)(suggesting that although incontestable status is a factor in the likelihood of confusion analysis, it is not necessarily determinative of infringement).

is to bridge."[10] Likelihood of confusion can be decreased where the two marks in question are used before separate groups of consumers or where the distinct nature of the products clearly suggests that the two users are unrelated. Factors determinative of the competitive proximity of the products "include appearance, style, function, fashion appeal, advertising orientation and price."[11]

*Lois Sportswear*, by emphasizing the difference between designer and regular jeans, endorsed a rather narrow view regarding the similarity of the goods factor. But is that approach appropriate in the age of "lifestyle" marketing? Consider the following excerpt from an article in the New York Times on Levi's loss of market share in recent years:

> "Maybe one of Levi's problems is that it has no cola. It has no denim-toned house paint. Levi makes what is essentially a commodity: blue jeans. Its ads may evoke rugged outdoorsmanship, but Levi hasn't promoted any particular life style to sell other products. Once people get to know a brand's most famous product, the thinking goes, they will trust that brand to deliver any number of items, even if the original product has no relationship to the subsequent stuff the company hawks. To wit: Brooks Brothers now has its own line of wines and Jack Daniel's sells clothes. "Great marketers say the brand can be the thing that holds their group of consumers together," said Sam I. Hill, a principal partner at Helios Consulting in New York. The life-style label is an intelligent reaction by marketers who want a deeper relationship with consumers."[12]

Once consumers develop expectations that marketers will expand across categories, should the courts protect trademark holders more by taking greater liberties with these two factors? For further discussion, see Note 2 below.

  d.  *Consumer sophistication.* The concept of consumer sophistication encompasses a variety of factors including the price of the product, the potential for impulse purchasing, and the nature of the product itself. In general, courts take the view that the more sophisticated the consumer, the less the likelihood of confusion.[13] In contrast, in *Lois Sportswear*, the court found that in the post-sale context, sophisticated consumers are "more likely to be affected by the sight of appellee's stitching pattern on appellants' jeans and, consequently, to transfer goodwill." Do you agree with the analysis of *Lois Sportswear* on this point? How should this factor be evaluated in the context of the Principal Problem?

  e.  *Actual confusion.* Although proof of actual confusion need not be demonstrated, such proof can be extremely probative of likelihood of

---

[10] Jordache Enterprises, Inc. v. Levi Strauss & Co., 841 F.Supp. 506, 517 (S.D.N.Y.1993).

  [11] *Id.*

[12] Jennifer Steinhauer, That's Not a Skim Latte. It's a Way of Life, New York Times, March 21, 1999, at Sec. 4, p. 5, col. 1.

[13] Private Eyes Sunglass Corp. v. Private Eye Vision Center, 25 U.S.P.Q.2d (BNA) 1709, 1718 (D.Conn.1992).

confusion. Sometimes actual confusion is demonstrated by direct evidence such as testimonial or anecdotal evidence, but frequently proof of actual confusion stems from market research surveys. The following summarizes the governing principles regarding the admissibility of survey evidence:

> "The trustworthiness of surveys depends upon foundation evidence that (1) the 'universe' was properly defined, (2) a representative sample of that universe was selected, (3) the questions to be asked of interviewees were framed in a clear, concise and nonleading manner, (4) sound interview procedures were followed by competent interviewers who had no knowledge of the litigation or the purpose for which the survey was conducted, (5) the data gathered was accurately reported, (6) the data was analyzed in accordance with accepted statistical principles and (7) objectivity of the entire process was assured."[14]

The term "universe" represents the portion of the population that possesses the characteristics required for making the critical mental association.[15] Frequently, the validity of the survey's universe is at issue.[16]

f. *Good faith.* The role of good faith in the likelihood of confusion analysis is, in and of itself, rather confusing Thus, some courts have held that intentional copying gives rise to a presumption of secondary meaning, while other courts treat a showing of intentional copying only as evidence of secondary meaning.[17] Some apply a presumption of likelihood of confusion in cases involving intentional copying.[18] Finally, there are courts that refuse to apply such a presumption and instead treat intentional copying as just one of the factors that must be considered in a likelihood of confusion analysis.[19] Is *Lois Sportswear* inconsistent with the application of a pre-

---

[14] Schieffelin & Co. v. Jack Company of Boca, 850 F.Supp. 232, 245 (S.D.N.Y.1994).

[15] *Id.*

[16] See, e.g., Sterling Drug, Inc. v. Bayer AG, USA, 14 F.3d 733, 741 (2d Cir.1994)(in case where "the relevant issue is whether consumers mistakenly believe that the senior user's products actually originate with the junior user, it is appropriate to survey the senior user's customers" rather than the junior user's consumer base); Jordache Enterprises, Inc. v. Levi Strauss & Co., 841 F.Supp. 506, 518–19 (S.D.N.Y.1993)(universe defective because it included only those who had worn jeans within the past six months, but failed to include potential purchasers of jeans).

[17] Compare Maryland Stadium Authority v. Becker, 806 F.Supp. 1236, 1241 (D.Md. 1992)(in the Fourth Circuit, evidence of intentional copying gives rise to a *"prima facie* case of secondary meaning sufficient to shift the burden of persuasion to the defendant") with Brooks Shoe Mfg. Co. v. Suave Shoe Corp., 716 F.2d 854, 860 (11th Cir.

1983)(although intentional copying is "probative evidence" of secondary meaning, the defendant may have had motivations other than capitalizing on the plaintiff's goodwill). See also Perfect Fit Industries, Inc. v. Acme Quilting Co., 618 F.2d 950 (2d Cir. 1980)(under New York law, intentional copying can substitute for secondary meaning).

[18] See, e.g., Anheuser–Busch, Inc. v. L. & L. Wings, Inc., 962 F.2d 316, 321 (4th Cir. 1992)(appearing to limit presumption to cases involving an intent to confuse); Academy of Motion Picture Arts and Sciences v. Creative House Promotions, Inc., 944 F.2d 1446, 1456 (9th Cir.1991); Chevron Chemical Co. v. Voluntary Purchasing Groups, 659 F.2d 695, 704 (5th Cir.1981); Maryland Stadium Authority v. Becker, 806 F.Supp. 1236, 1241 (D.Md.1992).

[19] Schwinn Bicycle Co. v. Ross Bicycles, Inc., 870 F.2d 1176, 1184–85 (7th Cir.1989). See also the Second Circuit's analysis in Perfect Fit Industries, Inc. v. Acme Quilting Co., 618 F.2d 950, 954 (2d Cir.1980).

sumption? Should intentional copying give rise to either a presumption of secondary meaning or likelihood of confusion? Can you think of any other measures a defendant can take to show its good faith?

Sometimes the good faith analysis comes up in relation to other issues, including the applicability of defenses, such as the defense of parody. Do you agree with the way the Wal–Mart adjudicator handled this point?

g. *Quality of the products/marketing channels.* Some courts do not consider the quality of the products explicitly and instead examine the marketing channels in which the product is distributed.[20] Although these appear to involve similar considerations, instances can arise in which the quality factor favors the plaintiff because the defendant is producing a cheap imitation, but the marketing channels factor will favor the defendant because cheaper imitations often are sold in different trade channels.

**2.** *Trademark infringement versus trademark registration.* The upshot of cases like *McDonald's* is that trademark holders can successfully assert rights against those with whom they do not compete. Doesn't this create a curious anomaly? Recall that one of the requirements for federal registration is use—or at least, the intent to use. At the registration stage, "use" is not measured in the abstract. Rather, the applicant is required to designate the goods on which the mark is or will be used; the validity of the mark is determined by its appropriateness for particular goods; and the issue whether the mark is likely to be confused with a previously registered mark is also determined with reference to the registered owner's and applicant's actual usage, see Assignment 2. Yet, despite this careful attention paid to use at the registration stage, cases like *McDonald's* allow mark holders to expand the reach of their marks to products that they do not sell or intend to sell. When a plaintiff is successful in such a case, what she has managed to do is create a right to a mark that she has not "used" within the meaning of the Lanham Act.

What is the justification for treating the registration and infringement contexts so differently? One possibility is that the law is being used to give trademark holders a zone of expansion. That is, the law is construed so that once a merchant develops a successful business in one kind of goods, she can use the goodwill that the mark has developed to enter into a new field. This is socially desirable from the customer's point of view because a consumer who likes the first product can use the mark on the new one as an indication that he is likely to be satisfied with it as well.[21] And as the N.Y. Times quotation in Note 1 makes clear, the ability to expand is also valuable to merchants and provides added incentives to create goodwill in the first place.

This justification cannot, however, explain all of the cases. As *McDonald's* and the cases cited therein indicate, McDonald's has managed to

---

[20] See, e.g., *Ferrari*, 944 F.2d at 1242.

[21] For example, it is said that Coca Cola did not use the Coke trademark in connection with its first entry into the diet soda business because it did not think its first soda (Tab) was good enough for the mark. When Diet Coke was finally introduced, customers were especially eager to try it.

prevent use of its mark in the dentistry, bagel, and motel fields—even though it is not too likely that the company would consider entering all (or any) of these businesses. Thus, it is likely that the law is doing something more than simply protecting the trademark holder's ability to expand into new fields. Is the law, in essence, taking a right to a *signal* and converting it into something more closely akin to *property*? If the point is only to protect the integrity of the signal—the cachet of the mark—then would it not make more sense to protect the merchant through dilution law? That way, the added scope is provided only to marks that are famous, and thus likely to be valuable enough to exploit across many marketing categories.[22]

**3.** *The family-of-marks doctrine.* Another way to limit the reach of infringement actions is to confine *McDonald's* to its particular facts—to the situation in which a merchant is trying to transfer goodwill in one good to other products by using a common element in all of its marks, thereby creating a "family."

The "family of marks" doctrine arises most often in opposition proceedings: someone tries to register a mark with the common element, and the trademark holder opposes. As a general matter, when the applicant's goods are very different from those of the trademark holder, the Patent and Trademark Office will dismiss the opposition and register the mark. The PTO's justification is that permitting these oppositions would allow trademark holders to own their rights "in gross"—that is, unconnected with the mark's use as a signal on particular goods or services.[23] However, there are cases where particular features of marks take on such a strong association for consumers that the PTO is willing to protect the trademark holder. Examples include the "Mc" prefix for food items,[24] and the "to" suffix for snacks.[25] The Federal Circuit, the court that reviews the registration decisions of the PTO, has clarified the circumstances where a family-of-marks argument should succeed. According to the court, the issue is whether the group of goods for which the common element is registered has a recognizable common characteristic that is associated by the public with the common element and is considered indicative of the common origin of the goods.[26] Should common elements in a company's trade dress—such as similar stitching designs across an entire line of products—also be protectable on a "family" theory or does the public's right to coordinate their purchases trump the trademark holder's interests?[27]

[22] See generally, Mark A. Lemley, The Modern Lanham Act And The Death Of Common Sense,108 Yale L.J. 1687 (1999).

[23] See, e.g., Bissell, Inc. v. Easy Day Mfg. Co., 130 U.S.P.Q. (BNA) 485 (T.T.A.B. 1958).

[24] J & J Snack Foods Corp. v. McDonald's Corporation, 932 F.2d 1460 (Fed. Cir.1991)(upholding refusal to register "McPretzel" for pretzels).

[25] The Frito Co. v. Buckeye Foods, 130 U.S.P.Q. (BNA) 347 (T.T.A.B. 1961).

[26] J & J Snack Foods Corp. v. McDonald's Corporation, 932 F.2d 1460, 1462 (Fed.Cir.1991).

[27] Compare Imagineering, Inc. v. Van Klassens, Inc., 53 F.3d 1260 (Fed. Cir.)(protecting a furniture design on a finding that it possessed "a coherent total image, comprising wide slats, scooped seat boards and arms, rounded edges, notched and curved legs, and angled backrests, among other distinctive attributes," id. at 1263), cert. denied, 516 U.S. 909 (1995) with Industria Arredam-

**4.** *Reverse confusion.* The typical type of confusion that can support a claim of trademark infringement or unfair competition under § 43(a) occurs when consumers have the misimpression that the senior user is the source of the junior's product. Another form of confusion, called reverse confusion, exists when consumers have the misimpression that the junior user is the source of the senior user's product.

Reverse confusion cases typically involve a smaller senior user and a larger junior user. For example, in Banff, Ltd. v. Federated Department Stores, Inc.,[28] the owner of the unregistered trademark "Bee Wear" for clothing brought suit against the renowned department store Bloomingdale's for the use of "B Wear" in various typestyles for a line of women's clothing. In recognizing a cause of action for reverse confusion, the Second Circuit stated: "The objectives of [the Lanham Act]—to protect an owner's interest in its trademark by keeping the public free from confusion as to the source of goods and ensuring fair competition—are as important in a case of reverse confusion as in typical trademark infringement. Were reverse confusion not a sufficient basis to obtain Lanham Act protection, a larger company could with impunity infringe the senior mark of a smaller one."[29]

Absent the doctrine of reverse confusion, a junior user would be able to overwhelm the senior user by saturating the market with a similar trademark, so that the public would eventually believe that the senior user's products are really the junior user's, or that the senior user has become connected to or associated with, the junior user. The result of this unchecked saturation could be the senior user's loss of the value of its trademark, its product and corporate identity, the control over its goodwill, and reputation, and the ability to move into new markets.[30] Should the test for infringement be applied differently in reverse confusion cases? Reverse confusion should be distinguished from reverse passing off, which is discussed in Note 11(b).

**5.** *The temporal component of confusion.* At common law, the essence of trademark infringement was passing off—the sale of a product to a consumer who believed he was buying the product of a different merchant. Courts accordingly focused on the likelihood of confusion at the time of sale. In several of the cases in this Assignment, however, the chronology is quite different.

a. *Post-sale confusion.* In *Lois Sportswear*, a strong argument can be made that consumers were not likely to be confused *at the time of purchase* because they can see the trademarks clearly enough to perceive the differences. Nonetheless, the court was concerned with the fact that the marks appear different "at significant distance," making the issue the

enti Fratelli Saporiti v. Charles Craig, Ltd., 725 F.2d 18 (2d Cir. 1984)(finding an interlocking pillow design on modular furniture functional and unprotectable).

[28] 841 F.2d 486 (2d Cir.1988).

[29] Id. at 490–491.

[30] See Fisons Horticulture, Inc. v. Vigoro Industries, Inc., 30 F.3d 466, 474–475 (3d Cir.1994)(quoting Ameritech, Inc. v. American Information Technologies Corp., 811 F.2d 960, 964 (6th Cir.1987)).

possibility that the jeans will confuse people *who see them after they are sold*. This is not an uncommon problem. A good example is Ferrari, S.P.A. v. Roberts,[31] where the defendant sold body shells in the shape of the famous (and expensive) Daytona Spyder. Buyers understood that the kits could be driven only if bolted onto cars that had engines, wheels, gasoline tanks, etc.: no consumer was confused. But as in *Lois Sportswear*, infringement was found on a theory of post-sale confusion. Does it make sense to worry about post-sale events? While it is true that wearing Lois jeans communicates information about Lois Sportswear to anyone who sees the jeans, is enough information communicated to give the trademark holder a right of control? One of the authors of this book is a devoted fan of Coach bags and uses them until they fall apart. Those who observe a bag in a state of disrepair may not fully appreciate the sturdiness of the exterior binding and seams. Should Coach be permitted to stop this use of the bag on a post-sale confusion rationale? Obviously, the author's property right in the bag will trump here. But if that is so, shouldn't courts assume that people who view trademarked products after they are sold take what they see with a grain of salt—that is, shouldn't we assume that consumers will not attribute every characteristic they see to the trademark holder? If that is the case, why extend the reach of infringement to the post-sale context?

b.   *Initial interest confusion.* Some courts characterize the metatag problem in *Welles* as involving confusion before the time of purchase. For example, in Brookfield Communications, Inc. v. West Coast Entertainment Corp.,[32] both defendant and plaintiff used the Internet to offer products and services to people interested in the film industry. The defendant, West Coast, used Brookfield's trademark, ''Movie Buff'' as a metatag. In enjoining this activity, the court said:

> ''West Coast's use of 'moviebuff.com' in metatags will ... result in what is known as initial interest confusion. Web surfers looking for Brookfield's 'MovieBuff' products who are taken by a search engine to 'westcoastvideo.com' will find a database similar enough to 'MovieBuff' such that a sizeable number of consumers who were originally looking for Brookfield's product will simply decide to utilize West Coast's offerings instead. Although there is no source confusion in the sense that consumers know they are patronizing West Coast rather than Brookfield, there is nevertheless initial interest confusion in the sense that, by using 'moviebuff.com' or 'MovieBuff' to divert people looking for 'MovieBuff' to its web site, West Coast improperly benefits from the goodwill that Brookfield developed in its mark.''

Are courts right to extend the temporal reach of trademark law this way? Economists argue that trademarks are valuable because they reduce search costs. That is, customers who can rely on a trademark do not need to engage in detailed examination of every purchase to discern its source and quality. But the emphasis here is on saving search *costs*, not eliminating the search all together. Can the marketplace function efficiently if it is

---

[31] 944 F.2d 1235 (6th Cir. 1991).      [32] 174 F.3d 1036 (9th Cir.1999).

not possible for competitors to make customers aware of the alternatives available to them? Does a theory of initial interest confusion eliminate the ability effectively to discuss the trademark holder on the Internet?[33]

In considering these temporal issues, is it significant that when the Lanham Act was amended in 1967, Congress specifically deleted the statute's reference to confusion among *purchasers*, thus broadening the scope of the statute?[34]

**6.** *Dilution: § 43(c).* As noted in the Introduction, dilution is intended to cover activities that impair the value of the mark *outside* the context of consumer confusion as to source or origin. As can be seen from the Court's discussion in *Moseley*, dilution is a purely legislative creation. In sharp derogation from the common law, it reflects a trend that only about half of the states were pursuing at the time that the federal provision was enacted.

Under the Court's interpretation of the federal legislation, how much protection does § 43(c) actually provide? In states that had enacted dilution protection, it was regarded as encompassing two components, blurring and tarnishment. Tarnishment has always been thought relatively easy to understand as an association that brings the mark into disrepute. The quintessential example is Dallas Cowboys Cheerleaders, Inc. v. Pussycat Cinema, Ltd.,[35] where the movie's protagonist, Debbie, "dons a uniform strikingly similar to that worn by the Dallas Cowboy Cheerleaders and for approximately twelve minutes of film footage engages in various sex acts while clad or partially clad in the uniform."[36] Since there are many people who might object to watching this sort of activity, it is obvious why the Cowboys would think that reputational interests were at stake. In contrast, the concept of blurring has always been contested. Because many words have multiple meanings, people are well versed in resolving ambiguities. Families, for example, have ways of identifying which "David" is meant when both father and son share that name. Thus, is it possible that Dupont or Buick or Kodak would be less effective as signals for particular chemicals, cars, or cameras if the terms also appeared in conjunction with shoes, aspirin, or pianos? Indeed, isn't it possible that consumers will become better acquainted with a mark if they encounter it more often and have to think about it carefully?[37]

[33] See also Promatek Industries, Ltd. v. Equitrac Corp., 300 F.3d 808 (7th Cir. 2002), prohibiting the defendant from using its competitor's trademark, Copitrak, as a metatag on an initial-interest confusion theory. The court acknowledged that web users would quickly understand that Equitrac used the trademark to describe its business, which included maintaining and servicing Copitrak equipment. However, the court reasoned: "What is important is not the duration of the confusion, it is the misappropriation of Promatek's goodwill."

[34] See *Ferrari*, 944 F.2d at 1245.

[35] 604 F.2d 200 (2d Cir.1979).

[36] 604 F.2d at 202–03 (footnote omitted).

[37] For example, in the *Ringling Bros–Barnum & Bailey* case discussed in *Moseley*, which involved Utah's slogan "the greatest snow on earth," a survey was conducted that showed that "consumer familiarity with Ringling's mark was greater in Utah (46%), where Utah's mark was well-known, than in the rest of the country (41%), where Utah's mark was virtually unknown," 170 F.3d at 463. For an economic basis for skepticism about the doctrine of dilution, see Ty Inc. v. Perryman, 306 F.3d 509 (7th Cir. 2002).

Given that background, it is interesting that the *Moseley* Court called the tarnishment aspect of dilution into question by asking, in Part IV of the opinion, "whether it is actually embraced by the statutory text." At the same time, the Court required proof of actual dilution—by which it seems to mean blurring, the component that is so poorly understood. What kind of evidence can be mustered to meet the Court's standard? The Court mentions surveys, but what exactly would a survey test? The Court also suggests that dilution may be obvious when junior and senior marks are the same. Is that now the only situation where a dilution claim will be successful?[38] Won't many instances of identical marks be actionable as confusion anyway? Does Justice Kennedy's concurrence shed light on how dilution might be proved?

Also, what is required to prove that the mark is famous? The *Moseley* Court did not confront that issue. However, the lower courts have been giving it an interpretation that is helpful to trademark owners. For instance, in Times Mirror Magazines, Inc. v. Las Vegas Sports News,[39] the court held that the mark, "The Sporting News" for a weekly publication on sports was famous enough:

> We are persuaded that a mark not famous to the general public is nevertheless entitled to protection from dilution where both the plaintiff and defendant are operating in the same or related markets, so long as the plaintiff's mark possesses a high degree of fame in its niche market.

The defendant was preliminarily enjoined from using the mark, "Las Vegas Sporting News" for a magazine on sports betting. In dissent, Judge Barry argued that the fame element was an important way to limit the reach of § 43(c) claims, and Congress meant to protect only marks that are famous nationally.[40] Given *Moseley*, which opinion—the majority or the dissent—is more likely to receive the Supreme Court's support?

**7.** *Cybersquatting: § 43(d) and the UDRP.* When the Internet first became popular, only traditional causes of action were available to trademark holders. In situations where both the trademark holder and the alleged infringer were selling similar products or services, standard passing off claims could be successfully pursued under § 1114 or analogous state law.[41] However, if the alleged infringer was selling in a category far removed from that of the trademark holder, or if the website was not being used to sell goods at all, § 1114 and state analogues were unavailing. Dilution claims were sometimes successful on a blurring rationale, but only in cases where the trademark was sufficiently famous to merit this protection.[42] These

---

[38] See Maureen Morrin and Jack Jacoby, Trademark Dilution: Empirical Measures for an Elusive Concept, 19 J. Public Pol'y & Marketing, 19 (2) 265–276 (2000).

[39] 212 F.3d 157 (3d Cir.2000), cert. denied, 531 U.S. 1071 (2001).

[40] See also Thane Intern., Inc. v. Trek Bicycle Corp., 305 F.3d 894, 907–09 (9th Cir. 2002).

[41] See, e.g., Brookfield Communications, Inc. v. West Coast Entertainment Corp., 174 F.3d 1036 (9th Cir.1999).

[42] See, e.g., Avery Dennison Corp. v. Sumpton, 189 F.3d 868 (9th Cir.

limitations created a serious problem. Trademark holders who had not quickly acted to reserve the domain names corresponding to their marks sometimes found that others had moved in. Some registrants used the trademark holder's domain name to conduct their own business, but others used it to gripe about the trademark or parody it or to hold the site hostage until the trademark holder paid a hefty ransom.

Congress responded to this concern with the Anticybersquatting Consumer Protection Act (ACPA) § 43(d), which allows trademark holders to remove domain names corresponding to their marks from the hands of cyberpirates. However, it provides a limited remedy. The ACPA deals only with problems arising from the use of domain names, not with problems created by the use of a trademark within the text of a website or as a metatag. Furthermore, as the *Wal–Mart* case explains, the trademark holder must demonstrate bad faith. The statute sets out a host of factors to consider, but the list is not meant to be exclusive and the statute does not explain how the factors should be weighed. Thus, the meaning of bad faith awaits further judicial elaboration. Should courts consider the factors used in bad faith analysis under § 1114 or in assessing statutory damages under § 1117(c)? What else should be considered? In Eurotech, Inc. v. Cosmos European Travels, EG,[43] one factor that the court found significant was that the defendants had failed to conduct a trademark search before obtaining the domain name. Is this an appropriate criterion, given the expense of trademark searches relative to the cost of obtaining a domain name?

**8.** *Jurisdiction over cybersquatters.* Because only minimal information needs to be provided to register and maintain a domain name, trademark holders have found that it is not always easy to find the people who have claimed their marks. To deal with that problem the ACPA permits the owner of a trademark to file an *in rem* action against the domain name itself, in the judicial district in which "the domain name registrar, domain name registry, or other domain name authority that registered or assigned the domain name is located." Since Network Solutions, Inc. (now a part of Verisign, Inc.) was for a long time the only registrar, as a practical matter, may of these actions must be brought where it is located—the Eastern District of Virginia.

Is this provision constitutional? In Shaffer v. Heitner,[44] the Supreme Court held that Delaware could not assert jurisdiction over the directors of Greyhound, a Delaware corporation, simply because they held Greyhound stock. The Court applied the same minimum contacts analysis it would have applied to an *in personam* action and looked for volitional conduct that foreseeably connected the defendants to Delaware. Since stock is essentially intangible, its ownership could not provide the nexus for the suit. Domain names are similarly intangible. As they can be registered via

1999)(denying that trademarks "Avery" and "Dennison" for office products were industrial fasteners were diluted under § 43(c)).

[43] 213 F.Supp.2d 612 (E.D.Va. 2002).

[44] 433 U.S. 186 (1977).

the Internet, registrants do not have to physically visit the registry. Furthermore, for those who registered when NSI was the only registry, contact with Virginia was not entirely volitional. Thus, it can be argued that cybersquatters do not have the minimum contacts necessary to maintain a suit against them in Virginia. On the other hand, because of the peculiarities of Delaware law, the directors in *Shaffer* subjected themselves to the courts *in personam* power as soon as they chose to defend themselves—thus, they were liable not just for the value of their shares, but for the entire value of the judgment. In contrast, the ACPA limits the remedy to loss of the domain name, unless bad faith is shown.[45] The ACPA has other safeguards as well: the procedure can be used only when the defendant cannot otherwise be found, and it requires the assent of a court. Moreover, now that there are other registrars, the use of any particular one can be considered voluntary contact with the state in which it is located. Courts that have considered this provision have upheld its constitutionality.[46]

Trademark holders who have been unable to locate the domain name holder or who want a remedy other than that contemplated by the in rem action, have tried to sue domain-name registries—that is, the organizations that permitted the domain name to be registered and that maintain the registration. A variety of theories have been used, including trademark infringement, breach of contract, breach of a third party beneficiary contract, and conversion. So far, these cases for so called "domain name poaching" have had mixed results.[47]

**9.** *ICANN and cybersquatters. Wal-mart* demonstrates another alternative for trademark holders. The Internet Corporation for Assigned Names and Numbers (ICANN) is a private body incorporated in California that operates under the auspices of the U.S. Commerce Department.[48] Although ICANN's duties focus mainly on the structure of Internet communication and domain name registration, it promulgated the UDRP to deal with hijacked domain names.[49] This system, which covers the domain names that ICANN controls along with a few others, is cheaper than adjudication. Moreover, it arguably avoids the jurisdiction problem because everyone who registers a domain name is required, as a condition of registration, to

---

[45] At least one court has, however, held that all rights of the domain name holder can be pursued in rem, see Harrods Ltd. v. Sixty Internet Domain Names, 302 F.3d 214 (4th Cir. 2002).

[46] See, e.g., Caesars World, Inc. v. Caesars-Palace.Com., 112 F.Supp.2d 502 (E.D.Va. 2000).

[47] See Kremen v. Cohen, 337 F.3d 1024 (9th Cir. 2003), finding that Network Solutions, Inc., which had transferred the domain name sex.com without the authorization of the registrant, could be liable for conversion, but not on other theories. See also Dluhos v.

Strasberg, 2001 WL 1720272 (D.N.J. 2001), *aff'd in part, rev'd in part,* 321 F.3d 365 (3d Cir. 2003) ; Virtual Works, Inc. v. Network Solutions, Inc., 106 F.Supp.2d 845 (E.D. Va. 2000).

[48] For a general critique of ICANN's control over the Internet, see Michael Froomkin, Wrong Turn In Cyberspace: Using ICANN To Route Around The APA And The Constitution, 50 Duke L.J. 17 (2000).

[49] The managers of certain country codes have also made submission to dispute resolution a condition of registration.

submit to the authority of a dispute resolution provider. Further, complainants who utilize the dispute resolution system must agree to submit to the jurisdiction of the courts of the place of domain name registration or of the domain name holder.

This procedure has several problems, however. As with § 43(d), it is limited to domain name disputes created by bad faith. It is said to work best for fairly well-known marks. Further, since the only remedy available is transfer of the mark to the trademark holder, it cannot be used if monetary damages are claimed. When the system was first created, there was also strong suspicion that it would be heavily biased in favor of trademark holders, who are, after all, repeat players and, as complainants, have the power to choose which of the authorized dispute resolution providers to use. In fact, trademark holders do tend to win most cases.[50]

Interestingly, an unforeseen phenomenon may be providing an antidote to the bias concern. Some of the dispute resolution providers have chosen law professors to act as adjudicators. *Wal–Mart*, for example, was decided by Henry Perritt, then dean and cyberlaw professor at Chicago–Kent College of Law. Although his decision to refuse relief to Wal–Mart smacks of radical academic thinking and is somewhat unusual in outcome (most sucks.com registrants have lost), the thoroughness of the decision has clarified and publicized the public interest side of the domain name problem.[51] Indeed, decisions like this one have led some to argue that other intellectual property problems created by the Internet, such as the problems in *Welles*, or widespread copyright infringement, could also be dealt with through alternative means of dispute resolution.[52]

Finally, the relationship between the Lanham Act and the UDRP requires further elaboration. By its terms, use of the UDRP system does not preclude litigation. Thus a U.S. trademark holder who loses her UDRP case can sue in a U.S. court claiming all possible theories of relief. By the same token, domain name holders who are stripped of their rights (in a ploy called reverse domain name hijacking) can seek reactivation of the domain name through an action under § 1114(2)(D)(v).[53] The issues that

[50] See, e.g., Milton Mueller, Rough Justice: An Analysis of ICANN's Dispute Resolution Policy, http://dcc.syr.edu/roughjustice.htm (comparing dispute resolution providers' outcomes).

[51] For a court opinion similarly holding a sucks.com cite was not infringement for reasons similar to Perritt's, see Taubman Co. v. Webfeats, 319 F.3d 770 (6th Cir. 2003)("Taubman concedes that Mishkoff is 'free to shout "Taubman Sucks!" from the rooftops....'" " ... Essentially, this is what he has done in his domain name," id. at 777). For a WIPO panel decision reaching the opposite conclusion from Perritt's, see The Royal Bank of Scotland Group plc v. Personal and Pedro Lopez, WIPO Domain Name Dispute Case No. D2003–0166 (ordering that the domain name natwestbanksucks.com be transferred to the holder of the natwest family of trademarks).

[52] See Andrew Christie, The ICANN Domain Name Dispute Resolution System as a Model for Resolving other Intellectual Property Disputes on the Internet, 5 J. World Intell. Prop'y No. 1 (Jan. 2002); Laurence R. Helfer and Graeme B. Dinwoodie, Designing Non–National Systems: The Case of the Uniform Domain Name Dispute Resolution Policy 43 Wm. & Mary L. Rev. 141 (2001).

[53] See, e.g., Sallen v. Corinthians Licenciamentos LTDA, 273 F.3d 14 (1st Cir. 2001)(suit also brought as a declaratory judg-

arise in these suits are well illustrated by the Fourth Circuit's Barcelo-na.com v. Excelentisimo Ayuntamiento De Barcelona.[54] In that case, a private individual registered the domain name "barcelona.com," planning to use it on behalf of Bcom, a company formed under Delaware law to offer commercial services such as webhosting. After Bcom contacted the City Council of Barcelona, Spain with a "proposal for financing," the City Council demanded transfer of the domain name and brought action under the UDRP when Bcom refused to relinquish the registration. A WIPO panel was convened in Switzerland; it found that the mark was confusingly similar to various Spanish trademarks owned by the City Council and that the financing proposal was a bad-faith attempt to sell it the mark. Bcom was ordered to transfer the domain name to the City Council. Bcom then filed an action against the City Council in the Eastern District of Virginia, seeking restoration of its domain name and a declaratory judgment that barcelona.com did not infringe any rights owned by the City Council.

The first question was *in personam* jurisdiction. The City Council claimed that the court lacked authority because it did not do business in the United States. That defense was rejected because, as noted above, use of the UDRP requires the complainant to submit to the jurisdiction of the place where the domain name was registered. The second issue was whether the panel decision was entitled to deference. Some have argued that panelists (like Perritt) have greater expertise in Internet matters than courts do, and thus their decisions should be given considerable weight. In this case, however, the City Council made a different argument: it claimed that because jurisdiction was based on its use of the dispute resolution system, the court must defer to the panel decision. That argument was rejected on a ground that is probably also applicable to the claim concerning expertise: according to the Fourth Circuit, "recourse to full-blown adjudication under a particular nation's law is necessary to prevent abuse of the UDRP process."[55] The final issue was choice of law. The panel had recognized the City Council's trademark rights under *Spanish* law. However, the Fourth Circuit held that under § 1114(2)(D)(v), only rights "under this chapter"—i.e. under the Lanham Act—are relevant. Since the City Council had not registered its marks in the United States, Bcom was held to have done nothing unlawful by registering barcelona.com.

The upshot of this case is curious: only U.S. trademark rights are protectable, even though the domain name system is international and foreign trademark holders can be hailed into U.S. courts. Could the City Council have avoided this result? Its trademark rights would have been recognized in a Spanish court, but it had won the UDRP action, and so had no complaint on which to base a lawsuit. Could it have argued in the U.S. court that it had common law trademark rights protectable under the

---

ment of noninfringement); Weber–Stephen Products Co. v. Armitage Hardware and Bldg. Supply, Inc., 54 U.S.P.Q.2d 1766 (N.D.Ill.2000) (holding that federal courts are not bound to stay ACPA actions when the same dispute is pending in a UDRP proceeding).

[54] 330 F.3d 617 (4th Cir. 2003).

[55] Id., at 624.

Lanham Act? See International Bancorp v. Society des Bains de Mer,[56] providing factors for determining when a mark has been sufficiently used in interstate commerce and in the United States to be protected by federal trademark law.

**10.** *Disclaimers.* Could Levi or Druck & Gerner or the registrants of wallmartcanadasucks.com or barcelona.com avoid trademark infringement problems by putting a sign on their product, office, or website stating that it is not associated with the trademark owner? In general, courts disfavor the use of disclaimers, mainly because they do not believe that consumers read or understand them and thus, they doubt that these messages allevi-ate the possibility of confusion[57] or dilution.[58] Moreover, disclaimers on websites are seen too late to dissipate initial interest confusion.[59] However, it has been suggested that some form of disclaimer practice may be the only solution to confusion on the Internet. The reason is that, so long as entities are operating in different countries, it is entirely possible for each to hold trademark rights to the same mark for the same product. For example, there are two Budweiser beers, one in the United States and the other in the Czech Republic. Of course, only one of the parties can register the analog domain name in a particular top level domain. That registrant will not have acted in bad faith, and so cannot be ousted under the UDRP or § 43(d). Yet consumer confusion is likely to result. The only solution may be for the registrant to put a disclaimer on its site, or better yet, a link to the other party's website.[60]

**11.** *Other § 43(a) claims.* In addition to claims of likelihood of confusion arising from false designation of origin or false description or representa-tion, § 43(a) covers at least three other important claims.

a. *False endorsements.* Many countries recognize rights of integrity and paternity which can be used to prevent the use of an individual's persona in a context that suggests endorsement, approval, or sponsorship. Several recent cases use section § 43(a) to achieve similar protection.[61]

---

[56] 329 F.3d 359 (4th Cir. 2003).

[57] See, e.g., Jacob Jacoby & Maureen Morrin, "Not Manufactured or Authorized By ... ": Recent Federal Cases Involving Trademark Disclaimers, 17 J. Pub. Pol'y & Marketing 97 (1998). For example, the *Brook-field* court did not believe that initial interest confusion could be dispelled by posting a dis-claimer on West Coast's main web page, Brookfield Communications, Inc. v. West Coast Entertainment Corp., 174 F.3d 1036 (9th Cir. 1999).

[58] Jacob Jacoby, Is It Rational To As-sume Consumer Rationality? Some Consumer Psychological Perspectives on Rational Choice Theory, 6 Roger Williams U. L. Rev. 81 (2000).

[59] See, e.g., PACCAR Inc. v. TeleScan Technologies, L.L.C., 319 F.3d 243, 253 (6th Cir. 2003).

[60] See, e.g., Mark Sableman, Link Law Revisited: Internet Linking Law At Five Years, 16 Berkeley Tech. L.J. 1273 (2001).

[61] See, e.g., Waits v. Frito–Lay, Inc., 978 F.2d 1093 (9th Cir.1992), cert. denied, 506 U.S. 1080 (1993)(singer prevailed in a § 43(a) action against an advertising agency for us-ing a sound-alike imitating his distinctive voice in a commercial for chips); White v. Samsung Electronics America, Inc., 971 F.2d 1395 (9th Cir.1992), cert. denied, 508 U.S. 951 (1993)(holding actress Vanna White raised a genuine issue of material fact regard-ing likelihood of confusion stemming from defendant's advertisement for VCRs featur-ing a robot dressed in a wig, gown and jewel-

b. *Reverse passing off.* Closely related to some of the claims about association are actions to enjoin reverse passing off. This occurs when the defendant sells plaintiff's goods, representing their source or origin as with the defendant.[62] In academia, this sort of activity (claiming someone else's work is one's own) is known as plagiarism. However, it is important to see that rights under the Lanham are distinct from allocating appropriate credit for creative input. In Dastar Corp. v. Twentieth Century Fox Film Corp.,[63] the Supreme Court stressed that the "source" or "origin" of goods for Lanham Act purposes is the manufacturer of the goods (in the case of the video at issue in that case, the vendor of the DVDs, tapes, etc.). Accreditation for authorship is not otherwise controlled by federal law for most works, with the exception of certain types of visual art, see Assignment 9.

c. *False Advertising.* False advertising, the defendant's representation that his goods or services have characteristics or qualities they do not have, always has been actionable under § 43(a). In 1988, Congress amended § 43(a) to expressly include trade disparagement, the defendant's misrepresentation of the quality of the plaintiff's goods.

Avon Products v. S.C. Johnson & Son[64] illustrates the issues arising in these cases. It involved Skin–So–Soft, a bath oil product, which users had long considered an effective insect repellent. Skin–So–Soft was not registered with the Environmental Protection Agency as is required for inspect

---

ry suggestive of White and posed next to the Wheel of Fortune game board); Allen v. National Video, Inc., 610 F.Supp. 612 (S.D.N.Y. 1985)(actor Woody Allen obtained summary judgment on § 43(a) claim in case where defendant hired a look-alike to pose in an advertisement for its national video rental chain). But see Advanced Resources Int'l, Inc. v. Tri–Star Petroleum Co., 4 F.3d 327, 335 (4th Cir.1993)(refusing to extend the rationale of "courts that have found protectable interests in voices, likenesses and images, and to interpret § 43(a) to prohibit the use of a commissioned, signed, unaltered report when that use implies an unauthorized and false endorsement"). See also King v. Innovation Books, 976 F.2d 824 (2d Cir.1992)(court affirmed preliminary injunction of use of possessory credit in § 43(a) action where the plaintiff writer was neither involved in nor approved of a movie that was loosely based on his short story); Smith v. Montoro, 648 F.2d 602 (9th Cir.1981)(sustaining plaintiff actor's § 43(a) claim where defendant film distributor removed plaintiff's name from the film credits and advertising materials and substituted the name of another actor); Gilliam v. American Broadcasting Companies, Inc., 538 F.2d 14 (2d Cir.1976)(plaintiff group

of writers and performers stated a § 43(a) claim based on the defendant network's broadcasting of a program truthfully designated as having been written and performed by the plaintiffs but which had been edited, without plaintiffs' consent, into a mutilated and distorted form that substantially departed from the original work). See also Cleary v. News Corp., 30 F.3d 1255, 1260–61 (9th Cir. 1994)(raising, but not deciding, whether "the Lanham Act protects an author against an inaccurate designation of authorship despite the fact that the author expressly contracted away the right to attribution").

[62] See, e.g., Smith v. Montoro, 648 F.2d 602 (9th Cir.1981). In Cleary v. News Corp., 30 F.3d 1255, 1261–62 (9th Cir.1994), the court noted that the test for reverse passing off differs among the circuits. The Ninth Circuit uses a demanding standard which requires a reverse passing off plaintiff to show that the material in question was "bodily appropriated," whereas in the Second Circuit, the less rigorous "consumer confusion" standard is invoked.

[63] 539 U.S. 23 (2003).

[64] 32 U.S.P.Q.2d 1001 (S.D.N.Y. 1994).

repellents, and Avon did not itself promote it for that use. Avon did, however, register another repellent, Avon Herbal Fresh Skin–So–Soft Moisturizing Suncare Mosquito, Flea, & Deer Tick Repellant. Nonetheless, Johnson, producer of the insect repellent Off! Skintastic, initiated an advertising campaign that featured the claim that "Avon Skin–So–Soft is not EPA-registered for use as an insect repellent." It also ran a commercial stating: "I used to use Avon Skin–So–Soft but Off! Skintastic is just a hundred times better . . . It's not greasy . . . That's why 4 out of 5 Avon users prefer the feel of Off! Skintastic." Avon sued under § 43(a) and the case was decided at the preliminary injunction phase.

Recovery for false advertising requires a plaintiff to demonstrate either that the defendant's advertising is literally false, or that, while literally true, it is nevertheless likely to mislead and confuse consumers. As to literal falsity, the court easily found Johnson's contention concerning EPA registration actionable. However, Avon lost on the literal falsity of the other elements of Johnson's ad. Its attack on the "4 out of 5" language was rejected because Johnson showed that oiliness and greasiness is important to consumers and Avon could not disprove that assertion. The "hundred times better" contention was dismissed as "puffery." Avon also lost its argument that the commercial was implicitly misleading. In such cases, the plaintiff must introduce extrinsic evidence, usually in the form of consumer surveys, showing that the advertisement tends to mislead or confuse consumers.[65] Avon did not meet this burden of proof.

Was this case rightly decided? When numbers are thrown around, don't consumers believe that actual testing occurred? If such testing did not occur, isn't the ad false? The *Avon* court followed a general rule that round numbers like 100 or 1000 are understood by consumers as exaggeration. But what about the 4 out of 5 claim? In general, the plaintiff's burden in a literal falsity case varies according to whether the defendant's advertising includes tests that purport to prove the superiority of the defendant's product: "Where the defendant's advertisement claims that its product is superior plaintiff must affirmatively prove defendant's product equal or inferior. Where . . . the defendant's ad explicitly or implicitly represents that tests or studies prove its product superior, plaintiff satisfies its burden by showing that the tests did not establish the proposition for which they were cited."[66] If a plaintiff satisfies this burden, a court will enjoin the advertisement without evaluating the advertisement's impact on the public.[67] For advertisements that are alleged to be literally false but which do not rely upon tests, how can a plaintiff prove the literal falsity? Is this issue raised in the Principal Problem? In reality, how easy is it to make

---

[65] See Tyco Industries, Inc. v. Lego Systems, Inc., 5 U.S.P.Q.2d (BNA) 1023, 1035–36 (D.N.J.1987)(court found misleading toy company's claim that its pre-school and standard-size blocks "connect" to each other accompanied by illustration of blocks directly connecting because the need to use an adapter block was not disclosed).

[66] Castrol, Inc. v. Quaker State Corp., 977 F.2d 57, 62–63 (2d Cir.1992).

[67] Id. at 62.

distinctions between advertisements that are literally false and those that are implicitly false?

Is this the best way to protect consumers from false and misleading advertising? The Federal Trade Commission maintains a Bureau of Consumer Protection to exercise its authority under the Federal Trade Commission Act, 15 U.S.C. §§ 41–58. Many states also maintain consumer protection agencies. Some commentators believe it is necessary to give trademark holders a private right of action to deal with situations where the government fails to act. However, the burdens of proof that may of the § 43(a) cases impose make the cases costly to litigate. Moreover, courts that are too quick to find consumers misled wind up enjoining the distribution of information that is true, and which may be helpful to some consumers.

**12.** *Consumer standing.* The issue of whether consumers and non-competitors have standing to sue in false endorsement and false advertising cases currently is quite problematic. Many courts take the position that § 43(a) only applies to commercial parties, and thus exclude consumers.[68] At least one court allowed consumers standing.[69] Recently, the Ninth Circuit reconciled conflicting authority there by holding that competition in the traditional sense is not required for a plaintiff to bring a false endorsement action under § 43(a), although a discernible competitive interest is required in false advertising actions.[70] The 1988 amendments to the Lanham Act left this difficult issue unresolved. Should consumers be allowed to bring a § 43(a) action for either false endorsement or false advertising?

**13.** *Contributory infringement.* As in many areas of the law, aiding and abetting the unlawful conduct of another can be actionable under a theory of contributory or vicarious liability. The Supreme Court had occasion to deal with the subject of contributory trademark infringement in Inwood Laboratories, Inc. v. Ives Laboratories, Inc.[71] In that case, the manufacturer of a drug marketed under a registered trademark sued the manufacturers of a generic version of that drug on the theory that the defendants should be vicariously liable for trademark infringement by the pharmacists who dispensed the generic drug. The district court in that case had ruled in favor of the generic drug manufacturers because it found that they had not suggested, or even implied, that pharmacists should dispense the generic drugs incorrectly identified with the plaintiff's trademark.[72] The Second

---

[68] See, e.g., Serbin v. Ziebart International Corp., 11 F.3d 1163 (3d Cir.1993); Colligan v. Activities Club of New York, Ltd., 442 F.2d 686, 692 (2d Cir.), cert. denied, 404 U.S. 1004 (1971); Ortho Pharmaceutical Corp. v. Cosprophar Inc., 828 F.Supp. 1114, 1124 (S.D.N.Y.1993)(commercial plaintiff need not be in competition with defendant, but must have a "reasonable interest to be protected" against the false advertising).

[69] Arnesen v. The Raymond Lee Organization, Inc., 333 F.Supp. 116 (C.D.Cal.1971).

[70] Waits v. Frito–Lay, Inc., 978 F.2d 1093, 1107–10 (9th Cir.1992), cert. denied, 506 U.S. 1080 (1993). See also American Ventures, Inc. v. Post, Buckley, Schuh & Jernigan, Inc., 27 U.S.P.Q.2d (BNA) 1587, 1590–91 (W.D.Wash.1993).

[71] 456 U.S. 844 (1982).

[72] See Ives Laboratories, Inc. v. Darby Drug Co., 488 F.Supp. 394 (E.D.N.Y.1980).

Circuit reversed,[73] and the Supreme Court reversed the Second Circuit on the ground that it had set aside factual findings by the district court that were not clearly erroneous. In the course of its opinion, the Court articulated the following standard for contributory trademark infringement: "[I]f a manufacturer or distributor intentionally induces another to infringe a trademark, or if it continues to supply its product to one whom it knows or has reason to know is engaging in trademark infringement, the manufacturer or distributor is contributorially responsible for any harm done as a result of the deceit."[74] This standard is a more narrow one than that which is applied for copyright infringement. See Sony Corp. of America v. Universal City Studios, Inc., reprinted in Assignment 11.

There are now some claims about domain name poaching that have been brought against domain name registrars on a theory that they contributed to the infringing activity. However, in Lockheed Martin Corp. v. Network Solutions, Inc.,[75] the Ninth Circuit held that NSI lacked the requisite control over the means of infringement to be considered contributorily liable.

[73] See Ives Laboratories, Inc. v. Darby Drug Co., 638 F.2d 538 (2d Cir.1981).

[74] 456 U.S. at 854.

[75] 194 F.3d 980 (9th Cir. 1999).

# ASSIGNMENT 4

# THE INTEREST IN PUBLIC ACCESS

The last Assignment demonstrated the usages of a trademark that its owner can control through actions for trademark infringement, dilution, and unfair competition. This Assignment is designed to look explicitly at the other side of the coin, the uses of the trademark that remain within the control of the public. These matters are, of course, intimately connected. Indeed, several of the main protections of public access were discussed in prior Assignments: the doctrines of genericity and functionality, which keep signals necessary for competition in the public domain; the secondary meaning requirement, which allows subject matter such as colors and descriptive marks to remain as available to the public as is feasible; the requirement that plaintiffs in dilution cases show actual reduction in signaling capacity, which provides the public with some leeway to utilize protected marks. Furthermore, trademarks are subject to a series of defenses grounded in expressive values. As you saw in the previous Assignment, some of these defenses are crafted to facilitate effective discussion of the *trademark holder*. These include the nominative use defense discussed in *Welles*, which permits others to utilize the trademark in order to identify the trademark holder; and the defense discussed in *Wal–Mart* permitting utilization of the trademark for the purposes of parodying or criticizing the trademark holder. In this Assignment, we will examine defenses that are largely aimed at allowing competitors to discuss *themselves, their businesses and their products*: the fair use defense found in § 1115(b)(4) and the first sale doctrine discussed in *Davidoff*. This Assignment rounds out the discussion of expressive concerns by looking, in the *L.L. Bean* case, at the relationship between defenses to trademark law and the free-speech guarantees of the First Amendment, and in *Quality Inns v. McDonald's*, at the problem of determining what the public understands when viewing the mark.

There is, however, another important dimension to public access: the temporal dimension. Unlike copyright and patent rights, which protect newly-created works, trademark rights can remove existing material from the public domain. As a result, there is not only a question of *what* can be protected (the content-based issues discussed in the previous paragraph), but also of *when* protection kicks in—when it is that the public retains the right to use a signal, and when it is that the trademark owner takes control. As *Dawn Donut* shows, the ability to enjoin others from using a protected mark is not triggered by registration alone. While it is true that registration gives others constructive (if not actual) notice of the registered owner's claim, the ability to actually stop unauthorized use may accrue only when the registered owner enters—or plans to enter—the unauthorized user's trading region.

By the same token, trademark rights continue to be enforceable only as long as the holder maintains the mark. As noted in Assignment 1, certificates of registration must be renewed every ten years, at which time a fee must be paid and an averment of use must be filed.[1] Beyond these technical requirements for registered marks, trademark rights can be lost through abandonment. There are two types of abandonment: first, commisive or omisive conduct that causes the mark to lose its distinctiveness; second, discontinuation of the mark with the intent not to resume use.[2] Trademark abandonment is usually raised as an affirmative defense in an infringement suit, but it can also be the basis for a petition to cancel a trademark.[3]

## 1. PRINCIPAL PROBLEM

Our client, Kathleen Boddie, has been a masseuse since October, 1988, when she opened a small massage parlor, "Boddie Workers," in Greenwich Village, New York City. Kathleen uses all her own massage oils, which are made of plants, herbs, fruits, flowers, and seeds. Because she cares about nature, she has carefully avoided ingredients that have been tested on animals. When massage became popular, Kathleen decided to expand her business to the greater New York area. In January, 1990, she opened a second parlor in Westport, Connecticut, which is a very wealthy community about 50 miles from the Greenwich Village location.

Both parlors are managed from Kathleen's tiny headquarters in Greenwich Village and are staffed by masseuses and masseurs that she has personally trained. Ads run in New York Magazine (which also did a small feature on her parlors), The Connecticut Shopper, and The National Body Builder Newsletter.

Kathleen's problems began in March 1990, when The Body Works, Ltd., an English company that manufactures and sells soaps, perfumes, bath oils, and cosmetics, opened its first American store, Body Works, in Deerfield, Illinois. Since that time, the company has expanded across the Midwest and the West Coast. It has recently opened a store in New York City and is looking for sites in Boston, Massachusetts and in Westport, Connecticut.

Kathleen's operation came to the English company's attention in an unusual way. The Body Works, Ltd. advertises extensively in national papers such as the Chicago Tribune, the New York Times and the Wall Street Journal. The ads, which feature a cute little bunny rabbit, claim that the products sold are made of natural ingredients and that no animals have been used to test them. As soon as she saw the first ad, Kathleen's

---

[1] § 1058.

[2] See § 1127 (defining when a mark is considered "abandoned"). Three years of nonuse is considered prima facie evidence of abandonment.

[3] §§ 1064 (cancellation of registration permissible at any time if the mark has been abandoned); 1115(b) (incontestable status subject to abandonment defense).

professional interest was piqued. On a trip to Chicago, she stopped in Deerfield, purchased a bottle of bath oil, and then had it analyzed. When it turned out to contain a synthetic color that Kathleen knew had been tested on rabbits, she changed her ads to include a cartoon strongly resembling the Body Works' bunny. Enfeebled and dressed in a hospital gown, the bunny has a word balloon overhead with the words, "WHAT'S UP NOW, DOC?" Underneath, the ad says:

BODDIE WORKERS: FOR PEOPLE WHO CARE
BODY WORKS: FOR PEOPLE WHO DON'T

The ads then list the addresses of Kathleen's parlors. The enfeebled version of the Body Works bunny has proved popular with animal-rights advocates. To publicize the issue further, Kathleen now sells mugs and tee shirts featuring the same cartoon as her ads. She's also started buying a few products from Body Works, which she resells, she says, "for comparative purposes." She's carefully labeled them with stickers of the sickly bunny.

The Body Works, Ltd. has sued Kathleen under the Lanham Act, seeking to enjoin her from using the name "Boddie Workers" for her parlors, from using the words "Body Works" and the sickly bunny in her ads and on her mugs and tee-shirts, and from selling Body Works products. In thinking about how to defend this suit, keep in mind that Body Works applied to federally register the term "Body Works" and the bunny in November 1988 based on its own prior registration in the United Kingdom. The marks were placed on the Principal Register in December 1989. Kathleen has never registered "Boddie Workers."

## 2.   MATERIALS FOR SOLUTION OF PRINCIPAL PROBLEM

A.   STATUTORY MATERIALS: §§ 1057, 1060, 1064–1065, 1072, 1114–1115, 1125(C)(4) & 1126–1127

B.   CASES: Review: Playboy Enterprises v. Welles and Wal–Mart Stores, Inc. v. Wallmartcanadasucks.com

## Dawn Donut Company, Inc. v. Hart's Food Stores, Inc.

United States Court of Appeals, Second Circuit, 1959.
267 F.2d 358.

■ LUMBARD, CIRCUIT JUDGE.

The principal question is whether the plaintiff, a wholesale distributor of doughnuts and other baked goods under its federally registered trademarks "Dawn" and "Dawn Donut," is entitled under the provisions of the Lanham Trade–Mark Act to enjoin the defendant from using the mark "Dawn" in connection with the retail sale of doughnuts and baked goods entirely within a six county area of New York State surrounding the city of Rochester. The primary difficulty arises from the fact that although plaintiff licenses purchasers of its mixes to use its trademarks in connection with the retail sales of food products made from the mixes, it has not licensed or otherwise exploited the mark at the retail level in defendant's market area for some thirty years.

We hold that because no likelihood of public confusion arises from the concurrent use of the mark in connection with retail sales of doughnuts and other baked goods in separate trading areas, and because there is no present likelihood that plaintiff will expand its retail use of the mark into defendant's market area, plaintiff is not now entitled to any relief under the Lanham Act, 15 U.S.C.A. § 1114. Accordingly, we affirm the district court's dismissal of plaintiff's complaint.

This is not to say that the defendant has acquired any permanent right to use the mark in its trading area. On the contrary, we hold that because of the effect of the constructive notice provision of the Lanham Act, should the plaintiff expand its retail activities into the six county area, upon a proper application and showing to the district court, it may enjoin defendant's use of the mark.

With respect to defendant's counterclaim to cancel plaintiff's registration on the ground that its method of licensing its trademarks violates the Lanham Act, a majority of the court holds that the district court's dismissal of defendant's counterclaim should be affirmed. They conclude that the district court's finding that the plaintiff exercised the degree of control over the nature and quality of the products sold by its licensees required by the Act was not clearly erroneous, particularly in view of the fact that the defendant had the burden of proving its claim for cancellation. I dissent from this conclusion because neither the finding of the trial judge nor the undisputed evidence in the record indicates the extent of supervision and control actually exercised by the plaintiff.

Plaintiff, Dawn Donut Co., Inc., of Jackson, Michigan since June 1, 1922 has continuously used the trademark 'Dawn' upon 25 to 100 pound bags of doughnut mix which it sells to bakers in various states, including New York, and since 1935 it has similarly marketed a line of sweet dough mixes for use in the baking of coffee cakes, cinnamon rolls and oven goods in general under that mark. In 1950 cake mixes were added to the company's line of products. Dawn's sales representatives call upon bakers to solicit orders for mixes and the orders obtained are filled by shipment to the purchaser either directly from plaintiff's Jackson, Michigan plant, where the mixes are manufactured, or from a local warehouse within the customer's state. For some years plaintiff maintained a warehouse in Jamestown, New York, from which shipments were made, but sometime prior to the commencement of this suit in 1954 it discontinued this warehouse and has since then shipped its mixes to its New York customers directly from Michigan.

Plaintiff furnishes certain buyers of its mixes, principally those who agree to become exclusive Dawn Donut Shops, with advertising and packaging material bearing the trademark 'Dawn' and permits these bakers to sell goods made from the mixes to the consuming public under that trademark.

These display materials are supplied either as a courtesy or at a moderate price apparently to stimulate and promote the sale of plaintiff's mixes.

The district court found that with the exception of one Dawn Donut Shop operated in the city of Rochester, New York during 1926–27, plaintiff's licensing of its mark in connection with the retail sale of doughnuts in the state of New York has been confined to areas not less than 60 miles from defendant's trading area. The court also found that for the past eighteen years plaintiff's present New York state representative has, without interruption, made regular calls upon bakers in the city of Rochester, N.Y., and in neighboring towns and cities, soliciting orders for plaintiff's mixes and that throughout this period orders have been filled and shipments made of plaintiff's mixes from Jackson, Michigan into the city of Rochester. But it does not appear that any of these purchasers of plaintiff's mixes employed the plaintiff's mark in connection with retail sales.

The defendant, Hart Food Stores, Inc., owns and operates a retail grocery chain within the New York counties of Monroe, Wayne, Livingston, Genesee, Ontario and Wyoming. The products of defendant's bakery, Starhart Bakeries, Inc., are distributed through these stores, thus confining the distribution of defendant's product to an area within a 45 mile radius of Rochester. Its advertising of doughnuts and other baked products over television and radio and in newspapers is also limited to this area. Defendant's bakery corporation was formed on April 13, 1951 and first used the imprint "Dawn" in packaging its products on August 30, 1951. The district court found that the defendant adopted the mark "Dawn" without any actual knowledge of plaintiff's use or federal registration of the mark, selecting it largely because of a slogan "Baked at midnight, delivered at Dawn" which was originated by defendant's president and used by defendant in its bakery operations from 1929 to 1935. Defendant's president testified, however, that no investigation was made prior to the adoption of the mark to see if anyone else was employing it. Plaintiff's marks were registered federally in 1927, and their registration was renewed in 1947. Therefore by virtue of the Lanham Act, 15 U.S.C.A. § 1072, the defendant had constructive notice of plaintiff's marks as of July 5, 1947, the effective date of the Act.

Defendant's principal contention is that because plaintiff has failed to exploit the mark "Dawn" for some thirty years at the retail level in the Rochester trading area, plaintiff should not be accorded the exclusive right to use the mark in this area.

We reject this contention as inconsistent with the scope of protection afforded a federal registrant by the Lanham Act.

Prior to the passage of the Lanham Act courts generally held that the owner of a registered trademark could not sustain an action for infringement against another who, without knowledge of the registration, used the mark in a different trading area from that exploited by the registrant so that public confusion was unlikely. By being the first to adopt a mark in an area without knowledge of its prior registration, a junior user of a mark could gain the right to exploit the mark exclusively in that market.

But the Lanham Act, 15 U.S.C.A. § 1072, provides that registration of a trademark on the principal register is constructive notice of the registrant's claim of ownership. Thus, by eliminating the defense of good faith and lack of knowledge, § 1072 affords nationwide protection to registered marks, regardless of the areas in which the registrant actually uses the mark.

That such is the purpose of Congress is further evidenced by 15 U.S.C.A. § 1115(a) and (b) which make the certificate of registration evidence of the registrant's "exclusive right to use the ... mark in commerce." "Commerce" is defined in 15 U.S.C.A. § 1127 to include all the commerce which may lawfully be regulated by Congress. These two provisions of the Lanham Act make it plain that the fact that the defendant employed the mark "Dawn," without actual knowledge of plaintiff's registration, at the retail level in a limited geographical area of New York state before the plaintiff used the mark in that market, does not entitle it either to exclude the plaintiff from using the mark in that area or to use the mark concurrently once the plaintiff licenses the mark or otherwise exploits it in connection with retail sales in the area.

Plaintiff's failure to license its trademarks in defendant's trading area during the thirty odd years that have elapsed since it licensed them to a Rochester baker does not work an abandonment of the rights in that area. We hold that 15 U.S.C.A. § 1127, which provides for abandonment in certain cases of non-use, applies only when the registrant fails to use his mark, within the meaning of § 1127, anywhere in the nation. Since the Lanham Act affords a registrant nationwide protection, a contrary holding would create an insoluble problem of measuring the geographical extent of the abandonment.

Accordingly, since plaintiff has used its trademark continuously at the retail level, it has not abandoned its federal registration rights even in defendant's trading area.

[We next] turn to the question of whether on this record plaintiff has made a sufficient showing to warrant the issuance of an injunction against defendant's use of the mark "Dawn" in a trading area in which the plaintiff has for thirty years failed to employ its registered mark.

The Lanham Act, 15 U.S.C.A. § 1114, sets out the standard for awarding a registrant relief against the unauthorized use of his mark by another. It provides that the registrant may enjoin only that concurrent use which creates a likelihood of public confusion as to the origin of the products in connection with which the marks are used. Therefore if the use of the marks by the registrant and the unauthorized user are confined to two sufficiently distinct and geographically separate markets, with no likelihood that the registrant will expand his use into defendant's market, so that no public confusion is possible, then the registrant is not entitled to enjoin the junior user's use of the mark.

As long as plaintiff and defendant confine their use of the mark "Dawn" in connection with the retail sale of baked goods to their present separate trading areas it is clear that no public confusion is likely.

The district court took note of what it deemed common knowledge, that "retail purchasers of baked goods, because of the perishable nature of such goods, usually make such purchases reasonably close to their homes, say within about 25 miles, and retail purchases of such goods beyond that distance are for all practical considerations negligible." No objection is made to this finding and nothing appears in the record which contradicts it as applied to this case.

Moreover, we note that it took plaintiff three years to learn of defendant's use of the mark and bring this suit, even though the plaintiff was doing some wholesale business in the Rochester area. This is a strong indication that no confusion arose or is likely to arise either from concurrent use of the marks at the retail level in geographically separate trading areas or from its concurrent use at different market levels, viz. retail and wholesale in the same area.

The decisive question then is whether plaintiff's use of the mark "Dawn" at the retail level is likely to be confined to its current area of use or whether in the normal course of its business, it is likely to expand the retail use of the mark into defendant's trading area. If such expansion were probable, then the concurrent use of the marks would give rise to the conclusion that there was a likelihood of confusion.

The district court found that in view of the plaintiff's inactivity for about thirty years in exploiting its trademarks in defendant's trading area at the retail level either by advertising directed at retail purchasers or by retail sales through authorized licensed users, there was no reasonable expectation that plaintiff would extend its retail operations into defendant's trading area. There is ample evidence in the record to support this conclusion and we cannot say that it is clearly erroneous.

However, because of the effect we have attributed to the constructive notice provision of the Lanham Act, the plaintiff may later, upon a proper showing of an intent to use the mark at the retail level in defendant's market area, be entitled to enjoin defendant's use of the mark.

The final issue presented is raised by defendant's appeal from the dismissal of its counterclaim for cancellation of plaintiff's registration on the ground that the plaintiff failed to exercise the control required by the Lanham Act over the nature and quality of the goods sold by its licensees.

We are all agreed that the Lanham Act places an affirmative duty upon a licensor of a registered trademark to take reasonable measures to detect and prevent misleading uses of his mark by his licensees or suffer cancellation of his federal registration. § 1064, provides that a trademark registration may be canceled because the trademark has been "abandoned." And "abandoned" is defined in § 1127 to include any act or omission by the registrant which causes the trademark to lose its significance as an indication of origin.

Prior to the passage of the Lanham Act many courts took the position that the licensing of a trademark separately from the business in connection with which it had been used worked an abandonment. The theory of these cases was that:

> "A trade-mark is intended to identify the goods of the owner and to safeguard his good will. The designation if employed by a person other than the one whose business it serves to identify would be misleading. Consequently, a right to the use of a trade-mark or a trade-name cannot be transferred in gross." American Broadcasting Co. v. Wahl Co., 121 F.2d 412, 413 (2d Cir.1941).

Other courts were somewhat more liberal and held that a trademark could be licensed separately from the business in connection with which it had been used provided that the licensor retained control over the quality of the goods produced by the licensee. E. I. duPont De Nemours & Co. v. Celanese Corporation of America, 167 F.2d 484 (1948). But even in the *duPont* case the court was careful to point out that naked licensing, viz. the grant of licenses without the retention of control, was invalid. E. I. DuPont de Nemours & Co. v. Celanese Corporation of America, 167 F.2d, at 489.

The Lanham Act clearly carries forward the view of these latter cases that controlled licensing does not work an abandonment of the licensor's registration, while a system of naked licensing does. § 1055 provides:

> "Where a registered mark or a mark sought to be registered is or may be used legitimately by related companies, such use shall inure to the benefit of the registrant or applicant for registration, and such use shall not affect the validity of such mark or of its registration, provided such mark is not used in such manner as to deceive the public."

And § 1127 defines "related company" to mean "any person who legitimately controls or is controlled by the registrant or applicant for registration in respect to the nature and quality of the goods or services in connection with which the mark is used."

Without the requirement of control, the right of a trademark owner to license his mark separately from the business in connection with which it has been used would create the danger that products bearing the same trademark might be of diverse qualities. If the licensor is not compelled to take some reasonable steps to prevent misuses of his trademark in the hands of others the public will be deprived of its most effective protection against misleading uses of a trademark. The public is hardly in a position to uncover deceptive uses of a trademark before they occur and will be at best slow to detect them after they happen. Thus, unless the licensor exercises supervision and control over the operations of its licensees the risk that the public will be unwittingly deceived will be increased and this is precisely what the Act is in part designed to prevent. See Sen. Report No. 1333, 79th Cong., 2d Sess. (1946). Clearly the only effective way to protect the public, where a trademark is used by licensees, is to place on the licensor the affirmative duty of policing in a reasonable manner the activities of his licensees.

The critical question on these facts therefore is whether the plaintiff sufficiently policed and inspected its licensees' operations to guarantee the quality of the products they sold under its trademarks to the public. The trial court found that: "By reason of its contacts with its licensees, plaintiff exercised legitimate control over the nature and quality of the food products on which plaintiff's licensees used the trademark 'Dawn.' Plaintiff and its licensees are related companies within the meaning of Section 45 of the Trademark Act of 1946." It is the position of the majority of this court that the trial judge has the same leeway in determining what constitutes a reasonable degree of supervision and control over licensees under the facts and circumstances of the particular case as he has on other questions of fact; and particularly because it is the defendant who has the burden of proof on this issue they hold the lower court's finding not clearly erroneous.

I dissent from the conclusion of the majority that the district court's findings are not clearly erroneous because while it is true that the trial judge must be given some discretion in determining what constitutes reasonable supervision of licensees under the Lanham Act, it is also true that an appellate court ought not to accept the conclusions of the district court unless they are supported by findings of sufficient facts. It seems to me that the only findings of the district judge regarding supervision are in such general and conclusory terms as to be meaningless. In the absence of supporting findings or of undisputed evidence in the record indicating the kind of supervision and inspection the plaintiff actually made of its licensees, it is impossible for us to pass upon whether there was such supervision as to satisfy the statute. There was evidence before the district court in the matter of supervision, and more detailed findings thereon should have been made.

Plaintiff's licensees fall into two classes: (1) those bakers with whom it made written contracts providing that the baker purchase exclusively plaintiff's mixes and requiring him to adhere to plaintiff's directions in using the mixes; and (2) those bakers whom plaintiff permitted to sell at retail under the "Dawn" label doughnuts and other baked goods made from its mixes although there was no written agreement governing the quality of the food sold under the Dawn mark.[a]

[a] On cross-examination plaintiff's president conceded that during 1949 and 1950 the company in some instances, the number of which is not made clear by his testimony, distributed its advertising and packaging material to bakers with whom it had not reached any agreement relating to the quality of the goods sold in packages bearing the name "Dawn". It also appears from plaintiff's list of the 16 bakers who were operating as exclusive Dawn shops at the time of the trial that plaintiff's contract with 3 of these shops had expired and had not been renewed and that in the case of 2 other such shops the contract had been renewed only after a substantial period of time had elapsed since the expiration of the original agreement. The record indicates that these latter 2 bakers continued to operate under the name "Dawn" and purchase "Dawn" mixes during the period following the expiration of their respective franchise agreements with the plaintiff. Particularly damaging to plaintiff is the fact that one of the 2 bakers whose franchise contracts plaintiff allowed to lapse for a substantial period of time has also been permitted by plaintiff to sell doughnuts made from a mix other than plaintiff's in packaging labeled with plaintiff's trademark.

The contracts that plaintiff did conclude, although they provided that the purchaser use the mix as directed and without adulteration, failed to provide for any system of inspection and control. Without such a system plaintiff could not know whether these bakers were adhering to its standards in using the mix or indeed whether they were selling only products made from Dawn mixes under the trademark "Dawn".

The absence, however, of an express contract right to inspect and supervise a licensee's operations does not mean that the plaintiff's method of licensing failed to comply with the requirements of the Lanham Act. Plaintiff may in fact have exercised control in spite of the absence of any express grant by licensees of the right to inspect and supervise.

The question then, with respect to both plaintiff's contract and non-contract licensees, is whether the plaintiff in fact exercised sufficient control.

Here the only evidence in the record relating to the actual supervision of licensees by plaintiff consists of the testimony of two of plaintiff's local sales representatives that they regularly visited their particular customers and the further testimony of one of them, Jesse Cohn, the plaintiff's New York representative, that "in many cases" he did have an opportunity to inspect and observe the operations of his customers. The record does not indicate whether plaintiff's other sales representatives made any similar efforts to observe the operations of licensees.

Moreover, Cohn's testimony fails to make clear the nature of the inspection he made or how often he made one. His testimony indicates that his opportunity to observe a licensee's operations was limited to "those cases where I am able to get into the shop" and even casts some doubt on whether he actually had sufficient technical knowledge in the use of plaintiff's mix to make an adequate inspection of a licensee's operations.

The fact that it was Cohn who failed to report the defendant's use of the mark "Dawn" to the plaintiff casts still further doubt about the extent of the supervision Cohn exercised over the operations of plaintiff's New York licensees.

Thus I do not believe that we can fairly determine on this record whether plaintiff subjected its licensees to periodic and thorough inspections by trained personnel or whether its policing consisted only of chance, cursory examinations of licensees' operations by technically untrained salesmen. The latter system of inspection hardly constitutes a sufficient program of supervision to satisfy the requirements of the Act.

Therefore it is appropriate to remand the counterclaim for more extensive findings on the relevant issues rather than hazard a determination on this incomplete and uncertain record. I would direct the district court to order the cancellation of plaintiff's registrations if it should find that the plaintiff did not adequately police the operations of its licensees.

But unless the district court finds some evidence of misuse of the mark by plaintiff in its sales of mixes to bakers at the wholesale level, the cancellation of plaintiff's registration should be limited to the use of the mark in connection with sale of the finished food products to the consuming public. Such a limited cancellation is within the power of the court. Section 1119 specifically provides that "In any action involving a registered mark the court may . . . order the cancellation of registrations, in whole or in part, . . . ". Moreover, partial cancellation is consistent with § 1051(a)(1), governing the initial registration of trademarks which requires the applicant to specify "the goods in connection with which the mark is used and the mode or manner in which the mark is used in connection with such goods . . . ".

The district court's denial of an injunction restraining defendant's use of the mark "Dawn" on baked and fried goods and its dismissal of defendant's counterclaim are affirmed.

## L.L. Bean, Inc. v. Drake Publishers, Inc.

United States Court of Appeals, First Circuit, 1987.
811 F.2d 26.

■ Bownes, Circuit Judge.

Imitation may be the highest form of flattery, but plaintiff-appellee L.L. Bean, Inc., was neither flattered nor amused when High Society magazine published a prurient parody of Bean's famous catalog. Defendant-appellant Drake Publishers, Inc., owns High Society, a monthly periodical featuring adult erotic entertainment. Its October 1984 issue contained a two-page article entitled "L.L. Beam's Back–To–School–Sex–Catalog." The article was labelled on the magazine's contents page as "humor" and "parody." The article displayed a facsimile of Bean's trademark and featured pictures of nude models in sexually explicit positions using "products" that were described in a crudely humorous fashion.

L.L. Bean sought a temporary restraining order to remove the October 1984 issue from circulation. The complaint alleged trademark infringement, unfair competition, trademark dilution, deceptive trade practices, interference with prospective business advantage and trade libel. [Among other things, the district court granted] Bean summary judgment with respect to the trademark dilution claim raised under Maine law. Me.Rev. Stat.Ann. tit. 10, § 1530 (1981). It ruled that the article had tarnished Bean's trademark by undermining the goodwill and reputation associated with the mark. The court also held that enjoining the publication of a parody to prevent trademark dilution did not offend the first amendment. An injunction issued prohibiting further publication or distribution of the "L.L. Beam Sex Catalog." [Drake appealed.]

I

A trademark is a word, name or symbol adopted and used by a manufacturer or merchant to identify goods and distinguish them from those manufactured by others. 15 U.S.C.A. § 1127 (1985 Supp.). One need only open a magazine or turn on television to witness the pervasive influence of trademarks in advertising and commerce. Designer labels appear on goods ranging from handbags to chocolates to every possible form of clothing. Commercial advertising slogans, which can be registered as trademarks, have become part of national political campaigns. "Thus, trademarks have become a natural target of satirists who seek to comment on this integral part of the national culture." Dorsen, Satiric Appropriation and the Law of Libel, Trademark and Copyright: Remedies Without Wrongs, 65 B.U.L.Rev. 923, 939 (1986); Note, Trademark Parody: A Fair Use and First Amendment Analysis, 72 Va.L.Rev. 1079 (1986).

The ridicule conveyed by parody inevitably conflicts with one of the underlying purposes of the Maine anti-dilution statute, which is to protect against the tarnishment of the goodwill and reputation associated with a particular trademark. The court below invoked this purpose as the basis for its decision to issue an injunction. The issue before us is whether enjoining the publication of appellant's parody violates the first amendment guarantees of freedom of expression.

## II

The district court disposed of the first amendment concerns raised in this matter by relying on the approach taken in Dallas Cowboys Cheerleaders, Inc. v. Pussycat Cinema, Ltd., 604 F.2d 200 (2d Cir.1979). In rejecting Drake's claim that the first amendment protects the unauthorized use of another's trademark in the process of conveying a message, the district court cited the following language from Dallas Cowboys Cheerleaders: "Plaintiff's trademark is in the nature of a property right, . . . and as such it need not 'yield to the exercise of First Amendment rights under circumstances where adequate alternative avenues of communication exist.' Lloyd Corp. v. Tanner, 407 U.S. 551 [92 S.Ct. 2219, 33 L.Ed.2d 131] (1972)."

We do not believe that the first amendment concerns raised here can be resolved as easily as was done in Dallas Cowboys Cheerleaders. Aside from our doubts about whether there are alternative means of parodying plaintiff's catalog, we do not think the court fully assessed the nature of a trademark owner's property rights.

The limits on the scope of a trademark owner's property rights was considered recently in Lucasfilm Ltd. v. High Frontier, 622 F.Supp. 931 (D.D.C.1985). In that case, the owners of the trademark "Star Wars" alleged injury from public interest groups that used the term in commercial advertisements presenting their views on President Reagan's Strategic Defense Initiative. Judge Gesell stressed that the sweep of a trademark owner's rights extends only to injurious, unauthorized commercial uses of the mark by another. 622 F.Supp. at 933–35. Trademark rights do not entitle the owner to quash an unauthorized use of the mark by another who is communicating ideas or expressing points of view. Id.

III

The district court's opinion suggests that tarnishment may be found when a trademark is used without authorization in a context which diminishes the positive associations with the mark. Neither the strictures of the first amendment nor the history and theory of anti-dilution law permit a finding of tarnishment based solely on the presence of an unwholesome or negative context in which a trademark is used without authorization. Such a reading of the anti-dilution statute unhinges it from its origins in the marketplace. A trademark is tarnished when consumer capacity to associate it with the appropriate products or services has been diminished. The threat of tarnishment arises when the goodwill and reputation of a plaintiff's trademark is linked to products which are of shoddy quality or which conjure associations that clash with the associations generated by the owner's lawful use of the mark: "[T]he risk may be that of detracting from the plaintiff's good will by the possibility that a defendant's use of plaintiff's unique mark will tarnish plaintiff's trade name by reason of public dissatisfaction with defendant's product and a resultant holding of this dissatisfaction against plaintiff. An alternative to this . . . risk is the danger of public identification of plaintiff's trade name or mark with a product or service of a type incompatible with the quality and prestige previously attached by the public to the plaintiff's product." Tiffany & Co. v. Boston Club, Inc., 231 F.Supp. 836, 844 (D.Mass.1964).

As indicated by Judge Caffrey in Tiffany, the dilution injury stems from an unauthorized effort to market incompatible products or services by trading on another's trademark. The Constitution is not offended when the anti-dilution statute is applied to prevent a defendant from using a trademark without permission in order to merchandise dissimilar products or services. Any residual effect on first amendment freedoms should be balanced against the need to fulfill the legitimate purpose of the anti-dilution statute. The law of trademark dilution has developed to combat an unauthorized and harmful appropriation of a trademark by another for the purpose of identifying, manufacturing, merchandising or promoting dissimilar products or services. The harm occurs when a trademark's identity and integrity—its capacity to command respect in the market—is undermined due to its inappropriate and unauthorized use by other market actors. When presented with such circumstances, courts have found that trademark owners have suffered harm despite the fact that redressing such harm entailed some residual impact on the rights of expression of commercial actors. See, e.g., Chemical Corp. of America v. Anheuser–Busch, Inc., 306 F.2d 433 (5th Cir.1962), cert. denied, 372 U.S. 965, 83 S.Ct. 1089, 10 L.Ed.2d 129 (1963)(floor wax and insecticide maker's slogan, "Where there's life, there's bugs," harmed strength of defendant's slogan, "Where there's life, there's Bud."); Original Appalachian Artworks, Inc. v. Topps Chewing Gum, 642 F.Supp. 1031 (N.D.Ga.1986)(merchandiser of "Garbage Pail Kids" stickers and products injured owner of Cabbage Patch Kids mark); General Electric Co. v. Alumpa Coal Co., 205 U.S.P.Q. (BNA) 1036 (D.Mass.1979)("Genital Electric" monogram on underpants and T-shirts harmful to plaintiff's trademark).

While the cases cited above might appear at first glance to be factually analogous to the instant one, they are distinguishable for two reasons. First, they all involved unauthorized commercial uses of another's trademark. Second, none of those cases involved a defendant using a plaintiff's trademark as a vehicle for an editorial or artistic parody. In contrast to the cases cited, the instant defendant used plaintiff's mark solely for noncommercial purposes. Appellant's parody constitutes an editorial or artistic, rather than a commercial, use of plaintiff's mark. The article was labelled as "humor" and "parody" in the magazine's table of contents section; it took up two pages in a one-hundred-page issue; neither the article nor appellant's trademark was featured on the front or back cover of the magazine. Drake did not use Bean's mark to identify or promote goods or services to consumers; it never intended to market the "products" displayed in the parody.

We think the Constitution tolerates an incidental impact on rights of expression of commercial actors in order to prevent a defendant from unauthorizedly merchandising his products with another's trademark.[a] In such circumstances, application of the anti-dilution statute constitutes a legitimate regulation of commercial speech, which the Supreme Court has defined as "expression related solely to the economic interests of the speaker and its audience." Central Hudson Gas & Elec. v. Public Serv. Comm'n, 447 U.S. 557, 561, 100 S.Ct. 2343, 2348, 65 L.Ed.2d 341 (1980). It offends the Constitution, however, to invoke the anti-dilution statute as a basis for enjoining the noncommercial use of a trademark by a defendant engaged in a protected form of expression.

Our reluctance to apply the anti-dilution statute to the instant case also stems from a recognition of the vital importance of parody. Although, as we have noted, parody is often offensive, it is nevertheless "deserving of substantial freedom—both as entertainment and as a form of social and literary criticism." Berlin v. E.C. Publications, Inc., 329 F.2d 541 (2d Cir.), cert. denied, 379 U.S. 822, 85 S.Ct. 46, 13 L.Ed.2d 33 (1964). It would be anomalous to diminish the protection afforded parody solely because a parodist chooses a famous trade name, rather than a famous personality, author or creative work, as its object.[b]

[a] We have no occasion to consider the constitutional limits which might be imposed on the application of anti-dilution statutes to unauthorized uses of trademarks on products whose principal purpose is to convey a message. Mutual of Omaha Ins. Co. v. Novak, 775 F.2d 247 (8th Cir.1985) (plaintiff entitled to preliminary injunction against peace activist protesting nuclear weapons proliferation by marketing "Mutant of Omaha" T-shirts). Such a situation undoubtedly would require a balancing of the harm suffered by the trademark owner against the benefit derived by the parodist and the public from the unau-thorized use of a trademark on a product designed to convey a message.

[b] We recognize that the plaintiffs in Pillsbury Co. v. Milky Way Productions, Inc., 215 U.S.P.Q. (BNA) 124 (N.D.Ga.1981), obtained injunctive relief against Screw magazine, which had published pictures of facsimiles of Pillsbury's trade characters, "Poppin Fresh" and "Poppie Fresh," engaged in sexual intercourse and fellatio. The pictorial also featured plaintiff's trademark and the refrain of its jingle, "The Pillsbury Baking Song." While the district court granted relief under Georgia's anti-dilution statute, 215 U.S.P.Q.

The district court's injunction falls not only because it trammels upon a protected form of expression, but also because it depends upon an untoward judicial evaluation of the offensiveness or unwholesomeness of the appellant's materials. The Supreme Court has recognized the threat to free speech inherent in sanctioning such evaluations. Cohen v. California, 403 U.S. 15, 25, 91 S.Ct. 1780, 1788, 29 L.Ed.2d 284 (1971).

Reversed and remanded.

■ LEVIN H. CAMPBELL, CHIEF JUDGE (dissenting)[omitted].

# Quality Inns International, Inc. v. McDonald's Corp.

United States District Court for the District of Maryland, 1988.
695 F.Supp. 198.

■ NIEMEYER, DISTRICT JUDGE.

On September 21, 1987, Quality Inns International, Inc. announced a new chain of economy hotels to be marketed under the name "McSleep Inn." The response of McDonald's Corporation was immediate. It demanded by letter sent three days later that Quality International not use the name "McSleep" because it infringed on McDonald's family of marks that are characterized by the use of the prefix "Mc" combined with a generic word. [Quality Inns then filed this declaratory judgment action.]

## QUALITY INTERNATIONAL

Quality International is a Delaware corporation with its principal offices in Silver Spring, Maryland. It is engaged in the lodging business, particularly in inns, hotels, suites, and resorts.

Having no product to compete in the economy segment, Quality International designed a concept for a hotel with a smaller basic room which would rent for between $20 and $29 per night. Each room would have a queen size bed, plush carpeting, color TV, and a contiguous bathroom. There would be no conference rooms, food or other amenities on the premises, except a swimming pool in certain geographical areas. These economy hotels would all be of new construction and a consistent architecture. The name selected by Mr. Hazard for this product was "McSleep Inn." The first McSleep Inn is scheduled to open in December, 1988.

## MCDONALD'S CORPORATION

McDonald's Corporation is a Delaware corporation with its principal offices in Oak Brook, Illinois. Founded by Ray A. Kroc, it opened its first

at 135, it did so only after specifically declining to consider whether defendants' presentation constituted a parody. Id. at 129–30. The defendants in Pillsbury had tried to proffer parody as a defense to plaintiff's copyright infringement claim; they did not assert it as a defense to the dilution claim. Pillsbury, therefore, does not stand for the proposition that the publication of a parody properly may be enjoined under an anti-dilution statute, since the court never considered whether defendants had presented a parody, and defendants never asserted parody as a defense to the dilution claim.

restaurant in April, 1955, in Des Plaines, Illinois. It is now the largest fast food business in the world, with over 10,000 restaurants in 45 countries and over $14 billion in sales annually.

In recent years, McDonald's began to focus on a long distance travel market, defined by customers traveling on the road who are more than 30 miles from home when they use the service. Pursuing this market, McDonald's took over numerous tollway restaurants and converted them to McDonald's restaurants. After the first year of conversion, the increased sales at all of the restaurants that were converted averaged over three times the previous year's sales, and indeed the sale of gas at the neighboring gas station increased significantly, although not as much. McDonald's attributes these successes to its recognition.

The attribution to McDonald's, however, has not been totally under its control. Journalists have created their own words by adding "Mc" to a generic word. The Court was presented with literally hundreds of such uses, such as McLaw, McTax, McNews, McPaper, McSurgery, McArt, even McGod. Since the issue is raised in this action that "Mc" words have become generic, the Court will address the scope of this usage more fully below.

As part of its promotion, McDonald's created a language that it called "McLanguage" from which it developed a family of marks for its products such as McChicken, McNugget, McPizza, as well as marks outside the food area related to its business such as McStop, McKids, and McShuttle. There is no evidence that this language or these marks existed before McDonald's created them or that, outside of McDonald's sphere of promotion and presence, anyone would understand these words to mean anything. "Mc" obviously is a Scottish or Irish surname used in proper names. The use to form words, however, was unique at the time. The marks that are owned by McDonald's and that were formulated by combining "Mc" and a generic word are fanciful and enjoy a meaning that associates the product immediately with McDonald's and its products and service.

They also constitute a family of marks that is enforceable against infringing uses, and since they are fanciful they will be given the strongest protection. McDonald's Corp. v. McBagel's, Inc., 649 F.Supp. 1268 (S.D.N.Y.1986).

THIRD–PARTY USES OF "MC"

Quality International has pointed out that there are a substantial number of third-party uses of "Mc" with a generic word that would give rise to infringement to the same extent as would the mark McSleep Inn. Quality International urges that these uses by third parties are so pervasive that McDonald's should now be denied the right to enforce its marks against McSleep Inn.

The evidence established that there are many third-party uses. McHappy and McDonuts are used for baked goods and doughnuts in Ohio and the midwest area. McMaid is used for maid service franchising in various midwestern states. McDivots is used for golf accessories in the Colorado area. McFranchise is used for management consulting in the northeast. McMoose is used in Heritage Park on the east coast. McWest is used for contracting. McSports is used for a sports store in a strip shopping center. McPrint is used for franchised printing in the New York area. McQuick is used for quick change lubrications in the midwest area, mostly Indiana. McBud is a florist in the midwest. [The court went on to provide many other examples of third-party uses, both present and past.]

Permitting the use by third parties of infringing marks can be relevant to three specific issues in a trademark case. If a trademark owner has expressly or impliedly given an assurance to another user that he will not assert his trademark rights, he may be barred from enforcing his mark against that user, by reason of estoppel by acquiescence. Sweetheart Plastics, Inc. v. Detroit Forming, Inc., 743 F.2d 1039 (4th Cir.1984).

Acquiescence may be inferred from conduct as well. Thus, delay in enforcement of a mark against a defendant may become relevant to the question of estoppel by acquiescence. Whether a trademark owner delayed in enforcing its trademark rights against others, however, is not relevant to establishing an estoppel defense, since estoppel by acquiescence focuses on a plaintiff's acts toward the defendant, not toward others. Acquiescence is a personal defense that merely results in a loss of rights against the defendant.

Third-party uses permitted by the owner of a mark may also be probative of the abandonment of a mark by the owner. A mark is abandoned when any course of conduct of the owner, including acts of omission as well as commission, causes the mark to lose its significance as an indication of origin. See 15 U.S.C.A. § 1127(b). Failing to take action against an infringer has been held to be such an "act of omission." Once a mark has been held abandoned, it is free for all to use and falls into the public domain. It may be seized by another, and the person doing so gains rights against the whole world. 15 U.S.C.A. § 1115. However, as the court in Sweetheart Plastics emphasized, "[t]he issue is hardly ever 'abandonment,' because that requires proof that the mark has lost all significance as an indication of origin" and is "completely without signs of life." 743 F.2d at 1047–48.

So long as there is no abandonment or estoppel by acquiescence, a trademark owner's tolerance of third-party uses of his marks will not bar enforcement of his rights against an infringing user. It may, however, bear on the issue of the strength of his mark. The damage that third-party users of a mark can cause an owner who seeks to enforce his mark is the weakening of the mark's strength. Failure to take reasonable steps to prevent third-party uses of the mark may weaken a mark to the point where it is entitled to only a narrow scope of enforcement, and ultimately the question may become one of abandonment. However, where the owner of the mark has been reasonably diligent in protecting his rights, even though infringements exist, no intent to abandon will be inferred.

In this case Quality International does not contend that McDonald's has abandoned its family of marks or that McDonald's has acquiesced in Quality International's use of McSleep Inn. The Court likewise reaches those same conclusions based on the evidence presented. McDonald's gave no assurances, expressly or impliedly, to Quality International that it could use McSleep Inn, and McDonald's did not delay in pursuing enforcement of its marks. The evidence of third-party uses introduced by Quality Inns therefore is probative only of the strength and scope of McDonald's family of marks. These uses will not preclude the enforcement of those marks against Quality International.

The Court can point to no evidence that public awareness of Mc-Donald's family of marks and their attribution of source to McDonald's has been lessened by the third-party uses. The more important question, and probably the only relevant one, is whether third-party uses are so prevalent that the public would not likely confuse McSleep Inn with McDonald's. The Court found no evidence to suggest impact by third-party uses on this question of confusion. Although the question is more fully encompassed in the answer to the issue whether McSleep Inn is likely to cause confusion, which is discussed below, suffice it to conclude at this point that third-party uses do not preclude McDonald's enforcement of its family of marks.

GENERIC DEFENSE

Both Mr. Hazard, Quality International's CEO, and Mr. Mosser, its vice president in charge of franchising, urged at trial that "Mc" has become a generic prefix meaning thrifty, consistent, and perhaps convenient. They urge that the notion of thriftiness comes from the association with the Scots and the perception that the Scots are thrifty. The Court was directed to the writings of H.L. Mencken, the famous Baltimore journalist and writer, who said: Nearly all the English words and phrases based on Scotch embody references to the traditional penuriousness of the Scots, for example Scotch coffee, hot water flavored with burnt biscuit; to play the Scotch organ, to put money in a cash register; Scotch pint, a two-quart bottle; Scotch sixpence, a threepence; and the Scotchman's cinema, Piccadilly Circus, because it offers many free attractions. The American Language by H.L. Mencken (4th Ed. Abridged with Annotations and Material by Raven I. [appropriately] McDavid, Jr.), at pages 388–89.

Both Mr. Hazard and Mr. Mosser acknowledge that the aspect of "Mc" that includes consistency and convenience derives from McDonald's and its extensive promotional efforts. They urge, however, that any such association with McDonald's is now lost to the public domain by common usage.

In support of the contention that "Mc" as a prefix has derived a singular meaning and become part of the language, Dr. Roger W. Shuy, a linguist from Georgetown University, reviewed hundreds of journalistic uses of the prefix "Mc" for purposes of deriving its meaning and to evidence it common usage. Several examples will give a sampling of the broad range of his findings.

The term "McFood" has been used as follows: "It's a push-button, do-it-yourself, convenience-oriented world.... Why cook when we can zap a Lean Cuisine in the micro, or order McFood from a drive-in McSpeaker." Similarly, the word McLunch has been used for what kids are eating in school.

In the area of clothes, McFashion has been used in connection with smaller, specialized express stores for kids, imitating the concept of a fast food outlet.

McMedicine has been used to refer to prompt, inexpensive medical care centers, and McSurgery becomes surgery without overnight hospital stays.

McLaw has been used to describe the legal franchise phenomenon, suggesting that legal advice is dispensed through drive-in windows. Describing franchising in other areas have been McFuneral for funeral operations; McLube or McOil Change for the fast, little drive-in shops offering ten-minute oil changes; and McMiz for franchising of the Broadway musical "Les Miserables." Even the franchising of local post office branches has been suggested to become McMail, and franchised tax preparation as McTax.

In the news and media area, USA Today has been characterized as McPaper, "fast news for the fast-food generation." There was even a book called The Making of McPaper. The distillation of books or books without substance has been referred to as McBook, and similar characterizations have been made about digested news stories, McNews.

Even culture that has been subjected to mass marketing has been characterized with the prefix "Mc." The proliferation of low-cost mass-produced art is McArt. One article even referred to McMozart.

Movies that are analogized to fast food which satisfy the appetite and taste good have been called McMovies or McCinemas. Similarly, there is McTelevision, McTelecast, and McVideo.

No subject seems to have been excluded. In connection with religion there has been a reference to McGod: "It was a difficult year for the McGod family network. [Jimmy Baker, Jimmy Swaggart, and Jerry Falwell] fought a major turf battle over control of the PTL McTelevangelism."

One article perhaps summarized it all, "This is the era of instant gratification, of poptops, quick wash, fast fix, frozen foods, McEverything."

A news report placed into evidence referred to the trial before this Court as taking place in the McCourt, which, of course, would make the judge the McJudge. While the Court understood that association with the Courthouse in Baltimore, it could not come to grips with the suggestion that the trial was before a McJudge. The Court could find few, if any, of the attributes of "Mc" used by McDonald's or by the journalists otherwise to fit. Perhaps this McPinion will fulfill that prophecy.

After reviewing these articles and numerous others, Dr. Shuy reviewed the context of the "Mc" word and derived a list of 27 definitions for the prefix "Mc": highly advertised; franchise; easy access; inexpensive; high volume; lacks prestige, comfort, cost; everyday; prepackaged; specialty chain; quick; convenient; reduces choices; self-service; mass merchandising; standardized; state of the art marketing; low brow; assembly line precision; uniform; market dominance formula; handy location; positive attitude; simple; comfortable; honest; looks okay; and working man. He reduced these to four terms which he characterizes as the definition of "Mc," that is, "basic, convenient, inexpensive, and standardized."

McDonald's retained an outside firm to do its own internal marketing research into the public perception of the meaning of "Mc" and the conclusions reached were similar to those reached by Dr. Shuy. McDonald's list, which was much shorter, distilled the following definitions: (1) "reliable at a good price," (2) "prepackaged, consistent, fast, and easy" (3) "a prefix McDonald's adds to everything it does," and (4) "processed, simplified, has the punch taken out of it."

Dr. David W. Lightfoot, a linguist from the University of Maryland, testified at trial on behalf of McDonald's. He took no issue with the meanings derived by Dr. Shuy and by McDonald's own internal survey. However, he disputed vigorously any notion that "Mc" is a generic word. He pointed out that "Mc" does not have a single easy identifiable meaning. For instance, of the 27 or so definitions derived by Dr. Shuy from the journalistic uses, many were not incorporated into Dr. Shuy's condensed definition. Dr. Lightfoot concluded that all the meanings derived by Dr. Shuy, by McDonald's and by him were essentially descriptive of McDonald's Corporation and the reputation it has earned over the years. He concluded that whether or not there was a specific reference to McDonald's Corporation in each article, in every case the allusion was to McDonald's and its family of marks in a manner that was intended to be cute and playful.

The Court concludes that indeed the uses in the press of "Mc" plus a generic word are coined and novel to each article for the playful use by the author. In each case the allusion, whether express or implied, was to McDonald's, sometimes flattering and sometimes pejorative. There was no single independent meaning of "Mc" understood in the language and its uses have been created to convey any one of several attributes that the author makes to McDonald's.

This is not analogous to a circumstance where a product is referred to so frequently by brand name that even competitive brands are called by the one name and the brand identity is lost. On the contrary, the attribution of source to McDonald's in the use of "Mc" is strong and persists. The Court notes that while most of the articles used by Dr. Shuy did not contain express allusions to McDonald's, a very similar group of articles that he did not use in his analysis, but which conveyed the same meanings, made express allusions to McDonald's. The Court therefore rejects any contention that McDonald's has lost its right to enforce its marks because "Mc" has become a prefix with a single meaning that has become part of the English language and beyond McDonald's control.

[Finding that there is sufficient likelihood that consumers will be confused, the court declared that McSleep would infringe McDonald's trademarks and permanently enjoined Quality Inns from utilizing that term.]

# Davidoff & Cie, S.A v. PLD International Corp.

United States Court of Appeals, Eleventh Circuit, 2001.
263 F.3d 1297.

■ ANDERSON, CHIEF JUDGE:

This case appears to be the first time that this circuit has addressed the circumstances under which the resale of a genuine product with a registered trademark can be considered infringement. We recognize the general rule that a trademark owner's authorized initial sale of its product exhausts the trademark owner's right to maintain control over who thereafter resells the product; subsequent sales of the product by others do not constitute infringement even though such sales are not authorized by the trademark owner. However, we adopt from our sister circuits their exception to this general rule—i.e., the unauthorized resale of a materially different product constitutes infringement. Because we conclude that the resold products in the instant case are materially different, we affirm.

## I. BACKGROUND

Davidoff & Cie, S.A., a Swiss corporation, is the manufacturer of DAVIDOFF COOL WATER fragrance products and owns the U.S. trademark. Davidoff & Cie, S.A. exclusively licenses Lancaster Group US LLC (collectively "Davidoff") to distribute its products to retailers in the United States. Working outside of this arrangement, PLD International Corporation ("PLD") acquires DAVIDOFF fragrances that are intended for overseas sale or that are sold in duty-free sales. PLD then distributes them to discount retail stores in the United States.

At the time that PLD acquires the product, the original codes on the bottom of the boxes are covered by white stickers, and batch codes on the bottles themselves have been obliterated with an etching tool. The etching leaves a mark on the bottle near its base on the side opposite the DAVIDOFF COOL WATER printing. The mark is approximately one and one-eighth inches in length and one-eighth of an inch wide. The batch codes are removed, according to PLD, to prevent Davidoff from discovering who sold the fragrances to PLD because Davidoff would stop selling to those vendors.

## II. DISTRICT COURT PROCEEDINGS

Davidoff filed a complaint seeking, *inter alia,* a preliminary injunction against PLD for infringement of its trademark under the Lanham Trade-Mark Act, 15 U.S.C. § 1051 *et seq.* Davidoff alleged that PLD's distribution of the fragrances with the batch codes removed and obliterated constituted infringement. The district court held that PLD's distribution of DAVIDOFF fragrances constituted infringement by creating a likelihood of consumer confusion. In reaching this conclusion, the district court found that the product distributed by PLD differed from the genuine DAVIDOFF product because the removal of the batch code from the bottle by etching the glass "constitutes alteration of a product," which would create a likelihood of consumer confusion. A consumer might believe that a product had been harmed or tampered with.[a] Based on the infringement finding, the district court granted a preliminary injunction, prohibiting PLD from selling, repackaging or altering any product with the name "DAVIDOFF" and/or "COOL WATER" with an obliterated batch code. This appeal followed.

## III.  CONTENTIONS

PLD argues that it is selling genuine DAVIDOFF fragrances and that as a result no consumer can be confused. Therefore, it claims that it cannot be considered an infringer under the Lanham Act. PLD asserts that "[w]ith or without a manufacturer or batch code on its packaging, the product is absolutely the same." PLD states that the district court incorrectly relied on cases where the product itself and not just the packaging was altered.

Davidoff urges us to adopt a material difference test whereby a material difference between goods sold under the same trademark warrants a finding of consumer confusion. Davidoff argues that the obliteration of batch codes by PLD transforms the appearance of its product into a materially different, infringing product, which is likely to confuse consumers.

## IV.  PRELIMINARY INJUNCTION POSTURE

We review a district court's order granting or denying a preliminary injunction for abuse of discretion. A party seeking a preliminary injunction for trademark infringement must establish four elements: (1) substantial likelihood of success on the merits; (2) that it would be irreparably harmed if injunctive relief were denied; (3) that the threatened injury to the trademark owner outweighs whatever damage the injunction may cause to the alleged infringer; (4) that the injunction, if issued, would not be adverse to the public interest. The issues raised by PLD in this case primarily address the first element: substantial likelihood of success on the merits.

## V.  TRADEMARK INFRINGEMENT: LAW

In order to succeed on the merits of a trademark infringement claim, a plaintiff must show that the defendant used the mark in commerce without its consent and "that the unauthorized use was likely to deceive, cause

---

[a] The district court also based its finding of infringement on the fact that the removal of the batch code interfered with DAVI-DOFF's quality control system. Although the lack of quality control can rise to the level of a material difference from the trademark owner's product and create a likelihood of confusion, *see* Warner–Lambert Co. v. North-side Dev. Corp., 86 F.3d 3, 7 (2d Cir.1996), we need not address the district court's findings in this regard because we conclude that the physical differences in PLD's product create a likelihood of consumer confusion and support the district court's infringement finding. *See* Part VI.

confusion, or result in mistake." Generally speaking, the determination boils down to the existence *vel non* of "likelihood of confusion."

A. *Purpose*

To understand what type of consumer confusion is actionable under the Lanham Trade–Mark Act, it is useful to review Congress' purposes for enacting trademark legislation. Congress sought to protect two groups: consumers and registered trademark owners. *See* S.Rep. No. 1333, 19th Cong.2d Sess., *reprinted in* 1946 U.S.Code Cong. Serv. 1274. In protecting these groups lawmakers recognized that "[e]very product is composed of a bundle of special characteristics." *Societe Des Produits Nestle, S.A. v. Casa Helvetia, Inc.,* 982 F.2d 633, 636 (1st Cir.1992) ("Nestle"). Consumers who purchase a particular product expect to receive the same special characteristics every time. *See id.* The Lanham Act protects these expectations by excluding others from using a particular mark and making consumers confident that they can purchase brands without being confused or misled. *See* 15 U.S.C. § 1114(1); S.Rep. No. 100–515, at 4 (1988), *reprinted in* 1988 U.S.C.C.A.N. 5577, 5580. Thus trademark law ensures consistency for the benefit of consumers. *See Nestle,* 982 F.2d at 636; *Original Appalachian Artworks, Inc. v. Granada Electronics, Inc.,* 816 F.2d 68, 75 (2d Cir.1987) (Cardamone, J., concurring).

The Lanham Act also protects trademark owners. *See* S.Rep. No. 100–515 at 4. A trademark owner has spent time, energy and money in presenting a product to the public and building a reputation for that product. The Act prevents another vendor from acquiring a product that has a different set of characteristics and passing it off as the trademark owner's product. *See Two Pesos, Inc. v. Taco Cabana, Inc.,* 505 U.S. 763, 778, 112 S.Ct. 2753, 2762, 120 L.Ed.2d 615 (1992) (Stevens, J., concurring) (noting that passing off is a form of infringement prohibited by the Lanham Act). This would potentially confuse consumers about the quality and nature of the trademarked product and erode consumer goodwill.

B. *Resale of a Genuine Trademarked Product and the Material Difference Exception*

The resale of genuine trademarked goods generally does not constitute infringement. This is for the simple reason that consumers are not confused as to the origin of the goods: the origin has not changed as a result of the resale. Under what has sometimes been called the "first sale" or "exhaustion" doctrine, the trademark protections of the Lanham Act are exhausted after the trademark owner's first authorized sale of that product. Therefore, even though a subsequent sale is without a trademark owner's consent, the resale of a genuine good does not violate the Act.

This doctrine does not hold true, however, when an alleged infringer sells trademarked goods that are materially different than those sold by the trademark owner. Our sister circuits have held that a materially different product is not genuine and therefore its unauthorized sale constitutes trademark infringement. We follow our sister circuits and hold that the resale of a trademarked product that is materially different can constitute a trademark infringement.[b] This rule is consistent with the purposes behind the Lanham Act, because materially different products that have the same trademark may confuse consumers and erode consumer goodwill toward the mark.

Not just any difference will cause consumer confusion. A material difference is one that consumers consider relevant to a decision about whether to purchase a product. Because a myriad of considerations may influence consumer preferences, the threshold of materiality must be kept low to include even subtle differences between products.

The caselaw supports the proposition that the resale of a trademarked product that has been altered, resulting in physical differences in the product, can create a likelihood of consumer confusion. Such alteration satisfies the material difference exception and gives rise to a trademark infringement claim. *Nestle,* 982 F.2d at 643–44 (applying the material difference exception, e.g., differences in the composition, presentation and shape of premium chocolates); *Original Appalachian Artworks,* 816 F.2d at 73 (applying the material difference exception where the infringing Cabbage Patch Kids dolls had Spanish language adoption papers and birth certificates, rather than English).

## VI. APPLICATION OF THE EXCEPTION IN THIS CASE

The district court found that etching the glass to remove the batch code degrades the appearance of the product and creates a likelihood of confusion. In addition, the court credited testimony of the marketing vice-president that the etching may make a consumer think that the product had been harmed or tampered with. We defer to the district court's finding that the etching degrades the appearance of the bottle. This finding is not clearly erroneous in light of the stylized nature of the fragrance bottle, which has an otherwise unblemished surface. Indeed, based on our own examination and comparison of the genuine fragrance bottle and the bottle sold by PLD, we agree with the district court that a consumer could very likely believe that the bottle had been tampered with. We agree with the district court that this alteration of the product could adversely affect Davidoff's goodwill, creates a likelihood of consumer confusion, satisfies the material difference exception to the first sale doctrine, and thus constitutes

[b] PLD argues that the material difference test only applies to so-called gray-market goods: foreign made goods bearing a trademark and intended for sale in a foreign country, but that are subsequently imported into the United States without the consent of the U.S. trademark owner. We reject this argument and join the Third Circuit in noting that infringement by materially different products "is not limited to gray goods cases.... The same theory has been used to enjoin the sale of domestic products in conditions materially different from those offered by the trademark owner." Iberia Foods Corp. v. Romeo, 150 F.3d 298, 302 (3d Cir.1998). Indeed, several courts have held that the purchase and resale of goods solely within the United States may constitute infringement when differences exist in quality control or the products themselves. *See* Enesco Corp. v. Price/Costco Inc., 146 F.3d 1083 (9th Cir. 1998); Warner–Lambert Co. v. Northside Dev. Corp., 86 F.3d 3 (2d Cir.1996); Matrix Essentials, Inc. v. Emporium Drug Mart, Inc., 988 F.2d 587 (5th Cir.1993); Shell Oil Co. v. Commercial Petroleum Inc., 928 F.2d 104 (4th Cir.1991).

a trademark infringement. We believe that the material difference in this case is comparable to, or more pronounced than, the product differences in *Nestle* and *Original Appalachian Artworks* where the First and Second Circuits applied the material difference exception and found trademark infringement.

PLD directs us to two cases, *Graham Webb International Ltd. Partnership v. Emporium Drug Mart, Inc.,* 916 F.Supp. 909 (E.D.Ark.1995), and *John Paul Mitchell Systems v. Randalls Food Markets, Inc.,* 17 S.W.3d 721 (Tex.App.2000), where courts have held that the removal of batch codes on hair care products does not constitute infringement. They are both distinguishable from the instant case. Neither court found that the removal affected the overall appearance of the product to the extent that it might be material to a consumer decision to purchase the product.

PLD also attempts to cast the effect of the etching as minimal. PLD argues that the etching is on the back side of the bottle beneath several lines of printing that identifies the manufacturer and distributor, country of origin and volume, while the front side contains the trademarks in gold and black script letters. This may be true, but the etching is clearly noticeable to a consumer who examines the bottle. At oral argument, PLD argued that only the packaging but not the product itself—i.e., the liquid fragrance inside the bottle—had been altered by the etching. In marketing a fragrance, however, a vendor is not only selling the product inside the bottle, it is also selling the "commercial magnetism" of the trademark that is affixed to the bottle. The appearance of the product, which is associated with the trademark, is important to establishing this image. This makes the appearance of the bottle material to the consumer decision to purchase it. Because the etching degrades the appearance of the bottles, the DAVIDOFF fragrance that PLD distributes is materially different from that originally sold by Davidoff. Therefore, we agree with the district court that PLD's sale of this materially different product creates a likelihood of confusion, and satisfies Davidoff's burden of establishing a likelihood of success on the merits.

The district court correctly decided that Davidoff demonstrated a substantial likelihood of success on the merits by showing a likelihood of consumer confusion. Davidoff has also met the other three elements necessary for a preliminary injunction. Accordingly, the district court's order granting a preliminary injunction is AFFIRMED.

NOTES

**1.** *Cancellation.* As noted in Assignment 2, Note 10, public access to symbols of expressive concern is enhanced by the right in § 1064 to have a mark cancelled from the Principal Register. This procedure is cheaper and faster than litigation, but it is not an appropriate vehicle for making the sorts of claims involved in *Welles* or *L.L.Bean.* That is, it is not the place for a challenger to argue that she is using a registered mark in a manner that is not infringing.

**2.** *Defenses to infringement and incontestability.* Assignment 2, Note 11 covers a somewhat converse situation from that described in Note 1: public access to marks is inhibited after the mark has been in use for five years. Pursuant to § 1065, defenses to infringement that are based on the possibility of confusion with marks in use at the time of registration and certain defenses based on the mark's lack of inherent distinctiveness can no longer be raised.

**3.** *Geographic limitations.* The timing problems to which the Introduction referred can, alternatively, be conceptualized as geographic boundary problems. There are two variations:

a. *Market entry by the registered owner.* Under the geographic approach, *Dawn Donut*'s holding is that the enforcement of trademark rights is geographically bounded by the territory in which the mark is in actual use. The theory is that before a trademark holder enters a particular marketing region, it is unlikely that consumers within the market would be confused by use of the mark by another. Accordingly, prior to entry into a territory, there is no basis for bringing an infringement action.

This view of trademark protection is rather close to the common law of unfair competition that existed prior to the adoption of registration systems. Under the so-called *Rectanus* doctrine, named after United Drug Co. v. Theodore Rectanus Co.,[4] the first merchant to use a mark in any particular marketing region earned the exclusive right to use the mark in that location on similar goods—irrespective of who, on an absolute basis, was the first to adopt the mark for those goods.[5] Priority was, in short, determined by who was first in a particular geographic locality, not by who was first to adopt a particular mark.

So long as most commerce was local, the *Rectanus* doctrine was acceptable. However, as it became more common for merchants to market in more than one region, the inability to reserve marks on a nationwide basis became problematic. The solution to this problem is what national registration systems are all about, see Assignment 1 (which also discusses this same problem in relation to international marketing). Under the Lanham Act, a merchant who plans to market nationwide can register her mark, thereby giving constructive notice to future merchants that the mark is taken. Anyone who adopts a similar mark for similar goods after registration can be ousted under § 1114(1).

Given that the intent of federal registration is to reduce consumer confusion and to give registered owners the ability to use their marks to expand geographically, is *Dawn Donut* rightly decided? Why require a

---

[4] 248 U.S. 90 (1918).

[5] An example: A is the first merchant in the United States to adopt the mark "Willie" for widgets. A operates exclusively in New York State. B later adopts the same mark for widgets and operates in Illinois. B then expands her business to Ohio. If A later enters Ohio, who has the right to use Willie for widgets in the state? Under the Rectanus doctrine, the answer is B. Although A was first on an absolute basis (the first in the United States), B was the first to use Willie for widgets in Ohio, and so has priority in that location.

registered owner to wait until she enters a marketing region before she can enforce her rights? Won't consumers who travel across marketing regions be confused during the period of dual use? Won't local consumers who are acquainted with the local producer become confused when use of the mark shifts to the registered owner? Furthermore, how should a court determine when a registered owner has made the expansion efforts required to trigger the right to sue? These difficult problems have led some courts to allow trademark owners to enjoin junior users as soon as their marks are registered.[6] Many courts do, however, follow *Dawn Donut*.[7] Indeed, a similar principle is used in connection with intent-to-use registrations. A merchant who has received a Notice of Allowance is not been permitted to enjoin junior users until after her own use has begun and the mark has been registered.[8]

b. *Section 1115(b)(5): market retention by an unregistered senior user.* Geography and timing combine to create another way for members of the public to utilize a mark without the authority of its registered owner—and to foster yet another source of confusion. Since notice (constructive or otherwise) can operate only against those who adopt a mark *after* the notice is given, a trademark holder cannot acquire rights over merchants who used the mark before it was registered. In such cases, all that registration can do is freeze the prior-user's rights—that is, confine the prior user to the geographic location where he was using the mark at the time it was registered, § 1115(b)(5). Some courts will, in addition, provide a modest zone of expansion.[9]

Section 1115(b)(5) may be the most equitable way to deal with those who used a mark prior to its registration. However, it has the side-effect of creating localities where a registered mark is in the exclusive possession of someone other than its registered owner. Consider, for example, Thrifty Rent–A–Car System, Inc. v. Thrift Cars, Inc.,[10] which involved the service

---

[6] See, e.g., Sterling Brewing, Inc. v. Cold Spring Brewing Corp., 100 F.Supp. 412 (D.Mass.1951). An alternative approach confines Dawn Donut to cases involving products, like donuts, that are consumed close to their source, see, e.g., Gastown, Inc. of Delaware v. Gastown, Inc., 331 F.Supp. 626, 632 (D.Conn.1971)("The American motorist is no longer subject to the limitations of provincial or state line horizons. Transportation, advertising, and communication have regionalized or in some instances nationalized the general public's exposure to tradenames, especially in the field of gasoline products.").

[7] See, e.g., Minnesota Pet Breeders, Inc. v. Schell & Kampeter, Inc., 41 F.3d 1242 (8th Cir.1994); Armand's Subway, Inc. v. Doctor's Assocs., Inc., 604 F.2d 849 (4th Cir.1979); Mister Donut of America, Inc. v. Mr. Donut, Inc., 418 F.2d 838 (9th Cir.1969).

[8] See, e.g., Talk To Me Products, Inc. v. Larami Corp., 804 F.Supp. 555, 559 (S.D.N.Y. 1992), aff'd, 992 F.2d 469 (2d Cir.1993). Cf. Fila Sport, S.p.A v. Diadora America, Inc., 141 F.R.D. 74 (N.D.Ill.1991)(finding no basis for federal jurisdiction without actual registration). See also Report of the Trademark Review Comm'n, 77 Trademark Rep. 375, 403 (1987).

[9] See, e.g., Wiener King, Inc. v. The Wiener King Corp., 407 F.Supp. 1274 (D.N.J. 1976). Indeed, some courts give junior users not only a modest right to expand geographically, but also a margin in which to expand from one category of goods to another, see, e.g., Rodeo Collection, Ltd. v. West Seventh, 812 F.2d 1215, 1219 (9th Cir.1987).

[10] 831 F.2d 1177 (1st Cir.1987).

mark, "Thrifty Rent-a-Car System." The predecessor of the registered owner (Thrifty) began using the mark in Tulsa, Oklahoma in March, 1958. The mark was registered in July, 1964. Thrifty's national expansion efforts led it to enter the car rental market in Massachusetts in December, 1967.

The defendant (Thrift) was a much smaller company. Its main operations, which began in October 1962, were limited to East Taunton, Cape Cod, Massachusetts. However, it advertised all over the Cape Cod region: in the Taunton yellow pages, in the Taunton Daily Gazette, in The Cape Cod Times, in The Anchor (the newspaper of the local Roman Catholic Diocese), and in The Inquirer and Mirror (a Nantucket newspaper). These uses of the mark were initially tolerated by Thrifty. However, when Thrift tried to open a car rental facility at the Nantucket airport, where Thrifty had a facility of its own, Thrifty sued. It sought to limit Thrift to car rentals in East Taunton, and to prevent it from doing business in Taunton or to directly advertise to the Cape Cod community.

The district court enjoined Thrift Cars from using "Thrift" in conducting a car rental business outside of Taunton and from advertising in media directed outside of East Taunton. However, the court allowed Thrift to continue to advertise in publications where it had placed ads prior to Thrifty's registration. In addition, it ordered the *plaintiff*, Thrifty, to refrain from operating in East Taunton and from advertising in any media principally intended to target the East Taunton area. Both sides appealed. In affirming, the First Circuit held that the "limited area" defense of § 1115(b)(5) required Thrift to demonstrate "(1) that it adopted its mark before Thrifty's 1964 registration under the Lanham Act, and without knowledge of Thrifty's prior use; (2) the extent of the trade area in which Thrift Cars used the mark prior to Thrifty's registration; and (3) that Thrift Cars has continuously used the mark in the pre-registration trade area." Since Thrift could make this showing with respect to East Taunton, it was permitted to continue to use the mark there. However, it was not permitted to expand:

> "The limited advertising Thrift Cars had done was not deemed sufficient to establish a presence outside East Taunton; nor were Thrift Cars' sporadic rentals in Nantucket and elsewhere in southeastern Massachusetts enough to sustain Thrift Cars' claim that it had already expanded out of East Taunton prior to Thrifty's federal registration.

> "We also note that the fact that Thrift Cars had desired to expand into the Nantucket market prior to July 1964 by unsuccessfully applying for a license to operate at the airport is not sufficient to meet the requirements of § 1115(b)(5). A mere desire, without more, will not confer upon Thrift Cars the ability to exclude Thrifty from Nantucket."

As to the advertising issue, the First Circuit said:

> "Thrifty now urges that the court allowed Thrift Cars too broad an advertising distribution base, because it extended outside East Taunton to Cape Cod and Nantucket. Thrifty says that by permitting both

parties to advertise in the major resort area publications, the court abused its discretion because substantial consumer confusion is likely to result.

"We reject Thrifty's arguments and agree with the district court that to contract Thrift Cars' advertising base would be a punitive move. The district court did not allow Thrift Cars to advertise in any publications that it had not used prior to Thrifty's registration. On the contrary, the court simply authorized Thrift Cars to use only the same newspapers it had used prior to that critical date. While we recognize that some consumer confusion may result because there will be some overlap in advertising, the Lanham Act does not require the complete elimination of all confusion. We think, moreover, that the confusion spawned as a result of Thrift Cars' advertising will be minimal and should not significantly interfere with Thrifty's proprietary rights in its mark. See Burger King of Florida, Inc. v. Hoots, 403 F.2d 904, 908–09 (7th Cir.1968)."

**4.** *Geographic expansion and product expansion.* Compare *Dawn Donut* to *Lois Sportswear* and the other cases in Assignment 3. Allowing a merchant to control the use of his mark on noncompeting goods facilitates product expansion. The product category is "reserved" in the sense that consumers do not build an association between the mark for that category and another producer. When the trademark holder eventually enters the field, consumers automatically draw a connection between the goodwill he has built up in his old line and the new goods. (For instance, the consumer who liked her Sony TV will be more willing to buy a Sony DVD if she is sure it is manufactured by the same producer).

Why is geographic expansion not treated in the same way as product expansion? Why was Dawn Donut required to wait until it penetrated northern New York before it could reserve its mark for baked goods? Why was its opportunity to transfer the goodwill it developed in one region of the country to another region hampered? Or, if the *Dawn Donut* rule is right, why not require trademark owners to enter a product category before they are permitted to enjoin other competitors in that category from using their marks?

**5.** *The expressive dimension of trademarks.* Consider this quotation from a biography of Senator Edward (Ted) Kennedy's first wife, Joan:

> "When I campaign alone I'm approachable. Women talk to me, complain, but when I'm with Ted I'm a Barbie doll."[11]

Is this use of the term "Barbie" the same as the use made of the trademark in *L.L. Bean, Welles,* or *Lois Sportswear?* Trademark usages can be arranged on a spectrum. At one end, are cases like *Lois Sportswear,* where the defendant is using the mark purely in its signaling sense, to communi-

---

[11] Marcia Chellis, The Joan Kennedy Story: Living With the Kennedys 191 (Jove ed. 1986). Along the same lines: "Betsy McCaughey, Lieutenant Governor of New York, once described herself as Barbie and Gov. George Pataki as Ken." N.Y. Times Magazine, June 4, 1995 at 18, col. 1.

cate with customers about the defendant's own goods. At the other end are expressive uses such as the one in the quotation, where the trademark "Barbie" was not used to sell dolls, but rather to convey an image that readers understand because of their familiarity with the product with which the mark is associated. Between the polls, are hybrid uses of the types exemplified by the cases in this and the previous Assignment.

Should the difference in the way a mark is used influence the outcome of infringement actions? Because every successful infringement action limits someone's ability to utilize communicative symbols, trademark law always implicates expressive concerns. However, a strong argument can be made that when the defendant is using the mark as a signal, interference with free speech does not rise to the level of a constitutional violation. The signaling function is purely commercial, and commercial speech has sometimes received limited First Amendment protection.[12] Accordingly, when courts balance the value in giving merchants an unambiguous avenue with which to communicate with customers against the interest in commercial expression, trademark interests win.

What about nonsignaling uses? Pure expression is entitled to the highest level of constitutional scrutiny. Accordingly, it can be argued that purely expressive uses of trademarks should never be enjoined. In fact, most courts do side with purely-expressive users. However, most manage to avoid constitutional adjudication by considering these nonsignaling usages as outside the purview of trademark law,[13] or as unlikely to give rise to a consumer confusion.[14] For Lanham Act claims, these uses are sometimes found to be within the "fair use" defense of § 1115(b)(4).

But this leaves some problem cases, where the mark is used expressively, but for the purpose of selling goods. An example is Prestonettes, Inc. v. Coty,[15] where the Court allowed the defendant, a manufacturer of scented face powders, to use on its labels the trademarks of the perfumes used as ingredients. According to Justice Holmes:

> "A trade mark only gives the right to prohibit the use of it so far as to protect the owner's good will against the sale of another's product as his.... When the mark is used in a way that does not deceive the public we see no such sanctity in the word as to prevent its being used to tell the truth. It is not taboo."[16]

---

[12] See, e.g., Posadas de Puerto Rico Assoc. v. Tourism Company of Puerto Rico, 478 U.S. 328, 340 (1986); Central Hudson Gas & Electric Corp. v. Public Service Comm'n of New York, 447 U.S. 557, 562–563 (1980).

[13] See, e.g., Restatement Third Unfair Competition, § 25(2) and Comment i.

[14] An example here is Reddy Communications, Inc. v. Environmental Action Foundation, 477 F.Supp. 936 (D.D.C.1979), where plaintiffs, investor-owned public utilities, had sued the defendant under traditional trade-

mark law for caricaturing their cartoon-figure trademark, Reddy Kilowatt, on brochures criticizing the electric power industry. On a finding that the text surrounding the caricature eliminated any likelihood of consumer confusion, the court held for defendant.

[15] 264 U.S. 359 (1924).

[16] Id. at 368. Another oft-cited example is Champion Spark Plug Co. v. Sanders, 331 U.S. 125 (1947), allowing a spark plug reconditioner to use the trademark of the reconditioned spark plug on its products, so long as

More recently, however, the Court has shown less sympathy for the expressive dimension of a defendant's usage. In San Francisco Arts & Athletics Inc. (SFAA) v. United States Olympic Committee (USOC),[17] a gay-rights group sponsored a series of international athletic competitions. To evoke the tenets of ancient Greece, including its spirit of cooperation, mutual acceptance and international friendship, and to make the point that sexual preference is unrelated to athleticism, the group called its events the "Gay Olympic Games" and used that title on its letterheads and promotional materials, including advertising, tee shirts, buttons, and bumper stickers. The USOC sued, claiming infringement of its trademark rights and its right under 36 U.S.C.A. § 380(a), which provides special protection for the words "Olympic," "Olympiad," "Citius Altius Fortius," and for the five interlocking olympic rings. The Supreme Court agreed with the USOC. After noting that § 380 did not require a showing of consumer confusion,[18] the Court stated:

> "One reason for Congress to grant the USOC exclusive control of the word 'Olympic,' as with other trademarks, is to ensure that the USOC receives the benefit of its own efforts so that the USOC will have an incentive to continue to produce a 'quality product' that, in turn, benefits the public."[19]

This part of the Court's rationale seems to be that if there is a benefit to using the trademark, it should flow to its holder. Should this rationale be extended to prohibit the hybrid usages in all of the cases in this and the previous Assignment? Was the problem that the SFAA was earning too much through the sale of shirts, buttons, and such, thereby making untenable their claim to be using the mark expressively?

**6.** *Genericity.* We saw in Assignment 2 that generic words are not eligible for trademark registration or protection. However, as *Quality Inns* demonstrates, the meaning of words is a function of their use. As the public becomes acquainted with a mark, the mark can become so closely associated with a category of goods that everyone who markets goods in the category needs to use the word to compete. At that point, the symbol, even it was once considered capable of distinguishing goods, becomes unprotectable. Aspirin, thermos, cellophane, shredded wheat, and escalator are all examples of trademarks that were lost in this way.

A finding that a mark is generic is a calamity to its owner. The entire investment in the old mark is lost and new efforts must be undertaken to educate the public about a new one. In fact, many companies work hard to make sure their marks do not become generic. Xerox sends requests to its shareholders to use the word "photocopy" in their workplaces. It has also published advertisements depicting graveyards of generic marks and asking the public to use the word "photocopy" rather than "Xerox." Sanka began calling itself "Sanka *brand* decaffeinated coffee" after it became clear that

the word "repaired" or "used" was stamped on the plug in a visible fashion.

[17] 483 U.S. 522 (1987).

[18] Id. at 530–31.

[19] Id. at 537.

customers were ordering "sanka" when they meant decaf. And no one does more to establish the term "plastic strips" than Johnson & Johnson, which is trying to protect its trademark rights in "Band-aid."

These efforts are not, however, determinative of the genericity of a mark. In Judge Learned Hand's words, the test for genericity is:

> "What do the buyers understand by the word for whose use the parties are contending? If they understand by it only the kind of goods sold, then, I take it, it makes no difference whatever what efforts the plaintiff has made to get them to understand more."[20]

Note, however, that the category—"the kind of goods sold"—must be defined with care. Every merchant tries to create a unique niche for her goods. If each niche were considered a category, then success in creating a niche would divest the merchant of trademark protection.[21] To counter this problem, the Trademark Clarification Act of 1984[22] amended the Lanham Act to specify that genericity is determined by the "primary significance of the registered mark to the relevant public" and not by "purchaser motivation" to buy goods within the niche.[23]

Review G. Heileman Brewing Company, Inc. v. Anheuser–Busch, Inc. in Assignment 2. Given that "LA" became generic for low alcohol beer in Australia, was Anheuser–Busch wise to try to acquire trademark rights for it in the United States?

**7.** *Dilution and expressive interests.* Arguably, dilution claims are more intrusive into expressive interests than standard trademark claims. There is (apparently) no need for the trademark holder to enter a particular trading region or to produce a particular product before bringing suit; nor is necessary to establish that consumers will likely be confused by the usage made of the mark. On the other hand, the dilution provision has defenses of its own. The mark must be famous nationally or within the niche market that the trademark holder and unauthorized user share.[24] Moreover, fame must have been acquired before the challenged usage began. This means that anyone who used the mark before it became famous can continue in that use.[25] Finally, the right of action applies only to "commercial uses in commerce;"[26] specifically exempted are uses in

---

[20] Bayer v. United Drug Co., 272 Fed. 505, 509 (2d Cir.1921). See also Kellogg Co. v. National Biscuit Co., 305 U.S. 111 (1938)("shredded wheat"), King–Seeley Thermos Co. v. Aladdin Industries, Inc., 321 F.2d 577 (2d Cir.1963).

[21] See, for example, Anti–Monopoly, Inc. v. General Mills Fun Group, 684 F.2d 1316 (9th Cir.1982), cert. denied, 459 U.S. 1227 (1983), where the court defined the category in which plaintiff was marketing monopoly-type games rather than board games, and proceeded to hold the word "Monopoly" generic for the category.

[22] P.L. 98–620, 98 Stat. 3335 (1984).

[23] § 1064(c).

[24] See, e.g., Thane Int'l, Inc. v. Trek Bicycle Corp., 305 F.3d 894, 907–912 (9th Cir. 2002).

[25] Cf. Enterprise Rent–A–Car Co. v. Advantage Rent–A–Car, Inc., 330 F.3d 1333 (Fed. Cir. 2003)(barring an opposition based on dilution, on the ground that the registering party used the mark before it became famous).

[26] § 43(c)(1).

comparative commercial advertising, news reporting and commentary, and noncommercial uses of the mark.[27]

Mattel, Inc. v. MCA Records, Inc.[28] exemplifies the delicate line that courts must draw. In that case, the holder of the Barbie mark sued MCA, the producer and distributor of a song called Barbie Girl in which members of the band, Aqua, impersonated Barbie and her consort, Ken.[29] On the claim of trademark infringement, the Ninth Circuit held for the defendant on the grounds that the work was a parody and also involved a nominative use of the name Barbie. As to dilution, the court acknowledged Barbie's fame ("the ideal American woman and a bimbo; . . . a symbol of American girlhood, a public figure . . . not just a toy but a cultural icon.") Because the song sold records, the court regarded Aqua's use as a "commercial use in commerce" and it also found that the use diluted the mark. However—and despite the fact that it had just found the use "commercial"—the court held that the use was "noncommercial" for purposes of the statutory defense. The court reasoned that "noncommercial use refers to a use that consists of entirely noncommercial, or fully constitutionally protected, speech." Quoting earlier cases, it held:

> "[T]he core notion of commercial speech is that it does no more than propose a commercial transaction . . . If speech is not 'purely commercial'—that is, if it does more than propose a commercial transaction—then it is entitled to full First Amendment protection."[30]

The court concluded:

> "Barbie Girl is not purely commercial speech, and is therefore fully protected. To be sure, MCA used Barbie's name to sell copies of the song. However . . . the song also lampoons the Barbie image and comments humorously on the cultural values Aqua claims she represents. Use of the Barbie mark in the song Barbie Girl therefore falls within the noncommercial exemption to the [dilution provision.]"[31]

Is simultaneously finding a use commercial and noncommercial the best way to deal with dilution of hybrid signals? Note that the commercial/noncommercial distinction plays an important role in other areas of intellectual property law, see, for example Assignments 11, on fair use in copyright, and 13, on state-based rights of publicity. Should courts instead apply the parody defense and other standard trademark defenses?

Note also that the statute attempts to diminish the impact of dilution claims by providing for only injunctive relief, unless the court finds that the user "willfully intended to trade on the owner's reputation or to cause dilution. . . . "[32] Does a limit on monetary damages actually alleviate

[27] § 43(c)(4).

[28] 296 F.3d 894 (9th Cir. 2002).

[29] Impersonated is the court's term. Your authors understand that Barbie and Ken are not really persons.

[30] Id. at 906(quoting Hoffman v. Capital Cities/ABC, Inc., 255 F.3d 1180, 1184 (9th Cir. 2001) and Bolger v. Youngs Drug Prods. Corp., 463 U.S. 60, 66 (1983)).

[31] Id. at 906–07.

[32] § 43(c)(2).

expressive concerns—indeed. might not some potential users prefer monetary damages to having their uses enjoined?

**8.** *The first sale doctrine.* This common law principle, which is also
applicable to copyrighted and patented materials, has traditionally acted as
an important vehicle for expanding public access to protected works. It
creates a nice balance between public and proprietary needs: the right
holder can profit by the sale of embodiments of his work, but once the sale
of an embodiment is made, the right holder's interest is exhausted; subsequent sellers do not need authorization—unless, in trademark contexts
such as the one presented in *Davidoff*, the public is likely to be confused by
the subsequent use of the trademark. The public benefits because (as those
of you who purchased a used copy of this casebook already know) the resale
usually occurs at a lower price.

Why did Davidoff care that PLD had scratched off the coding under its
bottles? Was it really concerned that consumers would think less of the
goods? Was it, as a footnote suggests, because it needed the codes to control
the quality of its products? Or was the court right in thinking that it
wanted to figure out which of its vendors was selling to PLD? If it
identified that vendor, what would it do? It might cut the vendor off from
future supplies. Moreover, it is likely to have had a contract with the
vendor that limited the terms of the sale (to specific countries or stores, to
end-users, or the like); once Davidoff identified the vendor it could sue for
breach of contract and recover on the sales that it didn't manage to enjoin.

Are these machinations in the public interest? Obviously, they protect
the trademark holder's reputation. Control over resale preserves the cachet
of the mark by allowing the trademark holder to bar distribution in down-
market locations, such as discount stores. It also allows the trademark
holder to exert some control over the retail price. But isn't the effect on
price worrisome? Should the court have allowed Davidoff to end-run the
first sale doctrine on a theory of consumer confusion? Don't consumers who
buy in discount stores understand that there is a reason that they are
paying less? If so, are they likely to attribute the scratch marks to
Davidoff? Note that at one time, the antitrust laws prohibited manufacturers from setting the price at which distributors could resell the manufacturers' products, in part to encourage retail price competition.[33] That policy
has also given way to an approach that grants manufacturers more freedom
of movement.

Many first-sale cases involve gray goods (also called parallel imports)—
that is, goods sold under the right holder's authority in one country (where
the price is low) and resold in a second country (where the trademark
holder or his licensee is selling at a much higher price). If the right holder
can prevent resale, then he is, in effect, price discriminating—setting the
price by local, rather than global, demand. In both international and

---

[33] See, e.g., Federal Trade Comm'n v.
Beech-Nut Packing Co., 257 U.S. 441
(1922)(prohibiting manufacturer from re-straining discounters (also through the use of
a code number tracking system)).

domestic cases, the effect of price discrimination on social welfare is complex and varies from context to context. The issue will be revisited in Assignments 5, 13, and 24.

**9.** *Abandonment.* As noted in the Introduction, there are two ways that a mark can be abandoned: by allowing the mark to lose distinctiveness or by discontinuing use with intent not to resume.

a.   *Loss of distinctiveness.* A key difference between trademarks on the one hand, and copyrights and patents on the other, is that trademarks require an ongoing business enterprise. Section 1060 codifies the common law rule that a trademark cannot be assigned apart from "the goodwill of the business in which the mark is used." This also is true with respect to the trademark of an insolvent or bankrupt. Thus, if the buyer of the bankrupt's assets fails to continue the business, abandonment of the mark will result and anyone, including the bankrupt, is free to use the trademark.[34] As *Dawn Donut* indicates, uncontrolled licensing of a trademark also can result in abandonment because the mark no longer be performing the function of indicating source or quality.[35]

Abandonment for loss of distinctiveness is said to protect the public because it assures that marks send consistent messages. But is the doctrine actually welfare enhancing? Restrictions on licensing and the loss effectuated by bankruptcy hurt the trademark owner because these rules reduce the value of marks as instruments for raising capital. For example, even a valuable trademark cannot easily be used as a security interest for a loan because the creditor cannot utilize the mark without the defaulting debtor's cooperation. Nor is it clear that *trademark holders* always choose to use their marks consistently. For instance, national and international businesses, such as restaurants, often conform their products to local preferences and to the stock of local suppliers, see, e.g., the Principal Problem in Assignment 5. Are trademark holders who tailor their goods to specific markets in danger of losing their marks?

Is there really a need for courts to supervise the use of marks in this way? How much supervision should be required? Note that this is the crux of the split between Judge Lumbard's own dissenting views and the majority decision that he wrote for the *Dawn Donut* court.[36] Are courts capable of deciding when supervision is adequate? Absent a quality control requirement, would licensees or franchisees really fail to exercise quality control—isn't it in their economic interest to do so?

It should not be surprising that there are other courts that take the same relaxed approach of the *Dawn Donut* majority. Consider, for example, the Fifth Circuit's views in Taco Cabana Int'l, Inc. v. Two Pesos, Inc.[37] In

---

[34] See J. Thomas McCarthy, 2 McCarthy on Trademarks and Unfair Competition § 18.09 [1] (3d ed. 1992).

[35] See also Restatement (Third) of Unfair Competition § 33, comment b (1994).

[36] Your editors agree: it is very strange to see a judge dissent from his own opinion.

[37] 932 F.2d 1113 (5th Cir. 1991). The Supreme Court reviewed this case on other issues, see Assignment 2.

that case, two brothers had founded the Taco Cabana chain of restaurants. Six days before they sued Two Pesos for trademark infringement, the brothers had divided up the restaurants in the Taco Cabana chain, each retaining rights to utilize the chain's distinctive trade dress. Two Pesos then defended against the claim of infringement on the ground that the division was a naked license that amounted to an abandonment of rights in the trade dress. The Fifth Circuit disagreed:

> "The purpose of the quality-control requirement is to prevent the public deception that would ensue from variant quality standards under the same mark or dress. Where the particular circumstances of the licensing arrangement persuade us that the public will not be deceived, we need not elevate form over substance and require the same policing rigor appropriate to more formal licensing and franchising transactions. Where the license parties have engaged in a close working relationship, and may justifiably rely on each parties' intimacy with standards and procedures to ensure consistent quality, and no actual decline in quality standards is demonstrated, we would depart from the purpose of the law to find an abandonment simply for want of all the inspection and control formalities."[38]

b. *Abandonment based on non-use.* The non-use prong of abandonment is intended to replenish the public domain by returning to the public those marks that are no longer used for source and quality identification.

Trademark holders sometimes have legitimate business reasons for shelving their marks and the statute takes this into account by defining abandonment as discontinuation coupled with an intent not to resume use. Under federal law, three years of non-use creates a prima facie case of abandonment.[39] However, the trademark holder is permitted to rebut the presumption of abandonment by offering evidence of intent to resume. Of course, even if there is non-use for less than three years, abandonment still can be established if it can be proven that a trademark owner has no intent to resume use. The bottom line is that in many cases under this prong of abandonment, the main issue is one of intent. It is determined on an objective, rather than a subjective, standard, utilizing a "totality of the objective evidence."[40]

Silverman v. CBS, Inc.[41] demonstrates how difficult it can be to determine intent. That case concerned rights to the names, characters, and other features of "Amos 'n' Andy," a radio show and later a television program about a set of memorable Black characters. The series was on the radio from 1928–1955. It ran on CBS TV from 1951–1953, after which it was shown in syndication. It was finally taken off the air in 1966, in

[38] Id. at 1121.

[39] § 1127, definition of "abandoned."

[40] EH Yacht, LLC v. Egg Harbor, LLC, 84 F.Supp.2d 556 (D.N.J. 2000). Courts have also noted the impropriety of determining "intent not to resume use" on a motion for summary judgment. See Cline v. 1–888–PLUMBING Group, Inc., 146 F.Supp.2d 351, 364 (S.D.N.Y. 2001).

[41] 870 F.2d 40 (2d Cir. 1989).

response to complaints by civil rights organizations, including the NAACP, that the programs were demeaning to Blacks.

By 1981, times had changed: "Amos 'n' Andy" came to be regarded as a classic. Silverman, a playwright, began a Broadway musical based on the characters and planned to incorporate the phrase, "Amos 'n' Andy" into the title. To make sure he could utilize the names and characters freely, he brought an action against CBS seeking a declaratory judgment that CBS had no rights under any body of law, including trademark law. After a bench trial on the issue of abandonment, the court ruled that CBS had not abandoned its marks. On appeal, the Second Circuit disagreed. Among other things, the court said:

> Ordinarily, 21 years of non-use would easily surpass the non-use requirement for finding abandonment. The District Court concluded, however, that CBS had successfully rebutted the presumption of abandonment arising from its prolonged non-use by offering a reasonable explanation for its decision to keep the programs off the air and by asserting its intention to resume use at some indefinite point in the future. This conclusion raises a question as to the proper interpretation of the statutory phrase "intent not to resume": Does the phrase mean intent never to resume use or does it merely mean intent not to resume use within the reasonably foreseeable future?
>
> We conclude that the latter must be the case. The statute provides that intent not to resume may be inferred from circumstances, and two consecutive years of non-use is prima facie abandonment.[a] Time is thereby made relevant. Indeed, if the relevant intent were intent never to resume use, it would be virtually impossible to establish such intent circumstantially. Even after prolonged non-use, and without any concrete plans to resume use, a company could almost always assert truthfully that at some point, should conditions change, it would resume use of its mark.
>
> We do not think Congress contemplated such an unworkable standard. More likely, Congress wanted a mark to be deemed abandoned once use has been discontinued with an intent not to resume within the reasonably foreseeable future. This standard is sufficient to protect against the forfeiture of marks by proprietors who are temporarily unable to continue using them, while it also prevents warehousing of marks, which impedes commerce and competition.
>
> We are buttressed in this conclusion by the fact that the statute requires proof of "intent not to resume," rather than "intent to abandon." The statute thus creates no state of mind element concerning the ultimate issue of abandonment. On the contrary, it avoids a subjective inquiry on this ultimate question by setting forth the circumstances under which a mark shall be "deemed" to be abandoned. Of course, one of those circumstances is intent not to resume use,

---

[a] [Prior to January 1, 1996, the statutory period was two years. It was changed to three in order to conform to the TRIPS Agreement—eds.]

which is a matter of subjective inquiry. But we think the provision, by introducing the two concepts of "deemed" abandonment and intent not to resume use, contemplates a distinction, and it is a distinction that turns at least in part on duration of the contemplated non-use.

Congress's choice of wording appears to have been deliberate. One early version of what became section 45 of the Lanham Act had provided that "intent to *abandon* may be inferred from the circumstances." H.R. Rep. 4744, 76th Cong., 1st Sess. (1939)(emphasis added). However, shortly thereafter a new bill modified this phrase by substituting "intent not to resume" for "intent to abandon." H.R. Rep. 6618, 76th Cong., 1st Sess. (1939). Though it has been suggested that the phrases are interchangeable, see Note, 56 Fordham L. Rev. 1003, 1020 n.113 (1988), we agree with the Fifth Circuit that the phrases are better understood as having distinct meanings. See Exxon Corp. v. Humble Exploration Co., 695 F.2d 96, 102, 103 n.7 (5th Cir.1983). "Abandonment" connotes permanent relinquishment. See Webster's Third New International Dictionary 2 (1981)(defining "abandon" to mean "to cease to assert ... an interest ... esp. with the intent of *never* again resuming or reasserting it")(emphasis added). We think that Congress, by speaking of "intent not to resume" rather than "intent to abandon" in this section of the Act meant to avoid the implication that intent never to resume use must be shown.

\* \* \*

A proprietor who temporarily suspends use of a mark can rebut the presumption of abandonment by showing reasonable grounds for the suspension and plans to resume use in the reasonably foreseeable future when the conditions requiring suspension abate. But a proprietor may not protect a mark if he discontinues using it for more than 20 years and has no plans to use or permit its use in the reasonably foreseeable future. A bare assertion of possible future use is not enough.

\* \* \*

An adjudication of trademark rights often involves a balancing of competing interests. In weighing the competing interests and reaching our conclusion concerning abandonment, we are influenced in part by the context in which this dispute arises—one in which the allegedly infringing use is in connection with a work of artistic expression. Just as First Amendment values inform application of the idea/expression dichotomy in copyright law, in similar fashion such values have some bearing upon the extent of protection accorded a trademark proprietor against use of the mark in works of artistic expression.

*Silverman* raises the issue of what type of use is sufficient to preserve an owner's rights in a mark. Must it be the kind of use that satisfies the bona fide use requirement for registration?[42] Should the practice of chal-

---

[42] See Kellogg Co. v. Exxon Corp., 209 F.3d 562, 575–76 (6th Cir. 2000).

lenging unauthorized uses count as use? (The *Silverman* court held it did not.) Should it matter if the failure to use was involuntary? If so, should CBS's failure to use its "Amos 'n' Andy" marks be considered involuntary?

A finding of abandonment in a given situation is very much a factual issue. For example, one court held that summary judgment for the defendants on plaintiff's claim for trade dress infringement of its car body style (the Ferrari) was not warranted even though the plaintiff had not manufactured cars with that body style for over thirteen years and had no intention of resuming production of such cars. This holding was based on the plaintiff's showing of goodwill associated with its vehicle and "evidence of ongoing parts support for the vehicle."[43] Another court held that sales of ninety-eight units of a product per year over a five to six year period provided sufficient use to preclude abandonment.[44] Is a finding of abandonment warranted if a trademark owner modifies its trademark? Once a mark has been abandoned, what should be the result if the trademark owner resumes use?

[43] Ferrari S.p.A. Esercizio Fabbriche Automobili E Corse v. McBurnie Coachcraft Inc., 10 U.S.P.Q.2d (BNA) 1278, 1282 (S.D.Cal.1988).

[44] Bishop v. Equinox Int'l Corp., 154 F.3d 1220, 1222 (10th Cir. 1998).

# ASSIGNMENT 5

# REMEDIES

## 1. INTRODUCTION

Remedies for trademark infringement, as is true of copyright and patent infringement, are statutorily based and include injunctive relief as well as various forms of monetary relief. The remedial provisions of the Lanham Act apply not only to trademark infringement under § 1114(1) but also to violations of § 43(a).[1] Section 1116(a) of the Lanham Act provides that courts can grant injunctions "according to the principles of equity."[2] This means that successful plaintiffs must show that they lack an adequate remedy at law or that they will be irreparably harmed absent an injunction. With respect to the availability of preliminary injunctions, a plaintiff also must establish a likelihood of success on the merits.[3] Sometimes courts also will order a freezing of the defendant's assets in conjunction with the entry of preliminary injunctive relief if such is believed to be necessary to insure the availability of permanent relief.[4]

Section 1117(a) of the Lanham Act, which provides for monetary relief, states that successful plaintiffs can obtain the specified monetary relief of defendant's profits, damages sustained by the plaintiff, and the statute indicates that principles of equity also may apply.[5] Thus, equitable considerations play a pivotal role in awarding these monetary remedies under trademark law.[6] In addition, there are two instances in which the Lanham

---

[1] See §§ 1116, 1117, 1118, & 1125(b)(prohibiting the importation of goods violating § 43(a)). Of course, § 1119, which grants courts the authority to take certain actions with respect to registrations, is limited in application to registered trademarks.

[2] § 1116(a).

[3] See, e.g., Dial–A–Mattress Operating Corp. v. Mattress Madness, Inc., 841 F.Supp. 1339, 1345, reconsideration denied 847 F.Supp. 18 (E.D.N.Y.1994).

[4] See, e.g., Levi Strauss & Co. v. Sunrise International Trading Inc., 51 F.3d 982, 987 (11th Cir.1995); Reebok International Ltd. v. Marnatech, 970 F.2d 552, 560 (9th Cir.1992).

[5] § 1117(a). Monetary recovery by the plaintiff generally is viewed as cumulative, so that a plaintiff may receive both damages and defendant's profits as long as there is no

double recovery. See, e.g., Babbit Electronics, Inc. v. Dynascan Corp., 38 F.3d 1161, 1183 (11th Cir.1994); J. Thomas McCarthy, 4 McCarthy on Trademarks and Unfair Competition § 30:27[1][a] (3rd ed. 1992)(both damages and profits "will be appropriate in a case where the parties do not compete, since in that case defendant's profits are granted under the theory of unjust enrichment, which does not attempt to measure plaintiff's actual loss"). But see Nintendo of America, Inc. v. Dragon Pacific International, 40 F.3d 1007, 1010 (9th Cir.1994), cert. denied, Sheng v. Nintendo of America, 515 U.S. 1107 (1995)(recovery of both damages and defendant's profits is generally considered double recovery).

[6] See Brown, Civil Remedies for Intellectual Property Invasions: Themes and Variations, 55 L. & Contemp. Probs. 45, 65 (1992).

Act authorizes an award of statutory damages. The Anticybersquatting Consumer Protection Act, *see* Assignment 3 and the discussion of § 43(d) of the Lanham Act supra, provides for the availability of statutory damages of between $1000 and $100,000 per domain name, based on the court's discretion.[7] Statutory damages also can be awarded under the Lanham Act pursuant to the Anti–Counterfeiting Consumer Protection Act, *see* infra Note 6.

The Lanham Act also precludes recovery of monetary remedies in certain instances. For example, a registrant's failure to provide the appropriate notice of registration will preclude an award of profits and damages "unless the defendant had actual notice of the registration."[8] Moreover, § 1114(1)(b) provides that infringers who merely reproduce a registered mark on labels or packaging "intended to be used in commerce," as opposed to those who infringe by using the marks in commerce, are not liable for profits or damages "unless the acts have been committed with knowledge that such imitation is intended to be used to cause confusion...."[9] Additionally, § 1114(2) specifies that printers and publishers who qualify as innocent infringers are subject only to injunctive relief.

Other remedies provided in the Lanham Act include treble damages (see infra Note 5) and attorneys fees (see infra Note 4),[10] cancellation and restoration of registrations,[11] the destruction of infringing articles,[12] and the prohibition of importation of goods that "copy or simulate" a registered trademark.[13] One issue that arises in conjunction with the prohibition on importation is whether the Lanham Act is violated by the importation of gray market goods (goods that are manufactured and sold abroad under a valid license but imported into the United States without the permission of the owner of the United States' trademark rights in the identical mark[14]). This issue is explored further in the Principal Problem and the accompanying materials, which also treat some of the other interesting issues that arise in connection with the imposition of trademark remedies.

## 2. PRINCIPAL PROBLEM

Plaintiffs Nestle, S.A., the registered owner of the trademark PERUGINA for chocolate candy in the United States and Puerto Rico, and its wholly owned subsidiary Nestlé Puerto Rico, Inc., the exclusive distributor in Puerto Rico, are suing Casa Helvetia based on the defendant's unauthorized importation and distribution of PERUGINA chocolates in Puerto

[7] § 1117(d).
[8] § 1111.
[9] § 1114(1)(b).
[10] § 1117(a).
[11] § 1119.
[12] § 1118.
[13] § 1124.

[14] See Vivitar Corp. v. United States, 761 F.2d 1552, 1555 (Fed.Cir.1985), cert. denied 474 U.S. 1055 (1986). Where the United States' trademark owner also imports goods into this country, the grey market goods are called "parallel importations." Id. at 1555.

Rico. Plaintiffs' chocolates are made in Italy, and the defendant's chocolates are made in Venezuela but are nonetheless genuine PERUGINA
candies that have been purchased by defendant from Nestle's official
licensee and authorized distributor in Venezuela of the PERUGINA candies. Plaintiffs are suing for trademark infringement under § 1114(1),
unfair competition under § 43(a), and violating § 1124 for importing a
materially different product.

The respective candies are similar in color and have an identical
appearance, both inside and out. Both come in boxes that display the
PERUGINA logo and the same logo type; both have Pegasus symbols and a
picture of the product on the back of the box. Still, certain differences exist
between the Italian and Venezuelan chocolates and their packaging. First,
the Venezuelan chocolate is made from domestic beans, and the Italian
chocolate is made from Ecuadorian and African beans. The Italian chocolate is produced from cane sugar while the Venezuelan chocolate is sweet-
ened with corn syrup. The Italian chocolate contains five per cent more
milk fat to prolong shelf life. The Venezuelan chocolate contains imported
hazelnuts and the Italian chocolate has fresh hazelnuts. The Italian candies
come in a wider variety of shapes than the Venezuelan products.

With respect to the packaging of the two products, the Italian candies
come in a box that has a glossy wax finish with a silver tray, whereas the
Venezuelan candy comes in a more ordinary-looking box with a transparent
tray. The Italian product is described on the box in English and French,
whereas the Venezuelan product displays Spanish and English. Both products clearly identify the different places of manufacture of the respective
products. Moreover, the Italian chocolates cost over $5.00 more per box
than the Venezuelan chocolates.

There is no dispute that the Venezuelan products are genuine PERU-
GINA products that are manufactured under Nestle's authorization, and
there is no evidence as to whether the Venezuelan products fail to satisfy
any required quality control standards. The shipping and handling procedures of the two products are, however, markedly different. Moreover, the
testimony of the plaintiffs' witnesses at the trial conveyed the impression
that the plaintiffs were inferring that the Venezuelan product is an inferior
chocolate in commonplace packaging.

The district court dismissed the plaintiffs' complaint and held that the
defendant's unauthorized distribution of the Venezuelan chocolates in
Puerto Rico did not violate the Lanham Act. Plaintiffs have hired you as
their attorney for the appeal, and have offered to provide you with as many
free samples of both products as you can consume. Now comes the not-so-
fun part. Your clients want to know your opinion as to the merits of their
case and the likelihood that the appellate court will reverse. They also want
to know what remedies they can obtain under the Lanham Act, and if you
foresee any difficulties with obtaining any particular remedies in the event
they prevail on appeal.

3. MATERIALS FOR SOLUTION OF PRINCIPAL PROBLEM

A. STATUTORY MATERIALS: §§ 1114, 1116, 1117, 1118, 1119, 1120, 1122, 1124, 1125(b), & 18 U.S.C. § 2320

B. CASES:

# George Basch Co. v. Blue Coral, Inc.

United States Court of Appeals, Second Circuit, 1992.
968 F.2d 1532.

■ WALKER, CIRCUIT JUDGE.

Along with several issues regarding the particulars of injunctive relief, this case presents the general question of whether, in an action for trade dress infringement, a plaintiff may recover a defendant's profits without establishing that the defendant engaged in deliberately deceptive conduct. The district court concluded that bad faith was not a necessary predicate for an accounting. We disagree. Accordingly, we hold that in order to justify an award of profits, a plaintiff must establish that the defendant engaged in willful deception.

Background

The George Basch Co., Inc., ("Basch") manufactures and distributes NEVR–DULL, a cotton wadding metal polish. NEVR–DULL is packaged in a five ounce cylindrical metal can, about 3–1/2 inches high by 3–1/2 inches in diameter, and navy blue in color. Along with a product description and directions, the product's name is printed on the can in white block lettering. On either side of the product's name there are two red and white icons that depict what the product may be used for: the radiator grill of a car, silverware, a brass lamp, and a motor boat on a trailer.

Appellants, Blue Coral, Inc., its subsidiary Simoniz Canada Ltd., and their mutual president, Michael Moshontz (hereafter collectively referred to as "Blue Coral") manufacture and distribute a line of automotive wheel cleaning and polishing products. In both the United States and Canada, Blue Coral markets these products under the trademark ESPREE. In 1987, Blue Coral approached Basch with respect to becoming Basch's exclusive NEVR–DULL distributor in Canada. By agreement of the parties, effective July 28, 1987, Blue Coral became NEVR–DULL's exclusive Canadian distributor. NEVR–DULL was not sold under the ESPREE mark, and its Canadian trade dress remained substantially the same as the United States' version, with the exception that the French language was employed on the front of the can.

In April 1988, Blue Coral asked Basch to produce a wadding metal polish for Blue Coral to market in the United States. Blue Coral intended to add the polish to its line of ESPREE products. The parties negotiated through August of that year, at which time they ended their talks unsuc-

cessfully due to an impasse regarding price. Blue Coral ultimately contracted with another manufacturer of metal polish.

On July 25, 1988, Blue Coral introduced EVER BRITE—the new
ESPREE wadding metal polish—into the United States market. EVER
BRITE was packaged in the same size cylindrical metal can used by Basch
to package NEVR–DULL. The base color of the EVER BRITE can was
black. On its front appeared an angled silver grid-like background. Super-
imposed over the center of the grid, also on an angle, were large white
block letters which read "EVER BRITE." Five different types of wheel
faces were depicted in the upper right hand corner of the grid. To the right
of the wheel faces appeared six red and white icons that represented
silverware, chrome wheels, brassware, brass beds, copperware, and car
bumpers and trim.

Relations between Basch and Blue Coral turned bleak. In March 1989,
Basch terminated Blue Coral's Canadian distributorship. Approximately
one year later, Blue Coral introduced EVER BRITE into the Canadian
market. Blue Coral's Canadian trade dress was also substantially the same
as its United States' version—merely substituting French print in some
places on the can where English had been used, and placing a hyphen
between EVER and BRITE where none had been before.

On March 7, 1989, Basch brought this action in the United States
District Court for the Eastern District of New York. In its complaint, Basch
alleged trade dress infringement in violation of § 43(a) of the Lanham Act.
Blue Coral moved for summary judgment which the district court denied.

The action was tried to a jury in July 1991. The district court ruled
that, as a matter of law, Basch was precluded from receiving damages on its
trade dress infringement claim because it had failed to produce any
evidence regarding actual consumer confusion or that Blue Coral acted
with intent to deceive the public.

The district court concluded, however, that despite Basch's failure to
introduce evidence on either of these points, Basch could recover Blue
Coral's profits if it succeeded on its trade dress infringement claim. The
case was submitted to the jury by special verdict. The jury found against
Blue Coral on Basch's trade dress infringement claim. Accordingly, it
awarded Basch $200,000 in Blue Coral's profits, allegedly stemming from
Blue Coral's wrongful use of its EVER BRITE trade dress.

Blue Coral timely moved for judgment n.o.v. In its motion, Blue Coral
argued that: (1) Basch had failed to prove that its NEVR–DULL trade dress
enjoyed secondary meaning; (2) since Basch had not shown actual consumer confusion, or deceptive conduct on Blue Coral's part, Basch could not
recover any of Blue Coral's profits; (3) it was for the district judge sitting as
a court in equity, and not the jury, to make an award of profits; and (4) in
any event, the $200,000 award was grossly in excess of its actual profits.

The district court denied Blue Coral's motion, and entered its judgment which included the $200,000 jury award. The judgment also con-
tained an injunction allowing Blue Coral to sell off its remaining inventory

of infringing cans, but prohibiting any future use of the existing trade dress in the United States market. The district court also denied Basch's application for attorney fees. This appeal followed.

Discussion

[W]e affirm the district court's judgment that Basch sufficiently established the necessary elements to support the jury's finding of liability.

Grounds for Awarding Profits

We turn now to the issue of whether the district court correctly authorized an award of Blue Coral's profits. Section 35(a) of the Lanham Act generally provides that a successful plaintiff under the act shall be entitled, "subject to the principles of equity, to recover (1) defendant's profits, (2) any damages sustained by the plaintiff, and (3) costs of the action." 15 U.S.C.A. § 1117(a). Clearly, the statute's invocation of equitable principles as guideposts in the assessment of monetary relief vests the district court with some degree of discretion in shaping that relief. See *id.*, (both damage and profit awards may be assessed "according to the circumstances of the case"). Nevertheless, that discretion must operate within legally defined parameters.

For example, it is well settled that in order for a Lanham Act plaintiff to receive an award of damages the plaintiff must prove either "actual consumer confusion or deception resulting from the violation," Getty Petroleum Corp. v. Island Transportation Corp., 878 F.2d 650, 655 (2d Cir.1989)(quoting PPX Enterprises, Inc. v. Audiofidelity Enterprises, Inc., 818 F.2d 266, 271 (2d Cir.1987)), or that the defendant's actions were intentionally deceptive thus giving rise to a rebuttable presumption of consumer confusion. See Resource Developers, Inc. v. Statue of Liberty–Ellis Island Foundation, Inc., 926 F.2d 134, 140 (2d Cir.1991); *PPX Enterprises*, 818 F.2d at 273. Here, Basch failed to present any evidence regarding consumer confusion or intentional deception. Accordingly, prior to the jury's deliberation, the district court correctly decided that damages were not an available form of relief. Basch does not appeal from this ruling.

However, with respect to authorizing an award of Blue Coral's profits, the district judge concluded that § 35(a) affords a wider degree of equitable latitude. In denying its j.n.o.v. motion, the district court rejected Blue Coral's position that, absent a finding of defendant's willfully deceptive conduct, a court may not award profits. Rather, it relied upon contrary dictum in Louis Vuitton S.A. v. Lee, 875 F.2d 584, 588–89 (7th Cir.1989), in determining that a Lanham Act plaintiff may be entitled to the profits of an innocent infringer, i.e., one who inadvertently misappropriates the plaintiff's trade dress. To the extent that the cases are ambiguous as to whether deceptive conduct is a necessary basis for an accounting, we take this opportunity to clarify the law.

The rule in this circuit has been that an accounting for profits is normally available "only if the 'defendant is unjustly enriched, if the plaintiff sustained damages from the infringement, or if the accounting is necessary to deter a willful infringer from doing so again.' " *Burndy Corp. v. Teledyne Industries, Inc.*, 748 F.2d 767, 772 (2d Cir.1984) (quoting *W. E. Bassett Co. v. Revlon, Inc.*, 435 F.2d 656, 664 (2d Cir.1970)). Courts have interpreted the rule to describe three categorically distinct rationales. See e.g., *Cuisinarts, Inc. v. Robot–Coupe Intern. Corp.*, 580 F.Supp. 634, 637 (S.D.N.Y.1984)("These justifications are stated in the disjunctive. Any one will do.").

Thus, the fact that willfulness expressly defines the third rationale (deterrence) may suggest that the element of intentional misconduct is unnecessary in order to require an accounting based upon a theory of unjust enrichment or damages. However, the broad language contained in *Burndy Corp.* and *W. E. Bassett Co.* is in no way dispositive on this point. Indeed, a closer investigation into the law's historical development strongly supports our present conclusion that, under any theory, a finding of defendant's willful deceptiveness is a prerequisite for awarding profits.

*Unjust Enrichment*: The fact that an accounting may proceed on a theory of unjust enrichment is largely a result of legal institutional evolution. Prior to the fusion of law and equity under the Federal Rules of Civil Procedure, see Fed.R.Civ.P. 2., courts of law were the sole dispensary of damages, while the chancellor issued specific relief. However, in order to avoid piecemeal litigation, once a court of equity took jurisdiction over a case it would do complete justice—even if that entailed granting a monetary award. This resulted in the development of parallel remedial schemes.

Long ago, the Supreme Court explained the origin of profit awards in trademark infringement suits:

> The infringer is required in equity to account for and yield up his gains to the true owner [of the mark], upon a principle analogous to that which charges a trustee with the profits acquired by the wrongful use of the property of the *cestui que trust*. Not that equity assumes jurisdiction upon the ground that a trust exists. . . . The jurisdiction must be rested upon some other equitable ground—in ordinary cases, as in the present, the right to an injunction—but the court of equity, having acquired jurisdiction upon such a ground, retains it for the purpose of administering complete relief, rather than send the injured party to a court of law for his damages. And profits are then allowed as an equitable measure of compensation, on the theory of a trust *ex maleficio*.

*Hamilton–Brown Shoe Co. v. Wolf Brothers & Co.*, 240 U.S. 251, 259 (1916).

Thus, a defendant who is liable in a trademark or trade dress infringement action may be deemed to hold its profits in constructive trust for the injured plaintiff. However, this results only "when the defendant's sales 'were attributable to its infringing use' of the plaintiff's" mark, *Burndy Corp.*, 748 F.2d at 772 (quoting *W. E. Bassett Co.*, 435 F.2d at 664), and when the infringing use was at the plaintiff's expense. *Id.* at 773. In other words, a defendant becomes accountable for its profits when the plaintiff can show that, were it not for defendant's infringement, the defendant's sales would otherwise have gone to the plaintiff. *Id.* at 772.

At bottom, this is simply another way of formulating the element of consumer confusion required to justify a damage award under the Lanham Act. As such, it follows that a profits award, premised upon a theory of unjust enrichment, requires a showing of actual consumer confusion—or at least proof of deceptive intent so as to raise the rebuttable presumption of consumer confusion. See *Resource Developers*, 926 F.2d at 140; *PPX Enterprises*, 818 F.2d at 273.

Moreover, the doctrine of constructive trust has traditionally been invoked to defeat those gains accrued by wrongdoers as a result of fraud. See Latham v. Father Divine, 85 N.E.2d 168, 170 (1949)("A constructive trust will be erected whenever necessary to satisfy the demands of justice.... Its applicability is limited only by the inventiveness of men who find new ways to enrich themselves by grasping what should not belong to them."); Restatement of Restitution, § 160 cmt.d (1937); cf. Robert Stigwood Group Ltd. v. O'Reilly, 530 F.2d 1096, 1100–1101 & n.9 (2d Cir.), *cert. denied*, 429 U.S. 848 (1976)(recognizing that imposition of a constructive trust over defendant's profits may be an available remedy for willful copyright infringement).

The rationale underlying the Supreme Court's holding in *Hamilton Shoe Co.* reflects this purpose. There, the Court upheld a profits award for trademark infringement where the "imitation of complainant's mark was fraudulent, [and] the profits included in the decree [were] confined to such as accrued to the defendant through its persistence in the unlawful simulation...." 240 U.S. at 261. Thus, it would seem that for the defendant's enrichment to be "unjust" in terms of warranting an accounting, it must be the fruit of willful deception. See El Greco Leather Products Co. v. Shoe World, Inc., 726 F.Supp. 25, 29–30 (E.D.N.Y.1989).

*Where Plaintiff Sustains Damages*: Historically, an award of defendant's profits has also served as a rough proxy measure of plaintiff's damages. Champion Plug Co. v. Sanders, 331 U.S. 125, 131 (1947); Mishawaka Mfg. Co. v. S.S. Kresge Co., 316 U.S. 203, 206 (1942); *Hamilton Shoe Co.*, 240 U.S. at 261–62; see also, Restatement (Third) of Unfair Competition § 37 cmt.b (Tent. Draft No.3, 1991) ("Restatement"). Due to the inherent difficulty in isolating the causation behind diverted sales and injured reputation, damages from trademark or trade dress infringement are often hard to establish. Recognizing this, the Supreme Court has stated that, "infringement and damage having been found, the Act requires the trademark owner to prove only the sales of articles bearing the infringing mark." *Mishawaka Mfg. Co.*, 316 U.S. at 206.

Under this rule, profits from defendant's proven sales are awarded to the plaintiff unless the defendant can show "that the infringement had no relationship" to those earnings. *Id*. This shifts the burden of proving economic injury off the innocent party, and places the hardship of disproving economic gain onto the infringer. Of course, this "does not stand for the proposition that an accounting will be ordered merely because there has been an infringement." *Champion Plug Co.*, 331 U.S. at 131. Rather, in order to award profits there must first be "a basis for finding damage." *id*.;

*Mishawaka Mfg. Co.*, 316 U.S. at 206. While a plaintiff who seeks the defendant's profits may be relieved of certain evidentiary requirements otherwise carried by those trying to prove damages, a plaintiff must nevertheless establish its general right to damages before defendant's profits are recoverable.

Thus, under the "damage" theory of profits, a plaintiff typically has been required to show consumer confusion resulting from the infringement. Cf. *Perfect Fit Indus., Inc. v. Acme Quilting Co.*, 618 F.2d 950, 955 (2d Cir.), *cert. denied*, 459 U.S. 832 (1980)(New York law of unfair competition); *G.H. Mumm Champagne v. Eastern Wine Corp.*, 142 F.2d 499, 501 (2d Cir.), *cert. denied*, 323 U.S. 715 (1944)(L. Hand, J.). Whether a plaintiff also had to show willfully deceptive conduct on the part of the defendant is not so clear. While some courts "rejected good faith as a defense to an accounting for profits," *Burger King Corp. v. Mason*, 855 F.2d 779, 781 (11th Cir.1988)(citing *Wolfe v. National Lead Co.*, 272 F.2d 867, 871 (9th Cir.1959), *cert. denied*, 362 U.S. 950 (1960)), others have concluded that a defendant's bad faith is the touchstone of accounting liability. Cf. *Champion Plug Co.*, 331 U.S. at 131 (accounting was unavailable where "there had been no showing of fraud or palming off"); *Carl Zeiss Stiftung v. VEB Carl Zeiss Jena*, 433 F.2d 686, 706–08 (2d Cir.1970)(discussing monetary awards which are inclusive of both damages and profits).

*Deterrence*: Finally, we have held that a court may award a defendant's profits solely upon a finding that the defendant fraudulently used the plaintiff's mark. See *Monsanto Chemical Co. v. Perfect Fit Mfg. Co.*, 349 F.2d 389, 396 (2d Cir.1965), *cert. denied*, 383 U.S. 942 (1966). The rationale underlying this holding is not compensatory in nature, but rather seeks to protect the public at large. By awarding the profits of a bad faith infringer to the rightful owner of a mark, we promote the secondary effect of deterring public fraud regarding the source and quality of consumer goods and services. *id.*; *W. E. Bassett Co.*, 435 F.2d at 664.

\* \* \*

Although these three theories address slightly different concerns, they do share common ground. In varying degrees, a finding of defendant's intentional deceptiveness has always been an important consideration in determining whether an accounting was an appropriate remedy. In view of this, the American Law Institute has recently concluded that a finding of willful infringement is the necessary catalyst for the disgorgement of ill-gotten profits. See Restatement, § 37(1)(a)("One ... is liable for the net profits earned on profitable transactions resulting from [the infringement], if, but only if, the actor engaged in conduct with the intention of causing confusion or deception ... ").

We agree with the position set forth in § 37 of the Restatement and therefore hold that, under § 35(a) of the Lanham Act, a plaintiff must prove that an infringer acted with willful deception before the infringer's profits are recoverable by way of an accounting. Along with the Restatement's drafters, we believe that this requirement is necessary to avoid the conceivably draconian impact that a profits remedy might have in some cases. While damages directly measure the plaintiff's loss, defendant's profits measure the defendant's gain. Thus, an accounting may overcompensate for a plaintiff's actual injury and create a windfall judgment at the defendant's expense. See Restatement, § 37 at cmt.e. Of course, this is not to be confused with plaintiff's lost profits, which have been traditionally compensable as an element of plaintiff's damages.

So as to limit what may be an undue windfall to the plaintiff, and prevent the potentially inequitable treatment of an "innocent" or "good faith" infringer, most courts require proof of intentional misconduct before allowing a plaintiff to recover the defendant's profits. *id.*; see also ALPO Petfoods, Inc. v. Ralston Purina Co., 913 F.2d 958, 968 (D.C.Cir.1990); Frisch's Restaurants, Inc. v. Elby's Big Boy, 849 F.2d 1012, 1015 (6th Cir.1988); Schroeder v. Lotito, 747 F.2d 801, 802 (1st Cir.1984)(per curiam)(applying Rhode Island law). We underscore that in the absence of such a showing, a plaintiff is not foreclosed from receiving monetary relief. Upon proof of actual consumer confusion, a plaintiff may still obtain damages—which, in turn, may be inclusive of plaintiff's own lost profits. See *Getty Petroleum Corp.*, 878 F.2d at 655.

Neither *Burndy Corp.* or *W. E. Bassett Co.* rejects the notion that willful deceptiveness is a necessary predicate for an award of defendant's profits. See *El Greco Leather Products Co.*, 726 F.Supp. at 29. To the contrary, both cases reflect the centrality of this factor. For example, defendant's profits were denied in *Burndy Corp.* because the plaintiff failed to establish that its own sales were diverted as a result of the infringement and that the defendant acted willfully. This finding precluded both unjust enrichment and deterrence as available grounds for relief. See 748 F.2d at 773. On the other hand, an accounting was ordered in *W. E. Bassett Co.* solely because the defendant had "deliberately and fraudulently infringed Bassett's mark." 435 F.2d at 664. Finally, to the extent that these cases suggest that a defendant's profits are recoverable whenever a plaintiff may obtain damages, we conclude that the language of *Burndy Corp.* and *W. E. Bassett Co.* was simply imprecise on this point, and we reject such a reading. Cf. *Carl Zeiss Stiftung*, 433 F.2d at 706–08.

Having stated that a finding of willful deceptiveness is necessary in order to warrant an accounting for profits, we note that it may not be sufficient. While under certain circumstances, the egregiousness of the fraud may, of its own, justify an accounting, see *W. E. Bassett Co.*, 435 F.2d at 664, generally, there are other factors to be considered. Among these are such familiar concerns as: (1) the degree of certainty that the defendant benefited from the unlawful conduct; (2) availability and adequacy of other remedies; (3) the role of a particular defendant in effectuating the infringement; (4) plaintiff's laches; and (5) plaintiff's unclean hands. See generally Restatement, § 37(2) at cmt.f & cases cited in the reporter's notes. The district court's discretion lies in assessing the relative importance of these factors and determining whether, on the whole, the equities weigh in favor of an accounting. As the Lanham Act dictates, every award is "subject to equitable principles" and should be determined "according to the circumstances of the case." § 1117.

In light of the foregoing legal analysis, the district court's error becomes apparent. To begin with, the district judge concluded that an accounting was warranted in order to prevent Blue Coral's unjust enrichment. However, as stated earlier, Basch produced no evidence to suggest that the infringement caused any sales diversion. As a result, there is nothing to suggest that Blue Coral's EVER BRITE sales were at Basch's expense. It follows that "an accounting based on unjust enrichment is precluded." *Burndy Corp.*, 748 F.2d at 773.

Secondly, even if Basch had shown loss of sales, it still would not have been entitled to an accounting for profits under a theory of unjust enrichment—or any other theory. The jury made no finding to the effect that Blue Coral was a bad faith infringer. Indeed, one reason why the judge refused to let the jury assess damages was the fact that Basch failed to present any evidence regarding bad faith infringement. Nevertheless, Basch argues that the court's jury instruction on liability—which suggested that the jury consider whether Blue Coral intended "to benefit" from Basch's NEVR–DULL trade dress—taken in conjunction with the special verdict finding that Blue Coral "intended to imitate Basch's NEVR–DULL trade dress," results in a constructive finding that Blue Coral engaged in intentionally deceptive conduct. We disagree.

There is an "essential distinction . . . between a deliberate attempt to deceive and a deliberate attempt to compete. Absent confusion, imitation of certain successful features in another's product is not unlawful and to that extent a 'free ride' is permitted." *Norwich Pharmacal Co. v. Sterling Drug, Inc.*, 271 F.2d 569, 572 (2d Cir.1959) (citation omitted). Of course, even when a likelihood of confusion does arise, that does not inexorably lead to the conclusion that the defendant acted with deliberate deceit. Depending upon the circumstances, consumer confusion might as easily result from an innocent competitor who inadvertently crosses the line between a "free ride" and liability, as it could from a defendant's intentionally fraudulent conduct.

In this regard, we note that the jury specifically found that "the acts of [Blue Coral] in violation of Basch's rights [were not] done wantonly and maliciously and in reckless disregard of Basch's rights." This conclusion is buttressed by the fact this is not a case of a counterfeit trade dress from which a jury might infer that Blue Coral "intended to deceive the public concerning the origin of the goods." *WSM, Inc. v. Tennessee Sales Co.*, 709 F.2d 1084, 1087 (6th Cir.1983). Thus, we find no merit in Basch's contention that the jury effectively concluded that Blue Coral acted with wrongful intent.

Accordingly, we reverse the district court's denial of Blue Coral's j.n.o.v. motion, insofar as it related to the availability of an accounting in this case, and we vacate the jury's profits award. Because we hold that an accounting was not available in this case, we need not reach the issue of whether it was appropriate for the jury to calculate profits.

II. Basch's Cross–Appeal

A. The District Court's Injunction

The district court's injunction restrained Blue Coral from using the present EVER BRITE trade dress in the United States, but authorized the defendant

> to manufacture, sell and distribute metal polishing cleaners in the same shape and size containers as previously used in the infringing trade dress if the color of the can is either silver or red . . . with leave granted to plaintiff for additional relief based upon a showing of actual confusion.

The court's order also permitted Blue Coral to continue using its present trade dress outside of the United States, and to sell off its remaining inventory of infringing cans.

In its cross-appeal, Basch argues that this relief was insufficient. Specifically, Basch contends that: the substantive breadth of the injunction is too narrow—i.e., a can by any other color is likely to confuse; and, the court erred in allowing Blue Coral to sell off its remaining inventory without ordering the defendant to account for the profits obtained from those sales. We find no merit in any of these arguments.

It is axiomatic that the contours of an injunction are shaped by the sound discretion of the trial judge and, barring an abuse of that discretion, they will not be altered on appeal. Springs Mills, Inc. [v. Ultracashmere House, Ltd.], 724 F.2d [352], 355 [(2d Cir.1983)]. Moreover, "a finding of likelihood of confusion in an infringement action does not automatically compel the issuance of an injunction. . . . " Jim Beam Brands Co. v. Beamish & Crawford Ltd., 937 F.2d 729, 737 (2d Cir.1991), *cert. denied*, 112 S.Ct. 1169 (1992). If the trial judge ultimately determines that injunctive relief is warranted, "the relief granted should be no broader than necessary to cure the effects of the harm caused." Soltex Polymer Corp. [v. Fortex Industries, Inc.], 832 F.2d [1325], 1329 [(2d Cir.1987)].

The instant injunction is consistent with these principles. First, given the fact that the EVER BRITE trade dress is, at best, only moderately similar to the overall appearance of the NEVR–DULL can, we agree with the district court that there was no need for Blue Coral to make major aesthetic changes. Basch was unable to produce any evidence of actual consumer confusion between NEVR–DULL and EVER BRITE during the approximately three years that EVER BRITE used the infringing trade dress. This suggests to us that the likelihood of confusion created by Blue Coral was minimal, thereby requiring only minimal correction. The district court's assessment that a change of can color would supply the needed distinction between products seems reasonable. In any event, the district court granted Basch leave to apply for additional relief upon a future showing of actual confusion.

Finally, we cannot fault the district court for allowing Blue Coral to liquidate its remaining inventory of infringing cans without requiring the defendant to account for the profits on those sales. Our approval stems largely from the fact that Basch never moved for a preliminary injunction to restrain Blue Coral's use of the trade dress in question. Actions speak louder than words, and motions speak loudest of all. Since Basch itself apparently concluded that the economic loss it was suffering, if any, did not warrant a remedy from the outset of this action, we cannot say that the district court abused its discretion in allowing Blue Coral to sell off its remaining cans and retain the profits. Cf. E.I. Dupont De Nemours & Co. v. Yoshida Int'l, Inc., 393 F.Supp. 502, 528 (E.D.N.Y.1975)(in minimizing injury to good faith infringer, injunction may provide for a grace period before use of infringing mark is permanently restrained); Carling Brewing Co. v. L. Fatato, Inc., 305 F.Supp. 1070, 1071 (E.D.N.Y.1969)(use grace period incorporated into permanent injunction).

B.  Attorney Fees

The Lanham Act provides that "the court in exceptional cases may award reasonable attorney fees to the prevailing party." § 1117(a). The decision whether or not to award such fees also rests within the broad discretion of the district judge. Getty Petroleum Corp. v. Bartco Petroleum Corp., 858 F.2d 103, 114 (2d Cir.1988), *cert. denied*, 490 U.S. 1006 (1989). Basch argues that the district judge abused his discretion in denying its application for reasonable attorney fees. We disagree. In view of the fact that there was no finding of bad faith infringement in this case, indeed the jury specifically found that Blue Coral's actions in fashioning its EVER BRITE trade dress were not egregious, we find no abuse of discretion here. Orient Express Trading Co., Ltd. v. Federated Dep't Stores, Inc., 842 F.2d 650, 655 (2d Cir.1988).

Conclusion

Having reviewed the development of the relevant case law under §§ 43(a) and 35(a) of the Lanham Act, and having considered the underlying policies that the law seeks to implement, we conclude that before a defendant may be held to account for profits received in conjunction with a trade dress infringement, a plaintiff must first prove that the defendant acted with willful intent to deceive the public. Since the plaintiff in this case failed to establish this vital element, we partially reverse the district court's denial of Blue Coral's motion for judgment n.o.v., and vacate the jury award. We affirm the district court's grant of injunctive relief and denial of attorney fees.

Affirmed in part; reversed in part; and jury award vacated.

■ KEARSE, CIRCUIT JUDGE, dissenting in part.

I respectfully dissent from so much of the majority decision as reverses the monetary award to plaintiff George Basch Co. ("Basch") on account of the infringement by defendant Blue Coral, Inc. ("Blue Coral"), of the trade dress for Basch's product, NEVR–DULL. The district court, though finding that damages were unavailable because there was no proof of actual consumer confusion, determined that an award to Basch of Blue Coral's profits was appropriate because Blue Coral had been unjustly enriched by its infringement. The court had noted that if the question of profits was a matter to be decided by the court rather than the jury, the court would accept the jury's findings as advisory. See Fed.R.Civ.P. 39(c). Whether the final judgment reflects findings and conclusions by the court or a refusal to set aside the jury's verdict, I think the award of profits was a remedy permitted by law and was supported by the findings of a properly instructed jury.

The Lanham Act, § 1051 et seq. (1988), provides, in pertinent part, that when the plaintiff has established a violation of § 1125(a), which prohibits, *inter alia*, trade practices that falsely indicate a product's origin, the plaintiff is generally entitled, "subject to the principles of equity, to recover (1) defendant's profits, [and] (2) any damages sustained by the plaintiff." § 1117(a). The term "profits" is not coextensive with the term "damages," see, e.g., Monsanto Chemical Co. v. Perfect Fit Products Manufacturing Co., 349 F.2d 389 (2d Cir.1965) (affirming denial of damages, reversing denial of profits), *cert. denied*, 383 U.S. 942 (1966), and even where the plaintiff has not proven any loss of its own sales, and hence has not proven damages, an award of profits may be justified as an equitable remedy where the defendant has been unjustly enriched by his infringement, see *Id.* at 395; W. E. Bassett Co. v. Revlon, Inc., 435 F.2d 656, 664 (2d Cir.1970)("An accounting should be granted if the defendant is unjustly enriched . . . .").

In the present case, the evidence was that Blue Coral, having been the exclusive distributor of Basch's NEVR–DULL in Canada, asked Basch to produce a Blue Coral version of the product that Blue Coral could distribute in the United States under its own trademark. When negotiations failed to achieve agreement, Blue Coral set out to copy Basch's NEVR–DULL. (See, e.g., Plaintiff's Exhibit 34, a Blue Coral document dated March 28, 1988, entitled "LABORATORY MEMORANDUM NO. 19 [-] DUPLICATION OF NEVR–DULL," discussing "the feasibility of duplicating Nevr-Dull for manufacturing by Blue Coral.")

The jury was instructed, *inter alia*, that it could not find infringement of the NEVR–DULL trade dress simply on the basis that Blue Coral had intentionally copied it. Rather, it was told that if it found that Blue Coral had intentionally copied the NEVR–DULL trade dress, it could find infringement only if it also found a likelihood of confusion, which it might infer if it found "there was an intent to benefit from Basch's protectable right in its NEVR–DULL trade dress." The court also told the jury that the amount of monetary damages it could award for trade-dress infringement was "limited to what you find the defendant Blue Coral made as a result of the violation of Nevr–Dull trade dress." The court explained that the jury could properly award to Basch only the amount Blue Coral made that it would not be fair or equitable for Blue Coral to retain.

Having been thus instructed, the jury was asked the following questions and gave the following answers:

"Was Basch's trade dress for its NEVR–DULL product inherently distinctive? Yes."

"Did the trade dress for Basch's NEVR–DULL product acquire secondary meaning? Yes."

"Did defendants intend to imitate Basch's NEVR–DULL trade dress? Yes."

"Did defendants' use of its trade dress in marketing EVER BRITE create a likelihood of confusion among a substantial number of members of the consuming public as to the source of EVER BRITE, i.e., as to whether EVER BRITE was manufactured by the maker of NEVR–DULL? Yes."

"Did the violation of Basch's rights proximately cause damage to Basch? Yes."

The jury found that the "profits earned by Blue Coral due to trade dress infringement" totaled "$200,000."

These findings of Blue Coral's intentional copying of a distinctive trade dress that had acquired secondary meaning, thereby creating a likelihood of consumer confusion, in order to benefit from the breach of Basch's rights, and culminating in the unfair receipt by Blue Coral of $200,000 in profits due to the infringement, suffice, in my view, to support the conclusion that Blue Coral was unjustly enriched. I would affirm the district court's judgment that an award of profits was justified.

## Sands, Taylor & Wood Co. v. Quaker Oats Co.

United States Court of Appeals, Seventh Circuit, 1992.
978 F.2d 947, cert. denied 507 U.S. 1042, 113 S.Ct. 1879, 123 L.Ed.2d 497 (1993).

■ CUDAHY, CIRCUIT JUDGE.

Sands, Taylor & Wood Company (STW) brought this action against The Quaker Oats Company (Quaker) for federal trademark infringement and related state-law claims, alleging that Quaker's use of the words "Thirst Aid" in its advertising slogan "Gatorade is Thirst Aid" infringed STW's registered trademark for THIRST–AID. The district court agreed, and entered judgment for STW in the amount of $42,629,399.09, including prejudgment interest and attorney's fees. The court also permanently enjoined Quaker from using the words "Thirst Aid." Not surprisingly, Quaker appeals.

The district court awarded STW ten percent of Quaker's profits on sales of Gatorade for the period during which the "Thirst Aid" campaign ran—$24,730,000—based on its finding that Quaker had acted in bad faith. The court also ordered Quaker to pay STW's attorney's fees, again based on the finding of bad faith, as well as prejudgment interest on the award of profits beginning from May 12, 1984. Quaker challenges all three of these rulings.

A.  Profits

Quaker argues that an award of its profits was inappropriate here because there was no evidence that Quaker intended to trade on STW's good will or reputation; indeed, such an intent is necessarily absent in a reverse confusion case. According to Quaker, an award of the defendant's profits is justified only where the defendant has been unjustly enriched by appropriating the plaintiff's good will. There is some support for this position in the case law. "To obtain an accounting of profits, the courts usually require that defendant's infringement infer some connotation of 'intent,' or a knowing act denoting an intent, to infringe or reap the harvest of another's mark and advertising." [2 J. Thomas McCarthy, Trademarks and Unfair Competition § 30:25, at 498 (2d ed. 1984)]. The law of this circuit is not, however, so limited. As we stated in Roulo [v. Russ Berrie & Co., Inc.]:

> The Lanham Act specifically provides for the awarding of profits in the discretion of the judge subject only to principles of equity. As stated by this Court, "The trial court's primary function is to make violations of the Lanham Act unprofitable to the infringing party." [citation omitted] Other than general equitable considerations, there is no express requirement that the parties be in direct competition or that the infringer wilfully infringe the trade dress to justify an award of profits. [citation omitted] Profits are awarded under different rationales including unjust enrichment, deterrence, and compensation.

886 F.2d [931], 941 [(7th Cir.1989)]. This broader view seems to be more consistent with the language of the Lanham Act than is the narrower (though perhaps more logical) rule espoused by Quaker. 2 McCarthy, *supra* § 30:28, at 514–15. We decline to adopt Quaker's restrictive interpretation in light of Seventh Circuit precedent.

Nevertheless, we are mindful of the fact that awards of profits are to be limited by "equitable considerations." The district court justified the award of profits based on its finding that Quaker acted in bad faith. The evidence of bad faith in this case, however, is pretty slim. The court based its finding on (1) Quaker's "failure to conduct a basic trademark search until days before the airing of the Thirst Aid commercial," and its "anonymous, cursory investigations" of Karp's[a] use of the mark once it obtained such a search; (2) Quaker's decision to continue with the "Thirst Aid" campaign after it discovered Karp's registrations; (3) the fact that Quaker did not seek a formal legal opinion regarding potential trademark issues until after the first "Thirst Aid" commercials were aired; and (4) Quaker's failure to take "reasonable precautions" to avoid the likelihood of confusion. Sands, Taylor & Wood [v. The Quaker Oats Co.], 18 U.S.P.Q.2d [(BNA) 1457], 1472–73 [(N.D.Ill.1990)].

None of these facts is particularly good evidence of bad faith. For example, Quaker's in-house counsel, Lannin, testified at trial that his review of the "Thirst Aid" campaign in February or March of 1984 did not include a trademark search because he concluded that the proposed advertisements used the words "Thirst Aid" descriptively, and not as a trademark, and therefore did not raise any trademark issues. The district court apparently accepted this testimony, but nonetheless found Quaker's failure

[a] [Karp was the assignee of STW's registrations for THIRST–AID, but it entered into a licenseback agreement with STW, resulting in STW's ownership of the trademark registrations.]—eds.

to investigate indicative of bad faith. Further, the court stated that it is a "close question" whether "Thirst Aid" is a descriptive term. Indeed, this court has found that the district court erred in concluding that "Thirst Aid" was not descriptive as a matter of law. A party who acts in reasonable reliance on the advice of counsel regarding a close question of trademark law generally does not act in bad faith. Cuisinarts, Inc. v. Robot–Coupe Int'l Corp., 580 F.Supp. 634, 637 (S.D.N.Y.1984).

Nor does Quaker's decision to proceed with the "Thirst Aid" campaign once it learned of Karp's registrations necessarily show bad faith. Based both on his earlier conclusion that "Thirst Aid" was descriptive and on his investigation into Karp's use of the term, which revealed that Karp was not currently using the THIRST–AID mark on any products sold at retail, Lannin concluded that Quaker's ads did not infringe Karp's rights in its marks. That conclusion was confirmed by the opinion Quaker obtained a few weeks later from its outside counsel, which concluded that Quaker was making a fair use of "Thirst Aid" because "Thirst–Aid" [sic] is not used as a trademark on the product but rather clearly as a positioning statement or claim in advertising. It is used descriptively to inform the purchaser that the product will aid your thirst, and as a play on the words "First Aid." "The fact that one believes he has a right to adopt a mark already in use because in his view no conflict exists since the products are separate and distinct cannot, by itself, stamp his conduct as in bad faith." Nalpac, Ltd. v. Corning Glass Works, 784 F.2d 752, 755 (6th Cir.1986)(quoting Mushroom Makers, Inc. v. R.G. Barry Corp., 441 F.Supp. 1220, 1230 (S.D.N.Y.1977), aff'd, 580 F.2d 44 (2d Cir.1978)). Even the defendant's refusal to cease using the mark upon demand is not necessarily indicative of bad faith. Absent more, courts should "not make an inference of bad faith from evidence of conduct that is compatible with a good faith business judgment." Munters Corp. v. Matsui America, Inc., 730 F.Supp. 790, 799–800 (N.D.Ill.1989), aff'd, 909 F.2d 250 (7th Cir.1990).

Quaker's failure to obtain a formal legal opinion from outside counsel until after the "Thirst Aid" campaign began is similarly weak evidence of bad faith. Given Lannin's sincere, reasonable conclusion that Quaker's ads used "Thirst Aid" descriptively, so that no trademark issue was raised, Quaker had no reason to seek the opinion of outside trademark counsel. Similarly, Quaker had no reason to take any precautions to avoid likelihood of confusion; Quaker's research had revealed that there was no product about which people were likely to be confused.[b]

A determination of bad faith is a finding of fact subject to the clearly erroneous standard of review. Web Printing Controls Co. v. Oxy–Dry Corp.,

---

[b] The district court finds it indicative of bad faith that Quaker did not contact STW after receiving its trademark search, even though STW's name was "referenced on the trademark report." *Sands, Taylor & Wood,* 18 U.S.P.Q.2d at 1472. The reference to STW appears in a list of "Thirst Aid" uses found by searching various directories—in the case of STW, the *Thomas Grocer Register*. STW's name does not appear on any of the federal registrations that the search turned up, nor does it appear anywhere in conjunction with Karp's name. Quaker's failure to contact STW based on the reference in the trademark report is at best weak evidence of bad faith.

906 F.2d 1202, 1205 n.3 (7th Cir.1990). We cannot say on this record that the district court's conclusion was clearly erroneous. We do think, however, that the evidence of bad faith here is marginal at best. Further, this is not a case where the senior user's trademark is so well-known that the junior user's choice of a confusingly similar mark, out of the infinite number of marks in the world, itself supports an inference that the junior user acted in bad faith. 2 McCarthy, *supra* § 23:33, at 147. There is no question that Quaker developed the "Thirst Aid" campaign entirely independently, with no knowledge of STW's marks. In such a case, an award of $24 million in profits is not "equitable"; rather, it is a windfall to the plaintiff. Quaker may have been unjustly enriched by using STW's mark without paying for it, but the award of profits bears no relationship to that enrichment. A reasonable royalty, perhaps related in some way to the fee STW was paid by Pet, would more accurately reflect both the extent of Quaker's unjust enrichment and the interest of STW that has been infringed. We therefore reverse the district court's award of profits and remand for a redetermination of damages. A generous approximation of the royalties Quaker would have had to pay STW for the use of the THIRST–AID mark had it recognized the validity of STW's claims seems to us an appropriate measure of damages, although perhaps not the only one. In any event, we can conceive of no rational measure of damages that would yield $24 million.[c]

## B. Attorney's Fees

The Lanham Act provides for recovery of attorney's fees by the prevailing party in "exceptional cases." § 1117(a). The district court concluded that this was such an exceptional case based on its finding that Quaker acted in bad faith. Because we affirm that finding, we also affirm the award of attorney's fees. The "equitable considerations" which lead us to reverse the award of profits do not apply to this issue.

## C. Prejudgment Interest

As the district court noted, the Lanham Act is silent with respect to prejudgment interest. The court nevertheless decided to award such interest, relying on this Circuit's rule that "prejudgment interest should be presumptively available to victims of federal law violations. Without it, compensation is incomplete and the defendant has an incentive to delay." Gorenstein Enterprises, Inc. v. Quality Care–USA, Inc., 874 F.2d 431, 436 (7th Cir.1989). Quaker argues that the Lanham Act's silence means that

[c] Because neither Judge Ripple nor Judge Fairchild joins this part of the court's opinion, it expresses the individual views of Judge Cudahy. To enable this issue to be decided by majority vote, however, Judge Cudahy has no difficulty with deferring to Judge Ripple's view, expressed in his separate opinion, that the district court's award of damages should be reversed and remanded for "a more precise determination" not limited to a reasonable royalty. Thus, Judges Cudahy and Ripple agree that, in recalculating the award of damages, the district court should be guided by the following principles: (1) the court may not simply award STW a percentage of Quaker's profits; (2) the court should use a reasonable royalty as a baseline or sorting point for determining the appropriate award; (3) in determining the appropriate award, the court may take into account the possible need for deterrence, which may involve consideration of the amount of Quaker's profits.

prejudgment interest is not available in an action for infringement under the Act. No court of appeals has accepted this argument, and we decline to do so here. We do, however, vacate the award of prejudgment interest and remand for recalculation based on the redetermination of damages we have ordered.

For the foregoing reasons, the decision of the district court is AF-FIRMED in part, REVERSED in part and REMANDED for further proceedings.

■ RIPPLE, CIRCUIT JUDGE, concurring.

In my view, Quaker's corporate conduct in this matter deserves a somewhat less charitable appraisal than that presented. Therefore, in assessing damages, I believe the district court, in the exercise of its discretion, might well place substantial emphasis on deterrence. See Roulo v. Russ Berrie & Co., Inc., 886 F.2d 931, 941 (7th Cir.1989). Therefore, I doubt very much that damages measured by a "reasonable royalty"—a speculative approximation itself—necessarily would suffice in this case. Nevertheless, I agree with Judge Cudahy that the district court's use of a "percentage of profits" benchmark for the award of damages is difficult to sustain. I therefore concur in his conclusion that a more precise determination is appropriate.

■ FAIRCHILD, SENIOR CIRCUIT JUDGE, dissenting in part.

Twenty-four million dollars ($24 million) is, indeed, a big number. It is, however, only 10% of the profit realized by Quaker out of the product it marketed by using STW's mark. We are affirming the finding that Quaker used the mark in bad faith. The real question, it seems to me, is one of causation. What portion of Quaker's profit resulted from its use of THIRST AID, and therefore constituted unjust enrichment? I am unable to say that the district court's estimate of 10% was unreasonable or clearly erroneous. Quaker made no showing that it should have been a different number. The 90% ($216 million) of profit which Quaker retains is no paltry reward for everything it contributed to the success of the venture.

Therefore, I respectfully dissent from the decision to reverse the award.

## Lever Bros. Co. v. United States

United States Court of Appeals, District of Columbia, 1993.
981 F.2d 1330.

■ SENTELLE, CIRCUIT JUDGE.

The District Court entered a judgment invalidating the "affiliate exception" of 19 C.F.R. § 133.21(c)(2)(1988) as inconsistent with the statutory mandate of the Lanham Act of 1946, 15 U.S.C.A. § 1124 (1988), prohibiting importation of goods which copy or simulate the mark of a domestic manufacturer, and issued a nationwide injunction barring enforcement of the regulation with respect to any foreign goods bearing a valid United States trademark but materially and physically differing from the United States version of the goods. The United States appeals. We conclude that the District Court, obedient to our limited remand in a prior decision in this same cause, properly determined that the regulation is inconsistent with the statute. However, because we conclude that the remedy the District Court provided is overbroad, we vacate the judgment and remand for entry of an injunction against allowing the importation of the foreign-produced Lever Brothers brand products at issue in this case.

## I.  Background[a]

Lever Brothers Company ("Lever US" or "Lever"), an American company, and its British affiliate, Lever Brothers Limited ("Lever UK"), both manufacture deodorant soap under the "Shield" trademark and hand dishwashing liquid under the "Sunlight" trademark. The trademarks are registered in each country. The products have evidently been formulated differently to suit local tastes and circumstances. The U.S. version lathers more, the soaps smell different, the colorants used in American "Shield" have been certified by the FDA whereas the colorants in British "Shield" have not, and the U.S. version contains a bacteriostat that enhances the deodorant properties of the soap. The British version of "Sunlight" dishwashing soap produces less suds, and the American version is formulated to work best in the "soft water" available in most American cities, whereas the British version is designed for "hard water" common in Britain.

The packaging of the U.S. and U.K. products is also somewhat different. The British "Shield" logo is written in script form and is packaged in foil wrapping and contains a wave motif, whereas the American "Shield" logo is written in block form, does not come in foil wrapping and contains a grid pattern. There is small print on the packages indicating where they were manufactured. The British "Sunlight" comes in a cylindrical bottle labeled "Sunlight Washing Up Liquid." The American "Sunlight" comes in a yellow, hourglass-shaped bottle labeled "Sunlight Dishwashing Liquid."

Lever asserts that the unauthorized influx of these foreign products has created substantial consumer confusion and deception in the United States about the nature and origin of this merchandise, and that it has received numerous consumer complaints from American consumers who unknowingly bought the British products and were disappointed.

Lever argues that the importation of the British products was in violation of section 42 of the Lanham Act, which provides that with the exception of goods imported for personal use:

[a] We present an abbreviated background as we have already provided some detail in our prior opinion. Lever Bros. Co. v. United States, 877 F.2d 101 (D.C.Cir.1989)("*Lever I*").

[N]o article of imported merchandise which shall copy or simulate the name of the [sic] any domestic manufacture, or manufacturer ... or which shall copy or simulate a trademark registered in accordance with the provisions of this chapter ... shall be admitted to entry at any customhouse of the United States.

*Id*. The United States Customs Service ("Customs"), however, was allowing importation of the British goods under the "affiliate exception" created by 19 C.F.R. § 133.21(c)(2), which provides that foreign goods bearing United States trademarks are not forbidden when "the foreign and domestic trademark or tradename owners are parent and subsidiary companies or are otherwise subject to common ownership or control."[b]

In *Lever I*, we concluded that "the natural, virtually inevitable reading of section 42 is that it bars foreign goods bearing a trademark identical to the valid U.S. trademark but physically different," without regard to affiliation between the producing firms or the genuine character of the trademark abroad. 877 F.2d 101, 111 (D.C.Cir.1989). In so concluding, we applied the teachings of Chevron U.S.A. Inc. v. NRDC, 467 U.S. 837 (1984). Under the *Chevron* analysis, if Congress has clearly expressed an intent on a matter, we give that intent full effect (Step One of *Chevron*). If there is any ambiguity, we accept Customs' interpretation, provided only that it is reasonable (Step Two of *Chevron*). See *Lever I*, 877 F.2d at 105 (citing *Chevron* 467 U.S. at 842–43). The *Lever I* panel found the present controversy to survive barely *Chevron* Step One and "provisionally" concluded that the affiliate exception is inconsistent with section 42 with respect to physically different goods.[c] The "provisional" qualifier on our determination of the invalidity of the exception was a very limited one. Noting that "neither party has briefed the legislative history nor administrative practice in any detail," we adopted the apparently controlling reading of section 42 only "tentatively" and remanded the case to the District Court to allow the parties to "join issue on those points." *Lever I*, 877 F.2d at 111. The panel in *Lever I* thus created a very small window of opportunity for the government to establish that the affiliate exception regulation was consistent with section 42 of the Lanham Act. At that time we said, "subject to some persuasive evidence running against our tentative conclusion, we must say that Lever's probability of success on its legal argument is quite high." *Id*.

Our task today is clearly circumscribed. Under the "law of the case" doctrine, any determination as to an issue in the case which has previously been determined is ordinarily binding upon us. Because no reason exists in

---

[b] This case does not involve a dispute between corporate affiliates. Neither Lever US nor Lever UK has authorized the importation which is being conducted by third parties. See *Lever I*, 877 F.2d at 103.

[c] In *Lever I*, we expressly recognized that our decision was not in conflict with the Supreme Court's decision in K Mart Corp. v. Cartier Inc., 486 U.S. 281 (1988), which upheld the affiliate exception against a challenge based on section 526 of the Tariff Act of 1930, 19 U.S.C.A. § 1526 (1988), but "did not reach the question of the exception's validity under section 42 of the Lanham Act." *Lever I*, 877 F.2d at 108 & n.8.

this case to avoid application of the general rule, we are bound by this Court's prior determinations concerning the application of the *Chevron* doctrine.

After reviewing the submissions of the parties, the District Court found that Customs' administrative practice was "at best inconsistent" and, in any event, had "never addressed the specific question of physically different goods that bear identical trademarks." Lever Bros. Co. v. United States, 796 F.Supp. 1, 5 (D.D.C.1992). The District Court concluded that "section 42 ... prohibits the importation of foreign goods that ... are physically different, regardless of the validity of the foreign trademark or the existence of an affiliation between the U.S. and foreign markholders." *Id.* The court accordingly concluded that "neither the legislative history of the statute nor the administrative practice of the Customs Service clearly contradicts the plain meaning of section 42" and granted summary judgment against the government. *Id.* at 13.

By way of remedy, the District Court enjoined Customs "from enforcing 19 C.F.R. § 133.21(c)(2) as to foreign goods that bear a trademark identical to a valid United States trademark but which are materially, physically different." *Lever Bros. Co.*, 796 F.Supp. at 6.

II. Analysis

Here the specific question at Step Two of *Chevron* is whether the intended prohibition of section 42 admits of an exception for materially different goods manufactured by foreign affiliates. We apply a very limited Step Two *Chevron* analysis, see *Chevron*, 467 U.S. at 842–43, because we previously concluded that the intent of Congress is virtually plain. *Lever I*, 877 F.2d 101 at 104–05. The government bears a heavy burden in attempting to overcome the apparent meaning of the statute. A presumption in favor of reasonably clear statutory language will be disrupted only if there is a " 'clearly expressed legislative intention' contrary to that language." INS v. Cardoza–Fonseca, 480 U.S. 421, 432 n.12 (1987)(quoting United States v. James, 478 U.S. 597, 606 (1986)). When we remanded this case, we indicated that the Government could not prevail unless it produced "persuasive evidence" rebutting our tentative reading of the statute, *Lever I*, 877 F.2d at 111, because the affiliate exception appears to contradict the clear implication of the language of section 42. The legislative history and administrative practice before us, as before the District Court, will not perform that onerous task.

A. Legislative History and Administrative Practice Prior to Enactment of Lanham Act

The first federal statute regulating the importation of trademarked merchandise was enacted in 1871. It prohibited the importation of "watches, watch cases, watch movements, or parts of watch movements, of foreign manufacture, which shall copy or simulate the name or trade-mark of any domestic manufacturer," unless the domestic manufacturer was the importer. Act of March 3, 1871, ch.125, § 1, 16 Stat. 580. Little legislative history accompanied the 1871 Act as the final legislation was adopted without debate in either house of Congress. See Cong. Globe, 41st Cong., 3d Sess. 1926, 1994 (1871). The administrative record is also sparse, but it does make clear that the domestic manufacturer was to have complete control over the importation of watches bearing its trademark.

In 1883, Congress amended the law to extend trademark protection to all kinds of domestic merchandise. The amended statute provided that "no watches, watch-cases, watch-movements, or parts of watch-movements, or any other articles of foreign manufacture" that simulated or copied the trademark of a domestic manufacturer would be allowed entry. 22 Stat. 488, 490 (1883). Although the phrase "any other articles of foreign manufacture" was added at conference, the conference report does not explain the addition. See 14 Cong. Rec. 3713 (1883). The Treasury Department ("Treasury") interpreted the 1883 statute to prohibit foreign manufacturers from importing goods that an American manufacturer had requested to be manufactured abroad on its behalf and stamped with its trademark.

Section 7 of the Tariff Act of 1890 revised the protection accorded to domestic merchandise, providing in relevant part, that "no article of imported merchandise which shall copy or simulate the name or trademark of any domestic manufacture or manufacturer, shall be admitted to entry at any custom-house of the United States." 26 Stat. 567, 613 (1890). Unlike the earlier provisions, this statute did not include an exception for foreign merchandise imported by the domestic trademark owner, nor was any provision made for entry with the domestic trademark owner's consent. It is unclear from the legislative history why Congress did not include special language allowing importations by the domestic trademark owner. It is clear, however, that the domestic trademark owner still retained effective control over the importation of goods bearing its trademark since all foreign merchandise bearing its mark was barred from entry.

The 1890 trademark importation provision was reenacted with almost identical language in 1894. Tariff Act of 1894, § 6, 28 Stat. 547. An 1897 reenactment expanded the sweep of the provision to prohibit the entry of articles marked in a manner "calculated to induce the public to believe that the article is manufactured in the United States." Tariff Act of 1897, § 11, 30 Stat. 207. Although the legislative history is again sparse, it appears the language was added to provide further protection to the public against deceptive marks. See 4 Treas. Dec. 506, 508 (1901) (ruling that even if Customs found a recorded trademark to be invalid, foreign merchandise must nevertheless be excluded if bottled or labeled so as to lead public to believe it was manufactured in United States).

Section 27 of the Trade–Mark Act of 1905, 33 Stat. 724, 730 (1905), amplified governmental protection of trademarks against imports. Trademark protection was extended to all trademarks registered with the then Patent Office. Certain foreign interests were allowed to register their trademarks in the United States, and "traders" as well as manufacturers were given import protection. Again, however, there was no mention of anything akin to the affiliate exception.

In Fred Gretsch Manufacturing Co. v. Schoening, 238 F. 780 (2d Cir.1916), the Second Circuit held that section 27 did not prohibit a third party from importing violin strings manufactured in Germany that bore a trademark registered in the United States by an American who had contracted to be the exclusive agent for the sale of the strings in the United States. The Treasury Department interpreted this decision narrowly and instructed local customs officers that this opinion was "to be applied only to cases where the mark covered by the United States registration is one which was adopted and is used by a foreign manufacturer upon merchandise manufactured by him, and the registration of which in the United States is to protect and cover the foreign article when sold in this country." Treas. Dec. Int. Rev. 37021, 32 Treas. Dec. 203, 204 (1917).

The Supreme Court interpreted section 27 more broadly. In A. Bourjois & Co. v. Katzel, 260 U.S. 689 (1923), the Court held that a third party could not import a face powder manufactured in France when the plaintiff owned the United States trademarks for the product, even though the product sold was "the genuine product of the French concern.... " *Id.* at 691. The Supreme Court concluded that even an authentic foreign trademark on "genuine" merchandise may infringe a registered United States trademark. In another case that year involving the same Bourjois company, the Supreme Court held in a per curiam memorandum that third-party importation of goods bearing an authentic identical foreign trademark infringed the United States trademark owner's rights under section 27 and must be excluded from entry by Customs. A. Bourjois Co. v. Aldridge, 263 U.S. 675 (1923)(answering questions certified to it by the Second Circuit at 292 Fed. 1013 (2d Cir.1922)).

Until 1936, the regulations implementing section 27 quoted the statute, then provided for an absolute ban on imports bearing trademarks that copied or simulated United States marks. In 1936 the Treasury Department adopted new regulations implementing section 27 in light of *Aldridge.* See T.D. 48537, 70 Treas. Dec. 336 (1936). Section 518(b) of the regulations stated that a foreign mark, even if a "genuine trade-mark ... in a foreign country," shall be deemed to "copy or simulate" a United States mark if the foreign mark is "identical with a trade-mark ... protected by the laws of the United States." *Id.*

Section 518(b) of the 1936 regulations also included a "same person" exception, the first precursor of the affiliate exception:

> However, merchandise manufactured or sold in a foreign country under a trade-mark or trade name, which trade-mark is registered and recorded, shall not be deemed for the purpose of these regulations to copy or simulate such United States trade-mark or trade name if such foreign trade-mark or trade name and such United States trade-mark or trade name are owned by the same person, partnership, association, or corporation.

*Id.* The regulation did not explain the source of this exception, and there is no evidence that Customs considered the issue of physically different imports.

Several conclusions can be drawn from the pre-Lanham Act legislative history and administrative practice. First, at least until 1936, protection from unauthorized importation was consistently based upon ownership of a United States trademark, not upon the nature of the relationship between the trademark owner and the foreign producer. Second, as trademark law became more international, the trend was toward greater protection from foreign importation. Third, although the 1936 regulations implemented the first version of the affiliate exception, the specific question of materially different goods is nowhere addressed.

B.   Legislative History of Section 42 of Lanham Act

In the late 1930s and early 1940s, Congress considered a wholesale revision and codification of the United States trade-mark laws, resulting in the Lanham Trade–Mark Act of 1946. In 1944, the Tariff Commission submitted a memorandum to the Senate Subcommittee on Patents which, after discussing the legislative and administrative history of section 27, stated that "in the light of the Supreme Court's decision in the *Bourjois* case, . . . Section 27 of the Trade–Mark Act of 1905 prohibits the entry of all articles bearing marks which infringe registered trade-marks." Hearings on H.R. 82 Before the Subcomm. of the Senate Comm. on Patents, 78th Cong., 2d Sess. 86 (1944)(hereinafter "1944 Hearings"). The memorandum explicitly stated that the 1905 Act's phrase "all articles" included "articles identical with those sold by the registrant under his mark and bearing identical trade-marks." *Id*. The memorandum then added: "However, section 27 does not apply to the registrant's own merchandise, i.e., merchandise of the registrant bearing the registrant's mark, which mark has been applied by or for the account of the registrant." *Id*.

In *Lever I*, we concluded that the Tariff Commission's memorandum "falls far short of ratification of the affiliate exception, at least in the broad form applied by Customs here." 877 F.2d at 106. We noted two shortcomings with reliance on this memorandum. First, the memorandum refers to "articles identical to those sold by the registrant," but "makes no mention of the situation presented here, where a third party imports foreign goods bearing a valid foreign trademark identical to a US trademark but covering physically different goods." *Id*. Customs failed to respond to this point on remand, and for good reason: the 1944 memorandum does not address the distinction between identical and materially different merchandise.

Second, we stated that "we can find no indication that a single member of Congress, much less the committee, much less members speaking on the floor of either house, ever excavated these paragraphs from the mass in which they lay embedded." *Id*. The United States responds to this by noting that Senator Pepper, Chairman of the Subcommittee, requested the memorandum to be made part of the record, 1944 Hearings at 83, from which it infers congressional awareness of Customs' policy. We conclude that this evidence is insufficient to meet our earlier stated objection. The routine insertion into the record of an agency's prepared hearing testimony is at best minuscule evidence that this testimony reflected shared congressional intent at the time of enactment.

It is also noteworthy that the 1944 memorandum does not refer to "affiliates" or "closely affiliated" companies, but only to the importation of one's "own" merchandise. In short, there is nothing in the record concerning the Lanham Act indicating that Congress contemplated—much less intended to allow—an affiliate exception. More to the point, there is no evidence that Congress intended to allow third parties to import physically different trademarked goods that are manufactured and sold abroad by a foreign affiliate of the American trademark holder.

## C. Legislative History and Developments Since Passage of Lanham Act

The Treasury Department's administrative practice after passage of the Lanham Act has been inconsistent. The 1936 regulations remained in effect until 1953, when the Department briefly adopted a "related companies" exception. See T.D. 53399, 88 Treas. Dec. 376, 384 (1953). There was no indication that this regulation took cognizance of physically different goods. In any event, Treasury abandoned the related-companies exception in 1959 because it was inconsistent with section 42. Treas. Dec. Int. Rev. 54932, 94 Treas. Dec. 433 (1959), 24 FR 7522 (Sept. 18, 1959). There is some evidence that Customs continued to apply the related-companies exception, even after the Customs regulations were returned to their earlier formulation, although apparently only to identical "gray market" goods. See K Mart Corp. v. Cartier, Inc., 486 U.S. 281, 311 (1988).

In the 1950s, several attempts were made to enact the affiliate exception into law. None of these bills were passed; furthermore, none of them suggest that physically different infringing imports would be permitted.

After Congress repeatedly considered and failed to enact the affiliate exception, the Treasury Department revived the exception. In 1972 the affiliate exception was adopted in the form at issue here. See 37 FR 20677 (1972). Under the 1972 regulations, section 42's protections were rendered inapplicable where:

(1) Both the foreign and the U.S. trademark or trade name are owned by the same person or business entity;

(2) The foreign and domestic trademark or trade name owners are parent and subsidiary companies or are otherwise subject to common ownership or control;

(3) The articles of foreign manufacture bear a recorded trademark or trade name applied under authorization of the U.S. owner.

19 C.F.R. § 133.21(c)(citations omitted).[d]

[d] In K Mart Corp. v. Cartier, Inc., 486 U.S. 281 (1988), the Supreme Court struck down 19 C.F.R. § 133.21(c)(3), which allowed the importation of foreign-made goods where the United States trademark owner has authorized the use of the mark, as in conflict with the unequivocal language of section 526 of the Tariff Act. Section 526 prohibits the importation of "any merchandise of foreign manufacture" bearing a trademark "owned by" a citizen of, or by a "corporation ... organized within, the United States" unless

Neither the notice proposing the regulations, 35 FR 19269 (1970), nor the final notice adopting them, Treas. Dec. Int. Rev. 72–266, 6 Cust. B. & Dec. 538 (1972), explained their rationale. The statement accompanying the final rule contained no response to objections raised by several companies and associations.

Customs has not even adhered consistently to its own 1972 regulations. In Bell & Howell: Mamiya Co. v. Masel Supply Co., 719 F.2d 42 (2d Cir.1983), the Department of Justice and Customs filed an amicus curiae brief urging that import protection be provided to exclude parallel imports of identical foreign goods made by a company affiliated with the U.S. trademark owner. At that time, Customs took the position that "neither the legislative reports nor the congressional debate contain any clear evidence of a legislative intent to deny trademark protection where the owner of the U.S. mark is owned or controlled by the foreign manufacturer of the trademarked goods." Brief of the United States as Amicus Curiae at 8, Bell & Howell: Mamiya Co. v. Masel Supply Co., 719 F.2d 42 (2d Cir.1983).

The United States denounces its *Bell & Howell* brief now on the grounds that Customs signed the brief without the knowledge or approval of the Treasury Department, and deems it irrelevant because it never resulted in a change to the regulations at issue in this case. We stress that monumental inferences cannot be drawn from inconsistent litigating positions taken by a large agency, but the Customs Service's position in favor of excluding imports in *Bell & Howell* is evidence of Lever's claim that Customs' administrative policy has been inconsistent. And Customs' assertion in the *Bell & Howell* brief that the legislative history of the Lanham Act contains no clear evidence in support of the affiliate exception is undeniably relevant given that Customs defends the opposite position here.

In 1978, Congress added an exception to section 42 for goods imported for personal consumption. Customs Procedural Reform and Simplification Act of 1978, 19 U.S.C.A. § 1526(d)(1978). However, neither the 1978 amendment nor the accompanying legislative history sheds any light on the application of section 42 in general, or the affiliate exception in particular.

In 1984, Congress enacted the Trademark Counterfeiting Act of 1984, 18 U.S.C.A. § 2320 (1984). That statute, however, was a criminal statute and did not take the form of an amendment to section 42. Thus, any views expressed in the legislative history of that statute "form a hazardous basis for inferring the intent" of the Congress that enacted section 42. Consumer Prod. Safety Comm'n v. GTE Sylvania, Inc., 447 U.S. 102, 117 (1980). In any event, the legislative history accompanying the 1984 Act does not address the question of the importation of physically different trademarked goods manufactured by affiliated companies.

written consent of the trademark owner is produced at the time of entry. 19 U.S.C.A. § 1526. By a different majority, the Supreme Court upheld 19 C.F.R. § 133.21(c)(2), the regulation at issue here, as consistent with section 526. As we noted above, the *K Mart* case did not address the validity of these regulations under the Lanham Act. See *supra* n.c.

Customs' main argument from the legislative history is that section 42 of the Lanham Act applies only to imports of goods bearing trademarks that "copy or simulate" a registered mark. Customs thus draws a distinction between "genuine" marks and marks that "copy or simulate." A mark applied by a foreign firm subject to ownership and control common to that of the domestic trademark owner is by definition "genuine," Customs urges, regardless of whether or not the goods are identical. Thus, any importation of goods manufactured by an affiliate of a U.S. trademark owner cannot "copy or simulate" a registered mark because those goods are *ipso facto* "genuine."

This argument is fatally flawed. It rests on the false premise that foreign trademarks applied to foreign goods are "genuine" in the United States. Trademarks applied to physically different foreign goods are not genuine from the viewpoint of the American consumer. As we stated in *Lever I*:

> On its face ... section [42] appears to aim at deceit and consumer confusion; when identical trademarks have acquired different meanings in different countries, one who imports the foreign version to sell it under that trademark will (in the absence of some specially differentiating feature) cause the confusion Congress sought to avoid. The fact of affiliation between the producers in no way reduces the probability of that confusion; it is certainly not a constructive consent to importation.

877 F.2d at 111.

There is a larger, more fundamental and ultimately fatal weakness in Customs' position in this case. Section 42 on its face appears to forbid importation of goods that "copy or simulate" a United States trademark. Customs has the burden of adducing evidence from the legislative history of section 42 and its administrative practice of an exception for materially different goods whose similar foreign and domestic trademarks are owned by affiliated companies. At a minimum, this requires that the specific question be addressed in the legislative history and administrative practice. The bottom line, however, is that the issue of materially different goods was not addressed either in the legislative history or the administrative record. It is not enough to posit that silence implies authorization, when the authorization sought runs counter to the evident meaning of the governing statute. Therefore, we conclude that section 42 of the Lanham Act precludes the application of Customs' affiliate exception with respect to physically, materially different goods.

## IV. Scope of Injunction

The United States alternatively argues that this Court should vacate the District Court's injunction that applies to materially different goods other than those directly at issue in this case. The District Court's injunction provides that the Customs Service is "enjoined from enforcing [the common ownership or control provision] as to foreign goods that bear a trademark identical to a valid United States trademark but which are materially, physically different." Lever Bros. Co. v. United States, 796 F.Supp. 1, 5 (D.D.C.1992).

The United States points out that this suit was brought by a single company, proceeding solely on its own behalf, to protect two specific trademarks. Lever never asked the District Court to enjoin Customs from applying the affiliate exception to other trademarks or other companies, nor did Lever seek to certify this suit as a class action. In its prayer for relief, Lever asked only that the Customs Service be permanently enjoined "from enforcing said regulations with respect to plaintiff's 'Shield' and 'Sunlight' trademarks, and directing defendants to exclude from entry into the United States any foreign-manufactured merchandise and material bearing said trademarks." To be sure, Lever did include boilerplate language requesting that the court award "such other and further relief as the Court may deem just and proper," *id.* at 8, but this is too slender a reed upon which to rest a nationwide injunction under the facts of this case. We therefore conclude that Lever is entitled only to that relief specifically sought in its complaint, namely, that Customs be enjoined from allowing the importation of Lever's "Shield" and "Sunlight" trademarks.

V.   Conclusion

For the foregoing reasons, we affirm the District Court's ruling that section 42 of the Lanham Act, § 1124, bars the importation of physically different foreign goods bearing a trademark identical to a valid U.S. trademark, regardless of the trademark's genuine character abroad or affiliation between the producing firms. Injunctive relief, however, is limited to the two products which were the subject of this action. We therefore vacate the District Court's prior order to the extent that it renders global relief and remand for the entry of an injunction consistent with this opinion.

So ordered.

NOTES

**1.** *Injunctive relief.* Injunctive relief is the standard remedy in trademark cases and a plaintiff need only prove likelihood of confusion in order to obtain this remedy.[15] Still, courts do consider equitable defenses such as laches and estoppel in determining the propriety of injunctive relief.[16] Because likelihood of confusion is the touchstone in trademark litigation, an objectionable use may be infringing in some contexts, but not in others. Therefore, frequently injunctions are qualified so that they clearly specify the nature of the prohibited conduct. Another issue that arises in conjunction with the imposition of injunctive relief in trademark infringement

[15] See Brown, supra note 6, at 51, 65.

[16] See, e.g., Dial–A–Mattress Operating Corp. v. Mattress Madness, Inc., 841 F.Supp. 1339, 1355 (E.D.N.Y.1994)(laches and estoppel together will bar injunctive relief); Death Tobacco, Inc. v. Black Death USA, 31 U.S.P.Q.2d 1899, 1907 (C.D.Cal.1993)(court considering whether to grant injunctive relief "sits in equity and must take all equitable considerations into account").

actions was explored in Assignment 4. Recall the *Dawn Donut* case which held that the plaintiff could not obtain injunctive relief in a region that it had not yet physically entered. Courts which follow *Dawn Donut* hold that "the nationwide right conferred by registration does not entitle the owner to injunctive relief unless there is a present likelihood of confusion."[17]

**2.** *Compensatory damages.* Due to the ease with which injunctive relief is obtained in trademark infringement actions, damages are of secondary importance.[18] This is illustrated by the more restrictive requirements of actual confusion or bad faith which are imposed by some circuits. For example, *Basch* indicated that, to recover damages, a plaintiff must prove actual consumer confusion or that the defendant acted in an intentionally deceptive manner. As *Sands* observed, sometimes the reasonable royalty approach popular in patent law is invoked as a means of determining damages in trademark cases.[19] One form of monetary relief unique to trademark and unfair competition cases is the imposition on the defendants of the costs for corrective advertising.[20]

**3.** *Defendant's profits.* *Basch* highlights the distinction between an award of damages and profits by stating that "[w]hile damages directly measure the plaintiff's loss, defendant's profits measure the defendant's gain" and "[t]hus, an accounting may overcompensate for a plaintiff's actual injury and create a windfall judgment at the defendant's expense." The language of § 504(b) emphasizes that only those profits that are "not taken into account in computing the actual damages" can be awarded. This precludes the possibility of double counting so that defendants do not have to both disgorge their own profits and compensate plaintiffs for their lost profits on the identical set of sales. In contrast, in patent law only damages, as opposed to the other party's profits, are recoverable.[21] *Sands* and *Basch* illustrate that courts are split over whether to award the defendant's profits in the absence of bad faith.[22] If Nestle relies on *Sands* for an award of profits in the Principal Problem, what do you think the defendant would argue in response? When an award of profits is made, the plaintiff must only establish the defendant's sales, and the "defendant must prove all elements of cost or deduction."[23] Moreover, apportionment is appropriate with respect to those profits that are not attributable to the infringement.

The Lanham Act is unique in that it provides that the award of defendant's profits can be increased or decreased at the court's discretion. The statute also provides that such a sum "shall constitute compensation

---

[17] National Association for Healthcare Communications, Inc. v. Central Arkansas Area Agency on Aging, Inc., 257 F.3d 732 (8th Cir. 2001); Minnesota Pet Breeders Inc. v. Schell & Kampeter Inc., 41 F.3d 1242, 1246 (8th Cir.1994).

[18] Brown, supra note 6, at 65.

[19] Id.

[20] Id.

[21] See 35 U.S.C. § 284.

[22] For a discussion of the divergent case law, see Quick Technologies, Inc. v. The Sage Group PLC, 313 F.3d 338 (5th Cir. 2002)(concluding that although willful infringement is an important factor in determining whether to award an accounting of profits, it is not a prerequisite to such an award).

[23] § 1117(a).

and not a penalty."[24] Still, the statute does not provide a ceiling on the increase of profits.[25] How is an increased profit award different from punitive damages (see Note 5)? The profits adjustment clause has been used infrequently, and therefore its scope has not been defined.[26]

**4.** *Attorney's fees.* Section 1117(a) also provides that reasonable attorney's fees may be awarded to the prevailing party in "exceptional cases." Determining what constitutes an exceptional case often is difficult. Some courts follow the rule that a case is exceptional for this purpose when there is conduct that is "malicious, fraudulent, deliberate or willful."[27] Some courts also will refrain from awarding attorney's fees if the plaintiff fails to show any damages.[28] Other courts take a less restrictive approach and look to equitable considerations in making a determination whether a particular case is "exceptional."[29] What do you think of Judge Cudahy's resolution of the attorney's fees issue in Sands? Should a distinction be drawn between the awarding of attorney's fees to prevailing plaintiffs and to prevailing defendants? In National Association of Professional Baseball Leagues, Inc. v. Very Minor Leagues, Inc.,[30] the court concluded that because the underlying conduct under scrutiny is different for plaintiffs and defendants, there does not have to be perfect harmony between the standards for awarding attorney's fees to prevailing plaintiffs and prevailing defendants. Specifically, "[w]hen attorney fees are awarded against a defendant, the court looks to whether the defendant's acts of infringement were pursued in bad faith. When attorney fees are awarded against a plaintiff, the court looks to the plaintiff's conduct in bringing the lawsuit and the manner in which it is prosecuted."[31] When attorney's fees are awarded, how shall they be calculated? Should attorney's fees be awarded in cases involving the importation of gray market goods? What should be the standard for awarding attorney's fees on appeal?

**5.** *Treble/punitive damages.* Section 1117(a) provides that "[i]n assessing damages, the court may enter judgment, according to the circumstances of the case, for any sum above the amount found as actual damages, not exceeding three times such amount."[32] Thus § 1117(a) provides strictly capped compensatory relief and rejects the concept of punitive damages. How are treble damages different from punitive damages? In Thompson v. Haynes,[33] the court cautioned that there is no statutory authorization for

[24] Id.

[25] Id.

[26] Brown, supra note 6, at 74.

[27] Gordon and Breach Science Publishers S.A. v. American Institute of Physics, 166 F.3d 438, 439 (2d Cir. 1999); Gracie v. Gracie USA, 217 F.3d 1060, 1068 (9th Cir. 2000).

[28] See CJC Holdings, Inc. v. Wright & Lato, Inc., 979 F.2d 60, 66 (5th Cir.1992).

[29] Securacomm Consulting, Inc. v. Securacom Inc., 224 F.3d 273, 283 (3d Cir. 2000)(affirming district court's award of attorney's fees to plaintiff on the ground that

the defendant's conduct involved "a sweeping attempt to beat a financially weaker opponent through the use of vexatious litigation.").

[30] 223 F.3d 1143 (10th Cir. 2000).

[31] Id. at 1148.

[32] § 1117(a). See Larsen v. Terk Techs. Corp., 151 F.3d 140, 149–150 (4th Cir. 1998)(affirming lower court's award of treble damages).

[33] 305 F.3d 1369 (Fed. Cir. 2002).

trebling the award of profits, and that it was error for the lower court to combine the profits and damage award and enhance both in a similar fashion. Note that an award of treble damages is mandatory when the infringement is intentional and the use of a counterfeit trademark is involved. See Note 6 infra.

Following the *Sands* opinion reprinted in the casebook, the district court recalculated the plaintiff's damages in the amount of $20,656,822, which represented a doubling of the hypothetical base royalty of $10,328,411. This award was based on a deterrence rationale. On appeal, *Quaker* maintained that the doubling of the base royalty was a penalty which is prohibited by § 1117(a) of the Lanham Act. The court's opinion contains an excellent discussion of the tension between the provisions for enhancement damages, on the one hand, and the prohibition of punitive damages on the other.[34] It emphasized that the final remedy must "provide a sufficient deterrent to ensure that the guilty party will not return to its former ways and once again pollute the marketplace."[35] Royalty payments, without more, may not promote deterrence and therefore enhancement is appropriate. Ultimately, the court approved the base royalty rate but remanded the case so that the district court could state the basis of the award with more precision.[36]

**6.** *Trademark Counterfeiting Act and the Anti–Counterfeiting Consumer Protection Act.* Counterfeit goods are "made so as to imitate a well-known product in all details of construction and appearance so as to deceive customers into thinking that they are getting genuine merchandise."[37] The Trademark Counterfeiting Act of 1984 provides criminal penalties and enhanced civil remedies for anyone who "intentionally traffics or attempts to traffic in goods or services and knowingly uses a counterfeit mark on or in connection with such goods or services."[38] Thus, the dual mental-state of intention and knowing trafficking must be satisfied before liability can be imposed.[39] The term "traffic" is defined as "to transport, transfer, or otherwise dispose of, to another, as consideration for anything of value, or make or obtain control of with intent to transport, transfer or dispose."[40] The term "counterfeit" is defined in the statute as "a spurious mark" that is likely to cause confusion or to deceive and "(i) that is used in connection with trafficking in goods or services; [and] (ii) that is identical with, or substantially indistinguishable from, a mark registered for those goods or services on the principal register," regardless of whether the defendant knew of such registration.[41] The criminal penalties under the Act include maximum fines and/or prison terms for individuals, and even higher fines

---

[34] Sands, Taylor & Wood v. Quaker Oats Co., 34 F.3d 1340, 1346—50 (7th Cir.1994).

[35] Id. at 1348.

[36] Id. at 1352.

[37] 3 McCarthy § 25.01[5][a].

[38] 18 U.S.C. § 2320(a).

[39] See United States v. Sultan, 115 F.3d 321 (5th Cir. 1997)(reversing defendant's conviction of violating the Trademark Counterfeiting Act on ground that the government did not prove that the defendant knew that he was selling counterfeit goods).

[40] 18 U.S.C. § 2320(e)(2).

[41] 18 U.S.C. § 2320(d)(1).

for corporations.[42] The civil remedies include the seizure of goods and counterfeit marks upon an ex parte application,[43] and, under § 1117(b), a mandatory award of reasonable attorney's fees plus the greater of three times the defendant's profits or treble damages, absent "extenuating circumstances."[44] The mandatory aspect of damages under § 1117(b) underscores its strictly capped punitive nature.

In 1996, Congress passed the Anti–Counterfeiting Consumer Protection Act (ACCPA)[45] This statute increases the criminal and civil penalties for the counterfeiting of copyrighted and trademarked products and makes available statutory damages to plaintiff trademark owners for losses attributable to trademark counterfeiting. Statutory damages were included in the ACCPA because it is difficult, if not impossible, for the trademark owners to determine the amount of damages they suffer as a result of the defendant's deceptive practices.[46] The range of statutory damages is between $500 and $100,000 per counterfeit mark for each type of goods or services, and if the defendant's conduct was willful[47], statutory damages can be awarded up to $1,000,000 per counterfeit mark. In contrast to § 1117(a) & (b), § 1117(c) "looks to compensatory considerations (e.g., actual losses and trademark value)" as well as "punitive considerations (e.g. ... , deterrence of other infringers and redress of wrongful defense conduct)."[48] Thus, under § 1117(c), "there is no necessary mathematical relationship between the size of such an award and the extent or profitability of the defendant's wrongful activities."[49] Although the ACCPA does not outline factors courts should consider in determining an award of statutory damages, courts have looked to the Copyright Act for guidance.[50]

**7.** *Prejudgment interest. Sands* affirms the availability of prejudgment interest in trademark infringement actions, even though the Lanham Act does not expressly provide for this remedy. The availability of this remedy is completely within the court's discretion.

**8.** *Federal/state immunity.* Section 1122 of the Lanham Act expressly nullifies the federal government's immunity from suit, as well as the states' immunity under the Eleventh Amendment.[51] However, the issue whether states can be sued for trademark infringement is in flux in light of the

[42] 18 U.S.C. § 2320(a).

[43] 15 U.S.C. § 1116(d)(1)(A).

[44] 15 U.S.C. § 1117(b).

[45] 15 U.S.C. § 1117(c).

[46] Polo Ralph Lauren v. 3M Trading Co., 1999 WL 33740332 (S.D.N.Y. 1999); Sara Lee Corp. v. Bags of New York, Inc., 36 F.Supp.2d 161, 165 (S.D.N.Y. 1999).

[47] Polo Ralph Lauren v. 3M Trading Co., 1999 WL 33740332 (S.D.N.Y. 1999)("Willfulness in this context depends upon whether the defendant had actual or constructive knowledge that its conduct was infringing.").

[48] Polo Ralph Lauren v. 3M Trading Co., 1999 WL 33740332 (S.D.N.Y. 1999); Sara Lee Corp. v. Bags of New York, Inc., 36 F.Supp.2d 161, 165 (S.D.N.Y. 1999).

[49] Gucci America, Inc. v. Gold Ctr. Jewelry, 997 F.Supp. 399, 404 (S.D.N.Y.), *modified on other grounds,* 997 F.Supp. 409 (S.D.N.Y.), *rev'd on other grounds,* 158 F.3d 631 (2d Cir. 1998).

[50] Polo Ralph Lauren v. 3M Trading Co., 1999 WL 33740332 (S.D.N.Y. 1999); Sara Lee Corp. v. Bags of New York, Inc., 36 F.Supp.2d 161, 166 (S.D.N.Y. 1999).

[51] § 1122(a) & (b).

Supreme Court's decision in College Savings Bank v. Florida Prepaid Postsecondary Education Expense Board.[52] In that case, the Court affirmed the Third Circuit's ruling that the provision of the Lanham Act abrogating the states' Eleventh Amendment immunity was unconstitutional as applied in that case. The Court held that this provision does not permit a state to be sued for its alleged misrepresentation of its own product.[53] In the wake of this decision, bills have been introduced to restore state liability but thus far, efforts to enact such legislation have been unsuccessful.[54]

**9.** *Gray market goods.* In *Lever*, the court prohibited the importation of goods made by a foreign affiliate of a U.S. corporation where the foreign goods differed materially from the goods made by the U.S. company. Can you articulate an appropriate legal standard for determining materiality? One court has stated "[t]he courts have applied a low threshold of materiality, requiring no more than showing that consumers would be likely to consider the differences between the foreign and domestic products to be significant when purchasing the product, for such differences would suffice to erode the goodwill of the domestic source."[55] Should physical differences in the products be the only type of differences that matter in determining materiality?

In footnotes c and d of *Lever*, the court notes that the Supreme Court had upheld the affiliate exception against a challenge based on § 526 of the Tariff Act in K Mart Corp. v. Cartier Inc.[56] Section 526 bars the importation of "any merchandise of foreign manufacture if such merchandise ... bears a trademark owned by a citizen of, or by a corporation or association created or organized within, the United States, and registered ... by a person domiciled in the United States ... , unless written consent of the owner of such trademark is produced at the time of making entry."[57] Thus, *K Mart* approved "Customs' decision to permit third-party purchasers to buy goods produced abroad by a foreign subsidiary of a US firm and import them over the US firm's opposition."[58] In light of *Lever's* holding, what would be the result if *K Mart* were extended to allow importation under the affiliate exception where a U.S. firm's "*domestically* manufactured goods are identical to the imports?"[59] The court in *K Mart* did not reach, however, the validity of the affiliate exception under § 1124 of the Lanham Act.

---

[52] 527 U.S. 666 (1999).

[53] College Savings Bank v. Florida Prepaid Postsecondary Education Expense Board, 527 U.S. 666 (1999).

[54] See also GAO Report on State Immunity, October 12, 2001, available at http://www.gao.gov

[55] Gamut Trading Co. v. United States Int'l Trade Comm'n, 200 F.3d 775, 779 (Fed. Cir. 1999).

[56] 486 U.S. 281 (1988).

[57] 19 U.S.C.A. § 1526(a).

[58] Lever Brothers Co. v. U.S., 877 F.2d 101, 110–111 (D.C.Cir.1989)(Lever I).

[59] Id. at 111 (emphasis in original).

# ASSIGNMENT 6

# COPYRIGHT PROTECTION: INTRODUCTION

STATUTORY MATERIALS: §§ 104A, 401–412 & 701–710

The authority for the law discussed in this Copyright Unit and the Patent Unit which follows derives from the federal constitution, and in this respect copyright and patent law differs from trademark law which lacks a similar explicit constitutional foundation. In the United States, the need for a uniform federal law governing copyrights and patents is recognized in the Copyright Clause, Article I, Section 8, Clause 8 of the United States Constitution. Clause 8 grants Congress the power "to promote the progress of science and useful arts, by securing for limited times to authors and inventors the exclusive right to their respective writings and discoveries."[1] Pursuant to this constitutional authority, Congress enacted the first United States' copyright statute in 1790. Several revisions of and amendments to the statute subsequently ensued. The current copyright statute, the 1976 Copyright Act, became effective on January 1, 1978 and is codified at §§ 101 et seq.[2] The 1976 Act embodies a major substantive revision of its immediate predecessor, the 1909 Copyright Act, more about which will be said below.

Before delving into an exploration of copyright law, it is important to consider the underlying policies that have shaped the doctrines in this area. To realize the objective of the Copyright Clause, Congress has authorized limited monopolies for creators of copyrighted works. These monopolies contain limits on both the duration of the rights and their substantive exercise. After the period of copyright protection has expired, the property becomes part of the public domain, to be enjoyed freely by all. The copyright law also sanctions certain types of unauthorized uses of copyrighted property.[3] On numerous occasions, the Supreme Court has observed that the promotion of the arts and sciences is the primary purpose of the monopoly granted to copyright owners, with financial rewards to creators as a secondary concern.[4] This analysis of the Copyright Clause

---

[1] U.S. Const. art. I, § 8, cl. 8.

[2] Unless otherwise noted, all statutory citations in the Copyright Unit are to 17 U.S.C.

[3] See Assignment 11.

[4] See Fogerty v. Fantasy, Inc., 510 U.S. 517 (1994); Feist Publications, Inc. v. Rural Telephone Service Co., 499 U.S. 340, 349–50 (1991); Mazer v. Stein, 347 U.S. 201 (1954). See also H.R. Rep. No. 2222, 60th Cong., 2d Sess. 7 (1909).

suggests that the sovereign's duty to promote the public welfare must take precedence over the specific property rights enjoyed by copyright proprietors. Nevertheless, rewards to individuals under copyright law are essential to effectuating copyright law's major objective of enhancing societal progress, because an absence of monetary protections might well result in diminished creativity. Thus, copyright law represents a delicate balance between society's optimal use of resources and the optimal impetus for individual creativity.

The focus of our attention in the following Assignments will be on the provisions of the 1976 Act and the interpretative doctrines. Before you conclude that you can forget completely about the 1909 Act, however, you should know that its provisions still govern works created *prior* to January 1, 1978, the effective date of the 1976 Act. Therefore, students must be familiar with certain key aspects of the 1909 Act. Although the 1909 Act and the 1976 Act share certain features and frequently the case law decided under the 1909 Act bears some relevance to judicial interpretations of the 1976 Act, the two statutes also differ from one another in several critical respects. Two of the most important differences are the degree to which formalities are emphasized in these respective statutes and the duration of copyright protection.

Under the 1909 Act, federal copyright protection was available for works from the time of publication, and the state common law regime typically protected unpublished works. Prior to the 1909 Act, copyright protection was available only upon registration. Also, if the work was published without the proper notice, copyright protection was forfeited (more on this below). The length of protection under the 1909 Act was an initial 28–year term, with an optional renewal term of an additional 28 years.

The 1976 Act reduced the significance of formalities such as publication with the requisite notice. In fact, under the 1976 Act, a work receives protection as soon as it is created, regardless of whether it bears a copyright notice. Effectively, this aspect of the 1976 Act abolished the notion of state common law copyright, although we should add that state common law protections still are available for some types of works.[5] Part of the reason why Congress felt the need for de-emphasizing certain formalities for copyright protection stemmed from a prevalent sentiment that the United States should become a member of the Berne Convention. As will be discussed below, Berne is an international copyright treaty which espouses the view that copyright formalities should not be required in order to receive protection. Many of the provisions of the 1909 Act were inconsistent with Berne, and precluded our potential adherence to the treaty. The other reason for the declining focus on formalities undoubtedly was a response to certain real-world consequences. Compliance with formalities as a prerequisite for protection is far more problematic for copyright owners than for trademark owners and inventors. Unlike trademark holders who are in

---

[5] See Assignment 13 (preemption).

business and therefore have attorneys, or inventors who already have invested considerable resources in their inventions (and for whom attorney or agent fees are not so momentous), authors and artists often work in garrets with no money at all (hence the term "starving artist"). Uncounselled, they frequently lost their rights inadvertently. By providing protection for authors and artists from the moment of creation rather than upon publication with notice, the 1976 Act reduces this risk of loss. The declining importance of copyright formalities is even more apparent in certain amendments to the 1976 Act following our ultimate adherence to Berne in 1988. These amendments will be discussed below.

In addition to dispensing with certain formalities, the 1976 Act also abandoned the dual period of protection in favor of a single term of protection lasting generally for the duration of the author's life plus fifty years. In 1998, the Sony Bono Copyright Term Extension Act was passed, extending the copyright term for an additional twenty years. This new duration is, for the most part, consistent with the European Union's term of protection.[6]

Although compliance with copyright formalities is certainly not essential under the current copyright regime, we should nonetheless emphasize that such compliance is highly desirable for reasons that will be discussed below. Therefore, the following section examines the mechanics of the three significant copyright formalities: registration, deposit and notice. It also details briefly the application and judicial process.

## 1.   FEDERAL COPYRIGHT FORMALITIES

There is a government office for registering copyrights similar to that for trademarks and patents. The Copyright Office, part of the Library of Congress, is the principle source for copyright information and services. The primary functions of the Copyright Office include: 1) registering copyrights; 2) maintaining records pertinent to copyrights such as assignments and transfers of copyright ownership; 3) acquiring works for the Library of Congress; 4) furnishing information on copyright searches; and 5) advising Congress on proposed amendments to copyright law.[7]

### A.   REGISTRATION

The process of registering for a copyright involves depositing material with the Copyright Office to be reviewed by an examiner who decides whether to issue a registration certificate. Section 410 provides that "the Register [of Copyrights] shall register the claim and issue to the applicant a certificate of registration" where "the material deposited constitutes copyrightable subject matter and ... the other legal and formal requirements

---

[6] See Assignment 9 for a more detailed treatment of this issue.

[7] See Peters, The Copyright Office and the Formal Requirements of Registration of

Claims to Copyright, 17 U. Dayton L. Rev. 737, 737–38 (1992).

... have been met."[8] The material reviewed by the Copyright Office includes a completed application form (see Appendix for a sample application),[9] the appropriate deposit material,[10] and the filing fee.[11]

Registration, while not mandatory, affords the copyright claimant certain advantages. Most importantly, § 411 of the 1976 Act provides that registration is a prerequisite for instituting an infringement action for works originating in the United States, and § 412 provides that registration is a prerequisite for recovering statutory damages and attorney's fees (an exception is made for infringements occurring during the first three months after a work is published if registration is made before the end of the three months).[12] In addition, a registration certificate made before or within five years after first publication constitutes prima facie evidence of the validity of the copyright and of the facts stated in the certificate;[13] and registration is required before a document recorded with the Copyright Office provides constructive notice of the facts contained therein.[14]

## B. DEPOSIT

The deposit requirement is treated in § 407 of the 1976 Act. Although a copyright claimant is required to deposit two copies of her work in the Copyright Office, the statute provides that such deposit is not a condition of copyright protection. However, failure to satisfy the deposit requirement will result in a fine.[15] One court has held that the mandatory deposit requirement is not a "taking" requiring just compensation since Congress, in enacting the copyright law, is permitted to condition its protections upon satisfying certain requirements.[16]

## C. NOTICE

As discussed above, under the 1976 Act a creator receives copyright protection immediately upon the fixation of her work. Although publication with a copyright notice therefore is not currently required to obtain copyright protection, providing a copyright notice can be beneficial. For one thing, it provides psychological comfort to the creator who simply may not believe that copyright protection is automatic. Other reasons for providing a copyright notice will be explored in our subsequent discussion of the

[8] § 410(a).

[9] The requirements for this are detailed at § 409. Application forms are also available from the Copyright Office and may be ordered by telephoning the Forms and Circulars Hotline at (212) 707–9100. There are different application forms for different types of works. The application form reprinted is for nondramatic literary works, serials and periodicals. These documents also can be obtained on line at www.copyright.gov

[10] See § 408(b).

[11] The filing fee is currently thirty dollars as provided in 37 C.F.R. § 202.3(b)(4)(ii)(1991).

[12] § 412.

[13] § 410(c).

[14] § 205(c).

[15] See § 407(d).

[16] Ladd v. Law & Technology Press, 762 F.2d 809 (9th Cir.1985), cert. denied, 475 U.S. 1045 (1986).

Berne Convention.[17] In order to receive the benefits of notice, the proper statutory form of notice must be used.[18] There are three general components to proper notice: 1) the term "Copyright" or "Copr." or the symbol for copyright which is the letter "c" enclosed in a circle; 2) the copyright owner's name or a recognized designation or abbreviation thereof; and 3) the date of publication.[19]

## D. THE APPLICATION AND JUDICIAL PROCESS

The legislative history of the 1976 Copyright Act established "originality and fixation in a tangible form" as the fundamental criteria for copyright protection.[20] Once all the required materials are deposited, an examiner studies the record and determines whether the material falls within the subject matter of copyright and if it is an original work of authorship.[21] These two questions are asked regardless of the type of work for which a copyright is being sought. The subject matter question involves determining whether the work before the examiner falls within the categories listed in § 102(a) which include literary works; musical works; dramatic works; pantomimes and choreographic works; pictorial, graphic, and sculptural works; motion pictures and other audiovisual works; sound recordings; and architectural works.[22] The concept of originality is treated in the Originality Assignment. In making these decisions, examiners follow various guidelines. The first of these guidelines is found at 37 C.F.R. § 202 (1991) (Code of Federal Regulations). Another set of guidelines is found in the Compendium of Copyright Office Practices. Both of these are promulgated by the Copyright Office. Additionally, there are examining divisions which adhere to detailed practices and the Copyright Office also submits "Circulars" applicable to different categories of works.[23] Perhaps the most important rule examiners follow is the "rule of doubt," which provides that the Copyright Office should register the work if "a court could reasonably find that this work might be subject to copyright."[24]

If an author has completed the registration process and her work is infringed,[25] the next issue is determining what course of action the author

---

[17] See note 42 and accompanying text.

[18] § 401(b).

[19] Id. In some cases, "(c)" has been allowed as a valid substitute for the copyright symbol. See Videotronics, Inc. v. Bend Elec., 586 F.Supp. 478, 481 (D.Nev.1984). Additionally, the date may be omitted for certain works including some pictorial, graphic and sculptural works. § 401(b)(2).

[20] H.R. Rep. No. 1476, 94th Cong., 2d Sess. 51 (1976), reprinted in 1976 U.S.C.C.A.N. 5659, 5664. See § 102.

[21] See Peters, note 7, at 737–38.

[22] § 102(a).

[23] See Peters, note 7, at 739.

[24] Id. at 758. See also Syntek Semiconductor Co., Ltd. v. Microchip Technology Inc., 285 F.3d 857 (9th Cir. 2002), amended, 307 F.3d 775 (9th Cir. 2002)(upholding initial consideration by the Register of Copyrights under the doctrine of primary jurisdiction in case involving whether decompiled object code qualifies for registration as source code). But see Tanenbaum, An Analysis and Guide to the Berne Convention Implementation Act: Amendments to the United States Copyright Act, 13 Hamline L. Rev. 253, 269 (1990)("Some observers have concluded that the standards used by the Copyright Office to determine registrability may be more restrictive than those used by the courts to determine copyrightability.").

[25] Section 106 identifies the exclusive rights the copyright owner has in her work. These rights are subject to §§ 107–120.

should take to have the infringement rectified. For civil actions "arising under any Act of Congress relating to ... copyrights," the federal district courts have original jurisdiction which is exclusive of the state courts.[26] Even if a copyright claimant has been refused registration, she can maintain an infringement action under § 411(a), which allows an applicant to institute an action if "deposit, application and fee have been delivered to the Copyright Office in proper form and registration has been refused."[27] In these circumstances, the copyright claimant must notify the Register and serve a copy of the complaint on the Register. The Register of Copyrights has the option of intervening in the action with respect to the registrability of the work. Many courts hold that during the interim period between the filing of an application and a final decision respecting registration, no infringement action can be maintained by the copyright claimant in federal district court,[28] although there is some authority to the contrary.[29]

## 2.   The International Stage

United States' copyright law provides protection only against infringement in the United States,[30] but American books, films, and television

---

[26] 28 U.S.C. § 1338(a). An important issue is determining what "arising under" entails. See Cohen, "Arising Under" Jurisdiction and the Copyright Laws, 44 Hastings L.J. 337, 337 (1993).

Inconsistencies occur in cases involving contractual relations between authors and their assignees. The issue is whether suit should be brought in state court under state contract law or whether the appropriate forum is federal court as an action arising under copyright law. Id. at 340. Although the Supreme Court has not addressed this issue in the context of copyright law, lower courts have developed two different approaches to the question. Id. at 341. The first approach is to decide jurisdiction by determining what is the "principle and controlling issue." This requires the court to decide whether the case is really a contract dispute or rather a "genuine" copyright issue. Id. at 362. Professor Cohen identifies the problem with this approach as the lack of clear guidelines and inability to predict what the court will decide. Id. at 374. The second approach is to look "only to the language of the plaintiff's complaint." Id. at 341. Professor Cohen recognizes the advantages of this approach as "clarity and relative predictability" but thinks the disadvantage of deferring to the

plaintiff's choice outweighs these attributes. Id. at 372–73. She endorses the approach of identifying the relative weight of the federal and state interests involved and granting jurisdiction to the court with the outweighing interest. Id.

[27] § 411(a).

[28] Arthur Rutenberg Homes, Inc. v. Drew Homes, Inc., 29 F.3d 1529 (11th Cir. 1994); Strategy Source, Inc. v. Lee, 233 F.Supp.2d 1 (D.D.C. 2002); Villa v. Brady Publishing, 63 U.S.P.Q.2d 1601 (N.D. Ill. 2002); Denenberg v. Berman, 64 U.S.P.Q.2d 1054 (D. Neb. 2002); City Merchandise, Inc. v. Kings Overseas Corp., 64 U.S.P.Q.2d 1061 (S.D.N.Y. 2001); Hudson's Bay Co. of New York, Inc. v. Seattle Fur Exch., 15 U.S.P.Q.2d 1316 (S.D.N.Y.1990).

[29] Apple Barrel Prods., Inc. v. Beard, 730 F.2d 384 (5th Cir. 1984); International Kitchen Exhaust Cleaning Association v. Power Washers of North America, 81 F.Supp.2d 70 (D.D.C. 2000)(allowing a plaintiff to institute an action once the Copyright Office receives the application, work and filing fee to "best effectuate the interests of justice and promote judicial economy").

[30] Subafilms, Ltd. v. MGM–Pathe Communications Co., 24 F.3d 1088 (9th Cir.1994). Cf. Los Angeles News Service v. Reuters

shows are enjoyed internationally, so authors want protection all over the world. To ensure rights for Americans in foreign markets, the United States has entered into three multilateral conventions. The central thrust of these conventions is the principle of "national treatment": "A work of an American national first generated in America will receive the same protection in a foreign nation as that country accords to the works of its own nationals."[31]

The first of these conventions, the Universal Copyright Convention ("UCC"), took effect in 1955. It was originally conceived as a temporary measure to protect the interests of United States' copyright proprietors internationally until our copyright law could be revised to conform with the requirements of the Berne Convention, the second multilateral convention. As discussed earlier, the emphasis on formalities in the 1909 Act precluded our membership in the Berne Convention while that statute was in effect. As a result of the United States' adherence to the other two conventions, the UCC has receded in importance.

The United States joined the Berne Convention in 1988 via the Berne Convention Implementation Act of 1988 which became effective on March 1, 1989.[32] The Berne Convention, which is considered "the oldest and most comprehensive copyright convention,"[33] binds approximately ninety countries to a unitary copyright law system which is administered by the World Intellectual Property Organization (WIPO).[34] The primary motivation for the United States' adherence to Berne was to make an "international statement about our moral posture in adhering to the world's foremost multilateral copyright treaty."[35] While Berne was originally "an attempt to create a universal international copyright law,"[36] it has become a "minimum protection instrument with an emphasis on national treatment and independent protection."[37] Adherence to the Berne Convention is not self-executing in the United States which means copyright protection is still vindicated by bringing suit under the Copyright Act and not directly under

---

Television International Ltd., 149 F.3d 987 (9th Cir. 1998)(allowing recovery of damages for extraterritorial exploitation of a work that was initially reproduced without authorization in the United States).

[31] Id. at 1097.

[32] Berne Convention Implementation Act of 1988, Pub. L. No. 100–568, 102 Stat. 2853 (1988). See also D. Nimmer, Nation, Duration, Violation, Harmonization: An International Copyright Proposal for the United States, 55 Law & Contemp. Probs. 211, 217 (1992).

[33] See D. Nimmer, The Impact of Berne on United States Copyright Law, 8 Cardozo Arts & Ent. L.J. 27, 27–28 (1989).

[34] See Ricketson, The 1992 Horace S. Manges Lecture—People or Machines: The

Berne Convention and the Changing Concept of Authorship, 16 Colum.-VLA J.L. & Arts 1, 2 (1991). Our adherence to the Berne Convention does not affect our membership in the UCC, which is administered by the United Nations Educational Scientific and Cultural Organization (UNESCO). See Arden, The Questionable Utility of Copyright Notice: Statutory and Nonlegal Incentives in the Post–Berne Era, 24 Loy. U. Chi. L.J. 259, 277 (1993); Tanenbaum, note 24, at 253. See WIPO's website, www.wipo.int for an introduction to the Berne Convention.

[35] See Nimmer, note 31, at 29.

[36] Stanton, Comment, Development of the Berne International Copyright Convention and Implications of United States Adherence, 13 Hous. J. Int'l L. 149 (1990).

[37] Id.

the provisions of the Berne Convention.[38] Since the United States is one of the most influential world powers and is a major exporter of intellectual property, its adherence strengthens the Berne Convention.[39] The United States' membership in the Berne Convention means any work first published in the United States will automatically be protected in other Berne countries.[40]

As discussed above, one of the primary doctrines endorsed by Berne is the lack of formalities required in order to receive copyright protection.[41] One especially important aspect of Berne is that it has reduced significantly the importance of the notice requirement. Historically, a work would fall into the public domain unless a copyright notice appeared on publicly distributed copies of the work. Even before the adoption of Berne, however, the importance of notice had declined. Under the 1909 Act, publication with notice was still essentially a prerequisite for copyright protection. Under the 1976 Act, the notice requirements were liberalized, especially with respect to the measures a creator could take to rescue her copyright even after publication without notice.[42] Now, with the adoption of Berne, copyright notice is permissive rather than mandatory for works published after the effective date of Berne.[43] Nevertheless, Berne still provides an incentive to use notice by specifying that in the case of defendants who have access to copies bearing the proper notice, courts shall not give any weight to a claim of innocent infringement in mitigation of actual or statutory damages.[44]

Berne modified the existing law on registration by providing for a dual system under which registration is a prerequisite for bringing an infringement suit for works originating in the United States but not for Berne Convention works whose country of origin is *not* the United States. This dual system arguably is not unfair to American creators because presumably they are more familiar with American Copyright Office procedures.

[38] Berne Convention Implementation Act of 1988, § 2(1).

[39] See Stanton, note 34, at 177.

[40] See 37 Pat. Trademark & Copyright J. (BNA) 462 (1989).

[41] See 134 Cong. Rec. H3082 (daily ed. May 10, 1988) ("The central feature of Berne is its prohibition of formalities.") (statement of Rep. Robert Kastenmeier); Tanenbaum, note 24, at 256–57.

[42] See § 405(a)(2)(i.e., registration for work within 5 years and a reasonable effort to add notice to all copyrights distributed after the omission is discovered).

[43] See §§ 401(a) and 402(a) (providing that copyright notice *may* be placed on protected works) (emphasis added).

[44] See §§ 401(d) and 402(d) of the 1976 Act as amended by Berne.

In addition to providing benefits in the United States, notice confers copyright protection in countries that adhere to the UCC rather than Berne. Complying with the UCC notice requirements (which are virtually the same as the 1976 Act except that the copyright symbol must be used rather than the term "copyright" or abbreviation "copr.") exempts the copyright owner from meeting the requirements of the individual country adhering to the UCC. See Tanenbaum, note 24, at 263. Another way to receive protection in countries not adhering to Berne or the UCC is to include the phrase "All Rights Reserved." This phrase confers copyright protection in some South American and Latin American countries. Id. at 263 (referring to the hemispheric treaty known as the Copyright Convention Between the United States and Other American Republics).

Moreover, all creators are treated equally regarding the need to register in order to obtain the benefits of the presumptive validity of the copyright deriving from registration,[45] and awards of statutory damages and attorney's fees.

Additionally, Berne modified § 407(a) of the 1976 Act by making the mandatory deposit provisions applicable to all U.S. works, not just those works that display a copyright notice. This modification parallels the new optional nature of notice under Berne, and also was intended to expand the Library of Congress' collection.

Another change under Berne is the elimination of the requirement of recording assignments and other transactions prior to bringing an infringement suit.[46] This applies to both works of United States' origin and foreign works. However, like other post-Berne provisions, there are incentives for recording. Recording a transfer provides actual notice to persons who search the Copyright Office records and provides constructive notice even if the records are not searched.[47] Additionally, recording a transfer with the Copyright Office protects an assignee against subsequent transfers to third parties by creating statutory priority for the party who first records.[48]

The third convention is the TRIPS agreement, discussed in greater detail in connection with the trademark chapters. This convention was implemented in 1994 but became effective as of January 1, 1996. With respect to copyright law, TRIPS essentially incorporated Berne by reference.[49] Although other changes to the copyright law as a result of TRIPS are noted in the subsequent chapters of this unit, one in particular should be mentioned at this point. Section 104A now provides that copyright protection is automatically restored to certain foreign works that are still under foreign copyright protection but which have fallen into the public domain in the United States due to a lack of compliance with our formalities or for other specified reasons.[50] The duration of United States' protection for these restored works is equivalent to what they would have received had the United States' copyright remained in effect. Section 104A has significant ramifications for reliance parties currently using the restored works. Such parties are immunized for activities prior to the copyright restoration date, but are precluded from reproducing any restored work as of the date they have effective notice that an owner intends to enforce the restored work. See also Assignment 9.

---

[45] See § 410(c).

[46] § 205(a)(1988)("[a]ny transfer of copyright ownership or other document pertaining to a copyright *may* be recorded. . . . ") (emphasis added).

[47] § 205(c).

[48] § 205(d).

[49] Information about TRIPS is available at www.wto.org

[50] For applications of this section, see Alameda Films SA de CV v. Authors Rights Restoration Corp., 331 F.3d 472 (5th Cir. 2003); Dam Things from Denmark v. Russ Berrie & Co., 290 F.3d 548 (3d Cir. 2002).

# APPENDIX

**FORM TX**
UNITED STATES COPYRIGHT OFFICE

REGISTRATION NUMBER

TX            TXU

EFFECTIVE DATE OF REGISTRATION

Month          Day          Year

**DO NOT WRITE ABOVE THIS LINE. IF YOU NEED MORE SPACE, USE A SEPARATE CONTINUATION SHEET.**

**1**

**TITLE OF THIS WORK ▼**

**PREVIOUS OR ALTERNATIVE TITLES ▼**

**PUBLICATION AS A CONTRIBUTION** If this work was published as a contribution to a periodical, serial, or collection, give information about the collective work in which the contribution appeared.    **Title of Collective Work ▼**

If published in a periodical or serial give: **Volume ▼**      **Number ▼**      **Issue Date ▼**      **On Pages ▼**

**2**

**a**

**NAME OF AUTHOR ▼**

**DATES OF BIRTH AND DEATH**
Year Born ▼      Year Died ▼

Was this contribution to the work a "work made for hire"?
☐ Yes
☐ No

**AUTHOR'S NATIONALITY OR DOMICILE**
Name of Country
OR { Citizen of ▶
Domiciled in ▶

**WAS THIS AUTHOR'S CONTRIBUTION TO THE WORK**
Anonymous?    ☐ Yes ☐ No
Pseudonymous?    ☐ Yes ☐ No
If the answer to either of these questions is "Yes," see detailed instructions.

**NATURE OF AUTHORSHIP** Briefly describe nature of the material created by this author in which copyright is claimed. ▼

**NOTE**
Under the law, the "author" of a "work made for hire" is generally the employer, not the employee (see instructions). For any part of this work that was "made for hire" check "Yes" in the space provided, give the employer (or other person for whom the work was prepared) as "Author" of that part, and leave the space for dates of birth and death blank.

**b**

**NAME OF AUTHOR ▼**

**DATES OF BIRTH AND DEATH**
Year Born ▼      Year Died ▼

Was this contribution to the work a "work made for hire"?
☐ Yes
☐ No

**AUTHOR'S NATIONALITY OR DOMICILE**
Name of country
OR { Citizen of ▶
Domiciled in ▶

**WAS THIS AUTHOR'S CONTRIBUTION TO THE WORK**
Anonymous?    ☐ Yes ☐ No
Pseudonymous?    ☐ Yes ☐ No
If the answer to either of these questions is "Yes," see detailed instructions.

**NATURE OF AUTHORSHIP** Briefly describe nature of the material created by this author in which copyright is claimed. ▼

**c**

**NAME OF AUTHOR ▼**

**DATES OF BIRTH AND DEATH**
Year Born ▼      Year Died ▼

Was this contribution to the work a "work made for hire"?
☐ Yes
☐ No

**AUTHOR'S NATIONALITY OR DOMICILE**
Name of Country
OR { Citizen of ▶
Domiciled in ▶

**WAS THIS AUTHOR'S CONTRIBUTION TO THE WORK**
Anonymous?    ☐ Yes ☐ No
Pseudonymous?    ☐ Yes ☐ No
If the answer to either of these questions is "Yes," see detailed instructions.

**NATURE OF AUTHORSHIP** Briefly describe nature of the material created by this author in which copyright is claimed. ▼

**3**

**a** **YEAR IN WHICH CREATION OF THIS WORK WAS COMPLETED** This information must be given in all cases.
◀ Year

**b** **DATE AND NATION OF FIRST PUBLICATION OF THIS PARTICULAR WORK** Complete this information ONLY if this work has been published.
Month ▶          Day ▶          Year ▶          ◀ Nation

**4**

**COPYRIGHT CLAIMANT(S)** Name and address must be given even if the claimant is the same as the author given in space 2. ▼

See instructions before completing this space.

**TRANSFER** If the claimant(s) named here in space 4 are different from the author(s) named in space 2, give a brief statement of how the claimant(s) obtained ownership of the copyright. ▼

APPLICATION RECEIVED

ONE DEPOSIT RECEIVED

TWO DEPOSITS RECEIVED

REMITTANCE NUMBER AND DATE

DO NOT WRITE HERE OFFICE USE ONLY

**MORE ON BACK ▶** • Complete all applicable spaces (numbers 5-11) on the reverse side of this page.
• See detailed instructions.    • Sign the form at line 10.

DO NOT WRITE HERE
Page 1 of _____ pages

EXAMINED BY

**FORM TX**

CHECKED BY

☐ CORRESPONDENCE
Yes

FOR
COPYRIGHT
OFFICE
USE
ONLY

**DO NOT WRITE ABOVE THIS LINE. IF YOU NEED MORE SPACE, USE A SEPARATE CONTINUATION SHEET.**

**PREVIOUS REGISTRATION** Has registration for this work, or for an earlier version of this work, already been made in the Copyright Office?

☐ Yes  ☐ No  If your answer is "Yes," why is another registration being sought? (Check appropriate box) ▼

a. ☐ This is the first published edition of a work previously registered in unpublished form.

b. ☐ This is the first application submitted by this author as copyright claimant.

c. ☐ This is a changed version of the work, as shown by space 6 on this application.

If your answer is "Yes," give: **Previous Registration Number** ▼          **Year of Registration** ▼

**5**

**DERIVATIVE WORK OR COMPILATION** Complete both space 6a & 6b for a derivative work; complete only 6b for a compilation.

a. **Preexisting Material** Identify any preexisting work or works that this work is based on or incorporates. ▼

b. **Material Added to This Work** Give a brief, general statement of the material that has been added to this work and in which copyright is claimed. ▼

**6**

See instructions
before completing
this space

**—space deleted—**

**7**

**REPRODUCTION FOR USE OF BLIND OR PHYSICALLY HANDICAPPED INDIVIDUALS**          A signature on this form at space 10, and a check in one of the boxes here in space 8, constitutes a non-exclusive grant of permission to the Library of Congress to reproduce and distribute solely for the blind and physically handicapped and under the conditions and limitations prescribed by the regulations of the Copyright Office: (1) copies of the work identified in space 1 of this application in Braille (or similar tactile symbols); or (2) phonorecords embodying a fixation of a reading of that work; or (3) both.

a ☐ Copies and Phonorecords          b ☐ Copies Only          c ☐ Phonorecords Only

**8**

See instructions

**DEPOSIT ACCOUNT** If the registration fee is to be charged to a Deposit Account established in the Copyright Office, give name and number of Account.

Name ▼          **Account Number** ▼

**9**

**CORRESPONDENCE** Give name and address to which correspondence about this application should be sent.   Name/Address/Apt/City/State/Zip ▼

Area Code & Telephone Number ►

Be sure to
give your
daytime phone
◄ number

**CERTIFICATION*** I, the undersigned, hereby certify that I am the

Check one ►

☐ author
☐ other copyright claimant
☐ owner of exclusive right(s)
☐ authorized agent of _____

of the work identified in this application and that the statements made
by me in this application are correct to the best of my knowledge.

Name of author or other copyright claimant, or owner of exclusive right(s) ▲

**Typed or printed name and date ▼** If this application gives a date of publication in space 3, do not sign and submit it before that date.

_____ date ► _____

Handwritten signature (X) ▼

**10**

**MAIL
CERTIFI-
CATE TO**

Certificate
will be
mailed in
window
envelope

Name ▼

Number/Street/Apartment Number ▼

City/State/ZIP ▼

**YOU MUST:**
• Complete all necessary spaces
• Sign your application in space 10

**SEND ALL 3 ELEMENTS
IN THE SAME PACKAGE**
1. Application form
2. Nonrefundable $20 filing fee
   in check or money order
   payable to Register of Copyrights
3. Deposit material

**MAIL TO:**
Register of Copyrights
Library of Congress
Washington, D.C. 20559

**11**

September 1991—100,000                    ☆U.S. GOVERNMENT PRINTING OFFICE: 1991-282-170/40,005

# ASSIGNMENT 7

# THE REQUIREMENTS OF ORIGINALITY AND AUTHORSHIP

## 1. INTRODUCTION

Under the 1976 Copyright Act, copyright protection is accorded to "original works of authorship fixed in any tangible medium of expression."[1] This phrase encompasses three requirements: 1) originality; 2) authorship; and 3) fixation. This Assignment explores the parameters of originality and authorship (the statutory concept of fixation is discussed in Note 5). One easily stated rule is that a work is original if it is not copied from another work.[2] According to the legislative history accompanying the 1976 Act, the standard for original works of authorship, which was already established by the courts under the 1909 Copyright Act, "does not include requirements of novelty, ingenuity, or aesthetic merit."[3] Therefore, because material capable of copyright protection does not have to be new, just original, it is much easier to obtain copyright protection, as opposed to patent protection, which requires that the materials protected be both new and original (see Assignments 17 & 18).

The application of the originality standard in copyright law has given rise to much litigation, and, as the following materials suggest, can be extremely problematic. The originality requirement is especially difficult to apply with respect to two specific areas of works protected under copyright law, compilations and derivative works, because these works are, by definition, based on material already in existence. Section 101 of the statute defines a derivative work as "a work based upon one or more preexisting works" in any "form in which a work may be recast, transformed, or adapted."[4] Section 101 defines a compilation as "a work formed by the collection and assembling of preexisting materials or of data that are selected, coordinated, or arranged in such a way that the resulting work as a whole constitutes an original work of authorship." Compilations also can include "collective works" which consist of an assembly of "separate and

---

[1] § 102.

[2] See Sheldon v. Metro–Goldwyn Pictures Corp., 81 F.2d 49 (2d Cir. 1936), cert. denied, 298 U.S. 669 (1936).

[3] H.R. Rep. No. 1476, 94th Cong., 2d Sess. 51 (1976), reprinted in 1976 U.S.C.C.A.N. 5659, 5664.

[4] The underlying work upon which a derivative work is based must be copyrightable. Ets–Hokin v. Skyy Spirits, Inc., 225 F.3d 1068 (9th Cir. 2000).

independent works in themselves.''[5] Thus, the ''compilation'' category is broader than the ''collective work'' category because the component parts of a compilation, unlike a collective work, do not necessarily have to be independently copyrightable. Section 103 of the statute is clear that although copyright protection does extend to compilations and derivative works, such protection only applies to the material ''contributed by the author of such work.''[6] Thus, cases involving these works require a determination as to whether the author has made any contributions that can be deemed sufficiently original to merit copyright protection.

## 2. PRINCIPAL PROBLEM

Although much copyright litigation today involves glitzy new technology, this case involves something ancient and precious—the Dead Sea Scrolls. The first scroll was discovered accidentally in 1947. The scroll in question in this lawsuit, however, was discovered in Cave #4 of Qumran in the Judean Desert in the 1950's. Originally, access to and study of the scrolls found in the Qumran Caves were under the authority of the Jordanian government, pursuant to its jurisdiction over Qumran at the time the scrolls were discovered. Jordan, therefore, authorized a limited international team of researchers to study the scrolls. Following the Six Day War, the scrolls were transferred from the Rockefeller Museum in Jerusalem to the State of Israel, and the Antiquities Authority continued Jordan's policy of exclusivity regarding the number and identity of researchers allowed access to the scrolls.

Initially, Harvard Professor Strugnell attempted to compile the thousands of discovered fragments into one scroll. Although Strugnell was able to identify about a hundred fragments of the scroll and match them into between sixty-seventy fragments, the enormity of the task required an individual with linguistic and Halakhic (Jewish law) knowledge which Strugnell lacked. In 1981, Professor Elisha Qimron, a Professor of Hebrew Language at Ben–Gurion University in Be'er Sheeba, joined Strugnell. Professor Qimron is the plaintiff in this lawsuit. For 11 years, Qimron engaged in deciphering the scroll, ultimately compiling a text of 120 lines. This deciphered text is critical to the study of Jewish law at the turn of the era. It reveals the basis of the schism between the Dead Sea Scroll sectarians and the dominant Jewish authorities who controlled the Jerusalem Temple. It also helps explain a number of other major Dead Sea Scrolls. Additionally, the deciphered text is important to the study of the development of the Hebrew language. In 1990, Qimron and Strugnell reached an agreement with the English Oxford University Press regarding publication of the deciphered text, along with photographs of the scroll's fragments and interpretation.

Defendant Hershel Shanks is an attorney and editor of an archaeological review published by the Biblical Archaeological Society (''BAS''). In

[5] See § 101 (defining ''collective work'' and ''compilation'').  [6] § 103(b).

1991, prior to the publication of the deciphered text by the English Oxford University Press, Shanks and BAS published in the United States a book called "Facsimile Edition of the Dead Sea Scrolls." This book contained the 120 line deciphered text and a set of nearly 1,800 photos of unpublished scroll fragments. Many observers believe that it was the publication of this work that broke the monopoly held by the scholars assigned to publish the scrolls in the 1950's. Shanks maintains that he has been a voice to all those who remained outside the research cartel. In the BAS publication, the reconstruction and deciphered text was attributed to Professor Strugnell, working "with a colleague." At the time, Professor Qimron, the "unnamed" colleague, was a junior untenured academic.

Professor Qimron promptly filed a lawsuit, charging BAS and Shanks with copyright infringement based on the publication of the reconstructed deciphered text. The trial court found in his favor, and awarded $25,000. On appeal, the primary issue is whether the deciphered text is copyrightable. Please read the following materials before considering this issue.

## 3.  MATERIALS FOR SOLUTION OF PRINCIPAL PROBLEM

A.  STATUTORY MATERIALS: §§ 101 (all definitions), 102, & 103

B.  CASES:

## Feist Publications, Inc. v. Rural Telephone Service Co.

Supreme Court of the United States, 1991.
499 U.S. 340, 111 S.Ct. 1282, 113 L.Ed.2d 358.

■ JUSTICE O'CONNOR delivered the opinion of the Court.

This case requires us to clarify the extent of copyright protection available to telephone directory white pages.

I

Rural Telephone Service Company is a certified public utility that provides telephone service to several communities in northwest Kansas. It is subject to a state regulation that requires all telephone companies operating in Kansas to annually issue an updated telephone directory. Accordingly, as a condition of its monopoly franchise, Rural publishes a typical telephone directory, consisting of white pages and yellow pages. The white pages list in alphabetical order the names of Rural's subscribers, together with their towns and telephone numbers. The yellow pages list Rural's business subscribers alphabetically by category and feature classified advertisements of various sizes. Rural distributes its directory free of charge to its subscribers, but earns revenue by selling yellow pages advertisements.

Feist Publications, Inc., is a publishing company that specializes in area-wide telephone directories. Unlike a typical directory, which covers only a particular calling area, Feist's area-wide directories cover a much larger geographical range, reducing the need to call directory assistance or consult multiple directories. The Feist directory that is the subject of this litigation covers 11 different telephone service areas in 15 counties and contains 46,878 white pages listings—compared to Rural's approximately 7,700 listings. Like Rural's directory, Feist's is distributed free of charge and includes both white pages and yellow pages. Feist and Rural compete vigorously for yellow pages advertising.

As the sole provider of telephone service in its service area, Rural quite easily obtains subscriber information. Persons desiring telephone service must apply to Rural and provide their names and addresses; Rural then assigns them a telephone number. Feist is not a telephone company, let alone one with monopoly status, and therefore lacks independent access to any subscriber information. To obtain white pages listings for its area-wide directory, Feist approached each of the 11 telephone companies operating in northwest Kansas and offered to pay for the right to use its white pages listings.

Of the 11 telephone companies, only Rural refused to license its listings to Feist. Rural's refusal created a problem for Feist, as omitting listings would have left a gaping hole in its area-wide directory, rendering it less attractive to potential yellow pages advertisers. In a decision subsequent to that which we review here, the District Court determined that this was precisely the reason Rural refused to license its listings. The refusal was motivated by an unlawful purpose "to extend its monopoly in telephone service to a monopoly in yellow pages advertising." Rural Telephone Service Co. v. Feist Publications, Inc., 737 F.Supp. 610, 622 (D.Kan.1990).

Unable to license Rural's white pages listings, Feist used them without Rural's consent. Feist removed several thousand listings that fell outside the geographic range of its area-wide directory, then hired personnel to investigate the 4,935 that remained. These employees verified the data reported by Rural and sought to obtain additional information. As a result, a typical Feist listing includes the individual's street address, whereas most of Rural's listings do not. Notwithstanding these additions, however, 1,309 of the 46,878 listings in Feist's 1983 directory were identical to listings in Rural's 1982–1983 white pages. Four of these were fictitious listings that Rural had inserted into its directory to detect copying.

Rural sued for copyright infringement in the District Court for the District of Kansas taking the position that Feist, in compiling its own directory, could not use the information contained in Rural's white pages. Rural asserted that Feist's employees were obliged to travel door-to-door or conduct a telephone survey to discover the same information for themselves. Feist responded that such efforts were economically impractical and, in any event, unnecessary because the information copied was beyond the scope of copyright protection. The District Court granted summary judgment to Rural, explaining that "courts have consistently held that telephone directories are copyrightable" and citing a string of lower court decisions. 663 F.Supp. 214, 218 (1987). In an unpublished opinion, the Court of Appeals for the Tenth Circuit affirmed "for substantially the reasons given by the district court." [J]udgt. order reported at 916 F.2d 718 (1990). We granted certiorari, 498 U.S. 808 (1990), to determine whether the copyright in Rural's directory protects the names, towns, and telephone numbers copied by Feist.

II

A

This case concerns the interaction of two well-established propositions. The first is that facts are not copyrightable; the second, that compilations of facts generally are. Each of these propositions possesses an impeccable pedigree. The truism that facts cannot obtain a valid copyright is universally understood. The most fundamental axiom of copyright law is that "no author may copyright his ideas or the facts he narrates." Harper & Row, Publishers, Inc. v. Nation Enterprises, 471 U.S. 539, 556 (1985). Rural wisely concedes this point, noting in its brief that "facts and discoveries, of course, are not themselves subject to copyright protection." At the same time, however, it is beyond dispute that compilations of facts are within the subject matter of copyright. Compilations were expressly mentioned in the Copyright Act of 1909, and again in the Copyright Act of 1976.

There is an undeniable tension between these two propositions. Many compilations consist of nothing but raw data—i.e., wholly factual information not accompanied by any original written expression. On what basis may one claim a copyright in such a work? Common sense tells us that 100 uncopyrightable facts do not magically change their status when gathered together in one place. Yet copyright law seems to contemplate that compilations that consist exclusively of facts are potentially within its scope.

The key to resolving the tension lies in understanding why facts are not copyrightable. The sine qua non of copyright is originality. To qualify for copyright protection, a work must be original to the author. See *Harper & Row*, at 547–549. Original, as the term is used in copyright, means only that the work was independently created by the author (as opposed to copied from other works), and that it possesses at least some minimal degree of creativity. 1 M. Nimmer & D. Nimmer, Copyright §§ 2.01[A], [B] (1990) (hereinafter "Nimmer"). To be sure, the requisite level of creativity is extremely low; even a slight amount will suffice. The vast majority of works make the grade quite easily, as they possess some creative spark, "no matter how crude, humble or obvious" it might be. *id.*, § 1.08[C][1]. Originality does not signify novelty; a work may be original even though it closely resembles other works so long as the similarity is fortuitous, not the result of copying. To illustrate, assume that two poets, each ignorant of the other, compose identical poems. Neither work is novel, yet both are original and, hence, copyrightable. See Sheldon v. Metro–Goldwyn Pictures Corp., 81 F.2d 49, 54 (C.A.2 1936).

Originality is a constitutional requirement. The source of Congress' power to enact copyright laws is Article I, § 8, cl.8, of the Constitution, which authorizes Congress to "secure for limited Times to Authors ... the exclusive Right to their respective writings." In two decisions from the late

19th century—The Trade–Mark Cases, 100 U.S. 82 (1879); and Burrow–Giles Lithographic Co. v. Sarony, 111 U.S. 53 (1884)—this Court defined the crucial terms "authors" and "writings." In so doing, the Court made it unmistakably clear that these terms presuppose a degree of originality.

Two 19th century Supreme Court decisions were particularly influential in addressing the originality requirement. In the *Trade–Mark Cases*, the Supreme Court addressed the constitutional scope of "writings." For a particular work to be classified "under the head of writings of authors," the Court determined, "originality is required." 100 U.S., at 94. The Court explained that originality requires independent creation plus a modicum of creativity. In *Burrow–Giles*, the Court distilled the same requirement from the Constitution's use of the word "authors." The Court defined "author," in a constitutional sense, to mean "he to whom anything owes its origin; originator; maker." 111 U.S., at 58 (internal quotation marks omitted).

The originality requirement articulated by the Supreme Court in *The Trade–Mark Cases* and *Burrow–Giles* remains the touchstone of copyright protection today. See Goldstein v. California, 412 U.S. 546, 561–562 (1973). It is the very "premise of copyright law." Miller v. Universal City Studios, Inc., 650 F.2d 1365, 1368 (C.A.5 1981).

It is this bedrock principle of copyright that mandates the law's seemingly disparate treatment of facts and factual compilations. "No one may claim originality as to facts." [Nimmer] § 2.11[A], p. 2–157. This is because facts do not owe their origin to an act of authorship. The distinction is one between creation and discovery: The first person to find and report a particular fact has not created the fact; he or she has merely discovered its existence. Census takers, for example, do not "create" the population figures that emerge from their efforts; in a sense, they copy these figures from the world around them. Denicola, Copyright in Collections of Facts: A Theory for the Protection of Nonfiction Literary Works, 81 Colum. L. Rev. 516, 525 (1981)(hereinafter Denicola). Census data therefore do not trigger copyright because these data are not "original" in the constitutional sense. Nimmer § 2.03[E]. The same is true of all facts—scientific, historical, biographical, and news of the day. "They may not be copyrighted and are part of the public domain available to every person." *Miller*, at 1369.

Factual compilations, on the other hand, may possess the requisite originality. The compilation author typically chooses which facts to include, in what order to place them, and how to arrange the collected data so that they may be used effectively by readers. These choices as to selection and arrangement, so long as they are made independently by the compiler and entail a minimal degree of creativity, are sufficiently original that Congress may protect such compilations through the copyright laws. Nimmer §§ 2.11[D], 3.03; Denicola 523, n.38. Thus, even a directory that contains absolutely no protectible written expression, only facts, meets the constitutional minimum for copyright protection if it features an original selection or arrangement. See *Harper & Row*, 471 U.S., at 547. Accord, Nimmer § 3.03.

This protection is subject to an important limitation. The mere fact that a work is copyrighted does not mean that every element of the work may be protected. Originality remains the sine qua non of copyright; accordingly, copyright protection may extend only to those components of a work that are original to the author. Patterson & Joyce, Monopolizing the Law: The Scope of Copyright Protection for Law Reports and Statutory Compilations, 36 UCLA L. Rev. 719, 800–802 (1989) (hereinafter Patterson and Joyce); Ginsburg, Creation and Commercial Value: Copyright Protection of Works of Information, 90 Colum. L. Rev. 1865, 1868, and n.12 (1990)(hereinafter Ginsburg). Thus, if the compilation author clothes facts with an original collocation of words, he or she may be able to claim a copyright in this written expression. Others may copy the underlying facts from the publication, but not the precise words used to present them. Where the compilation author adds no written expression but rather lets the facts speak for themselves, the expressive element is more elusive. The only conceivable expression is the manner in which the compiler has selected and arranged the facts. Thus, if the selection and arrangement are original, these elements of the work are eligible for copyright protection. No matter how original the format, however, the facts themselves do not become original through association.

This inevitably means that the copyright in a factual compilation is thin. Notwithstanding a valid copyright, a subsequent compiler remains free to use the facts contained in another's publication to aid in preparing a competing work, so long as the competing work does not feature the same selection and arrangement.

It may seem unfair that much of the fruit of the compiler's labor may be used by others without compensation. As Justice Brennan has correctly observed, however, this is not "some unforeseen byproduct of a statutory scheme." *Harper & Row*, 471 U.S., at 589 (dissenting opinion). It is, rather, "the essence of copyright," *ibid.*, and a constitutional requirement. The primary objective of copyright is not to reward the labor of authors, but "to promote the Progress of Science and useful Arts." Art. I, § 8, cl.8. To this end, copyright assures authors the right to their original expression, but encourages others to build freely upon the ideas and information conveyed by a work. *Harper & Row*, at 556–557. This principle, known as the idea/expression or fact/expression dichotomy, applies to all works of authorship. As applied to a factual compilation, assuming the absence of original written expression, only the compiler's selection and arrangement may be protected; the raw facts may be copied at will. This result is neither unfair nor unfortunate. It is the means by which copyright advances the progress of science and art.

This, then, resolves the doctrinal tension: Copyright treats facts and factual compilations in a wholly consistent manner. Facts, whether alone or as part of a compilation, are not original and therefore may not be copyrighted. A factual compilation is eligible for copyright if it features an original selection or arrangement of facts, but the copyright is limited to the particular selection or arrangement. In no event may copyright extend to the facts themselves.

B

As we have explained, originality is a constitutionally mandated pre-requisite for copyright protection. The Court's decisions announcing this rule predate the Copyright Act of 1909, but ambiguous language in the 1909 Act caused some lower courts temporarily to lose sight of this requirement.

The 1909 Act embodied the originality requirement, but not as clearly as it might have. See Nimmer § 2.01. The subject matter of copyright was set out in §§ 3 and 4 of the Act. Section 4 stated that copyright was available to "all the writings of an author." 35 Stat. 1076. By using the words "writings" and "author"—the same words used in Article I, § 8, of the Constitution and defined by the Court in The *Trade–Mark Cases* and *Burrow–Giles*—the statute necessarily incorporated the originality require-ment articulated in the Court's decisions. It did so implicitly, however, thereby leaving room for error.

Section 3 was similarly ambiguous. It stated that the copyright in a work protected only "the copyrightable component parts of the work." It thus stated an important copyright principle, but failed to identify the specific characteristic—originality—that determined which component parts of a work were copyrightable and which were not. Most courts correctly construed the 1909 Act, notwithstanding the less-than-perfect statutory language. They understood from this Court's decisions that there could be no copyright without originality. See Patterson & Joyce 760–761. But some courts misunderstood the statute. See, e. g., Leon v. Pacific Telephone & Telegraph Co., 91 F.2d 484 (C.A.9 1937); Jeweler's Circular Publishing Co. v. Keystone Publishing Co., 281 F. 83 (C.A.2 1922). These courts ignored §§ 3 and 4, focusing their attention instead on § 5 of the Act. Section 5, however, was purely technical in nature: It provided that a person seeking to register a work should indicate on the application the type of work, and it listed 14 categories under which the work might fall. One of these categories was "books, including composite and cyclopaedic works, directories, gazetteers, and other compilations." § 5(a). Section 5 did not purport to say that all compilations were automatically copyrighta-ble. Indeed, it expressly disclaimed any such function, pointing out that "the subject-matter of copyright is defined in section four." Nevertheless, the fact that factual compilations were mentioned specifically in § 5 led some courts to infer erroneously that directories and the like were copy-rightable per se, "without any further or precise showing of original—personal—authorship." Ginsburg 1895.

Making matters worse, these courts developed a new theory to justify the protection of factual compilations. Known alternatively as "sweat of the brow" or "industrious collection," the underlying notion was that copy-right was a reward for the hard work that went into compiling facts. The classic formulation of the doctrine appeared in *Jeweler's Circular Publishing Co.*, 281 F. at 88:

> "The right to copyright a book upon which one has expended labor in its preparation does not depend upon whether the materials which he has collected consist or not of matters which are publici juris, or whether such materials show literary skill *or originality*, either in thought or in language, or anything more than industrious collection. The man who goes through the streets of a town and puts down the names of each of the inhabitants, with their occupations and their street number, acquires material of which he is the author" (emphasis added).

The "sweat of the brow" doctrine had numerous flaws, the most glaring being that it extended copyright protection in a compilation beyond selection and arrangement—the compiler's original contributions—to the facts themselves. Under the doctrine, the only defense to infringement was independent creation. A subsequent compiler was "not entitled to take one word of information previously published," but rather had to "independently work out the matter for himself, so as to arrive at the same result from the same common sources of information." *id.* at 88–89 (internal quotations omitted). "Sweat of the brow" courts thereby eschewed the most fundamental axiom of copyright law—that no one may copyright facts or ideas.

## C

"Sweat of the brow" decisions did not escape the attention of the Copyright Office. When Congress decided to overhaul the copyright statute and asked the Copyright Office to study existing problems, the Copyright Office promptly recommended that Congress clear up the confusion in the lower courts as to the basic standards of copyrightability. The Register of Copyrights explained in his first report to Congress that "originality" was a "basic requisite" of copyright under the 1909 Act, but that "the absence of any reference to [originality] in the statute seems to have led to misconceptions as to what is copyrightable matter." Report of the Register of Copyrights on the General Revision of the U.S. Copyright Law, 87th Cong., 1st Sess., p.9 (H. Judiciary Comm. Print 1961). The Register suggested making the originality requirement explicit. *ibid.*

Congress took the Register's advice. In enacting the Copyright Act of 1976, Congress dropped the reference to "all the writings of an author" and replaced it with the phrase "original works of authorship." § 102(a). In making explicit the originality requirement, Congress announced that it was merely clarifying existing law: "The two fundamental criteria of copyright protection [are] originality and fixation in tangible form.... The phrase 'original works of authorship,' which is purposely left undefined, is intended to incorporate without change *the standard of originality established by the courts under the present [1909] copyright statute*." H.R. Rep. No. 94–1476, p.51 (1976)(emphasis added)(hereinafter H. R. Rep.); S. Rep. No. 94–473, p.50 (1975)(emphasis added) (hereinafter S. Rep.). The Copyright Office echoed this sentiment: "Our intention here is to maintain the established standards of originality.... " Supplementary Report of the

Register of Copyrights on the General Revision of U.S. Copyright Law, 89th Cong., 1st Sess., pt.6, p.3 (H. Judiciary Comm. Print 1965) (emphasis added).

To ensure that the mistakes of the "sweat of the brow" courts would not be repeated, Congress took additional measures. For example, § 3 of the 1909 Act had stated that copyright protected only the "copyrightable component parts" of a work, but had not identified originality as the basis for distinguishing those copyrightable component parts from those that were not. The 1976 Act deleted this section and replaced it with § 102(b), which identifies specifically those elements of a work for which copyright is not available: "In no case does copyright protection for an original work of authorship extend to any idea, procedure, process, system, method of operation, concept, principle, or discovery, regardless of the form in which it is described, explained, illustrated, or embodied in such work." Section 102(b) is universally understood to prohibit any copyright in facts. As with § 102(a), Congress emphasized that § 102(b) did not change the law, but merely clarified it: "Section 102(b) in no way enlarges or contracts the scope of copyright protection under the present law. Its purpose is to restate . . . that the basic dichotomy between expression and idea remains unchanged." H.R. Rep., at 57; S. Rep., at 54.

Congress took another step to minimize confusion by deleting the specific mention of "directories . . . and other compilations" in § 5 of the 1909 Act. As mentioned, this section had led some courts to conclude that directories were copyrightable per se and that every element of a directory was protected. In its place, Congress enacted two new provisions. First, to make clear that compilations were not copyrightable per se, Congress provided a definition of the term "compilation." Second, to make clear that the copyright in a compilation did not extend to the facts themselves, Congress enacted § 103.

The definition of "compilation" is found in § 101 of the 1976 Act. It defines a "compilation" in the copyright sense as "a work formed by the collection and assembling of preexisting materials or of data that are selected, coordinated, or arranged *in such a way that* the resulting work as a whole constitutes an original work of authorship" (emphasis added).

The purpose of the statutory definition is to emphasize that collections of facts are not copyrightable per se. It conveys this message through its tripartite structure, as emphasized above by the italics. The statute identifies three distinct elements and requires each to be met for a work to qualify as a copyrightable compilation: (1) the collection and assembly of pre-existing material, facts, or data; (2) the selection, coordination, or arrangement of those materials; and (3) the creation, by virtue of the particular selection, coordination, or arrangement, of an "original" work of authorship.

At first glance, the first requirement does not seem to tell us much. It merely describes what one normally thinks of as a compilation—a collection of pre-existing material, facts, or data. What makes it significant is that it is not the sole requirement. It is not enough for copyright purposes that an author collects and assembles facts. To satisfy the statutory definition, the work must get over two additional hurdles. In this way, the plain language indicates that not every collection of facts receives copyright protection. Otherwise, there would be a period after "data."

The third requirement is also illuminating. It emphasizes that a compilation, like any other work, is copyrightable only if it satisfies the originality requirement ("an original work of authorship"). Although § 102 plainly states that the originality requirement applies to all works, the point was emphasized with regard to compilations to ensure that courts would not repeat the mistake of the "sweat of the brow" courts by concluding that fact-based works are treated differently and measured by some other standard. As Congress explained it, the goal was to "make plain that the criteria of copyrightable subject matter stated in section 102 apply with full force to works . . . containing preexisting material." H.R. Rep., at 57; S. Rep., at 55.

The key to the statutory definition is the second requirement. It instructs courts that, in determining whether a fact-based work is an original work of authorship, they should focus on the manner in which the collected facts have been selected, coordinated, and arranged. This is a straight-forward application of the originality requirement. Facts are never original, so the compilation author can claim originality, if at all, only in the way the facts are presented. To that end, the statute dictates that the principal focus should be on whether the selection, coordination, and arrangement are sufficiently original to merit protection.

Not every selection, coordination, or arrangement will pass muster. This is plain from the statute. It states that, to merit protection, the facts must be selected, coordinated, or arranged "in such a way" as to render the work as a whole original. This implies that some "ways" will trigger copyright, but that others will not. Otherwise, the phrase "in such a way" is meaningless and Congress should have defined "compilation" simply as "a work formed by the collection and assembly of preexisting materials or data that are selected, coordinated, or arranged." The fact that Congress did not do so is dispositive. In accordance with "the established principle that a court should give effect, if possible, to every clause and word of a statute," Moskal v. United States, 498 U.S. 103, 109–110 (1990)(internal quotation marks omitted), we conclude that the statute envisions that there will be some fact-based works in which the selection, coordination, and arrangement are not sufficiently original to trigger copyright protection.

As discussed earlier, however, the originality requirement is not particularly stringent. A compiler may settle upon a selection or arrangement that others have used; novelty is not required. Originality requires only that the author make the selection or arrangement independently (i.e., without copying that selection or arrangement from another work), and that it display some minimal level of creativity. Presumably, the vast majority of compilations will pass this test, but not all will. There remains a narrow category of works in which the creative spark is utterly lacking or so trivial as to be virtually nonexistent. For instance, merely changing the medium or scale of a work has been negated as an original work by many authorities. See Russ VerSteeg, Rethinking Originality, 34 Wm. & Mary L. Rev. 801, 805–11 (1993). Such works are incapable of sustaining a valid copyright.

Even if a work qualifies as a copyrightable compilation, it receives only limited protection. This is the point of § 103 of the Act. Section 103 explains that "the subject matter of copyright ... includes compilations," § 103(a), but that copyright protects only the author's original contributions—not the facts or information conveyed:

> "The copyright in a compilation ... extends only to the material contributed by the author of such work, as distinguished from the preexisting material employed in the work, and does not imply any exclusive right in the preexisting material." § 103(b).

As § 103 makes clear, copyright is not a tool by which a compilation author may keep others from using the facts or data he or she has collected. "The most important point here is one that is commonly misunderstood today: copyright ... has no effect one way or the other on the copyright or public domain status of the preexisting material." H.R. Rep., at 57; S. Rep., at 55. The 1909 Act did not require, as "sweat of the brow" courts mistakenly assumed, that each subsequent compiler must start from scratch and is precluded from relying on research undertaken by another. Rather, the facts contained in existing works may be freely copied because copyright protects only the elements that owe their origin to the compiler— the selection, coordination, and arrangement of facts.

In summary, the 1976 revisions to the Copyright Act leave no doubt that originality, not "sweat of the brow," is the touchstone of copyright protection in directories and other fact-based works. Nor is there any doubt that the same was true under the 1909 Act. The 1976 revisions were a direct response to the Copyright Office's concern that many lower courts had misconstrued this basic principle, and Congress emphasized repeatedly that the purpose of the revisions was to clarify, not change, existing law. The revisions explain with painstaking clarity that copyright requires originality, § 102(a); that facts are never original, § 102(b); that the copyright in a compilation does not extend to the facts it contains, § 103(b); and that a compilation is copyrightable only to the extent that it features an original selection, coordination, or arrangement, § 101.

III

There is no doubt that Feist took from the white pages of Rural's directory a substantial amount of factual information. At a minimum, Feist copied the names, towns, and telephone numbers of 1,309 of Rural's subscribers. Not all copying, however, is copyright infringement. To establish infringement, two elements must be proven: (1) ownership of a valid copyright, and (2) copying of constituent elements of the work that are original. The first element is not at issue here; Feist appears to concede that Rural's directory, considered as a whole, is subject to a valid copyright because it contains some foreword text, as well as original material in its yellow pages advertisements.

The question is whether Rural has proved the second element. In other words, did Feist, by taking 1,309 names, towns, and telephone numbers from Rural's white pages, copy anything that was "original" to Rural? Certainly, the raw data does not satisfy the originality requirement. Facts themselves are already in existence and the "finder" of the fact is merely a discoverer, nor an author with originality. Rural may have been the first to discover and report the names, towns, and telephone numbers of its subscribers, but this data does not "owe its origin" to Rural. *Burrow–Giles*, 111 U.S., at 58. Rather, these bits of information are uncopyrightable facts; they existed before Rural reported them and would have continued to exist if Rural had never published a telephone directory. The originality requirement "rules out protecting . . . names, addresses, and telephone numbers of which the plaintiff by no stretch of the imagination could be called the author." Patterson & Joyce 776.

Rural essentially concedes the point by referring to the names, towns, and telephone numbers as "preexisting material." Section 103(b) states explicitly that the copyright in a compilation does not extend to "the preexisting material employed in the work."

The question that remains is whether Rural selected, coordinated, or arranged these uncopyrightable facts in an original way. As mentioned, originality is not a stringent standard; it does not require that facts be presented in an innovative or surprising way, only that the author can show a limited level of creativity. It is equally true, however, that the selection and arrangement of facts cannot be so mechanical or routine as to require no creativity whatsoever. The standard of originality is low, but it does exist. As this Court has explained, the Constitution mandates some minimal degree of creativity, see *The Trade–Mark Cases*, 100 U.S., at 94; and an author who claims infringement must prove "the existence of . . . intellectual production, of thought, and conception." *Burrow–Giles*, at 59–60.

The selection, coordination, and arrangement of Rural's white pages do not satisfy the minimum constitutional standards for copyright protection. As mentioned at the outset, Rural's white pages are entirely typical. Persons desiring telephone service in Rural's service area fill out an application and Rural issues them a telephone number. In preparing its white pages, Rural simply takes the data provided by its subscribers and lists it alphabetically by surname. The end product is a garden-variety white pages directory, devoid of even the slightest trace of creativity.

Rural's selection of listings could not be more obvious: It publishes the most basic information—name, town, and telephone number—about each person who applies to it for telephone service. This is "selection" of a sort, but it lacks the modicum of creativity necessary to transform mere selection into copyrightable expression. Rural expended sufficient effort to make the white pages directory useful, but insufficient creativity to make it original.

We note in passing that the selection featured in Rural's white pages may also fail the originality requirement for another reason. Feist points out that Rural did not truly "select" to publish the names and telephone numbers of its subscribers; rather, it was required to do so by the Kansas Corporation Commission as part of its monopoly franchise. See 737 F.Supp., at 612. Accordingly, one could plausibly conclude that state law dictated this selection; Rural did not.

Nor can Rural claim originality in its coordination and arrangement of facts. The white pages do nothing more than alphabetically list Rural's subscribers. This arrangement may, technically speaking, owe its origin to Rural; no one disputes that Rural undertook the task of alphabetizing the names itself. However, there is nothing remotely creative about arranging names alphabetically in a white pages directory. It is an age-old practice, firmly rooted in tradition and so commonplace that it has come to be expected as a matter of course. It is not only unoriginal, it is practically inevitable. This time-honored tradition does not possess the minimal creative spark required by the Copyright Act and the Constitution.

We conclude that the names, towns, and telephone numbers copied by Feist were not original to Rural and therefore were not protected by the copyright in Rural's combined white and yellow pages directory. As a constitutional matter, copyright protects only those constituent elements of a work that possess more than a de minimis quantum of creativity. Rural's white pages, limited to basic subscriber information and alphabetically arranged, fall short of the mark. As a statutory matter, § 101 does not afford protection from copying to a collection of facts that are selected, coordinated, and arranged in a way that utterly lacks originality. Given that some works must fail, we cannot imagine a more likely candidate. Indeed, were we to hold that Rural's white pages pass muster, it is hard to believe that any collection of facts could fail.

Because Rural's white pages lack the requisite originality, Feist's use of the listings cannot constitute infringement. This decision should not be construed as demeaning Rural's efforts in compiling its directory, but rather as making clear that copyright rewards originality, not effort. As this Court noted more than a century ago, "great praise may be due to the plaintiffs for their industry and enterprise in publishing this paper, yet the law does not contemplate their being rewarded in this way." Baker v. Selden, 101 U.S. 99, 105 (1880).

The judgment of the Court of Appeals is Reversed.

## Kregos v. Associated Press

United States Court of Appeals, Second Circuit, 1991.
937 F.2d 700, cert. denied, 510 U.S. 1112, 114 S.Ct. 1056, 127 L.Ed.2d 376 (1994).

■ NEWMAN, CIRCUIT JUDGE.

The primary issue on this appeal is whether the creator of a baseball pitching form is entitled to a copyright. The appeal requires us to consider the extent to which the copyright law protects a compiler of information. George L. Kregos appeals from the April 30, 1990, judgment of the District Court for the Southern District of New York (Gerard L. Goettel, Judge) dismissing on motion for summary judgment his copyright and trademark claims against the Associated Press ("AP") and Sports Features Syndicate, Inc. ("Sports Features"). We affirm dismissal of the trademark claims, but conclude that Kregos is entitled to a trial on his copyright claim, though the available relief may be extremely limited.

Facts

The facts are fully set forth in Judge Goettel's thorough opinion, 731 F.Supp. 113 (S.D.N.Y.1990). The reader's attention is particularly called to the appendices to that opinion, which set forth Kregos' pitching form and the allegedly infringing forms. *Id*. at 122–24. Kregos distributes to newspapers a pitching form, discussed in detail below, that displays information concerning the past performances of the opposing pitchers scheduled to start each day's baseball games. The form at issue in this case, first distributed in 1983, is a redesign of an earlier form developed by Kregos in the 1970's. Kregos registered his form with the Copyright Office and obtained a copyright. Though the form, as distributed to subscribing newspapers, includes statistics, the controversy in this case concerns only Kregos' rights to the form without each day's data, in other words, his rights to the particular selection of categories of statistics appearing on his form.

In 1984, AP began publishing a pitching form provided by Sports Features. The AP's 1984 form was virtually identical to Kregos' 1983 form. AP and Sports Features changed their form in 1986 in certain respects, which are discussed in part I(D) below.

Kregos' 1983 form lists four items of information about each day's games—the teams, the starting pitchers, the game time, and the betting odds, and then lists nine items of information about each pitcher's past performance, grouped into three categories. Since there can be no claim of a protectable interest in the categories of information concerning each day's game, we confine our attention to the categories of information concerning the pitchers' past performances. For convenience, we will identify each performance item by a number from 1 to 9 and use that number whenever referring to the same item in someone else's form.

The first category in Kregos' 1983 form, performance during the entire season, comprises two items—won/lost record (1) and earned run average (2). The second category, performance during the entire season against the opposing team at the site of the game, comprises three items—won/lost record (3), innings pitched (4), and earned run average (5). The third category, performance in the last three starts, comprises four items— won/lost record (6), innings pitched (7), earned run average (8), and men on base average (9). This last item is the average total of hits and walks given up by a pitcher per nine innings of pitching.

It is undisputed that prior to Kregos' 1983 form, no form had listed the same nine items collected in his form. Kregos pulled his categories of data from a "universe of available data." It is also undisputed that some but not all of the nine items of information had previously appeared in other forms. In the earlier forms, however, the few items common to Kregos' form were grouped with items different from those in Kregos' form.

The District Court granted summary judgment for the defendants on both Kregos' copyright and trademark claims. On the copyright side of the case, the Court ruled that Kregos lacked a copyrightable interest in his pitching form on three grounds. First, the Court concluded that Kregos' pitching form was insufficiently original in its selection of statistics to warrant a copyright as a compilation. Second, the Court concluded that, in view of the limited space available for displaying pitching forms in newspapers, the possible variations in selections of pitching statistics were so limited that the idea of a pitching form had merged into its expression. Third, the Court ruled that Kregos' pitching form was not entitled to a copyright because of the so-called "blank form" doctrine.

Discussion

I. Copyright Claim

A. Copyright for a Compilation of Facts

The basic principles concerning copyright protection for compilations of facts are clear and have recently been authoritatively restated in the Supreme Court's decision rejecting copyright protection for telephone book white pages. Feist Publications, Inc. v. Rural Telephone Service Co., Inc., 499 U.S. 340 (1991)("*Feist*"). Thus, as to compilations of facts, independent creation as to selection and arrangement will not assure copyright protection; the requirement of minimal creativity becomes an important ingredient of the test for copyright entitlement.

Prior to *Feist*, we had applied these principles to require some minimal level of creativity in two fairly recent cases that illustrate compilations of facts one of which is and one of which is not entitled to a copyright, Eckes v. Card Prices Update, 736 F.2d 859 (2d Cir.1984), and Financial Information, Inc. v. Moody's Investors Service, 808 F.2d 204 (2d Cir.1986)("*FFI*"), *cert. denied*, 484 U.S. 820 (1987). In *Eckes* we upheld a District Court's finding, made after trial, that a selection of 5,000 out of 18,000 baseball cards to be considered "premium" was entitled to a copyright. *Eckes*, 736 F.2d, at 863. In *FFI* we upheld a District Court's finding, also made after trial, that the listing of five items of information concerning municipal bond calls lacked sufficient selection to warrant a copyright; in almost all instances, the five items for the various bond issues had all appeared in "tombstone" ads, and only "minor additional research" was needed to complete the listings. *FFI*, 808 F.2d, at 208.

Kregos' pitching form presents a compilation of facts that falls between the extremes illustrated by *Eckes* and *FFI*. Kregos has selected nine items of information concerning a pitcher's performance. "The universe of available data" available only from inspection of box scores of prior games is considerably greater than nine, though perhaps not as great as the quantity of 18,000 cards in *Eckes*. For example, Kregos could have selected past performances from any number of recent starts, instead of using the three most recent starts. And he could have chosen to include strikeouts, walks, balks, or hit batters. In short, there are at least scores of available statistics about pitching performance available to be calculated from the underlying data and therefore thousands of combinations of data that a selector can choose to include in a pitching form.[a]

It cannot be said as a matter of law that in selecting the nine items for his pitching form out of the universe of available data, Kregos has failed to display enough selectivity to satisfy the requirement of originality. Whether in selecting his combination of nine items he has displayed the requisite degree of creativity is a somewhat closer question. Plainly, he has done better than the compiler in *FFI* who "selected" only the five facts about bond calls already grouped together in nearly all tombstone ads. Judge Goettel was persuaded to rule against Kregos, at least in part, because "most of the statistics ... had been established in previously existing forms." 731 F.Supp., at 118. But that observation is largely irrelevant to the issue of whether Kregos' selection of statistics displays sufficient creativity to warrant a copyright. Nearly all copyrighted compilations of facts convey facts that have been published elsewhere. Each of the cards selected for the "premium" category in *Eckes* had previously been published. To hold a valid copyright, a compiler of facts need not be a discoverer of facts. Indeed, any discovered fact, or, in Kregos' case, any newly devised statistic, would not, in and of itself, be eligible for copyright protection. It's the originality shown what the finder does with the fact that allows for copyrightability.

[T]he record discloses no prior pitching form with more than three of the pitching performance statistics that are included in Kregos' selection of nine statistics. Neither a prior identical form to his nor one which varies in only a trival degree exists. The validity of his copyright in a compilation of facts cannot be rejected as a matter of law for lack of the requisite originality and creativity.

## B. Idea/Expression Merger

The fundamental copyright principle that only the expression of an idea and not the idea itself is protectable, see Mazer v. Stein, 347 U.S. 201, 217 (1954), has produced a corollary maxim that even expression is not protected in those instances where there is only one or so few ways of expressing an idea that protection of the expression would effectively accord protection to the idea itself. Our Circuit has considered this so-called "merger" doctrine in determining whether actionable infringement has occurred, rather than whether a copyright is valid, see Durham Industries, Inc. v. Tomy Corp., 630 F.2d 905, 916 (2d Cir.1980), an approach the

---

[a] If the universe of available data included even 20 items and a selector was limited to 9 items, there would be 167,960 combinations of items available.

Nimmer treatise regards as the "better view." See 3 Nimmer on Copyright § 13.03[B][3] at 13–58 (1990). Assessing merger in the context of alleged infringement will normally provide a more detailed and realistic basis for evaluating the claim that protection of expression would inevitably accord protection to an idea.

In this case, Judge Goettel understood Kregos' idea to be "to publish an outcome predictive pitching form." 731 F.Supp., at 119. In dissent, Judge Sweet contends that Kregos' idea is that the nine statistics he has selected are the most significant ones to consider when attempting to predict the outcome of a baseball game. Unquestionably, if that is the idea for purposes of merger analysis, then merger of that idea and its expression has occurred—by definition.

Though there is room for fair debate as to the identification of the pertinent idea whenever merger analysis is applied to a compilation of facts, we think the "idea" in this case is the one as formulated by Judge Goettel. Kregos has not devised a system that he seeks to withdraw from the public domain by virtue of copyright. He does not present his selection of nine statistics as a method of predicting the outcome of baseball games. His idea is that of "an outcome predictive pitching form" in the general sense that it selects the facts that he thinks newspaper readers should consider in making their own predictions of outcomes. He does not purport to weigh the nine statistics, much less provide a method for comparing the aggregate value of one pitcher's statistics against that of the opposing pitcher in order to predict an outcome or even its probability of occurring. He has not devised a system, as had the deviser of a bookkeeping system in Baker v. Selden, 101 U.S. 99 (1879). He has compiled facts, or at least categories of facts, and selected those facts from a vast pool of information.

Though formulating the idea as "an outcome predictive pitching form," Judge Goettel applied the merger doctrine, concluding that the idea of selecting outcome predictive statistics to rate pitching performance was capable of expression in only a very limited number of ways.

As the various pitching forms in the record indicate, the past performances of baseball pitchers can be measured by a variety of statistics. Kregos' selection of categories includes three statistics for the pitcher's current season performance against the day's opponent at the site of the day's game; other charts select "at site" performance against the opponent during the prior season, and some select performance against the opponent over the pitcher's career, both home and away. Some charts include average men on base per nine innings; others do not. The data for most recent starts could include whatever number of games the compiler thought pertinent. These variations alone (and there are others) abundantly indicate that there are a sufficient number of ways of expressing the idea of rating pitchers' performances; this variety of expression precludes a ruling that the idea has merged into its expression.

In reaching this conclusion, we confess to some unease because of the risk that protection of selections of data, or, as in this case, categories of data, have the potential for according protection to ideas. Our concern may be illustrated by an example of a doctor who publishes a list of symptoms that he believes provides a helpful diagnosis of a disease. There might be many combinations of symptoms that others could select for the same purpose, but a substantial question would nonetheless arise as to whether that doctor could obtain a copyright in his list, based on the originality of his selection. If the idea that the doctor is deemed to be expressing is the general idea that the disease in question can be identified by observable symptoms, then the idea might not merge into the doctor's particular expression of that idea by his selection of symptoms. That general idea might remain capable of many other expressions. But it is arguable that the doctor has conceived a more precise idea—namely, the idea that his selection of symptoms is a useful identifier of the disease. That more limited idea can be expressed only by his selection of symptoms, and therefore might be said to have merged into his expression.

As long as selections of facts involve matters of taste and personal opinion, there is no serious risk that withholding the merger doctrine will extend protection to an idea. That was surely the case with the selection of premium baseball cards in *Eckes* where the compiler selected 5,000 premium baseball cards from over 18,000 cards. It is also true of a selection of prominent families for inclusion in a social directory. See Social Register Ass'n v. Murphy, 128 F. 116 (C.C.R.I. 1904). However, where a selection of data is the first step in an analysis that yields a precise result or even a better-than-average probability of some result, protecting the "expression" of the selection would clearly risk protecting the idea of the analysis.

Kregos' pitching form is part way along the continuum spanning matters of pure taste to matters of predictive analysis. He is doing more than simply saying that he holds the opinion that his nine performance characteristics are the most pertinent. He implies that his selections have some utility in predicting outcomes. On the other hand, he has not gone so far as to provide a system for weighing the combined value of the nine characteristics for each of two opposing pitchers and determining a probability as to which is more likely to win. Like the compilers of horse racing statistics, Kregos has been content to select categories of data that he obviously believes have some predictive power, but has left its interpretation to all sports page readers as to the likely outcomes from the sets of data he has selected. His "idea," for purposes of the merger doctrine, remains the general idea that statistics can be used to assess pitching performance rather than the precise idea that his selection yields a determinable probability of outcome. Since there are various ways of expressing that general idea, the merger doctrine need not be applied to assure that the idea will remain in the public domain.

C.  "Blank Form" Doctrine

The District Court also ruled that Kregos could not obtain a valid copyright in his pitching form because of the so-called "blank form" doctrine. The doctrine derives from the Supreme Court's decision in Baker v. Selden. The Court there denied copyright protection to blank forms contained in a book explaining a system of double-entry bookkeeping. The forms displayed an arrangement of columns and headings that permitted entries for a day, a week, or a month to be recorded on one page or two facing pages. The Court made clear that the author could not obtain copyright protection for an "art" that "might or might not have been patented" and reasoned that since the "art" was available to the public, "the ruled lines and headings of accounts must necessarily be used as incident to it." *Id.* at 104. Then, in a concluding statement that is susceptible to overreading, the Court said that "blank account-books are not the subject of copyright." *Id.* at 107. Similarly, a check book account register, a baby book for growth information and measurements for cooking or otherwise probably will not be copyrightable. Simply stated, it depends upon the pool of information from which the selection is taken.

Though there are some statements suggesting broadly that no blank forms are copyrightable, many courts have recognized that there can be protectable elements of forms that include considerable blank space.[b]

The regulations of the Copyright Office are careful to preclude copyright registration to:

> Blank forms, such as ... account books, diaries, bank checks, scorecards, address books, report forms, order forms and the like, which are designed for recording information *and do not in themselves convey information.*

37 C.F.R. § 202.1(c)(1990)(emphasis added).

Of course, a form that conveys no information and serves only to provide blank space for recording information contains no expression or selection of information that could possibly warrant copyright protection. See, e.g., John H. Harland Co. v. Clarke Checks, Inc., 711 F.2d 966, 971–72 (11th Cir.1983)(check stubs). At the same time, it should be equally obvious that a writing that does contain a *selection* of categories of information worth recording, sufficiently original and creative to deserve a copyright as a compilation of facts, cannot lose that protection simply because the work also contains blank space for recording the information. When the Copyright Office denies a copyright to scorecards or diaries that "do not in themselves convey information," it must be contemplating works with headings so obvious that their selection cannot be said to satisfy even minimal creativity (a baseball scorecard with columns headed "innings" and lines headed "players"; a travel diary with headings for "cities" "hotels," and "restaurants"). Such a work conveys no information, not just because it contains blanks, but because its selection of headings is totally uninformative. On the other hand, if a scorecard or diary contained a group of headings whose selection (or possibly arrangement) displayed cognizable creativity, the author's choice of those headings would convey to users the information that this group of categories was something out of the ordinary. See 1 Nimmer on Copyright § 2.18[C][1] at 2–201 (1990)("Thus

[b] We are concerned with protectable elements in the selection (and perhaps arrangement) of the categories of information to be recorded on the forms. There is widespread agreement that a work containing a blank form may be copyrightable because of the protectable elements of the textual matter accompanying the form.

books intended to record the events of baby's first year, or a record of a European trip, or any one of a number of other subjects, *may* evince considerable originality in suggestions of specific items of information which are to be recorded, and in the arrangement of such items.") (emphasis added; footnote omitted).

The Ninth Circuit has rejected this approach. With deference, we suggest that this critique of cases recognizing a copyright in the selection of categories of information for forms is not well taken. All forms may convey that the information called for is important (or at least worth recording), but the form-maker does not necessarily display even minimal creativity by selecting categories of "important" information. [C]ourts are obliged to determine as to forms, as with all compilations of information, whether the author's selection of categories of data to be recorded displays at least minimal creativity. The check stub in Clarke Checks was plainly deficient in this regard. However, all forms need not be denied protection simply because many of them fail to display sufficient creativity.

In the pending case, once it is determined that Kregos' selection of categories of statistics displays sufficient creativity to preclude a ruling as a matter of law that it is not a copyrightable compilation of information, that same conclusion precludes rejecting his copyright as a "blank form."

## D. Extent of Protection

Our ruling that Kregos' copyright claim survives defendants' motion for summary judgment does not, of course, mean that he will necessarily obtain much of a victory. If Kregos prevails at trial on the factual issues of originality and creativity, he will be entitled to protection only against infringement of the protectable features of his form. Only the selection of statistics might be entitled to protection. We agree entirely with Judge Goettel that nothing in Kregos' arrangement of the selected statistics displays the requisite creativity. As to the arrangement, Kregos' form is surely a "garden-variety" pitching form. The statistics are organized into the "obvious" arrangement of columns, and the form follows the pattern of most other forms: the statistics are organized into three groups, first the statistics about each pitcher's performance for the season, then the statistics about the pitcher's performance against the day's opponent, and finally the statistics concerning the pitcher's recent starts.

Even as to the selection of statistics, if Kregos establishes entitlement to protection, he will prevail only against other forms that can be said to copy his selection. That would appear to be true of the AP's 1984 form, which, as Judge Goettel noted, is "identical in virtually every sense to plaintiff's form." 731 F.Supp., at 115. Whether it is also true of the AP's current form, revised in 1986, is far less certain. That form contains six of Kregos' nine items (1, 2, 6, 7, 8, 9). It also includes four items that Kregos does not have. Three of these items concern performance against the day's opposing team—won-lost record, innings pitched, and earned run average; though these three statistics appear on Kregos' form, the AP's 1986 form shows data for the current season both home and away, whereas Kregos' form shows data for the pitcher's current season at the site of that day's game. The fourth item on the AP's 1986 form and not on Kregos' form shows the team's record in games started by that day's pitcher during the season.

The reason for doubting that the AP's 1986 form infringes Kregos' form arises from the same consideration that supports Kregos' claim to a copyright. Kregos can obtain a copyright by displaying the requisite creativity in his selection of statistics. But if someone else displays the requisite creativity by making a selection that differs in more than a trivial degree, Kregos cannot complain. Kregos contends that the AP's 1986 form makes insignificant changes from its 1984 form. But Kregos cannot have it both ways. If his decision to select, in the category of performance against the opposing team, statistics for the pitcher's current season at the site of today's game displays, in combination with his other selections, enough creativity to merit copyright protection, then a competitor's decision to select in that same category performance statistics for the pitcher's season performance both home and away may well insulate the competitor from a claim of infringement. Thus, though issues remain to be explored before any determination can be made, it may well be that Kregos will have a valid claim only as to the AP's 1984 form.

[In part II of the opinion, the court affirmed the district court's grant of summary judgment for the defendants on the trademark claims because the plaintiff did not demonstrate secondary meaning in his form.]

# APPENDIX 1

(Kregos' 1983 Pitching Fora)

THE HARTFORD COURANT: Sunday, May 6, 1984

# SCOREBOARD

## Today's Games

| Team | Probable Pitcher (H) | Time | Odds | 1984 W/L | 1984 ERA | vs.team at site W/L | vs.team at site IP | vs.team at site ERA | Last 3 starts W/L | Last 3 starts IP | Last 3 starts ERA | MBA |
|---|---|---|---|---|---|---|---|---|---|---|---|---|
| | | | | AMERICAN LEAGUE | | | | | | | | |
| DET | Wilcox (R) | | Even–6 | 3–0 | 3.34 | 0–2 | 10 | 9.00 | 2–0 | 22 | 2.05 | 11.05 |
| CLEV | Blyleven (R) | 1:35 | * | 3–2 | 3.14 | 0–0 | 6 | 3.00 | 1–1 | 22 | 3.68 | 12.68 |
| K.C. | Gura (L) | | * | 4–0 | 2.55 | 0–2 | 9⅔ | 9.31 | 2–0 | 21⅓ | 1.69 | 9.28 |
| TORN | Alexander (R) | 1:35 | 5½–6½ | 1–1 | 3.82 | * | * | * | 1–1 | 21⅔ | 2.91 | 9.97 |
| CHIC | Bannister (L) | | Even–6 | 2–2 | 5.12 | 0–1 | 8 | 2.25 | 1–1 | 19⅔ | 5.03 | 15.10 |
| BOST | Hurst (L) | 2:05 | * | 3–3 | 2.02 | 1–1 | 13⅓ | 4.73 | 2–1 | 18 | 1.50 | 15.00 |
| OAK | Warren (R) | | Even–6 | 3–3 | 3.82 | * | * | * | 2–1 | 18 | 5.00 | 15.50 |
| MINN | Hodge (L) | 2:15 | * | 0–0 | 7.20 | * | * | * | 0–0 | 5 | 7.20 | 23.40 |
| N.Y. | Fontenot (L) | | * | 0–4 | 4.88 | 1–0 | 7 | 5.14 | 0–2 | 16⅓ | 2.76 | 13.22 |
| MIL | Cocanower (R) | 2:30 | 5½–6½ | 0–4 | 3.00 | * | * | * | 0–3 | 23⅔ | 1.90 | 12.55 |
| BALT | Boddicker (R) | | 6–7 | 1–3 | 3.19 | 1–0 | 6 | 4.50 | 1–1 | 23 | 1.57 | 10.17 |
| TEX | Darwin (R) | 3:05 | * | 3–0 | 2.40 | 1–0 | 6⅔ | 0.00 | 2–0 | 25 | 1.08 | 7.54 |
| CAL | John (L) | | 5½–6½ | 2–2 | 2.04 | * | * | * | 1–1 | 21⅓ | 2.11 | 11.39 |
| SEAT | Young (L) | 4:35 | * | 2–2 | 6.52 | 1–0 | 11⅔ | 0.77 | 0–1 | 11⅔ | 8.49 | 20.83 |
| | | | | NATIONAL LEAGUE | | | | | | | | |
| ATL | McMurtry (R) | | * | 2–3 | 3.58 | 1–0 | 7 | 3.86 | 1–1 | 20⅓ | 3.10 | 13.28 |
| MONT | Lea (R) | 1:05 | 6–7 | 4–1 | 2.61 | 0–1 | 7 | 6.43 | 2–0 | 20 | 2.70 | 13.05 |
| ATL | Camp (R) | | * | 2–0 | 2.31 | 0–1 | 4 | 4.50 | 2–0 | 11⅔ | 2.31 | 10.03 |
| MONT | Palmer (R) | | 6–7 | 2–0 | 2.29 | * | * | * | 1–0 | 14⅔ | 2.45 | 5.52 |
| L.A. | Pena (R) | | * | 4–1 | 1.41 | 0–0 | 7⅔ | 2.35 | 3–0 | 24⅔ | 1.11 | 7.40 |
| PITT | McWilliams (L) | 1:35 | Pick 'em | 0–3 | 3.24 | 0–0 | 8 | 2.25 | 0–2 | 17 | 3.18 | 12.18 |
| L.A. | Valenzuela (L) | | 5½–6½ | 3–2 | 2.93 | 0–0 | 7⅓ | 3.68 | 3–0 | 27 | 0.67 | 6.33 |
| PITT | Tudor (L) | | * | 1–1 | 2.91 | * | * | * | 0–1 | 19⅓ | 4.19 | 14.43 |
| CINN | Russell (R) | | * | 1–3 | 3.14 | * | * | * | 0–2 | 22 | 1.23 | 11.45 |
| PHIL | Carlton (L) | 1:35 | 7½–8½ | 1–1 | 2.50 | 1–0 | 8 | 4.50 | 0–1 | 21 | 2.14 | 11.57 |
| HOUS | Ryan (R) | | * | 1–2 | 3.65 | 2–0 | 15⅓ | 2.30 | 0–1 | 16 | 5.06 | 12.94 |
| METS | Gooden (R) | 1:35 | Pick 'em | 2–1 | 2.63 | * | * | * | 1–0 | 19 | 0.47 | 9.95 |
| S.F. | Laskey (R) | | * | 0–3 | 2.20 | * | * | * | 0–2 | 19⅔ | 2.29 | 10.98 |
| STL | Andujar (R) | 2:15 | 6½–7½ | 4–2 | 3.09 | 0–1 | 15⅔ | 2.87 | 2–1 | 25 | 3.24 | 10.08 |
| S.D. | Show (R) | | * | 4–1 | 1.89 | 2–0 | 14 | 1.93 | 2–1 | 17⅓ | 1.56 | 10.90 |
| CUBS | Ruthven (R) | 2:20 | Even–6 | 2–2 | 5.35 | * | * | * | 0–2 | 17⅓ | 7.79 | 12.98 |

Bottom team is home team. Favored team is designated by odds beside pitcher's name. All pitching data reflects the pitcher's past performance as a "starter." 1984—Pitcher's 1984 record as "starter." Vs Team at site—Pitcher's past performance vs. today's opponent at the site of today's game. Last 3 Starts—Reflects how pitcher is currently going. Details his performance over his last three starts. W/L—Won/lost record as a "starter". IP—Innings pitched. ERA—Earned run average. MBA—Men on base average. (Average number of men allowed to reach base via hits and walks per nine innings pitched.) The odds are estimated lines. Time is Eastern Daylight Time

# APPENDIX 2

(AP' s 1984 Pitching Fora)

## FRIDAY'S PITCHERS
### American

| Away Home | Probable Pitcher | Time | Line | 1983 W–L | ERA | vs. opp. at site W–L | IP | ERA | last 3 starts W–L | IP | ERA | AHWG |
|---|---|---|---|---|---|---|---|---|---|---|---|---|
| DET | Matt Wilcox (R) | | EV–6 | 11–10 | .397 | 0–0 | 90 | 0.00 | 0–0 | 00.0 | 0.00 | 0.0 |
| at CHI | Rich Dotson (R) | 1:30 | | 22–7 | 3.22 | 1–0 | 80 | 2.25 | 0–0 | 00.0 | 0.00 | 0.0 |
| NY | John Montefusco (R) | | 5.5–6.5 | 14–4 | 3.31 | 0–0 | 00 | 00 | 000 | 00.0 | 0.00 | 0.0 |
| at TEX | Frank Tanana (L) | 7:35 | | 7–9 | 3.05 | 0–1 | 71 | 6.14 | 0–0 | 00.0 | 0.00 | 0.0 |
| CLE | Bert Blyleven (R) | | | 7–10 | 3.91 | 0–0 | 00 | 00 | 00.0 | 0.00 | 0.00 | 0.0 |
| at KC | Mark Gubicza (R) | 7:35 | PK | 0–0 | 0–0 | 0.0 | 00 | 00.0 | 0.00 | 0.00 | 0.00 | 0.0 |
| BALT | Mike Boddiker (R) | | 5.5–6.5 | 16–8 | 2.77 | 1–0 | 70 | 0.0 | 0–0 | 00.0 | 0.00 | 0.0 |
| at MINN | Mike Smithson (R) | 7:35 | | 10–11 | 3.91 | 0–0 | 00 | 0–0 | 00.0 | 0.00 | 0.00 | 0.0 |
| TOR | Doyle Alexander (R) | | 5.5–6.5 | 7–8 | 4.41 | 1–0 | 111 | 1.59 | 0–0 | 00 | 0.00 | 0.0 |
| at CAL | Steve Brown (R) | 9:30 | | 3–4 | 4.50 | 1–1 | 32 | 7.36 | 0.0 | 00.0 | 0.00 | 0.0 |
| BOST | Dennis Boyd (R) | | | 4–8 | 3.34 | 0–0 | 00 | 0–0 | 00.0 | 00.0 | 0.00 | 0.0 |
| at OAK | Larry Sorensen (R) | 9:35 | EV–6 | 12–11 | 4.24 | 0–0 | 00 | 0–0 | 0.00 | 00.0 | 0.00 | 0.0 |
| MILW | Moose Haas (R) | | 7.5–8.5 | 13–3 | 3.27 | 0–0 | 70 | 129 | 0–0 | 00.0 | 0.00 | 0.0 |
| at SEA | Matt Young (L) | 9:35 | | 11–15 | 3.27 | 0–0 | 00 | 0–0 | 00.0 | 0.00 | 0.00 | 0.0 |

### National

| Away Home | Probable Pitcher | Time | Line | 1983 W–L | ERA | vs. opp. at site W–L | IP | ERA | last 3 starts W–L | IP | ERA | AHWG |
|---|---|---|---|---|---|---|---|---|---|---|---|---|
| PHIL | Charles Hudson (R) | | EV–6 | 8–8 | 3.35 | 0–0 | 52 | 9.53 | 0–0 | 00.0 | 0.00 | 0.0 |
| at CINN | Joe Price (L) | 6:35 | | 10–6 | 3.38 | 1–0 | 81 | 1.08 | 0–0 | 0.00 | 00.0 | 0.0 |
| MONT | Bryn Smith (R) | | | 6–11 | .349 | 0–0 | 12 | 5.40 | 0–0 | 00.0 | 0.00 | 0.0 |
| at ATL | Ken Dayley (L) | 6:40 | 6–7 | 5–8 | 4.30 | 0–1 | 61 | 2.84 | 0–0 | 00.0 | 0.00 | 0.0 |
| NY | Walt Terrell (R) | | | 8–8 | 3.50 | 1–0 | 60 | 1.50 | 0–0 | 00.0 | 0.00 | 0.0 |
| at HOU | Tony Scott (R) | 7:35 | 7.5–8.5 | 10–6 | 3.72 | 1–1 | 161 | 2.20 | 0–0 | 00.0 | 0.00 | 0.0 |
| CHI | Scott Sanderson (R) | | 6.5–7.5 | 6–7 | .445 | 0–0 | 10 | 27.00 | 0–0 | 00.0 | 0.00 | 0.0 |
| at SD | Tim Lollar (L) | 9:05 | | 7–12 | 4.58 | 1–1 | 131 | 3.38 | 0–0 | 00.0 | 0.00 | 0.0 |
| PITT | John Tudor (L) | | 6.5–7.5 | 13–12 | 4.05 | 0–3 | 00 | 0–0 | 00.0 | 0.00 | 0.00 | 0.0 |
| at LA | Bob Welch (R) | 9:35 | | 15–12 | 2.65 | 0–0 | 70 | 2.57 | 0–0 | 00.0 | 0.00 | 0.0 |
| ST L | Joaquin Andujar (R) | | EV–6 | 7–16 | 4.00 | 0–1 | 80 | 5.63 | 0–0 | 00.0 | 0.00 | 0.0 |
| at SF | Bill Laskey (R) | 10:05 | | 13–10 | 4.19 | 1–0 | 90 | 1.00 | 0–0 | 00.0 | 0.00 | 0.0 |

Legend W–L Won–Lost IP Innings pitched ERA Earned run average AHWG Average hits and walks per nine innings

# APPENDIX 3

(AP' s 1984 Pitching Fora)

| | PITCHERS | LINE | 1987 W–L | ERA | TEAM REC | 1987 W–L | VS IP | OPP ERA | LAST 3 STARTS W–L | IP | ERA | AHWG |
|---|---|---|---|---|---|---|---|---|---|---|---|---|
| Minnesota | Niekro (R) | 2:35p | 7–12 | 5.00 | 6–11 | 1–1 | 10.0 | 3.60 | 1–1 | 17.2 | 4.58 | 13.2 |
| Kansas City | Gubicza (R) | 6–7 | 12–18 | 4.10 | 14–20 | 0–1 | 6.0 | 7.50 | 1–2 | 23.0 | 2.35 | 12.1 |
| Seattle | Langston (L) | 3:05p | 18–13 | 3.86 | 20–14 | 2–0 | 18.0 | 1.00 | 1–2 | 21.0 | 3.00 | 15.4 |
| Texas | Hough (R) | 5½–6½ | 18–12 | 3.78 | 22–17 | 1–0 | 12.0 | 4.50 | 1–1 | 25.0 | 2.88 | 9.7 |
| Cleveland | Farrell (R) | 3:10p | 4–1 | 3.21 | 3–5 | No Record | | | 0–1 | 21.0 | 4.71 | 14.1 |
| California | Witt (R) | 6–7 | 16–13 | 3.85 | 18–17 | No Record | | | 1–1 | 23.0 | 3.91 | 11.3 |

KEY=
  TEAM REC—Team's record in games started by today's pitcher.
  AHWG—Average hits and walks allowed per 9 innings.
  VS OPP—Pitcher's record versus this opponent, 1987 statistics.
  Copyright 1987 Sports Features Syndicate, Inc. and Computer Sports World.
  AP–NY–01–25–89 1635 EST <

■ SWEET, DISTRICT JUDGE, concurring in part and dissenting in part.

While I concur in the majority's conclusion that Kregos has displayed sufficient creativity to satisfy the *Feist Publications* standard for copyright-ability, I would affirm the district court's grant of summary judgment because I conclude that Kregos' idea here has merged into his expression.

1. Kregos' Idea

I respectfully disagree with the majority's statement that Kregos' idea was the abstract "general idea that statistics can be used to assess pitching performance," because I do not believe that the majority has set forth convincing grounds for its determination as to the idea at issue here.

In my opinion, Kregos' form constitutes an explanation of his preferred system of handicapping baseball games, and he seeks to use his copyright here to prevent others from practicing that system.

The majority characterizes Kregos' work as dealing with "matters of taste and opinion," and therefore compares it to the list of baseball card prices in Eckes v. Card Prices Update, 736 F.2d 859 (2d Cir.1984) or to a listing of socially prominent families rather than to the hypothetical doctor's diagnostic chart. In my view, both the pitching form and the diagnostic chart are expressions intended to assist in predicting particular outcomes, with the data intended to be used as a basis for that prediction. In contrast, neither the card price list nor the social register is associated with any defined event or result, and the information reported—the card prices, the names of the families—is itself the primary feature or attraction.

Finally, in light of the majority's agreement with the district court that Kregos' arrangement of the statistics was not itself creative or original, and therefore that his particular ordering is not protected, it is difficult to grasp exactly what "expression" the majority intends to protect, if not the fundamental expression that these nine items are valuable in predicting games. This difficulty becomes apparent as the majority speculates about the extent of protection to be given to Kregos' form.

2. The Application of the Merger Doctrine

As a secondary matter, I disagree with the majority's characterization of how the merger doctrine is applied in this Circuit.

I believe the proper approach requires the court first to decide whether the copyrighted work satisfies the primary requirement of creativity, then to determine whether there is merger before extending copyright protection. This is based on the wording of § 102(b) of the Copyright Act, which provides

> In no case does copyright protection for an original work of authorship extend to any idea, procedure, process, system, method of operation, concept, principle, or discovery, regardless of the form in which it is described, explained, illustrated, or embodied in such work.

I interpret this language as indicating that protection cannot be given to a work which is inseparable from its underlying idea.

The Nimmer treatise supports the majority's approach, suggesting that merger must be considered in the context of determining whether infringement has occurred rather than in deciding the issue of copyrightability. Under this approach, a court which finds that merger exists should hold that the two works in question are not "substantially similar," even where they are in fact identical, a result which I view as a not useful variety of doublespeak.

Nimmer notwithstanding, the majority of cases have rejected this approach and instead followed the method in which merger becomes an issue only when the two works in question—the copyrighted one and the alleged infringement—appear on the surface to be similar, and under which merger is used as a reason for denying all copyright protection to the plaintiff and thereby excusing the defendant's use of a similar or even identical expression.

The difference in applying these two approaches is not insignificant. Nimmer's method lends itself much more readily to the erroneous conclusion that merger is only available where the defendant has independently created an expression which happens coincidentally to be similar to the plaintiff's work. Merger is then viewed as a means of explaining the unintentional similarity between the two works—thus Nimmer's characterization of it as a means of negating substantial similarity. In other words, if a defendant has actually copied the plaintiff's work, it is unlikely to be allowed to rely on merger to avoid liability. This approach owes little if anything to the strictures of § 102(b), and instead depends on the fundamental principle of copyright law that independent creation is never infringement.

The more common approach, in which merger is considered as part of the determination of copyrightability, absolves even a defendant who has directly copied the plaintiff's work if the idea of that work is merged into the expression. I believe this approach accords more fully with both the language and the purpose of § 102(b), and serves to focus consideration on the proper definition of the idea at the outset of the inquiry.

## Hearn v. Meyer

United States District Court, S.D. New York, 1987.
664 F.Supp. 832.

■ LEISURE, DISTRICT JUDGE.

The complaint in this action seeks monetary damages, recovery of printing plates and other printing materials, and other relief for alleged copyright infringement in connection with a book authored by defendant Susan Meyer and published in 1983 by co-defendant Harry N. Abrams, Inc., entitled "A Treasury of the Great Children's Illustrators" ("Treasury"). In particular, plaintiff Michael Patrick Hearn, the author of several books and a number of articles concerning children's illustrators, contends that certain reproductions in "Treasury" of original illustrations by W.W. Denslow which were also reproduced in plaintiff's book, entitled "The Annotated Wizard of Oz", infringe plaintiff's copyright on his reproductions.

Defendants now move for summary judgment seeking the dismissal of plaintiff's claims. Defendants contend that their reproductions of plaintiff's reproductions of the originally published illustrations of W.W. Denslow do not constitute violations of the law of copyright because plaintiff's reproductions of Denslow's illustrations are not original and, therefore, are not copyrightable. For the purposes of this motion, defendants concede access to plaintiff's work. Plaintiff cross-moves for summary judgment on his claims regarding the reproductions of the illustrations.

Discussion

The legal principles governing defendants' motion are well-settled. "[A] court may determine non-infringement as a matter of law on a motion for summary judgment, either because the similarity between two works concerns only '*non*-copyrightable elements of the plaintiff's work,' or because no reasonable jury, properly instructed, could find that the two works are substantially similar." Warner Bros. Inc. v. American Broadcasting Cos., Inc., 720 F.2d 231, 240 (2d Cir.1983)(citations omitted)(emphasis in original).

A.   Copyrightable Elements

When copyright infringement is alleged, "the analysis must first be to determine exactly what the [plaintiff's] copyright covers, and then to see if there has been an infringement thereof." Axelbank v. Rony, 277 F.2d 314, 317 (9th Cir.1960). The general rule is that "[a] copyright does not give to the owner thereof an exclusive right to use the basic material, but only the exclusive right to reproduce his individual presentation of the material." Rochelle Asparagus Co. v. Princeville Canning Co., 170 F.Supp. 809, 812 (S.D.Ill.1959). Accordingly, "the fact that the same subject matter may be present in two paintings does not prove copying or infringement." Franklin Mint Corp. v. National Wildlife Art Exchange, Inc., 575 F.2d 62, 65 (3d Cir.), *cert. denied*, 439 U.S. 880 (1978). As Justice Holmes stated: "Others are free to copy the original [subject matter]. They are not free to copy the copy." *Id.* (quoting Bleistein v. Donaldson Lithographing Co., 188 U.S. 239, 249 (1903)).

B.   Plaintiff Owns No Copyright in Copies of Public Domain Reproductions of Original Illustrations

Plaintiff is the author of a book which contains reproductions, Color Plates XXII, XXVII and XLI, of three illustrations drawn by W.W. Denslow which were reproduced originally in the famous children's book, "The Wonderful World of Oz." Plaintiff concedes that the reproductions of the original illustrations appearing in "The Wonderful World of Oz" are in the public domain, having been published originally in 1900. Plaintiff argues, however, that the reproductions of these illustrations appearing in his book "The Annotated Wizard of Oz" are entitled to their own copyrights as reproductions of works of art. Plaintiff alleges that defendants violated his purported copyright by making copies of his reproductions of the 1900 reproductions of the original illustrations. Defendants move for dismissal of this claim arguing that "[n]one of the illustrations ... upon which plaintiff sues are protected by copyright." In particular, defendants argue that plaintiff's work fails to satisfy " 'the one pervading element prerequisite to

copyright protection regardless of the form of the work' ... the requirement of originality—that the work be the original product of the claimant."
L. Batlin & Son, Inc. v. Snyder, 536 F.2d 486, 489–90 (2d Cir.), *cert. denied*,
429 U.S. 857 (1976)(quoting 1 M. Nimmer, The Law of Copyright § 10, at
32 (1975)).

The requirement of "originality" stems "from the fact that, constitutionally, copyright protection may be claimed only by 'authors.' " *L. Batlin*,
536 F.2d, at 490 (quoting U.S.Const., art. I, § 8; Burrow–Giles Lithographic
Co. v. Sarony, 111 U.S. 53, 58 (1884)). "Thus, '[o]ne who has slavishly or
mechanically copied from others may not claim to be an author.' " *L.
Batlin*, 536 F.2d, at 490 (quoting 1 M. Nimmer, § 6, at 10.2). Moreover,
"[s]ince the constitutional requirement must be read into the Copyright
Act, the requirement of originality is also a statutory one." *L. Batlin*, 536
F.2d, at 490 (citing Chamberlin v. Uris Sales Corp., 150 F.2d 512 (2d
Cir.1945)). "It has been the law of this circuit for at least 30 years that in
order to obtain a copyright upon a reproduction of a work of art ... that
the work 'contain[s] some substantial, not merely trivial originality.... ' "
*L. Batlin*, 536 F.2d, at 490 (quoting *Chamberlin*, 150 F.2d, at 513).

It is clear, therefore, that to rule upon any claim for infringement of
copyright, the Court must explore the concept of originality. The Second
Circuit has noted that "[t]he test of originality is concededly one with a low
threshold in that '[a]ll that is needed ... is that the "author" contributed
something more than a "merely trivial" variation, something recognizably
"his own." ' " *id.* (quoting Alfred Bell & Co. v. Catalda Fine Arts, Inc., 191
F.2d 99, 102–03 (2d Cir.1951)). However, as the Second Circuit has stated
"[w]hile a copy of something in the public domain will not, if it be merely a
copy, support a copyright, a distinguishable variation will ... " Gerlach–
Barklow Co. v. Morris & Bendien, Inc., 23 F.2d 159, 161 (2d Cir.1927)(cited
in *L. Batlin*, 536 F.2d, at 490). Finally, it is well settled that the foregoing
principles are applicable to both reproductions of a work of art and works
of art themselves. "The requirement of substantial as opposed to trivial
variation and the prohibition of mechanical copying, both of which are
inherent in and subsumed by the concept of originality, apply to both
statutory categories." *L. Batlin*, 536 F.2d, at 490.

The Second Circuit has applied this standard in a wide variety of cases.
It has held that "mass-produced commercial objects with a minimal element of artistic craftsmanship may satisfy the statutory requirement of
such a work." *id.* at 491 (citation omitted). Nevertheless, the Second
Circuit has held that "the mere reproduction of a work of art in a different
medium should not constitute the required originality.... " *id.* (quoting 1
M. Nimmer, § 20.2 at 94). Moreover, the Court of Appeals has stated that
"the requirement of originality [cannot] be satisfied simply by the demonstration of 'physical skill' or 'special training'.... A considerably higher
degree of skill is required, true artistic skill, to make the reproduction
copyrightable." *L. Batlin*, 536 F.2d, at 491 (emphasis in original). Finally,
the Second Circuit has recognized that although "the test of 'originality'

may leave a lot to be desired, ... it is the only one we have.... " *id*. at 492.

Mindful of the foregoing principles, the Court turns to the reproductions here in dispute. The Court examined the appearance of the reproductions contained in "The Annotated Wizard of Oz" and compared them to the original reproductions of the illustrations contained in "The Wonderful World of Oz." The Court agrees with plaintiff that:

> The "Witch of the North" plate in the Annotated Wizard is greener than the original and the witch's face has a deeper yellow. The colors in the "China" plate are lighter than the original, which has a bluer sky and a deeper brown in Dorothy's dress. The cowardly lion is browner in the reproduction than the original.

The Court, however, does not share plaintiff's conclusion that "[t]hese variations enhance the copyrightability of the reproductions."

The Court notes that plaintiff does not claim that these insignificant variations were created intentionally. Moreover, plaintiff fails to argue— and this Court fails to see—how these minor variations express the plaintiff's own artistic viewpoint. In short, the Court finds that, at least with respect to the works' appearance, plaintiff's reproductions are mere slavish copies of W.W. Denslow's illustrations, as reproduced originally in "The Wonderful World of Oz." Accordingly, the Court concludes that the appearance of plaintiff's reproductions is clearly insufficient to vest them with copyright protection.

Deprived of the assistance of the appearance of his reproductions, plaintiff turns, as he must, to the alleged difficulty of the copying process itself, as a way to satisfy the requirement of originality. Plaintiff claims that "the process by which he arranged for the reproduction of the five items at issue here involved a difficult, time-consuming and concentrated artistic effort to recreate the precise colors originally employed by Denslow in the first edition of the 'Wizard of Oz.' " Plaintiff noted the specific steps he took in order to produce the illustrations:

> 1.  Photograph the key block from the original illustration, dropping all of the other colors.
>
> 2.  Have each of the secondary colors hand-drawn on acetate which would require the tracing of the original plates in India ink or with coated mylar.
>
> 3.  Then each secondary color had to be photographed individually, and each printed in one color only.
>
> 4.  Then all the plates would be printed one on top of the other to give a variety of hue and color.

Plaintiff also described the process as follows:

> The work done by the various participants was long, time-consuming, and artistic in every sense of the word. The original drawings had to be retraced by hand in three separate stages to correspond to the three separate colors, red, yellow, and blue. Every bit of grass, every check on Dorothy's dress, every bit of shine on the Tin Woodman's body had to be redrawn with pen and ink on acetate and sometimes twice or more if it

involved a secondary color, green, orange or brown, because these colors were created only by the printing of two primary colors on top of one another.... This was time consuming, exacting work because no overlapping of colors could be accepted; any overlapping would result in peculiar rather than pure secondary colors. These errors could only be seen when the proofs of the separations were made, and if any errors were discovered, again retracing by hand was required to align all carelessnesses.

In support of his attempt to cast the above described effort in a manner which would satisfy the originality requirement, plaintiff relies heavily on Alfred Bell & Co., Ltd. v. Catalda Fine Arts, Inc., 74 F.Supp. 973 (S.D.N.Y.1947), aff'd 191 F.2d 99 (2d Cir.1951); Millworth Converting Corp. v. Slifka, 276 F.2d 443 (2d Cir.1960); and Alva Studios, Inc. v. Winninger, 177 F.Supp. 265 (S.D.N.Y.1959).

In *Alfred Bell*, plaintiff, "a British print producer and dealer, ... copyrighted in the United States eight mezzotint engravings of old masters produced at its order by three mezzotint engravers." 74 F.Supp., at 974–75. Plaintiff brought the action against "a color lithographer, a dealer in lithographs and the dealer's president, [who] produced and sold color lithographs of the eight mezzotints." *Id.* at 975. It was undisputed that the subjects of the eight engravings were all well-known works of art all in the public domain. *Id.* [The District Court found] that defendants had violated plaintiff's copyright. The Second Circuit affirmed. The Court of Appeals noted that the mezzotints " 'originated' with those who made them, and ... amply met the standards imposed by the Constitution and the statute." 191 F.2d, at 104. The Second Circuit then noted:

"Again, an engraver is almost invariably a copyist, but although his work may infringe copyright in the original painting if made without the consent of the owner of the copyright therein, his work may still be original in the sense that he has employed skill and judgment in its production. He produces the resemblance he is desirous of obtaining by means very different from those employed by the painter or draughtsman from whom he copies: means which require great labour and talent. The engraver produces his effects by the management of light and shade, or as the term of his art expresses it, the *chiarooscuro* [sic]. The due degrees of light and shade are produced by different lines and dots; he who is the engraver must decide on the choice of the different lines or dots for himself, and on his choice depends the success of his print."

*id.* at 104–05 n.22.

Plaintiff contends that:

The description of the mezzotint process matches precisely what was done in this case. Instead of working on copper, the modern artisan works with pen and ink on acetate. But he must hand-draw each and every mark that must be reproduced in a single color. Indeed in this case it had to be done two or three times. Every color had to be traced or redrawn individually on acetate. Primary colors were printed on top of each other to make secondary colors. Proofs had to be pulled at every stage to check the register and density of color. There was constant redrawing and reapplication of mylar—the gummed plastic that indicates the color. The process took over a year.

Plaintiff also seeks support from *Millworth Converting* in which Judge Friendly held that plaintiff was entitled to copyright a three-dimensional embroidered effect based on a public domain two-dimensional fabric design. Judge Friendly, relying on *Alfred Bell*, noted that the plaintiff "offered substantial evidence that its creation of a three-dimensional effect, giving something of the impression of embroidery on a flat fabric, required effort and skill." 276 F.2d, at 445. Accordingly, the Second Circuit found that "plaintiff's contribution to its reproduction of this design sufficed to meet the modest requirement of a copyright proprietor 'that his work contains some substantial, not merely trivial, originality. . . . ' " *Id.* (quoting *Chamberlin*, 150 F.2d, at 513).

Finally, plaintiff cites *Alva Studios* as support for his claim of originality. In *Alva Studios*, plaintiff was engaged in the business of reproducing "three-dimensional works of art, the originals of which [were] owned by various museums throughout the United States and several foreign countries." 177 F.Supp., at 266. The subject of the dispute in *Alva Studios* was plaintiff's reproduction of Auguste Rodin's sculpture, "Hand of God." Plaintiff copyrighted its reproduction; it then sued defendant for infringement because defendant was copying plaintiff's Rodin replica and marketing products embodying this copying through retail operation. It was undisputed that the original sculpture was in the public domain.

The District Court first examined whether plaintiff satisfied the requirement of originality. The Court found that plaintiff had done so because:

> [Plaintiff's] copyrighted work embodies and resulted from its skill and originality in producing an accurate scale reproduction of the original. In a work of sculpture, this reduction requires far more than an abridgment of a written classic; great skill and originality are called for when one seeks to produce a scale reduction of a great work with exactitude.

\* \* \*

The originality and distinction between the plaintiff's work and the original also lies in the treatment of the rear side of the base. The rear side of the original base is open; that of the plaintiff's work is closed. We find that this difference when coupled with the skilled scaled sculpture is itself creative. 177 F.Supp., at 267. In addition, the Court found "that the granting of approval by the Carnegie Institute's department of Fine Arts, experts in the field, to be extremely persuasive that the plaintiff's copyrighted work is in itself a work of art which bears the stamp of originality and of skill." *Id.* at 267. Accordingly, the Court found that plaintiff's work was original.

The Court has examined the aforementioned cases and finds that although, at first blush, they appear to support plaintiff's position, careful scrutiny and analysis reveals them to be inapposite. In *Alfred Bell* the District Court's finding of originality was based primarily on plaintiff's conversion of the original art work, oil paintings done on canvas, to mezzotint engravings. The District Court emphasized that "[w]hat is original ... is the handling of the painting in another medium.... It is only this treatment in another medium which is original...." 74 F.Supp., at 976. Moreover, in *Millworth Converting* the Court based its finding of originality on plaintiff's conversion of a two-dimensional fabric design into a three-dimensional embroidered effect. Finally, in *Alva Studios*, the District Court based its finding of originality on more than just the skill of the artisan doing the reproduction; the District Court noted that it took great creativity, as well as skill, to interpret, project and transpose the original Rodin work in order to create a scale model thereof. In addition, the Court relied on substantial differences in the appearance between the reproduction and the original. Finally, the District Court based its finding of originality on the accrediting of the reproduction by an expert.

In the instant action, plaintiff has not reproduced W.W. Denslow's illustrations in another medium or form. It is undisputed that the original illustrations were previously reproduced in the first edition of "The Wonderful World of Oz" and a scrapbook of the "Wizard of Oz" musical. The publisher of "The Wonderful World of Oz" was the first to reproduce W.W. Denslow's illustrations for a book. Plaintiff's contribution is merely the reproduction of the original reproductions.[a] Moreover, although it is undisputed that plaintiff expended great effort and time in reproducing the reproductions of W.W. Denslow's illustrations, such effort and time alone are not sufficient for a finding of originality. Accordingly, the Court finds that, as a matter of law, plaintiff's reproductions of the 1900 reproductions of W.W. Denslow's illustrations are not original and are therefore, not copyrightable.

Plaintiff's last claim for the copyrightability of his reproductions of the reproductions of W.W. Denslow's original illustrations stems from the alleged public benefit he has provided by making available to the public reproductions of rarely seen reproductions of original illustrations. It is undisputed that the original W.W. Denslow drawings are unavailable. It is also agreed that the original edition of "The Wonderful World of Oz" is a "rare work" and difficult to find in libraries. Therefore, plaintiff argues that his reproductions should be protected under the copyright law. Plaintiff also suggests that "defendants could have avoided the entire problem if they had bothered to find original illustrations by Denslow, as plaintiff Hearn did.... All they have to do is find the originals themselves, rather than appropriating the work of plaintiff here."

Although the Court agrees with plaintiff that, to some extent, defendants and the public have benefited from plaintiff's work, this, in and of itself, does not mandate copyright protection for the work. There are equally sound policy reasons—regarding these concededly rare and public domain reproductions of original illustrations—which militate against

[a] There is no evidence in the record regarding the skill and effort exercised by the original publisher in reproducing W. W. Denslow's illustrations for "The Wonderful World of Oz." Presumably, such effort and skill was equal to that allegedly displayed by plaintiff.

plaintiff's position. Plaintiff must not be permitted to "monopolize rights to reproduce what are concededly rare and public domain illustrations, and hence restrict public access to them." As the Second Circuit noted:

> Absent a genuine difference between the underlying work of art and the copy of it for which protection is sought, the public interest in promoting progress in the arts—indeed, the constitutional demand, could hardly be served. To extend copyrightability to minuscule variations would simply put a weapon for harassment in the hands of mischievous copiers intent on appropriating and monopolizing public domain work.

*L. Batlin*, 536 F.2d, at 492. Thus, the alleged public benefit conferred by plaintiff is not dispositive of this question.

Accordingly, the Court finds that plaintiff's reproductions of the reproductions of W.W. Denslow's illustrations do not satisfy the originality requirement under copyright law. Plaintiff's reproductions, therefore, are not protected, as a matter of law, by copyright. Plaintiff's claims in connection with said reproductions are thus dismissed.

NOTES

**1.** *Policies underlying the originality requirement.* Why do you suppose the originality requirement under copyright law is not more rigorous? Can the originality requirement as it is applied by the court in *Feist* be criticized for being too rigorous? What is the practical effect of the originality requirement as it is currently applied? Doesn't it call for difficult line-drawing on the part of the Register that might otherwise be unnecessary? Moreover, as *Feist* suggests, the level of originality present in a given work will determine the scope of protection for that work. Thus, during the course of an infringement suit, a court will be called upon to determine the appropriate scope of protection for a copyrighted work. If such is the case, why not allow all works to be registered, regardless of their originality, and have the courts determine the appropriate scope of copyright protection? The standard for originality varies considerably abroad, and some countries invoke standards requiring significantly more than independent selection and a minimal level of creativity.[7]

How broadly written is the opinion in *Feist?* Why does the Court engage in a protected discussion of the constitutional requirement of originality? Was this discussion necessary for the Court's ultimate decision?

Interestingly, two post-*Feist* cases involving yellow page directories have somewhat similar facts but opposite results. In BellSouth Advertising & Publishing Corporation v. Donnelley Information Publishing,[8] the Eleventh Circuit held that a plaintiff's coordination and arrangement of its yellow pages listings were not sufficiently original to merit copyright protection. The court explained that the plaintiff's alphabetized listing of

[7] See Herman Cohen Jehoram, *The EC Copyright Directives, Economics and Authors' Rights*, 25 Int'l Rev. Indus. Prop. & Copyright L. 821, 828–29 (1994).

[8] 999 F.2d 1436 (11th Cir. 1993), cert. denied, 510 U.S. 1101 (1994).

business categories, together with the individual businesses listed in alphabetical order under the relevant headings was "entirely typical" and "practically inevitable" for a business telephone directory, and that " '[b]ecause this is the one way to construct a useful business directory, the arrangement has "merged" with the idea of a business directory, and thus is uncopyrightable.' "[9] In contrast, the Second Circuit in Key Publications v. Chinatown Today Publishing Enterprises, Inc.[10] found that originality in plaintiff's yellow pages selection did exist and that the defendant's publication was infringing. The plaintiff's yellow pages directory was aimed at the Chinese American community in New York City and the court affirmed the district court's finding of originality in both the arrangement and the selection of the business listings targeted for Chinese American New Yorkers. What criteria do you think are appropriate for courts to consider when determining the originality of telephone directories?

**2.** *The essence of "authorship": originality, creativity, and idea vs. expression.* In order to receive protection, the 1976 Act states that a work must be an "original work of authorship." Is there a difference between originality and a "work of authorship"? Does the work of authorship requirement mandate that the creator infuse some of her own personality into the work? Can a work be original (i.e., not copied from another source) but lack the necessary degree of creative authorship for copyright protection? On the other hand, some scholars have argued that "authorship" is nothing more than a cultural or social construct that has been invoked inappropriately to justify too much authorial control. This position reflects the postmodern view which disputes that any one work can be attributable exclusively to an "author-genius."[11] What are the implications of this position for copyright law?

Sometimes courts invoke a higher originality standard for derivative works. The court in *Hearn* quotes from a Second Circuit opinion suggesting that with respect to reproductions of artistic works, a higher degree of skill, "true artistic skill", may be required to make a reproduction copyrightable (see Section B of case where the *L. Batlin* case is quoted). Should the originality requirement be applied differently to derivative works? What does *Hearn* suggest should be the appropriate standard for derivative works?

Section 102(b) of the Copyright Act provides that "[i]n no case does copyright protection for an original work of authorship extend to any idea, procedure, process, system, method of operation, concept, principle, or discovery, regardless of the form in which it is described, explained, illustrated, or embodied in such work."[12] Interestingly, despite the fact that the Patent Act does not specifically exclude principles, discoveries, etc., the courts have uniformly interpreted it as not extending to these things. See

[9] Id. at 1442.

[10] 945 F.2d 509 (2d Cir. 1991).

[11] For a discussion of this view, see Rochelle Cooper Dreyfuss, *Collaborative Research: Conflicts on Authorship, Ownership, and Accountability,* 53 Vand. L. Rev. 1161, 1215 (2000).

[12] § 102(b).

Assignment 15. However, many of the issues decided under the guise of "originality" and "authorship" in copyright law are decided as questions about "subject matter" in patent law.

The 1990's saw a race between two groups of researchers to map the human genome. This sequencing of the DNA will allow scientists to learn about how the body operates, and to identify and treat hereditary disorders. Should the sequences by copyrightable? Should a mapping of the entire human genome (all of the chromosomes, showing where each gene is located) be copyrightable? If so, who should own the copyright–the United States, who funded the research; the institute where the work was conducted; or the researchers? Is a genetic map different from a street map, which falls under § 101's definition of "pictorial, graphic, and sculptural works"? If maps and sequences were patentable, would your answer change? See Assignment 9 (discussing work for hire) and 15 (patents on sequences).

The line between idea and expression often is extremely difficult to draw, as the major cases suggest. In fact, this inquiry really is the bottom line in many of the originality cases. In Veeck v. Southern Building Code Congress International, Inc., [13] the Fifth Circuit ruled, en banc, that building codes are copyrightable until such time as they become enacted as law, after which they enter the public domain and are not subject to the copyright holder's exclusive use. Should the enactment of a building code render the code a fact? Does the enactment of the code as law dictate that there is only one way to express the meaning of the code, thus resulting in the "idea" embodied in the law merging with the original author's expression?

Consider this hypothetical. Plaintiff is the organizer of McDonald's Charity Christmas Parade in Chicago. Plaintiff sold exclusive Chicago broadcast rights to ABC. Defendant is WGN, a local television station, which intends to telecast the parade using its own personnel and equipment, simultaneously with ABC's telecast. Plaintiff argues that the production of the parade and the parade itself is a "compilation" of creative works under §§ 101 & 103(a) under the 1976 Act. How should the Court rule?

**3.** *Protection for star pagination.* In West Publishing Co. v. Mead Data Central,[14] West was seeking to enjoin Lexis' star pagination feature which inserts page numbers from West's reporters into the body of Lexis reports, providing "jump" citations to the location in West's reporters of the material viewed on Lexis. Through the use of star pagination, Lexis users would be able to obtain the exact West reporter page number of the material viewed on Lexis without having to open up a West volume. In granting West preliminary injunctive relief, the Federal Court of Appeals for the Eighth Circuit viewed the pagination of West's volumes as an expression of its case arrangements. According to the court in *West,* there is no per se rule excluding case arrangements from protection. Instead, the inquiry centers on whether the particular arrangement meets the "origi-

[13] 293 F.3d 791 (5th Cir. 2002).

[14] 799 F.2d 1219 (8th Cir.1986), cert. denied, 479 U.S. 1070 (1987).

nality and intellectual-creation standards."[15] The court concluded that West's arrangement process is the result of "considerable labor, talent, and judgment."[16] How different are West's arrangements from the alphabetical listings involved in *Feist*?

Subsequently, Mead and West arrived at a settlement under which Mead effectively recognized West's copyright in its page numbers and numbering systems in certain state code compilations. Still, West has been involved in similar litigation with other publishers more recently. In Oasis Publishing Co. v. West Publishing Co.,[17] a federal district court in Minnesota held that West's arrangement of its cases, including the internal pagination, is an original work of authorship entitled to copyright protection. The Second Circuit disagreed with this conclusion in Matthew Bender & Co. v. West Publishing Co.[18] In that case, the court affirmed a summary judgment for Matthew Bender and held that West's star pagination's volume and page numbers are unprotected information. Additionally, the Second Circuit issued a companion opinion affirming a decision following a bench trial which allowed Hyberlaw to scan cases in West Reporters (excluding the headnotes), thus rejecting West's argument that it has a protectable copyright interest in the decisions deriving from its various editorial steps.[19] Most recently, the district court in that case concluded that West should have to pay attorney's fees in part because West was not attempting to protect an "original work of authorship" in keeping with the policies underlying copyright law.[20]

**4.** *Database protection.* In the aftermath of *Feist,* concerns have been expressed as to the viability of the database industry. Compilers argue that the Supreme Court failed to appreciate that *Feist* presented a fairly unique set of facts: the plaintiff compiled the listings at issue as a side-effect of its telephone business. Thus, the database cost it almost nothing. In contrast, many databases can be very expensive to develop. If they can be copied easily, then compilers of data are vulnerable to free rider problems that ultimately may undermine their incentives to create. This concern has prompted considerable lobbying for database legislation that would, in effect, overrule *Feist*.

Indeed, such lobbying was successful in the European Union. In 1996, a directive was issued requiring all EU members to enact copyright legislation to protect those elements of a database with sufficient originality to be eligible for such protection,[21] and also to enact sui generis legislation recognizing the right:

[15] Id. at 1225.

[16] Id.

[17] 924 F.Supp. 918 (D. Minn. 1996).

[18] 158 F.3d 693 (2d Cir. 1998).

[19] Matthew Bender & Co. v. West Publishing Co., 158 F.3d 674 (2d Cir. 1998).

[20] Matthew Bender & Co. v. West Publishing Co., 53 U.S.P.Q.2d 1436, 1438 (S.D.N.Y. 1999)(noting that West was asserting a copyright in works "consisting predominantly" of the works of the courts, and failed to delineate which portion of the works at issue were not subject to copyright protection in violation of § 403 of the 1976 Act).

[21] Council Directive 96/9/EC of 11 March 1996, on the Legal Protection of Databases, 1996 O.J. (L 77) 20, art. 3.

"for the maker of a database which shows that there has been qualitatively and/or quantitatively a substantial investment in either the obtaining, verification or presentation of the contents to prevent extraction and/or re-utilization of the whole or of a substantial part, evaluated qualitatively and/or quantitatively, of the contents of that database."[22]

Protection lasts for 15 years, but there is also a rollover provision:

"Any substantial change, evaluated qualitatively or quantitatively, to the contents of a database, including any substantial change resulting from the accumulation of successive additions, deletions or alterations, which would result in the database being considered to be a substantial new investment, evaluated qualitatively or quantitatively, shall qualify the database resulting from that investment for its own term of protection."[23]

Significantly, there is also a reciprocity provision: protection is available to non-EU nationals only if their country offers comparable protection.[24] This provision has intensified efforts for similar legislation in the United States. Although bills have been introduced, the opposition is equally fierce and to date no legislation has been enacted. The opponents have several concerns. First, they are skeptical that legislation is needed (*Feist*, after all, is now over a decade old, and the database industry has not crumbled, nor has it succumbed to European competition). Second, they are worried about the anticompetitive effects of exclusive rights in so-called sole source databases—material that cannot feasibly be collected by a second-comer (the database in *Feist* and a database comprising material from Dead Sea Scrolls are two examples). Third, they believe the rollover provision has the potential for creating perpetual protection.[25]

On the other hand, there is clearly something to the argument that even low works of authorship need financial support.[26] Indeed, that may be the reason that courts stretch the concepts of originality and authorship to protect such works as yellow pages and star pagination. It may also be why courts are so willing to enforce contract restrictions on the use of databases.[27] As between eroding *Feist* and enacting database protection, there is much to recommend the legislative route. At least Congress has the tools to balance the public interest against the asserted needs of database compilers.[28] But does *Feist* make this approach unconstitutional? Can the impact

[22] Id., art 7.

[23] Id., art. 10.

[24] Id., recital 56.

[25] See, e.g., Jonathan Band and Makoto Kono, The Database Protection Debate in the 106th Congress, 62 Ohio St. L.J. 869 (2001); J.H. Reichman and Pamela Samuelson, Intellectual Property Rights in Data?, 50 Vand. L. Rev. 51 (1997).

[26] Jane C. Ginsburg, No "Sweat"? Copyright and Other Protection of Works of Infor-

mation After Feist v. Rural Telephone, 92 Colum. L. Rev. 338 (1992).

[27] See, e.g., ProCD, Inc. v. Zeidenberg, 86 F.3d 1447 (7th Cir. 1996). See Assignments 11 and 13. The validity of such contract restrictions under state law raises the issue of whether copyright law preempts the validity of state protection for this type of subject matter.

[28] See Jane C. Ginsburg, Copyright, Common Law, and Sui Generis Protection of

of *Feist* be eliminated if database protection ultimately is crafted under a misappropriation theory that does not rely on the Copyright Clause as its source of authority? Assignment 13 discussing preemption and misappropriation bears upon this issue.

**5.** *The "fixation" requirement.* The fixation requirement also derives from § 102 of the 1976 Act, which provides that "copyright protection subsists . . . in original works of authorship fixed in any tangible medium of expression, now known or later developed, from which they can be perceived, reproduced, or otherwise communicated, either directly or with the aid of a machine or device."[29] According to the definitions section of the 1976 Act, a work is " 'fixed' in a tangible medium of expression" when, "by or under the authority of the author," it is embodied in a copy or phonorecord that is "sufficiently permanent or stable to permit it to be perceived, reproduced, or otherwise communicated for a period of more than transitory duration."[30] That section also provides: "A work consisting of sounds, images, or both, that are being transmitted, is 'fixed' for purposes of this title if a fixation of the work is being made simultaneously with its transmission."[31] Interestingly, other countries protect unfixed as well as fixed works under their copyright laws.[32]

A genre of visual art has evolved that is not confined by the canvas and instead interacts directly with the viewer and the exhibition space. Ron Athey is an HIV-positive performance artist whose work features needles, razors, knives and much blood. In one four-minute bit, he sticks thirty hypodermic needles into his arm to recall his days as a junkie.[33] Obviously, this art form would not be considered copyrightable subject matter unless it were independently fixed in some manner.[34] What other types of works would not be considered "fixed" within the meaning of the statute? What about choreography? Consider also the McDonald's parade discussed in Note 2. Does a telecast of the parade satisfy the fixation requirement? Should WGN be prevented from telecasting the parade under the circumstances described in the Note?

TRIPS altered the application of the fixation requirement in one limited respect. Regarding live musical performances, the TRIPS amendments to the copyright statute have resulted in civil and criminal liability for fixations, reproductions, transmissions, and distributions of such performances without the consent of the performers.[35] Thus, even if such a performance is not fixed by or under the authority of the copyright owner,

Databases in the United States and Abroad, 66 U. Cin. L. Rev. 151(1997).

[29] § 102(a).

[30] § 101.

[31] Id.

[32] See Paul Kuruk, *Protecting Folklore Under Modern Intellectual Property Regimes: A Reappraisal of the Tensions Between Individual and Communal Rights in Africa and* the United States, 48 Am. U.L. Rev. 769, 814 (1999)(discussing the model in Tunis).

[33] See http://www.brightlightsfilm.com/24/athey.htm

[34] See Kwall, Copyright and the Moral Right: Is an American Marriage Possible?, 38 Vand. L. Rev. 1, 75 (1985) for additional examples of performance art.

[35] § 1101. See also 18 U.S.C. § 2319A (providing for criminal penalties).

the remedial provisions of the copyright statute will be applied regarding the prohibited activities. See also Assignment 13.

# SUBJECT MATTER: USEFUL ARTICLES AND PROTECTION FOR CHARACTERS

## 1.  INTRODUCTION

Sections 102–105 of the 1976 Act deal with copyrightable subject matter. We saw in the prior Assignment that § 103 provides copyright protection for two particular categories of works—compilations and derivative works. Section 102(a) specifically lists the following general categories of works of authorship that are eligible for copyright protection: literary works; musical works; dramatic works; pantomimes and choreographic works; pictorial, graphic, and sculptural works; motion pictures and other audiovisual works; sound recordings; and architectural works.[1]

Section 102(b), by precluding copyright protection for "any idea, procedure, process, system, method of operation, concept, principle, or discovery," excludes from copyright protection matter which is functional and must remain free for all to use. Of all the categories of "works of authorship" enumerated in § 102(a), the "pictorial, graphic, and sculptural works" category has spawned the most litigation involving the extent to which functional or "useful articles" should be protected. The 1976 Act defines a "useful article" as one with "an intrinsic utilitarian function that is not merely to portray the appearance of the article or to convey information."[2] This "useful article" definition is intended to provide an exception to the protection that otherwise would extend to "pictorial, graphic, and sculptural works."[3] Further, the definition of "pictorial, graphic, and sculptural works" in § 101 provides that "the design of a useful article . . . shall be considered a pictorial, graphic, or sculptural work only if, and only to the extent that, such design incorporates pictorial, graphic, or sculptural features that can be identified separately from, and are capable of existing independently of, the utilitarian aspects of the article."[4]

---

[1] Section 102 provides that "[w]orks of authorship *include* the following categories" (emphasis added). Under the definitions provided in § 101, the term "including" is "illustrative and not limitative." Thus, it is conceivable that other categories of "works of authorship" also could be protected by copyright law in addition to those specified in § 102.

[2] § 101.

[3] See Harper House, Inc. v. Thomas Nelson, Inc., 889 F.2d 197, 202 (9th Cir.1989).

[4] § 101.

Presumably, Congress' decision to allow three-dimensional works of art to be protected by copyright law but to disallow such protection for three-dimensional works of utility stems from a concern with restraining competition.[5] Although we might question whether it is more important for works of utility to remain freely available than works of art, this judgment is reflected not only in copyright law, but also in patent and trademark law.[6] Still, although the decision to disallow protection for functional or useful subject matter may be clear, the determination as to what constitutes such subject matter often is difficult. This is one of the themes explored in the materials which follow.

The second theme of this Assignment concerns the scope of copyright protection for fictional characters. Although fictional characters are not expressly protected in the 1976 Act under an independent subject matter category, they have received varying degrees of protection by the courts as components of the underlying works in which they appear. Some commentators have argued that express copyright protection for characters is necessary,[7] while others dispute this approach.[8] The question of copyright protection for fictional characters is not only a colorful, but also an increasingly important issue in light of the increased commercial value these characters possess as a result of the burgeoning entertainment industry. After reading the following materials, decide what degree of protection for characters you believe is most appropriate.

## 2.　PRINCIPAL PROBLEM

Barney Smith seeks a copyright registration for a children's Superman costume. Warner Brothers and D.C. Comics own the copyrights in various works embodying the character Superman. Since the creation of Superman in comics in 1938, Warner and D.C. have successfully exploited their rights to Superman in various media and have licensed the character in connection with a variety of merchandising efforts. Superman's familiar attire consists of a skin-tight blue leotard with red briefs, boots, a cape, and a large "S" emblazoned in red and gold upon the chest and cape.

Barney's costume consists of a very form-fitting blue leotard, the chest of which contains a large "S" emblazoned in red and gold. Although the leotard is not particularly comfortable to wear for long periods of time,

---

[5] See House Comm. On The Judiciary, 87th Cong., 1st Sess., Copyright Law Revision, Report of the Register of Copyrights of the General Revision on the U.S. Copyright Law 13 (Comm. Print 1961).

[6] Patent law, which typically protects useful subject matter, has a far shorter duration of protection than copyright law and the standards for patent law protection are far more rigorous. See Assignment 15 (discussing standards for design patent law protection). Moreover, under trademark law, protection for the functional features of an object's trade dress is disallowed. See Assignment 3. See also Lynch, Copyright in Utilitarian Objects: Beneath Metaphysics, 16 U. Dayton L. Rev. 647, 655–657 (1991).

[7] See, e.g., Comment, Finding a Home for Fictional Characters: A Proposal for Change in Copyright Protection, 78 Cal. L. Rev. 687 (1990).

[8] See, e.g., Nevins, Copyright + Character = Catastrophe, 39 J. Copyright Soc'y 303 (1992).

many children have become extremely attached to the costume and want to use the leotard as either sleepwear or as long underwear. The costume also comes with red briefs, boots, a cape displaying the same "S" as the leotard, and an ornate mask of Superman's face. Children who wear the costume outside do not need to wear regular clothes underneath the costume since the leotard is designed to cover all the necessary parts and to keep a child sufficiently warm even on chilly October Halloween days. The costume is rather expensive, selling for $60.00.

Barney wants to obtain copyright protection for the exterior appearance of the entire costume as an integrated ensemble of its component parts, which results in the portrayal of Superman. The Copyright Register, quoting its 1991 ruling on the Registrability of Costume Designs, has denied registration based on its position that "[f]anciful costumes will be registered only upon a finding of separately identifiable pictorial and/or sculptural authorship."[9] Warner and D.C. got wind of Barney's application and want to sue him for copyright infringement. Barney retains your services in dealing with Warner and D.C. and in appealing the registration decision to the federal district court. He wants you to explain to him all of the legal issues involved in this situation and wants your opinion as to how a court is likely to rule with respect to both the registration application and a potential infringement lawsuit.

## 3.　Materials for Solution of Principal Problem

A.　STATUTORY MATERIALS: §§ 102–104, 105, 113 (a)–(c), & 120

B.　CASES:

### Baker v. Selden

Supreme Court of the United States, 1879.
101 U.S. (11 Otto) 99, 25 L.Ed. 841.

■ Mr. Justice Bradley delivered the opinion of the Court.

Charles Selden, the testator of the complainant in this case, in the year 1859 took the requisite steps for obtaining the copyright of a book, entitled "Selden's Condensed Ledger, or Book-keeping Simplified," the object of which was to exhibit and explain a peculiar system of book-keeping. In 1860 and 1861, he took the copyright of several other books, containing additions to and improvements upon the said system. The bill of complaint was filed against the defendant, Baker, for an alleged infringement of these copyrights. The latter, in his answer, denied that Selden was the author or designer of the books, and denied the infringement charged, and contends on the argument that the matter alleged to be infringed is not a lawful subject of copyright.

[9] Vol. 56 Fed. Register, No 214, 56531̸0　(November 5, 1991).

A decree was rendered for the complainant, and the defendant appealed.

The book or series of books of which the complainant claims the copyright consists of an introductory essay explaining the system of book-keeping referred to, to which are annexed certain forms or blanks, consisting of ruled lines, and headings, illustrating the system and showing how it is to be used and carried out in practice. This system effects the same results as book-keeping by double entry; but, by a peculiar arrangement of columns and headings, presents the entire operation, of a day, a week, or a month, on a single page, or on two pages facing each other, in an account-book. The defendant uses a similar plan so far as results are concerned; but makes a different arrangement of the columns, and uses different headings. If the complainant's testator had the exclusive right to the use of the system explained in his book, it would be difficult to contend that the defendant does not infringe it, notwithstanding the difference in his form of arrangement; but if it be assumed that the system is open to public use, it seems to be equally difficult to contend that the books made and sold by the defendant are a violation of the copyright of the complainant's book considered merely as a book explanatory of the system. Where the truths of a science or the methods of an art are the common property of the whole world, any author has the right to express the one, or explain and use the other, in his own way. As an author, Selden explained the system in a particular way. It may be conceded that Baker makes and uses account-books arranged on substantially the same system; but the proof fails to show that he has violated the copyright of Selden's book, or that he has infringed Selden's right in any way, unless the latter became entitled to an exclusive right in the system.

The evidence of the complainant is principally directed to the object of showing that Baker uses the same system as that which is explained and illustrated in Selden's books. It becomes important, therefore, to determine whether, in obtaining the copyright of his books, he secured the exclusive right to the use of the system or method of book-keeping which the said books are intended to illustrate and explain. It is contended that he has secured such exclusive right, because no one can use the system without using substantially the same ruled lines and headings which he has appended to his books in illustration of it. In other words, it is contended that the ruled lines and headings, given to illustrate the system, are a part of the book, and, as such, are secured by the copyright; and that no one can make or use similar ruled lines and headings, or ruled lines and headings made and arranged on substantially the same system, without violating the copyright. And this is really the question to be decided in this case. Stated in another form, the question is, whether the exclusive property in a system of book-keeping can be claimed, under the law of copyright, by means of a book in which that system is explained? The complainant's bill, and the case made under it, are based on the hypothesis that it can be.

It cannot be pretended, and indeed it is not seriously urged, that the ruled lines of the complainant's account-book can be claimed under any special class of objects, other than books, named in the law of copyright existing in 1859. The law then in force was that of 1831, and specified only books, maps, charts, musical compositions, prints, and engravings. An account-book, consisting of ruled lines and blank columns, cannot be called by any of these names unless by that of a book.

There is no doubt that a work on the subject of book-keeping, though only explanatory of well-known systems, may be the subject of a copyright; but, then, it is claimed only as a book. Such a book may be explanatory either of old systems, or of an entirely new system; and, considered as a book, as the work of an author, conveying information on the subject of book-keeping, and containing detailed explanations of the art, it may be a very valuable acquisition to the practical knowledge of the community. But there is a clear distinction between the book, as such, and the art which it is intended to illustrate. The mere statement of the proposition is so evident, that it requires hardly any argument to support it. The same distinction may be predicated of every other art as well as that of book-keeping. A treatise on the composition and use of medicines, be they old or new; on the construction and use of ploughs or watches would be the subject of copyright; but no one would contend that the copyright of the treatise would give the exclusive right to the art or manufacture described therein. The copyright of the book, if not pirated from other works, would be valid without regard to the novelty, or want of novelty, of its subject-matter. The novelty of the art or thing described or explained has nothing to do with the validity of the copyright. To give to the author of the book an exclusive property in the art described therein, when no examination of its novelty has ever been officially made, would be a surprise and a fraud upon the public. That is the province of letters-patent, not of copyright. The claim to an invention or discovery of an art or manufacture must be subjected to the examination of the Patent Office before an exclusive right therein can be obtained; and it can only be secured by a patent from the government.

The difference between the two things, letters-patent and copyright, may be illustrated by reference to the subjects just enumerated. Take the case of medicines. Certain mixtures are found to be of great value in the healing art. If the discoverer writes and publishes a book on the subject (as regular physicians generally do), he gains no exclusive right to the manufacture and sale of the medicine; he gives that to the public. If he desires to acquire such exclusive right, he must obtain a patent for the mixture as a new art, manufacture, or composition of matter. He may copyright his book, if he pleases; but that only secures to him the exclusive right of printing and publishing his book. So of all other inventions or discoveries.

The copyright of a work on mathematical science cannot give to the author an exclusive right to the methods of operation which he propounds, or to the diagrams which he employs to explain them, so as to prevent an engineer from using them whenever occasion requires. The very object of publishing a book on science or the useful arts is to communicate to the world the useful knowledge which it contains. But this object would be frustrated if the knowledge could not be used without incurring the guilt of piracy of the book. And where the art it teaches cannot be used without employing the methods and diagrams used to illustrate the book, or such as are similar to them, such methods and diagrams are to be considered as necessary incidents to the art, and given therewith to the public; not given for the purpose of publication in other works explanatory of the art, but for the purpose of practical application.

Of course, these observations are not intended to apply to ornamental designs, or pictorial illustrations addressed to the taste. Of these it may be said, that their form is their essence, and their object, the production of pleasure in their contemplation. This is their final end. They are as much the product of genius and the result of composition, as are the lines of the poet or the historian's periods. On the other hand, the teachings of science and the rules and methods of useful art have their final end in application and use; and this application and use are what the public derive from the publication of a book which teaches them. But as embodied and taught in a literary composition or book, their essence consists only in their statement. This alone is what is secured by the copyright. The use by another of the same methods of statement, whether in words or illustrations, in a book published for teaching the art, would undoubtedly be an infringement of the copyright.

Recurring to the case before us, we observe that Charles Selden, by his books, explained and described a peculiar system of book-keeping, and illustrated his method by means of ruled lines and blank columns, with proper headings on a page, or on successive pages. Now, whilst no one has a right to print or publish his book, or any material part thereof, as a book intended to convey instruction in the art, any person may practice and use the art itself which he has described and illustrated therein. The use of the art is a totally different thing from a publication of the book explaining it. The copyright of a book on book-keeping cannot secure the exclusive right to make, sell, and use account-books prepared upon the plan set forth in such book. Whether the art might or might not have been patented, is a question which is not before us. It was not patented, and is open and free to the use of the public. And, of course, in using the art, the ruled lines and headings of accounts must necessarily be used as incident to it.

The plausibility of the claim put forward by the complainant in this case arises from a confusion of ideas produced by the peculiar nature of the art described in the books which have been made the subject of copyright. In describing the art, the illustrations and diagrams employed happen to correspond more closely than usual with the actual work performed by the operator who uses the art. Those illustrations and diagrams consist of ruled lines and headings of accounts; and it is similar ruled lines and headings of accounts which, in the application of the art, the book-keeper makes with his pen, or the stationer with his press; whilst in most other cases the diagrams and illustrations can only be represented in concrete forms of wood, metal, stone, or some other physical embodiment. But the principle is the same in all. The description of the art in a book, though entitled to the benefit of copyright, lays no foundation for an exclusive claim to the art itself. The object of the one is explanation; the object of the other is use. The former may be secured by copyright. The latter can only be secured, if it can be secured at all, by letters-patent.

Another case, that of Page v. Wisden (20 L.T.N.S. 435), which came before Vice–Chancellor Malins in 1869, has some resemblance to the present. There a copyright was claimed in a cricket scoring-sheet, and the Vice–Chancellor held that it was not a fit subject for copyright, partly because it was not new, but also because "to say that a particular mode of ruling a book constituted an object for a copyright is absurd."

The conclusion to which we have come is, that blank account-books are not the subject of copyright; and that the mere copyright of Selden's book did not confer upon him the exclusive right to make and use account-books, ruled and arranged as designated by him and described and illustrated in said book.

The decree of the Circuit Court must be reversed, and the cause remanded with instructions to dismiss the complainant's bill; and it is So ordered.

## Brandir International, Inc. v. Cascade Pacific Lumber Co.

United States Court of Appeals, Second Circuit, 1987.
834 F.2d 1142.

■ Oakes, Circuit Judge.

In passing the Copyright Act of 1976 Congress attempted to distinguish between protectable "works of applied art" and "industrial designs not subject to copyright protection." See H.R. Rep. No. 1476, 94th Cong., 2d Sess. 54, reprinted in 1976 U.S. Code Cong. & Admin. News 5659, 5667 (hereinafter H.R. Rep. No. 1476). The courts, however, have had difficulty framing tests by which the fine line establishing what is and what is not copyrightable can be drawn. Once again we are called upon to draw such a line, this time in a case involving the "RIBBON Rack," a bicycle rack made of bent tubing that is said to have originated from a wire sculpture. (A photograph of the rack is contained in the appendix to this opinion.) The Register of Copyright, named as a third-party defendant under the statute, 17 U.S.C. § 411, but electing not to appear, denied copyrightability. In the subsequent suit, the district court granted summary judgment on the copyright claim to defendant Cascade Pacific Lumber Co., d/b/a Columbia Cascade Co., manufacturer of a similar bicycle rack. We affirm as to the copyright claim.

Against the history of copyright protection well set out in the majority opinion in Carol Barnhart Inc. v. Economy Cover Corp., 773 F.2d 411, 415–18 (2d Cir.1985), and in Denicola, Applied Art and Industrial Design: A Suggested Approach to Copyright in Useful Articles, 67 Minn. L. Rev. 707, 709–17 (1983), Congress adopted the Copyright Act of 1976. The "works of art" classification of the Copyright Act of 1909 was omitted and replaced by reference to "pictorial, graphic, and sculptural works," § 102(a)(5). According to the House Report, the new category was intended to supply "as clear a line as possible between copyrightable works of applied art and uncopyrighted works of industrial design." H.R. Rep. No. 1476, at 55. The statutory definition of "pictorial, graphic, and sculptural works" states that "the design of a useful article, as defined in this section, shall be considered a pictorial, graphic, or sculptural work only if, and only to the extent that, such design incorporates pictorial, graphic, or sculptural features that can be identified separately from, and are capable of existing independently of, the utilitarian aspects of the article." § 101.[a] The legislative history added gloss on the criteria of separate identity and independent existence in saying:

> On the other hand, although the shape of an industrial product may be aesthetically satisfying and valuable, the Committee's intention is not to offer it copyright protection under the bill. Unless the shape of an automobile, airplane, ladies' dress, food processor, television set, or any other industrial product contains some element that, physically or conceptually, can be identified as separable from the utilitarian aspects of that article, the design would not be copyrighted under the bill.

H.R. Rep. No. 1476, at 55.

As courts and commentators have come to realize, however, the line Congress attempted to draw between copyrightable art and noncopyrightable design "was neither clear nor new." Denicola, 67 Minn. L. Rev. at 720. One aspect of the distinction that has drawn considerable attention is the reference in the House Report to "physically *or conceptually*" (emphasis added) separable elements. The District of Columbia Circuit in Esquire, Inc. v. Ringer, 591 F.2d 796, 803–04 (D.C.Cir.1978)(holding outdoor lighting fixtures ineligible for copyright), *cert. denied*, 440 U.S. 908 (1979), called this an "isolated reference" and gave it no significance. Professor Nimmer, however, seemed to favor the observations of Judge Harold Leventhal in his concurrence in *Esquire*, who stated that "the overall legislative policy ... sustains the Copyright Office in its efforts to distinguish between the instances where the aesthetic element is conceptually severable and the instances where the aesthetic element is inextricably interwoven with the utilitarian aspect of the article." 591 F.2d at 807; see 1 Nimmer on Copyright § 2.08[B] at 2–93 to 2–96.2 (1986). But see Gerber, Book Review, 26 U.C.L.A. L. Rev. 925, 938–43 (1979)(criticizing Professor Nimmer's view on conceptual separability). Looking to the section 101 definition of works of artistic craftsmanship requiring that artistic features be "capable of existing independently of the utilitarian aspects," Professor Nimmer queries whether that requires *physical* as distinguished from *conceptual* separability, but answers his query by saying "[t]here is reason

---

[a] The statute also defines "useful article" as one "having an intrinsic utilitarian function that is not merely to portray the appearance of the article or to convey information. An article that is normally a part of a useful article is considered a 'useful article.'" § 101.

to conclude that it does not." See 1 Nimmer on Copyright § 2.08[B] at 2–96.1. In any event, in Kieselstein–Cord v. Accessories by Pearl, Inc., 632 F.2d 989, 993 (2d Cir.1980), this court accepted the idea that copyrightability can adhere in the "conceptual" separation of an artistic element. Indeed, the court went on to find such conceptual separation in reference to ornate belt buckles that could be and were worn separately as jewelry. *Kieselstein–Cord* was followed in Norris Industries, Inc. v. International Telephone & Telegraph Corp., 696 F.2d 918, 923–24 (11th Cir.), *cert. denied*, 464 U.S. 818 (1983), although there the court upheld the Register's refusal to register automobile wire wheel covers, finding no "conceptually separable" work of art. See also Trans–World Mfg. Corp. v. Al Nyman & Sons, Inc., 95 F.R.D. 95 (D.Del.1982)(finding conceptual separability sufficient to support copyright in denying summary judgment on copyrightability of eyeglass display cases).

In Carol Barnhart Inc. v. Economy Cover Corp., 773 F.2d 411 (2d Cir.1985), a divided panel of this circuit affirmed a district court grant of summary judgment of noncopyrightability of four life-sized, anatomically correct human torso forms. *Carol Barnhart* distinguished *Kieselstein–Cord*, but it surely did not overrule it. The distinction made was that the ornamented surfaces of the *Kieselstein–Cord* belt buckles "were not in any respect required by their utilitarian functions," but the features claimed to be aesthetic or artistic in the *Carol Barnhart* forms were "inextricably intertwined with the utilitarian feature, the display of clothes." 773 F.2d at 419. But cf. Animal Fair, Inc. v. Amfesco Indus., Inc., 620 F.Supp. 175, 186–88 (D.Minn.1985)(holding bear-paw design conceptually separable from the utilitarian features of a slipper), aff'd mem., 794 F.2d 678 (8th Cir. 1986). As Judge Newman's dissent made clear, the *Carol Barnhart* majority did not dispute "that 'conceptual separability' is distinct from 'physical separability' and, when present, entitles the creator of a useful article to a copyright on its design." 773 F.2d at 420.

"Conceptual separability" is thus alive and well, at least in this circuit. The problem, however, is determining exactly what it is and how it is to be applied. Judge Newman's illuminating discussion in dissent in *Carol Barnhart*, see 773 F.2d at 419–24, proposed a test that aesthetic features are conceptually separable if "the article ... stimulate[s] in the mind of the beholder a concept that is separate from the concept evoked by its utilitarian function." *Id.* at 422. This approach has received favorable endorsement by at least one commentator, W. Patry, Latman's The Copyright Law 43–45 (6th ed. 1986), who calls Judge Newman's test the "temporal displacement" test. It is to be distinguished from other possible ways in which conceptual separability can be tested, including whether the primary use is as a utilitarian article as opposed to an artistic work, and whether the article is marketable as art, [neither] of which is very satisfactory. But Judge Newman's test was rejected outright by the majority as "a standard so ethereal as to amount to a 'nontest' that would be extremely difficult, if not impossible, to administer or apply." 773 F.2d at 419 n.5.

Perhaps the differences between the majority and the dissent in *Carol Barnhart* might have been resolved had they had before them the Denicola article on Applied Art and Industrial Design: A Suggested Approach to Copyright in Useful Articles. There, Professor Denicola points out that although the Copyright Act of 1976 was an effort "to draw as clear a line as possible," in truth "there is no line, but merely a spectrum of forms and shapes responsive in varying degrees to utilitarian concerns." 67 Minn. L. Rev. at 741. He suggests that "the dominant characteristic of industrial design is the influence of nonaesthetic, utilitarian concerns" and hence concludes that copyrightability "ultimately should depend on the extent to which the work reflects artistic expression uninhibited by functional considerations."[b] *Id.* To state the Denicola test in the language of conceptual separability, if design elements reflect a merger of aesthetic and functional considerations, the artistic aspects of a work cannot be said to be conceptually separable from the utilitarian elements. Conversely, where design elements can be identified as reflecting the designer's artistic judgment exercised independently of functional influences, conceptual separability exists.

We believe that Professor Denicola's approach provides the best test for conceptual separability and, accordingly, adopt it here for several reasons. First, the approach is consistent with the holdings of our previous cases. In *Kieselstein–Cord*, for example, the artistic aspects of the belt buckles reflected purely aesthetic choices, independent of the buckles' function, while in *Carol Barnhart* the distinctive features of the torsos—the accurate anatomical design and the sculpted shirts and collars—showed clearly the influence of functional concerns. Though the torsos bore artistic features, it was evident that the designer incorporated those features to further the usefulness of the torsos as mannequins. Second, the test's emphasis on the influence of utilitarian concerns in the design process may help, as Denicola notes, to "alleviate the de facto discrimination against nonrepresentational art that has regrettably accompanied much of the current analysis." *Id.* at 745.[c] Finally, and perhaps most importantly, we think Denicola's test will not be too difficult to administer in practice. The work itself will continue to give "mute testimony" of its origins. In

---

[b] Professor Denicola rejects the exclusion of all works created with some utilitarian application in view, for that would not only overturn Mazer v. Stein, 347 U.S. 201 (1954), on which much of the legislation is based, but also "a host of other eminently sensible decisions, in favor of an intractable factual inquiry of questionable relevance." 67 Minn. L. Rev. at 741. He adds that "any such categorical approach would also undermine the legislative determination to preserve an artist's ability to exploit utilitarian markets." *Id.* (citing § 113(a)(1976)).

[c] We are reminded not only by Judge Gesell in the district court in *Esquire*, 414 F.Supp. 939, 941 (D.D.C.1976), but by Holmes in Bleistein v. Donaldson Lithographing Co., 188 U.S. 239, 251–52 (1903), by Mazer v. Stein, 347 U.S. at 214, and by numerous other opinions, that we judges should not let our own view of styles of art interfere with the decisionmaking process in this area. Denicola suggests that the shape of a Mickey Mouse telephone is copyrightable because its form is independent of function, and "[a] telephone shape owing more to Arp, Brancusi, or Moore than Disney may be equally divorced from utilitarian influence." 67 Minn. L. Rev. at 746.

addition, the parties will be required to present evidence relating to the design process and the nature of the work, with the trier of fact making the determination whether the aesthetic design elements are significantly influenced by functional considerations.

Turning now to the facts of this case, we note first that Brandir contends, and its chief owner David Levine testified, that the original design of the RIBBON Rack stemmed from wire sculptures that Levine had created, each formed from one continuous undulating piece of wire. These sculptures were, he said, created and displayed in his home as a means of personal expression, but apparently were never sold or displayed elsewhere. He also created a wire sculpture in the shape of a bicycle and states that he did not give any thought to the utilitarian application of any of his sculptures until he accidentally juxtaposed the bicycle sculpture with one of the selfstanding wire sculptures. It was not until November 1978 that Levine seriously began pursuing the utilitarian application of his sculptures, when a friend, G. Duff Bailey, a bicycle buff and author of numerous articles about urban cycling, was at Levine's home and informed him that the sculptures would make excellent bicycle racks, permitting bicycles to be parked under the overloops as well as on top of the underloops. Following this meeting, Levine met several times with Bailey and others, completing the designs for the RIBBON Rack by the use of a vacuum cleaner hose, and submitting his drawings to a fabricator complete with dimensions. The Brandir RIBBON Rack began being nationally advertised and promoted for sale in September 1979.

In November 1982 Levine discovered that another company, Cascade Pacific Lumber Co., was selling a similar product. Thereafter, beginning in December 1982, a copyright notice was placed on all RIBBON Racks before shipment and on December 10, 1982, five copyright applications for registration were submitted to the Copyright Office. The Copyright Office refused registration by letter, stating that the RIBBON Rack did not contain any element that was "capable of independent existence as a copyrightable pictorial, graphic or sculptural work apart from the shape of the useful article." An appeal to the Copyright Office was denied by letter dated March 23, 1983, refusing registration on the above ground and alternatively on the ground that the design lacked originality, consisting of "nothing more than a familiar public domain symbol." In February 1984, after the denial of the second appeal of the examiner's decision, Brandir sent letters to customers enclosing copyright notices to be placed on racks sold prior to December 1982.

Between September 1979 and August 1982 Brandir spent some $38,500 for advertising and promoting the RIBBON Rack, including some 85,000 pieces of promotional literature to architects and landscape architects. Additionally, since October 1982 Brandir has spent some $66,000, including full-, half-, and quarter-page advertisements in architectural magazines such as Landscape Architecture, Progressive Architecture, and Architectural Record, indeed winning an advertising award from Progressive Architecture in January 1983. The RIBBON Rack has been featured in Popular

Science, Art and Architecture, and Design 384 magazines, and it won an Industrial Designers Society of America design award in the spring of 1980. In the spring of 1984 the RIBBON Rack was selected from 200 designs to be included among 77 of the designs exhibited at the Katonah Gallery in an exhibition entitled "The Product of Design: An Exploration of the Industrial Design Process," an exhibition that was written up in the New York Times.

Sales of the RIBBON Rack from September 1979 through January 1985 were in excess of $1,367,000. Prior to the time Cascade Pacific began offering for sale its bicycle rack in August 1982, Brandir's sales were $436,000. The price of the RIBBON Rack ranges from $395 up to $2,025 for a stainless steel model and generally depends on the size of the rack, one of the most popular being the RB–7, selling for $485.

Applying Professor Denicola's test to the RIBBON Rack, we find that the rack is not copyrightable. It seems clear that the form of the rack is influenced in significant measure by utilitarian concerns and thus any aesthetic elements cannot be said to be conceptually separable from the utilitarian elements. This is true even though the sculptures which inspired the RIBBON Rack may well have been—the issue of originality aside— copyrightable.

Brandir argues correctly that a copyrighted work of art does not lose its protected status merely because it subsequently is put to a functional use. The Supreme Court so held in Mazer v. Stein, 347 U.S. 201 (1954), and Congress specifically intended to accept and codify *Mazer* in section 101 of the Copyright Act of 1976. See H.R. Rep. No. 1476 at 54–55. The district court thus erred in ruling that, whatever the RIBBON Rack's origins, Brandir's commercialization of the rack disposed of the issue of its copyrightability.

Had Brandir merely adopted one of the existing sculptures as a bicycle rack, neither the application to a utilitarian end nor commercialization of that use would have caused the object to forfeit its copyrighted status. Comparison of the RIBBON Rack with the earlier sculptures, however, reveals that while the rack may have been derived in part from one of more "works of art," it is in its final form essentially a product of industrial design. In creating the RIBBON Rack, the designer has clearly adapted the original aesthetic elements to accommodate and further a utilitarian purpose. These altered design features of the RIBBON Rack, including the spacesaving, open design achieved by widening the upper loops to permit parking under as well as over the rack's curves, the straightened vertical elements that allow in-and above-ground installation of the rack, the ability to fit all types of bicycles and mopeds, and the heavy-gauged tubular construction of rustproof galvanized steel, are all features that combine to make for a safe, secure, and maintenance-free system of parking bicycles and mopeds. Its undulating shape is said in Progressive Architecture, January 1982, to permit double the storage of conventional bicycle racks. Moreover, the rack is manufactured from 2 3/8–inch standard steam pipe that is bent into form, the six-inch radius of the bends evidently resulting from bending the pipe according to a standard formula that yields bends having a radius equal to three times the nominal internal diameter of the pipe.

Brandir argues that its RIBBON Rack can and should be characterized as a sculptural work of art within the minimalist art movement. Minimalist sculpture's most outstanding feature is said to be its clarity and simplicity, in that it often takes the form of geometric shapes, lines, and forms that are pure and free of ornamentation and void of association. As Brandir's expert put it, "The meaning is to be found in, within, around and outside the work of art, allowing the artistic sensation to be experienced as well as intellectualized." People who use Foley Square in New York City see in the form of minimalist art the "Tilted Arc," which is on the plaza at 26 Federal Plaza. Numerous museums have had exhibitions of such art, and the school of minimalist art has many admirers.

It is unnecessary to determine whether to the art world the RIBBON Rack properly would be considered an example of minimalist sculpture. The result under the copyright statute is not changed. Using the test we have adopted, it is not enough that, to paraphrase Judge Newman, the rack may stimulate in the mind of the reasonable observer a concept separate from the bicycle rack concept. While the RIBBON Rack may be worthy of admiration for its aesthetic qualities alone, it remains nonetheless the product of industrial design. Form and function are inextricably intertwined in the rack, its ultimate design being as much the result of utilitarian pressures as aesthetic choices. Indeed, the visually pleasing proportions and symmetricalness of the rack represent design changes made in response to functional concerns. Judging from the awards the rack has received, it would seem in fact that Brandir has achieved with the RIBBON Rack the highest goal of modern industrial design, that is, the harmonious fusion of function and aesthetics. Thus there remains no artistic element of the RIBBON Rack that can be identified as separate and "capable of existing independently of the utilitarian aspects of the article." Accordingly, we must affirm on the copyright claim.

## APPENDIX 1

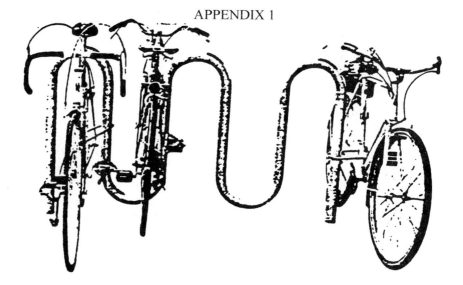

## APPENDIX 2

**Brandir Ribbon Bicycle Rack**
1979

Steven Levine worked in
wire to develop the basic
form

*The Design Problem*  To translate a sculpture into a working product design

Steven Levine started his career as an industrial engineer and computer analyst. Working with doodles, and then wire, he formed a sculptural piece. As he refined this form, he discovered that it could have a useful purpose as a bicycle and moped parking device. Aesthetics were the main concern how the size would relate to open spaces.

The rack is made of one piece of tubular construction 140 Steel Pipe and can be mounted below grace. Levine is both designer and manufacturer of the Ribbon Rack. He has stated that "the form was an inspiration that found a function."

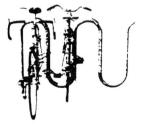

122

■ Winter, Circuit Judge, concurring in part and dissenting in part.

I respectfully dissent from the majority's discussion and disposition of the copyright claim.

My colleagues, applying an adaptation of Professor Denicola's test, hold that the aesthetic elements of the design of a useful article are not conceptually separable from its utilitarian aspects if "[f]orm and function are inextricably intertwined" in the article, and "its ultimate design [is] as much the result of utilitarian pressures as aesthetic choices." Applying the test to the instant matter, they observe that the dispositive fact is that "in creating the Ribbon Rack, [Levine] has clearly adapted the *original* aesthetic elements to accommodate and further a utilitarian purpose" (emphasis added). The grounds of my disagreement are that: (1) my colleagues' adaptation of Professor Denicola's test diminishes the statutory concept of "conceptual separability" to the vanishing point; and (2) their focus on the process or sequence followed by the particular designer makes copyright protection depend upon largely fortuitous circumstances concerning the creation of the design in issue.

With regard to "conceptual separability," my colleagues deserve considerable credit for their efforts to reconcile Carol Barnhart Inc. v. Economy Cover Corp., 773 F.2d 411 (2d Cir.1985) with Kieselstein–Cord v. Accessories by Pearl, Inc., 632 F.2d 989 (2d Cir.1980). In my view, these cases are not reconcilable. *Carol Barnhart* paid only lip service to the fact that the "conceptual separability" of an article's aesthetic utilitarian aspects may render the design of a "useful article" a copyrightable "sculptural work." § 101 (1982). Actually, the *Carol Barnhart* majority applied a test of physical separability. They thus stated:

> What distinguishes [the *Kieselstein–Cord*] buckles from the Barnhart forms is that the ornamented surfaces of the buckles were not in any respect required by their utilitarian functions; the artistic and aesthetic features could thus be conceived of as having been *added to, or superimposed upon,* an otherwise utilitarian article. The unique artistic design was wholly unnecessary to performance of the utilitarian function. In the case of the Barnhart forms, on the other hand, the features claimed to be aesthetic or artistic, e.g., the life-size configuration of the breasts and the width of the shoulders are inextricably intertwined with the utilitarian feature, the display of clothes.

773 F.2d at 419 (emphasis added). In contrast, *Kieselstein–Cord* focused on the fact that the belt buckles at issue could be perceived as objects other than belt buckles:

> We see in appellant's belt buckles conceptually separable sculptural elements, as apparently have the buckles' wearers who have used them as ornamentation for parts of the body other than the waist.

632 F.2d at 993.

My colleagues' adaptation of the Denicola test tracks the *Carol Barnhart* approach, whereas I would adopt that taken in *Kieselstein–Cord*, which allows for the copyrightability of the aesthetic elements of useful articles even if those elements simultaneously perform utilitarian functions. The latter approach received its fullest elaboration in Judge Newman's dissent in *Carol Barnhart*, where he explained that "[f]or the [artistic] design features to be 'conceptually separate' from the utilitarian aspects of the useful article that embodies the design, the article must stimulate in the mind of the beholder a concept that is separate from the concept evoked by its utilitarian function." 773 F.2d at 422 (Newman, J., dissenting).

In other words, the relevant question is whether the design of a useful article, however intertwined with the article's utilitarian aspects, causes an ordinary reasonable observer to perceive an aesthetic concept not related to the article's use. The answer to this question is clear in the instant case because any reasonable observer would easily view the Ribbon Rack as an ornamental sculpture.[d] Indeed, there is evidence of actual confusion over whether it is strictly ornamental in the refusal of a building manager to accept delivery until assured by the buyer that the Ribbon Rack was in fact a bicycle rack. Moreover, Brandir has received a request to use the Ribbon Rack as environmental sculpture, and has offered testimony of art experts who claim that the Ribbon Rack may be valued solely for its artistic features. As one of those experts observed: "If one were to place a Ribbon Rack on an island without access, or in a park and surround the work with a barrier, ... its status as a work of art would be beyond dispute."[e]

My colleagues also allow too much to turn upon the process or sequence of design followed by the designer of the Ribbon Rack. They thus suggest that copyright protection would have been accorded "had Brandir merely adopted ... as a bicycle rack" an enlarged version of one of David Levine's original sculptures rather than one that had wider upper loops and straightened vertical elements. I cannot agree that copyright protection for the Ribbon Rack turns on whether Levine serendipitously chose the final design of the Ribbon Rack during his initial sculptural musings or whether the original design had to be slightly modified to accommodate bicycles. Copyright protection, which is intended to generate incentives for designers by according property rights in their creations, should not turn on purely fortuitous events. For that reason, the Copyright Act expressly states that the legal test is how the final article is perceived, not how it was developed through various stages. It thus states in pertinent part:

> the design of a useful article ... shall be considered a ... sculptural work only if, and only to the extent that, such design incorporates ... *sculptural features that can be identified separately from, and are capable of existing independently of, the utilitarian aspects of the article.*

§ 101 (1982)(emphasis added).

I therefore dissent from the decision so far as it relates to copyrightability.

---

[d] The reasonable observer may be forgiven, however, if he or she does not recognize the Ribbon Rack as an example of minimalist art.

[e] The Copyright Office held that the Ribbon Rack was not copyrightable because it lacked originality. There may be some merit in that view in light of the Ribbon Rack's use of standard radii. This issue, however, was not raised in defendant's motion for summary judgment, was not addressed by the district court, and is not implicated here.

# Anderson v. Stallone

United States District Court, C.D. California, 1989.
11 U.S.P.Q.2d (BNA) 1161.

■ KELLER, JUDGE.

This matter came before the Court on the Motion for Summary Judgment of defendants Sylvester Stallone, Freddie Fields, Dean Stolber and MGM/UA Communications Co. Having reviewed the materials submitted and the arguments of counsel, the Court hereby orders the Motion granted in part and denied in part.

## Factual Background

The movies Rocky I, II, and III were extremely successful motion pictures. Sylvester Stallone wrote each script and played the role of Rocky Balboa, the dominant character in each of the movies. In May of 1982, while on a promotional tour for the movie Rocky III, Stallone informed members of the press of his ideas for Rocky IV. Although Stallone's description of his ideas would vary slightly in each of the press conferences, he would generally describe his ideas as follows:

> I'd do it [Rocky IV] if Rocky himself could step out a bit. Maybe tackle world problems.... So what would happen, say, if Russia allowed her boxers to enter the professional ranks? Say Rocky is the United States' representative and the White House wants him to fight with the Russians before the Olympics. It's in Russia with everything against him. It's a giant stadium in Moscow and everything is Russian Red. It's a fight of astounding proportions with 50 monitors sent to 50 countries. It's the World Cup—a war between 2 countries.

Waco Tribune Herald, May 28, 1982; Section D, p. 1.

In June of 1982, after viewing the movie Rocky III, Timothy Anderson wrote a thirty-one page treatment entitled "Rocky IV" that he hoped would be used by Stallone and MGM®R® UA Communications Co. (hereinafter "MGM") as a sequel to Rocky III. The treatment incorporated the characters created by Stallone in his prior movies and cited Stallone as a co-author.

In October of 1982, Mr. Anderson met with Art Linkletter, who was a member of MGM's board of directors. Mr. Linkletter set up a meeting on October 11, 1982, between Mr. Anderson and Mr. Fields, who was president of MGM at the time. Mr. Linkletter was also present at this October 11, 1982 meeting. During the meeting, the parties discussed the possibility that plaintiff's treatment would be used by defendants as the script for Rocky IV. At the suggestion of Mr. Fields, the plaintiff, who is a lawyer and was accompanied by a lawyer at the meeting, signed a release that purported to relieve MGM from liability stemming from use of the treatment. Plaintiff alleges that Mr. Fields told him and his attorney that "if they [MGM & Stallone] use his stuff [Anderson's treatment] it will be big money, big bucks for Tim."

On April 22, 1984, Anderson's attorney wrote MGM requesting compensation for the alleged use of his treatment in the forthcoming Rocky IV movie. On July 12, 1984, Stallone described his plans for the Rocky IV script on the Today Show before a national television audience. Anderson, in his deposition, states that his parents and friends called him to tell him that Stallone was telling "his story" on television. In a diary entry of July 12, 1984, Anderson noted that Stallone "explained my story" on national television.

Stallone completed his Rocky IV script in October of 1984. Rocky IV was released in November of 1985. The complaint in this action was filed on January 29, 1987.

### Defendants Are Entitled To Summary Judgment On Anderson's Copyright Infringement Claims

This Court finds that the defendants are entitled to summary judgment on plaintiff's copyright infringement claims on two separate grounds. First, Anderson's treatment is an infringing work that is not entitled to copyright protection. Second, Rocky IV is not substantially similar to Anderson's treatment, and no reasonable jury could find that Rocky IV is a picturization of Anderson's script.

### A. Defendants Are Entitled To Summary Judgment Because Anderson's Treatment Is An Infringing Work That Is Not Entitled To Copyright Protection

The Court finds that Anderson's treatment is not entitled to copyright protection. This finding is based upon the following determinations that will be delineated further below: (a) the Rocky characters developed in Rocky I, II and III constitute expression protected by copyright independent from the story in which they are contained; (b) Anderson's treatment appropriated these characters and created a derivative work based upon these characters without Stallone's permission in violation of Section 106(2); (c) no part of Anderson's treatment is entitled to copyright protection as his work is pervaded by the characters of the first three Rocky movies that are afforded copyright protection.

### 1. Visually Depicted Characters Can Be Granted Copyright Protection

The precise legal standard this Court should apply in determining when a character may be afforded copyright protection is fraught with uncertainty. The Second Circuit has followed Judge Learned Hand's opinion in Nichols v. Universal Pictures, 45 F.2d 119 (2d. Cir.1930), *cert. denied*, 282 U.S. 902 (1931). Judge Hand set forth a test, simple in theory but elusive in application, to determine when a character should be granted copyright protection. Essentially, under this test, copyright protection is granted to a character if it is developed with enough specificity so as to constitute protectable expression. *Id*. at 121.

This circuit originally created a more rigorous test for granting copyright protection to characters. In Warner Bros. Pictures, Inc. v. Columbia

Broadcasting System, Inc., (hereinafter the *"Sam Spade"* opinion) this circuit held that the literary character Sam Spade was not copyrightable, opining that a character could not be granted copyright protection unless it "constituted the story being told." 216 F.2d 945, 950 (9th Cir.1954). The *Sam Spade* case has not been explicitly overruled by this circuit and its requirement that a character "constitute the story being told" appears to greatly circumscribe the protection of characters in this circuit.

Subsequent decisions in the Ninth Circuit cast doubt on the reasoning and implicitly limit the holding of the *Sam Spade* case. In Walt Disney Productions v. Air Pirates, this circuit held that several Disney comic characters were protected by copyright. 581 F.2d 751, 755 (9th Cir.1978). In doing so the Court of Appeals reasoned that because "comic book characters ... are distinguishable from literary characters, the *Warner Bros.* language does not preclude protection of Disney's characters." *Id. Air Pirates* can be interpreted as either attempting to harmonize granting copyright protection to graphic characters with the "story being told" test enunciated in the *Sam Spade* case or narrowing the "story being told" test to characters in literary works. If *Air Pirates* is construed as holding that the graphic characters in question constituted the story being told, it does little to alter the *Sam Spade* opinion. However, it is equally as plausible to interpret *Air Pirates* as applying a less stringent test for protectability of graphic characters. Professor Nimmer has adopted the latter reading as he interprets *Air Pirates* as limiting the story being told requirement to word portraits. 1 M. Nimmer, THE LAW OF COPYRIGHT, § 2.12, p. 2–176 (1988).

This circuit's most recent decision on the issue of copyrightability of characters, Olson v. National Broadcasting Corporation, 855 F.2d 1446 (9th Cir.1988) does little to clarify the uncertainties in this circuit as to how the *Air Pirates* decision effects the continued viability of the *Sam Spade* test. In *Olson*, the Court of Appeals cited with approval the *Sam Spade* "story being told test" and declined to characterize this language as dicta. *Id.* at 1451–52 n.6. The Court then cited *Air Pirates* along with Second Circuit precedent and "recognize[d] that cases subsequent to *Warner Bros.* [*Sam Spade*] have allowed copyright protection for characters who are especially distinctive." *Id.* at 1452. *Olson* also stated definitively that "copyright protection may be afforded to characters visually depicted in a television series or in a movie." *Id.* But later in the opinion, the court in *Olson* distanced itself from the character delineation test that these cases employed, referring to it as "the more lenient standards adopted elsewhere". *Id.*

In an implicit acknowledgment of the unsettled state of the law, in considering the characters at issue in *Olson*, the circuit court evaluates the characters in the suit under *both tests. Id.* at 1452–53.

2.   The Rocky Characters Are Entitled To Copyright Protection As A Matter Of Law

*Olson*'s evaluation of literary characters is clearly distinguishable from the visually depicted characters of the first three Rocky movies for which the defendant seeks protection here. Thus, the more restrictive "story being told test" is inapplicable to the facts of this case. *Air Pirates*, 581 F.2d at 755, 1 M. Nimmer, § 2.12, p. 2–176. However, out of an abundance of caution this Court will determine the protectability of the Rocky characters under both tests. As shown below, the Rocky characters are protected from bodily appropriation under either standard.

The Rocky characters are one of the most highly delineated group of characters in modern American cinema. The physical and emotional characteristics of Rocky Balboa and the other characters were set forth in tremendous detail in the three Rocky movies before Anderson appropriated the characters for his treatment. The interrelationships and development of Rocky, Adrian, Apollo Creed, Clubber Lang, and Paulie are central to all three movies. Rocky Balboa is such a highly delineated character that his name is the title of all four of the Rocky movies and his character has become identified with specific character traits ranging from his speaking mannerisms to his physical characteristics. This Court has no difficulty ruling as a matter of law that the Rocky characters are delineated so extensively that they are protected from bodily appropriation when taken as a group and transposed into a sequel by another author. Plaintiff has not and cannot put before this Court any evidence to rebut the defendants' showing that Rocky characters are so highly delineated that they warrant copyright protection.

Plaintiff's unsupported assertions that Rocky is merely a stock character, made in the face of voluminous evidence that the Rocky characters are copyrightable, do not bar this Court from granting summary judgment on this issue. See Anderson v. Liberty Lobby, 477 U.S. 242, 247–48 (1986) ("the mere existence of *some* alleged factual dispute between the parties will not defeat an otherwise properly supported motion for summary judgment; the requirement is that there be no *genuine* issue of *material* fact")(emphasis in original). If any group of movie characters is protected by copyright, surely the Rocky characters are protected from bodily appropriation into a sequel which merely builds on the relationships and characteristics which these characters developed in the first three Rocky movies. No reasonable jury could find otherwise.

This Court need not and does not reach the issue of whether any single character alone, apart from Rocky, is delineated with enough specificity so as to garner copyright protection. Nor does the Court reach the issue of whether these characters are protected from less than bodily appropriation. See 1 M. Nimmer, § 2.12, p. 2–171 (copyrightability of characters is "more properly framed as relating to the degree of substantial similarity required to constitute infringement rather than in terms of copyrightability per se").

This Court also finds that the Rocky characters were so highly developed and central to the three movies made before Anderson's treatment that they "constituted the story being told." All three Rocky movies focused on the development and relationships of the various characters. The movies did not revolve around intricate plots or story lines. Instead, the focus of these movies was the development of the Rocky characters. The same evidence which supports the finding of delineation above is so extensive that it also warrants a finding that the Rocky characters—Rocky, Adrian, Apollo Creed, Clubber Lang, and Paulie—"constituted the story being told" in the first three Rocky movies.

3.   Anderson's Work Is An Unauthorized Derivative Work

Under Section 106(2), the holder of a copyright has the exclusive right to prepare derivative works based upon his copyrighted work. In this circuit a work is derivative *"only if it would be considered an infringing work if the material which it had derived from a prior work had been taken without the consent of the copyright proprietor of the prior work."* Litchfield v. Spielberg, 736 F.2d 1352, 1354 (9th Cir.1984)(emphasis in original), citing United States v. Taxe, 540 F.2d 961, 965 n.2 (9th Cir.1976). This Court must now examine whether Anderson's treatment is an unauthorized derivative work under this standard.

Usually a court would be required to undertake the extensive comparisons under the *Krofft* substantial similarity test to determine whether Anderson's work is a derivative work. [Sid and Marty Krofft Television Productions, Inc. v. McDonald's Corp., 562 F.2d 1157 (9th Cir.1977)]. See 1 M. Nimmer, § 3.01 at 3–3; p. 25–28. However, in this case, Anderson has bodily appropriated the Rocky characters in his treatment. This Court need not determine whether the characters in Anderson's treatment are substantially similar to Stallone's characters, as it is uncontroverted that the characters were lifted lock, stock, and barrel from the prior Rocky movies. Anderson retained the names, relationships and built on the experiences of these characters from the three prior Rocky movies. 1 M. Nimmer, § 2.12 at 2–177 (copying names of characters is highly probative evidence of infringement). His characters are not merely substantially similar to Stallone's, they *are* Stallone's characters. Anderson's bodily appropriation of these characters infringes upon the protected expression in the Rocky characters and renders his work an unauthorized derivative work. 1 Nimmer, § 2.12 at 2–171. By bodily appropriating the significant elements of protected expression in the Rocky characters, Anderson has copied protected expression and his treatment infringes on Stallone's copyrighted work.

4.   Since Anderson's Work Is An Unauthorized Derivative Work, No Part Of The Treatment Can Be Granted Copyright Protection

Stallone owns the copyrights for the first three Rocky movies. Under section 106(2), he has the exclusive right to prepare derivative works based on these copyrighted works. This Court has determined that Anderson's treatment is an unauthorized derivative work. Thus, Anderson has infringed upon Stallone's copyright. See section 501(a).

Nevertheless, plaintiff contends that his infringing work is entitled to copyright protection and he can sue Stallone for infringing upon his treatment. Plaintiff relies upon section 103(a) as support for his position that he is entitled to copyright protection for the non-infringing portions of his treatment. Section 103(a) reads:

> The subject matter of copyright as specified by section 102 includes compilations and derivative works, but protection for a work employing preexisting material in which copyright subsists does not extend to any part of the work in which the material has been used unlawfully.

Plaintiff has not argued that section 103(a), on its face, requires that an infringer be granted copyright protection for the non-infringing portions of his work. He has not and cannot provide this Court with a single case that has held that an infringer of a copyright is entitled to sue a third party for infringing the original portions of his work. Nor can he provide a single case that stands for the extraordinary proposition he proposes here, namely, allowing a plaintiff to sue the party whose work he has infringed upon for infringement of his infringing derivative work.

Instead, Anderson alleges that the House Report on section 103(a) indicates that Congress intended protection for the non-infringing portions of derivative works such as his treatment. The House Report for section 103(a) first delineates the difference between compilations and derivative works. H.R. Rep. No. 1476, 94th Cong., 2d Sess. at 57–58 (1976). The House Report then reads as follows:

> The second part of the sentence that makes up section 103(a) deals with the status of a compilation or derivative work unlawfully employing preexisting copyrighted material. In providing that protection does not extend to "any part of the work in which such material has been used unlawfully," the bill prevents an infringer from benefiting, through copyright protection, from committing an unlawful act, but preserves protection for those parts of the work that do not employ the preexisting work. Thus, an unauthorized translation of a novel could not be copyrighted at all, but the owner of copyright in an anthology of poetry could sue someone who infringed the whole anthology, even though the infringer proves that publication of one of the poems was unauthorized.

The Court recognizes that the House Report language is muddled. It makes a general statement that non-infringing portions of a work should be granted protection if these portions do not employ the pre-existing work. The report then provides two examples: one involving a compilation where the noninfringing portion was deemed protected, and another involving a derivative work where no part of the work could be protected. The general statement, when taken in the context of the comparison of compilations and derivative works in the section and the two examples given, is best understood as applying only to compilations. Although it is not crystal clear, it appears that the Committee assumed that in a derivative work the underlying work is "employed" throughout.

Professor Nimmer also interprets the House Report language as generally denying copyright protection to any portion of an unauthorized derivative work. After setting forth some of the language from the House Report regarding section 103(a) he states,

> the effect [of section 103(a)] generally would be to deny copyright to derivative works, in which the preexisting work tends to pervade the entire derivative work, but not to collective works, where the infringement arises from the copying of the selection and arrangement of a number of preexist-

ing works, and not per se from the reproduction of any particular prior work.

1 M. Nimmer, § 3.06, p. 3–22.3 thru 3–22.4.

Like the House Report, Nimmer also preceded his conclusion that no part of [a] derivative work unlawfully employing preexisting material should be copyrightable with a general statement that "only that portion of a derivative or collective work which employs the preexisting work would be denied copyright." 1 M. Nimmer, § 3.06, p. 3–22.3. At first blush, both Nimmer's and the Committee's language are internally inconsistent. Both start with a general proposition that only the portion of a work which unlawfully employs the prior work should be denied copyright protection. Both then appear to conclude that no part of an infringing derivative work should be granted copyright protection. Only if a derivative work is assumed to employ the infringing work throughout do these passages read coherently.

The case law interpreting section 103(a) also supports the conclusion that generally no part of an infringing derivative work should be granted copyright protection. In Eden Toys, Inc. v. Florelee Undergarment Co., the circuit court dealt primarily with the question of whether an authorized derivative work contained sufficient originality to gain copyright protection. 697 F.2d 27, 34–35 (2d. Cir.1982). However, in dicta the court opined on what result would be warranted if the derivative work had been made without the permission of the original author. The Court cited to the aforementioned passages from Professor Nimmer's treatise and the House Report and *assumed* without discussion that the "derivative copyrights would be invalid, since the preexisting illustration used without permission would tend to pervade the entire work." *Id.* at 34 n.6. In Gracen v. Bradford, the Seventh Circuit also dealt primarily with whether plaintiff's derivative work had sufficient originality to comply with [the] requirements of section 103. 698 F.2d 300, 302–303 (7th Cir.1983). *Gracen* also discussed the issue of the copyrightability of an unauthorized derivative work. The Court stated "if Miss Gracen had no authority to make derivative works from the movie, she could not copyright the painting and drawings, and she infringed MGM's copyright by displaying them publicly." *Id.* at 303. Once again, the Circuit court *assumed* that no part of an unlawful derivative work could be copyrighted.

Plaintiff has written a treatment which is an unauthorized derivative work. This treatment infringes upon Stallone's copyrights and his exclusive right to prepare derivative works which are based upon these movies. § 106(2). Section 103(a) was not intended to arm an infringer and limit the applicability of section 106(2) on unified derivative works. As the House Report and Professor Nimmer's treatise explain, 103(a) was not intended to apply to derivative works and most certainly was not an attempt to modify section 106(2). Section 103(a) allows an author whose authorship essentially is the arrangement or ordering of several independent works to keep the copyright for his arrangement even if one of the underlying works he arranged is found to be used unlawfully. The infringing portion would be easily severable and the scope of the compilation author's own work would be easily ascertainable. Even if this Court were to interpret section 103(a) as allowing an author of an infringing derivative work to sue third parties based on the non-infringing portions of his work, section 106(2) most certainly precludes the author of an unauthorized infringing derivative work from suing the author of the work which he has already infringed. Thus, the Court holds that the defendants are entitled to summary judgment on plaintiff's copyright claims as the plaintiff cannot gain copyright protection for any portion of his work under section 103(a). In addition, Anderson is precluded by section 106(2) from bringing an action for copyright infringement against Stallone and the other defendants.

## NOTES

**1.** *Functional subject matter. Baker* is the core of the separability doctrine and its application will be revisited in Assignment 10, which treats the copyrightability of computer programs. What is the relevance of Baker v. Selden to the Principal Problem?

Although many proposals have been introduced in Congress to provide a form of protection analogous to copyright law for the designs of useful articles, none of these legislative attempts have ever fared successfully (with the exception of protection for vessel hulls, *see* note 6). The Principal Problem involves a costume. Should the analysis differ if a dress design, historical period piece, or theatrical costume were involved? The Copyright Register's 1991 ruling on the Registrability of Costume Designs,[10] concludes that although "fanciful costumes will be registered [only] if they contain separable pictorial or sculptural authorship," "[g]arment designs (excluding separately identifiable pictorial representations of designs imposed upon the garment) will not be registered even if they contain ornamental features, or are intended to be used as historical or period dress."[11] The ruling also states that this "general policy of nonregistrability of garment designs will be applied not only to ordinary wearing apparel, but also to period and historical dress, and uniforms."[12] Moreover, "[w]earing apparel incorporated into theatrical productions will likewise be treated under the standards applying to garment designs in general."[13]

**2.** *Conceptual separability.* Which test for conceptual separability discussed in *Brandir* is the most theoretically satisfying? The majority in *Brandir* adopts Professor Denicola's test whereas the dissent endorses Judge Newman's "temporal displacement" test. Which of these tests allows greater latitude for registrability? The *Brandir* majority also notes that its application will require the parties to present evidence relating to the "design process and the nature of the work." According to the majority, such a test would not be difficult to apply since "the work itself will continue to give 'mute testimony' of its origins." The dissent disagrees with

[10] Vol. 56 Fed. Register, No. 214, 56531 (November 5, 1991).

[11] Id. at 56531–56532.

[12] Id. at 56532.

[13] Id.

this approach because, in his view, copyrightability should not be made to depend upon the fortuitous design process. Should *Brandir* have relied upon the sequences of actions or decisions in the design process? Is the majority or the dissent more persuasive? Why should a creator's intent be relevant? What if a creator does not fulfill her actual intent? Several years after *Brandir*, the Second Circuit upheld the copyrightability of a fish mannequin used to mount animal skins. In Hart v. Dan Chase Taxidermy Supply Co., Inc.,[14] the court concluded that any utilitarian feature of the mannequin merely serves to portray the appearance of the animal, and therefore the mannequin should be considered a sculptural work rather than a useful article. Is this approach consistent with *Brandir*?

*Brandir* supports the idea that a finding of copyrightability can be sustained with a showing of either physical or conceptual separability. Should a copyright claimant have to meet both tests in order to have a valid copyright? What is the difference in application between physical and conceptual separability? In addition to the tests discussed in *Brandir*, Professor Goldstein has proposed a different test positing that a particular "feature incorporated in the design of a useful article is conceptually separable if it can stand on its own as a work of art traditionally conceived, and if the useful article in which it is embodied would be equally useful without it."[15] The Goldstein test has been adopted by several district courts in recent years.[16] Does the Goldstein test have the potential for blurring the distinction between physical and conceptual separability? Who should have the ultimate responsibility for determining whether a particular work possesses the requisite degree of artistic merit "to stand on its own as a work of art traditionally conceived?" This concern is also evident in footnote c of *Brandir* which mentions Bleistein v. Donaldson Lithographing Co.[17] In that case, Justice Holmes made the now famous observation that "[i]t would be a dangerous undertaking for persons trained only to the law to constitute themselves final judges of the worth of pictorial illustrations, outside of the narrowest and most obvious limits."[18]

**3.** *Compilations vs. derivative works.* In *Anderson*, the court draws a distinction between compilations and derivative works, concluding that although protection can be obtained for the noninfringing portions of a compilation, similar protection is inappropriate for such portions of a derivative work.[19] How persuasive is this part of the court's discussion? Note that the court was apparently outraged by the defendant's attempt to sue the author of the work which the defendant had infringed. Would a

---

[14] 86 F.3d 320 (2d Cir. 1996).

[15] Paul Goldstein, *Copyright: Principles, Law & Practice*, 109.

[16] *See, e.g.,* Collezione Europa U.S.A., Inc. v. Hillsdale House, Ltd., 243 F.Supp.2d 444 (M.D. N.C. 2003); Celebration International, Inc. v. Chosun International, Inc., 234 F.Supp.2d 905 (S. D. Ind. 2002); Pivot Point International v. Charlene Products, Inc., 170 F.Supp.2d 828 (N.D. Ill. 2001).

[17] 188 U.S. 239 (1903).

[18] Id. at 251.

[19] See also Sobhani v. @Radical.Media, 257 F.Supp.2d 1234 (C.D. Cal. 2003)(denying copyright protection for original elements of plaintiff's unauthorized derivative commercial since the underlying work pervaded the entire derivative work).

better approach be to give each "author" a copyright in his material? That way, Anderson could not use the Rocky character without Stallone's permission and Stallone could not use the new story without Anderson's authorization. The two would be forced to bargain, and allocate the expected return in accordance with their perception of each author's contribution. This system of "blocking" rights is used in patent law, see Assignment 21.

**4.** *Protection for characters.* One of the germinal cases discussing whether characters should receive copyright protection is Warner Bros. v. Columbia Broadcasting System, a 1954 opinion from the Ninth Circuit.[20] In that case, the plaintiff was Warner Brothers, who had entered into an agreement with the defendant, Dashiel Hammett, author of "The Maltese Falcon." The agreement granted the plaintiff the right to use the "The Maltese Falcon" in movies, radio and television. Plaintiff claimed that this grant also entitled it to use the individual characters in "The Maltese Falcon" and their names. The defendant argued that the plaintiff's rights were limited to those contained in the agreement, which failed to grant any rights to the use of the characters and their names. Thus, the defendant was free to use these characters in his other works and could license the rights in the characters to third parties. The court found for the defendant as a matter of contract law. As noted in *Anderson,* however, the *Warner Brothers* court also indicated that a character is not copyrightable unless it "constitute[s] the story being told." When does a character constitute "the story being told?" Should comic book characters be judged under a more liberal standard than literary characters? If so, what about characters in movies or television? In *MGM v. American Honda Motor Co.,*[21] a district court in California relied on *Anderson* in concluding that, despite the constant change in actors, James Bond and his character traits are copyrightable under either "story being told" test or the character delineation test. Does this approach lead to more favorable treatment for cartoon characters (which are necessarily "delineated") as compared with literary characters?

What does the *Anderson* court ultimately conclude regarding the protectability of the Rocky characters? Should it make a difference whether the creator is trying to protect his own character (essentially this is *Anderson*) or whether someone other than the creator is trying to prevent the creator from using his own creation (as in *Warner Brothers*)? The Anderson court quotes Nimmer for the proposition that the question whether characters are copyrightable is "more properly framed [in terms of] . . . the degree of substantial similarity required to constitute infringement rather than in terms of copyrightability per se."[22] What does this quote mean?

---

[20] 216 F.2d 945 (9th Cir.1954), cert. denied, 348 U.S. 971 (1955).

[21] 900 F.Supp. 1287 (C.D. Cal. 1995).

[22] See Section IV(A)(2) of *Anderson,* quoting 1 M. Nimmer, § 2.12, p. 2–171.

In addition to determining the appropriate test for copyright protection of fictional characters, courts wanting to protect characters under copyright law must confront additional difficult questions. For example, what aspects of a character should be protected by copyright? With respect to comic book characters specifically, should the protection be limited to graphic depictions or should additional aspects of the character be considered? Should Barney be allowed to manufacture the costume without a license from Warner and D.C.? What would you tell a client who wanted to market a superhero costume? What if your client wanted to market a video game featuring a graphical depiction of a superhero, or a television program featuring a superhero? Attorneys desiring assistance in determining the copyright status of particular characters can order a Copyright Character Search & Report from an independent research company. These reports search a number of sources such as the records of the U.S. Copyright Office, the U.S. Patent and Trademark Office, state trademark registrations, newspaper and trade notices, an international licensing directory, and the case law.

Another difficult issue involves the appropriate degree of protection for series characters. The problem in this regard is that some of the works in which a character appears may have fallen into the public domain, while others remain protected under copyright law. In Silverman v. CBS, Inc.,[23] an excerpt from which appears in Part B of Assignment 4, the Second Circuit held that a producer of a Broadway musical based on the series characters "Amos 'n' Andy" could use any aspects of the characters that were sufficiently delineated in radio scripts currently in the public domain, but that any aspects of these characters that were further delineated in subsequent works still protected by copyright could not be used.[24] Is this a viable solution? Can you think of any other resolutions to this problem?

What is the legal status of fan fiction? This is a genre of literature found mainly on the Internet, in which amateur authors write their own stories utilizing characters from famous books, movies, and television shows.[25]

Frequently, a license involving the right to use a character is merely the right to make new works deriving from the original, underlying work in which the character first appears. To the extent these derivative rights in characters involve use of the characters on clothing, games, toys, and even food, merchandising rights typically covered by unfair competition or trademark law are being implicated as well copyright law. From the standpoint of copyright law, how significant is the appropriation of the character's name as well as its appearance?

*Query.* Does your local grocery store commit copyright infringement under § 106(2) if it markets a cake in the shape and appearance of Mickey

---

[23] 870 F.2d 40 (2d Cir.1989).

[24] Id. at 49–50.

[25] See, e.g., Rebecca Tushnet, Legal Fictions: Copyright, Fan Fiction, and a New Common Law, 17 Loy. L.A. Ent. L.J. 651 (1997).

Mouse without a license from Disney? Can the cake be considered a "derivative work" within the meaning of the statute?

**5.** *Architectural works.* As of 1990, copyright law specifically protects architectural works. The Architectural Works Copyright Protection Act ("AWCPA"), which applies to works created on or after December 1, 1990, and to unconstructed works embodied in unpublished plans created before this date,[26] amended the copyright statute by adding architectural works as a specific subject matter category in § 102. Other additions to the statute include a definition of "architectural work" in § 101 and certain limitations on the scope of protection for such works in § 120. The definition of "architectural work" covers the "design of a building as embodied in any tangible medium of expression, including a building, architectural plans, or drawings." How should the term "building" be interpreted? In Hunt v. Pasternack,[27] the Ninth Circuit held that copyright protection for architectural works is not limited to works that have actually been constructed.

Prior to the AWCPA, only the plans could be protected as "pictorial, graphic, and sculptural works" under § 102(a)(5). Thus, the construction of a building from copyrighted plans was not considered infringement.[28] Now it appears as though the plans enjoy a dual form of protection, as do nonfunctional monuments that qualify as "sculptures."[29] What are the consequences of this dual protection? One caveat imposed by § 120(a) is that if a building is "visible from a public place," a copyright owner cannot "prevent the making, distributing, or public display of pictures, paintings, photographs, or other pictorial representations of the work." What do you think is the purpose of this qualification? What limitations does § 120(b) provide? Why do you think the AWCPA crafted relatively narrow protections for architectural works? In Leicester v. Warner Brothers,[30] the Ninth Circuit concluded that the four towers forming a streetwall of the building that became the Second Bank of Gotham in the movie *Batman Forever* were part of the architectural work and therefore, subject to being photographed pursuant to § 120(a).[31] The court also affirmed the lower court's finding that the streetwall towers were not "conceptually separate" from the building and therefore were not entitled to independent copyright protection.[32] The dissent, however, argued that the conceptual separability test should continue to apply to pictorial, graphic and sculptural works incorporated into architectural buildings and thus would accord conceptual-

[26] Architectural Works Copyright Protection Act, Pub. L. No. 101–650, tit. 7, § 706(1) & (2), 104 Stat. 5133, 5134 (1990). Under the Act, the protection afforded to works in unpublished plans not constructed as of 1990 will expire on December 31, 2002, unless the work has been constructed by this date.

[27] 192 F.3d 877 (9th Cir. 1999).

[28] See, e.g., Imperial Homes Corp. v. Lamont, 458 F.2d 895, 899 (5th Cir.1972).

[29] See H.R. Rep. No. 735, 101st Cong., 2d Sess. 18, 20 n.43 (1990), reprinted in 1990

U.S.C.C.A.N. 6935, 6951 n.43 ("Monumental, nonfunctional works of architecture are currently protected under section 102(a)(5) of title 17 as sculptural works. These works are, nevertheless, architectural works, and as such, will not be protected exclusively under section 102(a)(8).").

[30] 232 F.3d 1212 (9th Cir. 2000).

[31] Id. at 1219.

[32] Id. at 1219.

ly separate elements full copyright protection as sculptural works under 17 U.S.C. § 102(5).[33] Recall from Note 15 in Assignment 2 that buildings can be protected by trademark law.

**6.** *Protection for Vessel Hulls.* As part of the Digital Millennium Copyright Act ("DMCA"), which was signed into law in October, 1998, Congress created a new form of protection for the design of vessel hulls by adding chapter 13 to the copyright statute.[34] Some observers believe that this new protection might be used as a model for more widespread design protection sometime in the future. Chapter 13 provides for a ten year term of protection, which begins upon the earlier of the "date of publication of the registration ... or the date the design is first made public."[35] If registration "for the design is not made within two years after the date on which the design is first made public," the protection under this chapter is lost.[36] Infringement under this chapter includes making or importing for sale or for use in trade any infringing article; and the selling or distributing for sale or for use in trade any infringing information.[37] The chapter provides for a variety of remedies including injunctive relief; damages; infringer's profits; and attorney's fees.[38] In 2003, the Copyright Office and the Patent and Trademark Office submitted a joint report to Congress concluding that it is too soon to determine whether this statute has had a significant impact on the boat building industry, and maintaining that the responsibility for promoting the statutory registration system lies with the industry, rather than the Copyright Office.[39] The DMCA is treated more extensively in Assignment 11.

**7.** *The New Hague Agreement.* In 1925, the Hague Agreement Concerning the International Deposit of Industrial Designs was completed by WIPO. The treaty intended to establish a process for obtaining protection of industrial designs at an international level. The treaty was revised in 1934 and again in 1960, and currently has over thirty signatories. The United States did not join the earlier versions of the Hague Agreement because many of its provisions were inconsistent with U.S. law.

In 1991, an expert committee began to revise the Hague Agreement in order to remove the barriers that prevented nations such as the United States from joining the agreement. The New Hague Agreement establishes a central filing system administered by WIPO for foreign design protection. The entire process for acquiring this protection would be streamlined and made less expensive to industrial design owners. The Draft Treaty was finalized by a Diplomatic Conference convened in Geneva in the summer of 1999. It will become effective after April 1, 2004.[40]

[33] Id. at 1235.
[34] 17 U.S.C. § 1301 et. seq.
[35] 17 U.S.C. §§ 1304; 1305(a).
[36] 17 U.S.C. § 1310(a).
[37] 17 U.S.C. § 1309(a).
[38] 17 U.S.C. §§ 1322 & 1323.
[39] See http://pubs.bna.com/ip/BNA/ptc.nsf/is/a0a7u1d1a9
[40] See *http://wipo.org/eng/main/htm,* http://wip.int/treaties/genaral/parties.html#1, and www.wipo.int./edocs/hag-docs/en/2003/hague_2003_12.pdf

Under the New Hague Agreement, WIPO determines whether an international application meets all minimum requirements, assigns the filing date, registers the application and forwards the application to the parties involved. WIPO then publishes the international registration and the signatories have a limited time to decide whether to register or grant protection to the industrial design. The term of protection is 15 years from the date of registration of the industrial design.

Under the new treaty, an applicant can file one English-language application with the PTO and will receive protection in all signatories to the New Hague Agreement. Currently, owners wishing to protect their industrial designs must file an application in each of the individual states where their designs are utilized. Implementation of this treaty in the U.S. would be through design patent law.

# THE RECIPIENTS OF COPYRIGHT'S INCENTIVES: OWNERSHIP, THE WORK FOR HIRE DOCTRINE, RENEWAL AND TERMINATION RIGHTS, AND MORAL RIGHTS

## 1. INTRODUCTION

An initial question concerning the recipients of copyright's incentives is the identity of the copyright owner. In this regard, there are several possibilities, including: an original author of the work; a party to whom the work is licensed; a party who contributes authorship material; or a party who commissions the work or for whom the author is working. The copyright statute provides a variety of possible answers to the ownership issue depending on the circumstances. Section 201(a) of the 1976 Copyright Act provides that the copyright in a protected work "vests initially in the author or authors of the work." The authors of a "joint work," which is defined in § 101 as "a work prepared by two or more authors with the intention that their contributions be merged into inseparable or interdependent parts of a unitary whole," are considered co-owners of the copyright, and essentially are viewed as tenants in common with respect to the work. Each co-owner has the unilateral right to use or license the work, as long as an accounting of profits is made to the other co-owners. Section 201(b) of the Act provides that "[i]n the case of a work made for hire, the employer or other person for whom the work was prepared is considered the author ... unless the parties have expressly agreed otherwise in a written instrument signed by them...." Thus, the work for hire doctrine is an exception to the rule that copyright ownership vests initially in the work's creator, and in recognizing this doctrine, the United States allows the employer of a work's creator to obtain "authorship" status.

A second question concerning incentives is the duration of copyright protection. The "Sonny Bono Copyright Term Extension Act" ("CTEA,")[1] whose constitutionality was affirmed by the Supreme Court in *Eldred v. Ashcroft*, reprinted herein, extended the copyright term for an additional twenty years. This extension, applicable to both existing and future copy-

[1] This amendment to the 1976 Copyright Act became the law in 1998.

rights, not only impacts the length of copyright protection generally, but also the length of protection for works made for hire and for joint works. For works generally, copyright protection currently extends for the life of the author plus seventy years (see § 302(a)). For works made for hire, the copyright now lasts for a term of ninety-five years from the year of the work's first publication, or a term of one hundred and twenty years from the year of its creation, whichever expires first (see § 302(c)). In the case of joint works, the period of protection lasts for seventy years after the death of the last surviving author's death (see § 302(b)).

This chapter focuses on several specific topics in conjunction with the broader issue of the recipients of copyright's incentives. One important focus of this chapter is the work for hire doctrine. The importance of determining whether a particular work is a work for hire is manifest, as this determination dictates who is the initial owner of the copyright, and how long copyright protection lasts. Other consequences also attach to a determination that a work is a work made for hire, all of which are relevant to the topics discussed in this Assignment. For example, when a work for hire has been licensed, that license is not subject to termination under §§ 203 & 304(c) of the Act.[2] Also, the employer of a work for hire can exercise the renewal right under § 304(a), as opposed to the actual author or her statutory successors. Moreover, the moral rights protections for visual art discussed below do not apply to works made for hire (see § 106A and the definition of "work of visual art" in § 101).

The renewal and termination provisions also are related to the topic of the recipients of copyright's incentives. As discussed in Assignment 6, under the 1909 Act federal copyright protection was available for an initial 28–year term, with an optional renewal term of an additional 28 years. The 1976 Act had to deal with renewal procedures for those works created prior to the effective date of that statute. Some of the issues pertaining to renewal rights are explored in this Assignment. In addition, this Assignment explores the statute's provisions for terminating a copyright license. Section 201(d) of the Act provides that the copyright owner can transfer any or all of the rights safeguarded by the 1976 Act. Section 106 of the statute assures the copyright owner the exclusive rights to reproduce and distribute the original work, to prepare derivative works, and to perform and display publicly certain types of copyrighted works. Each of these rights can be transferred by the copyright owner and separately owned. Since the 1976 Act generally does not purport to protect the author, but rather the copyright owner, if the original author of a work assigns all of her rights under § 106 to another party, traditionally the author no longer retains any rights with respect to her work. One exception to this general rule appears in the termination provisions in § 203 of the statute, which

---

[2] See Marvel Characters, Inc. v. Simon, 310 F.3d 280, 291 (2d Cir. 2002)(noting that because the statutory author of a work for hire historically was an employer-publisher, the original rationale underlying the termination provisions of providing additional benefits to authors is not as directly applicable since an "an employer-publisher does not face the same potential unequal bargaining position as an individual author.").

allow an author to terminate transfers and licenses after a period of time, but the author must wait a minimum of thirty-five years after the execution of the grant to exercise this right.

Finally, this Assignment addresses the topic of moral rights ("droit moral"). In contrast to the pecuniary rights protected under § 106 that are detailed in the foregoing paragraph, moral rights protect the personal rights of authors. Authors in the United States do not enjoy substantial moral rights protections, unlike authors in many other nations. In those countries that have moral rights protection, the doctrine essentially is said to encompass three major components: the right of disclosure, the right of attribution, and the right of integrity. Underlying the right of disclosure is the idea that the creator, as the sole judge of when a work is ready for public dissemination, is the only one who can possess any rights in an uncompleted work. The right of attribution, as its name suggests, safeguards a creator's right to compel recognition for her work and to prevent others from naming anyone else as the creator. It also protects a creator's negative rights of anonymity and pseudonymity. The right of integrity lies at the heart of the moral right doctrine, as it prohibits any alterations of a creator's work that will destroy the spirit and character of the creator's work. Although adaptations of a work from one medium to another present the most obvious potential for violations of a creator's right of integrity, in reality any modification of a work can be problematic from an integrity standpoint.[3]

In 1988, the United States joined the Berne Convention for the Protection of Literary and Artistic Works, the oldest multilateral treaty governing copyright protection. As a result, American creators can now obtain increased copyright protection internationally (see generally Assignment 6). Section 6bis of the Berne Convention recognizes a right of attribution and a right of integrity, but the treaty contemplates that the specific legislation of the respective Union members will govern substantive applications of these rights within each member country. When the United States joined the Convention, Congress believed that no additional moral rights protections were needed in this country given federal protections such as § 43(a) of the Lanham Act (see Assignment 3) and § 106(2) of the 1976 Copyright Act (governing the right to prepare derivative works), as well as the existing common law doctrines such as unfair competition, breach of contract, defamation and invasion of privacy law that had been used to redress moral rights violations.[4] In addition, several states provided

---

[3] Some formulations of the moral right doctrine also include the right to withdraw one's work from the public, the right to prevent excessive criticism, and the right to prevent assaults upon one's personality. See generally Roberta Rosenthal Kwall, Copyright and the Moral Right: Is an American Mar- riage Possible?, 38 Vand. L. Rev. 1, 5–16 (1985).

[4] See Final Report of Ad Hoc Working Group on U.S. Adherence to the Berne Convention, 10 Colum.-VLA J.L. & Arts 513, 555 (1986); H.R. Rep. No. 609, 100th Cong., 2d Sess. 38 (1988).

specific statutory moral rights protections for certain types of works, notably visual art.[5]

Still, in 1990 Congress amended the 1976 Copyright Act by adding the Visual Artists Rights Act ("VARA,") which provides relatively circumscribed federal rights of attribution and integrity for certain visual artists. These protections are discussed further in Note 5. As that Note and the other materials on moral rights contained in this Assignment illustrate, numerous problems exist with respect to VARA's scope and implementation.[6]

The issues surrounding the recipients of copyright's incentives present several difficult issues. Some of these issues revolve around identifying the original copyright owners. In general, these questions involve applications of the work for hire and joint authorship doctrines. Other doctrines explored in this Assignment are designed to determine, in various contexts, the rights of the original authors versus subsequent copyright assignees. The following Principal Problem is a comprehensive one that provides an opportunity to work through some of these important aspects of copyright law.

## 2. PRINCIPAL PROBLEM

David writes dual-language dictionaries of street slang English words that are intended to be used by people who are learning English. He is very well known for this endeavor and enjoys an international reputation, since he has written such dictionaries for people who speak Spanish, German, French, and Russian. All of his dictionaries contain groupings by categories of expressions (i.e., expressions relating to eating and food, expressions relating to recreational activities, etc.). He now wants to do an English–

---

[5] See, e.g., Cal. Civ. Code §§ 987–90 (West 1982 & Supp. 1993 & 2004); Conn. Gen. Stat. Ann. §§ 42–116s to 42–116t (West 2003); La. Rev. Stat. Ann. §§ 2151–56 (West 2003); Me. Rev. Stat. Ann. tit. 27, § 303 (West 2003); Mass. Gen. Laws Ann. ch. 231, § 85S (West Supp. 2000); Nev. Rev. Stat. §§ 597.720 (2003); N.J. Stat. Ann. §§ 2A:24A–1 to 2A:24A–8 (West 2000); N.M. Stat. Ann. §§ 13–4B–1 to 13–4B–3 (Michie 2003); N.Y. Arts & Cult. Aff. Law §§ 14.01–.08 (McKinney 1984 & Supp. 2003); Pa. Stat. Ann. tit. 73, §§ 2101–10 (2003); R.I. Gen. Laws §§ 5–62–2 to 5–62–6 (2000). The specific content of these statutes varies. Some statutes such as those in California, Connecticut, Massachusetts, and Pennsylvania provide relief for the actual commission of an alteration, while other statutes such as those in Louisiana, Maine, Nevada, New Jersey, New York, and Rhode Island provide relief for the display or publication of an altered work. The definitions of protected works also vary among the states. Compare California's definition of protected "fine art" ("an original painting, sculpture, or drawing . . . of recognized quality," § 987(b)(2)) with the extremely detailed and broad definition of "fine art" in the Connecticut statute (see § 42–116s(2)). Some of the state statutes offer more extensive protections than VARA. For example, California, Massachusetts, and New Mexico apparently presume that any alteration will harm a creator's honor or reputation. Massachusetts and New Mexico allow relief for alterations resulting from gross negligence. The provisions in Louisiana, Maine, New Jersey, New York, and Rhode Island extend to reproductions of protected works. These differences are significant with respect to the issue of preemption. See Note 5 in the text.

[6] Interestingly, TRIPs did not embrace a moral rights requirement.

Hebrew dictionary. To assist him with this project, he enters into agreements with Sam and Rivkah. Rivkah was an art major in college and did the illustrations for all of David's other dictionaries. For this dictionary, David wants her to draw illustrations of famous Israeli and American scenes and sights. Since Rivkah never has been to Israel, David sends her to Israel for two weeks so that she can make preliminary sketches of the sights to be included in the book. David pays for all of her travel and living expenses while Rivkah is in Israel, including the medical bills she incurred when she injured her ankle and had to be taken to a hospital emergency room. After Rivkah returned from Israel, she did most of the work on the illustrations at her own home, using her own art supplies.

Sam is an Israeli living in America who currently is looking for a job teaching Hebrew at an American university. He has never before worked with David, and his job is to provide assistance with translating the English expressions into Hebrew. David gave Sam an office to use in his office suite and they had daily contact during the period of time the dictionary was being prepared. David did all of the groupings and generally decided which English expressions should be included in the dictionary. Sam did all of the actual translations.

The agreement that David entered into with both Sam and Rivkah provided that they agreed to work "with and for" David on the street slang English–Hebrew dictionary. Both were paid in cash, based on an hourly wage.

While they were in the process of writing the dictionary, David decided that the collection of illustrations Rivkah had created for his series of dictionaries would make an interesting addition to his website, and would also help to promote his dictionaries. He sent illustrations from each of the dictionaries to his website's management company, with a letter authorizing the reproduction of the illustrations for the purpose of posting on his website. He did not indicate that Rivkah had created the illustrations, and the website does not designate her as the author of the illustrations.

At the same time, David entered into an agreement with Chaim Corp., who agreed to publish the English–Hebrew dictionary on the condition that Chaim can also create and market an audio cassette of the dictionary so that people can play it in their cars. Without consulting Sam or Rivkah, David granted Chaim the right to publish the dictionary and the right to make a derivative work of the dictionary. Unfortunately, when David hears the completed cassette, he is shocked by the strange background music, the annoying tone of the announcer, the re-ordering of the categories of his expressions, and the inclusion of a category of sex-related expressions. The cover of the cassette states that it is "based upon" David's English–Hebrew dictionary.

David retains you as his lawyer. Believing that the cassette is a perversion of his artistic integrity and his original creative vision, David wants to sue Chaim. He wants your advice with respect to what causes of action he can bring against Chaim for mutilating his work. David also wants to terminate Chaim's license immediately, and if this is not possible,

David wants to know when he can and if such a termination of Chaim's rights also will terminate Chaim's right to produce and market the cassette. Moreover, David has just learned that Rivkah and Sam have filed for a declaratory judgment that they are joint authors of the copyright in the dictionary. They want to join in David's lawsuit against Chaim, and also sue David for failing to get their permission to license the work to Chaim. David is vigorously disputing their joint authorship claim. David also wants advice on whether Rivkah can maintain any other lawsuits against him for reproducing her pictures on his website without her authorization.

What are the legal issues raised by the foregoing set of circumstances and how do you think all of these issues are likely to be resolved? Before giving your answers, consider the following materials.

## 3.   MATERIALS FOR SOLUTION OF PRINCIPAL PROBLEM

A.   STATUTORY MATERIALS: §§ 101 (definitions of "work made for hire," "joint work," & "work of visual art"), 106, 106A, 201–205, 301(f), & 302–305

B.   CASES:

## Eldred v. Ashcroft

Supreme Court of the United States, 2003.
537 U.S. 186, 123 S.Ct. 769, 154 L.Ed.2d 683.

■ JUSTICE GINSBURG delivered the opinion of the Court.

This case concerns the authority the Constitution assigns to Congress to prescribe the duration of copyrights. The Copyright and Patent Clause of the Constitution, Art. I, § 8, cl. 8, provides as to copyrights: "Congress shall have Power ... to promote the Progress of Science ... by securing [to Authors] for limited Times ... the exclusive Right to their ... Writings." In 1998, in the measure here under inspection, Congress enlarged the duration of copyrights by 20 years. Copyright Term Extension Act (CTEA), § 102(b) and (d), (amending 17 U.S.C. §§ 302, 304). As in the case of prior extensions, principally in 1831, 1909, and 1976, Congress provided for application of the enlarged terms to existing and future copyrights alike.

Petitioners are individuals and businesses whose products or services build on copyrighted works that have gone into the public domain. They seek a determination that the CTEA fails constitutional review under the Copyright Clause's "limited Times" prescription. Under the 1976 Copyright Act, copyright protection generally lasted from the work's creation until 50 years after the author's death. Under the CTEA, most copyrights now run from creation until 70 years after the author's death. 17 U.S.C. § 302(a). Petitioners do not challenge the "life-plus–70–years" time span itself. "Whether 50 years is enough, or 70 years too much," they acknowledge, "is not a judgment meet for this Court." Congress went awry, petitioners maintain, not with respect to newly created works, but in enlarging the term for published works with existing copyrights. The "limited Time" in effect when a copyright is secured, petitioners urge, becomes the constitutional boundary, a clear line beyond the power of Congress to extend.

In accord with the District Court and the Court of Appeals, we reject petitioners' challenges to the CTEA. In that 1998 legislation, as in all previous copyright term extensions, Congress placed existing and future copyrights in parity. In prescribing that alignment, we hold, Congress acted within its authority and did not transgress constitutional limitations.

## I

## A

We evaluate petitioners' challenge to the constitutionality of the CTEA against the backdrop of Congress' previous exercises of its authority under the Copyright Clause. The Nation's first copyright statute, enacted in 1790, provided a federal copyright term of 14 years from the date of publication, renewable for an additional 14 years if the author survived the first term. The 1790 Act's renewable 14-year term applied to existing works (*i.e.*, works already published and works created but not yet published) and future works alike. Congress expanded the federal copyright term to 42 years in 1831 (28 years from publication, renewable for an additional 14 years), and to 56 years in 1909 (28 years from publication, renewable for an additional 28 years). Both times, Congress applied the new copyright term to existing and future works.

In 1976, Congress altered the method for computing federal copyright terms. 1976 Act §§ 302–304. For works created by identified natural persons, the 1976 Act provided that federal copyright protection would run from the work's creation, not—as in the 1790, 1831, and 1909 Acts—its publication; protection would last until 50 years after the author's death. § 302(a). In these respects, the 1976 Act aligned United States copyright terms with the then-dominant international standard adopted under the Berne Convention for the Protection of Literary and Artistic Works. For anonymous works, pseudonymous works, and works made for hire, the 1976 Act provided a term of 75 years from publication or 100 years from creation, whichever expired first. § 302(c).

These new copyright terms, the 1976 Act instructed, governed all works not published by its effective date of January 1, 1978, regardless of when the works were created. §§ 302–303. For published works with existing copyrights as of that date, the 1976 Act granted a copyright term of 75 years from the date of publication, § 304(a) and (b), a 19-year increase over the 56-year term applicable under the 1909 Act.

The measure at issue here, the CTEA, installed the fourth major duration extension of federal copyrights. Retaining the general structure of the 1976 Act, the CTEA enlarges the terms of all existing and future copyrights by 20 years. For works created by identified natural persons, the term now lasts from creation until 70 years after the author's death. 17 U.S.C. § 302(a). This standard harmonizes the baseline United States copyright term with the term adopted by the European Union in 1993. For anonymous works, pseudonymous works, and works made for hire, the term is 95 years from publication or 120 years from creation, whichever expires first. 17 U.S.C. § 302(c).

Paralleling the 1976 Act, the CTEA applies these new terms to all works not published by January 1, 1978. §§ 302(a), 303(a). For works published before 1978 with existing copyrights as of the CTEA's effective date, the CTEA extends the term to 95 years from publication. §§ 304(a) and (b). Thus, in common with the 1831, 1909, and 1976 Acts, the CTEA's new terms apply to both future and existing copyrights.

**B**

We granted certiorari to address whether the CTEA's extension of existing copyrights exceeds Congress' power under the Copyright Clause.

**II**

**A**

We address first the determination of the courts below that Congress has authority under the Copyright Clause to extend the terms of existing copyrights. Text, history, and precedent, we conclude, confirm that the Copyright Clause empowers Congress to prescribe "limited Times" for copyright protection and to secure the same level and duration of protection for all copyright holders, present and future.

The CTEA's baseline term of life plus 70 years, petitioners concede, qualifies as a "limited Time" as applied to future copyrights. Petitioners contend, however, that existing copyrights extended to endure for that same term are not "limited." Petitioners' argument essentially reads into the text of the Copyright Clause the command that a time prescription, once set, becomes forever "fixed" or "inalterable." The word "limited," however, does not convey a meaning so constricted. At the time of the Framing, that word meant what it means today: "confined within certain bounds," "restrained," or "circumscribed." *S. Johnson, A Dictionary of the English Language* (7th ed. 1785). Thus understood, a time span appropriately "limited" as applied to future copyrights does not automatically cease to be "limited" when applied to existing copyrights.

Congress' consistent historical practice of applying newly enacted copyright terms to future and existing copyrights reflects a judgment stated concisely by Representative Huntington at the time of the 1831 Act: "Justice, policy, and equity alike forbid" that an "author who had sold his [work] a week ago, be placed in a worse situation than the author who should sell his work the day after the passing of [the] act." 7 Cong. Deb. 424 (1831). The CTEA follows this historical practice by keeping the duration provisions of the 1976 Act largely in place and simply adding 20 years to each of them. Guided by text, history, and precedent, we cannot agree with petitioners' submission that extending the duration of existing copyrights is categorically beyond Congress' authority under the Copyright Clause.

Satisfied that the CTEA complies with the "limited Times" prescription, we turn now to whether it is a rational exercise of the legislative authority conferred by the Copyright Clause. On that point, we defer substantially to Congress.

The CTEA reflects judgments of a kind Congress typically makes, judgments we cannot dismiss as outside the Legislature's domain. As respondent describes, a key factor in the CTEA's passage was a 1993 European Union (EU) directive instructing EU members to establish a copyright term of life plus 70 years. *EU Council Directive 93/98, p. 4; see 144 Cong. Rec. S12377–S12378* (daily ed. Oct. 12, 1998) (statement of Sen. Hatch). Consistent with the Berne Convention, the EU directed its members to deny this longer term to the works of any non-EU country whose laws did not secure the same extended term. See Berne Conv. Art. 7(8). By extending the baseline United States copyright term to life plus 70 years, Congress sought to ensure that American authors would receive the same copyright protection in Europe as their European counterparts. The CTEA may also provide greater incentive for American and other authors to create and disseminate their work in the United States.

In addition to international concerns, Congress passed the CTEA in light of demographic, economic, and technological changes, and rationally credited projections that longer terms would encourage copyright holders to invest in the restoration and public distribution of their works. Congress also heard testimony from Register of Copyrights Marybeth Peters and others regarding the economic incentives created by the CTEA. According to the Register, extending the copyright for existing works "could ... provide additional income that would finance the production and distribution of new works. Authors would not be able to continue to create," the Register explained, "unless they earned income on their finished works. The public benefits not only from an author's original work but also from his or her further creations. Although this truism may be illustrated in many ways, one of the best examples is Noah Webster[,] who supported his entire family from the earnings on his speller and grammar during the twenty years he took to complete his dictionary." *House Hearings 158–165.*

In sum, we find that the CTEA is a rational enactment; we are not at liberty to second-guess congressional determinations and policy judgments of this order, however debatable or arguably unwise they may be. Accordingly, we cannot conclude that the CTEA—which continues the unbroken congressional practice of treating future and existing copyrights in parity for term extension purposes—is an impermissible exercise of Congress' power under the Copyright Clause.

**IV**

As we read the Framers' instruction, the Copyright Clause empowers Congress to determine the intellectual property regimes that, overall, in that body's judgment, will serve the ends of the Clause. Beneath the facade of their inventive constitutional interpretation, petitioners forcefully urge that Congress pursued very bad policy in prescribing the CTEA's long terms. The wisdom of Congress' action, however, is not within our province to second guess. Satisfied that the legislation before us remains inside the domain the Constitution assigns to the First Branch, we affirm the judgment of the Court of Appeals.

**[Dissenting opinion by Justice Stevens omitted]**

**DISSENT:**

■ JUSTICE BREYER, dissenting.

The Constitution's Copyright Clause grants Congress the power to "*promote* the *Progress* of Science . . . by securing for *limited* Times to *Authors* . . . the exclusive Right to their respective Writings." Art. I, § 8, cl. 8 (emphasis added). The statute before us, the 1998 Sonny Bono Copyright Term Extension Act, extends the term of most existing copyrights to 95 years and that of many new copyrights to 70 years after the author's death. The economic effect of this 20–year extension—the longest blanket extension since the Nation's founding—is to make the copyright term not limited, but virtually perpetual. Its primary legal effect is to grant the extended term not to authors, but to their heirs, estates, or corporate successors. And most importantly, its practical effect is not to promote, but to inhibit, the progress of "Science"—by which word the Framers meant learning or knowledge.

The majority believes these conclusions rest upon practical judgments that at most suggest the statute is unwise, not that it is unconstitutional. Legal distinctions, however, are often matters of degree. And in this case the failings of degree are so serious that they amount to failings of constitutional kind. Although the Copyright Clause grants broad legislative power to Congress, that grant has limits. And in my view this statute falls outside them.

**I**

The "monopoly privileges" that the Copyright Clause confers "are neither unlimited nor primarily designed to provide a special private benefit." *Sony Corp. of America v. Universal City Studios, Inc.*, 464 U.S. 417, 429 (1984). This Court has made clear that the Clause's limitations are judicially enforceable. *E.g., Trade–Mark Cases*, 100 U.S. 82, 93–94, 25 L. Ed. 550, 1879 Dec. Comm'r Pat. 619 (1879). And, in assessing this statute for that purpose, I would take into account the fact that the Constitution is a single document, that it contains both a Copyright Clause and a First Amendment, and that the two are related.

The Copyright Clause and the First Amendment seek related objectives—the creation and dissemination of information. When working in tandem, these provisions mutually reinforce each other, the first serving as an "engine of free expression", *Harper & Row, Publishers, Inc. v. Nation Enterprises*, 471 U.S. 539, 558 (1985), the second assuring that government throws up no obstacle to its dissemination. At the same time, a particular statute that exceeds proper Copyright Clause bounds may set Clause and

Amendment at cross-purposes, thereby depriving the public of the speech-related benefits that the Founders, through both, have promised.

Consequently, I would review plausible claims that a copyright statute seriously, and unjustifiably, restricts the dissemination of speech somewhat more carefully than reference to this Court's traditional Commerce Clause jurisprudence might suggest. Rather, it is necessary only to recognize that this statute involves not pure economic regulation, but regulation of expression, and what may count as rational where economic regulation is at issue is not necessarily rational where we focus on expression—in a Nation constitutionally dedicated to the free dissemination of speech, information, learning, and culture. In this sense only, and where line-drawing among constitutional interests is at issue, I would look harder than does the majority at the statute's rationality—though less hard than precedent might justify.

I would find that the statute lacks the constitutionally necessary rational support (1) if the significant benefits that it bestows are private, not public; (2) if it threatens seriously to undermine the expressive values that the Copyright Clause embodies; and (3)if it cannot find justification in any significant Clause-related objective. Where, after examination of the statute, it becomes difficult, if not impossible, even to dispute these characterizations, Congress' "choice is clearly wrong." *Helvering v. Davis*, 301 U.S. 619, 640 (1937).

## II

### A

The Constitution itself describes the basic Clause objective as one of "promoting the Progress of Science," *i.e.*, knowledge and learning. The Clause exists not to "provide a special private benefit," *Sony*, 464 U.S. at 429, but "to stimulate artistic creativity for the general public good". *Twentieth Century Music Corp. v. Aiken*, 422 U.S. 151, 156 (1975). It does so by "motivating the creative activity of authors" through "the provision of a special reward." *Sony*, 464 U.S. at 429. The "reward" is a means, not an end. And that is why the copyright term is limited. It is limited so that its beneficiaries—the public—"will not be permanently deprived of the fruits of an artist's labors." *Stewart v. Abend*, 495 U.S. at 228.

Madison, like Jefferson and others in the founding generation, warned against the dangers of monopolies. *See, e.g., Monopolies. Perpetuities. Corporations. Ecclesiastical Endowments. in J. Madison, Writings* 756 (J. Rakove ed. 1999); *Letter from Thomas Jefferson to James Madison* (July 31, 1788), *in 13 Papers of Thomas Jefferson* 443 (J. Boyd ed. 1956)(arguing against even copyright monopolies); 2 Annals of Cong. 1917 (Gales and Seaton eds. 1834) (statement of Rep. Jackson in the First Congress, Feb. 1791) ("What was it drove our forefathers to this country? Was it not the ecclesiastical corporations and perpetual monopolies of England and Scotland?"). Madison noted that the Constitution had "limited them to two cases, the authors of Books, and of useful inventions." *[Madison]* id. at 756. He thought that in those two cases monopoly is justified because it amounts to "compensation for" an actual community "benefit" and because the monopoly is "temporary"—the term originally being 14 years (once renewable).

For present purposes, then, we should take the following as well established: that copyright statutes must serve public, not private, ends; that they must seek "to promote the Progress" of knowledge and learning; and that they must do so both by creating incentives for authors to produce and by removing the related restrictions on dissemination after expiration of a copyright's "limited Time". I would examine the statute's effects in light of these well-established constitutional purposes.

## C

What copyright-related benefits might justify the statute's extension of copyright protection? First, no one could reasonably conclude that copyright's traditional economic rationale applies here. The extension will not act as an economic spur encouraging authors to create new works. No potential author can reasonably believe that he has more than a tiny chance of writing a classic that will survive commercially long enough for the copyright extension to matter. * * * [I]n respect to works already created—*the statute creates no economic incentive at all.*

Second, the Court relies heavily for justification upon international uniformity of terms. Although it can be helpful to look to international norms and legal experience in understanding American law, in this case the justification based upon foreign rules is surprisingly weak. Those who claim that significant copyright-related benefits flow from greater international uniformity of terms point to the fact that the nations of the European Union have adopted a system of copyright terms uniform among themselves. And the extension before this Court implements a term of life plus 70 years that appears to conform with the European standard. But how does "uniformity" help to justify this statute?

Despite appearances, the statute does *not* create a uniform American–European term with respect to the lion's share of the economically significant works that it affects—*all* works made "for hire" and *all* existing works created prior to 1978. With respect to those works the American statute produces an extended term of 95 years while comparable European rights in "for hire" works last for periods that vary from 50 years to 70 years to life plus 70 years. *Compare 17 U.S.C. §§ 302(c), 304(a)–(b) with Council Directive 93/98/EEC of 29 October 1993 Harmonizing the Term of Protection of Copyright and Certain Related Rights, Arts. 1–3, 1993 Official J. Eur. Cmty. 290 (hereinafter EU Council Directive 93/98).* Neither does the statute create uniformity with respect to anonymous or pseudonymous works. *Compare 17 U.S.C. §§ 302(c), 304(a)–(b) with EU Council Directive 93/98, Art. 1.*

The statute does produce uniformity with respect to copyrights in new, post–1977 works attributed to natural persons. *Compare 17 U.S.C. § 302(a) with EU Council Directive 93/98, Art. 1(1).* But these works constitute only a subset (likely a minority) of works that retain commercial value after 75 years. And the fact that uniformity comes so late, if at all, means that bringing American law into conformity with this particular aspect of European law will neither encourage creation nor benefit the long-dead author in any other important way.

But if there is no incentive-related benefit, what is the benefit of the future uniformity that the statute only partially achieves? European and American copyright law have long coexisted despite important differences, including Europe's traditional respect for authors' "moral rights" and the absence in Europe of constitutional restraints that restrict copyrights to "limited Times." *See, e.g., Roberta Rosenthal Kwall, Copyright and the Moral Right: Is an American Marriage Possible?*, 38 Vand. L. Rev. 1, 1–3 (1985) (moral rights).

In sum, the partial, future uniformity that the 1998 Act promises cannot reasonably be said to justify extension of the copyright term for new works. And concerns with uniformity cannot possibly justify the extension of the new term to older works, for the statute there creates no uniformity at all.

## Community for Creative Non–Violence v. Reid

Supreme Court of the United States, 1989.
490 U.S. 730, 109 S.Ct. 2166, 104 L.Ed.2d 811.

■ JUSTICE MARSHALL delivered the opinion of the Court.

In this case, an artist and the organization that hired him to produce a sculpture contest the ownership of the copyright in that work. To resolve this dispute, we must construe the "work made for hire" provisions of the Copyright Act of 1976 (Act or 1976 Act), 17 U.S.C. §§ 101 and 201(b), and in particular, the provision in § 101, which defines as a "work made for hire" a "work prepared by an employee within the scope of his or her employment" (hereinafter § 101(1)).

I

Petitioners are the Community for Creative Non–Violence (CCNV), a nonprofit unincorporated association dedicated to eliminating homelessness in America, and Mitch Snyder, a member and trustee of CCNV. In the fall of 1985, CCNV decided to participate in the annual Christmastime Pageant of Peace in Washington, D.C., by sponsoring a display to dramatize the plight of the homeless. As the District Court recounted:

"Snyder and fellow CCNV members conceived the idea for the nature of the display: a sculpture of a modern Nativity scene in which, in lieu of the traditional Holy Family, the two adult figures and the infant would appear as contemporary homeless people huddled on a streetside steam grate. The family was to be black (most of the homeless in Washington being black); the figures were to be life-sized, and the steam grate would be positioned atop a platform 'pedestal,' or base, within which special-effects equipment would be enclosed to emit simulated 'steam' through the grid to swirl about the figures. They also settled upon a title for the work—'Third World

America'—and a legend for the pedestal: 'and still there is no room at the inn.' " 652 F.Supp. 1453, 1454 (D.C.1987).

Snyder made inquiries to locate an artist to produce the sculpture. He was referred to respondent James Earl Reid, a Baltimore, Maryland, sculptor. In the course of two telephone calls, Reid agreed to sculpt the three human figures. CCNV agreed to make the steam grate and pedestal for the statue. Reid proposed that the work be cast in bronze, at a total cost of approximately $100,000 and taking six to eight months to complete. Snyder rejected that proposal because CCNV did not have sufficient funds, and because the statue had to be completed by December 12 to be included in the pageant. Reid then suggested, and Snyder agreed, that the sculpture would be made of a material known as "Design Cast 62," a synthetic substance that could meet CCNV's monetary and time constraints, could be tinted to resemble bronze, and could withstand the elements. The parties agreed that the project would cost no more than $15,000, not including Reid's services, which he offered to donate. The parties did not sign a written agreement. Neither party mentioned copyright.

After Reid received an advance of $3,000, he made several sketches of figures in various poses. At Snyder's request, Reid sent CCNV a sketch of a proposed sculpture showing the family in a creche-like setting: the mother seated, cradling a baby in her lap; the father standing behind her, bending over her shoulder to touch the baby's foot. Reid testified that Snyder asked for the sketch to use in raising funds for the sculpture. Snyder testified that it was also for his approval. Reid sought a black family to serve as a model for the sculpture. Upon Snyder's suggestion, Reid visited a family living at CCNV's Washington shelter but decided that only their newly born child was a suitable model. While Reid was in Washington, Snyder took him to see homeless people living on the streets. Snyder pointed out that they tended to recline on steam grates, rather than sit or stand, in order to warm their bodies. From that time on, Reid's sketches contained only reclining figures.

Throughout November and the first two weeks of December 1985, Reid worked exclusively on the statue, assisted at various times by a dozen different people who were paid with funds provided in installments by CCNV. On a number of occasions, CCNV members visited Reid to check on his progress and to coordinate CCNV's construction of the base. CCNV rejected Reid's proposal to use suitcases or shopping bags to hold the family's personal belongings, insisting instead on a shopping cart. Reid and CCNV members did not discuss copyright ownership on any of these visits.

On December 24, 1985, 12 days after the agreed-upon date, Reid delivered the completed statue to Washington. There it was joined to the steam grate and pedestal prepared by CCNV and placed on display near the site of the pageant. Snyder paid Reid the final installment of the $15,000. The statue remained on display for a month. In late January 1986, CCNV members returned it to Reid's studio in Baltimore for minor repairs. Several weeks later, Snyder began making plans to take the statue on a tour of several cities to raise money for the homeless. Reid objected, contending that the Design Cast 62 material was not strong enough to withstand the ambitious itinerary. He urged CCNV to cast the statue in bronze at a cost of $35,000, or to create a master mold at a cost of $5,000. Snyder declined to spend more of CCNV's money on the project.

In March 1986, Snyder asked Reid to return the sculpture. Reid refused. He then filed a certificate of copyright registration for "Third World America" in his name and announced plans to take the sculpture on a more modest tour than the one CCNV had proposed. Snyder, acting in his capacity as CCNV's trustee, immediately filed a competing certificate of copyright registration.

Snyder and CCNV then commenced this action against Reid, seeking return of the sculpture and a determination of copyright ownership. The District Court granted a preliminary injunction, ordering the sculpture's return. After a 2–day bench trial, the District Court declared that "Third World America" was a "work made for hire" under § 101 of the Copyright Act and that Snyder, as trustee for CCNV, was the exclusive owner of the copyright in the sculpture. 652 F.Supp., at 1457. The court reasoned that Reid had been an "employee" of CCNV within the meaning of § 101(1) because CCNV was the motivating force in the statue's production. Snyder and other CCNV members, the court explained, "conceived the idea of a contemporary Nativity scene to contrast with the national celebration of the season," and "directed enough of [Reid's] effort to assure that, in the end, he had produced what they, not he, wanted." *Id.* at 1456.

The Court of Appeals for the District of Columbia Circuit reversed and remanded, holding that Reid owned the copyright because "Third World America" was not a work for hire. 846 F.2d 1485, 1494 (1988). Adopting what it termed the "literal interpretation" of the Act as articulated by the Fifth Circuit in Easter Seal Society for Crippled Children and Adults of Louisiana, Inc. v. Playboy Enterprises, 815 F.2d 323, 329 (1987), *cert. denied*, 485 U.S. 981 (1988), the court read § 101 as creating "a simple dichotomy in fact between employees and independent contractors." 846 F.2d, at 1492. Because, under agency law, Reid was an independent contractor, the court concluded that the work was not "prepared by an employee" under § 101(1). *Id.* at 1494. Nor was the sculpture a "work made for hire" under the second subsection of § 101 (hereinafter § 101(2)): sculpture is not one of the nine categories of works enumerated in that subsection, and the parties had not agreed in writing that the sculpture would be a work for hire. *Ibid.* The court suggested that the sculpture nevertheless may have been jointly authored by CCNV and Reid, *id.* at 1495, and remanded for a determination whether the sculpture is indeed a joint work under the Act, *id.*, 1498–1499.

We granted certiorari to resolve a conflict among the Courts of Appeals over the proper construction of the "work made for hire" provisions of the Act.[a] 488 U.S. 940 (1988). We now affirm.

[a] Compare Easter Seal Society for Crippled Children and Adults of Louisiana, Inc. v. Playboy Enterprises, 815 F.2d 323 (C.A.5 1987), *cert. denied*, 485 U.S. 981 (1988)(agen-

II

A

The Copyright Act of 1976 provides that copyright ownership "vests initially in the author or authors of the work." § 201(a). As a general rule, the author is the party who actually creates the work, that is, the person who translates an idea into a fixed, tangible expression entitled to copyright protection. § 102. The Act carves out an important exception, however, for "works made for hire."[b] If the work is for hire, "the employer or other person for whom the work was prepared is considered the author" and owns the copyright, unless there is a written agreement to the contrary. § 201(b). Classifying a work as "made for hire" determines not only the initial ownership of its copyright, but also the copyright's duration, § 302(c), and the owners' renewal rights, § 304(a), termination rights, § 203(a), and right to import certain goods bearing the copyright, § 601(b)(1). The contours of the work for hire doctrine therefore carry profound significance for freelance creators-including artists, writers, photographers, designers, composers, and computer programmers-and for the publishing, advertising, music, and other industries which commission their works.

Section 101 of the 1976 Act provides that a work is "for hire" under two sets of circumstances:

> "(1) a work prepared by an employee within the scope of his or her employment; or
>
> (2) a work specially ordered or commissioned for use as a contribution to a collective work, as a part of a motion picture or other audiovisual work, as a translation, as a supplementary work, as a compilation, as an instructional text, as a test, as answer material for a test, or as an atlas, if the parties expressly agree in a written instrument signed by them that the work shall be considered a work made for hire."[c]

Petitioners do not claim that the statue satisfies the terms of § 101(2). Quite clearly, it does not. Sculpture does not fit within any of the nine categories of "specially ordered or commissioned" works enumerated in that subsection, and no written agreement between the parties establishes "Third World America" as a work for hire.

The dispositive inquiry in this case therefore is whether "Third World America" is "a work prepared by an employee within the scope of his or her employment" under § 101(1). The Act does not define these terms. In

---

cy law determines who is an employee under § 101), with Brunswick Beacon, Inc. v. Schock–Hopchas Publishing Co., 810 F.2d 410 (C.A.4 1987)(supervision and control standard determines who is an employee under § 101); Evans Newton, Inc. v. Chicago Systems Software, 793 F.2d 889 (CA7), *cert. denied*, 479 U.S. 949 (1986) (same); and Aldon Accessories Ltd. v. Spiegel, Inc., 738 F.2d 548 (CA2), *cert. denied*, 469 U.S. 982 (1984)(a multifactor formal, salaried employee test determines who is an employee under § 101).

[b] We use the phrase "work for hire" interchangeably with the more cumbersome statutory phrase "work made for hire."

[c] Section 101 of the Act defines each of the nine categories of "specially ordered or commissioned" works.

the absence of such guidance, four interpretations have emerged. The first holds that a work is prepared by an employee whenever the hiring party[d] retains the right to control the product. See Peregrine v. Lauren Corp., 601 F.Supp. 828, 829 (D.Colo.1985); Clarkstown v. Reeder, 566 F.Supp. 137, 142 (S.D.N.Y.1983). Petitioners take this view. A second, and closely related, view is that a work is prepared by an employee under § 101(1) when the hiring party has actually wielded control with respect to the creation of a particular work. This approach was formulated by the Court of Appeals for the Second Circuit, Aldon Accessories Ltd. v. Spiegel, Inc., 738 F.2d 548, *cert. denied*, 469 U.S. 982 (1984), and adopted by the Fourth Circuit, Brunswick Beacon, Inc. v. Schock–Hopchas Publishing Co., 810 F.2d 410 (1987), the Seventh Circuit, Evans Newton, Inc. v. Chicago Systems Software, 793 F.2d 889, *cert. denied*, 479 U.S. 949 (1986), and, at times, by petitioners. A third view is that the term "employee" within § 101(1) carries its common-law agency law meaning. This view was endorsed by the Fifth Circuit in Easter Seal Society for Crippled Children and Adults of Louisiana, Inc. v. Playboy Enterprises, 815 F.2d 323 (1987), and by the Court of Appeals below. Finally, respondent and numerous amici curiae contend that the term "employee" only refers to "formal, salaried" employees. The Court of Appeals for the Ninth Circuit recently adopted this view. See Dumas v. Gommerman, 865 F.2d 1093 (1989).

The starting point for our interpretation of a statute is always its language. The Act nowhere defines the terms "employee" or "scope of employment." It is, however, well established that "where Congress uses terms that have accumulated settled meaning under . . . the common law, a court must infer, unless the statute otherwise dictates, that Congress means to incorporate the established meaning of these terms." NLRB v. Amax Coal Co., 453 U.S. 322, 329 (1981). In the past, when Congress has used the term "employee" without defining it, we have concluded that Congress intended to describe the conventional master-servant relationship as understood by common-law agency doctrine. [Citations omitted.] Nothing in the text of the work for hire provisions indicates that Congress used the words "employee" and "employment" to describe anything other than "the conventional relation of employer and employe[e]." [Citation omitted.] [C]ompare NLRB v. Hearst Publications, 322 U.S. 111, 124–132 (1944)(rejecting agency law conception of employee for purposes of the National Labor Relations Act where structure and context of statute indicated broader definition). On the contrary, Congress' intent to incorporate the agency law definition is suggested by § 101(1)'s use of the term, "scope of employment," a widely used term of art in agency law. See Restatement (Second) of Agency § 228 (1958)(hereinafter Restatement).

In past cases of statutory interpretation, when we have concluded that Congress intended terms such as "employee," "employer," and "scope of employment" to be understood in light of agency law, we have relied on the

---

[d] By "hiring party," we mean to refer to the party who claims ownership of the copyright by virtue of the work for hire doctrine.

general common law of agency, rather than on the law of any particular State, to give meaning to these terms. [Citations omitted.] This practice reflects the fact that "federal statutes are generally intended to have uniform nationwide application." Mississippi Band of Choctaw Indians v. Holyfield, 490 U.S. 30, 43 (1989). Establishment of a federal rule of agency, rather than reliance on state agency law, is particularly appropriate here given the Act's express objective of creating national, uniform copyright law by broadly pre-empting state statutory and common-law copyright regulation. See § 301(a). We thus agree with the Court of Appeals that the term "employee" should be understood in light of the general common law of agency.

In contrast, neither test proposed by petitioners is consistent with the text of the Act. The exclusive focus of the right to control the product test on the relationship between the hiring party and the product clashes with the language of § 101(1), which focuses on the relationship between the hired and hiring parties. The right to control the product test also would distort the meaning of the ensuing subsection, § 101(2). Section 101 plainly creates two distinct ways in which a work can be deemed for hire: one for works prepared by employees, the other for those specially ordered or commissioned works which fall within one of the nine enumerated categories and are the subject of a written agreement. The right to control the product test ignores this dichotomy by transforming into a work for hire under § 101(1) any "specially ordered or commissioned" work that is subject to the supervision and control of the hiring party. Because a party who hires a "specially ordered or commissioned" work by definition has a right to specify the characteristics of the product desired, at the time the commission is accepted, and frequently until it is completed, the right to control the product test would mean that many works that could satisfy § 101(2) would already have been deemed works for hire under § 101(1). Petitioners' interpretation is particularly hard to square with § 101(2)'s enumeration of the nine specific categories of specially ordered or commissioned works eligible to be works for hire, e.g., "a contribution to a collective work," "a part of a motion picture," and "answer material for a test." The unifying feature of these works is that they are usually prepared at the instance, direction, and risk of a publisher or producer. By their very nature, therefore, these types of works would be works by an employee under petitioners' right to control the product test.

The actual control test, articulated by the Second Circuit in *Aldon Accessories*, fares only marginally better when measured against the language and structure of § 101. Under this test, independent contractors who are so controlled and supervised in the creation of a particular work are deemed "employees" under § 101(1). Thus work for hire status under § 101(1) depends on a hiring party's *actual* control of, rather than *right to* control, the product. *Aldon Accessories*, 738 F.2d, at 552. Under the actual control test, a work for hire could arise under § 101(2), but not under § 101(1), where a party commissions, but does not actually control, a product which falls into one of the nine enumerated categories. Nonetheless, we agree with the Fifth Circuit Court of Appeals that "[t]here is simply no way to milk the 'actual control' test of *Aldon Accessories* from the language of the statute." *Easter Seal Society*, 815 F.2d, at 334. Section 101 clearly delineates between works prepared by an employee and commissioned works. Sound though other distinctions might be as a matter of copyright policy, there is no statutory support for an additional dichotomy between commissioned works that are actually controlled and supervised by the hiring party and those that are not.

We therefore conclude that the language and structure of § 101 of the Act do not support either the right to control the product or the actual control approaches.[e] The structure of § 101 indicates that a work for hire can arise through one of two mutually exclusive means, one for employees and one for independent contractors, and ordinary canons of statutory interpretation indicate that the classification of a particular hired party should be made with reference to agency law.

This reading of the undefined statutory terms finds considerable support in the Act's legislative history. The Act, which almost completely revised existing copyright law, was the product of two decades of negotiation by representatives of creators and copyright-using industries, supervised by the Copyright Office and, to a lesser extent, by Congress. Despite the lengthy history of negotiation and compromise which ultimately produced the Act, two things remained constant. First, interested parties and Congress at all times viewed works by employees and commissioned works by independent contractors as separate entities. Second, in using the term "employee," the parties and Congress meant to refer to a hired party in a conventional employment relationship. These factors militate in favor of the reading we have found appropriate.

In 1955, when Congress decided to overhaul copyright law, the existing work for hire provision was § 62 of the 1909 Copyright Act. It provided that "the word 'author' shall include an employer in the case of works made for hire." Because the 1909 Act did not define "employer" or "works made for hire," the task of shaping these terms fell to the courts. They concluded that the work for hire doctrine codified in § 62 referred only to works made by employees in the regular course of their employment. As for commissioned works, the courts generally presumed that the commissioned

---

[e] We also reject the suggestion of respondent and amici that the § 101(1) term "employee" refers only to formal, salaried employees. While there is some support for such a definition in the legislative history, the language of § 101(1) cannot support it. The Act does not say "formal" or "salaried" employee, but simply "employee." Moreover, respondent and those amici who endorse a formal, salaried employee test do not agree upon the content of this test. Compare, e.g., Brief for Respondent 37 (hired party who is on payroll is an employee within § 101(1)) with Tr. of Oral Arg. 31 (hired party who receives a salary or commissions regularly is an employee within § 101(1)); and Brief for Volunteer Lawyers for the Arts Inc. et al. as Amici Curiae 4 (hired party who receives a salary *and* is treated as an employee for Social Security and tax purposes is an employee within § 101(1)). Even the one Court of Appeals to adopt what it termed a formal, salaried employee test in fact embraced an approach incorporating numerous factors drawn from the agency law definition of employee which we endorse. See *Dumas*, 865 F.2d at 1104.

party had impliedly agreed to convey the copyright, along with the work itself, to the hiring party. [Citations omitted.]

In 1961, the Copyright Office's first legislative proposal retained the distinction between works by employees and works by independent contractors. See Report of the Register of Copyrights on the General Revision of the U.S. Copyright Law, 87th Cong., 1st Sess., Copyright Law Revision 86–87 (H. Judiciary Comm. Print 1961). After numerous meetings with representatives of the affected parties, the Copyright Office issued a preliminary draft bill in 1963. Adopting the Register's recommendation, it defined "work made for hire" as "a work prepared by an employee within the scope of the duties of his employment, but not including a work made on special order or commission." Preliminary Draft for Revised U.S. Copyright Law and Discussions and Comments on the Draft, 88th Cong., 2d Sess., Copyright Law Revision, Part 3, p.15, n.11 (H. Judiciary Comm. Print 1964)(hereinafter Preliminary Draft).

In response to objections by book publishers that the preliminary draft bill limited the work for hire doctrine to "employees," the 1964 revision bill expanded the scope of the work for hire classification to reach, for the first time, commissioned works. The bill's language, proposed initially by representatives of the publishing industry, retained the definition of work for hire insofar as it referred to "employees," but added a separate clause covering commissioned works, without regard to the subject matter, "if the parties so agree in writing." S. 3008, H.R. 11947, H.R. 12354, 88th Cong., 2d Sess., § 54 (1964), reproduced in 1964 Revision Bill with Discussions and Comments, 89th Cong., 1st Sess., Copyright Law Revision, pt.5, p.31 (H. R. Judiciary Comm. Print 1965). Those representing authors objected that the added provision would allow publishers to use their superior bargaining position to force authors to sign work for hire agreements, thereby relinquishing all copyright rights as a condition of getting their books published. See Supplementary Report, at 67.

In 1965, the competing interests reached an historic compromise, which was embodied in a joint memorandum submitted to Congress and the Copyright Office,[f] incorporated into the 1965 revision bill, and ultimately enacted in the same form and nearly the same terms 11 years later, as § 101 of the 1976 Act. The compromise retained as subsection (1) the language referring to "a work prepared by an employee within the scope of his employment." However, in exchange for concessions from publishers on provisions relating to the termination of transfer rights, the authors consented to a second subsection which classified four categories of commissioned works as works for hire if the parties expressly so agreed in writing: works for use "as a contribution to a collective work, as a part of a motion picture, as a translation, or as supplementary work." S. 1006, H.R.

---

[f] The parties to the joint memorandum included representatives of the major competing interests involved in the copyright revision process: publishers and authors, composers, and lyricists. See Copyright Law Revision: Hearings on H.R. 4347, 5680, 6831, 6835 before Subcommittee No. 3 of the House Committee on the Judiciary, 89th Cong., 1st Sess., pt.1, p.134 (1965).

4347, H.R. 5680, H.R. 6835, 89th Cong., 1st Sess., § 101 (1965). The interested parties selected these categories because they concluded that these commissioned works, although not prepared by employees and thus not covered by the first subsection, nevertheless should be treated as works for hire because they were ordinarily prepared "at the instance, direction, and risk of a publisher or producer." Supplementary Report of the Register of Copyrights on the General Revision of the U.S. Copyright Law: 1965 Revision Bill, 89th Cong., 1st Sess., Copyright Law Revision, 67 (H.R. Judiciary Comm. Print 1965)(hereinafter Supplementary Report). The Supplementary Report emphasized that only the "four special cases specifically mentioned" could qualify as works made for hire; "other works made on special order or commission would not come within the definition." *Id.* at 67–68.

In 1966, the House Committee on the Judiciary endorsed this compromise in the first legislative report on the revision bills. See H.R. Rep. No. 2237, 89th Cong., 2d Sess., 114, 116 (1966). Retaining the distinction between works by employees and commissioned works, the House Committee focused instead on "how to draw a statutory line between those works written on special order or commission that should be considered as works made for hire, and those that should not." *Id.* at 115. The House Committee added four other enumerated categories of commissioned works that could be treated as works for hire: compilations, instructional texts, tests, and atlases. *Id.* at 116. With the single addition of "answer material for a test," the 1976 Act, as enacted, contained the same definition of works made for hire as did the 1966 revision bill, and had the same structure and nearly the same terms as the 1966 bill.[g] Indeed, much of the language of the 1976 House and Senate Reports was borrowed from the Reports accompanying the earlier drafts.

Thus, the legislative history of the Act is significant for several reasons. First, the enactment of the 1965 compromise with only minor modifications demonstrates that Congress intended to provide two mutually exclusive ways for works to acquire work for hire status: one for employees and the other for independent contractors. Second, the legislative history underscores the clear import of the statutory language: only enumerated categories of commissioned works may be accorded work for hire status. The hiring party's right to control the product simply is not determinative. Indeed, importing a test based on a hiring party's right to

---

[g] An attempt to add "photographic or other portrait[s]," S. Rep. No. 94–473, p. 4 (1975), to the list of commissioned works eligible for work for hire status failed after the Register of Copyrights objected:

"The addition of portraits to the list of commissioned works that can be made into 'works made for hire' by agreement of the parties is difficult to justify. Artists and photographers are among the most vulnerable and poorly protected of all the beneficiaries of the copyright law, and it seems clear that, like serious composers and choreographers, they were not intended to be treated as 'employees' under the carefully negotiated definition in section 101."

Second Supplementary Report of the Register of Copyrights on the General Revision of the U.S. Copyright Law: 1975 Revision Bill, Chapter XI, p. 12–13.

control, or actual control of, a product would unravel the "carefully worked out compromise aimed at balancing legitimate interests on both sides." H.R. Rep. No. 2237, at 114, quoting Supplemental Report, at 66.[h]

[P]etitioners' construction of the work for hire provisions would impede Congress' paramount goal in revising the 1976 Act of enhancing predictability and certainty of copyright ownership. See H.R. Rep. No. 94–1476, at 129. In a "copyright marketplace," the parties negotiate with an expectation that one of them will own the copyright in the completed work. *Dumas*, 865 F.2d, at 1104–1105, n.18. With that expectation, the parties at the outset can settle on relevant contractual terms, such as the price for the work and the ownership of reproduction rights.

To the extent that petitioners endorse an actual control test,[i] CCNV's construction of the work for hire provisions prevents such planning. Because that test turns on whether the hiring party has closely monitored the production process, the parties would not know until late in the process, if not until the work is completed, whether a work will ultimately fall within § 101(1). Under petitioners' approach, therefore, parties would have to predict in advance whether the hiring party will sufficiently control a given work to make it the author. "If they guess incorrectly, their reliance on 'work for hire' or an assignment may give them a copyright interest that they did not bargain for." *Easter Seal Society*, 815 F.2d, at 333; accord, *Dumas*, 865 F.2d, at 1103. This understanding of the work for hire provisions clearly thwarts Congress' goal of ensuring predictability through advance planning. Moreover, petitioners' interpretation "leaves the door open for hiring parties, who have failed to get a full assignment of copyright rights from independent contractors falling outside the subdivision (2) guidelines, to unilaterally obtain work-made-for-hire rights years after the work has been completed as long as they directed or supervised the work, a standard that is hard not to meet when one is a hiring party." Hamilton, Commissioned Works as Works Made for Hire Under the 1976 Copyright Act: Misinterpretation and Injustice, 135 U. Pa. L. Rev. 1281, 1304 (1987).

In sum, we must reject petitioners' argument. Transforming a commissioned work into a work by an employee on the basis of the hiring party's right to control, or actual control of, the work is inconsistent with the language, structure, and legislative history of the work for hire provisions. To determine whether a work is for hire under the Act, a court first should ascertain, using principles of general common law of agency, whether the work was prepared by an employee or an independent contractor. After making this determination, the court can apply the appropriate subsection of § 101.

---

[h] Strict adherence to the language and structure of the Act is particularly appropriate where, as here, a statute is the result of a series of carefully crafted compromises.

[i] Petitioners concede that, as a practical matter, it is often difficult to demonstrate the existence of a right to control without evidence of the actual exercise of that right.

B

We turn, finally, to an application of § 101 to Reid's production of "Third World America." In determining whether a hired party is an employee under the general common law of agency, we consider the hiring party's right to control the manner and means by which the product is accomplished. Among the other factors relevant to this inquiry are the skill required; the source of the instrumentalities and tools; the location of the work; the duration of the relationship between the parties; whether the hiring party has the right to assign additional projects to the hired party; the extent of the hired party's discretion over when and how long to work; the method of payment; the hired party's role in hiring and paying assistants; whether the work is part of the regular business of the hiring party; whether the hiring party is in business; the provision of employee benefits; and the tax treatment of the hired party. See Restatement § 220(2)(setting forth a nonexhaustive list of factors relevant to determining whether a hired party is an employee).[j] No one of these factors is determinative.

Examining the circumstances of this case in light of these factors, we agree with the Court of Appeals that Reid was not an employee of CCNV but an independent contractor. 846 F.2d, at 1494, n.11. True, CCNV members directed enough of Reid's work to ensure that he produced a sculpture that met their specifications. 652 F.Supp., at 1456. But the extent of control the hiring party exercises over the details of the product is not dispositive. Indeed, all the other circumstances weigh heavily against finding an employment relationship. Reid is a sculptor, a skilled occupation. Reid supplied his own tools. He worked in his own studio in Baltimore, making daily supervision of his activities from Washington practicably impossible. Reid was retained for less than two months, a relatively short period of time. During and after this time, CCNV had no right to assign additional projects to Reid. Apart from the deadline for completing the sculpture, Reid had absolute freedom to decide when and how long to work. CCNV paid Reid $15,000, a sum dependent on "completion of a specific job, a method by which independent contractors are often compensated." Holt v. Winpisinger, 811 F.2d 1532, 1540 (1987). Reid had total discretion in hiring and paying assistants. "Creating sculptures was hardly 'regular business' for CCNV." 846 F.2d, at 1494, n.11. Indeed, CCNV is not a business at all. Finally, CCNV did not pay payroll or Social Security taxes, provide any employee benefits, or contribute to unemployment insurance or workers' compensation funds.

Because Reid was an independent contractor, whether "Third World America" is a work for hire depends on whether it satisfies the terms of § 101(2). This petitioners concede it cannot do. Thus, CCNV is not the author of "Third World America" by virtue of the work for hire provisions of the Act. However, as the Court of Appeals made clear, CCNV nevertheless may be a joint author of the sculpture if, on remand, the District Court

[j] In determining whether a hired party is an employee under the general common law of agency, we have traditionally looked for guidance to the Restatement of Agency.

determines that CCNV and Reid prepared the work "with the intention that their contributions be merged into inseparable or interdependent parts of a unitary whole." § 101.[k] In that case, CCNV and Reid would be co-owners of the copyright in the work. See § 201(a).

For the aforestated reasons, we affirm the judgment of the Court of Appeals for the District of Columbia Circuit.

It is so ordered.

---

[k] Neither CCNV nor Reid sought review of the Court of Appeals' remand order. We therefore have no occasion to pass judgment on the applicability of the Act's joint authorship provisions to this case.

"Third World America." Reprinted with the permission of James Earl Reid, sculptor and Community for Creative Non–Violence. Photography by Ron Portee. Print supplied by James Earl Reid and Ron Portee.

AND STILL THERE IS NO ROOM AT THE INN

## Childress v. Taylor

United States Court of Appeals, Second Circuit, 1991.
945 F.2d 500.

■ NEWMAN, CIRCUIT JUDGE.

This appeal requires consideration of the standards for determining when a contributor to a copyrighted work is entitled to be regarded as a joint author. The work in question is a play about the legendary Black comedienne Jackie "Moms" Mabley. The plaintiff-appellee Alice Childress claims to be the sole author of the play. Her claim is disputed by defendant-appellant Clarice Taylor, who asserts that she is a joint author of the play. Taylor, Paul B. Berkowsky, Ben Caldwell, and the "Moms" Company appeal from the February 21, 1991, judgment of the District Court for the Southern District of New York (Charles S. Haight, Jr., Judge) determining, on motion for summary judgment, that Childress is the sole author. We affirm.

Facts

Defendant Clarice Taylor has been an actress for over forty years, performing on stage, radio, television, and in film. After portraying

"Moms" Mabley in a skit in an off-off-Broadway production ten years ago, Taylor became interested in developing a play based on Mabley's life. Taylor began to assemble material about "Moms" Mabley, interviewing her friends and family, collecting her jokes, and reviewing library resources.

In 1985, Taylor contacted the plaintiff, playwright Alice Childress, about writing a play based on "Moms" Mabley. Childress had written many plays, for one of which she won an "Obie" award. Taylor had known Childress since the 1940s when they were both associated with the American Negro Theatre in Harlem and had previously acted in a number of Childress's plays.

When Taylor first mentioned the "Moms" Mabley project to Childress in 1985, Childress stated she was not interested in writing the script because she was too occupied with other works. However, when Taylor approached Childress again in 1986, Childress agreed, though she was reluctant due to the time constraints involved. Taylor had interested the Green Plays Theatre in producing the as yet unwritten play, but the theatre had only one slot left on its summer 1986 schedule, and in order to use that slot, the play had to be written in six weeks.

Taylor turned over all of her research material to Childress, and later did further research at Childress's request. It is undisputed that Childress wrote the play, entitled "Moms: A Praise Play for a Black Comedienne." However, Taylor, in addition to providing the research material, which according to her involved a process of sifting through facts and selecting pivotal and key elements to include in a play on "Moms" Mabley's life, also discussed with Childress the inclusion of certain general scenes and characters in the play. Additionally, Childress and Taylor spoke on a regular basis about the progress of the play.

Taylor identifies the following as her major contributions to the play: (1) she learned through interviews that "Moms" Mabley called all of her piano players "Luther," so Taylor suggested that the play include such a character; (2) Taylor and Childress together interviewed Carey Jordan, "Moms" Mabley's housekeeper, and upon leaving the interview they came to the conclusion that she would be a good character for the play, but Taylor could not recall whether she or Childress suggested it; (3) Taylor informed Childress that "Moms" Mabley made a weekly trip to Harlem to do ethnic food shopping; (4) Taylor suggested a street scene in Harlem with speakers because she recalled having seen or listened to such a scene many times; (5) the idea of using a minstrel scene came out of Taylor's research; (6) the idea of a card game scene also came out of Taylor's research, although Taylor could not recall who specifically suggested the scene; (7) some of the jokes used in the play came from Taylor's research; and (8) the characteristics of "Moms" Mabley's personality portrayed in the play emerged from Taylor's research. Essentially, Taylor contributed facts and details about "Moms" Mabley's life and discussed some of them with Childress. However, Childress was responsible for the actual structure of the play and the dialogue.

Childress completed the script within the six-week time frame. Childress filed for and received a copyright for the play in her name. Taylor produced the play at the Green Plays Theatre in Lexington, New York, during the 1986 summer season and played the title role. After the play's run at the Green Plays Theatre, Taylor planned a second production of the play at the Hudson Guild Theatre in New York City.

At the time Childress agreed to the project, she did not have any firm arrangements with Taylor, although Taylor had paid her $2,500 before the play was produced. On May 9, 1986, Taylor's agent, Scott Yoselow, wrote to Childress's agent, Flora Roberts, stating:

> Per our telephone conversation, this letter will bring us up-to-date on the current status of our negotiation for the above mentioned project:
>
> 1) CLARICE TAYLOR will pay ALICE CHILDRESS for her playwriting services on the MOMS MABLEY PROJECT the sum of $5,000.00, which will also serve as an advance against any future royalties.
>
> 2) The finished play shall be equally owned and be the property of both CLARICE TAYLOR and ALICE CHILDRESS. It is my understanding that Alice has commenced writing the project. I am awaiting a response from you regarding any additional points we have yet to discuss.

Flora Roberts responded to Yoselow in a letter dated June 16, 1986:

> As per our recent telephone conversation, I have told Alice Childress that we are using your letter to me of May 9, 1986 as a partial memo preparatory to our future good faith negotiations for a contract. There are two points which I include herewith to complete your two points in the May 9th letter, i.e.:
>
> 1) The $5,000 advance against any future royalties being paid by Clarice Taylor to Alice Childress shall be paid as follows. Since $1,000 has already been paid, $1,500 upon your receipt of this letter and the final $2,500 to be paid upon submission of the First Draft, but in no event later than July 7, 1986.
>
> 2) It is to be understood that pending the proper warranty clauses to be included in the contract, Miss Childress is claiming originality for her words only in said script.

After the Green Plays Theatre production, Taylor and Childress attempted to formalize their relationship. Draft contracts were exchanged between Taylor's attorney, Jay Kramer, and Childress's agent, Roberts. During this period, early 1987, the play was produced at the Hudson Guild Theatre with the consent of both Taylor and Childress. Childress filed for and received a copyright for the new material added to the play produced at the Hudson Guild Theatre.

In March 1987, Childress rejected the draft agreement proposed by Taylor,[a] and the parties' relationship deteriorated. Taylor decided to mount

---

[a] The preamble to this draft agreement stated:

The Producer [Taylor] wishes to acquire from the Author [Childress] the rights to produce and present a dramatic play written by Author and heretofore presented at the Hudson Guild Theatre

another production of the play without Childress. Taylor hired Ben Caldwell to write another play featuring "Moms" Mabley; Taylor gave Caldwell a copy of the Childress script and advised him of elements that should be changed.

The "Moms" Mabley play that Caldwell wrote was produced at the Astor Place Theatre in August 1987.[b] No reference to Childress was made with respect to this production. However, a casting notice in the trade paper "Back Stage" reported the production of Caldwell's play and noted that it had been "presented earlier this season under an Equity LOA at the Hudson Guild Theatre."

Flora Roberts contacted Jay Kramer to determine whether this notice was correct. Kramer responded:

> Ben Caldwell has written the play which I will furnish to you when a final draft is available. We have tried in every way to distinguish the new version of the play from what was presented at the Hudson Guild, both by way of content and billing.
>
> Undoubtedly, because of the prevalence of public domain material in both versions of the play, there may be unavoidable similarities. Please also remember that Alice was paid by Clarice for rights to her material which we have never resolved.

Kramer never sent a copy of Caldwell's play. Childress's attorney, Alvin Deutsch, sent Kramer a letter advising him of Childress's rights in the play as produced at the Hudson Guild and of her concerns about the advertising connecting Caldwell's play to hers. For example, one advertisement for Caldwell's play at the Astor Place Theatre quoted reviews referring to Childress's play. Other advertisements made reference to the fact that the play had been performed earlier that season at the Hudson Guild Theatre.

Childress sued Taylor and other defendants alleging violations of the Copyright Act. Taylor contended that she was a joint author with Childress, and therefore shared the rights to the play. Childress moved for summary judgment, which the District Court granted. The Court concluded that Taylor was not a joint author of Childress's play and that Caldwell's play was substantially similar to and infringed Childress's play. In rejecting Taylor's claim of joint authorship, Judge Haight ruled (a) that a work qualifies as a "joint work" under the definition section of the Copyright Act, § 101, only when *both* authors intended, at the time the work was created, "that their contributions be merged into inseparable or interdependent parts of a unitary whole," *id.*, and (b) that there was insufficient evidence to permit a reasonable trier to find that Childress had the requisite intent. The Court further ruled that copyright law requires the contributions of both authors to be independently copyrightable, and that Taylor's contributions, which consisted of ideas and research, were not copyrightable.

based on the life and career of Moms Mabley....

[b] The Caldwell play was billed as being "based on a concept by Clarice Taylor." Taylor was not listed as an author of that play.

Discussion

In common with many issues arising in the domain of copyrights, the determination of whether to recognize joint authorship in a particular case requires a sensitive accommodation of competing demands advanced by at least two persons, both of whom have normally contributed in some way to the creation of a work of value. Care must be taken to ensure that true collaborators in the creative process are accorded the perquisites of co-authorship and to guard against the risk that a sole author is denied exclusive authorship status simply because another person rendered some form of assistance. Copyright law best serves the interests of creativity when it carefully draws the bounds of "joint authorship" so as to protect the legitimate claims of both sole authors and co-authors.

Co-authorship was well known to the common law. An early formulation, thought by Learned Hand to be the first definition of "joint authorship," see Edward B. Marks Music Corp. v. Jerry Vogel Music Co., 140 F.2d 266, 267 (2d Cir.1944) ("Marks"), is set out in Levy v. Rutley, L.R., 6 C.P. 523, 529 (Keating, J.)(1871): "a joint laboring in furtherance of a common design." Three decades later, he adopted the formulation of this Circuit in *Marks*, determining that the words and music of a song ("December and May") formed a work of joint authorship even though the lyricist wrote the words before he knew the identity of the composer who would later write the music.

Though the early case law is illuminating, our task is to apply the standards of the Copyright Act of 1976 and endeavor to achieve the results that Congress likely intended.

The Copyright Act defines a "joint work" as:

> a work prepared by two or more authors with the intention that their contributions be merged into inseparable or interdependent parts of a unitary whole.

§ 101. The definition concerns the *creation* of the work by the joint authors, not the circumstances, in addition to joint authorship, under which a work may be *jointly owned*, for example, by assignment of an undivided interest. The distinction affects the rights that are acquired. Joint authors hold undivided interests in a work, like all joint owners of a work, but joint authors, unlike other joint owners, also enjoy all the rights of authorship, including the renewal rights applicable to works in which a statutory copyright subsisted prior to January 1, 1978. See § 304.

Some aspects of the statutory definition of joint authorship are fairly straightforward. Parts of a unitary whole are "inseparable" when they have little or no independent meaning standing alone. That would often be true of a work of written text, such as the play that is the subject of the pending litigation. By contrast, parts of a unitary whole are "interdependent" when they have some meaning standing alone but achieve their primary significance because of their combined effect, as in the case of the words and music of a song. Indeed, a novel and a song are among the examples offered by the legislative committee reports on the 1976 Copyright Act to illustrate the difference between "inseparable" and "interdependent" parts. See H.R. Rep. No. 1476, 94th Cong., 2d Sess. 120 (1976)("House Report"), reprinted in 1976 U.S.C.C.A.N. 5659, 5736; S. Rep. No. 473, 94th Cong., 2d Sess. 103–04 (1975)("Senate Report").

The legislative history also clarifies other aspects of the statutory definition, but leaves some matters in doubt. Endeavoring to flesh out the definition, the committee reports state:

> [A] work is "joint" if the authors collaborated with each other, or if *each* of the authors prepared his or her contribution with the knowledge and *intention* that it would be merged with the contributions of other authors as "inseparable or interdependent parts of a unitary whole." The touchstone here is the *intention, at the time the writing is done*, that the parts be absorbed or combined into an integrated unit. . . .

House Report at 120; Senate Report at 103 (emphasis added). This passage appears to state two alternative criteria—one focusing on the act of collaboration and the other on the parties' intent. However, it is hard to imagine activity that would constitute meaningful "collaboration" unaccompanied by the requisite intent on the part of both participants that their contributions be merged into a unitary whole, and the case law has read the statutory language literally so that the intent requirement applies to all works of joint authorship. See, e.g., Weissmann v. Freeman, 868 F.2d 1313, 1317–19 (2d Cir.1989); Eckert v. Hurley Chicago Co., Inc., 638 F.Supp. 699, 702–03 (N.D.Ill.1986).

A more substantial issue arising under the statutory definition of "joint work" is whether the contribution of each joint author must be copyrightable or only the combined result of their joint efforts must be copyrightable. The Nimmer treatise argues against a requirement of copyrightability of each author's contribution, see 1 Nimmer on Copyright § 6.07; Professor Goldstein takes the contrary view, see 1 Paul Goldstein, Copyright: Principles, Law and Practice § 4.2.1.2 (1989), with the apparent agreement of the Latman treatise, see William F. Patry, Latman's The Copyright Law 116 (6th ed. 1986)(hereinafter "Latman"). The case law supports a requirement of copyrightability of each contribution. [Citations omitted.] The Register of Copyrights strongly supports this view, arguing that it is required by the statutory standard of "authorship" and perhaps by the Constitution. See Moral Rights in Our Copyright Laws: Hearings on S. 1198 and S. 1253 Before the Subcomm. on Patents, Copyrights and Trademarks of the Senate Comm. on the Judiciary, 101st Cong., 1st Sess. 210–11 (1989)(statement of Ralph Oman).

The issue, apparently open in this Circuit, is troublesome. If the focus is solely on the objective of copyright law to encourage the production of creative works, it is difficult to see why the contributions of all joint authors need be copyrightable. An individual creates a copyrightable work by combining a non-copyrightable idea with a copyrightable form of expression; the resulting work is no less a valuable result of the creative process simply because the idea and the expression came from two different individuals. Indeed, it is not unimaginable that there exists a skilled writer who might never have produced a significant work until some other person supplied the idea. The textual argument from the statute is not convincing. The Act surely does not say that each contribution to a joint work must be copyrightable, and the specification that there be "authors" does not necessarily require a copyrightable contribution. "Author" is not defined in the Act and appears to be used only in its ordinary sense of an originator. The "author" of an uncopyrightable idea is nonetheless its author even though, for entirely valid reasons, the law properly denies him a copyright on the result of his creativity. And the Register's tentative constitutional argument seems questionable. It has not been supposed that the statutory grant of "authorship" status to the employer of a work made for hire exceeds the Constitution, though the employer has shown skill only in selecting employees, not in creating protectable expression.[c]

Nevertheless, we are persuaded to side with the position taken by the case law and endorsed by the agency administering the Copyright Act. The insistence on copyrightable contributions by all putative joint authors might serve to prevent some spurious claims by those who might otherwise try to share the fruits of the efforts of a sole author of a copyrightable work. More important, the prevailing view strikes an appropriate balance in the domains of both copyright and contract law. In the absence of contract, the copyright remains with the one or more persons who created copyrightable material. Contract law enables a person to hire another to create a copyrightable work, and the copyright law will recognize the employer as "author." § 201(b). Similarly, the person with non-copyrightable material who proposes to join forces with a skilled writer to produce a copyrightable work is free to make a contract to disclose his or her material in return for assignment of part ownership of the resulting copyright. *Id.* § 201(d). And, as with all contract matters, the parties may minimize subsequent disputes by formalizing their agreement in a written contract. It seems more consistent with the spirit of copyright law to oblige all joint authors to make copyrightable contributions, leaving those with non-copyrightable contributions to protect their rights through contract.

There remains for consideration the crucial aspect of joint authorship-the nature of the intent that must be entertained by each putative joint author at the time the contribution of each was created. The wording of the statutory definition appears to make relevant only the state of mind

---

[c] Judge Friendly has suggested that the concept of authorship in the constitutional grant implies some limitations. "It would thus be quite doubtful that Congress could grant employers the exclusive right to the writings of employees regardless of the circumstances." Scherr v. Universal Match Corp., 417 F.2d 497, 502 (2d Cir.1969) (Friendly, J., dissenting), *cert. denied*, 397 U.S. 936 (1970). He suggested that the "work for hire" doctrine, whether applied to employees or independent contractors (commissioned works) squares with the constitutional concept because vesting rights of authorship in the employer is what the parties "contemplated at the time of the contracting, or at least what they probably would have contemplated if they had thought about it." *Id.* However, this seems more like a justification for transfer of ownership than for recognition of authorship. Though the United States is perhaps the only country that confers "authorship" status on the employer of the creator of a work made for hire, see Latman at 114 n.2, its decision to do so is not constitutionally suspect.

regarding the unitary nature of the finished work-an intention "that their contributions be merged into inseparable or interdependent parts of a unitary whole." However, an inquiry so limited would extend joint author status to many persons who are not likely to have been within the contemplation of Congress. For example, a writer frequently works with an editor who makes numerous useful revisions to the first draft, some of which will consist of additions of copyrightable expression. Both intend their contributions to be merged into inseparable parts of a unitary whole, yet very few editors and even fewer writers would expect the editor to be accorded the status of joint author, enjoying an undivided half interest in the copyright in the published work. Similarly, research assistants may on occasion contribute to an author some protectable expression or merely a sufficiently original selection of factual material as would be entitled to a copyright, yet not be entitled to be regarded as a joint author of the work in which the contributed material appears. What distinguishes the writer-editor relationship and the writer-researcher relationship from the true joint author relationship is the lack of intent of both participants in the venture to regard themselves as joint authors.[d]

Focusing on whether the putative joint authors regarded themselves as joint authors is especially important in circumstances, such as the instant case, where one person (Childress) is indisputably the dominant author of the work and the only issue is whether that person is the sole author or she and another (Taylor) are joint authors. This concern requires less exacting consideration in the context of traditional forms of collaboration, such as between the creators of the words and music of a song.

In this case, appellant contends that Judge Haight's observation that "Childress never shared Taylor's notion that they were co-authors of the play" misapplies the statutory standard by focusing on whether Childress "intended the legal consequences which flowed from her prior acts." We do not think Judge Haight went so far. He did not inquire whether Childress intended that she and Taylor would hold equal undivided interests in the play. But he properly insisted that they entertain in their minds the concept of joint authorship, whether or not they understood precisely the legal consequences of that relationship. Though joint authorship does not require an understanding by the co-authors of the legal consequences of their relationship, obviously some distinguishing characteristic of the relationship must be understood in order for it to be the subject of their intent. In many instances, a useful test will be whether, in the absence of contractual agreements concerning listed authorship, each participant intended that all would be identified as co-authors. Though "billing" or "credit" is not decisive in all cases and joint authorship can exist without

[d] In some situations, the editor or researcher will be the employee of the primary author, in which event the copyright in the contributions of the editor or researcher would belong to the author, under the "work made for hire" doctrine. But in many situations the editor or researcher will be an independent contractor or an employee of some person or entity other than the primary author, in which event a claim of joint authorship would not be defeated by the "work made for hire" doctrine.

any explicit discussion of this topic by the parties,[e] consideration of the topic helpfully serves to focus the fact-finder's attention on how the parties implicitly regarded their undertaking.

An inquiry into how the putative joint authors regarded themselves in relation to the work has previously been part of our approach in ascertaining the existence of joint authorship. In Gilliam v. American Broadcasting Companies, Inc., 538 F.2d 14 (2d Cir.1976), we examined the parties' written agreements and noted that their provisions indicated "that the parties *did not consider themselves joint authors* of a single work." *Id.* at 22 (emphasis added). This same thought is evident in Judge Leval's observation that "[i]t is only where the dominant author *intends to be sharing authorship* that joint authorship will result." Fisher v. Klein, 16 U.S.P.Q.2d (BNA) 1795 at 1798 (S.D.N.Y.1990)(emphasis added). See also Weissmann v. Freeman, 868 F.2d at 1318 (each of those claiming to be joint authors "must intend to contribute to a joint work."). Judge Haight was entirely correct to inquire whether Childress ever shared Taylor's "notion that they were co-authors of the Play."

Examination of whether the putative co-authors ever shared an intent to be co-authors serves the valuable purpose of appropriately confining the bounds of joint authorship arising by operation of copyright law, while leaving those not in a true joint authorship relationship with an author free to bargain for an arrangement that will be recognized as a matter of both copyright and contract law. Joint authorship entitles the co-authors to equal undivided interests in the work, see § 201(a). That equal sharing of rights should be reserved for relationships in which all participants fully intend to be joint authors. The sharing of benefits in other relationships involving assistance in the creation of a copyrightable work can be more precisely calibrated by the participants in their contract negotiations regarding division of royalties or assignment of shares of ownership of the copyright, see § 201(d).

In this case, the issue is not only whether Judge Haight applied the correct standard for determining joint authorship but also whether he was entitled to conclude that the record warranted a summary judgment in favor of Childress. We are satisfied that Judge Haight was correct as to both issues. We need not determine whether we agree with his conclusion that Taylor's contributions were not independently copyrightable since, even if they were protectable as expression or as an original selection of facts, we agree that there is no evidence from which a trier could infer that Childress had the state of mind required for joint authorship. As Judge Haight observed, whatever thought of co-authorship might have existed in Taylor's mind "was emphatically not shared by the purported co-author." There is no evidence that Childress ever contemplated, much less would

---

[e] Obviously, consideration of whether the parties contemplated listed co-authorship (or would have accepted such billing had they thought about it) is not a helpful inquiry for works written by an uncredited "ghost writer," either as a sole author, as a joint author, or as an employee preparing a work for hire.

have accepted, crediting the play as "written by Alice Childress and Clarice Taylor."

Childress was asked to write a play about "Moms" Mabley and did so. To facilitate her writing task she accepted the assistance that Taylor provided, which consisted largely of furnishing the results of research concerning the life of "Moms" Mabley. As the actress expected to portray the leading role, Taylor also made some incidental suggestions, contributing ideas about the presentation of the play's subject and possibly some minor bits of expression. But there is no evidence that these aspects of Taylor's role ever evolved into more than the helpful advice that might come from the cast, the directors, or the producers of any play. A playwright does not so easily acquire a co-author.

Judge Haight was fully entitled to bolster his decision by reliance on the contract negotiations that followed completion of the script. Though his primary basis for summary judgment was the absence of any evidence supporting an inference that Childress shared "Taylor's notion that they were co-authors," he properly pointed to the emphatic rejection by Childress of the attempts by Taylor's agent to negotiate a co-ownership agreement and Taylor's acquiescence in that rejection. Intent "at the time the writing is done" remains the "touchstone," House Report at 120; Senate Report at 103, but subsequent conduct is normally probative of a prior state of mind.

Taylor's claim of co-authorship was properly rejected, and with the rejection of that claim, summary judgment for Childress was properly entered. The judgment of the District Court is affirmed.

## Stewart v. Abend

Supreme Court of the United States, 1990.
495 U.S. 207, 110 S.Ct. 1750, 109 L.Ed.2d 184.

■ JUSTICE O'CONNOR delivered the opinion of the Court.

The author of a pre-existing work may assign to another the right to use it in a derivative work. In this case the author of a pre-existing work agreed to assign the rights in his renewal copyright term to the owner of a derivative work, but died before the commencement of the renewal period. The question presented is whether the owner of the derivative work infringed the rights of the successor owner of the pre-existing work by continued distribution and publication of the derivative work during the renewal term of the pre-existing work.

I

Cornell Woolrich authored the story "It Had to Be Murder," which was first published in February 1942 in Dime Detective Magazine. The magazine's publisher, Popular Publications, Inc., obtained the rights to magazine publication of the story and Woolrich retained all other rights. Popular

Publications obtained a blanket copyright for the issue of Dime Detective Magazine in which "It Had to Be Murder" was published.

The Copyright Act of 1909 (1909 Act) provided authors a 28–year initial term of copyright protection plus a 28–year renewal term. In 1945, Woolrich agreed to assign the rights to make motion picture versions of six of his stories, including "It Had to Be Murder," to B. G. DeSylva Productions for $9,250. He also agreed to renew the copyrights in the stories at the appropriate time and to assign the same motion picture rights to DeSylva Productions for the 28–year renewal term. In 1953, actor Jimmy Stewart and director Alfred Hitchcock formed a production company, Patron, Inc., which obtained the motion picture rights in "It Had to Be Murder" from DeSylva's successors in interest for $10,000.

In 1954, Patron, Inc., along with Paramount Pictures, produced and distributed "Rear Window," the motion picture version of Woolrich's story "It Had to Be Murder." Woolrich died in 1968 before he could obtain the rights in the renewal term for petitioners as promised and without a surviving spouse or child. He left his property to a trust administered by his executor, Chase Manhattan Bank, for the benefit of Columbia University. On December 29, 1969, Chase Manhattan Bank renewed the copyright in the "It Had to Be Murder" story. Chase Manhattan assigned the renewal rights to respondent Abend for $650 plus 10% of all proceeds from exploitation of the story.

"Rear Window" was broadcast on the ABC television network in 1971. Respondent then notified petitioners Hitchcock (now represented by cotrustees of his will), Stewart, and MCA Inc., the owners of the "Rear Window" motion picture and renewal rights in the motion picture, that he owned the renewal rights in the copyright and that their distribution of the motion picture without his permission infringed his copyright in the story. Hitchcock, Stewart, and MCA nonetheless entered into a second license with ABC to rebroadcast the motion picture. In 1974, respondent filed suit against these same petitioners, and others, in the United States District Court for the Southern District of New York, alleging copyright infringement. Respondent dismissed his complaint in return for $25,000.

Three years later, the United States Court of Appeals for the Second Circuit decided Rohauer v. Killiam Shows, Inc., 551 F.2d 484, *cert. denied*, 431 U.S. 949 (1977), in which it held that the owner of the copyright in a derivative work may continue to use the existing derivative work according to the original grant from the author of the pre-existing work even if the grant of rights in the pre-existing work lapsed. 551 F.2d, at 494. Several years later, apparently in reliance on *Rohauer*, petitioners re-released the motion picture in a variety of media, including new 35 and 16 millimeter prints for theatrical exhibition in the United States, videocassettes, and videodiscs. They also publicly exhibited the motion picture in theaters, over cable television, and through videodisc and videocassette rentals and sales.

Respondent then brought the instant suit in the United States District Court for the Central District of California against Hitchcock, Stewart, MCA, and Universal Film Exchanges, a subsidiary of MCA and the distributor of the motion picture. Respondent's complaint alleges that the release of the motion picture infringes his copyright in the story because petitioners' right to use the story during the renewal term lapsed when Woolrich died before he could register for the renewal term and transfer his renewal rights to them. Respondent also contends that petitioners have interfered with his rights in the renewal term of the story in other ways. He alleges that he sought to contract with Home Box Office (HBO) to produce a play and television version of the story, but that petitioners wrote to him and HBO stating that neither he nor HBO could use either the title, "Rear Window" or "It Had to Be Murder." Respondent also alleges that petitioners further interfered with the renewal copyright in the story by attempting to sell the right to make a television sequel and that the re-release of the original motion picture itself interfered with his ability to produce other derivative works.

Petitioners filed motions for summary judgment based on the decision in *Rohauer*. Respondent moved for summary judgment on the ground that petitioners' use of the motion picture constituted copyright infringement. The District Court granted petitioners' motions for summary judgment based on *Rohauer*. Respondent appealed to the United States Court of Appeals for the Ninth Circuit.

The Court of Appeals reversed. 863 F.2d 1465 (1988). The issue before the court was whether petitioners were entitled to distribute and exhibit the motion picture without respondent's permission despite respondent's valid copyright in the pre-existing story. Relying on the renewal provision of the 1909 Act, § 24 (1976 ed.), respondent argued before the Court of Appeals that because he obtained from Chase Manhattan Bank, the statutory successor, the renewal right free and clear of any purported assignments of any interest in the renewal copyright, petitioners' distribution and publication of "Rear Window" without authorization infringed his renewal copyright. Petitioners responded that they had the right to continue to exploit "Rear Window" during the 28-year renewal period because Woolrich had agreed to assign to petitioners' predecessor in interest the motion picture rights in the story for the renewal period.

Petitioners also relied, as did the District Court, on the decision in Rohauer v. Killiam Shows, Inc. ... In *Rohauer*, the Court of Appeals for the Second Circuit held that statutory successors to the renewal copyright in a pre-existing work under § 24 could not "depriv[e] the proprietor of the derivative copyright of a right ... to use so much of the underlying copyrighted work as already has been embodied in the copyrighted derivative work, as a matter of copyright law." *Id.* at 492. The Court of Appeals in the instant case rejected this reasoning, concluding that even if the pre-existing work had been incorporated into a derivative work, use of the pre-existing work was infringing unless the owner of the derivative work held a valid grant of rights in the renewal term.

The court relied on Miller Music Corp. v. Charles N. Daniels, Inc., 362 U.S. 373 (1960), in which we held that assignment of renewal rights by an author before the time for renewal arrives cannot defeat the right of the author's statutory successor to the renewal rights if the author dies before the right to renewal accrues. An assignee of the renewal rights takes only an expectancy. The Court of Appeals reasoned that "[i]f *Miller Music* makes assignment of the full renewal rights in the underlying copyright unenforceable when the author dies before effecting renewal of the copyright, then a fortiori, an assignment of part of the rights in the underlying work, the right to produce a movie version, must also be unenforceable if the author dies before effecting renewal of the underlying copyright." 863 F.2d, at 1476. Finding further support in the legislative history of the 1909 Act and rejecting the *Rohauer* court's reliance on the equities and the termination provisions of the 1976 Act, §§ 203(b)(1), 304(c)(6)(A)(1988 ed.), the Court of Appeals concluded that petitioners received from Woolrich only an expectancy in the renewal rights that never matured; upon Woolrich's death, Woolrich's statutory successor, Chase Manhattan Bank, became "entitled to a renewal and extension of the copyright," which Chase Manhattan secured "within one year prior to the expiration of the original term of copyright." § 24 (1976 ed.). Chase Manhattan then assigned the existing rights in the copyright to respondent.

We granted certiorari to resolve the conflict between the decision in *Rohauer*, and the decision below. 493 U.S. 807 (1989).

## II

### A

Petitioners would have us read into the Copyright Act a limitation on the statutorily created rights of the owner of an underlying work. They argue in essence that the rights of the owner of the copyright in the derivative use of the pre-existing work are extinguished once it is incorporated into the derivative work, assuming the author of the pre-existing work has agreed to assign his renewal rights. Because we find no support for such a curtailment of rights in either the 1909 Act or the 1976 Act, or in the legislative history of either, we affirm the judgment of the Court of Appeals.

Petitioners and amicus Register of Copyrights assert, as the Court of Appeals assumed, that § 23 of the 1909 Act, § 24 (1976 ed.), and the case law interpreting that provision, directly control the disposition of this case. Respondent counters that the provisions of the 1976 Act control, but that the 1976 Act re-enacted § 24 in § 304 and, therefore, the language and judicial interpretation of § 24 are relevant to our consideration of this case. Under either theory, we must look to the language of and case law interpreting § 24.

The right of renewal found in § 24 provides authors a second opportunity to obtain remuneration for their works. Section 24 provides:

> "[T]he author of [a copyrighted] work, if still living, or the widow, widower, or children of the author, if the author be not living, or if such author, widow, widower, or children be not living, then the author's executors, or in the absence of a will, his next of kin shall be entitled to a renewal and extension of the copyright in such work for a further term of

twenty-eight years when application for such renewal and extension shall have been made to the copyright office and duly registered therein within one year prior to the expiration of the original term of copyright." § 24 (1976 ed.).

Since the earliest copyright statute in this country, the copyright term of ownership has been split between an original term and a renewal term. Originally, the renewal was intended merely to serve as an extension of the original term; at the end of the original term, the renewal could be effected and claimed by the author, if living, or by the author's executors, administrators, or assigns. In 1831, Congress altered the provision so that the author could assign his contingent interest in the renewal term, but could not, through his assignment, divest the rights of his widow or children in the renewal term. "The evident purpose of [the renewal provision] is to provide for the family of the author after his death. Since the author cannot assign his family's renewal rights, [it] takes the form of a compulsory bequest of the copyright to the designated persons." DeSylva v. Ballentine, 351 U.S. 570, 582 (1956).

In its debates leading up to the Copyright Act of 1909, Congress elaborated upon the policy underlying a system comprised of an original term and a completely separate renewal term. The renewal term permits the author, originally in a poor bargaining position, to renegotiate the terms of the grant once the value of the work has been tested. With these purposes in mind, Congress enacted the renewal provision of the Copyright Act of 1909, § 24 (1976 ed.). With respect to works in their original or renewal term as of January 1, 1978, Congress retained the two-term system of copyright protection in the 1976 Act. See §§ 304(a) and (b)(1988 ed.) (incorporating language of § 24 (1976 ed.)).

Applying these principles in Miller Music Corp. v. Charles N. Daniels, Inc., 362 U.S. 373 (1960), this Court held that when an author dies before the renewal period arrives, his executor is entitled to the renewal rights, even though the author previously assigned his renewal rights to another party. Thus, the renewal provisions were intended to give the author a second chance to obtain fair remuneration for his creative efforts and to provide the author's family a "new estate" if the author died before the renewal period arrived.

An author holds a bundle of exclusive rights in the copyrighted work, among them the right to copy and the right to incorporate the work into derivative works. By assigning the renewal copyright in the work without limitation, as in *Miller Music*, the author assigns all of these rights. After *Miller Music*, if the author dies before the commencement of the renewal period, the assignee holds nothing. If the assignee of all of the renewal rights holds nothing upon the death of the assignor before arrival of the renewal period, then, a fortiori, the assignee of a portion of the renewal rights, e.g., the right to produce a derivative work, must also hold nothing. Therefore, if the author dies before the renewal period, then the assignee may continue to use the original work only if the author's successor transfers the renewal rights to the assignee. This is the rule adopted by the

Court of Appeals below and advocated by the Register of Copyrights. Application of this rule to this case should end the inquiry. Woolrich died before the commencement of the renewal period in the story, and, therefore, petitioners hold only an unfulfilled expectancy. Petitioners have been "deprived of nothing. Like all purchasers of contingent interests, [they took] subject to the possibility that the contingency may not occur." *Miller Music*, at 378.

B

The reason that our inquiry does not end here, and that we granted certiorari, is that the Court of Appeals for the Second Circuit reached a contrary result in Rohauer v. Killiam Shows, Inc., 551 F.2d 484 (1977). Petitioners' theory is drawn largely from *Rohauer*. The Court of Appeals in *Rohauer* attempted to craft a "proper reconciliation" between the owner of the pre-existing work, who held the right to the work pursuant to *Miller Music*, and the owner of the derivative work, who had a great deal to lose if the work could not be published or distributed. 551 F.2d, at 490. Addressing a case factually similar to this case, the court concluded that even if the death of the author caused the renewal rights in the pre-existing work to revert to the statutory successor, the owner of the derivative work could continue to exploit that work. The court reasoned that the 1976 Act and the relevant precedents did not preclude such a result and that it was necessitated by a balancing of the equities:

> "[T]he equities lie preponderantly in favor of the proprietor of the derivative copyright. In contrast to the situation where an assignee or licensee has done nothing more than print, publicize and distribute a copyrighted story or novel, a person who with the consent of the author has created an opera or a motion picture film will often have made contributions literary, musical and economic, as great as or greater than the original author.... [T]he purchaser of derivative rights has no truly effective way to protect himself against the eventuality of the author's death before the renewal period since there is no way of telling who will be the surviving widow, children or next of kin or the executor until that date arrives." *Id.* at 493.

The Court of Appeals for the Second Circuit thereby shifted the focus from the right to use the pre-existing work in a derivative work to a right inhering in the created derivative work itself. By rendering the renewal right to use the original work irrelevant, the court created an exception to our ruling in *Miller Music* and, as petitioners concede, created an "intrusion" on the statutorily created rights of the owner of the pre-existing work in the renewal term.

Though petitioners do not, indeed could not, argue that its language expressly supports the theory they draw from *Rohauer*, they implicitly rely on § 6 of the 1909 Act, § 7 (1976 ed.), which states that "dramatizations ... of copyrighted works when produced with the consent of the proprietor of the copyright in such works ... shall be regarded as new works subject to copyright under the provisions of this title." Petitioners maintain that the creation of the "new," i.e., derivative, work extinguishes any right the owner of rights in the pre-existing work might have had to sue for infringement that occurs during the renewal term.

We think that . . . aspects of a derivative work added by the derivative author are that author's property, but the element drawn from the pre-existing work remains on grant from the owner of the pre-existing work. So long as the pre-existing work remains out of the public domain, its use is infringing if one who employs the work does not have a valid license or assignment for use of the pre-existing work. It is irrelevant whether the pre-existing work is inseparably intertwined with the derivative work. Indeed, the plain language of § 7 supports the view that the full force of the copyright in the pre-existing work is preserved despite incorporation into the derivative work. See § 7 (1976 ed.) (publication of the derivative work "shall not affect the force or validity of any subsisting copyright upon the matter employed"). This well-settled rule also was made explicit in the 1976 Act:

> "The copyright in a compilation or derivative work extends only to the material contributed by the author of such work, as distinguished from the pre-existing material employed in the work, and does not imply any exclusive right in the pre-existing material. The copyright in such work is independent of, and does not affect or enlarge the scope, duration, ownership, or subsistence of, any copyright protection in the pre-existing material." § 103(b)(1988 ed.).

Properly conceding there is no explicit support for their theory in the 1909 Act, its legislative history, or the case law, petitioners contend, as did the court in *Rohauer*, that the termination provisions of the 1976 Act, while not controlling, support their theory of the case. For works existing in their original or renewal terms as of January 1, 1978, the 1976 Act added 19 years to the 1909 Act's provision of 28 years of initial copyright protection and 28 years of renewal protection. See §§ 304(a) and (b)(1988 ed.). For those works, the author has the power to terminate the grant of rights at the end of the renewal term and, therefore, to gain the benefit of that additional 19 years of protection. See § 304(c). In effect, the 1976 Act provides a third opportunity for the author to benefit from a work in its original or renewal term as of January 1, 1978. Congress, however, created one exception to the author's right to terminate: The author may not, at the end of the renewal term, terminate the right to use a derivative work for which the owner of the derivative work has held valid rights in the original and renewal terms. See § 304(c)(6)(A). The author, however, may terminate the right to create new derivative works. *Ibid.* For example, if petitioners held a valid copyright in the story throughout the original and renewal terms, and the renewal term in "Rear Window" were about to expire, petitioners could continue to distribute the motion picture even if respondent terminated the grant of rights, but could not create a new motion picture version of the story. Both the court in *Rohauer* and petitioners infer from this exception to the right to terminate an intent by Congress to prevent authors of pre-existing works from blocking distribution of derivative works. In other words, because Congress decided not to permit authors to exercise a third opportunity to benefit from a work incorporated into a derivative work, the Act expresses a general policy of undermining the author's second opportunity. We disagree.

The process of compromise between competing special interests leading to the enactment of the 1976 Act undermines any such attempt to draw an overarching policy out of § 304(c)(6)(A), which only prevents termination with respect to works in their original or renewal copyright terms as of January 1, 1978, and only at the end of the renewal period.

In fact, if the 1976 Act's termination provisions provide any guidance at all in this case, they tilt against petitioners' theory. The plain language of the termination provision itself indicates that Congress assumed that the owner of the pre-existing work possessed the right to sue for infringement even after incorporation of the pre-existing work in the derivative work.

> "A derivative work *prepared* under authority of the grant before its termination may continue to be utilized under the terms of the grant after its termination, but this privilege does not extend to the preparation after the termination of other derivative works based upon the copyrighted work covered by the terminated grant." § 304(c)(6)(A)(emphasis added).

Congress would not have stated explicitly in § 304(c)(6)(A) that, at the end of the renewal term, the owner of the rights in the pre-existing work may not terminate use rights in existing derivative works unless Congress had assumed that the owner continued to hold the right to sue for infringement even after incorporation of the pre-existing work into the derivative work. Cf. Mills Music, Inc. v. Snyder, 469 U.S. 153, 164 (1985) (§ 304(c)(6)(A) "carves out an exception from the reversion of rights that takes place when an author exercises his right to termination").

Accordingly, we conclude that neither the 1909 Act nor the 1976 Act provides support for the theory set forth in *Rohauer*. And even if the theory found some support in the statute or the legislative history, the approach set forth in *Rohauer* is problematic. While the result in *Rohauer* might make some sense in some contexts, it makes no sense in others. In the case of a condensed book, for example, the contribution by the derivative author may be little, while the contribution by the original author is great. Yet, under the *Rohauer* "rule," publication of the condensed book would not infringe the pre-existing work even though the derivative author has no license or valid grant of rights in the pre-existing work. Thus, even if the *Rohauer* "rule" made sense in terms of policy in that case, it makes little sense when it is applied across the derivative works spectrum.

Finally, petitioners urge us to consider the policies underlying the Copyright Act. They argue that the rule announced by the Court of Appeals will undermine one of the policies of the Act—the dissemination of creative works—by leading to many fewer works reaching the public. These arguments are better addressed by Congress than the courts.

In any event, the complaint that respondent's monetary request in this case is so high as to preclude agreement fails to acknowledge that an initially high asking price does not preclude bargaining. Presumably, respondent is asking for a share in the proceeds because he wants to profit from the distribution of the work, not because he seeks suppression of it.

Moreover, although dissemination of creative works is a goal of the Copyright Act, the Act creates a balance between the artist's right to control the work during the term of the copyright protection and the public's need for access to creative works. The copyright term is limited so that the public will not be permanently deprived of the fruits of an artist's labors. But nothing in the copyright statutes would prevent an author from hoarding all of his works during the term of the copyright. In fact, this Court has held that a copyright owner has the capacity arbitrarily to refuse to license one who seeks to exploit the work. See Fox Film Corp. v. Doyal, 286 U.S. 123, 127 (1932).

The limited monopoly granted to the artist is intended to provide the necessary bargaining capital to garner a fair price for the value of the works passing into public use. When an author produces a work which later commands a higher price in the market than the original bargain provided, the copyright statute is designed to provide the author the power to negotiate for the realized value of the work. That is how the separate renewal term was intended to operate. At heart, petitioners' true complaint is that they will have to pay more for the use of works they have employed in creating their own works. But such a result was contemplated by Congress and is consistent with the goals of the Copyright Act.

With the Copyright Act of 1790, Congress provided an initial term of protection plus a renewal term that did not survive the author. In the Copyright Act of 1831, Congress devised a completely separate renewal term that survived the death of the author so as to create a "new estate" and to benefit the author's family, and, with the passage of the 1909 Act, his executors. The 1976 Copyright Act provides a single, fixed term, but provides an inalienable termination right. See §§ 203, 302. This evolution of the duration of copyright protection tellingly illustrates the difficulties Congress faces in attempting to "secur[e] for limited Times to Authors ... the exclusive Right to their respective Writings." U.S. Const., Art. I, § 8, cl.8. Absent an explicit statement of congressional intent that the rights in the renewal term of an owner of a pre-existing work are extinguished upon incorporation of his work into another work, it is not our role to alter the delicate balance Congress has labored to achieve.

[Affirmed.]

# New York Times Co., Inc., et al. v. Jonathan Tasini, et al.[7]

Supreme Court of the United States, 2001.
533 U.S. 483, 121 S.Ct. 2381, 150 L.Ed.2d 500.

■ JUSTICE GINSBURG delivered the opinion of the Court.

This copyright case concerns the rights of freelance authors and a presumptive privilege of their publishers. The litigation was initiated by six free-

[7] Editors Note: For an interesting symposium devoted to *Tasini* and related issues, see *The Law, Technology & The Arts Sympo-* *sium: Copyright in the Digital Age: Reflections on Tasini and Beyond,* 53 Case Western L. Rev. 601 (2003).

lance authors and relates to articles they contributed to three print periodicals (two newspapers and one magazine). Under agreements with the periodicals' publishers, but without the freelancers' consent, two computer database companies placed copies of the freelancers' articles—along with all other articles from the periodicals in which the freelancers' work appeared—into three databases. Whether written by a freelancer or staff member, each article is presented to, and retrievable by, the user in isolation, clear of the context the original print publication presented.

The freelance authors' complaint alleged that their copyrights had been infringed by the inclusion of their articles in the databases. The publishers, in response, relied on the privilege of reproduction and distribution accorded them by § 201(c) of the Copyright Act, which provides:

> "Copyright in each separate contribution to a collective work is distinct from copyright in the collective work as a whole, and vests initially in the author of the contribution. In the absence of an express transfer of the copyright or of any rights under it, the owner of copyright in the collective work is presumed to have acquired only the privilege of reproducing and distributing the contribution as part of that particular collective work, any revision of that collective work, and any later collective work in the same series." 17 U.S.C. 201(c).

Specifically, the publishers maintained that, as copyright owners of collective works, *i.e.,* the original print publications, they had merely exercised "the privilege" § 201(c) accords them to "reproduce and distribute" the author's discretely copyrighted contribution.

In agreement with the Second Circuit, we hold that § 201(c) does not authorize the copying at issue here. The publishers are not sheltered by § 201(c), we conclude, because the databases reproduce and distribute articles standing alone and not in context, not "as part of that particular collective work" to which the author contributed, "as part of . . . any revision" thereof, or "as part of . . . any later collective work in the same series." Both the print publishers and the electronic publishers, we rule, have infringed the copyrights of the freelance authors.

## I

### A

Respondents Jonathan Tasini [and others] are authors (Authors). Between 1990 and 1993, they wrote the 21 articles (Articles) on which this dispute centers. [The Authors] contributed 12 Articles to The New York Times, the daily newspaper published by petitioner The New York Times Company (Times); Newsday, another New York daily paper, published by petitioner Newsday, Inc. (Newsday); [and] Sports Illustrated, a weekly magazine published by petitioner Time, Inc. (Time). The Authors registered copyrights in each of the Articles. The Times, Newsday, and Time (Print Publishers) registered collective work copyrights in each periodical edition in which an Article originally appeared. The Print Publishers engaged the Authors as independent contractors (freelancers) under contracts that in no instance secured consent from an Author to placement of an Article in an electronic database.

At the time the Articles were published, all three Print Publishers had agreements with petitioner LEXIS/NEXIS (formerly Mead Data Central Corp.), owner and operator of NEXIS, a computerized database that stores information in a text-only format. NEXIS contains articles from hundreds of journals (newspapers and periodicals) spanning many years. The Print Publishers have licensed to LEXIS/NEXIS the text of articles appearing in the three periodicals. The licenses authorize LEXIS/NEXIS to copy and sell any portion of those texts.

Pursuant to the licensing agreements, the Print Publishers regularly provide LEXIS/NEXIS with a batch of all the articles published in each periodical edition. The Print Publisher codes each article to facilitate computerized retrieval, then transmits it in a separate file. After further coding, LEXIS/NEXIS places the article in the central discs of its database.

Subscribers to NEXIS, accessing the system through a computer, may search for articles by author, subject, date, publication, headline, key term, words in text, or other criteria. Responding to a search command, NEXIS scans the database and informs the user of the number of articles meeting the user's search criteria. The user then may view, print, or download each of the articles yielded by the search. The display of each article includes the print publication (*e.g.*, The New York Times), date (September 23, 1990), section (Magazine), initial page number (26), headline or title ("Remembering Jane"), and author. Each article appears as a separate, isolated "story"—without any visible link to the other stories originally published in the same newspaper or magazine edition. NEXIS does not contain pictures or advertisements, and it does not reproduce the original print publication's formatting features such as headline size, page placement (e.g., above or below the fold for newspapers), or location of continuation pages.

The Times (but not Newsday or Time) also has licensing agreements with petitioner University Microfilms International (UMI). The agreements authorize reproduction of Times materials on two CD–ROM products, the New York Times OnDisc (NYTO) and General Periodicals OnDisc (GPO).

Like NEXIS, NYTO is a text-only system. Unlike NEXIS, NYTO, as its name suggests, contains only the Times. Pursuant to a three-way agreement, LEXIS/NEXIS provides UMI with computer files containing each article as transmitted by the Times to LEXIS/NEXIS. Like LEXIS/NEXIS, UMI marks each article with special codes. UMI also provides an index of all the articles in NYTO. Articles appear in NYTO in essentially the same way they appear in NEXIS, i.e., with identifying information (author, title, etc.), but without original formatting or accompanying images.

GPO contains articles from approximately 200 publications or sections of publications. Unlike NEXIS and NYTO, GPO is an image-based, rather than a text-based, system. The Times has licensed GPO to provide a facsimile of the Times' Sunday Book Review and Magazine. UMI "burns" images of each page of these sections onto CD–ROMs. The CD–ROMs show each article exactly as it appeared on printed pages, complete with photographs, captions, advertisements, and other surrounding materials. UMI provides an index and abstracts of all the articles in GPO. Articles are accessed through NYTO and GPO much as they are accessed through NEXIS.

B

On December 16, 1993, the Authors filed this civil action in the United States District Court for the Southern District of New York. The Authors alleged that their copyrights were infringed when, as permitted and facilitated by the Print Publishers, LEXIS/NEXIS and UMI (Electronic Publishers) placed the Articles in the NEXIS, NYTO, and GPO databases (Databases). The Authors sought declaratory and injunctive relief, and damages. In response to the Authors' complaint, the Print and Electronic Publishers raised the reproduction and distribution privilege accorded collective work copyright owners by 17 U.S.C. 201(c). After discovery, both sides moved for summary judgment.

The District Court granted summary judgment for the Publishers, holding that § 201(c) shielded the Database reproductions. 972 F. Supp. 804, 806 (1997). The privilege conferred by § 201(c) is transferable, the court first concluded, and therefore could be conveyed from the original Print Publishers to the Electronic Publishers. Id. at 816. Next, the court determined, the Databases reproduced and distributed the Authors' works, in § 201(c)'s words, "as part of ... [a] revision of that collective work" to which the Authors had first contributed. To qualify as "revisions," according to the court, works need only "preserve some significant original aspect of [collective works]—whether an original selection or an original arrangement." Id. at 821. This criterion was met, in the District Court's view, because the Databases preserved the Print Publishers' "selection of articles" by copying all of the articles originally assembled in the periodicals' daily or weekly issues. Id. at 823. The Databases "highlighted" the connection between the articles and the print periodicals, the court observed, by showing for each article not only the author and periodical, but also the print publication's particular issue and page numbers. Id. at 824 ("The electronic technologies not only copy the publisher defendants' complete original 'selection' of articles, they tag those articles in such a way that the publisher defendants' original selection remains evident online.").

The Authors appealed, and the Second Circuit reversed. 206 F.3d 161 (1999). The Court of Appeals granted summary judgment for the Authors on the ground that the Databases were not among the collective works covered by § 201(c), and specifically, were not "revisions" of the periodicals in which the Articles first appeared. Id. at 167–170. Just as § 201(c) does not "permit a Publisher to sell a hard copy of an Author's article directly to the public even if the Publisher also offered for individual sale all of the other articles from the particular edition," the court reasoned, so § 201(c) does not allow a Publisher to "achieve the same goal indirectly" through computer databases. Id. at 168. In the Second Circuit's view, the Databases effectively achieved this result by providing multitudes of "individually retrievable" articles. *Ibid.* As stated by the Court of Appeals, the Databases might fairly be described as containing "new anthologies of innumerable" editions or publications, but they do not qualify as "revisions" of particular editions of periodicals in the Databases. Id. at 169. Having concluded that § 201(c) "does not permit the Publishers," acting without the author's consent, "to license individually copyrighted works for inclusion in the electronic databases," the court did not reach the question whether the § 201(c) privilege is transferable. Id. at 165, and n. 2.

We granted certiorari to determine whether the copying of the Authors' Articles in the Databases is privileged by 17 U.S.C. 201(c). 531 U.S. 978 (2000). Like the Court of Appeals, we conclude that the § 201(c) privilege does not override the Authors' copyrights, for the Databases do not reproduce and distribute the Articles as part of a collective work privileged by § 201(c). Accordingly, and again like the Court of Appeals, we find it unnecessary to determine whether the privilege is transferable.

## II

When, as in this case, a freelance author has contributed an article to a "collective work" such as a newspaper or magazine, see § 101 (defining "collective work"), the statute recognizes two distinct copyrighted works: "Copyright in *each separate contribution to a collective work is distinct from copyright in the collective work as a whole....* " § 201(c) (emphasis added). Copyright in the separate contribution "vests initially in the author of the contribution" (here, the freelancer). *Ibid.* Copyright in the collective work vests in the collective author (here, the newspaper or magazine publisher) and extends only to the creative material contributed by that author, not to "the preexisting material employed in the work," § 103(b).

Prior to the 1976 revision, as the courts below recognized, authors risked losing their rights when they placed an article in a collective work. Pre–1976 copyright law recognized a freelance author's copyright in a published article only when the article was printed with a copyright notice in the author's name. See Copyright Act of 1909, § 18, 35 Stat. 1079.

In the 1976 revision, Congress acted to "clarify and improve [this] confused and frequently unfair legal situation with respect to rights in contributions." H. R. Rep. No. 94–1476, p. 122 (1976) (hereinafter H. R. Rep.). The 1976 Act recast[ed] the copyright as a bundle of discrete "exclusive rights," 17 U.S.C. 106 (1994 ed. and Supp. V), each of which "may be transferred ... and owned separately," § 201(d)(2). Congress also provided, in § 404(a), that "a single notice applicable to the collective work as a whole is sufficient" to protect the rights of freelance contributors. And in § 201(c), Congress codified the discrete domains of "copyright in each separate contribution to a collective work" and "copyright in the collective work as a whole." Together, § 404(a) and § 201(c) "preserve the author's copyright in a contribution even if the contribution does not bear a separate notice in the author's name, and without requiring any unqualified transfer of rights to the owner of the collective work." H. R. Rep. 122.

Section 201(c) both describes and circumscribes the "privilege" a publisher acquires regarding an author's contribution to a collective work:

> "In the absence of an express transfer of the copyright or of any rights under it, the owner of copyright in the collective work is presumed to have acquired *only* the privilege of reproducing and distributing the contribution as part of that particular collective work, any revision of that collective work, and any later collective work in the same series." (Emphasis added.)

A newspaper or magazine publisher is thus privileged to reproduce or distribute an article contributed by a freelance author, absent a contract otherwise providing, only "as part of" any (or all) of three categories of collective works: (a) "that collective work" to which the author contributed her work, (b) "any revision of that collective work," or (c) "any later collective work in the same series." In accord with Congress' prescription, a "publishing company could reprint a contribution from one issue in a later issue of its magazine, and could reprint an article from a 1980 edition of an encyclopedia in a 1990 revision of it; the publisher could not revise the contribution itself or include it in a new anthology or an entirely different magazine or other collective work." H. R. Rep. 122–123.

Essentially, § 201(c) adjusts a publisher's copyright in its collective work to accommodate a freelancer's copyright in her contribution. If there is demand for a freelance article standing alone or in a new collection, the Copyright Act allows the freelancer to benefit from that demand; after authorizing initial publication, the freelancer may also sell the article to others. Cf. Stewart v. Abend, 495 U.S. 207, 229, 109 L. Ed. 2d 184, 110 S. Ct. 1750 (1990) ("when an author produces a work which later commands a higher price in the market than the original bargain provided, the copyright statute [i.e., the separate renewal term of former 17 U.S.C. 24] is designed to provide the author the power to negotiate for the realized value of the work"); id. at 230 (noting author's "inalienable termination right" under current 17 U.S.C. 203, 302). It would scarcely "preserve the author's copyright in a contribution" as contemplated by Congress, H. R. Rep. 122, if a newspaper or magazine publisher were permitted to reproduce or distribute copies of the author's contribution in isolation or within new collective works.

### III

In the instant case, the Authors wrote several Articles and gave the Print Publishers permission to publish the Articles in certain newspapers and magazines. It is undisputed that the Authors hold copyrights and, therefore, exclusive rights in the Articles.[a] It is clear, moreover, that the

---

[a] The Publishers do not claim that the Articles are "work[s] made for hire." 17 U.S.C. § 201(b). The Print Publishers neither engaged the Authors to write the Articles as "employees[s]" nor "commissioned" the Authors through "a written instrument signed by [both parties]" indicating that the Articles shall be considered "work[s] made for hire." § 101 (1994 ed., Supp. V)(defining "work made for hire").

Print and Electronic Publishers have exercised at least some rights that § 106 initially assigns exclusively to the Authors.

Against the Authors' charge of infringement, the Publishers do not here contend the Authors entered into an agreement authorizing reproduction of the Articles in the Databases. See at 3, n. 1. Nor do they assert that the copies in the Databases represent "fair use" of the Authors' Articles. Instead, the Publishers rest entirely on the privilege described in § 201(c). Each discrete edition of the periodicals in which the Articles appeared is a "collective work," the Publishers agree. They contend, however, that reproduction and distribution of each Article by the Databases lie within the "privilege of reproducing and distributing the [Articles] as part of . . . [a] revision of that collective work," § 201(c). The Publishers' encompassing construction of the § 201(c) privilege is unacceptable, we conclude, for it would diminish the Authors' exclusive rights in the Articles.

In determining whether the Articles have been reproduced and distributed "as part of" a "revision" of the collective works in issue, we focus on the Articles as presented to, and perceptible by, the user of the Databases. The Databases first prompt users to search the universe of their contents: thousands or millions of files containing individual articles from thousands of collective works. When the user conducts a search, each article appears as a separate item within the search result. [W]e cannot see how the Database perceptibly reproduces and distributes the article "as part of" either the original edition or a "revision" of that edition.

One might view the articles as parts of a new compendium—namely, the entirety of works in the Database. In that compendium, each edition of each periodical represents only a miniscule fraction of the ever-expanding Database. The Database no more constitutes a "revision" of each constituent edition than a 400–page novel quoting a sonnet in passing would represent a "revision" of that poem. "Revision" denotes a new "version," and a version is, in this setting, a "distinct form of something regarded by its creators or others as one work." Webster's Third New International Dictionary 1944, 2545 (1976). The massive whole of the Database is not recognizable as a new version of its every small part.

Alternatively, one could view the Articles in the Databases "as part of" no larger work at all, but simply as individual articles presented individually. That each article bears marks of its origin in a particular periodical suggests that the article was *previously* part of that periodical. But the markings do not mean the article is *currently* reproduced or distributed as part of the periodical. The Databases' reproduction and distribution of individual Articles—simply *as individual Articles*—would invade the core of the Authors' exclusive rights under § 106.

We therefore affirm the judgment of the Court of Appeals.

■ DISSENT: JUSTICE STEVENS, with whom JUSTICE BREYER joins, dissenting.

This case raises an issue of first impression concerning the meaning of the word "revision" as used in § 201(c) of the 1976 revision of the Copyright Act of 1909 (1976 Act). Ironically, the Court today seems unwilling to acknowledge that changes in a collective work far less extensive than those made to prior copyright law by the 1976 "revision" do not merit the same characterization.

Two analytically separate questions are blended together in the Court's discussion of revisions. The first is whether the electronic versions of the collective works created by the owners of the copyright in those works are "revision[s]" of those works within the meaning of 17 U.S.C. § 201(c). In my judgment they definitely are. The second is whether the aggregation of LEXIS/NEXIS and UMI of the revisions with other editions of the same periodical or with other periodicals within a single database changes the equation. I think it does not.

The 1976 Act's extensive revisions of the copyright law had two principal goals with respect to the rights of freelance authors whose writings appeared as part of larger collective works. First, as the legislative history of § 201(c) unambiguously reveals, one of its most significant aims was to "preserve the author's copyright in a contribution even if the contribution does not bear a separate notice in the author's name, and without requiring any unqualified transfer of rights to the owner of the collective work." H. R. Rep. No. 94–1476, p. 122 (1976) (hereinafter H. R. Rep.) (discussing the purpose of § 201(c)). Indeed, § 404(a) states that "a single notice applicable to the collective work as a whole is sufficient" to protect the author's rights.

The second significant change effected by the 1976 Act clarified the scope of the privilege granted to the publisher of a collective work. While pre–1976 law had the effect of encouraging an author to transfer her *entire* copyright to the publisher of a collective work, § 201(c) creates the opposite incentive, stating that, absent some agreement to the contrary, the publisher acquires from the author only "the privilege of reproducing and distributing the contribution as part of that particular collective work, any revision of that collective work, and any later collective work in the same series." Congress intended this limitation on what the author is presumed to give away primarily to keep publishers from "revising the contribution itself or including it in a new anthology or an *entirely different magazine or other collective work.*" H. R. Rep. 122–123.

The majority is surely correct that the 1976 Act's new approach to collective works was an attempt to " 'clarify and improve the . . . confused and frequently unfair legal situation' " that existed under the prior regime. Id. at 122. It does not follow, however, that Congress' efforts to "preserve the author's copyright in a contribution," H. R. Rep. 122, can only be honored by a finding in favor of the respondent authors.

Indeed, the conclusion that the petitioners' actions were lawful is fully consistent with both of Congress' principal goals for collective works in the

1976 Act. First, neither the publication of the collective works by the Print Publishers, nor their transfer to the Electronic Databases had any impact on the legal status of the copyrights of the respondents' individual contributions. By virtue of the 1976 Act, respondents remain the owners of the copyright in their individual works. Moreover, petitioners neither modified respondents' individual contributions nor published them in a "new anthology or *an entirely different magazine or other collective work.*" H. R. Rep. 122–123 (emphasis added). Because I do not think it is at all obvious that the decision the majority reaches today is a result clearly intended by the 1976 Congress, I disagree with the Court's conclusion.

NOTE: In a later suit, Tasini sued The New York Times for interfering with the ability of freelance writers to obtain relief from the infringement of their copyrights especially as it concerned a release agreement. The case was dismissed for lack of subject matter jurisdiction pursuant to Fed. R. Civ. P. 12(b)(1).

## Dastar Corp. v. Twentieth Century Fox Film Corp.

Supreme Court of the United States, 2003.
539 U.S. 23, 123 S.Ct. 2041, 156 L.Ed.2d 18.

■ JUSTICE SCALIA delivered the opinion of the Court.

I

In 1948, three and a half years after the German surrender at Reims, General Dwight D. Eisenhower completed Crusade in Europe, his written account of the allied campaign in Europe during World War II. Doubleday published the book, registered it with the Copyright Office in 1948, and granted exclusive television rights to an affiliate of respondent Twentieth Century Fox Film Corporation (Fox). Fox, in turn, arranged for Time, Inc., to produce a television series, also called Crusade in Europe, based on the book, and Time assigned its copyright in the series to Fox. The television series, consisting of 26 episodes, was first broadcast in 1949. In 1975, Doubleday renewed the copyright on the book as the " 'proprietor of copyright in a work made for hire.' " Fox, however, did not renew the copyright on the Crusade television series, which expired in 1977, leaving the television series in the public domain.

In 1988, Fox reacquired the television rights in General Eisenhower's book, including the exclusive right to distribute the Crusade television series on video and to sub-license others to do so. Respondents SFM Entertainment and New Line Home Video, Inc., in turn, acquired from Fox the exclusive rights to distribute Crusade on video. SFM obtained the negatives of the original television series, restored them, and repackaged the series on videotape; New Line distributed the videotapes.

Enter petitioner Dastar. In 1995, Dastar decided to expand its product line from music compact discs to videos. Anticipating renewed interest in World War II on the 50th anniversary of the war's end, Dastar released a video set entitled World War II Campaigns in Europe. To make Campaigns,

Dastar purchased eight beta cam tapes of the *original* version of the Crusade television series, which is in the public domain, copied them, and then edited the series. Dastar's Campaigns series is slightly more than half as long as the original Crusade television series. Dastar substituted a new opening sequence, credit page, and final closing for those of the Crusade television series; inserted new chapter-title sequences and narrated chapter introductions; moved the "recap" in the Crusade television series to the beginning and retitled it as a "preview"; and removed references to and images of the book. Dastar created new packaging for its Campaigns series and (as already noted) a new title.

Dastar manufactured and sold the Campaigns video set as its own product. The advertising states: "Produced and Distributed by: *Entertainment Distributing*" (which is owned by Dastar), and makes no reference to the Crusade television series. Similarly, the screen credits state "DASTAR CORP presents" and "an ENTERTAINMENT DISTRIBUTING Production," and list as executive producer, producer, and associate producer, employees of Dastar. The Campaigns videos themselves also make no reference to the Crusade television series, New Line's Crusade videotapes, or the book. Dastar sells its Campaigns videos to Sam's Club, Costco, Best Buy, and other retailers and mail-order companies for $25 per set, substantially less than New Line's video set.

In 1998, respondents Fox, SFM, and New Line brought this action alleging that Dastar's sale of its Campaigns video set infringes Doubleday's copyright in General Eisenhower's book and, thus, their exclusive television rights in the book. Respondents later amended their complaint to add claims that Dastar's sale of Campaigns "without proper credit" to the Crusade television series constitutes "reverse passing off"[a] in violation of § 43(a) of the Lanham Act, 15 U.S.C. § 1125(a). On cross-motions for summary judgment, the District Court found for respondents.

The Court of Appeals for the Ninth Circuit affirmed the judgment for respondents on the Lanham Act claim, but reversed as to the copyright claim and remanded. 34 Fed. Appx. 312, 316 (2002).[b] We granted certiorari. *Dastar Corp. v. Twentieth Century Fox Film Corp.*, 537 U.S. 1099 (2003).

## II

While much of the Lanham Act addresses the registration, use, and infringement of trademarks and related marks, § 43(a), 15 U.S.C. § 1125(a) is one of the few provisions that goes beyond trademark protec-

---

[a] Passing off (or palming off, as it is sometimes called) occurs when a producer misrepresents his own goods or services as someone else's. "Reverse passing off," as its name implies, is the opposite: The producer misrepresents someone else's goods or services as his own.

[b] As for the copyright claim, the Ninth Circuit held that the tax treatment General Eisenhower sought for his manuscript of the book created a triable issue as to whether he intended the book to be a work for hire. The copyright issue is still the subject of litigation, but is not before us. We express no opinion as to whether petitioner's product would infringe a valid copyright in General Eisenhower's book.

tion. [E]very Circuit to consider the issue found § 43(a) broad enough to encompass reverse passing off. [citations omitted]. *The Trademark Law Revision Act of 1988* made clear that § 43(a) covers origin of production as well as geographic origin. Its language is amply inclusive, moreover, of reverse passing off—if indeed it does not implicitly adopt the unanimous court-of-appeals jurisprudence on that subject. See, *e.g., Alpo Petfoods, Inc. v. Ralston Purina Co.*, 286 U.S. App. D.C. 192, 913 F.2d 958, 963–964, n. 6 (CADC 1990) (Thomas, J.).

Thus, as it comes to us, the gravamen of respondents' claim is that, in marketing and selling Campaigns as its own product without acknowledging its nearly wholesale reliance on the Crusade television series, Dastar has made a "false designation of origin, false or misleading description of fact, or false or misleading representation of fact, which ... is likely to cause confusion ... as to the origin ... of his or her goods." See, *e.g.,* Brief for Respondents 8, 11. That claim would undoubtedly be sustained if Dastar had bought some of New Line's Crusade videotapes and merely repackaged them as its own. Dastar's alleged wrongdoing, however, is vastly different: it took a creative work in the public domain—the Crusade television series—copied it, made modifications (arguably minor), and produced its very own series of videotapes. If "origin" refers only to the manufacturer or producer of the physical "goods" that are made available to the public (in this case the videotapes), Dastar was the origin. If, however, "origin" includes the creator of the underlying work that Dastar copied, then someone else (perhaps Fox) was the origin of Dastar's product. At bottom, we must decide what § 43(a)(1)(A) of the Lanham Act means by the "origin" of "goods."

III

The dictionary definition of "origin" is "the fact or process of coming into being from a source," and "that from which anything primarily proceeds; source." Webster's New International Dictionary 1720–1721 (2d ed. 1949). And the dictionary definition of "goods" (as relevant here) is "wares; merchandise." *Id.*, at 1079. We think the most natural understanding of the "origin" of "goods"—the source of wares—is the producer of the tangible product sold in the marketplace, in this case the physical Campaigns videotape sold by Dastar. The concept might be stretched (as it was under the original version of § 43(a)) n5 to include not only the actual producer, but also the trademark owner who commissioned or assumed responsibility for ("stood behind") production of the physical product. But as used in the Lanham Act, the phrase "origin of goods" is in our view incapable of connoting the person or entity that originated the ideas or communications that "goods" embody or contain. Such an extension would not only stretch the text, but it would be out of accord with the history and purpose of the Lanham Act and inconsistent with precedent.

It could be argued, perhaps, that the reality of purchaser concern is different for what might be called a communicative product—one that is valued not primarily for its physical qualities, such as a hammer, but for the intellectual content that it conveys, such as a book or, as here, a video. The purchaser of a novel is interested not merely, if at all, in the identity of the producer of the physical tome (the publisher), but also, and indeed primarily, in the identity of the creator of the story it conveys (the author). And the author, of course, has at least as much interest in avoiding passing-off (or reverse passing-off) of his creation as does the publisher. For such a communicative product (the argument goes) "origin of goods" in § 43(a) must be deemed to include not merely the producer of the physical item (the publishing house Farrar, Straus and Giroux, or the video producer Dastar) but also the creator of the content that the physical item conveys (the author Tom Wolfe, or—assertedly—respondents).

The problem with this argument according special treatment to communicative products is that it causes the Lanham Act to conflict with the law of copyright, which addresses that subject specifically. Thus, in construing the Lanham Act, we have been "careful to caution against misuse or over-extension" of trademark and related protections into areas traditionally occupied by patent or copyright. *TrafFix Devices, Inc. v. Marketing Displays, Inc.*, 532 U.S., 23, 29 (2001). Assuming for the sake of argument that Dastar's representation of itself as the "Producer" of its videos amounted to a representation that it originated the creative work conveyed by the videos, allowing a cause of action under *§ 43(a)* for that representation would create a species of mutant copyright law that limits the public's "federal right to 'copy and to use,'" expired copyrights, *Bonito Boats, Inc. v. Thunder Craft Boats, Inc.*, 489 U.S. 141, 165 (1989).

When Congress has wished to create such an addition to the law of copyright, it has done so with much more specificity than the Lanham Act's ambiguous use of "origin." The *Visual Artists Rights Act of 1990*, § 603(a), 104 Stat. 5128, provides that the author of an artistic work "shall have the right ... to claim authorship of that work." 17 U.S.C. § 106A(a)(1)(A). That express right of attribution is carefully limited and focused: It attaches only to specified "works of visual art," § 101, is personal to the artist, §§ 106A(b) and (e), and endures only for "the life of the author," at § 106A(d)(1). Recognizing in § 43(a) a cause of action for misrepresentation of authorship of noncopyrighted works (visual or otherwise) would render these limitations superfluous. A statutory interpretation that renders another statute superfluous is of course to be avoided. *E.g., Mackey v. Lanier Collection Agency & Service, Inc.*, 486 U.S. 825, 837, 100 L. Ed. 2d 836, 108 S. Ct. 2182, and n. 11 (1988).

Reading "origin" in § 43(a) to require attribution of uncopyrighted materials would pose serious practical problems. Without a copyrighted work as the basepoint, the word "origin" has no discernable limits. A video of the MGM film Carmen Jones, after its copyright has expired, would presumably require attribution not just to MGM, but to Oscar Hammerstein II (who wrote the musical on which the film was based), to Georges Bizet (who wrote the opera on which the musical was based), and to Prosper Merimee (who wrote the novel on which the opera was based). In many cases, figuring out who is in the line of "origin" would be no simple task. Indeed, in the present case it is far from clear that respondents have that status. Neither SFM nor New Line had anything to do with the production of the Crusade television series—they merely were licensed to distribute the video version. While Fox might have a claim to being in the line of origin, its involvement with the creation of the television series was limited at best. Time, Inc., was the principal if not the exclusive creator, albeit under arrangement with Fox. And of course it was neither Fox nor Time, Inc., that shot the film used in the Crusade television series. Rather, that footage came from the United States Army, Navy, and Coast Guard, the British Ministry of Information and War Office, the National Film Board of Canada, and unidentified "Newsreel Pool Cameramen." If anyone has a claim to being the *original* creator of the material used in both the Crusade television series and the Campaigns videotapes, it would be those groups, rather than Fox. We do not think the Lanham Act requires this search for the source of the Nile and all its tributaries.

Another practical difficulty of adopting a special definition of "origin" for communicative products is that it places the manufacturers of those products in a difficult position. On the one hand, they would face Lanham Act liability for *failing* to credit the creator of a work on which their lawful copies are based; and on the other hand they could face Lanham Act liability for *crediting* the creator if that should be regarded as implying the creator's "sponsorship or approval" of the copy, 15 U.S.C. § 1125(a)(1)(A). In this case, for example, if Dastar had simply "copied [the television series] as Crusade in Europe and sold it as Crusade in Europe," without changing the title or packaging (including the original credits to Fox), it is hard to have confidence in respondents' assurance that they "would not be here on a Lanham Act cause of action," Tr. of Oral Arg. 35.

In sum, reading the phrase "origin of goods" in the Lanham Act in accordance with the Act's common-law foundations (which were *not* designed to protect originality or creativity), and in light of the copyright and patent laws (which *were*), we conclude that the phrase refers to the producer of the tangible goods that are offered for sale, and not to the author of any idea, concept, or communication embodied in those goods. To hold otherwise would be akin to finding that § 43(a) created a species of perpetual patent and copyright, which Congress may not do. See *Eldred v. Ashcroft*, 537 U.S. 186, 208, 154 L. Ed. 2d 683, 123 S. Ct. 769 (2003).

Because we conclude that Dastar was the "origin" of the products it sold as its own, respondents cannot prevail on their Lanham Act claim. The judgment of the Court of Appeals for the Ninth Circuit is reversed, and the case is remanded for further proceedings consistent with this opinion.

## Excerpts From Roberta Kwall, Copyright and the Moral Right: Is an American Marriage Possible?

38 Vanderbilt L. Rev. 1 (1985).
Copyright © 1985 by Roberta Rosenthal Kwall and Vanderbilt University School of Law. Reprinted by permission. Footnotes omitted.

\* \* \*

III. The Copyright–Moral Right Interface

A. Copyright Law as a Limited Substitute for the Moral Right

Courts and commentators have posited copyright law as a substitute theory for the moral right doctrine, but traditional copyright law is of limited utility in vindicating all of the interests protected by moral rights. The court in Gilliam v. American Broadcasting Companies, Inc., [538 F.2d 14 (2d Cir.1976)] applied the 1909 Copyright Act in a novel fashion to grant relief to the plaintiffs, a group of British writers and performers whose scripts had been edited extensively after they were produced into British television programs but prior to their broadcast on defendant's American television network. The court ultimately concluded that the defendant, a remote sublicensee of the British Broadcasting Corporation (BBC), committed copyright infringement as a result of the extensive editing because the contract between the plaintiffs and BBC did not grant specifically to BBC the right to edit the programs once they had been recorded. BBC, therefore, could not grant rights that it did not possess to benefit its sublicensee. Critical to the court's ruling was its finding that the group had retained a common-law copyright in their original, unpublished scripts upon which BBC based the recorded television programs. Analogizing the situation to one in which a user licensed to create certain derivative works from a copyrighted script exceeds the media or time restrictions of his license in the production of a derivative work, the court held that the extensive editing exceeded the scope of any license that BBC was entitled to grant.

The peculiar fact situation in *Gilliam* arguably militates against the decision's application in a broad range of copyright cases concerning aspects of the moral right. In *Gilliam* the court relied heavily upon the agreement between the plaintiffs and BBC which provided that all rights which were not granted to BBC were retained by the plaintiffs. Thus, *Gilliam*'s ultimate moral right significance may be that in the face of a silent contract, an artist will not be held to have granted his licensee the right to perform extensive editing.

\* \* \*

The economic interests protected by the copyright laws are intertwined substantially with the personal interests that are the focus of the moral right doctrine. Indeed, if the moral right doctrine were to become a part of our jurisprudence in the future, its scope would be influenced significantly by the 1976 Act. The relationship between the 1976 Act and the moral right doctrine must be examined, therefore, to assess any future development of the doctrine in the United States.

B.  The 1976 Copyright Act

\* \* \*

1.  The Act's Potential for Safeguarding Moral Rights

The 1976 Act does contain several provisions that could have a significant effect upon the scope of a moral right doctrine in this country. As the following discussion demonstrates, some of these provisions have a sizable potential for vindicating the personal rights of creators. One of the most important provisions in this regard is section 106(2), which grants to the copyright owner the exclusive right to prepare and to authorize the preparation of "derivative works based upon the copyrighted work." Section 101 defines a "derivative work" as one that "represent[s] an original work of authorship" but is "based upon one or more preexisting works."

A creator can prevent unauthorized alterations and modifications of his work by invoking section 106(2), for such actions presumably would result in an unauthorized derivative work. In this situation the effect of section 106(2) is most obvious because there is no dispositive contractual arrangement between the creator and the entity making the unauthorized alterations. In addition, however, the copyright proprietor's exclusive rights relating to the preparation of derivative works raises a fascinating issue concerning a creator's paternity and integrity interests in authorized derivative works. For purposes of illustration, [consider a] playwright [who] authorizes a motion picture company to produce a movie based on her work, but has retained all other rights in her play. In the playwright's opinion, however, the motion picture company's final product, which is publicized as "based upon" her play, is a substantial distortion of her original theme and story line. Does the playwright have any recourse in this situation under section 106(2) of the 1976 Act?

The playwright could rely upon the *Gilliam* rationale by asserting that the movie company has violated the scope of their agreement. Specifically, she could argue that in the agreement, she assigned to the company her right under section 106(2) to prepare a derivative work based upon her play, and to use her name in connection therewith, but that the company violated this agreement because the movie ultimately produced was so extensively altered that it was not "based upon" her play within the meaning of section 106(2). Of course, the situations in *Gilliam* and our hypothetical case are not identical. In *Gilliam* a licensee of the creators authorized the defendants to reproduce the work, but due to the contractual agreement between the licensee and the creators, the licensee could not have authorized the defendants to perform the type of editing at issue. In our hypothetical case, the playwright authorized the movie company to prepare a derivative work, which authorization in itself necessitates a certain number of changes. Although *Gilliam* does not hold explicitly that copyright ownership includes the right to prohibit mutilating changes in a work, the *Gilliam* opinion relied upon the existence of an implied condition of assignment that would preclude the defendants from exercising the reproduction and performance rights which they were granted if they made material changes in the work. Similarly, when the right to prepare a derivative work is at issue, the *Gilliam* rationale supports an inferred condition that the right cannot be exercised if the changes which are made constitute mutilation and the derivative work is billed as "based upon" the creator's underlying work. Hence, the performance of such alterations and resulting false attribution constitute an infringement under section 106(2), just as the performance of the unauthorized editing in *Gilliam* violated the rights granted to the defendants in that case.

The ultimate success of the *Gilliam* argument depends upon the interpretation of the phrase "derivative works *based upon* the copyrighted work" as it is used in section 106(2). Although the phrase "based upon" may, at first glance, appear self-explanatory, application of the phrase in this context is difficult because it requires a determination of the degree of creative liberty that is properly exercisable by one who transforms a preexisting work into another medium. No court has had occasion to interpret section 106(2) in this particular context, but decisions exist in which the import of the phrase "based upon" was explored in analogous circumstances. At least one court, in determining whether a defendant's movie was "based upon" a particular book in the context of plaintiffs' allegation that the movie infringed the book, invoked the "substantial similarity" test used by the courts in deciding copyright infringement actions. The court ultimately concluded, as a matter of law, that the film was not "based upon" the book because a reasonable jury could not find that the two works were "substantially similar beyond the level of generalized ideas or themes." [See Burroughs v. Metro–Goldwyn–Mayer, Inc., 683 F.2d 610, 623–24 (2d Cir.1982).]

On balance, the "substantial similarity" test is the appropriate standard to judge whether a derivative work is "based upon" a preexisting work within the meaning of section 106(2). In providing that the copyright owner has the exclusive right to prepare or authorize the preparation of any derivative works based upon the copyrighted work, Congress, in section 106(2), contemplated that the preparation of an unauthorized derivative work constitutes copyright infringement. Although the legislative history discloses no specific guidelines for determining when an unauthorized derivative work infringes the original work, most courts would invoke the "substantial similarity" test to determine infringement. Therefore, if our playwright had never entered into an agreement with the movie company, the playwright would have an action for copyright infringement under section 106(2), perhaps with a corresponding right to compel recognition for her work, assuming she could prove that the movie company's product was substantially similar to her own. Logically, courts should apply the same standard in the converse situation presented by the hypothetical case. If the movie company's product can satisfy the "substantial similarity" test, the playwright should not be able to rely successfully on *Gilliam* to support her claim under section 106(2). The alterations of the play would not be sufficiently extreme to warrant a holding that the movie company had exceeded its derivative rights assignment. If, however, the movie is not substantially similar to the play, the playwright should prevail.

Application of the "substantial similarity" test, however, is extremely problematic, particularly in the context of adaptations. One popular method for determining substantial similarity is the "ordinary observation or impression" test. This test requires the ordinary observer to perceive a substantial similarity between the two works in question, "so that the alleged copy comes so near to the original as to give the audience the idea created by the original." The use of this test with respect to derivative and preexisting works requires caution, however, because the technical requirements of a different medium usually necessitate certain changes, which could lull an ordinary observer into believing that no substantial similarity exists. In commenting on this problem, one court noted the importance of educating the trier of fact with respect to any differences that are mandated by the adaptation process so as to preserve the creator's valuable rights under section 106(2).

Although section 106(2) does not mention moral rights, the foregoing analysis illustrates how section 106(2) can be utilized by a creator to protect certain aspects of his moral rights, assuming that he has retained some copyright in his work. In our hypothetical situation, if the movie company had exceeded the scope of its rights under section 106(2) by virtue of its distorted use of the playwright's underlying work, the company would be liable to the playwright assuming she had retained all of her other rights under the copyright laws. Suppose, however, that the playwright had transferred to the movie company her other rights in her work, including her right to authorize all derivative works. In this situation would the playwright be able to safeguard her personal interest in preventing an unwarranted mutilation of her work by the movie company?

Section 501(b) of the 1976 Act provides that the "legal or beneficial owner of an exclusive right under a copyright is entitled . . . to institute an action for any infringement of that particular right committed while he or she is the owner of it." Although section 501(b) does not define the term "beneficial owner," the legislative history states that a " 'beneficial owner' for this purpose would include, for example, an author who had parted with legal title to the copyright in exchange for percentage royalties based on sales or license fees." Consistent with this interpretation, courts have allowed creators, who have assigned copyrights in their works in exchange for royalties, to maintain infringement actions, regardless of whether the legal owners of the copyrights also are parties to the actions.

This analysis of section 501(b) suggests that even creators who no longer own the copyrights in their works can maintain infringement actions to protect aspects of their moral rights by using section 106(2), assuming they have transferred their copyright interests in exchange for a share of royalties. Most creators presumably would not transfer these valuable rights absent some type of royalty arrangement. Nevertheless, a strong argument can be made that all creators who have transferred their copyrights should be deemed beneficial owners within the meaning of section 501(b), regardless of whether their transfer agreements contemplate royalties. Although no court has had the opportunity to review this issue, a grant of standing to all creators is consistent with the legislative history, which speaks of an author who parts with legal title in exchange for royalties merely *as an example* of a "beneficial owner."

On the other hand, one can argue that a creator who retains no economic ties to his copyrighted work should not receive the protections afforded by the statute, which exist to safeguard economic rights. This argument, however, ignores the application of the termination provisions of the 1976 Act, under which all creators retain a potential economic interest in their works. In fact, the termination provisions codified in section 203, which govern all copyrights executed on or after the effective date of the 1976 Act, and section 304(c), the comparable provision for subsisting copyrights, have been hailed as a departure from our copyright tradition of subordinating the author's interests to those of the publisher. Section 203 provides that an author, except an author of a work made for hire, may terminate any grant of a copyright or any right under a copyright "at any time during a period of five years beginning at the end of thirty-five years from the date of execution of the grant," provided he complies with the stipulated notice requirements. If an author is dead, his termination interest may be exercised by his spouse and his children or grandchildren in accordance with the terms of the termination statute. The legislative history for this provision discloses an intent to safeguard authors against unremunerative transfers. Similarly, section 304(c) details the circumstances in which a transfer or license of a 1909 Act copyright may be terminated by the author or those entitled to exercise his interest if he is dead. Section 304(c) closely tracks section 203. According to the legislative history, the arguments for granting rights of termination under section 304 are even stronger than they are under section 203 because section 304(b) also creates a new property right by adding nineteen years "to the duration of any renewed copyright whose second term started during the twenty-eight years immediately preceding the effective date of the Act." Thus, the author, as "the fundamental beneficiary of copyright under the Constitution," should have an opportunity to share in this new property right.

The foregoing analysis suggests that even an author who has transferred his copyright interest without a royalty arrangement retains some economic and beneficial interest in the copyright. One commentator has suggested that section 203 might allow an author to terminate his copyright grant if the transferee has violated any of the creator's moral rights. Although this position is consistent with the legislative history's emphasis on the creator's economic needs, no court yet has linked personal rights with the additional economic safeguards offered to creators by these provisions. Courts easily could make this correlation in an appropriate case, however, given that a creator's economic interests in his work can be threatened by violations of his personal rights that impair the work's marketability.

NOTES

**1.** *Ownership vs. authorship.* Should the sculpture at issue in *Community for Creative Non–Violence* be considered a joint work? Note that the Court of Appeals remanded on this issue. If the sculpture was determined to be a joint work, could Reid object to CCNV's proposed tour? Could Reid stop the tour if Reid were declared the sole owner of the copyright (see §§ 109(a) & (c) of the 1976 Copyright Act)? Who would have the right to any profits from the tour if Reid was the sole copyright owner? Should Reid have to give the sculpture back to CCNV regardless of the determination of copyright ownership (see § 202)? If the sculpture had been protected under VARA (§ 106A), could CCNV destroy the sculpture if Reid were declared the sole owner of the copyright?

*Childress* notes the distinction between joint authorship and joint ownership of a copyrighted work, and observes that only joint authors can invoke the rights of authorship such as exercise of the renewal rights pursuant to § 304. Can you think of any other rights that a joint author, but not co-owner, of a copyrighted work can exercise? Given these distinctions, how persuasive is the court's conclusion that parties who make non-copyrightable contributions to works should resort to contract law to protect their interests? Will reliance on contract law always be a feasible option?

Appellate decisions in both the Seventh[8] and Ninth[9] Circuits adhere to the test for joint authorship endorsed in *Childress* requiring both independent copyrightability of each contribution and intent by all putative authors at the time of the collaboration that they be co-authors. This standard departs from the statutory definition of a "joint work" that asks whether the authors have "the intention to merge" their respective contributions into a unitary whole. In interpreting this statutory language, these circuits evince concern with the prospect that, notwithstanding the provision of a relatively minor contribution, a party can be deemed a joint author under the statutory definition as long as all parties to the work intended to merge their contributions into a unitary whole. Therefore, these courts endorse a more rigorous test for determining joint authorship than appears to be statutorily mandated. Both authors of this casebook have criticized the "independent copyrightability" and "mutual intent to be joint authors" requirements for joint authorship invoked by these influential appellate courts.[10]

The Second Circuit subsequently applied the joint authorship test announced in *Childress* in an interesting suit by a dramaturg against the playwright of the critically acclaimed Broadway musical *Rent*. In Thomson v. Larson[11] the court interpreted the intention standard announced in *Childress* to mean more than a consideration of the parties' words or their "professed state of mind." Instead, *Childress* "suggested a more nuanced inquiry into factual indicia of ownership and authorship, such as how a

---

[8] Erickson v. Trinity Theatre, Inc., 13 F.3d 1061 (7th Cir. 1994)(affirming injunction against theater company from performing plays to which plaintiff playwright owned the copyrights).

[9] Aalmuhammed v. Lee, 202 F.3d 1227 (9th Cir. 2000)(denying plaintiff film advisor's joint authorship claim to movie *Malcolm X*).

[10] See Roberta Rosenthal Kwall, *"Author–Stories": Narrative's Implications for* *Moral Rights and Copyright's Joint Authorship Doctrine*, 75 S. Cal. L. Rev. 1 (2001); Rochelle Cooper Dreyfuss, *Collaborative Research: Conflicts on Authorship, Ownership, and Accountability*, 53 Vand. L. Rev. 1161 (2000). For an interesting English case explicitly rejecting the mutual intent for joint authorship test, see Beckingham v. Hodgens [2003] E.M.L.R. 18/376.

[11] 147 F.3d 195 (2d Cir.1998).

collaborator regarded herself in relation to the work in terms of billing and credit, decisionmaking, and the right to enter into contracts."[12] After evaluating this evidence, the Second Circuit affirmed the district court's judgment that the dramaturg was not a joint author.

*Thomson v. Larson* also raised the interesting question as to whether the dramaturg could retain the copyright in her contribution to the play even if the court finds that the mutual intent requirement for joint authorship is lacking. Since the dramaturg raised this issue for the first time on appeal to the Second Circuit, however, the court refused to decide this matter. Note that this issue also is raised in the Principal Problem.

**2.**   *Work for hire.* How well does the Supreme Court's decision in *Community for Creative Non–Violence* accomplish "Congress' paramount goal in revising the 1976 Act of enhancing predictability and certainty of copyright ownership" (see Section II(A) of case)? Are there any other approaches which the Court could have adopted that would have been more consistent with this goal?[13] Does David have a stronger work for hire argument with respect to Rivkah or Sam under the second subpart of the work for hire definition dealing with specifically commissioned works? How would you analyze whether their respective works should be considered works for hire under both subparts of the statutory definition?[14]

**3.**   *Termination provisions.* Section 304(c) provides a mechanism whereby an author, or her statutory successors, can terminate transfers and licenses covering the extended renewal term for copyrights in works created before the effective date of the 1976 Act. According to § 304(c)(3), "[t]ermination of the grant may be effected at any time during a period of five years beginning at the end of fifty-six years from the date copyright was originally secured, or beginning on January 1, 1978, whichever is later." Section 304(c)(6)(D) provides that after the copyright owner terminates a grant pursuant to § 304(c), any further grant of any rights covered under the terminated grant can only be made after the effective date of the termination, although an agreement of a further grant between the author (or her successors) and the original grantee (or its successors) can be made after a notice of termination has been served. This provision gives the original grantee a bit of an advantage from a negotiation standpoint. As part of the CTEA, a new subsection (d) was added to § 304 which provides that for copyrights already in their renewal terms at the effective date of

---

[12] Id. at 1070.

[13] Cf. Estate of Burne Hogarth v. Edgar Rice Burroughs, Inc., 342 F.3d 149 (2d Cir. 2003)(reaffirming, for 1909 Act works, that as long as the "instance and expense" test is satisfied, the work is a work for hire and the commissioning party is deemed the author).

[14] In 1999, Congress added sound recordings to the list of commissioned works that can qualify as works made for hire under subpart (2) of the statutory definition. This amendment was extremely controversial among musicians and ultimately was repealed, perhaps illustrating that some artists do indeed have strong lobbying power. Cf. Morrill v. The Smashing Pumpkins, 157 F.Supp.2d 1120, 1125 (C.D. Cal. 2001)(noting that in the case of sound recordings, the law is clear that absent an employment relationship or express assignment, the copyright is either with the performing artist exclusively or held jointly by the performing artist and record producer).

the CTEA, the termination right can still be exercised by appropriate persons if the termination right period already has expired. This amendment allows for termination during a period of 5 years beginning at the end of 75 years from the date the copyright originally was secured as long as the author or owner of the termination right has not previously exercised the termination right. Works made for hire are, of course, expressly exempted from this provision.

Section 203 incorporates the termination provisions for works created after the effective date of the 1976 Act. Since, as originally enacted, the 1976 Act eliminated the two successive 28–year periods of protection in favor of a single term consisting of the life of the author plus 50 years, the period in which a notice of termination can be served was modified so that it could "be effected at any time during a period of five years beginning at the end of thirty-five years from the date of execution of the grant; or, if the grant covers the right of publication of the work, the period begins at the end of thirty-five years from the date of publication of the work under the grant or at the end of forty years from the date of execution of the grant, whichever term ends earlier" (see § 203(a)(3)). The CTEA, which extended the copyright term for an additional twenty years, did not alter the time frame in which the termination provisions could be exercised. Why do you think the statute draws a distinction between grants covering the right of publication and all other works?

Section 203(b)(1) mirrors § 304(C)(6)(A), which was discussed in *Stewart*, in that it provides that upon termination, the owner of a derivative work prepared under a grant of the underlying work may continue to utilize the derivative work after termination, but the owner of the derivative work cannot prepare new derivative works of the underlying work once the initial grant has been terminated. See also Note 4. How do the provisions in § 203 relate to the Principal Problem? What issues in the Problem are left unanswered by § 203?

In Mills Music, Inc. v. Snyder,[15] the Supreme Court had occasion to consider another novel question concerning the application of the derivative works exception in § 304(c)(6)(A). In *Mills,* the author of a copyrighted song assigned to a music publishing company the rights to the renewal term for the song in exchange for a share of royalties from mechanical reproductions of the song (i.e., records as opposed to sheet music). The music publishing company then issued licenses to record companies pursuant to this renewal right authorizing the use of the song by the record companies in mechanical reproductions. These agreements required the record companies to pay royalties to the music publishing company, who in turn was contractually required to pay royalties to the song's author. After the author's death, the widow and son of the song's author terminated the grant to the music publishing company of rights in the renewal copyright, pursuant to § 304(c). Termination did not, however, affect rights to sell recordings prepared under the original grant, nor did it affect the grantees'

---

[15] 469 U.S. 153 (1985).

obligation to pay royalties. Thus, the issue in *Mills* was to whom should the royalties be paid: to the middleman music publishing company, as the grantee of the original creator, or to the heirs of the author. In reversing the Second Circuit, the Supreme Court recognized that although § 304 was enacted to benefit authors, the derivative works exception contained in § 304(c)(6)(A) was nonetheless sufficiently broad to support the music publisher's right to royalties. In what respect is the rationale of *Mills* inconsistent with *Stewart?*

**4.** *Renewal rights. Stewart* deals with one of the sticky issues pertaining to renewal rights in that it focuses on a grantee's continued right to use a derivative work that is based on the copyrighted work subject to the renewal right. *Stewart* was decided in 1990, and as of that year, the ramifications of the opinion were confined to underlying works published between 1962 and January 1, 1978 (the latter being the effective date of the 1976 Act). The renewal right is inapplicable to any work created after the effective date of the 1976 Act. Moreover, any work published before 1962 would have already entered its renewal period before 1990. Is *Stewart* a good decision from a policy standpoint? Why or why not?

Under the pre-amended § 304(a), the author, if living, or her statutory renewal successors had to apply for and register the renewal right in the year prior to the expiration of the first 28–year period of protection, and, in the absence of this application for renewal, the copyright terminated at the end of the first 28–year period of protection. Section § 304(a) was amended in 1992 to provide that registration of the renewal interest was no longer required. This section provided that the copyright was automatically extended for a 47–year renewal period at the end of the original 28–year term, and technically there was no need to register an application to extend the term. In light of the CTEA's lengthening of the renewal extension by twenty years, § 304(a) now provides that the copyright automatically is extended for a 67–year renewal period at the end of the original 28–year term. Still, if an author survives into the 28th year of the first term of copyright protection and files a renewal registration before dying, the renewal right will vest in the author rather than the statutory renewal successors. If the author has filed such a renewal registration, any assignments made by the author of the renewal term will continue to be honored. On the other hand, if the author does not survive into the 28th year or dies in the 28th year but fails to file a renewal before dying, the renewal right vests automatically in the statutory renewal successors of the author (i.e., those who would have been entitled to claim renewal as of the last day of the original 28–year copyright term). The 1992 Amendment did not change the identity of the statutory renewal successors (the specific order of the statutory renewal successors is discussed below).

Nevertheless, incentives exist for filing an application to renew during the 28th year of the original term. For example, registration for renewal made during the 28th year of the original term will affect the right to utilize a derivative work prepared under authority of a grant in the first copyright term. If a statutory renewal claimant (including the author) registers a renewal within the 28th year, the claimant can terminate an assignment made by the author that authorizes the exploitation of a derivative work in the renewal term. If the renewal is not made by the statutory claimant in the 28th year, then the statutory claimant cannot prevent the continued exploitation, in the renewal term, of a derivative work created during the first 28–year term (note that since the author is considered a statutory claimant, an author who fails to register the renewal will lose the right to prevent the exploitation of the derivative work in the renewal term just like all other statutory claimants). However, there still is no authorization to create or prepare new derivative works based on the copyrighted work subject to the grant. This amendment does not affect the operation of § 203. It is intended to parallel the derivative works clauses of § 203(b)(1) and § 304(c)(6)(A) (see Note 3). The new amendment also leaves undisturbed the *Stewart* decision, since in that case the copyright owner's successor renewed in the 28th year of the original term.

The Court's opinion in *Stewart* also explores the rationale underlying the renewal right in general as a means of safeguarding the economic interests of an author and her family. Section 304(a) mandates the following order of statutory successors of the renewal right, in the event the author is deceased: the author's widow, widower, or children; the author's executor; or in the absence of a will, the author's next of kin. Should the government have the right to mandate the recipients of an author's renewal rights in "the form of a compulsory bequest of the copyright to the designated persons" (see Section II(A) of *Stewart*)? Can you think of any other instances where the government mandates the recipient of an individual's property upon death, notwithstanding contrary provisions in a will?

**5.** *Moral rights under VARA and otherwise.* VARA grants authors of certain works of visual arts three rights: the right of integrity, the right of attribution, and, in the case of works of visual art of "recognized stature," the right to prevent destruction. The statute also contains special provisions for works of visual art that have become part of buildings.[16] Under VARA, the right of integrity includes the right to prevent any intentional distortion, mutilation, or other modification of an author's work of visual art that would be prejudicial to the artist's honor or reputation.[17] Regrettably, the statute fails to define or provide any guidance with respect to how a determination of prejudice, honor, or reputation should be made.[18] Further, VARA does not provide a way to obtain damages due to modifications resulting from the passage of time or the inherent nature of the materials, or due to conservation efforts.[19]

[16] 17 U.S.C. § 113(d).

[17] 17 U.S.C. § 106A(a)(3)(A).

[18] See Carter v. Helmsley–Spear, Inc., 861 F.Supp. 303, 323 (S.D.N.Y. 1994), rev'd, 71 F.3d 77 (2d Cir. 1995), cert. denied, 517 U.S. 1208 (1996)(applying these terms in light of "readily understood meanings" such as whether the proposed alteration "would cause injury or damage to plaintiffs' good name, public esteem, or reputation in the artistic community.")

[19] 17 U.S.C. § 106A(c)(2)(only modifications resulting from grossly negligent conservations are actionable). See Flack v.

With respect to the right of attribution, VARA guarantees the author the rights "to claim authorship" of a covered work, to prevent attribution in connection with a work not created by the author,[20] and to prevent use of the author's name in conjunction with a work in the event it is distorted, mutilated or otherwise modified in a manner that will prejudice the artist's honor or reputation.[21] The right of attribution in VARA, while unlike the right of integrity in that it is not limited to intentional alterations, does not include the negative rights of anonymity or pseudonymity.[22] Regarding the prohibition of the destruction of works of "recognized statute," the statute covers both intentional and grossly negligent destructions, but it fails to define the term "recognized stature."[23]

One significant problem with VARA is that the statute only applies to a very narrow category of visual art which includes "a painting, drawing, print, or sculpture, . . . or a still photographic image produced for exhibition purposes only existing in a single copy . . . , or in a limited edition of 200 copies or fewer that are signed and consecutively numbered by the author."[24] VARA also specifically excludes protection for reproductions of works,[25] and fails to provide any remedy when works are used in a context found objectionable or distasteful by the author.[26]

The duration of the rights specified in § 106A varies, depending on when the work was created with respect to the effective date of VARA (June 1, 1991). Section 106A(d) provides that the moral rights safeguarded by the statute expire with the death of the author for works created on or after the effective date of VARA. For works created before the effective date of VARA, but title to which has not been transferred at the time of the effective date, the duration of rights under § 106A is co-extensive with those under copyright law. Neither the statute nor the legislative history

---

Friends of Queen Catherine Inc., 139 F.Supp.2d 526 (S.D.N.Y. 2001)(dismissing plaintiff's allegation that damage due to defendant's placement of head of clay sculpture outdoors constituted an intentional modification actionable under VARA).

[20] 106A(a)(1).

[21] See § 106A(a)(2)(1994).

[22] See generally Edward Damich, The Visual Artists Rights Act of 1990: Toward a Federal System of Moral Rights Protection for Visual Art, 39 Cath. U. L. Rev. 945 (1990).

[23] 17 U.S.C. § 106A(a)(3)(B). *See* Carter v. Helmsley–Spear, Inc., 861 F.Supp. 303, 325 (S.D.N.Y. 1994), rev'd, 71 F.3d 77 (2d Cir. 1995), cert. denied, 517 U.S. 1208 (1996)(interpreting the "recognized stature" requirement as "a gate-keeping mechanism" affording protection only to art work "that art experts, the art community, or society in general views as possessing stature.").

[24] See § 101 (definition of a "work of visual art"). Compare the statutes in Maine, New Jersey, Nevada, and Rhode Island which define the protected works as including limited editions of no more than three hundred copies.

Although models are excluded from the definition of a "work of visual art," one court has determined that a clay sculpture from which a bronze statute was to be cast should be considered a work covered under VARA rather than an excluded "model." See Flack v. Friends of Queen Catherine Inc., 139 F.Supp.2d 526 (S.D.N.Y. 2001) (applying the standards of the artistic community in making this determination).

[25] 17 U.S.C. § 106A(c)(3).

[26] For a full treatment of these problems, see Roberta Rosenthal Kwall, *"Author–Stories": Narrative's Implications for Moral Rights and Copyright's Joint Authorship Doctrine*, 75 S. Cal. L. Rev. 1, 33 (2001).

offers any explanation for this strange dichotomy, but in its original form VARA provided a duration equal to that of copyright law. The current duration for works created on or after the effective date of VARA was a result of a last-minute amendment by the Senate. VARA also provides that the rights in joint works last until the death of the last surviving author.

Other countries that recognize the moral rights doctrine can be divided into two groups with respect to the question of duration. The first group, which includes Germany and the Netherlands, follows the approach advocated by the Berne Convention and simultaneously terminates a creator's moral rights and copyright. The second group adheres to the French view that moral rights are perpetual.[27] What arguments support limiting the existence of moral rights to the creator's life and what arguments support their survival beyond the creator's death? If they do survive the creator's death, who should be able to exercise them?

Professor Kwall's excerpt discusses the compatibility between the moral rights doctrine and the 1976 Copyright Act. Her analysis is especially relevant for evaluating how works not covered by VARA can be afforded some type of moral rights protection in this country. *Dastar* also bears on the issue of exercising moral rights protection for non-VARA works. What is the impact of *Dastar* on David's attempt to safeguard his moral right of integrity? Aside from § 43(a), how can David attempt to protect his right of integrity? How successful will Rivkah be in her suit against David for using her illustrations in her website without appropriate attribution?

Although Professor Kwall suggests that certain provisions of the 1976 Act have the potential for assisting creators seeking to vindicate aspects of their moral rights, the statute contains other provisions that pose both impediments to and limitations upon the enforcement of a creator's personal interests. Can you think of specific provisions of the 1976 Copyright Act that directly circumscribe moral rights protection in this country for works not covered by VARA? Keep this question in mind as you study the provisions of the 1976 Copyright Act which are treated in the subsequent assignments.

One particularly complicated problem raised by VARA is the preemptive effect of the statute with respect to state moral rights statutes such as those detailed in footnote 5. VARA provides that state law actions are not preempted if they 1) arise "from undertakings commenced before the effective date" of VARA; or 2) stem from activities violating rights that are not equivalent to those provided in § 106A; or 3) arise from "activities violating ... rights which extend beyond the life of the author."[28] Note that by virtue of this last preemption exemption, states are free to protect a creator's moral rights posthumously. Many state moral rights statutes do, in fact, provide protection for the life of the author plus fifty years.[29] In

---

[27] See Kwall, Copyright and the Moral Right: Is an American Marriage Possible?, 38 Vand. L. Rev. 1, 15 (1985).

[28] See § 301(f)(2).

[29] California, Connecticut, Massachusetts, New Mexico, and Pennsylvania provide protection for the life of the author plus fifty years. Louisiana's statute says that "[t]he

light of these preemption exemptions, how should we analyze whether the state moral rights statutes such as those discussed in footnote 5 should be preempted under VARA?[30] The subject of preemption under the 1976 Act in general is treated in Assignment 13.

Some people believe that, on a federal level, moral rights protections in addition to VARA are embodied in the "copyright management information" provisions of the Digital Millennium Copyright Act, which create a de facto right of attribution in the Internet environment. Section 1202(a) prohibits the knowing provision or distribution of false copyright management information if done "knowingly and with the intent to induce, enable, facilitate, or conceal infringement." Section 1202(b) prohibits the intentional removal or alteration of copyright management information, and the distribution of such altered works.[31]

**6.** *International uniformity.* Ironically, the cases in this chapter present some interesting issues regarding the United States' willingness to adhere to global norms in the area of intellectual property. Notwithstanding Justice Breyer's criticisms of the *Eldred* majority's reliance on the uniformity rationale for upholding the CTEA, Congress' decision to enact this amendment to the 1976 Copyright Act was influenced by the EU's directive to establish a life plus seventy (70) year copyright term.[32] In contrast, the United States' reluctance to enact moral rights protections consistent with those of other nations is important because this disparity probably reflects the last significant gap in the rights of authors here and abroad.[33]

provisions of this Chapter apply to any works of fine art regardless of when created." *La. Rev. Stat. Ann. § 2155Gb (2003)* La. R.S. 51:2155 (2003). This language suggests that protection may be perpetual in that state. California also provides that a public interest organization can obtain injunctive relief to preserve the integrity of a covered work, see Cal. Civ. Code § 989(c) (2004), and at least one commentator has suggested that this public enforcement right should be perpetual. See Joseph Zuber, The Visual Artists Rights Act of 1990—What it Does, and What it Preempts, 23 Pac. L.J. 445, 456–57 (1992).

[30] In Board of Managers of Soho International Arts Condominium v. New York, the district court held that VARA preempted New York's Artists' Authorship Rights Act. 2003 WL 21403333 (S.D.N.Y. 2003).

[31] See generally Jane Ginsburg, Symposium: II, Art and the Law, *Suppression and Liberty: Have Moral Rights Come of (Digital) Age in the United States?*, 19 Cardozo Arts &

Ent. L.J. 9 (2001); Justin Hughes, Symposium: II., Art and the Law, *Suppression and Liberty: The Line Between Work and Framework, Text and Context*, 19 Cardozo Arts & Ent. L.J. 19 (2001); Roberta Kwall, *Moral Rights for University Employees and Students: Can Educational Institutions Do Betterthan U.S. Copyright Law?*, 27 J.C. & U.L. 53 (2000).

[32] Significantly, however, the EU grants protection for "neighboring rights" (e.g., performers' rights in sound recordings) only for life plus fifty years because such rights are not considered within the scope of copyright. In the United States, however, these rights are considered within the scope of copyright and now receive protection for life plus seventy years.

[33] See Michael Gunlicks, *A Balance ofInterests: The Concordance of Copyright Lawand Moral Rights in the Worldwide Economy*, 11 Fordham Intell. Prop. Media & Ent. L.J. 601, 606 (2001).

# ASSIGNMENT 10

# THE SCOPE OF THE COPYRIGHT HOLDER'S RIGHTS: INFRINGEMENT

## 1. INTRODUCTION

The essential predicate of copyright protection is that the copyright proprietor has the exclusive right to engage in certain activities with respect to the copyrighted work. Section 106 of the 1976 Act provides the copyright owner with the exclusive rights to reproduce, distribute, publicly perform and publicly display the protected work, as well as the rights to prepare derivative works based on the underlying protected work and publicly perform sound recordings through a digital audio transmission.[1] In addition, the Visual Artists Rights Act provides limited rights of attribution and integrity applicable to certain works of authorship.[2] The copyright owner's exclusive ability to exercise and to authorize the exercise of this bundle of rights enables her to safeguard, in large measure, the pecuniary value of the copyrighted work. As such, copyright law promotes the creative process by providing financial incentives to creators.

This Assignment will explore the unauthorized uses of copyrighted property in different contexts such as literature, music, art, and even computer programs. It illustrates that the application of the test for copyright infringement presents some troublesome issues. It is not always easy to decide when one work is based so heavily upon another that the substantial similarity between them should be infringement. Moreover, it is difficult to implement the idea/expression and fact/expression dichotomies that are at the core of the protectability requirements. Finally, one of the most important issues that must be addressed is whether the test for copyright infringement should vary according to the type of work at issue. The Principal cases offer several different approaches to these issues.

## 2. PRINCIPAL PROBLEM

Your client, William Dawson, is the copyright owner of an arrangement of the spiritual "Ezekiel Saw De Wheel," many copies of which have been sold over the years in the form of sheet music. In 1987, Gilbert M. Martin composed an arrangement of the spiritual, and subsequently granted Hinshaw Music, Inc. the exclusive rights to publish, distribute, and sell his arrangement in the form of sheet music. Dawson sued Martin and Hinshaw

---

[1] § 106.

[2] § 106A. VARA is covered extensively in Assignment 9.

for copyright infringement. The district court held for the defendants after a bench trial.

The court found that reasonable minds might conclude that the idea of the defendants' work was substantially similar to the idea of the plaintiff's work. According to the court, the pattern, theme and organization of the plaintiff's arrangement is unique among any other arrangement of this spiritual, and substantial similarities could be found to exist between the plaintiff's and defendants' arrangements with respect to this unique pattern. Still, the court ruled against the plaintiff because it felt that no reasonable jury could find that, in comparing the "total concept and feel" of the two works, the expression of ideas in defendants' work was substantially similar to the expression of ideas in plaintiff's work. In applying this test, the court relied only on the sheet music of the two arrangements since the plaintiff did not present recordings of performances of the two arrangements.

Dawson wants you to appeal the district court's ruling. He wants to know what the test for copyright infringement is and whether the district court applied the correct test. Before advising him, consider the following materials.

## 3. Materials for Solution of Principal Problem

A. STATUTORY MATERIALS: § 501(a) & (b)

B. CASES:

# Nichols v. Universal Pictures Corporation

United States Court of Appeals, Second Circuit, 1930.
45 F.2d 119.

■ L. Hand, Circuit Judge.

The plaintiff is the author of a play, "Abie's Irish Rose", which it may be assumed was properly copyrighted under section five, subdivision (d), of the Copyright Act, 17 USCA § 5(d). The defendant produced publicly a motion picture play, "The Cohens and The Kellys", which the plaintiff alleges was taken from it. As we think the defendant's play too unlike the plaintiff's to be an infringement, we may assume, arguendo, that in some details the defendant used the plaintiff's play, as will subsequently appear, though we do not so decide. It therefore becomes necessary to give an outline of the two plays.

"Abie's Irish Rose" presents a Jewish family living in prosperous circumstances in New York. The father, a widower, is in business as a merchant, in which his son and only child helps him. The boy has philandered with young women, who to his father's great disgust have always been Gentiles, for he is obsessed with a passion that his daughter-in-law shall be an orthodox Jewess. When the play opens the son, who has been courting a young Irish Catholic girl, has already married her secretly before a Protestant minister, and is concerned to soften the blow for his father, by securing a favorable impression of his bride, while concealing her faith and race. To accomplish this he introduces her to his father at his home as a Jewess, and lets it appear that he is interested in her, though he conceals the marriage. The girl somewhat reluctantly falls in with the plan; the father takes the bait, becomes infatuated with the girl, concludes that they must marry, and assumes that of course they will, if he so decides. He calls in a rabbi, and prepares for the wedding according to the Jewish rite.

Meanwhile the girl's father, also a widower, who lives in California, and is as intense in his own religious antagonism as the Jew, has been called to New York, supposing that his daughter is to marry an Irishman and a Catholic. Accompanied by a priest, he arrives at the house at the moment when the marriage is being celebrated, but too late to prevent it, and the two fathers, each infuriated by the proposed union of his child to a heretic, fall into unseemly and grotesque antics. The priest and the rabbi become friendly, exchange trite sentiments about religion, and agree that the match is good. Apparently out of abundant caution, the priest celebrates the marriage for a third time, while the girl's father is inveigled away. The second act closes with each father, still outraged, seeking to find some way by which the union, thus trebly insured, may be dissolved.

The last act takes place about a year later, the young couple having meanwhile been abjured by each father, and left to their own resources. They have had twins, a boy and a girl, but their fathers know no more than that a child has been born. At Christmas each, led by his craving to see his grandchild, goes separately to the young folks' home, where they encounter each other, each laden with gifts, one for a boy, the other for a girl. After some slapstick comedy, depending upon the insistence of each that he is right about the sex of the grandchild, they become reconciled when they learn the truth, and that each child is to bear the given name of a grandparent. The curtain falls as the fathers are exchanging amenities, and the Jew giving evidence of an abatement in the strictness of his orthodoxy.

"The Cohens and The Kellys" presents two families, Jewish and Irish, living side by side in the poorer quarters of New York in a state of perpetual enmity. The wives in both cases are still living, and share in the mutual animosity, as do two small sons, and even the respective dogs. The Jews have a daughter, the Irish a son; the Jewish father is in the clothing business; the Irishman is a policeman. The children are in love with each other, and secretly marry, apparently after the play opens. The Jew, being in great financial straits, learns from a lawyer that he has fallen heir to a large fortune from a great-aunt, and moves into a great house, fitted luxuriously. Here he and his family live in vulgar ostentation, and here the Irish boy seeks out his Jewish bride, and is chased away by the angry father. The Jew then abuses the Irishman over the telephone, and both become hysterically excited. The extremity of his feelings makes the Jew sick, so that he must go to Florida for a rest, just before which the daughter discloses her marriage to her mother.

On his return the Jew finds that his daughter has borne a child; at first he suspects the lawyer, but eventually learns the truth and is overcome with anger at such a low alliance. Meanwhile, the Irish family who have been forbidden to see the grandchild, go to the Jew's house, and after a violent scene between the two fathers in which the Jew disowns his daughter, who decides to go back with her husband, the Irishman takes her back with her baby to his own poor lodgings. The lawyer, who had hoped to marry the Jew's daughter, seeing his plan foiled, tells the Jew that his fortune really belongs to the Irishman, who was also related to the dead woman, but offers to conceal his knowledge, if the Jew will share the loot. This the Jew repudiates, and, leaving the astonished lawyer, walks through the rain to his enemy's house to surrender the property. He arrives in great dejection, tells the truth, and abjectly turns to leave. A reconciliation ensues, the Irishman agreeing to share with him equally. The Jew shows some interest in his grandchild, though this is at most a minor motive in the reconciliation, and the curtain falls while the two are in their cups, the Jew insisting that in the firm name for the business, which they are to carry on jointly, his name shall stand first.

It is of course essential to any protection of literary property, whether at common-law or under the statute, that the right cannot be limited literally to the text, else a plagiarist would escape by immaterial variations. That has never been the law, but, as soon as literal appropriation ceases to be the test, the whole matter is necessarily at large, so that, as was recently well said by a distinguished judge, the decisions cannot help much in a new case. When plays are concerned, the plagiarist may excise a separate scene, or he may appropriate part of the dialogue. Then the question is whether the part so taken is "substantial"; it is the same question as arises in the case of any other copyrighted work. But when the plagiarist does not take out a block in situ, but an abstract of the whole, decision is more troublesome. Upon any work, and especially upon a play, a great number of patterns of increasing generality will fit equally well, as more and more of the incident is left out. The last may perhaps be no more than the most general statement of what the play is about, and at times might consist only of its title; but there is a point in this series of abstractions where they are no longer protected, since otherwise the playwright could prevent the use of his "ideas", to which, apart from their expression, his property is never extended. Nobody has ever been able to fix that boundary, and nobody ever can. In some cases the question has been treated as though it were analogous to lifting a portion out of the copyrighted work, but the analogy is not a good one, because, though the skeleton is a part of the body, it pervades and supports the whole. In such cases we are rather concerned with the line between expression and what is expressed. As respects plays, the controversy chiefly centers upon the characters and sequence of incident, these being the substance.

[W]e do not doubt that two plays may correspond in plot closely enough for infringement. How far that correspondence must go is another matter. Nor need we hold that the same may not be true as to the characters, quite independently of the "plot" proper, though, as far as we know, such a case has never arisen. If Twelfth Night were copyrighted, it is quite possible that a second comer might so closely imitate Sir Toby Belch or Malvolio as to infringe, but it would not be enough that for one of his characters he cast a riotous knight who kept wassail to the discomfort of the household, or a vain and foppish steward who became amorous of his mistress. These would be no more than Shakespeare's "ideas" in the play, as little capable of monopoly as Einstein's Doctrine of Relativity, or Darwin's theory of the Origin of Species. It follows that the less developed the characters, the less they can be copyrighted; that is the penalty an author must bear for marking them too indistinctly.

In the two plays at bar we think both as to incident and character, the defendant took no more—assuming that it took anything at all—than the law allowed. The stories are quite different. One is of a religious zealot who insists upon his child's marrying no one outside his faith; opposed by another who is in this respect just like him, and is his foil. Their difference in race is merely an obbligato to the main theme, religion. They sink their differences through grandparental pride and affection. In the other, zealotry is wholly absent; religion does not even appear. It is true that the parents are hostile to each other in part because they differ in race; but the marriage of their son to a Jew does not apparently offend the Irish family at all, and it exacerbates the existing animosity of the Jew, principally because he has become rich, when he learns it. They are reconciled through the honesty of the Jew and the generosity of the Irishman; the grandchild has nothing whatever to do with it. The only matter common to the two is a quarrel between a Jewish and an Irish father, the marriage of their children, the birth of grandchildren and a reconciliation.

If the defendant took so much from the plaintiff, it may well have been because her amazing success seemed to prove that this was a subject of enduring popularity. Even so, granting that the plaintiff's play was wholly original, and assuming that novelty is not essential to a copyright, there is no monopoly in such a background. Though the plaintiff discovered the vein, she could not keep it to herself; so defined, the theme was too generalized an abstraction from what she wrote. It was only a part of her "ideas".

Nor does she fare better as to her characters. It is indeed scarcely credible that she should not have been aware of those stock figures, the low comedy Jew and Irishman. The defendant has not taken from her more than their prototypes have contained for many decades. If so, obviously so to generalize her copyright, would allow her to cover what was not original with her. But we need not hold this as matter of fact, much as we might be justified. Even though we take it that she devised her figures out of her brain de novo, still the defendant was within its rights.

There are but four characters common to both plays, the lovers and the fathers. The lovers are so faintly indicated as to be no more than stage properties. They are loving and fertile; that is really all that can be said of them, and anyone else is quite within his rights if he puts loving and fertile lovers in a play of his own, wherever he gets the cue. The plaintiff's Jew is quite unlike the defendant's. His obsession is his religion, on which depends such racial animosity as he has. He is affectionate, warm and patriarchal. None of these fit the defendant's Jew, who shows affection for his daughter only once, and who has none but the most superficial interest in his grandchild. He is tricky, ostentatious and vulgar, only by misfortune redeemed into honesty. Both are grotesque, extravagant and quarrelsome; both are fond of display; but these common qualities make up only a small part of their simple pictures, no more than any one might lift if he chose. The Irish fathers are even more unlike; the plaintiff's a mere symbol for religious fanaticism and patriarchal pride, scarcely a character at all. Neither quality appears in the defendant's, for while he goes to get his grandchild, it is rather out of a truculent determination not to be forbidden, than from pride in his progeny. For the rest he is only a grotesque hobbledehoy, used for low comedy of the most conventional sort, which any one might borrow, if he chanced not to know the exemplar.

We assume that the plaintiff's play is altogether original, even to an extent that in fact it is hard to believe. We assume further that, so far as it has been anticipated by earlier plays of which she knew nothing, that fact is immaterial. Still, as we have already said, her copyright did not cover everything that might be drawn from her play; its content went to some extent into the public domain. We have to decide how much, and while we are as aware as any one that the line, wherever it is drawn, will seem arbitrary, that is no excuse for not drawing it; it is a question such as courts must answer in nearly all cases. Whatever may be the difficulties a priori, we have no question on which side of the line this case falls. A comedy based upon conflicts between Irish and Jews, into which the marriage of their children enters, is no more susceptible of copyright than the outline of Romeo and Juliet.

We cannot approve the length of the record, which was due chiefly to the use of expert witnesses. Argument is argument whether in the box or at the bar, and its proper place is the last. The testimony of an expert upon such issues, especially his cross-examination, greatly extends the trial and contributes nothing which cannot be better heard after the evidence is all submitted. It ought not to be allowed at all; and while its admission is not a ground for reversal, it cumbers the case and tends to confusion, for the more the court is led into the intricacies of dramatic craftsmanship, the less likely it is to stand upon the firmer, if more naive, ground of its considered impressions upon its own perusal. We hope that in this class of cases such evidence may in the future be entirely excluded, and the case confined to the actual issues; that is, whether the copyrighted work was original, and whether the defendant copied it, so far as the supposed infringement is identical.

Decree affirmed.

# Computer Associates International, Inc. v. Altai, Inc.

United States Court of Appeals, Second Circuit, 1992.
982 F.2d 693.

■ WALKER, CIRCUIT JUDGE.

In recent years, the growth of computer science has spawned a number of challenging legal questions, particularly in the field of copyright law. As scientific knowledge advances, courts endeavor to keep pace, and some-times—as in the area of computer technology—they are required to venture into less than familiar waters. This is not a new development, though. "From its beginning, the law of copyright has developed in response to significant changes in technology." Sony Corp. v. Universal City Studios, Inc., 464 U.S. 417, 430 (1984).

[T]he copyright law seeks to establish a delicate equilibrium. On the one hand, it affords protection to authors as an incentive to create, and, on the other, it must appropriately limit the extent of that protection so as to avoid the effects of monopolistic stagnation. In applying the federal act to new types of cases, courts must always keep this symmetry in mind.

Among other things, this case deals with the challenging question of whether and to what extent the "non-literal" aspects of a computer program, that is, those aspects that are not reduced to written code, are protected by copyright. While a few other courts have already grappled with this issue, this case is one of first impression in this circuit. As we shall discuss, we find the results reached by other courts to be less than satisfactory. Drawing upon long-standing doctrines of copyright law, we take an approach that we think better addresses the practical difficulties embedded in these types of cases. In so doing, we have kept in mind the necessary balance between creative incentive and industrial competition.

This appeal comes to us from the United States District Court for the Eastern District of New York, the Honorable George C. Pratt, Circuit Judge, sitting by designation. By Memorandum and Order, Judge Pratt found that defendant Altai, Inc.'s ("Altai"), OSCAR 3.4 computer program had infringed plaintiff Computer Associates' ("CA"), copyrighted computer program entitled CA–SCHEDULER. Accordingly, the district court award-ed CA $364,444 in actual damages and apportioned profits. Altai has abandoned its appeal from this award. With respect to CA's second claim for copyright infringement, Judge Pratt found that Altai's OSCAR 3.5 program was not substantially similar to a portion of CA–SCHEDULER called ADAPTER, and thus denied relief.

Because we are in full agreement with Judge Pratt's decision and in substantial agreement with his careful reasoning, we affirm the judgment of the district court in its entirety.

Background

I.  Computer Program Design

Certain elementary facts concerning the nature of computer programs are vital to the following discussion. The Copyright Act defines a computer program as "a set of statements or instructions to be used directly or indirectly in a computer in order to bring about a certain result". 17 U.S.C. § 101. In writing these directions, the programmer works "from the general to the specific". Whelan Associates, Inc. v. Jaslow Dental Laboratory, Inc., 797 F.2d 1222, 1229 (3d Cir.1986), cert. denied, 479 U.S. 1031 (1987).

The first step in this procedure is to identify a program's ultimate function or purpose. An example of such an ultimate purpose might be the creation and maintenance of a business ledger. Once this goal has been achieved, a programmer breaks down or "decomposes" the program's ultimate function into "simpler constituent problems or 'subtasks,' " Englund, at 870, which are also known as subroutines or modules. See Spivack, at 729. In the context of a business ledger program, a module or subroutine might be responsible for the task of updating a list of outstanding accounts receivable. Sometimes, depending upon the complexity of its task, a subroutine may be broken down further into sub-subroutines.

Having sufficiently decomposed the program's ultimate function into its component elements, a programmer will then arrange the subroutines or modules into what are known as organizational or flow charts. Flow charts map the interactions between modules that achieve the program's end goal. See Kretschmer, at 826.

In order to accomplish these intra-program interactions, a programmer must carefully design each module's parameter list. A parameter list, according to the expert appointed and fully credited by the district court, Dr. Randall Davis, is "the information sent to and received from a subroutine". The term "parameter list" refers to the form in which information is passed between modules (e.g. for accounts receivable, the designated time frame and particular customer identifying number) and the information's actual content (e.g. 8/91–7/92; customer No. 3). With respect to form, interacting modules must share similar parameter lists so that they are capable of exchanging information.

"The functions of the modules in a program together with each module's relationships to other modules constitute the 'structure' of the program". Englund, at 871. Additionally, the term structure may include the category of modules referred to as "macros". A macro is a single instruction that initiates a sequence of operations or module interactions within the program. Very often the user will accompany a macro with an instruction from the parameter list to refine the instruction (e.g. current total of accounts receivable (macro), but limited to those for 8/91 to 7/92 from customer No. 3 (parameters)).

In fashioning the structure, a programmer will normally attempt to maximize the program's speed, efficiency, as well as simplicity for user operation, while taking into consideration certain externalities such as the memory constraints of the computer upon which the program will be run. See *id.*; Kretschmer, at 826; Menell, at 1052. "This stage of program design often requires the most time and investment". Kretschmer, at 826.

Once each necessary module has been identified, designed, and its relationship to the other modules has been laid out conceptually, the resulting program structure must be embodied in a written language that the computer can read. This process is called "coding", and requires two steps. *Whelan*, 797 F.2d at 1230. First, the programmer must transpose the program's structural blue-print into a source code. This step has been described as "comparable to the novelist fleshing out the broad outline of his plot by crafting from words and sentences the paragraphs that convey the ideas". Kretschmer, at 826. The source code may be written in any one of several computer languages, such as COBAL, FORTRAN, BASIC, EDL, etc., depending upon the type of computer for which the program is intended. *Whelan*, 797 F.2d at 1230. Once the source code has been completed, the second step is to translate or "compile" it into object code. Object code is the binary language comprised of zeros and ones through which the computer directly receives its instructions. *Id.*, at 1230–31; Englund, at 868 & n.13.

After the coding is finished, the programmer will run the program on the computer in order to find and correct any logical and syntactical errors. This is known as "debugging" and, once done, the program is complete. See Kretschmer, at 826–27.

II.  Facts

CA is a Delaware corporation, with its principal place of business in Garden City, New York. Altai is a Texas corporation, doing business primarily in Arlington, Texas. Both companies are in the computer software industry—designing, developing and marketing various types of computer programs.

The subject of this litigation originates with one of CA's marketed programs entitled CA–SCHEDULER. CA–SCHEDULER is a job scheduling program designed for IBM mainframe computers. Its primary functions are straightforward: to create a schedule specifying when the computer should run various tasks, and then to control the computer as it executes the schedule. CA–SCHEDULER contains a sub-program entitled ADAPTER, also developed by CA. ADAPTER is not an independently marketed product of CA; it is a wholly integrated component of CA–SCHEDULER and has no capacity for independent use.

Nevertheless, ADAPTER plays an extremely important role. It is an "operating system compatibility component", which means, roughly speaking, it serves as a translator. An "operating system" is itself a program that manages the resources of the computer, allocating those resources to other programs as needed. The IBM's System 370 family of computers, for which CA–SCHEDULER was created, is, depending upon the computer's size, designed to contain one of three operating systems: DOS/VSE, MVS, or CMS. As the district court noted, the general rule is that "a program written for one operating system, e.g., DOS/VSE, will not, without modification, run under another operating system such as MVS". Computer Associates Int'l, Inc. v. Altai, Inc., 775 F.Supp. 544, 550 (E.D.N.Y.1991). ADAPTER's function is to translate the language of a given program into the particular language that the computer's own operating system can understand.

The district court succinctly outlined the manner in which ADAPTER works within the context of the larger program. In order to enable CA–SCHEDULER to function on different operating systems, CA divided the CA–SCHEDULER into two components:

— a first component that contains only the task-specific portions of the program, independent of all operating system issues, and

— a second component that contains all the interconnections between the first component and the operating system.

In a program constructed in this way, whenever the first, task-specific, component needs to ask the operating system for some resource through a "system call", it calls the second component instead of calling the operating system directly.

The second component serves as an "interface" or "compatibility component" between the task-specific portion of the program and the operating system. It receives the request from the first component and translates it into the appropriate system call that will be recognized by whatever operating system is installed on the computer, e.g., DOS/VSE, MVS, or CMS. Since the first, task-specific component calls the adapter component rather than the operating system, the first component need not be customized to use any specific operating system. The second interface component insures that all the system calls are performed properly for the particular operating system in use.

*Id.* at 551. ADAPTER serves as the second, "common system interface" component referred to above.

A program like ADAPTER, which allows a computer user to change or use multiple operating systems while maintaining the same software, is highly desirable. It saves the user the costs, both in time and money, that otherwise would be expended in purchasing new programs, modifying existing systems to run them, and gaining familiarity with their operation. The benefits run both ways. The increased compatibility afforded by an ADAPTER-like component, and its resulting popularity among consumers, makes whatever software in which it is incorporated significantly more marketable.

Starting in 1982, Altai began marketing its own job scheduling program entitled ZEKE. The original version of ZEKE was designed for use in conjunction with a VSE operating system. By late 1983, in response to customer demand, Altai decided to rewrite ZEKE so that it could be run in conjunction with an MVS operating system.

At that time, James P. Williams ("Williams"), then an employee of Altai and now its President, approached Claude F. Arney, III ("Arney"), a computer programmer who worked for CA. Williams and Arney were longstanding friends, and had in fact been co-workers at CA for some time before Williams left CA to work for Altai's predecessor. Williams wanted to recruit Arney to assist Altai in designing an MVS version of ZEKE.

At the time he first spoke with Arney, Williams was aware of both the CA–SCHEDULER and ADAPTER programs. However, Williams was not involved in their development and had never seen the codes of either program. When he asked Arney to come work for Altai, Williams did not know that ADAPTER was a component of CA–SCHEDULER.

Arney, on the other hand, was intimately familiar with various aspects of ADAPTER. While working for CA, he helped improve the VSE version of ADAPTER, and was permitted to take home a copy of ADAPTER's source code. This apparently developed into an irresistible habit, for when Arney left CA to work for Altai in January, 1984, he took with him copies of the source code for both the VSE and MVS versions of ADAPTER. He did this in knowing violation of the CA employee agreements that he had signed.

Once at Altai, Arney and Williams discussed design possibilities for adapting ZEKE to run on MVS operating systems. Williams, who had created the VSE version of ZEKE, thought that approximately 30% of his original program would have to be modified in order to accommodate MVS. Arney persuaded Williams that the best way to make the needed modifications was to introduce a "common system interface" component into ZEKE. He did not tell Williams that his idea stemmed from his familiarity with ADAPTER. They decided to name this new component-program OSCAR.

Arney went to work creating OSCAR. No one at Altai, including Williams, knew that he had the ADAPTER code, and no one knew that he was using it to design OSCAR/VSE. In three months, Arney successfully completed the OSCAR/VSE project. In an additional month he developed an OSCAR/MVS version. When the dust finally settled, Arney had copied approximately 30% of OSCAR's code from CA's ADAPTER program.

The first generation of OSCAR programs was known as OSCAR 3.4. From 1985 to August 1988, Altai used OSCAR 3.4 in its ZEKE product, as well as in programs entitled ZACK and ZEBB. In late July 1988, CA first learned that Altai may have appropriated parts of ADAPTER. After confirming its suspicions, CA secured copyrights on its 2.1 and 7.0 versions of CA–SCHEDULER. CA then brought this copyright action against Altai.

Apparently, it was upon receipt of the summons and complaint that Altai first learned that Arney had copied much of the OSCAR code from ADAPTER. After Arney confirmed to Williams that CA's accusations of copying were true, Williams immediately set out to survey the damage. Without ever looking at the ADAPTER code himself, Williams learned from Arney exactly which sections of code Arney had taken from ADAPTER.

Upon advice of counsel, Williams initiated OSCAR's rewrite. The project's goal was to save as much of OSCAR 3.4 as legitimately could be used, and to excise those portions which had been copied from ADAPTER. Arney was entirely excluded from the process, and his copy of the ADAPTER code was locked away. Williams put eight other programmers on the project, none of whom had been involved in any way in the development of OSCAR 3.4. Williams provided the programmers with a description of the ZEKE operating system services so that they could rewrite the appropriate code. The rewrite project took about six months to complete and was finished in mid-November 1989. The resulting program was entitled OS-CAR 3.5.

From that point on, Altai shipped only OSCAR 3.5 to its new customers. Altai also shipped OSCAR 3.5 as a "free upgrade" to all customers that had previously purchased OSCAR 3.4. While Altai and Williams acted responsibly to correct what Arney had wrought, the damage was done. CA's lawsuit remained.

Discussion

CA contends that the district court applied an erroneous method for determining whether there exists substantial similarity between computer programs, and thus, erred in determining that OSCAR 3.5 did not infringe the copyrights held on the different versions of its CA–SCHEDULER program. CA asserts that the test applied by the district court failed to account sufficiently for a computer program's non-literal elements.

I.   Copyright Infringement

In any suit for copyright infringement, the plaintiff must establish its ownership of a valid copyright, and that the defendant copied the copyrighted work. The plaintiff may prove defendant's copying either by direct evidence or, as is most often the case, by showing that (1) the defendant had access to the plaintiff's copyrighted work and (2) that defendant's work is substantially similar to the plaintiff's copyrightable material.

For the purpose of analysis, the district court assumed that Altai had access to the ADAPTER code when creating OSCAR 3.5. See *Computer Associates*, 775 F.Supp., at 558. Thus, in determining whether Altai had unlawfully copied protected aspects of CA's ADAPTER, the district court narrowed its focus of inquiry to ascertaining whether Altai's OSCAR 3.5 was substantially similar to ADAPTER. Because we approve Judge Pratt's conclusions regarding substantial similarity, our analysis will proceed along the same assumption.

As a general matter, and to varying degrees, copyright protection extends beyond a literary work's strictly textual form to its non-literal components. As we have said, "[i]t is of course essential to any protection of literary property . . . that the right cannot be limited literally to the text, else a plagiarist would escape by immaterial variations". Nichols v. Universal Pictures Corp., 45 F.2d 119, 121 (2d Cir.1930) (L. Hand, J.), *cert. denied*, 282 U.S. 902 (1931). Thus, where "the fundamental essence or structure of one work is duplicated in another", 3 Nimmer, [Nimmer on Copyright] § 13.03[A][1], at 13–24, courts have found copyright infringement. This black letter proposition is the springboard for our discussion.

A.   Copyright Protection for the Non-literal Elements of Computer Programs

It is now well settled that the literal elements of computer programs, i.e., their source and object codes, are the subject of copyright protection. See *Whelan*, 797 F.2d at 1233. Here, as noted earlier, Altai admits having copied approximately 30% of the OSCAR 3.4 program from CA's ADAPTER source code, and does not challenge the district court's related finding of infringement.

In this case, the hotly contested issues surround OSCAR 3.5. As recounted above, OSCAR 3.5 is the product of Altai's carefully orchestrated rewrite of OSCAR 3.4. After the purge, none of the ADAPTER source code remained in the 3.5 version; thus, Altai made sure that the literal elements of its revamped OSCAR program were no longer substantially similar to the literal elements of CA's ADAPTER.

According to CA, the district court erroneously concluded that Altai's OSCAR 3.5 was not substantially similar to its own ADAPTER program. CA argues that this occurred because the district court "committed legal error in analyzing [its] claims of copyright infringement by failing to find that copyright protects expression contained in the non-literal elements of computer software". We disagree.

CA argues that, despite Altai's rewrite of the OSCAR code, the resulting program remained substantially similar to the *structure* of its ADAPTER program. As discussed above, a program's structure includes its non-literal components such as general flow charts as well as the more specific organization of inter-modular relationships, parameter lists, and macros. In addition to these aspects, CA contends that OSCAR 3.5 is also substantially similar to ADAPTER with respect to the list of services that both ADAPTER and OSCAR obtain from their respective operating systems. We must decide whether and to what extent these elements of computer programs are protected by copyright law.

The statutory terrain in this area has been well explored. See Lotus Dev. Corp. v. Paperback Software Int'l, 740 F.Supp. 37, 47–51 (D.Mass. 1990); see also *Whelan*, 797 F.2d at 1240–42; Englund, at 885–90; Spivack, at 731–37. The Copyright Act affords protection to "original works of authorship fixed in any tangible medium of expression". § 102(a). This broad category of protected "works" includes "literary works", *id.*, which are defined by the act as

> works, other than audiovisual works, expressed in words, numbers, or other verbal or numerical symbols or indicia, regardless of the nature of the material objects, such as books, periodicals, manuscripts, phonorecords, film tapes, disks, or cards, in which they are embodied.

Section 101. While computer programs are not specifically listed as part of the above statutory definition, the legislative history leaves no doubt that Congress intended them to be considered literary works. See H.R. Rep. No. 1476, 94th;Cong., 2d Sess. 54 (hereinafter "House Report"); *Whelan*, 797 F.2d at 1234; Apple Computer, Inc. v. Franklin Computer Corp., 714 F.2d 1240, 1247 (3d Cir.1983), *cert. dismissed*, 464 U.S. 1033 (1984).

The syllogism that follows from the foregoing premises is a powerful one: if the non-literal structures of literary works are protected by copyright; and if computer programs are literary works, as we are told by the legislature; then the non-literal structures of computer programs are protected by copyright. See *Whelan*, 797 F.2d at 1234 ("By analogy to other literary works, it would thus appear that the copyrights of computer programs can be infringed even absent copying of the literal elements of the program."). We have no reservation in joining the company of those courts that have already ascribed to this logic. [Citations omitted.] However, that conclusion does not end our analysis. We must determine the scope of copyright protection that extends to a computer program's non-literal structure.

As a caveat, we note that our decision here does not control infringement actions regarding categorically distinct works, such as certain types of screen displays. These items represent products of computer programs, rather than the programs themselves, and fall under the copyright rubric of audiovisual works. If a computer audiovisual display is copyrighted separately as an audiovisual work, apart from the literary work that generates it (i.e., the program), the display may be protectable regardless of the underlying program's copyright status. Of course, the copyright protection that these displays enjoy extends only so far as their expression is protectable. In this case, however, we are concerned not with a program's display, but the program itself, and then with only its non-literal components. In considering the copyrightability of these components, we must refer to venerable doctrines of copyright law.

1.  Idea vs. Expression Dichotomy

It is a fundamental principle of copyright law that a copyright does not protect an idea, but only the expression of the idea. This axiom of common law has been incorporated into the governing statute. See § 102(b). See also House Report, at 5670 ("Copyright does not preclude others from using ideas or information revealed by the author's work.").

Congress made no special exception for computer programs. To the contrary, the legislative history explicitly states that copyright protects computer programs only "to the extent that they incorporate authorship in programmer's expression of original ideas, as distinguished from the ideas themselves". *Id.* at 5667; see also *id.* at 5670 ("Section 102(b) is intended . . . to make clear that the expression adopted by the programmer is the copyrightable element in a computer program, and that the actual processes or methods embodied in the program are not within the scope of copyright law.").

Similarly, the National Commission on New Technological Uses of Copyrighted Works ("CONTU") established by Congress to survey the issues generated by the interrelationship of advancing technology and copyright law, see Pub. L. 93–573, § 201, 88 Stat. 1873 (1974), recommended, inter alia, that the 1976 Copyright Act "be amended . . . to make it explicit that computer programs, to the extent that they embody the author's original creation, are proper subject matter for copyright". See National Commission on New Technological Uses of Copyrighted Works, Final Report 1 (1979)(hereinafter "CONTU Report"). To that end, Congress adopted CONTU's suggestions and amended the Copyright Act by adding, among other things, a provision to § 101 which defined the term "computer program". See Pub. L. No. 96–517, § 10(a), 94 Stat. 3028 (1980). CONTU also "concluded that the idea-expression distinction should be used to determine which aspects of computer programs are copyrightable". *Lotus Dev. Corp.*, 740 F.Supp., at 54 (citing CONTU Report, at 44).

Drawing the line between idea and expression is a tricky business. Judge Learned Hand noted that "[n]obody has ever been able to fix that boundary, and nobody ever can". *Nichols*, 45 F.2d at 121. Thirty years later his convictions remained firm. "Obviously, no principle can be stated as to when an imitator has gone beyond copying the 'idea,' and has borrowed its 'expression,' " Judge Hand concluded. "Decisions must therefore inevitably be ad hoc". Peter Pan Fabrics, Inc. v. Martin Weiner Corp., 274 F.2d 487, 489 (2d Cir.1960).

The essentially utilitarian nature of a computer program further complicates the task of distilling its idea from its expression. In order to describe both computational processes and abstract ideas, its content "combines creative and technical expression". See Spivack, at 755. The variations of expression found in purely creative compositions, as opposed to those contained in utilitarian works, are not directed towards practical application. For example, a narration of Humpty Dumpty's demise, which would clearly be a creative composition, does not serve the same ends as, say, a recipe for scrambled eggs—which is a more process oriented text. Thus, compared to aesthetic works, computer programs hover even more closely to the elusive boundary line described in § 102(b).

The doctrinal starting point in analyses of utilitarian works is the seminal case of Baker v. Selden, 101 U.S. 99 (1879). In *Baker*, the Supreme Court faced the question of "whether the exclusive property in a system of bookkeeping can be claimed, under the law of copyright, by means of a book in which that system is explained[.]" *Id.* at 101. The Supreme Court found nothing copyrightable in Selden's bookkeeping system, and rejected his infringement claim regarding the ledger sheets.

To the extent that an accounting text and a computer program are both "a set of statements or instructions ... to bring about a certain result", § 101, they are roughly analogous. In the former case, the processes are ultimately conducted by human agency; in the latter, by electronic means. In either case, as already stated, the processes themselves are not protectable. But the holding in *Baker* goes farther. The Court concluded that those aspects of a work, which "must necessarily be used as incident to" the idea, system or process that the work describes, are also not copyrightable. 101 U.S., at 104. Selden's ledger sheets, therefore, enjoyed no copyright protection because they were "necessary incidents to" the system of accounting that he described. *Id.* at 103. From this reasoning, we conclude that those elements of a computer program that are necessarily incidental to its function are similarly unprotectable.

While Baker v. Selden provides a sound analytical foundation, it offers scant guidance on how to separate idea or process from expression, and moreover, on how to further distinguish protectable expression from that expression which "must necessarily be used as incident to" the work's underlying concept.

2. Substantial Similarity Test for Computer Program Structure: Abstraction—Filtration—Comparison

As discussed herein, we think that district courts would be well-advised to undertake a three-step procedure, based on the abstractions test utilized by the district court, in order to determine whether the non-literal elements of two or more computer programs are substantially similar. This approach breaks no new ground; rather, it draws on such familiar copyright doctrines as merger, scenes a faire, and public domain. In taking this approach, however, we are cognizant that computer technology is a dynamic field which can quickly outpace judicial decisionmaking. Thus, in cases where the technology in question does not allow for a literal application of the procedure we outline below, our opinion should not be read to foreclose the district courts of our circuit from utilizing a modified version.

In ascertaining substantial similarity under this approach, a court would first break down the allegedly infringed program into its constituent structural parts. Then, by examining each of these parts for such things as incorporated ideas, expression that is necessarily incidental to those ideas, and elements that are taken from the public domain, a court would then be able to sift out all non-protectable material. Left with a kernel, or possibly kernels, of creative expression after following this process of elimination, the court's last step would be to compare this material with the structure of an allegedly infringing program. The result of this comparison will determine whether the protectable elements of the programs at issue are substantially similar so as to warrant a finding of infringement. It will be helpful to elaborate a bit further.

Step One: Abstraction

As the district court appreciated, see *Computer Associates*, 775 F.Supp., at 560, the theoretic framework for analyzing substantial similarity expounded by Learned Hand in the *Nichols* case is helpful in the present context.

While the abstractions test was originally applied in relation to literary works such as novels and plays, it is adaptable to computer programs. [T]he abstractions test "implicitly recognizes that any given work may consist of a mixture of numerous ideas and expressions". 3 Nimmer § 13.03[F] at 13–62.34–63.

As applied to computer programs, the abstractions test will comprise the first step in the examination for substantial similarity. Initially, in a manner that resembles reverse engineering on a theoretical plane, a court should dissect the allegedly copied program's structure and isolate each level of abstraction contained within it. This process begins with the code and ends with an articulation of the program's ultimate function. Along the way, it is necessary essentially to retrace and map each of the designer's steps—in the opposite order in which they were taken during the program's creation.

## Step Two: Filtration

Once the program's abstraction levels have been discovered, the substantial similarity inquiry moves from the conceptual to the concrete. Professor Nimmer suggests, and we endorse, a "successive filtering method" for separating protectable expression from non-protectable material. See generally 3 Nimmer § 13.03[F]. This process entails examining the structural components at each level of abstraction to determine whether their particular inclusion at that level was "idea" or was dictated by considerations of efficiency, so as to be necessarily incidental to that idea; required by factors external to the program itself; or taken from the public domain and hence is nonprotectable expression. See also Kretschmer, at 844–45 (arguing that program features dictated by market externalities or efficiency concerns are unprotectable). The structure of any given program may reflect some, all, or none of these considerations. Each case requires its own fact specific investigation.

Strictly speaking, this filtration serves "the purpose of defining the scope of plaintiff's copyright". Brown Bag Software v. Symantec Corp., No. 89–16239, slip op. 3719, 3738 (9th Cir. April 7, 1992)(endorsing "analytic dissection" of computer programs in order to isolate protectable expression). By applying well developed doctrines of copyright law, it may ultimately leave behind a "core of protectable material". 3 Nimmer § 13.03[F][5], at 13–72. Further explication of this second step may be helpful.

### (a) Elements Dictated by Efficiency

The portion of Baker v. Selden, discussed earlier, which denies copyright protection to expression necessarily incidental to the idea being expressed, appears to be the cornerstone for what has developed into the doctrine of merger. See Morrissey v. Procter & Gamble Co., 379 F.2d 675, 678–79 (1st Cir.1967)(relying on *Baker*;for the proposition that expression embodying the rules of a sweepstakes contest was inseparable from the idea of the contest itself, and therefore were not protectable by copyright). The doctrine's underlying principle is that "[w]hen there is essentially only one way to express an idea, the idea and its expression are inseparable and copyright is no bar to copying that expression". Concrete Machinery Co. v. Classic Lawn Ornaments, Inc., 843 F.2d 600, 606 (1st Cir.1988). Under these circumstances, the expression is said to have "merged" with the idea itself. In order not to confer a monopoly of the idea upon the copyright owner, such expression should not be protected.

CONTU recognized the applicability of the merger doctrine to computer programs. In its report to Congress it stated that:

> [C]opyrighted language may be copied without infringing when there is but a limited number of ways to express a given idea.... In the computer context, this means that when specific instructions, even though previously

> copyrighted, are the only and essential means of accomplishing a given task, their later use by another will not amount to infringement.

CONTU Report at 20. While this statement directly concerns only the application of merger to program code, that is, the textual aspect of the program, it reasonably suggests that the doctrine fits comfortably within the general context of computer programs.

Furthermore, when one considers the fact that programmers generally strive to create programs "that meet the user's needs in the most efficient manner", Menell, at 1052, the applicability of the merger doctrine to computer programs becomes compelling. In the context of computer program design, the concept of efficiency is akin to deriving the most concise logical proof or formulating the most succinct mathematical computation. Thus, the more efficient a set of modules are, the more closely they approximate the idea or process embodied in that particular aspect of the program's structure.

While, hypothetically, there might be a myriad of ways in which a programmer may effectuate certain functions within a program,—i.e., express the idea embodied in a given subroutine—efficiency concerns may so narrow the practical range of choice as to make only one or two forms of expression workable options. Of course, not all program structure is informed by efficiency concerns. It follows that in order to determine whether the merger doctrine precludes copyright protection to an aspect of a program's structure that is so oriented, a court must inquire "whether the use of *this particular set* of modules is necessary efficiently to implement that part of the program's process" being implemented. Englund, at 902. If the answer is yes, then the expression represented by the programmer's choice of a specific module or group of modules has merged with their underlying idea and is unprotected. *Id.* at 902–03.

Another justification for linking structural economy with the application of the merger doctrine stems from a program's essentially utilitarian nature and the competitive forces that exist in the software marketplace. See Kretschmer, at 842. Working in tandem, these factors give rise to a problem of proof which merger helps to eliminate.

Efficiency is an industry-wide goal. Since, as we have already noted, there may be only a limited number of efficient implementations for any given program task, it is quite possible that multiple programmers, working independently, will design the identical method employed in the allegedly infringed work. Of course, if this is the case, there is no copyright infringement.

Under these circumstances, the fact that two programs contain the same efficient structure may as likely lead to an inference of independent creation as it does to one of copying. Thus, since evidence of similarly efficient structure is not particularly probative of copying, it should be disregarded in the overall substantial similarity analysis. See 3 Nimmer § 13.03[F][2], at 13–65.

We conclude that application of the merger doctrine in this setting is an effective way to eliminate non-protectable expression contained in computer programs.

(b)  Elements Dictated By External Factors

We have stated that where "it is virtually impossible to write about a particular historical era or fictional theme without employing certain 'stock' or standard literary devices", such expression is not copyrightable. Hoehling v. Universal City Studios, Inc., 618 F.2d 972, 979 (2d Cir.), cert. denied, 449 U.S. 841 (1980). For example, the Hoehling case was an infringement suit stemming from several works on the Hindenberg disaster. There we concluded that similarities in representations of German beer halls, scenes depicting German greetings such as "Heil Hitler", or the singing of certain German songs would not lead to a finding of infringement because they were "indispensable, or at least standard, in the treatment of" life in Nazi Germany. Id. (quoting Alexander v. Haley, 460 F.Supp. 40, 45 (S.D.N.Y.1978). This is known as the scenes a faire doctrine, and like "merger", it has its analogous application to computer programs.

Professor Nimmer points out that "in many instances it is virtually impossible to write a program to perform particular functions in a specific computing environment without employing standard techniques". 3 Nimmer § 13.03[F][3], at 13–65. This is a result of the fact that a programmer's freedom of design choice is often circumscribed by extrinsic considerations such as (1) the mechanical specifications of the computer on which a particular program is intended to run; (2) compatibility requirements of other programs with which a program is designed to operate in conjunction; (3) computer manufacturers' design standards; (4) demands of the industry being serviced; and (5) widely accepted programming practices within the computer industry. Id. at 13–66–71.

Courts have already considered some of these factors in denying copyright protection to various elements of computer programs. In the Plains Cotton case, the Fifth Circuit refused to reverse the district court's denial of a preliminary injunction against an alleged program infringer because, in part, "many of the similarities between the . . . programs [were] dictated by the externalities of the cotton market". Plains Cotton Co-op v. Goodpasture Computer Service, Inc., 807 F.2d 1256, 1262 (5th Cir.), cert. denied, 484 U.S. 821 (1987). [T]he district court in Q–Co Industries, [Inc. v. Hoffman], rested its holding on what, perhaps, most closely approximates a traditional scenes a faire rationale. There, the court denied copyright protection to four program modules employed in a teleprompter program. This decision was ultimately based upon the court's finding that "the same modules would be an inherent part of any prompting program". 625 F.Supp. 608, 616 (S.D.N.Y.1985). Building upon this existing case law, we conclude that a court must also examine the structural content of an allegedly infringed program for elements that might have been dictated by external factors.

(c) Elements Taken From the Public Domain

Closely related to the non-protectability of scenes a faire, is material found in the public domain. Such material is free for the taking and cannot be appropriated by a single author even though it is included in a copyrighted work. We see no reason to make an exception to this rule for elements of a computer program that have entered the public domain by virtue of freely accessible program exchanges and the like. Thus, a court must also filter out this material from the allegedly infringed program before it makes the final inquiry in its substantial similarity analysis.

Step Three: Comparison

The third and final step of the test for substantial similarity that we believe appropriate for non-literal program components entails a comparison. Once a court has sifted out all elements of the allegedly infringed program which are "ideas" or are dictated by efficiency or external factors, or taken from the public domain, there may remain a core of protectable expression. In terms of a work's copyright value, this is the golden nugget. At this point, the court's substantial similarity inquiry focuses on whether the defendant copied any aspect of this protected expression, as well as an assessment of the copied portion's relative importance with respect to the plaintiff's overall program. See 3 Nimmer § 13.03[F][5].

3. Policy Considerations

We are satisfied that the three step approach we have just outlined not only comports with, but advances the constitutional policies underlying the Copyright Act. Since any method that tries to distinguish idea from expression ultimately impacts on the scope of copyright protection afforded to a particular type of work, "the line [it draws] must be a pragmatic one, which also keeps in consideration 'the preservation of the balance between competition and protection.'" *Apple Computer*, 714 F.2d at 1253 (citation omitted).

CA and some amici argue against the type of approach that we have set forth on the grounds that it will be a disincentive for future computer program research and development. At bottom, they claim that if programmers are not guaranteed broad copyright protection for their work, they will not invest the extensive time, energy and funds required to design and improve program structures. While they have a point, their argument cannot carry the day. The interest of the copyright law is not in simply conferring a monopoly on industrious persons, but in advancing the public welfare through rewarding artistic creativity, in a manner that permits the free use and development of non-protectable ideas and processes.

Recently, the Supreme Court has emphatically reiterated that "[t]he primary objective of copyright is not to reward the *labor* of authors...." Feist Publications, Inc. v. Rural Telephone Service Co., 111 S.Ct. 1282, 1290 (1991) (emphasis added). While the *Feist* decision deals primarily with the copyrightability of purely factual compilations, its underlying tenets apply to much of the work involved in computer programming. *Feist* put to rest the "sweat of the brow" doctrine in copyright law. *Id*. at 1295. The

Court flatly rejected this justification for extending copyright protection, noting that it "eschewed the most fundamental axiom of copyright law—that no one may copyright facts or ideas". *Id.* [at 1291].

*Feist* teaches that substantial effort alone cannot confer copyright status on an otherwise uncopyrightable work. As we have discussed, despite the fact that significant labor and expense often goes into computer program flow-charting and debugging, that process does not always result in inherently protectable expression. In view of the Supreme Court's recent holding, however, we must reject the legal basis of CA's disincentive argument.

Furthermore, we are unpersuaded that the test we approve today will lead to the dire consequences for the computer program industry that plaintiff and some amici predict. To the contrary, serious students of the industry have been highly critical of the sweeping scope of copyright protection in that it "enables first comers to 'lock up' basic programming techniques as implemented in programs to perform particular tasks". Menell, at 1087.

To be frank, the exact contours of copyright protection for non-literal program structure are not completely clear. We trust that as future cases are decided, those limits will become better defined. Indeed, it may well be that the Copyright Act serves as a relatively weak barrier against public access to the theoretical interstices behind a program's source and object codes. This results from the hybrid nature of a computer program, which, while it is literary expression, is also a highly functional, utilitarian component in the larger process of computing.

In the meantime, Congress has made clear that computer programs are literary works entitled to copyright protection. Of course, we shall abide by these instructions, but in so doing we must not impair the overall integrity of copyright law. While incentive based arguments in favor of broad copyright protection are perhaps attractive from a pure policy perspective, see *Lotus Dev. Corp.*, 740 F.Supp., at 58, ultimately, they have a corrosive effect on certain fundamental tenets of copyright doctrine. If the test we have outlined results in narrowing the scope of protection, as we expect it will, that result flows from applying, in accordance with Congressional intent, long-standing principles of copyright law to computer programs. Of course, our decision is also informed by our concern that these fundamental principles remain undistorted.

B.   The District Court Decision

We turn now to our review of the district court's decision in this particular case. At the outset, we must address CA's claim that the district court erred by relying too heavily on the court appointed expert's "personal opinions on the factual and legal issues before the court".

1.   Use of Expert Evidence in Determining Substantial Similarity Between Computer Programs

Pursuant to Fed.R.Evid. 706, and with the consent of both Altai and CA, Judge Pratt appointed and relied upon Dr. Randall Davis of the

Massachusetts Institute of Technology as the court's own expert witness on the issue of substantial similarity. Dr. Davis submitted a comprehensive written report that analyzed the various aspects of the computer programs at issue and evaluated the parties' expert evidence. At trial, Dr. Davis was extensively cross-examined by both CA and Altai.

The well-established general rule in this circuit has been to limit the use of expert opinion in determining whether works at issue are substantially similar. As a threshold matter, expert testimony may be used to assist the fact finder in ascertaining whether the defendant had copied any part of the plaintiff's work. See Arnstein v. Porter, 154 F.2d 464, 468 (2d Cir.1946). To this end, "the two works are to be compared in their entirety . . . [and] in making such comparison resort may properly be made to expert analysis. . . . " 3 Nimmer § 13.03[E][2], at 13–62.16.

However, once some amount of copying has been established, it remains solely for the trier of fact to determine whether the copying was "illicit", that is to say, whether the "defendant took from plaintiff's works so much of what is pleasing to [lay observers] who comprise the audience for whom such [works are] composed, that defendant wrongfully appropriated something which belongs to the plaintiff". Arnstein, 154 F.2d at 473. Since the test for illicit copying is based upon the response of ordinary lay observers, expert testimony is thus "irrelevant" and not permitted. Id. at 468, 473. We have subsequently described this method of inquiry as "merely an alternative way of formulating the issue of substantial similarity". Ideal Toy Corp. v. Fab–Lu Ltd. (Inc.), 360 F.2d 1021, 1023 n.2 (2d Cir.1966).

Historically, Arnstein's ordinary observer standard had its roots in "an attempt to apply the 'reasonable person' doctrine as found in other areas of the law to copyright". 3 Nimmer § 13.03 [E][2], at 13–62.10–11. That approach may well have served its purpose when the material under scrutiny was limited to art forms readily comprehensible and generally familiar to the average lay person. However, in considering the extension of the rule to the present case, we are reminded of Holmes' admonition that, "[t]he life of the law has not been logic: it has been experience". O.W. Holmes, Jr., THE COMMON LAW 1 (1881).

Thus, in deciding the limits to which expert opinion may be employed in ascertaining the substantial similarity of computer programs, we cannot disregard the highly complicated and technical subject matter at the heart of these claims. Rather, we recognize the reality that computer programs are likely to be somewhat impenetrable by lay observers—whether they be judges or juries—and, thus, seem to fall outside the category of works contemplated by those who engineered the Arnstein test. As Judge Pratt correctly observed:

> In the context of computer programs, many of the familiar tests of similarity prove to be inadequate, for they were developed historically in the context of artistic and literary, rather than utilitarian, works.

Computer Associates, 775 F.Supp., at 558.

In making its finding on substantial similarity with respect to computer programs, we believe that the trier of fact need not be limited by the strictures of its own lay perspective. Rather, we leave it to the discretion of the district court to decide to what extent, if any, expert opinion, regarding the highly technical nature of computer programs, is warranted in a given case.

In so holding, we do not intend to disturb the traditional role of lay observers in judging substantial similarity in copyright cases that involve the aesthetic arts, such as music, visual works or literature.

In this case, Dr. Davis' opinion was instrumental in dismantling the intricacies of computer science so that the court could formulate and apply an appropriate rule of law. While Dr. Davis' report and testimony undoubtedly shed valuable light on the subject matter of the litigation, Judge Pratt remained, in the final analysis, the trier of fact. The district court's use of the expert's assistance, in the context of this case, was entirely appropriate.

2. Evidentiary Analysis

The district court had to determine whether Altai's OSCAR 3.5 program was substantially similar to CA's ADAPTER. We note that Judge Pratt's method of analysis effectively served as a road map for our own, with one exception—Judge Pratt filtered out the non-copyrightable aspects of OSCAR 3.5 rather than those found in ADAPTER, the allegedly infringed program. We think that our approach—i.e., filtering out the unprotected aspects of an allegedly infringed program and then comparing the end product to the structure of the suspect program—is preferable, and therefore believe that district courts should proceed in this manner in future cases.

The fact that the district court's analysis proceeded in the reverse order, however, had no material impact on the outcome of this case. Since Judge Pratt determined that OSCAR effectively contained no protectable expression whatsoever, the most serious charge that can be levelled against him is that he was overly thorough in his examination.

Moving to the district court's evaluation of OSCAR 3.5's structural components, we agree with Judge Pratt's systematic exclusion of non-protectable expression. With respect to code, the district court observed that after the rewrite of OSCAR 3.4 to OSCAR 3.5, "there remained virtually no lines of code that were identical to ADAPTER". *Id.* at 561. Accordingly, the court found that the code "present[ed] no similarity at all". *Id.* at 562.

Next, Judge Pratt addressed the issue of similarity between the two programs' parameter lists and macros. [T]he district court reasonably found that, for lack of persuasive evidence, CA failed to meet its burden of proof on whether the macros and parameter lists at issue were substantially similar. See *Computer Associates*, 775 F.Supp., at 562.

The district court also found that the overlap exhibited between the list of services required for both ADAPTER and OSCAR 3.5 was "determined by the demands of the operating system and of the applications program to which it [was] to be linked through ADAPTER or OSCAR''. *Id.* In other words, this aspect of the program's structure was dictated by the nature of other programs with which it was designed to interact and, thus, is not protected by copyright.

Finally, in his infringement analysis, Judge Pratt accorded no weight to the similarities between the two programs' organizational charts, ''because [the charts were] so simple and obvious to anyone exposed to the operation of the program[s]''. *Id.* CA argues that the district court's action in this regard ''is not consistent with copyright law''—that ''obvious'' expression is protected, and that the district court erroneously failed to realize this. However, to say that elements of a work are ''obvious'', in the manner in which the district court used the word, is to say that they ''follow naturally from the work's theme rather than from the author's creativity''. 3 Nimmer § 13.03[F][3], at 13–65. This is but one formulation of the scenes a faire doctrine, which we have already endorsed as a means of weeding out unprotectable expression.

Since we accept Judge Pratt's factual conclusions and the results of his legal analysis, we affirm his dismissal of CA's copyright infringement claim based upon OSCAR 3.5. We emphasize that, like all copyright infringement cases, those that involve computer programs are highly fact specific. The amount of protection due structural elements, in any given case, will vary according to the protectable expression found to exist within the program at issue.

Conclusion

In adopting the above three step analysis for substantial similarity between the non-literal elements of computer programs we seek to insure two things: (1) that programmers may receive appropriate copyright protection for innovative utilitarian works containing expression; and (2) that non-protectable technical expression remains in the public domain for others to use freely as building blocks in their own work. At first blush, it may seem counterintuitive that someone who has benefited to some degree from illicitly obtained material can emerge from an infringement suit relatively unscathed. However, so long as the appropriated material consists of non-protectable expression, ''[t]his result is neither unfair nor unfortunate. It is the means by which copyright advances the progress of science and art''. *Feist*, 111 S.Ct., at 1290.

Accordingly, we affirm the judgment of the district court in all respects.

# Apple Computer, Inc. v. Microsoft Corp.

United States Court of Appeals, Ninth Circuit, 1994.
35 F.3d 1435, cert. denied, 513 U.S. 1184, 115 S.Ct. 1176, 130 L.Ed.2d 1129 (1995).

■ RYMER, CIRCUIT JUDGE.

Lisa and Macintosh are Apple computers. Each has a graphical user interface (''GUI'') which Apple Computer, Inc. registered for copyright as an audiovisual work. Both GUIs were developed as a user-friendly way for ordinary mortals to communicate with the Apple computer; the Lisa Desktop and the Macintosh Finder[a] are based on a desktop metaphor with windows, icons and pull-down menus which can be manipulated on the screen with a hand-held device called a mouse. When Microsoft Corporation released Windows 1.0, having a similar GUI, Apple complained. As a result, the two agreed to a license giving Microsoft the right to use and sublicense derivative works generated by Windows 1.0 in present and future products. Microsoft released Windows 2.03 and later, Windows 3.0; its licensee, Hewlett–Packard Company (HP), introduced NewWave 1.0 and later, New-Wave 3.0, which run in conjunction with Windows to make IBM-compatible computers easier to use. Apple believed that these versions exceed the license, make Windows more "Mac-like", and infringe its copyright. This action followed.

In a series of published rulings,[b] the district court construed the agreement to license visual displays in the Windows 1.0 interface, not the interface itself; determined that all visual displays in Windows 2.03 and 3.0 were in Windows 1.0 except for the use of overlapping windows[c] and some changes in the appearance and manipulation of icons; dissected the Macintosh, Windows and NewWave interfaces based on a list of similarities submitted by Apple to decide which are protectable; and applied the limiting doctrines of originality, functionality, standardization, scenes a faire and merger to find no copying of protectable elements in Windows 2.03 or 3.0, and to limit the scope of copyright protection to a handful of individual elements in NewWave.[d] The court then held that those elements in NewWave would be compared with their equivalent Apple elements for substantial similarity, and that the NewWave and Windows 2.03 and 3.0

---

[a] The Macintosh Finder is registered as a derivative work of the Lisa Desktop. Although the district court dismissed the Finder as a work in suit, the Macintosh interface has been referred to interchangeably with the Lisa during the course of this litigation.

[b] Apple Computer, Inc. v. Microsoft Corp., 709 F.Supp. 925 (N.D.Cal.1989)(*Apple I*); Apple Computer, Inc. v. Microsoft Corp., 717 F.Supp. 1428 (N.D.Cal.1989)(*Apple II*); Apple Computer, Inc. v. Microsoft Corp., 759 F.Supp. 1444 (N.D.Cal.1991)(*Apple III*); Apple Computer, Inc. v. Microsoft Corp., 779 F.Supp. 133 (N.D.Cal.1991)(*Apple IV*); Apple Computer, Inc. v. Microsoft Corp., 799 F.Supp. 1006 (N.D.Cal.1992)(*Apple V*); Apple Computer, Inc. v. Microsoft Corp., 821 F.Supp. 616 (N.D.Cal.1993)(*Apple VI*). The first two published opinions were rendered by Hon. William S. Schwarzer; after his appointment as Director of the Federal Judicial Cen-

ter, this matter was reassigned to the calendar of Hon. Vaughn R. Walker.

Our treatment of facts throughout is truncated because the district court's is so extensive.

[c] Windows 1.0 had a tiled windowing system in which the windows were connected together in a fixed pattern such that all open windows were simultaneously visible. An overlapping system allows windows to be stacked on top of one another and moved around the screen individually.

[d] These items relate to the "zooming rectangle" animation associated with the opening or closing of an icon into a window, the "dimming" of a folder icon that has been opened into a window, and the use of a trash can icon to depict the discard function. Each appears in both versions 1.0 and 3.0 of New-Wave, but none is in any version of Windows.

works as a whole would be compared with Apple's works for virtual identity. When Apple declined to oppose motions for summary judgment of noninfringement for lack of virtual identity, however, judgments in favor of Microsoft and HP were entered.

Apple asks us to reverse because of two fundamental errors in the district court's reasoning. First, Apple argues that the court should not have allowed the license for Windows 1.0 to serve as a partial defense. Second, Apple contends that the court went astray by dissecting Apple's works so as to eliminate unprotectable and licensed elements from comparison with Windows 2.03, 3.0 and NewWave as a whole, incorrectly leading it to adopt a standard of virtual identity instead of substantial similarity. We disagree.

The district court's approach was on target. In so holding, we readily acknowledge how much more complex and difficult its task was than ours. The district court had to grapple with graphical user interfaces in the first instance—and for the first time, with a claim of copying a computer program's artistic look as an audiovisual work instead of program codes registered as a literary work. In this case there is also the unusual, added complexity of a license that arguably covers some or most of the allegedly infringing works. The district court therefore had to cut new paths as it went along; we have the luxury of looking at the case at the end of the trip. From this vantage point, it is clear that treatment of Apple's GUIs, whose visual displays are licensed to a great degree and which are a tool for the user to access various functions of a computer in an aesthetically and ergonomically pleasing way, follows naturally from a long line of copyright decisions which recognizes that works cannot be substantially similar where analytic dissection demonstrates that similarities in expression are either authorized, or arise from the use of common ideas or their logical extensions.

We therefore hold:

(1) Because there was an agreement by which Apple licensed the right to make certain derivative works, the district court properly started with the license to determine what Microsoft was permitted to copy. Infringement cannot be founded on a licensed similarity. We read Microsoft's license as the district court did, to cover visual displays—not the Windows 1.0 interface itself. That being so, the court correctly decided first to identify which visual displays in Windows 2.03, 3.0 and NewWave are licensed and which are not.

(2) The district court then properly proceeded to distinguish ideas from expression, and to "dissect" unlicensed elements in order to determine whether the remaining similarities lack originality, flow naturally from basic ideas, or are one of the few ways in which a particular idea can be expressed given the constraints of the computer environment. Dissection is not inappropriate even though GUIs are thought of as the "look and feel" of a computer, because copyright protection extends only to protectable elements of expression.

(3) Having found that the similarities in Windows 2.03 and 3.0 consist only of unprotectable or licensed elements, and that the similarities be-

tween protectable elements in Apple's works and NewWave are de minimis, the district court did not err by concluding that, to the extent there is creative expression left in how the works are put together, as a whole they can receive only limited protection. When the range of protectable and unauthorized expression is narrow, the appropriate standard for illicit copying is virtual identity. For these reasons, the GUIs in Windows 2.03, 3.0 and NewWave cannot be compared for substantial similarity with the Macintosh interface as a whole. Instead, as the district court held, the works must be compared for virtual identity.[e]

The fact that Apple licensed the right to copy almost all of its visual displays fundamentally affects the outcome of its infringement claims. Authorized copying accounts for more than 90% of the allegedly infringing features in Windows 2.03 and 3.0, and two-thirds of the features in NewWave. More than that, the 1985 Agreement and negotiations leading up to Microsoft's license left Apple no right to complain that selection and arrangement of licensed elements make the interface as a whole look more ''Mac-like'' than Windows 1.0.

Thus, we do not start at ground zero in resolving Apple's claims of infringement. Rather, considering the license and the limited number of ways that the basic ideas of the Apple GUI can be expressed differently, we conclude that only ''thin'' protection, against virtually identical copying, is appropriate. Apple's appeal, which depends on comparing its interface as a whole for substantial similarity, must therefore fail.

To prevail, Apple must show ownership of a valid copyright in the Macintosh GUI and that Microsoft and HP copied unlicensed, protected elements of its copyrighted audiovisual works. Brown Bag Software v. Symantec Corp., 960 F.2d 1465, 1472 (9th Cir.), *cert. denied*, 113 S.Ct. 198 (1992). Copying may be shown by circumstantial evidence of access and substantial similarity of both the general ideas and expression between the copyrighted work and the allegedly infringing work. *Id.*

We have traditionally determined whether copying sufficient to constitute infringement has taken place under a two-part test having ''extrinsic'' and ''intrinsic'' components. As originally adopted in Sid & Marty Krofft Television Productions, Inc. v. McDonald's Corp., 562 F.2d 1157, 1164 (9th Cir.1977), the extrinsic prong was a test for similarity of ideas based on external criteria; analytic dissection and expert testimony could be used, if helpful. The intrinsic prong was a test for similarity of expression from the standpoint of the ordinary reasonable observer, with no expert assistance. *Id.* As it has evolved, however, the extrinsic test now objectively considers whether there are substantial similarities in both ideas and expression, whereas the intrinsic test continues to measure expression subjectively. *Brown Bag*, 960 F.2d at 1475; Shaw v. Lindheim, 919 F.2d 1353, 1357 (9th Cir.1990). Because only those elements of a work that are protectable and used without the author's permission can be compared when it comes to the ultimate question of illicit copying, we use analytic dissection to determine the scope of copyright protection before works are considered ''as a whole''. See, e.g., *Brown Bag*, 960 F.2d at 1475–76 (explaining that

[e] Since Apple contests only the legal standard of virtual identity, we do not consider whether summary judgment was appropriately entered on the merits under that standard.

purpose of analytic dissection is to define scope of copyright protection); *Pasillas v. McDonald's Corp.*, 927 F.2d 440, 443 (9th Cir.1991)(copyright holder cannot rely on standard elements to show substantial similarity of expression); *Harper House, Inc. v. Thomas Nelson, Inc.*, 889 F.2d 197, 207–08 (9th Cir.1989)(trier of fact cannot base infringement decision on unprotectable aspects of plaintiff's work).

Although this litigation has raised difficult and interesting issues about the scope of copyright protection for a graphical user interface, resolving this appeal is a matter of applying well-settled principles. In this, as in other cases, the steps we find helpful to follow are these:

(1) The plaintiff must identify the source(s) of the alleged similarity between his work and the defendant's work.

(2) Using analytic dissection, and, if necessary, expert testimony, the court must determine whether any of the allegedly similar features are protected by copyright. Where, as in this case, a license agreement is involved, the court must also determine which features the defendant was authorized to copy. Once the scope of the license is determined, unprotectable ideas must be separated from potentially protectable expression; to that expression, the court must then apply the relevant limiting doctrines in the context of the particular medium involved, through the eyes of the ordinary consumer of that product.

(3) Having dissected the alleged similarities and considered the range of possible expression, the court must define the scope of the plaintiff's copyright—that is, decide whether the work is entitled to "broad" or "thin" protection. Depending on the degree of protection, the court must set the appropriate standard for a subjective comparison of the works to determine whether, as a whole, they are sufficiently similar to support a finding of illicit copying.

\* \* \*

## B

It is not easy to distinguish expression from ideas, particularly in a new medium. However, it must be done, as the district court did in this case. *Baker v. Selden*, 101 U.S. 99 (1879). Well-recognized precepts guide the process of analytic dissection. First, when an idea and its expression are indistinguishable, or "merged", the expression will only be protected against nearly identical copying. *Krofft*, 562 F.2d at 1167–68; *Kalpakian*, 446 F.2d at 742. For example, in this case, the idea of an icon in a desktop metaphor representing a document stored in a computer program can only be expressed in so many ways. An iconic image shaped like a page is an obvious choice.

The doctrine of scenes a faire is closely related. In this case, for example, use of overlapping windows inheres in the idea of windows. A programmer has only two options for displaying more than one window at a time: either a tiled system, or an overlapping system. As demonstrated by Microsoft's scenes a faire video, overlapping windows have been the clear preference in graphic interfaces. Accordingly, protectable substantial similarity cannot be based on the mere use of overlapping windows, although, of course, Apple's particular expression may be protected.

Apple suggests that scenes a faire should not limit the scope of its audiovisual copyright, or at least that the interactive character of GUIs and their functional purpose should not outweigh their artistry. While user participation may not negate copyrightability of an audiovisual work, the district court did not deny protection to any aspect of Apple's works on this basis. In any event, unlike purely artistic works such as novels and plays, graphical user interfaces generated by computer programs are partly artistic and partly functional. They are a tool to facilitate communication between the user and the computer; GUIs do graphically what a character-based interface, which requires a user to type in alphanumeric commands, does manually. Thus, the delete function is engaged by moving an icon on top of a trash can instead of hitting a "delete" key. In Apple's GUI, the ability to move icons to any part of the screen exemplifies an essentially functional process, indispensable to the idea of manipulating icons by a mouse.

To the extent that GUIs are artistic, there is no dispute that creativity in user interfaces is constrained by the power and speed of the computer. See Manufacturers Technologies, Inc. v. Cams, Inc., 706 F.Supp. 984, 994–95 (D.Conn.1989)(denying protection to formatting style of plaintiff's screen displays because of constraints on viable options available to programmers). For example, hardware constraints limit the number of ways to depict visually the movement of a window on the screen; because many computers do not have enough power to show the entire contents of the window as it is being moved, the illusion of movement must be shown by using the outline of a window or some similar feature. Design alternatives are further limited by the GUI's purpose of making interaction between the user and the computer more "user-friendly". These, and similar environmental and ergonomic factors which limit the range of possible expression in GUIs, properly inform the scope of copyright protection.

Originality is another doctrine which limits the scope of protection. As the Supreme Court recently made clear, protection extends only to those components of a work that are original to the author, although original selection and arrangement of otherwise uncopyrightable components may be protectable. Feist Publications, Inc. v. Rural Tel. Serv. Co., 499 U.S. 340, 348–51 (1991). Apple's argument that components should not be tested for originality because its interface as a whole meets the test is therefore misplaced.

In sum, the district court's analytic dissection was appropriately conducted under the extrinsic portion of our test for whether sufficient copying to constitute infringement has taken place. We are not persuaded to the contrary by Apple's arguments that the district court shouldn't have dissected at all, or dissected too much; that it "filtered out" unprotectable and licensed elements instead of viewing the Macintosh interface as a whole; and that it should have recognized protectability of arrangements and the "total concept and feel" of the works under a substantial similarity standard.

As we made clear in *Aliotti*, the party claiming infringement may place "no reliance upon any similarity in expression resulting from" unprotectable elements. *Id.* (emphasis added)(similarities between competing stuffed dinosaur toys on account of posture and body design, and being cuddly, stem from the physiognomy of dinosaurs or from the nature of stuffed animals and are thus unprotectable). Otherwise, there would be no point to the extrinsic test, or to distinguishing ideas from expression. In this case, it would also effectively rescind the 1985 Agreement. This does not mean that at the end of the day, when the works are considered under the intrinsic test, they should not be compared as a whole. See McCulloch v. Albert E. Price, Inc., 823 F.2d 316, 321 (9th Cir.1987) (contrasting artistic work at issue, where decorative plates were substantially similar in more than the one unprotectable element (text), with factual works which have many unprotectable elements and very little protectable expression). Nor does it mean that infringement cannot be based on original selection and arrangement of unprotected elements. However, the unprotectable elements have to be identified, or filtered, before the works can be considered as a whole. See *Harper House*, 889 F.2d at 207–08 (reversing because "total impact and effect" test of jury instruction did not distinguish between protectable and unprotectable material, thereby improperly making it possible for jury to find copying based on unprotected material instead of selection and arrangement); see also *Pasillas*, 927 F.2d at 443 (copyright holder could not rely on unprotectable elements to show substantial similarity of expression); *Frybarger*, 812 F.2d at 529 (to extent that similarities between works were confined to ideas and general concepts, they were noninfringing).

### C

The district court's conclusion that the works as a whole are entitled only to limited protection and should be compared for virtual identity follows from its analytic dissection. By virtue of the licensing agreement, Microsoft and HP were entitled to use the vast majority of features that Apple claims were copied. Of those that remain, the district court found no unauthorized, protectable similarities of expression in Windows 2.03 and 3.0, and only a handful in NewWave. Thus, any claim of infringement that Apple may have against Microsoft must rest on the copying of Apple's unique selection and arrangement of all of these features. Under *Harper House* and *Frybarger*, there can be no infringement unless the works are virtually identical.

We therefore hold that the district court properly identified the sources of similarity in Windows and NewWave, determined which were licensed, distinguished ideas from expression, and decided the scope of Apple's copyright by dissecting the unauthorized expression and filtering out unprotectable elements. Having correctly found that almost all the similarities spring either from the license or from basic ideas and their obvious expression, it correctly concluded that illicit copying could occur only if the works as a whole are virtually identical.

# Michael Stillman v. Leo Burnett Co.

United States District Court, N.D. Illinois, 1989.
720 F.Supp. 1353.

■ DUFF, DISTRICT JUDGE.

Plaintiff Michael Stillman has sued defendants Leo Burnett Company, Inc. ("Burnett") and United Airlines, Inc. ("United") for copyright infringement under the Copyright Act, 17 U.S.C. § 501. Stillman alleges that the defendants copied a "silent" television commercial he had created for Eastern Airlines, Inc. ("Eastern"), and then misrepresented that they had created their commercial through lucky inspiration. The defendants have moved to dismiss. For the reasons set forth below, the motion will be denied.

Facts

For the purposes of this motion, the court accepts as true the allegations of the complaint, the facts contained within the complaint's exhibits, and the videotapes (with accompanying storyboards) of the two commercials.[a] Stillman is a creative advertising consultant, and the creator and producer of television commercials. In late 1981, he created a commercial for Eastern's Canadian airline passenger market, which aired on Canadian television during 1982 and 1983.

The commercial employed silence as a way of attracting viewer attention to the screen. Of the nine screens in the commercial, the first eight were black with white reverse-type writing. The writing faded in and out from screen to screen—with the exception of the Eastern name and logo, which remained on the screen—and read as follows:

Screen 1:

A SILENT COMMERCIAL FOR EASTERN SUPER 7'S

Screen 2:

MIAMI EASTERN SUPER 7'S

Screen 3:

7 NIGHTS 8 DAYS CHOICE HOTEL
EASTERN SUPER 7'S

Screen 4:

SCHEDULED ROUND TRIP FLIGHTS
EASTERN SUPER 7'S

[a] In an earlier ruling, this court converted the defendants' motion to dismiss to one for summary judgment.

Screen 5:

> RENTAL CAR UNLIMITED
> MILEAGE (AND MORE)
> EASTERN SUPER 7'S

Screen 6:

> ONLY $370 PER PERSON
> DOUBLE OCCUPANCY
> EASTERN SUPER 7'S

Screen 7:

> WHY SO QUIET?
> EASTERN SUPER 7'S

Screen 8:

> BECAUSE THE COMPETITION IS SLEEPING
> EASTERN SUPER 7'S

The last screen suddenly broke into color and sound, showing a picture of a sunset and containing a voice-over explaining the point of the silent commercial. The commercial was hugely successful and profitable for Eastern, and was widely discussed in Canadian and American advertising industry circles.

In 1986, after Eastern (inexplicably) decided not to use the silent commercial for its American market, Stillman, who owned the right to it, wrote two letters to United's president suggesting that United engage Stillman to produce silent commercials for United's American market. With the letters, he enclosed copies of the Eastern storyboard, and some ideas about how the silent commercial could be used for United.

United never hired Stillman, but in 1987 it did air a "silent" commercial on American television. This commercial, like the Eastern commercial, contained nine screens, the first eight of which were black with white reverse-type writing fading in and out from screen to screen and reading as follows:

Screen 1:

> This is a silent commercial

Screen 2:

> The money we saved on sound

Screen 3:

> Helps keep our air fares this low:

Screen 4:

> United's Chicago $89 from New York
> UNITED AIRLINES

Screen 5:

> United's Miami $89 from New York
> UNITED AIRLINES

Screen 6:

United's Los Angeles $99
from New York UNITED AIRLINES

Screen 7:

United's San Francisco $99
from New York UNITED AIRLINES

Screen 8:

Call Now 212–867–3000 718–803–2200
201–624–1500 or your travel agent

Fares shown are each way with round trip—Restrictions apply. Seats are limited. The last screen broke into color, showing an airplane taking off over the word "Roarrrrr", but maintaining silence.

The creator and producer of United's silent commercial was Leo Burnett. At the time Leo Burnett created the commercial, it was aware of Stillman's silent commercial for Eastern. Nevertheless, in interviews following the airing of the United commercial, Leo Burnett represented that it had created the silent commercial and that the creation resulted from "lucky inspiration".

In 1988, Stillman applied for and received a Certificate of Registration for his silent commercial from the United States Register of Copyrights. Shortly thereafter, he filed this lawsuit.

Discussion

Courts frequently have said that a copyright claim contains only two elements: (1) the plaintiff's ownership of a valid copyright in a work; and (2) the defendant's copying of this work in creating another one. See, e.g., Atari, Inc. v. North American Philips Consumer Electronics Corp., 672 F.2d 607, 614 (7th Cir.1982). In *Atari*, the Seventh Circuit elaborated on the second element. According to the Court of Appeals, a plaintiff can establish copying by showing (1) that the defendant had access to the plaintiff's work, and (2) that the two works are substantially similar. 672 F.2d at 614. Further, the Court of Appeals stated, a plaintiff establishes substantial similarity by showing (1) that "the defendant copied from the plaintiff's work and (2) [that] the copying, if proven, went so far as to constitute an improper appropriation". *Id.*

At first blush, this framework appears circular: To prove copying, the plaintiff must prove substantial similarity; and to prove substantial similarity, he must prove copying. See Nash v. CBS, Inc., 704 F.Supp. 823, 826 (N.D.Ill.1989). The confusion lies in the different meaning of the word "copying" in copyright law.

Copying, as an element of a copyright claim, refers to the ultimate legal issue of whether the defendant violated the copyright laws by reproducing protectible expression from the plaintiff's work. Copying as a prong of substantial similarity, by contrast, is limited to the purely factual issue of whether the defendant used the plaintiff's work as a starting point for his own. See Arnstein v. Porter, 154 F.2d 464 (2d Cir.1946). Thus, a defendant who has copied from a plaintiff's work as a factual matter—that is, by employing the plaintiff's ideas, procedures or techniques—may not have copied as a legal matter; the difference between the two lies in the second prong of the substantial similarity inquiry—i.e., unlawful appropriation. If a defendant has not copied something protected by the copyright laws—specifically, the plaintiff's expression of his ideas—then his copying will not subject him to liability. Sid & Marty Krofft Television v. McDonald's Corp., 562 F.2d 1157, 1163–64 (9th Cir.1977). Thus, when the Seventh Circuit stated in *Atari* that, in effect, a plaintiff must establish copying in order to prove copying, what it must have meant was that the plaintiff must establish at least permissible copying as a prerequisite to proving illicit copying.

Yet, with this inexactitude in the *Atari* framework resolved, others emerge. If a defendant must prove copying in order to prove substantial similarity, why must he then prove access in order to establish an infringement? After all, copying, even in the permissible sense, clearly requires that the defendant have had access to—indeed, have relied upon—the plaintiff's work in creating the new one. Moreover, although it is clear why a plaintiff must show improper appropriation in order to prove a copyright violation, it is difficult to see why such appropriation stands as a prong of substantial similarity, rather than as a separate element of the copyright cause of action. Substantial similarity, in the context of the *Atari* framework (672 F.2d at 614), is merely one of two elements—the other being access—that must be proved in order to permit an inference that the defendant usurped material from the plaintiff's work; this inference arises, however, upon proof of substantial similarity between even nonprotectible elements of the two works, without any need to prove that what was taken amounted to an unlawful appropriation of the plaintiff's expression. See *Arnstein*, 154 F.2d at 469.

These difficulties arise out of the dual usages of another term—substantial similarity. As just noted, substantial similarity can refer to the likeness between two works sufficient to give rise to an inference, when supported by evidence of access, that the defendant took ideas from the plaintiff's work. Substantial similarity, however, is also used as a term of art relating to the unlawful nature of the similarities between two works. See Roth Greeting Cards v. United Card Co., 429 F.2d 1106, 1110 (9th Cir.1970); Nimmer on Copyright § 13.03[A] at 13–22.1 (1988)(similarity is not "substantial" if what was copied was nonprotectible).

*Atari* creates obfuscation because it refers to substantial similarity in its former usage, but then sets forth the test necessary to establish the latter. Proof of both copying and unlawful appropriation are necessary to establish substantial similarity when that term is used as a term of art; a copy that does not unlawfully appropriate protectible expression cannot be substantially similar in the sense required to establish a violation. See *Atari*, 672 F.2d at 614. They are not necessary, however, when substantial similarity is used in the sense of a factual predicate for an inference of copying. On the contrary, when the phrase is used in this sense, it is not copying which is necessary to establish substantial similarity, but rather substantial similarity which is necessary to prove copying.

This discussion suggests that some clarification of the *Atari* logic is needed. To prevail on a copyright claim, a plaintiff must prove (1) a valid copyright, and (2) illicit copying. To prove illicit copying, he must establish both (1) copying, and (2) unlawful appropriation. To establish copying, a plaintiff must show (1) access, and (2) substantial similarity between the works "when compared in their entirety including both protectible and unprotectible material". 3 Nimmer on Copyright § 13.03[e] at 13–55 (1988). Finally, to show unlawful appropriation (i.e., substantial similarity as a matter of law), the plaintiff must demonstrate that the defendant's copying extended to the plaintiff's protectible expression.

The defendants have conceded, for the purposes of this motion, both the validity of the plaintiff's copyright and their permissible copying of the Eastern commercial. Their only argument at this stage is that, even assuming such copying, they are entitled to judgment because the United silent commercial did not copy any protectible material from the Eastern commercial. This argument requires a further analysis of how a plaintiff establishes the copying of protectible expression.

As noted above, the copying/unlawful appropriation dichotomy simply reflects the fact that the copyright laws do not protect ideas, procedures, and concepts, but only the expressions of ideas. Copying occurs when a defendant usurps the former; unlawful appropriation, however, requires the purloining of expression as well. In *Krofft*, the Ninth Circuit, building on Arnstein v. Porter, articulated a bifurcated test for proving copying and unlawful appropriation.

The first test, the so-called extrinsic test, permits a plaintiff to prove copying by showing, through analytic dissection and (if necessary) expert testimony, that the similarities between the two works—when viewed in terms of their protectible and nonprotectible elements—are so substantial as to warrant a finding that the defendant usurped, at least, the plaintiff's ideas. 562 F.2d at 1164. The second, or intrinsic, test addresses the indeterminate boundary between ideas and their expression. Because the infringement of expression occurs when "the ordinary observer, unless he set out to detect the disparities [in two works], would be disposed to overlook them, and regard [the works'] aesthetic appeal as the same", Peter Pan Fabrics, Inc. v. Martin Weiner Corp., 274 F.2d 487, 489 (2d Cir.1960)(Hand, J.), the intrinsic test precludes reference to objective criteria and expert testimony, and requires instead an inquiry into whether an ordinary observer experiencing the two works would conclude that "the accused work has captured the 'total concept and feel' of the copyrighted work". *Atari*, 672 F.2d at 614 (quoting Roth Greeting Cards v. United Card Co., 429 F.2d 1106, 1110 (9th Cir.1970); *Krofft*, 562 F.2d at 1164; Arnstein v. Porter, 154 F.2d at 468.

*Krofft* further explained that summary judgment is rarely appropriate under the intrinsic test, since laymen are as qualified as judges to determine the reactions of an ordinary observer. 562 F.2d at 1166. If an ordinary observer could conclude that the defendant copied the plaintiff's expression (by using the plaintiff's work to create another work evoking a similar response in an ordinary observer), then, *Krofft* instructed (and *Atari* purported to follow, 672 F.2d at 614), the case should go to the jury.

Under *Krofft*'s extrinsic-intrinsic tests, this court could not grant the defendants' motion for summary judgment. As the defendants acknowledge, under the extrinsic test a question of fact exists as to whether they copied Stillman's work: the commercials both use silence as the means of attracting viewer attention to the screen; they both begin with a screen stating that they are silent commercials; they both contain eight screens with black background and white lettering; they both break into color in the final screen; and they both tie their silence into the low fares of their respective airlines. Further, under the intrinsic test, a reasonable jury could find similarity of expression in the two commercials. Although the commercials have a different pace, a different message, and a different final frame, these differences do not so undermine the similarities as to render implausible a jury finding that the United commercial exudes the same total concept and feel as does the Eastern commercial. See *Atari*, 672 F.2d at 618 (focus of ordinary observer test is on similarities rather than differences).

The intrinsic-extrinsic analysis, however, does not fully encompass the infringement inquiry. See *Krofft*, 562 F.2d at 1167. The intrinsic test, by focusing on the response of the ordinary observer, follows the accepted view that ordinarily a plaintiff can establish copying of expression even in the absence of identical copying. *Id.* Yet, because this test eschews analytic dissection, it fails to account for the possibility that the similarity of expression may fall within the category of what is known as nonprotectible expression. Specifically, when the expression is indistinguishable from the idea, the copyright laws prohibit only identical copying because to protect more would be to grant a monopoly over the idea. In the same vein, when the similarity between two works arises exclusively from the use of the same process or technique it cannot form the basis for a copyright claim. See Baker v. Selden, 101 U.S. (11 Otto) 99, 101 (1879). Finally, "similarity of expression, whether literal or non-literal, which necessarily results from the fact that the common idea is only capable of expression in more or less stereotyped form will preclude a finding of actionable similarity". 3 Nimmer on Copyright § 13.03[A] at 13–21–13–33 (1988). Stated in terms of the intrinsic test, a non-identical work that would evoke a similar response in an ordinary observer as does another work does not violate the latter's copyright if the similar response arises solely from the similarities of the nonprotectible elements of the two works.

The defendants insist that a comparison of the United commercial with the Eastern commercial reveals that all they copied are the nonprotectible elements of Stillman's work. They first contend that the idea of using a silent commercial to attract viewer attention to the screen is indistinguishable from the expression of that idea through the use of silence, so that their use of silence per se cannot give rise to liability. They next assert that the use of black screens with white lettering and of color screens at the end are all audio-visual techniques which similarly cannot render them liable absent identical copying. Lastly, they urge that their copying of Stillman's use of a first screen stating that the commercial is silent is necessary to the expression of a silent commercial (i.e., to inform the viewers that their sets are not broken), and thus cannot form the basis for a copyright claim. Since any similarity in the total concept and feel of the two commercials results from these nonprotectible elements, and since the two commercials are not identical, the defendants conclude that no illicit copying has occurred.

The defendants are correct insofar as they argue that, in order to determine whether all of the similarities between two works result from the copying of nonprotectible expression, the court may undertake an analytic dissection of the two works. The extrinsic and intrinsic tests both involve findings of fact, but the issue of protectibility/nonprotectibility is an issue of law. Thus, before a court may send a copyright case to the jury, it must satisfy itself that, even assuming copying of an idea and its expression, at least some of what the defendant copied falls into the area of protectible expression.[b]

The defendants, however, misapply this inquiry in the instant case. Although a plaintiff can protect neither his ideas nor his use of procedures and techniques to express these ideas, he can protect the creative arrangement and interaction of the techniques composing the expression. As *Krofft* noted in countenancing limited analytic dissection for the purpose of ensuring some copying of protectible expression, "it is the *combination* of many different elements which may command copyright protection because of its particular subjective quality". 562 F.2d at 1169 (original emphasis). When this combination of elements is used in a way that is not "indispensable, or at least standard in the treatment of a given topic", *Atari*, 672 F.2d at 616, no idea-expression unity exists, and the requirement of near-identical similarity does not come into play.

Standing on their own, Stillman's use of an initial screen announcing that the commercial was a silent commercial, eight black screens with white lettering, and a color screen at the end, do not amount to protectible expression. Yet, the synergy of these nonprotectible elements in the East-

[b] In Olson v. National Broadcasting Co., 855 F.2d 1446 (9th Cir.1988), the Ninth Circuit (without saying so) appears to have incorporated this requirement—that, if copying occurred, it extended to protectible expression—into the extrinsic test. In *Olson*, the Court affirmed a j.n.o.v. for the defendants under the extrinsic test after analytically dissecting the two works and determining that all of their similarities resulted from similarities in nonprotectible elements of the plaintiff's work. See *id.* at 1450–53. This approach, however, loses sight of the function of the extrinsic test, which is to determine not whether illicit copying occurred, but rather whether any copying occurred. Since the Court does not appear to have questioned the jury's determination that the defendants copied from the plaintiff, see *id.* at 1448, *Krofft* should have led the *Olson* Court to find the extrinsic test satisfied, and to confine itself to reviewing the jury's verdict under the intrinsic test and, if necessary, under the idea-expression unity limitation on this test, see *id.* at 1453.

ern commercial creates a whole that is greater than the sum of its parts. Each of the nonprotectible elements of the commercial may have been quite indispensable to a silent commercial, but Stillman's actual arrangement of these elements in the creation of his commercial was in no sense dictated by the idea of a silent commercial, and therefore renders the idea-expression unity limitation inapplicable here. Should a jury find that the defendants copied the Eastern commercial in making the United commercial, and that in doing so they created a commercial that evokes a similar response in ordinary observers, this court could not say that the defendants' copying fell exclusively within the realm of the nonprotectible. Accordingly, the defendants' motion for summary judgment must be denied.

## Louis M. Kohus v. John V. Mariol

United States Court of Appeals, Sixth Circuit, 2003.
328 F.3d 848.

■ Opinion by ALICE M. BATCHELDER, CIRCUIT JUDGE.

Louis Kohus ("Kohus") appeals the district court's grant of summary judgment in favor of defendants John Mariol, James Mariol, and JVM Innovation & Design ("Defendants"), on Kohus's claims for copyright infringement. Kohus argues that the district court applied the wrong legal standard, and that the court erred by refusing to consider expert testimony. Having concluded that the Sixth Circuit [**2] does not have a settled legal standard in this area, we set out a standard below and remand so the district court may apply that standard.

Statement of Facts

Kohus invents and designs consumer products, including children's items. In 1987 he formed Kohus/Mariol, Inc. ("KMI") with John Mariol ("Mariol"). They developed a number of products, including product 11–KMI86 , a portable children's playyard, which included drawings for a latch that would lock the upper rails in place for use. This latch ("the 11–KMI86 latch") was unlike others on the market in that it had two flippers, or hinges, instead of one, and this gave it a two-step [*852] function that could make it safer than comparable latches.

By August of 1988 a serious disagreement had developed between KMI's shareholders, and Kohus and KMI sued Mariol and his father James (who was also an inventor, and worked with Kohus) in Ohio court. The lawsuit remained unresolved for some six years, though the court did order that in the interim James should maintain control of all KMI's products and assets. The parties parted ways, and Mariol acted as his father's agent in handling KMI's products and assets.

In November of 1994 the KMI litigation finally ended in a settlement. Paragraph two of the settlement agreement provided that "JAMES MARIOL hereby assigns to KOHUS all rights, title and interest, whether known or unknown, that he may now have or hereafter acquire in those . . .

products identified in Exhibit B . . . , including without limitation any . . . design drawings[.]" Exhibit B included product 11–KMI86. Consequently, after November of 1994 Mariol no longer had the right to develop or market the 11–KMI86 latch.

In February of 1995 Mariol, who was consulting with Evenflo Juvenile Furniture Co. ("Evenflo") on a project to develop a collapsible playyard, faxed Evenflo a latch drawing entitled "Joint Version No. 2." Kohus alleges that this drawing is substantially similar to the 11–KMI86 latch.

In January of 1996 Mariol became a contractor for Kolcraft Enterprises, Inc., where he was assigned to assist another engineer in developing a collapsible playyard. Mariol and his co-engineer subsequently obtained two patents from the United States Patent and Trademark Office ("PTO") on playyards they developed at Kolcraft: Patent No. 5,826,285 ("the '285 Patent"), and Patent No. 5,867,851 ("the '851 Patent"). Both of the patent documents present identical drawings of a latch that Kohus alleges was derived from, and substantially similar to, the 11–KMI86 latch. In 1999 Kohus discovered the '285 and '851 Patents while conducting patent searches on the internet, and he then applied for and received a certificate of registration on the 11–KMI86 latch.

Mariol had, in his patent applications, attempted to establish a claim for the allegedly infringing latch, but the patent examiner had not allowed this and had required him to file that claim separately. Mariol subsequently did so, though he amended the patent application with a supplemental information disclosure statement in which he explained to the PTO that Kohus had filed suit against him. In the supplemental disclosure Mariol included the original drawings of the 11–KMI86 latch, though he had not asked Kohus's permission. The PTO nevertheless rejected the latch-related claims in the patent application, finding that they were "anticipated" by the original drawings of the 11–KMI86 latch.

Kohus filed this lawsuit on October 1, 1999, contending Joint Version No. 2 [was] substantially similar to the 11–KMI86 latch drawing, and that these [this] drawing violated his right to create derivatives of the 11–KMI86 latch drawing. The Defendants subsequently filed for summary judgment, arguing that even if the drawing [was] substantially similar, Kohus's claim should fail because the Defendants did not have access to the 11–KMI86 latch drawing. After the district court found that they did have access and rejected this motion, the Defendants filed another motion for summary judgment, this time arguing that their drawing [was] not substantially similar to the 11–KMI86 latch drawing. The district court compared the drawings, and refused to consider the conflicting testimony of experts proffered by each side. It concluded that no reasonable trier of fact could find that the Defendants' drawings were substantially similar to the 11–KMI86 latch drawing, and held that since Kohus's substantial similarity argument failed, his derivative copying argument should also fail. Kohus now appeals.

Analysis

I.   *Whether the Latches Depicted in the Defendants' Drawings Substantially Similar to the Latch in Kohus's Copyrighted Drawing*

A.   The Applicable Legal Standard

In copyright infringement cases "granting summary judgment, particularly in favor of a defendant, is a practice to be used sparingly," but "a court may compare the two works and render a judgment for the defendant on the ground that as a matter of law a trier of fact would not be permitted to find substantial similarity." *Wickham v. Knoxville Int'l Energy Exposition, Inc.*, 739 F.2d 1094, 1097 (6th Cir. 1984) (citations omitted); *see also Hoehling v. Universal City Studios, Inc.*, 618 F.2d 972, 977 (2d Cir. 1980) ("Because substantial similarity is customarily an extremely close question of fact, summary judgment has traditionally been frowned upon in copyright litigation[.]") (citing *Arnstein v. Porter*, 154 F.2d 464, 468 & 474 (2d Cir. 1946)).

To succeed in a copyright infringement action, a plaintiff must establish that he or she owns the copyrighted creation, and that the defendant copied it. *Wickham*, 739 F.2d at 1097. In the present case Kohus's ownership of the 11–KMI86 latch drawing is not disputed, and copying is the sole issue.

Not all "copying" is actionable, however: it is a constitutional requirement that a plaintiff bringing an infringement claim must prove "copying of constituent elements of the work *that are original.*" *Feist Publ'ns, Inc. v. Rural Tel. Serv. Co.*, 499 U.S. 340, 361, 113 L. Ed. 2d 358, 111 S. Ct. 1282 (1991) (emphasis added). Consequently, before comparing similarities between two works a court should first identify and eliminate those elements that are unoriginal and therefore unprotected.

For cases like the one before us here, where there is no direct evidence of copying, a plaintiff may establish "an inference of copying by showing (1) access to the allegedly-infringed work by the defendant(s) and (2) a substantial similarity between the two works at issue." *Ellis v. Diffie*, 177 F.3d 503, 506 (6th Cir. 1999). In this case access has been established, and only substantial similarity is at issue.

Courts have established various tests for the substantial similarity finding. The traditional approach is the "ordinary observer" or "audience" test, which "requires the trier of fact to gauge the similarities of the two works solely on the basis of his 'net impression' and without relying on expert analysis or dissection." *Id.* at 506 n.2 (citation omitted); *see also* 4 Melville B. Nimmer & David Nimmer, Nimmer on Copyright § 13.03[E][1] (1991) (hereinafter "Nimmer"). There are a number of difficulties with this approach, *see* 4 Nimmer § 13.03[E][2], and courts have undertaken various modifications—typically, by adding a prior step that does allow expert testimony and analytic dissection. *See Arnstein*, 154 F.2d at 468 (distinguishing two essential elements in a substantial similarity suit—"(a) that defendant copied from plaintiff's copyrighted work and (b) that the copying (assuming it to be proved) went so far as to constitute improper appropriation"—and holding that expert testimony is appropriate under the first prong, but not under the second because the determination is to be made from the viewpoint of the ordinary observer); *Sid & Marty Krofft Television Prods., Inc. v. McDonald's Corp.*, 562 F.2d 1157, 1163–64 (9th Cir. 1977) (creating an alternate two-part test: the "extrinsic test," in which expert testimony and analytic dissection may be employed to help the jury "determine whether there has been copying of the expression of an idea rather than just the idea itself"; and the "intrinsic test," in which expert testimony is not appropriate because the trier of fact must determine substantial similarity from the viewpoint of the ordinary reasonable person.)

The Sixth Circuit has thus far "not adopted a specific test for determining substantial similarity in copyright infringement cases," *Ellis*, 177 F.3d at 506 n.2, and this case presents an opportunity to do so. Our criteria in establishing a test are faithfulness to the law.

*Feist* favors an approach that involves reducing the comparison to elements that are original. The case does not mention the ordinary observer or audience test and it is not necessarily hostile to that test, but—as Nimmer observes—it requires that courts ask this question: "Does the audience test give content to the Court's definition of infringing conduct as 'copying of constituent elements of the work that are original?' " 4 Nimmer § 13.03[E][1][b]. We agree with Nimmer's conclusion: "to the extent that the audience test frustrates that goal, it must be discarded, limited, or tailored to meet the Supreme Court's formulation." *Id.*

Though the Sixth Circuit has not adopted a specific test for substantial similarity, the case *Monogram Models, Inc. v. Industro Motive Corp.*, 492 F.2d 1281 (6th Cir. 1974), obliquely endorsed a two-part test, similar to that in *Arnstein*: the first step allows expert evidence and dissection, and the second requires the trier of fact to evaluate similarity from the viewpoint of the ordinary observer.

[A] two-step approach that reconciles *Feist* and *Monogram Models* is found in *Sturdza v. United Arab Emirates*, 350 U.S. App. D.C. 154, 281 F.3d 1287 (D.C. Cir. 2002):[a] the first step "requires identifying which aspects of the artist's work, if any, are protectible by copyright," *id.* at 1295; the second "involves determining whether the allegedly infringing work is 'substantially similar' to protectible elements of the artist's work," *id.* at 1296. We approve this method, and adopt it.

The essence of the first step is to filter out the unoriginal, unprotectible elements—elements that were not independently created by the inventor, and that possess no minimal degree of creativity, *see Feist*, 499 U.S. at 345—through a variety of analyses. It is axiomatic, to begin with, that mere

[a] The *Sturdza* case followed the "abstraction-filtration-comparison" approach taken in Country Kids 'N City Slicks, Inc. v. Sheen, 77 F.3d 1280 (10th Cir. 1996), which itself adopted for ordinary purposes the specialized computer-software copyright infringement test set forth in Computer Assocs. Int'l, Inc. v. Altai, Inc., 982 F.2d 693 (2d Cir. 1992). *See also* 4 Nimmer § 13.03[E][1][b] (suggesting that courts apply the test in all substantial similarity cases, and not merely in computer software cases).

abstract ideas are not protectible, but the expression of an idea is. *See Mazer v. Stein*, 347 U.S. 201, 217, 98 L. Ed. 630, 74 S. Ct. 460, 1954 Dec. Comm'r Pat. 308 (1954) ("Unlike a patent, a copyright gives no exclusive right to the art disclosed; protection is given only to the expression of the idea—not the idea itself."); 17 U.S.C. § 102(b) ("In no case does copyright protection for an original work of authorship extend to any idea[.]"). Often helpful in distinguishing between the two is Judge Learned Hand's famous "abstractions test" formulated in *Nichols v. Universal Pictures Corp.*, 45 F.2d 119, 121 (2d Cir. 1930). This test of course does not identify the dividing line in individual cases, but rather constitutes a methodological tool courts can use to identify the spectrum of options. In the present case we do not presume to establish a scheme of abstractions, and we leave that issue for the parties to develop before the district court. Nevertheless, by way of example, an initial description of the 11–KMI86 latch would likely be quite detailed—a steel-enclosed hinge employing two banana-shaped flippers that cross over one another and share a common pivot point like scissors, each flipper fitting into a notch on the rail, and so on. In successive abstractions details like the shape of the steel enclosure would fall away, leaving the essentials, particularly the double-hinged feature, intact.

Next, in cases like this one, that involve a functional object rather than a creative work, it is necessary to eliminate those elements dictated by efficiency. *See Baker v. Selden*, 101 U.S. 99, 103, 25 L. Ed. 841, 1880 Dec. Comm'r Pat. 422 (1879) ("Where the art [that a science book] teaches cannot be used without employing the methods and diagrams used to illustrate the book, or such as are similar to them, such methods and diagrams are to be considered as *necessary incidents* to the art[.]") (emphasis added). To this end, the merger doctrine establishes that "when there is essentially only one way to express an idea, the idea and its expression are inseparable [i.e., they merge,] and copyright is no bar to copying that expression." *Concrete Mach. Co. v. Classic Lawn Ornaments, Inc.*, 843 F.2d 600, 606 (1st Cir. 1988). In the present case expert testimony will likely be required to establish what elements, if any, are necessary to the function of any latch designed for the upper arm of a collapsible playyard.

It is also important to filter out *scenes a faire*: "those elements that follow naturally from the work's theme, rather than from the author's creativity," 4 Nimmer § 13.03[F][3], or elements that [**16] are "dictated by external factors such as particular business practices," *Computer Mgmt. Assistance Co. v. Robert F. DeCastro, Inc.*, 220 F.3d 396, 401 (5th Cir. 2000). In the present case, possible external considerations could include standard industry practices for constructing latches, or safety standards established by organizations like the American Society for Testing Materials and the Juvenile Products Manufacturer's Association.

Once the unprotectible elements have been filtered out, the second step is to determine whether the allegedly infringing work is substantially similar to the protectible elements of the original. We noted above that our *Monogram Models* case establishes that this determination should be based on the judgment of the ordinary reasonable person (i.e., the ordinary lay observer). *See* 492 F.2d at 1286. This standard, however, is in need of modification.

The ordinary observer test is based on the economic incentive view of copyright law, that the "purpose of the copyright laws [is to] provide creators with a financial incentive to create for the ultimate benefit of the public." *Dawson v. Hinshaw Music, Inc.*, 905 F.2d 731, 733 (4th Cir. 1990); *see also Mazer*, 347 U.S. at 219 ("The economic philosophy behind the clause empowering Congress to grant patents and copyrights is the conviction that encouragement of individual effort by personal gain is the best way to advance public welfare through the talents of authors and inventors in 'Science and useful Arts.' "). The test was designed for cases where the lay audience purchases the product at issue, and where the lay audience's untutored judgment determines whether the product will sell. *See Arnstein*, 154 F.2d at 473 ("The question, therefore, is whether defendant took from plaintiff's works so much of what is pleasing to the ears of lay listeners, who comprise the audience for whom such popular music is composed, that defendant wrongfully appropriated something which belongs to the plaintiff.").

In cases where the target audience possesses specialized expertise, however, the specialist's perception of similarity may be much different from the lay observer's, and it is appropriate in such cases to consider similarity from the specialist's perspective. The larger principle here is that the inquiry in the second prong of the substantial similarity test should focus on the *intended audience*. This will ordinarily be the lay public, in which case the finder of fact's judgment should be from the perspective of the lay observer or, as *Monogram Models* put it, the ordinary reasonable person. But in cases where the audience for the work possesses specialized expertise that is relevant to the purchasing decision and lacking in the lay observer, the trier of fact should make the substantial similarity determination from the perspective of the intended audience. Expert testimony will usually be necessary to educate the trier of fact in those elements for which the specialist will look. *See Dawson*, 905 F.2d at 736 ("Such an inquiry [into the viewpoint of an observer with specialized expertise] may include, and no doubt in many cases will require, admission of testimony from members of the intended audience or, possibly, from those who possess expertise with reference to the tastes and perceptions of the intended audience.").

We also share *Dawson*'s concern that our holding should not be "read as an invitation to every litigant in every copyright case to put before the court the seemingly unanswerable question of whether a product's audience is sufficiently specialized to justify departure from the lay characterization of the ordinary observer test." 905 F.2d at 736. Consequently, we agree that

> in any given case, a court should be hesitant to find that the lay public does not fairly represent a work's intended audience. In our opinion, departure from the lay characterization is warranted only where the intended audi-

ence possesses "specialized expertise." We thereby pay heed to the need for hesitancy when departing from the indiscriminately selected lay public in applying the test. To warrant departure from the lay characterization of the ordinary observer test, "specialized expertise" must go beyond mere differences in taste and instead must rise to the level of the possession of knowledge that the lay public lacks.

*Id.* at 737.

### B.  The Legal Standard Applied

The district court in the present case applied the ordinary observer test, only, and on the basis of that test it rejected expert testimony proffered by both Kohus and the Defendants. Instead it analyzed the drawings of the latches on its own, concluding that no reasonable finder of fact could determine that they were substantially similar.

In light of our restated and modified substantial similarity determination procedure, however, it is evident that the district court must conduct its proceedings anew. The first prong of the inquiry will almost certainly require expert testimony, because the drawings are technical in nature and a lay person is unlikely to understand what constitutes creativity in this area, which elements are standard for the industry, and which elements are dictated by efficiency or by external standards. In conducting the second prong, the district court should consider substantial similarity from the viewpoint of the intended audience, the nature of which the court must determine. This appears to be one of those rare cases where the intended audience is not the lay public: the drawings are technical and are appropriate for patent treatment; interpretational guidance is needed for the lay viewer to imagine the structure and function of the device that the drawings depict; and the initial purchasers of the device would probably be trained engineers, capable of discerning technical niceties that the ordinary person would not detect, and likely to base their purchasing decision on such details.

### Conclusion

We vacate the judgment of the district court, and remand for further proceedings in accordance with this opinion.

### NOTES

**1.**  *Tests for infringement.* Arnstein v. Porter[3] is the seminal copyright infringement decision in the Second Circuit. In that case, the court held that a copyright infringement plaintiff must prove a) copying; and b) improper appropriation. The first element, copying, could be proved by the defendant's direct admission or by circumstantial evidence such as evidence of access and similarities between the two works that are sufficient to prove copying. The *Arnstein* court also held that expert testimony could be resorted to by the trier of fact to aid in this analysis. Absent evidence of access, the existing similarities must be so striking "as to preclude the

[3] 154 F.2d 464 (2d Cir.1946).

possibility that the plaintiff and defendant independently arrived at the same result."[4] Once copying is established, the plaintiff must then prove improper appropriation by showing substantial similarity to protected expression. Satisfaction of this element is determined by the "ordinary lay hearer," and thus analytic dissection and "expert testimony are irrelevant."[5] How does this test compare with the tests invoked in *Nichols* and *Altai*? How would you compare the tests for infringement in the Second, Ninth, Seventh and Sixth Circuits? Are they markedly different or fairly consistent? Which test is best?

The court in *Apple* endorsed the "virtual identity" standard for infringement with respect to works with a narrow range of protectable and unauthorized expression. Most courts, however, invoke a more lenient standard which requires the defendant's work to be "substantially similar" to the plaintiff's if it is to be considered infringing. Why shouldn't the standard for copyright infringement for all types of works be virtual identity rather than substantial similarity? Would paraphrasing a work render it virtually identical to the original work? Should paraphrasing be considered infringement?

**2.** *Protected vs. unprotected material.* Part of the difficulty with the area of copyright infringement is that one of the main issues, namely, the extent to which unprotected subject matter should be considered in copyright determinations, arises in conjunction with the following three separate inquiries: (1) Should unprotected subject matter contained in a plaintiff's work be considered in the initial determination of the copyrightability of the plaintiff's work?; (2) Should unprotected subject matter be considered in the copying prong (generally the first prong) of an infringement inquiry?; and (3) Should unprotected subject matter be considered in the unlawful appropriation prong (generally the second prong) of an infringement inquiry? Note that this Assignment is concerned with the second and third inquiries, whereas Assignment 7 addresses the first inquiry. Of course, to the extent a defendant's alleged infringement stems from copying elements from the plaintiff's work that are not within the scope of the plaintiff's copyright, all three inquiries are related.

**3.** *Substantial similarity.* The dual meaning of substantial similarity is discussed in *Stillman*. The court in that case clarifies that substantial similarity can be used in a factual or evidentiary sense, which provides circumstantial evidence of copying when combined with evidence of access. In addition, substantial similarity also can be used to refer to the similarities existing between two works that render the defendant's work an unlawful appropriation of the plaintiff's work in the legal sense. In the view of the late Professor Alan Latman, the type of substantial similarities used to establish copying in a factual sense is simply intended to prove that independent creation is unlikely and therefore such similarities "may or may not be substantial." He suggested that since these similarities are "offered as probative of the act of copying," the test for this type of

---

[4] Id. at 468.                     [5] Id.

similarity should be renamed "probative similarity."[6] The Second Circuit expressly adopted Professor Latman's terminology in Laureyssens v. Idea Group, Inc.[7] and more recently reiterated the distinction between "probative similarity" and "substantial similarity" in Ringgold v. Black Entertainment Television, Inc.[8]

**4.** *Access.* Since direct evidence of copying by a defendant is rarely available,[9] the plaintiff may use circumstantial evidence to demonstrate that the defendant had access to the plaintiff's work. The relevant circumstantial evidence consists of both evidence of access and the existence of substantial similarities between the works in question. Regarding evidence of access, most courts conclude that a plaintiff must show that the defendant had a reasonable opportunity to view or hear the plaintiff's work, rather than that the infringer actually saw or heard the work.[10] Presence of access in conjunction with probative similarities between works allow the trier of fact to conclude that factual copying has occurred. Evidence that the defendant had the *reasonable opportunity* to view or hear the plaintiff's work (as opposed to actually viewing or hearing it) is usually adequate to prove access by the defendant.[11] However, *reasonable opportunity* to view does not mean *any possibility*. In Ellis v. Diffie[12] the Sixth Circuit refused to infer access through pure speculation,[13] where the defendant also provided evidence of independent creation. How would you distinguish speculation from reasonable opportunity? According to the Ninth Circuit, circumstantial evidence of reasonable access is proven by either: "(1) a particular chain of events established between the plaintiff's work and the defendant's access to that work, or (2) the plaintiff's work has been widely disseminated."[14]

Some courts, however, will permit an inference of access if the works in question are "strikingly similar."[15] According to this view, access remains an element of copyright infringement but the level of similarity

[6] Alan Latman, "Probative Similarity" As Proof of Copying: Toward Dispelling Some Myths in Copyright Infringement, 90 Colum. L. Rev. 1187, 1214 (1990).

[7] 964 F.2d 131, 140 (2d Cir.1992). *Laureyssens* originally was decided a month before *Altai*, but was amended two days after the *Altai* decision.

[8] 126 F.3d 70, 74 (2d Cir. 1997). Other courts also have adopted the term "probative similarity." See, e.g., Peel & Co., Inc. v. The Rug Market, 238 F.3d 391 (5th Cir. 2001).

[9] But see Segrets, Inc. v. Gillman Knitwear Co., Inc., 207 F.3d 56, 61–62 (1st Cir. 2000) (uncontradicted testimony of defendant's employee indicating purchase of plaintiff's works for use as models).

[10] See Bouchat v. Baltimore Ravens, Inc., 228 F.3d 489 (4th Cir. 2000)(upholding access based on the plaintiff's fax of a drawing to an intermediary who shared an office with the defendant).

[11] Three Boys Music Corp. v. Bolton, 212 F.3d 477, 481 (9th Cir. 2000).

[12] 177 F.3d 503 (6th Cir. 1999).

[13] Id. The recording artist alleged that defendant could have access to his song through the third party representing the recording company.

[14] Three Boys Music Corp. v. Bolton, 212 F.3d at 482.

[15] See, e.g., Bouchat v. Baltimore Ravens, Inc., 228 F.3d at 494; Gaste v. Kaiserman, 863 F.2d 1061, 1068 (2d Cir. 1988); Ty, Inc. v. GMA Accessories, Inc., 132 F.3d 1167, 1170 (7th Cir. 1997).

between the works in question can be used as evidence of access.[16] A few courts appear to go even farther by suggesting that when the similarities are so striking that the possibility of independent creation is precluded, access is an unnecessary element of copyright infringement.[17]

**5.**  *Unlawful appropriation.* Should the unlawful appropriation prong of the substantial similarity test consider only the similarity of protected expression, or should it also consider whether the "concept and feel" of the works at issue are similar? Can *Stillman* and *Apple* be reconciled? To what extent does the *Altai* court allow for protection of a unique arrangement of unprotectable material? The "total concept and feel" approach has received some acceptance among the courts,[18] although courts have refrained from invoking this test in instances involving wholesale and verbatim copying of original text, or works of different genres.[19] In the Ninth Circuit, courts seem inclined to apply the "total concept and feel" test as part of the subjective comparison undertaken in conjunction with the intrinsic test.[20]

In some cases the Second Circuit has adopted a test for unlawful appropriation that features both a qualitative and quantitative component. Specifically, the qualitative component concerns the copying of protectable elements. The quantitative component generally concerns the overall amount of the copyrighted work that is copied, and courts require more than a "de minimus" amount to satisfy this component.[21] The qualitative/quantitative test has been deemed especially useful in cases where the works in question are from different genres.[22]

Although in many cases the lay observer can determine the substantiality of the works in question, *Kohus* shows that this is not always the case. Who should make this determination in the Principal Problem?

[16] Bouchat v. Baltimore Ravens, Inc., 228 F.3d at 494; Repp & K & R Music, Inc. v. Webber, 132 F.3d 882 (2d Cir. 1997).

[17] Ferguson v. National Broadcasting Co., Inc., 584 F.2d 111, 113 (5th Cir. 1978). See also Bucklew v. Hawkins, 329 F.3d 923, 926 (7th Cir. 2003) (relying on *Ferguson* and observing that "it is more straightforward to say that in some cases proof of access isn't required"); Three Boys Music Corp. v. Bolton, 212 F.3d 477, 481 (9th Cir. 2000).

[18] See, e.g., Sturdza v. United Arab Emirates, 281 F.3d 1287 (D.C. Cir. 2002) (architectural designs); Boisson v. Banian, Ltd., 273 F.3d 262 (2d Cir. 2001) (quilt designs); Williams v. Crichton, 84 F.3d 581 (2d Cir. 1996) (noting that the test is especially appropriate in cases involving children's works due to their decreased complexity).

[19] See, e.g., Lynx Ventures LLC v. Miller, 45 Fed.Appx. 68 (2d Cir. 2002) ("Where the wholesale and verbatim copying of original text is at issue reliance on the total concept and feel test effectively immunizes the infringer who appends original material to plagiarized text."); Castle Rock Entertainment, Inc. v. Carol Publishing Group, Inc. v. Golub, 150 F.3d 132, 140 (2d Cir. 1998) ("The total concept and feel test is simply not helpful in analyzing works that, because of their different genres and media, must necessarily have a different concept and feel.").

[20] See, e.g., Cavalier v. Random House, Inc., 297 F.3d 815 (9th Cir. 2002); Three Boys Music Corp. v. Bolton, 212 F.3d 477, 481 (9th Cir. 2000).

[21] Castle Rock Entertainment, Inc. v. Carol Publishing Group, Inc. v. Golub, 150 F.3d 132, 138–39 (2d Cir. 1998) (involving a quiz book devoted to testing its readers' recall of the television show *Seinfeld*). See also On Davis v. The Gap, Inc., 246 F.3d 152, 172 (2d Cir. 2001) (noting generally the importance of the "rarely discussed" de minimis doctrine in copyright law).

[22] See Castle Rock Entertainment, *id.*

**6.** *Computer programs. Altai* observes that the case dealt with the extent to which the "non-literal" aspects of a computer program are copyrightable, and that this was a case "of first impression" in the Second Circuit. The first generation of computer cases typically dealt with whether the literal aspects of a computer program, such as the source or object code, are subject to copyright protection.[23] Currently there is no doubt that these literal aspects are protected. The second generation of computer cases deals with the non-literal aspects of computer programs. Litigation on this point has revolved around the structure, sequence, and organization of the source and object code; the structure of a program's command system; and the presentation of information on the screen (i.e., the user interface).[24] Are there any arguments against extending broad copyright protection to user interfaces? Can the three-step approach in *Altai* be applied to screen displays and user interfaces? What about a computer menu command hierarchy? The patentability of computer programs is treated in Assignment 15.

In a portion of *Altai* that does not appear in the text, the court also reversed the district court's determination that CA's trade secret misappropriation claim was preempted by § 301 of the 1976 Copyright Act and held that "with regard to OSCAR 3.5, CA has a viable trade secret claim against *Altai* that must be considered by the district court on remand."[25] The court further noted that if on remand "the district court finds that CA was injured by *Altai*'s unlawful use of CA's trade secrets in creating OSCAR 3.5, CA is entitled to an award of damages for trade secret misappropriation, as well as consideration by the district court of CA's request for injunctive relief on its trade secret claim."[26] What is the impact of this determination from the standpoint of providing relief for program developers? Trade secrets are covered in depth in Assignment 24.

In Computer Associates International, Inc. v. Altai, Inc.,[27] the Second Circuit held that *res judicata* and collateral estoppel do not bar the plaintiff's action for copyright infringement in France despite the U.S. ruling that OSCAR 3.5 does not violate the plaintiff's United States copyright. The court reached this conclusion regarding *res judicata* because the defendants' infringing conduct, which was the basis of the French action, occurred after the plaintiff had filed the lawsuit in the United States, and also because the New York district court lacked jurisdiction over one of the French defendants. With respect to the collateral estoppel

---

[23] See, e.g., Apple Computer, Inc. v. Franklin Computer Corp., 714 F.2d 1240, 1243 (3d Cir.1983), cert. dismissed, 464 U.S. 1033 (1984); Midway Mfg. Co. v. Strohon, 564 F.Supp. 741, 750 (N.D.Ill.1983).

[24] Lotus Dev. Corp. v. Paperback Software Int'l, 740 F.Supp. 37, 46 (D.Mass.1990) (holding that the user interface for the Lotus 1–2–3 spreadsheet program as a whole is copyrightable). This opinion also contains a good summary of the case law extending copyright protection to the non-literal components of computer programs. See id. at 55.

[25] 982 F.2d at 719.

[26] 982 F.2d at 721. Ultimately, the Second Circuit determined that the trade secret claim was barred by the Texas statute of limitations. See Computer Associates International, Inc. v. Altai, Inc., 61 F.3d 6 (2d Cir.1995).

[27] 126 F.3d 365 (2d Cir.1997).

issue, the court reasoned that Altai failed to show the copyright standards in France and the United States are sufficiently "identical" for purposes of applying that doctrine.

In MAI Systems Corp. v. Peak Computer, Inc.,[28] the Ninth Circuit held that a computer servicing company performing maintenance duties infringed the copyright in plaintiff's software by its unlicensed transfer of the computer programs from a permanent storage device such as a floppy disk to the computer's random access memory ("RAM"). According to the court, the defendant's loading the software into the RAM so that it is able to view the system error log and diagnose the computer's problem shows that the representation created in the RAM is sufficiently "fixed" for purposes of establishing copyright infringement.[29] Title III of the Digital Millennium Copyright Act amended § 117(c) of the 1976 Copyright Act to provide that "it is not an infringement for the owner or lessee of a machine to make or authorize the making of a copy of a computer program if such copy is made solely by virtue of the activation of a machine that lawfully contains an authorized copy of the computer program, for purposes only of maintenance or repair of that machine" as long as the new copy is not used in any other manner and is destroyed immediately after the maintenance or repair is finished. Other provisions of the Digital Millennium Copyright Act are treated in depth in Assignment 11.

**7.** *Visual art.* Note that § 501 of the copyright statute, which deals with infringement, specifically provides that a violation of the author's rights under the Visual Artists Rights Act ("VARA") constitutes infringement (VARA is discussed in Assignment 9). Although none of the major cases reproduced in this Assignment treat visual art, one of the more interesting infringement cases dealing with visual art is Steinberg v. Columbia Pictures Industries, Inc.[30] That case was an action by artist Saul Steinberg against the producers and advertisers of the movie "Moscow on the Hudson," stemming from their use of an illustration created to advertise the movie that allegedly infringed the plaintiff's famous picture. The plaintiff's picture, which had appeared on the cover of The New Yorker, depicted the world as viewed by a "typical" New Yorker. It showed minute details of a street in New York City, with a background consisting of the Hudson River, followed by tiny letters designating various major cities in the United States as well as other countries to the west (the idea being that the world pretty much revolves around New York City). The defendants' picture was similar, except that it had the Atlantic Ocean and locations in Europe as the background. What special difficulties are raised in cases involving infringements of visual art?

**8.** *Expert testimony.* In the traditional, bifurcated approach to infringement, expert testimony is allowed to be considered in the copying prong of

[28] 991 F.2d 511 (9th Cir.1993).

[29] Id. at 518. See also Advanced Computer Services of Michigan, Inc. v. MAI Systems Corp., 845 F.Supp. 356 (E.D.Va.1994); Triad Systems Corp. v. Southeastern Express Co.,

31 U.S.P.Q.2d 1239 (N.D.Cal.1994), affirmed in part, reversed in part 64 F.3d 1330 (9th Cir.1995).

[30] 663 F.Supp. 706 (S.D.N.Y.1987).

the inquiry, but disallowed in the unlawful appropriation prong. Why do you suppose the traditional bifurcated approach is wary of expert testimony in the unlawful appropriation prong of the infringement test? As *Altai* and *Kohus* illustrate, a new trend is emerging in which the trier of fact makes the ultimate infringement determination subject to information provided by expert testimony.[31] Courts and commentators have suggested that with respect to technically complex material, this new approach makes a good deal more sense because it is unrealistic to expect the trier of fact to be exposed to expert opinion in the copying, or extrinsic, prong of the infringement analysis, and then to forget that testimony in its unlawful appropriation analysis.[32] Does this issue have any relevance to the Principal Problem?

**9.** *Subconscious copying.* In Bright Tunes Music Corp. v. Harrisongs Music, Ltd.,[33] the district court ruled, and the Second Circuit affirmed, that George Harrison had committed infringement when he wrote his hit song, *My Sweet Lord,* around 1970. Harrison's defense was that his copying was subconscious, and therefore not actionable. The court rejected Harrison's argument. The song that was allegedly infringed, *He's So Fine,* had been on top of the billboard charts for several weeks in both the United States and England. Although the district court did not believe that Harrison deliberately used the music of *He's So Fine* in composing his song, the unquestionable access and the virtual identity of the songs compelled a finding of subconscious copying. The Second Circuit rejected Harrison's argument that the number of years between the time when the plaintiff's song was on the radio and the time when Harrison composed his song should preclude a finding of access, in light of the song's popularity and Harrison's admission that he remembered hearing the song. Harrison also argued before the Second Circuit that, as a policy matter, the doctrine of subconscious copying should not be recognized because it "brings the law of copyright improperly close to patent law, which imposes a requirement of novelty."[34] Do you agree? More recently, the Ninth Circuit affirmed a jury verdict of

[31] But see Sturdza v. United Arab Emirates, 281 F.3d 1287 (D.C.Cir. 2002) (disallowing expert testimony in comparing architectural designs and noting that reliance on expert testimony to show substantial similarity is largely confined to cases involving computer programs).

[32] See, e.g., Whelan Assoc., Inc. v. Jaslow Dental Lab., Inc., 797 F.2d 1222, 1233 (3d Cir.1986), cert. denied, 479 U.S. 1031 (1987) ("join[s] the growing number of courts which do not apply the ordinary observer test in copyright cases involving exceptionally difficult materials, like computer programs, but instead adopt[s] a single substantial similarity inquiry according to which both lay and expert testimony would be admissible"); *Note, The Role of the Expert Witness in Music*

*Copyright Infringement Cases,* 57 Fordham L. Rev. 127, 138–39 (1988) (criticizing application of test for infringement in Krofft that allows the factfinder to consider expert testimony in the first prong of the substantial similarity analysis but then requires it to disregard this testimony in the second prong in the context of music infringement cases). See also Brown Bag Software v. Symantec Corp., 960 F.2d 1465, 1474 n.3 (9th Cir.), cert. denied, 506 U.S. 869 (1992) (noting that the law in the Ninth Circuit "appears to be moving toward the test ... in which lay and expert testimony are uniformly admissible").

[33] 420 F.Supp. 177 (S.D.N.Y.1976), aff'd sub nom. ABKCO Music, Inc. v. Harrisongs Music, Ltd., 722 F.2d 988 (2d Cir.1983).

[34] 722 F.2d at 998.

subconscious infringement in favor of the Isley Brothers and against Michael Bolton and his writing partner based on the defendants' song "Love is a Wonderful Thing." In Three Boys Music Corp. v. Bolton,[35] the plaintiffs' song never made the top 100 Billboard charts and defendants denied ever hearing it. Despite admitting that "this may be a weak case of access," the court supported its affirmance by claiming that "it is entirely plausible that two Connecticut teenagers obsessed with rhythm and blues music could remember an Isley Brothers' song . . . and subconsciously copy it twenty years later."[36] Are there any other problems with allowing good faith to establish a defense to infringement? If good faith is not relevant to the ultimate infringement determination, to what should it pertain?

**10.** *Interim infringement (reverse engineering).* In Sega v. Accolade,[37] the court considered the legality of defendant's "reverse engineering" of plaintiff Sega's video game programs to discover the compatibility requirements for their own equipment. This process entailed the defendant Accolade's transformation of the "machine-readable object code contained in commercially available copies of [plaintiff's] game cartridges into human-readable source code using a process called 'disassembly' or 'decompilation.' "[38] From the disassembled code, the defendant discovered the interface specifications of the plaintiff's console. The defendant then created a development manual containing functional descriptions of these interface requirements. Subsequently, the defendant created its own games, relying on the information concerning the interface specifications contained in the development manual. Interestingly, the interface used the message "PRODUCED BY OR UNDER LICENSE FROM SEGA ENTERPRISES LTD." To achieve compatability, the defendant copied this portion of Sega's code into its own game programs with the result that they displayed the Sega trademark.

*Sega* held that such intermediate copying of a computer object code can constitute copyright infringement, and the court distinguished *Altai* on the ground that the "legality of the intermediate copying" was not "at issue."[39] Still, *Sega* ultimately concluded that the defendant's activity constituted fair use since disassembly was the only means through which Accolade could gain access to the unprotected aspects of the program and it had a legitimate reason for such access.[40] *Sega* thus raises the issues of whether intermediate copying in and of itself is lawful, and whether some instances of such copying can be excused as fair use. In Sony Computer Entertainment, Inc. v. Connectix Corp.,[41] the Ninth Circuit again concluded that intermediate copying was fair use in a case involving the defendant's copying of a software program that operates Sony's "PlayStation" video game system. The defendant's product emulated both the hardware and

[35] 212 F.3d 477 (9th Cir. 2000).

[36] Id. at 483.

[37] 977 F.2d 1510 (9th Cir.1992).

[38] Id. at 1514.

[39] Id. at 1518–19.

[40] Id. at 1520. The court also concluded that Sega's use of the trademark security code to gain access to the plaintiff's console did not constitute trademark infringement. Id. at 1528–32.

[41] 203 F.3d 596 (9th Cir.2000).

software components of Sony's console so that users could play Sony games on a computer instead of a television. Relying on *Sega* for the proposition that where disassembly is the only way to gain access to the functional elements in a computer program, and where legitimate reason exists for seeking such access, disassembly is fair use of a copyrighted work. Fair use is covered in Assignment 11. More recently, Judge Posner embraced the rationale of *Sega* in a case presenting the issue whether the copyright owner of a compilation can prevent its copyright licensees from disclosing the compiled, noncopyrighted data. In Assessment Technologies of WI, LLC v. WIREdata, Inc.,[42] the defendant was a multiple listing service that sought to obtain the plaintiff's data regarding specific real properties for use by real estate brokers. The data in question was not collected by the plaintiff but rather by tax assessors. The court concluded that even if the raw data were so entangled with the protected compilation that extraction of the data was not possible without making a copy of the program, the result in *Sega* would protect the defendant's ability to copy the entire compilation.

The facts of *Sega* also suggest the further issue of the "clean room" defense. That is, whether there should be infringement when a programmer other than the intermediate copier writes a new program using the intermediate copier's specifications, but never sees the original code. In *Altai*, in deciding whether OSCAR 3.5 infringed the plaintiff's copyright, should it have mattered that the defendant infringed the plaintiff's copyright in creating the prior version, OSCAR 3.4, even though the defendant took precautions not to use the plaintiff's work in the new version and none of the programmers who had been hired to create OSCAR 3.5 had been involved with the prior version?

**11.** *Defense summary judgments. Arnstein* also held that summary judgment could not be granted when there is the "slightest doubt" with respect to the facts, but this aspect of the case has been repudiated in the Second Circuit.[43] In the copyright context specifically, the Second Circuit has held that summary judgment for the defense may be warranted on the issue of improper appropriation if no reasonable jury could find that the works in question are substantially similar.[44] In Shaw v. Lindheim,[45] a case involving literary works, the Ninth Circuit held summary judgment for the defense must be denied when a comparison of works under the extrinsic test presents a triable issue of fact. Otherwise, a court would be granting the defendant summary judgment based exclusively "on a purely subjective determination of similarity" as a matter of law. Does *Stillman* follow the rule of *Shaw* regarding summary judgment?

---

[42] 350 F.3d 640 (7th Cir. 2003).

[43] See, e.g., Beal v. Lindsay, 468 F.2d 287, 291 (2d Cir.1972).

[44] See, e.g., Arpaia v. Anheuser–Busch Companies, Inc., 55 F.Supp.2d 151, 162 (W.D.N.Y. 1999); Denker v. Uhry, 820 F.Supp. 722, 728 (S.D.N.Y.1992), aff'd, 996 F.2d 301 (2d Cir.1993), and Second Circuit cases cited at p. 728 of the district court opinion.

[45] 919 F.2d 1353 (9th Cir.1990).

# ASSIGNMENT 11

# PUBLIC ACCESS CONSIDERATIONS AND THE FAIR USE DOCTRINE

## 1. INTRODUCTION

This Assignment addresses numerous facets of the public access debate in copyright law. The fair use doctrine, which is the focus of the Principal Problem and the major cases, is a key component of the law governing public access. As you will see, however, the Notes attempt to highlight several other significant current issues being discussed regarding the extent to which copyright can, and should, be privatized. These issues can be grouped collectively into a framework concerned with public access generally.

The fair use doctrine, a focal point of this chapter, has been called "the most troublesome" in all of copyright law.[1] In essence, the fair use doctrine of copyright law explicitly recognizes that some unauthorized uses of copyrighted property ought to be tolerated. In explaining the fair use doctrine, one court has observed that it "offers a means of balancing the exclusive rights of a copyright holder with the public's interest in dissemination of information affecting areas of universal concern, such as art, science and industry."[2] Thus, the doctrine seeks to achieve a balance between the optimal use by society of resources and the optimal level of creativity. You will recall that although the reward to creators is a secondary goal of copyright law's overall goal of promoting the progress of science and useful arts, such rewards are essential to effectuating copyright law's major objective of enhancing society's progress. Clearly an absence of monetary protections would result in diminished creativity. Therefore, the fair use doctrine is one way in which the copyright law attempts to strike a balance between the competing interests of the individual creator and that of society. Although there is a loose connection between the underpinnings of the fair use doctrine and the First Amendment in that fair use does protect First Amendment interests to some extent, no direct authority exists for the proposition that fair use is coextensive with the First Amendment.[3]

---

[1] Dellar v. Samuel Goldwyn, Inc., 104 F.2d 661, 662 (2d Cir.1939).

[2] Wainwright Sec., Inc. v. Wall St. Transcript Corp., 558 F.2d 91, 94 (2d Cir.1977), cert. denied, 434 U.S. 1014 (1978) (enjoining defendants from publishing abstracts of plaintiff's financial research reports).

[3] See the full text of United States v. Elcom, 203 F.Supp.2d 1111 n.4 (N.D. Cal. 2002) for a more complete treatment of this relationship.

The fair use doctrine also is supported by an economically-based policy justification. Specifically, it allows parties to avoid market exchange. Typically, copyright infringements will be enjoined unless the doctrine of fair use, or some other use exempted by the copyright law, applies in a given situation. Thus, aside from the application of the fair use doctrine, the lawful right to use copyrighted property typically can be secured only through market exchanges. The fair use doctrine thus can be viewed, at least in part, as a mechanism for allowing parties the lawful right to use copyrighted works in certain instances where they would not otherwise be able to obtain such lawful rights.

The fair use doctrine is used as an affirmative defense and the doctrine is usually applied once it is established that the defendant's work is, in fact, substantially similar to the plaintiff's. The doctrine is codified in § 107 of the 1976 Copyright Act, although the doctrine was already well-established by the judiciary at the time the 1976 statute was enacted. The fair use doctrine is extraordinarily flexible, and its application typically turns on the particular facts in issue. Section 107 does provide some guidance, however, in that it sets forth the following four factors for determining whether a particular use is a fair use.

1.  The purpose and character of the use, including whether such use is of a commercial nature or is for nonprofit educational purposes.

2.  The nature of the copyrighted work.

3.  The amount and substantiality of the portion used in relation to the copyrighted work as a whole.

4.  The effect of the use upon the potential market for or value of the copyrighted work. The fact that a work is unpublished shall not itself bar a finding of fair use if such finding is made upon consideration of all the above factors.[4]

All of these factors were widely used under the previously existing common law as well. Courts typically balance these four factors in determining whether a particular use of a work constitutes a fair use, although, as you shall see, there are other factors that often come into play in a fair use analysis. In fact, the legislative history to § 107 emphasizes that these factors are not to be considered definitive or determinative. The problem with such an ad hoc approach is that it is difficult to obtain much guidance from the existing fair use cases. This dilemma is illustrated by the fair use cases decided by the Supreme Court reprinted in this Assignment: Sony Corp. of America v. Universal City Studios, Inc.,[5] Harper & Row, Publishers, Inc. v. Nation Enterprises,[6] and Campbell v. Acuff–Rose Music, Inc.[7]

The Principal Problem and the accompanying materials also treat relevant provisions of the DMCA, particularly those provisions implicating fair use and other important public access concerns. Since its enactment, the scope of the DMCA has garnered an increasingly substantial degree of

[4] § 107.

[5] 464 U.S. 417 (1984).

[6] 471 U.S. 539 (1985).

[7] 510 U.S. 569 (1994).

attention, both in academic quarters and in the courts. The importance of the DMCA cannot be overstated because it has provided copyright owners with an unprecedented level of copyright protection. Critical to understanding the impact of the DMCA is a basic understanding of "digital rights management," ("DRM"). DRM refers to the technological tools used by the recording, software, and movie industries to insure that every user pay for digital enjoyment of copyrighted works. Encryption and watermarking represent two specific DRM tools. Encryption "refers to the process of inserting the digital data into a scrambler, resulting in gibberish that can be unscrambled only with a specific key."[8] In order to consume the content, users must have access to the key that decrypts the code, thus allowing the copyright owner control of the means of consumption.[9] Digital watermarks function similarly to paper watermarks in that they are ownership tags serving to validate authenticity and detect unauthorized copying. DRM technology is rapidly evolving, and newer applications promise copyright owners more affirmative, personalized control over their works through increased levels of monitoring and reporting of consumer behavior.[10] United States v. Elcom, Ltd.,[11] reprinted below, illustrates the connection between the DMCA and public access.

## 2.  PRINCIPAL PROBLEM

Bell Spree, a graduate film student at New York University ("N.Y.U."), learns of a legal controversy involving the books *Gone with the Wind* and *The Wind Done Gone*. *Gone with the Wind*, the classic Civil War epic written by Margaret Mitchell, was published in 1936 and is one of the best-selling books in the world. *The Wind Done Gone* is a recently authored novel that purports to critique *Gone with the Wind*'s depiction of slavery and the American South during the Civil War period. Suntrust Bank (the current copyright owner of *Gone with the Wind*) has recently released a limited edition DVD of *Gone with the Wind* containing new commentary from famous authors about how this story has affected their lives, writing careers, and society in general. Being a film student, Bell decides to watch the new DVD version of *Gone with the Wind* instead of reading it, so she orders the movie from Online Movies.

Online Movies provides customers with the ability to view movies from home by streaming the movie into the customer's computer. In order to view the movie, the customer initially must download a program created by Online Movies that both decrypts the movie, so it may be viewed, and prevents the movie from being copied onto the customer's hard drive. When ordering a movie, customers pay the rental fee and they have 30 days to

---

[8] Megan E. Gray & Will Thomas De-Vries, *The Legal Fallout From Digital Rights Management Technology*, 4 Computer & Internet Law 20, 22 (2002) (Arnold & Porter, Editor-in-Chief).

[9] Id.

[10] Id.

[11] 203 F.Supp.2d 1111 (N.D. Cal. 2002).

begin watching the movie. Once a customer begins to view the film, it will be erased from the customer's hard-drive within 24 hours.

After watching *Gone with the Wind*, Bell becomes highly offended not only by the racism in the movie, but also by the belittling portrayal of the female characters. She is so upset that she decides to make a movie that will be a feminist statement against the views depicted in *Gone with the Wind*. After further research and planning, Bell decides her best course of action would be to make a new work, using *Gone with the Wind* footage from the film she recently viewed. She also knows that a digital copy will allow her to manipulate easily the film. So, Bell tries to save a copy of the film onto her computer after ordering it again from Online Movies. Unfortunately, Bell does not possess the computer skills needed to defeat the technological protections Online Movies has placed on its streaming movies.

Not deterred, she asks her friend, Sue Lightning, a computer whiz, if Sue would be able to assist her in defeating the technological protections that Online Movies has placed on its movies through the program Bell downloaded. Bell once again orders the movie from Online and asks Sue to work at her computer. As a result of Sue's technological expertise, she is able to sidestep the protections against copying contained in the program. Sue downloads a digital file of *Gone with the Wind*, which she then gives to Bell.

Bell, now in possession of the digital file, uses the scenes from it as the basis for her film. She edits, manipulates, adds, and changes the limited edition film in order to create her work—namely the *Gone with the Wind* story as scene from the feminist point of view. Bell's version not only incorporates *Gone with the Wind* footage from the story itself (albeit much of it she manipulated digitally), but also about 30% of the new commentary in its entirety. Bell ends up using her film for a class project. Her work receives enormous attention—both within and outside of the N.Y.U. film academy. Bell is offered a tenure-track teaching position at a small college in California, and is the recipient of several invitations to appear on local and national talk shows. She makes her movie available for viewing by posting advertisements on feminist websites, and charges a modest fee to those who watch it. Bell's primary purpose in charging the fee is to recoup some of her costs.

Suntrust Bank learns of Bell's work and informs Online Movies of the breach of its technological protections. The two companies then file suit against Bell and Sue. Suntrust Bank argues that they have committed copyright infringement by making an unauthorized derivative work. Online Movies argues that they have violated the Digital Millennium Copyright Act. Both defendants raise the defense of fair use.

Assess the arguments each side will make regarding the fair use defense. Would the assessment of Sue's conduct change if she were not a friend, but instead had been hired by Bell to circumvent the technological protections?

## 3. MATERIALS FOR SOLUTION OF PRINCIPAL PROBLEM

A. STATUTORY MATERIALS: §§ 107–119; 512(a); 602(a); 1201 & 1202.

B. CASES:

## Sony Corp. of America v. Universal City Studios, Inc.

Supreme Court of the United States, 1984.
464 U.S. 417, 104 S.Ct. 774, 78 L.Ed.2d 574.

■ JUSTICE STEVENS delivered the opinion of the Court.

Petitioners manufacture and sell home video tape recorders. Respondents own the copyrights on some of the television programs that are broadcast on the public airwaves. Some members of the general public use video tape recorders sold by petitioners to record some of these broadcasts, as well as a large number of other broadcasts. The question presented is whether the sale of petitioners' copying equipment to the general public violates any of the rights conferred upon respondents by the Copyright Act.

Respondents commenced this copyright infringement action against petitioners in the United States District Court for the Central District of California in 1976. Respondents alleged that some individuals had used Betamax video tape recorders (VTR's) to record some of respondents' copyrighted works which had been exhibited on commercially sponsored television and contended that these individuals had thereby infringed respondents' copyrights. Respondents further maintained that petitioners were liable for the copyright infringement allegedly committed by Betamax consumers because of petitioners' marketing of the Betamax VTR's. Respondents sought no relief against any Betamax consumer. Instead, they sought money damages and an equitable accounting of profits from petitioners, as well as an injunction against the manufacture and marketing of Betamax VTR's.

After a lengthy trial, the District Court denied respondents all the relief they sought and entered judgment for petitioners. 480 F.Supp. 429 (1979). The United States Court of Appeals for the Ninth Circuit reversed the District Court's judgment on respondents' copyright claim. 659 F.2d 963 (1981). We granted certiorari. 457 U.S. 1116 (1982). We now reverse.

An explanation of our rejection of respondents' unprecedented attempt to impose copyright liability upon the distributors of copying equipment requires a quite detailed recitation of the findings of the District Court. In summary, those findings reveal that the average member of the public uses a VTR principally to record a program he cannot view as it is being televised and then to watch it once at a later time. This practice, known as "time-shifting," enlarges the television viewing audience. For that reason, a significant amount of television programming may be used in this manner without objection from the owners of the copyrights on the programs. For the same reason, even the two respondents in this case, who do assert objections to time-shifting in this litigation, were unable to prove that the practice has impaired the commercial value of their copyrights or has created any likelihood of future harm. Given these findings, there is no basis in the Copyright Act upon which respondents can hold petitioners liable for distributing VTR's to the general public. The Court of Appeals' holding that respondents are entitled to enjoin the distribution of VTR's, to collect royalties on the sale of such equipment, or to obtain other relief, if affirmed, would enlarge the scope of respondents' statutory monopolies to encompass control over an article of commerce that is not the subject of copyright protection. Such an expansion of the copyright privilege is beyond the limits of the grants authorized by Congress.

I

The two respondents in this action, Universal City Studios, Inc., and Walt Disney Productions, produce and hold the copyrights on a substantial number of motion pictures and other audiovisual works. In the current marketplace, they can exploit their rights in these works in a number of ways: by authorizing theatrical exhibitions, by licensing limited showings on cable and network television, by selling syndication rights for repeated airings on local television stations, and by marketing programs on prerecorded videotapes or videodiscs. Some works are suitable for exploitation through all of these avenues, while the market for other works is more limited.

The respondents and Sony both conducted surveys of the way the Betamax machine was used by several hundred owners during a sample period in 1978. Although there were some differences in the surveys, they both showed that the primary use of the machine for most owners was "time-shifting." Both surveys also showed, however, that a substantial number of interviewees had accumulated libraries of tapes. Sony's survey indicated that over 80% of the interviewees watched at least as much regular television as they had before owning a Betamax. Respondents offered no evidence of decreased television viewing by Betamax owners.

Sony introduced considerable evidence describing television programs that could be copied without objection from any copyright holder, with special emphasis on sports, religious, and educational programming. For example, their survey indicated that 7.3% of all Betamax use is to record sports events, and representatives of professional baseball, football, basketball, and hockey testified that they had no objection to the recording of their televised events for home use.

Respondents offered opinion evidence concerning the future impact of the unrestricted sale of VTR's on the commercial value of their copyrights. The District Court found, however, that they had failed to prove any likelihood of future harm from the use of VTR's for time-shifting. 480 F.Supp., at 469.

The District Court concluded that noncommercial home use recording of material broadcast over the public airwaves was a fair use of copyrighted works and did not constitute copyright infringement. The Court of Appeals reversed the District Court's judgment on respondents' copyright claim. It did not set aside any of the District Court's findings of fact. Rather, it concluded as a matter of law that the home use of a VTR was not a fair use because it was not a "productive use."[a] It therefore held that it was unnecessary for plaintiffs to prove any harm to the potential market for the copyrighted works, but then observed that it seemed clear that the cumulative effect of mass reproduction made possible by VTR's would tend to diminish the potential market for respondents' works. 659 F.2d, at 974.

\* \* \*

## III

The Copyright Act does not expressly render anyone liable for infringement committed by another. In contrast, the Patent Act expressly brands anyone who "actively induces infringement of a patent" as an infringer, 35 U.S.C. § 271(b), and further imposes liability on certain individuals labeled "contributory" infringers, § 271(c). The absence of such express language in the copyright statute does not preclude the imposition of liability for copyright infringements on certain parties who have not themselves engaged in the infringing activity.[b] For vicarious liability is imposed in virtually all areas of the law, and the concept of contributory infringement is merely a species of the broader problem of identifying the circumstances in which it is just to hold one individual accountable for the actions of another.

Such circumstances were plainly present in Kalem Co. v. Harper Brothers, 222 U.S. 55 (1911), the copyright decision of this Court on which respondents place their principal reliance. In *Kalem*, the Court held that the producer of an unauthorized film dramatization of the copyrighted book Ben Hur was liable for his sale of the motion picture to jobbers, who in turn arranged for the commercial exhibition of the film. Justice Holmes, writing for the Court, explained:

> "The defendant not only expected but invoked by advertisement the use of its films for dramatic reproduction of the story. That was the most conspicuous purpose for which they could be used, and the one for which especially they were made. If the defendant did not contribute to the infringement it is impossible to do so except by taking part in the final act. It is liable on principles recognized in every part of the law." *Id.* at 62–63.

The use for which the item sold in *Kalem* had been "especially" made was, of course, to display the performance that had already been recorded upon it. The producer had personally appropriated the copyright owner's

---

[a] "Without a 'productive use,' i.e. when copyrighted material is reproduced for its intrinsic use, the mass copying of the sort involved in this case precludes an application of fair use." 659 F.2d, at 971–972.

[b] As the District Court correctly observed, however, "the lines between direct infringement, contributory infringement and vicarious liability are not clearly drawn.... " 480 F.Supp., at 457–458. The lack of clarity in this area may, in part, be attributable to the fact that an infringer is not merely one who uses a work without authorization by the copyright owner, but also one who authorizes the use of a copyrighted work without actual authority from the copyright owner.

protected work and, as the owner of the tangible medium of expression upon which the protected work was recorded, authorized that use by his sale of the film to jobbers. But that use of the film was not his to authorize: the copyright owner possessed the exclusive right to authorize public performances of his work. Further, the producer personally advertised the unauthorized public performances, dispelling any possible doubt as to the use of the film which he had authorized.

Respondents argue that *Kalem* stands for the proposition that supplying the "means" to accomplish an infringing activity and encouraging that activity through advertisement are sufficient to establish liability for copyright infringement. This argument rests on a gross generalization that cannot withstand scrutiny. The producer in *Kalem* did not merely provide the "means" to accomplish an infringing activity; the producer supplied the work itself, albeit in a new medium of expression. Sony in the instant case does not supply Betamax consumers with respondents' works; respondents do. Sony supplies a piece of equipment that is generally capable of copying the entire range of programs that may be televised: those that are uncopyrighted, those that are copyrighted but may be copied without objection from the copyright holder, and those that the copyright holder would prefer not to have copied. The Betamax can be used to make authorized or unauthorized uses of copyrighted works, but the range of its potential use is much broader than the particular infringing use of the film Ben Hur involved in *Kalem*. *Kalem* does not support respondents' novel theory of 11 liability.

Justice Holmes stated that the producer had "contributed" to the infringement of the copyright, and the label "contributory infringement" has been applied in a number of lower court copyright cases involving an ongoing relationship between the direct infringer and the contributory infringer at the time the infringing conduct occurred. In such cases, as in other situations in which the imposition of vicarious liability is manifestly just, the "contributory" infringer was in a position to control the use of copyrighted works by others and had authorized the use without permission from the copyright owner.[c] This case, however, plainly does not fall in that category. The only contact between Sony and the users of the Betamax that is disclosed by this record occurred at the moment of sale. The District Court expressly found that "no employee of Sony ... had either direct involvement with the allegedly infringing activity or direct contact with purchasers of Betamax who recorded copyrighted works off-the-air." 480

---

[c] The so-called "dance hall cases," Famous Music Corp. v. Bay State Harness Horse Racing & Breeding Assn., Inc., 554 F.2d 1213 (C.A.1 1977) (racetrack retained infringer to supply music to paying customers); KECA Music, Inc. v. Dingus McGee's Co., 432 F.Supp. 72 (W.D.Mo.1977) (cocktail lounge hired musicians to supply music to paying customers); Dreamland Ball Room, Inc. v. Shapiro, Bernstein & Co., 36 F.2d 354 (C.A.7 1929) (dance hall hired orchestra to supply music to paying customers), are often contrasted with the so-called landlord-tenant cases, in which landlords who leased premises to a direct infringer for a fixed rental and did not participate directly in any infringing activity were found not to be liable for contributory infringement. E.g., Deutsch v. Arnold, 98 F.2d 686 (C.A.2 1938).

F.Supp., at 460. And it further found that "there was no evidence that any of the copies made by the other individual witnesses in this suit were influenced or encouraged by [Sony's] advertisements." *Ibid.*

If vicarious liability is to be imposed on Sony in this case, it must rest on the fact that it has sold equipment with constructive knowledge of the fact that its customers may use that equipment to make unauthorized copies of copyrighted material. There is no precedent in the law of copyright for the imposition of vicarious liability on such a theory. The closest analogy is provided by the patent law cases to which it is appropriate to refer because of the historic kinship between patent law and copyright law.[d]

In the Patent Act both the concept of infringement and the concept of contributory infringement are expressly defined by statute.[e] The prohibition against contributory infringement is confined to the knowing sale of a component especially made for use in connection with a particular patent. There is no suggestion in the statute that one patentee may object to the sale of a product that might be used in connection with other patents. Moreover, the Act expressly provides that the sale of a "staple article or commodity of commerce suitable for substantial noninfringing use" is not contributory infringement. 35 U.S.C. § 271(c).

When a charge of contributory infringement is predicated entirely on the sale of an article of commerce that is used by the purchaser to infringe a patent, the public interest in access to that article of commerce is necessarily implicated. A finding of contributory infringement does not, of course, remove the article from the market altogether; it does, however, give the patentee effective control over the sale of that item. Indeed, a

---

[d] E.g., United States v. Paramount Pictures, Inc., 334 U.S., at 158; Fox Film Corp. v. Doyal, 286 U.S., at 131; Wheaton v. Peters, 8 Pet. 591, 657–658 (1834). The two areas of the law, naturally, are not identical twins, and we exercise the caution which we have expressed in the past in applying doctrine formulated in one area to the other. See generally Mazer v. Stein, 347 U.S. 201, 217–218 (1954); Bobbs–Merrill Co. v. Straus, 210 U.S., at 345.

We have consistently rejected the proposition that a similar kinship exists between copyright law and trademark law, and in the process of doing so have recognized the basic similarities between copyrights and patents. The Trade–Mark Cases, 100 U.S. 82, 91–92 (1879); see also United Drug Co. v. Theodore Rectanus Co., 248 U.S. 90, 97 (1918) (trademark right "has little or no analogy" to copyright or patent). Given the fundamental differences between copyright law and trademark law, in this copyright case we do not look to the standard for contributory in-

fringement set forth in Inwood Laboratories, Inc. v. Ives Laboratories, Inc., 456 U.S. 844, 854–855 (1982), which was crafted for application in trademark cases. There we observed that a manufacturer or distributor could be held liable to the owner of a trademark if it intentionally induced a merchant down the chain of distribution to pass off its product as that of the trademark owner's or if it continued to supply a product which could readily be passed off to a particular merchant whom it knew was mislabeling the product with the trademark owner's mark. If *Inwood*'s narrow standard for contributory trademark infringement governed here, respondents' claim of contributory infringement would merit little discussion. Sony certainly does not "intentionally [induce]" its customers to make infringing uses of respondents' copyrights, nor does it supply its products to identified individuals known by it to be engaging in continuing infringement of respondents' copyrights, see *id.,* at 855.

[e] 35 U.S.C. § 271.

finding of contributory infringement is normally the functional equivalent of holding that the disputed article is within the monopoly granted to the patentee.[f]

For that reason, in contributory infringement cases arising under the patent laws the Court has always recognized the critical importance of not allowing the patentee to extend his monopoly beyond the limits of his specific grant. These cases deny the patentee any right to control the distribution of unpatented articles unless they are "unsuited for any commercial noninfringing use." Dawson Chemical Co. v. Rohm & Haas Co., 448 U.S. 176, 198 (1980).

We recognize there are substantial differences between the patent and copyright laws. But in both areas the contributory infringement doctrine is grounded on the recognition that adequate protection of a monopoly may require the courts to look beyond actual duplication of a device or publication to the products or activities that make such duplication possible. The staple article of commerce doctrine must strike a balance between a copyright holder's legitimate demand for effective-not merely symbolic-protection of the statutory monopoly, and the rights of others freely to engage in substantially unrelated areas of commerce. Accordingly, the sale of copying equipment, like the sale of other articles of commerce, does not constitute contributory infringement if the product is widely used for legitimate, unobjectionable purposes. Indeed, it need merely be capable of substantial noninfringing uses.

## IV

The question is thus whether the Betamax is capable of commercially significant noninfringing uses. In order to resolve that question, we need not explore all the different potential uses of the machine and determine whether or not they would constitute infringement. Rather, we need only consider whether on the basis of the facts as found by the District Court a significant number of them would be noninfringing. Moreover, in order to resolve this case we need not give precise content to the question of how much use is commercially significant. For one potential use of the Betamax plainly satisfies this standard, however it is understood: private, noncommercial time-shifting in the home. It does so both (A) because respondents have no right to prevent other copyright holders from authorizing it for their programs, and (B) because the District Court's factual findings reveal that even the unauthorized home time-shifting of respondents' programs is legitimate fair use.

\* \* \*

[f] It seems extraordinary to suggest that the Copyright Act confers upon all copyright owners collectively, much less the two respondents in this case, the exclusive right to distribute VTR's simply because they may be used to infringe copyrights. That, however, is the logical implication of their claim. The request for an injunction below indicates that respondents seek, in effect, to declare VTR's contraband. Their suggestion in this Court that a continuing royalty pursuant to a judicially created compulsory license would be an acceptable remedy merely indicates that respondents, for their part, would be willing to license their claimed monopoly interest in VTR's to Sony in return for a royalty.

B. Unauthorized Time–Shifting

Even unauthorized uses of a copyrighted work are not necessarily infringing. An unlicensed use of the copyright is not an infringement unless it conflicts with one of the specific exclusive rights conferred by the copyright statute. Moreover, the definition of exclusive rights in § 106 of the present Act is prefaced by the words "subject to sections 107 through 118." Those sections describe a variety of uses of copyrighted material that "are not infringements of copyright" "notwithstanding the provisions of section 106." The most pertinent in this case is § 107, the legislative endorsement of the doctrine of "fair use."[g]

That section identifies various factors that enable a court to apply an "equitable rule of reason" analysis to particular claims of infringement.[h] Although not conclusive, the first factor requires that "the commercial or nonprofit character of an activity" be weighed in any fair use decision.[i] If the Betamax were used to make copies for a commercial or profit-making

---

[g] The Copyright Act of 1909, 35 Stat. 1075, did not have a "fair use" provision. Although that Act's compendium of exclusive rights "to print, reprint, publish, copy, and vend the copyrighted work" was broad enough to encompass virtually all potential interactions with a copyrighted work, the statute was never so construed. The courts simply refused to read the statute literally in every situation. When Congress amended the statute in 1976, it indicated that it "intended to restate the present judicial doctrine of fair use, not to change, narrow, or enlarge it in any way." H. R. Rep. No. 94–1476, p.66 (1976).

[h] The House Report expressly stated that the fair use doctrine is an "equitable rule of reason" in its explanation of the fair use section:

"Although the courts have considered and ruled upon the fair use doctrine over and over again, no real definition of the concept has ever emerged. Indeed, since the doctrine is an equitable rule of reason, no generally applicable definition is possible, and each case raising the question must be decided on its own facts. . . .

The bill endorses the purpose and general scope of the judicial doctrine of fair use, but there is no disposition to freeze the doctrine in the statute, especially during a period of rapid technological change. Beyond a very broad statutory explanation of what fair use is and some of the criteria applicable to it, the courts

must be free to adapt the doctrine to particular situations on a case-by-case basis."

H.R. Rep. No. 94–1476, at 65–66.

The Senate Committee similarly eschewed a rigid, bright-line approach to fair use. The Senate Report endorsed the view "that off-the-air recording for convenience" could be considered "fair use" under some circumstances, although it then made it clear that it did not intend to suggest that off-the-air recording for convenience should be deemed fair use under any circumstances imaginable. S. Rep. No. 94–473, p. 65–66 (1975). The latter qualifying statement is quoted by the dissent, and if read in isolation, would indicate that the Committee intended to condemn all off-the-air recording for convenience. Read in context, however, it is quite clear that that was the farthest thing from the Committee's intention.

[i] "The Committee has amended the first of the criteria to be considered–'the purpose and character of the use'-to state explicitly that this factor includes a consideration of 'whether such use is of a commercial nature or is for non-profit educational purposes.' This amendment is not intended to be interpreted as any sort of not-for-profit limitation on educational uses of copyrighted works. It is an express recognition that, as under the present law, the commercial or non-profit character of an activity, while not conclusive with respect to fair use, can and should be weighed along with other factors in fair use decisions." H. R. Rep. No. 94–1476, at 66.

purpose, such use would presumptively be unfair. The contrary presumption is appropriate here, however, because the District Court's findings plainly establish that time-shifting for private home use must be characterized as a noncommercial, nonprofit activity. Moreover, when one considers the nature of a televised copyrighted audiovisual work, see § 107(2), and that time-shifting merely enables a viewer to see such a work which he had been invited to witness in its entirety free of charge, the fact that the entire work is reproduced, see § 107(3), does not have its ordinary effect of militating against a finding of fair use.

. . . .

This is not, however, the end of the inquiry because Congress has also directed us to consider "the effect of the use upon the potential market for or value of the copyrighted work." § 107(4). The purpose of copyright is to create incentives for creative effort. Even copying for noncommercial purposes may impair the copyright holder's ability to obtain the rewards that Congress intended him to have. But a use that has no demonstrable effect upon the potential market for, or the value of, the copyrighted work need not be prohibited in order to protect the author's incentive to create. The prohibition of such noncommercial uses would merely inhibit access to ideas without any countervailing benefit.

Thus, although every commercial use of copyrighted material is presumptively an unfair exploitation of the monopoly privilege that belongs to the owner of the copyright, noncommercial uses are a different matter. A challenge to a noncommercial use of a copyrighted work requires proof either that the particular use is harmful, or that if it should become widespread, it would adversely affect the potential market for the copyrighted work. Actual present harm need not be shown; such a requirement would leave the copyright holder with no defense against predictable damage. Nor is it necessary to show with certainty that future harm will result. What is necessary is a showing by a preponderance of the evidence that some meaningful likelihood of future harm exists. If the intended use is for commercial gain, that likelihood may be presumed. But if it is for a noncommercial purpose, the likelihood must be demonstrated.

In this case, respondents failed to carry their burden with regard to home time-shifting. There was no need for the District Court to say much about past harm. "Plaintiffs have admitted that no actual harm to their copyrights has occurred to date." *Id.* at 451.

On the question of potential future harm from time-shifting, the District Court offered a more detailed analysis of the evidence. It rejected respondents' "fear that persons 'watching' the original telecast of a program will not be measured in the live audience and the ratings and revenues will decrease," by observing that current measurement technology allows the Betamax audience to be reflected. *Id.* at 466.[j] It rejected

---

j "There was testimony at trial, however, that Nielsen Ratings has already developed the ability to measure when a Betamax in a sample home is recording the program. Thus, the Betamax owner will be measured as a part of the live audience. The later diary can

respondents' prediction "that live television or movie audiences will decrease as more people watch Betamax tapes as an alternative," with the observation that "[there] is no factual basis for [the underlying] assumption." *Ibid.* It rejected respondents' "fear that time-shifting will reduce audiences for telecast reruns", and concluded instead that "given current market practices, this should aid plaintiffs rather than harm them." *Ibid.* And it declared that respondents' suggestion that "theater or film rental exhibition of a program will suffer because of time-shift recording of that program" "lacks merit." *Id.* at 467.[k]

After completing that review, the District Court restated its overall conclusion several times, in several different ways. "Harm from time-shifting is speculative and, at best, minimal." *Ibid.* "The audience benefits from the time-shifting capability have already been discussed. It is not implausible that benefits could also accrue to plaintiffs, broadcasters, and advertisers, as the Betamax makes it possible for more persons to view their broadcasts." *Ibid.* "No likelihood of harm was shown at trial, and plaintiffs admitted that there had been no actual harm to date." *Id.* at 468–469. "Television production by plaintiffs today is more profitable than it has ever been, and, in five weeks of trial, there was no concrete evidence to suggest that the Betamax will change the studios' financial picture." *Ibid.*

The District Court's conclusions are buttressed by the fact that to the extent time-shifting expands public access to freely broadcast television programs, it yields societal benefits. In Community Television of Southern California v. Gottfried, 459 U.S. 498, 508, n.12 (1983), we acknowledged the public interest in making television broadcasting more available. Concededly, that interest is not unlimited. But it supports an interpretation of the concept of "fair use" that requires the copyright holder to demonstrate some likelihood of harm before he may condemn a private act of time-shifting as a violation of federal law.

When these factors are all weighed in the "equitable rule of reason" balance, we must conclude that this record amply supports the District Court's conclusion that home time-shifting is fair use. In light of the findings of the District Court regarding the state of the empirical data, it is

augment that measurement with information about subsequent viewing." *Id.* at 466.

In a separate section, the District Court rejected plaintiffs' suggestion that the commercial attractiveness of television broadcasts would be diminished because Betamax owners would use the pause button or fast-forward control to avoid viewing advertisements:

"It must be remembered, however, that to omit commercials, Betamax owners must view the program, including the commercials, while recording. To avoid commercials during playback, the viewer must fast-forward and, for the most part, guess as to when the commercial has

passed. For most recordings, either practice may be too tedious. As defendants' survey showed, 92% of the programs were recorded with commercials and only 25% of the owners fast-forward through them. Advertisers will have to make the same kinds of judgments they do now about whether persons viewing televised programs actually watch the advertisements which interrupt them." *Id.* at 468.

[k] "This suggestion lacks merit. By definition, time-shift recording entails viewing and erasing, so the program will no longer be on tape when the later theater run begins." J. Blackmun dissenting, 417 U.S., at 467.

clear that the Court of Appeals erred in holding that the statute as presently written bars such conduct.[1]

In summary, the record and findings of the District Court lead us to two conclusions. First, Sony demonstrated a significant likelihood that substantial numbers of copyright holders who license their works for broadcast on free television would not object to having their broadcasts time-shifted by private viewers. And second, respondents failed to demonstrate that time-shifting would cause any likelihood of nonminimal harm to the potential market for, or the value of, their copyrighted works. The Betamax is, therefore, capable of substantial noninfringing uses. Sony's sale of such equipment to the general public does not constitute contributory infringement of respondents' copyrights.

## V

One may search the Copyright Act in vain for any sign that the elected representatives of the millions of people who watch television every day have made it unlawful to copy a program for later viewing at home, or have enacted a flat prohibition against the sale of machines that make such copying possible.

It may well be that Congress will take a fresh look at this new technology, just as it so often has examined other innovations in the past.

---

[1] The Court of Appeals chose not to engage in any "equitable rule of reason" analysis in this case. Instead, it assumed that the category of "fair use" is rigidly circumscribed by a requirement that every such use must be "productive." It therefore concluded that copying a television program merely to enable the viewer to receive information or entertainment that he would otherwise miss because of a personal scheduling conflict could never be fair use. That understanding of "fair use" was erroneous.

Congress has plainly instructed us that fair use analysis calls for a sensitive balancing of interests. The distinction between "productive" and "unproductive" uses may be helpful in calibrating the balance, but it cannot be wholly determinative. Although copying to promote a scholarly endeavor certainly has a stronger claim to fair use than copying to avoid interrupting a poker game, the question is not simply two-dimensional. For one thing, it is not true that all copyrights are fungible. Some copyrights govern material with broad potential secondary markets. Such material may well have a broader claim to protection because of the greater potential for commercial harm. Copying a news broadcast may have a stronger claim to fair use than copying a motion picture. And, of course, not all uses are fungible. Copying for commercial gain has a much weaker claim to fair use than copying for personal enrichment. But the notion of social "productivity" cannot be a complete answer to this analysis. A teacher who copies to prepare lecture notes is clearly productive. But so is a teacher who copies for the sake of broadening his personal understanding of his specialty. Or a legislator who copies for the sake of broadening her understanding of what her constituents are watching; or a constituent who copies a news program to help make a decision on how to vote.

Making a copy of a copyrighted work for the convenience of a blind person is expressly identified by the House Committee Report as an example of fair use, with no suggestion that anything more than a purpose to entertain or to inform need motivate the copying. In a hospital setting, using a VTR to enable a patient to see programs he would otherwise miss has no productive purpose other than contributing to the psychological well-being of the patient. Virtually any time-shifting that increases viewer access to television programming may result in a comparable benefit. The statutory language does not identify any dichotomy between productive and nonproductive time-shifting, but does require consideration of the economic consequences of copying.

But it is not our job to apply laws that have not yet been written. Applying the copyright statute, as it now reads, to the facts as they have been developed in this case, the judgment of the Court of Appeals must be reversed.

It is so ordered.

■ JUSTICE BLACKMUN, with whom JUSTICE MARSHALL, JUSTICE POWELL, and JUSTICE REHNQUIST join, dissenting.

\* \* \*

## IV

Fair Use

Congress in the 1976 Act simply incorporated a list of factors "to be considered." No particular weight, however, was assigned to any of these, and the list was not intended to be exclusive.

## A

The monopoly created by copyright thus rewards the individual author in order to benefit the public. There are situations, nevertheless, in which strict enforcement of this monopoly would inhibit the very "Progress of Science and useful Arts" that copyright is intended to promote. An obvious example is the researcher or scholar whose own work depends on the ability to refer to and to quote the work of prior scholars. Obviously, no author could create a new work if he were first required to repeat the research of every author who had gone before him. The scholar, like the ordinary user, of course could be left to bargain with each copyright owner for permission to quote from or refer to prior works. But there is a crucial difference between the scholar and the ordinary user. When the ordinary user decides that the owner's price is too high, and forgoes use of the work, only the individual is the loser. When the scholar forgoes the use of a prior work, not only does his own work suffer, but the public is deprived of his contribution to knowledge. The scholar's work, in other words, produces external benefits from which everyone profits. In such a case, the fair use doctrine acts as a form of subsidy—albeit at the first author's expense—to permit the second author to make limited use of the first author's work for the public good.

A similar subsidy may be appropriate in a range of areas other than pure scholarship. The situations in which fair use is most commonly recognized are listed in § 107 itself. [O]ther examples may be found in the case law. Each of these uses, however, reflects a common theme: each is a productive use, resulting in some added benefit to the public beyond that produced by the first author's work. The fair use doctrine, in other words, permits works to be used for "socially laudable purposes." See Copyright Office, Briefing Papers on Current Issues, reprinted in 1975 House Hearings 2051, 2055. I am aware of no case in which the reproduction of a copyrighted work for the sole benefit of the user has been held to be fair use.

I do not suggest, of course, that every productive use is a fair use. A finding of fair use still must depend on the facts of the individual case, and on whether, under the circumstances, it is reasonable to expect the user to bargain with the copyright owner for use of the work. But when a user reproduces an entire work and uses it for its original purpose, with no added benefit to the public, the doctrine of fair use usually does not apply. There is then no need whatsoever to provide the ordinary user with a fair use subsidy at the author's expense.

The making of a videotape recording for home viewing is an ordinary rather than a productive use of the Studios' copyrighted works. The District Court found that "Betamax owners use the copy for the same purpose as the original. They add nothing of their own." 480 F.Supp., at 453. Although applying the fair use doctrine to home VTR recording, as Sony argues, may increase public access to material broadcast free over the public airwaves, I think Sony's argument misconceives the nature of copyright. Copyright gives the author a right to limit or even to cut off access to his work. A VTR recording creates no public benefit sufficient to justify limiting this right. Nor is this right extinguished by the copyright owner's choice to make the work available over the airwaves. Section 106 of the 1976 Act grants the copyright owner the exclusive right to control the performance and the reproduction of his work, and the fact that he has licensed a single television performance is really irrelevant to the existence of his right to control its reproduction. Although a television broadcast may be free to the viewer, this fact is equally irrelevant; a book borrowed from the public library may not be copied any more freely than a book that is purchased.

It may be tempting, as, in my view, the Court today is tempted, to stretch the doctrine of fair use so as to permit unfettered use of this new technology in order to increase access to television programming. But such an extension risks eroding the very basis of copyright law, by depriving authors of control over their works and consequently of their incentive to create. Even in the context of highly productive educational uses, Congress has avoided this temptation; in passing the 1976 Act, Congress made it clear that off-the-air videotaping was to be permitted only in very limited situations. See 1976 House Report 71; 1975 Senate Report 64. And, the Senate Report adds, "[the] committee does not intend to suggest . . . that off-the-air recording for convenience would under any circumstances, be considered 'fair use.'" *Id.* at 66. I cannot disregard these admonitions.

B

Courts should move with caution, however, in depriving authors of protection from unproductive "ordinary" uses. "[A] particular use which may seem to have little or no economic impact on the author's rights today can assume tremendous importance in times to come." Register's Supplementary Report 14. Although such a use may seem harmless when viewed in isolation, "[isolated] instances of minor infringements, when multiplied many times, become in the aggregate a major inroad on copyright that must be prevented." 1975 Senate Report 65.

I therefore conclude that, at least when the proposed use is an unproductive one, a copyright owner need prove only a potential for harm to the market for or the value of the copyrighted work. See 3 M. Nimmer, Copyright § 13.05[E][4][c], p. 13–84 (1983). Proof of actual harm, or even probable harm, may be impossible in an area where the effect of a new technology is speculative. Infringement thus would be found if the copyright owner demonstrates a reasonable possibility that harm will result from the proposed use. When the use is one that creates no benefit to the public at large, copyright protection should not be denied on the basis that a new technology that may result in harm has not yet done so.

The Studios have identified a number of ways in which VTR recording could damage their copyrights. VTR recording could reduce their ability to market their works in movie theaters and through the rental or sale of prerecorded videotapes or videodiscs; it also could reduce their rerun audience, and consequently the license fees available to them for repeated showings. Moreover, advertisers may be willing to pay for only "live" viewing audiences, if they believe VTR viewers will delete commercials or if rating services are unable to measure VTR use; if this is the case, VTR recording could reduce the license fees the Studios are able to charge even for first-run showings. Library-building may raise the potential for each of the types of harm identified by the Studios, and time-shifting may raise the potential for substantial harm as well.[a]

Although the District Court found no likelihood of harm from VTR use, 480 F.Supp., at 468, I conclude that it applied an incorrect substantive standard and misallocated the burden of proof. The District Court's reluctance to engage in prediction in this area is understandable, but, in my view, the court was mistaken in concluding that the Studios should bear the risk created by this uncertainty. The Studios have demonstrated a potential for harm, which has not been, and could not be, refuted at this early stage of technological development.

The District Court's analysis of harm, moreover, failed to consider the effect of VTR recording on "the potential market for or the value of the copyrighted work," as required by § 107(4). The requirement that a putatively infringing use of a copyrighted work, to be "fair," must not impair a "potential" market for the work has two implications. First, an infringer cannot prevail merely by demonstrating that the copyright holder suffered no net harm from the infringer's action. Indeed, even a showing

[a] A VTR owner who has taped a favorite movie for repeated viewing will be less likely to rent or buy a tape containing the same movie, watch a televised rerun, or pay to see the movie at a theater. Although time-shifting may not replace theater or rerun viewing or the purchase of prerecorded tapes or discs, it may well replace rental usage; a VTR user who has recorded a first-run movie for later viewing will have no need to rent a copy when he wants to see it. Both library-builders and time-shifters may avoid commercials; the library-builder may use the pause control to record without them, and all users may fast-forward through commercials on playback.

that the infringement has resulted in a net benefit to the copyright holder will not suffice. Rather, the infringer must demonstrate that he had not impaired the copyright holder's ability to demand compensation from (or to deny access to) any group who would otherwise be willing to pay to see or hear the copyrighted work. Second, the fact that a given market for a copyrighted work would not be available to the copyright holder were it not for the infringer's activities does not permit the infringer to exploit that market without compensating the copyright holder.

In this case, the Studios and their amici demonstrate that the advent of the VTR technology created a potential market for their copyrighted programs. That market consists of those persons who find it impossible or inconvenient to watch the programs at the time they are broadcast, and who wish to watch them at other times. These persons are willing to pay for the privilege of watching copyrighted work at their convenience, as is evidenced by the fact that they are willing to pay for VTR's and tapes; undoubtedly, most also would be willing to pay some kind of royalty to copyright holders. The Studios correctly argue that they have been deprived of the ability to exploit this sizable market.

It is thus apparent from the record and from the findings of the District Court that time-shifting does have a substantial adverse effect upon the "potential market for" the Studios' copyrighted works. Accordingly, even under the formulation of the fair use doctrine advanced by Sony, time-shifting cannot be deemed a fair use.

\* \* \*

## VI

The court has adopted an approach very different from the one I have outlined. There is no indication that the fair use doctrine has any application for purely personal consumption on the scale involved in this case, and the Court's application of it here deprives fair use of the major cohesive force that has guided evolution of the doctrine in the past.

[T]he Court purports to apply to time-shifting the four factors explicitly stated in the statute. The Court confidently describes time-shifting as a noncommercial, nonprofit activity. It is clear, however, that personal use of programs that have been copied without permission is not what § 107(1) protects. The intent of the section is to encourage users to engage in activities the primary benefit of which accrues to others. Time-shifting involves no such humanitarian impulse. Purely consumptive uses are certainly not what the fair use doctrine was designed to protect, and the awkwardness of applying the statutory language to time-shifting only makes clearer that fair use was designed to protect only uses that are productive.

The next two statutory factors are all but ignored by the Court-though certainly not because they have no applicability. The second factor—"the nature of the copyrighted work"—strongly supports the view that time-shifting is an infringing use. The rationale guiding application of this factor is that certain types of works, typically those involving "more of diligence than of originality or inventiveness," New York Times Co. v. Roxbury Data Interface, Inc., 434 F.Supp. 217, 221 (NJ 1977), require less copyright protection than other original works. Thus, for example, informational works, such as news reports, that readily lend themselves to productive use by other, are less protected than creative works of entertainment. Sony's own surveys indicate that entertainment shows account for more than 80% of the programs recorded by Betamax owners.

The third statutory factor—"the amount and substantiality of the portion used"—is even more devastating to the Court's interpretation. It is undisputed that virtually all VTR owners record entire works, see 480 F.Supp., at 454, thereby creating an exact substitute for the copyrighted original. Fair use is intended to allow individuals engaged in productive uses to copy small portions of original works that will facilitate their own productive endeavors. Time-shifting bears no resemblance to such activity, and the complete duplication that it involves might alone be sufficient to preclude a finding of fair use. It is little wonder that the Court has chosen to ignore this statutory factor.[b]

The fourth factor requires an evaluation of "the effect of the use upon the potential market for or value of the copyrighted work." This is the factor upon which the Court focuses, but once again, the Court has misread the statute. As mentioned above, the statute requires a court to consider the effect of the use on the potential market for the copyrighted work. The Court has struggled mightily to show that VTR use has not reduced the value of the Studios' copyrighted works in their present markets. Even if true, that showing only begins the proper inquiry. The development of the VTR has created a new market for the works produced by the Studios. That market consists of those persons who desire to view television programs at times other than when they are broadcast, and who therefore purchase VTR recorders to enable them to time-shift.[c] Because time-shifting of the Studios' copyrighted works involves the copying of them, however, the Studios are entitled to share in the benefits of that new market. Those benefits currently go to Sony through Betamax sales. Respondents therefore can show harm from VTR use simply by showing that the value of their copyrights would increase if they were compensated for the copies that are used in the new market. The existence of this effect is self-evident.

[b] The Court's one oblique acknowledgement of this third factor, *ante*, at [IV(B)], and n.[h], seems to suggest that the fact that time-shifting involves copying complete works is not very significant because the viewers already have been asked to watch the initial broadcast free. This suggestion misses the point. As has been noted, a book borrowed from a public library may not be copied any more freely than one that has been purchased. An invitation to view a showing is completely different from an invitation to copy a copyrighted work.

[c] The Court implicitly has recognized that this market is very significant. The central concern underlying the Court's entire opinion is that there is a large audience who would like very much to be able to view programs at times other than when they are broadcast. The Court simply misses the implication of its own concerns.

# Harper & Row v. Nation Enterprises

Supreme Court of the United States, 1985.
471 U.S. 539, 105 S.Ct. 2218, 85 L.Ed.2d 588.

■ JUSTICE O'CONNOR delivered the opinion of the Court.

This case requires us to consider to what extent the "fair use" provision of the Copyright Revision Act of 1976 (hereinafter the Copyright Act), sanctions the unauthorized use of quotations from a public figure's unpublished manuscript. In March 1979, an undisclosed source provided The Nation Magazine with the unpublished manuscript of "A Time to Heal: The Autobiography of Gerald R. Ford." Working directly from the purloined manuscript, an editor of The Nation produced a short piece entitled "The Ford Memoirs—Behind the Nixon Pardon." The piece was timed to "scoop" an article scheduled shortly to appear in Time Magazine. Time had agreed to purchase the exclusive right to print prepublication excerpts from the copyright holders, Harper & Row, Publishers, Inc. (hereinafter Harper & Row), and Reader's Digest Association, Inc. (hereinafter Reader's Digest). As a result of The Nation article, Time canceled its agreement. Petitioners brought a successful copyright action against The Nation. On appeal, the Second Circuit reversed the lower court's finding of infringement, holding that The Nation's act was sanctioned as a "fair use" of the copyrighted material. We granted certiorari, 467 U.S. 1214 (1984), and we now reverse.

I

In February 1977, shortly after leaving the White House, former President Gerald R. Ford contracted with petitioners Harper & Row and Reader's Digest, to publish his as yet unwritten memoirs. The memoirs were to contain "significant hitherto unpublished material" concerning the Watergate crisis, Mr. Ford's pardon of former President Nixon and "Mr. Ford's reflections on this period of history, and the morality and personalities involved." In addition to the right to publish the Ford memoirs in book form, the agreement gave petitioners the exclusive right to license prepublication excerpts, known in the trade as "first serial rights." Two years later, as the memoirs were nearing completion, petitioners negotiated a prepublication licensing agreement with Time, a weekly news magazine. Time agreed to pay $25,000, $12,500 in advance and an additional $12,500 at publication, in exchange for the right to excerpt 7,500 words from Mr. Ford's account of the Nixon pardon. The issue featuring the excerpts was timed to appear approximately one week before shipment of the full length book version to bookstores. Exclusivity was an important consideration; Harper & Row instituted procedures designed to maintain the confidentiality of the manuscript, and Time retained the right to renegotiate the second payment should the material appear in print prior to its release of the excerpts.

Two to three weeks before the Time article's scheduled release, an unidentified person secretly brought a copy of the Ford manuscript to Victor Navasky, editor of The Nation, a political commentary magazine.

Mr. Navasky knew that his possession of the manuscript was not authorized and that the manuscript must be returned quickly to his "source" to avoid discovery. 557 F.Supp. 1067, 1069 (S.D.N.Y.1983). He hastily put together what he believed was "a real hot news story" composed of quotes, paraphrases, and facts drawn exclusively from the manuscript. *Ibid.* Mr. Navasky attempted no independent commentary, research or criticism, in part because of the need for speed if he was to "make news" by "[publishing] in advance of publication of the Ford book." The 2,250–word article appeared on April 3, 1979. As a result of The Nation's article, Time canceled its piece and refused to pay the remaining $12,500.

Petitioners brought suit in the District Court for the Southern District of New York, alleging conversion, tortious interference with contract, and violations of the Copyright Act. After a 6-day bench trial, the District Judge found that "A Time to Heal" was protected by copyright at the time of The Nation publication and that respondents' use of the copyrighted material constituted an infringement under the Copyright Act. The District Court rejected respondents' argument that The Nation's piece was a "fair use" sanctioned by § 107. The court awarded actual damages of $12,500.

A divided panel of the Court of Appeals for the Second Circuit reversed. 723 F.2d 195 (1983). The Court of Appeals was especially influenced by the "politically significant" nature of the subject matter and its conviction that it is not "the purpose of the Copyright Act to impede that harvest of knowledge so necessary to a democratic state" or "chill the activities of the press by forbidding a circumscribed use of copyrighted words." *Id.* at 197, 209.

II

The Nation has admitted to lifting verbatim quotes of the author's original language totaling between 300 and 400 words and constituting some 13% of The Nation article. In using generous verbatim excerpts of Mr. Ford's unpublished manuscript to lend authenticity to its account of the forthcoming memoirs, The Nation effectively arrogated to itself the right of first publication, an important marketable subsidiary right. For the reasons set forth below, we find that this use of the copyrighted manuscript, even stripped to the verbatim quotes conceded by The Nation to be copyrightable expression, was not a fair use within the meaning of the Copyright Act.

III

A

Perhaps because the fair use doctrine was predicated on the author's implied consent to "reasonable and customary" use when he released his work for public consumption, fair use traditionally was not recognized as a defense to charges of copying from an author's as yet unpublished works. Under common-law copyright, "the property of the author ... in his intellectual creation [was] absolute until he voluntarily [parted] with the same." American Tobacco Co. v. Werckmeister, 207 U.S. 284, 299 (1907); 2

Nimmer § 8.23, at 8–273. This absolute rule, however, was tempered in practice by the equitable nature of the fair use doctrine. In a given case, factors such as implied consent through de facto publication on performance or dissemination of a work may tip the balance of equities in favor of prepublication use. But it has never been seriously disputed that "the fact that the plaintiff's work is unpublished . . . is a factor tending to negate the defense of fair use." *Ibid.* Publication of an author's expression before he has authorized its dissemination seriously infringes the author's right to decide when and whether it will be made public, a factor not present in fair use of published works. Respondents contend, however, that Congress, in including first publication among the rights enumerated in § 106, which are expressly subject to fair use under § 107, intended that fair use would apply in pari materia to published and unpublished works. The Copyright Act does not support this proposition.

The Copyright Act represents the culmination of a major legislative reexamination of copyright doctrine. Among its other innovations, it eliminated publication "as a dividing line between common law and statutory protection," H. R. Rep. No. 94–1476, at 129 (1976) extending statutory protection to all works from the time of their creation. It also recognized for the first time a distinct statutory right of first publication, which had previously been an element of the common-law protections afforded unpublished works.

Though the right of first publication, like the other rights enumerated in § 106, is expressly made subject to the fair use provision of § 107, fair use analysis must always be tailored to the individual case. The right of first publication implicates a threshold decision by the author whether and in what form to release his work. First publication is inherently different from other § 106 rights in that only one person can be the first publisher; as the contract with Time illustrates, the commercial value of the right lies primarily in exclusivity. Because the potential damage to the author from judicially enforced "sharing" of the first publication right with unauthorized users of his manuscript is substantial, the balance of equities in evaluating such a claim of fair use inevitably shifts.

The Senate Report confirms that Congress intended the unpublished nature of the work to figure prominently in fair use analysis. In discussing fair use of photocopied materials in the classroom the Committee Report states:

> "A key, though not necessarily determinative, factor in fair use is whether or not the work is available to the potential user. If the work is 'out of print' and unavailable for purchase through normal channels, the user may have more justification for reproducing it. . . . The applicability of the fair use doctrine to unpublished works is narrowly limited since, although the work is unavailable, this is the result of a deliberate choice on the part of the copyright owner. Under ordinary circumstances, the copyright owner's 'right of first publication' would outweigh any needs of reproduction for classroom purposes." S. Rep. No. 94–473 at 64 (1975).

Although the Committee selected photocopying of classroom materials to illustrate fair use, it emphasized that "the same general standards of fair use are applicable to all kinds of uses of copyrighted material." *Id.* at 65.

Even if the legislative history were entirely silent, we would be bound to conclude from Congress' characterization of § 107 as a "restatement" that its effect was to preserve existing law concerning fair use of unpublished works as of other types of protected works and not to "change, narrow, or enlarge it." House Report, at 66. We conclude that the unpublished nature of a work is "[a] key, though not necessarily determinative, factor" tending to negate a defense of fair use. Senate Report, at 64.

We also find unpersuasive respondents' argument that fair use may be made of a soon-to-be-published manuscript on the ground that the author has demonstrated he has no interest in nonpublication. The author's control of first public distribution implicates not only his personal interest in creative control but his property interest in exploitation of prepublication rights, which are valuable in themselves and serve as a valuable adjunct to publicity and marketing. Under ordinary circumstances, the author's right to control the first public appearance of his undisseminated expression will outweigh a claim of fair use.

B

Respondents, however, contend that First Amendment values require a different rule under the circumstances of this case. The thrust of the decision below is that "[the] scope of [fair use] is undoubtedly wider when the information conveyed relates to matters of high public concern." Consumers Union of the United States, Inc. v. General Signal Corp., 724 F.2d 1044, 1050 (C.A.2 1983)(construing 723 F.2d 195 (1983)(case below) as allowing advertiser to quote Consumer Reports), *cert. denied*, 469 U.S. 823 (1984). Respondents advance the substantial public import of the subject matter of the Ford memoirs as grounds for excusing a use that would ordinarily not pass muster as a fair use-the piracy of verbatim quotations for the purpose of "scooping" the authorized first serialization. Respondents explain their copying of Mr. Ford's expression as essential to reporting the news story it claims the book itself represents. In respondents' view, not only the facts contained in Mr. Ford's memoirs, but "the precise manner in which [he] expressed himself [were] as newsworthy as what he had to say." Respondents argue that the public's interest in learning this news as fast as possible outweighs the right of the author to control its first publication.

The Second Circuit noted, correctly, that copyright's idea/expression dichotomy "[strikes] a definitional balance between the First Amendment and the Copyright Act by permitting free communication of facts while still protecting an author's expression." 723 F.2d, at 203. No author may copyright his ideas or the facts he narrates. § 102(b). As this Court long ago observed: "[The] news element—the information respecting current events contained in the literary production—is not the creation of the writer, but is a report of matters that ordinarily are publici juris; it is the history of the day." International News Service v. Associated Press, 248 U.S. 215, 234 (1918). But copyright assures those who write and publish factual narratives such as "A Time to Heal" that they may at least enjoy the right to market the original expression contained therein as just compensation for their investment. Cf. Zacchini v. Scripps–Howard Broadcasting Co., 433 U.S. 562, 575 (1977).

Respondents' theory, however, would expand fair use to effectively destroy any expectation of copyright protection in the work of a public figure. Absent such protection, there would be little incentive to create or profit in financing such memoirs, and the public would be denied an important source of significant historical information. The promise of copyright would be an empty one if it could be avoided merely by dubbing the infringement a fair use "news report" of the book.

Nor do respondents assert any actual necessity for circumventing the copyright scheme with respect to the types of works and users at issue here.[a] Where an author and publisher have invested extensive resources in creating an original work and are poised to release it to the public, no legitimate aim is served by pre-empting the right of first publication. The fact that the words the author has chosen to clothe his narrative may of themselves be "newsworthy" is not an independent justification for unauthorized copying of the author's expression prior to publication. To paraphrase another recent Second Circuit decision:

> "The fair use doctrine is not a license for corporate theft, empowering a court to ignore a copyright whenever it determines the underlying work contains material of possible public importance." Iowa State University Research Foundation, Inc. v. American Broadcasting Cos., Inc., 621 F.2d 57, 61 (1980)(citations omitted).

In our haste to disseminate news, it should not be forgotten that the Framers intended copyright itself to be the engine of free expression. By establishing a marketable right to the use of one's expression, copyright supplies the economic incentive to create and disseminate ideas.

It is fundamentally at odds with the scheme of copyright to accord lesser rights in those works that are of greatest importance to the public. Such a notion ignores the major premise of copyright and injures author and public alike.

In view of the First Amendment protections already embodied in the Copyright Act's distinction between copyrightable expression and uncopyrightable facts and ideas, and the latitude for scholarship and comment traditionally afforded by fair use, we see no warrant for expanding the doctrine of fair use to create what amounts to a public figure exception to copyright. Whether verbatim copying from a public figure's manuscript in a

---

[a] It bears noting that Congress in the Copyright Act recognized a public interest warranting specific exemptions in a number of areas not within traditional fair use, see, e.g., § 115 (compulsory license for records); § 105 (no copyright in Government works). No such exemption limits copyright in personal narratives written by public servants after they leave Government service.

given case is or is not fair must be judged according to the traditional equities of fair use.

IV

*Purpose of the Use.* The Second Circuit correctly identified news reporting as the general purpose of The Nation's use. News reporting is one of the examples enumerated in § 107 to "give some idea of the sort of activities the courts might regard as fair use under the circumstances." Senate Report, at 61. This listing was not intended to be exhaustive, see *ibid.*; § 101 (definition of "including" and "such as"), or to single out any particular use as presumptively a "fair" use. The drafters resisted pressures from special interest groups to create presumptive categories of fair use, but structured the provision as an affirmative defense requiring a case-by-case analysis. The fact that an article arguably is "news" and therefore a productive use is simply one factor in a fair use analysis.

We agree with the Second Circuit that the trial court erred in fixing on whether the information contained in the memoirs was actually new to the public. The Nation has every right to seek to be the first to publish information. But The Nation went beyond simply reporting uncopyrightable information and actively sought to exploit the headline value of its infringement, making a "news event" out of its unauthorized first publication of a noted figure's copyrighted expression.

The fact that a publication was commercial as opposed to nonprofit is a separate factor that tends to weigh against a finding of fair use. In arguing that the purpose of news reporting is not purely commercial, The Nation misses the point entirely. The crux of the profit/nonprofit distinction is not whether the sole motive of the use is monetary gain but whether the user stands to profit from exploitation of the copyrighted material without paying the customary price.

In evaluating character and purpose we cannot ignore The Nation's stated purpose of scooping the forthcoming hardcover and Time abstracts. The Nation's use had not merely the incidental effect but the intended purpose of supplanting the copyright holder's commercially valuable right of first publication. Also relevant to the "character" of the use is "the propriety of the defendant's conduct." 3 Nimmer § 13.05[A], at 13–72. "Fair use presupposes 'good faith' and 'fair dealing.' " Time Inc. v. Bernard Geis Associates, 293 F.Supp. 130, 146 (S.D.N.Y.1968), quoting Schulman, Fair Use and the Revision of the Copyright Act, 53 Iowa L. Rev. 832 (1968). The trial court found that The Nation knowingly exploited a purloined manuscript. Unlike the typical claim of fair use, The Nation cannot offer up even the fiction of consent as justification. Like its competitor newsweekly, it was free to bid for the right of abstracting excerpts from "A Time to Heal."

*Nature of the Copyrighted Work.* Second, the Act directs attention to the nature of the copyrighted work. "A Time to Heal" may be characterized as an unpublished historical narrative or autobiography. The law generally recognizes a greater need to disseminate factual works than works of fiction or fantasy.

Some of the briefer quotes from the memoirs are arguably necessary adequately to convey the facts; for example, Mr. Ford's characterization of the White House tapes as the "smoking gun" is perhaps so integral to the idea expressed as to be inseparable from it. Cf. 1 Nimmer § 1.10[C]. But The Nation did not stop at isolated phrases and instead excerpted subjective descriptions and portraits of public figures whose power lies in the author's individualized expression. Such use, focusing on the most expressive elements of the work, exceeds that necessary to disseminate the facts.

The fact that a work is unpublished is a critical element of its "nature." Our prior discussion establishes that the scope of fair use is narrower with respect to unpublished works. While even substantial quotations might qualify as fair use in a review of a published work or a news account of a speech that had been delivered to the public or disseminated to the press, see House Report, at 65, the author's right to control the first public appearance of his expression weighs against such use of the work before its release. The right of first publication encompasses not only the choice whether to publish at all, but also the choices of when, where, and in what form first to publish a work.

In the case of Mr. Ford's manuscript, the copyright holders' interest in confidentiality is irrefutable; the copyright holders had entered into a contractual undertaking to "keep the manuscript confidential" and required that all those to whom the manuscript was shown also "sign an agreement to keep the manuscript confidential." While the copyright holders' contract with Time required Time to submit its proposed article seven days before publication, The Nation's clandestine publication afforded no such opportunity for creative or quality control. It was hastily patched together and contained "a number of inaccuracies." (testimony of Victor Navasky). A use that so clearly infringes the copyright holder's interests in confidentiality and creative control is difficult to characterize as "fair."

*Amount and Substantiality of the Portion Used.* Next, the Act directs us to examine the amount and substantiality of the portion used in relation to the copyrighted work as a whole. In absolute terms, the words actually quoted were an insubstantial portion of "A Time to Heal." The District Court, however, found that "[The] Nation took what was essentially the heart of the book." 557 F.Supp., at 1072. We believe the Court of Appeals erred in overruling the District Judge's evaluation of the qualitative nature of the taking. A Time editor described the chapters on the pardon as "the most interesting and moving parts of the entire manuscript." The portions actually quoted were selected by Mr. Navasky as among the most powerful passages in those chapters. He testified that he used verbatim excerpts because simply reciting the information could not adequately convey the "absolute certainty with which [Ford] expressed himself," or show that "this comes from President Ford," or carry the "definitive quality" of the original. In short, he quoted these passages precisely because they qualitatively embodied Ford's distinctive expression.

As the statutory language indicates, a taking may not be excused merely because it is insubstantial with respect to the infringing work. As Judge Learned Hand cogently remarked, "no plagiarist can excuse the wrong by showing how much of his work he did not pirate." Sheldon v. Metro–Goldwyn Pictures Corp., 81 F.2d 49, 56 (CA2), *cert. denied*, 298 U.S. 669 (1936). Conversely, the fact that a substantial portion of the infringing work was copied verbatim is evidence of the qualitative value of the copied material, both to the originator and to the plagiarist who seeks to profit from marketing someone else's copyrighted expression.

Stripped to the verbatim quotes, the direct takings from the unpublished manuscript constitute at least 13% of the infringing article. The Nation article is structured around the quoted excerpts which serve as its dramatic focal points. In view of the expressive value of the excerpts and their key role in the infringing work, we cannot agree with the Second Circuit that the "magazine took a meager, indeed an infinitesimal amount of Ford's original language." 723 F.2d, at 209.

*Effect on the Market.* Finally, the Act focuses on "the effect of the use upon the potential market for or value of the copyrighted work." This last factor is undoubtedly the single most important element of fair use.[b] See 3 Nimmer § 13.05[A], at 13–76, and cases cited therein. "Fair use, when properly applied, is limited to copying by others which does not materially impair the marketability of the work which is copied." 1 Nimmer § 1.10[D], at 1–87. The trial court found not merely a potential but an actual effect on the market. Time's cancellation of its projected serialization and its refusal to pay the $12,500 were the direct effect of the infringement. The Court of Appeals rejected this fact-finding as clearly erroneous, noting that the record did not establish a causal relation between Time's nonperformance and respondents' unauthorized publication of Mr. Ford's expression as opposed to the facts taken from the memoirs. We disagree. Rarely will a case of copyright infringement present such clear-cut evidence of actual damage. Petitioners assured Time that there would be no other authorized publication of any portion of the unpublished manuscript prior to April 23, 1979. Any publication of material from chapters 1 and 3 would permit Time to renegotiate its final payment. Time cited The Nation's article, which contained verbatim quotes from the unpublished manuscript, as a reason for its nonperformance. [O]nce a

---

[b] Economists who have addressed the issue believe the fair use exception should come into play only in those situations in which the market fails or the price the copyright holder would ask is near zero. See, e.g., T. Brennan, Harper & Row v. The Nation, Copyrightability and Fair Use, Dept. of Justice Economic Policy Office Discussion Paper 13–17 (1984); Gordon, Fair Use as Market Failure: A Structural and Economic Analysis of the Betamax Case and its Predecessors, 82 Colum. L. Rev. 1600, 1615 (1982). As the facts here demonstrate, there is a fully functioning market that encourages the creation and dissemination of memoirs of public figures. In the economists' view, permitting "fair use" to displace normal copyright channels disrupts the copyright market without a commensurate public benefit.

copyright holder establishes with reasonable probability the existence of a causal connection between the infringement and a loss of revenue, the burden properly shifts to the infringer to show that this damage would have occurred had there been no taking of copyrighted expression. See 3 Nimmer § 14.02, at 14–7–14–8.1. Petitioners established a prima facie case of actual damage that respondents failed to rebut.

More important, to negate fair use one need only show that if the challenged use "should become widespread, it would adversely affect the *potential* market for the copyrighted work." Sony Corp. of America v. Universal City Studios, Inc., 464 U.S., at 451 (emphasis added); *id.* at 484, and n.36 (collecting cases)(dissenting opinion). This inquiry must take account not only of harm to the original but also of harm to the market for derivative works. "If the defendant's work adversely affects the value of any of the rights in the copyrighted work (in this case the adaptation [and serialization] right) the use is not fair." 3 Nimmer § 13.05[B], at 13–77–13–78.

It is undisputed that the factual material in the balance of The Nation's article, besides the verbatim quotes at issue here, was drawn exclusively from the chapters on the pardon. The excerpts were employed as featured episodes in a story about the Nixon pardon-precisely the use petitioners had licensed to Time. The borrowing of these verbatim quotes from the unpublished manuscript lent The Nation's piece a special air of authenticity-as Navasky expressed it, the reader would know it was Ford speaking and not The Nation. Thus it directly competed for a share of the market for prepublication excerpts. The Senate Report states:

> "With certain special exceptions . . . a use that supplants any part of the normal market for a copyrighted work would ordinarily be considered an infringement." Senate Report, at 65.

Placed in a broader perspective, a fair use doctrine that permits extensive prepublication quotations from an unreleased manuscript without the copyright owner's consent poses substantial potential for damage to the marketability of first serialization rights in general.

## V

In sum, the traditional doctrine of fair use, as embodied in the Copyright Act, does not sanction the use made by The Nation of these copyrighted materials. Any copyright infringer may claim to benefit the public by increasing public access to the copyrighted work. See Pacific & Southern Co. v. Duncan, 744 F.2d 1490 at 1499–1500 (11th Cir.1984). But Congress has not designed, and we see no warrant for judicially imposing, a "compulsory license" permitting unfettered access to the unpublished copyrighted expression of public figures.

[T]he judgment of the Court of Appeals is reversed, and the case is remanded for further proceedings consistent with this opinion.

It is so ordered.

■ [The dissenting opinion of JUSTICE BRENNAN, joined by JUSTICE WHITE and JUSTICE MARSHALL, is omitted.]

# Campbell v. Acuff–Rose Music, Inc.

Supreme Court of the United States, 1994.
510 U.S. 569, 114 S.Ct. 1164, 127 L.Ed.2d 500.

■ JUSTICE SOUTER delivered the opinion of the Court.

We are called upon to decide whether 2 Live Crew's commercial parody of Roy Orbison's song, "Oh, Pretty Woman," may be a fair use within the meaning of the Copyright Act of 1976, 17 U.S.C. § 107 (1988 ed. and Supp. IV). Although the District Court granted summary judgment for 2 Live Crew, the Court of Appeals reversed, holding the defense of fair use barred by the song's commercial character and excessive borrowing. Because we hold that a parody's commercial character is only one element to be weighed in a fair use enquiry, and that insufficient consideration was given to the nature of parody in weighing the degree of copying, we reverse and remand.

II

The fair use doctrine thus "permits [and requires] courts to avoid rigid application of the copyright statute when, on occasion, it would stifle the very creativity which that law is designed to foster."

The task is not to be simplified with bright-line rules, for the statute, like the doctrine it recognizes, calls for case-by-case analysis. Nor may the four statutory factors be treated in isolation, one from another. All are to be explored, and the results weighed together, in light of the purposes of copyright.[a]

A

The first factor in a fair use enquiry draws on Justice Story's formulation, "the nature and objects of the selections made." *Folsom v. Marsh*, at

---

[a] Because the fair use enquiry often requires close questions of judgment as to the extent of permissible borrowing in cases involving parodies (or other critical works), courts may also wish to bear in mind that the goals of the copyright law, "to stimulate the creation and publication of edifying matter," Leval, [Toward a Fair Use Standard, 103 Harv. L. Rev. 1105,] 1134 [(1990)], are not always best served by automatically granting injunctive relief when parodists are found to have gone beyond the bounds of fair use. See 17 U.S.C. § 502(a) (court "*may* ... grant ... injunctions on such terms as it may deem reasonable to prevent or restrain infringement") (emphasis added); Leval 1132 (while in the "vast majority of cases, [an injunctive] remedy is justified because most infringements are simple piracy," such cases are "worlds apart from many of those raising reasonable contentions of fair use" where "there may be a strong public interest in the publication of the secondary work [and] the copyright owner's interest may be adequately protected by an award of damages for whatever infringement is found"); *Abend v. MCA, Inc.*, 863 F.2d 1465, 1479 (CA9 1988) (finding "special circumstances" that would cause "great injustice" to defendants and "public injury" were injunction to issue), aff'd *sub nom. Stewart v. Abend*, 495 U.S. 207, 109 L. Ed. 2d 184, 110 S. Ct. 1750 (1990).

348. The enquiry here may be guided by the examples given in the preamble to § 107, looking to whether the use is for criticism, or comment, or news reporting, and the like. The central purpose of this investigation is to see, in Justice Story's words, whether the new work merely "supersede[s] the objects" of the original creation, *Folsom v. Marsh*, at 348; or instead adds something new, with a further purpose or different character, altering the first with new expression, meaning, or message; it asks, in other words, whether and to what extent the new work is "transformative." Leval 1111. Although such transformative use is not absolutely necessary for a finding of fair use, *Sony*, at 455, n. 40, the goal of copyright, to promote science and the arts, is generally furthered by the creation of transformative works. Such works thus lie at the heart of the fair use doctrine's guarantee of breathing space within the confines of copyright, see, *e. g., Sony*, at 478–480 (BLACKMUN, J., dissenting), and the more transformative the new work, the less will be the significance of other factors, like commercialism, that may weigh against a finding of fair use.

This Court has only once before even considered whether parody may be fair use, and that time issued no opinion because of the Court's equal division. *Benny v. Loew's Inc.*, 239 F.2d 532 (CA9 1956), aff'd *sub nom. Columbia Broadcasting System, Inc. v. Loew's Inc.*, 356 U.S. 43, 2 L. Ed. 2d 583, 78 S. Ct. 667 (1958). Suffice it to say now that parody has an obvious claim to transformative value, as Acuff–Rose itself does not deny. Like less ostensibly humorous forms of criticism, it can provide social benefit, by shedding light on an earlier work, and, in the process, creating a new one. We thus line up with the courts that have held that parody, like other comment or criticism, may claim fair use under § 107.

For the purposes of copyright law, the heart of any parodist's claim to quote from existing material, is the use of some elements of a prior author's composition to create a new one that, at least in part, comments on that author's works. If, on the contrary, the commentary has no critical bearing on the substance or style of the original composition, which the alleged infringer merely uses to get attention or to avoid the drudgery in working up something fresh, the claim to fairness in borrowing from another's work diminishes accordingly (if it does not vanish), and other factors, like the extent of its commerciality, loom larger.[b] Parody needs to mimic an original to make its point, and so has some claim to use the creation of its victim's (or collective victims') imagination, whereas satire

[b] A parody that more loosely targets an original than the parody presented here may still be sufficiently aimed at an original work to come within our analysis of parody. If a parody whose wide dissemination in the market runs the risk of serving as a substitute for the original or licensed derivatives (see at 590–594, discussing factor four), it is more incumbent on one claiming fair use to establish the extent of transformation and the parody's critical relationship to the original. By contrast, when there is little or no risk of market substitution, whether because of the large extent of transformation of the earlier work, the new work's minimal distribution in the market, the small extent to which it borrows from an original, or other factors, taking parodic aim at an original is a less critical factor in the analysis, and looser forms of parody may be found to be fair use, as may satire with lesser justification for the borrowing than would otherwise be required.

can stand on its own two feet and so requires justification for the very act of borrowing.

The fact that parody can claim legitimacy for some appropriation does not, of course, tell either parodist or judge much about where to draw the line. Like a book review quoting the copyrighted material criticized, parody may or may not be fair use, and petitioners' suggestion that any parodic use is presumptively fair has no more justification in law or fact than the equally hopeful claim that any use for news reporting should be presumed fair, see *Harper & Row*, 471 U.S. at 561.

We have less difficulty in finding that critical element in 2 Live Crew's song than the Court of Appeals did, although having found it we will not take the further step of evaluating its quality. The threshold question when fair use is raised in defense of parody is whether a parodic character may reasonably be perceived.[c] Whether, going beyond that, parody is in good taste or bad does not and should not matter to fair use. As Justice Holmes explained, "it would be a dangerous undertaking for persons trained only to the law to constitute themselves final judges of the worth of [a work], outside of the narrowest and most obvious limits."

The Court of Appeals, however, immediately cut short the enquiry into 2 Live Crew's fair use claim by confining its treatment of the first factor essentially to one relevant fact, the commercial nature of the use. The court then inflated the significance of this fact by applying a presumption ostensibly culled from *Sony*, that "every commercial use of copyrighted material is presumptively ... unfair.... " *Sony*, 464 U.S. at 451. In giving virtually dispositive weight to the commercial nature of the parody, the Court of Appeals erred.

The language of the statute makes clear that the commercial or nonprofit educational purpose of a work is only one element of the first factor enquiry into its purpose and character. As we explained in *Harper & Row*, Congress resisted attempts to narrow the ambit of this traditional enquiry by adopting categories of presumptively fair use, and it urged courts to preserve the breadth of their traditionally ample view of the universe of relevant evidence. 471 U.S. at 561; House Report, p. 66. Accordingly, the mere fact that a use is educational and not for profit does not insulate it from a finding of infringement, any more than the commercial character of a use bars a finding of fairness. If, indeed, commerciality carried presumptive force against a finding of fairness, the presumption would swallow nearly all of the illustrative uses listed in the preamble paragraph of § 107, including news reporting, comment, criticism, teaching, scholarship, and research, since these activities "are generally conduct-

___

c The only further judgment, indeed, that a court may pass on a work goes to an assessment of whether the parodic element is slight or great, and the copying small or extensive in relation to the parodic element, for a work with slight parodic element and extensive copying will be more likely to merely "supersede the objects" of the original. See at 586–594, discussing factors three and four.

ed for profit in this country." *Harper & Row, at 592* (Brennan, J., dissenting). Congress could not have intended such a rule.

*Sony* itself called for no hard evidentiary presumption. There, we emphasized the need for a "sensitive balancing of interests," 464 U.S. at 455, n.40, noted that Congress had "eschewed a rigid, bright-line approach to fair use," *id.*, at 449, n.31, and stated that the commercial or nonprofit educational character of a work is "not conclusive," *id.*, at 448–449, but rather a fact to be "weighed along with other[s] in fair use decisions," *id.*, at 449, n.32 (quoting House Report, p. 66). The Court of Appeals's elevation of one sentence from *Sony* to a *per se* rule thus runs as much counter to *Sony* itself as to the long common-law tradition of fair use adjudication. Rather, as we explained in *Harper & Row, Sony* stands for the proposition that the "fact that a publication was commercial as opposed to nonprofit is a separate factor that tends to weigh against a finding of fair use." 471 U.S. at 562. But that is all, and the fact that even the force of that tendency will vary with the context is a further reason against elevating commerciality to hard presumptive significance.

B

The second statutory factor draws on Justice Story's expression, the "value of the materials used." *Folsom v. Marsh*, 9 F. Cas. at 348. We agree with both the District Court and the Court of Appeals that the Orbison original's creative expression for public dissemination falls within the core of the copyright's protective purposes. 754 F. Supp. at 1155–1156; 972 F.2d at 1437. This fact, however, is not much help in this case, or ever likely to help much in separating the fair use sheep from the infringing goats in a parody case, since parodies almost invariably copy publicly known, expressive works.

C

The third factor asks whether, in Justice Story's words, "the quantity and value of the materials used," are reasonable in relation to the purpose of the copying.

The District Court considered the song's parodic purpose in finding that 2 Live Crew had not helped themselves overmuch. 754 F. Supp. at 1156–1157. The Court of Appeals disagreed, stating that "while it may not be inappropriate to find that no more was taken than necessary, the copying was qualitatively substantial. . . . We conclude that taking the heart of the original and making it the heart of a new work was to purloin a substantial portion of the essence of the original." 972 F.2d at 1438.

The Court of Appeals is of course correct that this factor calls for thought not only about the quantity of the materials used, but about their quality and importance, too. We also agree with the Court of Appeals that whether "a substantial portion of the infringing work was copied verbatim" from the copyrighted work is a relevant question, see *id.*, at 565.

Where we part company with the court below is in applying these guides to parody, and in particular to parody in the song before us. When parody takes aim at a particular original work, the parody must be able to "conjure up" at least enough of that original to make the object of its critical wit recognizable. See, *e.g., Elsmere Music*, 623 F.2d at 253, n.1; *Fisher v. Dees*, 794 F.2d at 438–439. What makes for this recognition is quotation of the original's most distinctive or memorable features, which the parodist can be sure the audience will know. Once enough has been taken to assure identification, how much more is reasonable will depend, say, on the extent to which the song's overriding purpose and character is to parody the original or, in contrast, the likelihood that the parody may serve as a market substitute for the original. But using some characteristic features cannot be avoided.

We think the Court of Appeals was insufficiently appreciative of parody's need for the recognizable sight or sound when it ruled 2 Live Crew's use unreasonable as a matter of law. Copying does not become excessive in relation to parodic purpose merely because the portion taken was the original's heart. If 2 Live Crew had copied a significantly less memorable part of the original, it is difficult to see how its parodic character would have come through.

This is not, of course, to say that anyone who calls himself a parodist can skim the cream and get away scot free. In parody, as in news reporting, see *Harper & Row*, context is everything, and the question of fairness asks what else the parodist did besides go to the heart of the original. It is significant that 2 Live Crew not only copied the first line of the original, but thereafter departed markedly from the Orbison lyrics for its own ends.

D

In assessing the likelihood of significant market harm, the Court of Appeals quoted from language in *Sony* that " 'if the intended use is for commercial gain, that likelihood may be presumed. But if it is for a noncommercial purpose, the likelihood must be demonstrated.' " 972 F.2d at 1438, quoting *Sony*, 464 U.S. at 451. The court reasoned that because "the use of the copyrighted work is wholly commercial, . . . we presume that a likelihood of future harm to Acuff–Rose exists." 972 F.2d at 1438. In so doing, the court resolved the fourth factor against 2 Live Crew, just as it had the first, by applying a presumption about the effect of commercial use, a presumption which as applied here we hold to be error.

No "presumption" or inference of market harm that might find support in *Sony* is applicable to a case involving something beyond mere duplication for commercial purposes. But when the second use is transformative, market substitution is at least less certain, and market harm may not be so readily inferred. Indeed, as to parody pure and simple, it is more likely that the new work will not affect the market for the original in a way cognizable under this factor, that is, by acting as a substitute for it ("superseding [its] objects"). See Leval 1125; Patry & Perlmutter 692, 697–698. This is so because the parody and the original usually serve different market functions. Bisceglia, ASCAP, Copyright Law Symposium, No. 34, at 23.

We do not, of course, suggest that a parody may not harm the market at all, but when a lethal parody, like a scathing theater review, kills demand for the original, it does not produce a harm cognizable under the Copyright Act. Because "parody may quite legitimately aim at garroting the original, destroying it commercially as well as artistically," B. Kaplan, An Unhurried View of Copyright 69 (1967), the role of the courts is to distinguish between "biting criticism [that merely] suppresses demand [and] copyright infringement[, which] usurps it." *Fisher v. Dees*, 794 F.2d at 438.

This distinction between potentially remediable displacement and un-remediable disparagement is reflected in the rule that there is no protecti-ble derivative market for criticism. The market for potential derivative uses includes only those that creators of original works would in general develop or license others to develop. Yet the unlikelihood that creators of imagina-tive works will license critical reviews or lampoons of their own productions removes such uses from the very notion of a potential licensing market.

2 Live Crew's song comprises not only parody but also rap music, and the derivative market for rap music is a proper focus of enquiry, see *Harper & Row*, at 568; Nimmer § 13.05B. Evidence of substantial harm to it would weigh against a finding of fair use, because the licensing of derivatives is an important economic incentive to the creation of originals. The fact that a parody may impair the market for derivative uses by the very effectiveness of its critical commentary is no more relevant under copyright than the like threat to the original market.

Although 2 Live Crew submitted uncontroverted affidavits on the question of market harm to the original, neither they, nor Acuff–Rose, introduced evidence or affidavits addressing the likely effect of 2 Live Crew's parodic rap song on the market for a nonparody, rap version of "Oh, Pretty Woman." [I]t is impossible to deal with the fourth factor except by recognizing that a silent record on an important factor bearing on fair use disentitled the proponent of the defense, 2 Live Crew, to summary judg-ment. The evidentiary hole will doubtless be plugged on remand.

## A & M Records, Inc. v. Napster, Inc.

United States Court of Appeals, Ninth Circuit 2001.
239 F.3d 1004.

■ BEEZER, CIRCUIT JUDGE.

Plaintiffs are engaged in the commercial recording, distribution and sale of copyrighted musical compositions and sound recordings. The com-plaint alleges that Napster, Inc. ("Napster") is a contributory and vicarious copyright infringer. The district court preliminarily enjoined Napster "from engaging in, or facilitating others in copying, downloading, uploading, transmitting, or distributing plaintiffs' copyrighted musical compositions and sound recordings, protected by either federal or state law, without express permission of the rights owner." A & M Napster, Inc., 114 F.

Supp.2d 896, 9927 (N.D.Cal.2000). We affirm in part, reverse in part and remand.

## I

We have examined the papers submitted in support of and in response to the injunction application and it appears that Napster has designed and operates a system which permits the transmission and retention of sound recordings employing digital technology.

In 1987, the Moving Picture Experts Group set a standard file format for the storage of audio recordings in a digital format called MPEG–3, abbreviated as "MP3." Digital MP3 files are created through a process colloquially called "ripping." Ripping software allows a computer owner to copy an audio compact disk ("audio CD") directly onto a computer's hard drive by compressing the audio information on the CD into the MP3 format. The MP3's compressed format allows for rapid transmission of digital audio files from one computer to another by electronic mail or any other file transfer protocol.

Napster facilitates the transmission of MP3 files between and among its users. Through a process commonly called "peer-to-peer" file sharing, Napster allows its users to: (1) make MP3 music files stored on individual computer hard drives available for copying by other Napster users; (2) search for MP3 music files stored on other users' computers; and (3) transfer exact copies of the contents of other users' MP3 files from one computer to another via the Internet. These functions are made possible by Napster's MusicShare software, available free of charge from Napster's Internet site, and Napster's network servers and server-side software. Napster provides technical support for the indexing and searching of MP3 files, as well as for its other functions, including a "chat room," where users can meet to discuss music, and a directory where participating artists can provide information about their music.

### A.  Accessing the System

In order to copy MP3 files through the Napster system, a user must first access Napster's Internet site and download the MusicShare software to his individual computer. See http://www.Napster.com Once the software is installed, the user can access the Napster system. A first-time user is required to register with the Napster system by creating a "user name" and password.

### B.  Listing Available Files

If a registered user wants to list available files stored in his computer's hard drive on Napster for others to access, he must first create a "user library" directory on his computer's hard drive. The user then saves his MP3 files in the library directory, using self-designated file names. He next must log into the Napster system using his user name and password. His MusicShare software then searches his user library and verifies that the available files are properly formatted. If in the correct MP3 format, the names of the MP3 files will be uploaded from the user's computer to the Napster servers. The content of the MP3 files remains stored in the user's computer.

Once uploaded to the Napster servers, the user's MP3 file names are stored in a server-side "library" under the user's name and become part of a "collective directory" of files available for transfer during the time the user is logged onto the Napster system. The collective directory is fluid; it tracks users who are connected in real time, displaying only file names that are immediately accessible.

C. Searching for Available Files

Napster allows a user to locate other users' MP3 files in two ways: through Napster's search function and through its "hotlist" function.

Software located on the Napster servers maintains a "search index" of Napster's collective directory. To search the files available from Napster users currently connected to the net-work servers, the individual user accesses a form in the MusicShare software stored in his computer and enters either the name of a song or an artist as the object of the search. The form is then transmitted to a Napster server and automatically compared to the MP3 file names listed in the server's search index. Napster's server compiles a list of all MP3 file names pulled from the search index which include the same search terms entered on the search form and transmits the list to the searching user. The Napster server does not search the contents of any MP3 file; rather, the search is limited to "a text search of the file names indexed in a particular cluster. Those file names may contain typographical errors or otherwise inaccurate descriptions of the content of the files since they are designated by other users." *Napster*, 114 F. Supp. 2d at 906.

To use the "hotlist" function, the Napster user creates a list of other users' names from whom he has obtained MP3 files in the past. When logged onto Napster's servers, the system alerts the user if any user on his list (a "hotlisted user") is also logged onto the system. If so, the user can access an index of all MP3 file names in a particular hotlisted user's library and request a file in the library by selecting the file name. The contents of the hotlisted user's MP3 file are not stored on the Napster system.

D. Transferring Copies of an MP3 file

To transfer a copy of the contents of a requested MP3 file, the Napster server software obtains the Internet address of the requesting user and the Internet address of the "host user" (the user with the available files). The Napster servers then communicate the host user's Internet address to the requesting user. The requesting user's computer uses this information to establish a connection with the host user and downloads a copy of the contents of the MP3 file from one computer to the other over the Internet, "peer-to-peer." A downloaded MP3 file can be played directly from the user's hard drive using Napster's Music–Share program or other software. The file may also be transferred back onto an audio CD if the user has access to equipment designed for that purpose. In both cases, the quality of the original sound recording is slightly diminished by transfer to the MP3 format.

This architecture is described in some detail to promote an understanding of transmission mechanics as opposed to the content of the transmissions. The content is the subject of our copyright infringement analysis.

. . . .

### III

Plaintiffs claim Napster users are engaged in the wholesale reproduction and distribution of copyrighted works, all constituting direct infringement.[a] The district court agreed. We note that the district court's conclusion that plaintiffs have presented a prima facie case of direct infringement by Napster users is not presently appealed by Napster.

. . . .

### B.   Fair Use

Napster contends that its users do not directly infringe plaintiffs' copyrights because the users are engaged in fair use of the material. See 17 U.S.C. § 107. Napster identifies specific alleged fair uses: sampling, where users make temporary copies of a work before purchasing; [and] space-shifting, where users access a sound recording through the Napster system that they already own in audio CD format.

The district court considered factors listed in 17 U.S.C. § 107, which guide a court's fair use determination. The district court first conducted a general analysis of Napster system uses under § 107, and then applied its reasoning to the alleged fair uses identified by Napster. The district court concluded that Napster users are not fair users. We agree. We first address the court's overall fair use analysis.

1.   Purpose and Character of the Use

This factor focuses on whether the new work merely replaces the object of the original creation or instead adds a further purpose or different character. In other words, this factor asks "whether and to what extent the new work is 'transformative.' " See *Campbell v. Acuff–Rose Music, Inc.,* 510 U.S. 569, 579 (1994).

The district court first concluded that downloading MP3 files does not transform the copyrighted work. *Napster,* 114 F. Supp. 2d at 912. This conclusion is supportable. Courts have been reluctant to find fair use when an original work is merely retransmitted in a different medium. [Citations omitted].

This "purpose and character" element also requires the district court to determine whether the allegedly infringing use is commercial or noncommercial. See *Campbell,* 510 U.S. at 584–85. A commercial use weighs against a finding of fair use but is not conclusive on the issue. *Id.* The

[a] Secondary liability for copyright infringement does not exist in the absence of direct infringement by a third party.

district court determined that Napster users engage in commercial use of the copyrighted materials largely because (1) "a host user sending a file cannot be said to engage in a personal use when distributing that file to an anonymous requester" and (2) "Napster users get for free something they would ordinarily have to buy." *Napster*, 114 F. Supp. 2d at 912. The district court's findings are not clearly erroneous.

Direct economic benefit is not required to demonstrate a commercial use. Rather, repeated and exploitative copying of copyrighted works, even if the copies are not offered for sale, may constitute a commercial use. See *Worldwide Church of God v. Philadelphia Church of God*, 227 F.3d 1110, 1118 (9th Cir.2000) (stating that church that copied religious text for its members "unquestionably profited" from the unauthorized "distribution and use of [the text] without having to account to the copyright holder").; *American Geophysical Union v. Texaco, Inc.*, 60 F.3d 913, 922 (2d Cir.1994) (finding that researchers at for-profit laboratory gained indirect economic advantage by photocopying copyrighted scholarly articles). In the record before us, commercial use is demonstrated by a showing that repeated and exploitative unauthorized copies of copyrighted works were made to save the expense of purchasing authorized copies. See *Worldwide Church*, 227 F.3d at 1117–18; *Sega Enters. Ltd. v. MAPHIA*, 857 F. Supp. 679, 687 (N.D.Cal.1994) (finding commercial use when individuals downloaded copies of video games "to avoid having to buy video game cartridges"). Plaintiffs made such a showing before the district court.[b]

2.   The Nature of the Use

Works that are creative in nature are "closer to the core of intended copyright protection" than are more fact-based works. See *Campbell*, 510 U.S. at 586. The district court determined that plaintiffs' "copyrighted musical compositions and sound recordings are creative in nature ... which cuts against a finding of fair use under the second factor." *Napster*, 114 F. Supp. 2d at 913. We find no error in the district court's conclusion.

3.   The Portion Used

While "wholesale copying does not preclude fair use per se", copying an entire work "militates against a finding of fair use." *Worldwide Church*, 227 F.3d at 1118 (quoting *Hustler Magazine, Inc. v. Moral Majority, Inc.*, 796 F.2d 1148, 1155 (9th Cir.1986)). The district court determined that Napster users engage in "wholesale copying" of copyrighted work because file transfer necessarily "involves copying the entirety of the copyrighted work." *Napster*, 114 F. Supp. 2d at 913. We agree. We note, however, that under certain circumstances, a court will conclude that a use is fair even when the protected work is copied in its entirety. See, e.g., *Sony Corp. v. Universal City Studios, Inc.*, 464 U.S. 417, 449–50 (1984) (acknowledging that fair use of time-shifting necessarily involved making a full copy of a protected work).

[b] Napster counters that even if certain users engage in commercial use by downloading instead of purchasing the music, space-shifting and sampling are nevertheless non-commercial in nature. We address this contention in our discussion of these specific uses.

that fair use of time-shifting necessarily involved making a full copy of a protected work).

4. Effect of Use on Market

"Fair use, when properly applied, is limited to copying by others which does not materially impair the marketability of the work which is copied." *Harper & Row Publishers, Inc. v. Nation Enters.*, 471 U.S. 539, 566–67, 85 L. Ed. 2d 588, 105 S. Ct. 2218 (1985). "The importance of this [fourth] factor will vary, not only with the amount of harm, but also with the relative strength of the showing on the other factors." *Campbell*, 510 U.S. at 591 n.21. The proof required to demonstrate present or future market harm varies with the purpose and character of the use:

> A challenge to a noncommercial use of a copy-righted work requires proof either that the particular use is harmful, or that if it should become wide-spread, it would adversely affect the potential market for the copyrighted work. ... If the intended use is for commercial gain, that likelihood [of market harm] may be presumed. But if it is for a noncommercial purpose, the likelihood must be demonstrated.

*Sony*, 464 U.S. at 451 (emphases added).

Addressing this factor, the district court concluded that Napster harms the market in "at least" two ways: it reduces audio CD sales among college students and it "raises barriers to plaintiffs' entry into the market for the digital downloading of music." *Napster*, 114 F. Supp. 2d at 913. The district court relied on evidence plaintiffs submitted to show that Napster use harms the market for their copyrighted musical compositions and sound recordings. In a separate memorandum and order regarding the parties' objections to the expert reports, the district court examined each report, finding some more appropriate and probative than others. *A & M Records, Inc. v. Napster, Inc.*, 114 F. Supp. 2d 896, 2000 WL 1170106 (N.D. Cal. 2000).

The district court's careful consideration of defendant's objections to ... [the plaintiffs'] reports and decision to rely on the reports for specific issues demonstrates a proper exercise of discretion in addition to a correct application of the fair use doctrine. Defendant has failed to show any basis for disturbing the district court's findings.

We, therefore, conclude that the district court made sound findings related to Napster's deleterious effect on the present and future digital download market. Moreover, lack of harm to an established market cannot deprive the copyright holder of the right to develop alternative markets for the works. See *L.A. Times v. Free Republic*, 54 U.S.P.Q.2d (BNA) 1453, 1469–71 (C.D.Cal.2000) (stating that online market for plaintiff newspapers' articles was harmed because plaintiffs demonstrated that "[defendants] are attempting to exploit the market for viewing their articles online"); see also *UMG Recordings*, 92 F. Supp. 2d at 352 ("Any allegedly positive impact of defendant's activities on plaintiffs' prior market in no way frees defendant to usurp a further market that directly derives from reproduction of the plaintiffs' copyrighted works."). Here, similar to *L.A.*

*Times* and *UMG Recordings*, the record supports the district court's finding that the "record company plaintiffs have already expended considerable funds and effort to commence Internet sales and licensing for digital downloads." 114 F. Supp. 2d at 915. Having digital downloads available for free on the Napster system necessarily harms the copyright holders' attempts to charge for the same downloads.

We next address Napster's identified uses of sampling and space-shifting.

### 5. Identified Uses

Napster maintains that its identified uses of sampling and space-shifting were wrongly excluded as fair uses by the district court.

### a. Sampling

Napster contends that its users download MP3 files to "sample" the music in order to decide whether to purchase the recording. Napster argues that the district court: (1) erred in concluding that sampling is a commercial use because it conflated a noncommercial use with a personal use; (2) erred in determining that sampling adversely affects the market for plaintiffs' copyrighted music, a requirement if the use is non-commercial; and (3) erroneously concluded that sampling is not a fair use because it determined that samplers may also engage in other infringing activity.

The district court determined that sampling remains a commercial use even if some users eventually purchase the music. We find no error in the district court's determination. Plaintiffs have established that they are likely to succeed in proving that even authorized temporary downloading of individual songs for sampling purposes is commercial in nature. See *Napster*, 114 F. Supp. 2d at 913. The record supports a finding that free promotional downloads are highly regulated by the record company plaintiffs and that the companies collect royalties for song samples available on retail Internet sites. *Id.* Evidence relied on by the district court demonstrates that the free downloads provided by the record companies consist of thirty-to-sixty second samples or are full songs programmed to "time out," that is, exist only for a short time on the downloader's computer. *Id.* at 913–14. In comparison, Napster users download a full, free and permanent copy of the recording. *Id.* at 914–15. The determination by the district court as to the commercial purpose and character of sampling is not clearly erroneous.

The district court further found that both the market for audio CDs and market for online distribution are adversely affected by Napster's service. As stated in our discussion of the district court's general fair use analysis: the court did not abuse its discretion when it found that, overall, Napster has an adverse impact on the audio CD and digital download markets. Contrary to Napster's assertion that the district court failed to specifically address the market impact of sampling, the district court determined that "even if the type of sampling supposedly done on Napster were a non-commercial use, plaintiffs have demonstrated a substantial likelihood that it would adversely affect the potential market for their copyrighted works if it became widespread." *Napster*, 114 F. Supp. 2d at 914. The record supports the district court's preliminary determinations that: (1) the more music that sampling users download, the less likely they are to eventually purchase the recordings on audio CD; and (2) even if the audio CD market is not harmed, Napster has adverse effects on the developing digital download market.

Napster further argues that the district court erred in rejecting its evidence that the users' downloading of "samples" increases or tends to increase audio CD sales. The district court, however, correctly noted that "any potential enhancement of plaintiffs' sales ... would not tip the fair use analysis conclusively in favor of defendant." *Id.* at 914. We agree that increased sales of copyrighted material attributable to unauthorized use should not deprive the copyright holder of the right to license the material. Nor does positive impact in one market, here the audio CD market, deprive the copyright holder of the right to develop identified alternative markets, here the digital download market. See 114 F. Supp. 2d at 1469–71.

We find no error in the district court's factual findings or abuse of discretion in the court's conclusion that plaintiffs will likely prevail in establishing that sampling does not constitute a fair use.

### b. Space–Shifting

Napster also maintains that space-shifting is a fair use. Space-shifting occurs when a Napster user downloads MP3 music files in order to listen to music he already owns on audio CD. See *Id.* at 915–16. Napster asserts that we have already held that space-shifting of musical compositions and sound recordings is a fair use. See *Recording Indus. Ass'n of Am. v. Diamond Multimedia Sys., Inc.*, 180 F.3d 1072, 1079 (9th Cir.1999) ("Rio [a portable MP3 player] merely makes copies in order to render portable, or 'space-shift', those files that already reside on a user's hard drive. ... Such copying is a paradigmatic noncommercial personal use."). See also generally *Sony*, 464 U.S. at 423 (holding that "time-shifting," where a video tape recorder owner records a television show for later viewing, is a fair use).

We conclude that the district court did not err when it refused to apply the "shifting" analyses of *Sony* and *Diamond*. Both *Diamond* and *Sony* are inapposite because the methods of shifting in these cases did not also simultaneously involve distribution of the copyrighted material to the general public; the time or space-shifting of copyrighted material exposed the material only to the original user. In *Diamond*, for example, the copyrighted music was transferred from the user's computer hard drive to the user's portable MP3 player. So too *Sony*, where "the majority of VCR purchasers ... did not distribute taped television broadcasts, but merely enjoyed them at home." *Napster*, 114 F. Supp. 2d at 913. Conversely, it is obvious that once a user lists a copy of music he already owns on the Napster system in order to access the music from another location, the song becomes "available to millions of other individuals," not just the original CD owner.

We find no error in the district court's determination that plaintiffs will likely succeed in establishing that Napster users do not have a fair use defense. Accordingly, we next address whether Napster is secondarily liable for the direct infringement under two doctrines of copyright law: contributory copyright infringement and vicarious copyright infringement.

## IV

We first address plaintiffs' claim that Napster is liable for contributory copyright infringement. Traditionally, "one who, with knowledge of the infringing activity, induces, causes or materially contributes to the infringing conduct of another, may be held liable as a 'contributory' infringer.". *Gershwin Publ'g Corp. v. Columbia Artists Mgmt., Inc.*, 443 F.2d 1159, 1162 (2d Cir.1971). Put differently, liability exists if the defendant engages in "personal conduct that encourages or assists the infringement." *Matthew Bender & Co. v. West Publ'g Co.*, 158 F.3d 693, 706 (2d Cir.1998).

The district court determined that plaintiffs in all likelihood would establish Napster's liability as a contributory infringer. The district court did not err; Napster, by its conduct, knowingly encourages and assists the infringement of plaintiffs' copyrights.

### A. Knowledge

Contributory liability requires that the secondary infringer "know or have reason to know" of direct infringement. [citations omitted]. The district court found that Napster had both actual and constructive knowledge that its users exchanged copyrighted music. The district court also concluded that the law does not require knowledge of "specific acts of infringement" and rejected Napster's contention that because the company cannot distinguish infringing from noninfringing files, it does not "know" of the direct infringement. 114 F. Supp. 2d at 917.

It is apparent from the record that Napster has knowledge, both actual and constructive,[c] of direct infringement. Napster claims that it is nevertheless protected from contributory liability by the teaching of *Sony Corp. v. Universal City Studios, Inc.*, 464 U.S. 417, 78 L. Ed. 2d 574, 104 S. Ct. 774 (1984). We disagree. We observe that Napster's actual, specific knowledge of direct infringement renders Sony's holding of limited assistance to Napster. We are compelled to make a clear distinction between the architecture of the Napster system and Napster's conduct in relation to the operational capacity of the system.

[c] The district court found actual knowledge because: (1) a document authored by Napster co-founder Sean Parker mentioned "the need to remain ignorant of users' real names and IP addresses 'since they are exchanging pirated music' "; and (2) the Recording Industry Association of America ("RIAA") informed Napster of more than 12,000 infringing files, some of which are still available. 114 F. Supp. 2d at 918. The district court found constructive knowledge because: (a) Napster executives have recording industry experience; (b) they have enforced intellectual property rights in other instances; (c) Napster executives have downloaded copyrighted songs from the system; and (d) they have promoted the site with "screen shots listing infringing files." *Id.* at 919.

The Sony Court refused to hold the manufacturer and retailers of video tape recorders liable for contributory infringement despite evidence that such machines could be and were used to infringe plaintiffs' copyrighted television shows. Sony stated that if liability "is to be imposed on petitioners in this case, it must rest on the fact that they have sold equipment with constructive knowledge of the fact that their customers may use that equipment to make unauthorized copies of copy-righted material." *Id.* at 439. The Sony Court declined to impute the requisite level of knowledge where the defendants made and sold equipment capable of both infringing and "substantial noninfringing uses." *Id.* at 442 (adopting a modified "staple article of commerce" doctrine from patent law).

We are bound to follow Sony, and will not impute the requisite level of knowledge to Napster merely because peer-to-peer file sharing technology may be used to infringe plaintiffs' copyrights. We depart from the reasoning of the district court that Napster failed to demonstrate that its system is capable of commercially significant noninfringing uses. See *Napster*, 114 F. Supp. 2d at 916, 917–18. The district court improperly confined the use analysis to current uses, ignoring the system's capabilities. See generally *Sony*, 464 U.S. at 442–43 (framing inquiry as whether the video tape recorder is "capable of commercially significant noninfringing uses") (emphasis added). Consequently, the district court placed undue weight on the proportion of current infringing use as compared to current and future noninfringing use. Nonetheless, whether we might arrive at a different result is not the issue here. The instant appeal occurs at an early point in the proceedings and "the fully developed factual record may be materially different from that initially before the district court. . . ." *Id.* at 753. Regardless of the number of Napster's infringing versus noninfringing uses, the evidentiary record here supported the district court's finding that plaintiffs would likely prevail in establishing that Napster knew or had reason to know of its users' infringement of plaintiffs' copyrights.

This analysis is similar to that of Religious Technology Center v. Netcom On–Line Communication Services, Inc., which suggests that in an online context, evidence of actual knowledge of specific acts of infringement is required to hold a computer system operator liable for contributory copyright infringement. 907 F. Supp. at 1371. Netcom considered the potential contributory copyright liability of a computer bulletin board operator whose system supported the posting of infringing material. *Id.* at 1374. The court found that a disputed issue of fact existed as to whether the operator had sufficient knowledge of infringing activity. *Id.* at 1374–75.

We agree that if a computer system operator learns of specific infringing material available on his system and fails to purge such material from the system, the operator knows of and contributes to direct infringement. See *Netcom*, 907 F. Supp. at 1374. Conversely, absent any specific information which identifies infringing activity, a computer system operator cannot be liable for contributory infringement merely because the structure of the system allows for the exchange of copyrighted material. See *Sony*, 464 U.S. at 436, 442–43. To enjoin simply because a computer network allows for infringing use would, in our opinion, violate Sony and potentially restrict activity unrelated to infringing use.

We nevertheless conclude that sufficient knowledge exists to impose contributory liability when linked to demonstrated infringing use of the Napster system. The record supports the district court's finding that Napster has actual knowledge that specific infringing material is available using its system, that it could block access to the system by suppliers of the infringing material, and that it failed to remove the material. See *Napster*, 114 F. Supp. 2d at 918, 920–21.

## B.   Material Contribution

Under the facts as found by the district court, Napster materially contributes to the infringing activity. Relying on *Fonovisa*, the district court concluded that "without the support services defendant provides, Napster users could not find and download the music they want with the ease of which defendant boasts." *Napster*, 114 F. Supp. 2d at 919–20. We agree that Napster provides "the site and facilities" for direct infringement. See *Fonovisa*, 76 F.3d at 264. The district court correctly applied the reasoning in *Fonovisa*, and properly found that Napster materially contributes to direct infringement.

We affirm the district court's conclusion that plaintiffs have demonstrated a likelihood of success on the merits of the contributory copyright infringement claim.

## V

We turn to the question whether Napster engages in vicarious copyright infringement. Vicarious copyright liability is an "outgrowth" of respondeat superior. *Fonovisa*, 76 F.3d at 262. In the context of copyright law, vicarious liability extends beyond an employer/employee relationship to cases in which a defendant "has the right and ability to supervise the infringing activity and also has a direct financial interest in such activities." *Id.* (quoting *Gershwin*, 443 F.2d at 1162).

## A.   Financial Benefit

The district court determined that plaintiffs had demonstrated they would likely succeed in establishing that Napster has a direct financial interest in the infringing activity. *Napster*, 114 F. Supp. 2d at 921–22. We agree. Financial benefit exists where the availability of infringing material "acts as a 'draw' for customers." *Fonovisa*, 76 F.3d at 263–64 (stating that financial benefit may be shown "where infringing performances enhance the attractiveness of a venue"). Ample evidence supports the district court's finding that Napster's future revenue is directly dependent upon "increases in user-base." More users register with the Napster system as the "quality and quantity of available music increases." 114 F. Supp. 2d at 902. We conclude that the district court did not err in determining that Napster financially benefits from the availability of protected works on its system.

## B. Supervision

The district court determined that Napster has the right and ability to supervise its users' conduct. *Napster*, 114 F. Supp. 2d at 920–21. We agree in part.

The ability to block infringers' access to a particular environment for any reason whatsoever is evidence of the right and ability to supervise. See *Fonovisa*, 76 F.3d at 262. Here, plaintiffs have demonstrated that Napster retains the right to control access to its system. Napster has an express reservation of rights policy, stating on its website that it expressly reserves the "right to refuse service and terminate accounts in [its] discretion, including, but not limited to, if Napster believes that user conduct violates applicable law ... or for any reason in Napster's sole discretion, with or without cause."

To escape imposition of vicarious liability, the reserved right to police must be exercised to its fullest extent. Turning a blind eye to detectable acts of infringement for the sake of profit gives rise to liability.

The district court correctly determined that Napster had the right and ability to police its system and failed to exercise that right to prevent the exchange of copyrighted material. The district court, however, failed to recognize that the boundaries of the premises that Napster "controls and patrols" are limited. Put differently, Napster's reserved "right and ability" to police is cabined by the system's current architecture. As shown by the record, the Napster system does not "read" the content of indexed files, other than to check that they are in the proper MP3 format.

Napster, however, has the ability to locate infringing material listed on its search indices, and the right to terminate users' access to the system. The file name indices, therefore, are within the "premises" that Napster has the ability to police. We recognize that the files are user-named and may not match copyrighted material exactly (for example, the artist or song could be spelled wrong). For Napster to function effectively, however, file names must reasonably or roughly correspond to the material contained in the files, otherwise no user could ever locate any desired music. As a practical matter, Napster, its users and the record company plaintiffs have equal access to infringing material by employing Napster's "search function."

Our review of the record requires us to accept the district court's conclusion that plaintiffs have demonstrated a likelihood of success on the merits of the vicarious copyright infringement claim. Napster's failure to police the system's "premises," combined with a showing that Napster financially benefits from the continuing availability of infringing files on its system, leads to the imposition of vicarious liability.

. . . .

## VIII

. . . .

The district court correctly recognized that a preliminary injunction against Napster's participation in copyright infringement is not only warranted but required. We believe, however, that the scope of the injunction needs modification in light of our opinion. Specifically, we reiterate that contributory liability may potentially be imposed only to the extent that Napster: (1) receives reasonable knowledge of specific infringing files with copyrighted musical compositions and sound recordings; (2) knows or should know that such files are available on the Napster system; and (3) fails to act to prevent viral distribution of the works. See *Netcom*, 907 F. Supp. at 1374–75. The mere existence of the Napster system, absent actual notice and Napster's demonstrated failure to remove the offending material, is insufficient to impose contributory liability. See *Sony*, 464 U.S. at 442–43.

Conversely, Napster may be vicariously liable when it fails to affirmatively use its ability to patrol its system and preclude access to potentially infringing files listed in its search index. Napster has both the ability to use its search function to identify infringing musical recordings and the right to bar participation of users who engage in the transmission of infringing files.

The preliminary injunction which we stayed is overbroad because it places on Napster the entire burden of ensuring that no "copying, downloading, uploading, transmitting, or distributing" of plaintiffs' works occur on the system. As stated, we place the burden on plaintiffs to provide notice to Napster of copyrighted works and files containing such works available on the Napster system before Napster has the duty to disable access to the offending content. Napster, however, also bears the burden of policing the system within the limits of the system. Here, we recognize that this is not an exact science in that the files are user named. In crafting the injunction on remand, the district court should recognize that Napster's system does not currently appear to allow Napster access to users' MP3 files.

AFFIRMED IN PART, REVERSED IN PART AND REMANDED.

## Suntrust Bank v. Houghton Mifflin Company

United States Court of Appeals, Eleventh Circuit, 2001.
268 F.3d 1257.

■ BIRCH, CIRCUIT JUDGE:

In this opinion, we decide whether publication of The Wind Done Gone ("TWDG"), a fictional work admittedly based on Margaret Mitchell's Gone With the Wind ("GWTW"), should be enjoined from publication based on alleged copyright violations. The district court granted a preliminary injunction against publication of TWDG because it found that Plaintiff–Appellee SunTrust Bank ("SunTrust") met the four-part test governing preliminary injunctions. We VACATE the injunction and REMAND for consideration of the remaining claims.

## I. BACKGROUND

A. Procedural History

SunTrust is the trustee of the Mitchell Trust, which holds the copyright in GWTW. Since its publication in 1936, GWTW has become one of the best-selling books in the world, second in sales only to the Bible. The Mitchell Trust has actively managed the copyright, authorizing derivative works and a variety of commercial items. It has entered into a contract authorizing, under specified conditions, a second sequel to GWTW to be published by St. Martin's Press. The Mitchell Trust maintains the copyright in all of the derivative works as well. See 17 U.S.C. § 103.

Alice Randall, the author of TWDG, persuasively claims that her novel is a critique of GWTW's depiction of slavery and the Civil–War era American South. To this end, she appropriated the characters, plot and major scenes from GWTW into the first half of TWDG. According to SunTrust, TWDG "(1) explicitly refers to [GWTW] in its foreword; (2) copies core characters, character traits, and relationships from [GWTW]; (3) copies and summarizes famous scenes and other elements of the plot from [GWTW]; and (4) copies verbatim dialogues and descriptions from [GWTW]." *SunTrust Bank v. Houghton Mifflin Co.*, 136 F. Supp. 2d 1357, 1364 (N.D.Ga. 2001), vacated, 252 F.3d 1165 (11th Cir. 2001). Defendant–Appellant Houghton Mifflin, the publisher of TWDG, does not contest the first three allegations,[a] but nonetheless argues that there is no substantial similarity between the two works or, in the alternative, that the doctrine of fair use protects TWDG because it is primarily a parody of GWTW.

## II. DISCUSSION

Our primary focus at this stage of the case is on the appropriateness of the injunctive relief granted by the district court. In our analysis, we must evaluate the merits of SunTrust's copyright infringement claim, including Houghton Mifflin's affirmative defense of fair use. As we assess the fair-use defense, we examine to what extent a critic may use a work to communicate her criticism of the work without infringing the copyright in that work.

[T]he narrower question in this case is to what extent a critic may use the protected elements of an original work of authorship to communicate her criticism without infringing the copyright in that work. As will be discussed below, this becomes essentially an analysis of the fair use factors.

Before considering a claimed fair-use defense based on parody, however, the Supreme Court has required that we ensure that "a parodic character may reasonably be perceived" in the allegedly infringing work. *Id.* at 582, 114 S. Ct. at 1173. The Supreme Court's definition of parody in Campbell, however, is somewhat vague. On the one hand, the Court suggests that the aim of parody is "comic effect or ridicule," but it then

[a] Houghton Mifflin denies that there are passages from GWTW copied verbatim in TWDG.

proceeds to discuss parody more expansively in terms of its "commentary" on the original. *Id.* at 580, 114 S. Ct. at 1172. In light of the admonition in Campbell that courts should not judge the quality of the work or the success of the attempted humor in discerning its parodic character, we choose to take the broader view. For purposes of our fair-use analysis, we will treat a work as a parody if its aim is to comment upon or criticize a prior work by appropriating elements of the original in creating a new artistic, as opposed to scholarly or journalistic, work. Under this definition, the parodic character of TWDG is clear. TWDG is not a general commentary upon the Civil–War-era American South, but a specific criticism of and rejoinder to the depiction of slavery and the relationships between blacks and whites in GWTW. The fact that Randall chose to convey her criticisms of GWTW through a work of fiction, which she contends is a more powerful vehicle for her message than a scholarly article, does not, in and of itself, deprive TWDG of fair-use protection. We therefore proceed to an analysis of the four fair-use factors.

i.  Purpose and Character of the Work

The first factor in the fair-use analysis, the purpose and character of the allegedly infringing work, has several facets. The first is whether TWDG serves a commercial purpose or nonprofit educational purpose. § 107(1). Despite whatever educational function TWDG may be able to lay claim to, it is undoubtedly a commercial product.[b] The fact that TWDG was published for profit is the first factor weighing against a finding of fair use. *Id.*, 105 S. Ct. at 2231. However, TWDG's for-profit status is strongly overshadowed and outweighed in view of its highly transformative use of GWTW's copyrighted elements.

The second factor in the "purpose and character" analysis relevant to this case is to what extent TWDG's use of copyrighted elements of GWTW can be said to be "transformative." The issue of transformation is a double-edged sword in this case. On the one hand, the story of Cynara and her perception of the events in TWDG certainly adds new "expression, meaning, [and] message" to GWTW. From another perspective, however, TWDG's success as a pure work of fiction depends heavily on copyrighted elements appropriated from GWTW to carry its own plot forward.

However, as noted above, TWDG is more than an abstract, pure fictional work. It is principally and purposefully a critical statement that seeks to rebut and destroy the perspective, judgments, and mythology of GWTW. Randall's literary goal is to explode the romantic, idealized portrait of the antebellum South during and after the Civil War.

In light of this, we find it difficult to conclude that Randall simply tried to "avoid the drudgery in working up something fresh." *Campbell*, 510 U.S. at 580, 114 S. Ct. at 1172. It is hard to imagine how Randall could have specifically criticized GWTW without depending heavily upon copyrighted

---

[b] Randall did not choose to publish her work of fiction on the internet free to all the world to read; rather, she chose a method of publication designed to generate economic profit.

ASSIGNMENT 11 PUBLIC ACCESS CONSIDERATIONS

elements of that book. A parody is a work that seeks to comment upon or criticize another work by appropriating elements of the original. Thus, Randall has fully employed those conscripted elements from GWTW to make war against it.

While "transformative use is not absolutely necessary for a finding of fair use, . . . the more transformative the new work, the less will be the significance of other factors." *Id.*, 114 S. Ct. at 1171 (internal citations omitted). In the case of TWDG, consideration of this factor certainly militates in favor of a finding of fair use, and, informs our analysis of the other factors, particularly the fourth, as discussed below.

ii. Nature of the Copyrighted Work

GWTW is undoubtedly entitled to the greatest degree of protection as an original work of fiction. This factor is given little weight in parody cases, however.

iii. Amount and Substantiality of the Portion Used

GWTW is one of the most famous, popular, and enduring American novels ever written. Given the fame of the work and its primary characters, SunTrust argues that very little reference is required to conjure up GWTW. As we have already indicated in our discussion of substantial similarity, TWDG appropriates a substantial portion of the protected elements of GWTW. Houghton Mifflin argues that TWDG takes nothing from GWTW that does not serve a parodic purpose, the crux of the argument being that a large number of characters had to be taken from GWTW because each represents a different ideal or stereotype that requires commentary, and that the work as a whole could not be adequately commented upon without revisiting substantial portions of the plot, including its most famous scenes. Houghton Mifflin's argument is similar to that made by the defendants in Harper & Row, who argued for "expanding the doctrine of fair use to create what amounts to a public figure exception to copyright." 471 U.S. at 560, 105 S. Ct. at 2230. To the extent Houghton Mifflin argues for extra latitude in copying from GWTW because of its fame, the Supreme Court has squarely foreclosed any such privilege. *Id.* at 559, 105 S. Ct. at 2229–30. Notably, however, the Court did not go so far as to grant well-known works a special, higher copyright status either.

There are numerous instances in which TWDG appropriates elements of GWTW and then transforms them for the purpose of commentary.

On the other hand, however, we are told that not all of TWDG's takings from GWTW are clearly justified as commentary. SunTrust contends that TWDG, at least at the margins, takes more of the protected elements of GWTW than was necessary to serve a parodic function.

[W]e are presented with conflicting and opposing arguments relative to the amount taken and whether it was too much or a necessary amount.

Based upon this record at this juncture, we cannot determine in any conclusive way whether " 'the quantity and value of the materials used' " are reasonable in relation to the purpose of the copying. *Cambpell*, 510 U.S. at 586, 114 S. Ct. at 1175 (quoting *Folsom*, 9 F. Cas. at 348).

iv. Effect on the Market Value of the Original

The final fair-use factor requires us to consider the effect that the publication of TWDG will have on the market for or value of SunTrust's copyright in GWTW, including the potential harm it may cause to the market for derivative works based on GWTW. *Campbell*, 510 U.S. at 590, 114 S. Ct. at 1177.

As for the potential market, SunTrust proffered evidence in the district court of the value of its copyright in GWTW. Several derivative works of GWTW have been authorized.

SunTrust focuses on the value of GWTW and its derivatives, but fails to address and offers little evidence or argument to demonstrate that TWDG would supplant demand for SunTrust's licensed derivatives.

In contrast, the evidence proffered in support of the fair use defense specifically and correctly focused on market substitution and demonstrates why Randall's book is unlikely to displace sales of GWTW. Thus, we conclude, based on the current record, that SunTrust's evidence falls far short of establishing that TWDG or others like it will act as market substitutes for GWTW or will significantly harm its derivatives. Accordingly, the fourth fair use factor weighs in favor of TWDG.

We reject the district court's conclusion that SunTrust has established its likelihood of success on the merits. To the contrary, based upon our analysis of the fair use factors we find, at this juncture, TWDG is entitled to a fair-use defense.

Accordingly, we vacate the district court's injunction.

■ MARCUS, CIRCUIT JUDGE, specially concurring:

I concur in Judge Birch's thoughtful and thorough opinion but write separately to emphasize that, on this limited record, SunTrust has fallen well short of establishing a likelihood of success on its copyright infringement claim. I stress three points. First, the district court erred by finding that the critical or parodic element of The Wind Done Gone is anything but clear-cut. Far from amounting to "unabated piracy," 136 F. Supp. 2d 1357, 1369 (N.D. Ga. 2001), The Wind Done Gone is unequivocally parody, as both Judge Birch and the Supreme Court in *Campbell v. Acuff–Rose Music, Inc.*, 510 U.S. 569, 127 L. Ed. 2d 500, 114 S. Ct. 1164 (1994), define that term. Indeed, the book is critical by constitution, its main aim being to shatter Gone With the Wind's window on life in the antebellum and Civil War South. Second, in service of this parodic design, Randall radically reshapes what she borrows from Mitchell. I would thus go even further than Judge Birch in underscoring the transformative nature of Randall's book; the "purpose and nature" prong of the fair use analysis is not a close call, in my view. Third, the preliminary record, if anything, suggests that The Wind Done Gone will not act as a substitute for Mitchell's original. What little evidence we have before us indicates that these two books aim at different readerships; to the extent that there is any overlap between these respective markets, further factfinding may well reveal that these two books will act as complements rather than substitutes.

The Wind Done Gone's critical nature is clearer than that of other works courts have found to be protected parodies. This case does not involve a pop song that simply "comments on the naivete of the original of an earlier day." *Campbell*, 510 U.S. at 583.

The two books' shared subject matter simply helps demonstrate how The Wind Done Gone's critical character is more pronounced than many protected parodies. Our analysis might have been different had we faced a conflict between two literary worldviews of less perfect polarity, for example, or two works that differed over a matter of less sharp controversy. As Judge Birch explains in detail, though, The Wind Done Gone's plain object is to make war on Gone with the Wind's specific outlook—on a topic that itself tends to elicit no small comment and criticism.

Had Randall chosen to write The Wind Done Gone from the point of view of one of Mitchell's original characters, for example, and done no more than put a new gloss on the familiar tale without criticizing or commenting on its fundamental theme and spirit, Houghton Mifflin's case would have been much tougher.[a]

The district court recognized that "the two works ... present polar viewpoints," yet concluded that The Wind Done Gone recreates "the same fictional world, described in the same way and inhabited by the same people, who are doing the same things." 136 F. Supp. 2d at 1369. Of course, both works are set in the antebellum South, but The Wind Done Gone creates an alter universe described in a wholly different style, and inhabited by shrewd slaves who manipulate incompetent masters and free blacks who thrive independent of the white plantation system. Like a political, thematic, and stylistic negative, The Wind Done Gone inverts Gone With the Wind's portrait of race relations of the place and era.

Given this stark contrast, I would go further than Judge Birch in stressing the transformative nature of Randall's book.

---

[a] It is hazardous to speculate too much about the legality of various hypothetical parodies, given the many forms literary parody may take, and the levels of sophistication it may reach. See Margaret A. Rose, Parody: Ancient, Modern, and Post–Modern 36–38 (1993) (describing an array of parodic literary techniques and "signals"). The irony and self-awareness common in contemporary literature, in particular, may one day pose difficulties for the fair use doctrine. It is not hard to imagine a copyrighted story that parodies itself by design, or an author who makes a career out of parodying his own work in each subsequent one. (Vladimir Nabokov, among others, hinted at the potential for such practices. See, e.g., Vladimir Nabokov, Pale Fire (1962) (a novel consisting of a poem and substantial prose commentary on that poem).) Suppose that this hypothetical author in turn becomes the target of parody by another. Could the second author's work be said to usurp demand for the original author's self-parody? Here, we face a much simpler problem: Gone With the Wind lacks any apparent self-directed irony, and Randall's attack on it is just as straight-forward.

# United States of America v. Elcom Ltd.

United States District Court, N.D. Cal., 2002.
203 F.Supp.2d 1111.

■ RONALD M. WHYTE

## BACKGROUND

1.   The Technology: eBooks and the AEBPR

Adobe Systems is a software company headquartered in San Jose, California. Adobe's Acrobat eBook Reader product provides the technology for the reading of books in digital form (i.e., electronic books, or "ebooks") on personal computers. Use of the Adobe eBook format allows publishers or distributors of electronic books to control the subsequent distribution of the ebook, typically by limiting the distribution to those who pay for a copy. These restrictions are imposed by the publisher's use of the Adobe Content Server, which allows the publisher to grant or withhold a range of privileges from the consumer. For example, the ebook publisher may choose whether the consumer will be able to copy the ebook, whether the ebook can be printed to paper (in whole, in part, or not at all), whether the "lending function" is enabled to allow the user to lend the ebook to another computer on the same network of computers, and whether to permit the ebook to be read audibly by a speech synthesizer program. Id. P8. When a consumer purchases an ebook formatted for Adobe Acrobat eBook Reader from an Internet website, the ebook is downloaded directly to the consumer's computer from the ebook distributor's Adobe Content Server.[a] The ebook is accompanied by an electronic "voucher" which is recognized and read by the Adobe Acrobat eBook Reader,[b] which then "knows" that the copy of the ebook can only be read on the computer onto which it has been downloaded. Id. P9. Thus, typically, the purchaser of an ebook may only read the ebook on the computer onto which the ebook was downloaded but may not e-mail or copy the ebook to another computer. The user may or may not be able to print the ebook in paper form or have it audibly read by the computer. Id. PP5–9.

The indictment alleges that "when an ebook purchased for viewing in the Adobe eBook Reader format was sold by the publisher or distributor, the publisher or distributor of the ebook could authorize or limit the purchaser's ability to copy, distribute, print, or have the text read audibly by the computer. Adobe designed the eBook Reader to permit the management of such digital rights so that in the ordinary course of its operation, the eBook Reader effectively permitted the publisher or distributor of the ebook to restrict or limit the exercise of certain copyright rights of an

---

[a] The purchases are frequently accompanied by an End User License Agreement which may contain contractual language limiting the user's rights to use the ebook, including the rights to sell or transfer the ebook or to copy or distribute the content of the ebook without the publisher's permission.

[b] Adobe distributes the eBook Reader program free of charge and users download the software directly from the Internet onto their computers.

owner of the copyright for an ebook distributed in the eBook Reader format." Indictment P1(g).

Defendant Elcomsoft Company Ltd. ("Elcomsoft") developed and sold a product known as the Advanced eBook Processor ("AEBPR"). AEBPR is a Windows-based software program that allows a user to remove use restrictions from Adobe Acrobat PDF files and files formatted for the Adobe eBook Reader. The program allows a purchaser of an eBook Reader formatted electronic book to convert the format to one that is readable in any PDF viewer without the use restrictions imposed by the publisher. Thus, the restrictions imposed by the publisher are stripped away, leaving the ebook in a "naked PDF" format that is readily copyable, printable, and easily distributed electronically. The conversion accomplished by the AEBPR program enables a purchaser of an ebook to engage in "fair use" of an ebook without infringing the copyright laws, for example, by allowing the lawful owner of an ebook to read it on another computer, to make a back-up copy, or to print the ebook in paper form. The same technology, however, also allows a user to engage in copyright infringement by making and distributing unlawful copies of the ebook. Defendant was indicted for alleged violations of Section 1201(b)(1)(A) and (C) of the Digital Millennium Copyright Act ("DMCA"), 17 U.S.C. § § 1201(b)(1)(A) and (C), for allegedly trafficking in and marketing of the AEBPR.

## 2. The DMCA

Congress enacted the DMCA following the adoption of the World Intellectual Property Organization Copyright Treaty as an expansion of traditional copyright law in recognition of the fact that in the digital age, authors must employ protective technologies in order to prevent their works from being unlawfully copied or exploited.

Through the DMCA, Congress sought to prohibit certain efforts to unlawfully circumvent protective technologies, while at the same time preserving users' rights of fair use. Some understanding of the interplay between copyright and fair use is essential to understanding the issues confronting Congress and the issues presented here. Fair use and copyright are discussed in more detail below, but in brief, copyright grants authors the exclusive right to make and distribute copies of their original works of authorship but the doctrine of fair use permits a certain amount of copying for limited purposes without infringing the copyright, notwithstanding the exclusive rights of the copyright owner.

As part of the balance Congress sought to strike in protecting the rights of copyright owners while preserving fair use, Congress enacted three new anti-circumvention prohibitions, Section 1201(a)(1), Section 1201(a)(2) and Section 1201(b). The first two provisions target circumvention of technological measures that effectively control access to a copyrighted work; the third targets circumvention of technological measures that impose limitations on the use of protected works.

With regard to the first category, Congress banned both the act of circumventing access control restrictions as well as trafficking in and marketing of devices that are primarily designed for such circumvention. Specifically, Section 1201(a)(1)(A) provides that "no person shall circumvent a technological measure that effectively controls access to a work protected under this title." Thereafter, Section 1201(a)(2) provides that:

> no person shall manufacture, import, offer to the public, provide or otherwise traffic in any technology, product, service, device, component, or part thereof, that—
>
> (A) is primarily designed or produced for the purpose of circumventing a technological measure that effectively controls access to a work protected under this title;
>
> (B) has only limited commercially significant purpose or use other than to circumvent a technological measure that effectively controls access to a work protected under this title [17 U.S.C. § 1 et seq.]; or
>
> (C) is marketed by that person or another acting in concert with that person with that person's knowledge for use in circumventing a technological measure that effectively controls access to a work protected under this title.

17 U.S.C. § 1201(a)(2).

The third prohibition, however, addresses a different circumvention, specifically, circumventing a technological measure that imposes limitations on the use of a copyrighted work, or in the words of the statute, that "effectively protects the right of a copyright owner." Using language quite similar to Section 1201(a)(2), the Act provides that:

> no person shall manufacture, import, offer to the public, provide or otherwise traffic in any technology, product, service, device, component, or part thereof, that—
>
> (A) is primarily designed or produced for the purpose of circumventing protection afforded by a technological measure that effectively protects a right of a copyright owner under this title [17 U.S.C.A. § 1 et seq.] in a work or a portion thereof;
>
> (B) has only limited commercially significant purpose or use other than to circumvent protection afforded by a technological measure that effectively protects a right of a copyright owner under this title in a work or a portion thereof; or
>
> (C) is marketed by that person or another acting in concert with that person with that person's knowledge for use in circumventing protection afforded by a technological measure that effectively protects a right of a copyright owner under this title in a work or a portion thereof.

*17 U.S.C. § 1201*(b). Unlike Section 1201(a), however, Congress did not ban the act of circumventing the use restrictions. Instead, Congress banned only the trafficking in and marketing of devices primarily designed to circumvent the use restriction protective technologies. Congress did not prohibit the act of circumvention because it sought to preserve the fair use rights of persons who had lawfully acquired a work. See H.R. Rep. 105–551, pt. 1, at 18 (1998); Exemption to Prohibition on Circumvention of Copyright Protection Systems for Access Control Technologies, 65 Fed. Reg. 64,557 (2000) (codified at 37 C.F.R. § 201)("The prohibition in section 1201(b) extends only to devices that circumvent copy control measures. The decision not to prohibit the conduct of circumventing copy controls was made, in part, because it would penalize some noninfringing conduct such as fair use."). In fact, Congress expressly disclaimed any intent to impair any person's rights of fair use: "Nothing in this section shall affect rights, remedies, or defenses to copyright infringement, including fair use, under this title [17 U.S.C.A. § 1 et seq.]." 17 U.S.C. § 1201(c)(1).[d] Thus, circumventing use restrictions is not unlawful, but in order to protect the rights of copyright owners while maintaining fair use, Congress banned trafficking in devices that are primarily designed for the purpose of circumventing any technological measure that "effectively protects a right of a copyright owner," or that have limited commercially significant purposes other than circumventing use restrictions, or that are marketed for use in circumventing the use restrictions.

The difficulty is created by Section 1201(b)'s use of the phrase "effectively protects a right of a copyright owner" to define the prohibited device because the rights of a copyright owner are intertwined with the rights of others. The rights of a copyright owner include the exclusive rights to reproduce the copyrighted work, to prepare derivative works based upon the copyrighted work, to distribute copies by sale or otherwise, to perform the copyrighted work publicly, and to display the copyrighted work publicly. See 17 U.S.C. § 106. Exceptions to the copyright owner's exclusive rights are set forth in 17 U.S.C. §§ 107–120. One of those exceptions is that the copyright owner loses control over the disposition of a copy of a work upon the sale or transfer of the copy. 17 U.S.C. § 109. Thus, once a published copy is sold, the copyright owner has no right to restrict the further sale or transfer of that copy. Id. In addition, one of the most significant exceptions to the rights of a copyright owner is the doctrine of fair use. 17 U.S.C. § 107.

The interplay between fair use and copyright weaves throughout defendant's motions to dismiss. The parties dispute whether Congress banned, or intended to ban, all circumvention tools or instead banned only those circumvention devices that would facilitate copyright infringement, and if, as a result, the DMCA is unconstitutionally vague.

**DISCUSSION**

Fifth Amendment Due Process Challenge

Defendant contends that Section 1201(b) is unconstitutionally vague as applied to Elcomsoft because it does not clearly delineate the conduct which it prohibits. Due Process Motion at 13. Defendant argues that the DMCA bans only those tools that are primarily designed to circumvent usage

---

[d] Congress also enacted specific provisions to protect certain uses, including exceptions for law enforcement, reverse engineering, encryption research and security testing. 17 U.S.C. § 1201(e)–(g) and 1201(f).

control technologies in order to enable copyright infringement. Defendant reaches this conclusion because Congress did not ban the act of circumventing use control technologies and expressly refused to do so in order to avoid treading on legitimate fair use. Defendant thus argues that:

> the legislative history and the language of the DMCA establish that Congress did not prohibit the act of circumventing usage control technologies. For reasons directly related to that decision, it also did not ban *all* tools which might be used to circumvent usage control technologies. Congress sought to prohibit only those tools which are intended to be used to circumvent usage control technologies for the purpose of copyright infringement. Section 1201(b) does not provide a constitutionally adequate notice of this prohibition.

Due Process Motion at 14. From the premise that Congress has banned only those tools that are intended to circumvent usage control technologies for the purpose of copyright infringement, defendant then argues that the statute is unconstitutionally vague. "Section 1201(b) is doomed to inherent vagueness because not all tools are banned, and the language of the statute renders it impossible to determine which tools it in fact bans." Id. at 15. Defendant argues that because of the nature of the interplay between copyright owners' rights and fair use, any circumvention of a usage control technology for a legitimate purpose—such as for a fair use—must invariably involve circumvention of a technology that "protects the right of a copyright owner." Accordingly, there is no way for a manufacturer to know whether its tool is lawful. Moreover, this statutory vagueness leads to arbitrary enforcement.

The government's opposition brief does not directly address defendant's argument that some circumvention tools are prohibited while other circumvention tools are allowed. At the hearing, however, the government contended that the DMCA imposes a blanket ban on all circumvention tools. According to the government, Section 1201(b) does not prohibit only those tools that circumvent usage controls for the purpose of facilitating copyright infringement; the statute also prohibits tools that circumvent usage controls for the purpose of enabling fair use. Thus, if all tools that are primarily designed or produced for the purpose of circumventing protections afforded by technological measures are banned, the statute is not impermissibly vague.

Thus, the court's initial task is to determine whether the DMCA bans trafficking in all circumvention tools, regardless of whether they are designed to enable fair use or to facilitate infringement, or whether instead the statute bans only those tools that circumvent use restrictions for the purpose of facilitating copyright infringement. If all circumvention tools are banned, defendant's void-for-vagueness challenge necessarily fails.

The court must first consider the statutory language enacted by Congress. Despite defendant's repeated citations to the legislative history, if the language of the statute is clear, there is no need to resort to the legislative history in order to determine the statute's meaning. Section 1201(b) provides that:

no person shall manufacture, import, offer to the public, provide or otherwise traffic in any technology, product, service, device, component, or part thereof, that—

(A) is primarily designed or produced for the purpose of circumventing protection afforded by a technological measure that effectively protects a right of a copyright owner under this title [17 U.S.C.A. § 1 et seq.] in a work or a portion thereof. . . .

17 U.S.C. § 1201(b). The section is comprised of three parts: 1) trafficking in "any technology," "product," "service," "device," "component" or "part thereof"; 2) that is "primarily designed or produced for the purpose of circumventing protection afforded by a technological measure"; and 3) a technological measure that "effectively protects a right of a copyright owner" under the copyright statute.

The first element targets "any technology, product, service, device, component, or part thereof." This language is not difficult to decipher and is all-encompassing: it includes any tool, no matter its form, that is primarily designed or produced to circumvent technological protection.

Next, the phrase "circumvent protection afforded by a technological measure" is expressly defined in the statute to mean: "avoiding, bypassing, removing, deactivating, or otherwise impairing a technological measure." 17 U.S.C. § 1201(b)(2)(A).

Finally, the statute provides that "a technological measure 'effectively protects a right of a copyright owner under this title' if the measure, in the ordinary course of its operation, prevents, restricts, or otherwise limits the exercise of a right of a copyright owner under this title." Id. § 1201(b)(2)(B). The rights of a copyright owner are specified in 17 U.S.C. § 106.

Putting Section 1201(b)(2)(B) together with Section 106, a technological measure "effectively protects the right of a copyright owner" if, in the ordinary course of its operation, it prevents, restricts or otherwise limits the exercise of any of the rights set forth in Section 106, such as the rights to reproduce the work, prepare derivative works, distribute copies of the work, perform the work publicly or by digital audio transmission, or display the work publicly.

In short, the statute bans trafficking in any device that bypasses or circumvents a restriction on copying or performing a work. Nothing within the express language would permit trafficking in devices designed to bypass use restrictions in order to enable a fair use, as opposed to an infringing use. The statute does not distinguish between devices based on the uses to which the device will be put. Instead, all tools that enable circumvention of use restrictions are banned, not merely those use restrictions that prohibit infringement. Thus, as the government contended at oral argument, Section 1201(b) imposes a blanket ban on trafficking in or the marketing of any device that circumvents use restrictions.

Because the statutory language is clear, it is unnecessary to consider the legislative history to determine congressional intent or the scope of the statute. Nevertheless, statements within the legislative history support the interpretation reached above. Congress was concerned with promoting electronic commerce while protecting the rights of copyright owners, particularly in the digital age where near exact copies of protected works can be made at virtually no cost and distributed instantaneously on a worldwide basis. S. Rep. No. 105–190, at 8 (1998). Congress recognized that "most acts of circumventing a technological copyright protection measure will occur in the course of conduct which itself implicates the copyright owners rights," i.e., acts of infringement. Id. at 29.

Congress recognized that most uses of tools to circumvent copy restrictions would be for unlawful infringement purposes rather than for fair use purposes and sought to ban all circumvention tools that "can be used" to bypass or avoid copy restrictions.

Defendant relies heavily on congressional intent to preserve fair use but that congressional intent does not change the analysis. The Act expressly disclaims any intent to affect the rights, remedies, limitations, or defenses to copyright infringement, including the right of fair use. 17 U.S.C. § 1201(c). Congress' expressed intent to preserve the right of fair use is not inconsistent with a ban on trafficking in circumvention technologies, even those that could be used for fair use purposes rather than infringement. Fair use of a copyrighted work continues to be permitted, as does circumventing use restrictions for the purpose of engaging in a fair use, even though engaging in certain fair uses of digital works may be made more difficult if tools to circumvent use restrictions cannot be readily obtained.

The inescapable conclusion from the statutory language adopted by Congress and the legislative history discussed above is that Congress sought to ban all circumvention tools because most of the time those tools would be used to infringe a copyright. Thus, while it is not unlawful to circumvent for the purpose of engaging in fair use, it is unlawful to traffic in tools that allow fair use circumvention. That is part of the sacrifice Congress was willing to make in order to protect against unlawful piracy and promote the development of electronic commerce and the availability of copyrighted material on the Internet.

Accordingly, there is no ambiguity in what tools are allowed and what tools are prohibited because the statute bans trafficking in or the marketing of *all* circumvention devices. Therefore, defendant's motion to dismiss the indictment on due process grounds is denied.

NOTES

*REGARDING THE FAIR USE FACTORS*

**1.** *Impact on the potential market.* Professor Nimmer suggests this is "the most important and indeed central fair use factor"[12] and that, in applying

---

[12] 4 M. Nimmer and D. Nimmer, Nimmer on Copyrights § 13.05[A][4] at 13–182 (2002).

it, we should look to whether the two works fulfill the same function in terms of actual or potential consumer demand. How did the majority in *Sony* apply this factor? Is the *Sony* Court's analysis regarding market impact sound? Who should have the burden of proof on this issue?

In analyzing the necessary adverse impact upon the potential market, what type of impact is significant? Do *Sony* and *Harper* differ on this point? In *Napster*, which view of market impact did the court adopt and on what market did the court focus? When looking at market impact, what is the relevant market? What do *Campbell* and *Suntrust* say about this issue in the context of parodies? In Núñez v. Caribbean International News Corp.,[13] the court upheld a fair use defense in the context of a newspaper's printing of plaintiff photographer's pictures of a beauty pageant winner who became controversial as a result of the plaintiff's suggestive photographs. The plaintiff's photographs of the pageant winner appeared in conjunction with articles about the winner's controversial poses. In applying the fourth fair use factor, the court noted that the newspaper's publishing of the pictures would not harm the plaintiff's market because a newspaper photograph is an inadequate substitute for the pictures themselves. Moreover, in applying this factor, the court also noted that the potential market for the photographs might also include the sale to newspapers for the purpose of illustrating the controversy, but that such a market was unlikely to be developed.[14] This case illustrates the circularity of the application of the fourth fair use factor. A holding of fair use always will result in some harm to plaintiff's potential market because, by virtue of the fair use conclusion, the plaintiff is foregoing a fee.[15] How should courts draw the line at what markets to consider? See also question 2 in Note 4.

**2.** *Purpose and character of the use: commercial vs. non-commercial uses.* In *Sony*, the Court observed that "the commercial or nonprofit character of an activity [is to] be weighed in any fair use decision," and that a commercial use renders the defendant's activity "presumptively" unfair (see Section IV(B)). The Court qualifies this statement substantially in *Acuff–Rose*, wherein it expressly states that "the more transformative the new work, the less will be the significance of other factors, like commercialism, that may weigh against a finding of fair use." What is the relevance of a transformative use? Under *Acuff*, what is the relevance of a noncommercial use? How is the term "commercial" defined in *Sony*, *Harper*, and *Acuff*? What definition of commercial use did the court in *Napster* adopt? What type of economic benefits did it state are required to find commercial use? Do you find the court's position convincing?[16]

---

[13] 235 F.3d 18, 25 (1st Cir. 2000).

[14] *Id.* at 25.

[15] See William W. Fisher, *Reconstructings the Fair Use Doctrine*, 101 Harv. L. Rev. 1659, 1672 (1988).

[16] See Raymond Ku, *The Creative Destruction of Copyright: Napster and the New Economics of Digital Technology*, 69 U. Chicago L. Rev. 263 (2002)(arguing against copyright protection for digital works).

**3.** *Purpose and character of the use: productivity.* According to the majority opinion in *Sony*, whether the defendant makes a productive use of the plaintiff's work is not especially significant (see footnote 1 in Section IV(B) of the case), but this requirement is of critical importance to the dissent's view of fair use. In *Acuff–Rose*, the Court emphasizes the importance of transformative value. Is a transformative use the same as a productive use? What test should be applied for determining what is a productive use? Which test did the court in *Napster* apply? What was the court's holding on whether a change in medium represents a transformative work? Compare the position espoused in Hearn v. Meyer, Assignment 7, on the issue of transposing a work into a new medium. What does the concurrence in the *Suntrust* case suggest regarding whether Bell's work in the Problem is as transformative as the defendant's in that case?

**4.** *Purpose and character of the use: teaching, scholarship and research.* In controversial decisions made by the Sixth and Second Circuits, the courts ignored customs of the academic and research communities, respectively, to hold that the photocopying of copyrighted works without compensating the copyright owners was not a fair use based on the facts of each case.

In American Geophysical Union v. Texaco Inc.,[17] the Second Circuit affirmed the holding that a researcher's photocopying of articles related to his work was not a fair use. The researcher's conduct was being used as representative of the 400+ researchers the defendant employed and the court assessed the conduct on the basis of the institution as a whole, as opposed to the individual researcher. The defendant had multiple subscriptions to journals and these journals were circulated amongst the researchers so that they could photocopy articles relating to their work. In some cases, the copies were placed in archival files for the "primary purpose of providing [the] scientists each with his or her own personal copy without having to purchase."[18] In other instances, the copies were used in the laboratories, so that the copy, rather than the entire journal, would be destroyed in the case of a lab accident.

Regarding the court's application of the first fair use factor, the court determined that it favored the plaintiff because the predominant purpose of the defendant's use was to multiply the number of available copies of the articles to the defendant institution, thus serving the same purposes as purchasing additional subscriptions. Also, and despite the use of the articles in laboratories for research purposes, the court found that the photocopying did not involve a transformative use.[19] Under the second factor, the court ruled that the scientific nature of the works rendered them clearly factual. In deciding the third factor, the court viewed each of the articles as an independent work, rather than as a portion of the larger journal. On this basis, the court concluded the researcher copied the entire article. In terms of the fourth factor, the court held the plaintiff's market for licensing

[17] 60 F.3d 913 (2d Cir. 1994).      [19] Id. at 923.
[18] Id. at 919.

fees would be harmed by the defendant's conduct if such conduct became widespread.

In Princeton University Press v. Michigan Document Services, Inc., the district court held that a copyshop's practice of failing to obtain permission for the photocopying of excerpts on a fee-per-page of copyrighted materials for inclusion in coursepacks sold to students was not fair use. The district court also awarded damages that may have been enhanced for willfulness.[20] A three-judge panel of the sixth circuit then reversed this ruling.[21] In the *en banc* opinion, the Sixth Circuit affirmed the district court's ruling as to liability but concluded that the district court erred in its finding of willfulness.[22] The *en banc* 8–5 ruling therefore vacated the district court's damage award on the ground that it may have been linked to its finding of willfulness. The Supreme Court's denial of *cert.* leaves the *en banc* opinion as the final word in this case.[23]

The *en banc* opinion relied in instances on the reasoning of *American Geophysical*. In analyzing what it deemed as the most critical factor, "the effect of the use upon the potential market for or value of the copyrighted work," the court ruled that the defendant's use was commercial even though the ultimate users were students, since the copyshop's failure to obtain permission gave it a competitive edge over other copyshops that did pay royalties. Even if the challenged use was noncommercial, however, the court felt that the publishers met their burden of proving that the copyshop's practice diminished the potential market value of their works since the publishers of the works in question were collecting permission fees in an amount of almost $500,000 per year. As to the remaining fair use factors, the court deemed them "considerably less important" in a case such as this, where the use was nontransformative.[24] Interestingly, the court held that the purpose and character of the use factor weighed against fair use in this case since the use was commercial. The court also concluded that from a policy standpoint, the publishers require incentives to continue their activities even if the authors themselves would continue to write scholarly pieces absent these incentives. Finally, the court concluded that in light of the controversy sparked by the litigation's history, the copyshop's belief that its conduct amounted to fair use was not so unreasonable as to constitute willfulness for purposes of determining the appropriate statutory damages.

Think about the following questions based on *Princeton University Press* and *American Geophysical Union* as they pertain to the fair use discussion in this chapter. 1) Would a student or independent researcher who copies articles be making a fair use? If so, how is this conduct any different from that in the cases? 2) Should the courts assess the market harm on the basis of lost permission fees? Is this a cognizable market? 3) Do these decisions make sense in light of the language in the preamble to

[20] 855 F.Supp. 905 (E.D.Mich.1994).

[21] 74 F.3d 1512 (6th Cir.1996).

[22] 99 F.3d at 1381.

[23] 520 U.S. 1156 (1997).

[24] 99 F.3d at 1388.

section 107, which explicitly mentions "teaching scholarship, or research" as possible fair uses? 4) Should it matter whether a market for copying could be created? 5) Do these decisions support or suppress the underlying goal of the Copyright Clause—"to promote the Progress of Science and useful Arts"?

**5.** *Nature of the copyrighted work: relevance of publication.* Prior to the 1976 Act, unpublished works were protected only by common law copyright. Now copyright protection is extended to unpublished works as well, and this represents a significant change wrought by the new statute. What does the Court in *Harper* mean when it says that "the scope of fair use is narrower with respect to unpublished works" (see Section IV of the case)? Should the scope of fair use be narrower regarding unpublished works? Should it ever be permissible to use unpublished material? Should it matter whether the alleged infringer directly quotes or paraphrases the unpublished material? In 1992, Congress added the following final sentence to § 107: "The fact that a work is unpublished shall not itself bar a finding of fair use if such finding is made upon consideration of all the above factors." The Committee Report to this amendment suggests reaffirmance of *Harper*'s rule that the unpublished nature of a work is a "key" but not "necessarily determinative" factor prohibiting fair use.[25]

**6.** *Nature of the copyrighted work: fact vs. fiction.* The fair use doctrine recognizes that there is a greater need to disseminate factual works. This is discussed by the dissent in *Sony*, who believed that the entertainment component of the programs weakened the fair use claim. In *Harper*, the Court recognized that a factual work was at issue, but essentially discounted the importance of this criterion in this particular case because direct quotation from such works should only be allowed when necessary to convey facts adequately. The Nation's use "focus[ed] on the most expressive elements of the work, [and] exceed[ed] that necessary to disseminate the facts" (see Section IV of the case). How often would it be necessary to use direct quotation to convey facts? Note that in both *Sony* and *Harper*, application of the fact vs. fiction distinction would have suggested opposite results. How much weight should this factor be given in the assessment of a parody? What is the court's reasoning in *Suntrust* on this point?

**7.** *Amount of copying.* The Court's finding of fair use in *Sony* despite the involvement of wholesale copying suggests that this factor retains little, if any, force.[26] However, the court in *Napster* did not find fair use in an arguably similar situation.[27] Essentially, application of this factor is difficult because it is amorphous. How much is too much? Do we consider

---

[25] See H.R. Rep. No. 836, 102d Cong., 2d Sess. 5 (1992).

[26] *See also* Ty, Inc. v. Publications Int'l Ltd., 292 F.3d 512 (7th Cir. 2002)(use of photographs of plaintiff's entire beanie baby line was a fair use in the context of its use in a collector's guide); Nuñez v. Caribbean Int'l News Corp., 235 F.3d 18 (1st Cir. 2000)(de-fendant's use of entire photograph for a newspaper article was a fair use because the photograph prompted the controversy that was the subject of the article.)

[27] *See also* Worldwide Church of God v. Philadelphia Church of God Inc., 227 F.3d 1110 (9th Cir. 2000)(defendant's copying of an entire religious work was not a fair use).

quantity or quality? How should quality be judged? Also, do we compare the amount taken with the size of the defendant's work or the plaintiff's work? What is the real importance of the third fair use factor?

What effect does a work's being a parody have on the court's assessment of this factor? In the legislative notes accompanying § 107, Congress specified parodies as an example "of the sort of activities the courts might regard as fair use,"[28] but refused to endorse a per se rule protecting parodies. In general, parodies are given a broad scope of protection because they foster creativity, but the fair use doctrine still must be applied to parodies. In *Acuff–Rose*, the Supreme Court observed that "[w]hen parody takes aim at a particular original work, the parody must be able to 'conjure up' at least enough of that original to make the object of its critical wit recognizable." Does the Court provide any further guidance on this point?

**8.** *Propriety and custom.* The fair use doctrine recognizes the importance of other equitable factors such as defendant's relative good faith. How important was this factor in the major cases? How can good faith and fair dealing be defined?

Can the Nation's conduct in *Harper* be equated with that of a parodist who uses a copyrighted work after being expressly denied permission by the copyright owner? Does a defendant's use of a copyrighted work subsequent to being denied permission always indicate bad faith?

## *REGARDING PUBLIC ACCESS AND COPYRIGHT LAW GENERALLY*

Although the fair use doctrine occupies a central place in the right versus access debate, there are numerous other important topics that should be considered in this Assignment. Some of these issues were treated to some extent in the foregoing major cases. The following Notes continue the themes of this chapter, and also raise some additional important issues regarding public access not yet addressed.

**1.** *Contributory infringement and vicarious liability.* Obviously there is a connection between the standard for copyright infringement generally and public access. This Assignment incorporates the doctrines of contributory infringement and vicarious liability in order to emphasize the impact of these doctrines on public access to copyrighted works. Under *Napster*, what is the impact of knowledge of the infringing use regarding the inquiry of contributory infringement? How does this relate to the contributory infringement issue in *Sony*? The vicarious liability section of *Napster* is important because this case is one of the first cases to set a standard of vicarious liability in the digital context. How does *Napster*'s standard apply to the Principal Problem? In Metro–Goldwyn–Mayer Studios, Inc. v. Grokster, Ltd.,[29] a federal district court attempted to curb the result in *Napster* by emphasizing that in the instant case, the defendants' distributed software that enabled users to exchange digital media through a peer-to-peer transfer network entirely outside of the defendants' control. Thus, the

28 § 107, historical and revision notes, H.R. 94–1476, page 5678.

29 259 F.Supp.2d 1029, 1045 (C.D. Cal. 2003).

court determined that the defendants lacked the ability to supervise and control the infringing conduct, all of which occurred after the products had passed to the end-users. Should liability be predicated on the decision to program the system to avoid direct ability to monitor infringement? The relevance of this issue will grow as services such as Gnutella, which do not depend upon a central server, become increasingly prevalent.

Title II of the DMCA adds a new section 512 to the Copyright Act which addresses vicarious liability for copyright infringement for online service providers. This new provision creates several "safe harbors" for IPS that limit liability for the following four categories of conduct by a service provider: 1) transitory communications—when providers merely act as data conduits by transmitting digital information from one point on a network to another at the request of a third party; 2) system caching—when providers, for a limited time period, store copies of material that has been made available online by someone other than the provider, and then transmitted to a subscriber at his or her direction; 3) when providers host systems with infringing materials, provided service providers do not have actual knowledge of the infringement and act immediately to remove the infringing material; and 4) when providers link users to a site containing infringing material by using information location tools such as hyperlinks, online directories and search engines (this fourth limitation is subject to the same types of conditions as the third limitation). All four limitations completely bar monetary damages and provide restrictions on the availability of injunctive relief. This provision also includes a section governing the limitation of liability for nonprofit educational institutions. The scope of these safe harbor provisions will, undoubtedly, present courts with future challenges. For example, should companies who offer online services as part of their regular businesses fall within the safe harbor protections?[30] It is interesting to note that the European Directive on Electronic Commerce, adopted by the European Community in 2000, adopts principles similar to those of Title II of the DMCA.[31]

In *Ellison v. Robertson*,[32] the court held that AOL's liability was limited under § 512(a), the first category listed above. In that case, Robertson uploaded a copyrighted work without permission onto USENET, so that anyone could access and copy the work. AOL was linked to USENET so the work became accessible to all of AOL's members. The court held that AOL qualified under the § 512(a) safe harbor because AOL's storage of the defendant's posts was an "intermediate and transient storage" that was not maintained on the system for a longer period than was reasonably necessary. [33]

**2.**   *Public Access and the First Sale Doctrine.* The first sale doctrine has spawned several interesting issues which are explored below.

---

[30] See Neil Benchell, *The Digital Millennium Copyright Act: A Review of the Law and the Court's Interpretation*, 21 J. Marshall J. Computer & Info. L. 1, 17 (2002).

[31] Directive 2000/31/EC of the European Parliament and of the Council, 17.7.200 EN L 178/1 (June 8, 2000).

[32] 189 F.Supp.2d 1051 (C.D.Cal. 2002).

[33] Id. at 1070.

a. *The "core" first sale concept.* The first sale doctrine, which is codified at § 109(a), provides that notwithstanding the distribution right guaranteed by § 106(3), "the owner of a particular copy or phonorecord lawfully made under this title, or any person authorized by such owner, is entitled, without the authority of the copyright owner, to sell or otherwise dispose of the possession of that copy or phonorecord."[34] Thus, once a lawfully made copy of a copyrighted work is sold, the copyright holder has no control over subsequent sales or dispositions of that particular copy. What policies do you suppose support this doctrine?

The first sale doctrine does not apply when a party licenses, rather than sells, its work.[35] Therefore, in the context of transfers of software, defendants will not be able to rely on the first sale doctrine to bypass restrictions on subsequent transfers of the software if the agreements at issue between the software manufacturers and initial purchasers are deemed "licenses" rather than "sales agreements."[36] See also Note 3d discussing extractions and price fixing. In its current form, § 109(a) does not specifically provide for a digital first sale right, although there has been discussion of the need for such an amendment on the ground that unless enacted, the first sale doctrine eventually will become obsolete in an environment in which the contents of copyrighted works are being disseminated more frequently through electronic means.[37] Upon its enactment, the DMCA required the Register of Copyrights and the Assistant Secretary of Commerce for Communications and Information to commission a study of the impact of the access circumvention provisions on both the first sale doctrine and § 117 (see note 2b). This study ultimately rejected the need for amending § 109 to incorporate a digital first sale doctrine.[38]

b. *The Record Rental Amendment Act and the Computer Software Rental Amendments Act as exemptions to the first sale doctrine.* Section 109(b) embodies the Record Rental Amendment Act of 1984, and the Computer Software Amendments Act of 1990. The Record Rental Amendment Act was passed to deter the practice of record shops encouraging unauthorized recordings of copyrighted music by renting records and selling blank cassette tapes. As such, it is an exception to the first sale doctrine because it restricts the use and disposition of individual phonorecords by precluding

---

[34] § 109(a).

[35] See Microsoft Corp. v. Software Wholesale Club, Inc., 129 F.Supp.2d 995, 1007 (S.D. Tex. 2000).

[36] See Adobe Systems, Inc. v. Stargate Software Inc., 216 F.Supp.2d 1051, 1059 (N.D.Cal. 2002)(holding that the first sale doctrine does not apply because the transfer at issue was a license, and noting the importance of enhanced copyright protection for software developers).

[37] Jessica Litman, The Exclusive Right to Read, 13 Card. Arts & Ent. L.J. 29 (1994); Jessica Litman, Copyright and Information

Policy, 55 Law & Contemp. Probs. 185, 188–89, 208 (1992) (recommending the development of new alternatives such as "compulsory licenses for secondary uses of electronically disseminated works" to effectuate more complete access to copyrighted works).

[38] U.S. Copyright Office, 107th Cong., DMCA Section 104 Report 97 (2001). The study did conclude, however, that Congress "either (1) amend section 109(a) to ensure that fair use copies are not subject to the first sale doctrine; or (2) create a new archival exemption that provides expressly that backup copies may not be distributed."

the rental, lease, or lending of such works for direct or indirect commercial advantage. What is the scope of this prohibition?

Despite the enactment of the Record Rental Amendment Act, home taping is even more prevalent because people simply use other sources rather than rely on rentals from commercial outlets. As Sony Corp. of America v. Universal City Studios, Inc.[39] held, making a home recording of a television show is a fair use. Should the same be true of home tapings of phonorecords?[40] In 1992, Congress enacted the Audio Home Recording Act ("AHRA")[41] which requires the inclusion of the Serial Copy Management System (SCMS) in digital audio tape recorders (DATs). The SCMS allows DATs to make direct, digital-to-digital copies of CD's and other pre-recorded cassettes, but precludes digital-to-digital copies of these copies. In other words, the Act sanctions an unlimited number of first-generation digital-to-digital copies of music, but outlaws second-generation copies of these works. The impact of the AHRA has been minimal, however, largely because DAT technology has never been a significant component of the consumer electronics marketplace.[42]

Subsequent to the Record Rental Amendment Act, the Copyright Act was amended to provide yet another exemption to the first sale doctrine. Pursuant to the Computer Software Rental Amendments Act of 1990, the renting of computer software without the permission of the copyright owner for purposes of "direct or indirect commercial advantage" constitutes copyright infringement. See § 109(b). The objective of this amendment is similar to that of the Record Rental Amendment Act of 1984, to bolster the rights of copyright proprietors by making unauthorized home duplication more difficult, thus fostering sales of the protected work. Why should commercial rentals of records and computer software be treated differently from videos? What exceptions are provided by the Computer Software Rental Amendments Act of 1990? The copyrights of owners of computer programs also are limited by § 117 of the statute which allows the owner of a copy of a computer program to make another copy of the program if such copy "is created as an essential step in the utilization of

---

[39] 464 U.S. 417 (1984).

[40] See generally David Nimmer, Copyright Liability for Audio Home Recording: Dispelling the "Betamax" Myth, 68 Va. L. Rev. 1505, 1534 (1982) (observing that "audio home recording of copyrighted works has never been protected by any special exemption, express or implied, from the scope of the copyright laws" and is "not defensible under the 'fair use' doctrine"; advocates the imposition of royalty payments on the sales of recording equipment).

[41] §§ 1001–1010.

[42] See Brian Leubitz, *Digital Millennium? Technological Protections for Copyright* on the Internet, 11 Tex. Intell.Prop. L.J. 417, 425 (2003). In 1999, the Ninth Circuit held that a portable music player called the Rio, which allows users to download MP3 audio files from a computer and listen to them elsewhere, is not a digital audio recording device subject to the restrictions of the AHRA. Recording Industry Association of America v. Diamond Multimedia Systems, 180 F.3d 1072 (9th Cir. 1999). The basis for the decision was that the Rio cannot reproduce a digital music recording, either directly or indirectly from a transmission, and therefore does not qualify as a digital audio recording device under the AHRA.

the computer program in conjunction with a machine and . . . is used in no other manner" or "is for archival purposes only."[43]

*Discussion question.* Should the exemptions from the first sale doctrine provided in § 109(b) be extended to library books? Specifically, should authors be compensated from public funds when their works are lent from libraries? This type of system is called a public lending right and it is operational in about twelve countries. How would such a system fare in this country?

c. *First sale and unauthorized importation.* What is the significance of the phrase "lawfully made under this title"?[44] In a decision resolving a conflict in the federal circuit courts, the United States Supreme Court held that Copyright Act does not bar the unauthorized importation of goods into the United States. In Quality King Distributors, Inc. v. L'anza Research International, Inc.,[45] a California manufacturer of hair care products unsuccessfully challenged the ability of a foreign company to import the domestically produced products back into the United States for resale at discount prices to unauthorized retailers. The domestic manufacturer, L'anza, sued a foreign distributor that had bought the goods abroad from one of L'anza's authorized foreign distributors. Affixed to the goods were copyrighted labels.

Section 602(a) provides that the unauthorized importation of copies that have been acquired outside the United States infringes the copyright owner's exclusive right to distribute under § 106. The question before the Court, then, was whether the first sale doctrine applies to imported copies sold abroad. The Supreme Court held that it does apply and reversed the lower courts. In an opinion written by Justice Stevens, the Court noted that a copyright owner's exclusive right to distribute is qualified by the first sale doctrine. Since the exclusive right to distribute does not encompass resales by lawful owners that come within the scope of the first sale doctrine, both domestic and foreign owners of L'anza products who import and then resell them in the United States do not violate the importation provision.[46] In rejecting L'anza's argument that § 602(a) is superfluous if limited by the first sale doctrine, the Court emphasized that § 602(a) is in fact broader than § 109(a) because the former also encompasses copies that are lawfully made in another country and therefore not subject to § 109(a).[47] Moreover, the Court concluded that even though § 501(a) of the Copyright Act defines an infringer by referring separately to violations of sections 106 and 602, the other provisions of the statute compel the conclusion that § 602(a) does not function independently of the first sale doctrine.[48] Most significantly, because § 106 is subject not only to § 109(a)

---

[43] § 117(a).

[44] The legislative history states that defendants should bear the burden of proving whether a particular copy was lawfully made or acquired. See H.R. Rep. No. 94–1476, 94th Cong., 2d Sess. 80–81, *reprinted in* 1976 U.S. CODE CONG. & AD. NEWS 5659, 5694–95.

[45] 523 U.S. 135 (1998).

[46] 523 U.S. at 145.

[47] Id. at 147.

[48] Id. at 150.

but also to §§ 107 to 120, the fair use defense codified in § 107 would also be unavailable to importers if § 602(a) were construed as a separate right not subject to the other statutory limitations. The Court found this interpretation untenable, particularly in light of the importance of the fair use defense and the unlikely event that Congress intended to ban completely all imports containing any copyrighted material protected by a United States copyright.[49]

The Court noted that this copyright case was unusual because L'anza was primarily interested in protecting the integrity of its marketing method rather protecting its right to prevent unauthorized reproduction of copyrighted labels.[50] However, the Court affirmed that its legal interpretation of the Copyright Act would apply as well to cases involving more traditional copyrighted subject matter such as books and sound recordings.[51] Although *L'anza* apparently resolves the application of the first sale doctrine and the importation prohibition in the context of domestically manufactured goods, the Supreme Court has yet to resolve definitely situations where the copies sought to be imported were produced abroad,[52] and thus were not made "under this title" within the meaning of § 109(a). See Assignment 5.

**3.** *Public Access and the Digital Millennium Copyright Act.* The Digital Millennium Copyright Act presents a host of issues involving public access considerations. A few are considered below.

   a. *General Public Access/DMCA issues:* As discussed in *Elcom*, § 1201(a) encompasses both a basic prohibition on access circumvention, as well as a provision prohibiting trafficking that facilitates access circumvention. The basic provision is described in the Nimmer Treatise as "equivalent to breaking into a castle," and the trafficking ban as targeting "those who facilitate the process."[53] In contrast, § 1201(b), the "additional violations" subsection, targets those who facilitate conduct amounting to circumventing protection afforded by a technological measure that protects a right of a copyright owner. The additional violations subsection does not address the conduct of someone who, having obtained lawful access to a copyrighted work, nevertheless engages in a prohibited use of that work. Such conduct is analyzed within the framework of copyright infringement generally, and the DMCA has no specific relevance to this situation. In contrast, only those who assist alleged infringers by publicly offering services or instruments designed to achieve the prohibited technological breach are within the scope of the additional violations prohibitions. Which provision of the DMCA is at issue in the Principal Problem?

   Some scholars have expressed concern about these provisions of the DMCA because they appear to facilitate the protection of works beyond the

---

[49] Id.

[50] Id. at 140.

[51] Id.

[52] See Lingo Corp. v. Topix, Inc., 2003 WL 223454, *4 (S.D.N.Y. 2003).

[53] 3 M. Nimmer and D. Nimmer, Nimmer on Copyrights § 12A.03[D][1] at 12A–33, 12A–34 (2002).

scope of copyright.[54] Thus, there is a critical connection between the DMCA, public access generally, and the fair use doctrine in particular. For example, it can be argued that the DMCA permits the encryption of fact works that do not meet the test of *Feist* (see Assignment 7), prevents the copying of works in the public domain, and prevents the decryption of material that can be fairly used under § 107. With respect to the issue of the DMCA's potential for protecting works in the public domain, the court in *Elcom* rejected this concern by concluding that copy protection measures employed by a publisher of an electronic work that is otherwise in the public domain only affords the publisher protection against copying that particular electronic version of the work.[55] Do you agree? In 2003, the Librarian of Congress created four narrow exceptions to the DMCA, thus legalizing the circumvention of copyright protections in these instances for an initial period of three years.[56]

b. *The DMCA and Fair Use.* Regarding the interplay between the DMCA and the fair use doctrine, Section 1201(c) (1) provides that "[n]othing in this section shall affect rights, remedies, limitations or defenses to copyright infringement, including fair use, under this title." The question thus arises whether this provision bars the application of the fair use doctrine when defendants are found liable for violating the DMCA. In one of the few cases to consider this issue, the Second Circuit, in *Universal City Studios, Inc. v. Corley,*[57] held fair use does not apply to an action in which the defendants were found liable for violating § 1201(a)(2) of the DMCA by trafficking a computer program that was designed to circumvent the technological measures protecting copyrighted works. In that case, the defendants had offered a computer program which could be used to decrypt CSS, a protective code included in digital versatile disk (DVD) motion picture recordings to prevent copying. Standard DVD players and Windows-

---

[54] *See generally* David Nimmer, A Riff on Fair Use in the Digital Millennium Copyright Act, 148 U. Pa. L. Rev. 673 (2000); Glynn Lunney, Jr. *The Death of Copyright: Digital Technology, Private Copying, and the Digital Millennium Copyright Act,* 87 Va. L. Rev. 813 (2001). For an interesting essay on the myths underlying concerns about copyrights on the Internet, see Cynthia Ho, *Attacking the Copyright Evildoers in Cyberspace,* 55 SMU L. Rev. 1561 (2002).

[55] 203 F.Supp.2d at 1131.

[56] These exceptions are: 1) lists of sites blocked by commercial Internet filtering software, but not spam-fighting lists; 2) computer programs protected by hardware dongles (anti-piracy devices) that prevent access due to damage or obsolescence; 3) computer programs or video games using obsolete formats or hardware; and 4) e books distributed in a format preventing read-aloud or other handicapped access formats from functioning. See also http://www.copyright.gov/1201/; 37 CFR

201.40. Previously, the following two additional narrow classes of works were exempt from § 1201(a) as well: "1) compilations consisting of lists of websites blocked by filtering software applications; and 2) literary works, including computer programs and databases, protected by access control mechanisms that fail to permit access because of malfunction, damage or obsoleteness." See 65 Fed. Reg. 64556 (61 PTCJ 4, 18, 11/3/00). Section 1201(a)(1)(C) allows the Librarian of Congress to exempt certain classes of works from the DMCA's operation every three years based on a recommendation by the Register of Copyrights if it is demonstrated that the users in question are adversely affected in their ability to make noninfringing uses. The exemptions operate for a period of three years and are subject to re-evaluation upon their expiration.

[57] 273 F.3d 429 (2d Cir. 2001).

based computers have their own way to decrypt CSS, allowing viewers to enjoy the encoded movies they buy or rent. The defendants' product permitted copying, but it was (according to defendants) really aimed at helping those who lawfully acquired DVD recordings to play them on computers that utilized the Linux operating system (this is a free system popular among computer buffs). Since these owners would not be violating copyright by playing their lawfully acquired DVDs, the defendants argued that their own activity was fair use under § 107 of the Copyright Act. In affirming the injunction issued against the defendants, the court rejected the defendants' argument that the district court's application of the DMCA unconstitutionally eliminated fair use of copyrighted materials:

> [T]he DMCA does not impose even an arguable limitation on the opportunity to make a variety of traditional fair uses of DVD movies. The fact that the resulting copy will not be as perfect or as manipulable as a digital copy obtained by having direct access to the DVD movie in its digital form, provides no basis for a claim of unconstitutional limitation of fair use. Fair use has never been held to be a guarantee of access to copyrighted material in order to copy it by the fair user's preferred technique or in the format of the original.[58]

In other words, *Corley* assumes that access circumvention is a separate violation from copyright infringement. A strong argument can be made, however, that the fair use defense can, and should, be preserved and applied in cases involving anti-circumvention on the ground that the fair use doctrine was designed to apply to all rights within the "penumbra of copyright, as well as to other intellectual property rights."[59] Is *Corley* relevant to the Principal Problem? How does *Elcom* apply to the problem? Should Sue be entitled to a fair use defense under the DMCA?

It is interesting to note a critical difference between the traditional fair use doctrine and the DRM technologies. From the standpoint of the copyright owner, fair use is a reactive doctrine in that it is invoked by a defendant as a defense to copyright infringement. In contrast, DRM technologies are proactive measures to the extent that the copyright owner maintains the ability to sanction the use before it commences.[60] In 2000 and 2003, the Copyright Office considered whether circumvention in the aid of fair use should be entitled to an exemption from the access circumvention provisions of the DMCA, but ultimately rejected the need for such a measure.[61]

c. *Encryption Research.* Another exemption rejected by the Copyright Office in 2000 would have broadened the encryption research exemption

---

[58] 37 273 F.3d at 459.

[59] *See* Jane C. Ginsburg, *From Having Copies to Experiencing Works: The Development of an Access Right in U.S. Copyright Law,* http//papers.ssrn.com/sol3/papers.cfm–abstract_id=222493 (advocating the application of specialized fair use defenses to cir-cumvention cases which are tailored to "the context of digital online distribution".)

[60] See generally Gray & DeVries, note 8, at 29.

[61] Rules and Regulations, Library of Congress, 37 CFR 201.40. See also http://www.copyright.gov/1201/.

contained in § 1201(g) of the DMCA in part so that authorization need not be attempted to be obtained from the copyright owner prior to circumvention.[62] Indeed, concern exists with respect to the DMCA's chilling impact on encryption research and scholarship generally. One illustrative case concerns the Secure Digital Music Initiative ("SDMI"), promoted by the recording industry for the purpose of creating technological standards designed to facilitate online distribution of music employing copy protection technology.[63] The SDMI announced a contest with a reward to anyone who could crack the content of its digital watermarks. Edward Felten, a professor at Princeton, did so and planned on presenting his findings at a conference. He was threatened with a lawsuit, based in part on the DMCA, by the developer of one of the watermarking technologies and the Recording Industry Association of America ("RIAA"). Felten sued for a declaratory judgment to determine the constitutionality of the DMCA. He claimed that "[w]ithout full and open access to research in areas potentially covered by the DMCA, scientists and programmers working in those areas cannot exchange ideas and fully develop their own research." [64] The court, however, granted the RIAA's motion to dismiss Felten's complaint based on the plaintiffs' lack of standing. Felten's website contains a song about the case.[65]

 d. *Extractions.* The DMCA was enacted primarily to address piracy in the digital environment. Still, one significant impact of the increased protection afforded to copyright owners under the statute is that they are in a position to obtain leverage from potential users in the form of promises (extractions). One example of such leverage is a promise requiring the user not to make a fair use of the work. Similarly, copyright owners could extract promises not to resell the work (even though resales are allowable pursuant to the first sale doctrine, see Note 2 above), or promises not to use the information learned from the work to manufacture competing products.[66] Is it socially desirable to facilitate the enforcement of such

---

[62] *Id.*

[63] See the Secure Digital Music Initiative homepage at http://www.sdmi.org/ (last updated May 18, 2001)

[64] See EFF Complaint, Felten v. RIAA (D.N.J. June 6, 2001), par. 68, quoted in Tieffa Harper, *Much Ado About the First Amendment—Does the Digital Millennium Copyright Act Impede the Right to Scientific Expression?: Felten v. Recording Association of America*, 12 DePaul–LCA J. Art & Ent. L. 3, 5 (2002).

[65] See http://www.cs.princeton.edu/?prc/AMTFelten.html

Felten did not appeal the dismissal of the case. See
http://www.eff.org/IP/DRM/DMCA/Felten_v_RIAA/20020206_eff_felten_pr.html

[66] For examples of such promises see Bowers v. Baystate Technologies, Inc., 320 F.3d 1316 (Mem) (Fed. Cir. 2003)(prohibition of reverse engineering in shrinkwrap license agreement); Lexmark International, Inc. v. Static Control Components, Inc., 253 F.Supp.2d 943 (E.D. Ky. 2003)(in exchange for a discount, consumer promised to use plaintiff's print toner cartridge only once and return the used cartridge to manufacturer); ProCD, Inc. v. Zeidenberg, 86 F.3d 1447 (7th Cir. 1996)(shrinkwrap license limiting application program to non-commercial purposes). See also Gray & DeVries, note 8 at 26–27 (discussing Microsoft's End User License Agreement for its Media Player allowing the company to install automatically in users' computers future technological updates that will safeguard the integrity of protected content). See generally Assignment 13 for a

promises? One argument for permitting them to be enforced is that they facilitate price discrimination whereby those users who do not wish to make a fair use of the work, or to resell it, would arguably pay less and those who wish to make such uses would pay more.[67] If copyright owners engaged in price discrimination absent the ability to enforce extractions, copyright users could engage in arbitrage (the ability to garner profits by acting as middle persons in an imperfect market) by reselling the works at issue to others for a higher price. Therefore, in order for price discrimination to be effective, there must be operative restrictions on the transfer of the work to other users. [68] That said, the desirability of price discrimination in this context is debatable. On the one hand, the ability to engage in price discrimination could provide creators with a greater return (thus enhancing the incentive to create), while simultaneously reducing the costs to marginal users (thus enhancing the work's dissemination). On the other hand, those who make fair uses cannot always fully capture the benefits their uses create, and therefore may not be able to afford to compensate authors an increased amount. Moreover, marginal users may not be in a position to afford to pay very much for the work at all and absent the protection of the first sale doctrine, cheap copies may become unavailable.[69] One significant issue underlying these concerns is whether the copyright doctrines of fair use and first sale preempt the effect of private contracts embodying extractions such as those discussed above. The issue of preemption is treated fully in Assignment 13.

e.  *Criminal Liability.* Elcom was a criminal action by the United States. It began when the United States arrested Dimitry Sklyarov, the Russian programmer who developed the decryption program for the defendant, for violating the DMCA's criminal provisions.[70] Sklyarov testified against his employer in exchange for being allowed to return to Russia. Although the court validated the DMCA's legality, the jury acquitted Elcomsoft of all criminal charges.[71] With respect to the issue of criminalization, the Convention on Cybercrime, to which the United States is now a party, exceeds the DMCA's criminal standards by making it a crime just to

---

treatment of the legality of such contractual promises.

[67] See Gray & DeVries, note 8, at 27 (discussing the potential for price discrimination in the context of a new DRM operating system being developed by Microsoft); Michael Meurer, *Copyright Law and Price Discrimination*, 23 Cardozo L. Rev. 55 (examining the connection between price discrimination and copyright law from a microeconomics perspective); Julie E. Cohen, *Copyright and the Perfect Curve,* 53 Vand. L. Rev. 1799 (2000)(questioning price discrimination's utility).

[68] See ProCD, Inc. v. Zeidenberg, 86 F.3d 1447, 1450 (7th Cir. 1996).

[69] For contrasting perspectives on price discrimination, see Julie Cohen, note 67, and William W. Fisher III, *Property and Contract on the Internet*, 73 Chi–Kent L. Rev. 1203 (1998).

[70] See § 1204 (allowing the imposition of a fine of not more than $500,000 or imprisonment for not more than 5 years, for a first offense).

[71] See Gray & Devries, note 8, at 24; Benchell, note 30, at 15 (noting that "[t]he fact that a computer programmer from another country could be arrested for writing a commercially available program, in his own country, sends a shiver down the collective spine of all people working in the digital industry.").

possess devices "designed or adapted primarily for the purpose of illegally accessing computers."[72]

**4.** *Public Performance.* The copyright owner's exclusive right to publicly perform her work is codified in § 106(4) of the statute. To fully explore the exemptions related to public performances, it is worth spending a moment considering what a public performance is. This is defined by § 101 of the statute, which provides that "[t]o perform or display a work 'publicly' means (1) to perform or display it at a place open to the public or at any place where a substantial number of persons outside of a normal circle of a family and its social acquaintances is gathered; or (2) to transmit or otherwise communicate a performance or display of the work to a place specified by clause (1) or to the public, by means of any device or process, whether the members of the public capable of receiving the performance or display receive it in the same place or in separate places and at the same time or at different times." [73] The first clause of this definition has been called the "public place" clause and the second clause, the "transmit" clause.[74]

Regarding the "transmit" clause, the Second Circuit has held that a copyrighted signal is publicly performed (or displayed) when it is captured and transmitted to a satellite, as opposed to being received by the viewing public.[75] Regarding the "public place" clause, in Columbia Pictures Industries, Inc. v. Redd Horne, Inc.,[76] the Third Circuit considered the defendant's operation of two stores in which videos were rented for in-store viewing in private booths. When the door to the private viewing room was closed, a signal in the counter area at the front of the stores was activated and one of the store's employees placed the selected cassette into a video machine in the front of the store and the picture was transmitted to the patron's private booth. The court ruled that the defendant's stores qualified as a "public place" under the first clause of the statutory definition because the stores were "open to the public." According to the court, the "relevant 'place' within the meaning of section 101['s definition of public performance] is each of Maxwell's two stores, not each individual booth within each store".[77] In contrast, in Columbia Pictures Industries v. Professional Real Estate Investors,[78] the court affirmed a grant of summary judgment in favor of the defendant hotel in a copyright infringement suit by movie companies against the defendant based on the hotel's practice of

---

[72] See CRS Report for Congress, Cybercrime: The Council of Europe Convention 2 (April 26, 2002) http://www,usembassy.it/pdf/other/RS21208.pdf art. 6(1)(a)(i).

[73] § 101.

[74] See Columbia Pictures Industries, Inc. v. Professional Real Estate Investors, Inc., 866 F.2d 278 (9th Cir.1989).

[75] See, e.g.,. National Football League v. Primetime 24 Joint Venture, 211 F.3d 10 (2d Cir. 2000)(rejecting the argument that any

public performance occurs during the downlink from the satellite to the home viewer).

[76] 749 F.2d 154 (3d Cir. 1984).

[77] See also Video Pipeline, Inc. v. Buena Vista Home Entertainment, Inc., 192 F.Supp.2d 321 (D.N.J. 2002)(transmission of film clip previews to individual computers owned by members of the public constitute public performance), aff'd on other grounds, 342 F.3d 191 (3d Cir. 2003), cert. denied 124 S.Ct. 1410 (2004).

[78] 866 F.2d 278 (9th Cir. 1989).

providing videodiscs for rent to its guests for viewing in their rooms. Can a meaningful distinction be made between the hotel rooms in *Professional Real Estate* and the viewing booths in *Redd Horne* for purposes of applying the "public place" clause of the statutory definition of public performance? What if the booths in *Redd Horne* contained equipment which allowed the patrons to operate the video cassettes themselves, rather than having to rely on an employee of the store to start the video? Recall the discussion in Note 1 regarding the relevance of a decentralized system in the context of file-sharing. How should other types of institutions such as prisons, day care centers, and hospitals be evaluated with respect to the application of the public performance exemption?

**5.** *Public Display.* Section 109(c) of the Copyright Act provides another limitation on a copyright owner's exclusive rights. That subsection states that the owner of a lawfully made copy of a copyrighted work can publicly display that copy, without the copyright owner's permission, "either directly or by the projection of no more than one image at a time, to viewers present at the place where the copy is located."[79] Does this provision strike a reasonable balance between the competing interests of copyright owners and copy owners? How, if at all, should the public display right be qualified in the digital era? Should the owner of a painting be allowed to post a picture of his work on the Internet without being subjected to liability for copyright infringement?[80] Should it matter whether the picture is being used to sell the item depicted? Another context in which the scope of the public display right may be tested in future litigation is framing, "the process whereby one Web site can be visited while remaining in a previous Web-site."[81]

Some commentators also have advocated the adoption of a right of private display for visual artists which would become operative upon the resale of the work.[82] Functionally, this right is equivalent to a resale royalty provision, which also is known as droit de suite. Under droit de suite, visual artists have a right to a percentage of the resale sales price of their works. Currently, California is the only state with such a statute,[83] and the Register of Copyrights has recommended against the adoption of resale

[79] § 109(c).

[80] See Video Pipeline, Inc. v. Buena Vista Home Entertainment, Inc., 192 F.Supp.2d 321 (D.N.J. 2002)(concluding, based on legislative history and the language of the statute, that such electronic transmission is prohibited because the people receiving the electronic transmission are not in the presence of the copy from which the image is derived), aff'd on other grounds, 342 F.3d 191 (3d Cir. 2003), cert. denied 124 S.Ct. 1410 (2004). *See also* R. Anthony Reese, *The Public Display Right: The Copyright Act's Neglected Solution to the Controversy Over RAM "Copies,"* 2001 U. Ill. L. Rev. 83(advocating reliance on the public display right to regulate the use of copyrighted works on computer networks).

[81] Digital Equipment Corp. v. AltaVista Technology, Inc., 960 F.Supp. 456, 461 n.12 (D. Mass. 1997).

[82] See Thomas Goetzl & Stuart Sutton, Copyright and the Visual Artist's Display Right: A New Doctrinal Analysis, 9 Colum.–VLA J.L. & Arts 15, 50, 53 (1984) (advocating the adoption of a compulsory license to effectuate this private right of display).

[83] Cal. Civ.Code § 986 (West Supp. 1993).

royalties at this time.[84]

**6.** *Section 110(5) and the Fairness in Music Licensing Act.* The purpose of § 110(5) is to exempt from copyright infringement liability anyone who simply turns on, in a public place, an ordinary radio or television. Until 1998, this section exempted from infringement the communication of a "transmission embodying a performance or display of work by the public reception of the transmission on a single receiving apparatus *of a kind commonly used in private homes....* " (emphasis supplied). Thus, proprietors of small commercial establishments who brought standard equipment onto their premises were exempt from liability. The legislative history to § 110(5) specified the following factors to consider in applying this exemption: "[T]he size, physical arrangement, and noise level of the areas within the establishment where the transmissions are made audible or visible, and the extent to which the receiving apparatus is altered or augmented for the purpose of improving the aural or visual quality of the performance for individual members of the public using those areas."[85] However, despite the guidelines provided by the statute, courts took different approaches both with respect to what factors should be considered, and how the relevant factors should be applied.[86]

In 1998, Congress enacted the Fairness in Music Licensing Act ("FIMLA") which defines the parameters of the "home-style" exemption in greater detail. Essentially, § 110(5)(B) of the statute exempts from liability

[84] Copyright Office Report Executive Summary, Droit de Suite: The Artist's Resale Royalty, 16 Colum.-VLA J.L. & Arts 381 (1992).

[85] H.R. Rep. No. 94–1476, 94th Cong.2d Sess. 87 (1976), reprinted in 1976 U.S. Code Cong. & Admin. News 5659, 5701 (1977).

[86] Cases finding an exception under § 110(5) include Broadcast Music, Inc. v. Claire's Boutiques, Inc., 949 F.2d 1482 (7th Cir.1991)(exemption found for company with more than 700 retail stores, each using two speakers hung from the ceiling, concealed speaker wire, and a receiver typically located in a closet or storage area); Edison Brothers Stores, Inc. v. Broadcast Music, Inc., 954 F.2d 1419 (8th Cir.), cert. denied, 504 U.S. 930 (1992)(holding that § 110(5) exempts large chain of clothing stores where each store had 2 speakers that were not recessed and were placed within 15 feet of the receiver). Cases failing to find an exemption include: Cass County Music Co. v. Muedini, 55 F.3d 263 (7th Cir.1995)(holding that § 110(5) did not apply to a restaurant using system with single receiver since it employed separate control panel with five selector switches, nine recessed speakers, and configuration allowing up to 40 speakers); Blue Seas Music, Inc. v. Fitness Surveys, Inc., 831 F.Supp. 863 (N.D.Ga.1993)(no § 110(5) exemption where fitness facility had 13 recessed ceiling speakers and several floor speakers); Prophet Music, Inc. v. Shamla Oil Co., 26 U.S.P.Q.2d (BNA) 1554 (D.Minn.1993)(no § 110(5) exemption for defendant's "music-on-hold" telephone system which used a receiving apparatus that was connected to sophisticated amplification and telecommunications equipment designed to retransmit the broadcasts over an unlimited number of callers' telephones); Red Cloud Music Co. v. Schneegarten, Inc., 27 U.S.P.Q.2d (BNA) 1319 (C.D.Cal. 1992)(no § 110(5) exemption for a restaurant using 8 ceiling recessed speakers with concealed wiring where the receiver/amplifier was located in a separate room and the restaurant was about 3,000 square feet); and U.S. Songs, Inc. v. Downside Lenox, Inc., 771 F.Supp. 1220 (N.D.Ga.1991)(§ 110(5) did not apply to establishment containing 20 ceiling mounted speakers attached to a radio receiver placed behind a bar because the system was not of a type commonly used in private homes and the sounds were further transmitted since they were dispersed throughout the establishment).

public performances of nondramatic musical works originated by a licensed radio or television station in bars and restaurants having less than 3750 square feet; other establishments are exempt if they have less than 2000 square feet. For an establishment with a greater gross square footage than these specified amounts, the exemptions are as follows: audio performances are exempt if there are no more than six total loudspeakers, of which not more than four are in any one room; audiovisual performances are exempt if the visual portion is displayed by not more than four total devices, of which only one is located in any single room and has a diagonal screen no greater than 55 inches.[87]

A World Trade Organization dispute settlement panel has concluded that § 110(5) violates the TRIPS Agreement by failing to adhere to Art. 11 of the Berne Convention. Art. 11, which is incorporated into the TRIPS Agreement via Art. 9.1 of TRIPS, gives authors of musical works the exclusive right to authorize public performances of their works and "any communication to the public of the performance of their works." Thus, a dispute settlement panel of the World Trade Organization ("WTO") has concluded that the current version of 110(5) violates the TRIPS Agreement by derogating from authors' exclusive rights to authorize performances and communications of their work to the public. Specifically, although the TRIPS Agreement is highly protective of authors' rights, it does contemplate limitations which are reserved for: 1) *special cases* which 2) *do not conflict with a normal exploitation* of the work and 3) *do not reasonably prejudice* the legitimate interests of the right holder," Art. 13 (emphasis supplied). The WTO decision explores at length the different methods of calculating lost revenue to the right holders under the new 110(5) invoked by the United States and the European Communities, respectively. Ultimately, the WTO concluded that subpart B of the current version of 110(5) violates the third condition noted above because the United States did not adequately demonstrate that the new provision "does not reasonably prejudice the legitimate interests of the right holder" in light of the actual and potential effects of the exemption.[88] As of this writing, the United States and the European Community have agreed to a three-year deal pursuant to which the United States will pay over a million dollars in annual compensation to European performance rights organizations, which will then be distributed to European Community music copyright holders. This amount was based on a determination by a World Trade Organization arbitration team in 2001.[89] The United States is also supposed to work toward repealing FIMLA.

[87] For a comprehensive critique of this provision, see Laurence Helfer, *World Music on a U.S. Stage: A Berne/TRIPS and Economic Analysis of the Fairness in Music Licensing Act*, 80 B.U. L. Rev. 93 (2000).

[88] The decision can be accessed at www. wto.org, followed by a document search for document number (00–2284).

[89] See Daniel Pruzin, *WTO Grants $1.1 Million in Damages to Artists in U.S. Music Licensing Complaint*, 18 International Trade Reporter No. 41, p. 1649 (Oct. 2001)(the specific amount was 1.2 million euros, which converts into about $1.1 million U.S. dollars).

**7.** *ASCAP AND BMI.* One may question how the holders of copyrights in musical compositions insure that their rights are not violated. ASCAP (American Society of Composers, Authors, and Publishers) and BMI (Broadcast Music, Inc.) illustrate the principle that there is strength in numbers. The idea underlying these organizations is that a centralized body is better able to represent the interests of its individual members with respect to recouping royalty fees for public performances of music.[90] Taken together, ASCAP and BMI control ninety-five percent of the United States market for performance rights to musical compositions. ASCAP represents more than 40,000 composers and publishers and controls a repertoire of about 3 million compositions and BMI represents more than 100,000 members and controls about 1.5 million compositions.[91] ASCAP and BMI are vigilant about protecting their members' interests. The Fairness in Musical Licensing Act, discussed in Note 6, added a new section to the Copyright Act which addresses the determination of reasonable license rates charged by performing rights societies.[92]

**8.** *The TEACH Act.* In 2002, Congress amended § 110(2) of the Copyright statute by enacting the TEACH Act. Generally speaking, the TEACH Act expands the scope of the rights of distance educators working at accredited nonprofit educational institutions so that their rights to perform and display works, and to make copies of works integral to such performances and displays, are more consistent with the rights enjoyed by educators involved in traditional classroom instruction. Under this provision, distance educators can transmit entire performances of non-dramatic literary or musical works, although other performances (such as films and videos) can be transmitted only in reasonable and limited portions. Displays of any work can be transmitted in amounts comparable to typical face-to-face displays. Significantly, the TEACH Act does not cover works produced or marketed primarily for use in the digital distance education market. Nor does it cover works that an educator wishes students to study on their own time outside of the classroom. Thus, the fair use doctrine will still continue to be of prime importance in light of the relatively limited exemptions provided by the TEACH Act. Also, a new provision was added (§ 112(f)) authorizing educators to copy digital works and to digitize portions of an analog work in an amount authorized under § 110(2) if no digital version is

---

[90] These organizations license only "non-dramatic" or small performing rights, as opposed to "dramatic" or grand rights. Dramatic rights typically are licensed by agents who act in the interest of the copyright proprietors. See Joseph P. Scorese, Performing Broadway Music: The Demon Grand Rights Traps, 13 Colum.–VLA J.L. & Arts 261, 267 (1989).

[91] See Janet Avery, The Struggle Over Performing Rights to Music: BMI and AS-CAP vs. Cable Television, 14 Hastings Comm. & Ent. L.J. 47, 51 (1991). The Copyright Clearance Center, which was estab-

lished in 1977, performs essentially the same function as ASCAP and BMI in the context of photocopying copyrighted materials that are registered with the Center. The Center, as agent for publishers, grants blanket advance permission to photocopy the registered materials for a fee and remits these fees to the copyright owners.

[92] See § 513. See United States v. Broadcast Music, Inc., 316 F.3d 189 (2d Cir. 2003)(first time Second Circuit was invited to review a district court rate-setting pursuant to the BMI Consent Decree).

available or the available digital version is subject to technological protection measures preventing its use for § 110(2).[93]

**9.** *Limited rights for Sound Recordings..* Section 114 of the Copyright Act defines the scope of exclusive rights in sound recordings. Note that the statutory definition of sound recordings provides that they "are works that result from the fixation of a series of musical, spoken, or other sounds ... regardless of the nature of the material objects, such as disks, tapes, or other phonorecords, in which they are embodied."[94] Section 114 of the statute states that the exclusive rights of the owner of a copyright in a sound recording are limited to the rights of reproduction, distribution, and preparation of derivative works under § 106, but do not include the exclusive rights to display the work and to perform it publicly (except for performances of sound recordings by means of a digital audio transmission under § 106(6) discussed below). Why does the statute makes this distinction?

Section 114 also provides that with respect to the rights of reproduction and preparation of derivative works, the copyright owner has the exclusive right to duplicate the recording in forms that directly or indirectly recapture "the actual sounds fixed in the recording", but her rights "do not extend to the making or duplication of another sound recording that consists entirely of an independent fixation of other sounds, even though such sounds imitate or simulate those in the copyrighted sound recording."[95]

Why does the statute adopt this "actual reproduction" standard for infringement for sound recordings, thereby differentiating sound recordings from other types of copyrighted works that are infringed when the unauthorized reproduction or derivative work is "substantially similar"? Is the need for public access greater with respect to sound recordings than for other types of copyrighted works? In light of the foregoing, how would you evaluate the legality of digital sampling—a technique that involves the following steps: the recordation of a sound, its analysis, decomposition, storage of the tonal qualities in a computer, possible electronic alteration, and playback. What copyright issues are necessary to resolve in determining the legality of digital sampling? [96]

In 1995, Congress enacted the Digital Performance Right in Sound Recordings Act which provides that copyright protection in sound recordings extends to performing "the copyrighted work publicly by means of a digital audio transmission" (§ 106(6)). The Act defines a "digital transmission" as "a transmission in whole or in part in a digital or other non-analog

[93] See generally http://www.unc.edu/¿unclng.TEACH.htm & http://www.utsystem.edu/ogc/intellectualproperty/teachact.htm

[94] § 101.

[95] § 114.

[96] Recent cases on digital sampling include: Newton v. Diamond, 204 F.Supp.2d 1244 (C.D. Cal. 2002)(rejecting originality of sequence sampled and concluding that defendant's use was de minimis); Bridgeport Music, Inc. v. Dimension Films LLC, 230 F.Supp.2d 830 (M.D.Tenn. 2002)(holding use de minimis).

format."[97] It also contains exemptions for certain transmissions and retransmissions,[98] as well as provisions for compulsory licensing.[99] The Digital Millennium Copyright Act further expands the relevant exemptions in connection with ephemeral recordings under § 112 of the Copyright Act to permit the making of a single ephemeral recording to facilitate the digital transmission of a sound recording permitted under the Digital Performance Right in Sound Recordings Act.

**10.** *Compulsory licensing.* The Copyright statute contains several provisions for compulsory licensing. Section 111(c) provides for compulsory licenses for secondary transmissions by cable systems; § 112 encompasses a license for making ephemeral recordings (this licensing provision was added by the Digital Millennium Copyright Act); § 114 covers digital subscription transmissions of sound recordings (pursuant to the Digital Performance Right in Sound Recordings Act); § 115 mandates compulsory licenses for making and distributing phonorecords and licenses for digital phonorecord deliveries; § 116 provides for compulsory licenses for jukeboxes; § 118 specifies compulsory licenses for public broadcasters; and § 119 requires compulsory licenses for satellite retransmissions to the public for private home viewing. In addition, the Digital Millennium Copyright Act added to § 114 a provision expanding the license for digital subscription transmissions to include webcasting as a new category of "eligible nonsubscription transmissions." Webcasting refers to the use of the Internet to make a digital transmission of a sound recording with streaming audio technology.[100]

The rates and terms of a compulsory license are determined in one of two ways, either through a process based upon voluntary negotiations,[101] or where necessary, by means of an arbitration proceeding as prescribed in Chapter 8 of the Copyright Act. Until 1993, the Copyright Royalty Tribunal ("CRT") was responsible for adjusting the rates and terms for the compulsory licenses and determining the distribution of those royalty fees collected pursuant to the Copyright Act. However, in 1993, Congress abolished the CRT with the passage of the Copyright Tribunal Reform Act of 1993, and vested authority for administering these proceedings in the Librarian of Congress.[102]

What effect do compulsory licenses have on the price the copyright holder obtains for the work? What are the policies favoring and disfavoring compulsory licenses?

---

[97] See § 101.

[98] See § 114(d).

[99] See §§ 114(d) & 115.

[100] The Copyright Office has resolved issues pertaining to the determination of reasonable rates and terms for the digital performance of sound recordings by webcasters and ephemeral recordings. See 67 FR 45240; 37 CFR § 261.1 (applying the "willing buyer/willing seller" standard).

[101] See, e.g., 17 U.S.C. §§ 111(d)(4)(A); 112(e)(3)(4)(6) & (7); 114(e) & (f); 115(c)(3)(B)–(F); 116(b); 118(b)–(d)(2); 119(c)(2). Many of these statutory provisions clarify that parties may enter into private agreements without raising antitrust concerns.

[102] See, e.g., Recording Industry Association of America v. Librarian of Congress, 176 F.3d 528 (D.C. Cir. 1999)(concluding that rate terms for a compulsory license under § 114 were not supported by the evidence).

**11.** *Other defenses.* Although the fair use doctrine is by far the most notable defense to copyright infringement, other defenses also can be invoked where appropriate. Equitable defenses such as laches, estoppel,[103] and unclean hands often are raised in copyright infringement actions. Laches is proven when a defendant establishes that the plaintiff *inexcusably or unreasonably* delayed in bringing suit and the defendant was prejudiced by this delay.[104] Estoppel requires the plaintiff to aid the defendant in committing the allegedly infringing acts, or to induce or cause their performance by the defendant.[105] Unclean hands require that the plaintiff either participated in the infringing acts or committed fraud or some other "transgression" which resulted "in harm or prejudice to the defendant."[106]

Perhaps the most controversial defense in recent years is copyright misuse, which has been explicitly rejected by several courts as a viable defense in copyright infringement litigation.[107] Other courts assumed that copyright misuse only can be established when a violation of antitrust law has been shown.[108] The Fourth Circuit, however, breathed new life into the copyright misuse defense in 1990 in Lasercomb v. Reynolds,[109] in which it endorsed the following broad version of the defense: "The question is not whether the copyright is being used in a manner violative of antitrust law . . . , but whether the copyright is being used in a manner violative of the public policy embodied in the grant of a copyright."[110] Since *Lasercomb*, numerous courts have explicitly accepted copyright misuse as a viable defense, even if no antitrust violation can be shown.[111] In Lexmark International, Inc. v. Static Control Components, Inc., the court held that the plaintiff's attempt to enforce rights under the DMCA does not constitute an unlawful act designed to stifle competition and cannot thereby be deemed misuse.[112] A likely area for future litigation is whether the use of private

---

[103] See, e.g., John G. Danielson, Inc. v. Winchester–Conant Properties, Inc., 322 F.3d 26 (1st Cir. 2003)(holding that evidence did not establish sufficient knowledge on the part of the plaintiff to support estoppel).

[104] See, e.g., See Jacobsen v. Deseret Book Company, 287 F.3d 936 (10th Cir. 2002)(reversing district court's issuance of summary judgement on the issue of laches); Danjaq LLC v. Sony Corp., 263 F.3d 942 (9th Cir. 2001) (affirming district court's application of laches to prevent resolution of a copyright infringement claim); Lyons Partnership, L.P. v. Morris Costumes, Inc., 243 F.3d 789 (4th Cir. 2001)(concluding that laches should not bar copyright infringement claim).

[105] Coleman v. ESPN, Inc., 764 F.Supp. 290, 295 (S.D.N.Y.1991).

[106] *Id.* at 296.

[107] *Id.* at 295.

[108] See, e.g., Bellsouth Advertising & Publishing Corp. v. Donnelley Info. Publish-ing., 933 F.2d 952, 960–61 (11th Cir. 1991)(apparently requiring an antitrust violation to sustain copyright misuse defense).

[109] 911 F.2d 970 (4th Cir.1990).

[110] *Id.* at 978 (holding that the anticompetitive clauses in plaintiff's standard licensing agreement constitute copyright misuse).

[111] See, e.g., Alcatel USA, Inc. v. DGI Technologies, Inc., 166 F.3d 772 (5th Cir. 1999); Practice Management Information Corp. v. American Medical Association, 121 F.3d 516, amended, 133 F.3d 1140 (9th Cir. 1998); Qad, Inc. v. ALN Assoc., Inc., 974 F.2d 834 (7th Cir. 1992).

[112] 253 F.Supp.2d 943, 966 (E.D. Ky. 2003). See also Sony Computer Entm't Am., Inc. v. Gamemasters, 87 F.Supp.2d 976 (N.D.Cal. 1999) (rejecting claim that Sony was "misusing" its copyright by invoking the DMCA).

enforcement mechanisms, combined with technologically based restrictions which serve to limit users' rights for the benefit of copyright owners, will be held violative of copyright law under the misuse doctrine. See Note 3d.

# ASSIGNMENT 12

# REMEDIES

## 1. INTRODUCTION

As the materials below demonstrate, a variety of remedies for copyright infringement are available. With respect to damages, the remedial provisions of the 1976 Act allow a copyright proprietor who establishes infringement the choice of recovering either 1) statutory damages, or 2) actual damages and any of the infringer's profits not factored into the actual damage award.[1] The limitations upon these awards and the manner in which they are calculated are explored in the materials which follow. In addition, a court may impound the infringing materials and order their destruction or other disposition.[2] Courts also have the discretion to award costs and attorney's fees to the prevailing party.[3] Although most copyright infringement actions are civil in nature, § 506 of the Act provides for criminal liability for "[a]ny person who infringes a copyright willfully and for purposes of commercial advantage or private financial gain."[4] Criminal penalties are treated specifically as part of the Piracy, Counterfeiting, and Bootlegging Amendments.[5] The government rarely prosecutes an infringer under the criminal provision, but when it is invoked, it usually is in connection with massive sound-recording or film piracy infringements.[6] The DMCA also contains provisions for criminal penalties.[7] Also, in 1997, Congress passed the No Electronic Theft Act.[8] This statute provides criminal penalties for willful copyright infringement through electronic and other avenues. Specifically, it defines criminal infringement as either 1) infringement "for purposes of commercial advantage or private financial gain" or 2) "the reproduction or distribution, including by electronic means, during any 180–day period of 1 or more copies or phonorecords of 1 or more copyrighted works", with a total retail value of more than $1000.[9]

---

[1] § 504.

[2] § 503.

[3] § 505.

[4] § 506(a). Sections 506(b) and 509 also provide for the seizure and forfeiture of infringing goods when a person is convicted of criminal copyright infringement.

[5] See § 2319, The Piracy and Counterfeiting Amendments Act of 1984, 18 U.S.C.A. §§ 2318–2319A.

[6] See 3 Melville B. Nimmer & David Nimmer, Nimmer on Copyright, 15.01[C] (1993).

[7] § 1204(a). In general, however, the remedies for violating the DMCA essentially comport with those for other copyright infringements. Section 1203 provides for an array of equitable and monetary relief. With respect to innocent infringers, courts have discretion to reduce or remit damages under § 1203(c)(5).

[8] Pub. L. No. 105–147; 111 Stat. 2678.

[9] § 506(a). See generally Lydia Pallas Loren, Digitization, Commodification, Criminalization: The Evolution of Criminal Copyright Infringement and the Importance of the

In 1998, Congress amended the definition of criminal infringement in § 506(a) to comport with the No Electronic Theft Act.

The 1976 Act also provides courts with the discretion to issue both temporary (preliminary) and final (permanent) injunctive relief.[10] A copyright plaintiff thus may attempt to obtain preliminary injunctive relief that will be effective during the course of litigation. Typically, such preliminary relief will be granted where a plaintiff establishes a likelihood of success on the merits and a showing of irreparable harm, which is presumed when a plaintiff establishes a *prima facie* case of copyright infringement.[11] The case law indicates that preliminary injunctions are generally issued liberally in copyright litigation.[12] A successful copyright plaintiff also may be entitled to permanent injunctive relief where there is a threat of continuing violations on the part of the defendant. Of course, injunctive relief is not an effective remedy against infringements that occurred prior to the institution of the lawsuit.

## 2. PRINCIPAL PROBLEM

Your law firm represents Kira Silver, the promoter of the famous boxer, Bobby "Boxem" Carter. Recently, Carter was in a boxing match with a formidable opponent, James "Knockemdead" Smith. The fight aired only on cable television, and Silver owns the copyright to that broadcast. Silver sent WJN, a local broadcasting station in a major city, a telegram prior to the fight warning the station against broadcasting any part of the fight. Still, upon advice of counsel, WJN picked up 22 seconds of the fight (15 action and 7 stillframe) from the cable broadcast and used this footage in its evening news broadcast. The entire fight was 13 rounds, and each round consisted of three minutes. In addition, Silver had sold the delayed broadcast rights to the fight to NBC for four million dollars. NBC is quite upset and is threatening to rescind its agreement with Silver.

Silver sued WJN for copyright infringement. The district court granted summary judgment for the defendant on the issue of liability, concluding that WJN's use was fair. Silver wants to appeal and you have been assigned the remedies portion of the case. Your colleagues tell you that the merits of the fair use claim present a close question, but you should assume Silver can prevail on appeal. In advising Silver, be sure to include your opinion on whether Silver would be entitled to prospective injunctive relief; statutory damages; actual damages and WJN's profits; and costs and attorney's fees.

Willfulness Requirement, 77 Wash. U.L.Q. 835 (1999).

[10] § 502 (a).

[11] Bourne Co. v. Tower Records, Inc., 976 F.2d 99, 101 (2d Cir.1992).

[12] See, e.g., MAI Systems Corp. v. Peak Computer, Inc., 1992 WL 159803 (C.D.Cal. 1992); E.F. Johnson Co. v. Uniden Corp., 623 F.Supp. 1485, 1490–91 (D.Minn.1985). See generally Ralph Brown, Civil Remedies for Intellectual Property Invasions: Themes and Variations, 55 Law & Contemp. Probs. 45, 46–49 (1992).

3.   MATERIALS FOR SOLUTION OF PRINCIPAL PROBLEM

A.   STATUTORY MATERIALS: §§ 412 & 501–511

B.   CASES:

# Universal City Studios, Inc. v. Ahmed

United States District Court, E.D. Pennsylvania, 1993.
29 U.S.P.Q.2D (BNA) 1775.

■ HUTTON, JUDGE.

I.   Factual Background

In their complaint, the plaintiffs allege that the defendants infringed the plaintiffs' copyright to the motion picture Jurassic Park by selling or holding for sale pirated videocassettes of the film. On June 18, 1993, this Court granted the plaintiffs' motion for preliminary injunctive relief and entered an Order permitting the plaintiffs to seize the counterfeit videocassettes and other merchandise from the defendants.

The Court scheduled a Return Hearing for June 28, 1993. At the Return Hearing, defendants agreed to the entry of a permanent injunction prohibiting them from ever selling any merchandise bearing the copyrights and/or trademarks of plaintiffs in and to Jurassic Park.

II.   Discussion

Motion for Default Judgment

The plaintiffs have moved the Court to enter a default judgment against the defendants because they failed to plead or otherwise defend the action. Rule 55 of the Federal Rules of Civil Procedure grants the Court the power to enter default judgments in such circumstances. Rule 55 also provides that, "if, in order to enable the court to enter judgment . . . , it is necessary to determine the amount of damages, . . . the court may conduct such hearings as it deems necessary and proper." Fed.R.Civ.P. 55(b)(2).

The plaintiffs do not simply seek to have judgment entered against the defendants, they also seek to recover statutory damages and attorney's fees. However, the present record before the Court does not provide an adequate factual basis to support the award of statutory damages. Under 17 U.S.C. § 504, the plaintiffs may recover statutory damages—

> for all infringements involved in the action, with respect to any one work, for which any one infringer is liable individually, or for which two or more infringers are liable jointly and severally, in a sum of not less than $500 or more than $20,000 as the court considers just.

Section 504(c)(1). In cases of "wilful" infringement, the court may increase the damages award beyond the $20,000 limit set forth in § 504(c)(1).[a]

---

[a] Although the plaintiffs assert in their Memorandum of Law that the court may award a maximum of $50,000, the statute was amended in 1989 to permit the court to award up to $100,000 in cases of wilful infringement. § 504(c)(2).

It is well established that the Court need not conduct an evidentiary hearing prior to awarding a plaintiff statutory damages pursuant to a default judgment. However, in the absence of an evidentiary hearing, a plaintiff must present sufficiently "detailed affidavits" to permit the court to apply the appropriate factors in awarding statutory damages. [Citations omitted.]

Because the plaintiffs have sought an amount in excess of that set forth in 504(c)(1), the first question the Court must address is whether the plaintiffs can sustain the burden of proving that the infringement was wilful. § 504(c)(2). The term "wilfully" is not defined in the Copyright Act. Courts that have considered the question have defined "wilfulness" as requiring plaintiffs to show that the infringer acted with "actual knowledge or reckless disregard for whether its conduct infringed upon the plaintiff's copyright." Original Appalachian Artworks, Inc. v. J.F. Reichert, Inc., 658 F.Supp. 458, 464 (E.D.Pa.1987). The defendants' knowledge need not be proven directly, but may be inferred from the defendant's conduct.

On the record currently before the Court, the plaintiffs sustain their burden of proving that the defendants wilfully infringed the plaintiffs' copyright to Jurassic Park. Jurassic Park was released in theaters in the Philadelphia metropolitan area on June 10, 1993. At the time the tapes were seized, the motion picture was not yet legally available on videocassettes. This is customary and it is common knowledge that films are not released on videocassette until many months or years after the film has appeared in movie theaters. Yet, between June 15, 1993 and June 17, 1993, less than one week after the film's release in movie theaters, the defendants were observed selling videocassettes of Jurassic Park. From this, it can be inferred that the defendants knew they were infringing the plaintiffs' copyright, or at the very least, they exhibited reckless disregard. Thus, the court may, in its discretion, award up to $100,000 for the infringement of the plaintiffs' copyright.

The court has broad discretion in determining the appropriate measure of statutory damages within the range permitted by the statute. The following three factors are relevant in determining the appropriate measure of statutory damages under § 504: (1) expenses saved and profits reaped by defendants in connection with the infringement; (2) revenues lost by the plaintiffs; and (3) whether the infringement was wilful and knowing, or whether it was accidental and innocent. The factors, however, are not of equal weight. As one court within this circuit has stated:

> "in weighing these factors, most courts that have pondered the issue do not attach great weight to profits gained or to income lost, because these amounts are difficult to monetize. . . . Courts thus have focused largely on the element of intent, and the per infringement award tends understandably to escalate, in direct proportion to the blameworthiness of the infringing conduct."

*Original Appalachian*, 658 F.Supp., at 465 (quotation omitted). Although statutory damages "should bear some relation to actual damages", Association of American Med. Colleges v. Mikaelian, 1986 W.L. 332 (E.D.Pa.1986), the court may award statutory damages even if there is no evidence whatsoever before the court as to the defendant's profits, the defendant's costs avoided, or the plaintiff's lost profits. See H.R. Rep. No. 1476, 94th Cong., 2d Sess. 161. This is because statutory damages are designed not solely to compensate the copyright owner for losses incurred, but also to deter future infringement. F.W. Woolworth Co. v. Contemporary Arts, 344 U.S. 228, 233 (1952).

The plaintiffs have provided absolutely no evidence as to the defendants' profits or costs avoided, or the plaintiffs' lost profits as a result of the infringements. The plaintiffs' attorney attempted to calculate lost profits in the plaintiffs' memorandum of law, but this is not evidence.[b] Although evidence as to the defendants' profits or costs avoided such as licensing fees and/or the plaintiffs' lost profits would be relevant to the court's consideration, there is a sufficient evidentiary basis to conclude that statutory damages in some amount would be appropriate.

Thus, if there was only one defendant in the present case, there would be an adequate factual basis to award statutory damages without the need for a hearing or additional affidavits. However, the current record does not permit the court to award damages where, as here, there are numerous defendants.

Moreover, as a matter of law, the plaintiffs are not entitled to the measure of damages that they seek. The plaintiffs seek one $50,000 statutory damages award against each defendant for each copyright violation, that is, for each tape that each defendant sold or held for sale. The express language of § 504(c) and the case law interpreting § 504 clearly preclude such a recovery.

In Walt Disney Co. v. Powell, the United States Court of Appeals for the District of Columbia Circuit reversed the district court's statutory damages award because the district court "mistakenly focused on the number of infringements rather than the number of works infringed." 897 F.2d 565, 569 (D.C.Cir.1990). Rather, according to the court, "only one penalty lies for multiple infringements of one work." *Id.* (citing H.R. Rep. No. 1476, 94th Cong., 2d Sess. 161 ("A single infringer of a single work is liable for a single amount ... no matter how many acts of infringement are involved in the action and regardless of whether the acts were separate, isolated, or occurred in a related series....")). Thus, the law is clear that

---

[b] Moreover, without further factual support, plaintiffs' counsel's estimate is not persuasive. He asserts that the average price of a movie ticket is $7.50. He further asserts that "each [counterfeit] film could be viewed on a daily basis by 25 (or more) people times 365 ..., that is $60,937.50 in direct losses for each one copy of the film in a year." Because Jurassic Park is almost two hours in length, it is difficult to understand how 25 or more people could view the film in a single day, unless the counterfeiter or the purchaser of the counterfeit film is publicly exhibiting it. There is no factual basis from which to draw such an inference.

no matter how many times a defendant infringed the plaintiffs' copyright to Jurassic Parks, the plaintiffs are entitled to only one statutory damages award.

Notably absent from the plaintiffs' memorandum of law is any reference to *Powell* or the House Report to § 504. Rather, the plaintiffs cite two cases, BMG Music v. Perez, 952 F.2d 318 (9th Cir.1991), and Flyte Tyme Tunes v. Miszkiewicz, 715 F.Supp. 919 (E.D.Wis.1989), to support their assertion that they are entitled to recover for each any every tape sold or held for sale.[c]

*Perez* and *Miszkiewicz* simply do not stand for the proposition for which they are cited. In both cases the courts did enter multiple statutory damages awards. However, in both cases, unlike the present case, more than one copyright was infringed. See *Perez*, 952 F.2d, at 319 (plaintiffs alleged that the defendant purchased plaintiffs' copyrighted sound recordings and sold them in violation of the Copyright Act); *Miszkiewicz*, 715 F.Supp., at 919 (plaintiffs sought damages based on defendant's unauthorized public performance of copyrighted musical compositions). In the present case, the express language of § 504, the legislative history [and] *Powell* delineate the applicable rule of law; this rule of law does not permit the plaintiffs to recover for each tape sold or held for sale because only one copyright was infringed.

For the foregoing reasons, the Court denies the plaintiffs' Motion for Default Judgment. The plaintiffs are granted leave to renew their motion in a manner consistent with this opinion.

An appropriate Order follows.

# On Davis v. The Gap, Inc.

United States Court of Appeals for the Second Circuit, 2001.
246 F.3d 152.

■ LEVAL, CIRCUIT JUDGE:

Plaintiff On Davis ("Davis") appeals from an order of the United States District Court for the Southern District of New York (Sweet, J.) granting summary judgment to the defendant, The Gap, Inc. ("the Gap"), dismissing plaintiff's claim of copyright infringement.

Davis is the creator and designer of nonfunctional jewelry worn over the eyes in the manner of eyeglasses. The Gap, Inc. is a major international retailer of clothing and accessories marketed largely to a youthful customer base with annual revenues of several billions of dollars. It operates several chains of retail stores, some under the name "Gap." It is undisputed that the Gap, without Davis's permission, used a photograph of an individual

[c] It is noteworthy that with respect to both *Perez* and *Miszkiewicz*, counsel for the plaintiffs failed to provide an accurate case name and failed to provide an accurate citation. In contrast, every other citation in the plaintiffs' memorandum of law is accurate as to the case name, and as to the book and page where the case can be found.

wearing Davis's copyrighted eyewear in an advertisement for the stores operating under the "Gap" trademark that was widely displayed throughout the United States. Davis brought this action seeking a declaratory judgment of infringement and damages, including $2,500,000 in unpaid licensing fees, a percentage of the Gap's profits, punitive damages of $10,000,000, and attorney's fees. The district court granted summary judgment for the Gap on the grounds that (1) Davis's claims for actual damages and profits under 17 U.S.C. § 504 (b) (1994) were too speculative to support recovery, or were otherwise barred by a prior ruling of this court, (2) he was not eligible for statutory damages or attorney's fees because he had not timely registered his copyright, and (3) the Copyright Act does not permit recovery of punitive damages. See Davis I, 1999 U.S. Dist. LEXIS 5689, 1999 WL 199005, at *3–8. We affirm in part and, in part, vacate and remand.

BACKGROUND

Davis has created at least fifteen different designs of eye jewelry, which he markets under the name "Onoculii Designs." Davis describes Onoculii eyewear as "sculptured metallic ornamental wearable art." Am. Compl. P 7. The particular piece that gives rise to this action consists of a horizontal bar at the level of the eyebrows from which are suspended a pair of slightly convex, circular discs of polished metal covering the eyes, perforated with dozens of tiny pinprick holes. Davis registered his copyright for the design at issue, effective May 16, 1997.

Davis sought to gain recognition for his Onoculii line by promoting and marketing his designs "in carefully chosen media settings." Am. Compl. P 13. As part of his marketing plan, Davis encouraged "known stylish and popular entertainers" to wear his creations in public settings.

While Davis initially sold his designs on the street, since about 1995 he has marketed his merchandise through boutiques and optical stores. The eyewear sold at a wholesale price of approximately $30–45 a pair. Evidence in the record indicates that it sold at retail for $65–100 a pair in 1995. See Am. Compl., Ex. B. Davis asserts he has earned approximately $10,000 from sales. He testified that on one occasion he received a $50 fee from Vibe magazine for the use of a photograph depicting the musician Sun Ra wearing an Onoculii piece.

In May 1996, prior to Davis's registration of his copyright, the defendant created a series of advertisements showing photographs of people of various lifestyles wearing Gap clothing. The campaign was designed to promote the concept that Gap merchandise is worn by people of all kinds. The ad in question, which bears the caption "fast" emblazoned in red (the "fast" ad), depicts a group of seven young people probably in their twenties, of Asian appearance, standing in a loose V formation staring at the camera with a sultry, pouty, provocative look. The group projects the image of funky intimates of a lively after-hours rock music club. They are dressed primarily in black, exhibiting bare arms and partly bare chests, goatees (accompanied in one case by bleached, streaked hair), large-brimmed, Western-style hats, and distinctive eye shades, worn either over their eyes, on their hats, or cocked over the top of their heads. The central figure, at the apex of the V formation, is wearing Davis's highly distinctive Onoculii eyewear; he peers over the metal disks directly into the camera lens.

The "fast" photograph was taken by the Gap in May 1996 during a photo shoot in the Tribeca area of Manhattan. The defendant provided the subjects with Gap apparel to wear for the shoot, and a trailer in which to change. The Gap claims that it did not furnish eyewear to any of the subjects, and that the subjects were told to wear their own eyewear, wristwatches, earrings, nose-rings or other incidental items, thereby "permitting each person to project accurately his or her own personal image and appearance." Def.'s 56.1(c) Statement, P18.

The Gap's "fast" advertisement was published in a variety of magazines, including W, Vanity Fair, Spin, Details, and Entertainment Weekly. Davis claims that the total circulation of these magazines was over 2,500,000. For five weeks during August and September of 1996, the advertisement was displayed on the sides of buses in New York, Boston, Chicago, San Francisco, Atlanta, Washington, D.C., and Seattle. The advertisement may also have been displayed on bus shelters. According to Davis, when used on buses the photograph was cropped so that only the heads and shoulders of the subjects were shown.

Davis submitted evidence showing that during the fourth quarter of 1996, the period that Davis asserts is relevant to the "fast" advertisement, the net annual sales of the parent company, Gap, Inc., increased by about 10 percent, compared to the fourth quarter of 1995, to $1.668 billion dollars. There was no evidence of what portion of the parent company's revenues were attributable to the stores operated under the Gap label, much less what portion was related to the ad in question.

Shortly after seeing the "fast" advertisement in October and November 1996, Davis contacted the Gap by telephone and in writing. The Gap's advertising campaign, which apparently ran during August and September of 1996, had been completed by the time Davis wrote. Davis stated that he had not authorized the use of his design and inquired whether the Gap might be interested in selling a line of his eyewear.

Davis filed this action on November 19, 1997. The Gap then filed a motion for summary judgment, arguing, inter alia, that Davis had no entitlement to damages and that his claims were barred by the de minimis and fair use doctrines.

On April 9, 1999, the district court granted summary judgment for the Gap. See Davis I, 1999 U.S. Dist. LEXIS 5689, 1999 WL 199005, at *10. The district court first noted that Davis was not eligible for "statutory damages" under 17 U.S.C. § 504 (c) due to the fact that he had not registered his copyright within three months of his first "publication" of his work or prior to the allegedly infringing use by the Gap.[a] As regards damages under 17 U.S.C. § 504 (b), the court rejected Davis's claim as unduly speculative and, insofar as it sought damages for Davis's failure to receive a license fee from the Gap, precluded by a prior decision of this court. See Davis I, 1999 U.S. Dist. LEXIS 5689, 1999 WL 199005, at *3–7. Since the court also found Davis ineligible for punitive damages, it concluded that he was not entitled to any form of damages, and thus dismissed his claims. See id. at *8, 10. Davis filed a motion for reconsideration on April 27, 1999, which was denied on June 16, 1999. See Davis II, 186 F.R.D. 322.

On appeal, Davis argues principally that (1) the district court erred by granting summary judgment without ruling on the merits of his claim for declaratory relief; and (2) he was entitled to both compensatory and punitive damages. The Gap defends the district court's judgment and argues in addition that the suit was subject to dismissal under the de minimis and fair use doctrines.

We affirm in part and reverse in part.

DISCUSSION

A.  Declaratory Relief

Davis contends that it was improper for the district court to grant summary judgment on his copyright claims without first determining whether the defendant infringed his copyright. The complaint expressly sought "a declaratory judgment in favor of Mr. Davis against GAP, declaring" that the Gap had infringed Davis's copyright by its reproduction of his eyewear in its advertisement. Am. Compl., P A. The district court granted the defendant's motion for summary judgment on the basis of a variety of theories that had no bearing on the demand for declaratory relief. No doubt because of the confusing and prolix nature of the complaint, this aspect of the relief sought was overlooked. The existence of damages suffered is not an essential element of a claim for copyright infringement. The owner of a copyright is thus entitled to prevail in a claim for declaratory judgment of infringement without showing entitlement to monetary relief. Insofar as the judgment dismissed the claim for declaratory relief without discussion, we are obliged to vacate the judgment and remand for consideration of that claim.

B.  Compensatory Damages

17 U.S.C. § 504 imposes two categories of compensatory damages. Taking care to specify that double recovery is not permitted where the two

---

[a] 17 U.S.C. § 412 specifies that a copyright holder is not entitled to elect statutory damages or receive attorney's fees under § § 504 and 505 if "any infringement of copyright commenced after first publication of the work and before the effective date of its registration, unless such registration is made within three months after the first publication of the work." Because the allegedly infringing use of Davis's eyewear occurred in the late summer of 1996, far more than three months after the first publication of the eyewear in 1991 but before registration of the copyright on May 16, 1997, Davis is ineligible for statutory damages or attorney's fees.

categories overlap, the statute provides for the recovery of both the infringer's profits and the copyright owner's "actual damages." It is important that these two categories of compensation have different justifications and are based on different financial data. The award of the infringer's profits examines the facts only from the infringer's point of view. If the infringer has earned a profit, this award makes him disgorge the profit to insure that he not benefit from his wrongdoing. The award of the owner's actual damages looks at the facts from the point of view of they copyright owner; it undertakes to compensate the owner for any harm he suffered by reason of the infringer's illegal act.

The district court granted summary judgment dismissing Davis's claims for damages. As for Davis's claim of entitlement to a part of the "infringer's profits," the district court believed Davis failed to show any causal connection between the infringement and the defendant's profits. With respect to Davis's claim of entitlement to "actual damages" based on the license fee he should have been paid for the Gap's unauthorized use of his copyrighted material, the district court believed that his evidence was too speculative.

We agree with the district court as to the defendant's profits, but not as to Davis's claim for damages based on the Gap's failure to pay him a reasonable license fee.

1. *Infringer's profits*

Davis submitted evidence that, during and shortly after the Gap's advertising campaign featuring the "fast" ad, the corporate parent of the Gap stores realized net sales of $1.668 billion, an increase of $146 million over the revenues earned in the same period of the preceding year. The district court considered this evidence inadequate to sustain a judgment in the plaintiff's favor because the overall revenues of the Gap, Inc. had no reasonable relationship to the act of alleged infringement. See Davis I, 1999 U.S. Dist. LEXIS 5689, 1999 WL 199005, at *6. Because the ad infringed only with respect to Gap label stores and eyewear, we agree with the district court that it was incumbent on Davis to submit evidence at least limited to the gross revenues of the Gap label stores, and perhaps also limited to eyewear or accessories. Had he done so, the burden would then have shifted to the defendant under the terms of § 504(b) to prove its deductible expenses and elements of profits from those revenues attributable to factors other than the copyrighted work.

It is true that a highly literal interpretation of the statute would favor Davis. It says that "the copyright owner is required to present proof only of the infringer's gross revenue," 17 U.S.C. § 504 (b), leaving it to the infringer to prove what portions of its revenue are not attributable to the infringement. Nonetheless we think the term "gross revenue" under the statute means gross revenue reasonably related to the infringement, not unrelated revenues.

Thus, if a publisher published an anthology of poetry which contained a poem covered by the plaintiff's copyright, we do not think the plaintiff's statutory burden would be discharged by submitting the publisher's gross revenue resulting from its publication of hundreds of titles, including trade books, textbooks, cookbooks, etc. In our view, the owner's burden would require evidence of the revenues realized from the sale of the anthology containing the infringing poem. The publisher would then bear the burden of proving its costs attributable to the anthology and the extent to which its profits from the sale of the anthology were attributable to factors other than the infringing poem, including particularly the other poems contained in the volume. The point would be clearer still if the defendant publisher were part of a conglomerate corporation that also received income from agriculture, canning, shipping, and real estate development. While the burden-shifting statute undoubtedly intended to ease plaintiff's burden in proving the defendant's profits, we do not believe it would shift the burden so far as to permit a plaintiff in such a case to satisfy his burden by showing gross revenues from agriculture, canning, shipping and real estate where the infringement consisted of the unauthorized publication of a poem. The facts of this case are less extreme; nonetheless, the point remains the same: the statutory term "infringer's gross revenue" should not be construed so broadly as to include revenue from lines of business that were unrelated to the act of infringement.

[W]e think the district court was correct in ruling that Davis failed to discharge his burden by submitting The Gap, Inc.'s gross revenue of $1.668 billion—revenue derived in part from sales under other labels within the Gap, Inc.'s corporate family that were in no way promoted by the advertisement, not to mention sales under the "Gap" label of jeans, khakis, shirts, underwear, cosmetics, children's clothing, and infantwear.

2. *The copyright owner's actual damages: Davis's failure to receive a reasonable licensing fee*

Among the elements Davis sought to prove as damages was the failure to receive a reasonable license fee from the Gap for its use of his copyrighted eyewear. The complaint asserted an entitlement to a $2.5 million licensing fee. [T]he court found that Davis's claim was too speculative—that is, insufficiently supported by evidence. See Davis I, 1999 U.S. Dist. LEXIS 5689, 1999 WL 199005, at *5.

*Was Davis's evidence too speculative?*

While there was no evidence to support Davis's wildly inflated claim of entitlement to $2.5 million, in our view his evidence did support a much more modest claim of a fair market value for a license to use his design in the ad. In addition to his evidence of numerous instances in which rock music stars wore Onoculii eyewear in photographs exhibited in music publications, Davis testified that on one occasion he was paid a royalty of $50 for the publication by Vibe magazine of a photo of the deceased musician Sun Ra wearing Davis's eyewear.

On the basis of this evidence, a jury could reasonably find that Davis established a fair market value of at least $50 as a fee for the use of an image of his copyrighted design. This evidence was sufficiently concrete to support a finding of fair market value of $50 for the type of use made by Vibe. And if Davis could show at trial that the Gap used the image in a wider circulation than Vibe, that might justify a finding that the market value for the Gap's use of the eyewear was higher than $50. Therefore, to the extent the district court dismissed the case because Davis's evidence of the market value of a license fee was too speculative, we believe this was error.

*Actual damages under § 504(a) and (b)*

Because [precedent in this Circuit does] not rule on, much less foreclose, the use of a reasonable license fee theory as the measure of damages suffered by Davis when the Gap used his material without payment, we proceed to consider whether that measure of damages is permissible under the statute.

The question is as follows: Assume that the copyright owner proves that the defendant has infringed his work. He proves also that a license to make such use of the work has a fair market value, but does not show that the infringement caused him lost sales, lost opportunities to license, or diminution in the value of the copyright. The only proven loss lies in the owner's failure to receive payment by the infringer of the fair market value of the use illegally appropriated. Should the owner's claim for "actual damages" under § 504(b) be dismissed? Or should the court award damages corresponding to the fair market value of the use appropriated by the infringer?

Neither answer is entirely satisfactory. If the court dismisses the claim by reason of the owner's failure to prove that the act of infringement cause economic harm, the infringer will get his illegal taking for free, and the owner will be left uncompensated for the illegal taking of something of value. On the other hand, an award of damages might be seen as a windfall for an owner who received no less than he would have if the infringer had refrained from the illegal taking. In our view, the more reasonable approach is to allow such an award in appropriate circumstances.

Section 504(a) and (b) employ the broad term "actual damages." Courts and commentators agree it should be broadly construed to favor victims of infringement. [citations omitted].

A principal objective of the copyright law is to enable creators to earn a living either by selling or by licensing others to sell copies of the copyrighted work. If a copier of protected work, instead of obtaining permission and paying the fee, proceeds without permission and without compensating the owner, it seems entirely reasonable to conclude that the owner has suffered damages to the extent of the infringer's taking without paying what the owner was legally entitled to exact a fee for. We can see no reason why, as an abstract matter, the statutory term "actual damages" should not cover the owner's failure to obtain the market value of the fee the owner was entitled to charge for such use. In our view, as between leaving the victim of the illegal taking with nothing, and charging the illegal taker with the reasonable cost of what he took, the latter, at least in some circumstances, is the preferable solution.

It is important to note that under the terms of § 504(b), unless such a foregone payment can be considered "actual damages," in some circumstances victims of infringement will go uncompensated. If the infringer's venture turned out to be unprofitable, the owner can receive no recovery based on the statutory award of the "infringer's profits." And in some instances, there will be no harm to the market value of the copyrighted work. The owner may be incapable of showing a loss of either sales or licenses to third parties. To rule that the owner's loss of the fair market value of the license fees he might have exacted of the defendant do not constitute "actual damages," would mean that in such circumstances an infringer may steal with impunity. We see no reason why this should be so. Of course, if the terms of the statute compelled that result, our perception of inequity would make no difference; the statute would control. But in our view, the statutory term "actual damages" is broad enough to cover this form of deprivation suffered by infringed owners.

We recognize that awarding the copyright owner the lost license fee can risk abuse. Once the defendant has infringed, the owner may claim unreasonable amounts as the license fee—to wit Davis's demand for an award of $2.5 million. The law therefore exacts that the amount of damages may not be based on "undue speculation." Abeshouse, 754 F.2d at 470. The question is not what the owner would have charged, but rather what is the fair market value. In order to make out his claim that he has suffered actual damage because of the infringer's failure to pay the fee, the owner must show that the thing taken had a fair market value. But if the plaintiff owner has done so, and the defendant is thus protected against an unrealistically exaggerated claim, we can see little reason not to consider the market value of the uncollected license fee as an element of "actual damages" under § 504(b).[b]

We recognize also that finding the fair market value of a reasonable license fee may involve some uncertainty. But that is not sufficient reason to refuse to consider this as an eligible measure of actual damages. Many of the accepted methods of calculating copyright damages require the court to make uncertain estimates in the realm of contrary to fact. A classic element of the plaintiff's copyright damages is the profits the plaintiff would have earned from third parties, were it not for the infringement. See 4 Nimmer § 14. 02 A, at 14–9 to 10. This measure requires the court to explore the counterfactual hypothesis of the contracts and licenses the plaintiff would have made absent the infringement and the costs associated with them. See Fitzgerald Publ'g, 807 F.2d at 1118 (actual damages measured by "the

[b] Furthermore, the fair market value to be determined is not of the highest use for which plaintiff might license but the use the infringer made. Thus, assuming the defendant made infringing use of a Mickey Mouse image for a single performance of a school play before schoolchildren, teachers and parents with tickets at $3, the fair market value would not be the same as the fee customarily charged by the owner to license the use of this image in a commercial production.

profits which the plaintiff might have earned were it not for the infringement"); Stevens Linen Assocs. v. Mastercraft Corp., 656 F.2d 11, 15 (2d Cir. 1981) (same). A second accepted method, focusing on the "infringer's profits," similarly requires the court to explore circumstances that are counterfactual. The owner's entitlement to the infringer's profits is limited to the profits "attributable to the infringement." 17 U.S.C. § 504(b). The court, therefore, must compare the defendant's actual profits to what they would have been without the infringement, awarding the plaintiff the difference. Neither of these approaches is necessarily any less speculative than the approach that requires the court to find the market value of the license fee for what the infringer took. Indeed, it may be far less so. Many copyright owners are represented by agents who have established rates that are regularly paid by licensees. In such cases, establishing the fair market value of the license fee of which the owner was deprived is no more speculative than determining the damages in the case of a stolen cargo of lumber or potatoes. Given our long-held view that in assessing copyright damages "courts must necessarily engage in some degree of speculation," id. at 14, some difficulty in quantifying the damages attributable to infringement should not bar recovery.

\* \* \*

Honest users can infringe by reason of oversight or good faith mistake. The infringer may have mistakenly believed in good faith that the work was in the public domain, that his licensor was duly licensed, or that his use was protected by fair use. On the record before us, there is no reason to believe the Gap had any intention to infringe a copyright.

\* \* \*

We conclude that Section 504(b) permits a copyright owner to recover actual damages, in appropriate circumstances, for the fair market value of a license covering the defendant's infringing use. Davis adduced sufficiently concrete evidence of a modest fair market value of the use made by the Gap. The Gap's use of the infringed matter was substantial. If Davis were not compensated for the market value of the use taken, he would receive no compensation whatsoever.

## C. Punitive Damages

The district court correctly held that Davis is not entitled to punitive damages under the Copyright Act. See Davis I, 1999 U.S. Dist. LEXIS 5689, 1999 WL 199005, at \*8. As a general rule, punitive damages are not awarded in a statutory copyright infringement action. See 4 Nimmer § 14.02 B, at 14–23 to 24; Oboler v. Goldin, 714 F.2d 211, 213 (2d Cir. 1983). The purpose of punitive damages—to punish and prevent malicious conduct—is generally achieved under the Copyright Act through the provisions of 17 U.S.C. § 504 (c)(2), which allow increases to an award of statutory damages in cases of willful infringement. In any event, the question need not detain us long because Davis has failed to show willfulness on the Gap's part.

E.   Fair Use

[In this part of the opinion, the court concluded that all of the fair use factors favored Davis, this rejecting the Gap's fair use defense.]

CONCLUSION

Finding no merit to the parties' other contentions, we affirm the grant of summary judgment in favor of the defendant denying Davis's claims for infringer's profits under 17 U.S.C. § 504 (b), and for punitive damages; as regards Davis's claims for declaratory relief and "actual damages" under § 504(b), the judgment of the district court is vacated and the case remanded for further proceedings.

## Abend v. MCA, Inc.

United States Court of Appeals, Ninth Circuit, 1988.
863 F.2d 1465, aff'd, 495 U.S. 207, 110 S.Ct. 1750, 109 L.Ed.2d 184 (1990).

■ PREGERSON, CIRCUIT JUDGE.

[The facts of the case are recounted in the Supreme Court's opinion reprinted in Assignment 9.]

\* \* \*

Neither the equities, precedent, nor Congressional intent justify us in changing the balance between owners of renewal copyrights in underlying works and owners of the copyright in derivative works when Congress has refrained from doing so. We therefore hold that defendants' continued exploitation of the "Rear Window" film without Abend's consent violates Abend's renewal copyright in the underlying story "It Had to Be Murder," unless the defendants can establish any affirmative defenses.[a]

Our holding does not mean, however, that the equities of this case have no bearing on its outcome. We are mindful that this case presents compelling equitable considerations which should be taken into account by the district court in fashioning an appropriate remedy in the event defendants fail to establish any equitable defenses. Defendants invested substantial money, effort, and talent in creating the "Rear Window" film. Clearly the tremendous success of that venture initially and upon re-release is attributable in significant measure to, inter alia, the outstanding performances of its stars—Grace Kelly and James Stewart—and the brilliant directing of Alfred Hitchcock. The district court must recognize this contribution in determining Abend's remedy.

The district court may choose from several available remedies for the infringement. Abend seeks first an injunction against the continued exploitation of the "Rear Window" film. § 502(a) provides that the court "may ... grant temporary and final injunctions on such terms as it may deem reasonable to prevent or restrain infringement of a copyright." Defendants

---

[a] For the reasons discussed in the next section, we hold that defendants cannot char- acterize their use of the underlying story as a "fair use" to avoid liability for infringement.

argue that a finding of infringement presumptively entitles the plaintiff to an injunction, citing Professor Nimmer. See 3 M. Nimmer, Nimmer on Copyright § 14.06[B] at 14–55 to 14–56.2 (1988). However, Professor Nimmer also states that "where great public injury would be worked by an injunction, the courts might ... award damages or a continuing royalty instead of an injunction in such special circumstances." *Id.* at 14–56.2.

We believe such special circumstances exist here. The "Rear Window" film resulted from the collaborative efforts of many talented individuals other than Cornell Woolrich, the author of the underlying story. The success of the movie resulted in large part from factors completely unrelated to the underlying story, "It Had To Be Murder." It would cause a great injustice for the owners of the film if the court enjoined them from further exhibition of the movie. An injunction would also effectively foreclose defendants from enjoying legitimate profits derived from exploitation of the "new matter" comprising the derivative work, which is given express copyright protection by section 7 of the 1909 Act. Since defendants could not possibly separate out the "new matter" from the underlying work, their right to enjoy the renewal copyright in the derivative work would be rendered meaningless by the grant of an injunction. We also note that an injunction could cause public injury by denying the public the opportunity to view a classic film for many years to come.

This is not the first time we have recognized that an injunction may be an inappropriate remedy for copyright infringement. In Universal City Studios v. Sony Corp. of Amer., 659 F.2d 963, 976 (9th Cir.1981), rev'd on other grounds, 464 U.S. 417 (1984), we stated that Professor Nimmer's suggestion of damages or a continuing royalty would constitute an acceptable resolution for infringement caused by in-home taping of television programs by VCR—"time-shifting."

As the district court pointed out in the *Sony* case, an injunction is a "harsh and drastic" discretionary remedy, never an absolute right. Universal City Studios v. Sony Corp. of Amer., 480 F.Supp. 429, 463, 464 (C.D.Cal.1979), rev'd on other grounds, 659 F.2d 963 (9th Cir.1981), aff'd 464 U.S. 417 (1984). Abend argues nonetheless that defendants' attempts to interfere with his production of new derivative works can only be remedied by an injunction. We disagree. Abend has not shown irreparable injury which would justify imposing the severe remedy of an injunction on defendants. Abend can be compensated adequately for the infringement by monetary compensation. § 504(b) provides that the copyright owner can recover actual damages and "any profits of the infringement that are *attributable to the infringement* and are not taken into account in computing the actual damages." (Emphasis added.)

The district court is capable of calculating damages caused to the fair market value of plaintiff's story by the re-release of the film. Any impairment of Abend's ability to produce new derivative works based on the story would be reflected in the calculation of the damage to the fair market value of the story. In Cream Records, Inc. v. Jos. Schlitz Brewing Co., 754 F.2d 826, 827 (9th Cir.1985), for example, the plaintiff presented evidence that defendants' unauthorized use of part of plaintiff's song in a commercial had "destroyed the value of the copyrighted work" to other advertisers. We held that the plaintiff could recover this lost value as damages. *Id.* at 827–28.

In addition to actual damages suffered, Abend would be entitled to profits attributable to the infringement. § 504(b). Defendants' fear that Abend could receive 100% of their profits is unfounded. Abend can receive only the profits attributable to the infringement. *Id.*; *Frank Music Corp.*, 772 F.2d 505, 518 (9th Cir.1985)("When an infringer's profits are attributable to factors in addition to use of [its] work, an apportionment of profits is proper."). Should the court find infringement because defendants have failed to establish any affirmative defenses, on remand it must apportion damages.

While apportioning profits is not always an easy task in these cases, neither is it a new or unusual one. In the landmark case of Sheldon v. Metro–Goldwyn–Mayer Pictures Corp., 106 F.2d 45 (2d Cir.1939), aff'd, 309 U.S. 390 (1940), Judge Learned Hand held that profits should be apportioned between the plaintiff and defendants, after finding that defendants' movie "Letty Lynton" infringed plaintiff's play "Dishonored Lady." *Sheldon*, 309 U.S., at 396. Judge Hand recognized that "no real standard" can govern this apportionment, but he "resolved to avoid the one certainly unjust course of giving the plaintiffs everything, because the defendants cannot with certainty compute their own share." *Sheldon*, 106 F.2d, at 51. The court then set plaintiffs' share of the profits at 20%, to "favor the plaintiffs in every reasonable chance of error." *Id.*

We likewise recognize that courts cannot be expected to determine with "mathematical exactness" an apportionment of profits. We require only a "reasonable and just apportionment." *Frank Music Corp.*, 772 F.2d, at 518. In *Frank*, the defendants infringed plaintiff's copyright in the play "Kismet?" by including parts of songs and six minutes of music from the play, and by using similar characters and setting in Act IV of a musical revue entitled "Hallelujah Hollywood." *Id.* at 510. We remanded to the district court for apportionment of profits using a reasonable formula.

We also required apportionment in *Cream Records*, 754 F.2d, at 828. In *Cream*, the plaintiff, owner of the copyright in "The Theme From Shaft," sought to recover all profits earned from a commercial produced by the defendants which infringed plaintiffs copyright by using a ten note ostinato from the song. *Id.* We held that "[i]n cases such as this where an infringer's profits are not entirely due to the infringement, and the evidence suggests some division which may rationally be used as a springboard, it is the duty of the court to make some apportionment." *Id.* at 828–29.

Because factors other than Woolrich's story clearly contributed to "Rear Window's" success, should the district court find that the defendants have failed to establish any affirmative defense to the infringement, the district court should award Abend actual damages and apportion profits between Abend and the defendants.

# A & M Records, Inc. v. Napster, Inc.

United States Court of Appeals, Ninth Circuit, 2001.
239 F.3d 1004.

[See Assignment 11 for an excerpt of this case treating fair use, contributory infringement, and vicarious liability].

We address Napster's remaining argument that the district court should have imposed a constructive royalty payment structure in lieu of an injunction.

Royalties

Napster contends that the district court should have imposed a monetary penalty by way of a compulsory royalty in place of an injunction. We are asked to do what the district court refused.

Napster tells us that "where great public injury would be worked by an injunction, the courts might ... award damages or a continuing royalty instead of an injunction in such special circumstances." *Abend v. MCA, Inc., 863 F.2d 1465, 1479 (9th Cir.1988)* (quoting 3 Melville B. Nimmer & David Nimmer, Nimmer On Copyright § 14.06[B] (1988)), aff'd, *495 U.S. 207 (1990).* We are at a total loss to find any "special circumstances" simply because this case requires us to apply well-established doctrines of copyright law to a new technology. Neither do we agree with Napster that an injunction would cause "great public injury." Further, we narrowly construe any suggestion that compulsory royalties are appropriate in this context because Congress has arguably limited the application of compulsory royalties to specific circumstances, none of which are present here. See *17 U.S.C. § 115.*

The Copyright Act provides for various sanctions for infringers. See, e.g., *17 U.S.C. §§ 502* (injunctions); 504 (damages); and 506 (criminal penalties); see also *18 U.S.C. § 2319A* (criminal penalties for the unauthorized fixation of and trafficking in sound recordings and music videos of live musical performances). These statutory sanctions represent a more than adequate legislative solution to the problem created by copyright infringement.

Imposing a compulsory royalty payment schedule would give Napster an "easy out" of this case. If such royalties were imposed, Napster would avoid penalties for any future violation of an injunction, statutory copyright damages and any possible criminal penalties for continuing infringement. The royalty structure would also grant Napster the luxury of either choosing to continue and pay royalties or shut down. On the other hand, the wronged parties would be forced to do business with a company that profits from the wrongful use of intellectual properties. Plaintiffs would lose the power to control their intellectual property: they could not make a business decision not to license their property to Napster, and, in the event they planned to do business with Napster, compulsory royalties would take away the copyright holders' ability to negotiate the terms of any contractual arrangement.

# Fogerty v. Fantasy, Inc.

Supreme Court of the United States, 1994.
510 U.S. 517, 114 S.Ct. 1023, 127 L.Ed.2d 455.

■ CHIEF JUSTICE REHNQUIST delivered the opinion of the Court.

The Copyright Act of 1976, 17 U.S.C. § 505, provides in relevant part that in any copyright infringement action "the court may ... award a reasonable attorney's fee to the prevailing party as part of the costs." The question presented in this case is what standards should inform a court's decision to award attorney's fees to a prevailing defendant in a copyright infringement action—a question that has produced conflicting views in the Courts of Appeals.

Petitioner John Fogerty is a successful musician, who, in the late 1960's, was the lead singer and songwriter of a popular music group known as "Creedence Clearwater Revival."[a] In 1970, he wrote a song entitled "Run Through the Jungle" and sold the exclusive publishing rights to predecessors-in-interest of respondent Fantasy, Inc., who later obtained the copyright by assignment. The music group disbanded in 1972 and Fogerty subsequently published under another recording label. In 1985, he published and registered a copyright to a song entitled "The Old Man Down the Road", which was released on an album distributed by Warner Brothers Records, Inc. Respondent Fantasy, Inc., sued Fogerty, Warner Brothers, and affiliated companies,[b] in District Court, alleging that "The Old Man Down the Road" was merely "Run Through the Jungle" with new words. The copyright infringement claim went to trial and a jury returned a verdict in favor of Fogerty.

After his successful defense of the action, Fogerty moved for reasonable attorney's fees pursuant to § 505. The District Court denied the motion, finding that Fantasy's infringement suit was not brought frivolously or in bad faith as required by circuit precedent for an award of attorney's fees to a successful defendant. The Court of Appeals affirmed, 984 F.2d 1524 (C.A.9 1993), and declined to abandon the existing Ninth Circuit standard for awarding attorney's fees which treats successful plaintiffs and successful defendants differently. Under that standard, commonly termed the "dual" standard, prevailing plaintiffs are generally awarded attorney's fees as a matter of course, while prevailing defendants must show that the original suit was frivolous or brought in bad faith.[c] In contrast, some courts

---

[a] Creedence Clearwater Revival (CCR), recently inducted into the Rock and Roll Hall of Fame, has been recognized as one of the greatest American rock and roll groups of all time. With Fogerty as its leader, CCR developed a distinctive style of music, dubbed "swamp rock" by the media due to its southern country and blues feel.

[b] Pursuant to an agreement between Fogerty and the Warner defendants, Fogerty indemnified and reimbursed the Warner defendants for their attorney's fees and costs incurred in defending the copyright infringement action.

[c] By predicating an award of attorney's fees to prevailing defendants on a showing of bad faith or frivolousness on the part of plaintiffs, the "dual" standard makes it more difficult for prevailing defendants to secure awards of attorney's fees than prevailing plaintiffs. The Ninth Circuit has explained that prevailing plaintiffs, on the other hand,

of appeals follow the so-called "evenhanded" approach in which no distinction is made between prevailing plaintiffs and prevailing defendants. The Court of Appeals for the Third Circuit, for example, has ruled that "we do not require bad faith, nor do we mandate an allowance of fees as a concomitant of prevailing in every case, but we do favor an evenhanded approach." Lieb v. Topstone Industries, Inc., 788 F.2d 151, 156 (C.A.3 1986).

We granted certiorari, 113 S.Ct. 2992 (1993), to address an important area of federal law and to resolve the conflict between the Ninth Circuit's "dual" standard for awarding attorney's fees under § 505, and the so-called "evenhanded" approach exemplified by the Third Circuit.[d] We reverse.

Respondent advances three arguments in support of the dual standard followed by the Court of Appeals for the Ninth Circuit in this case. First, it contends that the language of § 505, when read in the light of our decisions construing similar fee-shifting language, supports the rule. Second, it asserts that treating prevailing plaintiffs and defendants differently comports with the "objectives" and "equitable considerations" underlying the Copyright Act as a whole. Finally, respondent contends that the legislative history of § 505 indicates that Congress ratified the dual standard which it claims was "uniformly" followed by the lower courts under identical language in the 1909 Copyright Act. We address each of these arguments in turn.

The statutory language—"the court may also award a reasonable attorney's fee to the prevailing party as part of the costs"—gives no hint that successful plaintiffs are to be treated differently than successful defendants. But respondent contends that our decision in Christiansburg Garment Co. v. EEOC, 434 U.S. 412 (1978), in which we construed virtually identical language, supports a differentiation in treatment between plaintiffs and defendants.

*Christiansburg* construed the language of Title VII of the Civil Rights Act of 1964, which in relevant part provided that the court "in its discretion, may allow the prevailing party . . . a reasonable attorney's fee as part of the costs. . . ." § 2000e–5(k). We had earlier held, interpreting the cognate provision of Title II of that Act, 42 U.S.C. § 2000a–3(b), that a

---

should generally receive such awards absent special circumstances such as "the presence of a complex or novel issue of law that the defendant litigates vigorously and in good faith. . . . " McCulloch v. Albert E. Price, Inc., 823 F.2d 316, 323 (C.A.9 1987). In the instant case, the Court of Appeals explained: "The purpose of [the dual standard] rule is to avoid chilling a copyright holder's incentive to sue on colorable claims, and thereby to give full effect to the broad protection for copyrights intended by the Copyright Act." 984 F.2d, at 1532.

[d] In addition to the Ninth Circuit, the Second, Seventh, and District of Columbia Circuits have adopted a "dual" standard of awarding attorney's fees whereby a greater burden is placed upon prevailing defendants than prevailing plaintiffs. On the other hand, the Fourth and Eleventh Circuits have been identified as following an "evenhanded" approach similar to that of the Third Circuit. [Citations omitted.]

prevailing plaintiff "should ordinarily recover an attorney's fee unless some special circumstances would render such an award unjust." Newman v. Piggie Park Enterprises, Inc., 390 U.S. 400, 402 (1968). This decision was based on what we found to be the important policy objectives of the Civil Rights statutes, and the intent of Congress to achieve such objectives through the use of plaintiffs as "private attorneys general." *Ibid.* In *Christiansburg,* we determined that the same policy considerations were not at work in the case of a prevailing civil rights defendant. We noted that a Title VII plaintiff, like a Title II plaintiff in *Piggie Park,* is "the chosen instrument of Congress to vindicate 'a policy that Congress considered of the highest priority.' " 434 U.S., at 418. We also relied on the admittedly sparse legislative history to indicate that different standards were to be applied to successful plaintiffs than to successful defendants.

Respondent points to our language in Flight Attendants v. Zipes, 491 U.S. 754, 758, n.2 (1989), that "fee-shifting statutes' similar language is a 'strong indication' that they are to be interpreted alike." But here we think this normal indication is overborne by the factors relied upon in our *Christiansburg* opinion which are absent in the case of the Copyright Act.[e] The legislative history of § 505 provides no support for treating prevailing plaintiffs and defendants differently with respect to the recovery of attorney's fees. The attorney's fees provision § 505 of the 1976 Act was carried forward verbatim from the 1909 Act with very little discussion. The relevant House Report provides simply:

> "Under section 505 the awarding of costs and attorney's fees are left to the court's discretion, and the section also makes clear that neither costs nor attorney's fees can be awarded to or against 'the United States or an officer thereof.' " H. R. Rep. No. 94–1476, p. 163 (1976).[f]

The goals and objectives of the two Acts are likewise not completely similar. Oftentimes, in the civil rights context, impecunious "private attorney general" plaintiffs can ill afford to litigate their claims against defendants with more resources. Congress sought to redress this balance in part, and to provide incentives for the bringing of meritorious lawsuits, by treating successful plaintiffs more favorably than successful defendants in terms of the award of attorney's fees. The primary objective of the Copyright Act is to encourage the production of original literary, artistic, and musical expression for the good of the public. In the copyright context, it has been noted that "entities which sue for copyright infringement as plaintiffs can run the gamut from corporate behemoths to starving artists; the same is true of prospective copyright infringement defendants." Cohen

---

[e] Additionally, we note that Congress, in enacting § 505 of the 1976 Copyright Act, could not have been aware of the *Christiansburg* dual standard as *Christiansburg* was not decided until 1978.

[f] The 1976 Copyright did change, however, the standard for awarding costs to the prevailing party. The 1909 Act provided a mandatory rule that "full costs *shall* be allowed." § 116 (1976 ed.)(emphasis added). The 1976 Act changed the rule from a man-

datory one to one of discretion. As the 1909 Act indicates, Congress clearly knows how to use mandatory language when it so desires. That Congress did not amend the neutral language of the 1909 rule respecting attorney's fees lends further support to the plain language of § 505—district courts are to use their discretion in awarding attorney's fees and costs to the prevailing party.

v. Virginia Electric & Power Co., 617 F.Supp. 619, 622–623 (E.D.Va.1985), aff'd on other grounds, 788 F.2d 247 (C.A.4 1986).

We thus conclude that respondent's argument based on our fee-shifting decisions under the Civil Rights Act must fail.[g]

Respondent next argues that the policies and objectives of § 505 and of the Copyright Act in general are best served by the "dual approach" to the award of attorney's fees.[h] The most common reason advanced in support of the dual approach is that, by awarding attorney's fees to prevailing plaintiffs as a matter of course, it encourages litigation of meritorious claims of copyright infringement. Indeed, respondent relies heavily on this argument. We think the argument is flawed because it expresses a one-sided view of the purposes of the Copyright Act. While it is true that one of the goals of the Copyright Act is to discourage infringement, it is by no means the only goal of that Act. In the first place, it is by no means always the case that the plaintiff in an infringement action is the only holder of a copyright; often times, defendants hold copyrights too, as exemplified in the case at hand.

More importantly, the policies served by the Copyright Act are more complex, more measured, than simply maximizing the number of meritorious suits for copyright infringement. We have often recognized the monopoly privileges that Congress has authorized, while "intended to motivate the creative activity of authors and inventors by the provision of a special reward", are limited in nature and must ultimately serve the public good. Sony Corp. of America v. Universal City Studios, Inc., 464 U.S. 417, 429 (1984).

Because copyright law ultimately serves the purpose of enriching the general public through access to creative works, it is peculiarly important that the boundaries of copyright law be demarcated as clearly as possible. To that end, defendants who seek to advance a variety of meritorious copyright defenses should be encouraged to litigate them to the same extent that plaintiffs are encouraged to litigate meritorious claims of infringement. In the case before us, the successful defense of "The Old Man Down the Road" increased public exposure to a musical work that could, as a result, lead to further creative pieces. Thus a successful defense of a copyright infringement action may further the policies of the Copyright Act every bit as much as a successful prosecution of an infringement claim by the holder of a copyright.

Respondent finally urges that the legislative history supports the dual standard, relying on the principle of ratification. See, Lorillard v. Pons, 434

---

[g] We note that the federal fee-shifting statutes in the patent and trademark fields, which are more closely related to that of copyright, support a party-neutral approach. Those statutes contain language similar to that of § 505, with the added proviso that fees are only to be awarded in "exceptional cases." § 285 (patent). Consistent with the party-neutral language, courts have generally awarded attorney's fees in an evenhanded manner based on the same criteria.

[h] Respondent points to four important interests allegedly advanced by the dual standard: (1) it promotes the vigorous enforcement of the Copyright Act; (2) it distinguishes between the wrongdoers and the blameless; (3) it enhances the predictability and certainty in copyrights by providing a relatively certain benchmark for the award of attorney's fees; and (4) it affords copyright defendants sufficient incentives to litigate their defenses.

U.S. 575, 580 (1978)("Congress is presumed to be aware of an administrative or judicial interpretation of a statute and to adopt that interpretation when it re-enacts a statute without change . . . ''). Respondent surveys the great number of lower court cases interpreting the identical provision in the 1909 Act, § 116 (1976 ed.), and asserts that "it was firmly established" that prevailing defendants should be awarded attorney's fees only where the plaintiff's claim was frivolous or brought with a vexatious purpose. Furthermore, respondent claims that Congress was aware of this construction of former § 116 because of two Copyright Studies submitted to Congress when studying revisions to the Act. W. Strauss, Damage Provisions of the Copyright Law, Study No. 22 (hereinafter Strauss Study), and R. Brown, Operation of the Damage Provisions of the Copyright Law: An Exploratory Study, Study No. 23 (hereinafter Brown Study), Studies Prepared for Subcommittee on Patents, Trademarks, and Copyrights, 86th Cong., 2d Sess. (H. Judiciary Comm. Print 1960).

[T]he Strauss and Brown Copyright Studies deal only briefly with the provision for the award of attorney's fees. In the Strauss Study, the limited discussion begins with a quote to A. Weil, American Copyright Law 530–531 (1917) for an explanation of the "discretionary awarding of attorney's fees." The study then notes that the pending bills contemplate no change in the attorney's fees provision and concludes with the simple statement "the cases indicate that this discretion has been judiciously exercised by the courts." *Ibid*.[i] This limited discussion of attorney's fees surely does not constitute an endorsement of a dual standard.

The Brown Study was intended as a supplement to the Strauss Study and, inter alia, provides information from a survey distributed to practitioners about the practical workings of the 1909 Copyright Act.[j] It also does not endorse a standard of treating prevailing plaintiffs and defendants differently. At one point, the study notes that "courts do not usually make an allowance at all if an unsuccessful plaintiff's claim was not 'synthetic, capricious or otherwise unreasonable,' or if the losing defendant raised real issues of fact or law." Brown Study 85.

Our review of the prior case law itself leads us to conclude that there was no settled "dual standard" interpretation of former § 116 about which Congress could have been aware. We note initially that at least one reported case stated no reason in awarding attorney's fees to successful defendants. See, e.g., Marks v. Leo Feist, Inc., 8 F.2d 460, 461 (C.A.2 1925)(noting that the Copyright Act gave courts "absolute discretion", the court awarded attorney's fees to prevailing defendant after plaintiff voluntarily dismissed suit). More importantly, while it appears that the majority of lower courts exercised their discretion in awarding attorney's fees to prevailing defendants based on a finding of frivolousness or bad faith, not

---

[i] In a footnote, the Strauss Study lists several cases exemplifying the courts' use of discretion. None of these cases explicitly require a dual standard of awarding attorney's fees, but instead offer various reasons for awarding or not awarding attorney's fees to the prevailing party.

[j] To this extent, the Brown Study focuses more on the effect that the prospect of an award of attorney's fees has on decisions to litigate or to settle cases. Based on its interview sources, the study concluded that the likelihood of getting a fee award is so problematic that "it is not a factor" that goes into the decision to settle or litigate. Brown Study 85.

all courts expressly described the test in those terms.[k] In fact, only one pre–1976 case expressly endorsed a dual standard. Breffort v. I Had a Ball Co., 271 F.Supp. 623 (S.D.N.Y.1967). This is hardly the sort of uniform construction which Congress might have endorsed.

In summary, neither of the two studies presented to Congress, nor the cases referred to by the studies, support respondent's view that there was a settled construction in favor of the "dual standard" under § 116 of the 1909 Copyright Act.

We thus reject each of respondent's three arguments in support of the dual standard. We now turn to petitioner's argument that § 505 was intended to adopt the "British Rule." Petitioner argues that, consistent with the neutral language of § 505, both prevailing plaintiffs and defendants should be awarded attorney's fees as a matter of course, absent exceptional circumstances. For two reasons we reject this argument for the British Rule.

First, just as the plain language of § 505 supports petitioner's claim for disapproving the dual standard, it cuts against him in arguing for the British Rule. The statute says that "the court may also award a reasonable attorney's fee to the prevailing party as part of the costs." The word "may" clearly connotes discretion. The automatic awarding of attorney's fees to the prevailing party would pretermit the exercise of that discretion.

Second, we are mindful that Congress legislates against the strong background of the American Rule. Unlike Britain where counsel fees are regularly awarded to the prevailing party, it is the general rule in this country that unless Congress provides otherwise, parties are to bear their own attorney's fees. Alyeska Pipeline Co. v. Wilderness Society, 421 U.S. 240, 247–262 (1975)(tracing the origins and development of the American Rule). While § 505 is one situation in which Congress has modified the American Rule to allow an award of attorney's fees in the court's discretion, we find it impossible to believe that Congress, without more, intended to adopt the British Rule. Such a bold departure from traditional practice would have surely drawn more explicit statutory language and legislative

---

[k] See, e.g., Schroeder v. William Morrow & Co., 421 F.Supp. 372, 378 (N.D.Ill. 1976)(refusing to award prevailing defendant an attorney's fee because plaintiff's action was "prosecuted in good faith and with a reasonable likelihood of success"), rev'd on other grounds, 566 F.2d 3 (C.A.7 1977); Kinelow Publishing Co. v. Photography In Business, Inc., 270 F.Supp. 851, 855 (S.D.N.Y. 1967)(denying fee award to prevailing defendant because plaintiff's claims, while "lacking in merit," were not "unreasonable or capricious"); Burnett v. Lambino, 206 F.Supp. 517, 518–519 (S.D.N.Y. 1962)(granting fee award to prevailing defendant where "asserted claim of infringement was so demonstrably lacking in merit that bringing it was clearly unreasonable"); Cloth v. Hyman, 146 F.Supp. 185, 193 (S.D.N.Y. 1956)(noting that it is proper to award fees when a copyright action is brought in bad faith, with a motive to "vex and harass the defendant," or where plaintiff's claim utterly lacks merit); Loew's, Inc. v. Columbia Broadcasting System, Inc., 131 F.Supp. 165, 186 (S.D.Cal.1955)(denying prevailing defendant fee award where question presented in the case "was a nice one," and there are "no authorities squarely in point to guide the litigants or their counsel"), aff'd, 239 F.2d 532 (C.A.9 1956), aff'd, 356 U.S. 43 (1958); Krafft v. Cohen, 38 F.Supp. 1022, 1023 (E.D.Pa.1941)(denying fee award to prevailing defendant where claim brought "in good faith," and evidence demonstrated appropriation); Lewys v. O'Neill, 49 F.2d 603, at 618 (S.D.N.Y.1931) (awarding fees to prevailing defendant because plaintiff's case was "wholly synthetic").

comment. Cf., Isbrandtsen Co. v. Johnson, 343 U.S. 779, 783 (1952)("Statutes which invade the common law . . . are to be read with a presumption favoring the retention of long-established and familiar principles, except when a statutory purpose to the contrary is evident"). Not surprisingly, no court has held that § 505 (or its predecessor statute) adopted the British Rule.

Thus we reject both the "dual standard" adopted by several of the Courts of Appeals, and petitioner's claim that § 505 enacted the British Rule for automatic recovery of attorney's fees by the prevailing party. Prevailing plaintiffs and prevailing defendants are to be treated alike, but attorney's fees are to be awarded to prevailing parties only as a matter of the court's discretion. "There is no precise rule or formula for making these determinations", but instead equitable discretion should be exercised "in light of the considerations we have identified." Hensley v. Eckerhart, 461 U.S. 424, 436–437 (1983).[13] Because the Court of Appeals erroneously held petitioner, the prevailing defendant, to a more stringent standard than that applicable to a prevailing plaintiff, its judgment is reversed and the case is remanded for further proceedings consistent with this opinion.

It is so ordered.

## NOTES

**1.** *Statutory damages.* What advice would you give to Silver if she wanted to elect statutory damages? In addition to those factors mentioned by the court in *Ahmed*, can you think of any other factors that are relevant to calculating a statutory damage award? How would a court calculate the defendant's profits and savings and the plaintiff's lost revenues under the facts of the Principal Problem?

Where an infringer proves that she was not aware of and had no reason to believe that her acts constituted infringement, a statutory damages award can be reduced to an amount not less than $200. Conversely, a court can increase awards involving willful conduct on the part of the defendant to a sum of up to $150,000.[14] Do you think Silver would be able to get increased statutory damages on the grounds that WJN acted willfully? Aside from a showing of willfulness, can you think of any other factors that are relevant to a court's decision to increase the amount of statutory damages?

[13] Some courts following the evenhanded standard have suggested several nonexclusive factors to guide courts' discretion. For example, the Third Circuit has listed several nonexclusive factors that courts should consider in making awards of attorney's fees to any prevailing party. These factors include "frivolousness, motivation, objective unreasonableness (both in the factual and in the legal components of the case) and the need in particular circumstances to advance considerations of compensation and deterrence." Lieb v. Topstone Industries, Inc., 788 F.2d 151, 156 (C.A.3 1986). We agree that such factors may be used to guide courts' discretion, so long as such factors are faithful to the purposes of the Copyright Act and are applied to prevailing plaintiffs and defendants in an evenhanded manner.

[14] § 504(c).

Suppose CBS, rather than WJN, had broadcast 22 seconds of the fight. Should CBS' broadcast be regarded as a single infringement, notwithstanding the involvement of each local broadcasting station?

In Feltner, Jr. v. Columbia Pictures Television,[15] the United States Supreme Court held that § 504(c) of the statute does not, in and of itself, grant a defendant the right to a jury assessment of statutory damages, thus interpreting the word "court" as used in this provision to mean" judge" rather than "jury." Nonetheless, the Court went on to conclude that the right to a jury trial regarding statutory damages is mandated by the Seventh Amendment because a monetary remedy is legal in nature and not rendered equitable simply because such relief is not fixed or readily calculable. Perhaps the most interesting aspect of this opinion is Justice Scalia's concurrence on the ground that the statute itself should be interpreted to require a jury trial. In so concluding, Justice Scalia, a staunch proponent of the "textualist" school of statutory interpretation, resorts to legislative history to bolster his interpretation of the statute!

**2.** *Actual damages and infringer's profits.* If a plaintiff elects to recover actual instead of statutory damages, the statute provides that the plaintiff also can recover "any profits of the infringer that are attributable to the infringement and are not taken into account in computing the actual damages."[16] The theory behind allowing both actual damages and the infringer's profits is "that some types of infringement inflict more harm to the copyright owner than the benefit reaped by the infringer, for example, where the infringer's minimal use forecloses a broader market ... or where the copyright owner's provable profit margin is greater than the infringer's."[17] A double recovery, however, is strictly prohibited. Further, the statute provides that "[i]n establishing the infringer's profits, the copyright owner is required to present proof only of the infringer's gross revenue, and the infringer is required to prove his or her deductible expenses and the elements of profit attributable to factors other than the copyrighted work."[18] Note, however, that in applying § 504(b) of the copyright statute, the court in *Davis* concluded that since the ad "infringed only with respect to Gap label stores and eyewear," the district court was correct in concluding "that it was incumbent on Davis to submit evidence at least limited to the gross revenues of the Gap label stores, and perhaps also limited to eyewear or accessories." Moreover, some courts preclude a deduction of the defendant's overhead from its gross revenue in cases involving willful infringements.[19] When an infringer's profits are attributable to many

[15] 523 U.S. 340 (1998).

[16] § 504(b).

[17] Pfanenstiel Architects, Inc. v. Chouteau Petroleum Co., 978 F.2d 430, 432 (8th Cir.1992). This measure of recovery also insures "that infringers are not able to retain some benefit flowing from their wrongful conduct that is not fully taken into account in the award of actual damages." U.S. Payphone, Inc. v. Executives Unlimited of Durham, Inc., 781 F.Supp. 412, 413 (M.D.N.C. 1991).

[18] § 504(b).

[19] See, e.g., Saxon v. Blann, 968 F.2d 676, 681 (8th Cir.1992). See also Allen–Myland, Inc. v. International Business Machines Corp., 770 F.Supp. 1014, 1024–25 (E.D.Pa. 1991)(discussing pertinent authority on this point and examining the concept of "willfulness" in the statutory damage context as a

factors other than its infringement, apportionment can become a difficult task. The defendant maintains the burden of proving the contribution to profits of these additional elements.[20]

The statute neither defines "actual damages" nor mandates a formula for their computation. In calculating actual damages, the primary measure of recovery is the diminishment of the market value of the plaintiff's work as a result of the infringement. In some instances, the determination of this market value is relatively uncomplicated. For example, in Cream Records v. Jos. Schlitz Brewing Co.,[21] in which a brewing company infringed a copyrighted song by using it in a television commercial, the evidence disclosed that the market value of a one-year license to use the music in question was eighty thousand dollars. Frequently, however, cases present no clear-cut evidence, and courts must rely on more indirect means of computing actual damages.

As discussed in Davis, one common approach is to award a plaintiff the profits he would have received but for the defendant's infringement. Because the types of property subject to copyright protection vary considerably, courts have employed several different methods of computing a plaintiff's lost profits. When the infringed property is one of several similar items that a plaintiff produces, some courts have measured the plaintiff's lost profits by the difference between sales of the infringed item and the average sales of all of the plaintiff's other products.[22] Another means of computing a plaintiff's lost profits entails calculating the average revenue the plaintiff earned for a period of time prior to the infringement, and then subtracting from this amount the revenue actually earned during the period of infringement.[23] A court also can measure the plaintiff's lost profits by measuring the defendant's sales during the infringement period to customers that had purchased from both the plaintiff and the defendant.[24] What would be the best measure of Davis' lost profits under the facts of the Principal Problem?

---

basis for defining "willfulness" in the context of determining whether overhead should be deducted from a defendant's profits).

[20] See Cook v. Robbins, 232 F.3d 736 (9th Cir. 2001)(noting that the statute clearly places the burden on the defendant); Walker v. Forbes, Inc., 28 F.3d 409 (4th Cir. 1994)(noting that the "Copyright Act draws the line between under and overdeterrence by establishing the damages provided."); Frank Music Corp. v. Metro–Goldwyn–Mayer, Inc., 772 F.2d 505, 518 (9th Cir.1985)(in case under 1909 Act involving infringement of six minutes of music in a 100 minute musical revue, appellate court remanded to the district court to reconsider its apportionment of profits and to fully explain its methodology). Mathematical exactness is unnecessary, but "a reasonable and just apportionment of profits is required." Id. at 518. *Frank Music*

also allowed for the apportionment of both the direct profits from the revue as well as indirect profits from the hotel and casino sponsoring the revue. The Ninth Circuit also reviewed the district court's post-remand decision regarding profits (see 886 F.2d 1545 (9th Cir.1989)).

[21] 754 F.2d 826, 827 (9th Cir.1985).

[22] See Stevens Linen Assocs. v. Mastercraft Corp., 656 F.2d 11, 15 (2d Cir. 1981)(woven upholstery fabrics at issue); Big Seven Music Corp. v. Lennon, 554 F.2d 504, 509–12 (2d Cir.1977)(comparing sales of infringed album by John Lennon with sales of his other contemporary albums).

[23] See Taylor v. Meirick, 712 F.2d 1112, 1119–21 (7th Cir.1983).

[24] See Stevens Linen Assocs. v. Mastercraft Corp., 656 F.2d 11, 15 (2d Cir.1981).

As *Davis* suggests, sometimes other methods of ascertaining actual damages are more appropriate than a lost profits calculation. *Davis* affirms looking to a copyright holder's loss of a reasonable royalty or license fee as a measure of actual damages, and disregards the potentially speculative nature of such calculations as a significant problem. In these instances, the value of such use can be determined by what a willing buyer would be required to pay to a willing seller.[25] Courts also may consider any value the plaintiff and defendant placed on the infringed work in prior negotiations.[26] In addition, courts can focus on the value of the property to the plaintiff.[27] Would any of these measures be applicable to the Principal Problem? Do you think the approach taken by the court in *Davis* is sound?

Many types of copyrighted property not only have an immediate value but also are capable of generating future royalties. In making a damage determination, courts also must consider this contingent income as part of the overall award.

*Davis* also discusses punitive damages, and notes that typically the purpose of such an award is achieved through increased statutory damages in situations involving willful infringement. The court did not, however, foreclose the possibility of punitive damages being awarded in an appropriate case, and at least one district court in the Second Circuit has concluded that "claims for punitive damages for copyright infringement found to be willful are not precluded as a matter of law and can be presented to the jury."[28]

**3.** *Injunctive relief and the public interest.* As Abend v. MCA, Inc. suggests, a court's decision to grant injunctive relief must balance the public's interest in enjoying the protected work (or derivative works based on the protected work) against the property interest of the copyright owner. The Supreme Court in *Abend* affirmed the merits of the Ninth Circuit's decision with respect to the infringement issue (see Assignment 9), but the Court explicitly noted that certiorari was not granted on the issue of relief and it did not discuss the lower court's decision in that regard.[29] In New York Times Co., Inc. v. Tasini,[30] also reprinted in Assignment 9, the Supreme Court held that print publishers could not rely on § 201(c) of the Copyright Act to shield them from copyright infringement for facilitating the reproduction of authors' articles on electronic databases. Although the Court

[25] See Deltak, Inc. v. Advanced Systems, Inc., 767 F.2d 357 (7th Cir. 1985)(computing actual damages based on the value of use to the infringer, with the value of such use determined by what a willing buyer would be required to pay to a willing seller).

[26] See Szekely v. Eagle Lion Films, 242 F.2d 266, 268–69 (2d Cir. 1957)(holding that the agreed compensation was an appropriate amount on which to base a damage award for common-law copyright infringement action brought by a screenplay writer who retained all rights and title to a manuscript).

[27] See Universal Pictures Co. v. Harold Lloyd Corp., 162 F.2d 354, 369–70 (9th Cir. 1947)(observing that the owner of personal property, including literary property, may testify as to its value, and upholding the use of expert testimony to value copyrighted property).

[28] TVT Records v. Island Def Jam Music Group, 262 F.Supp.2d 185 (S.D.N.Y. 2003).

[29] See Stewart v. Abend, 495 U.S. 207, 216 (1990).

[30] 533 U.S. 483 (2001).

indicated that the remedial issues should be decided by the district court, it nonetheless questioned the propriety of issuing an automatic injunction against the inclusion of the articles in the databases. [31]

The public interest component can take on added significance when the defendant is a government entity. In 1990, the Copyright Remedy Clarification Act ("CRCA") was passed, which expressly eliminated state immunity for copyright infringement. The Act currently provides that states are not immune from suit and that all remedies, both at law and in equity, are available against a state or instrumentality of a state to the same extent as are available against any other "public or private entity."[32] Whether this provision continues to be enforceable, however, is open to question in light of the Supreme Court's decision in College Savings Bank v. Florida Prepaid Postsecondary Education Expense Board,[33] discussed in Assignment 5. Recall that in that case, the Court affirmed the Third Circuit's ruling that the provision of the Lanham Act abrogating the states' Eleventh Amendment immunity was unconstitutional as applied in that case. The Fifth Circuit has relied on the reasoning in *Florida Prepaid* in holding that the CRCA is unconstitutional.[34] Although bills have been introduced to restore state liability, no legislation has been enacted as of this writing. It is worth noting that prior to the enactment of the CRCA, several courts had held that the 1976 Act failed to waive the states' Eleventh Amendment immunity for being sued in federal court for damages.[35] Since federal courts have exclusive jurisdiction over copyrighted matters,[36] the immunity of state entities from copyright damage actions in federal court resulted in prospective injunctive relief against individual state officials as the only available remedy against state government defendants.[37] As an exclusive alternative, this remedy clearly was unsatisfactory since an award of prospective, injunctive relief in federal court against individual state officials required copyright owners to identify and sue the state officials before any significant damage occurred. The government's use could be complete by the time a lawsuit was brought, thus significantly diminishing the value of the copyrighted work.

---

[31] Id. at 505.

[32] See §§ 501(a) & 511. The trademark and patent statutes contain similar provisions. See 15 U.S.C. § 1122, discussed in Assignment 5, and 35 U.S.C. § 296, discussed in Assignment 23.

[33] 527 U.S. 666 (1999).

[34] Chavez v. Arte Publico Press, 204 F.3d 601 (5th Cir.2000). *See also* Rodriguez v. Texas Commission on the Arts, 199 F.3d 279 (5th Cir.2000) (noting that the interests Congress "sought to protect in each statute are substantially the same and the language of the respective abrogation provisions are virtually identical.").

[35] Richard Anderson Photography v. Brown, 852 F.2d 114, 120 (4th Cir.1988), cert. denied, 489 U.S. 1033 (1989); BV Engineering v. University of California, Los Angeles, 858 F.2d 1394, 1400 (9th Cir.1988).

[36] See 28 U.S.C. § 1338(a)(providing federal district courts with original and exclusive jurisdiction over civil actions arising under federal copyright laws) and § 301 (preempting all "equivalent" state laws).

[37] The Supreme Court relaxed the application of the Eleventh Amendment immunity doctrine with respect to actions seeking prospective, injunctive relief against a state official for violations of federal constitutional law. Ex parte Young, 209 U.S. 123 (1908).

With respect to infringements by the federal government, 28 U.S.C. § 1498(b) provides that a copyright owner has the exclusive remedy of suing the federal government in the Claims Court for damages.[38] Both the legislative history and judicial interpretations of this provision reveal that its theoretical basis derives from the Fifth Amendment's just compensation clause.[39] Research shows that both federal and state governmental entities frequently use copyrighted property without the owner's permission.[40] From a remedial standpoint, should a distinction be drawn between federal and state governmental entities? What about between governmental entities in general and private defendants?

**4.** *Attorney's fees.* Strictly speaking, *Fogerty* would not be relevant to the Principal Problem if Silver were to be the prevailing party. Still, does the Court provide any guidance regarding the question of when an award of attorney's fees is appropriate?[41] In the Principal Problem, should either Silver or WJN (assuming the court found the broadcast was fair use) be able to recover attorney's fees? How do you think courts actually compute awards of attorney's fees?

Following the Supreme Court's decision in *Feltner* (see Note 1), the Ninth Circuit held that the defendant's prevailing on the narrow issue of whether the Seventh Amendment entitled him to a jury determination on statutory damages deriving from his liability for copyright infringement does not qualify him as a prevailing party for purposes of an award of attorney's fees pursuant to § 505.[42] With respect to the question of when an award of attorney's fees is appropriate under *Fogerty,* the First Circuit in Lotus Development Corp. v. Borland International, Inc.[43], affirmed the district court's refusal to award the prevailing defendant attorney's fees in a case of first impression. In so holding, the appellate court stated that the lower court did not commit legal error by reasoning that "when a plaintiff prosecutes an action, in good faith, in an unsettled area of law, and with a reasonable likelihood of success, against a party with similar financial resources, the prevailing party's case for attorney's fees is weaker, whether it be a plaintiff or a defendant."[44]

**5.** *Prejudgment interest.* Some precedent exists for the award of prejudgment interest in copyright litigation, although the statute does not specifically provide for it. The theory underlying an award of interest is that such

---

[38] See also § 502(a)(providing that injunctive relief is "subject to the provisions of section 1498 of Title 28").

[39] 28 U.S.C. § 1498(a) provides analogous relief to the owners of patented property for unlicensed uses by the federal government. See Assignment 22.

[40] See Roberta Rosenthal Kwall, Governmental Use of Copyrighted Property: The Sovereign's Prerogative, 67 Tex. L. Rev. 685 (1989).

[41] See Fantasy, Inc. v. Fogerty, 94 F.3d 553 (9th Cir. 1996) (holding that "an award

of attorney's fees to a prevailing defendant that furthers the underlying purposes of the Copyright Act is reposed in the sound discretion of the district courts, and that such discretion is not cabined by a requirement of culpability on the part of the losing party").

[42] Columbia Pictures Television v. Krypton Broadcasting of Birmingham Inc., 152 F.3d 1171 (9th Cir.1998), cert. denied, 534 U.S. 1127 (2002).

[43] 140 F.3d 70 (1st Cir.1998).

[44] Id. at 1777.

is necessary to fulfill the restitutionary nature of the monetary awards under copyright law.[45] Some courts, however, have taken the position that prejudgment interest is unnecessary to deter copyright infringement given the other remedies available under the 1976 Act.[46] It is worth noting that the Supreme Court held, in a patent case, that prejudgment interest should be awarded, despite a similar lack of statutory direction, to "ensure that the patent owner would in fact receive full compensation for 'any damages' [the patentee] suffered as a result of the infringement."[47] See Assignment 23.

[45] See Frank Music Corp. v. Metro–Goldwyn–Mayer Inc., 886 F.2d 1545, 1552 (9th Cir.1989), cert. denied, 494 U.S. 1017 (1990) (awarding prejudgment interest on the apportioned share of defendant's profits under the 1909 Act: "For the restitutionary purpose of this remedy to be served fully, the defendant generally should be required to turn over to the plaintiff not only the profits made from the use of his property, but also the interest on these profits, which can well exceed the profits themselves."); Allen–Myland, Inc. v. International Business Machines Corp., 770 F.Supp. 1014, 1029 (E.D.Pa. 1991)(instructing special master to award prejudgment interest on damages in action involving infringement of computer microcode).

[46] See In Design v. K–Mart Apparel Corp., 13 F.3d 559, 569 (2d Cir.1994) (affirming district court's denial of prejudgment interest given the plaintiff's sizable damage award and its "lack of any initiative . . . to shorten this litigation"); Robert R. Jones Assocs. v. Nino Homes, 858 F.2d 274, 282 (6th Cir.1988) (vacating district court's award of prejudgment interest under the 1976 Act).

[47] General Motors Corp. v. Devex Corp., 461 U.S. 648, 654 (1983).

# ASSIGNMENT 13

# PREEMPTION OF STATE LAWS: THE RIGHT OF PUBLICITY AND MISAPPROPRIATION

## 1. INTRODUCTION

Parallel to the federal development of intellectual property law, states have created a variety of rights in intellectual property that are generally referred to under the rubric of unfair trade practice laws. Some of these state laws were explored in Assignment 3. This Assignment treats two specific state law doctrines with the potential for overlapping with copyright's coverage—the doctrine of misappropriation and the right of publicity. These doctrines thus provide an ideal vehicle for illustrating the operation of § 301 of the 1976 Act, which addresses preemption of state laws by the federal copyright statute.

Misappropriation owes its origins to state unfair competition laws aimed at preventing the practice of "passing off": supplying consumers who demand the goods of one manufacturer with products produced by a different manufacturer; or marketing goods with trademarks, logos, symbols and labels similar to those of a competitor. States were concerned with these practices because they harmed both consumers and producers. Consumers wound up with purchases that disappointed their expectations, and producers found their extensive investments in quality, advertising, and goodwill undermined. By creating a right of action against the sale of goods with confusingly similar markings, the states managed to deal with the consumers' interest rather well. The producers' interest was, however, only partially addressed because passing off claims reached only the investment captured in the product's specific marks and trade dress. To protect producers' other investments in their products against those who would reap where they had not sown, courts developed rights "against a defendant's competing use of a valuable product or idea created by the plaintiff through investment of time, effort, money and expertise."[1] Misappropriation is, in short, the intellectual property version of unjust enrichment. Although the origin of misappropriation was unfair competition, many current applications of the doctrine involve copyrightable property. Thus, it is explored in this Assignment addressing copyright preemption.

---

[1] See Mayer v. Josiah Wedgwood & Sons, Ltd., 601 F.Supp. 1523, 1534 (S.D.N.Y. 1985). Misappropriation also is discussed in the Re-statement (Third) of Unfair Competition § 38 (1995).

The right of publicity discussed in the major cases is similar to misappropriation in many respects. It too protects against attempts to utilize another's investment—this time investment in a person's individual characteristics: name, likeness, and other recognizable attributes. The right of publicity is sometimes confused with the right of privacy because both are aimed at controlling the extent to which one party can use the details of the life of another. But the claims can be fundamentally different: right-of-privacy plaintiffs want to be left out of the limelight—they do not want features of their lives exploited at all. In contrast, the question in many right-of-publicity cases is *who* has the right to enjoy the values inhering in these features, the plaintiff or members of the public at large (the defendant being one example).[2]

The observation at the end of the previous paragraph, that the defendant in these state law cases stands as a proxy for the public's interest in the free availability of personal attributes, leads directly to the subject of this Assignment, for it suggests the possibility that there may be a conflict between federal intellectual property law and these state-based rights. After all, the Constitution gave to *Congress* the authority to create intellectual property law. The Copyright Clause can therefore be read as excluding the states from undertaking any activity in this field, especially activity that would tend to privatize material that would otherwise fall into the public domain. This is a sort of "dormant Copyright Clause" argument, akin to the dormant Commerce Clause doctrine familiar to constitutional lawyers.

More often encountered are arguments to the effect that when Congress enacts copyright and patent legislation, it creates a dividing line between subject matter whose protection is in the public interest and subject matter whose lack of protection is in the public interest. If the second category of subject matter is supposed to be in the public domain, then any state's attempt to prevent free use of such subject matter must be viewed as preempted.

Although the dividing-line theory is appealing, it is equally plausible to assume that copyright and patent law were not meant to be the sole forms of protection for intellectual property rights, that states should have a role in protecting industries of local importance, and that it makes sense to offer more expansive protection—copyrights and patents—for major contributions, and less expansive state law protection for more minor contributions. The Supreme Court has vacillated somewhat on the appropriate scope of federal preemption. Two major cases, Sears, Roebuck & Co v. Stiffel Co.,[3] and Compco Co. v. Day–Brite Lighting, Inc.,[4] tend to support

---

[2] Many right of publicity cases, however, do involve an objection on the part of the plaintiff to the exploitation itself. See, e.g., Waits v. Frito–Lay, Inc., 978 F.2d 1093 (9th Cir.1992), cert. denied, 506 U.S. 1080 (1993), See also Roberta Rosenthal Kwall, The Right of Publicity v. The First Amendment: A Property and Liability Rule Analysis, 70 Ind. L.J. 47 (1994).

The Right of Publicity is the subject of Restatement (Third) Of Unfair Competition §§ 46–49 (1993).

[3] 376 U.S. 225 (1964).

[4] 376 U.S. 234 (1964).

the position that a state may not prohibit the copying of something that federal law has left unpatented or uncopyrighted. This approach, however, arguably was undermined by the Court's subsequent decision in Goldstein v. California,[5] which essentially allowed state law protection for material that "had not previously been protected under the federal copyright statute" on the theory that states should retain some control over protection of creative works of essentially local interest.[6]

*Sears*, *Compco*, and *Goldstein* were decided prior to the enactment of Section 301 of the Copyright Act which expressly sets out a test for determining whether a particular state law is preempted by the 1976 Act. The test under Section 301 has two parts. The first part of the preemption test focuses on the nature of the work protected by the state law. For example, preemption will not occur if the state law does not pertain to "works of authorship that are fixed in a tangible medium of expression and come within the subject matter of copyright."[7] The states, in other words, are free to regulate all works that are not protected by the copyright law because of their nature or form of expression. If a particular work is capable of copyright protection but is not fixed in a tangible medium of expression, protection may be obtained under state common law copyright. See Note 9 of Assignment 7 for a discussion of fixation.

The second part of the preemption test emphasizes the nature of the rights that the state law attempts to safeguard. If the state seeks to protect rights that are "not equivalent to any of the exclusive rights within the general scope of copyright," the state's law will not be preempted by section 301.[8] The application of the equivalency prong of the preemption test thus requires a determination whether a particular state law creates rights that are "equivalent" to any of the rights protected by section 106 of the 1976 Act. Note that preemption of a state law will occur only if both parts of the test in section 301 are satisfied. Therefore, if a state law grants "equivalent rights" to a work that does not come within the scope of federal copyright law, no preemption will result. Similarly, a state may protect federally copyrightable works as long as such protection does not encompass rights equivalent to 1976 Act protections.

Section 301 has not, however, obviated all preemption problems in copyright law. Although Congress purported to enact an unambiguous statutory mandate concerning the issue of preemption, the following cases and materials demonstrate that it can be exceedingly difficult to apply this provision. For example, what approach should be taken with respect to subject matter that the Act has specifically excluded from protection:

---

[5] 412 U.S. 546 (1973).

[6] Id. at 568 (*Goldstein* validated a California statute protecting sound recordings, which were not then copyrightable subject matter). For a good discussion of these three decisions, see Howard B. Abrams, Copyright, Misappropriation, and Preemption: Constitutional and Statutory Limits of State Law Protection, 1983 Sup. Ct. Rev. 509.

[7] § 301(a).

[8] Id.

should it be treated the same as subject matter that is simply omitted from statutory consideration, or should the express exclusion of certain categories of works be read as placing them irretrievably in the public domain? Similarly, what about rights specifically denied to particular categories of works: can the states substitute their own judgment or are they expressly excluded from acting? The issue of preemption under § 301 has been litigated in the context of general state based actions such as fraud, breach of contract,[9] conversion[10] and tortious interference with business relationships,[11] as well as state law actions that specifically cover intellectual property (e.g., unfair competition,[12] misappropriation,[13] and the right of publicity[14]). This Assignment illustrates the difficulties surrounding the application of § 301 when a plaintiff attempts to bring a misappropriation or right of publicity action involving copyrighted property. An understanding of the materials that follow will require you to master not only the copyright preemption issue, but also the important state-created rights discussed herein.

[9] See, e.g., Wrench LLC v. Taco Bell Corp., 256 F.3d 446 (6th Cir. 2001)(implied-in-fact contract action not preempted); ProCD, Inc. v. Zeidenberg, 86 F.3d 1447 (7th Cir. 1996)(action based on breach of written contract not preempted). But see Selby v. New Line Cinema Corp., 96 F.Supp.2d 1053 (C.D. Cal. 2000)(advocating a fact specific approach to preemption; court holds preempted implied-in-fact contract action). See also note 10.

[10] See, e.g., Murray Hill Publ'ns, Inc. v. ABC Communs., 264 F.3d 622 (6th Cir. 2001)(conversion action preempted); United States ex rel. Berge v. Board of Trustees of the Univ. of Ala., 104 F.3d 1453 (4th Cir. 1997)(conversion action preempted); Strauss v. The Hearst Corp., 8 U.S.P.Q.2d (BNA) 1832 (S.D.N.Y. 1988) (conversion action preempted); Mayer v. Josiah Wedgwood & Sons, Ltd., 601 F.Supp. 1523 (S.D.N.Y. 1985)(conversion action preempted).

[11] See, e.g., Ticketmaster Corp. v. Tickets.Com, Inc., 54 U.S.P.Q.2d 1344 (C.D. Cal. 2000)(deliberately disrupting business through hyperlinking provides the necessary extra element to avoid preemption); Telecomm Tech. Servs. v. Siemens Rolm Communs., Inc., 66 F.Supp.2d 1306 (N.D. Ga. 1998)(tortious interference via violation of software license provides extra element to avoid preemption); Titan Sports, Inc. v. Turner Broadcasting Sys., 981 F.Supp. 65 (D. Conn. 1997)(tortious interference claim not qualitatively different from copyright violation and therefore preempted).

[12] See, e.g., Scholastic, Inc. v. Stouffer, 124 F.Supp.2d 836 (S.D.N.Y. 2000)(unfair competition claim contains reverse passing off as the extra element to survive preemption); Richard Feiner and Co., Inc. v. Larry Harmon Pictures Corp., 38 F.Supp.2d 276 (S.D.N.Y. 1999)(no extra element in unfair competition action and therefore preempted); Goes Lithography Co. v. Banta Corp., 26 F.Supp.2d 1042 (N.D. Ill. 1998)(unfair competition claim preempted because it merely restates copyright infringement claim).

[13] See Dun & Bradstreet Software v. Grace Consulting, 307 F.3d 197 (3d Cir. 2002)(state law misappropriation of trade secrets claim requiring proof of breach of duty through improper disclosure not preempted); Alcatel USA, Inc. v. DGI Techs., Inc., 166 F.3d 772 (5th Cir. 1999)(state law misappropriation action preempted); Mayer v. Josiah Wedgwood & Sons, Ltd., 601 F.Supp. 1523 (S.D.N.Y. 1985)(preempting state law misappropriation action).

[14] Cf. Brown v. Ames, 201 F.3d 654 (5th Cir. 2000)(state claims based on misappropriation of plaintiff's name and likeness not preempted) with Toney v. L'Oreal USA, Inc., 64 U.S.P.Q.2d 1857 (N.D. Ill. 2002)(plaintiff's state law claim for right of publicity violation based on alleged unauthorized use of likeness preempted by copyright law); Baltimore Orioles, Inc. v. Major League Baseball Players Association, 805 F.2d 663 (7th Cir. 1986) (common law right of publicity claim preempted).

## 2.   PRINCIPAL PROBLEM

Your clients, Nisa, Shanna and Rachel Meller, are dance historians. Last March, they attended a live ballet in which the famous American dancer Ilana Kaye was the featured performer. This performance was particularly special, since it marked Ilana's 10th anniversary of her debut in Swan Lake with the renowned Chesterfield Ballet Company. Although Ilana was not the choreographer of this performance, she improvised liberally during the actual performance. Ilana has a policy of allowing people to videotape her performances as long as they get her permission in advance. The Mellers wrote to Ilana for permission to videotape the March performance, but they never received a response. Still they videotaped one of Ilana's solo numbers with a home-type video camera so that they could enjoy her performance at home in the future.

Several months later, the Mellers decided to create a documentary film on 20th century dance. The film was produced on DVD and video, and many more copies of each were sold than the Mellers anticipated. The film featured about 20 minutes of Ilana's two hour anniversary performance, and realistically, the inclusion of this performance contributed greatly to the commercial success of the videos and DVDs.

Ilana has just instituted a lawsuit against the Mellers based on copyright infringement, misappropriation, and violation of Ilana's right of publicity. Your clients now are very nervous and want your opinion on whether any of these actions could be successful. Before advising them, consider the following materials.

## 3.   MATERIALS FOR SOLUTION OF PRINCIPAL PROBLEM

A.   STATUTORY MATERIALS: §§ 106, 301, & 1101

B.   CASES:

# National Basketball Association and NBA Properties, Inc. v. Motorola, Inc.

United States Court of Appeals, Second Circuit, 1997.
105 F.3d 841.

■ WINTER, CIRCUIT JUDGE:

Motorola, Inc. and Sports Team Analysis and Tracking Systems ("STATS") appeal from a permanent injunction. The injunction concerns a handheld pager sold by Motorola and marketed under the name "SportsTrax," which displays updated information of professional basketball games in progress. The injunction prohibits appellants, absent authorization from the National Basketball Association and NBA Properties, Inc. (collectively the "NBA"), from transmitting scores or other data about NBA games in progress via the pagers, STATS's site on America On–Line's computer dial-up service, or "any equivalent means."

The crux of the dispute concerns the extent to which a state law "hot-news" misappropriation claim based on International News Service v. Associated Press, 248 U.S. 215 (1918) ("INS"), survives preemption by the federal Copyright Act and whether the NBA's claim fits within the surviving INS-type claims. We hold that a narrow "hot-news" exception does survive preemption. However, we also hold that appellants' transmission of "real-time" NBA game scores and information tabulated from television and radio broadcasts of games in progress does not constitute a misappropriation of "hot news" that is the property of the NBA.

## I.  BACKGROUND

The facts are largely undisputed. Motorola manufactures and markets the SportsTrax paging device while STATS supplies the game information that is transmitted to the pagers. The product became available to the public in January 1996, at a retail price of about $200. SportsTrax's pager has an inch-and-a-half by inch-and-a-half screen and operates in four basic modes: "current," "statistics," "final scores" and "demonstration." It is the "current" mode that gives rise to the present dispute. In that mode, SportsTrax displays the following information on NBA games in progress: (i) the teams playing; (ii) score changes; (iii) the team in possession of the ball; (iv) whether the team is in the free-throw bonus; (v) the quarter of the game; and (vi) time remaining in the quarter. The information is updated every two to three minutes, with more frequent updates near the end of the first half and the end of the game. There is a lag of approximately two or three minutes between events in the game itself and when the information appears on the pager screen.

SportsTrax's operation relies on a "data feed" supplied by STATS reporters who watch the games on television or listen to them on the radio. The reporters key into a personal computer changes in the score and other information such as successful and missed shots, fouls, and clock updates. The information is relayed by modem to STATS's host computer, which compiles, analyzes, and formats the data for retransmission. The information is then sent to a common carrier, which then sends it via satellite to various local FM radio networks that in turn emit the signal received by the individual SportsTrax pagers.

Finding Motorola and STATS liable for misappropriation, Judge Preska entered the permanent injunction, reserved the calculation of damages for subsequent proceedings, and stayed execution of the injunction pending appeal. Motorola and STATS appeal from the injunction.

## II.  THE STATE LAW MISAPPROPRIATION CLAIM

### A.  Summary of Ruling

Because our disposition of the state law misappropriation claim rests in large part on preemption by the Copyright Act, our discussion necessarily goes beyond the elements of a misappropriation claim under New York law, and a summary of our ruling here will perhaps render that discussion—or at least the need for it—more understandable.

The issues before us are ones that have arisen in various forms over the course of this century as technology has steadily increased the speed and quantity of information transmission. Today, individuals at home, at work, or elsewhere, can use a computer, pager, or other device to obtain highly selective kinds of information virtually at will. *INS* was one of the first cases to address the issues raised by these technological advances, although the technology involved in that case was primitive by contemporary standards. INS involved two wire services, the Associated Press ("AP") and International News Service ("INS"), that transmitted news stories by wire to member newspapers. *Id.* INS would lift factual stories from AP bulletins and send them by wire to INS papers. *Id.* at 231. INS would also take factual stories from east coast AP papers and wire them to INS papers on the west coast that had yet to publish because of time differentials. *Id.* at 238. The Supreme Court held that INS's conduct was a common-law misappropriation of AP's property. *Id.* at 242.

With the advance of technology, radio stations began "live" broadcasts of events such as baseball games and operas, and various entrepreneurs began to use the transmissions of others in one way or another for their own profit. In response, New York courts created a body of misappropriation law, loosely based on INS, that sought to apply ethical standards to the use by one party of another's transmissions of events.

Federal copyright law played little active role in this area until 1976. Before then, it appears to have been the general understanding—there being no caselaw of consequence—that live events such as baseball games were not copyrightable. Moreover, doubt existed even as to whether a recorded broadcast or videotape of such an event was copyrightable. In 1976, however, Congress passed legislation expressly affording copyright protection to simultaneously-recorded broadcasts of live performances such as sports events. See 17 U.S.C. § 101. Such protection was not extended to the underlying events.

The 1976 amendments also contained provisions preempting state law claims that enforced rights "equivalent" to exclusive copyright protections when the work to which the state claim was being applied fell within the area of copyright protection. See 17 U.S.C. § 301. Based on legislative history of the 1976 Amendments, it is generally agreed that a "hot-news" INS-like claim survives preemption. H.R. No. 94–1476 at 132 (1976), reprinted in 1976 U.S.C.C.A.N. 5659, 5748. However, much of New York misappropriation law after INS goes well beyond "hot-news" claims and is preempted.

B. Copyrights in Events or Broadcasts of Events

The NBA asserted copyright infringement claims with regard both to the underlying games and to their broadcasts. The district court dismissed these claims, and the NBA does not appeal from their dismissal. Nevertheless, discussion of the infringement claims is necessary to provide the framework for analyzing the viability of the NBA's state law misappropriation claim in light of the Copyright Act's preemptive effect.

### 1.  Infringement of a Copyright in the Underlying Games

In our view, the underlying basketball games do not fall within the subject matter of federal copyright protection because they do not constitute "original works of authorship" under 17 U.S.C. § 102(a). Sports events are not "authored" in any common sense of the word. There is, of course, at least at the professional level, considerable preparation for a game. However, the preparation is as much an expression of hope or faith as a determination of what will actually happen. Unlike movies, plays, television programs, or operas, athletic events are competitive and have no underlying script. Preparation may even cause mistakes to succeed, like the broken play in football that gains yardage because the opposition could not expect it. Athletic events may also result in wholly unanticipated occurrences, the most notable recent event being in a championship baseball game in which interference with a fly ball caused an umpire to signal erroneously a home run.

What "authorship" there is in a sports event, moreover, must be open to copying by competitors if fans are to be attracted. If the inventor of the T-formation in football had been able to copyright it, the sport might have come to an end instead of prospering. Even where athletic preparation most resembles authorship—figure skating, gymnastics, and, some would uncharitably say, professional wrestling—a performer who conceives and executes a particularly graceful and difficult—or, in the case of wrestling, seemingly painful—acrobatic feat cannot copyright it without impairing the underlying competition in the future. A claim of being the only athlete to perform a feat doesn't mean much if no one else is allowed to try.

For many of these reasons, Nimmer on Copyright concludes that the "far more reasonable" position is that athletic events are not copyrightable. 1 M. Nimmer & D. Nimmer, Nimmer on Copyright § 2.09[F] at 2–170.1 (1996). Nimmer notes that, among other problems, the number of joint copyright owners would arguably include the league, the teams, the athletes, umpires, stadium workers and even fans, who all contribute to the "work."

Concededly, caselaw is scarce on the issue of whether organized events themselves are copyrightable, but what there is indicates that they are not. See Prod. Contractors, Inc. v. WGN Continental Broad. Co., 622 F.Supp. 1500 (N.D.Ill.1985) (Christmas parade is not a work of authorship entitled to copyright protection). In claiming a copyright in the underlying games, the NBA relied in part on a footnote in Baltimore Orioles, Inc. v. Major League Baseball Players Assn., 805 F.2d 663, 669 n. 7 (7th Cir.1986), cert. denied, 480 U.S.941 (1987), which stated that the "players' performances" contain the "Modest Creativity Required for Copyrightability." However, the Court went on to state, "moreover, even if the players' performances were not sufficiently creative, the players agree that the cameramen and director contribute creative labor to the telecasts." Id. This last sentence indicates that the court was considering the copyrightability of telecasts—not the underlying games, which obviously can be played without cameras.

We believe that the lack of caselaw is attributable to a general understanding that athletic events were, and are, uncopyrightable. Indeed, prior to 1976, there was even doubt that broadcasts describing or depicting such events, which have a far stronger case for copyrightability than the events themselves, were entitled to copyright protection. Indeed, as described in the next subsection of this opinion, Congress found it necessary to extend such protection to recorded broadcasts of live events. The fact that Congress did not extend such protection to the events themselves confirms our view that the district court correctly held that appellants were not infringing a copyright in the NBA games.

2.   Infringement of a Copyright in the Broadcasts of NBA Games

As noted, recorded broadcasts of NBA games—as opposed to the games themselves—are now entitled to copyright protection. The Copyright Act was amended in 1976 specifically to insure that simultaneously-recorded transmissions of live performances and sporting events would meet the Act's requirement that the original work of authorship be "fixed in any tangible medium of expression." 17 U.S.C. § 102(a). Accordingly, Section 101 of the Act, containing definitions, was amended to read:

> A work consisting of sounds, images, or both, that are being transmitted, is "fixed" for purposes of this title if a fixation of the work is being made simultaneously with its transmission.

17 U.S.C. § 101. Congress specifically had sporting events in mind:

> [T]he bill seeks to resolve, through the definition of "fixation" in section 101, the status of live broadcasts—sports, news coverage, live performances of music, etc.—that are reaching the public in unfixed form but that are simultaneously being recorded.

H.R. No. 94–1476 at 52, reprinted in 1976 U.S.C.C.A.N. at 5665. The House Report also makes clear that it is the broadcast, not the underlying game, that is the subject of copyright protection. In explaining how game broadcasts meet the Act's requirement that the subject matter be an "original work[ ] of authorship," 17 U.S.C. § 102(a), the House Report stated:

> When a football game is being covered by four television cameras, with a director guiding the activities of the four cameramen and choosing which of their electronic images are sent out to the public and in what order, there is little doubt that what the cameramen and the director are doing constitutes "authorship."

H.R. No. 94–1476 at 52, reprinted in 1976 U.S.C.C.A.N. at 5665.

Although the broadcasts are protected under copyright law, the district court correctly held that Motorola and STATS did not infringe NBA's copyright because they reproduced only facts from the broadcasts, not the expression or description of the game that constitutes the broadcast. The "fact/expression dichotomy" is a bedrock principle of copyright law that "limits severely the scope of protection in fact-based works." Feist Publications, Inc. v. Rural Tel. Service Co., 499 U.S. 340 (1991). " 'No author may copyright facts or ideas. The copyright is limited to those aspects of the work—termed "expression"—that display the stamp of the author's originality.'" *Id.* (quoting Harper & Row, Inc. v. Nation Enter., 471 U.S. 539, 547–48 (1985)).

We agree with the district court that the "defendants provide purely factual information which any patron of an NBA game could acquire from the arena without any involvement from the director, cameramen, or others who contribute to the originality of a broadcast." 939 F. Supp. at 1094. Because the SportsTrax device and AOL site reproduce only factual information culled from the broadcasts and none of the copyrightable expression of the games, appellants did not infringe the copyright of the broadcasts.

## C. The State–Law Misappropriation Claim

The district court's injunction was based on its conclusion that, under New York law, defendants had unlawfully misappropriated the NBA's property rights in its games. The district court reached this conclusion by holding: (i) that the NBA's misappropriation claim relating to the underlying games was not preempted by Section 301 of the Copyright Act; and (ii) that, under New York common law, defendants had engaged in unlawful misappropriation. *Id.* at 1094–1107. We disagree.

### 1. Preemption Under the Copyright Act

#### a) Summary

When Congress amended the Copyright Act in 1976, it provided for the preemption of state law claims that are interrelated with copyright claims in certain ways. Under 17 U.S.C. § 301, a state law claim is preempted when: (i) the state law claim seeks to vindicate "legal or equitable rights that are equivalent" to one of the bundle of exclusive rights already protected by copyright law under 17 U.S.C. § 106—styled the "general scope requirement"; and (ii) the particular work to which the state law claim is being applied falls within the type of works protected by the Copyright Act under Sections 102 and 103—styled the "subject matter requirement."

The district court concluded that the NBA's misappropriation claim was not preempted because, with respect to the underlying games, as opposed to the broadcasts, the subject matter requirement was not met. 939 F.Supp. at 1097. The court dubbed as "partial preemption" its separate analysis of misappropriation claims relating to the underlying games and misappropriation claims relating to broadcasts of those games. *Id.* at 1098, n.24. The district court then relied on a series of older New York misappropriation cases involving radio broadcasts that considerably broadened INS. We hold that where the challenged copying or misappropriation relates in part to the copyrighted broadcasts of the games, the subject matter requirement is met as to both the broadcasts and the games. We therefore reject the partial preemption doctrine and its anomalous consequence that "it is possible for a plaintiff to assert claims both for infringement of its copyright in a broadcast and misappropriation of its rights in the underlying event." *Id.* We do find that a properly-narrowed INS "hot-news" misappropriation claim survives preemption because it fails the general scope requirement, but that the broader theory of the radio broadcast cases relied upon by the district court were preempted when Congress extended copyright protection to simultaneously-recorded broadcasts.

b) "Partial Preemption" and the Subject Matter Requirement

The subject matter requirement is met when the work of authorship being copied or misappropriated "falls within the ambit of copyright protection." Harper & Row, Inc. v. Nation Enter., 723 F.2d 195, 200 (1983), rev'd on other grounds, 471 U.S. 539 (1985). We believe that the subject matter requirement is met in the instant matter and that the concept of "partial preemption" is not consistent with section 301 of the Copyright Act. Although game broadcasts are copyrightable while the underlying games are not, the Copyright Act should not be read to distinguish between the two when analyzing the preemption of a misappropriation claim based on copying or taking from the copyrightable work. We believe that:

> [O]nce a performance is reduced to tangible form, there is no distinction between the performance and the recording of the performance for the purposes of preemption under § 301(a). Thus, if a baseball game were not broadcast [*23] or were telecast without being recorded, the Players' performances similarly would not be fixed in tangible form and their rights of publicity would not be subject to preemption. By virtue of being videotaped, however, the Players' performances are fixed in tangible form, and any rights of publicity in their performances that are equivalent to the rights contained in the copyright of the telecast are preempted.

Baltimore Orioles, 805 F.2d at 675 (citation omitted).

Copyrightable material often contains uncopyrightable elements within it, but Section 301 preemption bars state law misappropriation claims with respect to uncopyrightable as well as copyrightable elements. In Harper & Row, for example, we held that state law claims based on the copying of excerpts from President Ford's memoirs were preempted even with respect to information that was purely factual and not copyrightable. We stated:

> The [Copyright] Act clearly embraces "works of authorship," including "literary works," as within its subject matter. The fact that portions of the Ford memoirs may consist of uncopyrightable material . . . does not take the work as a whole outside the subject matter [*24] protected by the Act. Were this not so, states would be free to expand the perimeters of copyright protection to their own liking, on the theory that preemption would be no bar to state protection of material not meeting federal statutory standards.

723 F.2d at 200 (citation omitted). The legislative history supports this understanding of Section 301(a)'s subject matter requirement. The House Report stated:

> As long as a work fits within one of the general subject matter categories of sections 102 and 103, the bill prevents the States from protecting it even if it fails to achieve Federal statutory copyright because it is too minimal or lacking in originality to qualify, or because it has fallen into the public domain.

534 at 131, reprinted in 1976 U.S.C.C.A.N. at 5747. See also

H.R. No. 94–1476 at 131, reprinted in 1976 U.S.C.C.A.N. at 5747. See also Baltimore Orioles, 805 F.2d at 676 (citing excerpts of House Report 94–1476).

Adoption of a partial preemption doctrine—preemption of claims based on misappropriation of broadcasts but no preemption of claims based on misappropriation of underlying facts—would expand significantly the reach of state law claims and render the preemption intended by Congress unworkable. It is often difficult or impossible to separate the fixed copyrightable work from the underlying uncopyrightable events or facts. Moreover, Congress, in extending copyright protection only to the broadcasts and not to the underlying events, intended that the latter be in the public domain. Partial preemption turns that intent on its head by allowing state law to vest exclusive rights in material that Congress intended to be in the public domain and to make unlawful conduct that Congress intended to allow.

c) The General Scope Requirement

Under the general scope requirement, Section 301 "preempts only those state law rights that 'may be abridged by an act which, in and of itself, would infringe one of the exclusive rights' provided by federal copyright law." Computer Assoc. Int'l, Inc. v. Altai, Inc., 982 F.2d 693, 716 (2d Cir.1992) (quoting Harper & Row, 723 F.2d at 200). However, certain forms of commercial misappropriation otherwise within the general scope requirement will survive preemption if an "extra-element" test is met.

We turn, therefore, to the question of the extent to which a "hot-news" misappropriation claim based on INS involves extra elements and is not the equivalent of exclusive rights under a copyright. Courts are generally agreed that some form of such a claim survives preemption. This conclusion is based in part on the legislative history of the 1976 amendments. The House Report stated:

> "Misappropriation" is not necessarily synonymous with copyright infringement, and thus a cause of action labeled as "misappropriation" is not preempted if it is in fact based neither on a right within the general scope of copyright as specified by section 106 nor on a right equivalent thereto. For example, state law should have the flexibility to afford a remedy (under traditional principles of equity) against a consistent pattern of unauthorized appropriation by a competitor of the facts (i.e., not the literary expression) constituting "hot" news, whether in the traditional mold of International News Service v.Associated Press, 248 U.S. 215 (1918), or in the newer form of data updates from scientific, business, or financial data bases.

H.R. No. 94–1476 at 132, reprinted in 1976 U.S.C.C.A.N. at 5748 (footnote omitted). The crucial question, therefore, is the breadth of the "hot-news" claim that survives preemption.

In INS, the plaintiff AP and defendant INS were "wire services" that sold news items to client newspapers. AP brought suit to prevent INS from selling facts and information lifted from AP sources to INS-affiliated newspapers. One method by which INS was able to use AP's news was to lift facts from AP news bulletins. INS, 248 U.S. at 231. Another method was to sell facts taken from just-published east coast AP newspapers to west coast INS newspapers whose editions had yet to appear. *Id.* at 238. The Supreme Court held (prior to Erie R. Co. v. Tompkins, 304 U.S. 64 (1938)), that INS's use of AP's information was unlawful under federal common law. It characterized INS's conduct as

> amount[ing] to an unauthorized interference with the normal operation of complainant's legitimate business precisely at the point where the profit is to be reaped, in order to divert a material portion of the profit from those who have earned it to those who have not; with special advantage to defendant in the competition because of the fact that it is not burdened with any part of the expense of gathering the news.

INS, 248 U.S. at 240.

The theory of the New York misappropriation cases relied upon by the district court is considerably broader than that of INS. For example, the district court quoted at length from Metropolitan Opera Ass'n v. Wagner–Nichols Recorder Corp., 199 Misc. 786, 101 N.Y.S.2d 483 (N.Y.Sup.Ct. 1950), aff'd, 279 A.D. 632, 107 N.Y.S.2d 795 (1st Dep't 1951). Metropolitan Opera described New York misappropriation law as standing for the "broader principle that property rights of commercial value are to be and will be protected from any form of commercial immorality"; that misappropriation law developed "to deal with business malpractices offensive to the ethics of [ ] society"; and that the doctrine is "broad and flexible." 939 F. Supp. at 1098–1110 (quoting Metropolitan Opera, 101 N.Y.S.2d at 492, 488–89).

However, we believe that Metropolitan Opera's broad misappropriation doctrine based on amorphous concepts such as "commercial immorality" or society's "ethics" is preempted. Such concepts are virtually synonymous for wrongful copying and are in no meaningful fashion distinguishable from infringement of a copyright. The broad misappropriation doctrine relied upon by the district court is, therefore, the equivalent of exclusive rights in copyright law.

Most of the broadcast cases relied upon by the NBA are simply not good law. Those cases were decided at a time when simultaneously-recorded broadcasts were not protected under the Copyright Act and when the state law claims they fashioned were not subject to federal preemption. For example, Metropolitan Opera, 199 Misc. 786, 101 N.Y.S.2d 483, involved the unauthorized copying, marketing, and sale of opera radio broadcasts. As another example, in Mutual Broadcasting System v. Muzak Corp., 177 Misc. 489, 30 N.Y.S.2d 419 (Sup. Ct. 1941), the defendant simultaneously retransmitted the plaintiff's baseball radio broadcasts onto telephone lines. As discussed above, the 1976 amendments to the Copyright Act were specifically designed to afford copyright protection to simultaneously-recorded broadcasts, and Metropolitan Opera and Muzak could today be brought as copyright infringement cases. Moreover, we believe that they would have to be brought as copyright cases because the amendments affording broadcasts copyright protection also preempted the state law misappropriation claims under which they were decided.

Our conclusion, therefore, is that only a narrow "hot-news" misappropriation claim survives preemption for actions concerning material within the realm of copyright. In our view, the elements central to an INS claim are: (i) the plaintiff generates or collects information at some cost or expense, (ii) the value of the information is highly time-sensitive, (iii) the defendant's use of the information constitutes free-riding on the plaintiff's costly efforts to generate or collect it; (iv) the defendant's use of the information is in direct competition with a product or service offered by the plaintiff, [and] (v) the ability of other parties to free-ride on the efforts of the plaintiff would so reduce the incentive to produce the product or service that its existence or quality would be substantially threatened.

INS is not about ethics; it is about the protection of property rights in time-sensitive information so that the information will be made available to the public by profit-seeking entrepreneurs. If services like AP were not assured of property rights in the news they pay to collect, they would cease to collect it. The ability of their competitors to appropriate their product at only nominal cost and thereby to disseminate a competing product at a lower price would destroy the incentive to collect news in the first place. The newspaper-reading public would suffer because no one would have an incentive to collect "hot news."

We therefore find the extra elements—those in addition to the elements of copyright infringement—that allow a "hotnews" claim to survive preemption are: (i) the time-sensitive value of factual information, (ii) the free-riding by a defendant, and (iii) the threat to the very existence of the product or service provided by the plaintiff.

2. The Legality of SportsTrax

We conclude that Motorola and STATS have not engaged in unlawful misappropriation under the "hot-news" test set out above. To be sure, some of the elements of a "hot-news" INS-claim are met. The information transmitted to SportsTrax is not precisely contemporaneous, but it is nevertheless time-sensitive. Also, the NBA does provide, or will shortly do so, information like that available through SportsTrax. It now offers a service called "Gamestats" that provides official play-by-play game sheets and half-time and final box scores within each arena. It also provides such information to the media in each arena. In the future, the NBA plans to enhance Gamestats so that it will be networked between the various arenas and will support a pager product analogous to SportsTrax. SportsTrax will of course directly compete with an enhanced Gamestats.

However, there are critical elements missing in the NBA's attempt to assert a "hot-news" INS-type claim. As framed by the NBA, their claim compresses and confuses three different informational products. The first product is generating the information by playing the games; the second product is transmitting live, full descriptions of those games; and the third product is collecting and retransmitting strictly factual information about the games. The first and second products are the NBA's primary business: producing basketball games for live attendance and licensing copyrighted broadcasts of those games. The collection and retransmission of strictly factual material about the games is a different product: e.g., box-scores in newspapers, summaries of statistics on television sports news, and real-time facts to be transmitted to pagers. In our view, the NBA has failed to show any competitive effect whatsoever from SportsTrax on the first and second products and a lack of any free-riding by SportsTrax on the third.

With regard to the NBA's primary products—producing basketball games with live attendance and licensing copyrighted broadcasts of those games—there is no evidence that anyone regards SportsTrax as a substitute for attending NBA games or watching them on television. In fact, Motorola markets SportsTrax as being designed "for those times when you cannot be at the arena, watch the game on TV, or listen to the radio ... "

The NBA argues that the pager market is also relevant to a "hot-news" INS-type claim and that SportsTrax's future competition with Gamestats satisfies any missing element. We agree that there is a separate market for the real-time transmission of factual information to pagers or similar devices. However, we disagree that SportsTrax is in any sense free-riding off Gamestats.

An indispensable element of an INS "hot-news" claim is free-riding by a defendant on a plaintiff's product, enabling the defendant to produce a directly competitive product for less money because it has lower costs. SportsTrax is not such a product. The use of pagers to transmit real-time information about NBA games requires: (i) the collecting of facts about the games; (ii) the transmission of these facts on a network; (iii) the assembling of them by the particular service; and (iv) the transmission of them to pagers or an on-line computer site. Appellants are in no way free-riding on Gamestats. Motorola and STATS expend their own resources to collect purely factual information generated in NBA games to transmit to SportsTrax pagers. They have their own network and assemble and transmit data themselves.

SportsTrax and Gamestats are each bearing their own costs of collecting factual information on NBA games, and, if one produces a product that is cheaper or otherwise superior to the other, that producer will prevail in the marketplace. This is obviously not the situation against which INS was intended to prevent: the potential lack of any such product or service because of the anticipation of free-riding.

For the foregoing reasons, the NBA has not shown any damage to any of its products based on free-riding by Motorola and STATS, and the NBA's misappropriation claim based on New York law is preempted.

## IV.   CONCLUSION

We vacate the injunction entered by the district court and order that the NBA's claim for misappropriation be dismissed.

# Comedy III Productions, Inc. v. Gary Saderup, Inc.

Supreme Court of California, 2001.
25 Cal.4th 387, 106 Cal.Rptr.2d 126, 21 P.3d 797.

■ MOSK, JUDGE:

A California statute grants the right of publicity to specified successors in interest of deceased celebrities, prohibiting any other person from using a celebrity's name, voice, signature, photograph, or likeness for commercial purposes without the consent of such successors. (Former Civ. Code, § 990.) The United States Constitution prohibits the states from abridging, among other fundamental rights, freedom of speech. (U.S. Const., 1st and 14th Amends.) In the case at bar we resolve a conflict between these two provisions. The Court of Appeal concluded that the lithographs and silk-screened T-shirts in question here received no First Amendment protection simply because they were reproductions rather than original works of art. As will appear, this was error: reproductions are equally entitled to First Amendment protection. We formulate instead what is essentially a balancing test between the First Amendment and the right of publicity based on whether the work in question adds significant creative elements so as to be transformed into something more than a mere celebrity likeness or imitation. Applying this test to the present case, we conclude that there are no such creative elements here and that the right of publicity prevails. On this basis, we will affirm the judgment of the Court of Appeal.

## I. The Statute

Section 990 declares broadly that "Any person who uses a deceased personality's name, voice, signature, photograph, or likeness, in any manner, on or in products, merchandise, or goods, or for purposes of advertising or selling, or soliciting purchases of, products, merchandise, goods, or services, without prior consent from the person or persons specified in subdivision (c), shall be liable for any damages sustained by the person or persons injured as a result thereof." (Id., subd. (a).) The amount recoverable includes "any profits from the unauthorized use," as well as punitive damages, attorney's fees, and costs. (Ibid.)

The statute further declares that "The rights recognized under this section are property rights" that are transferable before or after the personality dies, by contract or by trust or will. (§ 990, subd. (b).)

The statute provides a number of exemptions from the requirement of consent to use. Thus a use "in connection with any news, public affairs, or sports broadcast or account, or any political campaign" does not require consent. (§ 990, subd. (j).) Finally, subdivision (n) provides that "a play, book, magazine, newspaper, musical composition, film, radio or television program" (id., subd. (n)(1)), work of "political or newsworthy value" (id., subd. (n)(2)), "[s]ingle and original works of fine art" (id., subd. (n)(3)), or "an advertisement or commercial announcement" for the above works (id., subd. (n)(4)) are all exempt from the provisions of the statute.

II. Facts

Plaintiff Comedy III Productions, Inc. (hereafter Comedy III), brought this action against defendants Gary Saderup and Gary Saderup, Inc. hereafter collectively Saderup), seeking damages and injunctive relief for violation of section 990 and related business torts. The parties waived the right to jury trial and the right to put on evidence, and submitted the case for decision on the following stipulated facts:

Comedy III is the registered owner of all rights to the former comedy act known as The Three Stooges, who are deceased personalities within the meaning of the statute.

Saderup is an artist with over 25 years' experience in making charcoal drawings of celebrities. These drawings are used to create lithographic and silkscreen masters, which in turn are used to produce multiple reproductions in the form, respectively, of lithographic prints and silkscreened images on T-shirts. Saderup creates the original drawings and is actively involved in the ensuing lithographic and silkscreening processes.

Without securing Comedy III's consent, Saderup sold lithographs and T-shirts bearing a likeness of The Three Stooges reproduced from a charcoal drawing he had made. These lithographs and T-shirts did not constitute an advertisement, endorsement, or sponsorship of any product.

Saderup's profits from the sale of unlicensed lithographs and T-shirts bearing a likeness of The Three Stooges was $75,000 and Comedy III's reasonable attorney fees were $150,000.

On these stipulated facts the court found for Comedy III and entered judgment against Saderup awarding damages of $75,000 and attorney's fees of $150,000 plus costs. The court also issued a permanent injunction restraining Saderup from violating the statute by use of any likeness of The Three Stooges in lithographs, T-shirts, "or any other medium by which the [Saderup's] art work may be sold or marketed." The injunction further prohibited Saderup from "Creating, producing, reproducing, copying, distributing, selling or exhibiting any lithographs, prints, posters, t-shirts, buttons, or other goods, products or merchandise of any kind, bearing the photograph, image, face, symbols, trademarks, likeness, name, voice or signature of The Three Stooges or any of the individual members of The Three Stooges." The sole exception to this broad prohibition was Saderup's original charcoal drawing from which the reproductions at issue were made.

Saderup appealed. The Court of Appeal modified the judgment by striking the injunction. The court reasoned that Comedy III had not proved a likelihood of continued violation of the statute, and that the wording of the injunction was overbroad because it exceeded the terms of the statute and because it "could extend to matters and conduct protected by the First Amendment...."

The Court of Appeal affirmed the judgment as thus modified, however, upholding the award of damages, attorney fees, and costs. In so doing, it rejected Saderup's contentions that his conduct (1) did not violate the terms of the statute, and (2) in any event was protected by the constitutional guaranty of freedom of speech.

We granted review to address these two issues.

III.   Discussion

A.   The Statutory Issue

Saderup contends the statute applies only to uses of a deceased personality's name, voice, photograph, etc., for the purpose of advertising, selling, or soliciting the purchase of, products or services. He then stresses the stipulated fact (and subsequent finding) that the lithographs and T-shirts at issue in this case did not constitute an advertisement, endorsement, or sponsorship of any product. He concludes the statute therefore does not apply in the case at bar. As will appear, the major premise of his argument—his construction of the statute—is unpersuasive.

We therefore give effect to the plain meaning of the statute: it makes liable any person who, without consent, uses a deceased personality's name, voice, photograph, etc., either (1) "on or in" a product, or (2) in "advertising or selling" a product. The two uses are not synonymous.

Applying this construction of the statute to the facts at hand, we agree with the Court of Appeal that Saderup sold more than just the incorporeal likeness of The Three Stooges. Saderup's lithographic prints of The Three Stooges are themselves tangible personal property, consisting of paper and ink, made as products to be sold and displayed on walls like similar graphic art. Saderup's T-shirts are likewise tangible personal property, consisting of fabric and ink, made as products to be sold and worn on the body like similar garments. By producing and selling such lithographs and T-shirts, Saderup thus used the likeness of The Three Stooges "on ... products, merchandise, or goods" within the meaning of the statute.

B.   The Constitutional Issue

Saderup next contends that enforcement of the judgment against him violates his right of free speech and expression under the First Amendment. He raises a difficult issue, which we address below.

The right of publicity is often invoked in the context of commercial speech when the appropriation of a celebrity likeness creates a false and misleading impression that the celebrity is endorsing a product. (See Waits v. Frito–Lay, Inc. (9th Cir. 1992) 978 F.2d 1093; Midler v. Ford Motor Co. (9th Cir. 1988) 849 F.2d 460.) Because the First Amendment does not protect false and misleading commercial speech (Central Hudson Gas & Elec. Corp. v. Public Ser v. Com'n. (1980) 447 U.S. 557, 563–564, 65 L. Ed. 2d 341, 100 S. Ct. 2343), and because even nonmisleading commercial speech is generally subject to somewhat lesser First Amendment protection (Central Hudson, at p. 566), the right of publicity may often trump the right of advertisers to make use of celebrity figures.

But the present case does not concern commercial speech. As the trial court found, Saderup's portraits of The Three Stooges are expressive works and not an advertisement for or endorsement of a product. Although his work was done for financial gain, "the First Amendment is not limited to those who publish without charge.... [An expressive activity] does not lose its constitutional protection because it is undertaken for profit." (Guglielmi v. Spelling–Goldberg Productions (1979) 25 Cal. 3d 860, 868, 160 Cal. Rptr. 352, 603 P.2d 454 (conc. opn. of Bird, C. J.) (Guglielmi).)[a]

Because celebrities take on public meaning, the appropriation of their likenesses may have important uses in uninhibited debate on public issues, particularly debates about culture and values. And because celebrities take on personal meanings to many individuals in the society, the creative appropriation of celebrity images can be an important avenue of individual expression.

Nor do Saderup's creations lose their constitutional protections because they are for purposes of entertaining rather than informing. As Chief Justice Bird stated in Guglielmi, invoking the dual purpose of the First Amendment: "Our courts have often observed that entertainment is entitled to the same constitutional protection as the exposition of ideas. '[T]he line between informing and entertaining is too elusive for the protection of the basic right. Everyone is familiar with instances of propaganda through fiction. What is one man's amusement, teaches another doctrine.' " (Guglielmi, 25 Cal. 3d at p. 867, fn. omitted.)

Nor does the fact that expression takes a form of nonverbal, visual representation remove it from the ambit of First Amendment protection. In Bery v. City of New York (2d Cir. 1996) 97 F.3d 689, the court overturned an ordinance requiring visual artists—painters, printers, photographers, sculptors, etc.—to obtain licenses to sell their work in public places, but exempted the vendors of books, newspapers or other written matter. As the court stated: "Both the [district] court and the City demonstrate an unduly restricted view of the First Amendment and of visual art itself. Such myopic vision not only overlooks case law central to First Amendment jurisprudence but fundamentally misperceives the essence of visual communication and artistic expression." Moreover, the United States Supreme Court has made it clear that a work of art is protected by the First Amendment even if it conveys no discernable message. Hurley v. Irish–American Gay, Lesbian and Bisexual Group of Boston, Inc. (1995) 515 U.S. 557, 569, 132 L. Ed. 2d 487, 115 S. Ct. 2338.

Nor does the fact that Saderup's art appears in large part on a less conventional avenue of communications, T-shirts, result in reduced First Amendment protection. As Judge Posner stated in the case of a defendant who sold T-shirts advocating the legalization of marijuana, "its T-shirts ...

---

[a] Chief Justice Bird's concurring opinion in *Guglielmi* was signed by Justices Tobriner and Manuel. The principles enunciated in her concurrence were also endorsed by Justice Newman, who nonetheless did not join the opinion because he shared the view of the majority that the common law right of public- ity was not descendible (the case predated the passage of section 990). (*Guglielmi*, at p. 876.) Therefore, Chief Justice Bird's views in *Guglielmi* commanded the support of the majority of the court. Hereinafter, all references to *Guglielmi* in this opinion will be to the Chief Justice's opinion.

are to [the seller] what the New York Times is to the Sulzbergers and the Ochses—the vehicle of her ideas and opinions." (Ayres v. City of Chicago (7th Cir. 1997) 125 F.3d 1010, 1017; see also Cohen v. California (1971) 403 U.S. 15, 29 L. Ed. 2d 284, 91 S. Ct. 1780 [jacket with words "Fuck the Draft" on the back is protected speech].) First Amendment doctrine does not disfavor nontraditional media of expression.

But having recognized the high degree of First Amendment protection for noncommercial speech about celebrities, we need not conclude that all expression that trenches on the right of publicity receives such protection. The right of publicity, like copyright, protects a form of intellectual property that society deems to have some social utility. "Often considerable money, time and energy are needed to develop one's prominence in a particular field. Years of labor may be required before one's skill, reputation, notoriety or virtues are sufficiently developed to permit an economic return through some medium of commercial promotion. [Citations.] For some, the investment may eventually create considerable commercial value in one's identity." (Lugosi, 25 Cal. 3d at pp. 834–835 (dis. opn. of Bird, C. J.).)

The present case exemplifies this kind of creative labor. Moe and Jerome (Curly) Howard and Larry Fein fashioned personae collectively known as The Three Stooges, first in vaudeville and later in movie shorts, over a period extending from the 1920's to the 1940's. (See Fleming, The Three Stooges: Amalgamated Morons to American Icons (1999) pp. 10–46.) The three comic characters they created and whose names they shared— Larry, Moe, and Curly—possess a kind of mythic status in our culture. Their journey from ordinary vaudeville performers to the heights (or depths) of slapstick comic celebrity was long and arduous. (Ibid.) Their brand of physical humor—the nimble, comically stylized violence, the "nyuk-nyuks" and "whoop-whoop-whoops," eye-pokes, slaps and head conks created a distinct comedic trademark. Through their talent and labor, they joined the relatively small group of actors who constructed identifiable, recurrent comic personalities that they brought to the many parts they were scripted to play. Publicity and Privacy (2d ed. 2000) §§ 2.2– 2.7, pp. 2–1 to 2–22 "Groucho Marx just being Groucho Marx, with his moustache, cigar, slouch and leer, cannot be exploited by others. Red Skelton's variety of self-devised roles would appear to be protectible, as would the unique personal creations of Abbott and Costello, Laurel and Hardy and others of that genre. 'We deal here with actors portraying themselves and developing their own characters.'" (Lugosi, 25 Cal. 3d at pp. 825–826 (conc. opn. of Mosk, J.).)

In sum, society may recognize, as the Legislature has done here, that a celebrity's heirs and assigns have a legitimate protectible interest in exploiting the value to be obtained from merchandising the celebrity's image, whether that interest be conceived as a kind of natural property right or as an incentive for encouraging creative work. (See 1 McCarthy, The Rights of (McCarthy).) Although critics have questioned whether the right of publicity truly serves any social purpose, (see, e.g., Madow, 81 Cal.

L.Rev. at pp. 178–238), there is no question that the Legislature has a rational basis for permitting celebrities and their heirs to control the commercial exploitation of the celebrity's likeness.

Although surprisingly few courts have considered in any depth the means of reconciling the right of publicity and the First Amendment, we follow those that have in concluding that depictions of celebrities amounting to little more than the appropriation of the celebrity's economic value are not protected expression under the First Amendment. We begin with Zacchini v. Scripps–Howard Broadcasting Co. (1977) 433 U.S. 562, 576, 53 L. Ed. 2d 965, 97 S. Ct. 2849 (Zacchini), the only United States Supreme Court case to directly address the right of publicity. Zacchini, the performer of a human cannonball act, sued a television station that had videotaped and broadcast his entire performance without his consent. The court held the First Amendment did not protect the television station against a right of publicity claim under Ohio common law. In explaining why the enforcement of the right of publicity in this case would not violate the First Amendment, the court stated: " 'The rationale for [protecting the right of publicity] is the straightforward one of preventing unjust enrichment by the theft of goodwill. No social purpose is served by having the defendant get free some aspect of the plaintiff that would have market value and for which he would normally pay.' " ( Id. at p. 576.) The court also rejected the notion that federal copyright or patent law preempted this type of state law protection of intellectual property: "[Copyright and patent] laws perhaps regard the 'reward to the owner [as] a secondary consideration,' [citation], but they were 'intended definitely to grant valuable, enforceable rights' in order to afford greater encouragement to the production of works of benefit to the public. [Citation.] The Constitution does not prevent Ohio from making a similar choice here in deciding to protect the entertainer's incentive in order to encourage the production of this type of work." ( Id. at p. 577.)

To be sure, *Zacchini* was not an ordinary right of publicity case: the defendant television station had appropriated the plaintiff's entire act, a species of common law copyright violation. Nonetheless, two principles enunciated in *Zacchini* apply to this case: (1) state law may validly safeguard forms of intellectual property not covered under federal copyright and patent law as a means of protecting the fruits of a performing artist's labor; and (2) the state's interest in preventing the outright misappropriation of such intellectual property by others is not automatically trumped by the interest in free expression or dissemination of information; rather, as in the case of defamation, the state law interest and the interest in free expression must be balanced, according to the relative importance of the interests at stake. (See Gertz v. Robert Welch, Inc., 418 U.S. at pp. 347–350.)

*Guglielmi* adopted a similar balancing approach. The purported heir of Rudolph Valentino filed suit against the makers of a fictional film based on the latter's life. *Guglielmi* concluded that the First Amendment protection of entertainment superseded any right of publicity. This was in contrast to the companion Lugosi case, in which Chief Justice Bird concluded in her dissenting opinion that there may be an enforceable right of publicity that would prevent the merchandising of Count Dracula using the likeness of Bela Lugosi, with whom that role was identified. (Lugosi, 25 Cal. 3d at pp. 848–849.) Guglielmi proposed a balancing test to distinguish protected from unprotected appropriation of celebrity likenesses: "an action for infringement of the right of publicity can be maintained only if the proprietary interests at issue clearly outweigh the value of free expression in this context." (Guglielmi, 25 Cal. 3d at p. 871.)

It is admittedly not a simple matter to develop a test that will unerringly distinguish between forms of artistic expression protected by the First Amendment and those that must give way to the right of publicity. Certainly, any such test must incorporate the principle that the right of publicity cannot, consistent with the First Amendment, be a right to control the celebrity's image by censoring disagreeable portrayals. Once the celebrity thrusts himself or herself forward into the limelight, the First Amendment dictates that the right to comment on, parody, lampoon, and make other expressive uses of the celebrity image must be given broad scope. The necessary implication of this observation is that the right of publicity is essentially an economic right. What the right of publicity holder possesses is not a right of censorship, but a right to prevent others from misappropriating the economic value generated by the celebrity's fame through the merchandising of the "name, voice, signature, photograph or likeness" of the celebrity. (§ 990.)

Beyond this precept, how may courts distinguish between protected and unprotected expression? Some commentators have proposed importing the fair use defense from copyright law (17 U.S.C. § 107), which has the advantage of employing an established doctrine developed from a related area of the law. Others disagree, pointing to the murkiness of the fair use doctrine and arguing that the idea/expression dichotomy, rather than fair use, is the principal means of reconciling copyright protection and First Amendment rights. (See Kwall, The Right of Publicity vs. The First Amendment: A Property and Liability Rule Analysis (1994) 70 Ind. L.J. 47, 58, fn. 54.)

We conclude that a wholesale importation of the fair use doctrine into right of publicity law would not be advisable. At least two of the factors employed in the fair use test, "the nature of the copyrighted work" and "the amount and substantiality of the portion used" (17 U.S.C. § 107(2), (3)), seem particularly designed to be applied to the partial copying of works of authorship "fixed in [a] tangible medium of expression" (17 U.S.C. § 102); it is difficult to understand why these factors would be especially useful for determining whether the depiction of a celebrity likeness is protected by the First Amendment.

Nonetheless, the first fair use factor—"the purpose and character of the use" (17 U.S.C. § 107(1))—does seem particularly pertinent to the task of reconciling the rights of free expression and publicity. As the Supreme Court has stated, the central purpose of the inquiry into this fair use factor "is to see, in Justice Story's words, whether the new work merely 'supersedes the objects' of the original creation [citations], or instead adds something new, with a further purpose or different character, altering the first with new expression, meaning, or message; it asks, in other words, whether and to what extent the new work is 'transformative.' [Citation.] Although such transformative use is not absolutely necessary for a finding of fair use, [citation] the goal of copyright, to promote science and the arts, is generally furthered by the creation of transformative works." (Campbell v. Acuff–Rose Music, Inc. (1994) 510 U.S. 569, 579, 127 L. Ed. 2d 500, 114 S. Ct. 1164, fn. omitted.)

This inquiry into whether a work is "transformative" appears to us to be necessarily at the heart of any judicial attempt to square the right of publicity with the First Amendment. As the above quotation suggests, both the First Amendment and copyright law have a common goal of encouragement of free expression and creativity, the former by protecting such expression from government interference, the latter by protecting the creative fruits of intellectual and artistic labor. The right of publicity, at least theoretically, shares this goal with copyright law. (1 McCarthy, § 2.6, pp. 2–14 to 2–19.) When artistic expression takes the form of a literal depiction or imitation of a celebrity for commercial gain, directly trespassing on the right of publicity without adding significant expression beyond that trespass, the state law interest in protecting the fruits of artistic labor outweighs the expressive interests of the imitative artist.

On the other hand, when a work contains significant transformative elements, it is not only especially worthy of First Amendment protection, but it is also less likely to interfere with the economic interest protected by the right of publicity. As has been observed, works of parody or other distortions of the celebrity figure are not, from the celebrity fan's viewpoint, good substitutes for conventional depictions of the celebrity and therefore do not generally threaten markets for celebrity memorabilia that the right of publicity is designed to protect. Accordingly, First Amendment protection of such works outweighs whatever interest the state may have in enforcing the right of publicity. The right-of-publicity holder continues to enforce the right to monopolize the production of conventional, more or less fungible, images of the celebrity.

Cardtoons , L.C. v. Major League Baseball Players Association (10th Cir. 1996) 95 F.3d 959, cited by Saderup, is consistent with this "transformative" test. There, the court held that the First Amendment protected a company that produced trading cards caricaturing and parodying well-known major league baseball players against a claim brought under the Oklahoma right of publicity statute. The court concluded that "the cards provide social commentary on public figures, major league baseball players, who are involved in a significant commercial enterprise, major league baseball," and that "the cards are no less protected because they provide humorous rather than serious commentary." (Cardtoons, at p. 969.) The Cardtoons court weighed these First Amendment rights against what it concluded was the less-than-compelling interests advanced by the right of publicity outside the advertising context—especially in light of the reality that parody would not likely substantially impact the economic interests of celebrities—and found the cards to be a form of protected expression. (Cardtoons, at pp. 973–976.)

We emphasize that the transformative elements or creative contributions that require First Amendment protection are not confined to parody and can take many forms, from factual reporting to fictionalized portrayal, from heavy-handed lampooning to subtle social criticism.

Another way of stating the inquiry is whether the celebrity likeness is one of the "raw materials" from which an original work is synthesized, or whether the depiction or imitation of the celebrity is the very sum and substance of the work in question. We ask, in other words, whether a product containing a celebrity's likeness is so transformed that it has become primarily the defendant's own expression rather than the celebrity's likeness. And when we use the word "expression," we mean expression of something other than the likeness of the celebrity.

We further emphasize that in determining whether the work is transformative, courts are not to be concerned with the quality of the artistic contribution—vulgar forms of expression fully qualify for First Amendment protection. On the other hand, a literal depiction of a celebrity, even if accomplished with great skill, may still be subject to a right of publicity challenge. The inquiry is in a sense more quantitative than qualitative, asking whether the literal and imitative or the creative elements predominate in the work.[b]

Furthermore, in determining whether a work is sufficiently transformative, courts may find useful a subsidiary inquiry, particularly in close cases: does the marketability and economic value of the challenged work derive primarily from the fame of the celebrity depicted? If this question is answered in the negative, then there would generally be no actionable right of publicity. When the value of the work comes principally from some source other than the fame of the celebrity—from the creativity, skill, and reputation of the artist—it may be presumed that sufficient transformative elements are present to warrant First Amendment protection. If the question is answered in the affirmative, however, it does not necessarily follow that the work is without First Amendment protection—it may still be a transformative work.

In sum, when an artist is faced with a right of publicity challenge to his or her work, he or she may raise as affirmative defense that the work is protected by the First Amendment inasmuch as it contains significant transformative elements or that the value of the work does not derive primarily from the celebrity's fame.

[b] Saderup also cites ETW Corp. v. Jireh Publishing, Inc. (N.D. Ohio 2000) 99 F.Supp.2d 829, 835–836, in which the court held that a painting consisting of a montage of likenesses of the well-known professional golfer Eldridge "Tiger" Woods, reproduced in 5000 prints, was a work of art and therefore protected under the First Amendment.

Turning to the present case, we note that the trial court, in ruling against Saderup, stated that "the commercial enterprise conducted by [Saderup] involves the sale of lithographs and T-shirts which are not original single works of art, and which are not protected by the First Amendment; the enterprise conducted by the [Saderup] was a commercial enterprise designed to generate profits solely from the use of the likeness of The Three Stooges which is the right of publicity . . . protected by section 990." Although not entirely clear, the trial court seemed to be holding that reproductions of celebrity images are categorically outside First Amendment protection. The Court of Appeal was more explicit in adopting this rationale: "Simply put, although the First Amendment protects speech that is sold [citation], reproductions of an image, made to be sold for profit do not per se constitute speech." But this position has no basis in logic or authority.

Because the statute evidently aims at preventing the illicit merchandising of celebrity images, and because single original works of fine art are not forms of merchandising, the state has little if any interest in preventing the exhibition and sale of such works, and the First Amendment rights of the artist should therefore prevail. But the inverse—that a reproduction receives no First Amendment protection—is patently false: a reproduction of a celebrity image that, as explained above, contains significant creative elements is entitled to as much First Amendment protection as an original work of art. The trial court and the Court of Appeal therefore erred in this respect.

Rather, the inquiry is into whether Saderup's work is sufficiently transformative. Correctly anticipating this inquiry, he argues that all portraiture involves creative decisions, that therefore no portrait portrays a mere literal likeness, and that accordingly all portraiture, including reproductions, is protected by the First Amendment. We reject any such categorical position. Without denying that all portraiture involves the making of artistic choices, we find it equally undeniable, under the test formulated above, that when an artist's skill and talent is manifestly subordinated to the overall goal of creating a conventional portrait of a celebrity so as to commercially exploit his or her fame, then the artist's right of free expression is outweighed by the right of publicity. As is the case with fair use in the area of copyright law, an artist depicting a celebrity must contribute something more than a " 'merely trivial' variation, [but must create] something recognizable 'his own' " (L. Batlin & Son, Inc. v. Snyder (2d Cir. 1976) 536 F.2d 486, 490), in order to qualify for legal protection.

On the other hand, we do not hold that all reproductions of celebrity portraits are unprotected by the First Amendment. The silkscreens of Andy Warhol, for example, have as their subjects the images of such celebrities as Marilyn Monroe, Elizabeth Taylor, and Elvis Presley. Through distortion and the careful manipulation of context, Warhol was able to convey a message that went beyond the commercial exploitation of celebrity images and became a form of ironic social comment on the dehumanization of celebrity itself. Such expression may well be entitled to First Amendment protection. Although the distinction between protected and unprotected expression will sometimes be subtle, it is no more so than other distinctions triers of fact are called on to make in First Amendment jurisprudence.

Turning to Saderup's work, we can discern no significant transformative or creative contribution. His undeniable skill is manifestly subordinated to the overall goal of creating literal, conventional depictions of The Three Stooges so as to exploit their fame. Indeed, were we to decide that Saderup's depictions were protected by the First Amendment, we cannot perceive how the right of publicity would remain a viable right other than in cases of falsified celebrity endorsements.

Moreover, the marketability and economic value of Saderup's work derives primarily from the fame of the celebrities depicted. While that fact alone does not necessarily mean the work receives no First Amendment protection, we can perceive no transformative elements in Saderup's works that would require such protection.

Saderup argues that it would be incongruous and unjust to protect parodies and other distortions of celebrity figures but not wholesome, reverential portraits of such celebrities. The test we articulate today, however, does not express a value judgment or preference for one type of depiction over another. Rather, it reflects a recognition that the Legislature has granted to the heirs and assigns of celebrities the property right to exploit the celebrities' images, and that certain forms of expressive activity protected by the First Amendment fall outside the boundaries of that right. Stated another way, we are concerned not with whether conventional celebrity images should be produced but with who produces them and, more pertinently, who appropriates the value from their production. Thus, under section 990, if Saderup wishes to continue to depict The Three Stooges as he has done, he may do so only with the consent of the right-of-publicity holder.

## IV. Disposition

The judgment of the Court of Appeal is affirmed.

# Dustin Hoffman v. Capital Cities/ABC, Inc.

United States Court of Appeals for the Ninth Circuit, 2001.
255 F.3d 1180.

■ BOOCHEVER, CIRCUIT JUDGE:

In 1982, actor Dustin Hoffman starred in the movie "Tootsie," playing a male actor who dresses as a woman to get a part on a television soap opera. One memorable still photograph from the movie showed Hoffman in character in a red long-sleeved sequined evening dress and high heels, posing in front of an American flag. The still carried the text, "What do you get when you cross a hopelessly straight, starving actor with a dynamite red sequined dress? You get America's hottest new actress."

In March 1997, Los Angeles Magazine ("LAM") published the "Fabulous Hollywood Issue!" An article from this issue entitled "Grand Illusions" used computer technology to alter famous film stills to make it appear that the actors were wearing Spring 1997 fashions. The sixteen familiar scenes included movies and actors such as "North by Northwest" (Cary Grant), "Saturday Night Fever" (John Travolta), "Rear Window" (Grace Kelly and Jimmy Stewart), "Gone with the Wind" (Vivian Leigh and Hattie McDaniel), "Jailhouse Rock" (Elvis Presley), "The Seven Year Itch" (Marilyn Monroe), "Thelma and Louise" (Susan Sarandon and Geena Davis), and even "The Creature from the Black Lagoon" (with the Creature in Nike shoes). The final shot was the "Tootsie" still. The American flag and Hoffman's head remained as they appeared in the original, but Hoffman's body and his long-sleeved red sequined dress were replaced by the body of a male model in the same pose, wearing a spaghetti-strapped, cream-colored, silk evening dress and high-heeled sandals. LAM omitted the original caption. The text on the page identified the still as from the movie "Tootsie," and read, "Dustin Hoffman isn't a drag in a butter-colored silk gown by Richard Tyler and Ralph Lauren heels."

LAM did not ask Hoffman for permission to publish the altered photograph. Nor did LAM secure permission from Columbia Pictures, the copyright holder. In April 1997, Hoffman filed a complaint in California state court against LAM's parent company, Capital Cities/ABC, Inc. (now ABC, Inc. or "ABC"). The complaint alleged that LAM's publication of the altered photograph misappropriated Hoffman's name and likeness in violation of (1) the California common law right of publicity; (2) the California statutory right of publicity, Civil Code § 3344; (3) the California unfair competition statute, Business and Professions Code § 17200; and (4) the federal Lanham Act, 15 U.S.C. § 1125(a).

ABC removed the case to federal court. Hoffman added LAM as a defendant. After a bench trial, the district court found for Hoffman and against LAM on all of Hoffman's claims, rejecting LAM's defense that its use of the photograph was protected by the First Amendment. The court awarded Hoffman $1,500,000 in compensatory damages, and held that Hoffman was entitled to punitive damages as well. Hoffman v. Capital Cities/ABC, Inc., 33 F. Supp. 2d 867 (C.D. Cal. 1999). After a hearing, the court awarded Hoffman $1,500,000 in punitive damages. It also held that ABC was not liable for any of LAM's actions.

Hoffman moved for an award of $415,755.41 in attorney fees. The district court granted the motion, but reduced the amount to $269,528.50.

In these appeals, LAM appeals the district court's judgment in Hoffman's favor, and the court's award of attorney fees.

ANALYSIS

California recognizes, in its common law and its statutes, "the right of a person whose identity has commercial value—most often a celebrity—to control the commercial use of that identity." Waits v. Frito-Lay, Inc., 978 F.2d 1093, 1098 (9th Cir. 1992) (as amended). Hoffman claims that LAM violated his state right of publicity by appropriating his name and likeness. He also claims that LAM violated his rights under the federal Lanham Act.

LAM replies that its challenged use of the "Tootsie" photo is protected under the First Amendment. We evaluate this defense aware of "the careful balance that courts have gradually constructed between the right of publicity and the First Amendment and federal intellectual property laws." Landham v. Lewis Galoob Toys, Inc., 227 F.3d 619, 626 (6th Cir. 2000).

The district court concluded that the magazine article was commercial speech not entitled to constitutional protection: "the First Amendment does not protect the exploitative commercial use of Mr. Hoffman's name and likeness." Hoffman, 33 F. Supp. 2d at 874. [Also] the court found that LAM acted with actual malice, and "the First Amendment does not protect knowingly false speech." Id. at 875.[a]

[a] In Comedy III Prods., Inc. v. Gary Saderup, Inc., 25 Cal. 4th 387, 21 P.3d 797 (Cal. 2001), the California Supreme Court held that there was no First Amendment defense

Commercial speech

The district court concluded that LAM's alteration of the "Tootsie" photograph was an "exploitative commercial" use not entitled to First Amendment protection. We disagree.

"Commercial speech" has special meaning in the First Amendment context. Although the boundary between commercial and noncommercial speech has yet to be clearly delineated, the "core notion of commercial speech" is that it "does no more than propose a commercial transaction." Bolger v. Youngs Drug Prods. Corp., 463 U.S. 60, 66, 77 L. Ed. 2d 469, 103 S. Ct. 2875 (1983) (quotations omitted). Such speech is entitled to a measure of First Amendment protection. See, e.g., Greater New Orleans Broad. Ass'n, Inc. v. United States, 527 U.S. 173, 183, 144 L. Ed. 2d 161, 119 S. Ct. 1923 (1999) (setting out fourpart test to evaluate constitutionality of governmental regulation of "speech that is commercial in nature"). Commercial messages, however, do not receive the same level of constitutional protection as other types of protected expression. See 44 Liquormart, Inc. v. Rhode Island, 517 U.S. 484, 498, 134 L. Ed. 2d 711, 116 S. Ct. 1495 (1996). False or misleading commercial speech is not protected. See Florida Bar v. Went For It, Inc., 515 U.S. 618, 623–24, 132 L. Ed. 2d 541, 115 S. Ct. 2371 (1995) (commercial speech receives limited amount of protection compared to speech at core of First Amendment and may freely be regulated if it is misleading).

In many right of publicity cases, the challenged use of the celebrity's identity occurs in an advertisement that" does no more that propose a commercial transaction" and is clearly commercial speech. See, e.g., Newcombe v. Adolph Coors Co., 157 F.3d 686, 691 (9th Cir. 1998) (use of pitcher's image in printed beer advertisement); Abdul–Jabbar v. Gen. Motors Corp., 85 F.3d 407, 409 (9th Cir. 1996) (use of basketball star's former name in television car commercial); Waits, 978 F.2d at 1097–98 (use of imitation of singer's voice in radio snack-food commercial); White v. Samsung Elecs. Am., Inc., 971 F.2d 1395, 1396 (9th Cir. 1992) (as amended) (use of game-show hostess's "identity" in print advertisements for electronic products); Midler v. Ford Motor Co., 849 F.2d 460, 461 (9th Cir. 1988) (use in television car commercial of "sound-alike" rendition of song singer had recorded). In all these

to a California right of publicity claim when "artistic expression takes the form of a literal depiction or imitation of a celebrity for commercial gain." 21 P.3d at 808. An artist who added "significant transformative elements" could still invoke First Amendment protection. Id.

Even if we were to consider LAM an "artist" and the altered "Tootsie" photograph "artistic expression" subject to the *Comedy III* decision, there is no question that LAM's publication of the "Tootsie" photograph contained "significant transformative elements." Hoffman's body was eliminated and a new, differently clothed body was substituted in its place. In fact, the entire theory of Hoffman's case rests on his allegation that the photograph is not a "true" or "literal" depiction of him, but a false portrayal. Regardless of the scope of Comedy III, it is clear to us that it does not strip LAM of First Amendment protection.

cases, the defendant used an aspect of the celebrity's identity entirely and directly for the purpose of selling a product. Such uses do not implicate the First Amendment's protection of expressions of editorial opinion. Cf. White, 971 F.2d at 1401(advertisement in which "spoof" is entirely subservient to primary message to "buy" identified product not protected by First Amendment).

Hoffman points out that the body double in the "Tootsie" photograph was identified as wearing Ralph Lauren shoes and that there was a Ralph Lauren advertisement (which does not feature shoes) elsewhere in the magazine. (Insofar as the record shows, Richard Tyler, the designer of the gown, had never advertised in LAM.) Hoffman also points to the "Shopper's Guide" in the back of the magazine, which provided stores and prices for the shoes and gown.

These facts are not enough to make the "Tootsie" photograph pure commercial speech. If the altered photograph had appeared in a Ralph Lauren advertisement, then we would be facing a case much like those cited above. But LAM did not use Hoffman's image in a traditional advertisement printed merely for the purpose of selling a particular product. Insofar as the record shows, LAM did not receive any consideration from the designers for featuring their clothing in the fashion article containing the altered movie stills. Nor did the article simply advance a commercial message. "Grand Illusions" appears as a feature article on the cover of the magazine and in the table of contents. It is a complement to and a part of the issue's focus on Hollywood past and present. Viewed in context, the article as a whole is a combination of fashion photography, humor, and visual and verbal editorial comment on classic films and famous actors. Any commercial aspects are "inextricably entwined" with expressive elements, and so they cannot be separated out "from the fully protected whole." Gaudiya Vaishnava Soc'y v. City & County of San Francisco, 952 F.2d 1059, 1064 (9th Cir. 1991) (as amended). "There are commonsense differences between speech that does no more than propose a commercial transaction and other varieties," Va. State Bd. of Pharmacy v. Va. Citizens Consumer Council, Inc., 425 U.S. 748, 771 n.24, 48 L. Ed. 2d 346, 96 S. Ct. 1817 (1976) (quotations and citation omitted), and common sense tells us this is not a simple advertisement.

The district court also concluded that the article was not protected speech because it was created to "attract attention." 33 F. Supp. 2d at 874. A printed article meant to draw attention to the for-profit magazine in which it appears, however, does not fall outside of the protection of the First Amendment because it may help to sell copies. Cf. Dworkin v. Hustler Magazine, Inc., 867 F.2d 1188, 1197–98 (9th Cir. 1989) (although defendant may have published feature solely or primarily to increase circulation and therefore profits, article is not thereby purely commercial or for purposes of advertising); Leidholdt v. L.F.P. Inc., 860 F.2d 890, 895 (9th Cir. 1988) (same). While there was testimony that the Hollywood issue and the use of celebrities was intended in part to "rev up" the magazine's profile, that does not make the fashion article a purely "commercial" form of expression.

We conclude that LAM's publication of the altered "Tootsie" photograph was not commercial speech.

[In the next part of the opinion, the court concluded that Hoffman did not prove that LAM acted with actual malice in publishing the altered "Tootsie" photograph, and thus reversed the district court's judgment in Hoffman's favor].

REVERSED.

NOTES

**1.** *Preemption: subject matter of copyright.* The legislative history is clear that as long as a particular work is within the subject matter of copyright, this preemption condition is satisfied even if the work is not sufficiently original to qualify for copyright protection or if it has entered the public domain. Should Congress's decision in § 102(b) to expressly exclude ideas from the scope of copyright protection (see Note 2 in Assignment 7) be considered differently from the Copyright Act's mere omission of certain other categories of subject matter? Can an argument be made that states should be prohibited from protecting subject matter specifically excluded by Congress since Congress thus showed its intent that such material remain in the public domain? See also Note 4 on conflict preemption. Does this issue have any relevance to the Principal Problem? Should a cause of action based on breach of an oral contract regarding copyrighted material be preempted?

*N.B.A. v. Motorola* rejected a partial preemption analysis when dealing with state law claims involving both non-copyrightable and copyrightable subject matter. The court determined that the misappropriation claims based on the non-copyrightable matter still could be preempted in situations where the non-copyrightable matter is fixed and the misappropriation claim is based on copying from the copyrighted work. The *Motorola* court bolstered its conclusion by saying that "partial preemption" allows "state law to vest exclusive rights in material that Congress intended to be in the public domain and to make unlawful conduct that Congress intended to allow."[15] Do you agree with this analysis?

**2.** *Preemption: equivalency.* The 1976 Act does not define the term "equivalent," but the legislative history indicates that a state cause of action will not be preempted if it contains elements that are "different in kind" from copyright infringement.[16] In applying this standard, several courts have

[15] 105 F.3d at 849. See also Baltimore Orioles, Inc. v. Major League Baseball Players Association, 805 F.2d 663, cert. denied, 480 U.S. 941 (1987) (holding ball clubs' ownership of the copyright in the telecasts of major league baseball games preempts the Players' right of publicity in their on-field performances).

[16] See H.R. Rep. No. 1476, 94th Cong., 2d Sess. 109, 132, reprinted in 1976 U.S.C.C.A.N. 5659, 5748.

followed the late Professor Nimmer's suggestion that an "equivalent" right "is one which is infringed by the mere act of reproduction, performance, distribution or display."[17] Essentially, this approach requires an analysis of the state law in question to determine what acts will constitute an infringement. If the exercise of one or more of the six rights protected by federal copyright law is all that is necessary to constitute an infringement of the state law[18], preemption will occur.[19] If, however, other elements also are required to infringe the state law, no preemption will result. Some courts have invoked a test for preemption that focuses on whether the extra element of the state law renders the state action qualitatively different from the copyright law.[20] What does the term "qualitatively different" mean? Should a state law claim of unfair competition involving the copying of material protected by the copyright statute be preempted? Is a state based right of publicity action equivalent to an action for copyright infringement?

Interestingly, some courts have relied on the "extra element" test invoked in state law preemption cases in determining whether a plaintiff should be allowed to bring a cause of action under § 43(a) of the Lanham Act if the subject matter of the lawsuit involves copyrightable property.[21] How defensible is this approach? Keep in mind that the legislative history to § 301(a) expressly states that the preemptive effect of that section is "limited to state laws."[22] Moreover, § 301(d) provides that "nothing contained in Title 17 annuls or limits any rights or remedies under any other Federal statute."[23]

A second approach to the "equivalency" dilemma focuses on the interests protected by the state law at issue. Specifically, a state law will not be preempted if it serves different interests from copyright law.[24] Can you think of any instances in which an "objectives" test would save a state law from preemption that would otherwise be vulnerable under Professor Nimmer's pure "elements" test? Which test for preemption is more workable?

**3.**   *Preemption and misappropriation.* In *N.B.A. v. Motorola,* the court provided clear guidance on when a misappropriation involving "hot-news" would escape preemption. Did you agree with the court's application of its exception to the facts at issue?

---

[17] 1 M. Nimmer, Nimmer on Copyright § 1.01[B][1] at 1–12 (2003).

[18] See § 106.

[19] See id.

[20] See, e.g., Mayer v. Josiah Wedgwood & Sons, Ltd., 601 F.Supp. 1523, 1535 (S.D.N.Y. 1985).

[21] See, e.g., Natkin v. Winfrey, 56 U.S.P.Q.2d 1594 (N.D. Ill. 2000)(holding that plaintiff's § 43(a) and state law claims relat-

ing to defendants' publication of plaintiffs' photographs are preempted under § 301(a)).

[22] H.R. Rep. No. 94–1476, at 131, 1976 U.S.C.C.A.N. at 5746.

[23] § 301(d).

[24] See Baltimore Orioles, Inc. v. Major League Baseball Players Association, 805 F.2d 663, 677–79 (7th Cir. 1986)(rejecting lack of equivalency between the right of publicity and copyright on this ground).

As originally drafted, § 301(b)(3) provided specific examples of "nonequivalent" rights that the states could continue to protect under common law or statute.[25] The stipulated rights were "breaches of contract, breaches of trust, invasion of privacy, defamation, and deceptive trade practices such as passing off and false representation,"[26] but the legislative history clearly states that the list was intended to be illustrative rather than exhaustive.[27] The version of the bill that was enacted did not contain any such examples, although this absence was not a result of a rejection of the foregoing examples but rather of a controversy generated by the subsequent inclusion of "misappropriation" in the House version of the bill. The court in Mayer v. Josiah Wedgwood & Sons, Ltd. summarized a bit of the legislative history in the House Report:

> "Noting that 'misappropriation' is not *necessarily* synonymous with copyright infringement," . . . the House Report used as an example of an unpreempted misappropriation action—International News Serv. v. Associated Press, 248 U.S. 215, 39 S.Ct. 68, 63 L.Ed. 211 (1918)("INS"). In INS, defendant was found to have taken the facts reported in plaintiff's transmissions of "hot news" and used them in its own competing news service. The other example advanced was of sanctions imposed on one who improperly invades another's computerized data base and gains access to the data. Both these examples involve subject matter other than copyright, specifically the facts and data as opposed to their expression. Thus, the House Report states that "a cause of action labelled as 'misappropriation' is not preempted if it is in fact based neither on a right within the general scope of copyright . . . not on a right equivalent thereto." (citation omitted). It is thus not surprising that the House Report considered misappropriation to survive preemption. The tort it had in mind was not equivalent to copyright infringement.[28]

Apparently, however, the Department of Justice vigorously objected to the inclusion of "misappropriation" in the enumerated examples of nonpreempted rights, and after a series of ambiguous exchanges the bill was passed in an amended version that deleted all of the proposed examples.[29] Can you think of an instance in which a cause of action based on misappropriation of a work of authorship fixed in a tangible medium of expression within the subject matter of copyright would escape preemption?

[25] See H.R. Rep. No. 1476, at 109, 1976 U.S.C.C.A.N. at 5747–48.

[26] H.R. Rep. No. 4347, 89th Cong., 2d Sess. (1966).

[27] H.R. Rep. No. 1476, at 131–32, 1976 U.S.C.C.A.N. at 5747–48.

[28] 601 F.Supp. 1523, 1534 (S.D.N.Y. 1985)(granting defendant's motion for summary judgment in misappropriation action by plaintiff artist on the ground that plaintiff's action was preempted even though the subject matter in question had entered the public domain).

[29] For a history of this aspect of the statute, see 1 M. Nimmer, § 1.01[B], at 1–14.3 to–16. See also Howard B. Abrams, Copyright, Misappropriation, and Preemption: Constitutional and Statutory Limits of State Law Protection, 1983 Sup. Ct. Rev. 509, 537–550 for a good discussion of the legislative history of § 301.

What would be the result in the Principal Problem if the choreographic work was never fixed?

As discussed in Note 4 of Assignment 7, increased protection for databases is a current debate in the United States. *Sui generis* legislation for protecting data bases has been proposed, but the constitutionality of such protection may be in question. Alternatively, federal protection has been suggested under a misappropriation theory.[30] Without the enactment of such federal protection, however, database publishers have only limited means of protecting their investment and work product. State misappropriation laws offer a possible means of protection but the viability of such protection centers on preemption. Will the "hot news" exception in *Motorola* prove too limiting in this regard?

**4.** *Conflict preemption.* Those portions of a state law that conflict with the protections granted by the 1976 Act also will be preempted. This type of preemption, called "conflict preemption," derives from a basis independent of § 301. Here, the appropriate inquiry is whether compliance with both the federal and state law is physically impossible or if the state law poses an obstacle to fulfilling the goals of Congress. For example, in Association of American Medical Colleges v. Carey,[31] the court relied on conflict preemption to conclude that a state law that required disclosure of medical school admission test questions and answers was preempted because it denied the plaintiff who owned the copyright to the tests benefits safeguarded by the copyright statute. Similarly, in Vault Corp. v. Quaid Software Limited,[32] the court held preempted the state License Enforcement Act which "permit[ed] a software producer to prohibit the adaptation of its licensed computer program by decompilation or disassembly" because this statute "conflict[ed] with the rights of computer program owners under § 117 and clearly 'touches upon an area' of federal copyright law."[33] In recent years, however, courts have become more sympathetic to proprietary interests. Does state protection for the right of publicity conflict with federal copyright law?

**5.** *Right of publicity: manner of protection, descendibility and duration.* About half of the states have recognized the right of publicity, and in at least 15 of these states, legislation exists that governs this area either partially or completely.[34] Many of these statutes, like the California statute

[30] See Jonathan Band & Makoto Kono, *The Database Protection Debate in the 106th Congress*, 62 Ohio St. L.J. 869 (2001).

[31] 728 F.Supp. 873, 879 (N.D.N.Y.1990).

[32] 847 F.2d 255 (5th Cir.1988).

[33] Id. at 270.

[34] See, e.g., Cal. Civ. Code §§ 990 & 3344 (West 2000); Fla. Stat. Ann. § 540.08 (West 1997 & Supp.2001); Ind. Code §§ 32–13–1 to 20 (West 2001); 756 Ill. Comp. Stat. Ann. 1075/1–60 (West Supp. 2001); Ky. Rev. Stat. Ann. § 391.170 (Banks–Baldwin 1988); Mass. Ann. Laws ch. 214, § 3A (West 1989); Neb. Rev. Stat. §§ 20–202 to 211(1997); Nev. Rev. Stat. Ann. §§ 597.770–.810 (Michie 1999); Ohio Rev. Code Ann. §§ 2741.01–.09 (Banks–Baldwin Supp. 2001); Okla. Stat. Ann. tit. 12, §§ 1448–1449, tit. 21, §§ 839.1–.2 (West 1993 & Supp. 2001); R.I. Gen. Laws § 9–1–28 (1997); Tenn. Code Ann. §§ 47–25–1101 to–1108 (1995); Tex. Prop. Code Ann. §§ 26.001–.015 (West 2001); Utah Code Ann. §§ 45–3–1 to–6 (1998 & Supp. 2001); Va. Code Ann. § 8.01–40 (Michie 2000); Wis. Stat. Ann. § 895.50 (West 1997 & Supp.

applied in *Saderup*, also recognize that the right against commercial exploitation of an individual's name or likeness is descendible, meaning that it can be exercised by the heirs and assignees of the person to whom the right originally attached.[35] In other jurisdictions the right of publicity is descendible as a matter of common law.[36] Some jurisdictions make the unauthorized appropriation of protected attributes actionable under its statutory right of privacy.[37] In New York, for example, the courts have held that the state's privacy law which does protect against the unauthorized use of a person's name or likeness for purposes of trade precludes a cause of action under state common law right of publicity.[38] Moreover, relatives of a deceased are precluded from suing under that statute since the right of privacy is held to be personal in nature.[39] The Virginia privacy statute specifically provides relief to the relatives of a decedent whose name or likeness is appropriated for commercial purposes,[40] while the Wisconsin privacy statute specifically limits the ability to recover for the unauthorized

2001). In addition, the New York privacy statute addresses some aspects of the right of publicity. N.Y. Civ. Rights Law §§ 50–51 (McKinney 1992 & Supp. 2001).

[35] In Illinois, Nevada, and Texas, statutory protection is granted for fifty years following a person's death. Kentucky also provides for fifty years of protection following death, but only for public figures. California provides protection for seventy years after a person's death. Ohio allows protection for sixty years following an individual's death. Florida allows protection for forty years after a person's death. The Virginia statute allows for twenty years of protection following death. The Tennessee statute provides for an initial ten year period following the individual's death. The right is then terminated by proof of non-use for a period of two years. Oklahoma and Indiana apparently grant protection for 100 years following a person's death.

[36] See also Prima v. Darden Restaurants, Inc., 78 F.Supp.2d 337, 345 (D. N.J. 2000)("New Jersey law recognizes a right of publicity that right is characterized as a property right and, as such can descend to the person's estate upon his death."); Nature's Way Products, Inc. v. Nature–Pharma, Inc., 736 F.Supp. 245, 252 (D.Utah 1990)(observing that the Utah Supreme Court would hold that "the common law right of publicity survives the death of the subject person in cases where he or she transferred or otherwise exploited such rights while alive"). Some courts hold the right of

publicity to be descendible only if the deceased commercially exploited the right while alive. See, e.g., Factors Etc., Inc. v. Creative Card Company, 444 F.Supp. 279 (S.D.N.Y. 1977). For a general discussion of the descendibility issue and the various positions taken by courts, see Kwall, Is Independence Day Dawning for the Right of Publicity?, 17 U.C. Davis L. Rev. 191, 207–228 (1983).

[37] Nebraska, Virginia, New York and Wisconsin take this approach.

[38] See, e.g., Ryan v. Volpone Stamp Co., 107 F.Supp.2d 369, 391 (S.D.N.Y. 2000)(noting that right of publicity is subsumed in the state statutory right of privacy); Stephano v. News Group Publications, Inc., 64 N.Y.2d 174, 485 N.Y.S.2d 220, 474 N.E.2d 580 (Ct.App.1984)(interpreting N.Y. Civ. Rights Law §§ 50 & 51).

[39] See Pirone v. MacMillan, Inc., 894 F.2d 579 (2d Cir.1990)(daughters of Babe Ruth could not bring action under state privacy law). There has been some discussion of codifying the right of publicity in New York. For a discussion of this movement, see Burnett, The Property Right of Publicity and The First Amendment: Popular Culture and the Commercial Persona, 3 Hofstra Prop. L.J. 171, 186 (1990).

[40] Va. Code Ann. § 8.01–40 (Michie 2000). The Nebraska privacy statute also allows an action for the unauthorized exploitation of a person's name or likeness which is part of its privacy statute to survive that person's death. See Neb. Rev. Stat. §§ 20–202, 20–205, 20–208 (2000).

commercial use of protected attributes to "living" people.[41] Thus, the manner in which the right of publicity is protected and the descendibility and durational issues are subject to a complete lack of uniformity, which can be problematic for lawyers attempting to advise clients interested in the extent of protection afforded on a national basis. This situation is most difficult when the clients are relatives of a deceased individual whose publicity rights have been appropriated.

**6.** *Right of publicity: rationales, attributes, and scope of protection.* What are the rationales that support protection for the right of publicity? Does everyone have a right of publicity or only celebrities? *Saderup* embraces the right of publicity as an economic right. Is this view too narrow? What attributes should be protected by the right of publicity? In Midler v. Ford Motor Co.,[42] discussed in *Saderup*, the court concluded that the distinctive and widely recognized voice of a professional singer is an attribute appropriately protected under the right of publicity.

What standard can be used to determine which attributes are properly protected under the right of publicity? In Carson v. Here's Johnny Portable Toilets, Inc.,[43] the Sixth Circuit held that a portable toilet manufacturer violated Johnny Carson's right of publicity when it used the phrase "Here's Johnny" in conjunction with the slogan, "The World's Foremost Commodian."[44] In so holding, the court observed that "a celebrity's legal right of publicity is invaded whenever his identity is intentionally appropriated for commercial purposes."[45] Other courts have approved equally expansive applications of the right of publicity by holding that it protects aspects of an individual's identity such as a nickname,[46] professional statistical information,[47] and a distinctive racing car.[48] In an opinion which proved to be controversial, the Ninth Circuit held that Vanna White had a common law right of publicity action against a company that used in an advertisement, without her consent, a robot attired to resemble White and posed next to a game board recognizable as the Wheel of Fortune game show set.[49] Can this case be distinguished from *Midler* and from *Carson?* What is the danger of too expansive an interpretation of the right of publicity?

[41] Wis. Stat. Ann. § 895.50 (2)(b)(West 1997 & Supp. 2000).

[42] 849 F.2d 460 (9th Cir. 1988).

[43] 698 F.2d 831 (6th Cir.1983).

[44] Id. at 837.

[45] Id.

[46] Hirsch v. S.C. Johnson & Son, 90 Wis.2d 379, 280 N.W.2d 129 (1979)(prominent athlete had right of publicity in his nickname "Crazylegs" and could bring an action against manufacturer for commercial misappropriation of his nickname on a shaving gel).

[47] Uhlaender v. Henricksen, 316 F.Supp. 1277 (D.Minn.1970)(baseball table game manufacturer violated baseball players' rights of publicity by the unauthorized appropriation of their names and playing statistics for commercial use).

[48] Motschenbacher v. R.J. Reynolds Tobacco Co., 498 F.2d 821 (9th Cir.1974)(in case involving television commercial featuring the unique and distinctive decorations of plaintiff's racing car, court held that California law protected an individual's proprietary interest in his identity).

[49] White v. Samsung Electronics America, Inc., 971 F.2d 1395 (9th Cir.1992), cert. denied, 508 U.S. 951 (1993).

**7.** *Right of Publicity and protection for characters.* Wendt v. Host International, Inc.[50] raised many interesting right of publicity issues before the Ninth Circuit. In that case, actors George Wendt and John Ratzenberger sued Host for violating their rights of publicity by creating animatronic robotic figures based upon their likenesses and placing these robots in airport bars that were modeled upon the set from the television program *Cheers*. The district court dismissed the action but the Ninth Circuit held that the likeness determination is an issue for resolution by the jury. In so holding, the court was persuaded by the plaintiffs' argument that although they do not have any rights to the characters themselves, the physical likeness of the robots to the actors is what has commercial value to Host. The court also rejected the defendants' argument that the plaintiffs cannot claim a right of publicity violation by relying on indicia such as the set of the *Cheers* Bar that are the property of Paramount, the producer of *Cheers* and owner of the copyright to the television program.

As *Saderup* and *Wendt* illustrate, several difficulties arise when right of publicity claims implicate the appropriation of characters portrayed by actors. Should the rights at issue be considered the property of the persona (Wendt and Ratzenberger) or the entity producing the work in which the persona appears (Paramount)? Does it depend upon how many other roles the persona in question has played? If protection is afforded to the persona in these instances, is there a risk that the law is overly protecting the persona's interest to the detriment of those who make considerable creative contributions to the work in which the persona appears? Should the persona's contribution be treated analogously to a work made for hire under copyright law? Should these claims be preempted under the 1976 Copyright Act? The question of preemption raises the additional issue of what is being protected in these instances—the persona or the underlying work in which it appears.

**8.** *Right of publicity and the First Amendment.* In Zacchini v. Scripps–Howard Broadcasting Co.,[51] the Supreme Court explicitly considered the interplay between the right of publicity and the First Amendment. *Zacchini* involved a television station's broadcast of the plaintiff's entire human cannonball act, without consent, on its nighttime newscast. The Court in *Zacchini* observed that had the television station "merely reported that the petitioner was performing at the fair and described or commented on his act, with or without showing his picture on television, we would have a very different case."[52] But the defendant's filming and display of the plaintiff's entire circus act went way beyond the reporting of a newsworthy event. As such, the defendant's use was not in keeping with a purely informational purpose, and this situation resulted in a great degree of unjust enrichment. Of course, the challenge remains of determining where "the line in particular situations is to be drawn between media reports that

---

[50] 125 F.3d 806 (9th Cir. 1997), cert. denied, 531 U.S. 811 (2000).

[51] 433 U.S. 562 (1977).

[52] Id. at 569.

are protected and those that are not."[53] For example, would the result in *Zacchini* have been the same had the defendant appropriated a smaller portion of the plaintiff's act?

The conflict between the right of publicity and the First Amendment likely will provide a fertile source for litigation for the foreseeable future. Although courts can create various tests for resolving these disputes, very often the cases turn on specific factual distinctions. In ETW Corp. v. Jireh Publishing, Inc.,[54] the Sixth Circuit was faced with a right of publicity claim by the licensing agent of golfer Tiger Woods based on a painting commemorating Woods's victory at the Masters Tournament in 1997. The painting contained three views of Woods in different poses, and also the likenesses of famous golfers in the background. The defendant sold limited edition prints of the painting. The Sixth Circuit relied on *Hoffman* in rejecting the plaintiff's claim, focusing on the painting's substantial "informational and creative content."[55] Although the court endorsed the transformative effects test adopted by the Supreme Court of California in *Saderup*, it found the facts of that case clearly distinguishable: "Unlike the unadorned, nearly photographic reproduction of the faces of The Three Stooges in *Comedy III*, Rush's work does not capitalize solely on literal depiction of Woods. Rather, [the artist's] work consists of a collage of images in addition to Wood's image which are combined to describe, in artistic form, a historic event in sports history and to convey a message about the significance of Woods's achievement in that event."[56]

*Saderup* suggests that the defendant's decision to charge is irrelevant to the determination of the appropriate line between actionable publicity violations and protected First Amendment uses. One indication of transformative value, a key point in *Saderup*, is whether the marketability of the challenged work derives from the fame of the celebrity depicted. Note that this issue is raised in the Principal Problem. Can you think of any other factors that ought to be relevant in drawing the line between right of publicity violations and uses that are protected by the First Amendment?

In the Principal Problem, what if the defendant had used statistics about Ilana Kaye in a board game about 20th century dance? What if the same statistics were used in a book?

State statutes that circumscribe the right of publicity when it conflicts with First Amendment interests exist in several states such as California, Florida, Illinois, Indiana, Nebraska, Nevada, Ohio, Oklahoma, Tennessee, Texas, and Wisconsin.[57] Although the statutes in California, Nevada and

[53] Id. at 574–75.

[54] 332 F.3d 915 (6th Cir. 2003).

[55] Id. at 937.

[56] Id. at 938.

[57] See, e.g., Cal. Civ. Code § 3344(d)-(f)(West Supp. 2000); Fla. Stat. Ann. § 540.08(3)(a)(West 1997); 765 Ill. Comp. Stat. Ann. 1075/35(b)(West Supp. 2001); Ind. Code § 32–13 (West 2001); Neb. Rev. Stat. §§ 20–202(1)(1997); Nev. Rev. Stat. Ann. § 597.790(2)(a)–(e) (Michie 1997); Ohio Rev. Code Ann. § 2741.09 (Banks–Baldwin Supp. 2001); Okla. Stat. Ann. tit. 12 § 1449 (D)-(E)(West 1993 & Supp. 2001); Tenn. Code Ann. § 47–25–1107 (1995); Tex. Prop. Code Ann. § 26.012 (West 2001; and Wis. Stat. § 895.50(3)(West 1997 & Supp. 2000).

Tennessee provide that it should be a question of fact whether a defendant's use of a plaintiff's protected attribute was sufficiently directly connected with commercial sponsorship so as to constitute a prohibited use, in general the statutory formulations tend to be insufficiently flexible to solve the problem. How should the potential for conflict between the right of publicity and the First Amendment be addressed?

**9.** *The Right of Publicity and the Digital Dilemma.* As *Hoffman* illustrates, digital technology is creating endless possibilities for right of publicity litigation. In 1999, the California legislature enacted the Astaire Celebrity Image Protection Act[58] which expanded the scope of publicity rights for deceased celebrities. Actor Richard Masur, former President of the Screen Actors Guild, testified before the California Senate that new digital technology adds greater urgency to the need for stronger publicity rights. Representative of this technology is a process called "morphing," computer manipulation of old images in which deceased individuals are transformed into live characters in films and videos (the movie *Forest Gump* invoked this technology). Opponents of this statute worry that its enactment will stifle creativity and cause much uncertainty regarding the scope of appropriate protection for celebrity.[59]

The unauthorized use of celebrity names and likenesses on the Internet also is becoming an increasingly unmanageable problem. Consider the plight of Pamela Anderson Lee, whose name allegedly appears on more than 145,000 web pages, most of which are marketing products or services with no legitimate relationship to the actress. As noted in Assignment 3, Internet technology makes it possible to embed hidden words-called "metatags" to make the site easy for search engines to find. Many web page creators elect to list "Pamela Anderson Lee" among the metatags regarding their site's actual topic, given the reality that her name will be a tremendous drawing card. Of course, there is a parallel between this practice and that of using celebrity names and likenesses without authorization on the cover of magazines or on T-shirts. The interesting twist regarding such usage in cyberspace, however, is that it can be accomplished with tremendous ease and on a large-scale.[60]

**10.** *Preemption and private alternatives to copyright protection.* The high cost of developing materials like databases and computer programs, which are either uncopyrightable or thinly copyrighted, has led to considerable interest in developing private alternatives to the protection afforded by statutory intellectual property laws. Assignment 11 discussed the relationship between the increased protections afforded to copyright owners under the DMCA and their ability to extract promises from users limiting rights that would otherwise be allowable under the law. Currently, copyright owners are invoking private contractual agreements to extract, and enforce,

[58] Ca. Civil Code Sec. 3344.1.

[59] Vincent J. Schodolski, *Heirs Seek Right to Screen Use of Celebrity Images*, Chi. Trib., Apr. 26, 1999 at 11.

[60] Thomas E. Weber, *Net of Fame: Who Rules the Web? Pamela Anderson Lee, The B–Movie Actress*, Wall St. J., April 13, 1999, at A1.

such promises. This situation raises the question of whether these private agreements are preempted by the copyright law.

Many of the cases involve the legality of the shrinkwrap (or end-use) license. This is an agreement that is encountered during the first use of a product. Typically, it is found on the wrapper of the product; with software, it will often appear on the first screen seen when the program is loaded onto a computer. Accessing the product—tearing the wrapper or clicking through the initial screen—is deemed to be consent to the terms of the agreement. When these agreements are enforceable, licensors can use them to acquire many of the advantages of copyright. They can, for example, secure payment for continued use of a work. They can also impose prohibitions on use that mirror activities that would be regarded as copyright infringement were the product copyrighted, such as limits on copying, distribution, or preparation of derivative works. Shrinkwrap license can also be used to restrict licensees in ways that are not contemplated by the Copyright Act. For instance, a license could prohibit uses that would be considered fair under § 107 (including reverse engineering), or compulsory under § 110. Further, since the product is considered sold rather than licensed, the licensor can also bar resales that would be permitted under § 109(a). See Assignment 11.

For a long time, shrinkwrap licenses were thought unenforceable on two grounds: first, as adhesive under traditional contracts law, or second, as preempted by federal copyright law. However, important decisions in both the Seventh Circuit[61] and the Federal Circuit[62] have upheld these licenses on the ground that they are "private contractual agreements supported by mutual assent and consideration."[63] As to preemption, the Seventh Circuit has ruled that the contract affected only the parties to the agreement and not the world at large. As such, its "rights" were not equivalent to copyright, and were therefore not preempted under § 301(a).[64] Should the enforcement of such shrinkwrap licenses or other private contracts regulating the use of copyrighted works be preempted?

In the late 1990's, there was significant activity on the part of the American Law Institute (ALI) and the National Conference of Commissioners on Uniform State Laws (NCCUSL) to adopt a new Article to be added to the Uniform Commercial Code. Denominated "2B," this Article was to cover the licensing of intangible products. The project began in an attempt

[61] ProCD, Inc. v. Zeidenberg, 86 F.3d 1447 (7th Cir. 1996) (shrinkwrap license limiting application program to non-commercial purposes).

[62] Bowers v. Baystate Technologies, Inc., 320 F.3d 1316 (Fed. Cir. 2003)(prohibition of reverse engineering in shrinkwrap license agreement).

[63] Bowers v. Baystate Technologies, Inc., 320 F.3d 1316 (Fed. Cir. 2003). See also Lexmark International, Inc. v. Static Control Components, 253 F.Supp.2d 943, 973 (E.D.

Ky. 2003)(in granting preliminary injunctive relief based on defendant's violating an agreement requiring consumers to use plaintiff's print toner cartridge only once in exchange for a discount, the court observed that it had "little sympathy for consumers that accept the up-front discount when purchasing [the] cartridges and are subsequently required to comply" with the agreement).

[64] ProCD, Inc. v. Zeidenberg, 86 F.3d 1447, 1454 (7th Cir. 1996).

to modify the UCC's requirements of writings, signatures, and the like to the on-line environment, where transactions are consummated electronically, at the click of a mouse. The initial work was later expanded to cover transactions in software, whether involving the exchange of hard copy or through electronic transmission. The theory was that Art. 2's heavy focus on such physical issues as delivery, inspection, and conformity make it inapposite to software transactions. Next, the drafters decided that this theory applied to all intangibles. Accordingly, they decided to broaden Art. 2B to all transactions in "information."

Article 2B adopted the core principles of the Uniform Commercial Code. As is the case with Art. 2 treating the sale of goods, Art. 2B was biased in favor of contract-formation and its guiding principle was party autonomy. Art. 2B was not intended to create intellectual property rights, but rather to facilitate licensing. Nonetheless, it came under heavy criticism as inconsistent with national innovation policy. Opponents of the Article worried that the Article would lead to an increase in the number of transactions that prevent usages that the public would otherwise enjoy at no (or reduced) cost. These concerns led to several changes. After NCCUSL decided against various amendments suggested by members of the ALI (largely related to public interest safeguards), the ALI pulled out of the project. But since the UCC has always been a joint effort of both of these organizations, Art. 2B could no longer be situated within the Uniform Commercial Code. NCCUSL therefore propounded it as a stand alone law, renamed "UCITA"—the Uniform Computer Information Transactions Act. UCITA was adopted in only two states, Maryland and Virginia.[65] In 2003, the NCCUSL discharged the UCITA committee, but the organization's President issued a statement indicating that UCITA "will remain in place as a resource for the American legal and political community, and for reference by the courts."[66]

---

[65] Va. Code Ann. §§ 59.1–501.1 to 509.2 (Michie 2001); Md. Code Ann. Com. Law. §§ 22–101 to 22–816 (Supp. 2002).

[66] Statement by NCCUSL President K. King Burnett. See www.nccusl.org/nccusl.Desktopmodules/ NewsDisplayasp–ITEMID=56. The discharge of the UCITA committee occurred at the 112th Annual Meeting in Washington of NCCUSL. Alorie Gilbert, CNET News.com, Aug. 7, 2003.

# ASSIGNMENT 14

# PATENT PROTECTION: INTRODUCTION

Article I, Section 8, Clause 8 of the United States Constitution, although usually referred to as the "Copyright Clause," nonetheless expressly creates the constitutional basis for patent law. The Patent Act of 1952, 35 U.S.C. §§ 1–376, has been in effect since 1953. It protects three types of discoveries: utility inventions, designs, and asexually reproduced plants.[1] Of the three, utility patents have the most economic significance and they are the main focus of this casebook.

In many ways, a patent is the most desirable form of federal intellectual property protection; it establishes a right to prevent others from making the patented product or process or using it, selling it, offering it for sale within the United States, or importing it into the United States.[2] Patentees can, in other words, bar unauthorized utilization of their inventions without the need to prove copying (as required by copyright law) or consumer confusion (as required by trademark law). At the same time, however, the term of patent protection is the shortest of the three federal regimes. For most patents filed on January 1, 1995 or later, the term of protection is 20 years from the date the patent application is filed. For patents filed prior to January 1, 1995 but which were in force on that date, the term is 17 years from the date of issuance or 20 years from the date of application, whichever is longer.[3] Moreover, patents are more difficult to secure than

---

[1] §§ 101, 102, 161, 171 (all citations in the Patent Unit are to 35 U.S.C. unless otherwise noted). Sexually reproduced plants also receive patent-like protection, albeit under the agricultural statutes, Plant Variety Protection Act, 7 U.S.C § 2402.

[2] § 271(a). Patent law also creates the right to prevent others from inducing domestic infringements, § 271(b); the right to prevent domestic contributory infringements, § 271(c); the right to prevent others from selling components for assembly of the patented invention abroad, § 271(f); and the right to prevent others from importing into the United States articles manufactured with a patented process, § 271(g).

[3] § 154. In addition, it should be noted that in 1999, Congress added a new provision § 154(b)(1)(A)(i)–(iv), which guarantees that

even patents filed after January 1, 1995 will enjoy at least 17 years of *effective* protection. Under this amendment, after an application is pending three years, the patentee will receive one day of term extension for each day the application remains in the PTO as a result of the PTO's own inaction. An applicant will not receive an extension for time in which the applicant failed to make reasonable efforts to conclude prosecution.

Special limitations on remedies apply during the extended term of such patents, § 154(c). The term of design patents is 14 years from the date the patent issues, § 173. There are transition provisions that deal with patents and patent applications that were pending when the law changed from 17 years from filing to 20 years from issuance.

either copyrights or trademarks. A higher level of ingenuity is required to merit protection and a more rigorous examination is conducted before issuance. As we will see, utility inventions are examined to determine that they are useful, original, and new. They must, in addition, be nonobvious—significant advances over earlier technologies.[4] Designs must be not only new, original, and ornamental, they too must be nonobvious.[5] To receive plant patent protection, a plant must be a distinct new variety.[6]

Before embarking on an exploration of this fairly complex statutory regime, explicit consideration should be devoted to policy. This is especially true because the current statute adopts an approach to protecting intellectual property that is different from that taken by most industrialized countries. With the emergence of a global marketplace, the United States will, in most observers' views, be under considerable pressure to enact conforming legislation. Thus, the student is well advised to concentrate principally on underlying policy considerations.

To those who have studied copyright law, these policies will not be surprising. The Patent Act emanates from the assumption that a period of exclusivity is needed to induce the optimum level of innovation. This assumption is based mainly on economic considerations. Inventive activities are costly. Often, expensive experimentation is required before a new idea works. Finding a commercial method for exploiting the idea also requires money, as does developing distribution channels. Sometimes, consumers need considerable education to understand both why they need and how to use the new development. Innovators must factor these costs into the price at which they sell or license. But since copyists do not incur these expenses, they could—absent patent protection—undercut the inventor in the marketplace and prevent her from recouping her costs or earning a profit. Other inventors will not be so keen to invest their efforts in developing new ideas if they know they will suffer the same fate.

At the same time, however, exclusivity is costly to society. A new invention is, of course, the output of the inventor's mind, but in some sense, it is also input. New ideas are the building blocks on which future developments depend. If they are exclusively owned, it will be difficult for others to push the frontiers of knowledge even further. Equally important, exclusivity permits the patentee to set prices that are in excess of marginal cost. Some people who would purchase the invention were it competitively priced will forgo use rather than pay this higher price. In such cases, there is a "deadweight loss"—everyone loses: the patentee does not make a sale; the non-purchaser does not enjoy the benefit of the new technology. Thus, much of patent law is, like copyright, an attempt to balance the private benefits of exclusivity against these social costs.

Given that copyright and patent law have the same basic goals, why are two regimes necessary? One answer is that while patents are occasionally granted on subject matter similar in character to the sorts of things

---

[4] §§ 101–103.

[5] §§ 171, 103.

[6] § 161.

protected by copyright (computer programs are an example), they mostly protect material that is quite different—so different that innovators require a distinct protective regime.

For example, an author usually cannot, as a practical matter, simultaneously distribute her work and keep it secret. But some inventions are "noninforming:" they can be sold *and* hidden. A new method for brewing coffee, for instance, cannot be discovered by one who observes only the brew, consequently the brewer can sell a product (brewed coffee) without endangering her secret (the brewing technique). Indeed, even some products that are informing in some respects may not reveal all of the technicalities involved in their discovery, use, or construction. Secrecy is thus a genuine choice for many inventors. Indeed, it is even supported by law. Assignment 24 examines state trade secrecy laws and demonstrates that, on the whole, these laws (like rights of publicity and causes of action against misappropriation) are not considered preempted by federal law. Thus, patent law has, in addition to the objectives set out above, the goal of inducing inventors to reveal their discoveries—that is, to choose patenting over trade secrecy.[7]

Conversely, inventors sometimes face a problem authors do not. Even the impecunious author can manage to find scraps of paper on which to scribble her insights. But such is not the case for all inventors. Some inventions are complex products that are extremely expensive to build; others are processes that cannot be effectuated without costly equipment. In the absence of adequate funding, innovations of this type remain inchoate. But fixation—the existence of a "hard copy" of the innovation—is extremely important when rights are negotiated. Even without formal federal protection, an author can negotiate the sale of her work to a publisher, for the fixed copy acts as a record of what was created. Its transfer is a basis for implying a contract that, if the work is found valuable enough to publish, the author will be paid. In contrast, it is notoriously difficult to negotiate the sale of inchoate ideas. No investor or manufacturer will agree to buy the idea without knowing what it is—after all, it may be valueless or already commercialized. But once the inventor explains the idea, there is nothing to stop the listener from simply using it without compensating the inventor.

Patent law solves this paradox, known as "Arrow's disclosure paradox" (after Kenneth Arrow, a noted economist), by creating a public registry. The public documents filed in this registry—"patents"—function like the fixed copy of a work of authorship, for they describe to the world the metes and bounds of the registered invention. Inventors can then engage in transactions without worrying that they will be unable to demonstrate that they have transferred valuable information. The registry also ameliorates the secrecy problem. Because patents are public documents, in theory they reveal to the public what the inventor has done, how the invention was

---

[7] For lawyers, this means that there are clients who must also be counseled on the choice between patent protection. As you go through these materials, consider the relative advantages of each regime.

constructed, and how it operates. Others can therefore avoid duplicating the work and can, instead, build upon it. When the patent term expires, people can learn enough about the invention to use it effectively. (Of course, practice can be different from theory: patentees arguably do their best to keep elements of their invention secret and to extend the period of exclusivity by acquiring patents on technologies that are needed to optimally utilize the invention described in an expiring patent).

This Introduction examines a typical patent and describes the application process. As noted, this process is rigorous. It is also costly, both to the applicant and to the government. Since applicants often seek protection in many countries, the per-invention cost of worldwide protection is high. It is therefore not surprising that there are many international treaties concerning patent rights. The ones of greatest significance to the United States are described below.

## 1.  A SAMPLE PATENT

STATUTORY MATERIAL: §§ 111–113, § 116

US005203579A

## United States Patent [19]

### Lipschitz

[11] Patent Number:   **5,203,579**

[45] Date of Patent:   **Apr. 20, 1993**

[54] **SHOP E Z CART**

[76] Inventor:   Sarah Lipschitz, 2021 84 St., Apt. 5D, Brooklyn, `I.Y.` 11214

[21] Appl. No.: **770,363**

[22] Filed:   **Oct. 3, 1991**

[51] Int. Cl.⁵ ................................................. **B62B 3/00**
[52] U.S. Cl. ................................. 280/33.991; 248/129; 280/DIG. 4
[58] Field of Search ...................... 280/33.991, 33.992, 280/33.995, 33.997, 35, DIG. 4, 659, 47.34–47.35, DIG. 3; 248/95, 97, 98, 128, 129; 224/273

[56] **References Cited**

### U.S. PATENT DOCUMENTS

| | | | |
|---|---|---|---|
| 2,762,669 | 9/1956 | Watson | 280/33.991 |
| 4,097,056 | 6/1978 | Castellano | 280/47.35 |
| 4,560,096 | 12/1985 | Lucas et al. | 280/33.992 |
| 4,601,479 | 7/1986 | Reinbold et al. | 280/47.35 |
| 4,678,195 | 7/1987 | Trabiano | 280/33.992 |

### FOREIGN PATENT DOCUMENTS

0070674   3/1991   Japan .............................. 280/33.992

*Primary Examiner*—Richard M. Camby
*Attorney, Agent, or Firm*—John P. Halvonik

[57]     **ABSTRACT**

The invention is a clothes shopping cart that is designed to hold a substantial number of clothing and accessory items for a shopper in department and clothing stores. The cart moves about easily and provides the shopper with the ability to load up the cart with goods as a shopper wheels the cart about through the department store aisles. The clothing shopping cart is designed for ease of parking in conjunction with other carts. The cart uses a U shaped base and a storage space that is oriented to allow the carts to nest with each other. The cart is constructed to permit a substantial number or items to be placed in the cart prior to purchase while allowing for an adequate amount of room between the cart and aisles of the ordinary department store, so that a plurality of cars can move in and about the department store.

**3 Claims, 3 Drawing Sheets**

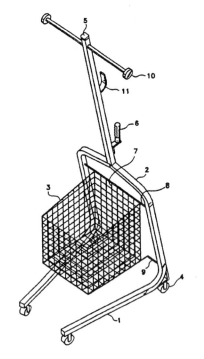

5,203,579

**1**

### SHOP E Z CART

#### BACKGROUND OF THE INVENTION

1. Field of the Invention

The invention relates to the field of shopping carts and, in particular, to a cart with a U shaped support structure and V shaped base legs that allows other shopping carts to nest with it. The handle of the cart is T shaped to allow one to place clothing and other items upon the handle for storage.

2. Description of the Prior Art

While there are other shopping carts, none that applicant is aware of has the unique construction of her particular shopping cart.

#### SUMMARY OF THE INVENTION

The invention comprises a shopping cart of unique construction comprising a support structure of inverted U shape bent in two planes. The upper plane represents the support for the storage basket suspended from the curved portion of the U shape. The lower plane defines the orientation of the ends of the U which serve as base legs for the rollers, wheels, etc. The cart may be used within department stores so that clothing and accessory items may be placed on the cart and stored prior to purchase. The upright handle of the cart has a T shaped construction and may be used to hold clothing, etc picked up in the store.

An object of the invention is to provide a shopping cart that readily nests in conjunction with other carts.

Another objective is to provide a shopping cart that allows one to store a considerable amount of clothing with a minimum of space.

Yet another objective is to provide a shopping cart that can readily move about crowded aisles.

Other advantages of the invention should be readily apparent to those skilled in the art once the invention has been described.

#### DESCRIPTION OF THE DRAWINGS

FIG. 1 shows overall construction of the Cart

FIG. 2A shows front view of cart

FIG. 2B shows side view of cart

FIG. 2C shows above view of the legs showing angled orientation

FIG. 3 shows the carts nested

#### DESCRIPTION OF THE PREFERRED EMBODIMENT

The shop EZ Cart is substantially as shown in FIG. 1. The base is of a U shaped construction with the ends 1 of the U serving as a wheeled support base that lies in a plane parallel to the floor. The support legs should have four rollers 4 or other wheeled means on the two ends for ease of movement, preferably 2 rollers per leg. The curved central portion 2 of the U is bent upward (i.e.: the U is inverted when the cart is in ordinary position) in a plane that is perpendicular to the first plane.

The plane with the legs is about parallel to the floor upon which the cart will move and toward that end rollers, casters, etc. designated 4 are mounted on the bottom surface of the legs. Two of each caster are preferably on each end.

The construction of the base should preferably be of metal rods, tubes, etc. that are typically used in the shopping cart industry.

The actual storage container 3 is preferably a wire basket suspended from the curved portion of the U. As the curved portion lies above the floor, the middle of

**2**

the U shape is actually the highest point of the base above the ground. The basket is suspended from the U shaped portion of the base, preferably near the highest standing parts of the base so that the basket rests above the plane of the floor.

The basket is preferably a wire basket of the kind that are commonly used in shopping carts. The basket is open at the top and the back wall 7 of the basket (that part of the basket that is closest to being directly below the curved part of the U) pivots upward so that other carts can nest with the subsequent baskets fitting inside the basket of the previous carts. The back wall of the basket forms a plane about perpendicular to the plane of the base and parallel to the plane of the upper part of the U. The basket is supported on the U shape by supports 8,9 in connection with the back wall. The upper part of the back wall should be pivotally connected to the upper support 8.

Goods are placed in the cart in the usually manner by depositing them into the open upper part, the back wall remains in place during use. The back wall pivots upward only when the carts are nested.

The storability of the cart is enhanced by the orientation of the container with the pivoting back wall. The baskets of the successive carts that are stacked adjacent will nest the basket portion of the next cart.

The bottom ends (legs) of the cart are slightly tapered inward so that they are converging. Thus the ends would form a V shape if they were extended all the way forward (which they are not). As it is, the angled ends enhance nesting because they allow successive, adjacent cart legs to fit within the space between the ends of the first cart.

The T shaped upper portion 5 should have rubberized ends 10 and these should be larger in diameter to prevent hangers from sliding off the upper handle. The upper portion is preferably of rounded construction and should allow hangers with clothing to hang from it. The rubber ends prevent hangers from falling off and will not snag clothing. Additional hooks 11 may be placed on the handle portion of the T to allow clothing, etc. to be stored.

A rubberized handle 6 may be placed in close connection with the upper part of the U to allow one to guide and push the vehicle.

I claim:

1. A shopping cart for the temporary storing of clothing comprising: base portion of substantially U shaped construction having two ends and a curved central portion connecting said ends, said U shape laying along two planes, said ends lying in a first plane and said curved portion lying in a second plane perpendicular to said first plane, said ends having roller means for movement, storage compartment in connection with said curved portion, said storage compartment having bottom wall, back and front walls and two side walls, said back wall located below said second portion of said U shape and about co-planar with said second plane, said back wall capable of pivoting upward so as to allow a plurality of said carts to nest alongside one another, said ends being slightly angled so as to facilitate nesting with other said carts, said cart having a handle portion in connection with said curved portion at about near the center of said curved portion, said handle having a T-shaped portion near said top end.

2. The apparatus of claim 1 wherein said handle means has a gripping portion.

3. The apparatus of claim 2 wherein each of said ends have two roller means for movement of said cart.

* * * * *

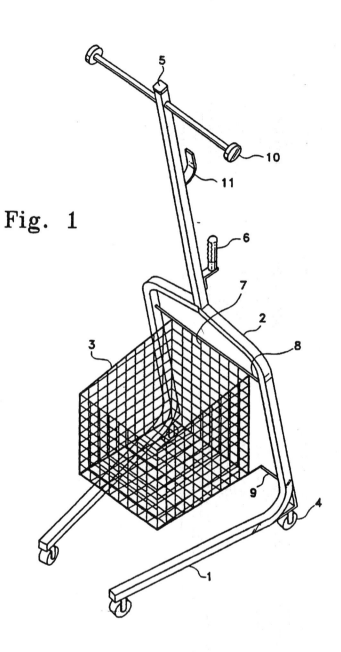

Fig. 1

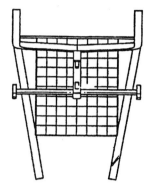

Fig. 2A

Fig. 2B

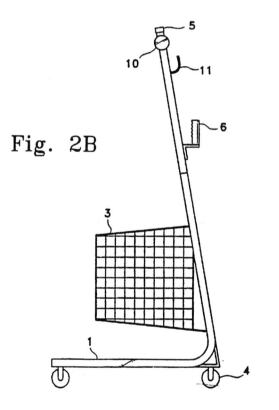

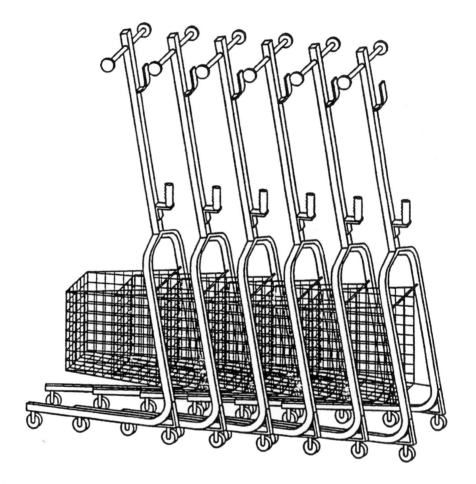

## Fig. 3

It is clear from its very first page that Patent 5,203,579 ameliorates many of the unique problems presented by the sort of innovations that patent law protects. It starts with two important dates: April 20, 1993, the date of issuance, and October 3, 1991, the date the application was filed. Since patents issued (or applied for) prior to 1995 and in force (or pending) on June 8, 1995, generally expire 17 years from the date of issuance or 20 years from the date of application, depending on which term is longer, § 154, these dates apprise the public of the time when this invention will be in the public domain, free for all to use. In this case, 20 years from filing would mean the patent expires on October 3, 2011; 17 years from issuance means expiration occurs on April 20, 2010. Since the 20–year term is longer, the actual expiration date is October 3, 2011.[8] (In the future, this calculation will be easier: a patent applied for after June 8, 1995 will remain in force for 20 years from the date of the application).

The patent also provides the name and address of the inventor, Sarah Lipschitz, the person who conceived the solution to the problem to which the patented invention was directed.[9] Had she assigned her rights to another, the assignee's name and address would also be recorded here. Members of the public who wish to use this invention before October 3, 2011 now know with whom to deal. Should they have any questions about, say, mechanical details of this cart, they know just who possesses the technical knowledge they need.

But what is the invention? An abstract is provided. As with abstracts in technical journals, this is a quick overview of what Ms. Lipschitz has constructed: a shopping cart for clothing (as opposed to groceries) that moves through crowded aisles easily and nests conveniently. Drawings are included if they are needed to insure understanding of the invention, § 113. For anyone interested in utilizing this invention, more information will be required: indeed, it is supplied—in the body of the document.

What would people reading patents wish to know? Surely, anyone interested in utilizing this cart will want to know if the patent is valid. There is no point, after all, in paying royalties to Ms. Lipschitz or waiting until the year 2011 if the patent is not enforceable. Thus, the patent contains whatever information Ms. Lipschitz possessed on the questions of usefulness, originality, novelty, and nonobviousness. The Background and Summary sections describe the problem she faced (building a nesting cart that carries clothing conveniently), the literature in the field, and explain why these older inventions were deficient. The patent also lists the "references"—documents on previous inventions—that Ms. Lipschitz showed the patent examiner, along with the examiner's own "Field of Search" in the materials on file in the Patent and Trademark Office (PTO).

Next, readers will want details on the invention. These are found in the main body of the patent, the "specification"—"a written description of

---

[8] There are a few exceptions to this term. For example, § 154(b) extends the term of protection for patents that have a long pendency in the Patent and Trademark Office due to delays attributable to the Office; §§ 155–156 extend the term of protection for substances that cannot be sold until they receive clearance from the Federal Food and Drug Administration (FDA) and are triggered by extensive delays between the time that clearance is sought and obtained. The term of a design patent is 14 years, § 173. Note also that special rules on remedies apply to patents subject to the interim term provision.

[9] See, e.g., Burroughs Wellcome Co. v. Barr Laboratories, Inc., 40 F.3d 1223, 1227 (Fed.Cir. 1994) .

the invention and of the manner and process of making and using it, in such full, clear, concise, and exact terms as to enable any person skilled in the art to which it pertains ... to make and use the same, and shall set forth the best mode contemplated by the inventor of carrying out his invention," § 112. This language is said to contain three separate requirements: enablement, best mode, and written description. Together, they form the quid pro quo of patent protection: in exchange for revealing information that might otherwise be kept secret, the government grants a legal right to exclude.

*Enablement.* The enablement requirement, which is found in the phrase that begins "to enable any person," § 112, is in some sense the most important. It requires the inventor to reveal all the information that the public will need to gain the full benefit of the invention after the patent expires, including information on how to construct and use the invention. Of course, the patentee is not required to write a primer on her field. Rather, the statute permits her to assume readers possess basic knowledge in the art to which the invention pertains. Ms. Lipschitz, for example, can use words like "rollers," "casters," and "U shaped construction" because people skilled in mechanicals already know these terms. Furthermore, courts construing this provision understand what anyone who has ever tried to assemble a bicycle knows: directions are never unambiguous and some experimentation will be necessary to convert what is on paper into a working version of the invention. However, if the amount of experimentation is "unduly extensive,"[10] or if the patentee has not provided enough information about the elements needed to construct the invention,[11] she will be regarding as not having fulfilled her duty and the patent will not be valid.

*Best mode.* The best mode requirement, found in the phrase beginning "and shall set forth," § 112, also focuses on the period after the patent expires. It aims at assuring effective competition. That is, while the

[10] See, e.g., Amgen, Inc. v. Chugai Pharmaceutical Co., Ltd., 927 F.2d 1200, 1213–14 (Fed.Cir.1991). In this case, the patent contained a broad claim for all possible DNA sequences capable of producing the protein that instructs bone marrow cells to increase production of red blood cells. The patentee had only isolated one such sequence—the DNA sequence encoding erythropoietin. Since the number of sequences that might encode erythropoietin or its analogs was in the millions, and the patentee had no way of specifying which ones would increase red blood cell production, the court held that "unduly extensive" experimentation would be required to find biologically active sequences. The broad claim was invalidated on enablement grounds.

[11] See, e.g., White Consolidated Industries, Inc. v. Vega Servo–Control, Inc., 713 F.2d 788 (Fed.Cir.1983). The invention was a system for controlling machine tools with a computer. The specification described one of the programs needed to run the computer as "The language TRANSLATOR used in the RUN mode may be a known translator capable of converting, in a single pass, a part program in programming language into a part program in machine language form, as for example, SPLIT." At the time, SPLIT was widely available for purchase, but it was held as a trade secret. Since its features were not disclosed, users could not create the program themselves, nor could they tell what other programs were sufficiently like SPLIT to substitute for it. Accordingly, the court held the patent invalid for lack of enablement. See also Union Pacific Resources Co. v. Chesapeake Energy Corp., 236 F.3d 684 (Fed. Cir. 2001).

enablement requirement will allow others to compete with the patentee (because they can build working versions of the invention), they may not be able to compete effectively if they do not know the most efficient way to utilize the invention. This provision deals with this problem by requiring the patentee to reveal the patentee's own—subjective—judgment as to the "preferred embodiment" of the invention. Compliance with the provision is determined by whether, from an objective point of view, that "preferred embodiment" has been well enough disclosed to enable a person with ordinary skill in the art.[12] Note that the best mode requirement works better in theory than in practice. It reveals what the patentee knew when the patent was filed.[13] By the time the patent expires, the patentee or her assignee will have enjoyed 20 years of experience with the invention. Although she will, presumably, have learned much more about utilizing it efficiently, there is no requirement that the patent be continuously updated.[14]

*Written Description.* The primary focus of the written description requirement is usually thought of as tied to the application process, where it is used to establish priority. In that role, the requirement of providing a "written description," § 112, pinpoints the time at which he applicant was "in possession of the invention," meaning the time when she fully recognized what it is that she had invented.[15] This use of the requirement is described below. In recent years, however, this provision has also come to be used (along with the enablement requirement) to prevent the patentee from overreaching—from claiming rights to technologies to which she did not significantly contribute. Used in this way, patents that fail to adequately describe the material the patentee has claimed may be held invalid.[16] Alternatively, products and processes that are not adequately described may not be regarded as infringing.[17] Some products—biologicals in particu-

[12] See, e.g., Wahl Instruments, Inc. v. Acvious, Inc., 950 F.2d 1575, 1579 (Fed.Cir. 1991)(the purpose of the requirement is "to restrain inventors from applying for a patent while at the same time concealing from the public preferred embodiments of their inventions which they have in fact conceived."); Chemcast Corp. v. Arco Industries Corp., 913 F.2d 923 (Fed.Cir.1990)(requiring that, in certain cases, patentee reveal not only the generic properties of material used in the invention, but also its trade name and supplier).

[13] See, e.g., Spectra–Physics, Inc. v. Coherent, Inc., 827 F.2d 1524, 1535 (Fed.Cir. 1987).

[14] There have, however, been a few lower court decisions requiring applicants who file continuations to reveal what they consider the best mode when the continuation is filed, see, e.g., Transco Prods. v. Performance Contracting, Inc., 821 F.Supp. 537 (N.D.Ill.1993) reversed & vacated 38 F.3d 551 (Fed.Cir.

1994). But no court has ever required updating after the patent has issued.

[15] Fiers v. Revel, 984 F.2d 1164 (Fed.Cir. 1993)(description of DNA must give its structure, not merely a potential method for isolating it); In re Gosteli, 872 F.2d 1008, 1012 (Fed.Cir.1989).

[16] See, e.g., Regents of the University of California v. Eli Lilly & Co., 119 F.3d 1559 (Fed.Cir. 1997), which held invalid a patent directed to a recombinant procaryotic microorganism modified to encode human insulin. The patent specification provided a written description of rat cDNA, but it included only a general method of producing human insulin cDNA, not a written description of human insulin cDNA, as per the asserted claim.

[17] See, e.g., Gentry Gallery, Inc. v. Berkline Corp., 134 F.3d 1473 (Fed.Cir.1998). Because the patent described a sectional sofa in which two independent reclining seats face in

lar—are very difficult to describe in words. In such cases, deposit of the material in a publicly-accessible depository is regarded as meeting the requirements of the Act.[18]

Finally, the reader will likely want to know what constitutes infringement. After all, the patent contains all sorts of information, including data on earlier technologies and details of construction that are not part of the invention itself.[19] Readers should not have to guess which bits of information are regarded by the patentee as proprietary. The storehouse of knowledge grows faster if information that the inventor does not consider part of the invention enters the public domain immediately and unequivocally. Accordingly, § 112 sets out a "peripheral claiming" regime that requires that "[t]he specification [] conclude with one or more claims particularly pointing out and distinctly claiming the subject matter which the applicant regards as his invention"—that is, that the patentee state precisely how to recognize the borders (periphery) of the claimed invention.[20]

In the shopping cart patent, this requirement is met with the language that begins "I claim:".[21] A few features of the claim are worth examining. First, note the format: three claims, one independent (Claim 1)[22] and two dependent (Claims 2 and 3).[23] The first claim broadly covers any shopping cart that contains a base with U-shaped construction of the specified type, with a pivoting back wall that makes nesting possible, and a T-shaped handle. This claim affords Ms. Lipschitz the most protection because many different shopping carts are likely to infringe it. However, it is also the most risky, for the claim is so broad, there is a real possibility that someone else may have previously invented a cart fitting this description. The earlier invention may not have been presented to the examiner and it will probably not have been known to Ms. Lipschitz either. However, if someone finds out about it, that person could go to court to have Claim 1 declared invalid for lack of novelty or for being obvious. There is no "blue penciling" of patent claims: if this claim is invalidated, it is struck in its entirety, even if a court could have edited the claim to transform it into a patentable claim of more modest dimensions.

Claims 2 and 3 are therefore important adjuncts to Claim 1. They describe these more modest inventions. They are called "dependent" claims

---

the same direction with the recliner controls on a console between them, it did not cover a reclining sofa whose controls were located in another location.

[18] Enzo Biochem, Inc. v. Gen–Probe Inc., 323 F.3d 956 (Fed.Cir. 2002).

[19] Indeed, patents sometimes contain information that, standing on its own, would be inventive enough to qualify for a patent, had the patentee recognized its significance.

[20] To understand peripheral claiming, it is helpful to consider the principal alternative: core claiming. In a core claiming system,

the patent lays out the central insight of the invention, deferring the determination of which extensions of that insight infringe to the time when such a determination is necessary (e.g. in an infringement suit). In peripheral claiming, it is the metes and bounds of the invention that are delineated.

[21] See Lipschitz Patent, p.2, col.2, line 45.

[22] Id. at line 46.

[23] Id. at lines 64 and 66.

because they incorporate "independent" Claim 1 by reference, and then contain language which usually serves to limit it. Claim 2 is limited to shopping carts of the Claim 1 type, that contain a handle that includes a grip. Claim 3 is even narrower: it is limited to Claim 1 shopping carts with the handle-gripping feature, which also have rollers. If the prior art does not contain these other features, Claims 2 and 3 will survive even if Claim 1 is struck. Some shopping carts will escape infringement, but Ms. Lipschitz will surely be happier with half a loaf than no loaf at all.

A second notable feature of this patent is the rather stilted language used to describe the cart. Remember, claims are significant not only because they define the invention, but also because they announce the boundaries of the public domain. Users of the patent system will pounce on the word choices made and on the punctuation utilized in an attempt to wrest as many inventive features as possible out of the patentee's hands. As a result, patent attorneys and agents have developed a formalized vocabulary with settled meaning. To give just one example, notice that Ms. Lipschitz's claim uses the word "comprising."[24] "Consisting of" may sound like a synonym, but it is not. Patent attorneys call "consisting of" a "close-ended phrase:" it implies that *only* shopping carts with exactly the features specified will infringe; shopping carts sporting features *in addition to* the ones described by Ms. Lipschitz will not infringe. In contrast, "comprising" is open-ended. Shopping carts with more features will infringe these claims, so long as they do, in fact, contain the features Ms. Lipschitz described. "Consisting of" is used to distinguish an invention from prior art that is somewhat similar. "Comprising" is used when the invention is so novel that there is no other art in the field that needs to be avoided.

Finally, notice that Ms. Lipschitz did not use the word "wheel" in describing the feature of Claim 3 that imparts mobility. Instead, she referred to "roller means for movement."[25] Claim 3 is drafted in what is called "means plus function form." Traditionally, this format has been extremely useful to patentees because it allowed them to extend the reach of their claims to embodiments that they cannot foresee at the time the patent issues. In this case, for example, Ms. Lipschitz's central insight is a movable shopping cart for clothing. It is irrelevant *how* motion is imparted because the method of creating movement is not the thing she has invented. Accordingly, anyone who uses a moving cart (with a handle with a grip) should be considered an infringer of Claim 3: it does not matter whether they use wheels similar to those in the diagram, casters, soda cans, hair curlers, roller blades, or some other wheel-like thing. By substituting "roller means for movement" for "wheel," Ms. Lipschitz creates a claim that is intended to cover all of these devices, and even to include means for movement that have yet to be invented. Means plus function claiming is specifically permitted by § 112 of the Act. However, as Assignment 21 will demonstrate, means plus function claims have, in recent years, come to be

---

[24] Id. at line 47.                    [25] Id. at line 67.

interpreted more restrictively than claims that avoid this format. As a result, this provision has become something of a trap for the unwary.[26]

## 2.   THE APPLICATION PROCESS

STATUTORY MATERIALS: §§ 122, 131–135, 141

Ms. Lipschitz filed her application on Oct. 3, 1991. It issued on April 20, 1993: what happened in the intervening 18 months? Patent applications are prosecuted by a small group of lawyers and patent agents who have passed a special examination administered by the PTO. Their practice is largely controlled by the Patent Rules of Practice, 37 C.F.R., and by the Manual of Patent Examining Procedure, which is published by the PTO. This is a highly specialized bar because, as noted above, language is critical and courts will not modify claims in order to save them. Drafting and prosecution are learned by apprenticeship to experienced drafters and are well beyond the scope of this casebook.[27]

In any event, the patent usually begins as an application in a form very similar to that of the issued patent.[28] It is submitted to the PTO in the name of the actual inventor or inventors, each of whom swears she believes herself to be the first inventor, §§ 111, 115, & 116. Note that this marks an important difference between patent and copyright law: the inventor is always named as a part of the patent application process, even if the invention was made for hire.[29] Inventions made pursuant to an employment relationship can be assigned to the employer. Indeed, many employers make the obligation to assign a part of the employment contract.[30] Howev-

---

[26] Of course, now that it is clear that the means plus function format can be limiting, there is litigation on what constitutes such a claim, see, e.g., Epcon Gas Systems, Inc. v. Bauer Compressors, Inc., 279 F.3d 1022 (Fed. Cir. 2002).

[27] Much of this material, including information on the qualifications for being admitted to practice before the PTO, is available at the PTO's website, www.uspto.gov.

[28] Alternatively, applicants can file provisional applications that conform only to § 112 ¶ 1 and § 113. If a full application is filed within 12 months, then the provisional application's date can be used for priority purposes, provided that the specification supports the claims, see §§ 111(b), 119(e). "Support" in this context apparently includes both an indication that the applicant was in possession of the invention and a written description in the *Enzo* sense, see New Railhead Mfg., L.L.C. v. Vermeer Mfg. Co., 298 F.3d 1290, 1296 (Fed.Cir. 2002). Note that the patent term will run from the date the

full application is filed and not the date of the provisional application.

[29] Compare § 201 of the Copyright Act, Assignment 9. In addition to creating a special rule of authorship for works made for hire, the Copyright Act also varies the substantive rules regarding such works. For example, there are no termination rights for such works, 17 U.S.C. § 203, nor are there moral rights in them, 17 U.S.C. § 106A. In contrast, all patents are equal, regardless of the circumstances in which the underlying inventions were created. Thus, patents belonging to employers by assignment are accorded the same rights as patents retained by the initial inventor(s).

[30] If the inventor becomes incapacitated or dies, or a recalcitrant inventor attempts to defeat the assignee's expectations by refusing to apply for a patent, the statute permits the legal representative or party to whom the invention is assigned to prosecute the application. The patent will, however, be granted to the actual inventor, § 118.

er, even in such circumstances, the employer will not be considered an inventor (or a joint inventor).[31]

After the application is filed, it is assigned a filing date, § 111,[32] and is then classified according to the technical art to which the invention belongs, assigned to an examining group, and ultimately given to an examiner experienced in that area. The examiner will review the application and, in all likelihood, will find some problems with it. Correspondence and/or personal interviews will follow, and the application will usually be amended. A record of each draft and the exchanges between examiner and attorney are kept for posterity in what is called the prosecution history or (for mysterious reasons) the "file wrapper." The file wrapper becomes part of the public record if the patent issues and is frequently consulted in infringement actions to interpret the claims.

Until 1999, if a patent did not issue, the application was never made public, § 122. That permitted a disappointed applicant to keep her invention as a trade secret. In 1999, however, Congress revised § 122 to provide that after 18 months' pendency, applications are to be promptly published.[33] This practice has the advantage of letting competitors and other inventors know what has already been invented and might be subject to patenting. And it does no great damage to most patentees' interests in that a similar publication practice exists in most other nations. Thus, anyone patenting abroad would eventually have her application disclosed in any event. However, inventors who do not patent abroad were concerned that early publication would eviscerate their ability to earn returns on their efforts. As a result, Congress compromised: an applicant can request secrecy in cases in which the invention will not be the subject of an application in another country or under a multinational agreement that requires 18 month publication. Also, if the invention is subject to an application only in countries with less extensive disclosure requirements, a redacted version of the application can be published instead.

There are several kinds of objections that the examiner can make. Possibly, the examiner will find that the application claims an invention that is the subject of another party's application or the subject of a patent currently in force. In that case, an interference will be declared, § 135, and

---

[31] This is not to say that the sort of employment problems that crop up in copyright and were treated in Assignment 9 do not exist in patent law as well. An employee who was hired for the specific purpose of solving a particular problem will generally find that the employment contract will be read as implying a duty to assign to the employer any patent rights created, see, e.g., Aero Bolt & Screw Co. v. Iaia, 180 Cal.App.2d 728, 5 Cal.Rptr. 53 (1960). Inventions made by employees hired for other purposes, but developed through the use of the employer's facilities, may be subject to a shop right—a right of the employer to a nonexclusive, royalty-free, nontransferable license to make and use the invention, cf. United States v. Dubilier Condenser Corp., 289 U.S. 178 (1933). See generally, Ronald B. Coolley, Recent Changes in Employee Ownership Laws, 41 Bus. Law. 57 (1985)(reviewing state statutes regulating these relationships).

[32] Applications must be accompanied by a fee; the fee schedule is set out in § 41.

[33] American Inventors Protection Act, Pub. L. 106–113, 113 Stat. 1501 (1999), codified at § 122(b).

both applicants (or the applicant and the patentee) will be given notice to appear before the Board of Patent Appeals and Interferences (BPAI), a legislative court administered within the PTO. The BPAI will then determine all issues of patentability and will also decide which of the parties has the right to the patent under the priority provision of the statute, § 102(g). The priority rule will be discussed in detail in Assignment 20. Oversimplified, the person who invents first receives the patent. Thus, an interference requires the parties to prove their dates of invention, with the burden of proof placed on the party who filed the later application. As with other civil litigation, settlements are permitted. However, because the settlement, like all agreements among competitors, implicates antitrust policy, it must be in writing and filed with the PTO, § 135(c).

Often, the examiner will reject claims for failure to comply with the substantive provisions of the Act, such as for inadequacies in the specification or because the invention is not novel or nonobvious under the requirements of §§ 102 and 103. The examiner must give the applicant notice and reasons for any rejection; the applicant is then permitted to amend her application and have it reexamined, § 132.

Sometimes, the applicant finds that her application requires a more fundamental change. If the application is found to claim more than one independent and distinct invention, the examiner has authority to require the applicant to prepare separate applications for each invention, § 121. It is here where the description requirement of § 112 becomes important. Although the applicant could start from scratch by filing a new application, she would have to relinquish the filing date of the first application. But the filing date is valuable. For example, it determines who bears the burden of proof in an interference. The applicant would therefore prefer to keep the original filing date, which she can do by filing what are called "divisional applications." A divisional will retain the filing date of the first—"parent"—application, so long as the applicant can show from the written description contained in the parent application that, on the earlier date, she was in possession of the invention disclosed in the divisional, § 120.

In addition, during the time that the application is pending in the PTO, the applicant may come to understand her initial insight better and discover it has other patentable features. Again, while she could file a brand new application, she would prefer to get the benefit of the filing date of the first application. A continuation, or continuation-in-part ("CIP"), application contains all of the information in the parent application and then adds new material. The matters disclosed in the parent's description will get the benefit of the earlier date, § 120, and the new material will be assigned a date that reflects when it was filed.[34]

[34] Continuations of continuations are also possible, without limit. Indeed, patentees have been known to drag the application process out for decades. When the term of protection began on issuance, this procedure led to the problem of the "submarine:" an application that lurked in the PTO, undetected by an industry that expanded in reliance on free access to the invention and that was profoundly undermined when the patent finally surfaced For more recent patent applications, the term begins to run from the time

Applicants dissatisfied with the decisions of the PTO have several levels of appeal. Parties to an interference can appeal the decision of the BPAI to the Court of Appeals for the Federal Circuit, the appellate court that hears appeals in all patent cases tried in federal courts, § 141. Alternatively, the applicant can seek review of the BPAI by suing the Commissioner of Patents in the United States District Court for the District of Columbia. Appeal from this court is to the Federal Circuit, § 146. A similar avenue for appeal is open after an application has been examined and rejected twice: the applicant can appeal to the BPAI, § 134, and can seek review of that decision in the Federal Circuit or bring a de novo action in district court, §§ 141, 145.

Of course, not all errors are the PTO's. After the patent issues, the patentee may, for example, find that she has omitted to claim part of her discovery, submitted a defective drawing, or failed to join an inventor. Errors committed without deceptive intent can be corrected through reissue, § 251, a procedure conducted along the same lines as the initial examination. Reissue is available at any time, except that the scope of the claims can be enlarged only within two years of the initial grant. Reissued patents have the same effect as initial patents with regard to claims contained in both. However, those who had begun to practice the inventions claimed only in the second patent enjoy "intervening rights"—the right to continue usages that began before the reissue took place, § 252.

In addition, a patentee occasionally discovers that the subject matter of an issued patent is covered by a patent that she already holds. There are two types of so-called "double patenting." "Same-invention type double patenting" occurs when a claim in the second patent turns out to cover exactly the same invention as that claimed in the first patent. "Obviousness type double patenting" occurs when a claim in the second patent is an obvious variation on a claim in the first patent.[35] In the case of same-invention double patenting, the offending claim of the second patent is invalid for, essentially, lack of novelty. In the case of obviousness type double patenting, however, the only problem is that the term of protection will be too long if both patents remain in force.[36] If double patenting occurred without deceptive intent, this problem can usually be cured by

of filing, which means that a long pendency will hurt the patentee: hopefully, that should end the problem. Moreover, the 18–month publication rule will substantially abate it as most applications will no longer be "submarines" (i.e. secret) for very long. Finally, the Federal Circuit has announced an equitable doctrine of laches, which renders a patent unenforceable if it was "issued after an unreasonable and unexplained delay in prosecution even though the applicant complied with pertinent statutes and rules," Symbol Technologies, Inc. v. Lemelson Medical, 277 F.3d 1361, 1363 (Fed.Cir. 2002).

[35] See, e.g., Gerber Garment Technology, Inc. v. Lectra Systems, Inc., 916 F.2d 683 (Fed.Cir.1990)(double patenting occurred when divisional application overlapped with parent application); In re Vogel, 422 F.2d 438 (C.C.P.A.1970)(method of packaging meat and beef obvious in light of previous patent for a method of packaging pork).

[36] For example, if the first patent issued in 1980 and the second patent issued in 1990, the latter patent would not expire until 2010, and the term for both combined would be 30 years (1980–2010).

simply disclaiming the part of the term that extends beyond the period of the first patent, § 253.[37]

Students are often puzzled by the parties' incentives during prosecution. At first blush, it would appear to be good strategy to reveal to the examiner as little as possible about the prior art. That way, the invention will be more likely to appear to meet the requirements of the Act. However, there are several features of the system that make this a poor way to proceed. First, an applicant bears a duty of candor—a duty to reveal to the PTO all of the information she possesses that is material to the question of patentability. If this duty is breached, the patent that issues will be unenforceable *in its entirety*—as to claims to which the hidden information pertained and as to all other claims in the patent as well.[38] Second, invalidity is always a valid defense. Unlike the case with trademarks, there is no time after which patents become incontestable.[39] Moreover, parties threatened with enforcement actions can ask for a declaratory judgment that the patent is invalid.[40] Validity determinations are made on the basis of all material presented in court, not just the art previously examined by the PTO. Although at this point the patent will be presumed valid, § 282, courts, as a practical matter, tend to give greater scrutiny to material that has not been passed on by the PTO. Finally, any party, including the Commissioner of Patents, can ask the PTO to reexamine the patent to determine the patentability of the invention in light of prior art, §§ 301–307. Thus, the victory obtained through breach of the duty to conduct examination equitably will be a hollow one.

## 3.   THE INTERNATIONAL STAGE

STATUTORY MATERIALS: §§ 104, 119, 351–376, Paris Convention, Arts. 2 and 4, TRIPS Agreement, Arts. 27–34.

A patent largely creates rights only within the nation that issued it. Inventors who wish to exploit their inventions globally will therefore often desire protection in other countries. The International Convention for the Protection of Industrial Property (the Paris Convention), and the Agreement on Trade–Related Aspects of Intellectual Property Rights (the TRIPS Agreement, which is a part of the General Agreement on Tariffs and

---

[37] In the example above, the disclaimer would produce the result that both patents expired in 2000.

[38] The leading case is J.P. Stevens & Co. v. Lex Tex Ltd., 747 F.2d 1553 (Fed.Cir. 1984). However, the standards enunciated there may somewhat overstate the parties' obligations as of more recent cases in which the court has emphasized the importance of proving intent, see, e.g., In re Harita, 847 F.2d 801 (Fed.Cir.1988); FMC Corp. v. Manitowoc Co., Inc., 835 F.2d 1411 (Fed.Cir.1987). The PTO from time to time promulgates its own standard of disclosure, 37 C.F.R. § 1.56.

Attorneys who engage in inequitable conduct of this type are, of course, subject to disciplinary action. See generally, Stanley L. Amberg, Evolution And Future Of New Rule 56 And The Duty Of Candor, The PTO's New Duty of Disclosure Rules May Be a Trap for Unwary Practitioners, 20 AIPLA Q.J. 163 (1992).

[39] 15 U.S.C. § 1065. See Assignment 2, Note 11.

[40] See, e.g., International Harvester Co. v. Deere & Co., 623 F.2d 1207 (7th Cir.1980).

Trade), provide the assurance that such protection will be obtainable in the countries that have signed these instruments. In addition, patentees seek to minimize the cost of obtaining global protection. The Patent Cooperation Treaty (PCT) is helpful in that respect.

a. *The Paris Convention*. This Convention was promulgated in 1883, adopted by the United States in 1887, and implemented through domestic legislation in 1903. It is recognized by well over 100 countries.[41] As it pertains to patent law, this Convention has two crucial features. First, under Art. 2 of the Convention:

> "[n]ationals of any country of the Union shall . . . enjoy in all the other countries of the Union the advantages that their respective laws now grant, or may hereafter grant, to nationals. . . . "

This "national treatment" provision assures inventors that the patents they acquire in a foreign country will be treated exactly the same as the patents acquired by nationals of that country. That way, all exploiters of patentable property compete in each country on a level playing field— French patentees do not enjoy special advantages in France any more than American patentees enjoy unique privileges in the United States. Note, however, that French patentees cannot enjoy in the United States privileges granted by France but not by the United States (and vice versa). Rather, within the borders of every country, patent holders are treated alike. The obligations undertaken by the United States through its adherence to the Convention are executed in § 119 of the Patent Act.

Second, Art. 4 of the Convention provides that:

> "Any filing that is equivalent to a national filing under the domestic legislation of any country of the Union . . . shall be recognized as giving rise to [a] right of priority."

The priority right is defined as up to 12 months for patents. Implemented in §§ 119 and 365 of the Patent Act, this provision means that when someone who has filed an application in one member country files a second application in another country, the filing date assigned to the latter application is the date of the first-filed application—as long as no more than 12 months have elapsed between filings.[42] For example, imagine an applicant files first in France on January 12, 1991. As long as she files her U.S. application by January 12, 1992, the U.S. filing date for most purposes will be considered January 12, 1991.

This ability to, essentially, predate a filing has been extremely important to foreign applicants, especially in the period prior to the adoption of NAFTA, and—later—the TRIPS Agreement. An applicant is always entitled to claim that her invention was reduced to practice on the filing date for purposes of determining (among other things) priority, novelty, and nonobviousness. Filing dates are also used to assign burdens of proof in

---

[41] A list of signatories is included in the Manual of Patent Examining Procedure § 201.13.

[42] The new provisional application process of § 111(b) may also trigger this requirement.

interferences. Since U.S. law once generally prohibited the use of foreign activities to establish the date on which an invention was reduced to practice, § 104(a), the ability of foreigners to rely on the date of their home-country filing often made the difference between winning a patent and becoming a licensee, an infringer, or a nonparticipant in the market for the invention. NAFTA, however, required the United States to treat Mexican and Canadian activity as equivalent to U.S. territory for the purpose of establishing invention dates, and the same is now also true for activity within the territory of all members of the TRIPS Agreement.[43] Accordingly, this advantage is not as important as it once was. Nonetheless, neither Agreement puts foreigners on an exactly equal footing with Americans: as you work your way through these materials, notice that foreign activities cannot as easily be used to *defeat* the patent rights of another as they are to *establish* the patent applicant's own right to a patent.

The 12–month grace period permitted between filings is in the nature of a compromise. On the one hand, it gives applicants time to determine whether it is worth spending the resources to seek foreign protection, hire international counsel, obtain translations of their applications, and conform their applications to the requirements of each member's law. On the other hand, it gives signatories some assurance that patent applications will be made promptly so that their nationals will quickly gain the benefit of the invention.[44]

It is also important to note the things that the Paris Convention does *not* do. It does not demand precisely equivalent treatment of foreign and domestic *applicants* (as opposed to patentees). Instead, each country is permitted to enact provisions aimed at further encouraging importation of new technologies.[45] Nor does the Convention create an international patent, good in all member states. Rather, each nation separately examines each application and entertains challenges to validity in accordance with domestic law. Finally, the Paris Convention does not create a unified international patent law. Indeed, signatories' laws differ in fundamental ways. In the United States, for example, the first person to invent an invention is generally awarded the patent, even if others filed applications earlier. In most other countries, the first to file is always the first in right.

b. *The General Agreement on Tariffs and Trade and the TRIPS Agreement.* Unlike the other international agreements discussed in this

---

[43] See § 104(a)(3).

[44] Signatories are permitted to go even further to encourage applicants to file their foreign applications within 12 months of the domestic application. As will be seen in Assignment 19, § 102(d) of the Patent Act punishes delay.

[45] For example, certain foreign applicants cannot rely on activities in their home country to demonstrate invention, § 104(a); it has been said that foreign patents are effective references only with respect to material in the claims, not in the remainder of the specification, Reeves Bros. v. United States Laminating Corp., 282 F.Supp. 118 (E.D.N.Y.1968); in some instances, foreign disclosures must be more complete than U.S. disclosures, In re Gosteli, 872 F.2d 1008 (Fed. Cir.1989), and issued foreign patents are not effective as references against co-pending applications from the date of application, In re Hilmer, 424 F.2d 1108 (C.C.P.A.1970).

Introduction, the General Agreement on Tariffs and Trade (the GATT) was not originally designed to deal with intellectual property. Instead, it is, as its name suggests, a general agreement designed to increase international commerce by reducing tariffs and other barriers to trade. When this Agreement went into force in 1948 with the United States as an original signatory, the parties to GATT focused on commerce in products like corn, chickens, lamps, and steel; it was only in 1986, during the so-called Uruguay Round of GATT trade negotiations, that intellectual property was introduced into the discussion. After a slow start in which the propriety of treating intellectual products as equivalent to grain and manufactured goods was questioned, the Uruguay Round ended with an agreement on a set of principles governing intellectual property protection in member states. The TRIPS Agreement, like the rest of the GATT, is administered by the World Trade Organization (WTO).

Two of the principles set out in the TRIPS Agreement mirror the Paris Convention: signatories to TRIPS agree to accord national treatment to foreign patent applicants and to accord priority according to the applicant's national filing date. A third extends the core principle of the GATT to intellectual property: it requires member countries to accord to other member nations most-favored-nation (MFN) treatment.[46] This means that any time one member of the GATT enters into an agreement related to intellectual property with any other member, the advantages of the agreement are generalized to apply to all other signatories.

A fourth significant feature of TRIPS is that it establishes a set of universal minimum standards governing the use of intellectual products. With respect to patent law, these standards include a prohibition against excluding from protection any particular field of technology;[47] a prohibition against discriminating among applications according to the place where invention occurred;[48] a requirement that applicants disclose their inventions "in a manner sufficiently clear and complete for the invention to be carried out by a person skilled in the art;"[49] a right in patentees to prevent third parties from "making, using, offering for sale, selling, or importing the patented invention";[50] and a period of protection that extends for at least 20 years from the date the application is filed.[51] Signatories retain the

---

[46] Id., Art. 4.

[47] Id., Art. 27(1). There are, however, some exceptions, including "diagnostic, therapeutic and surgical methods for the treatment of humans and animals," and "plants and animals other than microorganisms" Art. 27(3)(a).

[48] Id. This prohibition required a change in U.S. patent law, which, as we saw, generally does discriminate according to where an invention occurs, § 104. Thus, § 104 does not apply to signatories of GATT (or, for that matter, to Canada or Mexico, which negotiat-ed for exemptions under the North American Free Trade Agreement (NAFTA)).

[49] Id., at Art. 29(1).

[50] TRIPS Agreement, Art. 28(1).

[51] Id., at Art. 33. This too required a change in U.S. law, which formerly extended protection for 17 years from the date of issuance, which may or may not be longer, depending on the length of the examination procedure, see § 154. (It is because of this GATT-driven change that the calculation of Lipschitz's patent term was so complicated).

right to permit certain unauthorized uses of the patented invention, but only within narrow limits.[52]

c. *The Patent Cooperation Treaty.* The PCT is, like the TRIPS Agreement, a relatively recent development. Promulgated in 1970 and implemented (in stages) by the United States starting in 1975, see §§ 351–376,[53] the PCT is aimed at saving resources for both applicants and national patent offices through the elimination of duplicative examinations. An applicant can file an "international application" designating the countries in which patent protection is desired. Each member establishes a Receiving Office—generally the same agency that examines domestic applications—to receive applications, check their compliance with formalities, and forward copies to an International Searching Authority (ISA) and to the International Bureau (IB), which acts as a central repository. Several designated countries' patent offices, including the United States' PTO, act as ISAs; the World Intellectual Property Organization (WIPO) in Geneva, Switzerland currently serves as IB.

The ISA receiving an application conducts an international search aimed at discovering prior art that may be relevant in determining whether the invention is new and nonobvious. It transmits its Search Report to the IB and to the applicant. The applicant then has a number of options. She can have the IB transmit the application (which can be amended in light of the Search Report), along with the Report to the countries she designated, each of which will then determine patentability according to its own domestic law. Alternatively, the applicant can ask the IB to forward the application to an International Preliminary Examining Authority (once again, certain signatories' patent offices), which conducts an International Preliminary Examination, in a format similar to an examination within the PTO. This Examination results in a written opinion as to whether each claim is novel, involves an inventive step, and is industrially applicable. The International Preliminary Examination Report is forwarded to the IB, to the applicant, and to the patent offices of the designated countries. The Preliminary Examination Report is nonbinding; once it is received, domestic patent offices determine patentability under domestic law.

The PCT has certain advantages. The applicant can usually file a single application in her own country's Receiving Office, in the applicant's own language. Although translation into designated countries' languages may ultimately be necessary to obtain actual patents, the expense need not be incurred until after the Search Report and (if the applicant so desires) the International Preliminary Examination Report have provided the applicant with reason to believe that the invention is patentable. Although countries are free to differ with the opinion of the International Preliminary Examining Authority, its report will save local patent offices time and money. Furthermore, at least one patent office will certainly agree with its conclusions—namely, the one that conducted the examination. Thus, the

---

[52] Id., at Arts. 30 and 31.

[53] The signatories of the PCT are listed in the Manual of Patent Examining Procedure § 1870.

typical U.S. applicant will use the U.S. PTO as Receiving Office, ISA, and International Preliminary Examining Authority. She will conduct all her business in English, and have a good idea of what is patentable before she needs to hire translators and approach foreign offices. Simultaneously, she will have come close to finishing with the PTO's own examination of her application.

There are certain disadvantages to a PCT application, particularly for Americans. First, the PCT application must be drafted somewhat differently from purely domestic applications. There is a standardized format that must be utilized. There is also a "unity of invention" requirement which determines how inventions are split up for application purposes. This requirement is similar to that of most PCT members, but is significantly different from U.S. practice. Further, those who use the PCT cannot opt to keep the application secret until issuance. However, these disadvantages are not serious for most potential users of the system. They would file abroad anyway, where they would meet the same requirements.

Like the Paris Convention, the PCT does not go as far as many would like. The validity of a patent depends on the laws of each country where protection is sought; since patentability standards differ, the cost of obtaining world-wide protection is high and there remains the chance that some inventions will be patented by one party in one country and by a different party in other countries. To fully integrate world economies, it may be better for countries to agree to enact patent law that is, in all major respects, identical. Europe has been at the forefront of such efforts. Many European countries are members of the European Patent Convention (EPC). Although these countries (which are not coextensive with the countries of the European Union) maintain their own patent offices, they have all agreed to similar substantive patent law. They have also established a European Patent Office (EPO), where inventors can have their applications examined centrally. However, this central application and examination do not create a true Convention-wide patent. Rather, patentees essentially receive a bundle of individual national patents, which must be enforced and challenged separately in each nation's domestic courts.[54] The European Union is currently considering a true EU patent, which would provide exclusive rights in all members of the Union. Enforcement would be through a special court that would be established for that purpose.[55]

In the last decade, the number of patent applications world-wide has exploded to the point where there is reason to doubt that countries will be able to continue to afford the cost of providing timely examination. As a result, proposals for further widespread harmonization and standardized worldwide examination are now on the international agenda.[56] But true

[54] See generally, Victor Vandebeek, Realizing the European Common Market by Unifying Intellectual Property Law: Deadline 1992, 1990 B.Y.U. L. Rev. 1605.

[55] See Joseph Straus, Patent Litigation in Europe—A Glimmer of Hope? Present Status and Future Perspectives, 2 Wash. U. J.L. & Pol'y 403 (2000).

[56] See John R. Thomas, The Responsibil-

harmonization will require countries to compromise on fundamental issues, such as the first-to-invent or first-to-file priority rule. Further, countries will be called upon to abandon law that is particularly well adapted to their own cultural traditions. It remains to be seen whether the international community believes the benefits of harmonization will outweigh these costs.[57]

ity of The Rulemaker: Comparative Approaches To Patent Administration Reform, 17 Berkeley Tech. L.J. 727 (2002); Toshiko Takenaka, Rethinking The United States First-to-Invent Principle From A Comparative Law Perspective: A Proposal To Restructure § 102 Novelty And Priority Provisions, 39 Hous. L. Rev. 621 (2002); Harold Wegner, Patent Harmonization (1993).

[57] See generally, John F. Duffy, Harmony and Diversity In Global Patent Law, 17 Berkeley Tech. L.J. 685 (2002); Michael N.

Meller, Principles of Patentability and Some Other Basics for a Global Patent System, 83 J. Pat. & Trademark Office Soc'y 359 (2001); Keith Maskus, Lessons From Studying the International Economics of Intellectual Property Rights, 53 Vand. L. Rev. 2219 (2000); William T. Fryer, Patent Law Harmonization Treaty Decision is Not Far Off—What Course Should the U.S. Take?, 30 IDEA: J.L. & Tech. 309 (1990).

# ASSIGNMENT 15

# SUBJECT MATTER

## 1. INTRODUCTION

Sections 100 and 101 of the Patent Act together define the scope of patentable subject matter. Section 101, the more general provision, announces that patents are available for any "new and useful process, machine, manufacture, or composition of matter, or any useful improvement thereof." "New" and "useful" denote standards of inventiveness; they are discussed in Assignments 17 and 16. This Assignment is concerned only with the kinds of innovations that are eligible for utility patent protection: machines, manufactures, compositions of matter, processes, and improvements thereof.

Machines, manufactures, and compositions of matter are generally easy to recognize. They are things such as steam engines, pencils, and aspirin. "Process" requires slightly more exposition. One definition was provided in an early, much-cited case, Cochrane v. Deener:[1]

"A process is a mode of treatment of certain materials to produce a given result. It is an act, or a series of acts, performed upon the subject matter to be transformed and reduced to a different state of thing."

This definition works well when transformations are physical in nature. However, modern inventions often involve information products, such as computer or genetic code. Transformations of information are, as the Principal Problem makes clear, more difficult to analyze.

"Process" also has a second definition, provided by § 100:

"The term 'process' means process, art or method, and includes a new use of a known process, machine, manufacture, composition of matter, or material."

This provision is an important addition to patent law, for it enables the law to motivate the search for new ways to use old materials. Although an inventor cannot obtain a patent on the actual material (it is not "new"), a process patent can be obtained on the new way to use it. A process patent is not usually as valuable as a product patent because it is difficult to monitor its use. Nonetheless, it is better to have this limited right, than no legal ability to capture any of the benefits of inventing the new use. Moreover, in certain situations, a process patent can be as important as a product patent. U.S. patent law is mainly applicable to acts occurring on U.S. soil. Nonetheless, the importation into the United States of a nonpatented

---

[1] 94 U.S. 780, 788 (1876).

product manufactured abroad is considered infringement when the product is made with a process that is protected by a U.S. patent.[2] Rights over processes are particularly important in the biotechnology field, where standard (nonpatented) products can often be made more cheaply and at greater purity with new (and patented) biological processes.

Important economic consequences flow from the ability to acquire a patent on an improvement. It is important to understand that a patent on an improvement is distinct from rights to the technology that is being improved upon. Thus, if the underlying technology is in the public domain, only those who wish to practice the improved version need the patentee's permission. However, if the underlying technology is also patented, then it is sometimes the case that the two patents will block each other: that anyone who wishes to use the improved version will need permission from both patentees. By the same token, if the patentees themselves want to utilize the improvement or license others to do so, they will need each other's permission ("cross licenses").[3] The need for joint permission creates an opportunity for the two inventors to bargain with one another, hopefully in a manner that leads to an allocation of profits that reflects the contributions that each made to the field.[4]

But the real problem posed by §§ 100 and 101 lies not in what they do say so much as in what they omit. Compare these provisions with the definition of copyrightable subject matter in § 102 of the Copyright Act. In addition to providing a list of material that is copyrightable, the Copyright Act adds a definition of that which is not copyrightable. That is, § 102(b) expressly notes that copyright is not available for ideas, concepts, principles, and discoveries. At first blush, the express exclusions of the Copyright Act makes it appear that patent law is intended to cover ideas and principles. Indeed, early cases on the copyrightability of computer programs tended to assume that patent law picks up precisely where copyright leaves off.

On further thought, however, it is evident why this assumption could not be true. Copyright excludes ideas and principles because creating

---

[2] § 271(g). A product will not be considered made by a patented process if it is materially changed or if it becomes a trivial or nonessential component of another product.

[3] Compare this situation with the one encountered in Anderson v. Stallone, Assignment 8, where a work that used copyrighted material without authorization was considered not copyrightable under § 103(a) of the Copyright Act. Because copyright law apparently lacks a concept of blocking rights, there is little to compel holders to negotiate with those who would build on their work.

[4] For an interesting analysis of the importance of this kind of bargaining in areas

characterized by cumulative innovations, see Suzanne Scotchmer, Standing on the Shoulders of Giants: Cumulative Research and Patent Law, 5 J. Econ. Persps. 29 (1991). This discussion assumes that the work of improving on a patented invention is not itself infringing. That assumption is now in doubt, see, e.g., Integra Lifesciences I, Ltd. v. Merck KGaA, 331 F.3d 860, 874–77 (Fed.Cir. 2003)(Newman, J., dissenting in part). For a discussion of this issue in the context of computer technology, see Julie E. Cohen and Mark A. Lemley, Patent Scope and Innovation in the Software Industry, 89 Cal. L. Rev. 1 (2001).

exclusive rights in them would make it too difficult for others to make their own contributions to the storehouse of knowledge. The same concern necessarily animates patent law, for if the basic building blocks of science could be privately owned, innovation would certainly be slowed. As Assignment 7 made clear, copyright protects the public domain by drawing (with some difficulty) a line between ideas and expression. The analogue in patent law is the line between an idea and its embodiment:

> "While a scientific truth, or the mathematical expression of it, is not a patentable invention, a novel and useful structure created with the aid of knowledge of scientific truth may be."[5]

## 2.   PRINCIPAL PROBLEM

Gamma Biotech, Inc. is a biotechnology company that is trying to strike it rich on the tremendous commercial potential of proteins, which can be used for everything from pharmaceuticals to detergent. It has come to us for advice on a series of patent issues that it encountered in the course of identifying a protein implicated in the treatment of a particular form of brain cancer. Several independent laboratories were involved in this effort and each is trying to patent its contribution. The issue we need to address first is which (if any) of these discoveries is patentable subject matter.

This protein (like all proteins) is made by body cells under the direction of genes. In this case, the cells in question were first obtained by Dr. Alpha, who treated a certain Brenda Walsh for a fast-growing brain tumor. Dr. Alpha removed Walsh's tumor and then grew its cell line in his laboratory. He gave a sample of these cells to his friend, Professor Beta, who isolated and sequenced the genetic material and then published her findings. Gamma used this article to find the particular protein it believes can cure brain cancer. In the course of this work, Gamma also developed a method of evaluating sequencing information for promising leads, finding donors interested in developing these leads into cures, and matching their interest to the capabilities of particular scientists.

Gamma has several questions for us. First, can Alpha patent the cell line isolated from Brenda Walsh? Second, can Beta patent the cDNA generated from the cell line and then sequenced? Third, can Gamma patent the protein it identified or its new method of launching research projects?

Of course, to really understand what is going on here, you need to know a little biology. The nuclei of a plant or animal's cells contain chemicals that store the information necessary for the organism to function. These chemicals, called chromosomes, are made of double strands of deoxyribonucleic acid (DNA). The backbone of these strands is, in turn, made of combinations of four chemicals called adenine (A), guanine (G), cytosine (C) and thymine (T) arranged linearly. The strands are held together because pairs of these chemicals are complementary: the A's on one strand bond to the T's on the other. Similarly, the G's and C's bond.

[5] MacKay Radio & Telegraph Co. v. Radio Corp. of America, 306 U.S. 86, 94 (1939).

The order (or sequence) of these chemicals in the linear arrangement on the strands determines the structure of the proteins that the DNA programs the cells to create. Or, as biochemists would say, a particular piece of DNA "codes for," or "encodes," a particular protein.

Since DNA creates valuable proteins, and since the structure of these proteins depends on the structure of the DNA that created them, it would be nice to isolate DNA from cell lines that demonstrate interesting behavior, like the fast-growing cell line that Dr. Alpha started from Brenda Walsh's tumor. The DNA strands are, unfortunately, very long. Much of them have (so far as can be determined) no value at all. The 3% that is valuable codes for many different proteins. Accordingly, to get at interesting proteins, it is necessary to break the DNA up, get rid of the garbage, and then find the pieces of the sequence—the genes—that code for specific proteins.

One way to do that is to use standard, well known techniques to isolate an intermediate chemical, called messenger ribonucleic acid (mRNA), which a gene uses to convey its information to other processes within a cell. mRNA, which is single stranded, is also made from four chemicals with complementary aspects. Three are just like DNACG, C, and A, but in mRNA, T is replaced by Uracil (U). The order of these chemicals on each mRNA backbone is determined by the sequence of the specific gene that uses it. mRNA, though closer to the interesting protein than DNA, is, however, not quite close enough. That is because mRNA is not stable. However, there are techniques that can be used to convert mRNA into stable double-stranded DNA-like chemicals.

These techniques were used by Beta when she studied the Walsh cell line that her friend, Alpha, gave her. She isolated mRNA from the Walsh cell line and used standard laboratory techniques to eliminate the useless parts. Next, she exploited the fact that the G's on an mRNA will bind to C's and the A's will bind to U's and T's to make each strand of mRNA generate a complementary strand. The results were double-stranded molecules extremely similar to the genes of interest. In fact, they are identical to the original DNA in Walsh's body, except that they lack the noncoding parts. Called cDNA, these strands can be maintained for long periods of time and propagated.

Beta used her supply of cDNAs to isolate particular genes. Using standard techniques, she figured out the sequence of the chemicals and then published her results. Gamma saw the publication and requested supplies of her genes. Using well-known techniques, it caused the genes to generate the proteins they encode for, and found the one it suspects will cure cancer.

So, to return to the initial question: can Alpha patent the cell line isolated generated from the tumor in Brenda Walsh's head? Can Beta patent the cDNA she generated from the cell line and sequenced? Can Gamma patent the protein generated from the cDNA? Can Gamma patent its method of launching new research projects?

3.   MATERIALS FOR SOLUTION OF PRINCIPAL PROBLEM

A.   STATUTORY MATERIAL: § 101

B.   CASES:

# Diamond v. Chakrabarty

Supreme Court of the United States, 1980.
447 U.S. 303, 100 S.Ct. 2204, 65 L.Ed.2d 144.

■ MR. CHIEF JUSTICE BURGER delivered the opinion of the Court.

We granted certiorari to determine whether a live, human-made micro-organism is patentable subject matter under 35 U.S.C.A. § 101.

I

In 1972, respondent Chakrabarty, a microbiologist, filed a patent application, assigned to the General Electric Co. The application asserted 36 claims related to Chakrabarty's invention of "a bacterium from the genus Pseudomonas containing therein at least two stable energy-generating plasmids, each of said plasmids providing a separate hydrocarbon degradative pathway." This human-made, genetically engineered bacterium is capable of breaking down multiple components of crude oil. Because of this property, which is possessed by no naturally occurring bacteria, Chakrabarty's invention is believed to have significant value for the treatment of oil spills.

Chakrabarty's patent claims were of three types: first, process claims for the method of producing the bacteria; second, claims for an inoculum comprised of a carrier material floating on water, such as straw, and the new bacteria; and third, claims to the bacteria themselves. The patent examiner allowed the claims falling into the first two categories, but rejected claims for the bacteria. His decision rested on two grounds: (1) that micro-organisms are "products of nature," and (2) that as living things they are not patentable subject matter under 35 U.S.C. § 101.

Chakrabarty appealed the rejection of these claims to the Patent Office Board of Appeals, and the Board affirmed the Examiner on the second ground. Relying on the legislative history of the 1930 Plant Patent Act, in which Congress extended patent protection to certain asexually reproduced plants, the Board concluded that § 101 was not intended to cover living things such as these laboratory created micro-organisms.

The Court of Customs and Patent Appeals, by a divided vote, reversed.
* * *

II

The Constitution grants Congress broad power to legislate to "promote the Progress of Science and useful Arts, by securing for limited Times to Authors and Inventors the exclusive Right to their respective Writings and

Discoveries." Art. I, § 8, cl. 8. The patent laws promote this progress by offering inventors exclusive rights for a limited period as an incentive for their inventiveness and research efforts. The authority of Congress is exercised in the hope that "[t]he productive effort thereby fostered will have a positive effect on society through the introduction of new products and processes of manufacture into the economy, and the emanations by way of increased employment and better lives for our citizens." Kewanee Oil Co. v. Bicron Corp., 416 U.S.470, 480 (1974).

The question before us in this case is a narrow one of statutory interpretation requiring us to construe 35 U.S.C. § 101, which provides:

> "Whoever invents or discovers any new and useful process, machine, manufacture, or composition of matter, or any new and useful improvement thereof, may obtain a patent therefor, subject to the conditions and requirements of this title."

Specifically, we must determine whether respondent's micro-organism constitutes a "manufacture" or "composition of matter" within the meaning of the statute.

### III

In cases of statutory construction we begin, of course, with the language of the statute. And "unless otherwise defined, words will be interpreted as taking their ordinary, contemporary common meaning." We have also cautioned that courts "should not read into the patent laws limitations and conditions which the legislature has not expressed."

Guided by these canons of construction, this Court has read the term "manufacture" in § 101 in accordance with its dictionary definition to mean "the production of articles for use from raw or prepared materials by giving to these materials new forms, qualities, properties, or combinations, whether by hand-labor or by machinery." American Fruit Growers, Inc. v. Brogdex Co., 283 U.S. 1, 11 (1931). Similarly, "composition of matter" has been construed consistent with its common usage to include "all compositions of two or more substances and . . . all composite articles, whether they be the results of chemical union, or of mechanical mixture, or whether they be gases, fluids, powders or solids." Shell Development Co. v. Watson, 149 F.Supp. 279, 280 (D.D.C.1957). In choosing such expansive terms as "manufacture" and "composition of matter," modified by the comprehensive "any," Congress plainly contemplated that the patent laws would be given wide scope.

The relevant legislative history also supports a broad construction. The Patent Act of 1793, authored by Thomas Jefferson, defined statutory subject matter as "any new and useful art, machine, manufacture, or composition of matter, or any new or useful improvement [thereof]." Act of Feb. 21, 1793, § 1, 1 Stat. 319. The Act embodied Jefferson's philosophy that "ingenuity should receive a liberal encouragement." 5 Writings of Thomas Jefferson 75-76 (Washington ed. 1871). Subsequent patent statutes in 1836, 1870, and 1874 employed this same broad language. In 1952, when the patent laws were recodified, Congress replaced the word "art" with "process," but otherwise left Jefferson's language intact. The Committee Reports accompanying the 1952 Act inform us that Congress intended statutory subject matter to "include anything under the sun that is made by man." S. Rep. No. 1979, 82d Cong., 2d Sess., 5 (1952); HR Rep. No. 1923, 82d Cong., 2d Sess., 6 (1952).

This is not to suggest that § 101 has no limits or that it embraces every discovery. The laws of nature, physical phenomena, and abstract ideas have been held not patentable. Thus, a new mineral discovered in the earth or a new plant found in the wild is not patentable subject matter. Likewise, Einstein could not patent his celebrated law that $E=mc^2$; nor could Newton have patented the law of gravity. Such discoveries are "manifestations of . . . nature, free to all men and reserved exclusively to none." Funk Brothers Seed Co. v. Kalo Inoculant Co., 333 U.S. 127, 130 (1948).

Judged in this light, respondent's micro-organism plainly qualifies as patentable subject matter. His claim is not to a hitherto unknown natural phenomenon, but to a nonnaturally occurring manufacture or composition of matter—a product of human ingenuity "having a distinctive name, character [and] use." The point is underscored dramatically by comparison of the invention here with that in *Funk*. There, the patentee had discovered that there existed in nature certain species of root-nodule bacteria which did not exert a mutually inhibitive effect on each other. He used that discovery to produce a mixed culture capable of inoculating the seeds of leguminous plants. Concluding that the patentee had discovered "only some of the handiwork of nature," the Court ruled the product nonpatentable:

> "Each of the species of root-nodule bacteria contained in the package infects the same group of leguminous plants which it always infected. No species acquires a different use. The combination of species produces no new bacteria, no change in the six species of bacteria, and no enlargement of the range of their utility. Each species has the same effect it always had. The bacteria perform in their natural way. Their use in combination does not improve in any way their natural functioning. They serve the ends nature originally provided and act quite independently of any effort of the patentee."

Here, by contrast, the patentee has produced a new bacterium with markedly different characteristics from any found in nature and one having the potential for significant utility. His discovery is not nature's handiwork, but his own; accordingly it is patentable subject matter under § 101.

IV

Two contrary arguments are advanced, neither of which we find persuasive.

(A)

The petitioner's first argument rests on the enactment of the 1930 Plant Patent Act, which afforded patent protection to certain asexually reproduced plants, and the 1970 Plant Variety Protection Act, which authorized protection for certain sexually reproduced plants but excluded bacteria from its protection. In the petitioner's view, the passage of these Acts evidences congressional understanding that the terms "manufacture" or "composition of matter" do not include living things; if they did, the petitioner argues, neither Act would have been necessary.

We reject this argument. Prior to 1930, two factors were thought to remove plants from patent protection. The first was the belief that plants, even those artificially bred, were products of nature for purposes of the patent law. This position appears to have derived from the decision of the patent office in Ex parte Latimer, 1889 Dec.Com.Pat. 123, in which a patent claim for fiber found in the needle of the *Pinus australis* was rejected. The Commissioner reasoned that a contrary result would permit "patents [to] be obtained upon the trees of the forest and the plants of the earth, which of course would be unreasonable and impossible." The *Latimer* case, it seems, came to "se[t] forth the general stand taken in these matters" that plants were natural products not subject to patent protection. Thorne, Relation of Patent Law to Natural Products, 6 J. Pat.Off.Soc. 23, 24 (1923). The second obstacle to patent protection for plants was the fact that plants were thought not amenable to the "written description" requirement of the patent law. See 35 U.S.C. § 112. Because new plants may differ from old only in color or perfume, differentiation by written description was often impossible.

In enacting the Plant Patent Act, Congress addressed both of these concerns. It explained at length its belief that the work of the plant breeder "in aid of nature" was patentable invention. And it relaxed the written description requirement in favor of "a description ... as complete as is reasonably possible." 35 U.S.C. § 162. No Committee or Member of Congress, however, expressed the broader view, now urged by the petitioner, that the terms "manufacture" or "composition of matter" exclude living things. The sole support for that position in the legislative history of the 1930 Act is found in the conclusory statement of Secretary of Agriculture Hyde, in a letter to the Chairmen of the House and Senate Committees considering the 1930 Act, that "the patent laws ... at the present time are understood to cover only inventions or discoveries in the field of inanimate nature." Secretary Hyde's opinion, however, is not entitled to controlling weight. His views were solicited on the administration of the new law and not on the scope of patentable subject matter—an area beyond his competence. Moreover, there is language in the House and Senate Committee Reports suggesting that to the extent Congress considered the matter it found the Secretary's dichotomy unpersuasive. The Reports observe:

> "There is a clear and logical distinction *between the discovery of a new variety of plant and of certain inanimate things*, such, for example, as a new and useful natural mineral. The mineral is created wholly by nature unassisted by man.... On the other hand, a plant discovery resulting from cultivation is unique, isolated, and is not repeated by nature, nor can it be reproduced by nature unaided by man.... " (emphasis added).

Congress thus recognized that the relevant distinction was not between living and inanimate things, but between products of nature, whether living or not, and human-made inventions. Here, respondent's microorganism is the result of human ingenuity and research. Hence, the passage of the Plant Patent Act affords the Government no support.

Nor does the passage of the 1970 Plant Variety Protection Act support the Government's position. As the Government acknowledges, sexually reproduced plants were not included under the 1930 Act because new varieties could not be reproduced true-to-type through seedlings. By 1970, however, it was generally recognized that true-to-type reproduction was possible and that plant patent protection was therefore appropriate. The 1970 Act extended that protection. There is nothing in its language or history to suggest that it was enacted because § 101 did not include living things.

In particular, we find nothing in the exclusion of bacteria from plant variety protection to support the petitioner's position. The legislative history gives no reason for this exclusion. As the Court of Customs and Patent Appeals suggested, it may simply reflect congressional agreement with the result reached by that court in deciding In re Arzberger, 112 F.2d 834 (1940), which held that bacteria were not plants for the purposes of the 1930 Act. Or it may reflect the fact that prior to 1970 the Patent Office had issued patents for bacteria under § 101. In any event, absent some clear indication that Congress "focused on [the] issues . . . directly related to the one presently before the Court," there is no basis for reading into its actions an intent to modify the plain meaning of the words found in § 101.

(B)

The petitioner's second argument is that micro-organisms cannot qualify as patentable subject matter until Congress expressly authorizes such protection. His position rests on the fact that genetic technology was unforeseen when Congress enacted § 101. From this it is argued that resolution of the patentability of inventions such as respondent's should be left to Congress. The legislative process, the petitioner argues, is best equipped to weigh the competing economic, social, and scientific considerations involved, and to determine whether living organisms produced by genetic engineering should receive patent protection. In support of this position, the petitioner relies on our recent holding in Parker v. Flook, 437 U.S. 584 (1978), and the statement that the judiciary "must proceed cautiously when . . . asked to extend patent rights into areas wholly unforeseen by Congress." Id. at 596.

It is, of course, correct that Congress, not the courts, must define the limits of patentability; but it is equally true that once Congress has spoken it is "the province and duty of the judicial department to say what the law is." Marbury v. Madison, 1 Cranch 137, 177 (1803). Congress has performed its constitutional role in defining patentable subject matter in § 101; we perform ours in construing the language Congress has employed. In so doing, our obligation is to take statutes as we find them, guided, if ambiguity appears, by the legislative history and statutory purpose. Here, we perceive no ambiguity. The subject-matter provisions of the patent law have been cast in broad terms to fulfill the constitutional and statutory goal of promoting "the Progress of Science and the useful Arts" with all that means for the social and economic benefits envisioned by Jefferson. Broad general language is not necessarily ambiguous when congressional objectives require broad terms.

Nothing in *Flook* is to the contrary. That case applied our prior precedents to determine that a "claim for an improved method of calculation, even when tied to a specific end use, is unpatentable subject matter under § 101." The Court carefully scrutinized the claim at issue to determine whether it was precluded from patent protection under "the principles underlying the prohibition against patents for 'ideas' or phenomena of nature." We have done that here. *Flook* did not announce a new principle that inventions in areas not contemplated by Congress when the patent laws were enacted are unpatentable per se.

To read that concept into *Flook* would frustrate the purposes of the patent law. This Court frequently has observed that a statute is not to be confined to the "particular application[s] ... contemplated by the legislators." This is especially true in the field of patent law. A rule that unanticipated inventions are without protection would conflict with the core concept of the patent law that anticipation undermines patentability. Mr. Justice Douglas reminded that the inventions most benefiting mankind are those that "push back the frontiers of chemistry, physics, and the like." Great A. & P. Tea Co. v. Supermarket Corp., 340 U.S. 147, 154 (1950)(concurring opinion). Congress employed broad general language in drafting § 101 precisely because such inventions are often unforeseeable.

To buttress his argument, the petitioner, with the support of amicus, points to grave risks that may be generated by research endeavors such as respondent's. The briefs present a gruesome parade of horribles. Scientists, among them Nobel laureates, are quoted suggesting that genetic research may pose a serious threat to the human race, or, at the very least, that the dangers are far too substantial to permit such research to proceed apace at this time. We are told that genetic research and related technological developments may spread pollution and disease, that it may result in a loss of genetic diversity, and that its practice may tend to depreciate the value of human life. These arguments are forcefully, even passionately, presented; they remind us that, at times, human ingenuity seems unable to control fully the forces it creates—that with Hamlet, it is sometimes better "to bear those ills we have than fly to others that we know not of."

It is argued that this Court should weigh these potential hazards in considering whether respondent's invention is patentable subject matter under § 101. We disagree. The grant or denial of patents on microorganisms is not likely to put an end to genetic research or to its attendant risks. The large amount of research that has already occurred when no researcher had sure knowledge that patent protection would be available suggests that legislative or judicial fiat as to patentability will not deter the scientific mind from probing into the unknown any more than Canute could command the tides. Whether respondent's claims are patentable may determine whether research efforts are accelerated by the hope of reward or slowed by want of incentives, but that is all.

What is more important is that we are without competence to entertain these arguments—either to brush them aside as fantasies generated by fear of the unknown, or to act on them. The choice we are urged to make is a matter of high policy for resolution within the legislative process after the kind of investigation, examination, and study that legislative bodies can provide and courts cannot. That process involves the balancing of competing values and interests, which in our democratic system is the business of elected representatives. Whatever their validity, the contentions now pressed on us should be addressed to the political branches of the Government, the Congress and the Executive, and not to the courts.

We have emphasized in the recent past that "[o]ur individual appraisal of the wisdom or unwisdom of a particular [legislative] course . . . is to be put aside in the process of interpreting a statute." Our task, rather, is the narrow one of determining what Congress meant by the words it used in the statute; once that is done our powers are exhausted. Congress is free to amend § 101 so as to exclude from patent protection organisms produced by genetic engineering. Cf. 42 U.S.C. § 2181(a), exempting from patent protection inventions "useful solely in the utilization of special nuclear material or atomic energy in an atomic weapon." Or it may chose to craft a statute specifically designed for such living things. But, until Congress takes such action, this Court must construe the language of § 101 as it is. The language of that section fairly embraces respondent's invention.

Accordingly, the judgment of the Court of Customs and Patent Appeals is

Affirmed.

■ [The dissenting opinion of JUSTICE BRENNAN, joined by JUSTICES WHITE and MARSHALL, is omitted.]

# State Street Bank & Trust Co. v. Signature Financial Group, Inc.

United States Court of Appeals for the Federal Circuit, 1998.
149 F.3d 1368.

■ RICH, CIRCUIT JUDGE.

Signature Financial Group, Inc. (Signature) [assignee of U.S. Patent No. 5,193,056 (the '056 patent), which issued to R. Todd Boes] appeals from the decision of the United States District Court for the District of Massachusetts granting a motion for summary judgment in favor of State Street Bank & Trust Co. (State Street), finding the '056 invalid on the ground that the claimed subject matter is not encompassed by 35 U.S.C. § 101 (1994). See State Street Bank & Trust Co. v. Signature Financial Group, Inc., 927 F.Supp. 502, 38 USPQ2d 1530 (D.Mass.1996). We reverse and remand because we conclude that the patent claims are directed to statutory subject matter.

DISCUSSION

The following facts pertinent to the statutory subject matter issue are either undisputed or represent the version alleged by the nonmovant. The patented invention relates generally to a system that allows an administrator to monitor and record the financial information flow and make all calculations necessary for maintaining a partner fund financial services configuration. A partner fund financial services configuration essentially allows several mutual funds, or "Spokes," to pool their investment funds into a single portfolio, or "Hub," allowing for consolidation of, inter alia, the costs of administering the fund combined with the tax advantages of a partnership. In particular, this system provides means for a daily allocation of assets for two or more Spokes that are invested in the same Hub. The system determines the percentage share that each Spoke maintains in the Hub, while taking into consideration daily changes both in the value of the Hub's investment securities and in the concomitant amount of each Spoke's assets.

In determining daily changes, the system also allows for the allocation among the Spokes of the Hub's daily income, expenses, and net realized and unrealized gain or loss, calculating each day's total investments based on the concept of a book capital account. This enables the determination of a true asset value of each Spoke and accurate calculation of allocation ratios between or among the Spokes. The system additionally tracks all the relevant data determined on a daily basis for the Hub and each Spoke, so that aggregate year end income, expenses, and capital gain or loss can be determined for accounting and for tax purposes for the Hub and, as a result, for each publicly traded Spoke.

It is essential that these calculations are quickly and accurately performed. In large part this is required because each Spoke sells shares to the public and the price of those shares is substantially based on the Spoke's percentage interest in the portfolio. In some instances, a mutual fund administrator is required to calculate the value of the shares to the nearest penny within as little as an hour and a half after the market closes. Given the complexity of the calculations, a computer or equivalent device is a virtual necessity to perform the task.

The '056 patent application was filed 11 March 1991. It initially contained six "machine" claims, which incorporated means-plus-function clauses, and six method claims. According to Signature, during prosecution the examiner contemplated a § 101 rejection for failure to claim statutory subject matter. However, upon cancellation of the six method claims, the examiner issued a notice of allowance for the remaining present six claims on appeal. Only claim 1 is an independent claim.

The district court began its analysis by construing the claims to be directed to a process, with each "means" clause merely representing a step in that process. However, "machine" claims having "means" clauses may only be reasonably viewed as process claims if there is no supporting structure in the written description that corresponds to the claimed "means" elements. See In re Alappat, 33 F.3d 1526, 1540–41, 31 USPQ2d 1545, 1554 (Fed.Cir.1994) (in banc). This is not the case now before us.

When independent claim 1 is properly construed in accordance with § 112, ¶ 6, it is directed to a machine, as demonstrated below, where representative claim 1 is set forth, the subject matter in brackets stating the structure the written description discloses as corresponding to the respective "means" recited in the claims.

> 1. A data processing system for managing a financial services configuration of a portfolio established as a partnership, each partner being one of a plurality of funds, comprising:
>
> (a) computer processor means [a personal computer including a CPU] for processing data;
>
> (b) storage means [a data disk] for storing data on a storage medium;
>
> (c) first means [an arithmetic logic circuit configured to prepare the data disk to magnetically store selected data] for initializing the storage medium;
>
> (d) second means [an arithmetic logic circuit configured to retrieve information from a specific file, calculate incremental increases or decreases based on specific input, allocate the results on a percentage basis, and store the output in a separate file] for processing data regarding assets in the portfolio and each of the funds from a previous day and data regarding increases or decreases in each of the funds, [sic, funds'] assets and for allocating the percentage share that each fund holds in the portfolio;
>
> (e) third means [an arithmetic logic circuit configured to retrieve information from a specific file, calculate incremental increases and decreases based on specific input, allocate the results on a percentage basis and store the output in a separate file] for processing data regarding daily incremental income, expenses, and net realized gain or loss for the portfolio and for allocating such data among each fund;
>
> (f) fourth means [an arithmetic logic circuit configured to retrieve information from a specific file, calculate incremental increases and decreases based on specific input, allocate the results on a percentage basis and store the output in a separate file] for processing data regarding daily net unrealized gain or loss for the portfolio and for allocating such data among each fund; and
>
> (g) fifth means [an arithmetic logic circuit configured to retrieve information from specific files, calculate that information on an aggregate basis and store the output in a separate file] for processing data regarding aggregate year-end income, expenses, and capital gain or loss for the portfolio and each of the funds.

Each claim component, recited as a "means" plus its function, is to be read, of course, pursuant to § 112, & 6, as inclusive of the "equivalents" of the structures disclosed in the written description portion of the specification. Thus, claim 1, properly construed, claims a machine, namely, a data processing system for managing a financial services configuration of a portfolio established as a partnership, which machine is made up of, at the very least, the specific structures disclosed in the written description and corresponding to the means-plus-function elements (a)-(g) recited in the claim. A "machine" is proper statutory subject matter under § 101. We note that, for the purposes of a § 101 analysis, it is of little relevance whether claim 1 is directed to a "machine" or a "process," as long as it falls within at least one of the four enumerated categories of patentable subject matter, "machine" and "process" being such categories.

This does not end our analysis, however, because the court concluded that the claimed subject matter fell into one of two alternative judicially-created exceptions to statutory subject matter. The court refers to the first exception as the "mathematical algorithm" exception and the second exception as the "business method" exception. Section 101 reads:

> Whoever invents or discovers any new and useful process, machine, manufacture, or composition of matter, or any new and useful improvement thereof, may obtain a patent therefor, subject to the conditions and requirements of this title.

The plain and unambiguous meaning of § 101 is that any invention falling within one of the four stated categories of statutory subject matter may be patented, provided it meets the other requirements for patentability set forth in Title 35, i.e., those found in §§ 102, 103, and 112, & 2.

The repetitive use of the expansive term "any" in § 101 shows Congress's intent not to place any restrictions on the subject matter for which a patent may be obtained beyond those specifically recited in § 101. Indeed, the Supreme Court has acknowledged that Congress intended § 101 to extend to "anything under the sun that is made by man." Diamond v. Chakrabarty, 447 U.S. 303, 309, 100 S.Ct. 2204, 65 L.Ed.2d 144 (1980); see also Diamond v. Diehr, 450 U.S. 175, 182, 101 S.Ct. 1048, 67 L.Ed.2d 155 (1981). Thus, it is improper to read limitations into § 101 on the subject matter that may be patented where the legislative history indicates that Congress clearly did not intend such limitations.

The "Mathematical Algorithm" Exception

The Supreme Court has identified three categories of subject matter that are unpatentable, namely "laws of nature, natural phenomena, and abstract ideas." Diehr, 450 U.S. at 185, 101 S.Ct. 1048. Of particular relevance to this case, the Court has held that mathematical algorithms are not patentable subject matter to the extent that they are merely abstract ideas. See Diehr, 450 U.S. 175, 101 S.Ct. 1048, passim; Parker v. Flook, 437 U.S. 584, 98 S.Ct. 2522, 57 L.Ed.2d 451 (1978); Gottschalk v. Benson, 409 U.S. 63, 93 S.Ct. 253, 34 L.Ed.2d 273 (1972).[a] In Diehr, the Court explained that certain types of mathematical subject matter, standing alone, represent nothing more than abstract ideas until reduced to some type of

---

[a] [*Gottschalk, Parker,* and *Diehr*, the Supreme Court's three attempts to deal with the question whether computer programs are patentable subject matter, are also discussed in Note 2, along with the tests for patentability propounded in their aftermath by the lower courts.—eds.]

practical application, i.e., "a useful, concrete and tangible result." Alappat, 33 F.3d at 1544, 31 USPQ2d at 1557.[b]

Unpatentable mathematical algorithms are identifiable by showing they are merely abstract ideas constituting disembodied concepts or truths that are not "useful." From a practical standpoint, this means that to be patentable an algorithm must be applied in a "useful" way. In Alappat, we held that data, transformed by a machine through a series of mathematical calculations to produce a smooth waveform display on a rasterizer monitor, constituted a practical application of an abstract idea (a mathematical algorithm, formula, or calculation), because it produced "a useful, concrete and tangible result"—the smooth waveform.

Similarly, in Arrhythmia Research Technology Inc. v. Corazonix Corp., 958 F.2d 1053, 22 USPQ2d 1033 (Fed.Cir.1992), we held that the transformation of electrocardiograph signals from a patient's heartbeat by a machine through a series of mathematical calculations constituted a practical application of an abstract idea (a mathematical algorithm, formula, or calculation), because it corresponded to a useful, concrete or tangible thing—the condition of a patient's heart.

Today, we hold that the transformation of data, representing discrete dollar amounts, by a machine through a series of mathematical calculations into a final share price, constitutes a practical application of a mathematical algorithm, formula, or calculation, because it produces "a useful, concrete and tangible result"—a final share price momentarily fixed for recording and reporting purposes and even accepted and relied upon by regulatory authorities and in subsequent trades.

The district court erred by applying the Freeman–Walter–Abele test to determine whether the claimed subject matter was an unpatentable abstract idea. The Freeman–Walter–Abele test was designed by the Court of Customs and Patent Appeals, and subsequently adopted by this court, to extract and identify unpatentable mathematical algorithms in the aftermath of Benson and Flook. See In re Freeman, 573 F.2d 1237, 197 USPQ 464 (CCPA 1978) as modified by In re Walter, 618 F.2d 758, 205 USPQ 397 (CCPA 1980). The test has been thus articulated:

> First, the claim is analyzed to determine whether a mathematical algorithm is directly or indirectly recited. Next, if a mathematical algorithm is found, the claim as a whole is further analyzed to determine whether the algorithm is "applied in any manner to physical elements or process steps," and, if it is, it "passes muster under § 101."

In re Pardo, 684 F.2d 912, 915, 214 USPQ 673, 675–76 (CCPA 1982) (citing In re Abele, 684 F.2d 902, 214 USPQ 682 (CCPA 1982)).

After Diehr and Chakrabarty, the Freeman–Walter–Abele test has little, if any, applicability to determining the presence of statutory subject

---

[b] This has come to be known as the mathematical algorithm exception. This designation has led to some confusion, especially given the Freeman–Walter–Abele analysis. By keeping in mind that the mathematical algorithm is unpatentable only to the extent that it represents an abstract idea, this confusion may be ameliorated.

matter. As we pointed out in Alappat, 33 F.3d at 1543, 31 USPQ2d at 1557, application of the test could be misleading, because a process, machine, manufacture, or composition of matter employing a law of nature, natural phenomenon, or abstract idea is patentable subject matter even though a law of nature, natural phenomenon, or abstract idea would not, by itself, be entitled to such protection. The test determines the presence of, for example, an algorithm. Under Benson, this may have been a sufficient indicium of nonstatutory subject matter. However, after Diehr and Alappat, the mere fact that a claimed invention involves inputting numbers, calculating numbers, outputting numbers, and storing numbers, in and of itself, would not render it nonstatutory subject matter, unless, of course, its operation does not produce a "useful, concrete and tangible result." Alappat, 33 F.3d at 1544, 31 USPQ2d at 1557. After all, as we have repeatedly stated,

> every step-by-step process, be it electronic or chemical or mechanical, involves an algorithm in the broad sense of the term. Since § 101 expressly includes processes as a category of inventions which may be patented and § 100(b) further defines the word "process" as meaning "process, art or method, and includes a new use of a known process, machine, manufacture, composition of matter, or material," it follows that it is no ground for holding a claim is directed to nonstatutory subject matter to say it includes or is directed to an algorithm. This is why the proscription against patenting has been limited to mathematical algorithms. . . .

In re Iwahashi, 888 F.2d 1370, 1374, 12 USPQ2d 1908, 1911 (Fed.Cir. 1989).

The question of whether a claim encompasses statutory subject matter should not focus on which of the four categories of subject matter a claim is directed to—process, machine, manufacture, or composition of matter—but rather on the essential characteristics of the subject matter, in particular, its practical utility. Section 101 specifies that statutory subject matter must also satisfy the other "conditions and requirements" of Title 35, including novelty, nonobviousness, and adequacy of disclosure and notice. See In re Warmerdam, 33 F.3d 1354, 1359, 31 USPQ2d 1754, 1757–58 (Fed.Cir. 1994). For purpose of our analysis, as noted above, claim 1 is directed to a machine programmed with the Hub and Spoke software and admittedly produces a "useful, concrete, and tangible result." Alappat, 33 F.3d at 1544, 31 USPQ2d at 1557. This renders it statutory subject matter, even if the useful result is expressed in numbers, such as price, profit, percentage, cost, or loss.

The Business Method Exception

As an alternative ground for invalidating the '056 patent under § 101, the court relied on the judicially-created, so-called "business method" exception to statutory subject matter. We take this opportunity to lay this ill-conceived exception to rest. Since its inception, the "business method" exception has merely represented the application of some general, but no longer applicable legal principle, perhaps arising out of the "requirement for invention"—which was eliminated by § 103. Since the 1952 Patent Act, business methods have been, and should have been, subject to the same legal requirements for patentability as applied to any other process or method.

The business method exception has never been invoked by this court, or the CCPA, to deem an invention unpatentable. Application of this particular exception has always been preceded by a ruling based on some clearer concept of Title 35 or, more commonly, application of the abstract idea exception based on finding a mathematical algorithm.

State Street argues that we acknowledged the validity of the business method exception in Alappat when we discussed Maucorps and Meyer:

> Maucorps dealt with a business methodology for deciding how salesmen should best handle respective customers and Meyer involved a "system" for aiding a neurologist in diagnosing patients. Clearly, neither of the alleged "inventions" in those cases falls within any § 101 category.

Alappat, 33 F.3d at 1541, 31 USPQ2d at 1555. However, closer scrutiny of these cases reveals that the claimed inventions in both Maucorps and Meyer were rejected as abstract ideas under the mathematical algorithm exception, not the business method exception. See In re Maucorps, 609 F.2d 481, 484, 203 USPQ 812, 816 (CCPA 1979); In re Meyer, 688 F.2d 789, 796, 215 USPQ 193, 199 (CCPA 1982).

Even the case frequently cited as establishing the business method exception to statutory subject matter, Hotel Security Checking Co. v. Lorraine Co., 160 F. 467 (2d Cir.1908), did not rely on the exception to strike the patent. In that case, the patent was found invalid for lack of novelty and "invention," not because it was improper subject matter for a patent. The court stated "the fundamental principle of the system is as old as the art of bookkeeping, i.e., charging the goods of the employer to the agent who takes them." Id. at 469. "If at the time of [the patent] application, there had been no system of bookkeeping of any kind in restaurants, we would be confronted with the question whether a new and useful system of cash registering and account checking is such an art as is patentable under the statute." Id. at 472.

This case is no exception. The district court announced the precepts of the business method exception as set forth in several treatises, but noted as its primary reason for finding the patent invalid under the business method exception as follows:

> If Signature's invention were patentable, any financial institution desirous of implementing a multi-tiered funding complex modelled (sic) on a Hub and Spoke configuration would be required to seek Signature's permission before embarking on such a project. This is so because the '056 Patent is claimed [sic] sufficiently broadly to foreclose virtually any computer-implemented accounting method necessary to manage this type of financial structure.

927 F.Supp. 502, 516, 38 USPQ2d 1530, 1542. Whether the patent's claims are too broad to be patentable is not to be judged under § 101, but rather under §§ 102, 103 and 112. Assuming the above statement to be correct, it has nothing to do with whether what is claimed is statutory subject matter.

In view of this background, it comes as no surprise that in the most recent edition of the Manual of Patent Examining Procedures (MPEP) (1996), a paragraph of § 706.03(a) was deleted. In past editions it read:

> Though seemingly within the category of process or method, a method of doing business can be rejected as not being within the statutory classes. See Hotel Security Checking Co. v. Lorraine Co., 160 F. 467 (2nd Cir.1908) and In re Wait, 24 USPQ 88, 22 C.C.P.A. 822, 73 F.2d 982 (1934).

MPEP § 706.03(a) (1994). This acknowledgment is buttressed by the U.S. Patent and Trademark 1996 Examination Guidelines for Computer Related Inventions which now read:

> Office personnel have had difficulty in properly treating claims directed to methods of doing business. Claims should not be categorized as methods of doing business. Instead such claims should be treated like any other process claims.

Examination Guidelines, 61 Fed.Reg. 7478, 7479 (1996). We agree that this is precisely the manner in which this type of claim should be treated. Whether the claims are directed to subject matter within § 101 should not turn on whether the claimed subject matter does "business" instead of something else.

CONCLUSION

The appealed decision is reversed and the case is remanded to the district court for further proceedings consistent with this opinion.

NOTES

**1.** *Ideas vs. embodiments.* The difficulty in drawing a line between an idea, or a principle of nature, and its embodiment became evident early in patent law's history. In particular, consider two early cases, O'Reilly v. Morse,[6] involving the patent on the telegraph, and Dolbear v. American Bell Telephone Co. ("the Telephone Cases").[7] Commentators have long had difficulty explaining how the Supreme Court could have invalidated the eighth claim in Samuel F.B. Morse's patent on the telegraph on the ground that it claimed a principle rather than an embodiment, yet uphold the fifth claim of Alexander Graham Bell's patent on the telephone. Morse's claim read as follows:

> "Eighth. I do not propose to limit myself to the specific machinery ... described in the foregoing specification and claims; the essence of my invention being the use of the motive power of the electric or galvanic current, which I call electro-magnetism, however developed, for making or printing intelligible characters (letters or signs), at any distances ..."

Bell claimed:

[6] 56 U.S. (15 How.) 62 (1854).    [7] 126 U.S. 1 (1888).

"The method of, and apparatus for, transmitting vocal or other sounds telegraphically, as herein described, by causing electrical undulations, similar in form to the vibrations of the air accompanying the said vocal or other sounds, substantially as set forth."

As to *Morse,* the Supreme Court said:

"If this claim can be maintained, it matters not by what process or machinery the result is accomplished. For aught that we now know some future inventor, in the onward march of science, may discover a mode of writing or printing at a distance by means of the electric or galvanic current, without using any part of the process or combination set forth in the plaintiff's specification.... But yet if it is covered by this patent the inventor could not use it, nor the public have the benefit of it without the permission of this patentee."[8]

In contrast, in *The Telephone Cases,* the Court held:

"The patent for the art does not necessarily involve a patent for the particular means employed for using it. Indeed, the mention of any means ... is only necessary to show that the art can be used.... "[9]

Admittedly, Bell drafted his claim so that it would appear limited to "undulations." In contrast, Morse made very clear that his claim was meant to be broad. Yet in actual fact, both claims are equally drawn to principles, in Morse's case, the principle of using the wave properties of electromagnetism to transmit signs; in Bell's, the principle of using its oscillations to transmit sound. And so, the Supreme Court's concern that Morse was tying up basic building blocks of knowledge and extending the reach of his claim to those who were not utilizing his insight is equally applicable to Bell.

To be sure, *The Telephone Cases* tried to distinguish *Morse:*

"In the present case the claim is not for the use of a current of electricity in its natural state as it comes from the battery, but for putting a continuous current in a closed circuit into a certain specified condition suited to the transmission of vocal and other sounds, and using it in that condition for that purpose."[10]

However, the argument is somewhat less than convincing.[11]

Rather than indulge in similar talmudic distinctions,[12] the lower courts invented a series of "rules of thumb" to help draw the line between

[8] 56 U.S. (15 How.) at 113.

[9] 126 U.S. at 533.

[10] Id. at 534.

[11] See, e.g., Donald S. Chisum, Patents § 1.03[2].

[12] In In re Wait, 73 F.2d 982 (C.C.P.A. 1934), for example, the applicant claimed a process for the exchange of stocks and commodities that obviated the need for a broker. The court rejected the claims as drawn to non-statutory subject matter, holding:

The process, when analyzed carefully, appears to comprise, in its essence, nothing more than the advertising of, or giving publicity to, offers of purchase or sale by one party, the acceptance thereof by another, and the making of a record of the transaction followed by a withdrawal of the offer. Surely these are, and

principles and the embodiments. Among the inventions considered unpatentable were business systems,[13] printed matter,[14] functions-of-machines,[15] mental steps, and methods dependent on human reactions.[16] Although later courts rightly rejected these doctrines as too simplistic,[17] the cases cited in *State Street Bank* illustrate that line drawing remains a difficult problem.

**2.** *Computer Programs.* Because the mental-steps doctrine considered any series of steps that *could* be performed in a person's head unpatentable, it was clear from the dawn of the computer era that software would pose problems to patent law. But surprisingly, the first Court to consider them put its objection in more general terms. Thus, in Gottschalk v. Benson,[18] the issue was whether a computerized method for converting numerals

always have been, essential steps in all dealings of this nature, and even conceding, without holding, that some methods of doing business might present patentable novelty, we think such novelty is lacking here.

73 F.2d at 983. See also, e.g., Hotel Security Checking Co. v. Lorraine Co., 160 F. 467 (2d Cir.1908).

[13] See, e.g., Ex parte Gwinn, 112 U.S.P.Q. (BNA) 439 (P.Bd.App. 1955).

[14] Wyeth v. Stone, 30 F.Cas. 723 (No. 18,107) (C.C.D. Mass.1840) is a good example. The patentee had invented a new machine to cut ice. His patent read: "It is claimed, as new, to cut ice of a uniform size, by means of an apparatus worked by any other power than human." Justice Story (riding Circuit) invalidated the claim, stating:

It is a claim for an art or principle in the abstract, and not for any particular method of machinery, by which ice is to be cut. No man can have a right to cut ice by all means or methods, or by all or any sort of apparatus, although he is not the inventor of any or all such means, methods, or apparatus. A claim broader than the actual invention of the patentee is, for that very reason, upon the principles of the common law, utterly void ...

30 F.Cas. at 730. Later courts distinguished between claims drawn to particular machines and claims drawn to the "function of the machine," see, e.g., Corning v. Burden, 56 U.S. (15 How.) 252, 14 L.Ed. 683 (1853).

[15] Halliburton Oil Well Cementing Co. v. Walker, 146 F.2d 817 (9th Cir.1944), is most often cited. There, the court invalidated Walker's patent on a method for determining the location of an obstruction in a well, noting:

In substance, Walker's method here claimed consists in setting down three knowns in a simple equation and from them determining or computing an unknown. The three knowns are: (a) the distance from the well head to the tubing catcher (for example); (b) the length of time it takes an echo to return from that obstruction; and (c) the length of time it takes an echo to return from the fluid surface. From these three knowns can then be determined the distance of the fluid surface from the well head.

* * *

It must be remembered that this is purely a method patent. No apparatus is claimed. Given an apparatus for initiating an impulse wave in a well and a means for differentiating between and for recording echoes returned from obstruction in it, anybody with a rudimentary knowledge of arithmetic will be able to do what Walker claims a monopoly of doing. If his method were patentable it seems to us that the patentee would have a monopoly much broader than would the patentee of a particular apparatus....

146 F.2d at 821–22.

[16] See, e.g., Ex parte Turner, 1894 Comm'n Dec. 36.

[17] See, e.g., Application of Tarczy–Hornoch, 397 F.2d 856 (C.C.P.A.1968)(overruling the function-of-machine doctrine). Cf. Cincinnati Traction Co. v. Pope, 210 Fed. 443 (C.C.A.6 1913)(casting some doubt on the printed-matter doctrine and the business-method doctrine).

[18] 409 U.S. 63 (1972).

expressed as binary-coded decimals into pure binary numerals was a patentable process. The Court held it was not. Justice Douglas explained:

> "It is conceded that one may not patent an idea. But in practical effect, that would be the result if the formula for converting binary code to pure binary were patented in this case. The mathematical formula involved here has no substantial practical application except in connection with a digital computer, which means that if the judgment below is affirmed, the patent would wholly pre-empt the mathematical formula and in practical effect would be a patent on the algorithm itself."[19]

After the defeat in *Benson*, many patent applicants changed their strategy. Instead of applying for patents on mathematical manipulations, they tried to conform their claims to the process paradigm described by Cochrane v. Deener. That tack was first reviewed by the Supreme Court in Parker v. Flook.[20] In that case, the claims were drawn to a physical reaction: the catalytic conversion of hydrocarbons. The process used a computer program to continuously monitor a set of variables, compare changes in the variables, and signal abnormalities so that the reaction could be stopped. Flook was careful to stress the chemical changes occurring in the course of using his program rather than focus on the operation of the program itself. Nonetheless, the Court held the claim unpatentable, saying that a "conventional, post-solution application" that was well known in the art could not turn a rule of nature into patentable subject matter.

Four years later, in Diamond v. Diehr,[21] the Court returned to the question, but this time it provided an answer more favorable to those who thought patent rights necessary to the continued vitality of the computer field. The invention at issue in *Diehr* was a process for curing rubber in a mold. The essentials of the process were commonly used in the rubber manufacturing industry, but it was not efficient as it was difficult to calculate when the rubber should be released from the mold. Diehr's solution coupled a standard device for measuring temperature to a computer programmed to use the well-known Arrhenius rate equation to continuously calculate the curing time from the temperature and signal when the curing process was finished. The Court found that:

> "The 'Arrhenius' equation is not patentable in isolation, but when a process for curing rubber is devised which incorporates in it a more efficient solution of the equation, that process is at the very least not barred at the threshold by § 101."[22]

Despite the promise *Diehr* held for computer patents, implementing its holding proved difficult. The striking similarity between the processes at issue in *Flook* and *Diehr*, coupled with *Diehr*'s failure to articulate a standard for drawing the elusive line between ideas and embodiments,

---

[19] Id. at 71–72. Justice Douglas defined "algorithm" as "[a] procedure for solving a given type of mathematical problem," id. at 65.

[20] 437 U.S. 584 (1978).

[21] 450 U.S. 175 (1981).

[22] Id. at 188.

spawned much confusion and, as *State Street Bank* shows, several lines of cases. The *Freeman–Walter Abele* analysis was the product of the Court of Claims and Patent Appeals (CCPA), which at the time of the first generation of computer cases was the court that reviewed PTO decisions. Based on the language in *Benson*, it attempted to decide whether any algorithms recited in a claim in fact preempted a principle of nature. The Court of Appeals for the Federal Circuit, which replaced the CCPA in 1982, continued to cite this test, but also looked for specific limitations. In In re Alappat,[23] the limiting embodiment was the machine that executes the program. In In re Grams,[24] the embodiment was the physical process that the program mediates. The entire process was considered patentable, but only if it involved more than "mere" post-solution activity (the problem in *Flook*) or the gathering of data (which the court considered a problem in *Grams*). Dissatisfaction with these efforts was, however, rampant. The PTO released guidelines to help examiners (and the public); these have been updated and are available at the PTO website.

In fact, many observers thought the problem was not in articulating a way to decide when a patent preempts a principle, but rather in *Benson* itself. Some thought Justice Douglas incorrect in assuming that algorithms always recite rules of nature. In their view, mathematical notation is just a form of language; it is sometimes used to express principles of nature, but not always. Sometimes math expresses thoughts that could be said, albeit at greater length, in English.[25] When that is the case, there is no problem in allowing the patent to protect all uses of the algorithm. Others arrived at the same conclusion by noting that even programs that are about rules of nature rarely utilize the actual principles. That is because principles of nature are too complicated to use in commercially significant applications; the inventive feature may well be the way the program simplifies the actual principle without losing its relevance to the problem at hand. In a concurring opinion to the *Arrhythmia* decision discussed in *State Street Bank*, Judge Rader had the following to say about the patentability of a program that analyzes electrocardiograph signals in order to determine certain characteristics of heart function in the hours immediately after a heart attack:

> "While many ... steps involve the mathematical manipulation of data, the claims do not describe a law of nature or a natural phenomenon. Furthermore the claims do not disclose mere abstract ideas, but a practical and potentially life-saving process. Regardless of whether performed by computer, these steps comprise a 'process' within the meaning of § 101."[26]

*State Street Bank* was decided against this backdrop. How well does it deal with the problems that computer-implemented inventions have gener-

---

[23] 33 F.3d 1526 (Fed. Cir. 1994).

[24] 888 F.2d 835 (Fed. Cir. 1989).

[25] See, e.g., In re Meyer, 688 F.2d 789 (C.C.P.A. 1982).

[26] Arrhythmia Research Technology, Inc. v. Corazonix Corp., 958 F.2d 1053, 1060 (Fed. Cir. 1992).

ated? Has the Federal Circuit now rejected *Benson*? See also AT & T Corp. v. Excel Communications, Inc.[27] The patent in that case, entitled "Call Message Recording for Telephone Systems," covers methodology that aids long-distance carriers in providing differential billing treatment for subscribers, depending upon whether a subscriber calls someone with the same or a different long-distance carrier. Although the process basically involves plugging data about subscribers' and call recipients' primary interchange carriers (PICs) into an algebraic formula that then produces a billing record, the court upheld the patent. As to *Benson*, the court reasoned:

> "[The Court] never intended to create an overly broad, fourth category of [mathematical] subject matter excluded from § 101. Rather, at the core of the Court's analysis . . . lies an attempt by the Court to explain a rather straightforward concept, namely, that certain types of mathematical subject matter, standing alone, represent nothing more than abstract ideas until reduced to some type of practical application, and thus that subject matter is not, in and of itself, entitled to patent protection."[28]

On *Diehr*, the court stated:

> "The notion of 'physical transformation' can be misunderstood. In the first place, it is not an invariable requirement, but merely one example of how a mathematical algorithm may bring about a useful application."[29]

How well does the "useful, concrete, and tangible result" test for patentable subject matter deal the concern that fundamental relationships will become subject to private ownership? Does this liberal formulation do enough to prevent patentees from tying up applications of principles of nature, including applications they have not invented? In this connection, note that claims drafted in "means plus function" form allow a patentee to assert as infringing devices and practices utilizing an equivalent of the means shown, see the discussion of means plus function claiming in the Lipschitz patent in Assignment 14. Moreover, the patentee's right of action is not confined to literal infringement. As with copyright's substantial similarity test and trademark's confusing similarity test, patentees can assert rights against those who use "equivalents" of their inventions. See Assignment 21, Notes 2 and 7. Thus, it may be that claims meeting the requirements of *State Street Bank* will be quite broad.

At the same time, however, this test means that highly abstract lines will not need to be drawn at a time when the significance of the invention (both commercial and scientific) are unknowable. If it becomes clear that a patent is overly broad, the public domain can be protected in other ways. First, an application could be rejected for failure to meet the specification requirement: as the Introductory Assignment explained, § 112 requires the patentee to provide a written description of the invention and enough information about it to enable persons with skill in the art to practice the

---

[27] 172 F.3d 1352 (Fed. Cir. 1999).
[28] Id. at 1357.

[29] Id. at 1358.

invention. In Fiers v. Revel, the court held that a description of how to isolate DNA was inadequate as a "written description" within the meaning of the statute on the ground that a less stringent rule would allow patentees "to preempt the future before it has arrived."[30] Second, § 112 can be used to reject an attempt to enforce a patent against a later-discovered technology that was not enabled by the disclosure.[31] Third, narrow tests of infringement can be adopted. Nonetheless, problems in this area remain, see Note 5.

**3.** *Business methods. State Street Bank* is clearly of considerable importance to the computer industry. However, its real significance is to the business sector. As we saw, one of the old rules of thumb held business methods unpatentable. Although use of thumbs to decide abstract issues was long questionable, prior to the software cases, there was general agreement that business methods were not among the technologies at which patent law was directed. Once processes using programs became patentable, however, business methods dependant on software were drawn into the fold. In Paine, Webber, Jackson & Curtis, Inc. v. Merrill, Lynch, Pierce, Fenner & Smith, Inc.,[32] for example, the court upheld the patent on a "Cash Management Account" that used a computer to track clients' deposits in a brokerage securities account, a money market fund, and a Visa charge/checking account.

*State Street Bank* arguably takes this approach one step further: by unequivocally rejecting the business method exception, it appears to make *all* business methods susceptible to patenting, even those that do not involve computers. Is this wise? Michael Milken made a fortune selling high risk bonds offering substantial interest. These "junk bonds" proved very popular in the market; many acquisitions have been financed with them. How much more would Milken have made had he been able to patent junk bonds or the process of using them to raise capital? Could the airline that first thought up frequent flyer miles have gained an even greater competitive advantage by patenting the practice of awarding them? How about protection for the tools of other professions: should sports moves—pitches, end-zone wiggles, high jumps—be patentable? Novel legal theories?[33] The next technique for avoiding the strictures of campaign finance reform? A method of launching a research project?[34]

Judge Rich rejected both the mathematical algorithm and business method exceptions on the ground that they are not supported by § 101. But the prohibitions on patenting laws of nature, natural phenomena, or abstract ideas are not found in the statute either. Important policies

---

[30] 984 F.2d 1164, 1171 (Fed.Cir. 1993).

[31] Arguably, this is exactly how this problem is being handled in the biotechnology context, see, e.g., Enzo Biochem, Inc. v. Gen–Probe Inc., 323 F.3d 956 (Fed. Cir. 2002); Fiers v. Sugano, 984 F.2d 1164 (Fed. Cir. 1993).

[32] 564 F.Supp. 1358 (D.Del. 1983).

[33] See John R. Thomas, The Patenting of the Liberal Professions, 40 Boston College L. Rev. 1139(1999).

[34] Cf., e.g., U.S. Patent 6,584,450, Method and apparatus for renting items, which was awarded to Netflix for its method for renting a fixed number of items (such as three DVDs) at a time.

support these prohibitions: are there equally good reasons to leave business methods in the public domain, where all competitors can utilize them? Is the investment Milken made in convincing the market that junk bonds, though novel, are respectable investment vehicles, the kind of investment patent law is aimed at encouraging? Was the Supreme Court wise to deny *certiorari* in *State Street Bank*?[35] Can the problem of preserving business competition be solved by developing a narrow perspective on what is considered infringement of a business method patent?[36]

**4.** *Biologicals.* To a large extent, the patent problem facing biology mirrors the saga of computer programs. Cell lines and DNA (whether naturally occurring or artificially produced) are not only commercial products, they are also the tools of basic biological research. Indeed patents on biological products present obstacles to biologists. They may hinder innovation and ensnare inventors who use the product in ways not enabled by the patentee. In addition, as with the computer cases, applicants for patents on the "new" biologicals had to deal with some old "rules of thumb."

**a.** *Material derived from living organisms.* An early case here is Funk Brothers Seed Co. v. Kalo Inoculant Co.,[37] discussed in *Chakrabarty.* The invention was a culture of nitrogen-fixing bacteria used to inoculate plant seeds. Many strains of bacteria were prepared in a laboratory and combined in order to make a product useful to a broad range of plants. The Supreme Court held the preparation not patentable on the ground that each bacterium is a "manifestation of laws of nature, free to all men and reserved exclusively to none."[38]

*Funk*'s apparent unwillingness to extend patent protection to artificially-enhanced naturally occurring materials was, however, short lived. In 1947, after years of unsuccessful efforts, researchers of Merck & Co. isolated the active substance that gave cow liver its therapeutic benefits to anemia patients. A patent issued on the successful product, termed vitamin $B_{12}$. In Merck & Co. v. Olin Mathieson Chemical Corp.,[39] the Fourth Circuit upheld the validity of the patent over a challenge that the product was naturally occurring. In the course of the opinion, the court rejected the argument that vitamin $B_{12}$ was not patentable subject matter because it was merely a purification of living materials:

> "The fact ... that a new and useful product is the result of processes of extraction, concentration and purification of natural materials does not defeat its patentability.

. . . . .

[35] See 525 U.S. 1093 (1999). Now that the U.S. protects business method patents, the rest of the world also needs to consider them. For the European perspective, see http://europa.eu.int/eur-lex/en/com/pdf/2002/en_502PC0092.pdf.

[36] See, e.g., Wang Laboratories, Inc. v. America Online, Inc., 197 F.3d 1377 (Fed.Cir. 1999) and Note 5.

[37] 333 U.S. 127, 130 (1948).

[38] Id. at 130.

[39] 253 F.2d 156 (4th Cir.1958).

"The compositions of the patent here ... never existed before; there was nothing comparable to them. If we regard them as a purification of the active principle in natural fermentates, the natural fermentates are quite useless, while the patented compositions are of great medicinal and commercial value. The step from complete uselessness to great and perfected utility is a long one. That step is no mere advance in the degree of purity of a known product."[40]

Of course, prior to *Chakrabarty, Funk* could also have been read as prohibiting the patenting of living things. But since *Chakrabarty,* the PTO has taken the position that all non-human living things that are artificially produced are patentable.[41]

**b.** *Medicine.* The seminal case is Morton v. New York Eye Infirmary,[42] which invalidated the patent on ether as used to anesthetize surgical patients. This was probably the single most important discovery in the science of surgery, for no matter how successful a procedure, there had always been a danger that a patient would die of shock. In finding the patent invalid, the *Morton* court cited several grounds: ether was known, the effect of inhaling it was known, and the invention was dependent on human reaction. Furthermore, at the time of *Morton,* the Patent Act did not provide for process patents in the manner of § 101. Nonetheless, there is a strong suspicion that the real ground for *Morton* was the notion that life-saving procedures should not be privately owned. Indeed, one of the first significant medical substances to be patented was the scarlet fever vaccine, and the decision to patent it was greeted with substantial criticism on precisely this ground. Interestingly, the inventors, George and Gladys Dick, tried to defend their action on humanitarian grounds, claiming that the patent enabled them to control quality.[43] And although numerous decisions have upheld patents on medicines since *Morton,*[44] the debate over the propriety of patents in the field has not abated.[45]

**c.** *The property analogy.* Another manifestation of the concern over granting exclusive rights in biological materials is evident in the debate over whether the law should consider body parts as property. Some people

[40] 253 F.2d at 163. In support, the court quoted from Judge Learned Hand's opinion in Parke–Davis & Co. v. H. K. Mulford Co., 189 Fed. 95 (S.D.N.Y.1911), aff'd, 196 F. 496 (2d Cir.1912), upholding a patent on "Adrenalin," a substance isolated and purified from suprarenal glands of living animals.

[41] See, e.g., Ex parte Allen, 2 U.S.P.Q.2d (BNA) 1425 (Bd.Pat.App. & Int. 1987)(upholding a patent on a polyploid pacific oyster); U.S. Pat. No. 4,736,866 (patent on the so-called "Harvard mouse").

[42] 17 F.Cas. 879 (C.C.S.D.N.Y. 1862).

[43] See Charles Weiner, Patenting and Academic Research: Historical Case Studies, in Owning Scientific and Technical Information

(V. Weil and J. Snapper, eds.)(Rutgers Univ. Press 1989).

[44] See, e.g., Ex parte Scherer, 103 U.S.P.Q. (BNA) 107 (P.T.O. Bd. App.1954); Dick v. Lederle Antitoxin Laboratories, 43 F.2d 628 (S.D.N.Y.1930). See generally, Gregory Burch, Ethical Considerations in the Patenting of Medical Processes, 65 Tex. L. Rev. 1139 (1987).

[45] See, e.g., Bruce Nussbaum, Good Intentions: How Big Business and the Medical Establishment are Corrupting the Fight Against AIDS, Alzheimer's, Cancer, and More (Penguin Books 1990).

argue that recognizing such rights would be a species of slavery.[46] Another rationale for rejecting the property analogy is that ownership of rights to body parts will impede research.

Consider, for example, Moore v. University of California.[47] John Moore had had his spleen removed at UCLA Medical Center as part of his treatment for hairy-cell leukemia. Doctors required him to return to the Center from his home in Seattle on a number of occasions so they could take further samples of blood, blood serum, skin, bone marrow aspirate, and sperm. Unbeknownst to him, these samples were used not for treatment, but to grow a cell line of his T-lymphocytes, which was later patented and subject to lucrative licensing agreements. Moore sued on, among other things, a theory of tortious conversion, asserting that the samples and cell line were his property. In rejecting his claim, the court stated:

"The extension of conversion law into this area will hinder research by restricting access to the necessary raw materials. Thousands of human cell lines already exist in tissue repositories, such as the American Type Culture Collection and those operated by the National Institutes of Health and the American Cancer Society. These repositories respond to tens of thousands of requests for samples annually. Since the patent office requires the holders of patents on cell lines to make samples available to anyone, many patent holders place their cell lines in repositories to avoid the administrative burden of responding to requests. At present, human cell lines are routinely copied and distributed to other researchers for experimental purposes, usually free of charge. This exchange of scientific materials, which still is relatively free and efficient, will surely be compromised if each cell sample becomes the potential subject matter of a lawsuit.

"To expand liability by extending conversion law into this area would have a broad impact. The House Committee on Science and Technology of the United States Congress found that '49 percent of the researchers at medical institutions surveyed used human tissues or cells in their research.' Many receive grants from the National Institute of Health for this work. In addition, 'there are nearly 350 commercial biotechnology firms in the United States actively engaged in biotechnology research and commercial product development and approximately 25 to 30 percent appear to be engaged in research to develop a human therapeutic or diagnostic reagent.... Most, but not all, of the human

---

[46] Cf. Davis v. Davis, 842 S.W.2d 588 (Tenn.1992)(rejecting the notion that frozen embryos are property), cert. denied sub nom. Stowe v. Davis, 507 U.S. 911 (1993). See generally, Kevin D. DeBre', Note, Patents on People and the U.S. Constitution: Creating Slaves or Enslaving, 16 Hastings Const. L.Q. 221 (1989). Indeed, when the PTO announced that it would examine claims to non-

human animals, it stated that it regarded claims to human beings as prohibited by the Constitution, presumably the Thirteenth Amendment, see Nonnaturally Occurring Non–Human Animals are Patentable Under § 101, 33 Pat. Trademark & Copyright J. 884 (1987)

[47] 51 Cal.3d 120, 271 Cal.Rptr. 146, 793 P.2d 479 (1990)(en banc).

therapeutic products are derived from human tissues and cells, or human cell lines or cloned genes.' "

**5.** *Emerging problems.* The recognition of new categories of patentable subject matter can create significant transition problems. The PTO must hire examiners with enough experience in the new field to examine applications effectively. If the field is not new, then the PTO must also develop a library of prior art against which to determine claims of novelty and nonobviousness. Sometimes new examining approaches are also necessary. Because business methods are often put directly into practice (rather than described in journals), there is a paucity of public documentation available anywhere. As a result, the Office has been criticized for not citing relevant prior art and for issuing patents on methods long in use.[48] The PTO has instituted a series of checks to make sure examining in this field is accurate.[49] For a time, the industry took matters into its own hand and created a website that offered rewards for locating invalidating prior art. The site was apparently unsuccessful.[50] Commentators have suggested other changes in the patent-granting system to reduce the number of invalid or overbroad patents.[51]

In time, the problems in the new fields of software, business methods, and biotechnology will surely abate. However, in the interim, there is considerable uncertainty, and that has ramifications of its own. When the validity or the scope of issued patents is unclear, investors may hesitate to invest, for they would not want to find themselves on the wrong end of a successful infringement suit. Those who choose to participate in the field may begin to patent "defensively." That is, they may apply for patents not because they want to protect their investment in a technology they plan to use, but rather because they need bargaining chips—material that they can cross license, or counterclaims that they can assert, should anyone sue them for infringement. This vicious cycle of patenting and defensive patenting creates even more work for the PTO and—arguably—further chills entry into the field because every potential participant must then negotiate her way through a thicket of patents to determine whether she can freely pursue her business objectives. If she can't, then considerable negotiation may be required to put together the needed package of patent rights.[52]

New categories of invention also pose problems to lawmakers. Although patent law is nominally trans-substantive—the same rules apply to

---

[48] See, e.g., Rochelle Cooper Dreyfuss, Are Business Method Patents Bad For Business? 16 Santa Clara Computer & High Tech. L.J. 263 (2000). For a contrasting view on the value of business method patents, see Robert P. Merges, The Uninvited Guest: Patents on Wall Street, available at //papers.ssrn.com/sol3/papers.cfm?abstract_id=410900.

[49] See http://www.uspto.gov/web/offices/com/sol/actionplan.html.

[50] It was found at www.bountyquest.com.

[51] See, e.g., Robert P. Merges, As Many as Six Impossible Patents Before Breakfast: Property Rights for Business Concepts and Patent System Reform, 14 Berkeley Tech. L.J. 577 (1999).

[52] See Michael A. Heller & Rebecca S. Eisenberg, Can Patents Deter Innovation? The Anticommons in Biomedical Research, 280 Science 698 (1998).

every technology—in practice, the law takes the particularities of each field into account. For example, patent law determines inventiveness by looking at whether the invention could have been made by a person of ordinary skill in the art; infringement is partly determined by what a person with ordinary skill can figure out from the patent disclosure. In a field's early years, what the ordinary person knows changes rapidly and courts must keep up with that evolution. In biotechnology, courts may now have too low a conception of what the person knows, with the result that many patents issue, but they are not valuable enough to protect investors' legitimate interests. In contrast, it may be that in the computer industry, the level of knowledge is set too high.[53]

Finally, even after it is clear that a field should be the subject of patent protection, there may be specific issues meriting special treatment. For example, in the wake of recent cases expanding the subject matter of patents, Congress has enacted two provisions limiting their scope. To cope with the possibility that a business method patent will issue on a method already in use, Congress enacted the First Inventor Defense, also known as a prior user right. This is a defense to infringement in favor of any person who:

"acting in good faith, actually reduced the subject matter [of a business method patent] to practice at least one year before the effective filing date of such patent, and commercially used the subject matter before the effective filing date of such patent."[54]

In order to prevent the first inventor from competing away all patent profits, the defense can be asserted only by the party who established the defense and it can only be used with respect to the specific subject matter claimed.[55] How this defense will work in practice remains to be seen. Among other things, it will require courts to decide which inventions are business methods, thereby introducing into patent law a distinction that Judge Rich had hoped to obliterate.

Another example is a special provision enacted after it became clear that medical procedures (such as new types of incisions) are patentable subject matter. Congress became concerned that these patents would limit access to, and increase the price of, important medical methods, without any indication that physicians and surgeons needed a patent incentive to perfect their methods. Instead of changing the subject matter provisions of the statute, an amendment was made to the damages provision. It provides that a medical practitioner's performance of a medical activity that constitutes infringement cannot be the basis for monetary or injunctive relief against the medical practitioner or a health related care entity.[56]

In the same vein, some have argued that special legislation should be enacted to bar patents on biological research tools or to create a defense to

[53] See Dan L. Burk and Mark A. Lemley, Is Patent Law Technology–Specific?, 17 Berkeley Tech. L.J. 1155 (2002).

[54] § 273(b)(1).

[55] § 273(b)(6) & (b)(3)(C).

[56] § 287(c).

infringement when these tools are used for noncommercial purposes.[57] Others suggest that in the software and business method areas, special treatment should be accorded to industrial standards—inventions that an entire industry must share for compatibility or other reasons.[58]

**6.** *Non-utility patents.* The focus of this case book is on utility patents, but it is important to recognize that the law provides patent, or patent-like, protection to two other kinds of subject matter, plants and designs.

   a.  *Plants.* Plants are protected under two different statutes. The Plant Patent Act, §§ 161–164 of the Patent Act, creates rights in new and distinct plants that are asexually reproduced, while the Plant Variety Protection Act (PVPA), 7 U.S.C.A. §§ 2321–2583, creates rights in sexually reproduced plants. The PVPA is wholly administered by the Department of Agriculture, which assists the Commissioner of Patents with administering the Plant Patent Act. These statutes differ from standard patent law by substituting for the specification requirement of § 112, a requirement that the patentee place a sample of the protected plant on deposit, where it can be studied by others. The PVPA also differs from patent law in that it contains research and farmer's crop exemptions and a compulsory license provision. After *Chakrabarty,* there was a question whether the limitations of the PVPA can be avoided by applying for utility patents instead. In 2001, the Supreme Court answered that question in the affirmative.[59]

   b.  *Designs.* Sections 171–173 of the Patent Act create patent rights in new, original, and ornamental designs for articles of manufacture. The terms "new" and "original" have essentially the same meaning as they have for utility patents. Applications are scrutinized for nonobviousness and also to make sure that the design is ornamental rather than primarily functional. Infringement is determined in a manner rather similar to the way that copyright infringement is analyzed. However, the term of protection is shorter (14 years).

Design patents are sometimes thought of as protecting designs that are so inseparable from function that they cannot be protected by copyright, see Assignment 8. While it is nice to think that patent law takes up exactly where copyright leaves off, this notion is true to only a limited extent. First, § 171 specifies that a design must be "ornamental." Designs that are dictated purely by functional considerations are not any more eligible for patent protection than they are for copyright protection. Thus, purely functional designs—for instance, dashboards and refrigerator panels—receive no protection under U.S. patent law *or* copyright law.[60] The tendency

---

[57] See, e.g., Rebecca S. Eisenberg, Technology Transfer And The Genome Project: Problems With Patenting Research Tools, 5 Risk: Health Safety & Env't 163 (1994).

[58] See Janice M. Mueller, Patenting Industry Standards, 34 J. Marshall L. Rev. 897 (2001); Mark Lemley, Standardizing Government Standard–Setting Policy for Electronic

Commerce, 14 Berkeley Tech. L.J. 745 (1999).

[59] J.E.M. AG Supply, Inc. v. Pioneer Hi–Bred Intern., Inc., 534 U.S. 124 (2001).

[60] The exception is the boat hull, which since 1998 has its own statutory scheme in 17 U.S.C. §§ 1301–1332. Despite its narrow focus on boat hulls, this long and involved statute is entitled "Protection of Original De-

has been to try to acquire trademark rights in some feature of a successful design, but this is a problem too as it creates a term of protection that is far too long. In the view of many commentators, the absence of effective protection has put American designers and consumer product manufacturers in a competitively uncomfortable position.

Second, even for designs that fit within the legislative scheme, the general consensus is that the design statute does not work particularly well. The extensiveness of the examination system is a problem because a patent may not issue until after the popularity of the design has peaked. Moreover, decisions on what is nonobvious and what is an infringement tend to be very subjective. Congress has from time to time considered new design legislation, but has never acted.[61]

---

signs," and there is reason to believe that Congress is using this protection to test the waters for devising better protection for other functional designs. See Graeme B. Dinwoodie Essay: The Integration of International and Domestic Intellectual Property Lawmaking 23 Colum.-VLA J.L. & Arts 307 (2000) and Assignment 8.

[61] See William T. Fryer, Industrial Design Protection in the United States of America—Present Situation and Plans for Revision, 70 J.Pat.Off.Soc. 821 (1988); J.H. Reichman, Design Protection and the New Technologies: The United States Experience in a Transnational Perspective, 19 U.Balt.L.Rev. 6 (1991).

# ASSIGNMENT 16

# UTILITY

## 1. INTRODUCTION

In one sense, it is clear why the Patent Act would require an invention to be "useful," § 101. A patent is the quid pro quo for providing a social benefit; a useless invention provides no benefit, and so does not deserve a patent. In another sense, however, this requirement is somewhat mystifying. Since no one would waste time and money protecting an invention that has no use, there appears to be little reason to demand an inquiry into usefulness. Besides, what would it matter if a patent were granted on a useless invention? If the invention has no use, no one will use it and thus no one will pay the costs associated with exclusivity.

One explanation that has been offered for the utility requirement harkens back to trademark law. That is, the public may believe the United States to be certifying as wholesome those products that carry the federal government's own mark. Indeed, the term "patent medicine" derives from the practice of using a formulation's patent to imply therapeutic benefit.[1] Thus, it is not surprising that in some early cases, the utility requirement was used to deny patents to unwholesome—or immoral—products.[2] But imposing a requirement that the invention be nondeleterious—a requirement of "beneficial utility"—is problematic. The PTO does not have the expertise to test products for efficacy, safety, or morality. Nor would we want the PTO making decisions in conflict with those of agencies such as the Food and Drug Administration (FDA) and the Environmental Protection Agency (EPA), which have express authority over some of these issues. Moreover, wholesomeness is often contextual. A product that is considered immoral in one era may become indispensable to a new generation.[3] Thus,

---

[1] Cf. Board of Pharmacy v. Sherman, 74 N.J.Super. 417, 181 A.2d 418 (1962); Robert P. Merges, Intellectual Property in Higher Life Forms: The Patent System and Controversial Technologies, 47 Md.L.Rev. 1051 (1988). Even in this modern, technologically sophisticated era, patents are used in advertising everything from mattresses (Sealy Posturepedics) to makeup (Lancome).

[2] See, e.g., Rickard v. Du Bon, 103 Fed. 868 (2d Cir.1900)(process for flecking tobacco leafs); Meyer v. Buckley Mfg., 15 F.Supp. 640 (N.D.Ill.1936)(gambling machine). The same inclination can be observed in the Lanham Act, see 15 U.S.C. § 1052(a).

[3] Birth control methods furnish an example. It is also possible for a technology to be less dangerous than was initially thought. An example is the debate over hybridizing crop plants, see Frederick H. Buttel and Jill Belsky, Biotechnology, Plant Breeding, and Intellectual Property: Social and Ethical Dimensions, in Owning Scientific and Technical Information 110 (V. Weil and J.W. Snapper, eds. 1989); Zvi Griliches, Hybrid Corn: An Exploration in the Economics of Technological Change, 4 Econometrica 501 (1957).

it is not surprising that the Federal Circuit has firmly rejected this notion of utility.[4]

This leaves two other justifications for utility. One is that it serves as an adjunct to the specification requirement of § 112 in that it assures that the invention does what is claimed in the specification.[5] A second associates utility with problems akin to those addressed by the subject matter requirement. That is, the requirement that an invention have an end-use insures that the invention has *a* use—that it is more than just a principle of nature. Thus, the hurdle imposed by utility acts as another way to remove from the scope of patentability discoveries that are fundamental building blocks of science. More subtly, requiring a recitation of utility will tend to postpone the time when a patent application can be filed. As a result, fundamental insights will remain nonexclusive (for a while).[6]

## 2.  PRINCIPAL PROBLEM

Return to the facts of the Principal Problem in Assignment 15: Does Beta's cDNA sequence meet the requirement of utility?

## 3.  MATERIALS FOR SOLUTION OF PRINCIPAL PROBLEM

A.  STATUTORY MATERIAL: § 101

B.  CASES:

## Brenner v. Manson

Supreme Court of the United States, 1966.
383 U.S. 519, 86 S.Ct. 1033, 16 L.Ed.2d 69.

■ MR. JUSTICE FORTAS delivered the opinion of the Court.

In January 1960, respondent Manson, a chemist engaged in steroid research, filed an application to patent [an allegedly novel process for making certain known steroids;] precisely the same process described by Ringold and Rosenkranz [in an application filed on December 17, 1956]. He asserted that it was he who had discovered the process, and that he had done so before December 17, 1956. Accordingly, he requested that an "interference" be declared in order to try out the issue of priority between his claim and that of Ringold and Rosenkranz.

[4] Juicy Whip, Inc. v. Orange Bang, Inc., 185 F.3d 1364 (Fed. Cir. 1999) (upholding a patent on a juice dispenser, even though it was set up to mix water and syrup in a manner that makes it appear to be dispensing a constituted beverage).

[5] See, e.g., In re Ziegler, 992 F.2d 1197, 1200 (Fed. Cir. 1993)(polypropylene); Cusano v. Kotler, 159 F.2d 159 (3d Cir. 1947)(shuffleboard); Chicago Patent Corp. v. Genco, 124 F.2d 725 (7th Cir.1941)(pinball).

[6] See, e.g., Rebecca S. Eisenberg & Robert P. Merges, Opinion Letter as to the Patentability of Certain Inventions Associated With Identification of Partial cDNA Sequences, 23 AIPLA Q. J. 1 (1995).

A Patent Office examiner denied Manson's application, and the denial was affirmed by the Board of Appeals within the Patent Office. The ground for rejection was the failure "to disclose any utility for" the chemical compound produced by the process. Letter of Examiner, dated May 24, 1960. This omission was not cured, in the opinion of the Patent Office, by Manson's reference to an article in the November 1956 issue of the Journal of Organic Chemistry, 21 J.Org.Chem. 1333–1335, which revealed that steroids of a class which included the compound in question were undergoing screening for possible tumor-inhibiting effects in mice, and that a homologue[a] adjacent to Manson's steroid had proven effective in that role. Said the Board of Appeals, "It is our view that the statutory requirement of usefulness of a product cannot be presumed merely because it happens to be closely related to another compound which is known to be useful."

The Court of Customs and Patent Appeals (hereinafter CCPA) reversed, Chief Judge Worley dissenting. 52 C.C.P.A. (Pat.) 739, 745, 333 F.2d 234, 237–238. The court held that Manson was entitled to a declaration of interference since "where a claimed process produces a known product it is not necessary to show utility for the product," so long as the product "is not alleged to be detrimental to the public interest." Certiorari was granted, 380 U.S. 971, 85 S.Ct. 1334, 14 L.Ed.2d 267, to resolve this running dispute over what constitutes "utility" in chemical process claims. . . .

II

Our starting point is the proposition, neither disputed nor disputable, that one may patent only that which is "useful." In Graham v. John Deere Co., 383 U.S. 1, at 5–10, 86 S.Ct. 684, at 687–690, we have reviewed the history of the requisites of patentability, and it need not be repeated here. Suffice it to say that the concept of utility has maintained a central place in all of our patent legislation, beginning with the first patent law in 1790 and culminating in the present law's provision that

> "Whoever invents or discovers any new and useful process, machine, manufacture, or composition of matter, or any new and useful improvement thereof, may obtain a patent therefor, subject to the conditions and requirements of this title." [§ 101]

As is so often the case, however, a simple, everyday word can be pregnant with ambiguity when applied to the facts of life. That this is so is demonstrated by the present conflict between the Patent Office and the CCPA over how the test is to be applied to a chemical process which yields an already known product whose utility—other than as a possible object of scientific inquiry—has not yet been evidenced. It was not long ago that agency and court seemed of one mind on the question. In Application of

---

[a] "A homologous series is a family of chemically related compounds, the composition of which varies from member to member by $CH_2$ (one atom of carbon and two atoms of hydrogen). . . . Chemists knowing the proper-ties of one member of a series would in general know what to expect in adjacent members." Application of Henze, 181 F.2d 196, 200–201, 37 C.C.P.A. (Pat.) 1009, 1014.

Bremner, 182 F.2d 216, 217, 37 C.C.P.A. (Pat.) 1032, 1034 [1950], the court affirmed rejection by the Patent Office of both process and product claims. It noted that "no use for the products claimed to be developed by the processes had been shown in the specification." It held that "It was never intended that a patent be granted upon a product, or a process producing a product, unless such product be useful." Nor was this new doctrine in the court. See Thomas v. Michael, 166 F.2d 944, 946–947, 35 C.C.P.A. (Pat.) 1036, 1038–1039.

The Patent Office has remained steadfast in this view. The CCPA, however, has moved sharply away from Bremner. The trend began in Application of Nelson, 280 F.2d 172, 47 C.C.P.A. (Pat.) 1031. There, the court reversed the Patent Office's rejection of a claim on a process yielding chemical intermediates "useful to chemists doing research on steroids," despite the absence of evidence that any of the steroids thus ultimately produced were themselves "useful." The trend has accelerated, culminating in the present case where the court held it sufficient that a process produces the result intended and is not "detrimental to the public interest." 333 F.2d at 238, 52 C.C.P.A. (Pat.), at 745.

Respondent does not—at least in the first instance—rest upon the extreme proposition, advanced by the court below, that a novel chemical process is patentable so long as it yields the intended product and so long as the product is not itself "detrimental." Nor does he commit the outcome of his claim to the slightly more conventional proposition that any process is "useful" within the meaning of § 101 if it produces a compound whose potential usefulness is under investigation by serious scientific researchers, although he urges this position, too, as an alternative basis for affirming the decision of the CCPA. Rather, he begins with the much more orthodox argument that ... supporting affidavits ... reveal that an adjacent homologue of the steroid yielded by his process has been demonstrated to have tumor-inhibiting effects in mice, and that this discloses the requisite utility. We do not accept any of these theories as an adequate basis for overriding the determination of the Patent Office that the "utility" requirement has not been met.

Even on the assumption that the process would be patentable were respondent to show that the steroid produced had a tumor-inhibiting effect in mice, we would not overrule the Patent Office finding that respondent has not made such a showing. The Patent Office held that, despite the reference to the adjacent homologue, respondent's papers did not disclose a sufficient likelihood that the steroid yielded by his process would have similar tumor-inhibiting characteristics. Indeed, respondent himself recognized that the presumption that adjacent homologues have the same utility has been challenged in the steroid field because of "a greater known unpredictability of compounds in that field." In these circumstances and in this technical area, we would not overturn the finding of the Primary Examiner, affirmed by the Board of Appeals and not challenged by the CCPA.

The second and third points of respondent's argument present issues of much importance. Is a chemical process "useful" within the meaning of § 101 either (1) because it works—i.e., produces the intended product? or (2) because the compound yielded belongs to a class of compounds now the subject of serious scientific investigation? These contentions present the basic problem for our adjudication. Since we find no specific assistance in the legislative materials underlying § 101, we are remitted to an analysis of the problem in light of the general intent of Congress, the purposes of the patent system, and the implications of a decision one way or the other.

In support of his plea that we attenuate the requirement of "utility," respondent relies upon Justice Story's well-known statement that a "useful" invention is one "which may be applied to a beneficial use in society, in contradistinction to an invention injurious to the morals, health, or good order of society, or frivolous and insignificant"—and upon the assertion that to do so would encourage inventors of new processes to publicize the event for the benefit of the entire scientific community, thus widening the search for uses and increasing the fund of scientific knowledge. Justice Story's language sheds little light on our subject. Narrowly read, it does no more than compel us to decide whether the invention in question is "frivolous and insignificant"[b]—a query no easier of application than the one built into the statute. Read more broadly, so as to allow the patenting of any invention not positively harmful to society, it places such a special meaning on the word "useful" that we cannot accept it in the absence of evidence that Congress so intended. There are, after all, many things in this world which may not be considered "useful" but which, nevertheless are totally without a capacity for harm.

It is true, of course, that one of the purposes of the patent system is to encourage dissemination of information concerning discoveries and inventions. And it may be that inability to patent a process to some extent discourages disclosure and leads to greater secrecy than would otherwise be the case. The inventor of the process, or the corporate organization by which he is employed, has some incentive to keep the invention secret while uses for the product are searched out. However, in light of the highly developed art of drafting patent claims so that they disclose as little useful information as possible—while broadening the scope of the claim as widely as possible—the argument based upon the virtue of disclosure must be warily evaluated. Moreover, the pressure for secrecy is easily exaggerated, for if the inventor of a process cannot himself ascertain a "use" for that which his process yields, he has every incentive to make his invention known to those able to do so. Finally, how likely is disclosure of a patented process to spur research by others into the uses to which the product may be put? To the extent that the patentee has power to enforce his patent, there is little incentive for others to undertake a search for uses.

b Note on the Patent Laws, 3 Wheat.App. 13, 24. See also Justice Story's decisions on circuit in Lowell v. Lewis, 15 Fed.Cas. 1018 (No. 8568)(C.C.D.Mass.), and Bedford v. Hunt, 3 Fed.Cas. 37 (No. 1217)(C.C.D.Mass.).

Whatever weight is attached to the value of encouraging disclosure and of inhibiting secrecy, we believe a more compelling consideration is that a process patent in the chemical field, which has not been developed and pointed to the degree of specific utility, creates a monopoly of knowledge which should be granted only if clearly commanded by the statute. Until the process claim has been reduced to production of a product shown to be useful, the metes and bounds of that monopoly are not capable of precise delineation. It may engross a vast, unknown, and perhaps unknowable area. Such a patent may confer power to block off whole areas of scientific development, without compensating benefit to the public. The basic quid pro quo contemplated by the Constitution and the Congress for granting a patent monopoly is the benefit derived by the public from an invention with substantial utility. Unless and until a process is refined and developed to this point—where specific benefit exists in currently available form—there is insufficient justification for permitting an applicant to engross what may prove to be a broad field.

These arguments for and against the patentability of a process which either has no known use or is useful only in the sense that it may be an object of scientific research would apply equally to the patenting of the product produced by the process. Respondent appears to concede that with respect to a product, as opposed to a process, Congress has struck the balance on the side of nonpatentability unless "utility" is shown. Indeed, the decisions of the CCPA are in accord with the view that a product may not be patented absent a showing of utility greater than any adduced in the present case. We find absolutely no warrant for the proposition that although Congress intended that no patent be granted on a chemical compound whose sole "utility" consists of its potential role as an object of use-testing, a different set of rules was meant to apply to the process which yielded the unpatentable product. That proposition seems to us little more than an attempt to evade the impact of the rules which concededly govern patentability of the product itself.

This is not to say that we mean to disparage the importance of contributions to the fund of scientific information short of the invention of something "useful," or that we are blind to the prospect that what now seems without "use" may tomorrow command the grateful attention of the public. But a patent is not a hunting license. It is not a reward for the search, but compensation for its successful conclusion. "(A) patent system must be related to the world of commerce rather than to the realm of philosophy. * * *"[c]

The judgment of the CCPA is reversed.

■ JUSTICE HARLAN, concurring in part and dissenting in part.

[After explaining why most of the majority's arguments "have almost no force," Justice Harlan went on to say:]

[c] Application of Ruschig, 343 F.2d 965, 970, 52 C.C.P.A. (Pat.) 1238, 1245 (Rich, J.).

More to the point, I think, are the Court's remaining, prudential arguments against patentability; namely, that disclosure induced by allowing a patent is partly undercut by patent-application drafting techniques, that disclosure may occur without granting a patent, and that a patent will discourage others from inventing uses for the product. How far opaque drafting may lessen the public benefits resulting from the issuance of a patent is not shown by any evidence in this case but, more important, the argument operates against all patents and gives no reason for singling out the class involved here. The thought that these inventions may be more likely than most to be disclosed even if patents are not allowed may have more force; but while empirical study of the industry might reveal that chemical researchers would behave in this fashion, the abstractly logical choice for them seems to me to maintain secrecy until a product use can be discovered. As to discouraging the search by others for product uses, there is no doubt this risk exists but the price paid for any patent is that research on other uses or improvements may be hampered because the original patentee will reap much of the reward. From the standpoint of the public interest the Constitution seems to have resolved that choice in favor of patentability.

What I find most troubling about the result reached by the Court is the impact it may have on chemical research. Chemistry is a highly interrelated field and a tangible benefit for society may be the outcome of a number of different discoveries, one discovery building upon the next. To encourage one chemist or research facility to invent and disseminate new processes and products may be vital to progress, although the product or process be without "utility" as the Court defines the term, because that discovery permits someone else to take a further but perhaps less difficult step leading to a commercially useful item. In my view, our awareness in this age of the importance of achieving and publicizing basic research should lead this Court to resolve uncertainties in its favor and uphold the respondent's position in this case.

■ [JUSTICE DOUGLAS dissented in part, for substantially the reasons given by JUSTICE HARLAN.]

## Introduction of Legislation for a Moratorium on the Patenting of Genetically Engineered Animals

HON BENJAMIN L. CARDIN OF MARYLAND
138 Cong.Rec. E1117–02.

### Tuesday, April 28, 1992

Mr. Speaker, today I am introducing a bill to provide for a 5–year moratorium on the granting of patents on invertebrate or vertebrate animals, including those that have been genetically engineered. The availability of patents encourages the creation of genetically engineered animals, in most cases, animals whose genetic compositions have been manipulated by genetic engineering techniques to contain foreign genes from other animals, including humans. The resulting animals have combinations of genes and traits not found in nature. We have little experience in assessing the economic, ethical, and environmental consequences of the creation, release, and patenting of such creatures. The moratorium provided for in this bill would simply give the Congress the time to fully access, consider, and respond to the issues raised by the patenting of such animals.

At the outset, I want to make it clear this legislation is not intended to halt the promising field of biotechnology. The various techniques of biotechnology, when used responsibly have enormous potential to benefit society in a number of areas, including the creation of important new pharmaceutical and agricultural products. However, with the new benefits of biotechnology come risks. Genetic engineering allows scientists to take human genetic traits and insert them into the permanent genetic code of animals. Biotechnology is also becoming increasingly adept at mixing and matching the genetic traits of animals, insects, and plants to create new and different species. To suddenly and unconditionally grant patents for any and all of these genetic creations without a strict Federal review process would be irresponsible and impudent.

The bill I am introducing, which was introduced in the Senate on June 13, 1991, by Senator MARK HATFIELD of Oregon, will provide Congress the time to examine the risks of animal patenting. Specifically, the bill provides that no animal shall be patented until the commercialization and release of such an animal has been subjected to a Federal review process established to impose "environmental, health and safety, economic and ethical standards."

If patents are to be issued, we must ensure the patenting of genetically engineered animals will not cause economic harm to the Nation's farmers and researchers. In economic terms the Patent Office decision provides Government authority for the genetic manipulation, and ownership of all animal species. The use, enjoyment, and protection of animals, long a public right and responsibility, could be turned over to the public sector. In years to come there could be increasing competition for corporate control and ownership of the gene pool of animal species. The most immediate economic effect of this policy could be felt in agriculture, where the major chemical biotechnology, and pharmaceutical companies could conceivably position themselves to take over animal husbandry. The Patent Office has confirmed farmers will have to pay patent fees every time they breed a patented animal or sell part of their herds which contain such patented animals. This will also be true for researchers using patented laboratory animals. The economic consequences of animal patenting on small farmers and research institutions need to be carefully examined.

Unlike most intellectual property issues, the patenting of animals also creates a wide array of ethical concerns. The patent policy creates the need to establish reasonable limits to man's right to manipulate and refashion the biotic community to meet his industrial requirements. This includes the necessity of carefully examining the ethics of transferring of human genetic traits into animals. The potential for patenting and owning animals with human traits bring up an important public policy need to decide on how many, and what kind of, human genetic traits should be engineered into animals. Currently, thousands of animals have been created with human genes engineered into their permanent genetic code. There is a real urgency in regulating these transfers prior to further creation, patenting, and dissemination of these animals with human genes.

It is important to note that the patent decision, by encouraging genetic manipulation, could indirectly cause suffering to genetically engineered animals and extend that suffering through generations of the offspring of those altered animals.

Moreover, it is important to remember that even patenting laws have an influence on the way we think. Will future generations follow the ethics of this patent policy and view life as mere chemical manufacture and invention with no greater value or meaning than industrial products?

The patenting of animals could also indirectly cause environmental harm. The effect of species alteration could impact the delicate balance of the environment. The creation of new species and the effect of their release into their environment cannot be easily predicted, and should be carefully considered. Animals which are larger and have increased reproductivity could alter the depletion patterns of the ecosystem. Also, if the creation of new improved species leads to the popularization of that animal, valuable native gene pools could be lost. For example, salmon are currently being created with cattle genes to increase growth. When released into the environment these fish have the potential to invade new habitats and displace existing populations. If the genetically engineered salmon turn out to over populate or consume too much, they could cause irremediable damage to the environment. In addition, they could mate with native salmon and pollute the native gene pool forever. We must remember biological pollution cannot be recalled.

Despite the potential threat created by the release of genetically engineered animals, no Federal regulatory regime exists on the release of such animals. As long as this significant regulatory void exists, it is irresponsible to stimulate the creation of transgenic animals with the patent law. Moreover, this moratorium will provide the time and the incentive for industry, the public sector, and Congress to fashion appropriate safeguards.

The patenting of animals also brings up an important question about the role of Congress in extending patents into new areas of technology. In 1980 the Supreme Court opened the door to the patenting of animals with a 5 to 4 decision in Diamond versus Chakrabarty, which allowed the patenting of a genetically engineered microbe. In 1987, the Patent and Trademark Office (PTO), using a broad interpretation of the Chakrabarty case, announced it would consider applications for patents on genetically altered animals. One year later, in April 1988, PTO approved the first animal patent for the transgenic nonhuman mammals genetically engineered to contain a cancer causing gene (U.S. Patent No. 4,736,866). Presently, over 160 patent applications on animals are pending at the PTO.

It has been an established legal precedent for some time that Congress, not the PTO, makes decisions on extending patent coverage into the controversial areas. It is the duty of Congress, not the PTO, to determine whether living organisms, like plants and animals, are patentable. In the past, Congress actively participated in these types of decisions. For example, in 1930 Congress enacted the Plant Patent Act and, then, in 1970 enacted the Plant Variety Protection Act. In contrast, in 1987 with regard to the patenting of animals the PTO, not Congress, decided nonhuman animals constituted patentable subject matter.

As a result, one patent has been issued, the number of patent applications continues to grow, and no concrete progress has been made to ensure society will be able to deal with the unique ramifications of patenting genetically engineered animals. The economic, ethical, and environmental questions on animal patenting have been raised at a series of hearing conducted by the Intellectual Property and Administration of Justice Subcommittee. It is now imperative that Congress become more involved in this issue. A moratorium would provide the time necessary to conduct this vital public policy debate and to take regulatory steps needed to reap the benefits of this promising new technology, and avoid its risks.

NOTES

**1.** *Metes and bounds.* In *Brenner,* was Justice Fortas correct in thinking that without a specific use, "the metes and bounds of [the] monopoly are not capable of precise delineation?" The application was for a patent on a process; as with any other patented process, the boundaries are clearly confined to use of the process, § 271(a). Of course, uses not known to the inventor at the time of issuance would also be included, but this is true of every patent. The principal uses of the laser, for example, were found well after its inventor applied for patent protection, yet the inventor enjoys rights over all of these later-discovered applications.[7] If rights over uses not contemplated by the inventor are considered excessive, is not the remedy to confine *all* patents to the uses described in the specification? Why limit only those patentees who cannot articulate any use at the time of application? Furthermore, it is the *claiming* provision, not the *utility* provision, of the statute that is meant to delineate the metes and bounds of the invention.

**2.** *Patents as hunting licenses.* Justice Fortas is certainly right in thinking that the patentee in *Brenner* "flunked" the test of finding a use for the steroid he learned to synthesize. But should the Court have assumed that denying a patent will free—or encourage—others to seek a use for this steroid? What would be the reward? The inventor of the use could not patent the steroid. Unless the applicant kept the steroid secret, it became part of the public domain when the patent was rejected.[8] Although the use

[7] See, e.g., Gould v. General Photonics Corp., 534 F.Supp. 399 (N.D.Cal.1982).

[8] Indeed, the rush to patent c-DNA sequences derives from the fear that nothing

itself might be the subject of a process patent, the difficulty of monitoring usage makes process patents much less valuable than product patents. In contrast, granting the patent in the *Brenner* case would certainly have given the patentee incentive to encourage others to conduct research. Although the patentee would be forced to share royalties with the person who found a use, *some* profit is better than none at all.

**3.** *Proving utility.* In most cases, an applicant will assert a utility for the claimed invention and the PTO will then proceed on the assumption that the assertion is true, that the invention has both "general utility," the capacity to do *something*,[9] and "specific utility," the potential to work as claimed.[10] Sometimes, however, there is reason to doubt. In re Swartz, for example, involved claims related to cold fusion (a technique for creating a nuclear reaction using commonplace materials). The possibility of cold fusion has been rejected by the scientific community and the claims in the application were likewise rejected by the PTO. In the course of reviewing the applicant's appeal from the denial of a patent, the Federal Circuit had this to say on the procedure for determining utility:

> The PTO has the initial burden of challenging a patent applicant's presumptively correct assertion of utility. In re Brana, 51 F.3d 1560, 1566, 34 USPQ2d 1436, 1441 (Fed.Cir.1995). If the PTO provides evidence showing that one of ordinary skill in the art would reasonably doubt the asserted utility, however, the burden shifts to the applicant to submit evidence sufficient to convince such a person of the invention's asserted utility. Id. Here the PTO provided several references showing that results in the area of cold fusion were irreproducible. Thus the PTO provided substantial evidence that those skilled in the art would "reasonably doubt" the asserted utility and operability of cold fusion. The examiner found that Mr. Swartz had not submitted evidence of operability that would be sufficient to overcome reasonable doubt. After its review of the evidence, the Board found that Mr.

associated with the work will be patentable if the sequences fall into the public domain, see, e.g., Robin Herman, The Great Gene Gold Rush: U.S. Rankles Other Countries With Preemptive Strike in the Race to Patent Human Genes, The Washington Post, June 16, 1992, Health, p. z11 (describing National Institute of Health patent policy as an attempt to keep options open).

[9] See, e.g., In re Eltgroth, 419 F.2d 918, 922 (C.C.P.A.1970) ("Undoubtedly, the alleged utility of control of the aging process in living organisms and the significant beneficial results flowing therefrom is adequate [to satisfy the utility requirement.] Yet, there is a conspicuous absence of proof thereof ... [W]e find the instant record too speculative

to satisfy the requirement of 35 U.S.C. § 101."); In re Wooddy, 331 F.2d 636, 639–40 (C.C.P.A.1964)(claims to a method of forming underground caverns in salt formations with a nuclear explosion properly rejected as unenabled under § 112 and inoperative under § 101 because the method had never been carried out). This form of utility is sometimes called operability, see e.g. Donald S. Chisum, Patents § 4.04.

[10] See, e.g., Ex parte McKay, 200 U.S.P.Q. (BNA) 324 (PTO Bd. App. 1975)(patent on method for extracting oxygen from extraterrestrial materials upheld as potentially useful, even though "practical considerations would dictate against its commercial exploitation on earth").

Swartz had "produced no persuasive objective evidence, in our view, that overcomes the examiner's position."[11]

The Federal Circuit went on to uphold the PTO's rejection.

Cases involving pharmaceuticals are nominally handled the same way, although in practical effect, there are differences. Thus, applicants are asked to demonstrate that the assertion of utility is credible to a person with ordinary skill in the art. Because patent applications are filed long before the FDA has granted permission to use the invention on humans, applicants usually show utility by developing an animals or test tube model of the disease and its treatment, and then testing the product on this model. But because humans do not always respond the same way as animals or test tubes, the model itself must also be validated. In most cases, that can be done by showing that the same model worked in the past—that it correctly predicted the therapeutic value of other pharmaceuticals used to treat the same condition. In essence, the person with ordinary skill is deemed to reason that if there is a correlation between an animal or test tube model and human therapy for similar conditions, that same correlation will hold for the claimed product.[12]

For most medicines, this system has worked well. However, it can work only for conditions that have been treated in the past because it is only in such cases where there are models that have been validated. Some of the therapeutics discovered recently—such as new genetic therapies—treat conditions that have never been treated before. Thus, there is no validated animal or test tube model to work with. At first, the PTO rejected such applications on utility grounds. In the PTO's view, these inventors had to wait until the completion of human testing to file patent applications. This practice generated considerable controversy and led the PTO to hold hearings on the utility problem. Several speakers testified that the inability to secure patents on these new forms of therapy made it difficult for biotechnology start-up companies to attract investment capital, which, in turn, made it impossible to fund human testing. When it became clear that the new biotechnology industry was endangered by this vicious cycle (no patent without human tests, no money for human tests without a patent), the PTO quickly issued new guidelines which eased the burden of proving utility in these cases.[13]

**4.** *Use patents.* Commentators have proposed a solution to both the windfall problem identified in Note 1 and the incentive problem discussed in Note 2. They would divide utility patents into two categories and issue how-to-make patents to those, like the applicant in *Brenner,* who discover a

---

[11] In re Swartz, 232 F.3d 862, 864 (Fed. Cir.2000). See also Newman v. Quigg, 877 F.2d 1575 (Fed.Cir.1989)(upholding a finding that experiments by the National Bureau of Standards demonstrated that an "Energy Generation System Having Higher Energy Output Than Input" was not operable).

[12] See, e.g., In re Brana, 51 F.3d 1560 (Fed.Cir.1995).

[13] General utility guidelines as well as utility guidelines for gene-related inventions are available at the PTO website, www.uspto.gov.

method for synthesizing a new compound and how-to-use patents to those who discover new applications. How-to-make patents would be infringed only when the product is manufactured in the manner claimed by the patentee; how-to-use patents would be infringed only when the product is used in the specified manner. In this way, synthetic chemists would receive some reward for their efforts, but the incentive to find new uses would be preserved.[14]

**5.** *Rights to inventions made with federal assistance.* For many years, patent rights to inventions made under federal research grants were allocated by the federal agency responsible for the grants, with each agency having its own policy. Some agencies took the position that the public should hold the patents to government-funded inventions because it had paid for their development. Other agencies permitted the individual researchers to own rights to their inventions, but only if they agreed to grant the United States royalty-free licenses. However, there was long a suspicion that the commercial potential of government-sponsored inventions was underdeveloped. One explanation offered was similar to that discussed above: without strong private patent protection, no one has the incentive to make the effort to get the invention from the lab bench to the consumer.[15]

In 1980, Congress enacted the Bayh Dole Act, which allows federally-funded researchers to retain control over the patent rights to their inventions, unless the funding agency finds that exceptional circumstances mandate that the government retain these rights. To counteract the argument that the public would then pay twice for new inventions (once in funding their development, a second time through the high prices patents make possible), Congress limited the ability to acquire patent rights to nonprofit organizations, such as universities, and to small business firms. In that way, any overpayment by the public subsidizes activities that are in the public interest. To counteract the fear that such patents would block further developments, the agencies funding the research were given so-called "march-in rights"—rights to grant licenses in the event that the patentee fails to use the patent to "hunt" for uses for the invention. See §§ 200–211 of the Patent Act.

**6.** *"Utility . . . as a possible object of scientific inquiry".* Note that *Brenner* distinguishes between utility to researchers and utility to end-users, implying that only the latter qualifies as a specific utility under § 101. This distinction is even clearer in the case *Brenner* relied upon, Application of Bremner, which held that a chemical intermediate lacked utility. Intermediates have a transitory existence, and so are, indeed, of little use to consumers. However, they are of considerable interest to chemists, who use the structure of intermediates to understand, among other things, the mechanism and timing of reactions.

[14] For an example of such a proposal, see Paul H. Egger, Uses, New Uses and Chemical Patents—A Proposal, 51 J. Pat Off. Soc. 768, 784–87 (1969).

[15] See Jerome S. Gabig, Jr., Federal Research Grants: Who Owns the Intellectual Property, 9 Harv. J.L. & Pub. Pol. 639 (1986).

What explains this distinction? Perhaps the idea is that discoveries of interest only to scholars are similar in effect to principles of nature, that tying up the tools of inventiveness will block research or raise its costs to prohibitive levels. This would account for the hostility to patent protection in cases like *Brenner* and *Bremner;* it would also account for Congress's initial reluctance to grant patents on genetically-altered animals of use to researchers. But is this a cogent analysis? If these research tools are valued and needed, it would appear desirable for the patent system to encourage their development.

Could the problem of chilling research be solved in other ways? There is a common law defense to infringement for experiments conducted "for the gratification of scientific tastes, or for curiosity, or for amusement,"[16] but it is too narrow an exception to accommodate significant research efforts.[17] Some have suggested that a broader exception should be instituted, similar to copyright's fair use defense.[18] Others have noted that many of the patents that most seriously implicate research activity—patents on inventions that are close to fundamental principles of science or nature— are awarded to universities by virtue of the Bayh Dole Act, and then assigned on an exclusive basis. These observers suggest that the way to remedy the research problem is to amend Bayh Dole to make it easier for the government to "march in" in cases where researchers are unable to obtain licenses on reasonable terms.[19]

**7.** *The moral perspective.* The moratorium on animal patenting is no longer in place in the United States. However, the move to deny patents to socially dysfunctional products has not abated. Significantly, in 2002, the Canada Supreme Court held higher life forms unpatentable in a case involving a genetically engineered mouse bred for research purposes. The Court based its decision on the subject matter requirement of Canada's patent law, rather than on utility grounds. Nonetheless, the judges' decisions express many of the same concerns voiced by Cardin in the congressional debate on the moratorium reproduced in the readings above.[20] Would research on animals actually stop if patent protection is denied? If a field

[16] Roche Products, Inc. v. Bolar Pharmaceutical Co., Inc., 733 F.2d 858, 862 (Fed. Cir. 1984).

[17] See, e.g., Madey v. Duke University, 307 F.3d 1351 (Fed.Cir. 2002), cert. denied, ___ U.S. ___, 123 S.Ct. 2639 (2003).

[18] See, e.g., Janice M. Mueller, No "Dilettante Affair": Rethinking The Experimental Use Exception to Patent Infringement for Biomedical Research Tools, 76 Wash. L. Rev. 1 (2001); Maureen A. O'Rourke, Toward A Doctrine Of Fair Use In Patent Law, 100 Colum. L. Rev. 1177 (2000).

[19] See, e.g., Arti K. Rai and Rebecca S. Eisenberg, 2003 Bayh–Dole Reform and the Progress of Biomedicine, 66–SPG Law & Contemp. Probs. 289 (2003); Avital Bar-Sha-

lom and Robert Cook–Deegan, Patents and Innovation in Cancer Therapeutics: Lessons from CellPro, 80 The Milbank Quarterly, 637 (2002).

[20] President and Fellows of Harvard College v. Canada (Commissioner of Patents), 2002 SCC 76. The European Patent Office came down on the same side as the U.S., but only after explicitly considering whether the patent on the mouse would be "contrary to ordre public or morality," under art. 53(c) of the European Patent Convention, see In re President and Fellows of Harvard College, Examining Division of the European Patent Office, 1992 Official Journal EPO 558.

ASSIGNMENT 16  UTILITY

has enough potential, academic research—which has its own reward system—will certainly continue. Industrial research may also continue, with researchers counting on state-based trade secrecy protection as the vehicle for capturing financial reward. Is this a better state of affairs? As Justice Fortas noted, patents also encourage (or facilitate) publication of research results. Even if the public does not like the work, it can at least monitor the research for side effects and can take steps to assert direct control over further developments.

# ASSIGNMENT 17

# NOVELTY

## 1. INTRODUCTION

### A. SECTION 102

Among other things, § 102 refines the requirement, set out in § 101, that the invention be "new." Unfortunately, this section does several other things as well. Indeed, it is one of the most confusingly drafted provisions in the United States Code, laying out four distinct concepts in no discernable order. These are: novelty (newness),[1] statutory bar,[2] priority,[3] and originality.[4] Equally confusing is the fact that the novelty provisions of § 102 are not the only place in the Patent Act where "new" is interpreted. Section 103 provides further elaboration on the concept. It requires that the invention must be more than an obvious improvement over the technology that preceded it.

Because novelty is more closely related to the question of nonobviousness than it is to the other concepts in § 102, the next group of Assignments will depart from the order followed by the Patent Act. Immediately after this Assignment on novelty, § 103 will be examined. Originality will be discussed in Assignment 18, Note 7, and then the statutory bars (Assignment 19) and priority (Assignment 20) will be covered.

### B. NOVELTY

In some ways, the requirement that the invention be new is easy to justify. An old invention—or as patent lawyers say, an invention that is "anticipated by the prior art"—is a discovery that, in some sense, already exists in the storehouse of knowledge. People who work in the field know of it (or can find it), can use it, and can bring it to the public's attention. There is no need to encourage someone to invent this invention, and therefore there is no need to incur the costs associated with exclusivity. Moreover, if an invention is old, there may be people who are already relying on its free availability. Subsequent issuance of a patent covering the invention would frustrate these users' expectations.

The things considered relevant to the novelty inquiry go by a variety of names. The ones most often seen are: "prior art," "references," and "disclosures." What counts as a reference (prior art/disclosure) is enumerated in the provisions of § 102 that describe activity occurring "before the

---

[1] §§ 102(a), (e), and parts of (g).

[2] §§ 102(b), (c), and (d).

[3] § 102(g).

[4] § 102(f).

invention ... by the applicant." Under § 102(a), it includes knowledge or use of the invention by others in the United States, or publication or patenting anywhere in the world. Under § 102(e), it includes disclosures contained in an application for a U.S. patent—so long as the application eventually results in a patent. Finally, under the first sentence of § 102(g)(2), it includes inventions by another person in the United States— so long as that person has not abandoned, suppressed, or concealed the invention.[5] These provisions are not mutually exclusive. An invention can, all at the same time, be made by another (who does not abandon it), it can be disseminated within the United States, it can be described in print, and it can be disclosed in a pending application. However, if even only one of these events occurs, the applicant cannot receive a patent.

Despite the ease with which the novelty requirement can be justified, two anomalies remain. First, it is worth thinking about why patent law and copyright law take such different positions on novelty. Copyright requires only that the work be original; it is not disqualifying that a work is similar to another copyrighted work or to material already in the public domain. In contrast, originality, while a requirement of patent law,[6] is not sufficient. Once an invention runs afoul of the novelty requirement, its inventor is deprived of all rights, irrespective of the effort put into the work or the absence of public knowledge about the earlier technology.

What accounts for this difference? One possibility is that absolute rights are more necessary to reap the rewards of inventorship than authorship. In some sense, all works within the ambit of copyright are unique. After all, the proverbial monkeys with typewriters never have managed to duplicate Shakespeare. Moreover, a work acquires some of its value from the fact that it was written by a particular person. For example, no matter how accurate the historian, a study of the Ford presidency will never fully substitute for Gerald Ford's own account. Therefore, Ford's copyright will have value no matter how many other books are written about, say, the pardon of Richard Nixon. In contrast, inventions are fungible. The purchaser of the lightbulb cares only that it works; there is no value in using the specific bulb invented by Thomas Edison. Thus, if two inventors receive patents on the same invention, they will be in essentially perfect competition. Absent collusion, they will drive the price down to marginal cost and neither will capture the benefits patent law seeks to provide. Patent exclusivity must, in short, be just that: a right to exclude *all* others, even other independent inventors.[7]

First Amendment values may also account for part of the difference between copyright and patent law's positions on novelty. Because copyright is thought to further the interest in free expression,[8] denying copyright to

---

[5] §§ 102(e) and (g) include special rules for patents filed under the Patent Cooperation Treaty described in the Introduction to patent law, see also Note 2, below.

[6] As noted above, the originality requirement is set out in § 102(f), and is discussed in Assignment 18 at Note 7.

[7] But see Note 3 below.

[8] See, e.g., Assignment 11.

an independent author may raise constitutional concerns.[9] Although inventors have, from time to time, asserted First Amendment rights to conduct and publish research, these rights are not as well developed as they are in the copyright context.[10]

Finally, some commentators offer a "search model" that claims that the novelty requirement (or lack thereof) can be explained by examining the ratio between the cost of searching prior art to learn a particular innovation and the cost of developing that same innovation from scratch. When this ratio is low, the law encourages people to conduct a meticulous review of earlier work before they set out on expensive independent efforts. When this ratio is high, however, prior-art searches do not make economic sense, and so the law does not encourage them. In most of the patent industries, the literature is well indexed, there are abstracting services, and periodic articles that survey the field. Because this literature is conducive to efficient search, the novelty provisions require it. In many of the fields where copyright is pertinent—art, music, and poetry, for example—there is no systematic indexing or abstracting.[11] Since searching would be onerous, if not impossible, it is better if creators started fresh rather than do research. Accordingly, copyright law does not strip these creators of their rights when the works they produce turn out to be similar to material already in existence.[12]

The second anomaly surrounding novelty involves the choices Congress made in § 102. Not all bits of prior knowledge render an invention "not new." As the major cases in this Assignment demonstrate, some kinds of prior knowledge are not deemed anticipatory. Consider the extent to which the "search model" discussed in the previous paragraph helps decide which kinds of knowledge count for novelty purposes.

## 2. PRINCIPAL PROBLEM

Here is an oldie but goodie from our firm's case files. See if you think it was handled properly. Our clients were Larry Nichols and Moleculon Corporation, inventor and assignee of U.S. Letters Patent No. 3,655,201 (the § 201). They told us the following: It seems Nichols has been interested in puzzles since he was a youngster in the early 50's, when his mother gave him a number puzzle consisting of a two-dimensional square frame in which 15 numbered and interlocking (smaller) squares were fitted. A space,

---

[9] Cf. Rochelle C. Dreyfuss, A *Wiseguy's* Approach to Information Products: Muscling Copyright and Patent Into a Unitary Theory of Intellectual Property, 1992 S.Ct. Rev. 195.

[10] See, e.g., United States v. Progressive, Inc., 467 F.Supp. 990 (W.D.Wis.1979). See generally, Diane Leenheer Zimmerman, Scientific Speech in the 1990s, 2 N.Y.U. Envtl. L.J. 254 (1993); Gary Francione, Experimentation and the Marketplace Theory of the First Amendment, 136 U. Pa. L. Rev. 417 (1987).

[11] The Internet may some day make it possible to search for, say an iambic pentameter poem on the grace of a giraffe as easy as searching chemical abstracts for articles on ethyl alcohol, but such capacity is not available yet.

[12] Cf. John F. Duffy and Robert P. Merges, Patent Law and Policy: Cases and Materials 419–21 (3d ed. 2002).

which could theoretically hold another square, was left free so that the 15 existing squares could be moved about. The objective of the puzzle was to arrange the numbered squares in a variety of ways without removing them from the frame. Nichols had always felt a three-dimensional version of the puzzle was possible, and on a summer evening in 1957, the idea occurred to him for an assembly of eight cubes stacked in a 2x2x2 arrangement, with each of the six faces of the composite cube distinguished by a different color. He recognized that the smaller cubes could be rotated in sets of four around one of three mutually perpendicular axes and placed in a variety of arrangements.

Nichols very quickly realized that magnets could be used to hold the cubes in assembled form yet allow them rotational movement, but he had considerable difficulty translating his idea into a workable model. He played with the problem for many years, including the time when he was a graduate student in organic chemistry at Harvard. During that period, 1959–1962, he and a few close friends made many paper models that used a variety of construction techniques, such as tongue-in-groove and tab-and-slot arrangements. None of these worked in a truly satisfactory manner.

In 1962, Nichols received his Ph.D. and went to work for the Moleculon Research Corporation. In 1968, he happened on some small, strong magnets in a retail store and, using Moleculon's machine shop, he undertook to make a wood block model of his puzzle. Working after hours, he drilled holes in the internal faces of eight small wooden blocks, inserted the magnets, properly oriented them, and glued them in. He painted each face a different color and—low and behold—the puzzle worked. Nichols kept his creation in his office. In late 1968, Moleculon's principal shareholder and operating officer, Dr. Harold Obermayer, entered the office, saw the model on Nichols' desk, and began to play with it. Obermayer asked if he could buy a copy; Nichols told him it was not available commercially but allowed him to take the model home to play with.

Obermayer so enjoyed the puzzle that he offered to put Moleculon's efforts into its commercialization. On January 2, 1969, Nichols signed a written agreement assigning all his rights in the puzzle to Moleculon in return for a share of any proceeds. Moleculon assumed all expenses of commercializing the puzzle, initiated contacts with Parker Brothers, Ideal Corp., and other manufacturers of children's games, and hired an attorney to help Nichols prepare a patent application. Although none of Moleculon's contacts resulted in any kind of marketing agreement, the patent application was filed on January 12, 1970, and a patent issued on April 11, 1972, naming Larry D. Nichols as inventor and Moleculon Corp. as assignee and claiming rights to both the puzzle and its solution.[13]

[13] A representative claim to the puzzle reads as follows:

"A puzzle comprising at least eight pieces, visually distinguishable indicia on at least one face of each piece with the eight pieces together having at least two visually distinct indicia, means associated with each of the remaining faces only of each of the pieces releasably maintaining the pieces in assembled relationship forming a composite structure, said maintaining means enabling three inter-

In February, 1981, Obermayer became aware of a puzzle manufactured by the Ideal Corp. called Rubik's Cube, a 3x3x3 cube of rotating blocks painted six different colors. Obermayer immediately contacted Ideal to call its attention to the patent. Ideal's attorney invited Obermayer to a meeting at which the attorney explained that Ideal did not get the idea of the cube from Nichol's patent. Rather, one of its marketing agents on a trip to Eastern Europe saw some Hungarian children playing with a traditional folk puzzle of this type. The agent brought a copy to corporate headquarters, where the decision was made to rush it to market. It hit the stores in June, 1980 and was snapped up by puzzle lovers everywhere.

According to the attorney, Ideal never attempted to patent the puzzle. The patenting decision was made after Ideal's patent department found a patent ("Gustafson") issued in March 1963 describing a ball-shaped puzzle with an outer shell that rotated around an inner shell. The outer shell was divided into eight pieces, each painted with a bit of the map of the world; when purchased, the puzzle looked like a globe. Any four contiguous pieces could be rotated together around their center—for example, the northern hemisphere could be rotated around the North Pole so that Europe appeared above South America, or the western hemisphere could be rotated to make the U.S. level with Australia. If several rotations were made consecutively, the world could be entirely jumbled. Bringing it back into shape required the same type of reiterative solution used in Rubik's cube (that is, the solver places one piece in the right place, then must undo that solution to make room to position the next piece, resolve the puzzle for that piece, and then undo the solution to position the next piece . . . ).

Moleculon engaged us to sue Ideal for patent infringement. Of course, our first concern was whether the patent would hold up if challenged in litigation. What do you think?

affiliated groups of four contiguous pieces each to be rotated respectively about three mutually perpendicular aces, the two distinct indicia being so located on the respective pieces that the groups can be rotated to effect the display of at least two distinct indicia of the composite structure."

A representative claim to the puzzle's solution reads:

"A method for restoring a preselected pattern from sets of pieces which pieces have constantly exposed and constantly nonexposed surfaces, the exposed surfaces adapted to be combined to form the preselected pattern, which sets when in random engagement fail to display said preselected pattern which comprises:

a. engaging eight cube pieces as a composite cube;

b. rotating a first set of cube pieces comprising four cubes about a first axis;

c. rotating a second set of four cubes about a second axis; and

d. repeating steps (b) and (c) until the preselected pattern is achieved."

## 3.   Materials for Solution of Principal Problem

A.   STATUTORY MATERIAL: §§ 102 (a), (e), (g), & 104

B.   CASES:

# Gayler v. Wilder

Supreme Court of the United States, 1850.
51 U.S. (10 How.) 477, 13 L.Ed. 504.

■ Mr. Chief Justice Taney delivered the opinion of the Court.

[A patent was granted on June 1, 1843 to one Daniel Fitzgerald claiming "an improvement, new and useful, in the construction of iron chests, or safes, intended to resist the action of fire, and for the safe-keeping and preserving books and papers, and other valuables, from the destruction by fire."]

The remaining question is upon the validity of the patent an which the suit was brought.

It appears that James Conner, who carried on the business of a stereotype founder in the city of New York, made a safe for his own use between the years 1829 and 1832, for the protection of his papers against fire; and continued to use it until 1838, when it passed into other hands. It was kept in his counting-room and known to the persons engaged in the foundery; and after it passed out of his hands, he used others of a different construction.

It does not appear what became of this safe afterwards. And there is nothing in the testimony from which it can be inferred that its mode of construction was known to the person into whose possession it fell, or that any value was attached to it as a place of security for papers against fire; or that it was ever used for that purpose.

Upon these facts the court instructed the jury, "that if Connor had not made his discovery public, but had used it simply for his own private purpose, and it had been finally forgotten or abandoned, such a discovery and use would be no obstacle to the taking out of a patent by Fitzgerald or those claiming under him, if he be an original, though not the first, inventor or discoverer."

The instruction assumes that the jury might find from the evidence that Conner's safe was substantially the same with that of Fitzgerald, and also prior in time. And if the fact was so, the question then was whether the patentee was "the original and first inventor or discoverer," within the meaning of the act of Congress.

The act of 1836, ch. 357, § 6ᵃ authorizes a patent where the party has discovered or invented a new and useful improvement, "not known or used by others before his discovery or invention." And the 15th section provides

ᵃ [This is the predecessor to § 102(a)—
eds.]

that, if it appears on the trial of an action brought for the infringement of a patent that the patentee "was not the original and first inventor or discoverer of the thing patented," the verdict shall be for the defendant.

Upon a literal construction of these particular words, the patentee in this case certainly was not the original and first inventor or discoverer, if the Conner safe was the same with his, and preceded his discovery. But we do not think that this construction would carry into effect the intention of the legislature. It is not by detached words and phrases that a statute ought to be expounded. The whole act must be taken together, and a fair interpretation given to it, neither extending nor restricting it beyond the legitimate import of its language, and its obvious policy and object. And in the 15th section, after making the provision above mentioned, there is a further provision, that, if it shall appear that the patentee at the time of his application for the patent believed himself to be the first inventor, the patent shall not be void on account of the invention or discovery having been known or used in any foreign country, it not appearing that it had been before patented or described in any printed publication.

In the case thus provided for, the party who invents is not strictly speaking the first and original inventor. The law assumes that the improvement may have been known and used before his discovery. Yet his patent is valid if he discovered it by the efforts of his own genius, and believed himself to be the original inventor. The clause in question qualifies the words before used, and shows that by knowledge and use the legislature meant knowledge and use existing in a manner accessible to the public. If the foreign invention had been printed or patented, it was already given to the world and open to the people of this country, as well as of others, upon reasonable inquiry. They would therefore derive no advantage from the invention here. It would confer no benefit upon the community, and the inventor therefore is not considered to be entitled to the reward. But if the foreign discovery is not patented, nor described in any printed publication, it might be known and used in remote places for ages, and the people of this country be unable to profit by it. The means of obtaining knowledge would not be within their reach; and, as far as their interest is concerned, it would be the same thing as if the improvement had never been discovered. It is the inventor here that brings is to them, and places it in their possession. And as he does this by the effort of his own genius, the law regards him as the first and original inventor, and protects his patent, although the improvement had in fact been invented before, and used by others.

So, too, as to the lost arts. It is well known that centuries ago discoveries were made in certain arts the fruits of which have come down to us, but the means by which the work was accomplished are at this day unknown. The knowledge has been lost for ages. Yet it would hardly be doubted, if any one now discovered an art thus lost, and it was a useful improvement, that, upon a fair construction of the act of Congress, he would be entitled to a patent. Yet he would not literally be the first and original inventor. But he would be the first to confer on the public the benefit of the invention. He would discover what is unknown, and communicate knowledge which the public had not the means of obtaining without his invention.

Upon the same principle and upon the same rule of construction, we think that Fitzgerald must be regarded as the first and original inventor of the safe in question. The case as to this point admits, that, although Conner's safe had been kept and used for years, yet no test had been applied to it, and its capacity for resisting heat was not known; there was no evidence to show that any particular value was attached to it after it passed from his possession, or that it was ever afterwards used as a place of security for papers; and it appeared that he himself did not attempt to make another like the one he is supposed to have invented, but used a different one. And upon this state of the evidence the court put it to the jury to say, whether this safe had been finally forgotten or abandoned before Fitzgerald's invention, and whether he was the original inventor of the safe for which he obtained the patent; directing them, if they found these two facts, that their verdict must be for the plaintiff. We think there is no error in this instruction. For if the Conner safe had passed away from the memory of Conner himself, and of those who had seen it, and the safe itself had disappeared, the knowledge of the improvement was as completely lost as if it had never been discovered. The public could derive no benefit from it until it was discovered by another inventor. And if Fitzgerald made his discovery by his own efforts, without any knowledge of Conner's, he invented an improvement that was then new, and at that time unknown; and it was not the less new and unknown because Conner's safe was recalled to his memory by the success of Fitzgerald's.

We do not understand the Circuit Court to have said that the omission of Conner to try the value of his safe by proper tests would deprive it of its priority; nor his omission to bring it into public use. He might have omitted both, and also abandoned its use, and been ignorant of the extent of its value; yet, if it was the same with Fitzgerald's, the latter would not upon such grounds be entitled to a patent, provided Conner's safe and its mode of construction were still in the memory of Conner before they were recalled by Fitzgerald's patent.

The circumstances above mentioned, referred to in the opinion of the Circuit Court, appeared to have been introduced as evidence tending to prove that the Conner safe might have been finally forgotten, and upon which this hypothetical instruction was given. Whether this evidence was sufficient for that purpose or not, was a question for the jury, and the court left it to them. And if the jury found the fact to be so, and that Fitzgerald again discovered it, we regard him as standing upon the same ground with the discoverer of a lost art, or an unpatented and unpublished foreign invention, and like him entitled to a patent. For there was no existing and living knowledge of this improvement, or of its former use, at the time he made the discovery. And whatever benefit any individual may derive from it in the safety of his papers, he owes entirely to the genius and exertions of Fitzgerald.

Upon the whole, therefore, we think there is no error in the opinion of the Circuit Court, and the judgment is therefore affirmed.

■ Mr. Justice McLean, dissenting [omitted].

## Coffin v. Ogden

Supreme Court of the United States, 1873.
85 U.S. (18 Wall.) 120, 21 L.Ed. 821.

■ Mr. Justice Swayne stated the case, recited the evidence, and delivered the opinion of the Court.

The appellant was the complainant in the court below, and filed this bill to enjoin the defendants from infringing the patent upon which the bill is founded. The patent is for a door lock with a latch reversible, so that the lock can be applied to doors opening either to the right or the left hand. It was granted originally on the 11th of June, 1861, to Charles R. Miller, assignee of William S. Kirkham, [reissued and reassigned, ultimately to the complainant]. The answer alleges that the thing patented, or a material and substantial part thereof, had been, prior to the supposed invention thereof by Kirkham, known and used by divers persons in the United States, and that among them were Barthol Erbe, residing at Birmingham, near Pittsburg, and Andrew Patterson, Henry Masta, and Bernard Brossi, residing at Pittsburg, and that all these persons had such knowledge at Pittsburg. The appellees insist that Erbe was the prior inventor, and that this priority is fatal to the patent. This proposition, in its aspects of fact and of law, is the only one which we have found it necessary to consider.

Kirkham made his invention in March, 1861. This is clearly shown by the testimony, and there is no controversy between the parties on the subject.

It is equally clear that Erbe made his invention not later than January 1st, 1861. This was not controverted by the counsel for the appellant; but it was insisted that the facts touching that invention were not such as to make it available to the appellees, as against the later invention of Kirkham and the patent founded upon it. This renders it necessary to examine carefully the testimony upon the subject.

*Erbe*'s deposition was taken at Pittsburg upon interrogatories agreed upon by the parties and sent out from New York. He made the lock marked H. E. (It is the exhibit of the appellees, so marked). He made the first lock like it in the latter part of the year 1860. He made three such before he made the exhibit lock. The first he gave to Jones, Wallingford & Co. The second he sent to Washington, when he applied for a patent. The third he made for a friend of Jones. He thinks the lock he gave to Jones, Wallingford & Co. was applied to a door, but is not certain.

*Brossi.* In 1860 he was engaged in lockmaking for the Jones and Nimmick Manufacturing Company. He had known Erbe about seventeen years. In 1860 Erbe was foreman in the lock shop of Jones, Wallingford & Co., at Pittsburg. In that year, and before the 1st of January, 1861, he went to Erbe's house. Erbe there showed him a lock, and how it worked, so that it could be used right or left. He says: "He (Erbe) showed me the follower made in two pieces. One piece you take out when you take the knob away. The other part—the main part of the follower—slides forward in the case of the lock with the latch, so you can take the square part of the latch and turn it around left or right, whichever way a person wants to." He had then been a lockmaker eight years. He examined the lock carefully.

*Masta.* In 1860 he was a patternmaker for Jones, Wallingford & Co. Had known Erbe fourteen or fifteen years. Erbe showed him his improvement in reversible locks New Year's day, 1861. He examined the lock with the case open. "There is not a particle of difference between the exhibit and the original lock. It is all the same." He identifies the time by the facts that he commenced building a house in 1861, and that year is marked on the water conductor under the roof. [*Patterson* was deposed to similar effect.]

The case arose while the Patent Act of 1836 was in force, and must be decided under its provisions. The sixth section of that act requires that to entitle the applicant to a patent, his invention or discovery must be one "not known or used by others before his invention or discovery thereof." The fifteenth section allowed a party sued for infringement to prove, among other defences, that the patentee "was not the original and first inventor of the thing patented, or of a substantial and material part thereof claimed to be new."

The whole act is to be taken together and construed in the light of the context. The meaning of these sections must be sought in the import of their language, and in the object and policy of the legislature in enacting them. The invention or discovery relied upon as a defence, must have been complete, and capable of producing the result sought to be accomplished; and this must be shown by the defendant. The burden of proof rests upon him, and every reasonable doubt should be resolved against him. If the thing were embryotic or inchoate; if it rested in speculation or experiment; if the process pursued for its development had failed to reach the point of consummation, it cannot avail to defeat a patent founded upon a discovery or invention which was completed, while in the other case there was only progress, however near that progress may have approximated to the end in view. The law requires not conjecture, but certainty. If the question relate to a machine, the conception must have been clothed in substantial forms which demonstrate at once its practical efficacy and utility. The prior knowledge and use by a single person is sufficient. The number is immaterial. Until his work is done, the inventor has given nothing to the public. In Gayler v. Wilder the views of this court upon the subject were thus expressed: "We do not understand the Circuit Court to have said that the omission of Conner to try his safe by the proper tests would deprive it of its priority; nor his omission to bring in into public use. He might have omitted both, and also abandoned its use and been ignorant of the extent of its value; yet if it was the same with Fitzgerald's, the latter would not, upon such grounds, be entitled to a patent; provided Conner's safe and its mode of construction were still in the memory of Conner before they were recalled by Fitzgerald's patent." Whether the proposition expressed by the proviso in the last sentence is a sound one, it is not necessary in this case to consider.

Here it is abundantly proved that the lock originally made by Erbe "was complete and capable of working." The priority of Erbe's invention is clearly shown. It was known at the time to at least five persons, including Jones, and probably to many others in the shop where Erbe worked; and the lock was put in use, being applied to a door, as proved by Brossi. It was thus tested and shown to be successful. These facts bring the case made by the appellees within the severest legal tests which can be applied to them. The defence relied upon is fully made out.

## Scripps Clinic & Research Foundation v. Genentech, Inc.

United States Court of Appeals, Federal Circuit, 1991.
927 F.2d 1565.

■ PAULINE NEWMAN, CIRCUIT JUDGE.

The Invention

Factor VIII:C, called the clotting or procoagulant factor, is found in all mammals. It has been the subject of extensive scientific research, over many years. At the time the claimed invention was made, it was known that human Factor VIII:C is a complex protein produced by the Factor VIII:C gene and secreted into the blood stream. It occurs in normal blood plasma (plasma is the fluid fraction of blood) at a concentration of about 200 nanograms per milliliter. The total protein content of plasma is about 70 milligrams (0.070 gram) per milliliter; since a nanogram is one billionth of a gram, the total protein in plasma is 350,000 times greater than the Factor VIII:C protein in plasma. Most of the problems faced by researchers attempting to isolate Factor VIII:C were due to the amount and nature of the other proteins in the plasma.

It was known that in normal blood Factor VIII:C exists in complex association with another protein, named the "von Willebrand factor" or Factor VIII:RP (RP means "related protein").

Before the invention here at issue was made, scientists had succeeded in concentrating the Factor VIII:C in plasma. This concentrate has been used to replace transfusions of whole blood in the treatment of hemophilia. The process was expensive and, because of the large volume of whole blood needed as starting material, the possibility of contamination and disease from impurities in the source blood, the large amount of extraneous plasma proteins in the concentrate, and the large volume of concentrate that still had to be administered to the patient, there has been a continuing search for improvement. The record reflects the difficulties, over decades of research, in isolating and studying Factor VIII:C. Scripps reports that Genentech's scientists had been working in the field and had not isolated human Factor VIII:C in sufficient purity and amount to conduct successful characterization experiments.

At the Scripps Clinic & Research Foundation, Dr. Zimmerman and Dr. Fulcher were studying Factor VIII:C from human and porcine blood. These scientists succeeded in isolating and, for the first time, characterizing Factor VIII:C, by a process of chromatographic absorption of the Factor VIII:C complex using monoclonal antibodies specific to Factor VIII:RP, followed by separation of the Factor VIII:C.[a] Monoclonal antibodies are produced by the cloned copies of a single hybridoma cell. A hybridoma is a hybrid cell that is immortal: that is, it does not die as do normal cells, but continues to reproduce clones that in turn produce a specific antibody. As described in the R'011 patent, the hybridoma was made by fusing a mouse spleen cell that produced the desired antibody to Factor VIII:RP, with a mouse cancer cell, which contributed the immortality. The patent describes the method of assay for clones producing antibodies to VIII:RP, their isolation, and preparation of the monoclonal antibodies for use as the immunoadsorbent.

The claimed process whereby the Factor VIII:C/VIII:RP complex is separated from the other materials in blood, followed by separation of the VIII:C from the VIII:RP, is described in the R'011 patent and was summarized by Scripps as follows:

> The first step involves the application of a solution containing Factor VIII complex (Factor VIII:C/Factor VIII:RP) to a column packed with agarose beads. Attached to the beads is a monoclonal antibody to Factor VIII:RP. The monoclonal antibody binds and immobilizes the Factor VIII:RP part of the Factor VIII complex while the non-Factor VIII materials simply pass through the column. A calcium salt solution is then applied to break the bond between the Factor VIII:C and the Factor VIII:RP. The Factor VIII:C is eluted from the column while the Factor VIII:RP remains bound to the antibody.

The procedure produces purified but dilute Factor VIII:C:

> After this first step the Factor VIII:C is highly purified, but dilute. A second step to concentrate the Factor VIII:C solution may then be performed. This involves absorbing the Factor VIII:C on an aminohexylagarose column. The Factor VIII:C on the aminohexyl column is then eluted with a very small amount of calcium salt solution, resulting in a highly concentrated solution of highly purified Factor VIII:C.

Anticipation

The district court held, on cross-motions for summary judgment, that "it had been proved by clear and convincing evidence" that claims 24, 26,

[a] Drs. Zimmerman and Fulcher characterized the Factor VIII:C using a technique described as SDS-gel ("SDS" stands for sodium dodecyl sulfate) electrophoresis and production of a precipitating heterologous antibody. This work was reported in Fulcher and Zimmerman, Proc. Nat'l Acad. Sci. USA, "Characterization of the Human Factor VIII Procoagulant Protein with a Heterologous Precipitating Antibody", Vol. 79, pp. 1648–52, March, 1982. It is not disputed that this is the first time that human Factor VIII:C was sufficiently pure to be characterized scientifically, and that the Zimmerman/Fulcher characterization is now the generally recognized "fingerprint" of Factor VIII:C.

and 27 were invalid for anticipation, ... based on subject matter described in a 1979 dissertation by Robert B. Harris entitled "Isolation and Characterization of Low Molecular Weight, Non–Aggregated Antihemophilic Factor from Fresh Human Plasma."

A

Invalidity for anticipation requires that all of the elements and limitations of the claim are found within a single prior art reference. Carella v. Starlight Archery and Pro Line Co., 804 F.2d 135, 138, 231 U.S.P.Q. 644, 646 (Fed.Cir.1986); RCA Corp. v. Applied Digital Data Systems, Inc., 730 F.2d 1440, 1444, 221 U.S.P.Q. 385, 388 (Fed.Cir.1984). There must be no difference between the claimed invention and the reference disclosure, as viewed by a person of ordinary skill in the field of the invention.

It is sometimes appropriate to consider extrinsic evidence to explain the disclosure of a reference. Such factual elaboration is necessarily of limited scope and probative value, for a finding of anticipation requires that all aspects of the claimed invention were already described in a single reference: a finding that is not supportable if it is necessary to prove facts beyond those disclosed in the reference in order to meet the claim limitations. The role of extrinsic evidence is to educate the decision-maker to what the reference meant to persons of ordinary skill in the field of the invention, not to fill gaps in the reference. See Studiengesellschaft Kohle, mbH v. Dart Industries, Inc., 726 F.2d 724, 727, 220 U.S.P.Q. 841, 842 (Fed.Cir.1984)(although additional references may serve to reveal what a reference would have meant to a person of ordinary skill, it is error to build "anticipation" on a combination of these references). If it is necessary to reach beyond the boundaries of a single reference to provide missing disclosure of the claimed invention, the proper ground is not § 102 anticipation, but § 103 obviousness. Indeed, a publication on the Harris dissertation was included in the prior art statement filed by Scripps and was a cited reference under § 103.

B

In the summary judgment proceedings the parties filed three successive declarations of Dr. Harris, each explaining his dissertation. In the first declaration, filed by Miles, Inc., Harris stated that he isolated "a low molecular weight antihemophilic factor." In his second ("supplemental") declaration, filed by Scripps, Harris described this factor as not a naturally occurring substance, and of low specific activity:

6. The material I identified as low molecular weight antihemophilic factor (LMW–AHF) was not a naturally occurring substance. The material of my dissertation is the result of reacting plasma with a reducing agent called dithiothreitol (DTT) prior to purification. The reduced plasma is run through an initial purification step, and is then chemically reacted with radioactively labeled iodoacetamide (14C–IAA). This reduced and alkylated material was the LMWBAHF reported in my dissertation. After further purification, I obtained a maximum specific activity of 59.1 [units]/mg.

In the third Harris declaration, filed by Miles, Harris stated that his dissertation

> accurately reports on my work in which I was able to, and did, obtain a human VIII:C preparation having a potency of 193 [units]/ml and being substantially free of VIII:RP, the ratio of VIII:C to VIII:RP being greater than 100,000 times the ratio in plasma.

The third Harris declaration was cited by the district court in support of its finding of anticipation.

The parties debate whether Harris' statement in his second declaration that his product was chemically changed from naturally occurring VIII:C, is contradicted by the statement in his third declaration that he obtained a human VIII:C preparation. Scripps also points out that neither the potency value nor the ratio of VIII:C to VIII:RP described in the third Harris declaration appears in the Harris dissertation. Nor does the gel pattern evidence on which the district court found that:

> Harris also based his identification of his preparation upon sodium dodecyl sulfate polyacrylamide gel electrophoresis (SDSBPAGE) tests [the same tests used by Dr. Fulcher]. While Harris' gel patterns do not match the gel pattern found by Dr. Fulcher, there is no evidence that if he had VIII:C, it would necessarily have the gel pattern found by Dr. Fulcher.

Scripps, 707 F.Supp. 1547, 1551 n. 6 (N.D.Cal.1989), 11 U.S.P.Q.2d 1187, 1190 n. 6. Further, this finding that human Factor VIII:C, if obtained by Harris, would not necessarily have the "fingerprint" gel pattern of Dr. Fulcher, was not simply an adverse factual inference, improper on summary judgment; it was a finding of scientific fact contrary to the evidence. This finding also appears to be inconsistent with the court's finding that Dr. Harris had obtained purified Factor VIII:C because he based his identification on the same tests and gel patterns taught by Zimmerman and Fulcher. Also contradicting the court's conclusion was Scripps' evidence that the human Factor VIII:C SDS-gels of the inventors, the defendants, and non-parties to the litigation were the same, and that Dr. Harris' gel patterns were different.

To the extent that apparent inconsistencies among the three Harris declarations raise questions of credibility and weight, whether of witness or of interpretation of scientific data, they were improperly resolved on summary judgment.

Scripps also raised the question of whether the Harris dissertation was enabling and placed the purported anticipatory teaching of purified Factor VIII:C in possession of the public. Scripps pointed out that data in Harris' third declaration, on which the court relied, do not appear in his dissertation or in any other reference. See Akzo N.V. v. United States Int'l Trade Comm'n, 808 F.2d 1471, 1479, 1 U.S.P.Q.2d 1241, 1245 (Fed.Cir.1986), cert. denied, 482 U.S. 909, 107 S.Ct. 2490, 96 L.Ed.2d 382 (1987) (anticipatory reference must be enabling); In re Brown, 329 F.2d 1006, 1011, 141 U.S.P.Q. 245, 249 (CCPA 1964). The need to consider this issue, on disputed factual premises, also negates the propriety of the grant of summary judgment based on anticipation.

The grant of partial summary judgment of invalidity of claims 24, 26, and 27 for anticipation by the Harris dissertation is reversed. The issue is not amenable to summary disposition, and is remanded for trial.

# In re Cruciferous Sprout Litigation

United States Court of Appeals for the Federal Circuit, 2002.
301 F.3d 1343, cert. denied, 538 U.S. 907 (2003).

■ PROST, CIRCUIT JUDGE.

Brassica Protection Products LLC and Johns Hopkins University (collectively "Brassica") appeal from the decision of the United States District Court for the District of Maryland granting summary judgment that U.S. Patent Nos. 5,725,895 ("the '895 patent"), 5,968,567 ("the '567 patent"), and 5,968,505 ("the '505 patent") are invalid as anticipated by the prior art. We affirm the district court's ruling.

BACKGROUND

The three patents-in-suit relate to growing and eating sprouts to reduce the level of carcinogens in animals, thereby reducing the risk of developing cancer. Specifically, the patents describe methods of preparing food products that contain high levels of substances that induce Phase 2 enzymes. These enzymes are part of the human body's mechanism for detoxifying potential carcinogens. Thus, they have a chemoprotective effect against cancer. Foods that are rich in glucosinolates, such as certain cruciferous sprouts, have high Phase 2 enzyme-inducing potential. The inventors of the patents-in-suit recognized that the Phase 2 enzyme-inducing agents (or their glucosinolate precursors) are far more concentrated in certain sprouts (such as broccoli and cauliflower but not cabbage, cress, mustard or radish) that are harvested before the two-leaf stage than in corresponding adult plants. However, glucosinolate levels in cruciferous plants can be highly variable. According to the inventors, it is therefore desirable to select the seeds of those cruciferous plants which, when germinated and harvested before the two-leaf stage, produce sprouts that contain high levels of the desired enzyme-inducing potential.

The '895 patent was filed on September 15, 1995, and claims, *inter alia*, "A method of preparing a food product rich in glucosinolates, comprising germinated cruciferous seeds, with the exception of cabbage, cress, mustard and radish seeds, and harvesting sprouts prior to the 2–leaf stage, to form a food product comprising a plurality of sprouts." '895 patent, claim 1. The '567 patent is a continuation of the '895 application and it claims a "method of preparing a human food product" from sprouts. '567 patent, claims 1 and 9. The '505 patent is a divisional of the '895 application and it claims a "method of increasing the chemoprotective amount of Phase 2 enzymes in a mammal," as well as a "method of reducing the level of carcinogens in a mammal," by creating a "food product" from sprouts and then "administering said food product" to a mammal. '505 patent, claims 1 and 16.

The three patents-in-suit are owned by Johns Hopkins University and exclusively licensed to Brassica Protection Products LLC. Johns Hopkins and Brassica sued [a variety of defendants] in various district courts. Pursuant to 28 U.S.C. § 1407, the Judicial Panel on Multidistrict Litigation consolidated the various cases in the District of Maryland for pretrial proceedings. On June 7, 2001, the defendants filed a joint motion for partial summary judgment of invalidity, arguing that the patents were anticipated by prior art references disclosing growing and eating sprouts. Brassica filed a cross-motion for summary judgment that the patents are not invalid. On July 23, 2001, the district court held a *Markman* hearing to address claim construction issues and the parties' motions for summary judgment.

On August 10, 2001, the court granted defendants' motion for summary judgment of invalidity and denied Brassica's cross-motion for summary judgment. Brassica appeals the judgment of invalidity, arguing that the district court failed to properly construe the claims and did not apply the properly construed claims to the prior art when determining that the claims are anticipated under 35 U.S.C. § 102(b).[a]

## DISCUSSION

### I.

Brassica contends that the district court erroneously construed the claims by failing to treat the preamble of claim 1 of the '895 patent as a limitation of the claims.

No litmus test defines when a preamble limits claim scope. *Corning Glass Works v. Sumitomo Elec. U.S.A., Inc.*, 868 F.2d 1251, 1257, 9 USPQ2d 1962, 1966 (Fed.Cir.1989). Whether to treat a preamble as a limitation is a determination "resolved only on review of the entirety of the patent to gain an understanding of what the inventors actually invented and intended to encompass by the claim." *Id.* In general, a preamble limits the claimed invention if it recites essential structure or steps, or if it is "necessary to give life, meaning, and vitality" to the claim. Clear reliance on the preamble during prosecution to distinguish the claimed invention from the prior art may indicate that the preamble is a claim limitation because the preamble is used to define the claimed invention.

In this case, both the specification and prosecution history indicate that the phrase "rich in glucosinolates" helps to define the claimed invention and is, therefore, a limitation of claim 1 of the '895 patent. The specification, for example, states that "this invention relates to the production and consumption of foods which are rich in cancer chemoprotective compounds." '895 patent, col. 1, ll. 18–19. A stated object of the invention is "to provide food products and food additives that are rich in cancer chemoprotective compounds." *Id.* at col. 2, ll. 38–39. The specification

---

[a] [As we will see in Assignment 19, the determination of invalidity under § 102(b) is somewhat different from the analysis of § 102(a). However, for purposes of the issue here—identifying the contents of the prior art—the two provisions are treated the same—eds.]

therefore indicates that the inventors believed their invention to be making food products that are rich in chemoprotective compounds, or, in other words, food products "rich in glucosinolates." In addition, during reexamination[b] of the '895 patent the patentee argued as follows:

> Claim 1 of the patent, for example, is directed to "[a] method of preparing a food product rich in glucosinolates, ... and harvesting sprouts prior to the 2–leaf stage, to form a food product comprising a plurality of sprouts." ... Although "rich in glucosinolates" is recited in the preamble of the claim, the pertinent case law holds that the preamble is given weight if it breathes life and meaning into the claim.... Accordingly, the cited prior art does not anticipate the claims because it does not explicitly teach a method of preparing a food product comprising cruciferous sprouts that are rich in glucosinolates or contain high levels of Phase 2 inducer activity.

This language shows a clear reliance by the patentee on the preamble to persuade the Patent Office that the claimed invention is not anticipated by the prior art. As such, the preamble is a limitation of the claims.

## II.

Having construed the claim limitations at issue, we now compare the claims to the prior art to determine if the prior art anticipates those claims. In order to prove that a claim is anticipated under 35 U.S.C. § 102(b), defendants must present clear and convincing evidence that a single prior art reference discloses, either expressly or inherently, each limitation of the claim. *Minn. Mining & Mfg. Co. v. Johnson & Johnson Orthopaedics, Inc.,* 976 F.2d 1559, 1565, 24 USPQ2d 1321, 1326 (Fed.Cir.1992).

Brassica argues that the prior art does not expressly or inherently disclose the claim limitations of "preparing a food product rich in glucosinolates" (claims 1 and 9 of the '895 patent), or "identifying seeds which produce cruciferous sprouts ... containing high Phase 2 enzyme-inducing potential" (claims 1 and 16 of the '505 patent, claim 1 of the '567 patent). According to Brassica, the prior art merely discusses growing and eating sprouts without mention of any glucosinolates or Phase 2 enzyme-inducing potential, and without specifying that particular sprouts having these beneficial characteristics should be assembled into a "food product." Moreover, Brassica argues, the prior art does not inherently disclose these limitations because "at most, one following the prior art would have a possibility or probability of producing a food product high in Phase 2

---

[b] On December 6, 1999, the Patent Office granted a request for reexamination of the '895 patent. Claims 1–6 and 9–13 were rejected as anticipated by or obvious in light of many of the same prior art references relied on by the defendants in this case. After considering the patentee's arguments and declarations in support of patentability, the Patent Office issued a reexamination certificate and gave the following examiner's statement of reasons for patentability: "a method of preparing a food product wherein cruciferous sprouts, with the exception of cabbage, cress, mustard, and radish sprouts, that are rich in glucosinolates or contain high levels of phase 2 inducer activity are harvested prior to the 2–leaf stage is not taught or fairly suggested by the prior art or any combination thereof."

enzyme-inducing potential" and the "fact that one following the prior art might have selected seeds meeting the limitations of the claims is not sufficient to establish inherent anticipation."

It is well settled that a prior art reference may anticipate when the claim limitations not expressly found in that reference are nonetheless inherent in it. *See, e.g., Atlas Powder Co. v. Ireco Inc.*, 190 F.3d 1342, 51 USPQ2d 1943 (Fed.Cir.1999); *Titanium Metals Corp. v. Banner*, 778 F.2d 775, 227 USPQ 773 (Fed.Cir.1985). "Under the principles of inherency, if the prior art necessarily functions in accordance with, or includes, the claimed limitations, it anticipates." *MEHL/Biophile Int'l Corp. v. Milgraum*, 192 F.3d 1362, 1365, 52 USPQ2d 1303, 1305 (Fed.Cir.1999) (finding anticipation of a method of hair depilation by an article teaching a method of skin treatment but recognizing the disruption of hair follicles, citing *In re King*, 801 F.2d 1324, 1326, 231 USPQ 136, 138 (Fed.Cir.1986)). "Inherency is not necessarily coterminous with the knowledge of those of ordinary skill in the art. Artisans of ordinary skill may not recognize the inherent characteristics or functioning of the prior art." *MEHL/Biophile*, 192 F.3d at 1365, 52 USPQ2d at 1305–06; *Atlas Powder*, 190 F.3d at 1347, 51 USPQ2d at 1946–47.

Brassica does not claim to have invented a new kind of sprout, or a new way of growing or harvesting sprouts. Rather, Brassica recognized that some sprouts are rich in glucosinolates and high in Phase 2 enzyme-inducing activity while other sprouts are not. *See* '895 patent, col. 10, ll. 28–42 ("Sprouts suitable as sources of cancer chemoprotectants are generally cruciferous sprouts, with the exception of cabbage (Brassica olecracea capitata), cress (Lepidiumsativum), mustard (Sinapis alba and S. niger) and radish (Raphanus sativus) sprouts."). But the glucosinolate content and Phase 2 enzyme-inducing potential of sprouts necessarily have existed as long as sprouts themselves, which is certainly more than one year before the date of application at issue here. *See, e.g.,* Karen Cross Whyte, *The Complete Sprouting Cookbook* 4 (1973) (noting that in "2939 B.C., the Emperor of China recorded the use of health giving sprouts"). Stated differently, a sprout's glucosinolate content and Phase 2 enzyme-inducing potential are inherent characteristics of the sprout. *Cf.* Brian R. Clement, *Hippocrates Health Program* 8 (1989) (referring to "[i]nherent enzyme inhibitors, phytates (natural insecticides), oxalates, etc., present in every seed"). It matters not that those of ordinary skill heretofore may not have recognized these inherent characteristics of the sprouts. *MEHL/Biophile*, 192 F.3d at 1365, 52 USPQ2d at 1305.

*Titanium Metals Corp. v. Banner* is particularly instructive in this regard. In that case, the claim at issue recited:

> A titanium base alloy consisting essentially by weight of about 0.6% to 0.9% nickel, 0.2% to 0.4% molybdenum, up to 0.2% maximum iron, balance titanium, said alloy being characterized by good corrosion resistance in hot brine environments.

*Titanium Metals*, 778 F.2d at 776, 227 USPQ at 774. The prior art disclosed a titanium base alloy having the recited components of the claim, but the prior art did not disclose that such an alloy was "characterized by good corrosion resistance in hot brine environments." We nevertheless held that the claim was anticipated by the prior art, because "it is immaterial, on the issue of their novelty, what inherent properties the alloys have or whether these applicants discovered certain inherent properties." *Id.* at 782, 774 F.2d 483, 227 USPQ at 779. *Titanium Metals* explained the rationale behind this common sense conclusion:

> The basic provision of Title 35 applicable here is § 101, providing in relevant part: "Whoever invents or discovers any *new* . . . composition of matter, or any *new* . . . improvement thereof, may obtain a patent therefor, subject to the conditions and requirements of this title."
>
> . . . .
>
> . . . [C]ounsel never came to grips with the real issues: (1) what do the claims cover and (2) is what they cover new? Under the laws Congress wrote, they must be considered. Congress has not seen fit to permit the patenting of an old alloy, known to others through a printed publication, by one who has discovered its corrosion resistance or other useful properties, or has found out to what extent one can modify the composition of the alloy without losing such properties.

*Id.* at 780, 782, 778 F.2d 775, 227 USPQ at 777–78. Brassica has done nothing more than recognize properties inherent in certain prior art sprouts, just like the corrosion resistance properties inherent to the prior art alloy in *Titanium Metals*. While Brassica may have recognized something quite interesting about those sprouts, it simply has not invented anything new.

Brassica nevertheless argues that its claims are not anticipated because the prior art does not disclose selecting the particular seeds that will germinate as sprouts rich in glucosinolates and high in Phase 2 enzyme-inducing potential (as opposed to selecting other kinds of seeds to sprout) in order to form a food product. We disagree. The prior art teaches sprouting and harvesting the very same seeds that the patents recognize as producing sprouts rich in glucosinolates and having high Phase 2 enzyme-inducing potential.

Numerous prior art references identify these same sprouts as suitable for eating. *See, e.g.,* Stephen Facciola, *Cornucopia: A Source Book of Edible Plants* 47 (1990) (listing "Brassica oleracea Botrytis Group Cauliflower . . . Sprouted seeds are eaten"), Esther Munroe, *Sprouts to Grow and Eat* 9–14 (1974) (identifying "Broccoli, Brussels sprouts, Cabbage, Cauliflower, Collards and Kale"). These references therefore meet the claim limitation of identifying seeds to use in order to have sprouts with the inherent properties of glucosinolates and high Phase 2 enzyme-inducing activity. Despite the patents' admissions about the suitability of particular plant species found in these prior art references, Brassica argues that only specific cultivars of these plant species are rich in glucosinolates and high in Phase 2 enzyme-inducing activity. Thus, according to Brassica, the prior art fails to meet the "identifying" steps of the claims because it does not specify which cultivars should be sprouted. However, all of the appropriate cultivars that are identified in Brassica's patent are in the public domain. '895 patent, col. 10, ll. 43–65. Brassica cannot credibly maintain that no one has heretofore grown and eaten one of the many suitable cultivars identified by its patents. It is unnecessary for purposes of anticipation for the persons sprouting these particular cultivars to have realized that they were sprouting something rich in glucosinolates and high in Phase 2 enzyme-inducing potential. *Atlas Powder,* 190 F.3d at 1348, 51 USPQ2d at 1947 ("The public remains free to make, use, or sell prior art compositions or processes, regardless of whether or not they understand their complete makeup of the underlying scientific principles which allow them to operate.").

The prior art also discloses the remaining limitations of the claims....

CONCLUSION

For the foregoing reasons, we affirm the district court's summary judgment that the claims at issue are anticipated by the prior art. The prior art indisputably includes growing, harvesting and eating particular sprouts which Brassica has recognized as being rich in glucosinolates and high in Phase 2 enzyme-inducing potential. But the glucosinolate content and Phase 2 enzyme-inducing potential of these sprouts are inherent properties of the sprouts put there by nature, not by Brassica. Brassica simply has not claimed anything that is new and its claims are therefore invalid.

N O T E S

**1.** *The § 102(a) inquiry.* Most anticipation challenges claim that the patent should not issue (or is invalid) because one of the activities enumerated in § 102(a) had occurred before the applicant invented the invention. Note that although the section does not specifically require that the prior activity be "public," the cases construing this provision generally impute into it some level of publicity. For example, the safe in *Gayler* differed from the lock in *Ogden* in that its special characteristic—fireproofness—was hidden and could not be discerned or copied by mere inspection, whereas anyone viewing the *Ogden* lock could see it was reversible.

A consideration of the rationale underlying the novelty provision makes the reason for requiring some publicity clear. After all, if the prior activity does not inform the public of the invention, then the applicant *is* the one who is disseminating something new. Since the applicant provided the benefit patent law is aimed at producing, she should be entitled to receive the reward of a patent. Furthermore, awarding a patent to the applicant would not require people who were enjoying the invention for free to suddenly pay royalties. For example, no one could figure out how to practice the invention from the safe in *Gayler* because it was first hidden and then it was lost.

This analysis suggests that there are three inquiries at the heart of a § 102(a) case: first, whether the *contents* of the reference adequately gives the public the benefit of the invention; second, whether the reference is *accessible* to the public; third, whether the *date* of the reference actually precedes the date of the applicant's invention.

a. *Contents.* What must a reference teach in order to be considered anticipatory?

*(i) Enablement.* Because the novelty requirement is intended to prevent the patenting of inventions that are already available to the public, one content issue is straight forward: a reference will anticipate only if it contains enough information to allow the public to practice the invention. Thus, one reason why the Harris dissertation in *Scripps* was not anticipatory is because it was not enabling. Starting from Harris's manuscript, much more research is required to achieve the *Scripps* development.[14] It is precisely the promise of a patent that encourages this kind of work.

This statement of the justification for enablement highlights an important nuance in the way that patent law is construed. If the concept of "public" retained its ordinary meaning in the discussion of enablement, there would be few inventions that would be unpatentable. For instance, most disclosures are of a technical nature and could not, realistically speaking, enable the ordinary person to practice the invention. But, realistically speaking, what the ordinary person can do is not relevant. Only people who are trained in the field to which the invention pertains will read disclosures such as the Harris dissertation. Accordingly, it is the person *with ordinary skill in the art to which the invention pertains* who counts for § 102(a) purposes, and indeed, for most of patent law. Thus, the focus in *Scripps* is not on what Harris teaches the public at large, but on what Harris teaches the ordinary biochemist.

*(ii) The every element test.* Another way to look at the relationship between Harris and Scripps is to note that there are elements in the Scripps invention that are not described in the Harris dissertation. Since inventiveness was required to supply these missing elements, patent protection was warranted in the case. Thus, the "every element" test: anticipation under § 102(a) requires that the reference disclose *every* element (or, as in the *Sprout Litigation,* every limitation) of the applicant's invention.

The test for anticipation is sometimes expressed as: "That which infringes, if later, would anticipate, if earlier."[15] To see why anticipation is tied to infringement, focus on the party who invented the reference that is said to anticipate. (In the case of *Scripps,* this would be Harris.) Do we want to consider that person an infringer of the applicant's patent (i.e.: do we want Harris to be considered an infringer of Scripps' patent)? If the inventor of the reference had all the same insights as the patent applicant, we certainly would not want to do so. After all, the inventor of the reference may have relied on the continued free availability of his discovery

---

[14] See, e.g., Seymour v. Osborne, 78 U.S. (11 Wall.) 516 (1870); Pfizer, Inc. v. International Rectifier Corp., 545 F.Supp. 486 (C.D.Cal.1980).

[15] Knapp v. Morss, 150 U.S. 221, 228 (1893).

by committing time and effort into commercializing it. Since that is exactly the sort of activity society wants, this reliance interest deserves protection. Thus, if the inventor of the reference would be considered an infringer of the patent were it to issue, the patent should be denied: that which would infringe is deemed to anticipate. (Of course, in the actual *Scripps* case, Harris may not have had all of the applicants' insights. If that is the case, he had no reliance interest in the free availability of Scripps' invention, and so we do not mind if he is considered an infringer of the Scripps patent.)[16]

*(iii) Inherency.* Reconsider the facts of the Principal Problem. What if someone back in the early 1950's had invented a mechanical joint that effected a coupling similar to that found in Nichols' cube, and even utilized a color scheme similar to Nichols' to keep the sides of the coupling aligned: should the joint be considered anticipatory? On the one hand, nothing about the joint suggests it would make a fun puzzle; its intended function was never to amuse. On the other hand, the joint contains every element of the cube and enables the construction of the puzzle. Anyone with the idea of a three dimensional puzzle had only to look at this joint to fully effectuate the idea. Given that the goal of § 102(a) is to encourage the use of earlier work, § 102(a) prior art is said to encompass information of this type, information "inherent" in other works.

That said, determining inherency has proved highly contentious. As the *Sprout Litigation* court makes clear, the prior art must *necessarily* contain the inherent element—"invalidation based on inherency is not established by 'probabilities or possibilities.' "[17] Unfortunately, however, the Federal Circuit has not specified exactly what probability is sufficient. Since not *all* sprouts contain enough Phase 2 enzyme-inducing potential to protect against cancer, should inherency have been found in the *Sprout Litigation*?

---

[16] For another example, consider the *Titanium Metals* case, discussed in the *Sprout Litigation*. The prior art describing an alloy of titanium containing 0.25% molybdenum and 0.75% nickel. Someone later applied for a patent on titanium alloys containing anywhere between 0.2–0.4% molybdenum and 0.6–0.9% nickel. Should the reference be considered anticipatory? The person who authored the reference may well have put it to use. In order to avoid undermining the reliance interests of the author, the reference must be considered anticipatory.

Note, however, that a reference disclosing alloys in a range from 0.6–0.9% nickel would not necessarily anticipate an application for an alloy containing precisely 0.75% nickel. If the 0.75% alloy had surprisingly different characteristics, its identification may be considered a nonobvious improvement over prior art, see, e.g., In re Meyer, 599 F.2d 1026 (C.C.P.A.1979).

The results here could also be explained on the search cost model described in the Introduction. Under this approach, the issue is whether the law should encourage metallurgists interested in inventing new alloys of titanium to read this reference and explore its significance. Consider the reference discussed in the first paragraph (the .75% nickel alloy). Since reading about its existence should alert metallurgists to the possibility of other alloys with slightly different amounts of nickel, the law should regard the .75% nickel reference as anticipatory. But since the range reference in the second paragraph would not tell metallurgists about a surprisingly different characteristic of the .75% nickel alloy, there is no point in requiring them to read that reference first, and so that reference would not be regarded as anticipatory.

[17] Scaltech Inc. v. Retec/Tetra, L.L.C., 178 F.3d 1378, 1384 (Fed.Cir.1999).

Still harder is the question of what the person with ordinary skill must understand about the reference. The *Sprout Litigation* court states that "it matters not that those of ordinary skill heretofore may not have recognized the inherent characteristics of the sprouts." However, the court has flirted with other views. For example, Elan Pharmaceuticals, Inc. v. Mayo Foundation involved a patent on a "recipe" for producing mice engineered to contain a gene mutation associated with Alzheimer's disease. The prior art included a recipe that could have been used to produce mice with the same mutation, but it was not so recognized. In a decision that was later vacated, the court held that the reference was not anticipatory.[18] From a theoretical standpoint, which approach is better? The rule the court temporarily adopted in *Elan* encourages inventors to uncover previously unappreciated features of known art. On the other hand, if the goal is to protect the initial inventor and the public, then *Sprout Litigation* has it right. Remember, if a patent were to issue on an inherent feature of prior art, it would presumably cover the use made by the inventor of the prior art. Further, the *Elan* rule would permit an inventor to acquire successive periods of exclusivity— first on one invention, then on features inherent to that invention.[19]

b. *Accessibility*. A reference is able to teach the public the invention only if the public (the relevant public) is aware of its existence (or can make itself aware at reasonable cost). There are several dimensions to this issue.

*(i) Geography*. Section § 102(a) makes knowledge or use of the invention anticipatory only when it occurs in the United States. In contrast, any publication or patent is anticipatory, including those that are disseminated exclusively abroad.

What accounts for the difference in the way foreign events are treated? Here is a place where the search model discussed in the Introduction is especially useful. Because literature searches of both domestic and foreign journals, books, and patents are relatively inexpensive, the statute encourages them. Searching for "knowledge" (that is, unwritten knowledge) and "use" is, however, relatively expensive, especially if it involves activities occurring in far away places, among different cultures, and in different languages. Accordingly, the statute does not bar patents because of foreign knowledge or use. Alternatively, one could say that because foreign uses

---

[18] 304 F.3d 1221, 1227–28 (Fed. Cir. 2002), vacated, 314 F.3d 1299 (Fed. Cir. 2002). In a later decision, the Federal Circuit recharacterized the argument in *Elan* as going to the question whether the prior art *enabled* the invention at issue, not whether it inherently anticipated it, 346 F.3d 1051 (Fed. Cir. 2003). On inherency, see also ATD Corp. v. Lydall, Inc., 159 F.3d 534, 545 (Fed. Cir. 1998)("An anticipating reference must describe the patented subject matter with sufficient clarity and detail to establish that the subject matter existed and that its existence was recognized by persons of ordinary skill in the field of the invention.")

[19] See, e.g., Schering Corp. v. Geneva Pharmaceuticals, 339 F.3d 1373 (Fed.Cir. 2003), where the court found that DCL, an antihistamine, was anticipated by loratadine, better known as Claritin. Loratadine metabolized into DCL, although the ordinary artisan did not know it. Allowing Schering to patent DCL would have created strong incentives to investigate metabolites, but the patent would also have prevented generics from selling loratadine once the Claritin patent expired: had the DCL patent been valid, anyone who ingested Claritin would have infringed it.

and knowledge are hard to find, the public—the American public, that is—does not actually enjoy the benefit of the invention until the applicant re-invents it in the United States.

Cynics may have a different explanation. Section 102(a) is bolstered in an important way by § 104(a), which bars an applicant from establishing a date of invention through activity occurring abroad (unless a treaty declares otherwise).[20] That is, just as *challengers* to the patent cannot rely on foreign knowledge and use by virtue of § 102(a), *applicants* are barred from relying on foreign activities to establish invention by virtue of § 104(a). The net effect is to enhance the significance (for patent purposes) of work done in the United States, primarily by Americans, and to diminish the importance of work done abroad, primarily by foreigners. As international communication improves and the global market becomes the principal arena for patent exploitation, this parochialism becomes less tenable.[21] Indeed, § 104 once included all foreign countries. The North American Free Trade Agreement (NAFTA) and the TRIPS Agreement required the United States to amend it so that signatories of these treaties are treated as equivalent to the United States for purposes of establishing the date of invention. Many commentators believe that if world-wide harmonization of the patent laws is to be achieved, the United States will be required to eliminate the § 102(a) distinction as well.[22] One could even argue that § 102(a) violates the spirit of the TRIPS Agreement or the U.S. Constitution.[23]

*(ii) Dissemination.* The search model also suggests why it is that not every domestic use will be considered public enough to be anticipatory: some uses will be so hard to find, searching will not be cost effective. It is this problem which may account for the difference between *Gayler* and *Ogden*. Both inventions were in "use," but only one was disseminated enough to make search expedient—that is, enough to assure public availability. The lock, after all, was seen by several artisans, any one of whom could duplicate the invention and make it available to others; the applicant added nothing to the fund of knowledge. But the safe was never inspected. When its inventor stopped using it, its inventive feature was lost; the new

[20] The provision itself mentions NAFTA and GATT. The Paris Convention for the Protection of Industrial Property creates another important exception. It permits inventors to use as their date of invention the date on which they filed a patent application in another member state, so long as the U.S. application is filed within 12 months of the foreign filing, see Patent Act § 119. See generally, Section 3 of Assignment 14.

[21] Cf., e.g., Monaco v. Hoffman, 189 F.Supp. 474 (D.D.C.1960).

[22] See, e.g., Harold C. Wegner, Patent Law Simplification and the Geneva Patent Convention, 14 A.I.P.L.A. Q.J. 154 (1986).

[23] Article 27(1) of the TRIPS Agreement states that "patents shall be available ... without discrimination as to the place of invention." Although there is nothing in TRIPS that explicitly requires nondiscriminatory treatment of prior art, art. 27(1) can be read broadly as barring unequal treatment of those involved in the patent system. For specific examples of the effects of this distinction, see Margo A. Bagley, Patently Unconstitutional: The Geographic Limitation on Prior Art in a Small World, 87 Minn. L. Rev. 679 (2003)(arguing that barring the use of foreign knowledge violates the Copyright Clause because it permits the protection of material that is not inventive).

inventor enriched the storehouse of knowledge, and that contribution merits a patent. Alternatively, since no one saw the safe and relied on its status in the public domain, no one's interests would be frustrated by awarding the patent. In contrast, for all anyone knew, Brossi, Masta, or Patterson could have invested in efforts to commercialize the lock the moment they saw it.

Is it always the case that "patents" and "publications" will have achieved the level of dissemination required to effectively give the invention to the public? Desktop publishing and the Internet make it possible to disseminate information at low cost. However, it is not necessarily the case that the information will be widely seen or easy to find. Even before digitization, there were problems with these terms. Thus, dissertations are sometimes "printed," but distributed only within the degree-candidate's department. Only one copy may be retained by the University. Should the information in such a "publication" be considered to meet the "publicity" gloss of § 102(a)? Most courts decide that question by asking whether a researcher with ordinary skill in the art could have found the publication. Is it, for example, indexed or abstracted? If not, despite technical compliance with the "publication" requirement, such a work will not be considered anticipatory.[24] Printed documents that are marked "confidential" and distributed on a limited basis are similarly not considered to anticipate.[25]

Conversely, there are some documents that do not quite meet the definition of "patent" or "publication" that nonetheless have achieved the level of publicity necessary to find anticipation. For example, some countries have alternatives to patent protection that allow the inventor to avoid a rigorous examination if he is willing to accept less protection for a shorter term. The certificates issued under these regimes are available to the public just as patents are, but they go by names such as "inventor's certificates" or "petit patents." Should they be considered "patents" or "publications" for purposes of § 102(a)? Since they too encourage people to disclose new inventions and facilitate public dissemination, the answer is that they are considered "patents" for the purpose of § 102(a).[26]

Was *Gayler* rightly decided? The accessibility issue is of particular importance to the computer industry. Because it is possible to distribute programs in a way that makes the actual code almost impossible to read, software innovations can be protected as trade secrets.[27] However, if a

[24] See, e.g., Blandford v. Masco Industries, Inc., 799 F.Supp. 666 (N.D.Tex.1992); Jockmus v. Leviton, 28 F.2d 812 (2d Cir. 1928)(L. Hand, J.).

[25] Cf. Cooper Cameron Corp. v. Kvaerner Oilfield Products, Inc., 291 F.3d 1317 (Fed. Cir. 2002).

[26] See, e.g., Reeves Bros. v. United States Laminating Corp., 282 F.Supp. 118 (E.D.N.Y. 1968). Of course, the other elements of anticipation, including enablement, must be met; the fact that a disclosure meets these requirements to the satisfaction of a foreign patent examiner does not necessarily mean it meets the requirements of U.S. patent law, see, e.g., United States v. Adams, 383 U.S. 39 (1966). But see In re Carlson, 983 F.2d 1032 (Fed. Cir.1992)(holding a German "Geschmackmuster," a design registration, qualifies as a foreign patent under § 102(a) despite the fact that disclosure is available only in the city where the registered design is deposited).

[27] The Copyright Office facilitates the use of trade secrecy law by permitting deposit of only the first and last 25 pages of a pro-

reference must be genuinely accessible to the public in order to anticipate, keeping a program as a trade secret is risky. If the trade secret were, per *Gayler,* unavailable as a reference, then someone who re-invents the identical software would be able to patent it. The original innovator would then be required to get a license in order to continue to use the invention. Not surprisingly, there are patent lawyers in the software industry who maintain either that *Gayler* should, at the very least be confined to its facts, that it should be understood as creating a special rule for "lost art," that is, technologies that were not practiced in a way that revealed how they worked and are no longer practiced at all. In the alternative, it is argued that inventions that are being practiced in secret should count as effective prior art, either under § 102(a) or under the first sentence of § 102(g)(2), see Note 2(b).

*(iii) Operability.* There is another distinction between *Gayler* and *Ogden* that helps account for the difference in result. In *Ogden,* the latch was actually placed upon a door, where the operability of its special feature could be readily determined. In *Gayler,* however, the allegedly fire-proof safe was never exposed to fire. Thus, its inventive characteristic was never put to the test. Although § 102(a) does not expressly require proof that the prior art is operable, courts have construed it to impute such a requirement. Patents are considered operable because they must have met the requirement of utility in order to have issued. Printed publications are, in most technical fields, a good proxy for operability because articles are generally subjected to peer review prior to publication. Given the gloss of *Gayler,* inventions that are "used" in this country are also likely to have been operable. That leaves the category of "known," which has—interestingly—been interpreted as requiring some level of use.[28]

*(iv) Field of knowledge.* How far afield must the inventor cast the search net? In the inherency example, it was assumed that a mechanical joint could anticipate a child's puzzle, even though puzzle-makers are not likely to be acquainted with work in the mechanical arts. In fact, the novelty provisions are interpreted to charge the inventor with knowledge of the entire universe of prior art, including art in fields very different from their own specialities.[29] Does this make sense under the search model? Searching the entire domain of knowledge sounds extremely expensive. On the other hand, it is worth remembering that every element of the claimed invention must appear in the reference. It is not very likely that an entire invention will be duplicated in a field quite distant from the one to which the invention pertains.

**c.** *Dating invention.* The final question under the anticipation sections involves dating. That is, the *"effective date"* of the reference—the date the public received the benefit of the prior art—must precede the

---

gram, along with a statement that the rest is a trade secret, see U.S. Copyright Office, Circular 61, posted at www.copyright.gov/circs/circ61.html#computer1.

[28] See Donald S. Chisum, Patents § 3.05[3]; Westinghouse Machine Co. v. General Elec. Co., 207 F. 75 (2d Cir.1913).

[29] Chisum, at § 3.02[3].

*"critical date"*—in the case of § 102(a), the date on which the applicant invented the invention. In *Scripps,* for example, the Harris dissertation cannot function as prior art unless it was published (or at least indexed) before the date Scripps claims for the invention.

What should count as the *critical date*? In most cases, invention is not a sudden, one time event. As in the Principal Problem, the inventor has an idea that she ponders and experiments with for some time before it is fully realized. Should the conception of the idea be the critical date? The date on which the working model is finished? The date of first commercialization?

The practice in the PTO is that the critical date is assumed to be the date on which the applicant files a complete application disclosing the invention.[30] If the examiner cannot cite to prior art dating from an earlier time, the invention will be considered novel. If, however, the examiner finds a suitable reference, the inquiry goes to the next stage. To be anticipatory, a reference must predate the date of *invention* not *filing.* Thus, the applicant is permitted to establish that she invented the invention on an earlier date. The usual procedure is to "swear behind": to file an affidavit under Patent Office Rule 131 claiming "reduction to practice" on a date preceding the reference, or "conception" prior to that date, coupled with "due diligence" from before the reference's date and later "reduction to practice."[31] These technical terms, "conception," "reduction to practice" and "due diligence," are also utilized in determining priority and will be formally defined in Assignment 20. If the patent is challenged in litigation or in an interference, the patentee may be required to prove these dates and not merely swear to them.

What should count as the *effective date* of a reference? As with the other elements of novelty, it is the date on which an ordinary artisan in the field has effective access to the disclosure. For a patent, this is the date of issuance (except as explained in Note 2); for a book or journal article, it is the date of publication.[32] For publications that receive only modest circulation, it may be the date of indexing.[33]

**2.** §§ *102(e) and (g).* This Assignment focuses on § 102(a) because most cases involving novelty arise under § 102(a). However, the other novelty provisions deserve some attention.

a. § *102(e).* Consider this modification to the Principal Problem: what if a puzzlemaker had acquired a U.S. patent on a very different kind of three dimensional puzzle but in the course of describing the state of the art at the time of the invention, disclosed a puzzle much like Nichols'? If the patent issued before Nichols' invention, he would clearly lose under § 102(a). However, what if the patent had been *applied for* before Nichols invented his cube, but did not issue until *after* Nichols' critical date?

[30] See, e.g., Bates v. Coe, 98 U.S. 31 (1878).

[31] 37 C.F.R. § 1.131.

[32] See, e.g., In re Schlittler, 234 F.2d 882 (C.C.P.A.1956).

[33] Compare In re Hall, 781 F.2d 897 (Fed.Cir.1986), with In re Cronyn, 890 F.2d 1158 (Fed.Cir.1989).

In Alexander Milburn Co. v. Davis–Bournonville Co.,[34] the Supreme Court addressed this problem under an earlier patent statute. The Court recognized that because the patent application was secret at the time that the second invention was made,[35] there was a sense in which the second inventor had done everything necessary to be entitled to a patent. However, the Court also thought that the second inventor should not profit (and the public should not be made to pay) because of delays in the Patent Office. Accordingly, it interpreting "patent" to cover applications that eventually result in issued patents, that is, it made the effective date of an issued patent the date on which the application was filed.

This holding is now codified in § 102(e). Thus, whereas § 102(a) deals with public prior art, § 102(e) provides that in one particular circumstance, secret prior art will also be anticipatory. That circumstance is a disclosure in the patent pipeline at the time of the second invention. Note, however, that being in the pipeline is not sufficient, the application describing the invention must ultimately be disclosed. After all, if the application is dropped and never becomes public, then the second applicant (Nichols in our example) would be the one to make the invention public, and he should be entitled to a patent.

For two reasons, the current version of § 102(e) is more complicated than its original codification. First, at the time of *Milburn*, all patent applications were secret until they issued. Thus, the event triggering the application of § 102(e) was always issuance. Now, most applications are published 18 months after filing. As a result, publication is now the usual triggering event. For applications that are not subject to the publication requirement, issuance remains the trigger.

The second complication in 102(e) relates to the problem of foreign filings and filings under the Patent Cooperation Treaty (PCT).[36] Start with this question: what if Nichols' puzzle had been described in a *Hungarian* patent application? Clearly, if the patent had issued before Nichols' invention, § 102(a) would have prevented Nichols from acquiring a patent. But should the *Milburn* analysis also apply—that is, should Nichols' puzzle be regarded as anticipated if it is described in a Hungarian patent application filed before his critical date, but published after that date? Why should delays in the Hungarian patent office be any more helpful to Nichols than delays in the PTO?

Despite the logic of this position, *Milburn* has not been extended to this situation; § 102(e) is expressly limited to U.S. patent applications.[37] Perhaps this is another example of the protectionist slant of U.S. law. On the other hand, it makes sense to limit the situations in which secret art is anticipatory, for it is information that no amount of searching could have revealed to the second inventor. Furthermore, no one could have relied on

---

[34] 270 U.S. 390 (1926).

[35] § 122.

[36] The PCT application is described in Assignment 14.

[37] See In re Hilmer, 359 F.2d 859 (C.C.P.A.1966)(Hilmer I) and In re Hilmer, 424 F.2d 1108 (C.C.P.A.1970)(Hilmer II), discussed in Assignment 20 Note 7.

this invention being freely available. Indeed, efforts to extend § 102(e) in most other circumstances—such as manuscripts in the publication pipeline—have also, generally, failed.[38]

The one exception relates to PCT applications. These are not pure U.S. patent applications—some are filed abroad and do not even designate the United States as a country where a patent will be sought, some are filed abroad and do designate the United States, and some are filed in the U.S. PTO, but pursuant to requirements different from those of pure U.S. applications. Should these applications get the benefit of *Milburn*? Barring applications filed in the United States is a trap for the unwary, who may believe that because they are filing in the PTO, they are filing U.S. applications within the meaning of § 102(e). However, recognizing all PCT applications would improperly give some wholly foreign patents the benefit of § 102(e). Much of the complication in § 102(e) is intended to deal with this problem. Unfortunately, the language is difficult to parse (and it changes frequently). Apparently, the intent is to give only those PCT applications that are in English and designate the United States, the benefit of the *Milburn* rule.

b.  § *102(g)*. At its core, this provision sets the priority rule—that is, it determines who, among several independent inventors, is entitled to the patent. The complication in the language of § 102(g)(1) comes as a result of the § 104 problem described above, in connection with § 102(a): it is an attempt to implement the TRIPS and NAFTA requirements that foreign art from TRIPS and NAFTA countries count for the purpose of acquiring patent rights, but to prevent the use of foreign art to defeat patent rights. This function of § 102(g) will be discussed in Assignment 20.

For purposes of this Assignment, the part of this provision that is of interest is the first sentence of § 102(g)(2), which can be read as a novelty provision. It appears to deem anticipatory *any* invention made in the United States that has not been abandoned, suppressed, or concealed. Thus, § 102(g)—like § 102(e)—allows certain secret art to block the award of a patent. Indeed, at first blush, this provision appears to eviscerate § 102(a), or at least the gloss that assures that knowledge and/or use of the invention has enough publicity to enable an ordinary artisan to search for it easily. After all, *some* non-abandoned inventions may be extremely difficult to find. An example is an innovation in a computer program that is kept as a trade secret.

But closer inspection reveals that § 102(g) does not entirely eviscerate § 102(a). To see the difference, ask why should a patent ever be blocked by genuinely secret art? Certainly, it is not easy to explain this with the search model. The answer here lies in focusing on the first inventor, who has not "abandoned, suppressed or concealed" the invention. The definition of this phrase will be discussed in Assignment 20. For now, it is enough to

---

[38] See, e.g., In re Schlittler, 234 F.2d 882 (C.C.P.A.1956); Protein Foundation, Inc. v. Brenner, 260 F.Supp. 519 (D.D.C. 1966)(§ 102(b)); Ex parte Osmond, Smith, and Waite, 191 U.S.P.Q. (BNA) 334 (Pat.Off. Bd.App. 1973)

understand that an invention that has not been abandoned, suppressed, or concealed is one that is either in use (albeit, so secretly, it does not qualify as § 102(a) art), or is in the process of being patented or commercialized. If the second applicant's patent issues, the person using or developing that invention is suddenly an infringer. Yet she did nothing wrong: there is no requirement that inventors obtain patents.[39] Trade secrecy law is not preempted by the Patent Act,[40] and the first inventor may have been expecting to patent her invention or to capture her rewards through secrecy. Alternatively, she may have tried hard, but unsuccessfully, to disseminate the invention more broadly or even patent it. Section 102(g) protects such an inventor's reliance interest in the continued free availability of her invention. Thus, § 102(g) differs from § 102(a) in that it requires proof of continued use by the inventor.[41] In contrast, § 102(a) requires publicity, but not a continuation of use by the inventor (or by anyone else). Furthermore, § 102(g) entails proof positive that the invention is operable (otherwise, how could its inventor be using it?). As we saw, the interpretation of § 102(a) tends to require some suggestion of operability, but the provision does not explicitly require actual proof.

**3.** *Prior user rights.* As suggested earlier, the computer industry is particularly concerned about the accessibility issue in § 102(a) and the use of § 102(g)(2) as a novelty provision. The industry relies on trade secrecy protection and it wants to make sure that the use of a secret program is enough to defeat a second inventor's claim to a patent on the same technology. However, some argue that it is inappropriate to remove the publicity requirement from § 102(a) or to use § 102(g)(2) as a novelty provision, that focusing on the first inventor has the unfortunate effect of frustrating the second inventor's interests. Although that inventor may have searched prior art diligently and invested in development in reliance on the fact that the invention was not known, she is nonetheless barred from obtaining a patent.

Is there a way to accommodate the interests of both the first and the second inventors? In some countries, secret art is never anticipatory. Accordingly, the second inventor's expectations are fulfilled with a patent. However, the first inventor is also protected: she enjoys a "prior user

---

[39] See, e.g., Checkpoint Systems, Inc. v. U.S. ITC, 54 F.3d 756 (Fed.Cir.1995).

[40] See Assignment 24.

[41] See, e.g., E.I. du Pont de Nemours & Co. v. Phillips Petroleum Co., 849 F.2d 1430, 1437 (Fed.Cir.)("the requirement of proving no abandonment, suppression, or concealment does mollify somewhat the 'secret' nature of § 102(g) prior art"), cert. denied, 488 U.S. 986 (1988). See also Dow Chemical Co. v. Astro–Valcour, Inc., 267 F.3d 1334 (Fed. Cir. 2001); Dunlop Holdings v. Ram Golf Corp., 524 F.2d 33 (7th Cir.1975). But see Gillman v. Stern, 114 F.2d 28 (2d Cir. 1940)(L. Hand, J.), holding that a machine is not anticipated under § 102(g) by sales of its output, so long as the sales are "noninforming"—they do not reveal how the machine itself was made. The case is discussed in Assignment 19, Note 1. See also Frank E. Robbins, The Rights of a First Inventor–Trade Secret User as Against Those of the Second Inventor–Patentee (Part I), 61 J.Pat. Off.Soc. 574 (1979); Karl F. Jorda, The Rights of a First Inventor–Trade Secret User as Against Those of the Second Inventor–Patentee (Part II), 61 J.Pat.Off.Soc. 593 (1979).

right," which is the right to use the invention without paying royalties, limited to the uses being made at the time of the second invention.[42] U.S. law does not include a general prior user right. However, after the *State Street* case was decided, see Assignment 15, many patents issued on business methods long in use, but not recorded in the sort of reference that patent lawyers and the PTO could easily find. To save those who were already using a business method at the time it was patented the cost of going to court to invalidate the patent, Congress passed the "First Inventor Defense Act," which creates a defense to infringement in favor of any person who:

> "acting in good faith, actually reduced the subject matter [of a method patent] to practice at least one year before the effective filing date of such patent, and commercially used the subject matter before the effective filing date of such patent."[43]

To prevent corrosive competition between the patentee and the first inventor, the defense is specifically nominated as "Not a general license."[44] It is just a defense to a claim of infringement regarding the specific use that began before the filing date. "Method" is defined as "a method of doing or conducting business."[45] However, "business" is not defined, and there is reason to believe that this provision may eventually have fairly broad application.

Is this the better approach? It neatly balances both sets of interests, but there is real question whether the interests of trade secret holders deserve the accommodation. Trade secrecy is associated with significant public cost. Trade secrets can last longer than patents, they do not reveal information that could be used to further knowledge in its field, and inventors may waste resources reinventing something already known. Perhaps society is better off tolerating trade secrets, but requiring those who opt for trade secrets to bear the risk that they may find themselves infringers. In that way, innovators will be more likely to utilize the patent system. We will return to this issue in Assignment 24.

---

[42] See, e.g., William T. Fryer, Patent Law Harmonization Treaty Decision is Not Far Off—What Course Should the U.S. Take? : A Review of the Current Situation and Alternatives Available, 30 IDEA 309 (1990).

[43] § 273(b)(1).

[44] § 273(b)(3)(C).

[45] § 273(a)(3).

# ASSIGNMENT 18

# NONOBVIOUSNESS AND ORIGINALITY

## 1. INTRODUCTION

When the patent law was recodified in 1952, nonobviousness was set out as a statutory requirement for the first time. The new provision, § 103, did not, however, mark a major change in the law, for the courts had long imposed as a matter of common law a requirement of "invention" closely akin to what is now called nonobviousness.[1]

A moment's thought reveals why an intellectual property system that requires novelty might also impose a condition of nonobviousness. The novelty provision is intended to secure to the public domain inventions that were effectively available to the public prior to the intervention of the applicant. However, the test for novelty is rather limited. After all, every element of the invention must be revealed in a single prior disclosure.[2] This limitation means that some innovations that are arguably available to the public escape the novelty requirement. These are the inventions that, while not revealed in a single source, are either effectively disclosed in a series of references or represent minor changes in existing technology. It is not unreasonable (or, in the search model, overly costly) to expect ordinary artisans to pull together the things they learn, and even to make modest advances. The nonobviousness requirement makes these kinds of advances unpatentable.

Understanding the need to augment the novelty requirement does not, unfortunately, provide an easy test for determining which advances are so available to the public they should not be patentable. Prior to the 1952 Act, the courts experimented with a variety of formulations. In Hotchkiss v. Greenwood,[3] the Supreme Court held unpatentable inventions that could have been constructed with the "skill ... possessed by an ordinary mechanic acquainted with the business." Some courts enunciated a series of negative tests of invention. For example, changes in form, proportions, or degree and aggregations of old elements were held unpatentable.[4] Other

---

[1] See, e.g., Edmund Kitch, Graham v. John Deere Co: New Standards for Patents, 1966 S.Ct. Rev. 303.

[2] See Note 1(a)(ii) of Assignment 17.

[3] 52 U.S. (11 How.) 248 (1850).

[4] See, e.g., Carbice Corp. v. American Patents Dev. Corp., 283 U.S. 420 (1931); Dunbar v. Myers, 94 U.S. (4 Otto) 187 (1876).

courts looked to external signs of inventiveness, such as commercial success and the failure of others, especially in the face of long-felt need.[5]

The trend of using inventiveness to enhance the standard of patentability culminated in two cases heavily influenced by Justice William O. Douglas, who was always highly skeptical of patents. Writing for the Court in Cuno Engineering Corp. v. Automatic Devices Corp.,[6] he held that in order to be patentable, a "new device, however useful it may be, must reveal [a] flash of creative genius, not merely the skill of the calling."[7] *Cuno Engineering* was followed by Great Atlantic & Pacific Tea Co. v. Supermarket Equipment Corp.,[8] which involved the patent on a three-sided frame that was used to push groceries along the counter toward the checkout clerk before the invention of the conveyer belt. The majority opinion, authored by Justice Jackson, considered the device to be a combination of known elements. According to the Court, "[t]he conjunction or concert of known elements must contribute something; only when the whole in some way exceeds the sum of its parts is the accumulation of old devices patentable."[9] No patent was available for this device because "two and two have been added together, and still they make only four."[10] Concurring, Justice Douglas added:

> "Every patent is the grant of a privilege of exacting tolls from the public. The Framers plainly did not want those monopolies freely granted. The invention, to justify a patent, had to serve the ends of science—to push back the frontiers of chemistry, physics, and the like; to make a distinctive contribution to scientific knowledge. That is why through the years the opinions of the Court commonly have taken 'inventive genius' as the test. It is not enough that an article is new and useful. The Constitution never sanctioned the patenting of gadgets. Patents serve a higher end—the advancement of science."[11]

Given that genuine advances in science are usually in the nature of unpatentable discoveries of nature,[12] that geniuses are born rather infrequently, that most inventions combine known elements, and that two plus two invariably equals four, *Cuno Engineering* and *Great A & P* together created chaos in the law of patentability. Decisions of lower courts became difficult to reconcile and there was a great deal of forum shopping. More important, as validity became increasingly difficult to predict, patents lost value. The Supreme Court simply retreated from the fray; from 1950, when *Great A & P* was decided, until 1966, it did not review any patent cases on this issue.

The field was therefore left to Congress, which responded with the formulation now found in § 103(a). Harkening back to *Hotchkiss*, the

---

[5] See, e.g., Smith v. Goodyear Dental Vulcanite Co., 93 U.S. (3 Otto) 486 (1876).

[6] 314 U.S. 84 (1941).

[7] Id. at 90–92.

[8] 340 U.S. 147 (1950).

[9] Id. at 152.

[10] Id.

[11] Id. at 154–155 (footnotes omitted)(Douglas, J., concurring).

[12] See Assignment 15.

statute renders unpatentable inventions that "would have been obvious at the time the invention was made to a person having ordinary skill in the art." Patentability could no longer be negated by "the manner in which the invention was made," § 103(c).

Because the availability of a reference as prior art for nonobviousness purposes sometimes turns on the identity of the inventor (or inventive entity), the issue of originality is also covered in this Assignment.

## 2.   PRINCIPAL PROBLEMS

### (i)   PROBLEM A

Return to the facts of the Principal Problem of Assignment 17: is Nichols' cube nonobvious? If the cube was nonobvious, why didn't Ideal try to patent it?

### (ii)   PROBLEM B

Return to the facts of the Principal Problem of Assignment 15: is the protein manufactured by Gamma nonobvious even though Dr. Beta had previously determined the DNA sequence that encoded it? Is the genetic sequence nonobvious? In the original problem, you were told that Beta used standard techniques to determine the sequence. Now the information can be obtained with automatic sequencing devices. Would the knowledge that Beta used such equipment change your answer?

### (iii)   PROBLEM C

A public interest organization composed of scientists and medical researchers called the Coalition to Fight Terminal Diseases (CFTD) has come to us for advice. Drug X is currently the only drug on the market effective in treating a certain terminal contagious disease. The Alpha Company patented this drug in 1998. Pleased with its profits, Alpha has done no further research with it. CFTD has. It discovered a more purified version of Drug X which has fewer side effects and more therapeutic potential. CFTD has asked us for advice on whether it can patent its purified version.

To really understand what is going on here, you need to know a little chemistry. What CFTD discovered was that Drug X (like many drugs) actually exists in two structural forms, a so-called "(R)" form [here, (R)-X] and an "(S)" form [(S)-X]. These have identical chemical constitutions (the same atoms appear in the same order), but the structures are mirror images of each other, much like left and right hands. These mirror-image structures are called "enantiomers" and it is well known in pharmacological circles that despite being structurally identical, enantiomers do not usually have the same biological activity. Commonly, only one of the two provides therapeutic benefit; the other may be inactive or cause undesirable side effects.

Clinical experience showed that although X was useful in controlling the progression of disease, treatment had to be terminated at the end stage because of side effects. This is where CFTD stepped in. First, after determining that Alpha was selling X as a mixture of the two enantiomeric forms, it set out to purify the product so that the biologically beneficial enantiomer could be administered alone. A 1965 article in the Journal of the Australian Chemical Society on "Differential Solubility of Enantiomers" listed a group of solvents in which R-and S-enantiomers generally tend to have different solubilities. When none of the solvents listed in the article worked for X, CFTD scientists instead tried solvents that were known to dissolve the same sorts of things as the ones on the list. After several months' experimentation, one solvent was found that provided some separation. Further isolation was achieved by following a 1984 article in the New Zealand Journal of Solid State Chemistry on "Isolation through Adsorption," which described techniques for purifying chemical compounds by pouring them down columns packed with solids to which they adsorb (i.e. cling). CFTD researchers again spent many months finding just the right solid. Using a combination of these two techniques, 99% separation was achieved, and each enantiomer was further purified with standard purification methods.

(R)-X and (S)-X were then tested using procedures suggested by the FDA for a period of two years. In early 2003, (R)-X was identified as the therapeutic enantiomer. Use of (R)-X alone caused no new side effects, reduced the known side effects, and effectively controlled the disease. (S)-X was found to cause the side effects that require termination of treatment. CFTD published its research results immediately and has had an extraordinary number of requests for treatment doses of (R)-X.

As noted, CFTD has come to us for advice. Although its primary mission is to cure this terrible disease, it needs money to pursue its objectives and would like to secure a patent on both (R)-X itself and on its method of purification. What is your view on the patentability of any of the discoveries made by CFTD?

## 3. MATERIALS FOR SOLUTION OF PRINCIPAL PROBLEMS

A. STATUTORY MATERIAL: §§ 103 & 102(f)

B. CASES:

## Graham v. John Deere Co.

Supreme Court of the United States, 1966.
383 U.S. 1, 86 S.Ct. 684, 15 L.Ed.2d 545.

■ MR. JUSTICE CLARK delivered the opinion of the Court.

After a lapse of 15 years, the Court again focuses its attention on the patentability of inventions under the standard of Art. I, § 8, cl. 8, of the Constitution and under the conditions prescribed by the laws of the United States. Since our last expression on patent validity, Great A. & P. Tea Co. v. Supermarket Equipment Corp., 340 U.S. 147, 71 S.Ct. 127, 95 L.Ed. 162 (1950), the Congress has for the first time expressly added a third statutory dimension to the two requirements of novelty and utility that had been the sole statutory test since the Patent Act of 1793. This is the test of obviousness, i.e., whether "the subject matter sought to be patented and the prior art are such that the subject matter as a whole would have been obvious at the time the invention was made to a person having ordinary skill in the art to which said subject matter pertains. Patentability shall not be negatived by the manner in which the invention was made." § 103 of the Patent Act of 1952, 35 U.S.C. § 103 (1964 ed.).

The questions, involved in each of the companion cases before us, are what effect the 1952 Act had upon traditional statutory and judicial tests of patentability and what definitive tests are now required. We have concluded that the 1952 Act was intended to codify judicial precedents embracing the principle long ago announced by this Court in Hotchkiss v. Greenwood, 11 How. 248, 13 L.Ed. 683 (1851), and that, while the clear language of § 103 places emphasis on an inquiry into obviousness, the general level of innovation necessary to sustain patentability remains the same.

## I

The Cases

(a). No. 11, Graham v. John Deere Co., an infringement suit by petitioners, presents a conflict between two Circuits over the validity of a single patent on a "Clamp for vibrating Shank Plows." The invention, a combination of old mechanical elements, involves a device designed to absorb shock from plow shanks as they plow through rocky soil and thus to prevent damage to the plow. In 1955, the Fifth Circuit had held the patent valid under its rule that when a combination produces an "old result in a cheaper and otherwise more advantageous way," it is patentable. Jeoffroy Mfg., Inc. v. Graham, 219 F.2d 511, cert. denied, 350 U.S. 826, 76 S.Ct. 55, 100 L.Ed. 738. In 1964, the Eighth Circuit held, in the case at bar, that there was no new result in the patented combination and that the patent was, therefore, not valid. 333 F.2d 529, reversing D.C., 216 F.Supp. 272. We granted certiorari, 379 U.S. 956, 85 S.Ct. 652, 13 L.Ed.2d 553. Although we have determined that neither Circuit applied the correct test, we conclude that the patent is invalid under § 103 and, therefore, we affirm the judgment of the Eighth Circuit.

[(b). Omitted is a discussion of Calmar, Inc. v. Cook Chemical Co., and No. 43, Colgate–Palmolive Co. v. Cook Chemical Co., involving the invention of a finger-operated sprayer with a "hold down" cap that enables containers to be shipped without spillage.—eds.]

## II

At the outset it must be remembered that the federal patent power stems from a specific constitutional provision which authorizes the Congress "To promote the Progress of * * * useful Arts, by securing for limited Times to * * * Inventors the exclusive Right to their * * * Discoveries." Art. I, § 8, cl. 8. The clause is both a grant of power and a limitation. This qualified authority, unlike the power often exercised in the sixteenth and seventeenth centuries by the English Crown, is limited to the promotion of advances in the "useful arts." It was written against the backdrop of the practices—eventually curtailed by the Statute of Monopolies—of the Crown in granting monopolies to court favorites in goods or businesses which had long before been enjoyed by the public. See Meinhardt, Inventions, Patents and Monopoly, pp. 30–35 (London, 1946). The Congress in the exercise of the patent power may not overreach the restraints imposed by the stated constitutional purpose. Nor may it enlarge the patent monopoly without regard to the innovation, advancement or social benefit gained thereby. Moreover, Congress may not authorize the issuance of patents whose effects are to remove existent knowledge from the public domain, or to restrict free access to materials already available.

Congress quickly responded to the bidding of the Constitution by enacting the Patent Act of 1790 during the second session of the First Congress. It created an agency in the Department of State headed by the Secretary of State, the Secretary of the Department of War and the Attorney General, any two of whom could issue a patent for a period not exceeding 14 years to any petitioner that "hath * * * invented or discovered any useful art, manufacture, * * * or device, or any improvement therein not before known or used" if the board found that "the invention or discovery (was) sufficiently useful and important * * *." 1 Stat. 110. This group, whose members administered the patent system along with their other public duties, was known by its own designation as "Commissioners for the Promotion of Useful Arts."

Thomas Jefferson, who as Secretary of State was a member of the group, was its moving spirit and might well be called the "first administrator of our patent system." See Federico, Operation of the Patent Act of 1790, 18 J.Pat.Off.Soc. 237, 238 (1936). He was not only an administrator of the patent system under the 1790 Act, but was also the author of the 1793 Patent Act. In addition, Jefferson was himself an inventor of great note. His unpatented improvements on plows, to mention but one line of his inventions, won acclaim and recognition on both sides of the Atlantic. Because of his active interest and influence in the early development of the patent system, Jefferson's views on the general nature of the limited patent monopoly under the Constitution, as well as his conclusions as to conditions for patentability under the statutory scheme, are worthy of note.

Jefferson, like other Americans, had an instinctive aversion to monopolies. It was a monopoly on tea that sparked the Revolution and Jefferson certainly did not favor an equivalent form of monopoly under the new government. His abhorrence of monopoly extended initially to patents as well. From France, he wrote to Madison (July 1788) urging a Bill of Rights provision restricting monopoly, and as against the argument that limited monopoly might serve to incite "ingenuity," he argued forcefully that "the benefit even of limited monopolies is too doubtful to be opposed to that of their general suppression," V Writings of Thomas Jefferson, at 47 (Ford ed., 1895).

His views ripened, however, and in another letter to Madison (Aug. 1789) after the drafting of the Bill of Rights, Jefferson stated that he would have been pleased by an express provision in this form: "Art. 9. Monopolies may be allowed to persons for their own productions in literature, & their own inventions in the arts, for a term not exceeding—years, but for no longer term & no other purpose." Id., at 113. And he later wrote: "Certainly an inventor ought to be allowed a right to the benefit of his invention for some certain time. * * * Nobody wishes more than I do that ingenuity should receive a liberal encouragement." Letter to Oliver Evans (May 1807), V Writings of Thomas Jefferson, at 75–76 (Washington ed.).

The patent monopoly was not designed to secure to the inventor his natural right in his discoveries. Rather, it was a reward, an inducement, to bring forth new knowledge. The grant of an exclusive right to an invention was the creation of society—at odds with the inherent free nature of disclosed ideas—and was not to be freely given. Only inventions and discoveries which furthered human knowledge, and were new and useful, justified the special inducement of a limited private monopoly. Jefferson did not believe in granting patents for small details, obvious improvements, or frivolous devices. His writings evidence his insistence upon a high level of patentability.

As a member of the patent board for several years, Jefferson saw clearly the difficulty in "drawing a line between the things which are worth to the public the embarrassment of an exclusive patent, and those which are not." The board on which he served sought to draw such a line and formulated several rules which are preserved in Jefferson's correspondence. Despite the board's efforts, Jefferson saw "with what slow progress a system of general rules could be matured." Apparently Congress agreed with Jefferson and the board that the courts should develop additional conditions for patentability. Although the Patent Act was amended, revised or codified some 50 times between 1790 and 1950, Congress steered clear of a statutory set of requirements other than the bare novelty and utility tests reformulated in Jefferson's draft of the 1793 Patent Act.

III

The difficulty of formulating conditions for patentability was heightened by the generality of the constitutional grant and the statutes implementing it, together with the underlying policy of the patent system that "the things which are worth to the public the embarrassment of an exclusive patent," as Jefferson put it, must outweigh the restrictive effect of the limited patent monopoly. The inherent problem was to develop some means of weeding out those inventions which would not be disclosed or devised but for the inducement of a patent.

This Court formulated a general condition of patentability in 1851 in Hotchkiss v. Greenwood, 11 How. 248, 13 L.Ed. 683. The patent involved a mere substitution of materials—porcelain or clay for wood or metal in doorknobs—and the Court condemned it, holding:

"(U)nless more ingenuity and skill * * * were required * * * than were possessed by an ordinary mechanic acquainted with the business, there was an absence of that degree of skill and ingenuity which constitute essential elements of every invention. In other words, the improvement is the work of the skilful mechanic, not that of the inventor." At p. 267.

The Hotchkiss test laid the cornerstone of the judicial evolution suggested by Jefferson and left to the courts by Congress. The language in the case, and in those which followed, gave birth to "invention" as a word of legal art signifying patentable inventions. The Hotchkiss formulation, however, lies not in any label, but in its functional approach to questions of patentability. In practice, Hotchkiss has required a comparison between the subject matter of the patent, or patent application, and the background skill of the calling. It has been from this comparison that patentability was in each case determined.

## IV

### The 1952 Patent Act

The Act sets out the conditions of patentability in three sections. An analysis of the structure of these three sections indicates that patentability is dependent upon three explicit conditions: novelty and utility as articulated and defined in § 101 and § 102, and nonobviousness, the new statutory formulation, as set out in § 103. The first two sections, which trace closely the 1874 codification, express the "new and useful" tests which have always existed in the statutory scheme and, for our purposes here, need no clarification. The pivotal section around which the present controversy centers is § 103.

It is undisputed that this section was, for the first time, a statutory expression of an additional requirement for patentability, originally expressed in Hotchkiss. It also seems apparent that Congress intended by the last sentence of § 103 to abolish the test it believed this Court announced in the controversial phrase "flash of creative genius," used in Cuno Engineering Corp. v. Automatic Devices Corp., 314 U.S. 84, 62 S.Ct. 37, 86 L.Ed. 58 (1941).

It is contended, however, by some of the parties and by several of the amici that the first sentence of § 103 was intended to sweep away judicial precedents and to lower the level of patentability. Others contend that the Congress intended to codify the essential purpose reflected in existing judicial precedents—the rejection of insignificant variations and innovations of a commonplace sort—and also to focus inquiries under § 103 upon nonobviousness, rather than upon "invention," as a means of achieving more stability and predictability in determining patentability and validity.

The Reviser's Note to this section, with apparent reference to Hotchkiss, recognizes that judicial requirements as to "lack of patentable novelty (have) been followed since at least as early as 1850." The note indicates that the section was inserted because it "may have some stabilizing effect, and also to serve as a basis for the addition at a later time of some criteria which may be worked out." To this same effect are the reports of both

Houses, which state that the first sentence of the section "paraphrases language which has often been used in decisions of the courts, and the section is added to the statute for uniformity and definiteness."

We believe that this legislative history, as well as other sources, shows that the revision was not intended by Congress to change the general level of patentable invention. We conclude that the section was intended merely as a codification of judicial precedents embracing the Hotchkiss condition, with congressional directions that inquiries into the obviousness of the subject matter sought to be patented are a prerequisite to patentability.

V

Approached in this light, the § 103 additional condition, when followed realistically, will permit a more practical test of patentability. The emphasis on non-obviousness is one of inquiry, not quality, and, as such, comports with the constitutional strictures.

While the ultimate question of patent validity is one of law, Great A. & P. Tea Co. v. Supermarket Equipment Corp., 340 U.S. at 155, 71 S.Ct. at 131, the § 103 condition, which is but one of three conditions, each of which must be satisfied, lends itself to several basic factual inquiries. Under § 103, the scope and content of the prior art are to be determined; differences between the prior art and the claims at issue are to be ascertained; and the level of ordinary skill in the pertinent art resolved. Against this background, the obviousness or nonobviousness of the subject matter is determined. Such secondary considerations as commercial success, long felt but unsolved needs, failure of others, etc., might be utilized to give light to the circumstances surrounding the origin of the subject matter sought to be patented. As indicia of obviousness or nonobviousness, these inquiries may have relevancy. See Note, Subtests of "Nonobviousness": A Nontechnical Approach to Patent Validity, 112 U.Pa.L.Rev. 1169 (1964).

This is not to say, however, that there will not be difficulties in applying the nonobviousness test. What is obvious is not a question upon which there is likely to be uniformity of thought in every given factual context. The difficulties, however, are comparable to those encountered daily by the courts in such frames of reference as negligence and scienter, and should be amenable to a case-by-case development. We believe that strict observance of the requirements laid down here will result in that uniformity and definiteness which Congress called for in the 1952 Act.

VI

We now turn to the application of the conditions found necessary for patentability to the cases involved here:

This patent, No. 2,627,798 (hereinafter called the '798 patent) relates to a spring clamp which permits plow shanks to be pushed upward when they hit obstructions in the soil, and then springs the shanks back into normal position when the obstruction is passed over.

Background of the Patent

Chisel plows, as they are called, were developed for plowing in areas where the ground is relatively free from rocks or stones. Originally, the shanks were rigidly attached to the plow frames. When such plows were used in the rocky, glacial soils of some of the Northern States, they were found to have serious defects. As the chisels hit buried rocks, a vibratory motion was set up and tremendous forces were transmitted to the shank near its connection to the frame. The shanks would break. Graham, one of the petitioners, sought to meet that problem, and in 1950 obtained a patent, U.S. No. 2,493,811 (hereinafter '811), on a spring clamp where solved some of the difficulties. Graham and his companies manufactured and sold the '811 clamps. In 1950, Graham modified the '811 structure and filed for a patent. That patent, the one in issue, was granted in 1953. This suit against competing plow manufacturers resulted from charges by petitioners that several of respondents' devices infringed the '798 patent.

The Prior Art

We confine our discussion to the prior patent of Graham, '811, [which was] among the references asserted by respondents. The Graham '811 and '798 patent devices are similar in all elements, save two: (1) the stirrup and the bolted connection of the shank to the hinge plate do not appear in '811; and (2) the position of the shank is reversed, being placed in patent '811 above the hinge plate, sandwiched between it and the upper plate. The shank is held in place by the spring rod which is hooked against the bottom of the hinge plate passing through a slot in the shank. Other differences are of no consequence to our examination. In practice the '811 patent arrangement permitted the shank to wobble or fishtail because it was not rigidly fixed to the hinge plate; moreover, as the hinge plate was below the shank, the latter caused wear on the upper plate, a member difficult to repair or replace.

Graham's '798 patent application contained 12 claims. All were rejected as not distinguished from the Graham '811 patent. The inverted position of the shank was specifically rejected as was the bolting of the shank to the hinge plate. The Patent Office examiner found these to be "matters of design well within the expected skill of the art and devoid of invention." Graham withdrew the original claims and substituted the two new ones which are substantially those in issue here. His contention was that wear was reduced in patent '798 between the shank and the heel or rear of the upper plate. He also emphasized several new features, the relevant one here being that the bolt used to connect the hinge plate and shank maintained the upper face of the shank in continuing and constant contact with the underface of the hinge plate.

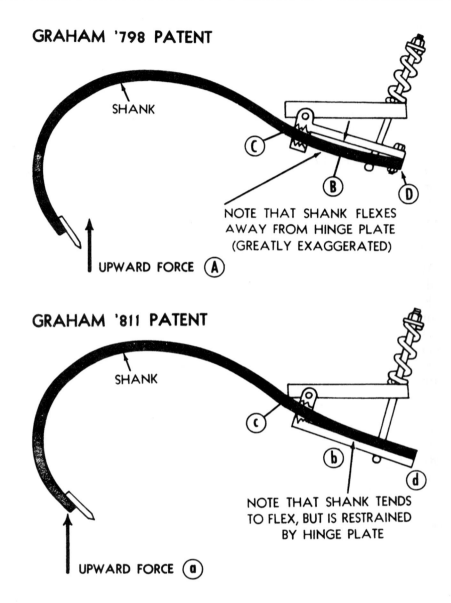

## GRAHAM '798 PATENT

SHANK

NOTE THAT SHANK FLEXES
AWAY FROM HINGE PLATE
(GREATLY EXAGGERATED)

UPWARD FORCE (A)

## GRAHAM '811 PATENT

SHANK

NOTE THAT SHANK TENDS
TO FLEX, BUT IS RESTRAINED
BY HINGE PLATE

UPWARD FORCE (a)

Graham did not urge before the Patent Office the greater "flexing" qualities of the '798 patent arrangement which he so heavily relied on in the courts. The sole element in patent '798 which petitioners argue before us is the interchanging of the shank and hinge plate and the consequences flowing from this arrangement. The contention is that this arrangement—which petitioners claim is not disclosed in the prior art—permits the shank to flex under stress for its entire length. As we have sketched (see sketch, "Graham '798 Patent" in Appendix), when the chisel hits an obstruction the resultant force (A) pushes the rear of the shank upward and the shank pivots against the rear of the hinge plate at (C). The natural tendency is for that portion of the shank between the pivot point and the bolted connection (i.e., between C and D) to bow downward and away from the hinge plate. The maximum distance (B) that the shank moves away from the plate is slight—for emphasis, greatly exaggerated in the sketches. This is so because of the strength of the shank and the short—nine inches or so—length of that portion of the shank between (C) and (D). On the contrary, in patent '811 (see sketch, "Graham '811 Patent" in Appendix), the pivot point is the upper plate at point (c); and while the tendency for the shank to bow between points (c) and (d) is the same as in '798, the shank is restricted because of the underlying hinge plate and cannot flex as freely. In practical effect, the shank flexes only between points (a) and (c), and not along the entire length of the shank, as in '798. Petitioners say that this difference in flex, though small, effectively absorbs the tremendous forces of the shock of obstructions whereas prior art arrangements failed.

The Obviousness of the Differences

We cannot agree with petitioners. We assume that the prior art does not disclose such an arrangement as petitioners claim in patent '798. Still we do not believe that the argument on which petitioners' contention is bottomed supports the validity of the patent. The tendency of the shank to flex is the same in all cases. If free-flexing, as petitioners now argue, is the crucial difference above the prior art, then it appears evident that the desired result would be obtainable by not boxing the shank within the confines of the hinge. The only other effective place available in the arrangement was to attach it below the hinge plate and run it through a stirrup or bracket that would not disturb its flexing qualities. Certainly a person having ordinary skill in the prior art, given the fact that the flex in the shank could be utilized more effectively if allowed to run the entire length of the shank, would immediately see that the thing to do was what Graham did, i.e., invert the shank and the hinge plate.

# Sakraida v. Ag Pro, Inc.

Supreme Court of the United States, 1976.
425 U.S. 273, 96 S.Ct. 1532, 47 L.Ed.2d 784.

■ MR. JUSTICE BRENNAN delivered the opinion of the Court.

Respondent Ag Pro, Inc., filed this action against petitioner Sakraida on October 8, 1968, in the District Court for the Western District of Texas for infringement of United States Letters Patent 3,223,070, entitled "Dairy Establishment," covering a water flush system to remove cow manure from the floor of a dairy barn. The patent was issued December 14, 1965, to Gribble and Bennett, who later assigned it to respondent.

Systems using flowing water to clean animal wastes from barn floors have been familiar on dairy farms since ancient times.[a] The District Court

[a] Among the labors of Hercules is the following: "Heracles now set out to perform his fifth Labour, and this time his task was to cleanse the stables of Augeas in a single day. Augeas was a rich king of Elis, who had three thousand cattle. At night the cattle always

found, and respondent concedes, that none of the 13 elements of the Dairy Establishment combination is new, and many of those elements, including storage of the water in tanks or pools, appear in at least six prior patented systems. The prior art involved spot delivery of water from tanks or pools to the barn floor by means of high pressure hoses or pipes. That system required supplemental hand labor, using tractor blades, shovels, and brooms, and cleaning by these methods took several hours. The only claimed inventive feature of the Dairy Establishment combination of old elements is the provision for abrupt release of the water from the tanks or pools directly onto the barn floor, which causes the flow of a sheet of water that washes all animal waste into drains within minutes and requires no supplemental hand labor. As an expert witness for respondent testified concerning the effect of Dairy Establishment's combination: "(W)ater at the bottom has more friction than this water on the top and it keeps moving ahead and as this water keeps moving ahead we get a rolling action of this water which produced the cleaning action.... You do not get this in a hose.... (U)nless that water is continuously directed toward the cleaning area the cleaning action almost ceases instantaneously.... "

[The District Court found the patent invalid on the ground that "(T)o those skilled in the art, the use of the old elements in combination was not an invention by the obvious-nonobvious standard. Even though the dairy barn in question attains the posture of a successful venture, more than that is needed for invention." The Court of Appeals reversed, concluding that "although the (respondent's) flush system does not embrace a complicated technical improvement, it does achieve a synergistic result through a novel combination."]

We cannot agree that the combination of these old elements to produce an abrupt release of water directly on the barn floor from storage tanks or pools can properly be characterized as synergistic, that is, "result(ing) in an effect greater than the sum of the several effects taken separately." Anderson's–Black Rock v. Pavement Salvage Co., 396 U.S. 57, 61, 90 S.Ct. 305, 308, 24 L.Ed.2d 258, 261 (1969). Rather, this patent simply arranges

stood in a great court surrounded with walls, close to the king's palace, and as it was quite ten years since the servants had cleaned it out, there was enough refuse in the court to build up a high mountain. Heracles went to Augeas and asked if he would give him the tenth part of his flocks if he thoroughly cleansed his stables in a single day. The king looked upon this as such an absolutely impossible feat that he would not have minded promising his kingdom as a reward for it, so he laughed and said, 'Set to work, we shall not quarrel about the wages,' and he further promised distinctly to give Heracles what he asked, and this he did in the presence of Phyleus, his eldest son, who happened to be there. The next morning Heracles set to work, but even his strong arms would have failed to accomplish the task if they had not been aided by his mother-wit. He compelled a mighty torrent to work for him, but you would hardly guess how he did it. First he opened great gates on two opposite sides of the court, and then he went to the stream, and when he had blocked up its regular course with great stones, he conducted it to the court that required to be cleansed, so that the water streamed in at one end and streamed out at the other, carrying away all the dirt with it. Before evening the stream had done its work and was restored to its usual course." C. Witt, Classic Mythology 119–120 (1883).

old elements with each performing the same function it had been known to perform, although perhaps producing a more striking result than in previous combinations. Such combinations are not patentable under standards appropriate for a combination patent. Exploitation of the principle of gravity adds nothing to the sum of useful knowledge where there is no change in the respective functions of the elements of the combination; this particular use of the assembly of old elements would be obvious to any person skilled in the art of mechanical application.

Though doubtless a matter of great convenience, producing a desired result in a cheaper and faster way, and enjoying commercial success, Dairy Establishment "did not produce a 'new or different function' . . . within the test of validity of combination patents." Anderson's–Black Rock v. Pavement Co., 396 U.S., at 60, 90 S.Ct., at 308, 24 L.Ed.2d, at 261. These desirable benefits "without invention will not make patentability." Great A. & P. Tea Co. v. Supermarket Corp., 340 U.S., at 153, 71 S.Ct., at 130, 95 L.Ed., at 167.

# Stratoflex, Inc. v. Aeroquip Corp.

United States Court of Appeals, Federal Circuit, 1983.
713 F.2d 1530.

■ MARKEY, CHIEF JUDGE.

## II.   Background

## A.   The Technology

Stratoflex and Aeroquip manufacture electrically conductive polytetrafluoroethylene (PTFE)[a] tubing used in the aircraft and missile industry to convey pressurized fuel, lubricants, and other fluids.

PTFE has replaced organic and synthetic rubbers and plastic in fuel hoses because it has a number of superior characteristics. Though pure PTFE is dielectric (non-conductive), it can be made with fillers to make it conductive, though the "filled" tubing is more susceptible to leakage when voids form between the PTFE and filler particles.

## B.   The Invention

The Slade invention relates to a composite PTFE tubing, formed of an inner layer of electrically conductive PTFE having particles such as carbon black uniformly distributed in it and an outer layer of essentially pure nonconductive PTFE. Claim 1 [is] representative:

> 1.   A tubular extrudate formed of attached concentric tubular extrusions, the inner tubular extrusion comprising associated particles of unsintered tetrafluoroethylene polymer and pulverulent, inert, electrically conductive particles, and the outer tubular extrusion comprising associated particles of unsintered tetrafluoroethylene polymer.

[a] The parties refer to polytetrafluoroethylene also as "Teflon," a registered trademark of the E.I. Dupont de Nemours Company.

The particles in the inner layer of the claimed tubing dissipate electrostatic charges built up on the inner surface of the tubing, conducting them lengthwise of the tubing to grounded metal fittings at the ends of a hose assembly of which the tubing is part, to prevent arcing or discharging through the tubing wall to the surrounding metal braid. Arcing causes "pin holes" through which fuel can leak. The outer layer is coextruded or bonded around the inner layer to contain any fuel leaking through the inner layer. The composite tubing has excellent conductivity, while retaining the desirable characteristics of PTFE tubing.

## C. Events Leading to the '087 Patent

Pure PTFE tubing had been used successfully in aircraft engines since at least 1956. In 1959, with the introduction of hydrocarbon jet fuels, leaks were noticed. Aeroquip assigned two staff engineers, Abbey and Upham, to determine the cause. They found the problem to be the arcing of electrostatic charges through the wall of the pure dielectric PTFE tubing to create "pin holes" as described above.

Abbey and Upham found the "pin hole" phenomenon exhibited by all three types of PTFE (White–Titeflex; Pink/Red–Aeroquip; Black–Goodrich) used in aircraft engines. The black tubing appeared superior because the carbon black it contained gave it an intermittent conductivity. The carbon black took the form of discontinuous strings and arcing across the spaces between string ends conveyed charges to the ends of the tubing. Electrical erosion of the strings, however, widened the spaces, destroying conductivity and leading to the "pin hole" phenomenon. Abbey and Upham concluded that susceptibility of PTFE tubing to "pin holing" was proportional to its conductivity, and that carbon black increased the conductivity of PTFE tubing.

In early 1960, having determined the cause of leaking, Aeroquip approached Raybestos–Manhattan (Raybestos), a PTFE hose manufacturer, for a solution. Aeroquip later purchased the hose section of Raybestos, obtaining the Slade patent by mesne assignment.

Raybestos assigned the project to the inventor, Winton Slade, who prepared several samples of conductive PTFE tubing (powdered lead, copper, chemically etched, and carbon black) and sent them for testing to Aeroquip in the summer of 1960. In the Fall, Aeroquip ordered a small production quantity of carbon black tubing. That tubing was not a composite and the carbon black was not uniformly distributed in it.

Slade conceived of the composite tube of the invention as early as August 5, 1960 and reduced it to practice in November of 1961. He filed a patent application on May 22, 1962, with claims directed to the composite tubing and also to various processes for making it. [After an interference that led to agreements to grant Titeflex royalty-free licenses,] Slade's original application issued with its product claims as the '087 patent on October 1, 1969.

D. Stratoflex Actions

From 1962 to 1970, Stratoflex purchased PTFE tubing containing carbon black from B.F. Goodrich. When Goodrich ceased production, Stratoflex purchased conductive PTFE tubing made by Titeflex under its license. Stratoflex then began manufacturing and selling its own "124" and "127" composite tubing having an inner layer with conductive carbon black uniformly dispersed throughout, and an outer layer that is essentially nonconductive, though that outer layer includes a small amount of carbon black to color the tubing and to aid extrusion.

On December 8, 1978, Aeroquip charged that Stratoflex's unauthorized manufacture and sale of "124" and "127" tubing infringed its rights under the '087 patent.

E. Trial and Opinion

Trial was held on December 15, 16, 18, 19 and 22, 1980. Stratoflex alleged that the '087 patent was invalid. On August 16, 1982, Judge Boyle issued judgment and an accompanying opinion [holding the patent invalid under § 103].

Obviousness

The declaration that claim[] 1 of the '087 patent [is] invalid was based on a conclusion that the inventions set forth in those claims would have been obvious under 35 U.S.C. § 103, in the light of facts found in the course of following the guidelines set forth in Graham v. John Deere Co., 383 U.S. 1, 17, 86 S.Ct. 684, 693, 15 L.Ed.2d 545 (1966).

Scope and Content of the Prior Art

Aeroquip contends that the scope of the relevant prior art excludes rubber hose because PTFE is a unique material, possessing properties that differ significantly from rubber, and that, because the claims are limited to PTFE, the rubber hose art could at most be peripherally relevant as background information.

The scope of the prior art has been defined as that "reasonably pertinent to the particular problem with which the inventor was involved." In re Wood, 599 F.2d 1032, 1036, 202 U.S.P.Q. 171, 174 (Cust. & Pat.App. 1979), see Weather Engineering Corp. of America v. United States, 614 F.2d 281, 222 Ct.Cl. 322, 204 U.S.P.Q. 41 (Ct.Cl.1980). The problem confronting Slade was preventing electrostatic buildup in PTFE tubing caused by hydrocarbon fuel flow while precluding leakage of fuel. None of the unique properties of PTFE would change the nature of that problem. Nor would anything of record indicate that one skilled in the art would not include the rubber hose art in his search for a solution to that problem.

Indeed, Slade himself referred to a standard textbook on conductive carbon black in rubber when he began his search for a solution. Judge Boyle correctly found Slade's act an acknowledgement by the problem solver of what he considered relevant prior art.

The examiner cited two prior art references in the rubber hose art, one disclosing the problem of electrostatic buildup caused by fuel flow. The Abbey–Upham report, though concerned with PTFE, included a conductivity comparison with carbon black filled rubber hose, and its bibliography listed several articles on electrostatic buildup in rubber. The record reflects that PTFE and rubber are used by the same hose manufacturers to make hoses and that the same and similar problems have been experienced with both. There is no basis for finding that a solution found for a problem experienced with one material would not be looked to when facing a problem with the other. The finding that the rubber hose art is relevant and thus within the scope of the art was not clearly erroneous.

The content of the prior art included the Abbey–Upham Report and several patents relating to conductive and composite rubber hose and to PTFE tubing.

The Abbey–Upham Report, as above indicated, discloses the cause of PTFE tubing "pin holes" as the arcing of electrostatic charges laterally through the non-conductive PTFE tubing wall to the surrounding metal braid, that carbon black increases conductivity of PTFE, and that susceptibility of PTFE tubing to "pinholing" is directly proportional to its conductivity. Judge Boyle correctly found the report to have disclosed the basic concepts underlying the claimed invention, but not that of forming PTFE tubing as a composite having a conductive inner layer and a nonconductive outer layer.

United States Patent No. 2,341,360 ('360 patent) teaches composite tubing having carbon black in one layer to make it electrically conductive for dissipation of static electricity.

U.S. Patent No. 2,781,288 ('288 patent) teaches a composite rubber hose with each layer arranged to take advantage of its particular properties. It suggests carbon black as a filler, but not as a conductor.

Aeroquip's attack on the content-of-the-prior-art findings is limited to its argument that rubber hose should be excluded. That argument having been found wanting, the findings on the content of the prior art cannot be viewed as clearly erroneous.

Consideration of the scope and content of the prior art tilts the scales of decision toward a conclusion of obviousness. Thus the Abbey–Upham report teaches use of carbon black to increase conductivity of PTFE tubing to reduce the chance of electrostatic buildup on the tubing wall. It would appear to have been obvious to one skilled in the art to place the conductive material in the wall where the electrostatic buildup occurs (here the inner wall subjected to electrostatic buildup by fuel flow) as suggested by the '360 patent. It would appear to have been obvious from the '288 patent to form a composite tubing with layers arranged to take advantage of their physical and chemical properties. On this record, consideration of the prior art as a whole, and in the absence of evidence that any special problem in following its teachings was created by the unique properties of PTFE, it would appear to have been obvious to place a conductive PTFE layer inside an essentially non-conductive outer PTFE layer to prevent fuel seepage associated with the conductive layer.

Differences Between the Claimed Invention and the Prior Art

Aeroquip concedes that pure PTFE had been known to be dielectric, that carbon black was known to be conductive, and that PTFE had been made into tubing containing at least a small amount of carbon black. It alleges that the prior art does not show the composite tubing set forth in the claims, specifically a composite PTFE tubing with its inner layer formed of uniformly distributed carbon black and PTFE, to provide conductivity sufficient to dissipate electrostatic buildup, and an outer layer of relatively pure PTFE that prevents fuel leakage. It is true that no single reference shows all elements of the claims, but the holding here is one of invalidity for obviousness, not for anticipation. The question, therefore, is whether the invention set forth in claims 1, as a whole, would have been obvious to one of ordinary skill in the art when made, in view of the teachings of the prior art as a whole.

Though findings on the "differences" from the prior art are suggested by Graham v. John Deere, the question under 35 U.S.C. § 103 is not whether the differences themselves would have been obvious. Consideration of differences, like each of the findings set forth in Graham, is but an aid in reaching the ultimate determination of whether the claimed invention as a whole would have been obvious.

Judge Boyle found that the differences between the claimed invention and the prior art were use of PTFE in concentric tubes and the "salt and pepper" process of forming the inner layer. The first difference would indicate a mere change of material.

With respect to use of a different material, the problem (leakage) and the cause ("pin holes" from electrostatic charges) were known with respect to that material (PTFE). A solution for the electrostatic charge problems, i.e., dissipation of charges lengthwise of the tubing, was known. Nothing in the first difference found would indicate that it would have been nonobvious to transfer that solution from tubing formed of other materials to tubing formed of PTFE. As above indicated, no special problem needed to be or was overcome in substituting a different material (PTFE) for the materials (rubber and plastics) of the prior art.

Aeroquip challenges the finding that the Abbey–Upham report does not teach away from use of carbon black in PTFE tubing, citing this language in the report: "The possibility of establishing continuous longitudinal strings of carbon particles during extrusion, especially in view of the relatively small percentage of carbon black used in Teflon hose seemed remote."

In the sentence following that cited to us by Aeroquip, the Abbey–Upham report describes uneven spacing between carbon black particles as a possible cause of intermittent conductivity. Far from "teaching away," therefore, the report may be viewed as pointing in the direction of uniform dispersion of such particles, as set forth in claim 7, to produce less intermittent conductivity.

The findings that the differences here were use of a different material and uniform dispersion of carbon black particles were not clearly erroneous. Those differences do not tilt the scales toward a conclusion of nonobviousness of the invention as a whole in light of all prior art teachings summarized above.

Level of Ordinary Skill

The district court found the level of ordinary skill to be that of a chemical engineer or equivalent, having substantial experience in the extrusion arts. Aeroquip says that was too high, suggesting that of an engineer or technician in the PTFE art, as described by its expert, Townsend Beaman. The suggestion is but another effort to limit the prior art to PTFE tubing and avoid inclusion of the art of making fuel hoses of other materials.

The level of ordinary skill may be determined from several factors. Orthopedic Equipment Company v. United States, 702 F.2d 1005, 217 USPQ 193 (Fed.Cir.1983) see Jacobson Brothers Inc. v. United States, 512 F.2d 1065, 206 Ct.Cl. 518 (Ct.Cl.1975). Slade had the level of skill set by the district court. Stratoflex witness Linger was a mechanical engineer with years of experience in the rubber and PTFE hose art. Mr. Beaman was patent counsel for Aeroquip. Judge Boyle correctly viewed Beaman as an observer of, not a worker in, the relevant art.

The statute, 35 U.S.C. § 103, requires that a claim be declared invalid only when the invention set forth in that claim can be said to have been obvious "to one of ordinary skill in the art." As an aid in determining obviousness, that requirement precludes consideration of whether the invention would have been obvious (as a whole and just before it was made) to the rare genius in the art, or to a judge or other layman after learning all about the invention.

Aeroquip has not shown the finding on the level of ordinary skill in the art to have been erroneous here.

Secondary Considerations

It is jurisprudentially inappropriate to disregard any relevant evidence on any issue in any case, patent cases included. Thus evidence rising out of the so-called "secondary considerations" must always when present be considered en route to a determination of obviousness. Indeed, evidence of secondary considerations may often be the most probative and cogent evidence in the record. It may often establish that an invention appearing to have been obvious in light of the prior art was not. It is to be considered as part of all the evidence, not just when the decisionmaker remains in doubt after reviewing the art.

Judge Boyle made findings on secondary considerations, but said she did not include them in her analysis because she believed the claimed inventions were plainly obvious and "those matters without invention will not make patentability" and should be considered only in a close case. That was error.

Enroute to a conclusion on obviousness, a court must not stop until all pieces of evidence on that issue have been fully considered and each has been given its appropriate weight. Along the way, some pieces will weigh more heavily than others, but decision should be held in abeyance, and doubt maintained, until all the evidence has had its say. The relevant evidence on the obviousness-nonobviousness issue, as the Court said in Graham, and as other courts had earlier emphasized, includes evidence on what has now been called "secondary considerations." It is error to exclude that evidence from consideration.

The evidence and findings on secondary considerations being present in the record, the interests of judicial economy dictate its consideration and evaluation on this appeal. The result being unchanged, a remand for reconsideration of the evidence would in this case constitute a waste of resources for the courts and the parties.

A nexus is required between the merits of the claimed invention and the evidence offered, if that evidence is to be given substantial weight enroute to conclusion on the obviousness issue. Solder Removal Co. v. USITC, 582 F.2d 628, 637, 65 CCPA 120, 199 U.S.P.Q. 129, 137 (CCPA 1978) and cases cited therein.

Aeroquip says commercial success is shown because: the "entire industry" makes the tubing claimed in the '087 patent; only Stratoflex is not licensed. We are not persuaded.

Recognition and acceptance of the patent by competitors who take licenses under it to avail themselves of the merits of the invention is evidence of nonobviousness. Here, however, Aeroquip does not delineate the make-up of the "entire industry." The record reflects only two manufacturers, Titeflex and Resistoflex, in addition to the parties. Titeflex has a royalty-free license, resulting from the interference settling agreement described above. Resistoflex has a license that includes several other patents and the right to use the trademark "HIBPAC" for complete hose assemblies. Aeroquip has shown neither a nexus between the merits of the invention and the licenses of record, nor that those licenses arose out of recognition and acceptance of the patent.

The military specifications were promulgated after the claimed invention was known. Thus the invention did not meet a longfelt but unfilled need expressed in the specifications. Moreover, the record does not support Aeroquip's assertion that the specifications can be met only by tubing covered by the claims of the '087 patent. The nexus required to establish commercial success is therefore not present with respect to the military specifications.

Nor is there evidence that others skilled in the art tried and failed to find a solution for the problem. Aeroquip cites Abbey and Upham, but their effort was limited to investigation of the problem and its cause, and was not directed to its solution.

Upon full consideration of the evidence respecting the secondary considerations in this case, and of Aeroquip's arguments, we are persuaded that nonobviousness is not established by that evidence. Judge Boyle's error in refusing to include that evidence in her analysis was therefore in this case harmless.

"Synergism" and "Combination Patents"

Judge Boyle said "synergism" is "a symbolic reminder of what constitutes nonobviousness when a combination patent is at issue," and that under "either standard (Graham analysis or synergism) the combination ... simply lacks the unique essence of authentic contribution to the Teflon art which is the heart of invention."

A requirement for "synergism" or a "synergistic effect" is nowhere found in the statute, 35 U.S.C. When present, for example in a chemical case, synergism may point toward nonobviousness, but its absence has no place in evaluating the evidence on obviousness. The more objective findings suggested in Graham, are drawn from the language of the statute and are fully adequate guides for evaluating the evidence relating to compliance with 35 U.S.C. § 103. Bowser, Inc. v. United States, 388 F.2d 346, 181 Ct.Cl. 834, 156 U.S.P.Q. 406 (Ct.Cl.1967). Judge Boyle treated synergism as an alternative consideration. Hence the error of its analytical inclusion is harmless in view of Judge Boyle's employment of the Graham aids.

The reference to a "combination patent" is equally without support in the statute. There is no warrant for judicial classification of patents, whether into "combination" patents and some other unnamed and undefined class or otherwise. Nor is there warrant for differing treatment or consideration of patents based on a judicially devised label. Reference to "combination" patents is, moreover, meaningless. Virtually all patents are "combination patents," if by that label one intends to describe patents having claims to inventions formed of a combination of elements. It is difficult to visualize, at least in the mechanical-structural arts, a "non-combination" invention, i.e., an invention consisting of a single element. Such inventions, if they exist, are rare indeed. Again, however, Judge Boyle's inclusion in her analysis of a reference to the '087 patent as a "combination" patent was harmless in view of her application of Graham guidelines.

Similarly, Judge Boyle's reference to "the heart of invention" was here a harmless fall-back to the fruitless search for an inherently amorphous concept that was rendered unnecessary by the statute, 35 U.S.C. The Graham analysis here applied properly looked to patentability, not to "invention." [W]e affirm the judgment declaring claim 1 invalid for obviousness.

# In re Dillon

United States Court of Appeals, Federal Circuit, 1990.
919 F.2d 688.

■ LOURIE, CIRCUIT JUDGE.

Diane M. Dillon, assignor to Union Oil Company of California, appeals the November 25, 1987, decision of the Board of Patent Appeals and

Interferences (Board) of the United States Patent and Trademark Office (PTO), Appeal No. 87–0944, rejecting claims 2–14, 16–22, and 24–37, all the remaining claims of patent application Serial No. 671,570 entitled "Hydrocarbon Fuel Composition." We affirm the rejection of all of the claims.[a]

### The Invention

Dillon's patent application describes and claims her discovery that the inclusion of certain tetra-orthoester compounds in hydrocarbon fuel compositions will reduce the emission of solid particulates (i.e., soot) during combustion of the fuel. In this appeal Dillon asserts the patentability of claims to hydrocarbon fuel compositions containing these tetra-orthoesters, and to the method of reducing particulate emissions during combustion by combining these esters with the fuel before combustion.

The tetra-orthoesters are a known class of chemical compounds. It is undisputed that their combination with hydrocarbon fuel, for any purpose, is not shown in the prior art, and that their use to reduce particulate emissions from combustion of hydrocarbon fuel is not shown or suggested in the prior art.

### The Rejection

The Board held all of the claims to be unpatentable on the ground of obviousness, 35 U.S.C. § 103, in view of certain primary and secondary references. As primary references the Board relied on two Sweeney U.S. patents, 4,390,417 ('417) and 4,395,267 ('267). Sweeney '417 describes hydrocarbon fuel compositions containing specified chemical compounds, viz., ketals, acetals, and tri-orthoesters, used for "dewatering" the fuels, particularly diesel oil. Sweeney '267 describes three-component compositions of hydrocarbon fuels heavier than gasoline, immiscible alcohols, and tri-orthoesters, wherein the tri-orthoesters serve as cosolvents to prevent phase separation between fuel and alcohol. The Board explicitly found that the Sweeney patents do not teach the use of the tetra-orthoesters recited in appellant's claims.

The Board cited Elliott U.S. Patent 3,903,006 and certain other patents, including Howk U.S. Patent 2,840,613, as secondary references. Elliott describes tri-orthoesters and tetra-orthoesters for use as water scavengers in hydraulic (non-hydrocarbon) fluids. The Board stated that the Elliott reference shows equivalence between tetra-orthoesters and tri-orthoesters, and that "it is clear from the combined teachings of these references ... that [Dillon's tetra-orthoesters] would operate to remove

---

[a] A panel of this court heard this appeal and reversed the Board on December 29, 1989. 892 F.2d 1554, 13 U.S.P.Q.2d 1337. The PTO petitioned for rehearing and suggested rehearing in banc on February 12, 1990. Rehearing in banc was ordered on May 21, 1990, and the judgment which was entered on December 29, 1989, was vacated, the accompanying opinion being withdrawn.

water from non-aqueous liquids by the same mechanism as the orthoesters of Sweeney."

The Board stated that there was a "reasonable expectation" that the tri-and tetra-orthoester fuel compositions would have similar properties, based on "close structural and chemical similarity" between the tri-and tetra-orthoesters and the fact that both the prior art and Dillon use these compounds as "fuel additives." The Commissioner argues on appeal that the claimed compositions and method "would have been prima facie obvious from combined teachings of the references." On this reasoning, the Board held that unless Dillon showed some unexpected advantage or superiority of her claimed tetra-orthoester fuel compositions as compared with tri-orthoester fuel compositions, Dillon's new compositions as well as her claimed method of reducing particulate emissions are unpatentable for obviousness. It found that no such showing was made.

The Issue

The issue before this court is whether the Board erred in rejecting as obvious under 35 U.S.C. § 103 claims to Dillon's new compositions and to the new method of reducing particulate emissions, when the additives in the new compositions are structurally similar to additives in known compositions, having a different use, but the new method of reducing particulate emissions is neither taught nor suggested by the prior art.

The Broad Composition Claims

The Board found that the claims to compositions of a hydrocarbon fuel and a tetra-orthoester were prima facie obvious over Sweeney '417 and '267 in view of Elliott and Howk. We agree. Appellant argues that none of these references discloses or suggests the new use which she has discovered. That is, of course, true, but the composition claims are not limited to this new use; i.e., they are not physically or structurally distinguishable over the prior art compositions except with respect to the orthoester component. We believe that the PTO has established, through its combination of references, that there is a sufficiently close relationship between the tri-orthoesters and tetra-orthoesters (see the cited Elliott and Howk references) in the fuel oil art to create an expectation that hydrocarbon fuel compositions containing the tetra-esters would have similar properties, including water scavenging, to like compositions containing the tri-esters, and to provide the motivation to make such new compositions. Howk teaches use of both tri-and tetra-orthoesters in a similar type of chemical reaction. Elliott teaches their equivalence for a particular practical use. Our case law well establishes that such a fact situation gives rise to a prima facie case of obviousness.

Appellant cites In re Wright, 848 F.2d 1216, 1219, 6 U.S.P.Q.2d 1959, 1961 (Fed.Cir.1988), for the proposition that a prima facie case of obviousness requires that the prior art suggest the claimed compositions' properties and the problem the applicant attempts to solve. The earlier panel opinion in this case, In re Dillon, 892 F.2d 1554, 13 U.S.P.Q.2d 1337 (now withdrawn), in fact stated "a prima facie case of obviousness is not deemed made unless both (1) the new compound or composition is structurally similar to the reference compound or composition and (2) there is some suggestion or expectation in the prior art that the new compound or composition will have the same or a similar utility as that discovered by the applicant." Id. at 1560, 13 U.S.P.Q.2d at 1341 (emphasis added).

This court, in reconsidering this case in banc, reaffirms that structural similarity between claimed and prior art subject matter, proved by combining references or otherwise, where the prior art gives reason or motivation to make the claimed compositions, creates a prima facie case of obviousness, and that the burden (and opportunity) then falls on an applicant to rebut that prima facie case. Such rebuttal or argument can consist of a comparison of test data showing that the claimed compositions possess unexpectedly improved properties or properties that the prior art does not have (In re Albrecht, 514 F.2d 1389, 1396, 185 U.S.P.Q. 585, 590 (CCPA 1975)); that the prior art is so deficient that there is no motivation to make what might otherwise appear to be obvious changes (Albrecht, 514 F.2d at 1396, 185 U.S.P.Q. at 590; In re Stemniski, 444 F.2d 581, 58 CCPA 1410, 170 U.S.P.Q. 343 (CCPA 1971); In re Ruschig, 343 F.2d 965, 52 CCPA 1238, 145 U.S.P.Q. 274 (CCPA 1965)), or any other argument or presentation of evidence that is pertinent. There is no question that all evidence of the properties of the claimed compositions and the prior art must be considered in determining the ultimate question of patentability, but it is also clear that the discovery that a claimed composition possesses a property not disclosed for the prior art subject matter, does not by itself defeat a prima facie case. Shetty, 566 F.2d at 86, 195 U.S.P.Q. at 756. Each situation must be considered on its own facts, but it is not necessary in order to establish a prima facie case of obviousness that both a structural similarity between a claimed and prior art compound (or a key component of a composition) be shown and that there be a suggestion in or expectation from the prior art that the claimed compound or composition will have the same or a similar utility as one newly discovered by applicant. To the extent that Wright suggests or holds to the contrary, it is hereby overruled. In particular, the statement that a prima facie obviousness rejection is not supported if no reference shows or suggests the newly-discovered properties and results of a claimed structure is not the law.

Under the facts we have here, as described above, we have concluded that a prima facie case has been established. The art provided the motivation to make the claimed compositions in the expectation that they would have similar properties. Appellant had the opportunity to rebut the prima facie case. She did not present any showing of data to the effect that her compositions had properties not possessed by the prior art compositions or that they possessed them to an unexpectedly greater degree. She attempted to refute the significance of the teachings of the prior art references. She did not succeed and we do not believe the PTO was in error in its decision.

Appellant points out that none of the references relates to the problem she confronted, citing In re Wright, and that the combination of references is based on hindsight. It is clear, however, that appellant's claims have to be considered as she has drafted them, i.e., as compositions consisting of a fuel and a tetra-orthoester, and that Sweeney '417 and '267 describe the combination of a liquid fuel with a related compound, a tri-orthoester. While Sweeney does not suggest appellant's use, her composition claims are not limited to that use; the claims merely recite compositions analogous to those in the Sweeney patents, and appellant has made no showing overcoming the prima facie presumption of similar properties for those analogous compositions. The mention in the appealed claims that the amount of orthoester must be sufficient to reduce particulate emissions is not a distinguishing limitation of the claims, unless that amount is different from the prior art and critical to the use of the claimed composition. See In re Reni, 419 F.2d 922, 925, 57 CCPA 857, 164 U.S.P.Q. 245, 247 (CCPA 1970). That is not the case here. The amount of ester recited in the dependent claims can be from 0.05–49%, a very broad range; a preferred range is .05–9%, compared with a percentage in Sweeney '417 approximately equimolar to the amounts of water in the fuel which the ester is intended to remove (.01–5%).

Appellant attacks the Elliott patent as non-analogous art, being in the field of hydraulic fluids rather than fuel combustion. We agree with the PTO that the field of relevant prior art need not be drawn so narrowly. As this court stated in In re Deminski, 796 F.2d 436, 442, 230 U.S.P.Q. 313, 315 (Fed.Cir.1986)(quoting In re Wood, 599 F.2d 1032, 1036, 202 U.S.P.Q. 171, 174 (CCPA 1979)): [t]he determination that a reference is from a nonanalogous art is therefore two-fold. First, we decide if the reference is within the field of the inventor's endeavor. If it is not, we proceed to determine whether the reference is reasonably pertinent to the particular problem with which the inventor was involved. Following that test, one concerned with the field of fuel oils clearly is chargeable with knowledge of Sweeney '417, which discloses fuel compositions with tri-orthoesters for dewatering purposes, and chargeable with knowledge of other references to tri-orthoesters, including for use as dewatering agents for fluids, albeit other fluids. These references are "within the field of the inventor's endeavor." Moreover, the statement of equivalency between tri-and tetra-orthoesters in Elliott is not challenged. We therefore conclude that Elliott is not excludable from consideration as non-analogous art. It is evidence that supports the Board's holding that the prior art makes the claimed compositions obvious, a conclusion that appellant did not overcome.

Appellant urges that the Board erred in not considering the unexpected results produced by her invention and in not considering the claimed invention as a whole. The Board found, on the other hand, that no showing was made of unexpected results for the claimed compositions compared with the compositions of Sweeney. We agree. Clearly, in determining patentability the Board was obligated to consider all the evidence of the properties of the claimed invention as a whole, compared with those of the prior art. However, after the PTO made a showing that the prior art compositions suggested the claimed compositions, the burden was on the applicant to overcome the presumption of obviousness that was created, and that was not done. For example, she produced no evidence that her compositions possessed properties not possessed by the prior art compositions. Nor did she show that the prior art compositions and use were so lacking in significance that there was no motivation for others to make obvious variants. There was no attempt to argue the relative importance of the claimed compositions compared with the prior art. See In re May, 574 F.2d 1082, 1092–95, 197 U.S.P.Q. 601, 609–11 (CCPA 1978).

Appellant's patent application in fact included data showing that the prior art compositions containing tri-orthoesters had equivalent activity in reducing particulate emissions (she apparently was once claiming such compositions with either tri-orthoesters or tetra-orthoesters). She asserts that the examiner used her own showing of equivalence against her in violation of the rule of In re Ruff, 256 F.2d 590, 596, 45 CCPA 1037, 118 U.S.P.Q. 340, 346 (CCPA 1958). While we caution against such a practice, it is clear to us that references by the PTO to the comparative data in the patent application were not employed as evidence of equivalence between the tri-and tetra-orthoesters; the PTO was simply pointing out that the applicant did not or apparently could not make a showing of superiority for the claimed tetra-ester compositions over the prior art tri-ester compositions.

■ ARCHER, CIRCUIT JUDGE, with whom MARKEY and MICHEL, CIRCUIT JUDGES, join, joining-in-part [omitted].

■ NEWMAN, CIRCUIT JUDGE, with whom COWEN AND MAYER, JJ. join, dissenting.

[After an extensive review of precedent, the dissent concluded:]

The Merits

Applying the guidance of precedent to Dillon's invention: the compositions are new, and their property and use of reducing particulate emissions is not taught or suggested in the prior art. There is no objective teaching in the prior art that would have led one of ordinary skill to make this product in order to solve the problem that was confronting Dillon: to reduce soot from combustion of hydrocarbon fuels. There is no reasonable basis in the prior art for expecting that Dillon's new compositions would have the particulate-reducing property that she discovered. As shown in Part I, ante, structure, properties and use must be considered in determining whether a prima facie case under section 103 has been made.

The Sweeney references show the water-sequestration property of tri-orthoesters in hydrocarbon fuels, and the Elliott reference shows the water-sequestration property of tri-and tetra-orthoesters in hydraulic fluids (which are not hydrocarbons and not fuels). There is no suggestion in the prior art that would have led one of ordinary skill to make Dillon's new compositions in the expectation that they would reduce particulate emissions from combustion. No reference suggests any relationship between the properties of water-sequestration and soot-reduction. All this is undisputed.

Dillon raises the question of whether the Sweeney and Elliott references are properly combinable, arguing that they are not in analogous arts.

This question need not be decided, for even when combined these references offer no suggestion of the property of reducing particulate emissions from combustion. In re Naber, 494 F.2d 1405, 1407, 181 U.S.P.Q. 639, 641 (CCPA 1974)("even if one of ordinary skill in the art were moved to combine the references, there would be no recognition that the problem of combustible deposits had been solved").

The board stated that it is inherent in Dillon's compositions that they would reduce particulate emissions, that Dillon "merely recited a newly discovered function inherently possessed" by the prior art. Arguments based on "inherent" properties can not stand when there is no supporting teaching in the prior art. Inherency and obviousness are distinct concepts. In re Spormann, 363 F.2d 444, 448, 53 CCPA 1375, 150 U.S.P.Q. 449, 452 (CCPA 1966):

> [T]he inherency of an advantage and its obviousness are entirely different questions. That which may be inherent is not necessarily known. Obviousness cannot be predicated on what is unknown.

When the PTO asserts that there is an explicit or implicit teaching or suggestion in the prior art, the PTO must produce supporting references. In re Yates, 663 F.2d 1054, 1057, 211 U.S.P.Q. 1149, 1151 (CCPA 1981).

The applicant's newly discovered properties must be considered in determining whether a prima facie case of unpatentability is made, along with all the other evidence. Neither structure nor properties can be ignored; they are essential to consideration of the invention as a whole. But Dillon's own discovery of the soot-reducing property of the tri-orthoester fuel composition is not evidence against her in determining whether the prior art makes a case of prima facie obviousness. In re Wertheim, 541 F.2d 257, 269, 191 U.S.P.Q. 90, 102 (CCPA 1976)(applicant's own disclosures can not be used to support a rejection of the claims "absent some admission that matter disclosed in the specification is in the prior art"); In re Ruff, 256 F.2d at 598, 118 U.S.P.Q. at 347 ("The mere statement of this proposition reveals its fallaciousness").

In view of the complete absence of any suggestion in the prior art that Dillon's new compositions would have her newly discovered and unobvious property and use of soot reduction, I would reverse the rejection of the composition and the use claims.

The Commissioner raised the policy argument that Dillon is simply removing from the public an obvious variant of Sweeney's and Elliott's compositions, one that might be useful to scavenge water in fuels. In Ruschig the court had considered the argument, and remarked that the provision of adequate patent protection for the applicant's new compounds, not previously in existence and having a new and unobvious use, was favored over the "mere possibility that someone might wish to use some of them for some such [other] purpose." 343 F.2d at 979, 145 U.S.P.Q. at 286. This practical wisdom has been tested by long experience. It accords with judicial recognition that: Although there is a vast amount of knowledge about general relationships in the chemical arts, chemistry is still largely empirical, and there is often great difficulty in predicting precisely how a given compound will behave. In re Carleton, 599 F.2d 1021, 1026, 202 U.S.P.Q. 165, 170 (CCPA 1979).

Granting Dillon a patent on her invention takes away nothing that the public already has; and the public receives not only the knowledge of Dillon's discovery, for abandoned patent applications are maintained in secrecy, but Dillon is not deprived of an incentive to discover and to commercialize this new product for this new use.

# In re Bell

United States Court of Appeals, Federal Circuit, 1993.
991 F.2d 781.

■ Lourie, J.

Applicants Graeme I. Bell, Leslie B. Rall, and James P. Merryweather (Bell) appeal from the March 10, 1992 decision of the U.S. Patent and Trademark Office (PTO) Board of Patent Appeals and Interferences, Appeal No. 91–1124, affirming the examiner's final rejection of claims 25–46 of application Serial No. 065,673, entitled "Preproinsulin–Like Growth Factors I and II," as unpatentable on the ground of obviousness under 35 U.S.C. Section 103 (1988). Because the Board erred in concluding that the claimed nucleic acid molecules would have been obvious in light of the cited prior art, we reverse.

## BACKGROUND

The claims of the application at issue are directed to nucleic acid molecules (DNA and RNA)[a] containing human sequences which code for human insulin-like growth factors I and II (IGF), single chain serum proteins that play a role in the mediation of somatic cell growth following the administration of growth hormones.[b]

[a] A basic familiarity with recombinant DNA technology is presumed. For a general discussion, see In re O'Farrell, 853 F.2d 894, 895–99, 7 U.S.P.Q.2d 1673, 1674–77 (Fed.Cir. 1988).

[b] Claim 25 is conceded to be representative of the claims at issue:

A composition comprising nucleic acid molecules containing a human sequence encoding insulin-like growth factor (hIGF) substantially free of nucleic acid molecules not containing said hIGF sequence, wherein said hIGF sequence is selected from the group consisting of:

(a) 5 "-GGA CCG GAG ACG CUC UGC GGG GCU GAG CUG GUG GAU GCU CUU CAG UUC GUG UGU GGA GAC AGG GGC UUU UAU UUC AAC AAG CCC ACA GGG UAU GGC UCC AGC AGU CGG AGG GCG CCU CAG ACA GGU AUC GUG GAU GAG UGC UGC UUC CGG AGC UGU GAU CUA AGG AGG CUG GAG AUG UAU UGC GCA CCC CUC AAG CCU GCC AAG UCA GCUB3", wherein U can also be T;

(b) 5 "-GCU UAC CGC CCC AGU GAG ACC CUG UGC GGC GGG GAG CUG GUG GAC ACC CUC CAG UUC GUC UGU GGG GAC CGC GGC UUC UAC UUC AGC AGG CCC GCA AGC CGU GUG AGC CGU CGC AGC CGU GGC AUC GUU GAG GAG UGC UGU UUC CGC AGC UGU GAC CUG GCC CUC CUG GAG ACG UAC UGU GCU ACC CCC GCC AAG UCC GAGB3", wherein U can also be T;

(c) nucleic acid sequences complementary to (a) or (b); and

(d) fragments of (a), (b) or (c) that are at least 18 bases in length and which will selec-

The relevant prior art consists of two publications by Rinderknecht disclosing amino acid sequences for IGFBI and -II and U.S. Patent 4,394,-443 to Weissman et al., entitled "Method for Cloning Genes." Weissman describes a general method for isolating a gene for which at least a short amino acid sequence of the encoded protein is known. The method involves preparing a nucleotide probe corresponding to the known amino acid sequence and using that probe to isolate the gene of interest. It teaches that it is advantageous to design a probe based on amino acids specified by unique codons.[c] The Weissman patent specifically describes the isolation of a gene which codes for human histocompatibility antigen, a protein unrelated to IGF. It describes the design of the probe employed, stating that it was based on amino acids specified by unique codons.

The examiner rejected the claims as obvious over the combined teachings of Rinderknecht and Weissman. She determined that it would have been obvious, "albeit tedious," from the teachings of Weissman to prepare probes based on the Rinderknecht amino acid sequences to obtain the claimed nucleic acid molecules. According to the examiner, "it is clear from [Weissman] that the ordinary artisan knows how to find the nucleic acid when the amino acid sequence is known" and that "the claimed sequences and hosts would have been readily determinable by and obvious to those of ordinary skill in the art at the time the invention was made."

The Board affirmed the examiner's rejection, holding that the examiner had established a prima facie case of obviousness for the claimed sequences "despite the lack of conventional indicia of obviousness, e.g., structural similarity between the DNA which codes for IGFBI and the amino acid sequence of the polypeptide which constitues [sic] IGFBI." Slip op. at 6. The Board reasoned that "although a protein and its DNA are not structurally similar, they are correspondently linked via the genetic code." Id. at 4 n.1. In view of Weissman, the Board concluded that there was no evidence "that one skilled in the art, knowing the amino acid sequences of the desired proteins, would not have been able to predictably clone the desired DNA sequences without undue experimentation." Id. at 8.

The issue before us is whether the Board correctly determined that the amino acid sequence of a protein in conjunction with a reference indicating a general method of cloning renders the gene prima facie obvious.

## DISCUSSION

We review an obviousness determination by the Board de novo. In re Vaeck, 947 F.2d 488, 493, 20 U.S.P.Q.2d 1438, 1442 (Fed.Cir.1991). Bell argues that the PTO has not shown how the prior art references, either

---

tively hybridize to human genomic DNA encoding hIGF.

[c] A sequence of three nucleotides, called a codon, codes for each of the twenty natural amino acids. Since there are twenty amino acids and sixty-four possible codons, most amino acids are specified by more than one codon. This is referred to as "degeneracy" in the genetic code. The term "unique" refers to an amino acid coded for by a single codon. See Amgen Inc. v. Chugai Pharmaceutical Co., 927 F.2d 1200, 1207-08 n.4, 18 U.S.P.Q.2d 1016, 1022 n.4 (Fed.Cir.), cert. denied, 112 S.Ct. 169 (1991).

alone or in combination, teach or suggest the claimed invention, and thus that it has failed to establish a prima facie case of obviousness.

We agree. The PTO bears the burden of establishing a case of prima facie obviousness. In re Fine, 837 F.2d 1071, 1074, 5 U.S.P.Q.2d 1596, 1598 (Fed.Cir.1988). "A prima facie case of obviousness is established when the teachings from the prior art itself would appear to have suggested the claimed subject matter to a person of ordinary skill in the art." In re Rinehart, 531 F.2d 1048, 1051, 189 U.S.P.Q. 143, 147 (CCPA 1976).

The Board supported the examiner's view that the "correspondent link" between a gene and its encoded protein via the genetic code renders the gene obvious when the amino acid sequence is known. In effect, this amounts to a rejection based on the Rinderknecht references alone. Implicit in that conclusion is the proposition that, just as closely related homologs, analogs, and isomers in chemistry may create a prima facie case, see In re Dillon, 919 F.2d 688, 696, 16 U.S.P.Q.2d 1897, 1904 (Fed.Cir.1990)(in banc), cert. denied, 111 S.Ct. 1682 (1991), the established relationship in the genetic code between a nucleic acid and the protein it encodes also makes a gene prima facie obvious over its correspondent protein.

We do not accept this proposition. It may be true that, knowing the structure of the protein, one can use the genetic code to hypothesize possible structures for the corresponding gene and that one thus has the potential for obtaining that gene. However, because of the degeneracy of the genetic code, there are a vast number of nucleotide sequences that might code for a specific protein. In the case of IGF, Bell has argued without contradiction that the Rinderknecht amino acid sequences could be coded for by more than 1036 different nucleotide sequences, only a few of which are the human sequences that Bell now claims. Therefore, given the nearly infinite number of possibilities suggested by the prior art, and the failure of the cited prior art to suggest which of those possibilities is the human sequence, the claimed sequences would not have been obvious.

Bell does not claim all of the 1036 nucleic acids that might potentially code for IGF. Neither does Bell claim all nucleic acids coding for a protein having the biological activity of IGF. Rather, Bell claims only the human nucleic acid sequences coding for IGF. Absent anything in the cited prior art suggesting which of the 1036 possible sequences suggested by Rinderknecht corresponds to the IGF gene, the PTO has not met its burden of establishing that the prior art would have suggested the claimed sequences.

This is not to say that a gene is never rendered obvious when the amino acid sequence of its coded protein is known. Bell concedes that in a case in which a known amino acid sequence is specified exclusively by unique codons, the gene might have been obvious. Such a case is not before us.[d] Here, where Rinderknecht suggests a vast number of possible nucleic acid sequences, we conclude that the claimed human sequences would not have been obvious.

---

[d] We also express no opinion concerning the reverse proposition, that knowledge of the structure of a DNA, e.g., a cDNA, might make a coded protein obvious.

Combining Rinderknecht with Weissman does not fill the gap. Obvious-ness "cannot be established by combining the teachings of the prior art to produce the claimed invention, absent some teaching or suggestion support-ing the combination." In re Fine, 837 F.2d at 1075, 5 U.S.P.Q.2d at 1598 (citing ACS Hosp. Sys. v. Montefiore Hosp., 732 F.2d 1572, 1577, 221 U.S.P.Q. 929, 933 (Fed.Cir.1984)). What a reference teaches and whether it teaches toward or away from the claimed invention are questions of fact. See Raytheon Co. v. Roper Corp., 724 F.2d 951, 960–61, 220 U.S.P.Q. 592, 599–600 (Fed.Cir.1983), cert. denied, 469 U.S. 835 [225 U.S.P.Q. 232] (1984).

While Weissman discloses a general method for isolating genes, he appears to teach away from the claimed invention by emphasizing the importance of unique codons for the amino acids. Weissman suggests that it is generally advantageous to design a probe based on an amino acid sequence specified by unique codons, and also teaches that it is "counter-productive" to use a primer having more than 14–16 nucleotides unless the known amino acid sequence has 4–5 amino acids coded for by unique codons. Bell, in contrast, used a probe having 23 nucleotides based on a sequence of eight amino acids, none of which were unique. Weissman therefore tends to teach away from the claimed sequences since Rinderk-necht shows that IGF–I has only a single amino acid with a unique codon and IGF–II has none.

The PTO, in urging us to affirm the Board, points to the suggestion in Weissman that the disclosed method can "easily" be applied to isolate genes for an array of proteins including peptide hormones. The PTO thus argues that in view of Weissman, a gene is rendered obvious once the amino acid sequence of its translated protein is known. We decline to afford that broad a scope to the teachings of Weissman. While "a reference must be considered not only for what it expressly teaches, but also for what it fairly suggests," In re Burckel, 592 F.2d 1175, 1179, 201 U.S.P.Q. 67, 70 (CCPA 1979), we cannot say that Weissman "fairly suggests" that its teachings should be combined with those of Rinderknecht, since it nowhere suggests how to apply its teachings to amino acid sequences without unique codons.

We conclude that the Board clearly erred in determining that Weiss-man teaches toward, rather than away from, the claimed sequences. There-fore, the requisite teaching or suggestion to combine the teachings of the cited prior art references is absent, see In re Fine, 837 F.2d 1075, 5 U.S.P.Q.2d at 1599 , and the PTO has not established that the claimed sequences would have been obvious over the combination of Rinderknecht and Weissman.

# Oddzon Products, Inc. v. Just Toys, Inc.

United States Court of Appeals for the Federal Circuit, 1997.
122 F.3d 1396.

■ LOURIE, CIRCUIT JUDGE.

OddzOn Products, Inc. appeals from the decision of the United States District Court for the Northern District of California granting summary judgment in favor of defendants Just Toys, Inc., Lisco, Inc., and Spalding & Evenflo Companies, Inc. (collectively "Just Toys") on OddzOn's claims of design patent infringement, trade dress infringement, and state-law unfair competition. Just Toys cross-appeals from the decision granting summary judgment in favor of the patentee OddzOn on Just Toys' claim of patent invalidity.

## BACKGROUND

OddzOn is a toy and sporting goods company that sells the popular "Vortex" tossing ball, a foam football-shaped ball with a tail and fin structure. The Vortex ball is OddzOn's commercial embodiment of its design patent, U.S. Patent D 346,001, which issued on April 12, 1994. Figure 1 of the patent is shown below:

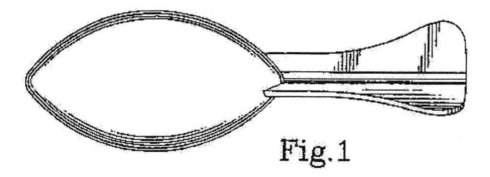

Fig.1

Just Toys, Inc., another toy and sporting goods company, sells a competing line of "Ultra Pass" balls. Two versions of the allegedly infringing Ultra Pass balls are shown below:

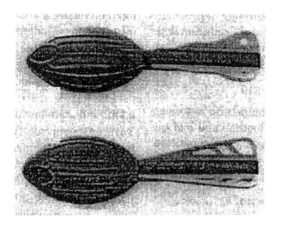

OddzOn sued Just Toys for design patent infringement, trade dress infringement, and state-law unfair competition, asserting that the Ultra Pass line of tossing balls was likely to be confused with OddzOn's Vortex ball, and that the Ultra Pass packaging was likely to be confused with the Vortex packaging. Just Toys denied infringement and asserted that the patent was invalid. On cross-motions for summary judgment, the district court held that the patent was not shown to be invalid and was not infringed. The court also held that Just Toys did not infringe OddzOn's trade dress.

The district court determined that two confidential designs that had been disclosed to the inventor qualified as subject matter encompassed within the meaning of 35 U.S.C. § 102(f) (1994) and concluded that these designs could be combined with other prior art designs for purposes of a challenge to the validity of the patent under 35 U.S.C. § 103 (1994). * * *

DISCUSSION

A.   The Prior Art Status of § 102(f) Subject Matter

The district court ruled that two confidential ball designs (the "disclosures") which "inspired" the inventor of the OddzOn design were prior art for purposes of determining obviousness under § 103. The district court noted that this court had recently declined to rule definitively on the relationship between § 102(f) and § 103, see Lamb–Weston, Inc. v. McCain Foods, Ltd., 78 F.3d 540, 544, 37 USPQ2d 1856, 1858–59 (Fed.Cir.1996), but relied on the fact that the United States Patent and Trademark Office (PTO) interprets prior art under § 103 as including disclosures encompassed within § 102(f). OddzOn challenges the court's determination that subject matter encompassed within § 102(f) is prior art for purposes of an obviousness inquiry under § 103. OddzOn asserts that because these disclosures are not known to the public, they do not possess the usual hallmark of prior art, which is that they provide actual or constructive public knowledge. OddzOn argues that while the two disclosures constitute patent-defeating subject matter under 35 U.S.C. § 102(f), they cannot be combined with "real" prior art to defeat patentability under a combination of § 102(f) and § 103.

The prior art status under § 103 of subject matter derived by an applicant for patent within the meaning of § 102(f) has never expressly been decided by this court. We now take the opportunity to settle the persistent question whether § 102(f) is a prior art provision for purposes of § 103. As will be discussed, although there is a basis to suggest that § 102(f) should not be considered as a prior art provision, we hold that a fair reading of § 103, as amended in 1984, leads to the conclusion that § 102(f) is a prior art provision for purposes of § 103.

Section 102(f) provides that a person shall be entitled to a patent unless "he did not himself invent the subject matter sought to be patented." This is a derivation provision, which provides that one may not obtain a patent on that which is obtained from someone else whose possession of the subject matter is inherently "prior." It does not pertain only to public knowledge, but also applies to private communications between the inventor and another which may never become public. Subsections (a), (b), (e), and (g), on the other hand, are clearly prior art provisions. They relate to knowledge manifested by acts that are essentially public. Subsections (a) and (b) relate to public knowledge or use, or prior patents and printed publications; subsection (e) relates to prior filed applications for patents of others which have become public by grant; and subsection (g) relates to prior inventions of others that are either public or will likely become public in the sense that they have not been abandoned, suppressed, or concealed. Subsections (c) and (d) are loss-of-right provisions. Section 102(c) precludes the obtaining of a patent by inventors who have abandoned their invention. Section 102(d) causes an inventor to lose the right to a patent by delaying the filing of a patent application too long after having filed a corresponding patent application in a foreign country. Subsections (c) and (d) are therefore not prior art provisions.

In In re Bass, 59 C.C.P.A. 1342, 474 F.2d 1276, 1290, 177 USPQ 178, 189 (CCPA 1973), the principal opinion of the Court of Customs and Patent Appeals held that a prior invention of another that was not abandoned, suppressed, or concealed (102(g) prior art) could be combined with other prior art to support rejection of a claim for obviousness under § 103. The principal opinion noted that the provisions of '102 deal with two types of issues, those of novelty and loss-of-right. It explained: "Three of [the subsections,] (a), (e), and (g), deal with events prior to applicant's invention date and the other, (b), with events more than one year prior to the U.S. application date. These are the 'prior art' subsections." Id. (emphasis in original). The principal opinion added, in dictum (§ 102(f) not being at issue), that "[o]f course, (c), (d), and (f) have no relation to § 103 and no relevancy to what is 'prior art' under § 103." Id. There is substantial logic to that conclusion. After all, the other prior art provisions all relate to subject matter that is, or eventually becomes, public. Even the "secret prior art" of § 102(e) is ultimately public in the form of an issued patent before it attains prior art status.

Thus, the patent laws have not generally recognized as prior art that which is not accessible to the public. It has been a basic principle of patent law, subject to minor exceptions, that prior art is:

> technology already available to the public. It is available, in legal theory at least, when it is described in the world's accessible literature, including patents, or has been publicly known or in ... public use or on sale "in this country." That is the real meaning of "prior art" in legal theory—it is knowledge that is available, including what would be obvious from it, at a given time, to a person of ordinary skill in the art.

Kimberly–Clark Corp. v. Johnson & Johnson, 745 F.2d 1437, 1453, 223 USPQ 603, 614 (Fed.Cir.1984) (citations omitted).

Moreover, as between an earlier inventor who has not given the public the benefit of the invention, e.g., because the invention has been abandoned without public disclosure, suppressed, or concealed, and a subsequent inventor who obtains a patent, the policy of the law is for the subsequent inventor to prevail. See W.L. Gore & Assocs., Inc. v. Garlock, Inc., 721 F.2d 1540, 1550, 220 USPQ 303, 310 (Fed.Cir.1983) ("Early public disclosure is a linchpin of the patent system. As between a prior inventor [who does not disclose] and a later inventor who promptly files a patent application ... , the law favors the latter."). Likewise, when the possessor of secret art (art that has been abandoned, suppressed, or concealed) that predates the critical date is faced with a later-filed patent, the later-filed patent should not be invalidated in the face of this "prior" art, which has not been made available to the public. Thus, prior, but non-public, inventors yield to later inventors who utilize the patent system.

However, a change occurred in the law after Bass was decided. At the time Bass was decided, § 103 read as follows:

> A patent may not be obtained though the invention is not identically disclosed or described as set forth in section 102 of this title, if the differences between the subject matter sought to be patented and the prior art are such that the subject matter as a whole would have been obvious at the time the invention was made to a person having ordinary skill in the art to which said subject matter pertains. Patentability shall not be negatived by the manner in which the invention was made.

35 U.S.C. § 103. The prior art being referred to in that provision arguably included only public prior art defined in subsections 102(a), (b), (e), and (g).

In 1984, Congress amended § 103, adding the following paragraph:

> Subject matter developed by another person, which qualifies as prior art only under subsection (f) or (g) of section 102 of this title, shall not preclude patentability under this section where the subject matter and the claimed invention were, at the time the invention was made, owned by the same person or subject to an obligation of assignment to the same person.

35 U.S.C. § 103 (now § 103(c)) (emphasis added). It is historically very clear that this provision was intended to avoid the invalidation of patents under § 103 on the basis of the work of fellow employees engaged in team research. See Section-by-Section Analysis: Patent Law Amendments Act of 1984, 130 Cong. Rec. 28069, 28071 (Oct. 1, 1984), reprinted in 1984 U.S.C.C.A.N. 5827, 5833 (stating that the amendment, which encourages communication among members of research teams, was a response to Bass and In re Clemens, 622 F.2d 1029, 206 USPQ 289 (CCPA 1980), in which "an earlier invention which is not public may be treated under Section 102(g), and possibly under 102(f), as prior art"). There was no clearly apparent purpose in Congress's inclusion of § 102(f) in the amendment other than an attempt to ameliorate the problems of patenting the results of team research. However, the language appears in the statute; it was enacted by Congress. We must give effect to it.

The statutory language provides a clear statement that subject matter that qualifies as prior art under subsection (f) or (g) cannot be combined with other prior art to render a claimed invention obvious and hence unpatentable when the relevant prior art is commonly owned with the claimed invention at the time the invention was made. While the statute does not expressly state in so many words that § 102(f) creates a type of prior art for purposes of § 103, nonetheless that conclusion is inescapable; the language that states that § 102(f) subject matter is not prior art under limited circumstances clearly implies that it is prior art otherwise. That is what Congress wrote into law in 1984 and that is the way we must read the statute.

This result is not illogical. It means that an invention, A', that is obvious in view of subject matter A, derived from another, is also unpatentable. The obvious invention, A', may not be unpatentable to the inventor of A, and it may not be unpatentable to a third party who did not receive the disclosure of A, but it is unpatentable to the party who did receive the disclosure.

The PTO's regulations also adopt this interpretation of the statute. 37 C.F.R. § 1.106(d) (1996) ("Subject matter which is developed by another person which qualifies as prior art only under 35 U.S.C. § 102(f) or (g) may be used as prior art under 35 U.S.C. § 103."). Although the PTO's interpretation of this statute is not conclusive, we agree with the district court that it is a reasonable interpretation of the statute.

It is sometimes more important that a close question be settled one way or another than which way it is settled. We settle the issue here (subject of course to any later intervention by Congress or review by the Supreme Court), and do so in a manner that best comports with the voice of Congress. Thus, while there is a basis for an opposite conclusion, principally based on the fact that § 102(f) does not refer to public activity, as do the other provisions that clearly define prior art, nonetheless we cannot escape the import of the 1984 amendment. We therefore hold that subject matter derived from another not only is itself unpatentable to the party who derived it under § 102(f), but, when combined with other prior art, may make a resulting obvious invention unpatentable to that party under a combination of §§ 102(f) and 103. Accordingly, the district court did not err by considering the two design disclosures known to the inventor to be prior art under the combination of §§ 102(f) and 103.

[The remainder of the opinion is omitted. In it, the court found that the invention was nonobvious.]

NOTES

**1.** *The § 103(a) inquiry.* In theory, the inquiry here is quite similar to the examination for novelty. References are found and dated to determine whether effective dates precede the critical date, the adequacy of dissemination is determined, and the contents of the art are scrutinized. Although § 103 does not list the activities that come within its scope, it is universally assumed that the same art that is pertinent to nonobviousness is also the art that is relevant to novelty. This includes § 102(a) art—information known or used in the United States as well as both domestic and foreign patents and printed publications. It also includes § 102(e) art—information contained in patent applications, so long as the patent eventually issues. And as *OddzOn* demonstrates, it also includes secret art under § 102(g)— inventions made in this country that have not been abandoned, suppressed, or concealed, and—under § 102(f)—information communicated to the applicant.[13] As with novelty, the critical date is the date on which the invention is reduced to practice; the effective date is the date on which the reference is considered accessible.

At this point, however, the analyses diverge, for while novelty is rigidly defined by the every-element test, the nonobviousness inquiry is far more open ended. The flexible nature of § 103 raises difficult issues for the courts.

a. *Policy considerations.* First, there is a pure policy question: how large a contribution must an inventor make to merit a patent? Justice Douglas thought the advance ought to be of major scientific significance; although the *Graham* Court read § 103 as adopting the less formidable *Hotchkiss* formulation, it was not willing to say that Congress had lowered the standard of patentability. This creates problems for inventions that are not deeply insightful, yet require considerable funds and efforts to make. As In re Dillon and In re Bell demonstrate, this is particularly a concern in chemical and biochemical cases. In both fields, theory is well enough advanced to predict the advantages of yet-unsynthesized structures. However, bringing these structures into being requires costly research. Absent a legal right—a patent right—to recapture the expense, it is not clear that the work will be done.

b. *Practical application.* Even if there were agreement on the level of contribution required, there would still be practical problems of implementation. Although the § 103 inquiry requires comparisons between sophisticated technologies, it is conducted by judges with no more training in technical matters than a law student, and by lay jurors, some of whom know more, but most of whom know a great deal less, than even law students know. As the major cases in this Assignment indicate, there has been much experimentation here as courts have searched for ways to formulate a clear test for nonobviousness.

*(i) Teaching away.* Some cases are made easy by the fact that the prior art "teaches away" from the invention in the sense that it discourages doing what the inventor has done. Such was claimed for certain of the references in *Stratoflex* and *Bell*. Indeed, on the same day that the Supreme Court invalidated the plow patent in *Graham*, it decided United States v.

---

[13] See, e.g., Hazeltine Research, Inc. v. Brenner, 382 U.S. 252 (1965); In re Bartfeld, 925 F.2d 1450 (Fed.Cir.1991)(§ 102(e)); Hybritech Inc. v. Monoclonal Antibodies, Inc., 802 F.2d 1367 (Fed.Cir.1986)(§ 102(g)). In addition, as *OddzOn* makes clear, information derived from another under § 102(f) is included as prior art for § 103 purposes.

Adams,[14] which upheld the patent on a battery utilizing plain water as the electrolyte. Although wet batteries were well known and every element of the invention could be found in other batteries, the Court found that long-accepted theories in the art should have deterred anyone from trying to put together the battery at issue in the case. "[K]nown disadvantages in old devices which would naturally discourage the search for new inventions may be taken into account in determining obviousness."[15] Accordingly, the patent in *Adams* was upheld. One must be careful here, however. The mere fact that an experiment fails is not reason enough to discard the reference. If it provides a basis for the applicant's work, it might nonetheless be considered relevant.[16]

Prior work may also obscure the problem the inventor needs to resolve. In Eibel Process Co. v. Minnesota & Ontario Paper Co.,[17] for example, the invention was in the field of paper making. At the time, paper was made by pouring wet stock onto a conveyer belt ("wire") which moved it through a drying environment. The industry had tried to speed up operations by moving the wire quickly, but if it moved too fast, the product turned out to be uneven. The inventor found a solution: he changed the pitch of the container from which the stock was poured. The Court held the invention nonobvious, stating that "[t]he invention was not the mere use of a high or substantial pitch to remedy a known source of trouble. It was the discovery of the source not before known and the application of the remedy for which Eibel was entitled to be rewarded in his patent."[18] The industry had not understood that the stock needed to be moving at a speed close to that of the wire when it hit the wire; Eibel's discovery of the problem merited a patent even though the solution was trivial once the problem was understood.

*(ii) Secondary considerations.* The so-called secondary considerations are factors external to the invention itself that demonstrate its inventiveness. They include long-felt need for a solution to the problem the invention addresses, the failure of others to find such a solution, the commercial success of the invention in the marketplace, and acquiescence—the willingness of others to accept the patent as valid and take a license or forgo use of the invention. Their use represents another attempt to find an objective test for nonobviousness, although they too have met with considerable controversy.

On the one hand, it does seem that these are signs that the invention is a significant advance. If need for the innovation existed for a long time, it can be assumed that others would have invented it had this been easy to do. Since the need persisted until this applicant came along, he must have made the kind of breakthrough necessary to earn a patent. Similarly, if others tried to invent and failed, but the applicant tried and succeeded, her

[14] 383 U.S. 39 (1966).

[15] Id. at 52.

[16] See Bristol–Myers Squibb Co. v. Ben Venue Laboratories, 246 F.3d 1368 (Fed. Cir. 2001).

[17] 261 U.S. 45 (1923).

[18] Id. at 68.

contribution must not have been obvious. By the same token, there are many entrepreneurs ready to earn an easy dollar. If the invention is a great commercial success, one of them would have brought it to market sooner if it was obvious to make. Finally, acquiescence is an indication that the people who *do* know the technology agree that the advance merits a patent.

On the other hand, these factors may be present for reasons other than the intrinsic creativity of the invention. Developments in other fields may make easy something that was formerly difficult. Suddenly, long-felt need will be met and failure will be overcome by a commercially successful new product. Furthermore, if the inventor charges licensees less than the cost of challenging the patent, there will be acquiescence rather than litigation. As *Stratoflex* makes clear, the Federal Circuit's response here is to recognize both the value and the danger of relying on these factors. It requires the lower courts to look at secondary considerations in every case, but also to consider whether there is a nexus between the invention and the factor. Absent a showing that the factor is present because of inventiveness, the consideration will not be taken into account in determining nonobviousness. While this resolution may not be theoretically satisfying, it does focus the lower courts on issues that can be measured without a high level of technological skill.[19]

*(iii) Combination patents.* As *Ag Pro* demonstrates, "combinations" were at one time split out for separate consideration. Because combination inventions are clearly made up of known elements, they were considered likely to be obvious. Thus, a special showing of synergy (or as the case puts it, synergistic results) was required. In theory, synergy should have been as easy to spot as teaching away. In practice, however, such was not the case.

One difficulty with the formulation was that there was considerable controversy over what should be considered a combination. Close inspection of any invention will reveal how it works: two things never add up to more than the sum of their parts. Moreover, at some level of particularity, every advance is a combination because innovation is largely a process of analogizing to earlier work, borrowing relevant bits and pieces from several sources. Indeed, an inventor's special gift may well be the ability to appreciate the benefits of combining disparate elements.[20] For these reason, it is appropriate that *Stratoflex* ultimately rejected the combination-patent idea along with the search for synergy.

*(iv) Motivation to combine.* In recent years, the Federal Circuit has emphasized the need for evidence of "a teaching, motivation, or suggestion to select and combine the references relied on as evidence of obvious-

---

[19] For further discussion, compare Rochelle C. Dreyfuss, The Federal Circuit: A Case Study in Specialized Courts, 64 N.Y.U. L. Rev. 1 (1989)(delineating the benefits of secondary considerations) with Robert P. Merges, Economic Perspectives on Innovation: Patent Standards and Commercial Suc- cess, 76 Cal. L. Rev. 803 (1988)(noting their disadvantages).

[20] For vivid examples of how inventions build upon each other, see Henry Petroski, The Evolution of Useful Things (Alfred A. Knopf 1992).

ness."[21] For example, the invention in In re Lee was a method of automatically displaying the functions of a video display device and demonstrating how to select and adjust the functions to facilitate the user's response. The prior art consisted of two references. One was a patent describing a television set with a menu display by which the user could adjust various picture and audio functions; it did not include a demonstration of how to adjust the functions. The other was a handbook for video games which described the video display as having a "demonstration mode" showing how to play the game; it made no mention of the adjustment of picture or audio functions. The Board of Patent Appeals and Interferences held that it would have been obvious for a person of ordinary skill to combine the teachings of the references to produce the Lee system. The Federal Circuit rejected the finding, saying:

> The Board's findings must extend to all material facts and must be documented on the record, lest the "haze of so-called expertise" acquire insulation from accountability. "Common knowledge and common sense," even if assumed to derive from the agency's expertise, do not substitute for authority when the law requires authority.[22]

Is it a good idea to impose a requirement that there be a reference suggesting the combination? This approach makes the determination of obviousness less subjective and it also recognizes that part of inventiveness is finding productive combinations. But isn't it odd to reject common knowledge and common sense? If something is common knowledge or common sense is it likely that anyone would take the time to write it down in a reference that meets the requirements of §§ 102 and 103? What is left of the notion that advances that could be accomplished by a person of ordinary skill should remain in the public domain?

Is the Federal Circuit moving away from the stringent requirement of *Lee*? In a recent opinion reviewing a finding of obviousness by the PTO, the court said:

> As persons of scientific competence in the fields in which they work, examiners and administrative patent judges on the Board are responsible for making findings, informed by their scientific knowledge, as to the meaning of prior art references to persons of ordinary skill in the art and the motivation those references would provide to such persons. Absent legal error or contrary factual evidence, those findings can establish a prima facie case of obviousness. In this case, the appellants have not pointed to any legal error affecting the Board's obviousness analysis. Nor have they pointed to sufficient factual grounds, either in the record or in any judicially noticeable sources, to question the

---

[21] In re Lee, 277 F.3d 1338, 1343 (Fed. Cir. 2002).

[22] Id. at 1344–45. See also In re Rouffet, 149 F.3d 1350, 1359 (Fed.Cir.1998) ("even when the level of skill in the art is high, the Board must identify specifically the principle, known to one of ordinary skill, that suggests the claimed combination. In other words, the Board must explain the reasons one of ordinary skill in the art would have been motivated to select the references and to combine them to render the claimed invention obvious.").

findings made by the examiner and the Board as to the teachings of the prior art and the motivation that the prior art references would give to a skilled artisan to make the claimed invention. We therefore sustain the Board's conclusion that the recited prior art references established a prima facie case of obviousness with respect to the appealed claims.[23]

*(v) Obvious-to-try.* As fields of knowledge grow, particular approaches and experiments can become obvious. For example, once a device for sequencing genes is invented, it is obvious to use it to find interesting genomic material and information. Should the *scientific* obviousness of an experiment render its result *legally* obvious? The Federal Circuit says no: " 'Obvious to try' has long been held not to constitute obviousness. A general incentive does not make obvious a particular result, nor does the existence of techniques by which those efforts can be carried out."[24] Instead, the court asks whether there was a reasonable expectation of success. If there were many approaches to choose from, if there were many pitfalls along the way, the successful outcome will be deemed nonobvious:

> An 'obvious-to-try' situation exists when a general disclosure may pique the scientist's curiosity, such that further investigation might be done as a result of the disclosure, but the disclosure itself does not contain a sufficient teaching of how to obtain the desired result, or that the claimed result would be obtained if certain directions were pursued.[25]

**2.** *The Court of Appeals for the Federal Circuit.* Interestingly, the Federal Circuit was itself a response to the § 103 problem. In the early 1970's, Congress had created a commission to make recommendations for improving the administration of federal justice. The Hruska Commission that was formed identified patent law as one of the areas in which the delivery of justice could be improved. It suggested that Congress create a specialized court with the technical expertise and experience necessary to decide difficult technological issues expediently.[26] The Federal Circuit was established in 1982 to hear patent appeals from the district courts in all of the federal circuits. It was no surprise to the patent bar that *Stratoflex* appeared so soon after the court was established, for the judges of the new court took the resolution of the nonobviousness problem as their premier challenge.[27]

The Federal Circuit has two important advantages over the regional circuits that previously decided patent appeals. First, it can require all the district courts to use the same objective tests of nonobviousness. Second, because every patent appeal winds up in this court, there is no longer an

---

[23] In re Berg, 320 F.3d 1310, 1315 (Fed. Cir.2003).

[24] In re Deuel, 51 F.3d 1552, 1559 (Fed. Cir. 1995), citing In re O'Farrell, 853 F.2d 894, 903 (Fed.Cir.1988).

[25] In re Eli Lilly & Co., 902 F.2d 943, 945 (Fed. Cir. 1990).

[26] See Commission on Revision of the Federal Court Appellate System, Structure and Internal Procedures: Recommendations for Change, reprinted in 67 F.R.D. 195 (1975).

[27] See, e.g., Howard T. Markey, The Phoenix Court, 10 AIPLA Q.J. 227 (1982).

incentive to shop for a forum with a higher or lower standard of nonobviousness. Cases like *Graham*, where the same patent was upheld on one circuit and invalidated on another, can no longer occur. The law on nonobviousness may not be theoretically perfect, but it is at least administered equitably.[28]

**3.** *Does § 103 render the § 102 inquiry superfluous?* Since § 103 looks at the same art as § 102, but lacks its rigidity of application, it is easy to fall into the trap of thinking that § 103 renders § 102 superfluous, for anything that is not new also appears to be obvious. Close attention to the details of the nonobviousness inquiry makes the independent significance of § 102 clearer.

*(i) Inherency.* In Assignment 17, we saw that information inherent in a reference counts for novelty purposes, even if use of the information is not specifically indicated. But as Judge Newman's dissent in *Dillon* makes clear, inherency is not sufficient for nonobviousness. In order for a reference to be utilized, the element of interest must be expressly pointed out. In terms of the search-model discussed in the Introduction to Assignment 17, it is clear why this is so. It would be too costly to require inventors to research all prior art with enough insight to appreciate every scrap of information inherent in it, and then combine all of this learning to produce the invention. But it is cost-effective to look for an *entirely* effectuated invention in earlier work. Accordingly, inherency is a feature of § 102(a) jurisprudence, but it is not used in the § 103 analysis.

*(ii) Field of reference.* Note 1(b)(iv) in Assignment 17 discussed the fact that every field is considered fair game when novelty is the issue. But such is not the case in § 103. As *Dillon* discusses, the information that is relevant to the nonobviousness inquiry must either be "within the field of the inventor's endeavor" or in an analogous art, that is, in a field "reasonably pertinent to the particular problem with which the inventor was involved."[29]

The analysis of a case involving analogous art is highly sensitive to the way that the problem is characterized and the fields the PTO (or court) believes the inventor would consult to solve that problem. For example, in In re Clay,[30] the invention was a way to store liquid hydrocarbon in a partially empty tank by filling the dead space with a gel. The prior art taught the use of gel to improve oil well production by filling subterranean cavities as they were emptied of petroleum. The court rejected use of this art on the ground that it was not analogous. Although it too was in the

---

[28] See, e.g., Rochelle C. Dreyfuss, The Federal Circuit: A Case Study in Specialized Courts, 64 N.Y.U. L. Rev. 1 (1989). For a more recent (and less sanguine) study of the court, see Arti K. Rai, Engaging Facts and Policy: A Multi–Institutional Approach to Patent System Reform, 103 Colum. L. Rev. 1035 (2003).

[29] See, e.g., Union Carbide Corp. v. American Can Co., 724 F.2d 1567 (Fed.Cir. 1984); In re Wood, 599 F.2d 1032 (C.C.P.A. 1979).

[30] 966 F.2d 656 (Fed. Cir. 1992).

petroleum field, Clay was trying to prevent the loss of liquid stored in a partly empty tank; the reference was about maximizing oil production.

**4.** *Process patents.* Note that the applicant in *Dillon* sought a product patent, a patent on a fuel additive. The application was rejected because the additive was, essentially, old news. But Dillon was using the additive to do something different from what the prior art additives did. While they scavenged water, hers reduced soot. Would she have had more success applying for a *process* patent on a method for using her additive to reduce soot? Section 100(b) of the Patent Act defines processes to include new methods for using known compositions of matter. Since Dillon had developed a new method (soot reduction) for using an old composition (the additive), her application would appear to exemplify exactly the situation § 100(b) was designed to address. Awarding Dillon a patent would compensate for the inventive work she did without removing a known product from the public domain.

Until 1985, Dillon's process application would probably have met with success. However, in that year, the Federal Circuit decided In re Durden,[31] which raised the standard for patenting processes. *Durden* rejected a patent on a method claim whose only inventive feature was that a starting material (i.e. one of the ingredients) was new. The court reasoned that since the method itself was known in the prior art, the invention was obvious. Given *Durden,* Dillon's process claim would be problematic because she is using an old method (adding an additive to fuel); only her starting material is new, and under *Durden,* that is not enough.

*Durden* was greeted with much criticism in the patent bar,[32] especially in that part of the bar concerned with biotechnology patents. Process patents are sometimes important to this industry for the same reasons they are important to Dillon: to create a financial return on researching new uses for known materials. However, the industry also needs process protection for another reason. Some of the commercially significant research in biotechnology involves the isolation and characterization of naturally occurring genes and the use of these genes to manufacture known proteins. Although the genes themselves are often patented, competitors can take them out of the country, where their use will not infringe the patent. The proteins produced are then re-imported into this country. Since the proteins were known and were not patentable, there is still no infringement. However, importation into the United States of a product manufactured by a process patented in the United States *is* an infringement, § 271(g). Hence, the special need for process patents. If the genetic researcher can get a patent on the *process* for using the gene, she is protected. She can sue the importer of the protein under § 271(g) for importing a product (the protein) that is manufactured by a process patented in the United States.

[31] 763 F.2d 1406 (Fed.Cir.1985).

[32] See, e.g., Harold C. Wegner, Much Ado About Durden, 71 J.Pat.Off.Soc., 785 (1985); Harold C. Wegner, Biotechnology Process Patents: Judicial or Legislative Remedy, 73 J.Pat.Off.Soc. 24 (1991).

At the behest of the biochemistry industry, Congress amended § 103 to add § 103(b).[33] This subsection creates a special rule for any biotechnological process on which a patent application is filed simultaneously with an application for a patent on a composition of matter that is either a starting material in the process or the end product of the process. Section 103(b) provides that if this composition of matter is found to be novel and nonobvious, then the process will also be considered nonobvious.

Section 103(b) has not proved as valuable as Congress hoped. First, it applies only to biotechnology processes and so would not change the result in a case like Dillon's, which involved a process for using a fuel additive. Second, the process and product claims must be made at the same time (indeed, both must, at the time they were invented, have been owned by the same person or subject to an obligation of assignment to the same person) and the validity of the claims rise and fall together. In any event, the Federal Circuit has since retreated from *Durden*. For example, in In re Ochiai,[34] the court was again faced with a question about the nonobviousness of a known process using and resulting in new compounds. The applicant had claimed a method for reacting a newly discovered (and patented) acid with other chemicals to produce a new member of the "cephem" family of compounds having antibiotic properties. The examiner and the Board rejected the process claim, claim 6, on *Durden* grounds. The Federal Circuit reversed, stating:

> The process invention Ochiai recites in claim 6 specifically requires use of none other than its new, nonobvious acid as one of the starting materials. One having no knowledge of this acid could hardly find it obvious to make any cephem using this acid as an acylating agent, much less the particular cephem recited in claim 6.
>
> * * *
>
> In addition, although the prior art references the examiner discussed do indeed teach the use of various acids to make various cephems, they do not define a class of acids the knowledge of which would render obvious the use of Ochiai's specifically claimed acid. The Board noted that Ochiai's specifically claimed acid is 'similar' to the acids used in the prior art. Likewise, the examiner asserted that the claimed acid was 'slightly different' from those taught in the cited references. Neither characterization, however, can establish the obviousness of the use of a starting material that is new and nonobvious, both in general and in the claimed process. The mere chemical possibility that one of those prior art acids could be modified such that its use would lead to the particular cephem recited in claim 6 does not make the process recited in claim 6 obvious 'unless the prior art suggested the desirability of [such a] modification.' In re Gordon, 733 F.2d 900, 902, 221 U.S.P.Q. 1125, 1127 (Fed.Cir.1984).

---

[33] The paragraphs of § 103 were also, for the first time, separately designated with letters.

[34] 71 F.3d 1565 (Fed.Cir.1995).

It remains to be seen whether § 103(b) or *Durden* retains vitality.

**5.**   *Presumption of Validity.* In an omitted section of *Stratoflex,* the Federal Circuit discussed § 282 of the Act, which creates a presumption that a patent is valid. As we have seen, similar presumptions exist in both copyright and trademark law. In both systems, the presumption has the effect of requiring the challenger to disprove validity, cf. Assignments 6 and 2. In *Stratoflex,* however, the district court had held that the presumption of patent validity applied only with respect to material that had been reviewed by the PTO; since material introduced for the first time by Stratoflex had never been scrutinized, the patentee, Aeroflex, bore the burden of showing that its invention was nonobvious over this art. The Federal Circuit reversed:

> Introduction of more pertinent prior art than that considered by the examiner does not ... 'weaken' or 'destroy' the presumption. Nor does such introduction 'shift' the burden of persuasion. The presumption continues its procedural burden-assigning role throughout the trial.[35]

Given that patent applications are much more rigorously examined than copyright and trademark applications, does it make sense to treat the presumptions in the same way in all three areas?

Issues concerning the presumption of validity generally arise in the course of litigating patentability in proceedings between private parties. A related question concerns the degree of deference that should be given to PTO fact finding.[36] The Federal Circuit had been using the "clearly erroneous" test, a stricter standard than the "arbitrary and capricious" and "unsupported by substantial evidence" tests set out in the Administrative Procedure Act, which governs the review of agency action generally.[37] In part, the court reasoned that the stricter standard was consonant with historical practice. And, since the PTO's decisions can be challenged in two ways—by direct review to the Federal Circuit or by filing an original action in the district court, the Federal Circuit also considered it necessary to examine PTO fact finding on the same standard used for reviewing lower court decisions.[38]

However, the Supreme Court disagreed. Dickinson v. Zurko[39] was a challenge to the PTO's denial of a patent on a method for increasing computer security. The Federal Circuit used the "clearly erroneous" test to set aside the factual findings underlying the determination of obviousness. The Supreme Court reversed, holding that the APA standard applied. After brushing aside the historical argument, the Court suggested that the anomaly created by reviewing district court decisions and PTO decisions on different standards could be handled by allowing the Federal Circuit to "adjust related review standards where necessary." Since the Supreme Court has not allowed the Federal Circuit to adjust reviewing standards in

---

[35] *Stratoflex,* 713 F.2d at 1534.

[36] See 35 U.S.C. § 141.

[37] 5 U.S.C. § 706(2)(A) and (E).

[38] In re Zurko, 142 F.3d 1447 (Fed.Cir. 1998).

[39] 527 U.S. 150 (1999).

the past, this language is something of a surprise.[40] Moreover, the deference that will now be accorded to the PTO contrasts rather starkly with the way that the Court treated its decisions in the cases in this Assignment. Could it be that the Court was influenced by the fact that the PTO *denied* Zurko's patent, whereas the patents in *Graham* and *Sakraida* had both been *granted*? Will the Court come to regret its decision in *Zurko*? Or, will *Zurko* encourage the PTO to bring its practice in line with that of other administrative agencies?

**6.** *The Person of Ordinary Skill in the Art.* Note the importance of the "ordinary artisan" standard to the determination of nonobviousness. It not only protects the public domain by rendering unpatentable inventions that are effectively available to ordinary people in the field, it also tailors patent law to particular fields. That is, it makes the standard for patentability turn on the depth of knowledge in each field: it is easier to patent in arts that are less advanced, and harder to patent in areas that are more sophisticated. As a result, the lure of patents is likely to attract more capital to fields where more work is required.

Does the Federal Circuit pay enough attention to determinations of the skill of ordinary artisans? There are surprisingly few opinions on this issue. Moreover, the court seems to consider itself bound by its prior determinations of the state of knowledge in a field. Thus, the standard in biotechnology was set by In re Bell, even though the case was decided over a decade ago and the work at issue was completed long before that—and long before the advent of sequencing devices and other genomic research innovations. By the same token, some observers suggest that the level of skill the court imputes to the software industry is too high in light of the complexity of modern computer science.[41]

**7.** *Originality (derivation).* As in copyright, patent protection is available only to the original creator of the work. The clearest statement of this requirement is found in § 102(f), which bars a patent if the subject matter was not invented by the applicant. See also § 111, which requires that the application be made by the inventor, and §§ 115–116, requiring applicants to swear that they believe themselves to be the original and first inventors of the subject matter of the application. Because the applicant who runs afoul of these provisions can be said to have "derived" the invention from another, patent attorneys usually speak of "derivation" rather than "originality." Traditionally, derivation requires evidence of conception by another and evidence from which it can be inferred that there was a communication to the inventor that was complete enough to enable one with ordinary skill to practice the invention.

[40] See Dennison Manufacturing Co. v. Panduit Corp., 475 U.S. 809 (1986)(per curiam).

[41] For discussions of these issues, see Dan L. Burk and Mark A. Lemley, Is Patent Law Technology–Specific?, 17 Berkeley Tech L.J. 1155 (2002); Lawrence M. Sung, On Treating Past as Prologue, 2001 J. L. Tech & Pol'y; Joseph P. Meara, Just Who Is The Person Having Ordinary Skill In The Art? Patent Law's Mysterious Personage, 77 Wash. L. Rev. 267 (2002).

Despite the clear bar on inventions derived from others, there are rather few cases decided on pure originality grounds. Proof of communication can be hard to come by. Moreover, it is often much easier to simply consider the first inventor's work as part of the prior art, and then reject the second inventor's application on the ground that the invention is obvious or not novel in light of the earlier work. For example, consider the case in which A invents a widget in the United States and shows it to B, who then applies for a patent. Derivation requires a showing that the invention was conceived by the first inventor (here, A) and the complete conception was communicated in an enabling way to the applicant (B).[42] It is often easier to simply show that the invention was used by another (namely, A) in the United States (§ 102(a)) or invented in this country by another who did not abandon, suppress, or conceal it (§ 102(g)(2)). If B did not brazenly apply for a patent on A's precise invention but instead made some minor changes, the application could be rejected on § 103 grounds.

Why, then, is § 102(f) broken out as a separate section? One answer is evident from *OddzOn,* which involved confidential ball designs, a type of secret art that would not defeat a patent under § 102(a), which is limited to inventions that are somewhat public, or under § 102(g)(2), where the "not abandoned, suppressed, or concealed" language means that the art must be in use or in the process of being patented or commercialized. Second, under § 102(f), foreign knowledge can defeat a patent. That is not possible under § 102(a) or § 102(g)(2) because these provisions are limited to material known, used, or made "in this country." Thus, an invention known only to, let us say, one other American or to a foreigner may not be effective anticipation. However, the applicant will nonetheless be unable to receive a patent if, instead of inventing the invention herself, this other American—or the foreigner—told her about it.[43]

Note that the last part of the traditional test for derivation was missing in *OddzOn*: the confidential ball designs did not enable an ordinary artisan to make the Vortex ball. Do you agree with the court's decision to combine § 102(f) with § 103 and to reject the patent on the ground that the secret information, when added to publicly available information, rendered the Vortex ball obvious? These §§ 102(f)/103 rejections blur the distinction between provisions that maintain the integrity of the public domain and provisions that insure that the patent is awarded to a true inventor. They also raise litigation costs. The distinction is blurred because information told only to an applicant is not really available to the world. As a result, the applicant accomplished something that no ordinary artisan could have done. Costs increase because the possibility of such a rejection creates incentives to investigate everything the applicant ever heard or saw, and require a court or the PTO to indulge in complicated determinations about the interaction between public material and information whose exact scope is uncertain. Significantly, other patent systems consider secret

[42] See, e.g., Johnson & Johnson v. W.L. Gore Assoc., 436 F.Supp. 704, 711 (D.Del. 1977).

[43] Section 102(f) is also not affected by § 104's bar on using foreign inventive activities.

art that is fully enabling to be patent defeating, but generally do not use secret art in combination with other references for nonobviousness purposes. Some of the Federal Circuit judges have urged their colleagues to take a similar approach here.[44] Assignment 20 takes up other issues involving secret art.

8. *The last sentence of § 103(c): common ownership.* Prior to 1984, the combination of § 103 with §§ 102(f) or (g) sometimes worked considerable mischief in large research organizations. Imagine, for example, that a scientist is assigned to develop a new product. After working on the project for a while, he comes up with a key insight. However, before he can bring the invention to the point where it can be practiced, priorities within the firm change, and the scientist is assigned to another task. Some years later, interest is rekindled. But since the first scientist is busy, a second scientist takes over the project. The second scientist combines the earlier insight with her own findings and completes the project. What happens when the firm tries to get a patent? The first researcher's work may be deemed to render the invention obvious on the basis of §§ 102(f)/103, or possibly §§ 102(g)/103.[45]

This state of affairs was highly inefficient as it led firms to institute procedures to prohibit their employees from sharing information. Finding this practice a waste of expensive talent, Congress enacted the second paragraph of § 103(c), which prevents the work of one inventor from being considered in reviewing the patent application of another when both did the work that is the subject of the application for the same company or when their work was subject to an obligation of assignment to the same entity.[46] Some claim that Congress has not gone far enough, and that other joint research efforts, such as collaborative academic work, also need special treatment.[47] Would a better approach be to overrule *OddzOn*?

---

[44] See, e.g., Lamb–Weston, Inc. v. McCain Foods, Ltd., 78 F.3d 540, 546 (Fed. Cir. 1996)(Newman, J., dissenting); Gambro Lundia AB v. Baxter Healthcare Corp., 110 F.3d 1573 (Fed. Cir. 1997).

[45] See, e.g., Kimberly–Clark Corp. v. Johnson and Johnson, 745 F.2d 1437 (Fed. Cir.1984). Section 102(g) is in the picture because it too permits invalidation based on secret art. That is, in the hypothetical, the work of the first researcher could be considered an invention invented by another in the United States. Even if not communicated to the second researcher, it could be disqualifying.

[46] At the same time, § 116, was modified so that successive researchers will sometimes be considered joint inventors.

[47] See, e.g., The Cooperative Research and Technology Enhancement (CREATE) Act of 2003, H.R. 2391, 18th Cong., 1st Sess. (2003).

# ASSIGNMENT 19

# STATUTORY BARS

## 1. INTRODUCTION

Unlike the novelty and nonobviousness provisions of §§ 102(a), (e), (g), and § 103, which are directed to events preceding invention, the statutory bars focus on events preceding the filing of a patent application. These provisions augment § 101 by adding new conditions for acquiring a patent. They enumerate activities that are regarded as so antithetical to the policies underlying patent law that their existence will bar a patent even if the invention is otherwise innovative enough to deserve one. Consequently, they are sometimes referred to as "loss of right" provisions.

The statutory bars are enumerated in those provisions of § 102 that describe activity occurring *before*—in most cases, more than a year before—the application was filed: under § 102(b), public use or sale of the invention in the United States more than a year before filing, or publication or patenting anywhere in the world more than a year before filing; under § 102(c), abandonment; under § 102(d), the issuance of an applicant's foreign patent before a U.S. application is filed, if the foreign patent was applied for more than a year before the U.S. filing.

The statutory bars can be thought of as statutes of limitation. The patent system is aimed at encouraging more than merely invention: it is also intended to promote dissemination. The costs of exclusivity are balanced out only if the social benefits provided by the invention are in fact captured through its widespread use. Thus, the inventor who keeps the invention to herself should not always be eligible to receive a patent. Furthermore, patents are time-bound: with some exceptions, they last no more than 20 years. The inventor who enjoys exclusive benefits of the invention before applying for a patent should be penalized for, in effect, trying to extend the term of protection beyond the limit set by Congress.

Because the policies underlying the statutory bars are so strong, it is somewhat surprising that some of the subsections provide for a one-year grace period—that is, public use, sale, publication, and patenting bar a patent only if they occurred *more* than a year before the application is filed. In many countries, these events would bar a patent even if they occurred the day before filing.[1] The United States, however, recognizes that in many areas, the PTO is not the most efficient vehicle for disseminating inventions. For example, academic researchers rely much more on research conferences than patents to learn and exchange information; industrial

---

[1] See, e.g., European Patent Convention, art. 54(1)(1977).

innovators use trade fairs. If these avenues could not be pursued until the application is filed, dissemination will be delayed rather than encouraged. Accordingly, so long as these activities do not go on for too long (defined as a year), the patent will not be barred.[2]

## 2. PRINCIPAL PROBLEM

Reconsider the Problem at issue in Assignment 17. Do any of the activities described raise a statutory bar?

## 3. MATERIALS FOR SOLUTION OF PRINCIPAL PROBLEM

A. STATUTORY MATERIALS: §§ 102(b), (c), & (d)

B. CASES:

## Egbert v. Lippmann

Supreme Court of the United States, 1881.
104 U.S.(14 Otto) 333, 26 L.Ed. 755.

■ MR. JUSTICE WOODS delivered the opinion of the Court.

This suit was brought for an alleged infringement of the complainant's reissued letters-patent, No. 5216, dated Jan. 7, 1873, for an improvement in corset-springs. The original letters bear date July 17, 1866, and were issued to Samuel H. Barnes. The reissue was made to the complainant, under her then name, Frances Lee Barnes, executrix of the original patentee.

The bill alleges that Barnes was the original and first inventor of the improvement covered by the reissued letters-patent, and that it had not, at the time of his application for the original letters, been for more than two years in public use or on sale, with his consent or allowance.[a] The answer takes issue on this averment. We have, therefore, to consider whether the defense that the patented invention had, with the consent of the inventor, been publicly used for more than two years prior to his application for the original letters, is sustained by the testimony in the record.

The evidence on which the defendants rely to establish a prior public use of the invention consists mainly of the testimony of the complainant.

She testifies that Barnes invented the improvement covered by his patent between January and May, 1855; that between the dates named the witness and her friend Miss Cugier were complaining of the breaking of their corset-steels. Barnes, who was present, and was an intimate friend of

---

[2] There are also countries that attempt to compromise these positions by providing a grace period, but only for narrow categories of dissemination, see, e.g., Toshiko Takenaka, The Substantial Identity Rule Under the Japanese Standard, 9 UCLA Pac. Basin L.J. 220, 224–25 (1991).

[a] [At that time, the Patent Act rendered a patent invalid if the invention was in public use, with the consent and allowance of the inventor, for more than two years prior to the application—eds.]

the witness, said he thought he could make her a pair that would not break. At their next interview he presented her with a pair of corset-steels which he himself had made. The witness wore these steels a long time. In 1858 Barnes made and presented to her another pair, which she also wore a long time. When the corsets in which these steels were used wore out, the witness ripped them open and took out the steels and put them in new corsets. This was done several times.

It is admitted, and, in fact, is asserted, by complainant, that these steels embodied the invention afterwards patented by Barnes and covered by the reissued letters-patent on which this suit is brought.

Joseph H. Sturgis, another witness for complainant, testifies that in 1863 Barnes spoke to him about two inventions made by himself, one of which was a corset-steel, and that he went to the house of Barnes to see them. Before this time, and after the transactions testified to by the complainant, Barnes and she had intermarried. Barnes said his wife had a pair of steels made according to his invention in the corsets which she was then wearing, and if she would take them off he would show them to witness. Mrs. Barnes went out, and returned with a pair of corsets and a pair of scissors, and ripped the corsets open and took out the steels. Barnes then explained to witness how they were made and used.

This is the evidence presented by the record, on which the defendants rely to establish the public use of the invention by the patentee's consent and allowance. The question for our decision is, whether this testimony shows a public use within the meaning of the statute.

We observe, in the first place, that to constitute the public use of an invention it is not necessary that more than one of the patented articles should be publicly used. The use of a great number may tend to strengthen the proof, but one well-defined case of such use is just as effectual to annul the patent as many. McClurg v. Kingsland, 1 How. 202; Consolidated Fruit–Jar Co. v. Wright, 94 U.S. 92; Pitts v. Hall, 2 Blatchf. 229. For instance, if the inventor of a mower, a printing-press, or a railway-car makes and sells only one of the articles invented by him, and allows the vendee to use it for two years, without restriction or limitation, the use is just as public as if he had sold and allowed the use of a great number.

We remark, secondly, that, whether the use of an invention is public or private does not necessarily depend upon the number of persons to whom its use is known. If an inventor, having made his device, gives or sells it to another, to be used by the donee or vendee, without limitation or restriction, or injunction of secrecy, and it is so used, such use is public, even though the use and knowledge of the use may be confined to one person.

We say, thirdly, that some inventions are by their very character only capable of being used where they cannot be seen or observed by the public eye. An invention may consist of a lever or spring, hidden in the running gear of a watch, or of a rachet, shaft, or cog-wheel covered from view in the recesses of a machine for spinning or weaving. Nevertheless, if its inventor sells a machine of which his invention forms a part, and allows it to be used without restriction of any kind, the use is a public one. So, on the other hand, a use necessarily open to public view, if made in good faith solely to test the qualities of the invention, and for the purpose of experiment, is not a public use within the meaning of the statute. Elizabeth v. American Nicholson Pavement Company, 97 U.S. 126; Shaw v. Cooper, 7 Pet. 292.

Tested by these principles, we think the evidence of the complainant herself shows that for more than two years before the application for the original letters there was, by the consent and allowance of Barnes, a public use of the invention, covered by them. He made and gave to her two pairs of corset-steels, constructed according to his device, one in 1855 and one in 1858. They were presented to her for use. He imposed no obligation of secrecy, nor any condition or restriction whatever. They were not presented for the purpose of experiment, nor to test their qualities. No such claim is set up in her testimony. The invention was at the time complete, and there is no evidence that it was afterwards changed or improved. The donee of the steels used them for years for the purpose and in the manner designed by the inventor. They were not capable of any other use. She might have exhibited them to any person, or made other steels of the same kind, and used or sold them without violating any condition or restriction imposed on her by the inventor.

According to the testimony of the complainant, the invention was completed and put into use in 1855. The inventor slept on his rights for eleven years. Letters-patent were not applied for till March, 1866. In the mean time, the invention had found its way into general, and almost universal, use. A great part of the record is taken up with the testimony of the manufacturers and venders of corset-steels, showing that before he applied for letters the principle of his device was almost universally used in the manufacture of corset-steels. It is fair to presume that having learned from this general use that there was some value in his invention, he attempted to resume, by his application, what by his acts he had clearly dedicated to the public.

"An abandonment of an invention to the public may be evinced by the conduct of the inventor at any time, even within the two years named in the law. The effect of the law is that no such consequence will necessarily follow from the invention being in public use or on sale, with the inventor's consent and allowance, at any time within the two years before his application; but that, if the invention is in public use or on sale prior to that time, it will be conclusive evidence of abandonment, and the patent will be void." Elizabeth v. Pavement Company.

We are of opinion that the defense of two years' public use, by the consent and allowance of the inventor, before he made application for letters-patent, is satisfactorily established by the evidence.

■ MR. JUSTICE MILLER dissenting [omitted.]

# Metallizing Engineering Co. v. Kenyon Bearing & Auto Parts Co.

United States Court of Appeals, Second Circuit, 1946.
153 F.2d 516.

■ L. HAND, CIRCUIT JUDGE.

The defendants appeal from the usual decree holding valid and infringed all but three of the claims of a reissued patent, issued to the plaintiff's assignor, Meduna; the original patent issued on May 25, 1943, upon an application filed on August 6, 1942. The patent is for the process of 'so conditioning a metal surface that the same is, as a rule, capable of bonding thereto applied spray metal to a higher degree than is normally procurable with hitherto known practices.'

The only question which we find necessary to decide is as to Meduna's public use of the patented process more than one year before August 6, 1942. The district judge made findings. The kernel of them is the following: "the inventor's main purpose in his use of the process prior to August 6, 1941, and especially in respect to all jobs for owners not known to him, was commercial." Upon this finding he concluded as matter of law that the use was not public but secret, and for that reason that its predominantly commercial character did prevent it from invalidating the patent. For the last he relied upon our decisions in Peerless Roll Leaf Co. v. Griffin & Sons, 29 F.2d 646, and Gillman v. Stern, 114 F.2d 28. We think that his analysis of Peerless Roll Leaf Co. v. Griffin & Sons, was altogether correct, and that he had no alternative but to follow that decision; on the other hand, we now think that we were then wrong and that the decision must be overruled for reasons we shall state. Gillman v. Stern, was, however, rightly decided.

So far as we can find, the first case which dealt with the effect of prior use by the patentee was Pennock v. Dialogue, 2 Pet. 1, 4, 7 L.Ed. 327, in which the invention had been completed in 1811, and the patent granted in 1818 for a process of making hose by which the sections were joined together in such a way that the joints resisted pressure as well as the other parts. It did not appear that the joints in any way disclosed the process; but the patentee, between the discovery of the invention and the grant of the patent, had sold 13,000 feet of hose; and as to this the judge charged: "If the public, with the knowledge and tacit consent of the inventor, be permitted to use the invention, without opposition, it is a fraud on the public afterwards to take out a patent." The Supreme Court affirmed a judgment for the defendant, on the ground that the invention had been "known or used before the application." "If an inventor should be permitted to hold back from the knowledge of the public the secrets of his invention; if he should * * * make and sell his invention publicly, and thus gather the whole profits, * * * it would materially retard the progress of science and the useful arts" to allow him fourteen years of legal monopoly "when the danger of competition should force him to secure the exclusive right" 2 Pet. at page 19, 7 L.Ed. 327. In Shaw v. Cooper, 7 Pet. 292, 8 L.Ed. 689, the public use was not by the inventory, but he had neglected to prevent it after he had learned of it, and this defeated the patent. "Whatever may be the intention of the inventor, if he suffers his invention to go into public use, through any means whatsoever, without an immediate assertion of his right, he is not entitled to a patent" 7 Pet. at page 323, 8 L.Ed. 689.

In the lower courts we may begin with the often cited decision in Macbeth–Evans Glass Co. v. General Electric Co., 6 Cir., 246 F. 695, which concerned a process patent for making illuminating glass. The patentee had kept the process as secret as possible, but for ten years had sold the glass, although this did not, so far as appears, disclose the process. The court held the patent invalid for two reasons, as we understand them: the first was that the delay either indicated an intention to abandon, or was of itself a forfeiture, because of the inconsistency of a practical monopoly by means of secrecy and of a later legal monopoly by means of a patent. So far, it was not an interpretation of "prior use" in the statute; but, beginning on page 702 of 246 F. 695 Judge Warrington seems to have been construing that phrase and to hold that the sales were such a use.

Coming now to our own decisions (the opinions in all of which I wrote), the first was Grasselli Chemical Co. v. National Aniline & Chemical Co., 2 Cir., 26 F.2d 305, in which the patent was for a process which had been kept secret, but the product had been sold upon the market for more than two years. We held that, although the process could not have been discovered from the product, the sales constituted a "prior use," relying upon Egbert v. Lippmann, 104 U.S. 333. There was nothing in this inconsistent with what we are now holding. But in Peerless Roll Leaf Co. v. Griffin & Sons, 2 Cir., 29 F.2d 646, where the patent was for a machine, which had been kept secret, but whose output had been freely sold on the market, we sustained the patent on the ground that "the sale of the product was irrelevant, since no knowledge could possibly be acquired of the machine in that way. In this respect the machine differs from a process * * * or from any other invention necessarily contained in a product" 29 F.2d at page 649. So far as we can now find, there is nothing to support this distinction in the authorities, and we shall try to show that we misapprehended the theory on which the prior use by an inventor forfeits his right to a patent. In Gillman v. Stern, 2 Cir., 114 F.2d 28, it was not the inventor, but a third person who used the machine secretly and sold the product openly, and there was therefore no question either of abandonment or forfeiture by the inventor. The only issue was whether a prior use which did not disclose the invention to the art was within the statute; and it is well settled that it is not. As in the case of any other anticipation, the issue of invention must then be determined by how much the inventor has contributed any new information to the art. Gayler v. Wilder, 10 How. 477, 496, 497, 13 L.Ed. 504; Tilghman v. Proctor, 102 U.S. 707, 711, 26 L.Ed. 279.

From the foregoing it appears that in Peerless Roll Leaf Co. v. Griffin & Sons, 2 Cir., 29 F.2d 646, we confused two separate doctrines: (1) The effect upon his right to a patent of the inventor's competitive exploitation of his machine or of his process; (2) the contribution which a prior use by another person makes to the art. Both do indeed come within the phrase, "prior use"; but the first is a defence for quite different reasons from the second. It had its origin—at least in this country—in the passage we have quoted from Pennock v. Dialogue, 2 Pet. 1, 7 L.Ed. 327; i.e., that it is a condition upon an inventor's right to a patent that he shall not exploit his discovery competitively after it is ready for patenting; he must content himself with either secrecy, or legal monopoly. It is true that for the limited period of two years he was allowed to do so, possibly in order to give him time to prepare an application; and even that has been recently cut down by half. But if he goes beyond that period of probation, he forfeits his right regardless of how little the public may have learned about the invention; just as he can forfeit it by too long concealment, even without exploiting the invention at all. Woodbridge v. United States, 263 U.S. 50, 44 S.Ct. 45, 68 L.Ed. 159; Macbeth–Evans Glass Co. v. General Electric Co., 6 Cir., 246 F. 695. Such a forfeiture has nothing to do with abandonment, which presupposes a deliberate, though not necessarily an express, surrender of any right to a patent. Although the evidence of both may at times overlap, each comes from a quite different legal source: one, from the fact that by renouncing the right the inventor irrevocably surrenders it; the other, from the fiat of Congress that it is part of the consideration for a patent that the public shall as soon as possible begin to enjoy the disclosure.

■ Judgment reversed; complaint dismissed.

## Pfaff v. Well Electronics, Inc.

Supreme Court of the United States, 1998.
525 U.S. 55, 119 S.Ct. 304, 142 L.Ed.2d 261.

■ JUSTICE STEVENS delivered the opinion of the Court.

Section 102(b) of the Patent Act of 1952 provides that no person is entitled to patent an "invention" that has been "on sale" more than one year before filing a patent application. We granted certiorari to determine whether the commercial marketing of a newly invented product may mark the beginning of the 1–year period even though the invention has not yet been reduced to practice.

I

On April 19, 1982, petitioner, Wayne Pfaff, filed an application for a patent on a computer chip socket. Therefore, April 19, 1981, constitutes the critical date for purposes of the on-sale bar of 35 U.S.C. § 102(b); if the 1–year period began to run before that date, Pfaff lost his right to patent his invention.

Pfaff commenced work on the socket in November 1980, when representatives of Texas Instruments asked him to develop a new device for mounting and removing semiconductor chip carriers. In response to this request, he prepared detailed engineering drawings that described the design, the dimensions, and the materials to be used in making the socket. Pfaff sent those drawings to a manufacturer in February or March 1981.

Prior to March 17, 1981, Pfaff showed a sketch of his concept to representatives of Texas Instruments. On April 8, 1981, they provided Pfaff with a written confirmation of a previously placed oral purchase order for 30,100 of his new sockets for a total price of $91,155. In accord with his normal practice, Pfaff did not make and test a prototype of the new device before offering to sell it in commercial quantities.[a] The manufacturer took several months to develop the customized tooling necessary to produce the device, and Pfaff did not fill the order until July 1981. The evidence therefore indicates that Pfaff first reduced his invention to practice in the summer of 1981. The socket achieved substantial commercial success before Patent No. 4,491,377 (the '377 patent) issued to Pfaff on January 1, 1985.[b]

After the patent issued, petitioner brought an infringement action against respondent, Wells Electronics, Inc., the manufacturer of a competing socket. Wells prevailed on the basis of a finding of no infringement. When respondent began to market a modified device, petitioner brought this suit, alleging that the modifications infringed six of the claims in the '377 patent. [The District Court held two claims invalid and upheld the rest, rejecting a defense based on § 102(b). The Court of Appeals reversed. It held two claims invalid on § 103 grounds and four claims invalid on § 102(b) grounds.] The conclusion [regarding § 102(b)] rested on the court's view that as long as the invention was "substantially complete at the time of sale," the 1–year period began to run, even though the invention had not yet been reduced to practice.

Because other courts have held or assumed that an invention cannot be "on sale" within the meaning of § 102(b) unless and until it has been reduced to practice, see, e.g., Timely Products Corp. v. Arron, 523 F.2d 288, 299–302 (C.A.2 1975); Dart Industries, Inc. v. E.I. du Pont De Nemours & Co., 489 F.2d 1359, 1365, n. 11 (C.A.7 1973), cert. denied, 417 U.S. 933, 94 S.Ct. 2645, 41 L.Ed.2d 236 (1974), and because the text of § 102(b) makes no reference to "substantial completion" of an invention, we granted certiorari. 523 U.S. ___, 118 S.Ct. 1183, 140 L.Ed.2d 315 (1998).

II

The primary meaning of the word "invention" in the Patent Act unquestionably refers to the inventor's conception rather than to a physical embodiment of that idea. The statute does not contain any express requirement that an invention must be reduced to practice before it can be patented. Neither the statutory definition of the term in § 100 nor the basic conditions for obtaining a patent set forth in § 101 make any mention

[a] At his deposition, respondent's counsel engaged in the following colloquy with Pfaff:

"Q. Now, at this time [late 1980 or early 1981] did we [sic] have any prototypes developed or anything of that nature, working embodiment?

"A. No.

"Q. It was in a drawing. Is that correct?

"A. Strictly in a drawing. Went from the drawing to the hard tooling. That's the way I do my business.

"Q. 'Boom-boom'?

"A. You got it.

"Q. You are satisfied, obviously, when you come up with some drawings that it is going to go—'it works'?

"A. I know what I'm doing, yes, most of the time." App. 96–97.

[b] Initial sales of the patented device were:

1981 $350,000

1982 $937,000

1983 $2,800,000

1984 $3,430,000

App. to Pet. for Cert. 223.

of "reduction to practice." The statute's only specific reference to that term is found in § 102(g), which sets forth the standard for resolving priority contests between two competing claimants to a patent. That subsection provides:

"In determining priority of invention there shall be considered not only the respective dates of conception and reduction to practice of the invention, but also the reasonable diligence of one who was first to conceive and last to reduce to practice, from a time prior to conception by the other."

Thus, assuming diligence on the part of the applicant, it is normally the first inventor to conceive, rather than the first to reduce to practice, who establishes the right to the patent.

It is well settled that an invention may be patented before it is reduced to practice. In 1888, this Court upheld a patent issued to Alexander Graham Bell even though he had filed his application before constructing a working telephone. Chief Justice Waite's reasoning in that case merits quoting at length:

"It is quite true that when Bell applied for his patent he had never actually transmitted telegraphically spoken words so that they could be distinctly heard and understood at the receiving end of his line, but in his specification he did describe accurately and with admirable clearness his process, that is to say, the exact electrical condition that must be created to accomplish his purpose, and he also described, with sufficient precision to enable one of ordinary skill in such matters to make it, a form of apparatus which, if used in the way pointed out, would produce the required effect, receive the words, and carry them to and deliver them at the appointed place. The particular instrument which he had, and which he used in his experiments, did not, under the circumstances in which it was tried, reproduce the words spoken, so that they could be clearly understood, but the proof is abundant and of the most convincing character, that other instruments, carefully constructed and made exactly in accordance with the specification, without any additions whatever, have operated and will operate successfully. A good mechanic of proper skill in matters of the kind can take the patent and, by following the specification strictly, can, without more, construct an apparatus which, when used in the way pointed out, will do all that it is claimed the method or process will do. . . .

"The law does not require that a discoverer or inventor, in order to get a patent for a process, must have succeeded in bringing his art to the highest degree of perfection. It is enough if he describes his method with sufficient clearness and precision to enable those skilled in the matter to understand what the process is, and if he points out some practicable way of putting it into operation." The Telephone Cases, 126 U.S. 1, 535–536, 8 S.Ct. 778, 31 L.Ed. 863 (1888).[c]

When we apply the reasoning of The Telephone Cases to the facts of the case before us today, it is evident that Pfaff could have obtained a

[c] This Court has also held a patent invalid because the invention had previously been disclosed in a prior patent application, although that application did not claim the invention and the first invention apparently had not been reduced to practice. Alexander Milburn Co. v. Davis–Bournonville Co., 270 U.S. 390, 401–402, 46 S.Ct. 324, 70 L.Ed. 651 (1926).

patent on his novel socket when he accepted the purchase order from Texas Instruments for 30,100 units. At that time he provided the manufacturer with a description and drawings that had "sufficient clearness and precision to enable those skilled in the matter" to produce the device. The parties agree that the sockets manufactured to fill that order embody Pfaff's conception as set forth in claims 1, 6, 7, and 10 of the '377 patent. We can find no basis in the text of § 102(b) or in the facts of this case for concluding that Pfaff's invention was not "on sale" within the meaning of the statute until after it had been reduced to practice.

## III

Pfaff nevertheless argues that longstanding precedent, buttressed by the strong interest in providing inventors with a clear standard identifying the onset of the 1–year period, justifies a special interpretation of the word "invention" as used in § 102(b). We are persuaded that this nontextual argument should be rejected.

As we have often explained, most recently in Bonito Boats, Inc. v. Thunder Craft Boats, Inc., 489 U.S. 141, 151, 109 S.Ct. 971, 103 L.Ed.2d 118 (1989), the patent system represents a carefully crafted bargain that encourages both the creation and the public disclosure of new and useful advances in technology, in return for an exclusive monopoly for a limited period of time. The balance between the interest in motivating innovation and enlightenment by rewarding invention with patent protection on the one hand, and the interest in avoiding monopolies that unnecessarily stifle competition on the other, has been a feature of the federal patent laws since their inception.

Consistent with these ends, § 102 of the Patent Act serves as a limiting provision, both excluding ideas that are in the public domain from patent protection and confining the duration of the monopoly to the statutory term. See, e.g., Frantz Mfg. Co. v. Phenix Mfg. Co., 457 F.2d 314, 320 (C.A.7 1972).

We originally held that an inventor loses his right to a patent if he puts his invention into public use before filing a patent application. "His voluntary act or acquiescence in the public sale and use is an abandonment of his right" Pennock v. Dialogue, 2 Pet. 1, 24, 7 L.Ed. 327 (1829) (Story, J.). A similar reluctance to allow an inventor to remove existing knowledge from public use undergirds the on-sale bar.

Nevertheless, an inventor who seeks to perfect his discovery may conduct extensive testing without losing his right to obtain a patent for his invention—even if such testing occurs in the public eye. The law has long recognized the distinction between inventions put to experimental use and products sold commercially. In 1878, we explained why patentability may turn on an inventor's use of his product.

> "It is sometimes said that an inventor acquires an undue advantage over the public by delaying to take out a patent, inasmuch as he thereby preserves the monopoly to himself for a longer period than is allowed by the policy of the law; but this cannot be said with justice when the delay is

occasioned by a bona fide effort to bring his invention to perfection, or to ascertain whether it will answer the purpose intended. His monopoly only continues for the allotted period, in any event; and it is the interest of the public, as well as himself, that the invention should be perfect and properly tested, before a patent is granted for it. Any attempt to use it for a profit, and not by way of experiment, for a longer period than two years before the application, would deprive the inventor of his right to a patent." Elizabeth v. American Nicholson Pavement Co., 97 U.S. 126, 137, 24 L.Ed. 1000 (1877) (emphasis added).

The patent laws therefore seek both to protect the public's right to retain knowledge already in the public domain and the inventor's right to control whether and when he may patent his invention. The Patent Act of 1836, 5 Stat. 117, was the first statute that expressly included an on-sale bar to the issuance of a patent. Like the earlier holding in Pennock, that provision precluded patentability if the invention had been placed on sale at any time before the patent application was filed. In 1839, Congress ameliorated that requirement by enacting a 2–year grace period in which the inventor could file an application. 5 Stat. 353.

In Andrews v. Hovey, 123 U.S. 267, 274, 8 S.Ct. 101, 31 L.Ed. 160 (1887), we noted that the purpose of that amendment was "to fix a period of limitation which should be certain"; it required the inventor to make sure that a patent application was filed "within two years from the completion of his invention," ibid. In 1939, Congress reduced the grace period from two years to one year. 53 Stat. 1212.

Petitioner correctly argues that these provisions identify an interest in providing inventors with a definite standard for determining when a patent application must be filed. A rule that makes the timeliness of an application depend on the date when an invention is "substantially complete" seriously undermines the interest in certainty.[d] Moreover, such a rule finds no support in the text of the statute. Thus, petitioner's argument calls into question the standard applied by the Court of Appeals, but it does not persuade us that it is necessary to engraft a reduction to practice element into the meaning of the term "invention" as used in § 102(b).

The word "invention" must refer to a concept that is complete, rather than merely one that is "substantially complete." It is true that reduction to practice ordinarily provides the best evidence that an invention is complete. But just because reduction to practice is sufficient evidence of completion, it does not follow that proof of reduction to practice is neces-

---

[d] The Federal Circuit has developed a multifactor, "totality of the circumstances" test to determine the trigger for the on-sale bar. See, e.g., Micro Chemical, Inc. v. Great Plains Chemical Co., 103 F.3d 1538, 1544 (C.A.Fed.1997) (stating that, in determining whether an invention is on sale for purposes of 102(b), " 'all of the circumstances surrounding the sale or offer to sell, including the stage of development of the invention and the nature of the invention, must be consid- ered and weighed against the policies underlying section 102(b)' "); see also UMC Electronics Co. v. United States, 816 F.2d 647, 656 (1987) (stating the on-sale bar "does not lend itself to formulation into a set of precise requirements"). As the Federal Circuit itself has noted, this test "has been criticized as unnecessarily vague." Seal–Flex, Inc. v. Athletic Track & Court Construction, 98 F.3d 1318, 1323, n. 2 (C.A.Fed.1996).

sary in every case. Indeed, both the facts of the Telephone Cases and the facts of this case demonstrate that one can prove that an invention is complete and ready for patenting before it has actually been reduced to practice.

We conclude, therefore, that the on-sale bar applies when two conditions are satisfied before the critical date. First, the product must be the subject of a commercial offer for sale. An inventor can both understand and control the timing of the first commercial marketing of his invention. The experimental use doctrine, for example, has not generated concerns about indefiniteness, and we perceive no reason why unmanageable uncertainty should attend a rule that measures the application of the on-sale bar of § 102(b) against the date when an invention that is ready for patenting is first marketed commercially. In this case the acceptance of the purchase order prior to April 8, 1981, makes it clear that such an offer had been made, and there is no question that the sale was commercial rather than experimental in character.

Second, the invention must be ready for patenting. That condition may be satisfied in at least two ways: by proof of reduction to practice before the critical date; or by proof that prior to the critical date the inventor had prepared drawings or other descriptions of the invention that were sufficiently specific to enable a person skilled in the art to practice the invention. In this case the second condition of the on-sale bar is satisfied because the drawings Pfaff sent to the manufacturer before the critical date fully disclosed the invention.

The evidence in this case thus fulfills the two essential conditions of the on-sale bar. As succinctly stated by Learned Hand:

"[I]t is a condition upon an inventor's right to a patent that he shall not exploit his discovery competitively after it is ready for patenting; he must content himself with either secrecy, or legal monopoly." Metallizing Engineering Co. v. Kenyon Bearing & Auto Parts Co., 153 F.2d 516, 520 (C.A.2 1946).

The judgment of the Court of Appeals finds support not only in the text of the statute but also in the basic policies underlying the statutory scheme, including § 102(b). When Pfaff accepted the purchase order for his new sockets prior to April 8, 1981, his invention was ready for patenting. The fact that the manufacturer was able to produce the socket using his detailed drawings and specifications demonstrates this fact. Furthermore, those sockets contained all the elements of the invention claimed in the '377 patent. Therefore, Pfaff's '377 patent is invalid because the invention had been on sale for more than one year in this country before he filed his patent application. Accordingly, the judgment of the Court of Appeals is affirmed.

# Baxter International, Inc. v. Cobe Laboratories, Inc.

United States Court of Appeals for the Federal Circuit, 1996.
88 F.3d 1054.

■ LOURIE, CIRCUIT JUDGE.

Baxter International, Inc. and Baxter Healthcare Corporation (collectively "Baxter") appeal from the decision of the United States District

Court for the Northern District of Illinois holding on summary judgment that the asserted claims of U.S. Patent 4,734,089 are invalid under 35 U.S.C. § 102(b) on the ground of a prior public use. Because the district court did not err in holding that there were no genuine issues of material fact regarding the disputed public use and because COBE was entitled to judgment as a matter of law, we affirm.

## BACKGROUND

The '089 patent concerns a sealless centrifuge for separating blood into its components. The application for the patent was filed on May 14, 1976 and it therefore had a critical date of May 14, 1975 for purposes of 35 U.S.C. § 102(b). The alleged prior public use involved the activities of Dr. Jacques Suaudeau, who was a research scientist for the National Institutes of Health (NIH). Suaudeau was studying isolated heart preservation by perfusion, which involved the pumping of whole blood and platelet-rich plasma that had been separated from whole blood through a heart. The centrifuge he had been using damaged platelets in the blood and he found that the damage was caused by rotating seals in the centrifuge. He approached Dr. Yoichiro Ito, another scientist at NIH, for advice in solving this problem, and Ito recommended that Suaudeau try using a sealless centrifuge that Ito had designed. Neither Suaudeau nor Ito had any relationship or connection with Herbert M. Cullis, the inventor named in the '089 patent.[a]

Suaudeau had the centrifuge built by the machine shop at NIH using Ito's drawings. Suaudeau balanced the centrifuge with water and then with blood, and tested it, all before the critical date. It was immediately apparent to Suaudeau that the centrifuge worked properly for its original purpose, as a separator, and that the centrifuge separated blood into its components. He also tested the suitability of the centrifuge for his own purposes, by performing experiments in order to determine if the centrifuge would produce platelet-rich plasma with a platelet count satisfactory for perfusion. These tests involved operating the centrifuge for as long as forty-three hours. All of this occurred in Suaudeau's laboratory at the NIH campus in Bethesda, Maryland. Suaudeau also balanced and tested the centrifuge at Massachusetts General Hospital, where he went to work after leaving NIH.

Baxter sued COBE Laboratories, Inc. for infringement of the '089 patent; it later amended its complaint to add COBE BCT, Inc. as a co-defendant (these companies will be collectively referred to as "COBE"). The representative claims read in pertinent part as follows:

10. A centrifugal blood processing apparatus for use in conjunction with a flow system including at least one blood processing chamber and a flexible

[a] [The Ito device was later made the subject of a patent application, and apparently after an interference with certain aspects of the Cullis application, a patent was granted to Ito.—eds.]

umbilical cable segment having a plurality of integral passageways for establishing fluid communication with said blood processing chamber, said apparatus comprising, in combination:

. . . .

17. The method of centrifugally processing biological fluid with reduced risk of contamination of the fluids of the outside environment using a closed leak-proof envelope which envelope includes an umbilical having input and output at one side thereof and defining passageways there through, which umbilical includes a flexible segment which is capable of repeated axial twisting and untwisting, and which envelope also includes at least one processing chamber connected at the other side of the umbilical which chamber is in communication with the passageways thereof, comprising the steps of:

. . . .

25. A disposable flow system for use in processing fluids in a centrifugal apparatus of the type having a stationary base, an orbiting assembly mounted to the base for orbiting about an axis at a first rotational speed, and a centrifugating rotor assembly for revolving about said axis at twice the rotational speed of said orbiting assembly, said unit comprising:

. . . .

COBE filed a motion for summary judgment of invalidity, asserting that there were no genuine issues of material fact and that the claimed invention had been in public use before the critical date. On December 21, 1994, the district court conducted a hearing on COBE's motion. It then held that Suaudeau had publicly used the claimed invention before the critical date and that the use was not experimental. The court stated that "a use by a single person not under the control of the inventor and in public, as that term of art is used, is a [use] sufficient" to invalidate a patent. The court found that the invention here had been reduced to practice before the critical date, and that others at NIH and Mass. General had observed the centrifuge in operation. Regarding Baxter's assertion that Suaudeau's use was experimental, the court stated that "the experimental use exception is limited to the inventor or people working for the inventor or under the direction and control of the inventor," but that neither Suaudeau nor Ito were acting under the direction or control of Cullis, the inventor. Furthermore, the court found that Suaudeau was not experimenting to perfect or test the invention but, rather, was making modifications for his own particular requirements. Accordingly, the district court held that there were no genuine issues of material fact, that the claimed invention had been in public use before the critical date, and that the asserted claims of the '089 patent were invalid. Baxter now appeals.

## DISCUSSION

Baxter argues that the district erred by not considering the totality of the circumstances or the policies underlying the public use bar. According to Baxter, Suaudeau's use of the centrifuge was not publicly known or accessible, and ethical constraints would have limited or precluded those who saw the centrifuge in operation from disclosing their knowledge of it. Baxter asserts that the most applicable policy involved here is the removal of inventions from the public domain that the public believes are freely available; according to Baxter, the public had no reason to believe that the centrifuge was freely available.

COBE responds that the district court correctly applied the law, considering the relevant policies underlying the public use bar. According to COBE, the centrifuge in Suaudeau's laboratory at NIH and at Mass. General was publicly accessible and those who saw it in operation were under no duty of confidentiality. Furthermore, COBE argues that the relevant policies support the district court's decision, as those who saw the centrifuge in operation would have reasonably believed the centrifuge was publicly available. COBE also asserts that NIH had an interest in continuing to use the technology that its employees, Ito and Suaudeau, began using without restriction before the critical date.

Under section 102, a person is entitled to a patent, *inter alia,* unless "the invention was ... in public use ... in this country, more than one year prior to the date of the application for patent in the United States." 35 U.S.C. § 102(b) (1994). We have described "public use" as including "any use of [the claimed] invention by a person other than the inventor who is under no limitation, restriction or obligation of secrecy to the inventor." *In re Smith,* 714 F.2d 1127, 1134, 218 USPQ 976, 983 (Fed.Cir.1983) (citing *Egbert v. Lippmann,* 104 U.S. 333, 336, 26 L.Ed. 755 (1881)). Whether a public use has occurred is a question of law. In considering whether a particular use was a public use within the meaning of section 102(b), we consider the totality of the circumstances in conjunction with the policies underlying the public use bar. These policies include:

> (1) discouraging the removal, from the public domain, of inventions that the public reasonably has come to believe are freely available; (2) favoring the prompt and widespread disclosure of inventions; (3) allowing the inventor a reasonable amount of time following sales activity to determine the potential economic value of a patent; and (4) prohibiting the inventor from commercially exploiting the invention for a period greater than the statutorily prescribed time.

We agree with COBE that there were no genuine issues of fact, that Suaudeau publicly used the invention before the critical date, and that COBE was entitled to judgment as a matter of law. We do agree with Baxter that the most applicable policy underlying the public use bar here is discouraging removal from the public domain of inventions that the public reasonably has come to believe are freely available. However, invalidation of the Cullis patent is not inconsistent with that policy. Suaudeau's use was public, and it was not experimental in a manner that saves Cullis's patent.

The centrifuge that Suaudeau was using met all the limitations of the representative claims of the '089 patent. Suaudeau testified that the centrifuge worked as a separator as soon as he operated it, which verified that it would work for its intended purpose as a centrifugal blood processing apparatus and method as recited in the claims. Suaudeau further testified that others at NIH came into his laboratory and observed the centrifuge in operation, including co-workers, who were under no duty to maintain it as confidential. Nor did Suaudeau make any discernible effort to maintain the centrifuge as confidential. His laboratory was located in a public building, and he testified that he recalled people coming and looking, people flowing into the lab before the critical date. He even testified that NIH had an anti-secrecy policy.

Suaudeau's lack of effort to maintain the centrifuge as confidential coupled with the free flow into his laboratory of people, including visitors to NIH, who observed the centrifuge in operation and who were under no duty of confidentiality supports only one conclusion: that the centrifuge was in public use. The record contains clear and convincing evidence to support the conclusion that the asserted claims of the '089 patent are invalid on the ground of Suaudeau's prior public use.

Baxter asserts that those who observed the centrifuge were under an ethical obligation to keep it secret. However, there was no evidence that this was so. According to unrefuted testimony by Suaudeau and Dr. Ronald Yankee, any relevant ethical obligation that existed was to refrain from taking credit for the work of others, or publishing the work of others without permission. Those who observed the centrifuge in operation were under no duty to maintain it as confidential.

Baxter also argues that Ito and NIH did not consider Suaudeau's use to have been a public use. Baxter cites the declaration in Ito's own patent application on the sealless centrifuge, filed under the auspices of NIH. In his declaration, Ito averred that the invention had not been in public use more than one year before the filing date of his patent application. The district court discounted the declaration, stating:

I regard Ito's declaration as a groundless statement insofar as the evidence before me bears upon its truth or falsity. I don't mean to say that Dr. Ito made a false declaration. That issue is not before me. All I can say is that on the basis of the evidence which is before me, which has been submitted by both sides here, he was clearly wrong when he said that there had been no use of the invention during the period exceeding a year prior to his own application.

The court was correct in discounting this declaration. Ito's averment was a statement of his own appraisal of the relevant facts, made in relation to his own application for patent. It does not bind a court later evaluating those facts, especially in relation to a third party's application for patent. Moreover, the declaration was only one factor to be considered under a totality of the circumstances evaluation. Ito's conclusory statement does not preclude the district court from deciding that the undisputed facts indicated a public use of the claimed invention before the critical date; the court thus did not err in discounting it.

Baxter argues that any alleged public use by Suaudeau is negated by the fact that it was experimental use. According to Baxter, Suaudeau's use was not for commercial purposes; it was to determine whether the invention would function as intended. Baxter also argues that Cullis was entitled to the benefit of Suaudeau's experimental use, even though Suaudeau was not acting under the control or direction of Cullis.

COBE responds that the totality of the circumstances does not support a conclusion of experimental use. COBE argues that Suaudeau reduced the invention to practice, which, according to COBE, ends experimental use. COBE argues that the fact that Suaudeau was not acting under the direction or control of the inventor also precludes a conclusion of experimental use. In addition, COBE argues that any testing of the invention by Suaudeau was for his own purposes and that Suaudeau was not experimenting with the claimed invention on behalf of the inventor.

Experimental use negates public use; when proved, it may show that particular acts, even if apparently public in a colloquial sense, do not constitute a public use within the meaning of section 102. *TP Labs., Inc. v. Professional Positioners, Inc.,* 724 F.2d 965, 971, 220 USPQ 577, 582 (Fed.Cir.), *cert. denied,* 469 U.S. 826, 105 S.Ct. 108, 83 L.Ed.2d 51 (1984). The Supreme Court has stated that "[t]he use of an invention by the inventor himself, or of any other person under his direction, by way of experiment, and in order to bring the invention to perfection, has never been regarded as [a public] use." *City of Elizabeth v. American Nicholson Pavement Co.,* 97 U.S. 126, 134, 24 L.Ed. 1000 (1877).

An analysis of experimental use, which is also a question of law, requires consideration of the totality of the circumstances and the policies underlying the public use bar. Evidentiary factors in determining if a use is experimental include the length of the test period, whether the inventor received payment for the testing, any agreement by the user to maintain the use confidential, any records of testing, whether persons other than the inventor performed the testing, the number of tests, and the length of the test period in relation to tests of similar devices. *TP Labs.,* 724 F.2d at 971–72, 220 USPQ at 582; *see also In re Brigance,* 792 F.2d 1103, 1108, 229 USPQ 988, 991 (Fed.Cir.1986).

The district court determined as a matter of law that Suaudeau's use was not experimental. It properly determined that Suaudeau was not experimenting with the basic features of the invention, stating:

> Furthermore, the work that they [Suaudeau and Ito] were doing was not experimental as to the invention. They were not trying to further refine the invention and prove that it would work for its intended purpose. They would not have been using it if it was not suitable for its intended purpose. They would have found something else to use instead. What they were doing was making modifications that would satisfy their particular requirements, much as one might modify the engine of an automobile to produce a speed greater than that afforded by the engine that came with the automobile. That doesn't mean that the modifier is experimenting with the basic invention represented by the engine, or at least not doing so within the meaning of the public use exception.

The district court did not err in this conclusion. Neither the basic purpose of the invention, which had previously been realized by others, nor the representative claims required obtaining platelet-rich plasma suitable for preservation of hearts, which was the purpose of Suaudeau's experiments. These experiments, which Baxter alleges constituted experimental use, were directed to fine-tuning the centrifuge to work for Suaudeau's particular purpose of heart preservation, not to determining if it would work as a centrifugal blood processing apparatus, or perform a method of centrifugally processing blood, as recited in the claims and which he had already verified. Further refinement of an invention to test additional uses is not the type of experimental use that will negate a public use.

The inventor's lack of direction or control over Suaudeau's use of the invention also supports a conclusion that the use was not experimental. One of the policies underlying experimental use as a negation of public use is allowing *an inventor* sufficient time to test an invention before applying for a patent. "The experimental use doctrine operates in the inventor's favor to allow *the inventor* to refine his invention or to assess its value relative to the time and expense of prosecuting a patent application. If it is not the inventor or someone under his control or 'surveillance' who does these things, there appears to us no reason why he should be entitled to rely upon them to avoid the statute." *See In re Hamilton*, 882 F.2d 1576, 1581, 11 USPQ2d 1890, 1894 (Fed.Cir.1989) (discussing experimental use in the context of the on-sale bar) (emphasis in original). Providing Cullis, the inventor, with the benefit of Suaudeau's testing is thus contrary to this policy, as Suaudeau was not using or testing the invention for Cullis. *Id.* Accordingly, we hold that public testing before the critical date by a third party for his own unique purposes of an invention previously reduced to practice and obtained from someone other than the patentee, when such testing is independent of and not controlled by the patentee, is an invalidating public use, not an experimental use.

## CONCLUSION

We conclude that the district court did not err in determining that there were no genuine issues of material fact, that Suaudeau publicly used the invention before the critical date, and that the use was not experimental. The district court thus did not err in holding that the asserted claims of the '089 patent are invalid.

■ PAULINE NEWMAN, CIRCUIT JUDGE, dissenting.

This case relates to the status as "public use" of unpublished information used for research purposes by a person who was completely independent of the inventor of the patent-in-suit. Can such private laboratory research use, if it occurs after a laboratory "reduction to practice," serve as an invalidating "public use" bar to the patented invention of another? The panel majority so holds.

The panel majority holds that since the reduction to practice of the similar device assertedly occurred more than a year before the filing date of the patent in suit, the ensuing laboratory use of that device was a "public use" and a bar under 35 U.S.C. § 102(b). This new rule of law, that unpublished laboratory use after a reduction to practice is a public use, creates a new and mischievous category of "secret" prior art. I respectfully dissent from the court's ruling, for it is contrary to, and misapplies, the law of 35 U.S.C. § 102.

## DISCUSSION

The panel majority holds that the Ito device was in "public use" as soon as the Ito centrifuge was reduced to practice. Assuming that there was an actual reduction to practice before the critical date—a strongly challenged assumption—the patent statute and precedent do not elevate private laboratory use after a reduction to practice to "public use" under § 102(b). When the public use is unknown and unknowable information in the possession of third persons, 35 U.S.C. § 102 accommodates such "secret prior art" only in the limited circumstances of § 102(e).

The issue here is not that of an Ito/Suaudeau personal defense as a prior user, a matter of current discussion among policy-makers. On the panel majority's ruling it is irrelevant whether Cullis or Ito was the first inventor, for the Cullis patent is now held to be barred by the Suaudeau laboratory use of the Ito device, before the date of any reference publication or the filing date of any patent application. This is not a correct reading of the law. Suaudeau's use in his laboratory did not become a public use under § 102(b) as soon as the Ito centrifuge was reduced to practice. *Cf. W.L. Gore & Assoc., Inc. v. Garlock Inc.,* 721 F.2d 1540, 1550, 220 USPQ 303, 310 (Fed.Cir.1983) (a third person's secret commercial activity, more than one year before the patent application of another, is not a § 102(b) bar to the patent of another), *cert. denied,* 469 U.S. 851, 105 S.Ct. 172, 83 L.Ed.2d 107 (1984).

### 35 U.S.C. § 102(a), (b)

The Ito device was described in a scientific publication, but the publication was not cited as prior art against the Cullis patent, apparently because of the publication date. The panel majority does not rely on any publication or patent as a prior art reference, but on the underlying laboratory development. This use of unknown, private laboratory work to create a new bar to patentability as of the date of laboratory reduction to practice is a distortion of the law and policy set forth in 35 U.S.C. § 102. Sections 102(a) and (b) establish that prior art is prior knowledge that meets specified requirements. This new category of internal laboratory use is immune to the most painstaking documentary search. The court thus produces a perpetual cloud on any issued patent, defeating the objective standards and policy considerations embodied in the § 102 definitions of prior art.

Precedent does not support the panel majority's ruling. For example, in *In re Smith,* 714 F.2d 1127, 218 USPQ 976 (Fed.Cir.1983), relied on by the majority and by the district court, it was held that public testing of the invention with over two hundred consumers was commercial activity and was a bar under § 102(b). It is an unwarranted leap from the context of *Smith* to the private laboratory use that here occurred. It is incorrect to hold that all use after reduction to practice is ipso facto a public use, even when conducted in a private laboratory.

## 35 U.S.C. § 102(e)

Heretofore, § 102(e) was the only source of so-called "secret prior art": the patent text remains secret while the patent application is pending, but after the patent is issued its subject matter is deemed to be prior art as of its filing date. *See Hazeltine Research v. Brenner*, 382 U.S. 252, 254–55, 86 S.Ct. 335, 337–38, 15 L.Ed.2d 304, 147 USPQ 429, 431 (1965) (under § 102(e) a patent is a reference as of its filing date, although its existence is not known until it issues). Thus the term "secret prior art" is used for prior art under § 102(e). This law reflects a careful balancing of public policies, for it is an exception to the rule that "prior art" is that which is available to the public. *Id.*

This retroactive effect does not reach back to the underlying research or to the date of reduction to practice of the reference patented invention. *See* § 102(e) (the patent applicant may show that his invention predates the filing date of the reference patent). It is irrelevant, as well as usually unknown, when the invention of the reference patent was reduced to practice. Such information is not discernable from the issued patent. Thus the court's ruling today adds an omnipresent pitfall to the complexities of the patent system.

## 35 U.S.C. § 102(c), (f)

There is no issue raised of abandonment under § 102(c) or derivation under § 102(f). My concern, as I have stressed, is that there is now created a new source of unknown and unknowable grounds of invalidity.

## 35 U.S.C. § 102(g)

Cullis and Ito were engaged in an interference proceeding in the PTO, in which Ito prevailed. Elaborate rules and extensive precedent govern the determination of reduction to practice under § 102(g). *See, e.g., Schendel v. Curtis*, 83 F.3d 1399, 38 USPQ2d 1743 (Fed.Cir.1996) (illustrating rigorous requirements for reduction to practice in patent interferences). Today's acquiescence in Suaudeau's purported reduction to practice, based on credibility determinations and other findings unwarranted in a summary proceeding, is unburdened by the usual rigors of this determination.

## SUMMARY

It is incorrect to interpret 35 U.S.C. § 102(b) to mean that laboratory use after a reduction to practice is a "public use," and thus a bar against any patent application filed, by anyone, more than a year thereafter. Section 102(b) was not intended to add to the bars based on information not published or publicly known or otherwise within the definition of prior art. A non-public use does not become a public use after a reduction to practice. It is simply incorrect to interpret the laboratory use in this case as a statutory bar to a patent. I can discern no benefit to society, or to the interest of justice, in this new unreliability of the patent grant.

## NOTES

**1.** *The § 102(b) inquiry.* The major cases in this Assignment deal mainly with the statutory bar of § 102(b)—that is, with the argument that the patent should not issue because one of the activities enumerated in this provision occurred more than a year before the applicant filed for a patent. The analysis looks at the same three issues examined in the novelty section: contents, accessibility, and dates. However, each of these prongs is evaluated quite differently, for the policies underlying novelty and bar differ in important respects.

    a. *Contents.* What must a reference teach in order to act as a bar? For novelty, where the issue was whether the inventor had made a new contribution to the storehouse of knowledge, the analysis looked at whether the public was able to practice the invention from the information in the prior art. Here, the focus is on the inventor and whether she waited too long. For that purpose, the prior art does not necessarily have to reveal every element of the claimed invention. Consider first the case in which the inventor was herself responsible for the prior art. She does not need enabling information to know that she ought to be applying for the patent—she already has the ability to practice the invention. Accordingly, an enablement-type requirement is not necessary in cases like *Egbert,* where the inventor created the prior art.

    Now consider the situation where the prior art belonged to another. If it fully reveals the invention, once again the inventor should know that the time to apply for a patent has arrived (or, will arrive within the year). What if the contents do not reveal the entire invention? This issue was considered in In re Foster.[3] The application on the invention, a rubber-like polymer, had been filed on August 21, 1956. The examiner found a reference partly revealing this polymer dated August 1954 (which, as we saw in Assignment 17, precedes the date the PTO takes as the date of invention). Since the invention would, per § 103, have been considered obvious in light of this reference, the applicant needed to establish an earlier date of invention. A Rule 131 affidavit was filed establishing an invention date of December 16, 1952. Since invention now predated this disclosure, the patent could not be denied on the ground that the invention was obvious when made. Still, the court viewed the claim as rather stale. Citing § 102(b), it stated:

> [S]ince the purpose of the statute has always been to require filing of the application within the prescribed period after the time the public came into possession of the invention, we cannot see that it makes any difference how it came into such possession, whether by a public use, a

    3 343 F.2d 980 (C.C.P.A.1965).

sale, a single patent or publication, or by combinations of one or more of the foregoing. In considering this principle, we assume, of course, that by these means the invention has become obvious to that segment of the 'public' having ordinary skill in the art. Once this has happened, the purpose of the law is to give the inventor only a year within which to file and this would seem to be liberal treatment.[4]

*Foster*-type rejections—so called "§§ 102(b)/103" rejections—have been affirmed as valid by the Federal Circuit with regard to prior art of the type involved in *Foster*. Should it be used in connection with other types of art, such as the rather secret information at issue in *Baxter*? Is that the real concern underlying Judge Newman's dissent in *Baxter*—that, as in the *OddzOn* case of the last Assignment, yet another category of secret art will be available to determine nonobviousness?[5]

b. *Accessibility.* As in § 102(a), this provision also distinguishes between activities occurring in the United States and abroad. Use or sale will bar a patent only if it took place in the United States, whereas patents and printed publications are effective as bars no matter where in the world they occurred. At this point, however, the similarity between these provisions ends, for despite the fact that only § 102(b) uses the word "public," *less* publicity is required to raise a statutory bar than to run afoul of the novelty provisions. As *Egbert* makes clear, since one issue for loss of right is what the *applicant* knew and enjoyed, it makes no difference that the *public* may never have seen an embodiment of the invention. Thus, the modesty of Ms. Barnes was quite irrelevant to the question whether her use barred the patent.

At the same time, however, it is important to note that there is a surviving doctrine of "noninforming public uses" that do not create statutory bars. For example, in Gillman v. Stern,[6] the patent on a new quilt-puffing machine was issued despite the fact that the output of a similar machine was sold by a third party for longer than the statutory period, the theory being that the quilts that were sold did not reveal the machine itself. Similarly, in W.L. Gore & Assoc. v. Garlock,[7] a patent issued on a method for stretching teflon to make the thread from which Gortex is manufactured, despite the fact that a tape using the thread, and a machine for making the tape, had been sold by someone other than the patentee for too long. Once again, the court reasoned that the thread and the machine had not revealed the process for making the thread. These cases are difficult to square with the general trend in § 102(b) cases to ignore enablement as a criterion for barring a patent. Furthermore, the results in these cases

---

[4] Id. at 988.

[5] Traditionally, §§ 102(b)/103 rejections had not been used in connection with any types of prior art other than patents and printed publications See D. Donald S. Chisum, Patents, § 5.03[2], citing In re Ownby, 471 F.2d 1233, 1236 (C.C.P.A.), cert. denied, 412 U.S. 950 (1973). Further, there appears to be no such thing as a §§ 102(e)/102(b) rejection (for inventions revealed in an application pending more than a year before this inventor's application was filed).

[6] 114 F.2d 28 (2d Cir.1940)(analyzed as a § 102(g) case).

[7] 721 F.2d 1540 (Fed.Cir.1983).

frustrate the interests of the people who were selling the noninforming products. If the second inventor's patent is not barred by § 102(b), they become infringers. Does *Baxter* support or undermine the continuing vitality of this doctrine? This issue is explored further in Note 2, below.

c. *Dating invention.* Notice that the critical date is different for 102(b) than for novelty. For novelty, the critical date is the date of invention; for § 102(b), it is one year preceding the date of application. The effective date of a patent or publication remains the same. The result is to put a limit on the use of Rule 131 affidavits. An inventor can "swear behind" a reference, but if the effective date of the reference is more than a year before the filing, swearing behind will not help: the patent will be barred by § 102(b).

**2.** *Third-party art.* Since § 102(b) is mainly intended to encourage inventors to apply for patents and to punish them for enjoying exclusive benefits in the invention for more than the statutory term, application of § 102(b) to prior articles, patents, and activities *of the inventor* makes sense, as does the lower level of dissemination and enablement required. However, under this approach, it seems curious to apply § 102(b) to the actions of parties other than the inventor. Commercial use of an invention by another does not implicate the applicant; he did not try to extend his rights beyond the term chosen by Congress, nor did he sit on his rights. If the other party's use is not publicly accessible, the applicant may not even have known that the grace period had begun.[8]

As is clear from *Metallizing Engineering*, Learned Hand would have drafted a much better statute. He would have distinguished between uses by the inventor and uses by third parties. He also would have drawn a distinction between informing and noninforming uses. In Hand's view, any use by the applicant, whether informing or not, should bar the issuance of the patent. Since the inventor knows what he invented and also what he is using the invention for, he needs no further information to realize that the time has come to file for the patent. Besides, why should the public's lack of knowledge save an inventor who is trying to extend the statutory term?

But third party uses can be a different matter. If the inventor knows a third party has begun to disseminate the information, he can rush right off to the PTO. As long as he applies within a year of this use, his patent will be granted. However, if the third party's use is noninforming, as in the case with the quilt and the Gortex thread described in Note 1(b), there is nothing to warn the first inventor. Therefore, he is in no way deficient for delaying his application and, in Hand's view, there is no reason to bar his patent.

From the public's point of view, the Hand approach also seems right. Although the principal thrust of § 102(b) is directed at the inventor, § 102(b) also protects the public domain, that is, the public's right to rely

---

[8] For an especially egregious decision, see Lorenz v. Colgate–Palmolive–Peet Co., 167 F.2d 423 (3d Cir.1948)(holding an applicant barred by the activity of a party who stole the invention from him); Evans Cooling Systems, Inc. v. General Motors Corp., 125 F.3d 1448 (Fed. Cir. 1997).

on the free availability of inventions that are known to the public (for more than a year) and not claimed. Informing public uses will always trigger this interest. Utilization of an invention for more than a year in a manner that enables others to learn how it works essentially "gives" the public the invention—puts it into the domain of public knowledge. But noninforming public uses do not do this: even if the invention is widely disseminated, no one can reverse engineer it or rely on its free availability. Thus, noninforming public uses do not jeopardize the public domain interest protected by § 102(b). Since, as the previous paragraph showed, third party uses also do not jeopardize the interest in regulating the inventor, Hand's formulation has a great deal to recommend it. Do you see any disadvantages? (Hint: consider the interests of Dr. Suaudeau in defeating the patent in *Baxter*).

**3.** *The Pfaff analysis.* Prior to *Pfaff*, there was considerable confusion over the meaning of "sale." Although the term is well understood in contract law, the Federal Circuit thought the goals of § 102(b) were too different from the policies underlying contracts to equate the definitions. For example, an invention that had never been completed (reduced to practice) could, in the Federal Circuit's view, still be considered on sale because the offer to sell meant that the patentee was trying to obtain a benefit outside the statutory term.[9] The problems with this analysis are first, that it makes it difficult to determine when the § 102(b) clock starts running. Second, it raises the possibility that an invention might never be made. After all, if no sale is consummated, the patentee may never create an embodiment. If the sale nonetheless bars a patent, no one will have the incentive to invent the innovation or reduce it to practice.

Does *Pfaff* provide a better approach? When is a product considered the "subject of a commercial offer for sale?" Must the seller appreciate the innovative character of the invention at the time of the sale?[10] Must the potential buyer? And what does "ready for patenting" mean: is it that the invention could be patented, or that the seller realizes that it is patentable?[11] Must the buyer be an unrelated third party?[12] Does an offer to sell include the distribution of data sheets, newsletters and other promotional material to potential distributors?[13] Would it be better to sacrifice the nicety of a test perfectly attuned to § 102(b) policies to regain the greater certainty of a contract-law approach?

One thing is clear: the "sale" must be of an embodiment, not of rights to the patent or rights to license the patent.[14] Patent rights are often sold

---

[9] See UMC Electronic Co. v. U.S., 816 F.2d 647 (Fed. Cir.1987).

[10] See, e.g., Scaltech v. Retec/Tetra, LLC, 269 F.3d 1321 (Fed. Cir. 2001)(no).

[11] See, e.g., Robotic Vision Systems, Inc. v. View Engineering, Inc., 249 F.3d 1307 (Fed. Cir. 2001)(on sale bar applies even when the inventor is skeptical about whether the invention works).

[12] See e.g., Special Devices, Inc. v. OEA, Inc., 270 F.3d 1353 (Fed. Cir. 2001)(no, sales to suppliers count as § 102(b) sales). See also

Netscape Comm'ns Corp. v. Konrad, 295 F.3d 1315 (Fed. Cir. 2002)(sales to entity funded by the same entity as the inventor is a sale under § 102(b)).

[13] See, e.g., Linear Technology Corp. v. Micrel, Inc., 275 F.3d 1040 (Fed. Cir. 2001)(not a sale).

[14] See e.g. In re Kollar, 286 F.3d 1326 (Fed. Cir. 2002)(also discussing application of these rules to process patents).

to support research; indeed, patent rights are created to attract capital to innovative activity.

**4.** *Experimental use: market vs. development testing.* The germinal case on experimental use is Elizabeth v. American Nicholson Pavement Co.,[15] where the inventor of a wooden pavement was granted a patent despite having installed it at a toll-gate a considerable time before filing the application. The Supreme Court agreed that the use, which was intended to test the usefulness and durability of the product, was in some sense public, but it reasoned that this sort of use should not defeat the patent:

> When the subject of invention is a machine, it may be tested and tried in a building, either with or without closed doors. In either case, such use is not a public use, within the meaning of the statute, so long as the inventor is engaged, in good faith, in testing its operation. He may see cause to alter it and improve it, or not. His experiments will reveal the fact whether any and what alterations may be necessary. If durability is one of the qualities to be attained, a long period, perhaps years, may be necessary to enable the inventor to discover whether his purpose is accomplished. And though, during all that period, he may not find that any changes are necessary, yet he may be justly said to be using his machine only by way of experiment; and no one would say that such a use, pursued with a bona fide intent of testing the qualities of the machine, would be a public use, within the meaning of the statute. So long as he does not voluntarily allow others to make it and use it, and so long as it is not on sale for general use, he keeps the invention under his own control, and does not lose his title to a patent.

Firms also engage in another type of experimentation: market testing. This research looks at how the product will be used by end-users and is intended to improve its user-friendliness, determine the proper positioning and pricing of the product in the market, and develop advertising strategies that will help consumers understand how the product will benefit them. Should this form of testing receive the benefit of the exception?

On the one hand, the objective of the patent laws is to produce products people can use. This testing is as important to useability as development testing. Furthermore, the law is intended to provide the inventor with approximately 20 years in which to earn a profit. This testing puts the inventor (or her successors in interest) in a position to begin to earn that profit on the day the patent issues. On the other hand, such testing has little to do with the inventive concept; it does not advance science or technology. Thus, it is no surprise that the courts have refused to give market research the benefit of the experimental use exception.[16] What about the third-party testing at issue in *Baxter*: does the Federal Circuit hold that the experiments there were not of the right sort or that inventors

[15] 97 U.S. 126, 137 (1877).

[16] See, e.g., In re Smith, 714 F.2d 1127 (Fed.Cir.1983)(market testing of carpet deodorizer).

should not be allowed to avail themselves of this exception when the experiments are by other parties?

**5.** *Pre-market clearance.* Some products are subject to federal or state requirements that manufacturers receive clearance before their products are put on the market. In the case of drugs, for example, the Federal Food and Drug Administration requires tests demonstrating safety and efficacy. Complying with these requirements can take a long time, yet § 102(b) appears to require an early filing. The result is that the owners of patents in areas requiring clearance may have less than the statutory period in which to recoup their costs. In the drug field, Congress has from time to time enacted private bills to extend rights on drugs that were subject to long delays in the FDA.[17] The Patent Act also contains provisions for extending or restoring patent terms in the case of certain products subject to regulatory review, see §§ 155–56.[18]

**6.** *Sections 102(c) and (d).* The other statutory bars are not the subject of significant amounts of litigation.

  a. *Section 102(c).* A much-cited case on abandonment is Macbeth–Evans Glass Co. v. General Electric Co.,[19] which is described in *Metallizing Engineering.* The invention was a "method ... for making glass for illuminating purposes such as in electric and other shades and globes." The applicant, Macbeth, had perfected the method in 1903 and began selling the glass immediately, keeping the method of manufacture secret. However, in May 1910, one of his employees quit. This employee then sold his knowledge to what later became GE. On May 9, 1913, Macbeth applied for a patent. The court held that Macbeth's actions in using the invention without benefit of a patent manifested an intent to forgo the right to a patent—to effectuate an abandonment to the public domain. According to the court, patent rights and trade secret rights are inconsistent in that the former rewards the inventor for revealing the invention to the public, while the latter hides the invention from the public. One can choose one or the other, not both. The court also noted the term-expanding effect of what Macbeth had tried to do.

  Two questions are raised by § 102(c). First, why is it so rarely used? The answer is that current understanding of the publicity requirement of § 102(b) makes subsection (c) largely superfluous. Almost any action that gives rise to an inference of abandonment also triggers § 102(b).[20] The only exceptions are acts of abandonment that occur within a year of filing. Because there is no grace period under subsection (c), patents in such cases

[17] See, e.g., S. Rep. 102–414, 102d Cong., 2d Sess. 1992 (Report on S 526, 1165, and 1506, to extend the patent term of the drugs Ethiofos and Ansaid, and the food additive, Olestra, respectively.)

[18] As a result of the legislation conforming U.S. patent law to the GATT, § 154 was amended to include a new term-extension provision.

[19] 246 Fed. 695 (6th Cir.1917).

[20] For example, if *Macbeth–Evans* arose today, it would probably be analyzed under § 102(b). As Notes 1(b) and 2 made clear, the fact that the glass does not enable the process for making it is not likely to be relevant, especially since the sale was by the inventor rather than a third party.

would be barred under (c), but not (b). However, abandonment is usually an inference based on action.[21] Unless the action goes on for some time—probably longer than a year, the inference cannot be drawn. Thus, the only pure abandonment cases are ones in which the inventor expressly states an intent to donate the invention to the public and changes his mind within the year—not a common occurrence.

The second question is what is the difference between abandonment in § 102(g) and § 102(c)? Section 102(c) is concerned with abandoning the *right to a patent*, for instance, practicing the invention as a trade secret (*Macbeth* is an example). Section 102(g) is about abandoning the *invention*, for example, putting it in the bottom drawer of a desk.

   b.  *Section 102(d).* Section 102(d) is aimed at encouraging foreign inventors to patent their inventions in the United States. It is difficult to apply for protection in several countries simultaneously. Each country examines applications under its own law, charges a fee, and many will review only applications written in the official language of the country. Compliance is costly, and the applicant may not want to incur these costs until commercial value is assured. At the same time, the United States created patent law in order to encourage dissemination of advances to its own citizens. Inventors who disseminate only abroad are ignoring this interest and may even put the United States in a competitively inferior position.

   Section 102(d) attempts to find a comfortable middle position between forcing people to invest in a U.S. patent before they are ready and allowing them to impose on Americans the costs of delay. It bars a patent on an invention for which a patent was applied for abroad under the authority of the U.S. applicant, but only if the foreign application is filed more than a year before the U.S. application is filed and only in the event that the foreign patent issues before the U.S. patent filing. In other words, two things are required to trigger § 102(d): first, a foreign filing more than a year before the U.S. filing; second, foreign issuance before U.S. filing.

   Why is § 102(d) used infrequently? First, the bar is relatively easy to avoid. All one has to do is file in the U.S. within a year of the foreign filing. Moreover, delays in foreign patent offices are as rampant as delays in the PTO. Unless the foreign application is filed a very long time before the U.S. application, it is not likely to issue before the applicant is ready to file in the United States. Finally, in the past, § 102(d) was interpreted as requiring that the U.S. and foreign applications claim identical inventions, which allowed an applicant who missed the filing date to avoid subsection (d) by carefully drafting the U.S. claims so they are not identical to the foreign claims. However, that interpretation is changing.[22]

---

[21] Cf. Assignment 4, Note 9.

[22] Compare General Electric Co. v. Alexander, 280 F. 852 (2d Cir.1922)(decided under the predecessor of § 102(d)) with In re Kathawala, 9 F.3d 942 (Fed. Cir. 1993)(interpreting "invention" in a manner that fulfills the goals underlying the provision).

# ASSIGNMENT 20

# PRIORITY

## 1. INTRODUCTION

A patent is a genuinely exclusive right: only one patent will be awarded for any given invention. Since it is sometimes the case that more than one entity independently invents the same invention, the patent system needs a priority rule to determine which inventor is entitled to the patent. The primary function of § 102(g) is to set out this rule. It establishes a modified "first to invent" system under which the first party to invent the invention receives the patent, unless that entity engages in certain disqualifying acts.

What are the disqualifying acts? Abandonment, suppression or concealment are the simple cases: as between someone who quickly brings his invention to the PTO for dissemination and someone who allows it to languish on a back burner, the law prefers the party who is eager. But the statute also creates a more intricate form of disqualification, a form that takes into account the complex nature of invention. This test breaks the inventive act into three steps: conception (i.e. thinking up the new idea), diligence (i.e. industrious experimentation), and reduction to practice (i.e. creating a physical rendition that works). Of these steps, conception is the most valued. Accordingly, the first inventor to conceive the invention is the one who generally wins the patent race. But the statute recognizes that the public cannot do very much with raw ideas; benefits flow mainly from the working rendition. Accordingly, if the first to conceive does not reduce to practice first, the statute looks into the cause of the delay. If it is lack of diligence, defined as failure to work on the concept from just before the second inventor conceived it, then the first to conceive is disqualified, and the second inventor—the first to reduce to practice—gets the patent.

This is a complicated rule. Hopefully, it will become clearer after the Principal Problem and major cases are analyzed. To begin, it is helpful to think about why simpler rules were rejected. The statute could create an absolute first-to-invent rule. But as the previous paragraph indicates, awarding strictly according to the time of conception would divest the system of the ability to motivate inventors to translate their ideas into viable applications. Thus, the statute needs to include a role for reduction to practice.

Of course, reduction could have the starring role. There would be much more motivation to reduce quickly if reduction were the sole criterion of priority. Indeed, virtually the entire patent world uses a simple variant of a reduction-based rule by awarding the patent to the first to file the patent application. The United States's unique position is usually explained by reference to the high respect paid here to the small inventor, who is regarded as a principal source of American ingenuity. Since the small inventor could never outcompete a major research corporation in preparing the patent application, it has always been considered inequitable to have the race turn solely on reduction to practice or on its substitute, filing.

Moreover, there may be such a thing as inventing too soon. Some ideas may be difficult to bring to fruition when first conceived, but become easier to utilize after collateral developments are made. In such instances, it would waste resources to "encourage" the inventor to make a working model quickly—a phenomenon economists call "dissipation of rents." On this theory, a priority test based exclusively on reduction to practice may be unwise.[1] The result is a test that takes both conception and reduction to practice into account and links them through a requirement of diligence.

But why is diligence required only from the time that the second inventor enters the picture—why not require diligence from the time of conception? Again, the reason may have to do with rent dissipation: there is no point in requiring the first inventor to incur the costs of diligence if a later collateral development makes his work superfluous. Of course, the statute could demand diligence from the time that working hard becomes cost-effective, but that rule would be difficult to administer since it would require resolution of complex factual questions. Requiring diligence from the time another inventor enters the race is, however, a good proxy for cost-effective diligence. The entry of others into a field is some indication that others consider the area ripe for development. Hence, the complicated priority rule of § 102(g).

Priority disputes are resolved within the PTO under its interferences procedure, which is described in Note 6.

## 2.   PRINCIPAL PROBLEM

In 1975, M. Palin, an amateur train buff living in Massachusetts, discovered a device that, when mounted on the last car in a train, stabilizes its motion. Traditionally, railroads use cabooses for this purpose, but cabooses weigh a great deal and their shape makes them unsuitable for carrying any sort of load. Experimenting on a miniature train set of his own construction, Palin quickly realized that his device made the use of

[1] See, e.g., Yoram Barzel, Optimal Timing of Innovations, 50 Rev. Econ. & Stat. 348 (1968). The gasoline-powered internal combustion engine, which was conceived in 1879 and awarded a patent in 1895, may be an example of an invention that was delayed in order to take advantage of collateral developments, see Electric Vehicle Co. v. C.A. Duerr & Co., 172 Fed. 923, 935 (S.D.N.Y. 1909)("Selden did not overstep the law. He did delay. He was not in a hurry. He could not get any one to back him, and doubtless appreciated that, if he was ahead of the times, it was wise not to let his patent get ahead, too. If he had gotten his grant in 1880, without a moneyed backer, the patent might and probably would have expired, or nearly so, before any one saw its possibilities; and, if the business world had seen them within 17 years, that term would then so nearly have expired that Selden would never have been able to get to final hearing before it ran out. At best, an accounting and not an injunction would have been his lot. The difference he may well have considered as a lawyer, and personally I believe he did think of it.").

cabooses unnecessary. But since he liked their look, he decided not to notify any railroad companies of his new discovery.

By the late 1980s, railroads found themselves locked in such keen competition with trucking companies that it became imperative to search for more economical ways of running trains. On February 1, 1991, Edward (Ned) Kelly, an individual who, at varying times in his checkered and highly successful career had worked with various railway companies, formulated the idea of a device that, when mounted on the end of a train instead of the caboose, would stabilize the train enough so that it would be unnecessary to use a caboose. A week later, Kelly drew his girlfriend a diagram of the invention to explain why he spent all his time playing around in the basement workroom of his Virginia home. He worked on the invention off and on, but on the first weekend in June, he married his friend and went on a long honeymoon. When he returned, he realized he didn't know enough about making machines to construct his device. On January 2, 1992, he hired a machinist who manufactured the device immediately. Kelly quickly engaged an attorney to prepare a patent application, but the lawyer was not convinced the device worked or was worth the cost of patenting. She spent several months urging Kelly to try it out, and then some more time was spent convincing a railway to overcome their past, very bad, experiences with Kelly and work with him. A small railroad finally cooperated, and the device was tried on February 1, 1993 by mounting it to the end of a caboose. With some substantial fiddling, it worked as predicted on its second run, and the patent application was filed the next day.

Meanwhile, work on similar fronts was afoot at other locations. During the summer of 1991, Professor Dina Wontchablow, a mechanical engineering professor at Kitchen University, in Kitchen, Texas had the idea for something she called the "Stabilitator." However, she was in the middle of another project, one that she needed to finish in order to apply for tenure. On June 15, 1991, she made an entry in her laboratory notebook explaining, from the theoretical perspective, how the idea would work, and went back to her other research. Even after her tenure was granted in October, 1991 she put off working on the Stabilitator, first to take a well-earned vacation, and second, because Kitchen U. gives tenured professors support to hire a masters degree student, and Wontchablow thought someone would really enjoy this subject. In the spring semester beginning January 10, 1992, someone did sign up to work under her supervision, and Wontchablow's assessment proved correct. The graduate student succeeded in building a prototype by the end of the semester. Over the summer, the model was tested by a railroad owned by an alumna of Kitchen University, and the patent application was prepared by a patent law professor at Kitchen University Law School and filed on January 2, 1993.

Then there is Watty Piper, owner of a single-engine train company that specializes in carrying donated toys from Knoxville to Appalachian mountain children. Piper's caboose was old and malfunctioned in a storm on January 5, 1992. While struggling with the caboose during the storm,

Piper envisioned a stabilizing device that would perform much better. He worked like a man possessed, muttering "I think I can, I think I can" as he slaved away in his machine shop. By March he had substituted his new device for the old caboose. As the good little children of Appalachia soon knew, it worked just fine, and Piper immediately contacted a patent attorney. The attorney did not take Piper very seriously, and put off work on the application until June. He finally got around to working on it that fall, and, after asking Piper to conduct some additional tests, and working through several drafts of the application, managed to file it on March 1, 1993.

All three applications were presented to the same examiner, who immediately declared an interference. A story about the interference was published in the June, 1993 Railroad Engineering News, M. Palin's favorite magazine. Seeing that cabooses would soon be a thing of the past anyway, Palin decided that he might as well benefit from his discovery. He filed a patent application on his invention that same July.

QUESTION: To whom should the patent be awarded?

## 3.   MATERIALS FOR SOLUTION OF PRINCIPAL PROBLEM

A.   STATUTORY MATERIAL: § 102(g)

B.   CASES:

## Townsend v. Smith

Court of Customs and Patent Appeals, 1929.
36 F.2d 292.

■ GRAHAM, PRESIDING JUDGE.

Harry P. Townsend, the appellant, presented his application to the Patent Office on January 13, 1922, praying that a patent might be issued to him on improvements in machines for cutting multiple threads on wood screws. On December 8, 1924, an interference proceeding was instituted and declared between his application and a patent issued to one Henry L. Smith, the appellee, No. 1,452,986, granted April 24, 1923, for a similar invention.

The sole question at issue in this case is the question of priority as between the appellant and appellee. Townsend claims to have conceived the idea of his invention on or about June 1, 1921. The Examiner of Interferences found that he had done so, while the Board of Examiners in Chief and the Commissioner of Patents, respectively, held that he had not proved such conception by such clear and convincing evidence as is required in such cases.

As both applications were co-pending at the time of the inadvertent issuance of the patent to appellee, and as but a short time intervened between the respective dates of application, the burden upon the appellant to prove prior conception is slight, and it is sufficient if he establish his case by a mere preponderance of the evidence. Having this rule, which we consider to be a reasonable one, in mind, we have examined the record carefully to ascertain what the facts are in this regard.

Townsend testifies that, while building wood screw threaders for the Ewing Bolt & Screw Company, on or about June 1, 1921, there was trouble with one of his screw threading machines. Townsend was an experienced builder of such machines, and understood them thoroughly at that time. He states that one of the gears had been cut with the wrong number of teeth, with the result that the threading tool, on the moment of initiating each cut on the screw blank, did not start in the same spot that it formerly did, and made a new mark each time the tool passed over the screw. He conceived the idea at the time, and mentioned it to the workmen around him, that this was the way to make a double threaded screw. At that time he was well acquainted with the Caldwell invention of double threaded wood screws. He says he explained it to two workmen, Pond and Clark, but that these men did not recollect it, except Clark recollected that some of the gears were cut wrong. He changed the machine at that time, putting on another gear, after which it cut single threaded screws, as it should have. He states that he thought nothing more about it until October 21, 1921, when he visited Smith and Caldwell at Providence, in answer to a letter informing him that they were interested in a machine for cutting a double threaded screw. He then promised them he would change one of his single threaded wood screw machines, which he was building for a Japanese order, and make it into a double threaded screw machine; that he did this on or about the 10th or 11th of November, 1921, and wrote to Swift November 14th to come and see the machine. On the same day he wrote out the details of his invention for his attorney, for the purpose of making application for a patent. On November 21st the machine was demonstrated, and was afterwards changed back to a single thread machine and shipped to Japan on November 30, 1921.

It is said by the Board of Examiners in Chief and the Commissioner that this testimony lacks corroboration of any kind. Townsend testifies that he did not know that a man by the name of Oscar J. Reeves had witnessed his occurrence of June 1st until about six weeks before the time of the hearing in May, 1925, but that Reeves, at that time, told him he had been present. The Board of Examiners in Chief and the Commissioner both reject the testimony of Reeves on the ground that it is not in harmony with Townsend's testimony, and is not to be relied upon as corroborative. Reeves is not related to either of the parties, and has no interest in the result of the proceeding. He testifies he was not well, and, in order to put in the time, on frequent occasions visited Townsend's shop where he was much interested in the operation of automatic machinery; that some time before June 17, 1921, which date he fixes by the fact that a short time thereafter he purchased a car and went to the country for his health, staying all summer, he was in Townsend's shop, and Townsend and his helpers were having trouble with a screw threading machine; that they had a wrong set of gearing in the machine which caused it to cut a double thread screw instead of a single thread; that Townsend made adjustments on the machine, and explained each adjustment to those about the machine; that he said at that time the trouble was caused by a wrong set of gears in the machine; that he explained to the men the changes he would have to make on the machine before it was ready for shipment, and so adjusted it that it worked before the witness left, making a single threaded screw after adjustment. Reeves testified, on being shown the drawings, that the adjustments were made on gears No. 42 and No. 43, which are the gears involved in the issue before us. On cross-examination he stated that double threaded screws were made with the machine, at that time, before the gears were changed, and that some of these were distributed among the bystanders.

It is said that, because Reeves goes further in this matter than Townsend, and states that double threaded screws were actually made and distributed at that time, that he must be in error; that his testimony is in conflict with that of Townsend in this respect; and that therefore it should be rejected as corroboration.

The rule is well settled in this jurisdiction as to what is required to constitute a conception and disclosure of an invention. It is well stated in Mergenthaler v. Scudder, 11 App.D.C. 264. A complete conception as defined in an issue of priority of invention is a matter of fact, and must be clearly established by proof. The conception of the invention consists in the complete performance of the mental part of the inventive art. All that remains to be accomplished in order to perfect the act or instrument belongs to the department of construction, not invention. It is therefore the formation in the mind of the inventor of a definite and permanent idea of the complete and operative invention as it is thereafter to be applied in practice that constitutes an available conception within the meaning of the patent laws. A priority of conception is established when the invention is made sufficiently plain to enable those skilled in the art to understand it.

Does the alleged conception and disclosure of Townsend, in June, meet these requirements? We are inclined to the belief that it does. It will be remembered that Townsend, accidentally, it is true, had before him, at the time he claims to have conceived the invention, a machine which was actually cutting the threads upon the screw blank in the same manner as the final invention. The only thing required to change the single thread screw machine to a double thread screw machine was the change in gears, which was already an accomplished fact by the error that had occurred. There can be no doubt that Townsend, and those about him, understood perfectly, at that time, just how such a machine could be constructed. This is not such a case as arises when an alleged inventor mentally conceives of some invention and makes an oral disclosure to another, which disclosure may or may not be complete. Here the parties had a complete working model, and there was nothing left to the imagination. The demonstration and disclosure were complete. We can see no reason for discarding the testimony of Reeves on the theory that he testifies screws were made and distributed, while Townsend does not. Townsend did not deny that this happened, nor did any one else. The fact that Reeves went further than

Townsend in this regard is not a sufficient fact upon which we should conclude that he committed perjury or was totally mistaken in all that he said.

Another circumstance which leads us to believe Townsend's story has foundation is the fact that, when he was finally called upon to construct a machine on the Swift and Caldwell order, Townsend disclosed fully to those men just how he proposed to make the machine. He went to his shop, according to the testimony of Clark, and informed him that he wanted to set up one of the machines in the shop to cut a double thread; that thereupon the witness Clark and Townsend, "simply took the machine we had, cut a new cam, changed the gears, and cut a double thread on our regular machine." This was but a few days after his interview with Swift and Caldwell, and at this time the idea was so well developed in Townsend's mind that there were no preliminary difficulties in the preparation of the double threaded screw machine. In Townsend's explanation to Swift, according to the testimony of the witness, John W. Caldwell, Townsend was definite and clear as to the method of converting one of his own machines for this purpose.

For these reasons we conclude that the Examiner of Interference correctly held that Townsend had established conception of this invention in June, 1921. It is agreed that Townsend reduced to practice on November 14, 1921, when he prepared and operated his machine. It is held by all the tribunals in the Patent Office that appellee, Smith, conceived the invention on the 19th or 20th of October, 1921. Appellee does not insist upon any earlier date. Whether this was the exact date of conception we are not now called upon to say, in view of our conclusion in the matter generally. After Smith's conception, no question is raised as to his diligence. He made the necessary drawings and started construction of his machine. According to the preliminary statement in this interference, the appellee, Smith, completed a fully operative machine and operated the same on or about December 12, 1921. This, appellee concedes in his argument, he must rely upon as his date for formal reduction to practice. His preliminary statement is his pleading and he is bound by it. Lindmark v. De Ferranti, 34 App.D.C. 445; Browne v. Dyson, 39 App.D.C. 415. Appellant, Townsend, filed his application for a patent in the Patent Office on January 13, 1922. The Smith application was made on January 3, 1922. No question arises in the case as to the diligence of either Townsend or Smith after October, 1921, when they were each.requested to prepare plans for double threaded screw machines by the Commercial Service Company. From that time forward each party moved with all the diligence required by the law.

From what has been said it appears that the appellant, Townsend, was the first to conceive and the first to reduce to practice. This being so, and there being no abandonment or negligence since reduction to practice, Townsend is entitled to priority. It has been argued that after Townsend's conception in June, 1921, he did nothing until October 21, 1921, and that this should be considered such failure to act promptly as to deprive him of the benefit of a claim of priority of conception. We do not understand this to be the law. Where an inventor has established priority of conception, disclosure and reduction to practice, in the absence of any clearly proved abandonment, his right to a patent has not become forfeited either to the public or to his rival. It has been held that a lapse of two years between a reduction to practice and the filing of an application, does not, in itself, constitute an abandonment. Rolfe v. Hoffman, 26 App.D.C. 336.

## Griffith v. Kanamaru

United States Court of Appeals, Federal Circuit, 1987.
816 F.2d 624.

■ NICHOLS, SENIOR CIRCUIT JUDGE.

Background

This patent interference case involves the application of Griffith, an Associate Professor in the Department of Biochemistry at Cornell University Medical College, for a patent on an aminocarnitine compound, useful in the treatment of diabetes, and a patent issued for the same invention to Kanamaru, an employee of Takeda Chemical Industries.

Griffith had established conception by June 30, 1981, and reduction to practice on January 11, 1984. Kanamaru filed for a United States patent on November 17, 1982. The board found, however, that Griffith failed to establish reasonable diligence [and decided that he] failed to establish a prima facie case for priority against Kanamaru's filing date. This result was based on the board's conclusion that Griffith's explanation for inactivity between June 15, 1983, and September 13, 1983, failed to provide a legally sufficient excuse to satisfy the "reasonable diligence" requirement of 35 U.S.C. § 102(g). Griffith appeals on the issue of reasonable diligence.

Analysis

I

Griffith must establish a prima facie case of reasonable diligence, as well as dates of conception and reduction to practice, to avoid summary judgment on the issue of priority. As a preliminary matter we note that, although the board focused on the June 1983 to September 1983 lapse in work, and Griffith's reasons for this lapse, Griffith is burdened with establishing a prima facie case of reasonable diligence from immediately before Kanamaru's filing date of November 17, 1982, until Griffith's reduction to practice on January 11, 1984. 35 U.S.C. § 102(g); 37 C.F.R. § 1.617(a).

On appeal, Griffith presents two grounds intended to justify his inactivity on the aminocarnitine project between June 15, 1983, and September 13, 1983. The first is that, notwithstanding Cornell University's extraordinary endowment, it is reasonable, and as a policy matter desirable, for Cornell to require Griffith and other research scientists to obtain funding from outside the university. The second reason Griffith presents is that he reasonably waited for Ms. Debora Jenkins to matriculate in the Fall of 1983 to assist with the project. He had promised her she should have that task which she needed to qualify for her degree. We reject these arguments and conclude that Griffith has failed to establish grounds to excuse his inactivity prior to reduction to practice.

## II

The reasonable diligence standard balances the interest in rewarding and encouraging invention with the public's interest in the earliest possible disclosure of innovation. 6 C. Gholz, I. Kayton, D. Conlin & R. Schwaab, Patent Practice 24–9 (1985) citing Hull v. Davenport, 90 F.2d 103, 105, 24 CCPA 1194, 1196, 33 U.S.P.Q. 506, 508 (1937). Griffith must account for the entire period from just before Kanamaru's filing date until his reduction to practice. 3 D. Chisum, Patents § 10.07 at 10–120 (1986). As one of our predecessor courts has noted: Public policy favors the early disclosure of inventions. This underlies the requirement for "reasonable diligence" in reducing an invention to practice, not unlike the requirement that, to avoid a holding of suppression or concealment, there be no unreasonable delay in filing an application once there has been a reduction to practice.

The board in this case was, but not properly, asked to pass judgment on the reasonableness of Cornell's policy regarding outside funding of research. The correct inquiry is rather whether it is reasonable for Cornell to require the public to wait for the innovation, given the well settled policy in favor of early disclosure. As the board notes, Chief Judge Markey has called early public disclosure the "linchpin of the patent system." Horwath v. Lee, 564 F.2d 948, 950, 195 U.S.P.Q. 701, 703 (CCPA 1977). A review of caselaw on excuses for inactivity in reduction to practice reveals a common thread that courts may consider the reasonable everyday problems and limitations encountered by an inventor. See, e.g., Bey v. Kollonitsch, 806 F.2d 1024, 231 U.S.P.Q. 967 (Fed.Cir.1986)(delay in filing excused where attorney worked on a group of related applications and other applications contributed substantially to the preparation of Bey's application); Reed v. Tornqvist, 436 F.2d 501, 168 U.S.P.Q. 462 (CCPA 1971)(concluding it is not unreasonable for inventor to delay completing a patent application until after returning from a three week vacation in Sweden, extended by illness of inventor's father); Keizer v. Bradley, 270 F.2d 396, 47 CCPA 709, 123 U.S.P.Q. 215 (1959)(delay excused where inventor, after producing a component for a color television, delayed filing to produce an appropriate receiver for testing the component); Courson v. O'Connor, 227 F. 890, 894 (7th Cir.1915)("exercise of reasonable diligence * * * does not require an inventor to devote his entire time thereto, or to abandon his ordinary means of livelihood"); De Wallace v. Scott, 15 App.D.C. 157 (1899)(where applicant made bona fide attempts to perfect his invention, applicant's poor health, responsibility to feed his family, and daily job demands excused his delay in reducing his invention to practice); Texas Co. v. Globe Oil & Refining Co., 112 F.Supp. 455, 98 U.S.P.Q. 312 (N.D.Ill.1953)(delay in filing application excused because of confusion relating to war).

Griffith argues that the admitted inactivity of three months between June 15, 1983, and September 13, 1983, which he attributes to Cornell's "reasonable" policy requiring outside funding and to Griffith's "reasonable" decision to delay until a graduate student arrived, falls within legal precedent excusing inactivity in the diligence context. We disagree. We first note that, in regard to waiting for a graduate student, Griffith does not even suggest that he faced a genuine shortage of personnel. He does not suggest that Ms. Jenkins was the only person capable of carrying on with the aminocarnitine experiment. We can see no application of precedent to suggest that the convenience of the timing of the semester schedule justifies a three-month delay for the purpose of reasonable diligence. Neither do we believe that this excuse, absent even a suggestion by Griffith that Jenkins was uniquely qualified to do his research, is reasonable.

Griffith's second contention that it was reasonable for Cornell to require outside funding, therefore causing a delay in order to apply for such funds, is also insufficient to excuse his inactivity. The crux of Griffith's argument is that outside funding is desirable as a form of peer review, or monitoring of the worthiness of a given project. He also suggests that, as a policy matter, universities should not be treated as businesses, which ultimately would detract from scholarly inquiry. Griffith states that these considerations, if accepted as valid, would fit within the scope of the caselaw excusing inactivity for "reasonable" delays in reduction to practice and filing.

These contentions on delay do not fit within the texture and scope of the precedent cited by the parties or discussed in this opinion. Griffith argues this case is controlled by the outcome of Litchfield v. Eigen, 535 F.2d 72, 190 U.S.P.Q. 113 (CCPA 1976). We disagree. In Litchfield, Judge Rich held that the inventors failed to establish due diligence because of their inactivity between April 1964 and September 1965. Id. at 76–77, 190 U.S.P.Q. at 116. The court based this conclusion on the finding that the inventors possessed the capacity to test the invention and chose instead to test other compounds. Id. Judge Rich did not reach the issue of the alleged budgetary limitations imposed by the sponsor and stated that the inventors failed to show any evidence of such financial limitations and that, therefore, the court could not consider this contention. Id.

Griffith's excuses sound more in the nature of commercial development, not accepted as an excuse for delay, than the "hardship" cases most commonly found. Delays in reduction to practice caused by an inventor's efforts to refine an invention to the most marketable and profitable form have not been accepted as sufficient excuses for inactivity. D. Chisum, Patents § 10.07[2] at 10–122 & n. 4 (1986)(citations omitted).

Cornell University has made a clear decision against funding Griffith's project in order to avoid the risks and distractions, albeit different in each case, that would result from directly financing these inventions. Griffith has placed in the record, and relies on, an able article by President Bok of Harvard, Business and the Academy, Harvard Magazine, May–June 1981, 31, App. at 81. Bok is explaining the policy issues respecting academic funding of scientific research, for the benefit of Harvard's alumni who must, of course, make up by their contributions the University's annual deficit. While much academic research could produce a profit, pursuit of such profit may be business inappropriate for a university though it would be right and proper for a commercial organization. For example, it might produce conflicts between the roles of scientists as inventors and developers against their roles as members of the university faculty. However large the university's endowment may be, it may be better to enlist private funding and let this source of funds develop the commercial utilization of any invention as perhaps, the beneficial owner. If there is a patent, the source of funds may end up assignee of the patent. It seems also implicit in this policy choice that faculty members may not be allowed single-minded pursuit of reduction to practice whenever they conceive some idea of value, and at times the rights of other inventors may obtain a priority that a single-minded pursuit would have averted. Bok says diligent reduction to practice, to satisfy the patent laws, may interfere with a faculty member's other duties. Bok is asking the approval of his alumni, not of the courts. The management of great universities is one thing, at least, the courts have not taken over and do not deem themselves qualified to undertake. Bok does not ask that the patent laws or other intellectual property law be skewed or slanted to enable the university to have its cake and eat it too, i.e., to act in a noncommercial manner and yet preserve the pecuniary rewards of commercial exploitation for itself.

If, as we are asked to assume, Cornell also follows the policy Bok has so well articulated, it seems evident that Cornell has consciously chosen to assume the risk that priority in the invention might be lost to an outside inventor, yet, having chosen a noncommercial policy, it asks us to save it the property that would have inured to it if it had acted in single-minded pursuit of gain.

## III

The record reveals that from the relevant period of November 17, 1982 (Kanamaru's filing date), to September 13, 1983 (when Griffith renewed his efforts towards reduction to practice), Griffith interrupted and often put aside the aminocarnitine project to work on other experiments. Between June 1982 and June 1983 Griffith admits that, at the request of the chairman of his department, he was primarily engaged in an unrelated research project on mitochondrial glutathione metabolism. Griffith also put aside the aminocarnitine experiment to work on a grant proposal on an unrelated project. Griffith's statement in the record that his unrelated grant application, if granted, might "support" a future grant request directed to the aminocarnitine project does not overcome the conclusion that he preferred one project over another and was not "continuously" or "reasonably" diligent. Griffith made only minimal efforts to secure funding directly for the aminocarnitine project.

The conclusion we reach from the record is that the aminocarnitine project was second and often third priority in laboratory research as well as the solicitation of funds. We agree that Griffith failed to establish a prima facie case of reasonable diligence or a legally sufficient excuse for inactivity to establish priority over Kanamaru.

## Paulik v. Rizkalla

United States Court of Appeals, Federal Circuit, 1985.
760 F.2d 1270.

■ PAULINE NEWMAN, CIRCUIT JUDGE.

This appeal is from the decision of the United States Patent and Trademark Office Board of Patent Interferences (Board), awarding priority of invention to the senior party[a] Nabil Rizkalla and Charles N. Winnick (Rizkalla), on the ground that the junior party and de facto first inventors Frank E. Paulik and Robert G. Schultz (Paulik) had suppressed or concealed the invention within the meaning of 35 U.S.C. § 102(g). We vacate this decision and remand to the Board.

I

Rizkalla's patent application has the effective filing date of March 10, 1975. Paulik's patent application was filed on June 30, 1975. The interference count is for a catalytic process for producing alkylidene diesters. Paulik presented deposition testimony and exhibits in support of his claim to priority; Rizkalla chose to rely solely on his filing date.

The Board held and Rizkalla does not dispute that Paulik reduced the invention of the count to practice in November 1970 and again in April 1971. On about November 20, 1970 Paulik submitted a "Preliminary Disclosure of Invention" to the Patent Department of his assignee, the Monsanto Company. The disclosure was assigned a priority designation of "B", which Paulik states meant that the case would "be taken up in the ordinary course for review and filing."

Despite occasional prodding from the inventors, and periodic review by the patent staff and by company management, this disclosure had a lower priority than other patent work. Evidence of the demands of other projects on related technology was offered to justify the patent staff's delay in acting on this invention, along with evidence that the inventors and assignee continued to be interested in the technology and that the invention disclosure was retained in active status.

In January or February of 1975 the assignee's patent solicitor started to work toward the filing of the patent application; drafts of the application were prepared, and additional laboratory experiments were requested by the patent solicitor and were duly carried out by an inventor. The Board held that "even if Paulik demonstrated continuous activity from prior to the Rizkalla effective filing date to his filing date ... such would have no

---

[a] [Note that in interference practice, the first party to file is called the "senior party," irrespective of the order of invention. The second to file, the junior party, bears the burden of proof—eds.]

bearing on the question of priority in this case", and cited 35 U.S.C. § 102(g) as authority for the statement that "[w]hile diligence during the above noted period may be relied upon by one alleging prior conception and subsequent reduction to practice, it is of no significance in the case of the party who is not the last to reduce to practice." The Board thus denied Paulik the opportunity to antedate Rizkalla, for the reason that Paulik was not only the first to conceive but he was also the first to reduce to practice.

The Board then held that Paulik's four-year delay from reduction to practice to his filing date was prima facie suppression or concealment under the first clause of § 102(g), that since Paulik had reduced the invention to practice in 1971 and 1972 he was barred by the second clause of section 102(g) from proving reasonable diligence leading to his 1975 filing, and that in any event the intervening activities were insufficient to excuse the delay. The Board refused to consider Paulik's evidence of renewed patent-related activity.

## II

The Board's decision converted the case law's estoppel against reliance on Paulik's early work for priority purposes, into a forfeiture encompassing Paulik's later work, even if the later work commenced before the earliest activity of Rizkalla. According to this decision, once the inference of suppression or concealment is established, this inference cannot be overcome by the junior party to an interference. There is no statutory or judicial precedent that requires this result, and there is sound reason to reject it.

United States patent law embraces the principle that the patent right is granted to the first inventor rather than the first to file a patent application.[b] The law does not inquire as to the fits and starts by which an invention is made. The historic jurisprudence from which 35 U.S.C. § 102(g) flowed reminds us that "the mere lapse of time" will not prevent the inventor from receiving a patent. Mason v. Hepburn, 13 App.D.C. 86, 91, 1898 C.D. 510, 513 (1898). The sole exception to this principle resides in § 102(g) and the exigencies of the priority contest.

There is no impediment in the law to holding that a long period of inactivity need not be a fatal forfeiture, if the first inventor resumes work on the invention before the second inventor enters the field. We deem this result to be a fairer implementation of national patent policy, while in full accord with the letter and spirit of § 102(g).

The Board misapplied the rule that the first inventor does not have to show activity following reduction to practice to mean that the first inventor will not be allowed to show such activity. Such a showing may serve either of two purposes: to rebut an inference of abandonment, suppression, or

[b] As observed by the Industrial Research Institute, a first-to-invent system "respects the value of the individual in American tradition and avoids inequities which can result from a 'race to the Patent Office'." Final Report of the Advisory Committee on Industrial Innovation, U.S. Dept. of Commerce, Sept. 1979, p. 174.

concealment; or as evidence of renewed activity with respect to the invention. Otherwise, if an inventor were to set an invention aside for "too long" and later resume work and diligently develop and seek to patent it, according to the Board he would always be worse off than if he never did the early work, even as against a much later entrant.

Such a restrictive rule would merely add to the burden of those charged with the nation's technological growth. Invention is not a neat process. The value of early work may not be recognized or, for many reasons, it may not become practically useful, until months or years later. Following the Board's decision, any "too long" delay would constitute a forfeiture fatal in a priority contest, even if terminated by extensive and productive work done long before the newcomer entered the field.

We do not suggest that the first inventor should be entitled to rely for priority purposes on his early reduction to practice if the intervening inactivity lasts "too long," as that principle has evolved in a century of judicial analysis. Precedent did not deal with the facts at bar. There is no authority that would estop Paulik from relying on his resumed activities in order to pre-date Rizkalla's earliest date. We hold that such resumed activity must be considered as evidence of priority of invention. Should Paulik demonstrate that he had renewed activity on the invention and that he proceeded diligently to filing his patent application, starting before the earliest date to which Rizkalla is entitled—all in accordance with established principles of interference practice—we hold that Paulik is not prejudiced by the fact that he had reduced the invention to practice some years earlier.

## III

This appeal presents a question not previously treated by this court or, indeed, in the historical jurisprudence on suppression or concealment. We take this opportunity to clarify an apparent misperception of certain opinions of our predecessor court which the Board has cited in support of its holding.

There is over a hundred years of judicial precedent on the issue of suppression or concealment due to prolonged delay in filing. From the earliest decisions, a distinction has been drawn between deliberate suppression or concealment of an invention, and the legal inference of suppression or concealment based on "too long" a delay in filing the patent application. Both types of situations were considered by the courts before the 1952 Patent Act, and both are encompassed in 35 U.S.C. § 102(g). The result is consistent over this entire period—loss of the first inventor's priority as against an intervening second inventor—and has consistently been based on equitable principles and public policy as applied to the facts of each case.

The earliest decisions dealt primarily with deliberate concealment. In 1858, the Supreme Court in Kendall v. Winsor, 62 U.S. (21 How.) 322, 328, 16 L.Ed. 165 (1858) held that an inventor who "designedly, and with the view of applying it indefinitely and exclusively for his own profit, withholds his invention from the public" impedes "the progress of science and the useful arts."

In Mason v. Hepburn, the classical case on inferred as contrasted with deliberate suppression or concealment, Hepburn was granted a patent in September 1894. Spurred by this news Mason filed his patent application in December 1894. In an interference, Mason demonstrated that he had built a working model in 1887 but showed no activity during the seven years thereafter. The court held that although Mason may have negligently rather than willfully concealed his invention, the "indifference, supineness, or wilful act" of a first inventor is the basis for "the equity" that favors the second inventor when that person made and disclosed the invention during the prolonged inactivity of the first inventor. 13 App.D.C. at 96, 1898 C.D. at 517.

The legislative history of section 102(g) makes clear that its purpose was not to change the law. As described in H.R.Rep. No. 1923, 82d Cong., 2d Sess. 17–18 (1951), section 102(g) "retains the present rules of [the case] law governing the determination of priority of invention." The pre–1952 cases all dealt with situations whereby a later inventor made the same invention during a period of either prolonged inactivity or deliberate concealment by the first inventor, after knowledge of which (usually, but not always, by the issuance of a patent to the second inventor) the first inventor was "spurred" into asserting patent rights, unsuccessfully.

The decisions after the 1952 Act followed a similar pattern, as the courts considered whether to extinguish a first inventor's priority under section 102(g). The cases show either intentional concealment or an unduly long delay after the first inventor's reduction to practice. Some cases excused the delay, and some did not. A few examples will illustrate the application of the statute:

In Gallagher v. Smith, 206 F.2d 939, 41 C.C.P.A. 734, 99 U.S.P.Q. 132 (1953), a seven-year delay (from 1938 to 1945) was excused in the absence of evidence of actual concealment or suppression, as against a later applicant who had a reduction to practice in 1943. Note that the applicant who had delayed was nonetheless the first to file.

Young v. Dworkin, 489 F.2d 1277, 180 U.S.P.Q. 388 (CCPA 1974), held that a 27–month delay amounted to suppression. Young had refrained from filing a patent application until he had acquired the machines to practice his invention commercially. Focusing on the character of Young's activity between his reduction to practice and filing date, the court found that during Young's prolonged period of inactivity Dworkin conceived the invention and filed his patent application. In concurrence, Judge Rich observed that "it is not the time elapsed that is the controlling factor but the total conduct of the first inventor," adding "[i]t may also be a relative matter, taking into account what the later inventor is doing too." 489 F.2d at 1285, 180 U.S.P.Q. at 395.

In Peeler v. Miller, 535 F.2d 647, 190 U.S.P.Q. 117 (CCPA 1976), relied on by the Board, Miller was inactive during the four-year period following his reduction to practice, and the proffered excuse (that work of higher priority was done in other areas) was found inadequate. As noted by the Board, there are many similarities with the case at bar. The difference, however, is significant: Peeler had entered the field and filed his patent application while Miller remained dormant; Rizkalla entered the field, according to the record before us, after Paulik had renewed activity on the invention.

IV

The decisions applying section 102(g) balanced the law and policy favoring the first person to make an invention, against equitable considerations when more than one person had made the same invention: in each case where the court deprived the de facto first inventor of the right to the patent, the second inventor had entered the field during a period of either inactivity or deliberate concealment by the first inventor. Often the first inventor had been spurred to file a patent application by news of the second inventor's activities. Although "spurring" is not necessary to a finding of suppression or concealment, see Young v. Dworkin, 489 F.2d at 1281, 180 U.S.P.Q. at 391–92 and citations therein, the courts' frequent references to spurring indicate their concern with this equitable factor.

This result furthers the basic purpose of the patent system. The exclusive right, constitutionally derived, was for the national purpose of advancing the useful arts—the process today called technological innovation. As implemented by the patent statute, the grant of the right to exclude carries the obligation to disclose the workings of the invention, thereby adding to the store of knowledge without diminishing the patent-supported incentive to innovate.

But the obligation to disclose is not the principal reason for a patent system; indeed, it is a rare invention that cannot be deciphered more readily from its commercial embodiment than from the printed patent. The reason for the patent system is to encourage innovation and its fruits: new jobs and new industries, new consumer goods and trade benefits. We must keep this purpose in plain view as we consider the consequences of interpretations of the patent law such as in the Board's decision.

A foreseeable consequence of the Board's ruling is to discourage inventors and their supporters from working on projects that had been "too long" set aside, because of the impossibility of relying, in a priority contest, on either their original work or their renewed work. This curious result is neither fair nor in the public interest. We do not see that the public interest is served by placing so severe a sanction on failure to file premature patent applications on immature inventions of unknown value. In reversing the Board's decision we do not hold that such inventions are necessarily entitled to the benefits of their earliest dates in a priority contest; we hold only that they are not barred from entitlement to their dates of renewed activity.

■ RICH, CIRCUIT JUDGE, concurring. [omitted]

■ MARKEY, CHIEF JUDGE, additional views.

I agree with the opinions of Judges Newman and Rich. I write only to explicate the importance, as I see it, of those opinions to the functioning of the patent system and the effect of our decision on inventors whether self-employed, employed by small businesses, or employed by large corporations.

The patent system does not operate in a vacuum. Patent applications are expensive. Nothing in the law precludes a pause in a series of steps taken to make an invention publicly known. The risk that another may file during a pause period is sufficient to discourage suppressors and concealers. For this court effectively to require that applications be filed on every shadow of a shade of an idea immediately upon its conception, or risk loss of the opportunity to patent (and potentially the right to make, use, or sell the invention), would impose a new and onerous rule. To render a restart after a pause meaningless does not contribute to a smooth working of the patent system. That result is neither required by statute nor intended by Congress. The rich corporation might well be able to flood the Patent Office with rushed applications and with refilings of those applications, avoiding all pauses on the way to filing a patent application. Less affluent businesses and individual inventors, however, would find it extremely difficult, if not impossible, to participate in a patent system so conducted.

On the other hand, I can see no harm to the patent system in a determination that a period of inactivity can be cured by a resumption of activity before the filing date of another and a requirement that the question of priority be then fought out on the basis of the date of renewed activity on the one side and whatever may be the earliest date established on the other side.

■ FRIEDMAN, CIRCUIT JUDGE (with whom Davis, Kashiwa, Bennett and Jack R. Miller, Circuit Judges, join), dissenting. [omitted]

## NOTES

**1.** *Conception.* In most cases, conception is purely a mental activity. "The test for conception is whether the inventor had an idea that was definite and permanent enough that one skilled in the art could understand the invention; the inventor must prove his conception by corroborating evidence, preferably by showing a contemporaneous disclosure. An idea is definite and permanent when the inventor has a specific, settled idea, a particular solution to the problem at hand, not just a general goal or research plan he hopes to pursue."[2] This does not mean that the invention must be operable. If that were the case, conception and reduction would be the same thing. Rather, the mental formulation must be complete enough so that only routine experimentation is needed to make the invention

[2] Burroughs Wellcome Co. v. Barr Laboratories, Inc., 40 F.3d 1223, 1227–28 (Fed. Cir. 1994).

operable.[3] Although there is older case law to the contrary,[4] the current rule seems to be that the inventor must appreciate what he did. Thus, in Estee Lauder Inc. v. L'Oreal, S.A. the court stated that "There must be contemporaneous recognition and appreciation of the invention . . . . . "[5]

**2.** *Reduction to practice: constructive vs. actual.* There are two ways to demonstrate that an invention has been reduced to practice. The inventor could prove that "(1) he constructed an embodiment or performed a process that met all the limitations of the interference count; and (2) he determined that the invention would work for its intended purpose."[6] Alternatively, the applicant can rely on her filing date. Since the invention must have specific utility to meet the "useful" standard of § 101, and since the application must provide a disclosure that enables others to use it, it can safely be assumed that once an application is made, the invention is reduced to practice. For obvious reasons, the first method (building an embodiment) is called "actual reduction to practice;" the second (relying on the filing date), "constructive reduction to practice." Applicants who rely on constructive reduction need never build a working model of their inventions unless requested to do so by the Commissioner, § 114.

Are conception and reduction to practice always as distinct as the major cases and these Notes imply? Conceiving the invention must be distinguished from conceiving of the idea for the invention. In biotechnology cases, for example, it is possible to conceive of a method for isolating particular genomic material without actually isolating it. Should the plan for isolating the material be considered "conception" and the actual isolation, "reduction to practice?" If so, then a researcher who did no more than design an experiment that *could* isolate genomic material would enjoy priority over the person who *actually* isolated the material. Thus, it is no wonder that the Federal Circuit has rejected this categorization. In Fiers v. Revel, which involved claims to the DNA that encodes for human fibroblast beta-interferon, a protein that promotes viral resistance in human tissues, the court said that "[c]onception of a substance claimed per se without reference to a process requires conception of its structure, name, formula, or definitive chemical or physical properties."[7] In other words, in some cases, conception can require reduction to practice.

[3] It can be helpful to think of a spectrum of experimentation. Small amounts of experimentation are consistent with conception, see, e.g., Summers v. Vogel, 332 F.2d 810 (C.C.P.A.1964); if serious levels of research are required, then the mental formulation will be considered more in the nature of a hope than a concept see, e.g., Fredkin v. Irasek, 397 F.2d 342 (C.C.P.A.1968), cert. denied, 393 U.S. 980 (1968).

[4] See, e.g., MacMillan v. Moffett, 432 F.2d 1237 (C.C.P.A.1970).

[5] Estee Lauder Inc. v. L'Oreal, S.A., 129 F.3d 588, 593 (Fed. Cir.1997) (emphasis in original) (citing Breen v. Henshaw, 472 F.2d 1398, 1401 (C.C.P.A. 1973). See also Dow Chem. Co. v. Astro–Valcour, Inc., 267 F.3d 1334, 1341 (Fed.Cir.2001) ("[T]here is no conception or reduction to practice where there has been no recognition or appreciation of the existence of the [invention].").

[6] Cooper v. Goldfarb, 154 F.3d 1321, 1327 (Fed.Cir.1998). See also Manning v. Paradis, 296 F.3d 1098 (Fed. Cir. 2002).

[7] Fiers v. Revel, 984 F.2d 1164, 1169 (Fed.Cir. 1993).

**3.** *Diligence.* Notice that the diligence cases are mainly about excuses—excuses for failing to work continuously on the invention from just before the time that the other party conceived the invention. Even very short delays must be accounted for. In In re Mulder,[8] for example, the first-to-invent had only two days to account for, but he lost nonetheless.

What counts as an excuse? As the major cases indicate, commercial considerations will not do; neither will doubts about the value of the enterprise.[9] But the demands of the inventor's day job,[10] poverty,[11] and illness,[12] will be accepted as excusing lack of diligence. Curiously, in the case of constructive reductions to practice, the patent attorney's other workload also counts.[13] Corroboration is required.[14]

What about personal excuses? Illness is clearly acceptable. What about marriage, child birth, or childcare duties? Now that it is becoming more common for academic institutions to seek patent rights, should the courts be more charitable to delays caused by the academic calendar and duties to students?

**4.** *Abandonment, suppression, or concealment.* Mason v. Hepburn[15] is the germinal case. Mason had built a working model of a gun clip in 1887 and hid it away, revealing it only after he had heard that Hepburn had obtained a patent on the same invention in 1894. The interference wound up in court and Hepburn, the second inventor, won. The court reasoned that as between Hepburn and Mason, Hepburn was the more deserving as it was he who had brought the invention to the public. Mason did not care about the public; he was merely spurred by Hepburn. Subsection 102(g)(1) and the first sentence of § 102(g)(2) capture the equitable notion that as between two inventors, the one who abandoned it should not later obtain the patent on it. But the codification is not complete. Section 102(g) says nothing about spurring, and as Paulik v. Rizkalla makes clear, this had given rise to doubt as to its significance in certain contexts.[16]

Students often expect three definitions, one each for abandonment, suppression, and concealment. In fact, courts do not tend to parse the phrase, although there are two sorts of activities that qualify:

> Our case law distinguishes between two types of abandonment, suppression, or concealment. The first is implicated when an inventor actively abandons, suppresses, or conceals his invention from the public. The second occurs when abandonment, suppression, or concealment may be inferred based upon the prior inventor's unreasonable delay in making the invention publicly known.... The failure to file a

[8] 716 F.2d 1542 (Fed.Cir.1983).

[9] Christie v. Seybold, 55 Fed. 69 (6th Cir.1893) is an oft-cited case.

[10] See, e.g., Courson v. O'Connor, 227 Fed. 890 (C.C.A.7 1915).

[11] See *Christie*.

[12] See, e.g., De Wallace v. Scott, 15 App. D.C. 157 (1899).

[13] See, e.g., *Courson*.

[14] See, e.g., Gould v. Schawlow, 363 F.2d 908 (C.C.P.A.1966).

[15] 13 App. D.C. 86, 1898 C.D. 510 (1898).

[16] See, e.g., the discussion of Young v. Dworkin, 489 F.2d 1277 (C.C.P.A.1974), recounted in *Paulik*.

patent application, to describe the invention in a published document, or to use the invention publicly, within a reasonable time after first making the invention may constitute abandonment, suppression, or concealment.[17]

**5.** *Corroboration.* Note the stress that is placed on corroborating conception. This is not unusual in patent practice. Indeed, in most situations, once issues relating to invention arise, the proponent must corroborate his allegations. Simply put, it's just too easy to tell a good—self-serving—story. However, corroboration requirements may present formidable barriers to small inventors. Large research and development firms require their researchers to record faithfully all of their work on the pages of dated and numbered laboratory notebooks, which are never torn out and regularly countersigned. But not all inventors are so sophisticated. The Federal Circuit has adopted a rule of reason approach that looks to individual circumstances, but nonetheless requires some independent evidence of the facts that need to be proved in an interference.[18]

**6.** *Interference practice.* Section 135 of the Patent Act controls priority practice. It gives the Commissioner of Patents the authority to declare an interference whenever an application claims the same thing as is claimed in a pending application or in an unexpired patent. The Board of Patent Appeals and Interferences decides priority (as well as issues of patentability) in an inter partes proceeding between the affected parties. In the proceeding, the senior party (first to file) enjoys the presumption of having invented first. Junior parties bear the burden of demonstrating their earlier dates of invention.[19]

It is important to consider the parties' motivations in an interference. Each party's main objective is to prove it should be the one to receive the patent. But once it becomes clear that the other side will win, the next-best result is usually to convince the PTO that the invention is not patentable by anyone, for example, by demonstrating that the party likely to win learned enough from another to render the invention obvious, §§ 102(f)/103. That way, the losers avoid becoming infringers. But there is sometimes another alternative. As with other lawsuits, parties can settle interferences privately, agreeing, for example, that one applicant will be awarded the patent and the others will receive licenses on favorable terms,[20] or that all the applicants will apply together as joint inventors.[21]

[17] Dow Chemical Co. v. Astro–Valcour, Inc., 267 F.3d 1334, 1342 (Fed. Cir. 2001). See also Apotex USA, Inc. v. Merck & Co., Inc., 254 F.3d 1031 (Fed. Cir. 2001)(dissemination of information in Canada and France before the patent owner's entry into the field demonstrates that the invention has not been abandoned, suppressed, or concealed).

[18] See, e.g., Coleman v. Dines, 754 F.2d 353 (Fed.Cir.1985).

[19] For an example of such a case, see Hahn v. Wong, 892 F.2d 1028 (Fed.Cir.1989).

[20] Stratoflex v. Aeroquip was such a case, see Assignment 18.

[21] A well-known example of an interference settled this way concerned patent rights to the method for testing the blood supply for the AIDS virus. Dr. Luc Montagnier of Paris' Pasteur Institute and Dr. Robert Gallo of the National Cancer Institute, two pioneers in AIDS research, had worked cooperatively in the past, but each applied for a patent on the

Such settlements save PTO resources, but they can work against the public interest. They eliminate the incentive to bring to the PTO's attention information on which to reject all the applications. They are also wonderful vehicles for dividing up markets and engaging in other forms of anticompetitive conduct. Accordingly, agreements to settle interferences must be placed on public record in the PTO, § 135(c).

At first blush, it may appear that there is yet another strategy, which is to tie the patentee up in an interference and eat up the 20 years of the patent term.[22] This approach is, however, of somewhat marginal utility. First, § 154(b) extends the term for up to five years to compensate for delays caused by an interference. Second, most applications are published 18 months after filing.[23] Once published, the applicant acquires provisional patent rights, which entitle him to a reasonable royalty on infringements that occur between the time of publication and issuance. The infringer must be given actual notice of the application and the right cannot be asserted until after the patent issues, § 154(d). As a result, the losing party in an interference may be able to utilize the invention while the patent is pending, but it will have to pay back royalties once the patent issues.

**7.** *International considerations.* In the *Griffith* case, why do you suppose Kanamaru relied on the date that he filed his U.S. application (his constructive reduction to practice date)? At the time of the case, § 104 prevented a foreign applicant from relying on inventive activities undertaken abroad; these applicants were essentially "stuck" with their U.S. filing dates. The one exception was under § 119, the provision of the Patent Act that executes the United States's international patent obligations. Thus, had Kanamaru filed a Japanese patent on say, June 29, 1981 and then filed his U.S. application by June 29, 1982, he could have established invention before Griffith's date of conception: § 119 provides that the U.S. application "shall have the same effect as the application would have if filed in this country on the date on which the application for patent for the same invention was first filed in such foreign country," so long as the U.S. application is within 12 months of the foreign application.

For applications from members of the TRIPS Agreement, the picture is now considerably different. TRIPS members are required to make patents

---

test claiming to be the true inventor. Jonas Salk (developer of the polio vaccine) stepped in to mediate on the theory that the dispute was "unhealthy" to science. He persuaded the parties to seek the patent jointly and to use 80% of the royalties to create a new center for AIDS-related research, see Yalta of AIDS: Ending a Bitter Feud, 129 TIME, April 13, 1987, at p. 57(1). But see Jon Cohen, Pasteur Wants More HIV Blood Test Royalties, 255 Science 792, Feb. 14, 1992 (reporting on a demand by the Pasteur Institute for a restructuring of the agreement in light of evidence that Gallo's work was based on sam-ples "remarkably similar" to samples that Montagnier had sent him.).

[22] Recall that for applications made after June 8, 1995, the term runs for 20 years from application, not issuance. There are transition rules in effect for patent applications pending or issued at that time: they run the longer of 20 years from application or 17 years from issuance, but they are subject to special remedies limitations, § 154(c).

[23] § 122(b). The exceptions are wholly domestic applications which the applicant has requested to keep confidential.

available "without discrimination as to the place of invention."[24] Thus, foreign activity—such as Kanamaru's work in his Japanese laboratory—could now be used to establish a date of invention in an interference, § 102(g)(1).

In the *Griffith* case, both sides were trying to obtain patent rights. As you know, once a party finds he will not be awarded the patent, the next strategy is to try to defeat the other party's patent. Could Kanamaru use his foreign activity for that purpose? At the time of the case, the answer was definitely no: § 102(g) acts as a novelty provision only with respect to inventions "made in this country." What if he had filed a foreign patent on June 29, 1981 and then filed in the U.S. within the year: could he have used the date of the foreign application for patent-defeating purposes? In re Hilmer involved just such an attempt based on pre-TRIPS law. In two opinions, the court rejected the arguments that § 119 made a foreign patent the equivalent of a U.S. patent and therefore effective on its filing date (as per § 102(e)), and that § 119 made information in a foreign patent the equivalent of an "invention ... made in this country" as of its filing date.[25]

Does TRIPS change this result? It imposes an obligation to make patents *available* without discrimination; nothing is said about allowing foreign work to *defeat* a patent application. The reason that § 102(g) is now so complicated is so that only work in this country can be used for that purpose, § 102(g)(2). Does this position undermine the spirit of the TRIPS Agreement?[26]

**8.** *First to file and international harmonization.* Reconsider the point made in the Introduction: the United States is now the only country in the world with a priority rule that turns on who invented first. Every other nation awards the patent to the first to file.[27] The advantages to first-to-file are obvious. There is no interference practice, no need to prove the dates of conception and reduction to practice, no need for corroboration, no need to excuse delay. Moreover, this rule provides more motivation to make the invention useable than the diligence requirement of § 102(g) because U.S. applicants can always hope no one else will be able to prove a conception date falling in the period of inactivity, and—if that fails—that the delay will be excused. In other countries, inventors know that all is lost if they don't file first.

[24] TRIPS Agreement, art. 27(1). NAFTA contains a similar requirement.

[25] In re Hilmer, 359 F.2d 859 (C.C.P.A. 1966)(Hilmer I) and In re Hilmer, 424 F.2d 1108 (C.C.P.A.1970)(Hilmer II).

[26] There is also at least one case that is somewhat inconsistent with *Hilmer*, raising the suggestion that the Federal Circuit means to overrule *Hilmer*, In re Deckler, 977 F.2d 1449 (Fed. Cir. 1992). Curiously, foreign activity can be used to rebut an presumption of abandonment, suppression, or conceal-ment, Apotex USA, Inc. v. Merck & Co., Inc. 254 F.3d 1031 (Fed. Cir.2001) (dissemination of information in Canada and France).

[27] See generally, Charles R.B. Macedo, First-to-File: Is American Adoption of the International Standard in Patent Law Worth the Price, 18 AIPLA Q.J. 193 (1990), noting that Canada and the Philippines were the only two holdouts until 1997, when Canada changed to a first to file system. The Philippines has now changed as well.

What prevents the U.S. from changing § 102(g) to conform to the law of other nations? It may seem that the change is constitutionally impermissible. After all, Congress's power is limited to the protection of "inventors," not "filers." But the first-to-file is an "inventor," she's just not necessarily the *first* inventor. That is, changing the priority rule does not entail a change in the originality requirement of § 102(f): if the applicant did not invent the invention, she cannot acquire a patent.

Another version of the constitutionality claim derives from language in Graham v. John Deere stating that Congress cannot use its patent power to remove inventions from the public domain, see Assignment 18. The argument here is that if the first to invent does not apply for a patent, the invention falls into the hands of the public, and the first to file cannot take it back. However, if this argument were true, then the *current* law would also be in trouble. Remember, §§ 102(a), (e), and (g) do not impose a requirement of *absolute* novelty. There are many kinds of references that are not considered anticipatory even though they fully reveal the invention.

If the obstacle to changing the law is not constitutional, then it must be based on policy. As noted in the Introduction, one policy justification for the current system is that first-to-invent is more responsive to small inventors. But isn't the effort to protect these inventors misguided? The evidence is that most interferences are won by the first party to file because that party enjoys a presumption in its favor that is difficult to overcome.[28] Moreover, the Notes on conception and reduction to practice attest to the many disadvantages under which small inventors operate now.

The theoretical explanation offered in the Introduction, that it is better if things are not invented too soon, is also inadequate to justify retention of the current system. First, it does not square with the diligence cases, which do not excuse waiting for collateral developments. Second, the common intuition is that all-out efforts do produce superior results. Third, it can be argued that the best way to compensate for the rent dissipation problem is to encourage early patenting. That way, the patent will expire sooner and the invention will go into the public domain at an earlier point in time.[29]

There are two more plausible explanations for the status quo. One is that U.S. patent attorneys are nervous about moving to first-to-file. Currently, they can save a late filing with proof of conception and diligence, using their own workload as an excuse; under first-to-file, a day's delay could mean that the client loses the patent right. Since malpractice litigation is not as well developed in other countries as it is here, the loss of a patent in this manner could be more costly to U.S. lawyers than it is to

[28] See Gerald J. Mossinghoff, The U.S. First–To–Invent System Has Provided No Advantage To Small Entities, 84 J. Pat. & Trademark Off. Soc'y 425 (2002); News & Comments, 34 Pat. Trademark & Copyright J. (BNA) 403, (Aug. 20, 1987)(quoting Richard Witte, chairman of the ABA–PTC Committee No. 108 on Patent System Policy Planning)(citing a figure of 75% for the percent of interferences won by the senior applicant).

[29] Cf. John F. Duffy, A Minimum Optimal Patent Term, available at http://papers.ssrn.com/sol3/papers.cfm?abstract_id=354282.

their foreign counterparts. However, as world markets become more important to U.S. companies, this objection is weakening. U.S. patent attorneys currently prepare their clients' foreign applications knowing that priority will be determined by filing date; all they need do is treat the U.S. application the same way. Second, it is claimed that applications under a first-to-file system are likely to be less informative because applicants are forced to prepare their applications more quickly.

Are these good enough reasons to put up with the labyrinth of § 102(g)? Even if you believe that they are, consider also the advantages of harmonizing U.S. law with that of the rest of the world. While differences among nations may make the adoption of a universal patent system unwise, it could be useful to harmonize on the main issues involved in examination. As innovation increases in economic importance and as patentees seek to protect their inventions in multiple markets, patent offices around the world are beginning to be inundated with applications. If the aspects of patent law that are relevant to examination were harmonized, these offices could share the workload.[30]

**9.** *Provisional applications.* In 1995, § 111 of the Patent Act was amended to permit the filing of provisional applications. Provisionals must include only the information required by § 112 ¶ 1 and by § 113. If an application that meets all the filing requirements is filed within 12 months, the date of the provisional will be used for priority purposes. However, the patent term will begin to run from the date of the filing of the full application. Will this provision help or hurt small inventors?

---

[30] See, e.g., John F. Duffy, Harmony and Diversity in Global Patent Law, 17 Berkeley Tech. L.J. 685 (2002); Toshiko Takenaka, Rethinking the United States First-to-Invent Principle From a Comparative Law Perspective: A Proposal To Restructure § 102 Novelty And Priority Provisions, 39 Hous. L. Rev. 621 (2002); Michael N. Meller, Planning For a Global Patent System, 80 J. Pat. & Trademark Off. Soc'y 379 (1998).

# THE SCOPE OF THE PATENT HOLDER'S RIGHTS: INFRINGEMENT AND CONTRIBUTORY INFRINGEMENT

## 1. INTRODUCTION

The Patent Act does not provide the patentee with any affirmative rights, such as to sell or license her invention. Rather, the Act gives to the patentee only the right to exclude others: a cause of action against those who make, use, sell, offer for sale, or import the patented invention in (or into) the United States. In addition to this action for infringement, the patentee can also recover from anyone who induces or contributes to infringement by others in the United States, imports into the United States products made abroad using a patented process, or distributes components for the assembly of a patented product abroad.

Because the patent holder is the only one who can exploit the invention free of the risk of being sued for infringement, ownership of a patent does, as a practical matter, represent a potentially significant income stream. If the invention is unique in the sense that there is nothing roughly comparable to it, the patentee is something of a monopolist, with the power to control the price and quantity of goods on the market. As a result, that price may be higher than the competitive price would be and the quantity available for sale may be lower than the competitive quantity would be. In effect, the value the public attaches to the invention (as measured by the difference between the marginal cost of the product and the price at which the public is willing to purchase it) is converted into profit for the patentee.

In many ways, this is exactly how the statute should work: the supracompetitive profit that the patentee earns compensates her for the investment she made and the risks she took in conceiving the inventive idea and bringing it to fruition. It is the opportunity for such reward that motivates others to undertake similar risks and investments in the future. Courts, therefore, are careful to interpret the scope of the patent broadly enough to insure that the patent does, in fact, cut off the ability of others to market inventions similar to the patented invention and drive the price the patentee can charge down to competitive levels.

There are, however, ways in which a patent monopoly is troublesome—indeed, as troublesome as any other monopoly. Output is restricted and prices are high; the patentee may be able to use control over the invention to restrain trade in other markets. Sometimes everyone loses: a deadweight social loss is produced when the patentee does not make a sale to a potential user who sets a value on the invention that is lower than the price the patentee is charging, but higher than the price at which the invention would be sold in a competitive market. Furthermore, invention often occurs sequentially: the frontiers of knowledge expand more rapidly if one person's insight can be used as a building block for future developments by another. If the right to exclude is interpreted to include a right to prevent others from experimenting with the patented invention, patentees could block superceding technologies and impede progress.

Because of these competing considerations, courts entertaining infringement actions must draw fine lines between undercompensating the patentee and shortchanging the public. Copyrights present some of these same problems, but §§ 107–120 of the Copyright Act, which limit exclusive rights, provide considerable guidance. There is nothing comparable in the Patent Act, and so courts must fall back on common law and other statutory regimes. This Assignment focuses on the patentee and demonstrates how infringement is defined to assure an adequate return. The next Assignment focuses on the public-interest side of the equation, describing the mechanisms that cabin the manner in which the patent is exploited. It is, however, important to appreciate that the division in these two Assignments is somewhat arbitrary. When deciding a case, a court will always consider both the private and public perspective.

## 2. PRINCIPAL PROBLEM

This Problem requires us to give more advice to the Coalition to Fight Diseases (CFTD), who was the client in Problem C of Assignment 18 that figured out a new way to treat a disease using a purified version of a known and patented drug, X. CFTD now wants to know whether it will commit patent infringement if it distributes its purified versions of X.

Now that I have a better idea of the whole story, let me recount it from the top. In 1998, the Alpha Company obtained U.S. Patent 1,ZZZ,ZZZ. It consists of two claims: Claim 1 is on "Chemical X" whose structure is depicted in the patent (but omitted here). Claim 2 is on the process for using X to treat a certain terminal contagious disease. In 2001, the Food and Drug Administration (FDA) approved the use of X for the treatment of this disease. The FDA's approval is limited: because X produces side effects that grow increasingly severe with use and debilitation, it is unsuitable to, and therefore not approved for, the end stage of illness. X is currently the only known treatment for this disease. Accordingly, Alpha has been able to establish a price for each dose of X that is well above the marginal cost of production.

It was out of concern for the victims of this disease, that a group of public-interest researchers organized our client, CFTD. CFTD knew that many chemicals to which the body is responsive are actually mixtures of two substances of identical chemical constitution and essentially identical structural form. The two substances, called "enantiomers," are mirror images of each other—much like left and right hands. Despite their identical constitutions and structures, it is often the case that each enantiomer will work differently in the body: one may have no effect or a deleterious effect, and the other a beneficial effect. For example, one enantiomer may treat disease while the other causes severe side effects.

CFTD suspected that X is, in fact, this sort of mixture. Initially, it asked Alpha for permission to work with X, but Alpha refused. CFTD then got samples of X through a physician's prescription. Using this sample, CFTD managed to separate X into its enantiomers, (R)-X and (S)-X, and to identify R-(X) as the biologically beneficial enantiomer. It then figured out how to manufacture (R)-X in commercial amounts and now it is ready for distribution. As I said, it is interested in knowing whether distribution of R-(X) in the future will be considered infringement.

## 3. Materials for Solution of Principal Problem

A. STATUTORY MATERIAL: § 271

B: CASES:

## Fromson v. Advance Offset Plate, Inc.

United States Court of Appeals, Federal Circuit, 1983.
720 F.2d 1565.

■ MARKEY, CHIEF JUDGE.

Appeal from four judgments of the U.S. District Court for the District of Massachusetts holding that claims 1, 4, 6, 7, 12 and 16 of U.S. Patent 3,181,461 issued to Fromson are not infringed. We vacate and remand.

BACKGROUND

A. The Technology

The Fromson patent involves a process for making a photographic printing plate for use in the art of lithography. The art involves creation on a printing surface of certain areas that are hydrophilic (water attracting) and organophobic (ink repelling) and other areas that are organophilic (ink attracting) and hydrophobic (water repelling).

At the time of the Fromson invention, the state of the art was depicted generally by U.S. Patent 2,714,006, issued on July 26, 1955 to Jewett and Case (Jewett). Jewett teaches the preparation of a presensitized lithographic plate. [These plates are made out of aluminum sheets that are treated with diazo coatings to make them them light-sensitive. Using stencils, appropriate areas are then exposed to light, washed with water and wiped with image developer or printer's developing ink. The resulting plates have ink—and water—attracting and repelling portions that recreate the stencil's image when the plates are used for printing.]

### B.   The Fromson Patent

In the 1950's, Fromson was in the business of selling metals and began, through Ano–Coil Corporation, to manufacture and sell anodized aluminum. In anodization, aluminum is coated with oxide while it is the anode in an electrolytic bath wherein it is subjected to an electric current, whence the term "anodized." The anodized aluminum was used in articles such as television antennas, furniture tubing, and nameplates.

Fromson, with no background in lithography, conceived of using anodized aluminum as a replacement for non-anodized aluminum in the plate taught by Jewett. His invention according to the Fromson patent improves the Jewett plate in a number of ways. It enables use in preparation of the plate of light-sensitive compounds other than diazo compounds. It enables the coating to absorb nitrogen-containing materials released by the light-sensitive compounds when exposed to light. Also, as the district court found, the Fromson plate enjoys improved corrosion resistance and a longer press life.

Fromson filed his application for patent in May, 1963, and the patent issued in May, 1965, containing eleven product and five process claims. Claim 1 is representative of the product claims:

> 1.   A sensitized photographic printing plate comprising an aluminum sheet having a surface which has been treated to form an aluminum oxide coating on said surface, a water-insoluble, hydrophilic, organophobic layer on said sheet resulting from the reaction of the aluminum oxide coating and an alkali metal silicate applied to said coating, and a light-sensitive coating over said layer [e.g., diazo resin] having one solubility in relation to a solvent in a state before exposure to light and another solubility in relation to said solvent in another state after exposure to light, said light-sensitive material being soluble in said solvent in one of said states and being insoluble in said solvent and in water, hydrophobic and organophilic in its other state.

### C.   The Advance Plate

After issuance of his patent, Fromson's invention enjoyed extensive commercial success and was the subject of licensing agreements with several companies. Fromson sued Advance Offset Plate, Inc. ("Advance"), charging it with infringement and of product claims 1, 4, 6 and 7, and process claims 12 and 16.

Though preparation of the Advance plate involves treatment of anodized aluminum with an aqueous solution of alkali metal silicate to yield a water-insoluble, hydrophilic layer, as set forth in the claims, Advance den[ies] infringement on the sole ground that there is no "reaction" between the aluminum oxide and sodium silicate. It is undisputed that Advance do[es] what the claims say, i.e., appl[ies] a water solution of an alkali metal silicate to an oxide coated aluminum sheet to produce a layer, but it is argued that the layer does not result from a "reaction" as we are asked by Advance to define that term.

Issue

Whether the district court erred in finding no infringement of claims 1, 4, 6, 7, 12, and 16.

Opinion

The issue of infringement raises at least two questions: (1) what is patented, and (2) has what is patented been made, used or sold by another. SSIH Equipment S.A. v. USITC, 718 F.2d 365, 376, 218 U.S.P.Q. 678, 688 (Fed.Cir.1983). The first is a question of law; the second a question of fact. Id.; Kalman v. Kimberly–Clark Corp., 713 F.2d 760, 771, 218 U.S.P.Q. 781, 788, 789 (Fed.Cir.1983). The present decision of the district court turned on the first question, which we review as a matter of law.

A.   Contentions of the Parties

Advance contend[s] that "the Court was totally convinced, based on the evidence presented, that Fromson was indeed referring to and claiming a 'reaction product' formed by the reaction of an aluminum oxide with sodium silicate, i.e., an aluminosilicate compound." Fromson argues that "reaction" in the claims should be interpreted to cover the claimed treatment of an oxide coated aluminum sheet with an aqueous solution of alkali metal silicate to form a water insoluble, hydrophilic, organophobic layer on the sheet, and that whether the layer is an aluminosilicate compound is irrelevant, there being no reference to any such compound in the asserted claims. We agree.

B.   Claim Construction—The Specification

In Autogiro Co. of America v. United States, 384 F.2d 391, 397, 155 U.S.P.Q. 697, 702 (Ct.Cl.1967), our predecessor court recognized that patentees are not confined to normal dictionary meanings: The dictionary does not always keep abreast of the inventor. It cannot. Things are not made for the sake of words but words for things. To overcome this lag, patent law allows the inventor to be his own lexicographer. (Citations omitted.) A patentee's verbal license "augments the difficulty of understanding the claims", and to understand their meaning, they must be construed "in connection with the other parts of the patent instrument and with the circumstances surrounding the inception of the patent application." Id. Accord, General Electric Co. v. United States, 572 F.2d 745, 751–53, 198 U.S.P.Q. 65, 70–73 (Ct.Cl.1978).

This appeal hinges on construction of "reaction." The specification discloses a new and improved method of forming plates for use in lithography. Fromson discovered that the treatment of anodized aluminum with an aqueous solution of water soluble alkali metal silicate produces a water insoluble, hydrophilic, organophobic layer on the aluminum, a layer having exceptional lithography-related properties. Fromson's invention included the formation of the layer, not its exact structure. Though Fromson referred to the disclosed treatment as involving a "reaction", he also referred to it in the specification as an "application" and as "adsorption."

Not all references to "reaction" were accompanied by a reference to formation of an aluminosilicate.

Fromson did theorize that his new, improved layer was an aluminosilicate believed "to be in the nature of a commercial zeolite", having "properties of a molecular sieve", but expressed that theory as merely a "belief." There is no basis or warrant for incorporating that belief as a limitation in the claims. It is undisputed that inclusion of Fromson's theory and belief was unnecessary to meet the enablement requirement of 35 U.S.C. § 112 (that a patentee describe how to make and use the invention). Moreover, it is axiomatic that an inventor need not comprehend the scientific principles on which the practical effectiveness of his invention rests. See, e.g., Diamond Rubber Co. v. Consolidated Rubber Co., 220 U.S. 428, 435–36, 31 S.Ct. 444, 447–48, 55 L.Ed. 527 (1911).

### C.   Claim Construction—The Claims

Significant evidence of the scope of a particular claim can be found on review of other claims. General Electric v. United States, 572 F.2d at 752, 198 U.S.P.Q. at 70. Here, claim 5 (not asserted) limits the layer described in claim 1 to "an aluminosilicate structure in the nature of a zeolite molecular sieve", i.e., to Fromson's theory of what is formed. In Kalman v. Kimberly–Clark Corp., 713 F.2d at 770, 218 U.S.P.Q. at 788, this court said "where some claims are broad and others narrow, the narrow claim limitations cannot be read into the broad whether to avoid invalidity or to escape infringement." Accord, Environmental Designs, Ltd. v. Union Oil Co. of California, 713 F.2d 693, 699, 218 U.S.P.Q. 865, 871 (Fed.Cir.1983); Caterpillar Tractor Co. v. Berco, S.P.A., 714 F.2d 1110, 1115, 219 U.S.P.Q. 185, 188 (Fed.Cir.1983). The aluminosilicate limitation of narrow claim 5 cannot, therefore, be read into broader claim 1.

### D.   Claim Construction—Prosecution History

The district court noted some of Fromson's arguments during prosecution of his application, in which he stressed the importance of "reacting" anodized aluminum with alkali metal silicate. However, whether the interaction of these two materials was a "reaction" or something else was immaterial to consideration of the prior art. It does not appear, moreover, that Fromson used "reacting" in his arguments any differently than he had in the specification and claims, i.e., to describe what he believed the interaction was between oxide coated aluminum and an aqueous solution of alkali metal silicate. Thus, Fromson's arguments focused on the fact of an interaction and production of a new layer with particular properties, not on the specific nature of the interaction or on any chemical structure of the layer.

That Fromson speculated, on one page of a response to a rejection, that the reaction layer is "believed to be in the nature of a commercial zeolite" is of no moment, in view of the total absence from the other thirteen pages in that response of any reference to formation of an aluminosilicate or zeolite, and in view of his clear labeling of the zeolite statement as a "belief." Instead, Fromson referred in those thirteen pages to an aluminum oxide-sodium silicate reaction surface or layer, indicating that he did not know, and did not care, what the "reaction" or the structure of the resulting product might be.

E.   Claim Construction—Other Considerations

That "reaction" in the claims need not be confined to production of an aluminosilicate is consistent with the dictionary definition. That in Webster's New Collegiate Dictionary (1974) includes both "chemical transformation or change", and "interaction of chemical entities", which are consistent with the definitions appearing in Hackh's Chemical Dictionary (1969) and the American Heritage Dictionary (1970).

When an oxide coated aluminum surface is contacted with an aqueous solution of water soluble alkali metal silicate, chemical change occurs in at least two ways. First, ions or other chemical units in solution have somehow interacted to form a solid structure. Second, the water insoluble solid structure, whatever may be its precise nature (e.g., silica or aluminosilicate), is not identical to the water soluble alkali metal silicate and oxidized aluminum that interacted to produce it. Moreover, there is clearly present an "interaction of chemical entities."

The foregoing is fully consistent with long-standing use of "reaction" in the lithography art. Claims are normally construed as they would be by those of ordinary skill in the art. See e.g., Schenck v. Nortron Corp., 713 F.2d 782, 785, 218 U.S.P.Q. 698, 701–02 (Fed.Cir.1983). Jewett interchangeably uses terms such as "treating", "treatment", and "react", to describe a lithographic plate producing process. Jewett's claims use "reacting", "treatment", and "reaction product." Jewett makes no attempt to define the structure of the layer there disclosed (as an aluminosilicate compound or otherwise), although it does mention the hydrophilic layer as being chemically bonded to the aluminum surface. Jewett refers to the layer as "silicate treatment", as "silicate or silicon containing" film, or as "an inorganic material such as silicate." It is not unreasonable to conclude that one of ordinary skill in the lithography art would interpret "react" in Fromson to mean the same thing it appears to mean in Jewett, i.e., the treatment of a metal substrate with an aqueous solution to yield a layer, regardless of the chemical structure of the layer or the proper label for the phenomena that produced it.

CONCLUSION

We hold, therefore, that the district court erred as a matter of law in interpreting the claims as limited to the product of a chemical reaction producing a new chemical compound in the restrictive sense of those terms.

# Graver Tank & Manufacturing Co. v. Linde Air Products Co.

Supreme Court of the United States, 1950.
339 U.S. 605, 70 S.Ct. 854, 94 L.Ed. 1097.

■ MR. JUSTICE JACKSON delivered the opinion of the Court.

Linde Air Products Co., owner of the Jones patent for an electric welding process and for fluxes to be used therewith, brought an action for infringement against Lincoln and the two Graver companies. The trial court held four flux claims valid and infringed and certain other flux claims and all process claims invalid. The Court of Appeals affirmed findings of validity and infringement as to the four flux claims but reversed the trial court and held valid the process claims and the remaining contested flux claims. We granted certiorari and reversed the judgment of the Court of Appeals insofar as it reversed that of the trial court, and reinstated the District Court decree. Rehearing was granted, limited to the question of infringement of the four valid flux claims and to the applicability of the doctrine of equivalents to findings of fact in this case.

At the outset it should be noted that the single issue before us is whether the trial court's holding that the four flux claims have been infringed will be sustained. Any issue as to the validity of these claims was unanimously determined by the previous decision in this Court and attack on their validity cannot be renewed now by reason of limitation on grant of rehearing. The disclosure, the claims, and the prior art have been adequately described in our former opinion and in the opinions of the courts below.

In determining whether an accused device or composition infringes a valid patent, resort must be had in the first instance to the words of the claim. If accused matter falls clearly within the claim, infringement is made out and that is the end of it.

But courts have also recognized that to permit imitation of a patented invention which does not copy every literal detail would be to convert the protection of the patent grant into a hollow and useless thing. Such a limitation would leave room for—indeed encourage—the unscrupulous copyist to make unimportant and insubstantial changes and substitutions in the patent which, though adding nothing, would be enough to take the copied matter outside the claim, and hence outside the reach of law. One who seeks to pirate an invention, like one who seeks to pirate a copyrighted book or play, may be expected to introduce minor variations to conceal and shelter the piracy. Outright and forthright duplication is a dull and very rare type of infringement. To prohibit no other would place the inventor at the mercy of verbalism and would be subordinating substance to form. It would deprive him of the benefit of his invention and would foster concealment rather than disclosure of inventions, which is one of the primary purposes of the patent system.

The doctrine of equivalents evolved in response to this experience. The essence of the doctrine is that one may not practice a fraud on a patent. Originating almost a century ago in the case of Winans v. Denmead, 15 How. 330, 14 L.Ed. 717, it has been consistently applied by this Court and the lower federal courts, and continues today ready and available for utilization when the proper circumstances for its application arise. "To temper unsparing logic and prevent an infringer from stealing the benefit of the invention" a patentee may invoke this doctrine to proceed against the producer of a device "if it performs substantially the same function in substantially the same way to obtain the same result." Sanitary Refrigerator Co. v. Winters, 280 U.S. 30, 42, 50 S.Ct. 9, 13, 74 L.Ed. 147. The theory on which it is founded is that "if two devices do the same work in substantially the same way, and accomplish substantially the same result, they are the same, even though they differ in name, form or shape." Union Paper–Bag Machine Co. v. Murphy, 97 U.S. 120, 125, 24 L.Ed. 935. The wholesome realism of this doctrine is not always applied in favor of a patentee but is sometimes used against him. Thus, where a device is so far changed in principle from a patented article that it performs the same or a similar function in a substantially different way, but nevertheless falls within the literal words of the claim, the doctrine of equivalents may be used to restrict the claim and defeat the patentee's action for infringement. Westinghouse v. Boyden Power–Brake Co., 170 U.S. 537, 568, 18 S.Ct. 707, 722, 42 L.Ed. 1136.

What constitutes equivalency must be determined against the context of the patent, the prior art, and the particular circumstances of the case. Equivalence, in the patent law, is not the prisoner of a formula and is not an absolute to be considered in a vacuum. It does not require complete identity for every purpose and in every respect. In determining equivalents, things equal to the same thing may not be equal to each other and, by the same token, things for most purposes different may sometimes be equivalents. Consideration must be given to the purpose for which an ingredient is used in a patent, the qualities it has when combined with the other ingredients, and the function which it is intended to perform. An important factor is whether persons reasonably skilled in the art would have known of the interchangeability of an ingredient not contained in the patent with one that was.

In the case before us, we have two electric welding compositions or fluxes: the patented composition, Unionmelt Grade 20, and the accused composition, Lincolnweld 660. The patent under which Unionmelt is made claims essentially a combination of alkaline earth metal silicate and calcium fluoride; Unionmelt actually contains, however, silicates of calcium and magnesium, two alkaline earth metal silicates. Lincolnweld's composition is similar to Unionmelt's, except that it substitutes silicates of calcium and manganese—the latter not an alkaline earth metal—for silicates of calcium and magnesium. In all other respects, the two compositions are alike. The mechanical methods in which these compositions are employed are similar. They are identical in operation and produce the same kind and quality of weld.

The question which thus emerges is whether the substitution of the manganese which is not an alkaline earth metal for the magnesium which is, under the circumstances of this case, and in view of the technology and the prior art, is a change of such substance as to make the doctrine of equivalents inapplicable; or conversely, whether under the circumstances the change was so insubstantial that the trial court's invocation of the doctrine of equivalents was justified.

Without attempting to be all-inclusive, we note the following evidence in the record: Chemists familiar with the two fluxes testified that manganese and magnesium were similar in many of their reactions (R. 287, 669). There is testimony by a metallurgist that alkaline earth metals are often found in manganese ores in their natural state and that they serve the same purpose in the fluxes (R. 831–832); and a chemist testified that 'in the sense of the patent' manganese could be included as an alkaline earth metal (R. 297). Much of this testimony was corroborated by reference to recognized texts on inorganic chemistry (R. 332). Particularly important, in addition, were the disclosures of the prior art, also contained in the record. The Miller patent, No. 1,754,566, which preceded the patent in suit, taught the use of manganese silicate in welding fluxes (R. 969, 971). Manganese was similarly disclosed in the Armor patent, No. 1,467,825, which also described a welding composition (R. 1346). And the record contains no evidence of any kind to show that Lincolnweld was developed as the result of independent research or experiments.

The trial judge found on the evidence before him that the Lincolnweld flux and the composition of the patent in suit are substantially identical in operation and in result. He found also that Lincolnweld is in all respects equivalent to Unionmelt for welding purposes. And he concluded that "for all practical purposes, manganese silicate can be efficiently and effectively substituted for calcium and magnesium silicates as the major constituent of the welding composition." These conclusions are adequately supported by the record; certainly they are not clearly erroneous.

Affirmed.

■ MR. JUSTICE MINTON took no part in the consideration or decision of this case.

■ MR. JUSTICE BLACK, with whom MR. JUSTICE DOUGLAS concurs, dissenting [omitted].

## Warner–Jenkinson Company, Inc. v. Hilton Davis Chemical Co.

Supreme Court of the United States, 1997.
520 U.S. 17, 117 S.Ct. 1040, 137 L.Ed.2d 146.

■ JUSTICE THOMAS delivered the opinion of the Court.

Nearly 50 years ago, this Court in Graver Tank & Mfg. Co. v. Linde Air Products Co., 339 U.S. 605, 70 S.Ct. 854, 94 L.Ed. 1097 (1950), set out the modern contours of what is known in patent law as the "doctrine of equivalents." Petitioner, which was found to have infringed upon respondent's patent under the doctrine of equivalents, invites us to speak the death of that doctrine. We decline that invitation. The significant disagreement within the Court of Appeals for the Federal Circuit concerning the application of Graver Tank suggests, however, that the doctrine is not free from confusion. We therefore will endeavor to clarify the proper scope of the doctrine.

I

The essential facts of this case are few. Petitioner Warner–Jenkinson Co. and respondent Hilton Davis Chemical Co. manufacture dyes. Impurities in those dyes must be removed. Hilton Davis holds United States Patent No. 4,560,746 ('746 patent), which discloses an improved purification process involving "ultrafiltration." The '746 process filters impure dye through a porous membrane at certain pressures and pH levels,[a] resulting in a high purity dye product.

The '746 patent issued in 1985. As relevant to this case, the patent claims as its invention an improvement in the ultrafiltration process as follows:

> "In a process for the purification of a dye ... the improvement which comprises: subjecting an aqueous solution ... to ultrafiltration through a membrane having a nominal pore diameter of 5–15 Angstroms under a hydrostatic pressure of approximately 200 to 400 p.s.i.g., *at a pH from approximately 6.0 to 9.0*, to thereby cause separation of said impurities from said dye...." App. 36–37 (emphasis added).

The inventors added the phrase "at a pH from approximately 6.0 to 9.0" during patent prosecution. At a minimum, this phrase was added to distinguish a previous patent (the "Booth" patent) that disclosed an ultrafiltration process operating at a pH above 9.0. The parties disagree as to why the low-end pH limit of 6.0 was included as part of the claim.[b]

In 1986, Warner–Jenkinson developed an ultrafiltration process that operated with membrane pore diameters assumed to be 5–15 Angstroms, at pressures of 200 to nearly 500 p.s.i.g., and at a pH of 5.0. Warner–Jenkinson did not learn of the '746 patent until after it had begun commercial use of its ultrafiltration process. Hilton Davis eventually learned of Warner–Jenkinson's use of ultrafiltration and, in 1991, sued Warner–Jenkinson for patent infringement.

As trial approached, Hilton Davis conceded that there was no literal infringement, and relied solely on the doctrine of equivalents. Over Warner–Jenkinson's objection that the doctrine of equivalents was an equitable doctrine to be applied by the court, the issue of equivalence was included

[a] The pH, or power (exponent) of Hydrogen, of a solution is a measure of its acidity or alkalinity. A pH of 7.0 is neutral; a pH below 7.0 is acidic; and a pH above 7.0 is alkaline. Although measurement of pH is on a logarithmic scale, with each whole number difference representing a ten-fold difference in acidity, the practical significance of any such difference will often depend on the context. Pure water, for example, has a neutral pH of 7.0, whereas carbonated water has an acidic pH of 3.0, and concentrated hydrochloric acid has a pH approaching 0.0. On the other end of the scale, milk of magnesia has a pH of 10.0, whereas household ammonia has a pH of 11.9. 21 Encyclopedia Americana 844 (Int'l ed.1990).

[b] Petitioner contends that the lower limit was added because below a pH of 6.0 the patented process created "foaming" problems in the plant and because the process was not shown to work below that pH level. Brief for Petitioner 4, n. 5, 37, n. 28. Respondent counters that the process was successfully tested to pH levels as low as 2.2 with no effect on the process because of foaming, but offers no particular explanation as to why the lower level of 6.0 pH was selected. Brief for Respondent 34, n. 34.

among those sent to the jury. The jury found that the '746 patent was not invalid and that Warner–Jenkinson infringed upon the patent under the doctrine of equivalents. The jury also found, however, that Warner–Jenkinson had not intentionally infringed, and therefore awarded only 20% of the damages sought by Hilton Davis. The District Court denied Warner–Jenkinson's post-trial motions, and entered a permanent injunction prohibiting Warner–Jenkinson from practicing ultrafiltration below 500 p.s.i.g. and below 9.01 pH. A fractured en banc Court of Appeals for the Federal Circuit affirmed. 62 F.3d 1512 (C.A.Fed.1995).

The majority below held that the doctrine of equivalents continues to exist and that its touchstone is whether substantial differences exist between the accused process and the patented process. The court also held that the question of equivalence is for the jury to decide and that the jury in this case had substantial evidence from which it could conclude that the Warner–Jenkinson process was not substantially different from the ultrafiltration process disclosed in the '746 patent. *Id.*, at 1525. There were three separate dissents, commanding a total of 5 of 12 judges.

We granted certiorari, and now reverse and remand.

### IIA

Petitioner's primary argument in this Court is that the doctrine of equivalents, as set out in Graver Tank in 1950, did not survive the 1952 revision of the Patent Act, 35 U.S.C. § 100 et seq., because it is inconsistent with several aspects of that Act. In particular, petitioner argues: (1) the doctrine of equivalents is inconsistent with the statutory requirement that a patentee specifically "claim" the invention covered by a patent, 35 U.S.C. § 112; (2) the doctrine circumvents the patent reissue process—designed to correct mistakes in drafting or the like—and avoids the express limitations on that process, 35 U.S.C. §§ 251–252; (3) the doctrine is inconsistent with the primacy of the Patent and Trademark Office (PTO) in setting the scope of a patent through the patent prosecution process; and (4) the doctrine was implicitly rejected as a general matter by Congress' specific and limited inclusion of the doctrine in one section regarding "means" claiming, 35 U.S.C. § 112, ¶ 6. All but one of these arguments were made in Graver Tank in the context of the 1870 Patent Act, and failed to command a majority.[c]

The 1952 Patent Act is not materially different from the 1870 Act with regard to claiming, reissue, and the role of the PTO. Compare, e.g., 35 U.S.C. § 112 ("The specification shall conclude with one or more claims

[c] Graver Tank was decided over a vigorous dissent. In that dissent, Justice Black raised the first three of petitioner's four arguments against the doctrine of equivalents. See 339 U.S., at 613–614, 70 S.Ct., at 858–859 (doctrine inconsistent with statutory requirement to "distinctly claim" the invention); *Id.*, at 614–615, 70 S.Ct., at 859–860 (patent reissue process available to correct mistakes); *Id.*, at 615, n. 3, 70 S.Ct., at 859, n. 3 (duty lies with the Patent Office to examine claims and to conform them to the scope of the invention; inventors may appeal Patent Office determinations if they disagree with result).

particularly pointing out and distinctly claiming the subject matter which the applicant regards as his invention") with The Consolidated Patent Act of 1870, ch. 230, § 26, 16 Stat. 198, 201 (the applicant "shall particularly point out and distinctly claim the part, improvement, or combination which he claims as his invention or discovery"). Such minor differences as exist between those provisions in the 1870 and the 1952 Acts have no bearing on the result reached in Graver Tank, and thus provide no basis for our overruling it.[d]

Petitioner's fourth argument for an implied congressional negation of the doctrine of equivalents turns on the reference to "equivalents" in the "means" claiming provision of the 1952 Act. Section 112, ¶ 6, a provision not contained in the 1870 Act, states:

> "An element in a claim for a combination may be expressed as a means or step for performing a specified function without the recital of structure, material, or acts in support thereof, and such claim shall be construed to cover the corresponding structure, material, or acts described in the specification and *equivalents thereof*." (Emphasis added.)

Thus, under this new provision, an applicant can describe an element of his invention by the result accomplished or the function served, rather than describing the item or element to be used (e.g., "a means of connecting Part A to Part B," rather than "a two-penny nail"). Congress enacted § 112, ¶ 6 in response to Halliburton Oil Well Cementing Co. v. Walker, which rejected claims that "do not describe the invention but use 'conveniently functional language at the exact point of novelty,'" 329 U.S. 1, 8, 67 S.Ct. 6, 9–10, 91 L.Ed. 3 (1946) (citation omitted). Section 112, ¶ 6 now expressly allows so-called "means" claims, with the proviso that application of the broad literal language of such claims must be limited to only those means that are "equivalent" to the actual means shown in the patent specification. This is an application of the doctrine of equivalents in a restrictive role, narrowing the application of broad literal claim elements. We recognized this type of role for the doctrine of equivalents in Graver Tank itself. The added provision, however, is silent on the doctrine of equivalents as applied where there is no literal infringement.

Because § 112, ¶ 6 was enacted as a targeted cure to a specific problem, and because the reference in that provision to "equivalents" appears to be no more than a prophylactic against potential side effects of that cure, such limited congressional action should not be overread for negative implications. Congress in 1952 could easily have responded to Graver Tank as it

---

[d] Petitioner argues that the evolution in patent practice from "central" claiming (describing the core principles of the invention) to "peripheral" claiming (describing the outer boundaries of the invention) requires that we treat Graver Tank as an aberration and abandon the doctrine of equivalents. Brief for Petitioner 43–45. We disagree. The suggested change in claiming practice predates Graver Tank, is not of statutory origin, and seems merely to reflect narrower inventions in more crowded arts. Also, judicial recognition of so-called "pioneer" patents suggests that the abandonment of "central" claiming may be overstated. That a claim describing a limited improvement in a crowded field will have a limited range of permissible equivalents does not negate the availability of the doctrine vel non.

did to the Halliburton decision. But it did not. Absent something more compelling than the dubious negative inference offered by petitioner, the lengthy history of the doctrine of equivalents strongly supports adherence to our refusal in Graver Tank to find that the Patent Act conflicts with that doctrine. Congress can legislate the doctrine of equivalents out of existence any time it chooses. The various policy arguments now made by both sides are thus best addressed to Congress, not this Court.

B

We do, however, share the concern of the dissenters below that the doctrine of equivalents, as it has come to be applied since Graver Tank, has taken on a life of its own, unbounded by the patent claims. There can be no denying that the doctrine of equivalents, when applied broadly, conflicts with the definitional and public-notice functions of the statutory claiming requirement. Judge Nies identified one means of avoiding this conflict:

> "[A] distinction can be drawn that is not too esoteric between substitution of an equivalent for a component *in* an invention and enlarging the metes and bounds of the invention *beyond* what is claimed.
>
> . . .
>
> "Where a claim to an invention is expressed as a combination of elements, as here, 'equivalents' in the sobriquet 'Doctrine of Equivalents' refers to the equivalency of an *element* or *part* of the invention with one that is substituted in the accused product or process.
>
> . . .
>
> "This view that the accused device or process must be more than 'equivalent' *overall* reconciles the Supreme Court's position on infringement by equivalents with its concurrent statements that 'the courts have no right to enlarge a patent beyond the scope of its claims as allowed by the Patent Office.' [Citations omitted.] The 'scope' is not enlarged if courts do not go beyond the substitution of equivalent elements." 62 F.3d, at 1573–1574 (Nies, J., dissenting) (emphasis in original).

We concur with this apt reconciliation of our two lines of precedent. Each element contained in a patent claim is deemed material to defining the scope of the patented invention, and thus the doctrine of equivalents must be applied to individual elements of the claim, not to the invention as a whole. It is important to ensure that the application of the doctrine, even as to an individual element, is not allowed such broad play as to effectively eliminate that element in its entirety. So long as the doctrine of equivalents does not encroach beyond the limits just described, or beyond related limits to be discussed, we are confident that the doctrine will not vitiate the central functions of the patent claims themselves.

III

Understandably reluctant to assume this Court would overrule Graver Tank, petitioner has offered alternative arguments in favor of a more restricted doctrine of equivalents than it feels was applied in this case. We address each in turn.

A

Petitioner first argues that Graver Tank never purported to supersede a well-established limit on non-literal infringement, known variously as "prosecution history estoppel" and "file wrapper estoppel." See Bayer Aktiengesellschaft v. Duphar Int'l Research B.V., 738 F.2d 1237, 1238 (C.A.Fed.1984). According to petitioner, any surrender of subject matter during patent prosecution, regardless of the reason for such surrender, precludes recapturing any part of that subject matter, even if it is equivalent to the matter expressly claimed. Because, during patent prosecution, respondent limited the pH element of its claim to pH levels between 6.0 and 9.0, petitioner would have those limits form bright lines beyond which no equivalents may be claimed. Any inquiry into the reasons for a surrender, petitioner claims, would undermine the public's right to clear notice of the scope of the patent as embodied in the patent file.

We can readily agree with petitioner that Graver Tank did not dispose of prosecution history estoppel as a legal limitation on the doctrine of equivalents. But petitioner reaches too far in arguing that the reason for an amendment during patent prosecution is irrelevant to any subsequent estoppel. In each of our cases cited by petitioner and by the dissent below, prosecution history estoppel was tied to amendments made to avoid the prior art, or otherwise to address a specific concern—such as obviousness—that arguably would have rendered the claimed subject matter unpatentable.

It is telling that in each case this Court probed the reasoning behind the Patent Office's insistence upon a change in the claims. In each instance, a change was demanded because the claim as otherwise written was viewed as not describing a patentable invention at all—typically because what it described was encompassed within the prior art. But, as the United States informs us, there are a variety of other reasons why the PTO may request a change in claim language. And if the PTO has been requesting changes in claim language without the intent to limit equivalents or, indeed, with the expectation that language it required would in many cases allow for a range of equivalents, we should be extremely reluctant to upset the basic assumptions of the PTO without substantial reason for doing so. Our prior cases have consistently applied prosecution history estoppel only where claims have been amended for a limited set of reasons, and we see no substantial cause for requiring a more rigid rule invoking an estoppel regardless of the reasons for a change.

In this case, the patent examiner objected to the patent claim due to a perceived overlap with the Booth patent, which revealed an ultrafiltration process operating at a pH above 9.0. In response to this objection, the phrase "at a pH from approximately 6.0 to 9.0" was added to the claim. While it is undisputed that the upper limit of 9.0 was added in order to distinguish the Booth patent, the reason for adding the lower limit of 6.0 is unclear. The lower limit certainly did not serve to distinguish the Booth patent, which said nothing about pH levels below 6.0. Thus, while a lower limit of 6.0, by its mere inclusion, became a material element of the claim, that did not necessarily preclude the application of the doctrine of equivalents as to that element.[e]

We are left with the problem, however, of what to do in a case like the one at bar, where the record seems not to reveal the reason for including the lower pH limit of 6.0. In our view, holding that certain reasons for a claim amendment may avoid the application of prosecution history estoppel is not tantamount to holding that the absence of a reason for an amendment may similarly avoid such an estoppel. Mindful that claims do indeed serve both a definitional and a notice function, we think the better rule is to place the burden on the patent-holder to establish the reason for an amendment required during patent prosecution. The court then would decide whether that reason is sufficient to overcome prosecution history estoppel as a bar to application of the doctrine of equivalents to the element added by that amendment. Where no explanation is established, however, the court should presume that the PTO had a substantial reason related to patentability for including the limiting element added by amendment. In those circumstances, prosecution history estoppel would bar the application of the doctrine equivalents as to that element. The presumption we have described, one subject to rebuttal if an appropriate reason for a required amendment is established, gives proper deference to the role of claims in defining an invention and providing public notice, and to the primacy of the PTO in ensuring that the claims allowed cover only subject matter that is properly patentable in a proffered patent application. Applied in this fashion, prosecution history estoppel places reasonable limits on the doctrine of equivalents, and further insulates the doctrine from any feared conflict with the Patent Act.

Because respondent has not proffered in this Court a reason for the addition of a lower pH limit, it is impossible to tell whether the reason for that addition could properly avoid an estoppel. Whether a reason in fact exists, but simply was not adequately developed, we cannot say. On remand, the Federal Circuit can consider whether reasons for that portion of the amendment were offered or not and whether further opportunity to establish such reasons would be proper.

### B

Petitioner next argues that even if Graver Tank remains good law, the case held only that the absence of substantial differences was a necessary element for infringement under the doctrine of equivalents, not that it was sufficient for such a result. Relying on Graver Tank's references to the problem of an "unscrupulous copyist" and "piracy," petitioner would require judicial exploration of the equities of a case before allowing applica-

---

[e] We do not suggest that, where a change is made to overcome an objection based on the prior art, a court is free to review the correctness of that objection when deciding whether to apply prosecution history estoppel. As petitioner rightly notes, such concerns are properly addressed on direct appeal from the denial of a patent, and will not be revisited in an infringement action. What is permissible for a court to explore is the reason (right or wrong) for the objection and the manner in which the amendment addressed and avoided the objection.

tion of the doctrine of equivalents. To be sure, Graver Tank refers to the prevention of copying and piracy when describing the benefits of the doctrine of equivalents. That the doctrine produces such benefits, however, does not mean that its application is limited only to cases where those particular benefits are obtained.

Elsewhere in Graver Tank the doctrine is described in more neutral terms. And the history of the doctrine as relied upon by Graver Tank reflects a basis for the doctrine not so limited as petitioner would have it. . . . If the essential predicate of the doctrine of equivalents is the notion of identity between a patented invention and its equivalent, there is no basis for treating an infringing equivalent any differently than a device that infringes the express terms of the patent. Application of the doctrine of equivalents, therefore, is akin to determining literal infringement, and neither requires proof of intent.

Petitioner also points to Graver Tank's seeming reliance on the absence of independent experimentation by the alleged infringer as supporting an equitable defense to the doctrine of equivalents. The Federal Circuit explained this factor by suggesting that an alleged infringer's behavior, be it copying, designing around a patent, or independent experimentation, indirectly reflects the substantiality of the differences between the patented invention and the accused device or process. According to the Federal Circuit, a person aiming to copy or aiming to avoid a patent is imagined to be at least marginally skilled at copying or avoidance, and thus intentional copying raises an inference—rebuttable by proof of independent development—of having only insubstantial differences, and intentionally designing around a patent claim raises an inference of substantial differences. This explanation leaves much to be desired. At a minimum, one wonders how ever to distinguish between the intentional copyist making minor changes to lower the risk of legal action, and the incremental innovator designing around the claims, yet seeking to capture as much as is permissible of the patented advance.

Although Graver Tank certainly leaves room for petitioner's suggested inclusion of intent-based elements in the doctrine of equivalents, we do not read it as requiring them. The better view, and the one consistent with Graver Tank's predecessors and the objective approach to infringement, is that intent plays no role in the application of the doctrine of equivalents.

\* \* \* \* \*

IV

[In this part, the Court defers to another day the issue of whether equivalence should be determined by the court or by the jury. Thus, it left standing the Federal Circuit's decision to allow a jury to apply the doctrine of equivalents.]

V

All that remains is to address the debate regarding the linguistic framework under which "equivalence" is determined. Both the parties and the Federal Circuit spend considerable time arguing whether the so-called "triple identity" test—focusing on the function served by a particular claim element, the way that element serves that function, and the result thus obtained by that element—is a suitable method for determining equivalence, or whether an "insubstantial differences" approach is better. There seems to be substantial agreement that, while the triple identity test may be suitable for analyzing mechanical devices, it often provides a poor framework for analyzing other products or processes. On the other hand, the insubstantial differences test offers little additional guidance as to what might render any given difference "insubstantial."

In our view, the particular linguistic framework used is less important than whether the test is probative of the essential inquiry: Does the accused product or process contain elements identical or equivalent to each claimed element of the patented invention? Different linguistic frameworks may be more suitable to different cases, depending on their particular facts. A focus on individual elements and a special vigilance against allowing the concept of equivalence to eliminate completely any such elements should reduce considerably the imprecision of whatever language is used. An analysis of the role played by each element in the context of the specific patent claim will thus inform the inquiry as to whether a substitute element matches the function, way, and result of the claimed element, or whether the substitute element plays a role substantially different from the claimed element. With these limiting principles as a backdrop, we see no purpose in going further and micro-managing the Federal Circuit's particular word-choice for analyzing equivalence. We expect that the Federal Circuit will refine the formulation of the test for equivalence in the orderly course of case-by-case determinations, and we leave such refinement to that court's sound judgment in this area of its special expertise.

VI

Today we adhere to the doctrine of equivalents. The determination of equivalence should be applied as an objective inquiry on an element-by-element basis. Prosecution history estoppel continues to be available as a defense to infringement, but if the patent-holder demonstrates that an amendment required during prosecution had a purpose unrelated to patentability, a court must consider that purpose in order to decide whether an estoppel is precluded. Where the patentholder is unable to establish such a purpose, a court should presume that the purpose behind the required amendment is such that prosecution history estoppel would apply. Because the Court of Appeals for the Federal Circuit did not consider all of the requirements as described by us today, particularly as related to prosecution history estoppel and the preservation of some meaning for each element in a claim, we reverse and remand for further proceedings consistent with this opinion.

■ JUSTICE GINSBURG, with whom JUSTICE KENNEDY joins, concurring.

I join the opinion of the Court and write separately to add a cautionary note on the rebuttable presumption the Court announces regarding prosecution history estoppel. I address in particular the application of the presumption in this case and others in which patent prosecution has already been completed. The new presumption, if applied woodenly, might in some instances unfairly discount the expectations of a patentee who had no notice at the time of patent prosecution that such a presumption would apply. Such a patentee would have had little incentive to insist that the reasons for all modifications be memorialized in the file wrapper as they were made. Years after the fact, the patentee may find it difficult to establish an evidentiary basis that would overcome the new presumption. The Court's opinion is sensitive to this problem, noting that "the PTO may have relied upon a flexible rule of estoppel when deciding whether to ask for a change" during patent prosecution.

Because respondent has not presented to this Court any explanation for the addition of the lower pH limit, I concur in the decision to remand the matter to the Federal Circuit. On remand, that court can determine— bearing in mind the prior absence of clear rules of the game—whether suitable reasons for including the lower pH limit were earlier offered or, if not, whether they can now be established.

## Festo Corp. v. Shoketsu Kinzoku Kogyo Kabushiki Co., Ltd.

Supreme Court of the United States, 2002.
535 U.S. 722, 122 S.Ct. 1831, 152 L.Ed.2d 944.

■ JUSTICE KENNEDY delivered the opinion of the Court.

This case requires us to address once again the relation between two patent law concepts, the doctrine of equivalents and the rule of prosecution history estoppel.

In the decision now under review the Court of Appeals for the Federal Circuit held that by narrowing a claim to obtain a patent, the patentee surrenders all equivalents to the amended claim element. Petitioner asserts this holding departs from past precedent in two respects. First, it applies estoppel to every amendment made to satisfy the requirements of the Patent Act and not just to amendments made to avoid pre-emption by an earlier invention, *i.e.,* the prior art. Second, it holds that when estoppel arises, it bars suit against every equivalent to the amended claim element. The Court of Appeals acknowledged that this holding departed from its own cases, which applied a flexible bar when considering what claims of equivalence were estopped by the prosecution history. Petitioner argues that by replacing the flexible bar with a complete bar the Court of Appeals cast doubt on many existing patents that were amended during the application process when the law, as it then stood, did not apply so rigorous a standard.

We granted certiorari to consider these questions.

I

Petitioner Festo Corporation owns two patents for an improved magnetic rodless cylinder, a piston-driven device that relies on magnets to move objects in a conveying system. The device has many industrial uses and has been employed in machinery as diverse as sewing equipment and the Thunder Mountain ride at Disney World. Although the precise details of the cylinder's operation are not essential here, the prosecution history must be considered.

Petitioner's patent applications, as often occurs, were amended during the prosecution proceedings. The application for the first patent, the Stoll Patent (U.S. Patent No. 4,354,125), was amended after the patent examiner rejected the initial application because the exact method of operation was unclear and some claims were made in an impermissible way. (They were multiply dependent.) 35 U.S.C. § 112. The inventor, Dr. Stoll, submitted a new application designed to meet the examiner's objections and also added certain references to prior art. The second patent, the Carroll Patent (U.S. Patent No. 3,779,401), was also amended during a reexamination proceeding. The prior art references were added to this amended application as well. Both amended patents added a new limitation—that the inventions contain a pair of sealing rings, each having a lip on one side, which would prevent impurities from getting on the piston assembly. The amended Stoll Patent added the further limitation that the outer shell of the device, the sleeve, be made of a magnetizable material.

After Festo began selling its rodless cylinder, respondents (whom we refer to as SMC) entered the market with a device similar, but not identical, to the ones disclosed by Festo's patents. SMC's cylinder, rather than using two one-way sealing rings, employs a single sealing ring with a two-way lip. Furthermore, SMC's sleeve is made of a nonmagnetizable alloy. SMC's device does not fall within the literal claims of either patent, but petitioner contends that it is so similar that it infringes under the doctrine of equivalents.

SMC contends that Festo is estopped from making this argument because of the prosecution history of its patents. The sealing rings and the magnetized alloy in the Festo product were both disclosed for the first time in the amended applications. In SMC's view, these amendments narrowed the earlier applications, surrendering alternatives that are the very points of difference in the competing devices—the sealing rings and the type of alloy used to make the sleeve. As Festo narrowed its claims in these ways in order to obtain the patents, says SMC, Festo is now estopped from saying that these features are immaterial and that SMC's device is an equivalent of its own.

The United States District Court for the District of Massachusetts disagreed. It held that Festo's amendments were not made to avoid prior art, and therefore the amendments were not the kind that give rise to estoppel. A panel of the Court of Appeals for the Federal Circuit affirmed. We granted certiorari, vacated, and remanded in light of our intervening decision in *Warner–Jenkinson*. After a decision by the original panel on remand, the Court of Appeals ordered rehearing en banc to address questions that had divided its judges since our decision in *Warner–Jenkinson*.

The en banc court reversed, holding that prosecution history estoppel barred Festo from asserting that the accused device infringed its patents under the doctrine of equivalents. The court held, with only one judge dissenting, that estoppel arises from any amendment that narrows a claim to comply with the Patent Act, not only from amendments made to avoid prior art. More controversial in the Court of Appeals was its further holding: When estoppel applies, it stands as a complete bar against any claim of equivalence for the element that was amended. Four judges dissented from the decision to adopt a complete bar [in four separate opinions].

## II

The patent laws "promote the Progress of Science and useful Arts" by rewarding innovation with a temporary monopoly. U.S. Const., Art. I, § 8, cl. 8. The monopoly is a property right; and like any property right, its boundaries should be clear. This clarity is essential to promote progress, because it enables efficient investment in innovation. A patent holder should know what he owns, and the public should know what he does not. For this reason, the patent laws require inventors to describe their work in "full, clear, concise, and exact terms," 35 U.S.C. § 112, as part of the delicate balance the law attempts to maintain between inventors, who rely on the promise of the law to bring the invention forth, and the public, which should be encouraged to pursue innovations, creations, and new ideas beyond the inventor's exclusive rights. Bonito Boats, Inc. v. Thunder Craft Boats, Inc., 489 U.S. 141, 150, 109 S.Ct. 971, 103 L.Ed.2d 118 (1989).

Unfortunately, the nature of language makes it impossible to capture the essence of a thing in a patent application. The inventor who chooses to patent an invention and disclose it to the public, rather than exploit it in secret, bears the risk that others will devote their efforts toward exploiting the limits of the patent's language:

> An invention exists most importantly as a tangible structure or a series of drawings. A verbal portrayal is usually an afterthought written to satisfy the requirements of patent law. This conversion of machine to words allows for unintended idea gaps which cannot be satisfactorily filled. Often the invention is novel and words do not exist to describe it. The dictionary does not always keep abreast of the inventor. It cannot. Things are not made for the sake of words, but words for things. Autogiro Co. of America v. United States, 181 Ct.Cl. 55, 384 F.2d 391, 397 (1967).

The language in the patent claims may not capture every nuance of the invention or describe with complete precision the range of its novelty. If patents were always interpreted by their literal terms, their value would be greatly diminished. Unimportant and insubstantial substitutes for certain elements could defeat the patent, and its value to inventors could be destroyed by simple acts of copying. For this reason, the clearest rule of patent interpretation, literalism, may conserve judicial resources but is not necessarily the most efficient rule. The scope of a patent is not limited to its literal terms but instead embraces all equivalents to the claims described. See *Winans v. Denmead,* 56 U.S. (15 How.) 330, 347, 14 L.Ed. 717 (1854).

It is true that the doctrine of equivalents renders the scope of patents less certain. It may be difficult to determine what is, or is not, an equivalent to a particular element of an invention. If competitors cannot be certain about a patent's extent, they may be deterred from engaging in legitimate manufactures outside its limits, or they may invest by mistake in competing products that the patent secures. In addition the uncertainty may lead to wasteful litigation between competitors, suits that a rule of literalism might avoid. These concerns with the doctrine of equivalents, however, are not new. Each time the Court has considered the doctrine, it has acknowledged this uncertainty as the price of ensuring the appropriate incentives for innovation, and it has affirmed the doctrine over dissents that urged a more certain rule.

## III

Prosecution history estoppel requires that the claims of a patent be interpreted in light of the proceedings in the PTO during the application process. Estoppel is a "rule of patent construction" that ensures that claims are interpreted by reference to those "that have been cancelled or rejected." *Schriber–Schroth Co. v. Cleveland Trust Co.,* 311 U.S. 211, 220–221, 61 S.Ct. 235, 85 L.Ed. 132 (1940). The doctrine of equivalents allows the patentee to claim those insubstantial alterations that were not captured in drafting the original patent claim but which could be created through trivial changes. When, however, the patentee originally claimed the subject matter alleged to infringe but then narrowed the claim in response to a rejection, he may not argue that the surrendered territory comprised unforeseen subject matter that should be deemed equivalent to the literal claims of the issued patent. On the contrary, "[b]y the amendment [the patentee] recognized and emphasized the difference between the two phrases[,] . . . and [t]he difference which [the patentee] thus disclaimed must be regarded as material." *Exhibit Supply Co. v. Ace Patents Corp.,* 315 U.S. 126, 136–137, 62 S.Ct. 513, 86 L.Ed. 736 (1942).

A rejection indicates that the patent examiner does not believe the original claim could be patented. While the patentee has the right to appeal, his decision to forgo an appeal and submit an amended claim is taken as a concession that the invention as patented does not reach as far as the original claim. Were it otherwise, the inventor might avoid the PTO's gatekeeping role and seek to recapture in an infringement action the very subject matter surrendered as a condition of receiving the patent.

Prosecution history estoppel ensures that the doctrine of equivalents remains tied to its underlying purpose. Where the original application once embraced the purported equivalent but the patentee narrowed his claims to obtain the patent or to protect its validity, the patentee cannot assert that he lacked the words to describe the subject matter in question. The doctrine of equivalents is premised on language's inability to capture the essence of innovation, but a prior application describing the precise element at issue undercuts that premise. In that instance the prosecution history has established that the inventor turned his attention to the subject matter in question, knew the words for both the broader and narrower claim, and affirmatively chose the latter.

### A

The first question in this case concerns the kinds of amendments that may give rise to estoppel. Petitioner argues that estoppel should arise when amendments are intended to narrow the subject matter of the patented invention, for instance, amendments to avoid prior art, but not when the amendments are made to comply with requirements concerning the form of the patent application.

Petitioner is correct that estoppel has been discussed most often in the context of amendments made to avoid the prior art. See *Exhibit Supply Co.,* at 137, 62 S.Ct. 513. Amendment to accommodate prior art was the emphasis, too, of our decision in *Warner–Jenkinson.* It does not follow, however, that amendments for other purposes will not give rise to estoppel. Prosecution history may rebut the inference that a thing not described was indescribable. That rationale does not cease simply because the narrowing amendment, submitted to secure a patent, was for some purpose other than avoiding prior art.

We agree with the Court of Appeals that a narrowing amendment made to satisfy any requirement of the Patent Act may give rise to an estoppel. As that court explained, a number of statutory requirements must be satisfied before a patent can issue. The claimed subject matter must be useful, novel, and not obvious. 35 U.S.C. §§ 101–103. In addition, the patent application must describe, enable, and set forth the best mode of carrying out the invention. § 112. These latter requirements must be satisfied before issuance of the patent, for exclusive patent rights are given in exchange for disclosing the invention to the public. What is claimed by the patent application must be the same as what is disclosed in the specification; otherwise the patent should not issue. The patent also should not issue if the other requirements of § 112 are not satisfied, and an applicant's failure to meet these requirements could lead to the issued patent being held invalid in later litigation.

Petitioner contends that amendments made to comply with § 112 concern the form of the application and not the subject matter of the invention. The PTO might require the applicant to clarify an ambiguous term, to improve the translation of a foreign word, or to rewrite a dependent claim as an independent one. In these cases, petitioner argues, the applicant has no intention of surrendering subject matter and should not be estopped from challenging equivalent devices. While this may be true in some cases, petitioner's argument conflates the patentee's reason for making the amendment with the impact the amendment has on the subject matter.

Estoppel arises when an amendment is made to secure the patent and the amendment narrows the patent's scope. If a § 112 amendment is truly cosmetic, then it would not narrow the patent's scope or raise an estoppel. On the other hand, if a § 112 amendment is necessary and narrows the patent's scope—even if only for the purpose of better description—estoppel may apply. A patentee who narrows a claim as a condition for obtaining a patent disavows his claim to the broader subject matter, whether the amendment was made to avoid the prior art or to comply with § 112. We must regard the patentee as having conceded an inability to claim the broader subject matter or at least as having abandoned his right to appeal a rejection. In either case estoppel may apply.

## B

Petitioner concedes that the limitations at issue—the sealing rings and the composition of the sleeve—were made for reasons related to § 112, if not also to avoid the prior art. Our conclusion that prosecution history estoppel arises when a claim is narrowed to comply with § 112 gives rise to the second question presented: Does the estoppel bar the inventor from asserting infringement against any equivalent to the narrowed element or might some equivalents still infringe? The Court of Appeals held that prosecution history estoppel is a complete bar, and so the narrowed element must be limited to its strict literal terms. Based upon its experience the Court of Appeals decided that the flexible-bar rule is unworkable because it leads to excessive uncertainty and burdens legitimate innovation. For the reasons that follow, we disagree with the decision to adopt the complete bar.

Though prosecution history estoppel can bar challenges to a wide range of equivalents, its reach requires an examination of the subject matter surrendered by the narrowing amendment. The complete bar avoids this inquiry by establishing a *per se* rule; but that approach is inconsistent with the purpose of applying the estoppel in the first place—to hold the inventor to the representations made during the application process and to the inferences that may reasonably be drawn from the amendment. By amending the application, the inventor is deemed to concede that the patent does not extend as far as the original claim. It does not follow, however, that the amended claim becomes so perfect in its description that no one could devise an equivalent. After amendment, as before, language remains an imperfect fit for invention. The narrowing amendment may demonstrate what the claim is not; but it may still fail to capture precisely what the claim is. There is no reason why a narrowing amendment should be deemed to relinquish equivalents unforeseeable at the time of the amendment and beyond a fair interpretation of what was surrendered. Nor is there any call to foreclose claims of equivalence for aspects of the invention that have only a peripheral relation to the reason the amendment was submitted. The amendment does not show that the inventor suddenly had more foresight in the drafting of claims than an inventor whose application was granted without amendments having been submitted. It shows only that he was familiar with the broader text and with the difference between the two. As a result, there is no more reason for holding the patentee to the literal terms of an amended claim than there is for abolishing the doctrine of equivalents altogether and holding every patentee to the literal terms of the patent.

Just as *Warner–Jenkinson* held that the patentee bears the burden of proving that an amendment was not made for a reason that would give rise to estoppel, we hold here that the patentee should bear the burden of showing that the amendment does not surrender the particular equivalent in question. The patentee, as the author of the claim language, may be expected to draft claims encompassing readily known equivalents. A patentee's decision to narrow his claims through amendment may be presumed to be a general disclaimer of the territory between the original claim and the amended claim. There are some cases, however, where the amendment cannot reasonably be viewed as surrendering a particular equivalent. The equivalent may have been unforeseeable at the time of the application; the rationale underlying the amendment may bear no more than a tangential relation to the equivalent in question; or there may be some other reason suggesting that the patentee could not reasonably be expected to have described the insubstantial substitute in question. In those cases the patentee can overcome the presumption that prosecution history estoppel bars a finding of equivalence.

This presumption is not, then, just the complete bar by another name. Rather, it reflects the fact that the interpretation of the patent must begin with its literal claims, and the prosecution history is relevant to construing those claims. When the patentee has chosen to narrow a claim, courts may presume the amended text was composed with awareness of this rule and that the territory surrendered is not an equivalent of the territory claimed. In those instances, however, the patentee still might rebut the presumption that estoppel bars a claim of equivalence. The patentee must show that at the time of the amendment one skilled in the art could not reasonably be expected to have drafted a claim that would have literally encompassed the alleged equivalent.

IV

On the record before us, we cannot say petitioner has rebutted the presumptions that estoppel applies and that the equivalents at issue have been surrendered. These matters should be determined in the first instance by further proceedings in the Court of Appeals or the District Court.

## Husky Injection Molding Systems Ltd. v. R & D Tool & Engineering Co.

United States Court of Appeals for the Federal Circuit, 2002.
291 F.3d 780.

■ DYK, CIRCUIT JUDGE.

Husky Injection Molding Systems Ltd. ("Husky") appeals from the decision of the United States District Court for the Western District of Missouri, granting the motion of R & D Tool & Engineering Co. ("R & D") for summary judgment of non-infringement of U.S. Patent No. Re. 33,237 (the " '237 patent"). Because we find that there were no genuine issues of material fact regarding infringement of the '237 patent and that the district court correctly concluded that R & D's replacement of the mold and carrier plate of the injection molding system was more akin to repair than reconstruction, we affirm.

## BACKGROUND

Husky manufactures and sells injection molding systems (the "X-series systems") that produce hollow plastic articles known as preforms. These preforms are subsequently reheated and blow molded into hollow plastic containers.

Husky is the assignee of the '237 patent, entitled "Apparatus for Producing Hollow Plastic Articles," which is directed to an injection molding machine that includes a carrier plate containing at least two sets of cavities for cooling the hollow plastic articles. The molds and carrier plates are not separately patented. The parties focus on claim 1 of the '237 patent, which provides:

> 1. An apparatus for producing hollow plastic articles which comprise [sic]:
>
> an injection molding machine including a first mold portion having at least one cavity therein and a second mold portion having at least one elongate core seating in said cavity in mold-closed position to form a first number of hot hollow plastic articles in an injection molding cycle, and means for reciprocating said mold portions form [sic] said mold-closed position to a mold-open position forming a gap between said mold portions;
>
> *a carrier plate having at least two sets of cavities therein for cooling said hollow plastic articles, with the number of cavities corresponding to a multiple of at least two times the number of hollow plastic articles produced in an injection molding cycle;*
>
> means for moving the carrier plate into and out of said gap;
>
> means for aligning one set at a time of said carrier plate cavities to juxtapose said aligned set of cavities with said hollow plastic articles formed in an injection molding cycle; and
>
> means for transferring said hollow plastic articles to said juxtaposed cavities.

'237 patent, col. 7, ll. 27–51 (emphasis added).

Generally preforms are made by injecting molten plastic into molds. One half of the mold contains at least one cavity; the other half contains a number of cores corresponding to the number of cavities. The cores engage with their respective cavities to form a closed mold and produce the shape of the hollow plastic articles. To prevent damage to the preforms, each article must be adequately cooled before it is handled. Traditionally the preforms were cooled in the molding machine, which was a time-consuming process. Having a lengthy cooling time in the molding machine was the limiting step in the production process of the articles and was at odds with the "high rate of production [that] is important in commercial operations. . . . " *Id.* at col. 1, ll. 20–24. Other injection molding systems have increased the speed of the molding cycle, although there have been corresponding increases in costs or risks of damage to the articles. According to the summary of the invention of the patent, the present invention economically allows a high rate of production while permitting the preforms to cool for an extended period of time inside the cavities of the carrier plate, rather than in the injection molds of the molding machine.

When a customer wishes to make a change in the preform design, it generally must buy a substitute mold and corresponding carrier plate in order to operate the Husky injection molding system as it was designed. Customers change the preform design on average after three to five years. When a system owner wants to make a different type of plastic article, it may purchase a replacement mold and carrier plate combination from Husky.

The alleged contributory infringer, R & D, makes molds and carrier plates, which substitute for components of Husky's injection molding system. To make the substitute molds and carrier plates, R & D purchased Husky's X-series system in 1997 without the mold or the carrier plate. At the time of the sale, R & D informed Husky's salesman of its intent to use the Husky system to make substitute molds. Moreover, all sales of X-series systems were without contractual restriction on the future purchase of molds or carrier plates.

In the summer of 2000, R & D shipped to Grafco, the owner of a Husky system, a new mold and carrier plate to allow Grafco to produce a different preform design. On June 9, 2000, Husky sued R & D for infringement of the '237 patent, urging that R & D had contributed to the infringement of the '237 patent. Husky concedes that the sale of the molds alone did not constitute contributory infringement because the molds were staple items. But Husky urged that R & D's sales to Husky's customers of a mold and carrier plate combination constituted contributory infringement because the substitution of a new carrier plate amounted to reconstruction of Husky's patented invention. R & D did not argue that the products it sold were outside the scope of the claims, but instead defended on the ground that its sales were akin to repair, and alternatively that Husky granted R & D an implied license to make and sell molds and carrier plates.[a]

On September 8, 2000, R & D filed a motion for summary judgment of non-infringement, which the district court granted on March 30, 2001. Based on Husky's own admission that "no reconstruction occurs if the customer replaces the combination for repair purposes," the Court focused on whether substitution of a new mold and carrier plate combination for an

[a] Husky also claimed that R & D induced infringement under 35 U.S.C. § 271(b). On appeal, Husky primarily focuses its claim on contributory infringement. The repair defense is equally applicable to inducement of infringement and contributory infringement.

unspent combination constituted reconstruction. In light of *Wilbur–Ellis Co. v. Kuther,* 377 U.S. 422, 84 S.Ct. 1561, 12 L.Ed.2d 419 (1964), the district court held that "the use of R & D's retrofit mold/carrier plate assembly to substitute for an unspent original mold/carrier plate assembly does not rise to the level of impermissible reconstruction set out by the Supreme Court in [*Aro Manufacturing Co. v. Convertible Top Replacement Co.,* 365 U.S. 336, 81 S.Ct. 599, 5 L.Ed.2d 592 (1961) (*'Aro I'*)]." The court noted that *Wilbur–Ellis* supports the holding that changing the shape of components to produce a different preform design is more akin to repair than reconstruction. The district court further held that "the use of a substitution mold/carrier plate assembly offered by R & D is within the rights of purchasers of a Husky X-series due to the Plaintiff's admission of its awareness of a replacement mold market. . . . " Alternatively, the court concluded that Husky's customers had an implied license to substitute the mold/carrier plate assembly in order to produce different preform designs because Husky had sold its system without restriction.

DISCUSSION

II

Here Husky alleges that R & D is a contributory infringer. The law of contributory infringement is well settled. Section 271 of title 35 provides in pertinent part:

   (a) Except as otherwise provided in this title, whoever *without authority makes, uses, offers to sell, or sells any patented invention,* within the United States or imports into the United States any patented invention during the term of the patent therefor, *infringes the patent.*

   \* \* \*

   (c) Whoever offers to sell or sells within the United States or imports into the United States a component of a patented machine, manufacture, combination or composition, or a material or apparatus for use in practicing a patented process, constituting a *material part of the invention, knowing the same to be especially made or especially adapted for use in an infringement of such patent,* and *not a staple article* or commodity of commerce suitable for substantial noninfringing use, shall be liable as a contributory infringer.

35 U.S.C. § 271 (1994) (emphases added).

   Thus, a seller of a "material part" of a patented item may be a contributory infringer if he makes a non-staple article that he knows was "especially made or especially adapted for use in an infringement of such patent." *Id.; Dawson Chem. Co. v. Rohm & Haas Co.,* 448 U.S. 176, 219, 100 S.Ct. 2601, 65 L.Ed.2d 696 (1980). For R & D to be liable as a contributory infringer, Husky's customers who purchased the replacement parts from R & D must be liable for direct infringement. 35 U.S.C. § 271(c) (1994); *Aro I,* 365 U.S. at 34, 81 S.Ct. 5991. Both an alleged direct infringer and an alleged contributory infringer benefit from the permissible repair exception.

III

The Supreme Court and this court have struggled for years to appropriately distinguish between repair of a patented machine and reconstruction. *See* Donald S. Chisum, 5 *Chisum on Patents* § 16.03[3], at 16–159 (1997) ("The line between permissible 'repair' and impermissible 'reconstruction' is a difficult one to draw and is the subject of numerous cases."). Based on those decisions, we can identify at least three primary repair and reconstruction situations.

First, there is the situation in which the entire patented item is spent, and the alleged infringer reconstructs it to make it useable again. This situation was first considered by the Supreme Court in *American Cotton–Tie Co. v. Simmons,* 106 U.S. (16 Otto) 89, 1 S.Ct. 52, 27 L.Ed. 79 (1882). *Cotton–Tie* involved a metallic cotton-bale tie consisting of a band and a buckle. After the cotton-bale tie was cut, it became scrap iron. The defendants subsequently purchased the scrap iron, riveted the pieces together, and recreated the bands. Although the defendants reused the original buckle, the Court found that the defendants "reconstructed [the band]," and thereby infringed the patent. Moreover, in *Morgan Envelope Co. v. Albany Perforated Wrapping Paper Co.,* 152 U.S. 425, 14 S.Ct. 627, 38 L.Ed. 500 (1894), the Court explained its decision in *Cotton–Tie.* Specifically, the Court noted that "the use of the tie was intended to be as complete a destruction of it as would be the explosion of a patented torpedo. In either case, the repair of the band or the refilling of the shell would be a practical reconstruction of the device."

Second, there is the situation in which a spent part is replaced. The Supreme Court first addressed this situation in *Wilson v. Simpson,* 50 U.S. (9 How.) 109, 13 L.Ed. 66 (1850). *Wilson* involved the replacement of cutter-knives in a wood-planing machine. In concluding that replacement of the cutter-knives was permissible repair, the Court stated that

> repairing partial injuries, whether they occur from accident or wear and tear, is only refitting a machine for use. And it is no more than that, though it shall be a replacement of an essential part of a combination. It is the use of the whole of that which a purchaser buys, when the patentee sells to him a machine; and when he repairs the damages which may be done to it, it is no more than the exercise of that right of care which every one may use to give duration to that which he owns, or has a right to use as a whole.

*Id.* at 123, 50 U.S. 109.

Subsequently, the Supreme Court set forth a definitive test in *Aro Manufacturing Co. v. Convertible Top Replacement Co.,* 365 U.S. 336, 81 S.Ct. 599, 5 L.Ed.2d 592 (1961) ("*Aro I*"). *Aro I* involved a combination patent on a convertible folding top of an automobile. The fabric of the convertible top had a shorter useful life than the other parts of the patented combination. In reaching the conclusion that replacement of the worn-out fabric of the convertible top was permissible repair, the Supreme Court adopted a bright-line test. Specifically, the Court concluded that replacement of a spent part of a combination patent, which is not separately patented, is not impermissible reconstruction no matter how "essential it may be to the patented combination and no matter how costly or difficult replacement may be." In adopting this bright-line test, the majority rejected Justice Brennan's suggestion in his concurrence that a multi-factor fact intensive test was appropriate to distinguish repair from reconstruction. Even if the owner sequentially replaces all of the worn-out parts of a patented combination, this sequential replacement does not constitute reconstruction. *See FMC Corp. v. Up–Right, Inc.,* 21 F.3d 1073, 1077, 30 USPQ2d 1361, 1363–64 (Fed.Cir.1994); *see also Surfco Hawaii v. Fin Control Sys. Pty, Ltd.,* 264 F.3d 1062, 1065, 60 USPQ2d 1056, 1058 (Fed.Cir.2001) ("Mere replacement of individual unpatented parts, one at a time, whether of the same part repeatedly or different parts successively, is no more than the lawful right of the owner to repair his property.") (quoting *Aro I,* 365 U.S. at 346, 81 S.Ct. 599). Moreover, in *Sage Products, Inc. v. Devon Industries, Inc.,* we held that replacement was not limited to worn out articles, but also included articles that were effectively spent. 45 F.3d 1575, 1578, 33 USPQ2d 1765, 1767 (Fed.Cir.1995).

Third, there is the situation in which a part is not spent but is replaced to enable the machine to perform a different function. This is a situation "kin to repair." In *Wilbur–Ellis,* the Supreme Court addressed whether changing the size of cans in fish-canning machines constituted reconstruction when the fish-canning machines were not spent, although they needed cleaning and repair. The Court concluded that the "[p]etitioners in adapting the old machine to a related use were doing more than repair in the customary sense; but what they did was kin to repair for it bore on the useful capacity of the old combination. . . . " This form of adaptation was within the scope of the purchased patent rights because the size of the cans was not "part of the invention."

This court has followed the holding of *Wilbur–Ellis* when addressing replacement of unpatented parts of a combination patent. For example, in *Surfco* we recently addressed a similar situation involving the modification of a surfboard. Surfco manufactured fins that had an additional safety feature and were interchangeable with the patentee's releasable fins on its surfboard. *Surfco,* 264 F.3d at 1064, 60 USPQ2d at 1057. This safety feature created an incentive to replace the patentee's fins with Surfco's fins. Once again we reiterated that permissible repair encompasses the situation where parts are replaced.

## IV

Despite the number of cases concerning repair and reconstruction, difficult questions remain. One of these arises from the necessity of determining what constitutes replacement of a part of the device, which is repair or akin to repair, and what constitutes reconstruction of the entire device, which would not be repair or akin to repair. Some few situations suggest an obvious answer. For example, if a patent is obtained on an automobile, the replacement of the spark plugs would constitute permissible repair, but few would argue that the retention of the spark plugs and the replacement of the remainder of the car at a single stroke was permissible activity akin to repair. Thus, there may be some concept of proportionality inherent in the distinction between repair and reconstruction.

Nonetheless, in *Aro I*, the Supreme Court explicitly rejected a "heart of the invention" standard, noting that no matter how essential an element of the combination is to the patent, "no element, separately viewed, is within the [patent] grant." *Aro I*, 365 U.S. at 344, 81 S.Ct. 599. Similarly, in *Dawson Chemical Co. v. Rohm & Haas Co.*, the Court noted that in *Aro I* it had "eschewed the suggestion that the legal distinction between 'reconstruction' and 'repair' should be affected by whether the element of the combination that has been replaced is an 'essential' or 'distinguishing' part of the invention." 448 U.S. 176, 217, 100 S.Ct. 2601, 65 L.Ed.2d 696 (1980).

However, *Aro I* itself was clearly dealing with "replaceable" parts, and we have interpreted *Aro I* as merely defining permissible repair in the context of "replaceable" parts, and as not foreclosing an inquiry into whether a particular part is replaceable. In *Sandvik Aktiebolag v. E.J. Co.*, the defendant offered a drill repair service that retipped the drill when it could no longer be resharpened. 121 F.3d 669, 671, 43 USPQ2d 1620, 1622 (Fed.Cir.1997), *cert. denied,* 523 U.S. 1040, 118 S.Ct. 1337, 140 L.Ed.2d 499 (1998). In that case, retipping did not involve "just attach[ing] a new part for a worn part," but instead required "several steps to replace, configure and integrate the tip onto the shank." We concluded that retipping the drill was impermissible reconstruction, applying the following test:

> There are a number of factors to consider in determining whether a defendant has made a new article, after the device has become spent, including the nature of the actions by the defendant, the nature of the device and how it is designed (namely, whether one of the components of the patented combination has a shorter useful life than the whole), whether a market has developed to manufacture or service the part at issue and objective evidence of the intent of the patentee.

In reaching the conclusion that reconstruction occurred, we noted that "[t]he drill tip was not manufactured to be a replaceable part;" "[i]t was not intended or expected to have a life of temporary duration in comparison to the drill shank;" and "the tip was not attached to the shank in a manner to be easily detachable." Difficult questions may exist as to the line between *Sandvik Aktiebolag* and *Wilbur–Ellis* where readily replaceable parts are not involved. We need not resolve those questions here. At a minimum, repair exists if the part being repaired is a readily replaceable part. *See generally* Donald S. Chisum, 5 *Chisum on Patents* § 16.03[3], at 16–163 (1997) ("Many decisions finding 'repair' involved soft or temporary parts clearly intended to be replaceable.").

We conclude that the same safe harbor exists where activity "akin to repair" is involved as when repair is involved. In both cases, there is no infringement if the particular part is readily "replaceable." For example, in *Surfco,* the patents in suit were directed to a surfboard having releasable fins. In describing *Aro I,* this court noted that "the concept of permissible 'repair' is directed primarily to the replacement of broken or worn parts. *However, permissible 'repair' also includes replacement of parts that are neither broken nor worn." Surfco,* 264 F.3d at 1065, 60 USPQ2d at 1058 (emphasis added). Accordingly, we held that "[t]he patented surf craft [was] not 'recreated' by the substitution of a different set of fins, even when the new fins [were] specifically adapted for use in the patented combination." Having determined that a part is readily replaceable, it is irrelevant whether the part was an essential element of the invention. We reject Husky's attempt to revive the heart of the invention standard in different words.

Husky also urges that the owner of a patented combination has no right to voluntarily replace an unspent part, unless there is a valid public policy justification for the replacement such as increased safety. This argument is directly inconsistent with both *Wilbur–Ellis* and *Surfco.*

In *Wilbur–Ellis,* the replacement of the 1 pound cans with 5 ounce cans did not enhance safety. In *Surfco,* we addressed whether a part needed to be spent or broken before there was a right to replace or modify it. We concluded that it was not a reconstruction to substitute different fins, even if the original fins were not in need of repair or replacement. Although the fins provided enhanced safety features, our holding in *Surfco* was not based on this policy justification, but instead on the right of a purchaser to modify a machine.

V

Here there is no question that the particular parts were readily "replaceable" parts. The design of the injection molding machine allowed replacement of the mold and carrier plates. Typically, after three to five years, a customer purchases a new mold and carrier plate in order to change the preform design. Moreover, Husky sold substitute molds and carrier plates, and provided separate quotations for the injection molding system and the mold/carrier plate assembly. We conclude that the carrier plates were readily replaceable.

In this case, the carrier plate is just one element of the patented combination and not separately patented, and selling replacement parts cannot constitute contributory infringement. We conclude that Husky's customers did not directly infringe the patent by replacing the molds and carrier plates; thus, R & D did not contributorily infringe the '237 patent.

# Paper Converting Machine Co. v. Magna–Graphics Corp.

United States Court of Appeals, Federal Circuit, 1984.
745 F.2d 11.

■ NICHOLS, SENIOR CIRCUIT JUDGE.[a]

This appeal is from a judgment of the United States District Court for the Eastern District of Wisconsin (Reynolds, C.J.), 576 F.Supp. 967, entered on December 1, 1983, and awarding plaintiff Paper Converting Machine Company (Paper Converting) $893,064 as compensation for defendant Magna–Graphics Corporation's (Magna–Graphics) willful infringement of United States Patent No. Re. 28,353. We affirm-in-part and vacate-in-part.

## I

Although the technology involved here is complex, the end product is one familiar to most Americans. The patented invention relates to a machine used to manufacture rolls of densely wound ("hard-wound") industrial toilet tissue and paper toweling. The machine, commonly known as an automatic rewinder, unwinds a paper web continuously under high tension at speeds up to 2,000 feet per minute from a large-diameter paper roll—known as the parent roll or bedroll—and simultaneously rewinds it onto paperboard cores to form individual consumer products.

Before the advent of automatic rewinders, toilet tissue and paper towel producers used "stop-start" rewinders. With these machines, the entire rewinding operation had to cease after a retail-sized "log" was finished so that a worker could place a new mandrel (the shaft for carrying the paperboard core) in the path of the paper web. In an effort to increase production, automatic rewinders were introduced in the early 1950's. These machines automatically moved a new mandrel into the path of the paper web while the machine was still winding the paper web onto another mandrel, and could operate at a steady pace at speeds up to about 1,200 feet per minute.

In 1962, Nystrand, Bradley, and Spencer invented the first successful "sequential" automatic rewinder, a machine which not only overcame previous speed limitations, but also could handle two-ply tissue. This rewinder simultaneously cut the paper web and impaled it on pins against the parent roll. Then, after a new mandrel was automatically moved into place, a "pusher" would move the paper web away from the parent roll and against a glue-covered paperboard core to begin winding a new paper log.

On April 20, 1965, United States Patent No. 3,179,348 (the '348 patent) issued, giving to Paper Converting (to whom rights in the invention had been assigned) patent protection for machines incorporating the sequential rewinding approach.

[a] Note that at the time this case was decided, § 271 did not provide patent holders with the right to prevent others from offering to sell the patented invention.

III

A

In early 1980 Fort Howard became interested in purchasing a new high-speed rewinder line. Both Paper Converting and Magna–Graphics offered bids. Because Magna–Graphics offered to provide an entire rewinder line for about 10 percent less than did Paper Converting, it won the contract. Delivery would have been before the '353 patent expired. Magna–Graphics began to build the contracted for machinery, but before it completed the rewinder, on February 26, 1981, the federal district court in Wisconsin determined that a similar Magna–Graphics' rewinder built for and sold to Scott infringed the '353 patent. The court enjoined Magna–Graphics from any future infringing activity. Because at the time of the federal injunction the rewinder intended for Fort Howard was only 80 percent complete, Magna–Graphics sought a legal way to fulfill its contract with Fort Howard rather than abandon its machine. First, [it tried to build a rewinder that did not infringe the patent, but counsel could not determine whether the new design would be infringing.]

Magna–Graphics thereafter continued to construct the Fort Howard machine, all the while staying in close consultation with its counsel. After finishing substantially all of the machine, Magna–Graphics tested it to ensure that its moving parts would function as intended at a rate of 1,600 feet of paper per minute. Although Magna–Graphics normally fully tested machines at its plant before shipment, to avoid infringement in this instance, Magna–Graphics ran its tests in two stages over a period of several weeks in July and August of 1981.

In the first stage of its test, Magna–Graphics checked the bedroll to determine whether the pushers actuated properly. During this stage of tests, no cutoff blades or pins were installed. In the second stage of the test, Magna–Graphics checked the cutoff roll to determine whether the cutting blade actuated as intended. During this phase of the testing, no pins or pusher pads were installed. At no time during the tests were the pins, pushers, and blade installed and operated together.

To further its scheme to avoid patent infringement, Magna–Graphics negotiated special shipment and assembly details with Fort Howard. Under the advice of counsel, Fort Howard and Magna–Graphics agreed that the rewinder's cutoff and transfer mechanism would not be finally assembled until April 22, 1982, two days after the expiration of the '353 patent. With this agreement in hand, Magna–Graphics shipped the basic rewinder machine to Fort Howard on September 17, 1981, and separately shipped the cutoff roll and bedroll on October 23, 1981. The rewinder machine was not assembled or installed at the Fort Howard plant until April 26, 1982.

B

With this case we are once again confronted with a situation which tests the temporal limits of the American patent grant. See Roche Products, Inc. v. Bolar Pharmaceutical Co., 733 F.2d 858, 221 U.S.P.Q. 937

(Fed.Cir.1984). We must decide here the extent to which a competitor of a patentee can manufacture and test during the life of a patent a machine intended solely for post-patent use. Magna–Graphics asserts that no law prohibits it from soliciting orders for, substantially manufacturing, testing, or even delivering machinery which, if completely assembled during the patent term, would infringe. We notice, but Magna–Graphics adds that it is totally irrelevant, that Paper Converting has lost, during the term of its patent, a contract for the patented machine which it would have received but for the competitor's acts.

The disjunctive language of the patent grant gives a patentee the "right to exclude others from making, using or selling" a patented invention during the 17 years of the patent's existence. 35 U.S.C. § 154. See also 35 U.S.C. § 271. Congress has never deemed it necessary to define any of this triad of excludable activities, however, leaving instead the meaning of "make," "use," and "sell" for judicial interpretation. See Roche Products, Inc. v. Bolar Pharmaceutical Co.

It is undisputed that Magna–Graphics intended to finesse Paper Converting out of the sale of a machine on which Paper Converting held a valid patent during the life of that patent. Given the amount of testing performed here, coupled with the sale and delivery during the patent-term of a "completed" machine (completed by being ready for assembly and with no useful noninfringing purpose), we are not persuaded that the district court committed clear error in finding that the Magna–Graphics' machine infringed the '353 patent.

To reach a contrary result would emasculate the congressional intent to prevent the making of a patented item during the patent's full term of 17 years. If without fear of liability a competitor can assemble a patented item past the point of testing, the last year of the patent becomes worthless whenever it deals with a long lead-time article. Nothing would prohibit the unscrupulous competitor from aggressively marketing its own product and constructing it to all but the final screws and bolts, as Magna–Graphics did here. We rejected any reduction to the patent-term in Roche; we cannot allow the inconsistency in the patent law which would exist if we permitted it here. Magna–Graphics built and tested a patented machine, albeit in a less than preferred fashion.

V

The judgment of the district court awarding damages and prejudgment interest for Paper Converting's lost profits on two automatic rewinder lines is affirmed.

■ NIES, CIRCUIT JUDGE, dissenting-in-part [omitted].


NOTES

**1.** *Literal infringement.* Literal infringement involves a two-part analysis. First, the claims are interpreted. Second, each claim is examined to see if it "reads on" (that is, describes) the so-called "accused device" (or the accused process). The patentee is not required to show copying: even an independent inventor who never heard of the patent or the patentee will be considered an infringer if he practices the invention described in any one of the claims.

a. *Claim interpretation.* As *Fromson* demonstrates, the claims, no matter how carefully drawn, can turn out to be ambiguous. After all, the patentee drafted the application when the discovery was in its infancy: she may not have completely understood what she was observing, and may not have had a literature from which to draw a vocabulary. By the time an infringement action is brought, her wording may not resonate with current understandings in the field, and so the claims may be difficult to interpret. Moreover, as Justice Kennedy makes clear in *Festo*, language does not always fully capture innovation.

Courts considering ambiguous claims will often rely on expert testimony. Experts in the field of the invention can testify on what the wording means to the person with ordinary skill in the art; experts in drafting patents can describe how similar wording is used in other applications. But the language of the cases in this Assignment on the doctrine of equivalents applies equally to literal infringement. The patent claims perform an important notice function. Thus, by far the most important evidence is what the patentee said, did, and wrote in her patent application, because this is what tells the public what she meant to keep and what she meant to release to the public domain. If other claims in the patent shed light on the meaning of particular language, that evidence will be regarded as significant. The prosecution history (the record of proceedings in the PTO, which is made available for issued patents) will also be examined with care, first to see whether words in claims that were cancelled reflect on the meaning of the claims that were allowed, and second, to determine whether the applicant said anything to the examiner that revealed her meaning. Furthermore, if the prosecution history reveals that the examiner regarded some aspect of the claims in the application as unpatentable, and the applicant in response relinquished that claim, the patentee will be estopped from later arguing for an interpretation of the allowed claims that will give her rights over the relinquished technology.

b. *Comparing the claims to the accused device.* Recall the test for novelty: "That which infringes, if later, would anticipate, if earlier."[1] *Fromson* demonstrates that courts do, indeed, apply a test for infringement that is akin to the test for novelty: they determine whether the accused device possesses every element of the claimed invention. Note, however, that this is the test for *literal* infringement. Accordingly, perhaps the test for novelty should be rephrased as "that which *literally* infringes, if later, would anticipate, if earlier."

**2.** *Infringement under the doctrine of equivalents.* The *Graver Tank* Court essentially saw the justification for the doctrine of equivalents as mirroring the policies that underlie the doctrines of consumer confusion and substan-

---

[1] Knapp v. Morss, 150 U.S. 221, 228 (1893). See Assignment 17.

tial similarity, that is, as another way to protect a right holder from trivial variations that could act as substitutes in the marketplace. Note, however, that copyrights arise automatically on fixation and trademarks are registered without an extensive examination. Patents, in contrast, are drafted and examined with care. In some sense then, the question is whether these differences in procedure should affect the decision on who bears the cost of failing to set out the bounds of the intellectual property claim with sufficient care. It could be argued that the patentee should not be "saved" from his mistakes by doctrine of equivalents because forcing him to bear their cost encourages thoroughness at the application stage.

Are the arguments in *Festo* and *Warner–Jenkinson* persuasive? While it is true that language is imperfect at capturing the "essence of a thing," the last paragraph of § 112 introduces flexibility into the drafting process. It allows patentees to claim inventions of more than one element ("combinations") by expressing "a means ... for performing a specified function." An illustration of "means plus function" claiming can be found in the Lipschitz patent of Assignment 14. It allows the patentee to extend the reach of her patent to *literally* cover other embodiments of the inventive concept, including some that could not have been foreseen at the time the claims were drafted. As Note 7 explains, the Federal Circuit has been interpreting means plus function language exceedingly narrowly, but might it not make more sense to restore flexibility there than to rely on the doctrine of equivalents, which creates so much unpredictability?

The Supreme Court also appears to be worried about unforeseeable developments, which the patentee could not have dealt with in drafting, but which make the literal language of a claim easy to circumvent. However, here too the statute has its own solution. The reissue provisions of §§ 251–252 give patentees a two-year window in which to expand the scope of the patent (and to correct for other errors). This provision has an important advantage over common law, for it also protects the public. Those who practiced the invention in reliance on the original scope enjoy "intervening rights," meaning the right to continue activity that began before the reissue. Of course, two years is not a long time. Would it be better to extend the time available for reissue than to rely on the doctrine of equivalents? In the Federal Circuit's consideration of *Warner–Jenkinson*, Judge Lourie had the clever idea of combining these approaches by depriving patentees who fail to seek reissue full recourse to the doctrine of equivalents.[2]

**3.** *The reverse doctrine of equivalents.* Note that *Graver Tank* also envisioned the possibility that an invention could be literally described by a claim, but be so far removed from the patented invention that it should not be considered infringing. Boyden Power–Brake Co. v. Westinghouse[3] is an example. The patentee had shown that a train could be made to brake

---

[2] Judge Lourie would also have penalized patentees who "impair the ability of the public to reasonably understand from the claims what is patented." Hilton Davis Chemical Co. v. Warner–Jenkinson Co., Inc., 62 F.3d 1512, 1547 (Fed. Cir.1995).

[3] 170 U.S. 537 (1898).

much faster if an auxiliary air supply is released against the wheels. The actual device that was patented did not, however, release air nearly fast enough to make much of a difference to railroad safety. The accused device got the air to the wheel effectively. Although this device was literally described by the patent, the Supreme Court found that it was utilizing a different insight, and so did not infringe under the reverse doctrine of equivalents.

The reverse doctrine is infrequently used. Some economists argue that it should be utilized more because it solves a persistent problem in patent law: providing enough incentive to make important improvements.[4] Current law may provide an improver with a patent right of his own, but the right is of limited value because the improver cannot use his improvement without a license from the patentee who has rights to the underlying invention. In theory, this principle of "blocking" patents should work well. The patentee should be willing to license the improver because the improvement makes his own invention more desirable; the two should agree on a royalty rate that reflects the relative benefit that each contributed to the improved device.[5] However, in practice parties have trouble achieving the optimal result. With a robust reverse doctrine of equivalents, improvers know that if they make a sufficiently important improvement, they may be "out from under" the patent. Thus, they have a greater incentive to invent.

**4.** *Delimiting the scope of patent rights.* The doctrines that define the scope of claims are in many ways the most important features of patent law. They set the level of reward (and hence incentive) and they also determine how much freedom the public has to utilize the information that the patentee discovered. Because scope indirectly controls the pace of innovation,[6] it is no wonder that the courts have worked hard to delineate the reach of both literal infringement and infringement under the doctrine of equivalents.

a. *Brakes on literal infringement.* As already noted, the reverse doctrine of equivalents is an important check on literal infringement because it prevents patentees from claiming rights in inventions that far supercede their original insights. However, the reverse doctrine of equivalents comes into play only when the technology of the accused device represents a large leap over the patented invention. Historically, the enablement requirement of § 112, which was discussed in Assignment 14, has been used in cases in which the defendant's technology lies closer to the patentee's. In that context, the enablement requirement limits the patentee by creating a

---

[4] See, e.g., Robert P. Merges and Richard R. Nelson, On the Complex Economics of Patent Scope, 90 Colum. L. Rev. 839 (1990).

[5] Suzanne Scotchmer, Standing on the Shoulders of Giants: Cumulative Research and the Patent Law, 5 J. Econ. Persp. 29 (1991); Jerry R. Green & Suzanne Scotchmer, On the Division of Profit in Sequential Innovation, 26 RAND J. Econ. 20, 21, 23 (1995).

[6] See, e.g., Pamela Samuelson and Suzanne Scotchmer, The Law and Economics of Reverse Engineering, 111 Yale L.J. 1575 (2002); Julie E. Cohen and Mark A. Lemley, Patent Scope and Innovation in the Software Industry, 89 Cal. L. Rev. 1 (2001); Ted O'Donoghue et al., Patent Breadth, Patent Life, and the Pace of Technological Progress, 7 J. Econ. & Mgmt. Strategy 1 (1998).

defense whenever a person with ordinary skill in the art could not have used the patent's disclosure to practice the defendant's technology without undue experimentation.[7]

More recently, the Federal Circuit has also begun to rely on the written description requirement of § 112 as a limit on scope. As noted in Assignment 14, that requirement is usually used in connection with interferences and claim amendments, to assure that the patentee was "in possession of the invention" as of the priority date claimed. In a new series of cases, it is also used as a defense to infringement. The leading case is Gentry Gallery, Inc. v. Berkline Corp.,[8] where a patent for sectional sofa with side-by-side recliners separated by a "fixed console" was held not to be infringed by a sectional sofa with recliners separated by a fold-down table top. The court reasoned that the patent specification "must clearly allow persons of ordinary skill in the art to recognize that [the inventor] invented what is claimed,"[9] and the specification failed to show that the patentee invented the sofa with the fold-down table.

A careful student of the § 112 cases will note that the Federal Circuit sometimes appears to use written description and enablement concepts interchangeably, thereby raising two questions. First, should two separate requirements be read into the language of § 112? If so, what exactly are the differences between them?[10] Furthermore, many of these cases arise in connection with patents on genetic sequences. In this context, they tend to limit patentees to almost the exact sequence recited in the claim. Is this too limiting a scope? After all, genetic sequences are not valuable for their structure per se (in the way that many chemical compounds are). Rather, their value lies in the information the sequence conveys to the body. That is, the value of the sequence is really in the protein that the sequence causes to be formed.[11] If a second comer can freely use the patent disclosure to manufacture a new sequence that conveys the same instructions—for instance, it instructs the body to produce the exact same protein—won't the patentee's market be undermined? Will patents susceptible to this kind of imitation retain enough value to motivate the optimum level of biotechnology research?

b. *Brakes on the doctrine of equivalents.* Reading between the lines of *Warner–Jenkinson* and *Festo*, you can see that the Federal Circuit has been very concerned that the doctrine of equivalents is unworkable, unpredictable, and takes too much of a role in determining patent scope. To curb these trends, the following issues have been emphasized:

---

[7] See, e.g., Fiers v. Revel, 984 F.2d 1164, 1171 (Fed.Cir.1993).

[8] 134 F.3d 1473 (Fed.Cir.1998).

[9] *Id.* at 1479, citing, In re Gosteli, 872 F.2d 1008, 1012 (Fed.Cir.1989).

[10] See, e.g., Arti K. Rai, Engaging Facts and Policy: A Multi–Institutional Approach to Patent System Reform, 103 Colum. L. Rev. 1035 (2003).

[11] Rebecca S. Eisenberg, Re–Examining The Role of Patents in Appropriating the Value of DNA Sequences, 49 Emory L.J. 783 (2000).

i. *Nonobviousness.* One of the oldest limits on the doctrine of equivalents is that the patentee cannot use it to stretch the patent to encompass activity that would have been considered obvious (or non-novel) at the time he made his invention. That is, the doctrine cannot be used to acquire exclusive rights over inventions that could not have been patented in the first place. In Wilson Sporting Goods Co. v. David Geoffrey & Assoc.,[12] Judge Rich attempted to make this analysis easier. He suggested constructing a hypothetical claim that would cover the accused product. Then, ask whether that claim could have been patented at the time the application on the patent in issue was pending.

ii. *Prosecution history estoppel.* Both *Warner–Jenkinson* and *Festo* focused on preventing patentees from using the doctrine of equivalents to recapture rights that were relinquished during prosecution. Thus, *Festo* stated that the "patentee's decision to narrow his claims through amendment may be presumed to be a general disclaimer of the territory between the original claim and the amended claim." This use of amendments raises several questions.

First, which amendments "count" for these purposes? Many patent lawyers had interpreted *Warner–Jenkinson* as applying prosecution history estoppel to an amendment only when it was *required* by the examiner, and then, only when it was aimed at *avoiding prior art.* However, when *Festo* was first decided in the Federal Circuit, that court was considerably more exacting. It held that both voluntary and involuntary amendments could estop the patentee, and that an amendment aimed at meeting *any* of the statutory requirements of patentability qualified. Presumably, even something as trivial as correcting a translation could give rise to estoppel. Although the Supreme Court's *Festo* decision noted that "truly cosmetic" amendments are not to be considered narrowing, it did not provide complete clarification of this issue. On remand, the Federal Circuit essentially reiterated its position. Thus, every "noncosmetic" amendment must now be scrutinized to determine whether it bars use of the doctrine of equivalents, no matter what its basis and, irrespective of whether the amendment was required by the PTO or was purely voluntary.[13]

The next issue is *when* a narrowing amendment bars use of the doctrine of equivalents. The *Festo* Court described three important situations when an amendment *cannot* be reasonably viewed as surrendering subject matter: 1) when the equivalent was "unforeseeable at the time of the application;" 2) when the rationale for the amendment "bear[s] no more than a tangential relation to the equivalent in question;" and 3) when there is "some other reason" to think that the "patentee could not reasonably be expected to have described the insubstantial substitute in question." If Justice Kennedy is right to think that language is too

---

[12] 904 F.2d 677 (Fed.Cir.1990).

[13] Festo Corp. v. Shoketsu Kinzoku Kogyo Kabushiki Co., Ltd., 344 F.3d 1359 (Fed. Cir. 2003).

imprecise to "capture the essence of a thing," how easy will it be to apply these exceptions?[14]

Once it is determined that an amendment is narrowing and not within one of the exceptions described above, the next issue is to determine the amendment's precise effect: how much territory it surrenders. In its first opinion in *Festo*, the Federal Circuit had adopted a *per se* rule—an absolute barrier to enlarging the scope of an element of a claim if that element had been the subject of a narrowing amendment. Apparently, the Federal Circuit was concerned that a more lenient rule would be difficult to apply, thereby making it impossible for competitors to know exactly what they can do by way of inventing around. That aspect of the Federal Circuit's decision was clearly reversed by the Supreme Court, which held that the doctrine of equivalents can be used, even on elements that were the subject of narrowing amendments, so long as nothing that was specifically relinquished is recovered. Again, given the difficulties of language, will it be easy to parse amendments so precisely?

In addition to reiterating its position on points that the Supreme Court left unclear, the Federal Circuit's remand decision in *Festo* set out the procedures to be used to determine the effect of amendments on the doctrine of equivalents. According to Judge Lourie, a court must first determine whether an amendment narrowed the literal scope of the claim. If it was narrowing, then the court decides whether the amendment was substantially related to patentability. If the prosecution history fails to reveal the reason for the amendment, then the court is to presume that the amendment was related to patentability, but the patentee must be given an opportunity to rebut the presumption. The patentee can do that by presenting expert testimony and extrinsic evidence on the factual question of whether the equivalent was unforeseeable, per the Supreme Court's first exception. The patentee could also use the record of the prosecution to show the amendment bore a tangential relationship to the equivalent, per the second exception. Further, the patentee can present reasons, such as shortcomings in language, or factors in the record, to show "some other reason" for the amendment, per the third exception. If the presumption cannot be rebutted in one of these ways, then the court must take up the question of the scope of the surrendered subject matter.

Is this standard too strict? In a concurring opinion, Judge Newman suggested that the framework developed is "one that few patentees can survive."[15] Is the test too complicated? Judge Rader's concurrence noted that patent prosecution is replete with amendments, and that "exceptions to an exception to an exception to the standard rule of infringement" will make it difficult for practitioners to predict the scope of patent claims.[16]

Will the emphasis on the amendment process put new pressures on the Patent Office? Will applicants now be less willing to amend their claims to meet examiners' objections and instead appeal rejections? Will they try to

---

[14] See, e.g., Bose Corp. v. JBL, Inc., 274 F.3d 1354 (Fed. Cir. 2001).

[15] 344 F.3d, at 1385.

[16] 344 F.3d, at 1374.

document the reason behind every change? Will they now file many narrow patent applications, hoping that some will not require amendment, and therefore avoid the uncertainties of *Festo*?

c. *The every-element test.* The Federal Circuit has stressed that a variation on the every-element test applies to a doctrine of equivalents analysis. In Pennwalt Corp. v. Durand–Wayland, Inc.,[17] for example, the court required that the accused device contain an equivalent to each and every element of the patented invention. In that case, both inventions sorted fruit by color and weight. The patented invention had discrete electrical components and the progress of the fruit through the sorter could be continuously observed on monitoring equipment. The accused device was computerized. Although it might have been possible to program the equipment to monitor the fruit's progress, it was not so programmed. The court held that there was no infringement under the doctrine of equivalents because the accused device did not have an equivalent to the patented invention's progress tracker.

This approach is supported by language in *Warner–Jenkinson,* but courts following *Pennwalt* have not found the "all-elements" test, as the Federal Circuit calls it, easy to apply. Because the Patent Act does not require patentees to separately identify the elements of their claims, there can be considerable uncertainty as to what features of the patented invention must be duplicated by the accused device. Further, the differences between the accused invention and the patented invention that make literal infringement unavailable, also tend to obscure the element by element comparison.[18] Note that application of the every-element test was also at issue in *Festo,* but the Federal Circuit avoided applying it (and the Supreme Court never considered it), even though there were dissenters who thought it would do a better job than prosecution history estoppel at narrowing the reach of the doctrine of equivalents. Is the problem that the court found the doctrine too hard to apply?

d. *Other factors.* As noted in *Warner–Jenkinson* and *Festo,* the Federal Circuit has also looked at the substantiality of the differences between the claim and the accused device, at the extent to which the infringer engaged in inventive activity as opposed to pure copying. These factors go to the question whether the infringer expended substantial resources on his version of the technology. To the extent the second comer did not free ride, there is less need to find infringement because even though there will be competition, it would not be ruinous competition. Did the Supreme Court pay enough attention to these factors, which level the playing field between the parties?[19]

[17] 833 F.2d 931 (Fed.Cir.1987), cert. denied, 485 U.S. 961 (1988).

[18] See, e.g., Corning Glass Works v. Sumitomo Electric U.S.A., Inc., 868 F.2d 1251 (Fed.Cir.1989); Catalina Marketing Int'l, Inc. v. Coolsavings.com, Inc., 289 F.3d 801 (Fed. Cir. 2002).

[19] *Festo* has spawned a considerable literature; for a small taste, see R. Polk Wagner, Reconsidering Estoppel: Patent Administration and the Failure of Festo, 151 U. Pa. L. Rev. 159 (2002); John F. Duffy, The Festo Decision and the Return of the Supreme Court to the Bar of Patents, 2002 Sup. Ct.

An axiom to parallel the one on literal infringement and anticipation has also been suggested: "that which infringes *under the doctrine of equivalents* if later, would render the invention *obvious*, if earlier." The idea is to make it possible to import some of the important work that the courts have done on the criteria for nonobviousness into the infringement analysis.

**5.** *The role of the jury.* At one time, patent disputes were usually tried to the bench. However, starting in the mid–1980's, parties began to exercise their Seventh Amendment rights to trials by jury. It is not clear why this change occurred. Arguably, it is related to the establishment of the Court of Appeals for the Federal Circuit. Because the standard for setting aside jury verdicts is somewhat more rigorous than the standard for setting aside judicial findings, it is possible that some attorneys have been using juries to insulate their trial-court "wins" from scrutiny by the patent experts who sit on the Federal Circuit. Another explanation is that patentees have discovered that juries tend to favor inventors over infringers, especially in the situation where the inventor is an American or an individual and the infringer is a foreigner or a corporation.

No matter what the explanation, this change in practice has been a major concern to both the Supreme Court and the Federal Circuit. Jury trials are more expensive and slower than bench trials. They also use up more judicial resources. In addition, there is a concern that jurors may be less able to cope with the technical issues raised by patent cases, leading to more incorrect and more unpredictable decisionmaking. In Markman v. Westview Instruments, Inc.,[20] the Supreme Court acknowledged some of these concerns, holding that even in jury-tried cases, the issue of claim interpretation—that is, the issue in *Fromson*—is to be decided by the judge. The Court reasoned that claim construction is neither strictly a question of law (which is always tried to the court) nor strictly a question of fact (which, under the Seventh Amendment, is within the province of the jury in actions at law). Accordingly, "functional considerations" should apply to determine the applicability of the Seventh Amendment. Since judges are better than juries at construing written instruments, the Court found that it makes sense to give judges the duty to interpret patent claims. That allocation of authority has the added benefit of allowing stare decisis to control claim interpretation, with the result that the same claim will usually be interpreted in the same way, thereby making for a more stable and predictable patent system.

*Markman* does, however, create two difficult procedural issues. First, pretrial hearings have proliferated. The attorneys need to develop their jury-trial strategy, so they push the court to construe the claims at an early stage, sometimes well before the presentation of evidence that could help

Rev. 273; Bruce M. Wexler and Henry Park, The Evolving Doctrines of Disclaimer And Prosecution Laches after Festo, 725 PLI/Pat 197 (2002); Anthony H. Azure, Festo's Effect on After–Arising Technology and the Doc-

trine of Equivalents, 76 Wash. L. Rev. 1153 (2001).

[20] 517 U.S. 370 (1996).

the court in understanding the patent.[21] Second, there is the matter of review. If the trial court does construe the claims pretrial (in what is now called a "*Markman* hearing"), should the Federal Circuit consider an appeal of the construction on an interlocutory basis? If the Federal Circuit waits until final judgment, and it turns out that the claims were interpreted incorrectly, then the jury part of the case may need to be repeated. For example, in the infringement part of the case, the jury will not have been comparing the accused device to the correct claims. So far, however, the Federal Circuit has rejected the possibility of an immediate appeal as counter to the usual federal practice of waiting for final judgment.[22]

*Markman* controls only claim construction—in other words, literal infringement. After it was decided, it was forcefully argued that another way to cabin the doctrine of equivalents would be to allocate that issue to the trial judge as well. Although the Supreme Court refused to consider this issue when it was presented in *Warner–Jenkinson*, the Federal Circuit took matters into its own hands on the remand in *Festo*, holding:

> [T]he presumption of surrender is a question of law to be determined by the court, not a jury. Prosecution history estoppel has traditionally been viewed as equitable in nature, its application being "guided by equitable and public policy principles." Loctite Corp. v. Ultraseal Ltd., 781 F.2d 861, 871 n. 7 (Fed.Cir.1985), overruled on other grounds by Nobelpharma AB v. Implant Innovations, Inc., 141 F.3d 1059, 1068 (Fed.Cir.1998). We have stated on numerous occasions that whether prosecution history estoppel applies, and hence whether the doctrine of equivalents may be available for a particular claim limitation, presents a question of law. The Supreme Court has recognized that, as a legal limitation on the application of the doctrine of equivalents, prosecution history estoppel is a matter to be determined by the court. Questions relating to the application and scope of prosecution history estoppel thus fall within the exclusive province of the court. Accordingly, the determinations concerning whether the presumption of surrender has arisen and whether it has been rebutted are questions of law for the court, not a jury, to decide.[23]

**6.** *Pioneer patents.* One reason that the doctrine of equivalents is controversial is that it is often invoked in connection with "pioneer patents," that is, patents on inventions that give birth to entirely new industries.[24] That it

---

[21] There is an interesting question whether judges actually are better than juries at construing claims, see Kimberly A. Moore, Judges, Juries, and Patent Cases—An Empirical Peek Inside the Black Box, 11 Fed. Circuit B.J. 209 (2001–2002). It isn't even clear that judges will be more consistent in their interpretation of patent claims. For example, compare CVI/Beta Ventures, Inc. v. Tura LP, 112 F.3d 1146 (Fed. Cir. 1997) with CVI/Beta Ventures, Inc. v. Custom Optical Frames, Inc., 92 F.3d 1203 (Fed. Cir. 1996)(interpreting the same claim in different ways).

[22] 28 U.S.C. § 1291. See Kimberly A. Moore, Are District Court Judges Equipped to Resolve Patent Cases?, 12 Fed. Circuit B.J. 1 (2002); Craig Allen Nard, Process Considerations in the Age of Markman and Mantras, 2001 U. Ill. L. Rev. 355.

[23] 344 F.3d, at 1367–68 (footnotes and citations omitted).

[24] See, e.g., Hilton Davis Chemical Co. v. Warner–Jenkinson Company, Inc., 62 F.3d

should be invoked in this context is not surprising. Of all inventors, pioneers should receive the largest opportunity for reward because they open new and fruitful directions for research, act as a basis for many other inventions, and, in the end, confer the greatest public benefit. Moreover, inventors who have a choice between working on something known and safe or working on something new and risky will choose the safer course, unless the rewards are structured to compensate for the extra risk. Giving a single entity (the patent holder) broad power over developments may also help a field develop in a more orderly fashion.[25] Further, patents facilitate negotiations among those who wish to participate in that development.[26]

Despite the cogency of these arguments, the view that pioneers should be given broad scope has been attacked. Thus, it has been argued that progress will be more rapid if the public has freedom of movement. That way, there will be competition to utilize the breakthrough insights. In contrast, a patentee with broad rights can refuse to permit others to work in the field. Besides, it can be argued that a broad scope is not necessary to assure an adequate return on investment, because the pioneer inventor has, in addition to the right to sue for literal patent infringement, significant first-mover advantages. That is, as the first on the market, he has a period of exclusivity in which to earn supracompetitive profits, create a loyal customer base, and establish a trademark.[27]

There is another, more subtle reason to give pioneer patents a strict interpretation. Reconsider Assignment 15 on patentable subject matter. There, we saw how difficult it is to draw a line between principles and embodiments. At that time, we saw this line-drawing as critical because we considered it important to make sure that principles remain in the public domain, where they can function as the spring boards for new inventions. In a sense, the issue concerning pioneers reprises that discussion. Indeed, the cases mentioned in that Assignment all involved pioneer inventions (the telephone, the telegraph, the earliest computer programs and biotechnologies), and the Courts' concern was that if the patents were upheld, research would be stifled. But if pioneer patents are given a narrow interpretation, the Courts' concerns would be substantially mitigated. Thus, it would not be so important to draw the difficult line between idea and embodiment absolutely accurately.

**7.** *The doctrine of equivalents and means plus function claiming.* Especially when used with the doctrine of equivalents, means plus function claiming can get out of hand and expand the scope of the patent to embodiments that the inventor did not enable. The last paragraph of § 112 can, however,

---

1512, 1539 (Fed.Cir.1995)(Lourie, J., dissenting). An omitted section of *Graver Tank* also referred to the pioneer patents as a special issue.

[25] See Edmund W. Kitch, The Nature and Function of the Patent System, 20 J.L. & Econ. 265 (1977).

[26] See, e.g., Robert P. Merges, Contracting Into Liability Rules: Intellectual Property Rights and Collective Rights Organizations, 84 Cal. L. Rev. 1293 (1996).

[27] See Nelson and Merges, note 4. See also John R. Thomas, The Question Concerning Patent Law and Pioneer Inventions, 10 High Tech. L.J. 35 (1995).

be read to limit the utility of this provision. It requires that means-plus-function claims "be construed to cover the corresponding structure ... described in the specification and equivalents thereof." According to the Federal Circuit, this language requires that means plus function claims be interpreted with reference to the specification as well as to the language of the claims. Thus, although the specification is usually used as an *example*—one particular embodiment of the claims, in means-plus-function cases, the court now considers the specification a *limit* on the claims. The accused product must duplicate every structure in the specification, or use an equivalent of that exact structure.[28] Furthermore, failure to disclose the structure corresponding to a means plus function clause renders the patent invalid.[29]

Because the Federal Circuit's interpretation of § 112 uses the word "equivalent," it is sometimes conflated with the doctrine of equivalents, but the two are different. *Graver Tank*'s doctrine of equivalents expands the scope of the claims; the requirement of structural equivalents shrinks the scope of claims. The question is whether it shrinks the value of means plus function claiming too much.

**8.** *Contributory infringement. Husky* illustrates one kind of issue arising in cases involving contributory infringement: distinguishing facilitation of repair from activities that enable infringement. Does the case create a useful line, or simply invite sharp practice, such as creative drafting of claims (so that parts are separately covered) and construction of embodiments (so that parts are difficult to change). The next Assignment will take up another vexing question, namely distinguishing actions for contributory infringement from attempts to leverage patent rights into fields where the patentee did not make a contribution. (Again, the question will be whether the courts create a useful line or invite sharp practice). In many of the cases addressing these problems, much turns on whether the item with which the defendant is dealing is a "stable article or commodity of commerce suitable for substantial noninfringing use," § 271(c). For patent law, the main case on that issue is Sony Corp. v. Universal City Studios, Inc.,[30] reproduced in Assignment 11, where the Supreme Court used the *patent* standard for contributory infringement because there was no contributory infringement provision in the copyright statute. Thus, everything that was said about the standard for infringement in *Sony* is directly applicable here.

**9.** *Extraterritoriality.* A U.S. patent is territorial in the sense that it provides for exclusivity only within the United States. If an inventor wants similar protection in another country, he must usually apply for patent protection there. Exceptions to that rule are cases where the patentee can claim that *foreign* activities affect *domestic* patent rights. In Deepsouth

[28] See, e.g., Intellicall, Inc. v. Phonometrics, Inc., 952 F.2d 1384 (Fed.Cir.1992).

[29] See, e.g., Cardiac Pacemakers, Inc. v. St. Jude Medical, Inc., 296 F.3d 1106 (Fed. Cir. 2002).

[30] 464 U.S. 417 (1984).

Packing Co. v. Laitram Corp.,[31] for example, the patent covered machinery for shrimp deveining. The alleged infringer was selling the machines in a disassembled form for export, with simple instructions allowing the foreign purchaser to put them together with about an hour's worth of work. The Supreme Court held that no infringement of the U.S. patent had occurred, partly because it considered the invention a combination, and thought that combinations could not be infringed until all elements are assembled; in part because it thought the patentee was trying to give extraterritorial application to the patent. The second part of the Court's reasoning was legislatively overruled in § 271(f). Recognizing the significance of foreign sales to the overall reward the patentee earns, Congress redefined conduct of the type at issue in *Deepsouth Packing* as infringing. Did the Federal Circuit effectively overrule the first part of the Court's reasoning in *Paper Converting*?

At the time of *Deepsouth Packing*, patentees had a second concern with foreign activities. Because U.S. process patents were only considered infringed by activity based in the United States, patented processes could be utilized abroad with impunity. The products made by the processes could then be imported into the United States, where they could be priced to undercut sales by domestic, royalty-paying producers. As a result, the income stream to the patentee was diminished and the rewards of innovation reduced. Section 271(g) brought an end to this practice by considering products made with patented processes to be infringing, even when manufacture occurs abroad. Section 103(b) was aimed at curing another extraterritoriality problem, see Assignment 18, Note 4.

**10.** *Exclusive rights to offer to sell and to import.* These two rights were added to the Patent Act in 1994 to conform it to the TRIPS Agreement. Neither has been the subject of significant dispute as yet, but there is reason to hope that they will take the pressure off the courts to construe activity such as that which took place is *Deepsouth Packing* and *Paper Converting* as "uses" of the patented work. Now some of that activity will probably be regarded as offering the patented invention for sale. However, one need only look at the cases on what is considered "on sale" for purposes of § 102(b), see Assignment 19, to realize that these provisions will probably breed extensive litigation of their own.[32]

---

[31] 406 U.S. 518 (1972).

[32] See, e.g., Timothy R. Holbrook, Liability for the "Threat Of A Sale": Assessing Patent Infringement for Offering to Sell an Invention and Implications For The On–Sale Patentability Bar and Other Forms of Infringement, 43 Santa Clara L. Rev. 751 (2003).

# THE INTEREST IN PUBLIC ACCESS

## 1. INTRODUCTION

The previous Assignment was principally aimed at demonstrating how infringement is defined to assure patentees an adequate return on investment. However, as with copyright and trademark, a mechanism is also needed to balance the competing interests of society so as to achieve optimal levels of creativity and usage. For patentable material, this adjustment is particularly critical because the patent right prohibits even independent inventors from exploiting their work. As we saw above, one way to protect the public interest lies in the definition of patent scope. In addition, *Husky*'s discussion of the right to repair began an investigation into judicially-created exceptions to the patent right. This Assignment examines other common law approaches to restraining the patentee, such as the right to experiment, patent misuse, and the first sale doctrine. It also looks at compulsory licensing and sovereign immunity as ways to promote public interests. Finally, as Note 1 indicates, the antitrust laws can also be to control the manner in which patentees exploit their unique positions in the marketplace.

## 2. PRINCIPAL PROBLEM

CFTD, the public interest organization of Assignments 18 and 21, is back in our office. Having just learned that it will probably be guilty of infringement if it distributes a purified component of patented Drug X, CFTD is now (somewhat belated) concerned about its past activities.

Here is what happened. CFTD was interested in Drug X, which is the only known treatment for a certain terminal disease, but which cannot be used in its end stages because of side effects. CFTD had the idea that purifying X could eliminate the material causing the side effects. It began its investigation by asking Alpha Co., the holder of the patent on X, for permission to use it. When Alpha refused, CFTD asked Dr. Beta to write it a prescription for X. Through ordinary market channels, CFTD used the prescription to purchase pills containing X. Ignoring the label on the bottle, "FOR MEDICINAL USE ONLY," CFTD scientists used a standard series of techniques to purify X from the tableting and coating materials used in fabrication. They quickly ascertaining that X is indeed made up of components. After CFTD identified the components as (R)-X and (S)-X, the scientists developed a method for separation, tested each, and found that only (R)-X actually treats the disease; (S)-X causes the side effects that require termination of treatment.

CFTD's foremost concern is to find out whether any of its activities infringed Alpha's patent. It is also planning for the future. (R)-X really is a better treatment for the disease. Accordingly, CFTD is asking other lawyers at our firm to seek FDA approval for (R)-X and to apply for similar regulatory approval in foreign countries.

Finally, CFTD notes that (R)-X is the only available therapy for the approximately 15,000 patients who, at any point in time, are in the end stage of disease. It has asked our associates to explore the possibility of applying for an exclusive right under the Orphan Drug Act, 21 U.S.C. §§ 360aa-dd, which is partially reproduced below. What CFTD needs from us is an assessment of whether these activities will infringe Alpha's patent on X.

## 21 U.S.C. § 360bb. Designation of drugs for rare diseases or conditions

(a) Request by sponsor; preconditions; "rare disease or condition" definition

(1) The manufacturer or the sponsor of a drug may request the Secretary to designate the drug as a drug for a rare disease or condition. . . .

(2) For purposes of paragraph (1), the term "rare disease or condition" means any disease or condition which (A) affects less than 200,000 persons in the United States, or (B) affects more than 200,000 in the United States and for which there is no reasonable expectation that the cost of developing and making available in the United States a drug for such disease or condition will be recovered from sales in the United States of such drug
. . .

## § 360cc. Protection for drugs for rare diseases or conditions

(a) Exclusive approval, certification, or license

Except as provided in subsection (b) of this section, if the Secretary—

(1) approves an application filed pursuant to § 355 of this title, or

(2) issues a certification under § 357 of this title, or

(3) issues a license under § 262 of Title 42

for a drug designated under § 360bb of this title for a rare disease or condition, the Secretary may not approve another application under § 355 of this title, issue another certification under § 262 of Title 42 for such drug for such disease or condition for a person who is not the holder of such approved application, of such certification, or of such license until the expiration of seven years from the date of the approval of the approved application, the issuance of the certification, or the issuance of the license. . . .

## 3. Materials for Solution of Principal Problem

A. STATUTORY MATERIAL: § 271

B. CASES:

## Special Equipment Co. v. Coe

Supreme Court of the United States, 1945.
324 U.S. 370, 65 S.Ct. 741, 89 L.Ed. 1006.

■ Mr. Chief Justice Stone delivered the opinion of the Court.

This is a suit in equity, brought in the District Court of the District of Columbia, under R.S. § 4915, 35 U.S.C.A. § 63, to compel respondent, the Commissioner of Patents, to issue a patent upon an application for a subcombination of the elements of a machine for which the inventor had previously filed a patent application. The district court gave judgment for respondent. The Court of Appeals for the District affirmed, 144 F.2d 497, 498, and we granted certiorari, 323 U.S. 697, 65 S.Ct. 120. The question is whether the Court of Appeals correctly rested its decision upon the ground that petitioner did not intend to make or use the invention and that the purpose of seeking the patent was to exploit and protect the combination invention embodied in the complete machine, of which the subcombination is a part.

The patent application for the complete machine discloses a highly ingenious device, which is said to have achieved a great advance in the art by increasing the speed and skill with which pears are prepared for canning, and to result in a great saving of manpower. The ... application for the subcombination specifies and claims the [complete] apparatus [which cleaves, cores, and pares pears], but without the splitting knife. In the operation of the device thus claimed the pears are pre-split by hand. [The Commissioner rejected this application].

The District Court sustained the Commissioner [and the Court of Appeals affirmed] for [among other reasons] that ... [i]t thought that the grant of a patent which the patentee has no intention of exploiting as a distinct invention "for the purpose of blocking the development of machines which might be constructed by others," is inconsistent with the constitutional requirement that the patent grant must "promote the Progress of Science and useful Arts."

Section 4886 of the Revised Statutes, 35 U.S.C.A. § 31, authorizes "any person who has invented * * * any new and useful * * * machine" to "obtain a patent." The patent grant is not of a right to the patentee to use the invention, for that he already possesses. It is a grant of the right to exclude others from using it.

It by no means follows that such a grant is an inconsistent or inappropriate exercise of the constitutional authority of Congress.... Congress, in the choice of means of promoting the useful arts by patent grants, could have provided that the grant should be conditioned upon the use of the patented invention, as in fact it did provide by the Act of 1832 (4 Stat. 577) authorizing the issue of patents to aliens conditioned upon the use of the invention, which provision was later repealed (5 Stat. 117, 125). But Congress was aware that an unpatented invention could be suppressed and the public thus deprived of all knowledge or benefit of it. It could have concluded that the useful arts would be best promoted by compliance with the conditions of the statutes which it did enact, which require that patents be granted only for a limited term upon an application fully disclosing the invention and the manner of making and using it. It thus gave to the inventor limited opportunity to gather material rewards for his invention and secured to the public the benefits of full knowledge of the invention and the right to use it upon the expiration of the patent.

[The Court goes on to find that the assumption that the patentee would suppress the second patent was not warranted by the record].

Reversed.

■ MR. JUSTICE DOUGLAS, with whom MR. JUSTICE BLACK and MR. JUSTICE MURPHY concur, dissenting.

It is a mistake ... to conceive of a patent as but another form of private property. The patent is a privilege "conditioned by a public purpose." Mercoid Corp. v. Mid–Continent Inv. Co., 320 U.S. 661, 666, 64 S.Ct. 268, 271, 88 L.Ed. 376. The public purpose is "to promote the Progress of Science and useful Arts." The exclusive right of the inventor is but the means to that end. That was early recognized by this Court ... See Pennock v. Dialogue, 2 Pet. 1, 19, 27 U.S. 1, 19, 7 L.Ed. 327; Kendall v. Winsor, 21 How. 322, 327, 328, 62 U.S. 322, 327, 328, 16 L.Ed. 165; Seymour v. Osborne, 11 Wall. 516, 533, 534, 78 U.S. 516, 533, 534, 20 L.Ed. 33. But the Paper Bag case [Continental Paper Bag Co. v. Eastern Paper Bag Co., 210 U.S. 405, 28 S.Ct. 748, 52 L.Ed. 1122 (1908)] marked a radical departure from that theory. It treated the "exclusive" right of the inventor as something akin to an "absolute" right. It subordinated the public purpose of the grant to the self-interest of the patentee.

The result is that suppression of patents has become commonplace. Patents are multiplied to protect an economic barony or empire, not to put new discoveries to use for the common good. "It is common practice to make an invention and to secure a patent to block off a competitor's progress. By studying his ware and developing an improvement upon it, a concern may 'fence in' its rival; by a series of such moves, it may pin the trade enemy within a technology which rapidly becomes obsolete. As often as not such maneuvers retard, rather than promote, the progress of the useful arts.... " Hamilton, Patents and Free Enterprise (1941), p. 161. The use of a new patent is suppressed so as to preclude experimentation which might result in further invention by competitors. A whole technology is blocked off. The result is a clog to our economic machine and a barrier to an economy of abundance.

It is difficult to see how ... suppression of patents can be reconciled with the provision of the statute which authorizes a grant of the "exclusive right to make, use, and vend the invention or discovery." Rev.Stat. § 4884, 35 U.S.C. § 40, 35 U.S.C.A. § 40. How may the words "to make, use, and vend" be read to mean "not to make, not to use, and not to vend?" Take the case of an invention or discovery which unlocks the doors of science and reveals the secrets of a dread disease. Is it possible that a patentee could be permitted to suppress that invention for seventeen years (the term of the letters patent) and withhold from humanity the benefits of the cure? But there is no difference in principle between that case and any case where a patent is suppressed because of some immediate advantage to the patentee.

■ MR. JUSTICE RUTLEDGE, dissenting (omitted).

## Adams v. Burke

Supreme Court of the United States, 1873.
84 U.S. (17 Wall.) 453, 21 L.Ed. 700.

■ MR. JUSTICE MILLER delivered the opinion of the court.

On the 26th day of May, 1863, letters-patent were granted to Merrill & Horner, for a certain improvement in coffinlids, giving to them the exclusive right of making, using, and vending to others to be used, the said improvement. On the 13th day of March, 1865, Merrill & Horner, the patentees, by an assignment duly executed and recorded, assigned to Lockhart & Seelye, of Cambridge, in Middlesex County, Massachusetts, all the right, title, and interest which the said patentees had in the invention described in the said letters-patent, for, to, and in a circle whose radius is ten miles, having the city of Boston as a centre. They subsequently assigned the patent, or what right they retained in it, to one Adams.

Adams now filed a bill in the court below, against a certain Burke, an undertaker, who used in the town of Natick (a town about seventeen miles from Boston, and therefore outside of the circle above mentioned) coffins with lids of the kind patented, alleging him to be an infringer of their patent, and praying for an injunction, discovery, profits, and other relief suitable against an infringer.

We have repeatedly held that where a person had purchased a patented machine of the patentee or his assignee, this purchase carried with it the right to the use of that machine so long as it was capable of use, and that the expiration and renewal of the patent, whether in favor of the original patentee or of his assignee, did not affect this right. The true ground on which these decisions rest is that the sale by a person who has the full right to make, sell, and use such a machine carries with it the right to the use of that machine to the full extent to which it can be used in point of time.

The right to manufacture, the right to sell, and the right to use are each substantive rights, and may be granted or conferred separately by the patentee.

But, in the essential nature of things, when the patentee, or the person having his rights, sells a machine or instrument whose sole value is in its use, he receives the consideration for its use and he parts with the right to restrict that use. The article, in the language of the court, passes without the limit of the monopoly. That is to say, the patentee or his assignee having in the act of sale received all the royalty or consideration which he claims for the use of his invention in that particular machine or instrument, it is open to the use of the purchaser without further restriction on account of the monopoly of the patentees.

It seems to us that, although the right of Lockhart & Seelye to manufacture, to sell, and to use these coffin-lids was limited to the circle of ten miles around Boston, that a purchaser from them of a single coffin acquired the right to use that coffin for the purpose for which all coffins are used. That so far as the use of it was concerned, the patentee had received his consideration, and it was no longer within the monopoly of the patent. It would be to engraft a limitation upon the right of use not contemplated by the statute nor within the reason of the contract to say that it could only be used within the ten-miles circle.

A careful examination of the plea satisfies us that the defendant, who, as an undertaker, purchased each of these coffins and used it in burying the body which he was employed to bury, acquired the right to this use of it freed from any claim of the patentee, though purchased within the ten-mile circle and used without it.

The decree of the Circuit Court dismissing the plaintiff's bill is, therefore, AFFIRMED.

■ MR. JUSTICE BRADLEY (with whom concurred JUSTICES SWAYNE and STRONG), dissenting (omitted).


# Madey v. Duke University

United States Court of Appeals for the Federal Circuit, 2002.
307 F.3d 1351.

■ GAJARSA, CIRCUIT JUDGE.

Dr. John M.J. Madey ("Madey") appeals from a judgment of the United States District Court for the Middle District of North Carolina. Madey sued Duke University ("Duke"), bringing claims of patent infringement and various other federal and state law claims. The district court dismissed-in-part certain patent infringement claims and dismissed certain other claims. After discovery, the district court granted summary judgment in favor of Duke on the remaining claims. For [one] set of alleged infringing acts, it held that the experimental use defense applied to Duke's use of Madey's patented laser technology.[a] The district court erred in its partial dismissal [and] erred in applying the experimental use defense. Accordingly, we reverse-in-part and remand.

---

[a] [The discussion on most of these claims, including certain patent claims, has been omitted because they raise issues irrelevant to this Assignment—eds.]

## BACKGROUND

In the mid–1980s Madey was a tenured research professor at Stanford University. At Stanford, he had an innovative laser research program, which was highly regarded in the scientific community. An opportunity arose for Madey to consider leaving Stanford and take a tenured position at Duke. Duke recruited Madey, and in 1988 he left Stanford for a position in Duke's physics department. In 1989 Madey moved his free electron laser ("FEL") research lab from Stanford to Duke. The FEL lab contained substantial equipment, requiring Duke to build an addition to its physics building to house the lab. In addition, during his time at Stanford, Madey had obtained sole ownership of two patents practiced by some of the equipment in the FEL lab.

At Duke, Madey served for almost a decade as director of the FEL lab. During that time the lab continued to achieve success in both research funding and scientific breakthroughs. However, a dispute arose between Madey and Duke. Duke contends that, despite his scientific prowess, Madey ineffectively managed the lab. Madey contends that Duke sought to use the lab's equipment for research areas outside the allocated scope of certain government funding, and that when he objected, Duke sought to remove him as lab director. Duke eventually did remove Madey as director of the lab in 1997. The removal is not at issue in this appeal, however, it is the genesis of this unique patent infringement case. As a result of the removal, Madey resigned from Duke in 1998. Duke, however, continued to operate some of the equipment in the lab. Madey then sued Duke for patent infringement of his two patents.

### The Patents and Infringing Equipment

One of Madey's patents, U.S. Patent No. 4,641,103 ("the '103 patent"), covers a "Microwave Electron Gun" used in connection with free electron lasers. The other patent, U.S. Patent No. 5,130,994 ("the '994 patent"), is titled "Free–Electron Laser Oscillator For Simultaneous Narrow Spectral Resolution And Fast Time Resolution Spectroscopy." The details of these two patents are not material to the issues on appeal. Their use in the lab, however, as embodied in certain equipment, is central to this appeal.

The equipment at the Duke FEL lab that practices the subject matter disclosed and claimed in the patents is set forth in the list below, which first lists the equipment and then the patent(s) it embodies.

—An infrared FEL called the "Mark III FEL," embodying the '994 patent and the '103 patent (by incorporating the microwave electron gun in the infrared FEL).

—A "Storage Ring FEL," embodying the same patents as the Mark III FEL because it incorporates a Mark III FEL.

The alleged infringing devices are the Mark III FEL [and] the Storage Ring FEL. Although it is not clear from the record, perhaps because Duke defended by asserting experimental use and government license defenses,

Duke seems to concede that the alleged infringing devices and methods read on the claims of the patents.

## The District Court's Dismissal Opinion

Duke moved to dismiss the infringement claims under the '103 patent under FRCP 12(b)(1) for lack of subject matter jurisdiction. [The district court analyzed the claims on which dismissal was sought as falling into two categories: (i) use in furtherance of an Office of Naval Research ("ONR") grant; and (ii) use that exceeds the authorized scope of the ONR grant. It then granted the motion in part. It reasoned that Madey bore the burden of setting forth specific evidence of "jurisdictional facts" to show that a genuine issue of fact exists. Uses "under the authority of the government research grant" were dismissed without prejudice on the ground that they qualified as uses "by or for the United States," and therefore jurisdiction was in the Court of Federal Claims, 28 U.S.C. § 1498.] The court acknowledged that discovery would be necessary to determine the nature and extent of Duke's private use.

## The District Court's Summary Judgment Opinion

*The Patent Motion and the Experimental Use Defense*

The district court acknowledged a common law "exception" for patent infringement liability for uses that, in the district court's words, are "solely for research, academic or experimental purposes." (citing *Deuterium Corp. v. United States,* 19 Cl.Ct. 624, 631, 14 USPQ2d 1636, 1642 (1990); *Whittemore v. Cutter,* 29 F. Cas. 1120 (C.C.D.Mass.1813) (No. 17,600); and citing two commentators[b]). The district court recognized the debate over the scope of the experimental use defense, but cited this court's opinion in *Embrex, Inc. v. Service Engineering Corp.,* 216 F.3d 1343, 1349, 55 USPQ2d 1161, 1163 (Fed.Cir.2000) to hold that the defense was viable for experimental, non-profit purposes. (Citing *Embrex,* noting that courts should not "construe the experimental use rule so broadly as to allow a violation of the patent laws in the guise of 'scientific inquiry,' when that inquiry has definite, cognizable, and not insubstantial commercial purposes" (quoting *Roche Prods., Inc. v. Bolar Pharm. Co.,* 733 F.2d 858, 863, 221 USPQ 937, 940 (Fed.Cir.1984))[c] ).

After having recognized the experimental use defense, the district court then fashioned the defense for application to Madey in the passage set forth below.

[b] Janice M. Mueller, No "Dilettante Affair": Rethinking the Experimental Use Exception to Patent Infringement for Biomedical Research Tools, 76 Wash. L.Rev. 1, 17 (2001); 5 Chisum on Patents § 16.03[1] (2000).

[c] The accused infringer in *Roche* sought to assert the experimental use defense to allow early development of a generic drug. After the *Roche* decision, however, Congress changed the law, overruling *Roche* in part, but without impacting the experimental use doctrine. Congress provided limited ability for a company to practice a patent in furtherance of a drug approval application. [See 35 U.S.C. § 271(e).]

Given this standard [for experimental use], for [Madey] to overcome his burden of establishing actionable infringement in this case, he must establish that [Duke] has not used the equipment at issue "solely for an experimental or other non-profit purpose." 5 Donald S. Chisum, *Chisum on Patents* § 16.03[1] (2000). More specifically, [Madey] must sufficiently establish that [Duke's] use of the patent had "definite, cognizable, and not insubstantial commercial purposes."

On appeal, Madey attacks this passage as improperly shifting the burden to the plaintiff to allege and prove that the defendant's use was not experimental.

Before the district court, Madey argued that Duke's research in its FEL lab was commercial in character and intent. Madey relied on *Pitcairn v. United States,* 212 Ct.Cl. 168, 547 F.2d 1106, 192 USPQ 612 (1976), where the government used patented rotor structures and control systems for a helicopter to test the "lifting ability" and other attributes of the patented technology. The *Pitcairn* court held that the helicopters were not built solely for experimental purposes because they were also built to benefit the government in its legitimate business. Based on language in Duke's patent policy, Madey argues that Duke is in the business of "obtaining grants and developing possible commercial applications for the fruits of its 'academic research.' "

The district court rejected Madey's argument, relying on another statement in the preamble of the Duke patent policy which stated that Duke was "dedicated to teaching, research, and the expansion of knowledge . . . [and] does not undertake research or development work principally for the purpose of developing patents and commercial applications." The district court reasoned that these statements from the patent policy refute any contention that Duke is "in the business" of developing technology for commercial applications. According to the district court, Madey's "evidence" was mere speculation,[d] and thus Madey did not meet his burden of proof to create a genuine issue of material fact. The court went on to state that "[w]ithout more concrete evidence to rebut [Duke's] stated purpose with respect to its research in the FEL lab, Plaintiff has failed to meet its burden of establishing patent infringement by a preponderance of the evidence."

Finally, under its discussion of the Patent Motion, the district court reasoned that Duke's argument that "essentially all" uses of the patents were covered by a license to the government was moot given the experimental use holding.

---

[d] Madey also argued that Duke's acceptance of funding from the government and private foundations was evidence of developing patented devices with commercial intent. The district court also rejected this proposition (citing Ruth v. Stearns–Roger Mfg. Co., 13 F.Supp. 697, 713 (D.Colo.1935) (concluding that the experimental use defense applies when a university uses a patented device in furtherance of its educational purpose); Ronald D. Hartman, Experimental Use as an Exception to Patent Infringement, 67 J. Pat. Off. Soc'y 617, 633 (1985) (concluding that *Ruth* supports application of the experimental use defense to a university's operations in furtherance of its educational function)).

## DISCUSSION

### The District Court's Dismissal Opinion

On appeal, Madey argues that the district court improperly applied 28 U.S.C § 1498(a) by failing to make sufficient supporting determinations. As a result, according to Madey, partial dismissal of the '103 patent infringement claim for Duke's use under the ONR grant was improper. Specifically, Madey argues that the court did not find that Duke's use was "by or for the United States," and that the use was with the "authorization or consent" of the United States. Madey makes the distinction that a research grant is different from a contract to acquire property or services for the government. Duke, on the other hand, attacks Madey's distinction as meaningless, arguing that either a grant or a contract can meet the prerequisites of § 1498(a).

Based on the district court's findings, we agree with Madey that the district court erred in granting the partial dismissal. Madey, however, also asserts that a research grant can never meet the requirements of § 1498(a). We disagree with this proposition.

In general, there are two important features of § 1498(a). It relieves a third party from patent infringement liability, and it acts as a waiver of sovereign immunity and consent to liability by the United States. This general mantra influences the application of § 1498(a) between private parties because in such a situation § 1498(a) is an affirmative defense. As a result, one possible consequence of dismissal based on this defense is a suit against the government in the Court of Federal Claims. In the sphere of this sovereign immunity influence on the defense, the [district court made two errors. First, because] § 1498(a) is not jurisdictional, the jurisdictional facts doctrine does not apply. Therefore, the basis for the district court's partial dismissal was improper.

Second, by failing to explain or demonstrate precisely how the ONR grant authorizes the government's consent to suit or authorizes Duke to use or manufacture the patented articles for the government, the district court has provided no findings or analysis upon which we can base our review of the issue appealed from the court's *Dismissal Opinion*. Although a research grant may not meet the requirements of § 1498(a), from the limited record presented by the parties, it cannot be determined whether the ONR grant may authorize the necessary predicates for § 1498(a).

### The District Court's Application of Experimental Use

On appeal, Madey asserts three primary errors related to experimental use. First, Madey claims that the district court improperly shifted the burden to Madey to prove that Duke's use was not experimental. Second, Madey argues that the district court applied an overly broad version of the very narrow experimental use defense inconsistent with our precedent. Third, Madey attacks the supporting evidence relied on by the district court as overly general and not indicative of the specific propositions and findings required by the experimental use defense, and further argues that there is no support in the record before us to allow any court to apply the very narrow experimental use defense to Duke's ongoing FEL lab operation. We substantially agree with Madey on all three points. In addition, Madey makes a threshold argument concerning the continued existence of the experimental use doctrine in any form, which we turn to first. Our precedent, to which we are bound, continues to recognize the judicially created experimental use defense, however, in a very limited form.

*The Experimental Use Defense*

Citing the concurring opinion in *Embrex,* Madey contends that the Supreme Court's opinion in *Warner–Jenkinson Co. v. Hilton Davis Chem. Co.,* 520 U.S. 17, 117 S.Ct. 1040, 137 L.Ed.2d 146 (1997) eliminates the experimental use defense. *Embrex,* 216 F.3d at 1352–53, 55 USPQ2d at 1166–67 (Rader, J., concurring). The Supreme Court held in *Warner–Jenkinson* that intent plays no role in the application of the doctrine of equivalents. Madey implicitly argues that the experimental use defense necessarily incorporates an intent inquiry, and thus is inconsistent with *Warner–Jenkinson.* Like the majority in *Embrex,* we do not view such an inconsistency as inescapable, and conclude the experimental use defense persists albeit in the very narrow form articulated by this court in *Embrex,* 216 F.3d at 1349, 55 USPQ2d at 1163, and in *Roche,* 733 F.2d at 863, 221 USPQ at 940.

*The District Court Improperly Shifted the Burden to Madey*

The district court held that in order for Madey to overcome his burden to establish actionable infringement, he must establish that Duke did not use the patent-covered free electron laser equipment solely for experimental or other non-profit purposes. Madey argues that this improperly shifts the burden to the patentee and conflates the experimental use defense with the initial infringement inquiry.

We agree with Madey that the district court improperly shifted the burden to him. The defense, if available at all, must be established by Duke.

*The District Court's Overly Broad Conception of Experimental Use*

Madey argues, and we agree, that the district court had an overly broad conception of the very narrow and strictly limited experimental use defense. The district court stated that the experimental use defense inoculated uses that "were solely for research, academic, or experimental purposes," and that the defense covered use that "is made for experimental, non-profit purposes only." Both formulations are too broad and stand in sharp contrast to our admonitions in *Embrex* and *Roche* that the experimental use defense is very narrow and strictly limited. In *Embrex,* we followed the teachings of *Roche* and *Pitcairn* to hold that the defense was very narrow and limited to actions performed "for amusement, to satisfy idle curiosity, or for strictly philosophical inquiry." Further, use does not qualify for the experimental use defense when it is undertaken in the "guise of scientific inquiry" but has "definite, cognizable, and not insubstantial commercial purposes." The concurring opinion in *Embrex* expresses a similar view: use is disqualified from the defense if it has the "slightest commercial implication." Moreover, use in keeping with the legitimate business of the alleged infringer does not qualify for the experimental use defense. The district court supported its conclusion with a citation to *Ruth v. Stearns–Roger Mfg. Co.,* 13 F.Supp. 697, 713 (D.Colo.1935), a case that is not binding precedent for this court.

The *Ruth* case represents the conceptual dilemma that may have led the district court astray. Cases evaluating the experimental use defense are few, and those involving non-profit, educational alleged infringers are even fewer. In *Ruth,* the court concluded that a manufacturer of equipment covered by patents was not liable for contributory infringement because the end-user purchaser was the Colorado School of Mines, which used the equipment in furtherance of its educational purpose. Thus, the combination of apparent lack of commerciality, with the non-profit status of an educational institution, prompted the court in *Ruth,* without any detailed analysis of the character, nature and effect of the use, to hold that the experimental use defense applied. This is not consistent with the binding precedent of our case law postulated by *Embrex, Roche* and *Pitcairn.*

Our precedent clearly does not immunize use that is in any way commercial in nature. Similarly, our precedent does not immunize any conduct that is in keeping with the alleged infringer's legitimate business, regardless of commercial implications. For example, major research universities, such as Duke, often sanction and fund research projects with arguably no commercial application whatsoever. However, these projects unmistakably further the institution's legitimate business objectives, including educating and enlightening students and faculty participating in these projects. These projects also serve, for example, to increase the status of the institution and lure lucrative research grants, students and faculty.

In short, regardless of whether a particular institution or entity is engaged in an endeavor for commercial gain, so long as the act is in furtherance of the alleged infringer's legitimate business and is not solely for amusement, to satisfy idle curiosity, or for strictly philosophical inquiry, the act does not qualify for the very narrow and strictly limited experimental use defense. Moreover, the profit or non-profit status of the user is not determinative.

In the present case, the district court attached too great a weight to the non-profit, educational status of Duke, effectively suppressing the fact that Duke's acts appear to be in accordance with any reasonable interpretation of Duke's legitimate business objectives.[e] On remand, the district court will have to significantly narrow and limit its conception of the experimental use defense. The correct focus should not be on the non-profit status of

[e] Duke's patent and licensing policy may support its primary function as an educational institution. See Duke University Policy on Inventions, Patents, and Technology Transfer (1996), available at http://www.ors.duke.edu/policies/patpol.htm (last visited Oct. 3, 2002). Duke, however, like other major research institutions of higher learning, is not shy in pursuing an aggressive patent licensing program from which it derives a not insubstantial revenue stream.

Duke but on the legitimate business Duke is involved in and whether or not the use was solely for amusement, to satisfy idle curiosity, or for strictly philosophical inquiry.

## Integra Lifesciences I, Ltd. v. Merck KGaA

United States Court of Appeals for the Federal Circuit, 2003.
331 F.3d 860.

[The owner of patents for pharmacologically useful peptides sued the defendant for using its inventions to find new drug treatments. The District Court held the patents infringed. The Federal Circuit affirmed, holding that the defendant's use did not qualify for protection under 35 U.S.C. § 271(e)(1) because that provision permits experimentation "solely for uses reasonably related to the development and submission of information" to the FDA. In the majority's view, finding new drugs is not *solely* aimed at FDA approval. In dissent, Judge Newman (who was not on the *Madey* court), took the opportunity to comment on the curtailment of the common law defense. The following is a short excerpt from her opinion.[a]]

■ NEWMAN, J., dissenting:

The purpose of a patent system is not only to provide a financial incentive to create new knowledge and bring it to public benefit through new products; it also serves to add to the body of published scientific/technologic knowledge. The requirement of disclosure of the details of patented inventions facilitates further knowledge and understanding of what was done by the patentee, and may lead to further technologic advance. The right to conduct research to achieve such knowledge need not, and should

---

[a] The majority (per Judge Rader) commented on Judge Newman's views in a footnote:

In her dissent, Judge Newman takes this opportunity to restate her dissatisfaction with this court's decision in Madey v. Duke Univ., 307 F.3d 1351, 64 USPQ2d 1737 (Fed.Cir.2002). However, the common law experimental use exception is not before the court in the instant case.

The issue before the jury was whether the infringing pre-clinical experiments are immunized from liability via the "FDA exemption," i.e., 35 U.S.C. § 271(e)(1). The district court did not instruct the jury on the common law research exemption with respect to the Merck's infringing activities. On appeal, Merck does not contend that the common law research exemption should apply to any of the infringing activities evaluated by the jury. Neither party has briefed this issue to this court. Moreover,

during oral arguments, counsel for Merck expressly stated that the common law research exemption is not relevant to its appeal. Judge Newman's dissent, however, does not mention that the Patent Act does not include the word "experimental," let alone an experimental use exemption from infringement. See 35 U.S.C. § 271 (2000). Nor does Judge Newman's dissent note that the judge-made doctrine is rooted in the notions of de minimis infringement better addressed by limited damages. Embrex v. Service Eng'g Corp., 216 F.3d 1343, 55 USPQ2d 1161 (Fed.Cir.2000) (Rader, J., concurring); see also Deuterium Corp. v. United States, 19 Cl.Ct. 624, 631, 14 USPQ2d 1636, 1642 (Cl.Ct.1990) ("This court questions whether any infringing use can be de minimis. Damages for an extremely small infringing use may be de minimis, but infringement is not a question of degree.").

not, await expiration of the patent. That is not the law, and it would be a practice impossible to administer. Yet today the court disapproves and essentially eliminates the common law research exemption. This change of law is ill-suited to today's research-founded, technology-based economy.

\* \* \*

The majority's prohibition of all research into patented subject matter is as impractical as it is incorrect. The information contained in patents is a major source of scientific as well as technologic knowledge. Indeed, in many areas of technology, technical information is not published outside of patent documents. A rule that this information cannot be investigated without permission of the patentee is belied by the routine appearance of improvements on patented subject matter, as well as the rapid evolution of improvements on concepts that are patented.

The subject matter of patents may be studied in order to understand it, or to improve upon it, or to find a new use for it, or to modify or "design around" it. Were such research subject to prohibition by the patentee the advancement of technology would stop, for the first patentee in the field could bar not only patent-protected competition, but all research that might lead to such competition, as well as barring improvement or challenge or avoidance of patented technology. Today's accelerated technological advance is based in large part on knowledge of the details of patented inventions and how they are made and used. Prohibition of research into such knowledge cannot be squared with the framework of the patent law.

In the framework of United States patent law there is no obligation that the patentee use the invention; the obligation is to disclose it and describe it and to provide enabling detail whereby it can be duplicated without undue experimentation. The patentee's permission is not required whenever a patented device or molecule is made or modified or investigated. Study of patented information is essential to the creation of new knowledge, thereby achieving further scientific and technologic progress.

Of course, the common law exemption is not unlimited. Indeed, it is a narrow exemption, for it must preserve the patentee's incentive to innovate, an incentive secured only by the right to exclude. It is the patentee who opened the door by providing the initial knowledge, without which there would be nothing to improve. Setting the boundaries of a common law exemption requires careful understanding of the mechanisms of the creation, development, and use of technical knowledge, and of today's complexity of interactions among invention and the innovating fruits of invention. It is the initial inventor whose rights must receive primary consideration in an effective patent law, for the public interest starts with the threshold invention. However, while that threshold invention may (as here) exact tribute from or enjoin commercial and pre-commercial activity, the patent does not bar all research that precedes such activity.

I do not here undertake to define the boundaries of the research exemption for all purposes and all activities, other than to observe that there is a generally recognized distinction between "research" and "development," as a matter of scale, creativity, resource allocation, and often the level of scientific/engineering skill needed for the project; this distinction may serve as a useful divider, applicable in most situations. Like "fair use" in copyright law, the great variety of possible facts may occasionally raise dispute as to particular cases. However, also like fair use, in most cases it will be clear whether the exemption applies.

\* \* \*

The panel majority states that acceptance of a common law research exemption would eliminate patents on "research tools." That is a misperception. There is a fundamental distinction between research into the science and technology disclosed in patents, and the use in research of patented products or methods, the so-called "research tools."

A research tool is a product or method whose purpose is use in the conduct of research, whether the tool is an analytical balance, an assay kit, a laser device (as in *Madey v. Duke University*),[b] or a biochemical method such as the PCR (polymerase chain reaction). It is as subject to the patent right as is any other device or method, whether it is used to conduct research or for any other purpose. Use of an existing tool in one's research is quite different from study of the tool itself.

## Dawson Chemical Co. v. Rohm & Haas Co.

Supreme Court of the United States, 1980.
448 U.S. 176, 100 S.Ct. 2601, 65 L.Ed.2d 696.

■ MR. JUSTICE BLACKMUN delivered the opinion of the Court.

This case presents an important question of statutory interpretation arising under the patent laws. The issue before us is whether the owner of a patent on a chemical process is guilty of patent misuse, and therefore is barred from seeking relief against contributory infringement of its patent rights, if it exploits the patent only in conjunction with the sale of an unpatented article that constitutes a material part of the invention and is not suited for commercial use outside the scope of the patent claims. The answer will determine whether respondent, the owner of a process patent on a chemical herbicide, may maintain an action for contributory infringement against other manufacturers of the chemical used in the process. To resolve this issue, we must construe the various provisions of 35 U.S.C. § 271, which Congress enacted in 1952 to codify certain aspects of the doctrines of contributory infringement and patent misuse that previously had been developed by the judiciary.

---

[b] Madey v. Duke University, 307 F.3d 1351 (Fed.Cir.2002) concerned the use of a patented laser device for the purpose for which it was made, not research into understanding or improving the design or operation of the machine. The facts of *Madey v. Duke* do not invoke the common law research exemption, despite the broad statement in that opinion. I do not disagree with that decision on its facts; I disagree only with its sweeping dictum, and its failure to distinguish between investigation into patented things, as has always been permitted, and investigation using patented things, as has never been permitted.

I

[Respondent, Rohm & Haas, is a manufacturer of chemicals and the holder of a patent ("the Wilson patent") on a method for using propanil (3,4–dichloropropionanilide) to kill weeds. Propanil was known before its herbicidal action was recognized. Accordingly, the chemical itself is not protected by a patent].

A

Petitioners, too, are chemical manufacturers. They have manufactured and sold propanil for application to rice crops since before Rohm & Haas received its patent. They market the chemical in containers on which are printed directions for application in accordance with the method claimed in the Wilson patent. Petitioners did not cease manufacture and sale of propanil after that patent issued, despite knowledge that farmers purchasing their products would infringe on the patented method by applying the propanil to their crops. Accordingly, Rohm & Haas filed this suit, in the United States District Court for the Southern District of Texas, seeking injunctive relief against petitioners on the ground that their manufacture and sale of propanil interfered with its patent rights.

The complaint alleged not only that petitioners contributed to infringement by farmers who purchased and used petitioners' propanil, but also that they actually induced such infringement by instructing farmers how to apply the herbicide. See 35 U.S.C. §§ 271(b) and (c). Petitioners responded to the suit by requesting licenses to practice the patented method. When Rohm & Haas refused to grant such licenses, however, petitioners raised a defense of patent misuse and counterclaimed for alleged antitrust violations by respondent.

B

For present purposes certain material facts are not in dispute. First, the validity of the Wilson patent is not in question at this stage in the litigation. We therefore must assume that respondent is the lawful owner of the sole and exclusive right to use, or to license others to use, propanil as a herbicide on rice fields in accordance with the methods claimed in the Wilson patent. Second, petitioners do not dispute that their manufacture and sale of propanil together with instructions for use as a herbicide constitute contributory infringement of the Rohm & Haas patent. Tr. of Oral Arg. 14. Accordingly, they admit that propanil constitutes "a material part of [respondent's] invention," that it is "especially made or especially adapted for use in an infringement of [the] patent," and that it is "not a staple article or commodity of commerce suitable for substantial noninfringing use," all within the language of 35 U.S.C. § 271(c).

As a result of these concessions, our chief focus of inquiry must be the scope of the doctrine of patent misuse in light of the limitations placed upon that doctrine by § 271(d). On this subject, as well, our task is guided by certain stipulations and concessions. The parties agree that Rohm & Haas makes and sells propanil; that it has refused to license petitioners or any others to do the same; that it has not granted express licenses either to retailers or to end users of the product; and that farmers who buy propanil from Rohm & Haas may use it, without fear of being sued for direct infringement, by virtue of an "implied license" they obtain when Rohm & Haas relinquishes its monopoly by selling the propanil. See App. 35–39. . . .

The parties disagree over whether respondent has engaged in any additional conduct that amounts to patent misuse. Petitioners assert that there has been misuse because respondent has "tied" the sale of patent rights to the purchase of propanil, an unpatented and indeed unpatentable article, and because it has refused to grant licenses to other producers of the chemical compound. They argue that § 271(d) does not permit any sort of tying arrangement, and that resort to such a practice excludes respondent from the category of patentees "otherwise entitled to relief" within the meaning of § 271(d). Rohm & Haas, understandably, vigorously resists this characterization of its conduct. It argues that its acts have been only those that § 271(d), by express mandate, excepts from characterization as patent misuse. It further asserts that if this conduct results in an extension of the patent right to a control over an unpatented commodity, in this instance the extension has been given express statutory sanction.

## II

[In this part of the opinion, the Court conducts an extensive review of cases involving contributory infringement and patent misuse. It concludes as follows:]

First, we agree with the Court of Appeals that the concepts of contributory infringement and patent misuse "rest on antithetical underpinnings." 599 F.2d, at 697. The traditional remedy against contributory infringement is the injunction. And an inevitable concomitant of the right to enjoin another from contributory infringement is the capacity to suppress competition in an unpatented article of commerce. See, e. g., Thomson–Houston Electric Co. v. Kelsey Electric R. Specialty Co., 72 F. 1016, 1018–1019 (C.C.Conn.1896). Proponents of contributory infringement defend this result on the grounds that it is necessary for the protection of the patent right, and that the market for the unpatented article flows from the patentee's invention. They also observe that in many instances the article is "unpatented" only because of the technical rules of patent claiming, which require the placement of an invention in its context. Yet suppression of competition in unpatented goods is precisely what the opponents of patent misuse decry.[a] If both the patent misuse and contributory infringement doctrines are to coexist, then, each must have some separate sphere of operation with which the other does not interfere.

[a] Even in the classic contributory infringement case of Wallace v. Holmes, 29 F.Cas. 74 (No. 17,100) (CC Conn.1871), the patentee's effort to control the market for the novel burner that embodied his invention arguably constituted patent misuse. If the patentee were permitted to prevent competitors from making and selling that element, the argument would run, he would have the power to erect a monopoly over the production and sale of the burner, an unpatented element, even though his patent right was limited to control over use of the burner in the claimed combination.

Second, we find that the majority of cases in which the patent misuse doctrine was developed involved undoing the damage thought to have been done by [Henry v]. A. B. Dick [Co., 224 U.S. 1 (1912)].[b] The desire to extend patent protection to control of staple articles of commerce died slowly, and the ghost of the expansive contributory infringement era continued to haunt the courts. As a result, among the historical precedents in this Court, only the Leeds & Catlin [Co. v. Victor Talking Machine Co, 213 U.S. 325 (1909)][c] and Mercoid [Corp. v. Mid–Continent Investment Co., 320 U.S. 661 (1944) and Mercoid Corp. v. Minneapolis–Honeywell Regulator Co., 320 U.S. 680 (1944)][d] cases bear significant factual similarity to the present controversy. Those cases involved questions of control over unpatented articles that were essential to the patented inventions, and that were unsuited for any commercial noninfringing use. In this case, we face similar questions in connection with a chemical, propanil, the herbicidal properties of which are essential to the advance on prior art disclosed by respondent's patented process. Like the record disc in Leeds & Catlin or the stoker switch in the Mercoid cases, and unlike the dry ice in Carbice [Corp. v. American Patents Development Corp., 283 U.S. 27 (1931)][e] or the bituminous emulsion in Leitch [Mfg. Co. v. Barber Co., 302 U.S. 458 (1938)][f], propanil is a nonstaple commodity which has no use except through practice of the patented method. Accordingly, had the present case arisen prior to Mercoid, we believe it fair to say that it would have fallen close to the wavering line between legitimate protection against contributory infringement and illegitimate patent misuse.

## III

### A

The critical inquiry in this case is how the enactment of § 271 affected the doctrines of contributory infringement and patent misuse. Viewed against the backdrop of judicial precedent, we believe that the language and structure of the statute lend significant support to Rohm & Haas' contention that, because § 271 (d) immunizes its conduct from the charge of patent misuse, it should not be barred from seeking relief. The approach that Congress took toward the codification of contributory infringement and patent misuse reveals a compromise between those two doctrines and

[b] [Holding that it was not misuse for the patentee of a printing press to require purchasers to buy all paper and ink supplies from the patentee—eds.].

[c] [Upholding an injunction against contributory infringement on a finding that it was not misuse for the patentees to bar others from manufacturing unpatented phonograph discs especially designed to be used in connection with a patented disc-and-stylus combination—eds.].

[d] [Substantially modifying A.B. Dick; holding that any attempt to control the market for unpatented goods constitutes misuse, even if the goods have no use outside a patented invention—eds.].

[e] [Finding it misuse for the patentee to authorize use of a patented design for a refrigeration package only to those who purchased dry ice refrigerant from a party designated by the patentee—eds.].

[f] [Finding misuse in an attempt to exploit a process patent for the curing of cement through sale of bituminous emulsion, an unpatented staple—eds.].

their competing policies that permits patentees to exercise control over nonstaple articles used in their inventions.

Section 271(c) identifies the basic dividing line between contributory infringement and patent misuse. It adopts a restrictive definition of contributory infringement that distinguishes between staple and nonstaple articles of commerce. It also defines the class of nonstaple items narrowly. In essence, this provision places materials like the dry ice of the Carbice case outside the scope of the contributory infringement doctrine. As a result, it is no longer necessary to resort to the doctrine of patent misuse in order to deny patentees control over staple goods used in their inventions.

The limitations on contributory infringement written into § 271(c) are counterbalanced by limitations on patent misuse in § 271(d). Three species of conduct by patentees are expressly excluded from characterization as misuse. First, the patentee may "deriv[e] revenue" from acts that "would constitute contributory infringement" if "performed by another without his consent." This provision clearly signifies that a patentee may make and sell nonstaple goods used in connection with his invention. Second, the patentee may "licens[e] or authoriz[e] another to perform acts" which without such authorization would constitute contributory infringement. This provision's use in the disjunctive of the term "authoriz[e]" suggests that more than explicit licensing agreements is contemplated. Finally, the patentee may "enforce his patent rights against . . . contributory infringement." This provision plainly means that the patentee may bring suit without fear that his doing so will be regarded as an unlawful attempt to suppress competition. The statute explicitly states that a patentee may do "one or more" of these permitted acts, and it does not state that he must do any of them.

In our view, the provisions of § 271(d) effectively confer upon the patentee, as a lawful adjunct of his patent rights, a limited power to exclude others from competition in nonstaple goods. A patentee may sell a nonstaple article himself while enjoining others from marketing that same good without his authorization. By doing so, he is able to eliminate competitors and thereby to control the market for that product. Moreover, his power to demand royalties from others for the privilege of selling the nonstaple item itself implies that the patentee may control the market for the nonstaple good; otherwise, his "right" to sell licenses for the marketing of the nonstaple good would be meaningless, since no one would be willing to pay him for a superfluous authorization. See Note, 70 Yale L.J. 649, 659 (1961).

Rohm & Haas' conduct is not dissimilar in either nature or effect from the conduct that is thus clearly embraced within § 271(d). It sells propanil; it authorizes others to use propanil; and it sues contributory infringers. These are all protected activities. Rohm & Haas does not license others to sell propanil, but nothing on the face of the statute requires it to do so. To be sure, the sum effect of Rohm & Haas' actions is to suppress competition in the market for an unpatented commodity. But as we have observed, in this its conduct is no different from that which the statute expressly protects.

The one aspect of Rohm & Haas' behavior that is not expressly covered by § 271(d) is its linkage of two protected activities—sale of propanil and authorization to practice the patented process—together in a single transaction. Petitioners vigorously argue that this linkage, which they characterize pejoratively as "tying," supplies the otherwise missing element of misuse. They fail, however, to identify any way in which this "tying" of two expressly protected activities results in any extension of control over unpatented materials beyond what § 271(d) already allows. Nevertheless, the language of § 271(d) does not explicitly resolve the question when linkage of this variety becomes patent misuse. In order to judge whether this method of exploiting the patent lies within or without the protection afforded by § 271(d), we must turn to the legislative history.

B

[In this section, the Court conducts a review of the legislative history of § 271]

C

[T]he materials that we have culled are exemplary, and they amply demonstrate the intended scope of the statute. It is the consistent theme of the legislative history that the statute was designed to accomplish a good deal more than mere clarification. It significantly changed existing law, and the change moved in the direction of expanding the statutory protection enjoyed by patentees. The responsible congressional Committees were told again and again that contributory infringement would wither away if the misuse rationale of the Mercoid decisions remained as a barrier to enforcement of the patentee's rights. They were told that this was an undesirable result that would deprive many patent holders of effective protection for their patent rights. They were told that Congress could strike a sensible compromise between the competing doctrines of contributory infringement and patent misuse if it eliminated the result of the Mercoid decisions yet preserved the result in Carbice. And they were told that the proposed legislation would achieve this effect by restricting contributory infringement to the sphere of nonstaple goods while exempting the control of such goods from the scope of patent misuse. These signals cannot be ignored. They fully support the conclusion that, by enacting §§ 271(c) and (d), Congress granted to patent holders a statutory right to control nonstaple goods that are capable only of infringing use in a patented invention, and that are essential to that invention's advance over prior art.

We find nothing in this legislative history to support the assertion that respondent's behavior falls outside the scope of § 271(d). To the contrary, respondent has done nothing that would extend its right of control over unpatented goods beyond the line that Congress drew.

[P]etitioners argue that respondent's unwillingness to offer similar licenses to its would-be competitors in the manufacture of propanil legally distinguishes this case and sets it outside § 271(d). To this argument, there are at least three responses. First, as we have noted, § 271(d) permits such licensing but does not require it. Accordingly, petitioners' suggestion would import into the statute a requirement that simply is not there. Second, petitioners have failed to adduce any evidence from the legislative history that the offering of a license to the alleged contributory infringer was a critical factor in inducing Congress to retreat from the result of the Mercoid decisions. Indeed, the Leeds & Catlin decision, which did not involve such an offer to license, was placed before Congress as an example of the kind of contributory infringement action the statute would allow. Third, petitioners' argument runs contrary to the long-settled view that the essence of a patent grant is the right to exclude others from profiting by the patented invention. 35 U.S.C. § 154; see Continental Paper Bag Co. v. Eastern Paper Bag Co., 210 U.S. 405, 424–425, 28 S.Ct. 748, 753–754, 52 L.Ed. 1122 (1908); Zenith Radio Corp. v. Hazeltine Research, Inc., 395 U.S. 100, 135, 89 S.Ct. 1562, 1582, 23 L.Ed.2d 129 (1969). If petitioners' argument were accepted, it would force patentees either to grant licenses or to forfeit their statutory protection against contributory infringement. Compulsory licensing is a rarity in our patent system,[g] and we decline to manufacture such a requirement out of § 271(d).

V

Under the construction of § 271(d) that petitioners advance, the rewards available to those willing to undergo the time, expense, and interim frustration of such practical research would provide at best a dubious incentive. Others could await the results of the testing and then jump on the profit bandwagon by demanding licenses to sell the unpatented, nonstaple chemical used in the newly developed process. Refusal to accede to such a demand, if accompanied by any attempt to profit from the invention through sale of the unpatented chemical, would risk forfeiture of any patent protection whatsoever on a finding of patent misuse. As a result, noninventors would be almost assured of an opportunity to share in the spoils, even though they had contributed nothing to the discovery. The incentive to await the discoveries of others might well prove sweeter than the incentive to take the initiative oneself.

■ Mr. Justice White, with whom Mr. Justice Brennan, Mr. Justice Marshall, and Mr. Justice Stevens join, dissenting. [omitted]

---

In 1988, Congress further clarified the reach of the misuse doctrine by amending the Act to include §§ 271(d)(4) and (5).

[g] Compulsory licensing of patents often has been proposed, but it has never been enacted on a broad scale. See, e. g., Compulsory Licensing of Patents under some Non–American Systems, Study of the Subcommittee on Patents, Trademarks, and Copyrights of the Senate Committee on the Judiciary, 85th Cong., 2d Sess., 1, 2 (Comm. Print 1959). Although compulsory licensing provisions were considered for possible incorporation into the 1952 revision of the patent laws, they were dropped before the final bill was circulated. See House Committee on the Judiciary, Proposed Revision and Amendment of the Patent Laws: Preliminary Draft, 81st Cong., 2d Sess., 91 (Comm. Print 1950).

# World Trade Organization

Ministerial Conference, 14 November 2001.
WT/MIN(01)/DEC/W/2, Doc. #01–5770

## DECLARATION ON THE TRIPS AGREEMENT AND PUBLIC HEALTH

### ("The Doha Declaration")

1. We recognize the gravity of the public health problems afflicting many developing and least-developed countries, especially those resulting from HIV/AIDS, tuberculosis, malaria and other epidemics.

2. We stress the need for the WTO Agreement on Trade–Related Aspects of Intellectual Property Rights (TRIPS Agreement) to be part of the wider national and international action to address these problems.

3. We recognize that intellectual property protection is important for the development of new medicines. We also recognize the concerns about its effects on prices.

4. We agree that the TRIPS Agreement does not and should not prevent Members from taking measures to protect public health. Accordingly, while reiterating our commitment to the TRIPS Agreement, we affirm that the Agreement can and should be interpreted and implemented in a manner supportive of WTO Members' right to protect public health and, in particular, to promote access to medicines for all.

In this connection, we reaffirm the right of WTO Members to use, to the full, the provisions in the TRIPS Agreement, which provide flexibility for this purpose.

5. Accordingly and in the light of paragraph 4 above, while maintaining our commitments in the TRIPS Agreement, we recognize that these flexibilities include:

(a) In applying the customary rules of interpretation of public international law, each provision of the TRIPS Agreement shall be read in the light of the object and purpose of the Agreement as expressed, in particular, in its objectives and principles.

(b) Each Member has the right to grant compulsory licences and the freedom to determine the grounds upon which such licences are granted.

(c) Each Member has the right to determine what constitutes a national emergency or other circumstances of extreme urgency, it being understood that public health crises, including those relating to HIV/AIDS, tuberculosis, malaria and other epidemics, can represent a national emergency or other circumstances of extreme urgency.

(d) The effect of the provisions in the TRIPS Agreement that are relevant to the exhaustion of intellectual property rights is to leave each Member free to establish its own regime for such exhaustion without challenge, subject to the MFN and national treatment provisions of Articles 3 and 4.

6. We recognize that WTO Members with insufficient or no manufacturing capacities in the pharmaceutical sector could face difficulties in making effective use of compulsory licensing under the TRIPS Agreement. We instruct the Council for TRIPS to find an expeditious solution to this problem and to report to the General Council before the end of 2002.

7. We reaffirm the commitment of developed-country Members to provide incentives to their enterprises and institutions to promote and encourage technology transfer to least-developed country Members pursuant to Article 66.2. We also agree that the least-developed country Members will not be obliged, with respect to pharmaceutical products, to implement or apply Sections 5 and 7 of Part II of the TRIPS Agreement or to enforce rights provided for under these Sections until 1 January 2016, without prejudice to the right of least-developed country Members to seek other extensions of the transition periods as provided for in Article 66.1 of the TRIPS Agreement. We instruct the Council for TRIPS to take the necessary action to give effect to this pursuant to Article 66.1 of the TRIPS Agreement.

NOTES

**1.** *The antitrust connection.* The Introduction mentioned that antitrust law provides a further check on the patentee. In Walker Process Equipment, Inc. v. Food Machinery & Chemical Corp.,[1] the Supreme Court held that if inequitable conduct in the Patent Office (then called fraud) renders the patent unenforceable, attempts to monopolize the subject matter (i.e. enforce the patent) may amount to a violation of the Sherman Act.[2] In addition, patent licensing arrangements are sometimes challenged for violating antitrust statutes. For instance, in Transparent–Wrap Machine Co. v. Stokes & Smith Co.,[3] the Supreme Court condemned a grant-back provision—that is, an arrangement requiring a licensee to grant to the patentee any rights acquired in improvements to the licensed invention; in Zenith Radio Corp. v. Hazeline Research Inc.,[4] package licensing (an agreement requiring licensees to pay for an entire package of patents, including ones the licensee did not need) was similarly found to violate the antitrust laws. In Hartford–Empire Co. v. United States,[5] the Sherman Act was deemed violated by a binding agreement between a group of competitors to pool their patent rights. In the context of the drug approval process, certain agreements between the holders of patents on prescription drugs and manufacturers of potential generic substitutes are also subject to scrutiny.[6]

Since the exclusive right of a patent is by its nature anticompetitive, the relationship between antitrust policy and patent law is necessarily fraught with difficulty. During times when competition is deemed more

[1] 382 U.S. 172 (1965).

[2] 15 U.S.C. §§ 15–16.

[3] 329 U.S. 637 (1947).

[4] 395 U.S. 100 (1969).

[5] 323 U.S. 386 (1945).

[6] See, e.g., In re Cardizem CD Antitrust Litigation, 105 F.Supp.2d 682 (E.D. Mich. 2000).

important than providing incentives to innovation, the business practices of patent holders come under considerable scrutiny. In the 1970's, for example, the Justice Department announced that nine specific licensing practices (the "Nine No–Nos") would be regarded as per se unlawful under the antitrust laws.[7]

In recent years, however, innovation has received renewed appreciation. Furthermore, strong arguments are now made that arrangements such as the No–Nos are not always anticompetitive. First, so long as patentees and licensees have equal bargaining power and engage in arms' length negotiations, the agreements that they reach are likely to be coincident with the public interest. After all, the licensee will pay no more for the patented invention than it is worth; the licensing provisions simply determine the form of payment. Second, certain concessions do no more than meter the use of the patented invention, thereby allowing the licensee to pay exactly what the patented invention is worth to that licensee. In *Dawson,* for example, tying sales of propanil to the right to practice the invention enabled the patentee to charge each farmer an amount commensurate with the use that farmer made of the weed-killing process. In the absence of tying, everyone would have had to pay the same price for a license. Farmers with small properties (and hence, few weeds), unable to afford the license at the single (supracompetitive) price, would have been foreclosed from using the process. In other words, tying can be socially beneficial: it eliminates the deadweight social loss discussed in the Introduction to the previous Assignment. For these reasons, the Justice Department has announced that its No–Nos will henceforth be judged under a rule of reason.[8]

Given the Justice Department's view, should the doctrine of misuse be reconsidered? As *Dawson* demonstrated, this doctrine is also intended to curb anticompetitive conduct. However, it takes a different approach from antitrust law. First, whereas antitrust law generally limits only those

---

[7] Remarks by Bruce Wilson, Department of Justice Luncheon Speech, Law on Licensing Practice: Myth or Reality (Jan. 21, 1975). These included tie-ins (which were in issue in Dawson), tie-outs (requirements that the licensee refrain from selling other products), resale restrictions, minimum price restraints, package licensing, grant-backs, royalties schedules not dependent on sales of the patented invention, restrictions on the sales of products made from the patented process, and restraints on the patentees's ability to grant licenses.

[8] See Roger B. Andewelt, Deputy Director of Operations, Antitrust Div., U.S. Dep't of Justice, The Antitrust Division's Perspective on Intellectual Property and Licensing—The Past, The Present, and the Future, Remarks to the American Bar Association, 30 Pat., Trademark, and Copyright J.

321 (1985); ., U.S. Dep't of Justice, Vertical Restraints Guidelines, 50 Fed. Reg. 6263, 6271 (1985); FTC/DOJ Antitrust Guidelines for the Licensing of Intellectual Property (1995), http://www.usdoj.gov/atr/public/guidelines/ipguide.htm. See generally, Robert H. Bork, The Antitrust Paradox 372 (1978); Ward S. Bowman, Jr., Patent and Antitrust Law 55 (1973); L. Schwartz, J. Flynn and H. First, Free Enterprise and Economic Organization: Antitrust (6th ed. 1983); Louis Kaplow, Extension of Monopoly Power Through Leverage, 85 Colum. L. Rev. 515 (1985); Louis Kaplow, The Patent–Antitrust Intersection: A Reappraisal, 97 Harv. L. Rev. 1813 (1984); William F. Baxter, Legal Restrictions on Exploitation of the Patent Monopoly: An Economic Analysis, 76 Yale L.J. 267 (1966).

competitors who have a dominant market position, application of the doctrine of patent misuse does not require a showing that the patentee has any special place in the industry. Thus, a patentee could be found guilty of misuse even if many other products compete with the patented invention. Second, where antitrust law imposes monetary liability on a losing defendant, the misuse doctrine renders her patent unenforceable until the misuse is "purged"—i.e. until the patentee stops engaging in the activity that amounted to misuse.

Jurisdictional issues further complicate the relationship between antitrust and patent law. The Federal Circuit's jurisdiction, like the jurisdiction of the district courts, is determined by the well pleaded complaint rule. This allows it to hear all pure patent cases because the patent claim will be on the face of the complaint. However, it will not have authority over patent/antitrust cases when the antitrust claim is the plaintiff's and the patent issue comes up as a defense. In those cases, the regional circuit will decide all issues (including patent issues). The Federal Circuit will, however, have authority over cases where the plaintiff is the patent holder and the antitrust claim is asserted as a defense or counterclaim.[9] Of course, this would not matter if all courts applied antitrust laws identically. But they do not. For example, in In re Independent Service Organizations Antitrust Litigation,[10] the Federal Circuit upheld a patentee's refusal to license patented parts against an antitrust challenge. In contrast, in Image Technical Services, Inc. v. Eastman Kodak Co.,[11] the Ninth Circuit found a patentee's refusal to license parts to be a violation of the antitrust law.

**2.** *Other limits on patent licenses.* The term of the patent is also an important limit on the patentee, and several cases have considered the extent to which a patentee can contractually obligate a licensee to continue paying royalties after the patent has expired or been found unenforceable by a court. In Brulotte v. Thys,[12] the Supreme Court held it misuse of a patent to make a contract binding a licensee to royalty payments extending beyond the patent's term. According to the Court, the patentee was using the patent as leverage to extract monopoly profits from an invention for a longer period than the patentee was entitled to protection, thereby attempting to secure a right denied by federal law. Similarly, in Lear v. Adkins,[13] the Court held unenforceable a contract provision requiring a licensee to pay royalties even if the patent was invalidated. The Court reasoned that any doctrine that effectively estops a licensee from challenging the validity of a patent is void on public policy grounds:

> "Licensees may often be the only individuals with enough economic incentive to challenge the patentability of an inventor's discovery. If they are muzzled, the public may continually be required to pay tribute to would-be monopolists without need or justification. We think it plain

---

[9] Holmes Group, Inc. v. Vornado Air Circulation Systems, Inc., 535 U.S. 826 (2002)(interpreting 28 U.S.C. § 1295(a)(1)).

[10] 203 F.3d 1322 (Fed. Cir. 2000).

[11] 125 F.3d 1195 (9th Cir. 1997).

[12] 379 U.S. 29 (1964).

[13] 395 U.S. 653 (1969).

that the technical requirements of contract doctrine must give way before the demands of the public interest ... "[14]

Because both of these cases involve a clash between state (contract) law and federal (patent) law, both can be analyzed as preemption cases under the analysis provided by the cases in Assignment 24?[15] Is the Justice Department's current analysis of licensing practices (see Note 1) pertinent here?[16] In Assignment 11, we saw the use of technological measures to restrict access to copyrightable materials. How should the use of such measures to restrict patented materials be analyzed? Is a contractual provisions like the one in the Principal Problem enforceable?[17]

**3.** *Patent law's influence on copyright: misuse.* Should the doctrine of misuse be imported into copyright law? Despite the declining viability of misuse defenses in patent law, litigants have begun to assert claims of misuse in copyright cases, see, e.g., Bellsouth Advertising & Publishing Corp. v. Donnelley Information Publishing, Inc.,[18] Lasercomb America, Inc. v. Reynolds,[19] and United Telephone Co. v. Johnson Publishing Co.[20]

**4.** *Copyright law's influence on patent law: compulsory licensing.* Should patent law incorporate the compulsory license approach taken by copyright, see Assignment 11? As the *Dawson* Court noted (and as is implied in *Coe*), the United States has consistently taken the position that there should be no compulsory licensing of patents. However, many countries think differently. One type of provision found in the law of several nations is a compulsory license that can be invoked in the event that the patentee refuses to engage in the activities required to fully disseminate the invention. For example, in Britain, the state is permitted to compel licensing if a patented invention is not commercialized "to the fullest extent that is reasonably practical" for three years.[21] German patent law provides for a compulsory license if the patentee is not willing to grant a license to someone who offers "reasonable compensation."[22] Although there has been little litigation under this provision in recent years, German practitioners claim it has a significant *in terrorem* effect on patentees.

Even in the United States, patents are sometimes subject to government control. Royalty-free licenses are occasionally used as a remedy in antitrust litigation, see, e.g., United States v. General Electric Co.[23] Com-

[14] Id. at 670–71.

[15] See Rochelle Cooper Dreyfuss, Dethroning Lear: Licensee Estoppel and the Incentive to Innovate, 72 Va. L. Rev. 677 (1986).

[16] For information on what the Federal Trade Commission and the Justice Department are now thinking about the interface between intellectual property and antitrust law, see FTC/DOJ Hearings on Competition and Intellectual Property Law in the Knowledge Based Economy, http://www.ftc.gov/opp/intellect/index.htm.

[17] See Monsanto Co. v. McFarling, 302 F.3d 1291 (Fed. Cir. 2002); Mallinckrodt, inc. v. Medipart, Inc., 976 F.2d 700 (Fed. Cir. 1992).

[18] 933 F.2d 952 (11th Cir.1991).

[19] 911 F.2d 970 (4th Cir.1990).

[20] 855 F.2d 604 (8th Cir.1988).

[21] Patents Act, 1977, c. 37 § 48.

[22] German Patent Act § 24 (Law of December 16, 1980, as amended Dec. 9, 1986).

[23] 115 F.Supp. 835 (D.N.J.1953). See also Charles Pfizer & Co. v. Federal Trade Comm'n, 401 F.2d 574 (6th Cir.

pulsory licenses have been created by statute when important national interests are at stake, see, e.g., the Clean Air Act, 42 U.S.C. § 7608. Furthermore, the government retains so-called march-in rights to inventions created with government funding. When the rights holder to such an invention fails to take steps to commercialize it within a reasonable time, the federal agency that provided the source of the funds may step in and grant licenses to parties who are willing to bring the invention into public use.[24]

Mostly at the behest of U.S. patent holders, the TRIPS Agreement incorporates specific limits on the ability of member states to resort to compulsory licensing. In particular, prior to TRIPS, many countries had working requirements: they would impose compulsory licenses in favor of domestic producers when a patentee refused to manufacture the patented product locally (and instead supplied the local market with products manufactured abroad). Article 27(1) prohibits this practice by barring members from discriminating "as to ... whether products are imported or locally produced." The Agreement does, however, permit members to uses compulsory licenses to control anti-competitive practices and to allow unauthorized uses on a case by case basis in specified circumstances.[25]

**5.** *Essential medicines: exhaustion, parallel importation, price discrimination, and compulsory licensing.* One problem that all countries must grapple with is the clash between relying on patents to encourage pharmaceutical research and putting the cost of medicines out of the reach of most patients. In some countries, including Canada, price controls or government purchase programs keep retail costs reasonable. Should Americans be permitted to buy their medication in Canada? Should they be allowed to order medicine abroad via the Internet? Should third parties be allowed to buy product in Canada and import it for resale in the United States? *Adams* creates patent law's analogue to the first sale doctrine of copyright law, holding that a patent holder's interest in a particular embodiment (e.g. a bottle of pills) is exhausted once it is sold under his authority. But *Adams* is a wholly domestic case: should exhaustion apply internationally? That is, is the U.S. patent holder's interest exhausted by a sale made in Canada? Arguably, it is not because the Canadian sale is at a price set by the Canadian government.[26] If so, then importation of (cheap) Canadian medicine should not be permitted. On the other hand, radically different prices within North America (or even within the developed world) strike many as grossly unfair.

As of this writing, Congress has pending before it legislation that would permit Americans to purchase prescription drugs abroad.[27] At the

---

1968)(requiring licensing at a reasonable royalty), cert. denied, 394 U.S. 920 (1969).

[24] § 203.

[25] TRIPS Agreement, arts. 40 and 31.

[26] See Jazz Photo Corp. v. International Trade Comm'n, 264 F.3d 1094, 1105 (Fed. Cir. 2001)(stating that international sales do not exhaust U.S. rights).

[27] The approach being considered in the House of Representatives is described on Rep. Rahm Emanuel's website, http://www.house.gov/apps/list/press/il05_emanuel/RxDrugBills.html. Safety issues stem-

same time, however, pharmaceutical companies have announced that they will track Canadian purchases of their products and cut off pharmacies that appear to be breaching their contractual agreements not to export to U.S. customers.[28] The problem raised by this activity is not, however, merely about the technicalities of the first sale doctrine. Pharmaceutical companies claim to earn half their revenue and most of their profits in the United States. Thus, the real issue is whether reduced prices will diminish incentives to undertake the substantial expense to bring new drugs to market. In other words, the question is whether Americans are willing to utilize their higher purchasing power to subsidize research that improves their own lives, but which the entire world then utilizes at significantly lower cost. Is there a way for countries to agree to share in the cost of health research? The TRIPS Agreement does not prevent members from controlling prices or barring parallel importation,[29] thus it does not currently deal with this issue.

How is your view of parallel importation affected by the problem of supplying essential medicines to less developed countries? For example, many African countries are struggling with HIV/AIDS and cannot afford to pay either the U.S. or the Canadian price for medication. The TRIPS Agreement's compulsory licensing provisions clearly permit African governments to authorize local manufacturers to make the medicines their citizens need.[30] Pharmaceuticals are, however, difficult to manufacture at the purity required and African countries lack the necessary infrastructure. There are nations (India and Brazil are examples) that are excellent generic drug manufacturers. Could they sell to Africa without the patent holder's authorization? Prior to the Doha Declaration, the answer was clearly no: unauthorized manufacture is permissible for health crises, but only to meet "predominantly" domestic needs. Thus, Indian generic producers could supply India, but not Botswana. The Doha Declaration recognized the problem, and in ¶ 6, promised to find a solution. But as of this writing (2003), no solution has been forthcoming. Patent owners are not so much worried about supplying product to Africa at prices that citizens there can afford; they are mainly worried that without clear rules against international exhaustion, the medicines they supply to Africa will be reimported into developed countries.[31]

ming from the lack of FDA supervision are also being explored.

[28] See, e.g., Gardiner Harris, Pfizer Moves to Stem Canadian Drug Imports, N.Y.Times, Sec. /cm p.1, col. 2 (Aug. 7, 2003).

[29] TRIPS Agreement, art. 6.

[30] TRIPS Agreement, art. 31(b) has a special provision for cases of "national emergency." Indeed, art. 27(2) permits members to exclude from patentability inventions necessary to protect human health. Moreover,

developing countries enjoy certain transition privileges that allow them to avoid patenting.

[31] For more on these issues, see Jean O. Lanjouw, A New Global Patent Regime For Diseases: U.S. and International Legal Issues, 16 Harv. J.L. & Tech. 85 (2002); Susan K. Sell, TRIPS and the Access to Medicines Campaign, 20 Wis. Int'l L.J. 481 (2002); Keith E. Maskus, Ensuring Access to Essential Medicines: Some Economic Considerations, 20 Wis. Int'l L.J. 563 (2002).

**6.** *Sovereign Immunity.* 28 U.S.C. § 1498, which was at issue in *Madey*, is also an interesting way to assure some public access. It permits the United States and those operating on its behalf, to use a patented invention without authorization but gives the patentee a right to "reasonable and entire compensation." Thus, it essentially operates as a limited exercise of the power of eminent domain in favor of federal employees and contractors. States also have some immunity to patent infringement by virtue of the Eleventh Amendment cases discussed in Assignment 5.[32] That protection is limited because long term usage could be stopped with an action for injunctive relief.[33] Nonetheless, it would promote access in cases where the intellectual property can be fully exploited through brief usage. For example, in some pharmaceutical research, potential medicines are tested against patented target molecules. Once the test is performed, the target is no longer needed.

**7.** *The common law experimental use defense.* Was *Madey* rightly decided? Judge Newman's footnote provides persuasive justification for the actual result in that case, but what about the broader language? Prior to that case, a line was drawn between commercial research (which required authorization) and noncommercial research (which was considered within the experimental use defense). *Madey* destroyed that line. It takes an approach similar to the one we saw in *Griffith,* the case in Assignment 20 which refused to grant a Cornell professor the flexibility to delay his work for academic reasons. In both, the rationale seems to be that if universities want to participate in the patent game, they must abide by the same rules as commercial players. But are universities the equivalent of commercial players? Can they devote all of their resources, or deploy all of their employees, to promising new research, or must they continue to educate students, staff English, Philosophy, Music, and Art Departments? Nonprofits often pursue fundamental research that will open new technological opportunities, and risky projects that profit-driven enterprises may be unwilling to tackle. Such research provides broad benefits to society: does it make sense to increase its cost?[34]

Many observers are not concerned about *Madey* because they believe that the public benefits of nonprofit research foster a norm against suing these institutions. The facts of *Madey* (which involve a disgruntled ex-employee) are certainly unique, but once it is understood that noncommercial research does not benefit from the exception, will this norm continue to

---

[32] Florida Prepaid Postsecondary Education Expense Board v. College Savings Bank, 527 U.S. 627 (1999); College Savings Bank v. Florida Prepaid Postsecondary Education Expense Board, 527 U.S. 666 (1999).

[33] Ex parte Young, 209 U.S. 123 (1908); *College Savings Bank*, 527 U.S., at 704 (Justice Breyer, dissenting).

[34] See Richard A. Epstein, Steady the Course: Property Rights in Genetic Material, http://papers.ssrn.com/sol3/papers.cfm?abstract_id=317101; Rochelle Cooper Dreyfuss, Varying the Course in Patenting Genetic Material: A Counter–Proposal to Richard Epstein's Steady Course, http://papers.ssrn.com/sol3/papers.cfm?abstract_id=394000; Rebecca S. Eisenberg, Patents and the Progress of Science: Exclusive Rights and Experimental Use, 56 U.Chi.L.Rev. 1017 (1989).

control? The Supreme Court denied certiorari in *Madey*.[35] Because the case was remanded and could be decided entirely on grounds related to the U.S. government's funding of the work, it may be a long time before the common law exception is revisited.

Is there another rationale that could be used to support an experimental use defense? Recall that ordinarily, an inventor who uses a patent for more than a year prior to applying for a patent is barred from receiving one under § 102(b). However, when the use is considered experimental, the § 102(b) bar does not apply, see Assignment 19. Section 102(b)'s experimental-use doctrine is, of course, different from the experimental use defense discussed in this Assignment. However, some argue that the two should be related: that if patentees are allowed (under § 102(b)) to *extend* their period of exclusivity in order to conduct experiments, then the public should be allowed (under the experimental use defense) to *contract* the exclusive right by engaging in experiments during the patent term.

**8.** *The statutory experimental use defense.* Congress tackled *Roche*, which was discussed in *Madey*, statutorily. In that case, generic drug companies used patented pharmaceuticals to generate data needed for FDA approval of their products while patents on these products were in force. They relied on the experimental use defense, arguing that they wanted to be able to market their products as soon as the patents covering them expired. When the Federal Circuit rejected the defense, Congress enacted with § 271(e) to provide a defense "solely for uses reasonably related to the development and submission of information under a Federal law which regulates drugs." In exchange, patentees received term extensions for delays in obtaining FDA approval. The exemption has been interpreted to cover medical devices as well as drugs.[36] However, *Integra* ended a lower court practice of permitting activities other than clinical testing.

**9.** *The remedial alternative.* As you will see in Assignment 23, another way a judge could promote access to an invention when important public interests are involved is to deny injunctive relief and instead award a right to continuing damages (that is, create a compulsory license judicially). The Federal Circuit has also fashioned a doctrine of prosecution laches whereby patents are not enforceable if there was an unreasonable delay in their prosecution. In essence, this defense recognizes that even when a patent application is filed, the public may gain a reliance interest in the free availability of the invention.[37]

---

[35] 123 S.Ct. 2639 (2003).

[36] Eli Lilly & Co. v. Medtronic, Inc., 496 U.S. 661 (1990).

[37] Symbol Technologies, Inc. v. Lemelson Medical, 277 F.3d 1361 (Fed. Cir. 2002).

ASSIGNMENT 23

# REMEDIES

## 1. INTRODUCTION

Because patents are intended to create financial incentives to invest in innovation, it should be no surprise that the Patent Act provides a right to damages "adequate to compensate for the infringement," § 284. As the following materials make clear, however, it is not always easy to determine the amount of compensation the patentee deserves. How does one determine the "but for" cause of the patentee's loss, on the standard familiar from tort law, or on another scale? Should the patentee be compensated for sales she was not, in fact, in a position to make? How should profits on such sales be determined? Should the patentee be compensated for losing the opportunity to sell materials that are used in conjunction with the patented product? It is easier by far to issue an injunction. And since a patent is the right to prevent others from dealing in the invention, injunctive relief is a key remedial device, § 283. A preliminary injunction prevents the alleged infringer from competing during the course of the litigation; a permanent injunction gives back to the patentee her exclusive market position for the remaining term of the patent.

Injunctions, however, pose problems of their own. First, an injunction cannot compensate for infringements that occurred before the suit was commenced. More important, injunctive relief can impose high social costs, especially when the patentee cannot keep up with demand, or refuses to license those who would engage in complementary activities (supplying demand in other markets, pursuing other research opportunities, and such). If the patent has important social benefits, such as curing disease or preventing bodily injury, the public cost of injunctive relief can be substantial. Private losses can also be high: the infringer will lose investments made in production and distribution facilities; workers may lose their jobs. Injunctions are, however, awarded "in accordance with the principles of equity." Thus, courts must balance the interests of the patentee in injunctive relief against the social costs entailed. The calculus may be different depending on whether the patentee is asking for preliminary or permanent relief.

One way to avoid these problems is to provide strong disincentives to infringement. If all that the Act did was give patentees the right to prevent future infringements and to receive a monetary award equivalent to what the infringer would have paid if she had received authorization, there would be many situations were there would be little reason *not to* infringe: the infringer would be no worse off than if she had bargained for a license.

Because of difficulties of proof, she may even be better off. To create the right incentives, the Patent Act gives the court power to award up to treble damages and to shift the costs of litigation on to the losing side. §§ 284, 285.

## 2.   PRINCIPAL PROBLEM

In 1944, Irwin Sea conceived of a camera that automatically produced a fully developed picture moments after the shutter clicked. Sea worked on his conception for a quarter of a century, founding a new company—Bolaroid—in the process. In 1974, Bolaroid produced the Quantro, the first instant camera with genuine consumer appeal. Patented in 1975, it went on the market in 1976 at a price of $60. The Quantro was an immediate success: it sold 500,000 units in the first year, along with other camera paraphernalia, such as the film the Quantro required, camera cases, lenses, lens cleaner, straps, tripods, and such.

Prior to Quantro's success, Zodak had been the largest producer of cameras for the amateur market in the United States. It first heard of Bolaroid in the early 1970's. Quickly recognizing the appeal of instant photography, it too entered the field, introducing its first instant camera, the EX, in 1980. The EX was not as good as the Quantro in terms of convenience of use or picture quality. However, Zodak did not want to lose market share. Accordingly, it took a very low profit on the EX, pricing it at $20 less than the Quantro. Because of this price differential, and because Zodak's name was much better known that Bolaroid's, Zodak ended 1980 with close to half the instant camera market, both companies selling about 300,000 units.

Zodak was not, however, pleased. Unable to manufacture an instant camera as good as Bolaroid's, it changed its strategy. It decided to portray instant photography as a gimmick, fun at carnivals and birthday parties, but unsuitable for any real photographic needs. In 1983, it came out with the Candle which produced fairly terrible pictures. The Candle sold in stores for $15. (This price represented Zodak's cost, although it did make money on Candle film, camera cases, etc.). The Candle could also be obtained from a certain cereal company for 50 labels and a $2.95 handling charge.

Needless to say, the Candle posed a real problem to Bolaroid. Because Zodak was so well identified with photography, the Candle capped consumers' expectations as to both price and quality. Bolaroid was forced to shelve its plans to create an instant camera for professional photographers and instead devote its resources to competing with the Candle. In 1985, it produced the One–Hop, which it sold (at a very low profit margin) for $28.00. This proved to be the most popular instant camera ever, selling 600,000 units in its first year and doubling that amount in the next year.

By 1987, new problems in this field emerged. The art of film development changed and developers were able to offer one-day, then 3–hour, and then 1–hour developing services. At the same time, the market for Quantros, One–Hops, EXs and Candles became saturated. Both Zodak and Bolaroid cut back on production.

Starting from the early 1980s, Bolaroid and Zodak were in negotiations over the question whether Zodak was infringing Bolaroid's patents. In 1988, these negotiations broke down completely. Bolaroid then sued Zodak in federal court, claiming that each and every Zodak camera infringed Bolaroid's Quantro patents. Zodak was initially unworried about the litigation. It had hired a well known patent attorney back in 1980, when it first marketed an instant camera. The attorney had found differences between Zodak's cameras and Bolaroid's claims. Although he thought that these differences were rather minor, he considered them strong enough to support a nonfrivolous argument that Zodak's cameras were noninfringing. Besides, the attorney reasoned that Zodak had the resources to appeal any adverse trial court decision to a court of appeals. At the time, the regional circuits rarely sustained holdings of patent validity.

Things did not work out as planned. As you know, the Federal Circuit was established in 1982 and began to uphold many more patents than the regional circuits had done. After years of procedural machinations, the trial court in Bolaroid v. Zodak decided the Quantro patents were valid and infringed by both the Candle and the EX. The Federal Circuit affirmed and returned the case to the district court to decide remedial issues:

First, should Zodak be enjoined from producing instant cameras and film? Hundreds of workers owe their jobs to the Zodak's instant photography line; Zodak has invested many thousands of dollars in the machinery that produces the cameras and films. Moreover, owners of Zodak cameras will not be able to use their cameras if film is unavailable. Second, how should Bolaroid be compensated for past infringements? Third, should Zodak be liable for treble damages or attorney's fees?

## 3.   MATERIALS FOR SOLUTION OF PRINCIPAL PROBLEM

A.   STATUTORY MATERIAL: §§ 281–287

B:   CASES:

# Rite–Hite Corporation v. Kelley Company, Inc.

United States Court of Appeals, Federal Circuit, 1995.
56 F.3d 1538.

[This case was decided by the Federal Circuit sitting in an en banc court of twelve judges. It produced a fractured result: six judges joined an opinion authored by Judge Lourie. As to one issue, they were joined by Judge Newman, writing for herself and one other judge. On a second issue, Judge Nies, writing for herself and three others, agreed with the result Judge Lourie reached, but not with his reasoning. Excepts from all three opinions are reproduced below.]

■ [LOURIE, CIRCUIT JUDGE:]

BACKGROUND

On March 22, 1983, Rite–Hite sued Kelley, alleging that Kelley's "Truk Stop" vehicle restraint infringed Rite–Hite's U.S. Patent 4,373,847 ("the '847 patent"). The '847 patent, issued February 15, 1983, is directed to a device for securing a vehicle to a loading dock to prevent the vehicle from separating from the dock during loading or unloading. Any such separation would create a gap between the vehicle and dock and create a danger for a forklift operator.

[After the district court's decision on liability was affirmed by the Federal Circuit and a permanent injunction issued], the damage issues were tried to the [district] court. Rite–Hite sought damages calculated as lost profits for two types of vehicle restraints that it made and sold: the "Manual Dok–Lok" model 55 (MDL–55), which incorporated the invention covered by the '847 patent, and the "Automatic Dok–Lok" model 100 (ADL–100), which was not covered by the patent in suit. The ADL–100 was the first vehicle restraint Rite–Hite put on the market and it was covered by one or more patents other than the patent in suit. The Kelley Truk Stop restraint was designed to compete primarily with Rite–Hite's ADL–100. Both employed an electric motor and functioned automatically, and each sold for $1,000–$1,500 at the wholesale level, in contrast to the MDL–55, which sold for one-third to one-half the price of the motorized devices. Rite–Hite does not assert that Kelley's Truk Stop restraint infringed the patents covering the ADL–100.

Of the 3,825 infringing Truk Stop devices sold by Kelley, the district court found that, "but for" Kelley's infringement, Rite–Hite would have made 80 more sales of its MDL–55; 3,243 more sales of its ADL–100; and 1,692 more sales of dock levelers, a bridging platform sold with the restraints and used to bridge the edges of a vehicle and dock. The court awarded Rite–Hite as a manufacturer the wholesale profits that it lost on lost sales of the ADL–100 restraints, MDL–55 restraints, and restraint-leveler packages. It also awarded to Rite–Hite as a retailer reasonable royalty damages on lost ADL–100, MDL–55, and restraint-leveler sales caused by Kelley's infringing sales.[a] Finally, prejudgment interest, calculated without compounding, was awarded. Kelley's infringement was found to be not willful.

On appeal, Kelley contends that the district court erred as a matter of law in its determination of damages. Kelley does not contest the award of damages for lost sales of the MDL–55 restraints; however, Kelley argues that the patent statute does not provide for damages based on Rite–Hite's lost profits on ADL–100 restraints because the ADL–100s are not covered by the patent in suit; lost profits on unpatented dock levelers are not attributable to demand for the '847 invention and, therefore, are not

---

[a] [Rite–Hite was a retailer of its own devices. It also distributed product through independent sales organizations (ISOs). The question whether the ISOs had standing to join in this suit is omitted from the opinions as reproduced above. It is discussed in Note 7—eds.]

recoverable losses; and the court erred in calculating a reasonable royalty based as a percentage of ADL–100 and dock leveler profits.

We affirm the damage award with respect to Rite–Hite's lost profits as a manufacturer on its ADL–100 restraint sales, affirm the court's computation of a reasonable royalty rate, [and] vacate the damage award based on the dock levelers.

DISCUSSION

A

I.   Lost Profits on the ADL–100 Restraints

[This portion of the opinion was joined by Judges Lourie, Rich, Michel, Plager, Clevenger, Schall, Newman, and Rader]

The district court's decision to award lost profits damages pursuant to 35 U.S.C. § 284 turned primarily upon the quality of Rite–Hite's proof of actual lost profits. The court found that, "but for" Kelley's infringing Truk Stop competition, Rite–Hite would have sold 3,243 additional ADL–100 restraints and 80 additional MDL–55 restraints. The court reasoned that awarding lost profits fulfilled the patent statute's goal of affording complete compensation for infringement and compensated Rite–Hite for the ADL–100 sales that Kelley "anticipated taking from Rite–Hite when it marketed the Truk Stop against the ADL–100." Rite–Hite, 774 F.Supp. 1514, 1540 (E.D. Wis. 1991). The court stated, "[t]he rule applied here therefore does not extend Rite–Hite's patent rights excessively, because Kelley could reasonably have foreseen that its infringement of the '847 patent would make it liable for lost ADL–100 sales in addition to lost MDL–55 sales." Id. The court further reasoned that its decision would avoid what it referred to as the "whip-saw" problem, whereby an infringer could avoid paying lost profits damages altogether by developing a device using a first patented technology to compete with a device that uses a second patented technology and developing a device using the second patented technology to compete with a device that uses the first patented technology.

Kelley maintains that Rite–Hite's lost sales of the ADL–100 restraints do not constitute an injury that is legally compensable by means of lost profits. It has uniformly been the law, Kelley argues, that to recover damages in the form of lost profits a patentee must prove that, "but for" the infringement, it would have sold a product covered by the patent in suit to the customers who bought from the infringer. Under the circumstances of this case, in Kelley's view, the patent statute provides only for damages calculated as a reasonable royalty. Rite–Hite, on the other hand, argues that the only restriction on an award of actual lost profits damages for patent infringement is proof of causation-in-fact. A patentee, in its view, is entitled to all the profits it would have made on any of its products "but for" the infringement. Each party argues that a judgment in favor of the other would frustrate the purposes of the patent statute. Whether the lost profits at issue are legally compensable is a question of law, which we review de novo.

The statute [35 U.S.C. § 284] mandates that a claimant receive damages "adequate" to compensate for infringement. Section 284 further instructs that a damage award shall be "in no event less than a reasonable royalty"; the purpose of this alternative is not to direct the form of compensation, but to set a floor below which damage awards may not fall. Thus, the language of the statute is expansive rather than limiting. It affirmatively states that damages must be adequate, while providing only a lower limit and no other limitation.

The Supreme Court spoke to the question of patent damages in General Motors Corp. v. Devex Corp., 461 U.S. 648, 654 (1983) stating that, in enacting § 284, Congress sought to "ensure that the patent owner would in fact receive full compensation for 'any damages' [the patentee] suffered as a result of the infringement." Thus, while the statutory text states tersely that the patentee receive "adequate" damages, the Supreme Court has interpreted this to mean that "adequate" damages should approximate those damages that will fully compensate the patentee for infringement. Further, the Court has cautioned against imposing limitations on patent infringement damages, stating: "When Congress wished to limit an element of recovery in a patent infringement action, it said so explicitly." General Motors, 461 U.S. at 653 (refusing to impose limitation on court's authority to award interest).

In Aro Mfg. Co. v. Convertible Top Replacement Co., 377 U.S. 476 (1964), the Court discussed the statutory standard for measuring patent infringement damages, explaining: The question to be asked in determining damages is "how much had the Patent Holder and Licensee suffered by the infringement. And that question [is] primarily: had the Infringer not infringed, what would the Patentee Holder–Licensee have made?" 377 U.S. at 507, (plurality opinion)(citations omitted). This surely states a "but for" test. In accordance with the Court's guidance, we have held that the general rule for determining actual damages to a patentee that is itself producing the patented item is to determine the sales and profits lost to the patentee because of the infringement. To recover lost profits damages, the patentee must show a reasonable probability that, "but for" the infringement, it would have made the sales that were made by the infringer. King Instrument Corp. v. Otari Corp., 767 F.2d 853, 863, (Fed.Cir.1985), cert. denied, 475 U.S. 1016 (1986).

Panduit Corp. v. Stahlin Bros. Fibre Works, Inc., 575 F.2d 1152 (6th Cir.1978), articulated a four-factor test that has since been accepted as a useful, but non-exclusive, way for a patentee to prove entitlement to lost profits damages. State Indus., Inc. v. Mor–Flo Indus., Inc., 883 F.2d 1573, 1577 (Fed.Cir.1989), cert. denied, 493 U.S. 1022 (1990). The Panduit test requires that a patentee establish: (1) demand for the patented product; (2) absence of acceptable non-infringing substitutes; (3) manufacturing and marketing capability to exploit the demand; and (4) the amount of the profit it would have made. Panduit, 575 F.2d at 1156. A showing under Panduit permits a court to reasonably infer that the lost profits claimed were in fact caused by the infringing sales, thus establishing a patentee's prima facie case with respect to "but for" causation. A patentee need not negate every possibility that the purchaser might not have purchased a product other than its own, absent the infringement. Id. The patentee need only show that there was a reasonable probability that the sales would have been made "but for" the infringement. Id. When the patentee establishes the reasonableness of this inference, e.g., by satisfying the Panduit test, it has sustained the burden of proving entitlement to lost profits due to the infringing sales. Id. at 1141. The burden then shifts to the infringer to show that the inference is unreasonable for some or all of the lost sales. Id.

Applying Panduit, the district court found that Rite–Hite had established "but for" causation. In the court's view, this was sufficient to prove entitlement to lost profits damages on the ADL–100. Kelley does not challenge that Rite–Hite meets the Panduit test and therefore has proven "but for" causation; rather, Kelley argues that damages for the ADL–100, even if in fact caused by the infringement, are not legally compensable because the ADL–100 is not covered by the patent in suit.

Preliminarily, we wish to affirm that the "test" for compensability of damages under § 284 is not solely a "but for" test in the sense that an infringer must compensate a patentee for any and all damages that proceed from the act of patent infringement. Notwithstanding the broad language of § 284, judicial relief cannot redress every conceivable harm that can be traced to an alleged wrongdoing. For example, remote consequences, such as a heart attack of the inventor or loss in value of shares of common stock of a patentee corporation caused indirectly by infringement are not compensable. Thus, along with establishing that a particular injury suffered by a patentee is a "but for" consequence of infringement, there may also be a background question whether the asserted injury is of the type for which the patentee may be compensated.

We believe that under § 284 of the patent statute, the balance between full compensation, which is the meaning that the Supreme Court has attributed to the statute, and the reasonable limits of liability encompassed by general principles of law can best be viewed in terms of reasonable, objective foreseeability. If a particular injury was or should have been reasonably foreseeable by an infringing competitor in the relevant market, broadly defined, that injury is generally compensable absent a persuasive reason to the contrary. Here, the court determined that Rite–Hite's lost sales of the ADL–100, a product that directly competed with the infringing product, were reasonably foreseeable. We agree with that conclusion. Being responsible for lost sales of a competitive product is surely foreseeable; such losses constitute the full compensation set forth by Congress, as interpreted by the Supreme Court, while staying well within the traditional meaning of proximate cause. Such lost sales should therefore clearly be compensable.

Recovery for lost sales of a device not covered by the patent in suit is not of course expressly provided for by the patent statute. Express language is not required, however. Statutes speak in general terms rather than specifically expressing every detail. Under the patent statute, damages should be awarded "where necessary to afford the plaintiff full compensation for the infringement." General Motors, 461 U.S. at 654. Thus, to refuse to award reasonably foreseeable damages necessary to make Rite–Hite whole would be inconsistent with the meaning of § 284.

Kelley asserts that to allow recovery for the ADL–100 would contravene the policy reason for which patents are granted: "[T]o promote the progress of . . . the useful arts." U.S. Const., art. I, § 8, cl. 8. Because an inventor is only entitled to exclusivity to the extent he or she has invented and disclosed a novel, nonobvious, and useful device, Kelley argues, a patent may never be used to restrict competition in the sale of products not covered by the patent in suit. In support, Kelley cites antitrust case law condemning the use of a patent as a means to obtain a "monopoly" on unpatented material. See, e.g., Ethyl Gasoline Corp. v. United States, 309 U.S. 436, 459 (1940)("The patent monopoly of one invention may no more be enlarged for the exploitation of a monopoly of another than for the exploitation of an unpatented article, or for the exploitation or promotion of a business not embraced within the patent.").

These cases are inapposite to the issue raised here. The present case does not involve expanding the limits of the patent grant in violation of the antitrust laws; it simply asks, once infringement of a valid patent is found, what compensable injuries result from that infringement, i.e., how may the patentee be made whole. Rite–Hite is not attempting to exclude its competitors from making, using, or selling a product not within the scope of its patent. The Truk Stop restraint was found to infringe the '847 patent, and Rite–Hite is simply seeking adequate compensation for that infringement; this is not an antitrust issue.

Kelley further asserts that, as a policy matter, inventors should be encouraged by the law to practice their inventions. This is not a meaningful or persuasive argument, at least in this context. A patent is granted in exchange for a patentee's disclosure of an invention, not for the patentee's use of the invention. There is no requirement in this country that a patentee make, use, or sell its patented invention. See Continental Paper Bag Co. v. Eastern Paper Bag Co., 210 U.S. 405, 424–30 (1908)(irrespective of a patentee's own use of its patented invention, it may enforce its rights under the patent). If a patentee's failure to practice a patented invention frustrates an important public need for the invention, a court need not enjoin infringement of the patent. See 35 U.S.C. § 283 (1988)(courts may grant injunctions in accordance with the principles of equity). Accordingly, courts have in rare instances exercised their discretion to deny injunctive relief in order to protect the public interest. See, e.g., Hybritech Inc. v. Abbott Lab., 4 U.S.P.Q.2d 1001 (C.D.Cal.1987)(public interest required that injunction not stop supply of medical test kits that the patentee itself was not marketing), aff'd, 849 F.2d 1446 (Fed.Cir.1988); Vitamin Technologists, Inc. v. Wisconsin Alumni Research Found., 64 U.S.P.Q. 285 (9th Cir. 1945)(public interest warranted refusal of injunction on irradiation of oleomargarine); City of Milwaukee v. Activated Sludge, Inc., 21 U.S.P.Q. 69 (7th Cir.1934)(injunction refused against city operation of sewage disposal plant because of public health danger). Whether a patentee sells its patented invention is not crucial in determining lost profits damages. Normally, if the patentee is not selling a product, by definition there can be no lost profits. However, in this case, Rite–Hite did sell its own patented products, the MDL–55 and the ADL–100 restraints.

Kelley has thus not provided, nor do we find, any justification in the statute, precedent, policy, or logic to limit the compensability of lost sales of a patentee's device that directly competes with the infringing device if it is proven that those lost sales were caused in fact by the infringement. Such lost sales are reasonably foreseeable and the award of damages is necessary to provide adequate compensation for infringement under 35 U.S.C. § 284. Thus, Rite–Hite's ADL–100 lost sales are legally compensable and we affirm the award of lost profits on the 3,283 sales lost to Rite–Hite's wholesale business in ADL–100 restraints.

II.   Damages on the Dock Levelers

[This portion of the opinion was joined by Judges Lourie, Rich, Michel, Plager, Clevenger, and Schall]

Based on the "entire market value rule," the district court awarded lost profits on 1,692 dock levelers that it found Rite–Hite would have sold with the ADL–100 and MDL–55 restraints. Kelley argues that this award must be set aside because Rite–Hite failed to establish that the dock levelers were eligible to be included in the damage computation under the entire market value rule. We agree.

When a patentee seeks damages on unpatented components sold with a patented apparatus, courts have applied a formulation known as the "entire market value rule" to determine whether such components should be included in the damage computation, whether for reasonable royalty purposes,[b] see Leesona Corp. v. United States, 599 F.2d 958, 974 (Ct.Cl.), cert. denied, 444 U.S. 991 (1979), or for lost profits purposes, see Paper Converting Machine Co. v. Magna–Graphics Corp., 745 F.2d 11, 23 (Fed. Cir.1984). Early cases invoking the entire market value rule required that for a patentee owning an "improvement patent" to recover damages calculated on sales of a larger machine incorporating that improvement, the patentee was required to show that the entire value of the whole machine, as a marketable article, was "properly and legally attributable" to the patented feature. Subsequently, our predecessor court held that damages for component parts used with a patented apparatus were recoverable under the entire market value rule if the patented apparatus "was of such paramount importance that it substantially created the value of the component parts." Marconi Wireless Telegraph Co. v. United States, 53 U.S.P.Q. 246, 250 (Ct. Cl.1942), aff'd in part and vacated in part, 320 U.S. 1 (1943). We have held that the entire market value rule permits recovery of damages based on the value of a patentee's entire apparatus containing

----

[b] This issue of royalty base is not to be confused with the relevance of anticipated collateral sales to the determination of a reasonable royalty rate. See Deere & Co. v. International Harvester Co., 710 F.2d 1551, 1559 (Fed.Cir.1983).

several features when the patent-related feature is the "basis for customer demand." State Indus., 883 F.2d at 1580.

The entire market value rule has typically been applied to include in the compensation base unpatented components of a device when the unpatented and patented components are physically part of the same machine. See, e.g., Western Elec. Co. v. Stewart–Warner Corp., 631 F.2d 333 (4th Cir.1980), cert. denied, 450 U.S. 971 (1981). The rule has been extended to allow inclusion of physically separate unpatented components normally sold with the patented components. See, e.g., Paper Converting, 745 F.2d at 23. However, in such cases, the unpatented and patented components together were considered to be components of a single assembly or parts of a complete machine, or they together constituted a functional unit.

In Paper Converting, this court articulated the entire market value rule in terms of the objectively reasonable probability that a patentee would have made the relevant sales. See 745 F.2d at 23. Furthermore, we may have appeared to expand the rule when we emphasized the financial and marketing dependence of the unpatented component on the patented component. See id. In Paper Converting, however, the rule was applied to allow recovery of profits on the unpatented components only because all the components together were considered to be parts of a single assembly. The references to "financial and marketing dependence" and "reasonable probability" were made in the context of the facts of the case and did not separate the rule from its traditional moorings.

Specifically, recovery was sought for the lost profits on sales of an entire machine for the high speed manufacture of paper rolls comprising several physically separate components, only one of which incorporated the invention. The machine was comprised of the patented "rewinder" component and several auxiliary components, including an "unwind stand" that supported a large roll of supply paper to the rewinder, a "core loader" that supplied paperboard cores to the rewinder, an "embosser" that embossed the paper and provided a special textured surface, and a "tail sealer" that sealed the paper's trailing end to the finished roll. Although we noted that the auxiliary components had "separate usage" in that they each separately performed a part of an entire rewinding operation, the components together constituted one functional unit, including the patented component, to produce rolls of paper. The auxiliary components derived their market value from the patented rewinder because they had no useful purpose independent of the patented rewinder.

Similarly, our subsequent cases have applied the entire market value rule only in situations in which the patented and unpatented components were analogous to a single functioning unit. See, e.g., Kalman v. Berlyn Corp., 914 F.2d 1473, 1485 (Fed.Cir.1990)(affirming award of damages for filter screens used with a patented filtering device); Kori Corp. v. Wilco Marsh Buggies & Draglines, Inc., 761 F.2d 649, 656 (Fed.Cir.)(affirming an award of damages for unpatented uppers of an improved amphibious vehicle having a patented pontoon structure), cert. denied, 474 U.S. 902 (1985).

Thus, the facts of past cases clearly imply a limitation on damages, when recovery is sought on sales of unpatented components sold with patented components, to the effect that the unpatented components must function together with the patented component in some manner so as to produce a desired end product or result. All the components together must be analogous to components of a single assembly or be parts of a complete machine, or they must constitute a functional unit. Our precedent has not extended liability to include items that have essentially no functional relationship to the patented invention and that may have been sold with an infringing device only as a matter of convenience or business advantage. We are not persuaded that we should extend that liability. Damages on such items would constitute more than what is "adequate to compensate for the infringement."

The facts of this case do not meet this requirement. The dock levelers operated to bridge the gap between a loading dock and a truck. The patented vehicle restraint operated to secure the rear of the truck to the loading dock. Although the two devices may have been used together, they did not function together to achieve one result and each could effectively have been used independently of each other. The parties had established positions in marketing dock levelers long prior to developing the vehicle restraints. Rite–Hite and Kelley were pioneers in that industry and for many years were primary competitors. Although following Rite–Hite's introduction of its restraints onto the market, customers frequently solicited package bids for the simultaneous installation of restraints and dock levelers, they did so because such bids facilitated contracting and construction scheduling, and because both Rite–Hite and Kelley encouraged this linkage by offering combination discounts. The dock levelers were thus sold by Kelley with the restraints only for marketing reasons, not because they essentially functioned together. We distinguish our conclusion to permit damages based on lost sales of the unpatented (not covered by the patent in suit) ADL–100 devices, but not on lost sales of the unpatented dock levelers, by emphasizing that the Kelley Truk Stops were devices competitive with the ADL–100s, whereas the dock levelers were merely items sold together with the restraints for convenience and business advantage. It is a clear purpose of the patent law to redress competitive damages resulting from infringement of the patent, but there is no basis for extending that recovery to include damages for items that are neither competitive with nor function with the patented invention.

III.   [Deleted: see Note 7—eds.]

IV.   Computation of Reasonable Royalty

[This portion of the opinion was joined by Judges Lourie, Rich, Michel, Plager, Clevenger and Schall]

The district court found that Rite–Hite as a manufacturer was entitled to an award of a reasonable royalty on 502 infringing restraint or restraint-leveler sales for which it had not proved that it contacted the Kelley customer prior to the infringing Kelley sale. Rite–Hite, 774 F.Supp. at 1534. The court awarded a royalty equal to approximately fifty percent of Rite–Hite's estimated lost profits per unit sold to retailers. Id. at 1535. Further, the court found that Rite–Hite as a retailer was entitled to a reasonable royalty amounting to approximately one-third its estimated lost distribution income per infringing sale. Kelley challenges the amount of the royalty as grossly excessive and legally in error.

A patentee is entitled to no less than a reasonable royalty on an infringer's sales for which the patentee has not established entitlement to lost profits. 35 U.S.C. § 284 (1988). The royalty may be based upon an established royalty, if there is one, or if not, upon the supposed result of hypothetical negotiations between the plaintiff and defendant.[c] The hypothetical negotiation requires the court to envision the terms of a licensing agreement reached as the result of a supposed meeting between the patentee and the infringer at the time infringement began.

The district court here conducted the hypothetical negotiation analysis. It determined that Rite–Hite would have been willing to grant a competitor a license to use the '847 invention only if it received a royalty of no less than one-half of the per unit profits that it was foregoing. In so determining, the court considered that the '847 patent was a "pioneer" patent with manifest commercial success; that Rite–Hite had consistently followed a policy of exploiting its own patents, rather than licensing to competitors; and that Rite–Hite would have had to forego a large profit by granting a license to Kelley because Kelley was a strong competitor and Rite–Hite anticipated being able to sell a large number of restraints and related products. It was thus not unreasonable for the district court to find that an unwilling patentee would only license for one-half its expected lost profits and that such an amount was a reasonable royalty. The fact that the award was not based on the infringer's profits did not make it an unreasonable award.

■ NIES, CIRCUIT JUDGE, with whom ARCHER, CHIEF JUDGE, SMITH, SENIOR CIRCUIT JUDGE, and MAYER, CIRCUIT JUDGE join, dissenting-in-part.

The majority uses the provision in 35 U.S.C. § 284 for "damages" as a tool to expand the property rights granted by a patent. I dissent.

I would hold that the diversion of ADL–100 sales is not an injury to patentee's property rights granted by the '847 patent. To constitute legal injury for which lost profits may be awarded, the infringer must interfere with the patentee's property right to an exclusive market in goods embodying the invention of the patent in suit. The patentee's property rights do

[c] The hypothetical negotiation is often referred to as a "willing licensor/ willing licensee" negotiation. However, this is an inaccurate, and even absurd, characterization when, as here, the patentee does not wish to grant a license. See Hanson v. Alpine Valley Ski Area, Inc., 718 F.2d 1075, 1081 (The willing licensee/licensor concept is "employed by the court as a means of arriving at reasonable compensation and its validity does not depend on the actual willingness of the parties to the lawsuit to engage in such negotiations[; t]here is, of course, no actual willingness on either side.").

not extend to its market in other goods unprotected by the litigated patent. Rite–Hite was compensated for the lost profits for 80 sales associated with the MDL–55, the only product it sells embodying the '847 invention. That is the totality of any possible entitlement to lost profits. Under 35 U.S.C. § 284, therefore, Rite–Hite is entitled to "damages" calculated as a reasonable royalty on the remainder of Kelley's infringing restraints.

I also disagree that the calculations of a reasonable royalty may be based on a percentage of Rite–Hite's lost profits. Under 35 U.S.C. § 284, a reasonable royalty must be attributed to Kelley's "use of the invention." A royalty must be based on the value of the patented hook, not on other features in the infringing device, e.g., the motors, which form no part of the patented invention used by Kelley.

LOST PROFITS

The Insufficiency of "But–For" as the Sole Test

The term "damages" in the patent statute must be interpreted in light of the familiar common law principles of legal or proximate cause associated generally with that term. In rejecting a "but-for" standard for determining "damages" in the Clayton Act, the Supreme Court observed: "[A] number of judge-made rules circumscribed the availability of damages recoveries in both tort and contract litigation—doctrines such as foreseeability and proximate cause, directness of injury, certainty of damages, and privity of contract.... " Associated Gen. Contractors, Inc. v. California State Council of Carpenters, 459 U.S. 519, 532–33 (1983) (citations omitted).

Under this Supreme Court precedent, the law is clear that proximate cause is applied as a legal limitation on "damages" in connection with the statutory torts which the Court has considered. A "but-for" test tells us nothing about whether the injury is legally one which is compensable. As above stated, the lack of proximate causation will preclude recovery for certain losses even though a "but-for" standard of injury in fact is satisfied.

Property Rights Granted by Patent

An inventor is entitled to a patent by meeting the statutory requirements respecting disclosure of the invention. Prior commercialization of the invention has never been a requirement in our law to obtain a patent. An inventor is merely required to teach others his invention in his patent application. Thus, when faced with the question of whether a patentee was entitled to enjoin an infringer despite the patentee's failure to use its invention, the Supreme Court held for the patentee. Congress provided a right to exclusive use and to deny that privilege would destroy that right. An injunction preserves the patentee's exclusive right to market embodiments of the patented invention.

These clearly established principles, however, do not lead to the conclusion that the patentee's failure to commercialize plays no role in determining damages. That the quid pro quo for obtaining a patent is disclosure of the invention does not dictate the answer to the question of the legal scope of damages. The patent system was not designed merely to build up a library of information by disclosure, valuable though that is, but to get new products into the marketplace during the period of exclusivity so that the public receives full benefits from the grant. The Congress of the fledgling country did not act so quickly in enacting the Patent Act of 1790 merely to further intellectual pursuits.

Thus, a patentee may withhold from the public the benefit of use of its invention during the patent term, and the public has no way to withdraw the grant for nonuse. Like the owner of a farm, a patentee may let his property lay fallow. But it is anomalous to hold that Congress, by providing an incentive for the patentee to enter the market, intended the patentee to be rewarded the same for letting his property lay fallow during the term of the patent as for making the investment necessary to commercializing a new product or licensing others to do so, in order that the public benefits from the invention.

Precedent Respecting the Apportionment of Profits and the Entire Market Value Rule

The patentee's willingness and ability to supply the patented invention during the period of infringement is the thread that runs through all precedent of this court respecting "lost profits" awards. See Kori Corp. v. Wilco Marsh Buggies & Draglines, Inc., 761 F.2d 649, 653 (Fed.Cir.), cert. denied, 474 U.S. 902 (1985)(Patentee "is entitled to be compensated [for its lost profits] on the basis of its ability to exploit the patent ")(emphasis added). While the majority does not specifically overturn any of our precedent, the basic premises expressed therein are eviscerated.

"Foreseeability" is not the Test for Patent Damages

In the majority's view, the consideration of patent rights ends upon a finding of infringement. The separate question of damages under its test does not depend on patent rights but only on foreseeable competitive injury. This position cannot be squared with the premise that compensation is due only for injury to patent rights. Thus, the majority's foreseeability standard contains a false premise, namely, that the "relevant market" can be "broadly defined" to include all competitive truck restraints made by the patentee. The relevant market for determining damages is confined to the market for the invention in which the patentee holds exclusive property rights.

The majority goes on to find the award of damages for lost sales of ADL–100s a foreseeable injury for infringement of the '847 patent. This is a remarkable finding. The facts are that Rite–Hite began marketing its ADL–100 motorized restraint in 1980. Kelley put out its Truk Stop restraint in June 1982. There is no dispute in this case that Kelley "designed around" the protection afforded by any patent related to the ADL–100 with which Kelley's Truk Stop restraint was intended to compete. Two years later, the '847 patent in suit issued on the later-developed alternative hook technology used in the MDL–55. Kelley would have to have had prescient vision to foresee that it would be held an infringer of the unknown claims of the subsequently issued '847 patent and that its lawful competition with the ADL–100 would be transformed into a compensable injury.

### The ADL–100 Patents

If nothing else, the patent term limit provision of 35 U.S.C. § 154 is skewed by protecting the profits on goods made under one patent for infringement of another. Under the majority's decision, the 17–year terms of the ADL–100 patents are meaningless. Rite–Hite is entitled to the add-on years provided by the later '847 patent after the terms of the ADL–100 patents expire. Congress has provided the term and the basis for protection of ADL–100 restraints. An award of damages on ADL–100s based on infringement of the '847 patent expands the term of protection as well as the basis for protection. Moreover, the majority would award damages for losses connected to the ADL–100 even if the patents on that device are invalid (albeit under a slight variation of a "but-for" test). If Rite–Hite had asserted infringement of the ADL–100 patents, it would receive no lost profits based on invalid ADL–100 patents but, nevertheless, is held entitled to lost profits on ADL–100s based on the '847 patent. This construction of the statute seems patently absurd.

No one argues that Rite–Hite is violating the antitrust laws. However, an award of damages for infringement of one patent based on losses of sales of a product not within the protected market violates antitrust policies. Under those policies, Rite–Hite is not entitled to tribute for infringement of one patent for losses in connection with a competitive product protected, if at all, only by other patents. This court has no license to elevate patent rights in the guise of damages over antitrust policies which preclude enlargement of the exclusive market provided by the '847 patent to promote and exploit the business of a patentee in goods not embraced within the patent.

### LEVELER SALES

I agree with the majority that under the entire market value rule, Rite–Hite is not entitled to lost profits on dock levelers, sold in conjunction with patented or unpatented restraints. However, I disagree with the majority's reasoning. The entire market value rule is based on a realistic evaluation of the commercial magnetism of the patented invention, not on whether components in a machine—or auxiliary goods—function together. I will not lengthen this already lengthy opinion but merely note that the majority proffers strained interpretations of the cited precedent. I would deny the award because the sales of levelers were not attributable to consumer demand for the invention of the '847 patent.

### CALCULATION OF A REASONABLE ROYALTY

The district court awarded damages in the form of a reasonable royalty for 502 infringing sales based on lost profits on Rite–Hite's restraints and restraint leveler packages. This "reasonable royalty," which totals $1,045.00 per infringing restraint, is more than the price of Rite–Hite's patented MDL–55, more than 75 percent of the average net sale price of Kelley's Truk–Stop, and 33 times greater than Kelley's net profit on its entire machine. If lost profits on ADL–100's were not recoverable as such, the court said it would have raised the amount of the reasonable royalty to include all of Rite–Hite's anticipated profits on ADL–100 units and packages. Rite–Hite, 774 F.Supp. at 1540 n. 22.

In determining a reasonable royalty, the district court started with basically wrong ideas even if ADL–100s and levelers were protected by the '847 patent. The court erroneously believed Kelley had to pay a reasonable royalty on ADL–100 sales if lost profits were not awarded. Id. This is a fundamental misunderstanding. Rite–Hite is entitled to a reasonable royalty on Kelley's sales of infringing devices. Rite–Hite would be entitled to a reasonable royalty on those sales even if it made no sales of a competing product. Further, where a patentee is not entitled to lost profit damages, lost profits may not, in effect, be awarded by merely labelling the basis of the award a reasonable royalty. See SmithKline Diagnostics, Inc. v. Helena Labs. Corp., 926 F.2d 1161, 1165, 1168 (Fed.Cir.1991)(rejecting SKD's proposed use of its lost profits figure as a "reasonable royalty").

■ NEWMAN, CIRCUIT JUDGE, with whom CIRCUIT JUDGE RADER joins, concurring in part and dissenting in part.

The court today takes an important step toward preserving damages as an effective remedy for patent infringement. Patent infringement is a commercial tort, and the remedy should compensate for the actual financial injury that was caused by the tort. Thus I concur in the majority's result with respect to entitlement to damages for lost sales of the ADL–100.

Yet the court draws a new bright line, adverse to patentees and the businesses built on patents, declining to make the injured claimants whole. The majority now restricts en banc the patentee's previously existing, already limited right to prove damages for lost sales of collateral items—the so-called "convoyed" sales. Such remedy is now eliminated entirely unless the convoyed item is "functionally" inseparable from the patented item. The court thus propounds a legally ambivalent and economically unsound policy, authorizing damages for the lost sales of the ADL–100 but not those dock levelers that were required to be bid and sold as a package with the MDL–55 and the ADL–100.

## I. THE LOST PROFITS FOR THE ADL–100

I agree that lost profits on the lost sales of the MDL–55 and the ADL–100 are the proper measure of compensatory damages for Kelley's infringement of Rite–Hite's '847 patent. The considerations with respect to the ADL–100 are those of general damages: directness, foreseeability, duty.

Patent damages must be viewed with a practical eye in order to implement the policy of damages law. It is not the usual situation that an infringing device takes sales from a patentee's line of more than one product, not all of which were made under the patent that is infringed. However, this does not change the application of 35 U.S.C. § 284. It may be simply differences in inventorship, or the timing of the discoveries, that places inventions in different patents of the same patent owner. Such a situation is not unusual. An example may be the case at bar, wherein Rite–Hite disclosed and claimed the infringed restraint in a later-filed patent having a different inventive entity than the patent on the ADL–100. Examples abound in the chemical field, where inventors may create related chemical compounds, obtain patents as the research progresses, and commercialize one of them. Should the infringer divert sales from another member of this series, according to Kelley, the only damages available would be a royalty at a sufficiently low rate to provide a profit to the infringer. The patent law is not prisoner of such irrational economics.

## II.   THE LOST CONVOYED SALES OF DOCK LEVELERS

### A.   Principles of Damages Law

The basic principle of damages law is that the injured party shall be made whole. On the facts on which the district court awarded damages for certain lost sales of dock levelers, the relationships were direct, causation was proved, the scope of recovery was narrow, and the circumstances were unusual. Reversing the district court, the majority holds that if the patented and convoyed items also have a separate market, there can never be recovery for the lost sales of the convoyed items. I do not believe that such a rule is necessary, or correct, in patent cases.

The majority adopts the rule for patent cases that lost "convoyed" sales can not be recompensed, whatever the directness of the injury and whatever the weight of the proof, unless the thing convoyed is a "functional" part of the thing patented. Heretofore, the question of recovery for lost sales of collateral items was a matter of fact and proof, the court looking at the closeness of the relationship between the items and the quality of the proof, cognizant of the policy of setting reasonable limits to liability.

A wrongdoer is, simply put, responsible for the direct, foreseeable consequences of the wrong. Indeed, in General Motors Corp. v. Devex Corp., 461 U.S. 648, 655 (1983), the Court referred to "Congress' overriding purpose of affording patent owners complete compensation," the Court observing that: When Congress wished to limit an element of recovery in a patent infringement action, it said so explicitly. 461 U.S. at 653. Thus the Court reiterated that limitations to recovery for patent infringement are not to be inferred.

### B.   The "Package" Sales of Dock Levelers and Truck Restraints

These dock leveler sales were as direct a target of the infringement as were the ADL–100 sales, and the quality of the proofs was equally high. The evidence shows the same transaction-by-transaction losses of sales to Kelley for the dock levelers as for the ADL–100 truck restraints, indeed in the same bid and sale packages. Precedent previously recognized that compensation may be appropriate when the items are sold together, whether or not they also have separate markets.

Recovery of damages for lost "convoyed" sales has always required a high standard of proof, lest remote and speculative claims be opportunistically pressed. However, it is not correct to hold that recovery is never possible unless the relationship of the patented and convoyed products is such that the only and necessary use is as a "single functioning unit." Indeed, even the majority's new requirement is met in this case. These specific dock levelers were not sold separately because the customer or Kelley required that they be sold together; and it is undisputed that they are used together.

The correct question is not whether the infringing truck restraint was part of a larger combination whereby the truck restraint could not function without the dock leveler, or whether the truck restraint or the dock leveler also had an independent market and use. The correct rule was stated in Leesona Corp. v. United States, 599 F.2d 958, 974 (Ct.Cl.), cert. denied, 444 U.S. 991 (1979), that it is not the physical joinder or separation of the contested items that determines their inclusion in or exclusion from the compensation base, so much as their financial and marketing dependence on the patented item under standard marketing procedures for the goods in question.

## Radio Steel & Mfg. Co. v. MTD Products, Inc.

United States Court of Appeals, Federal Circuit, 1986.
788 F.2d 1554.

■ FRIEDMAN, CIRCUIT JUDGE.

I

The case involves U.S. Patent No. 3,282,600, owned by Radio Steel & Mfg. Co. (Radio Steel). The patent covers an improved wheelbarrow. The complaint alleged that MTD Products, Inc. (MTD), had manufactured and sold wheelbarrows that infringed the patent. After trial, the district court held that the patent was valid but not infringed. Radio Steel & Mfg. Co. v. MTD Products, Inc., 566 F.Supp. 609 (N.D.Ohio 1983). In a previous appeal, 731 F.2d 840 (Fed.Cir.), cert. denied, 469 U.S. 831, 105 S.Ct. 119, 83 L.Ed.2d 62 (1984), we affirmed the district court's holding of patent validity, reversed its holding of noninfringement, and remanded the case for an accounting.

Following a trial in the accounting phase of the case, the district court awarded Radio Steel damages of $588,719.93 plus postjudgment interest and costs. The court found that "[t]he overwhelming majority of MTD's sales of the infringing wheelbarrows was to three retail store chains: White Stores, Montgomery Ward, and K–Mart." It determined that Radio Steel was entitled to recover lost profits on MTD's sales to K–Mart and the White Stores, which it calculated at $296,937.21. On MTD's sales to stores other than those two, the court ruled that Radio Steel was entitled to a reasonable royalty of ten percent, which amounted to $155,634.81.

The district court's combined damage award of $588,719.93 included prejudgment interest. The court rejected MTD's contention that Radio Steel was not entitled to prejudgment interest because it had allowed patent notices to remain on its wheelbarrows after the patent had expired.

The court held that MTD's infringement was not willful and therefore declined to enhance the damages or to award attorney fees.

II

In its appeal, MTD contends that (A) the award of lost profits was improper, (B) the ten percent royalty rate was excessive, and (C) Radio Steel's failure to remove patent markings from its wheelbarrows after the patent had expired barred the award to it of prejudgment interest.

A.  Lost Profits. In awarding lost profits, the district court applied the standard announced in Panduit Corp. v. Stahlin Bros. Fibre Works, Inc., 575 F.2d 1152 (6th Cir.1978), which we implicitly approved in Central Soya Co., Inc. v. George Hormel & Co., 723 F.2d 1573 (Fed.Cir.1983). Under Panduit, to receive lost profits a patent owner must prove: (1) demand for the patented product, (2) absence of acceptable noninfringing substitutes, (3) his manufacturing and marketing capability to exploit the demand, and (4) the amount of the profit he would have made. Panduit, at 1156. The district court found that Radio Steel had proved the four elements of Panduit with respect to sales MTD made to K–Mart and the White Stores.

On appeal, MTD challenges only the district court's finding that there were no acceptable noninfringing substitutes. That was a finding of fact that we can reverse only if it is clearly erroneous. MTD has not shown that the finding has that fatal flaw.

The district court found that the patented wheelbarrow has several attributes which demonstrate an absence of substitutes. The patented wheelbarrow could be shipped unassembled, thereby allowing more compact shipping with lower shipping costs. The wheelbarrows could be easily assembled at the stores.... The absence of the "shin scraper" brace along the rear of the legs, which was necessary in other wheelbarrows to achieve structural regidity [sic], also added to the popularity of the patented wheelbarrow.... Although other noninfringing contractor-type wheelbarrows exist in the market, such wheelbarrows are not acceptable substitutes for the patented product.

MTD contends, however, that wheelbarrows for many years past ... perform the same function of transporting a load contained in a bowl or tray on one wheel propelled by an operator holding the handles on which the bowl or tray is mounted and propelling the assembly on the single wheel. All wheelbarrows which have been on the market produce this result and are available acceptable substitutes. Some of these wheelbarrows ... have two-piece handles which facilitate packaging of the parts of the wheelbarrow, and these too are available acceptable non-infringing wheelbarrows.

This argument is another formulation of the contention, rejected twice by the district court and once by this court, that the patent simply was a combination of old elements. It ignores the district court's earlier ruling in the liability phase that "[i]t is the totality of all the elements and their interaction with each other which is the inventor's contribution to the art of wheelbarrow making." 566 F.Supp. at 619. It also ignores the statement in our prior opinion that "as the district court held, the '600 patent 'descri[bed] ... a new and improved complete wheelbarrow.'" 731 F.2d at 845. The various wheelbarrows to which MTD refers incorporate only some, but not all, of the elements of the patent. They do not establish that the district court's finding that these were not acceptable noninfringing substitutes is clearly erroneous.

B. *Reasonable Royalty.* The district court's determination that ten percent was a reasonable royalty on MTD's sales to stores other than K–Mart or White Stores reflected the court's own independent judgment and was not based upon the court's acceptance of the evidence of either party. Indeed, the court rejected the reasonable royalty figures of both parties.

The district court rejected MTD's estimate of two percent, stating that it did not find that figure to be a reasonable royalty. It observed that Radio Steel lost sales not only of the patented wheelbarrows, but also of collateral items that are normally attendant to the sales of wheelbarrows, such as garden carts and lawn mowers. The court also noted that MTD made substantial sales to White Stores, Montgomery Ward, and K–Mart of noninfringing wheelbarrows with the sale of the infringing wheelbarrows.

The court rejected Radio Steel's figure of twenty-one percent, indicating its view that that amount, which is two-thirds of Radio Steel's incremental profit, was too high a royalty for a patent that would expire in three years. The court also expressed concern that Radio Steel's twenty-one percent figure would allow the company to collect unreasonably high royalties from MTD's sales to Montgomery Ward, with whom Radio Steel had been unable to establish a regular and consistent merchandising arrangement. The court concluded that [c]onsidering the age of the patent, the patent's novelty and contribution to the industry, Radio Steel's unwillingness to license, the profit margin on the wheelbarrows, the availability of wheelbarrows from other manufacturers, and the collateral sale benefits, the Court finds 10% to be a reasonable royalty on MTD's sale of wheelbarrows to other than K–Mart and the White Stores.

MTD challenges the ten percent royalty on two grounds.

1. MTD asserts that ten percent is unreasonably high because it far exceeds the profit MTD actually made on the infringing wheelbarrows. It relies on testimony by its treasurer that the profit MTD made on the sale of infringing wheelbarrows was low, and that in one year it had a loss on those sales.

The determination of a reasonably royalty, however, is based not on the infringer's profit, but on the royalty to which a willing licensor and a willing licensee would have agreed at the time the infringement began.

Panduit, 575 F.2d at 1158. Moreover, the district court could well have discounted MTD's profit figures because the treasurer also testified that the infringing wheelbarrows might have been utilized as loss-leaders at various times during the period of infringement.

MTD contends that ten percent is not commensurate with the "patent's novelty and contribution" to the industry. MTD contends that the patent's "contribution, if any, consisted of forming channels on the ends of the cross-brace member as demonstrated at the trial on liability." MTD continues: [Radio Steel] did not invent the wheel, nor the bowl or tray, nor the supporting legs, nor the handles and certainly not two-piece handles which are useful in the packaging of the wheelbarrow parts. Wheelbarrows are extremely old and any contribution to the world's knowledge of wheelbarrows must of necessity be of a minute scale. The cost of forming channels on the ends of the cross-brace member, is to be compared to the cost of the wheel, the bowl or tray, the legs, and the handles. The value of each of the parts is commensurate with the cost. The importance of each of these parts is to be considered. The wheel is important; the bowl or tray is important; the legs are important; and the handles (one piece or two pieces) are important.

This is but another phrasing of the argument, which we have rejected in our discussion of lost profits, that the patent is only a combination of old elements and that their aggregation constituted a "minuscule" and "meager" contribution to the art.

The record fully supports the district court's selection of a ten percent reasonable royalty. MTD's treasurer testified that at the time of infringement, MTD expected to make a net profit of about six percent on its sale of infringing wheelbarrows. Radio Steel's vice president of finance testified that its net profit from its sales of patented wheelbarrows was ten plus-or-minus two percent. On this record we have no basis for rejecting the district court's selection of ten percent as a reasonable royalty rate. Deere & Co. v. International Harvester Co., 710 F.2d 1551 (Fed.Cir.1983).

## NTP, Inc. v. Research in Motion, Ltd.

United States District Court, E.D. Virginia, 2003.
270 F.Supp.2d 751.

[Plaintiff NTP, Inc. ("NTP") alleged that certain technology manufactured by Defendant Research In Motion, Ltd. ("RIM") directly and indirectly infringes upon thirty-one claims in seven patents (the "Campana patents"). The Campana patents sought to integrate electronic mail with wireless transmission. Prior to the Campana patents, the transfer of electronic mail was landline based. The Campana patents sought to increase the ability for individuals to gain access to their incoming and pending email, without requiring them to access a telephone line. The accused devices were the BlackBerry Pager, the BlackBerry Enterprise Server ("BES"), and the BlackBerry "wireless email solution." After the court denied defendant's motion for summary judgment, 261 F.Supp.2d 423 (E.D. Virginia, 2002), a jury trial was held.]

■ SPENCER, DISTRICT J.

At the conclusion of the trial, the jury returned a verdict in favor of NTP, finding that various RIM products and services infringed the Campana Patents. In addition, the jury made an express finding that RIM willfully infringed the Campana Patents. NTP has filed a series of post-trial motions seeking enhanced damages and attorney fees, as well as prejudgment and postjudgment interest.

II.

### A. Enhanced Damages

Upon a finding of infringement by the jury, "the court may increase the damages up to three times the amount found" if the jury also finds that the defendant willfully infringed the patents-in-suit. 35 U.S.C. § 284. Enhanced damages not only operate as a punitive measure against individual infringing defendants, but they also serve an overarching purpose as a deterrence of patent infringement. However, these damages are not meant to compensate the plaintiff. In assessing enhanced damages, it is first necessary that the fact-finder determine that the defendant is liable for willful infringement. Such a finding, however, does not mandate that the court award enhanced damages. Indeed, the court must engage in a separate analysis to determine whether the egregiousness of the defendant warrants enhanced damages, and if so, the extent of those damages. The decision whether to award enhanced damages is within the sound discretion of the court.

When addressing the issue of enhanced damages, courts "must consider factors that render defendant's conduct more culpable, as well as factors that are mitigating or ameliorating." *Read Corp. v. Portec, Inc.,* 970 F.2d 816, 826 (Fed.Cir.1992). A court is obliged to consider all relevant circumstances in reaching this determination. In *Read,* the Federal Circuit established that courts should consider the following factors together in determining the degree of the infringer's culpability: (1) whether the infringer deliberately copied the ideas or design of another; (2) whether the infringer, upon notice of the other's patent protection, investigated the scope of the patent and formed a good-faith belief that it was invalid or that it was not infringed; (3) the infringer's behavior as a party to the litigation; (4) the infringer's size and financial condition; (5) the closeness of the case; (6) the duration of the infringer's misconduct; (7) any remedial action by the infringer; (8) the infringer's motivation for harm; and (9) whether the infringer attempted to conceal its misconduct. After taking all of the *Read* factors into consideration, it is clear that enhanced damages are warranted. However, RIM's behavior does not warrant treble damages.

### 1. Whether RIM Deliberately Copied

RIM asserts that this factor should mitigate enhanced damages. There is no evidence that RIM copied any of the Campana Patents. Indeed, NTP concedes this much. It is apparent that RIM developed and conceived its BlackBerry products entirely independent of the Campana patents. Therefore, the absence of copying by RIM is a mitigating factor.

2. *Sufficiency of Investigation*

Possibly the most controverted issue with regards to enhanced damages is the sufficiency of RIM's investigation of the Campana Patents and whether its reliance on the oral opinion of Charles Meyer, RIM's lead in-house counsel, regarding infringement of those patents was in good faith and met RIM's duty of care. NTP is adamant that RIM's investigation was far from adequate, and as a result, RIM failed to satisfy its affirmative duty of care. RIM argues that, based on the totality of the circumstances, its investigation into the Campana Patents met its duty of care. However, RIM's argument as to the "totality of the circumstances"—namely, RIM's investigation *after* NTP filed suit—discounts the fact that NTP only asserted willfulness from the date of NTP's notice letter on January 27, 2000, to the day RIM received its oral opinion from Larry Nixon. Under these circumstances, it is more probative to evaluate RIM's actions immediately after it received the January 2000 notice letter from NTP.

Upon receiving actual notice of another's patent, a potential infringer "has an affirmative duty of care that normally requires the potential infringer to obtain competent legal advice before infringing or continuing to infringe." However, even if a potential infringer obtains legal advice, liability for willful infringement may still attach if that advice is not competent. Thus, the probative question is, whether "under all the circumstances, a reasonable person would prudently conduct himself with any confidence that a court might hold the patent invalid or not infringed." Whether an opinion is incompetent depends on an objective evaluation of the evidence. In order for an opinion to be effective and indicative of the defendant's good faith intent, it "must be premised upon the best information known to the defendant." Furthermore, the Federal Circuit has also noted that oral opinions, especially those that are not objective, carry little weight. However, even if an opinion incorrectly concludes that an infringer would not be liable for infringement, such opinion will mitigate enhanced damages if it is found to be competent.

The January 27, 2000 letter sent by NTP to RIM (the "Notice Letter") listed six patents owned by NTP and referred to a "distinct commercial advantage" available to RIM if it entered into a licensing agreement with NTP. The letter also included the following statement: "As you are aware, the patent laws cover direct infringement, contributory infringement, and inducement to infringe." Finally, the letter included documentation regarding the BlackBerry Desktop Software Installation Guide, the Getting Started Guide, and the BlackBerry solution. RIM adduced evidence that, upon receipt of the Notice Letter sometime during the first week of February 2000, some investigation was done by Charles Meyer with the assistance of in-house patent attorney Krishna Pathiyal, Director of Wireless Innovation Gary Mousseau, and Chief Executive Officer Mike Lazaridis. Both Lazaridis and Mousseau provided "technical assistance" to Meyer and Pathiyal as to how RIM's products worked. As part of his investigation, Meyer performed research to find out who NTP was, read the patent specifications, and reviewed all independent claims of each patent to see if RIM was somehow violating the patent. During the course of his investigation, Meyer met with Lazaridis three or four times and gave Lazaridis two oral reports that were not reduced to writing, because, as he surmised, "there was no need" to reduce them to writing. As a result of this investigation, Meyer concluded that, because one element of all the independent claims was missing, none of RIM's products infringed the six patents identified by NTP in the Notice Letter. On February 27, 2000, Meyer then sent a response to NTP (the "Response Letter") where he asked for more time to complete RIM's "due diligence," and he requested that NTP send a copy of the claims of the pending patent application as well as other documentation that led NTP to believe that RIM should take a license with respect to the Campana Patents. Meyer testified that, from the time he received the Notice Letter to the time he sent the Response Letter, he spent approximately 40 hours researching the patents. Meyer further testified that he spent an additional 10–20 hours with Lazaridis and Pathiyal discussing the patents.

Based on the evidence advanced at trial, it is difficult to determine whether RIM actually conducted any investigation at all. There were inconsistencies in the testimony of Charles Meyer, Krishna Pathiyal, Mike Lazaridis, and Gary Mousseau as to the amount of time spent investigating the Campana Patents, and who was involved in the investigation. Other circumstances that contributed to the doubt that any investigation was conducted include the demeanor of the witnesses, and the lack of any documentation of any aspect of the investigation whatsoever. For example, Charles Meyer's explanation concerning the failure to write notes on the face of the patents was implausible. Meyer's explanation was further undermined when he testified that, instead of writing on the patents, he took notes regarding the patents on separate sheets of paper, but later testified that he failed to locate any of those notes. Moreover, RIM could not locate its copy of the Notice Letter.

In any event, assuming that RIM conducted an investigation, it was not sufficient to meet its required duty of care because Meyer's oral opinion was not competent. A reasonably prudent person under these circumstances would not have confidence that a court would render a finding of non-infringement or invalidity. First, Neither Meyer nor Pathiyal were outside counsel. Therefore, it was more likely that any opinion issued by them would not be objective. Second, Meyer did not conduct a study of invalidity, order a copy of the prosecution history of the patents, or conduct a search of prior art. In addition, Meyer used both Lazaridis and Mousseau, interested parties, as technical resources.

*3. RIM's Litigation Behavior*

RIM consistently engaged in a variety of questionable litigation tactics throughout the course of this action. RIM's method of conducting discovery including its trickling of the delivery of documents, its failure to work with NTP to streamline document production, and its last-minute cancellation of a deposition scheduled to be taken in Waterloo, Ontario, made discovery unnecessarily arduous. Furthermore, RIM's decision to file premature motions for summary judgment before claim construction, and numerous summary judgment motions after construction, which essentially challenged the claim construction, was both wasteful of judicial resources and unduly burdensome to NTP. Along the same lines, RIM continued to improperly challenge the claim construction with the attempted proffering of Larry Nixon as an expert witness. The primary purpose of this testimony was to adduce evidence as to the perceived incorrect claim construction. Finally, RIM attempted to confuse and mislead the jury by conducting a demonstration of the TekNow! system which RIM asserted as prior art, by using updated software that did not exist at the time the system was used.

Accordingly, taking all these circumstances into consideration, RIM's litigation behavior was sufficiently egregious to be considered an enhancing factor.

### 4.   RIM's Size and Financial Condition

As RIM repeatedly acknowledged throughout its pleadings and its closing argument, NTP is a very small corporation, while RIM, in comparison, is a much larger entity. Thus, the primary consideration of this Court is the amount of enhanced damages that RIM can withstand. Such damages should not be awarded if it would severely affect the defendant's financial condition or unduly prejudice the defendant's non-infringing business. NTP argues that RIM received three billion dollars from investors, and according to co-CEO Jim Balsillie, the damages awarded by the jury represents a "small percentage" of RIM's cash reserves. RIM does not dispute that this statement was made, but instead focuses on other aspects of its financial condition. For example, RIM asserts that, on December 19, 2002, it reported a net loss of $92.3 million dollars for that quarter. RIM also asserts that $23.1 million represents a third of RIM's total revenue for its most recent fiscal quarter. RIM asserts that, as a result of its losses, it has had to announce employee layoffs. RIM surmises that, if damages are enhanced, it will result in larger losses and more layoffs.

The evidence established that the BlackBerry line of products is the core of RIM's business. Consequently, there will be little prejudice to RIM's non-infringing business. RIM will not be allowed to focus solely on its revenue and net loss on one hand, while discounting its considerable investment pool on the other. RIM is large enough to withstand enhanced damages in this case.

### 5.   Closeness of the Case

Enhanced damages should not be awarded if the defendant puts forth a "meritorious good faith defense and a substantial challenge to infringement." A case is close if it was "hard-fought" or the jury could have found for the defendant on the issues of infringement, validity, and willfulness, and could have awarded substantially less damages.

RIM argues that it raised substantial arguments with respect to claim construction, including whether the preambles of the claims were limiting;

the meaning of the term "originating processor"; whether the RF receiver and a destination processor can be a single device; whether certain claims require dual pathways; and the significance of the "in association with" and "responding to" limitations. RIM also asserts that it presented numerous prior art references such as ALOHAnet, the Zabarsky Patent, and the TekNow! system. However, in light of the fact that many of RIM's failed motions for summary judgment were aimed at challenging claim construction, RIM's argument here carries little weight. Moreover, RIM was not successful on any of its eight motions for summary judgment. RIM's infringement was clear. Indeed, it offered no real defense to NTP's infringement case at trial. RIM's evidence at trial further demonstrated that RIM's anticipation and obviousness defenses were not substantial. For example, Dr. Jeffrey Reed, RIM's own expert, was not able to correlate any piece of prior art to the specific elements and limitations of the asserted claims. Therefore, because RIM did not put forth a "meritorious good faith defense," or a "substantial challenge to infringement," this was not a close case.

### 6. Duration of RIM's Misconduct

NTP asserts that enhanced damages are appropriate due to RIM's infringement for well over three years, including two in which RIM willfully infringed the Campana Patents. RIM argues that the relevant period of any misconduct should be from the time this lawsuit was initiated until May 12, 2002, when it received its first oral opinion from Larry Nixon. NTP also notes that RIM continues to infringe the Campana Patents as evidenced by Chief Financial Officer Dennis Kavelman's statement during a post-verdict telephone conference that RIM's "products are unchanged." (NTP App. A, at 6.)

Under these circumstances, the duration of RIM's infringing activities was not so egregious to constitute an enhancing factor. However, the duration was too long to be mitigating. Therefore, this factor is neutral.

### 7. Remedial Action Taken by the Defendant

NTP asserts that, in light of Kavelman's assertion that RIM's products are "unchanged," that it has not undertaken any remedial action whatsoever. RIM counters this by stating that it is working on designing around the Campana Patents. (Lazaridis Decl. & 7.) However, RIM noted that such efforts have not been successful thus far. RIM's failed effort to design around the Campana Patents is not sufficient to constitute remedial action because it does not benefit NTP, the owner of the infringed patents, in any way. It is undisputed that, as of the conclusion of the trial, RIM has not engaged in any remedial action designed to benefit NTP by reducing RIM's infringing activities. Accordingly, RIM's failure to engage in such remedial action constitutes an enhancing factor.

### 8. Motivation for Harm

RIM had no motivation to harm NTP, and NTP concedes this point. Therefore, this is a basis for mitigating enhanced damages.

### 9. Concealment of Misconduct

Again, there is no evidence that RIM attempted to conceal any misconduct, and NTP concedes this. Therefore, this is also a basis for mitigating enhanced damages.

Based on the preceding discussion of the *Read* factors, enhanced damages are warranted in this case. However, RIM's conduct is not so egregious to warrant treble damages. Accordingly, the qualifying compensatory damages, as awarded by the jury, will be enhanced by a factor of 0.5. NTP has also asked this Court to enhance post-verdict compensatory damages. As discussed earlier, RIM has not taken any remedial measures to decrease its infringing activities. In fact, shortly after receiving an unfavorable jury verdict, it publicly announced that its products will remain "unchanged." Furthermore, it has stipulated to the infringement of four new models of BlackBerry handheld devices which it fully intends to market and sell. Therefore, there is a sufficient basis to enhance post-verdict damages. Accordingly, the post-verdict compensatory damages will also be enhanced by a factor of 0.5.

### B. Attorney's Fees

As a general rule, absent statutory authority, a "prevailing litigant is ordinarily not entitled to collect a reasonable attorneys' fee from the loser." *Alyeska Pipeline Service Co. v. Wilderness Society,* 421 U.S. 240, 247, 95 S.Ct. 1612, 44 L.Ed.2d 141 (1975). In patent infringement suits, district courts "in exceptional cases may award reasonable attorney fees to the prevailing party." 35 U.S.C. § 285 (2000). The purpose of this section is to award attorney fees in extraordinary cases where there is:

> [A] finding of unfairness or bad faith in the conduct of the losing party, or some other equitable consideration of similar force, which makes it grossly unjust that the winner of the particular law suit be left to bear the burden of his counsel fees which prevailing litigants normally bear.

*Machinery Corp. of America v. Gullfiber AB,* 774 F.2d 467, 471 (Fed.Cir. 1985).

When considering a request for attorney fees under § 285, "the trial judge undertakes a two-step inquiry: he or she must determine whether there is clear and convincing evidence that the case is 'exceptional,' and if so, whether an award of attorney fees to the prevailing party is warranted." *Interspiro USA, Inc. v. Figgie Int'l Inc.* 18 F.3d 927, 933 (Fed.Cir.1994). The first step is a question of fact reviewed for clear error. The second is within the discretion of the trial judge and is reviewed for abuse of discretion. The two steps are interrelated, as "the amount of the attorney fees depends on the extent to which the case is exceptional. In other words, the exceptionality determination highly influences the award setting."

An express finding of willfulness provides a sufficient basis for the award of attorney fees. As a general rule, attorneys fees under section 285 may be justified by any valid basis for awarding increased damages under section 284. Additional factors which may make a case exceptional include: actual wrongful intent or gross negligence, the closeness of the case and the parties' conduct, including evidence of bad faith, misconduct during litigation, fraud, and vexatious or frivolous litigation, inequitable conduct, and whether it would be grossly unfair for the prevailing party to bear the cost of litigation, or where the conduct of the losing party is marked by bad-faith or unfairness.

If this Court decides that this is an exceptional case, it must be determined "whether an award of attorney fees to the prevailing party is warranted." Courts may consider the litigation behavior of both the infringer and the patentee. To that end, "the trial judge is in the best position to weigh considerations such as the closeness of the case, the tactics of counsel, the conduct of the parties, and any other factors that may contribute to a fair allocation of the burdens of litigation as between winner and loser." In any event, an award for attorney's fees must be reasonable. *Gentry Gallery, Inc. v. Berkline Corp.*, 134 F.3d 1473, 1480 (Fed.Cir.1998).

Although the moving party must show that attorney fees are warranted, in the face of the jury's express finding of willful infringement, which, standing alone, is a sufficient basis to award attorney's fees, RIM must put forth a showing as to why attorney fees are not warranted in this case. RIM argues that this is not an exceptional case by asserting the closeness of the case, its own good faith defenses, and NTP's litigation conduct. However, based on the discussion of the *Read* factors, it is clear that this is an exceptional case. Again, there is substantial doubt as to whether any investigation of the Campana Patents occurred upon receipt of the Notice Letter. Even if an investigation was conducted, it was not sufficient to meet its duty of care. RIM's litigation behavior, including its discovery tactics, post-trial motions which rehashed issues previously dealt with on summary judgment, its attempt to advance evidence through an expert that the claim construction is erroneous, and its fraudulent demonstration of the Tek-Now! system with updated software installed by Gary Mousseau, also adds to the exceptionality of this case. Moreover, as discussed earlier, this was not a close case. Therefore, there is clear and convincing evidence that this case is sufficiently exceptional to warrant an award of attorney fees.

RIM advances a compelling argument regarding the difference between the number of patents and claims that NTP asserted in the beginning of the litigation, and the number asserted at trial. RIM notes that when NTP filed suit, it claimed infringement of eight patents having a combined total of over 2,400 claims. RIM further notes that NTP initially refused to limit the number of claims, first filing a "conditional" reduction of the asserted claims to 1,300, then to 500 shortly before the *Markman* hearing. Upon motion by RIM to compel NTP to further reduce its claims, the number of asserted claims was reduced to thirty-one. That number was finally reduced to sixteen claims on the eve of trial.

[I]n light of the fact that NTP slowly whittled down many of the asserted claims throughout the course of the case up until the eve of trial, it is appropriate to reduce the amount of this award. This Court, however, cannot determine to a mathematical certainty the portion of NTP's fees that was devoted to litigating claims that were not asserted. In any event, because NTP accumulated a majority of its fees with respect to other aspects of litigating the case, this Court will reduce NTP's award of attorney fees by 20%.

III.

NTP has also filed a motion for prejudgment and postjudgment interest. RIM does not oppose the award of postjudgment interest. RIM also does not oppose the award of prejudgment interest, or NTP's assertion that such interest should be compounded quarterly. RIM, however, disputes the award of prejudgment interest with respect to the appropriate interest rate. Therefore, the only remaining dispute with respect to prejudgment interest, is whether NTP should be awarded the prime rate of interest or the T-bill rate, as advanced by RIM.

Prejudgment interest is awarded pursuant to 35 U.S.C. § 284. The relevant language of that section states that "[u]pon finding for the claimant the court shall award the claimant damages adequate to compensate for the infringement, but in no event less than a reasonable royalty for the use made of the invention by the infringer, together with interest and costs as fixed by the court." "[P]rejudgment interest should ordinarily be awarded where necessary to afford the plaintiff full compensation for the infringement." *General Motors Corp. v. Devex Corp.*, 461 U.S. 648, 654, 103 S.Ct. 2058, 76 L.Ed.2d 211 (1983). Such interest must be applied only to the compensatory damages, not enhanced or other punitive damages. The determination of whether such interest is warranted, and the rate of interest, is within the ambit of the court's discretion. Typically, "an award of prejudgment interest is necessary to ensure that the patent owner is placed in as good a position as he would have been in had the infringer entered into a reasonable royalty agreement." *General Motors*, 461 U.S. at 655.

NTP asks the Court to apply the prime rate. The prime rate is the interest rate charged by banks to their most credit-worthy customers. The rate is almost always the same among major banks. The prime rate adjusts with changes by the Federal Reserve Board. RIM argues that using the prime rate would be punitive and asserts that it would be more appropriate for the Court to apply the one-year U.S. Treasury bill rate. Treasury bills are short-term securities that mature in one year or less from their issue date. Treasury bills are purchased for a price less than their face value, and when they mature investors may tender them for their face value. The interest is the difference between the purchase price and what is paid by the U.S. Treasury at maturity.

District courts, in their discretion, have selected various rates, including the prime rate, the prime rate plus a percentage, the U.S. Treasury bill rate, the state statutory rate, corporate bond rates, a set consumer credit rate, the rate the patentee actually paid for borrowed funds, and the rate the patentee actually earned on spare cash. 7 Donald S. Chisum, *Chisum on Patents* § 20.03 [4][a][v] (2002). NTP asserts that the prime rate is a fair rate for the use of its money. RIM, asserts that the purpose of prejudgment interest is to ensure that the patent owner is placed in as good a position as he would have been had the infringer entered into a reasonable royalty agreement, and thus, the prime rate will result in an excessive award. RIM argues that the one-year U.S. Treasury bill rate is sufficient to adequately compensate NTP.

To ensure that NTP is placed in as good a position as it would have been in had RIM entered into a reasonable royalty agreement, prejudgment interest will be calculated at the prime rate. Prejudgment interest will apply to compensatory damages only, and will not apply to attorney fees. The prime rate, compounded quarterly, is a conservative, middle-of-the road approach that takes into account normal market fluctuations. Thus, it more adequately places NTP in as good a position as it would have been in had RIM taken a license with NTP. The one-year U.S. Treasury bill rate is too low to accomplish this.

---

In an order issued August 5, 2003, the District Court awarded compensatory damages of $33,446,172.90; attorney's fees in the amount of $4,203,160.79; prejudgment interest of $2,022,838; and enhanced damages of $14,032,161. RIM was permanently enjoined from making, using, offering to sell, selling, or importing in or into the United States the Blackberry products found to infringe NTP's patents. The injunctive order was stayed pending appeal.

---

# Roche Products, Inc. v. Bolar Pharmaceutical Co., Inc.

United States Court of Appeals, Federal Circuit, 1984.
733 F.2d 858.

■ Nichols, Senior Circuit Judge.

[This case arose before Congress amended § 271 to permit certain uses of patented products to generate information required under federal laws regulating drugs. Bolar Pharmaceuticals, a manufacturer of generic drugs engaged, wished to sell Dalmane, a prescription sleeping medication, as soon as its patent term expired. To obtain the data it needed for FDA approval by the date of expiration, it engaged in research using Dalmane during the patent term. Roche Products, holder of the Dalmane patent, sued for infringement. Bolar defended on the ground that the use was experimental, and thus fell within the common law exception discussed in Assignment 22. After finding that Roche's valid was patent and infringed, and that Bolar's use did not qualify for the common law exception because it was commercial, the court went on to consider the issue of remedies:]

IV

The district court refused to grant a permanent injunction against Bolar because it believed the law did not require that it find infringement of the '053 patent. Since we hold that there is infringement, Roche is entitled to a remedy. We are not in a position, however, to decide the form of that remedy.

Roche requested us, at first, to remand this case to the district court with instructions to enter a permanent injunction against infringement by Bolar. [In addition], Roche requests ... an order to confiscate and destroy the data which Bolar has generated during its infringing activity, citing, Pfizer, Inc. v. International Rectifier Corp., 217 U.S.P.Q. 157 (C.D.Cal. 1982) (granting an injunction of that nature to remedy infringement done in contempt of a court order).

Statute provides the basis for Roche's request for injunctive relief, 35 U.S.C. § 283: The several courts having jurisdiction of cases under this title may grant injunctions in accordance with the principles of equity to prevent the violation of any right secured by patent, on such terms as the court deems reasonable.

Section 283, by its terms, clearly makes the issuance of an injunction discretionary: the court "may grant" relief "in accordance with the principles of equity." The trial court thus has considerable discretion in determining whether the facts of a situation require it to issue an injunction. The scope of relief, therefore, is not for us to decide at the first instance, nor is this the time or place for a discourse on the "principles of equity."

Whether an injunction should issue in this case, and of what form it should take, certainly depends on the equities of the case. Bolar, Roche, and amici Pharmaceutical Manufacturers Association and Generic Pharmaceutical Industry Association, each detail the "catastrophic" effect our decision for either party will have on the American public health system. It is true that it "is a principle of general application that courts, and especially courts of equity, may appropriately withhold their aid where the plaintiff is using the right asserted contrary to the public interest," Morton Salt Co. v. Suppiger Co., 314 U.S. 488, 492, 62 S.Ct. 402, 405, 86 L.Ed. 363 (1942), reh'g denied, 315 U.S. 826, 62 S.Ct. 620, 86 L.Ed. 1222 (1942). Since "the standards of the public interest, not the requirements of private litigation, measure the propriety and need for injunctive relief in these cases," Hecht Co. v. Bowles, 321 U.S. 321, 331, 64 S.Ct. 587, 592, 88 L.Ed. 754 (1944), rev'g Brown v. Hecht Co., 137 F.2d 689 (D.C.Cir.1943), we remand this case to the district court for further proceedings to consider what this interest is and what measures it calls for.

There are other aspects here that might make a tribunal reluctant to select, within the scope of its discretion, relief along the harsher side of the possible scale. The case clearly was regarded by both sides as a test. The good faith with which Bolar acted is undisputed, at least before us. Bolar says it did nothing clandestine, but notified Roche what it was going to do at all times before doing it, so Roche could act promptly to defend what it believed to be its rights. The case may be unlike Pfizer, Inc., in that Bolar scrupulously obeyed all court orders while they were in effect, or so it says, whereas in Pfizer, Inc., the infringer acted in defiance of court decrees. The destruction of material in Pfizer, Inc., was ordered after everything milder had proved useless. If other measures can be made sufficient, one might well be reluctant to order destruction of the records of research and tests that may embody information that would contribute to the health and happiness of the human race. All this is, of course, for the district judge to consider so far as he finds the factual predicates established.

The actual infringing acts are said to have all occurred in the relatively brief period between vacation of the lower court's restraining order and the expiration of the patent. Counsel for Roche was candid in explaining that he pushed so hard for the harsh relief he did because he thought any money damages would have to be nominal. The correctness of this belief has not been briefed or argued, and we hesitate to state a firm position, but tentatively, at least, we are skeptical. It is clear that the economic injury to Roche is, or is threatened to be, substantial, even though the amount of material used in the tests was small. If the patent law precludes substantial damages, there exists a strange gap in the panoply (in its proper meaning, a suit of armor) of protection the patent statutes place around an aggrieved and injured patentee. The district judge, before getting into the issue of equitable relief, must determine if he can deal with the case by adequate money damages. If he can, the predicate for equitable relief of a harsh, or even a mild, character is gone.

Counsel are equally mistaken in their apparent belief that once infringement is established and adjudicated, an injunction must follow. In Hecht Co. v. Bowles, the statute, unlike the one we have here, was seemingly mandatory by its language that once a violation was shown, an injunction must follow, and the D.C. Circuit had so held. But the circumstances made an injunction somewhat repugnant. Hecht Co., an unquestionably legitimate and long-established District of Columbia retailer, had got tangled up in the price control regulations of World War II, and its employees had in good faith unwittingly committed some violations. The situation was ironic in that the Hecht Co. had been a leader in extending the patriotic cooperation of the retail trade in application of the unpopular but necessary retail price controls, and had itself offered its own operation for study as illustrating the problems and how they could be solved.

After discovering some loopholes in the statute, in light of the legislative history, Justice Douglas continued at 329, 64 S.Ct. at 591–592: We are dealing here with the requirements of equity practice with a background of several hundred years of history. Only the other day we stated that "An appeal to the equity jurisdiction conferred on federal district courts is an appeal to the sound discretion which guides the determinations of courts of equity." Meredith v. Winter Haven, 320 U.S. 228, 235 [64 S.Ct. 7, 11, 88 L.Ed. 9]. The historic injunctive process was designed to deter, not to punish. The essence of equity jurisdiction has been the power of the Chancellor to do equity and to mould each decree to the necessities of the particular case. Flexibility rather than rigidity has distinguished it. The qualities of mercy and practicality have made equity the instrument for nice adjustment and reconciliation between the public interest and private needs as well as between competing private claims. We do not believe that such a major departure from that long tradition as is here proposed should be lightly implied. While two justices declined to join in the opinion, none expressed themselves in favor of affirming the D.C. Circuit. In short, if Congress wants the federal courts to issue injunctions without regard to historic equity principles, it is going to have to say so in explicit and even shameless language rarely if ever to be expected from a body itself made up very largely of American lawyers, having, probably, as much respect for traditional equity principles as do the courts. If an injunction was not mandatory in Hecht Co. v. Bowles, the more permissive statutory language here makes it a fortiori that an injunction is not mandatory now.

## V

Conclusion

The decision of the district court holding the '053 patent not infringed is reversed. The case is remanded with instructions to fashion an appropriate remedy. Each party to bear its own costs.

NOTES

**1.** *Monetary relief.* Prior to 1946, patent actions were regarded as sounding entirely in equity: the injunction is clearly an equitable remedy and monetary relief was conceptualized as an accounting for the profits that the defendant had earned through unauthorized use of the patented invention. At the time, courts encountered considerable difficulties with the accounting phase of the case because there was no accurate way to apportion the defendant's earnings between profit made on account of the invention, profits made on account of the defendant's own efforts (e.g. in marketing), and costs of production.[1] In 1946, Congress amended the statute to drop the reference to infringer's profits.[2] However, it was unclear whether Congress meant to restrict the patentee to an award of damages for his own lost profits or to give patentees a right to choose between compensation and an accounting. Some courts used defendant's profits as evidence of plaintiff's loss.[3] When the Patent Act was recodified in 1952, the entire monetary relief issue was reconsidered. Section 284 now indicates that the basic damage award is meant to compensate the patentee for the losses caused by the infringement. Compensation can be determined from the patentee's lost profits, or by establishing a royalty rate which is then applied to the sales price of the infringing articles.

a. *Lost profits.* As *Rite–Hite* demonstrates, one of the problems in a lost profit calculation is determining what is "lost." Are sales "lost" when the patentee is not, in fact, competing with the defendant in the market-

---

[1] See, e.g., Westinghouse Elec. & Mfg. Co. v. Wagner Elec. & Mfg. Co., 225 U.S. 604 (1912); Elizabeth v. American Nicolson Pavement Co., 97 U.S. (7 Otto) 126 (1877).

[2] Act of August 1, 1946, Ch. 726, § 1, 60 Stat. 778.

[3] For a discussion of both the pre-and post–1946 case law, see Judge Nies's full opinion in *Rite–Hite.*

place for the patented invention? Which of the *Rite–Hite* decisions on the ADL–100 restraint issue is the most defensible? The decisions of Judges Lourie and Newman create a remedy rule that maximizes the patentee's expected return, thus offering the greatest incentive to innovate. It also seems to mesh best with the rule in Special Equipment Co. v. Coe, Assignment 22, which allows patentees to refrain from exploiting the patented invention. Here, for example, the patentee apparently felt it would maximize its return by incorporating the patented invention into the cheaper restraint, while selling unpatented versions of the automatic restraint. Kelley interfered with that decision by marketing an automatic restraint that incorporated the patented invention. Accordingly, Judge Lourie's faction forced Kelley to pay for the business that Rite–Hite lost on both the patented and unpatented restraints.

In contrast, Judge Nies's rule, which would allow patentees to recover only in markets that it is exploiting, would reduce the patentee's flexibility and diminish the incentive to innovate. At the same time, however, it has the benefit of giving patentees strong incentives to bring their products to market. Here, for example, customers clearly wanted an automatic restraint that incorporated the patentee's invention. If the patentee had known that forgoing that market meant forgoing profits on automatic restraints, it probably would have chosen to sell an automatic version of the patented invention itself. Thus, this rule furthers the goal of fulfilling consumer demand for patented technologies.[4]

The discussion of the ADL–100 issue treats the question whether *substitute* technologies should be included in the base from which lost profits are calculated. A second question, the "entire market value rule" question, asks whether *complementary* products, which are generally sold at the same time as the patented item, should be included in the base. Courts—and panels of the Federal Circuit—have long disagreed on when such sales—called "collateral" or "convoyed" sales—should be included in the base. Indeed, *Rite–Hite* was probably accepted for en banc review mainly to consider this issue, which was raised by the dock levelers.

As a matter of patent policy, which opinion is best on this issue? Judge Newman tries to put the patentee in exactly the position it would have been in had the infringement not occurred. She, thus, once again would offer the largest reward, and so create the greatest incentive to innovate. However, it can be very difficult to determine what customers would have bought under other circumstances. In ordinary contract cases, such speculative injuries are rarely considered compensable. Of course, patentees could reduce the speculative nature of the inquiry by requiring customers

[4] Or does it? Would it not be better to permit Rite–Hite to collect damages but refuse to issue it an injunction? That way, consumer demand is satisfied (by Kelley), while Rite–Hite enjoys the tribute that its inventiveness earned. Economists have become interested in the question of the effect of various damage measures, see, e.g., Clement G. Krouse, But–For Markets and Reasonable Royalties: The Rite–Hite v. Kelley Misdirection, 43 Jurimetrics J. 229 (2003); Roger D. Blair and Thomas F. Cotter, Rethinking Patent Damages,10 Tex. Intell. Prop. L.J. 1 (2001).

for the patented item to purchase complementary products. But that requirement—tying the patented item to other products—could be considered a violation of the antitrust laws, see Assignment 22. Moreover, read broadly, the entire market value rule can compensate patentees for their marketing schemes rather than their inventiveness.

Because of these problems, the remainder of the court would not go as far as Judge Newman advocates. Judge Nies does not fully explain her position on this issue.[5] She would, apparently, repudiate the entire market value rule and limit patentees to lost profits on the patented invention. In contrast, Judge Lourie tries to find a happy medium. He would compensate patentees when the patented invention and the related item form a single "functional unit."

It remains to be seen whether the "functional unit" approach will work, but the prospects seem dim. First, why was the dock leveler and the restraint not considered part of a single functional unit? Second, this rule encourages patentees to engage in tying. Not, of course, through market tie-ins that would run afoul of the antitrust laws, but by so-called "technological tying." That is, patentees may well try to design the commercial embodiments of their patented inventions in a manner that forms a "functional unit" with other products. Third, the Lourie decision may be unstable because its two main parts are not completely consistent with one another. It is easy to *say* that products that substitute for the patented invention are included in the base on which profits are calculated, but that complementary products are not. What, however, is the overarching theory of this decision? If the idea is to return the patentee to the position it would have been in if the infringement had not occurred, or to compensate the patentee for all foreseeable injuries, then the patentee should be compensated for lost dock leveler sales as well as lost ADL–100 sales. If the idea is to compensate the patentee only for losing sales of the patented invention, then neither the ADL–100 nor the dock leveler sales should count. This opinion offers no real theory for splitting the difference. Finally, consider how royalties were determined in *Rite–Hite* and *Radio Steel:* do collateral sales sneak in through the back door? See Note 1(b).

Even after the base for calculating profits is determined, several difficult questions remain, for the patentee must establish what he would have earned if the infringement had not occurred. This is where the four-part test of Panduit Corp. v. Stahlin Bros. Fibre Works, Inc., discussed in both *Rite–Hite* and *Radio Steel,* comes in. Pre-infringement data can be used to make the showing required, but these must be adjusted for changes in the market for the patented item. And although courts do sometimes look at the defendant's profits in making this determination,[6] these data must also be corrected to account for sales attributable to the defendant's reputation, marketing scheme, production technique, and such. As with all

---

[5] Although most of Judge Nies's opinion was heavily edited, the dock leveler portion of it was reproduced in full.

[6] See, e.g., Velo–Bind, Inc. v. Minnesota Mining & Mfg. Co., 647 F.2d 965 (9th Cir.), cert. denied, 454 U.S. 1093 (1981).

torts, the infringement must be the "but for" cause of the patentee's loss. Thus, the award must also take account of the strategies that rivals would have employed had the infringement not occurred.[7]

b. *Royalties.* Courts can avoid the problem of computing the actual amount of lost profits by using the royalty method of awarding damages. In Georgia–Pacific Corp. v. U.S. Plywood–Champion Papers Inc.,[8] the court set out fifteen factors which remain the most comprehensive list of issues considered in determining a reasonable royalty:

(1) the royalties received by patentee for licensing of the patent;

(2) the rates paid by licensee for the use of comparable patents;

(3) the nature and scope of the license;

(4) the licensor's established policy to maintain its patent monopoly by not licensing to others or by granting licenses under conditions designed to preserve its monopoly;

(5) the commercial relationship between the licensor and licensee;

(6) the effect of selling the patented specialty in promoting the sale of other products;

(7) the duration of the patent and terms of the license;

(8) the established profitability of the patented product;

(9) the advantages of the patented product over old devices;

(10) the nature of the patented invention;

(11) the extent to which an infringer has used the invention;

(12) the portion of profit or selling price customary for use of the invention or analogous inventions;

(13) the portion of realizable profit that should be credited to the invention as distinguished from other factors;

(14) the opinion testimony of qualified experts; and

(15) the amount that a prudent licensee, desiring to obtain license, would have been willing to pay, and whereby the amount would have been acceptable by a prudent patentee who was willing to grant the license.[9]

Note that in *Radio Steel,* the court also enhanced the royalty rate to compensate the patentee for sales lost on related items. *Radio Steel* was decided before *Rite–Hite:* given the strict test that the *Rite–Hite* court

[7] See, e.g., Grain Processing Corp. v. American Maize–Products Co., 893 F.Supp. 1386 (N.D. Ind. 1995), aff'd in part, vacated in part, 108 F.3d 1392 (Fed. Cir. 1997), on remand, 979 F.Supp. 1233 (N.D. Ind. 1997), aff'd 185 F.3d 1341 (1999). See generally, John W. Schlicher, Measuring Patent Damages By the Market Value of Inventions—The Grain Processing, Rite–Hite, and Aro Rules, 82 J. Pat. & Trademark Off. Soc'y 503 (2000).

[8] 318 F.Supp. 1116 (S.D.N.Y. 1970), modified and aff'd, 446 F.2d 295 (2d Cir. 1971).

[9] Susan Perng Pan, Patent Damage Assessments After Rite–Hite and Grain Processing, 42 IDEA 481, 493–484 (2002).

articulated for deciding whether to include complementary products in the base used to calculate damages, is this decision still good law—does it make sense to include these items when determining the royalty rate? Did the *Rite–Hite* plurality in effect do the same thing?

**2.** *Willful infringement, attorney's fees and prejudgment interest.* These forms of relief are necessary for two reasons. First, to make the patentee whole. The *Devex* case cited in *NTP v. RIM* is a good example of the injury caused by protracted litigation. By the time the Supreme Court decided the case, it had been sub judice for 36 years; the trial court awarded damages equal to a reasonable royalty of $8,813,945.50 and prejudgment interest amounting to $11,022,854.97. The second reason for these remedies was suggested in the Introduction: unless the infringer faces the possibility of being put into a worse position by reason of the infringement than it would have been with a license, it would have a strong incentive to infringe. In effect, the infringer would be enjoying a compulsory license.

Nonetheless, there is reason to be concerned about enhanced royalties in cases where the defendant is providing the market with a popular (and, in *RIM,* an award-winning) product, and the plaintiff holds patents that it has never exploited. As the relief associated with patent infringement increases, so-called "patent trolls" are lured into the game.[10] These are companies whose business is to look for patents that are arguably being infringed, and then to file suits, mainly with the idea of securing settlements. Companies like RIM have little choice but to play hardball and refuse such settlements, otherwise large portions of their resources go to paying royalties as opposed to paying for research, development, and distribution of new products. When a court considers whether to award punitive damages against a company like RIM, which guessed wrong about whether it was infringing, should the court take into account the dynamics of trolling and the effect of its decision on the cost of doing business?

**3.** *Injunctive relief.* There are two types of injunctions: preliminary and permanent. In cases outside the patent area, preliminary relief is granted when the moving party proves a likelihood of success on the merits and irreparable injury. Prior to the establishment of the Federal Circuit, however, it was often harder to get preliminary relief in patent litigation. Courts reasoned that since patentees could be made whole with a monetary award, there was little point in enjoining the defendant preliminarily and force the public to suffer a diminution in output of the accused product before infringement was proven. Accordingly, they required the patentee to prove that the patent was unquestionably valid and that the infringement was clear.[11]

---

[10] See Brenda Sandburg, Battling the Patent Trolls, THE RECORDER, July 30, 2001, available at http://www.law.com/jsp/statearchive.jsp? type=Article & ol-did=ZZZ4DX7MSPC (noting that in 1999, patent claims against Intel totaled over $15 billion); Michael J. Meurer Controlling Opportunistic and Anti–Competitive Intellectual Property Litigation, 44 B.C. L. Rev. 509 (2003).

[11] See, e.g., Donald S. Chisum, Patents, § 20.04 (1987).

Initially, the Federal Circuit saw no reason to treat patentees this way. Because patent litigation often took many years, infringers could make large inroads into the patentee's business, establish customer loyalty, and enjoy a favorable marketing position when the patent expired. Furthermore, the goals of patent law and copyright are similar, and courts in copyright cases are fairly generous about granting preliminary relief on the presumption that the injury flowing from unauthorized usages of a protected work is irreparable. Early Federal Circuit cases suggested that the patentees should be treated just like holders of other intellectual property.[12] In later years, however, the court has shown some evidence of retreat from this position. In Illinois Tool Works, Inc. v. Grip–Pak, Inc.,[13] the Federal Circuit indicated that the presumption of irreparable injury is rebuttable, and in Chrysler Motors Corp. v. Auto Body Panels,[14] the Federal Circuit reinstated the requirement that patentees make a strong showing of validity. While it is impossible to know exactly what the Federal Circuit is thinking, it is likely that the court has become more sensitive to the public-interest side of the injunction issue. As noted in *Bolar,* injunctions—both preliminary and permanent—are matters of equity, and the equities can favor the public's interest in accessing the invention.

Consider also the effect of patent trolling—cases brought by patent holders who are not actively engaged in the defendant's business. In such cases, preliminary relief injures the defendant, but it does not provide any business-related benefits to the plaintiff. Instead, the threat of an injunction alters the power relationship between the parties, arguably forcing the defendant to improvidently settle with the "troll." For that reason, Congress is considering legislation to amend § 283 to list the following five factors for a court to consider in determining whether to bar the marketing of an allegedly infringing product: (1) whether the party seeking the injunction is marketing a product covered by the patent; (2) whether that party is engaging in activities to begin such marketing; (3) whether alternatives to the challenged product exist; (4) the adverse effects of removing that product; and (5) whether the party seeking the injunction will suffer harm not remedied by damages. Note that the *RIM* court was sensitive to this issue as well: it stayed its order of a permanent injunction pending appeal.

**4.** *Declaratory relief.* One way for a party starting a new venture to avoid patent infringement is to bring a suit for a declaration of patent invalidity, unenforceability, or noninfringement. Under the terms of the Declaratory Judgment Act, there must be a genuine case or controversy,[15] language that the Federal Circuit has interpreted as imposing a two-pronged require-

---

[12] See, e.g., Atlas Powder Co. v. Ireco Chems., 773 F.2d 1230 (Fed.Cir.1985); Smith Int'l v. Hughes Tool Co., 718 F.2d 1573 (Fed. Cir.), cert. denied, 464 U.S. 996 (1983).

[13] 906 F.2d 679 (Fed.Cir.1990).

[14] 908 F.2d 951 (Fed.Cir.1990). See also Amazon.com, Inc. v. Barnesandnoble.com, Inc., 239 F.3d 1343 (Fed. Cir. 2001)(refusing to enjoin Barnes and Noble's "shopping cart" check out system on the ground that Amazon.com's one-click patent was of dubious validity).

[15] 28 U.S.C. §§ 2201–02.

ment: "First, the defendant's conduct must have created on the part of the plaintiff a reasonable apprehension that the defendant will initiate suit if the plaintiff continues the allegedly infringing activity. Second, the plaintiff must actually have either produced the device [that is arguably infringing] or have prepared to produce that device."[16] Reasonableness is determined objectively, based on a totality of the circumstances. "Although the best evidence of a reasonable apprehension of suit comes in the form of an express threat of litigation, an express threat is not required.... [A] plaintiff must show more than the nervous state of mind of a possible infringer, but does not have to show that the patentee is poised on the courthouse steps."[17]

Should it be easier to bring a declaratory judgment action? Patentees know the standard; to avoid such suits, they sometimes write cease and desist letters that stop just short of raising a reasonable apprehension of suit under Federal Circuit case law. Nonetheless, the notice may be enough to meet the standard for willfulness. Congress is considering legislation that would tie the two standards together.

**5.** *Exclusion orders.* In addition to enjoining domestic usages of the patented invention, patentees can prevent importation of infringing articles under 19 U.S.C. § 1337(a), which makes unlawful:

(1)(B) The importation into the United States, the sale for importation, or the sale within the United States after importation ... of articles that—

  (i) infringe a valid and enforceable United States patent ... ; or

  (ii) are made, produced, processed, or mined under, or by means of, a process covered by claims of a valid and enforceable United States patent.

This statute has an important exception:

(2) Subparagraph (B) of paragraph (1) appl[ies] only if an industry in the United States, relating to the articles protected by the patent ... exists or is in the process of being established.

(3) For purposes of paragraph (2), an industry in the United States shall be considered to exist if there is in the United States, with respect to the articles protected by the patent ... concerned—

  (A) significant investment in plant and equipment;

  (B) significant employment of labor or capital; or

  (C) substantial investment in its exploitation, including engineering, research and development, or licensing.

The statute covers copyrighted and trademarked works as well as semiconductor chips (mask works).

---

[16] Goodyear Tire & Rubber Co. v. Releasomers, Inc., 824 F.2d 953 (Fed. Cir. 1987).

[17] Vanguard Research, Inc. v. Peat, Inc., 304 F.3d 1249, 1254–55 (Fed. Cir. 2002)(citations omitted).

**6.** *Time limitations.* Damages cannot be recovered for infringements that occurred before the infringer had notice of the patent. Marking patented articles with the word "patent" (or the abbreviation "pat.") followed by the number of the patent serves as constructive notice. If no goods are sold, if the patent is for a process, or if the patentee chooses not to mark her goods, then the patentee must prove actual notice, § 287. In addition, no recovery can be had for infringements that are more than six years old at the time of filing, § 286.

Finally, the defenses of laches and estoppel can also bar relief. Laches occurs when a patentee unreasonably delays filing suit after he knows or should have known of the infringement. It blocks relief for past infringements, but not an injunction to prevent future infringement. In contrast, estoppel, which occurs when an infringer reasonably relies on the patentee's representation that he will not enforce the patent, prevents the patentee from receiving all relief.

**7.** *Standing.* In an omitted portion of *Rite–Hite,* the court discussed whether independent sales organizations that sold the '847 and the ADL–100 through licensing agreements with Rite–Hite had standing to pursue their own actions against Kelley. Judge Lourie's plurality opinion, which, on this issue, was joined by Judges Archer, Smith, Nies and Mayer, said no. In their view, the only licensees who have sufficient interest in the patent to sue are those holding an exclusive right to practice the invention. Nonexclusive licensees (including those with exclusive licenses to particular territories) have received only a promise by the patentee to forebear from suing them for infringement. Judges Newman and Rader thought these organizations' injuries were directly and foreseeably caused by the infringement, giving them the right to sue along with Rite–Hite.

# PREEMPTION OF STATE LAW: TRADE SECRETS, COVENANTS NOT TO COMPETE, AND ECONOMIC ESPIONAGE

## 1. INTRODUCTION

This Assignment examines laws protecting information that can be exploited in secret. In a sense, this Assignment should be the introduction to the course in Intellectual Property. After all, when a creator first experiences an insight, it *is* a secret. For the creator, then, the initial question is how to proceed, whether to reveal the information and rely on patent or copyright law for market exclusivity, or whether to keep the invention confidential and rely on secrecy. The answer will depend on a variety of factors: whether the innovation can be adequately developed and utilized in secret; the availability of legal rights to buttress promises of confidentiality and deter breaches of security; and the costs and benefits of alternative intellectual property regimes.

For society, there is another set of questions. The costs of secrecy can be high. Because it can be difficult to license secrets without disclosing them, they may be significantly underutilized.[1] As important, if information is kept secret, then others will not know of it and will not be able to expand the knowledge base by building on it. Indeed, they may waste resources reinventing it themselves. The innovation may also pose health risks to employees or customers; its use may threaten the environment. Thus, society must ask whether it wishes to support the decision to keep innovation secret. Should confidentiality agreements be enforced; should laws be designed to deter security breaches? If creators are choosing secrecy because their innovations are not susceptible to patent or copyright protection, would it be better to enact sui generis regimes, tailored to the needs of the industries that fall between the cracks? To a large extent, trade secrecy and sui generis protections are creatures of state law. One must therefore ask whether these state laws are constitutional or preempted by federal intellectual property policy.

---

[1] See Note 3. To be sure, the exclusivity of patents and copyrights regime may also be used to restrict output, but these regimes are specifically designed to facilitate licensing. Thus, they enable rights holders to expand production through transactions with licensees.

State laws protecting secrecy can be divided into two categories: trade secrecy laws, and noncompete agreements. For trade secrecy, the common law was first summarized in the first Restatement of Torts, §§ 757–761, it was not addressed by the second Restatement of Torts, but is now a part of the Restatement of Unfair Competition Law, which was published in 1995.[2] In addition, in 1979, the National Conference of Commissioners on Uniform State Laws promulgated a Uniform Trade Secrets Act, which has been adopted by a majority of the states. Although the Restatement of Torts differed in some details from the Uniform Act, the new Restatement of Unfair Competition Law is intended to be "applicable to actions under the Uniform Trade Secrets Act as well as to actions at common law."[3]

These laws create rights of action against someone who acquires by improper means information that is valuable because it is not generally known, and then uses that information for economic benefit. Plaintiffs must have taken reasonable measures to keep the information confidential. "Improper means" covers a wide array of behavior, ranging from industrial espionage, bribery, and trespass, to breaches of duties of confidentiality. However, it does not include independent invention or reverse engineering (copying)—these are the main ways that secret innovations enter the public domain. From an economic perspective, this regime is generally effective. Innovations that are easy to reverse engineer or re-invent will usually enter the public domain quickly, and thus provide a lesser return to the initial innovator. Inventions that are difficult to create enter the public domain more slowly. During the extended period of exclusivity, the creator can recapture the costs of invention, build a reputation, and establish a base of loyal customers. Furthermore, by raising the costs of imitating successful innovations, trade secrecy law levels the playing field. Because the second comer must absorb the costs of reverse engineering or independently inventing, he cannot set prices low enough to undercut the initial innovator. In other words, there will ultimately be competition, but not competition so ruinous that the first mover cannot recover the costs of invention.

There are, however, at least three problems with trade secrecy protection. First, consider the problem of monitoring. Much of what is protected by trade secrecy law is industrial know-how: information about how to do things better. Since it is not possible to peer into rival factories to check whether competitors are using stolen secret processes, enforcement is often suboptimal. (To put this another way, if the creator thought he could practice the invention in secret, then so can anyone who appropriated the information improperly). Second, some products are very easy to figure out, even though they may have been hard to create. If it is too easy to reverse engineer the product, the innovator will not have the lead time needed to recoup costs. Third, trade secret holders are often reluctant to enforce their rights. Because trade secrecy litigation requires the plaintiff to tell the

[2] American Law Institute, Rest. 3d Unfair Competition Law (1995)(your editors have no explanation for why this Restatement is called "3d" when it is, in fact, the first independent Restatement of this area of the law and the second restatement over-all).

[3] Id. at § 39, Comment b.

court enough about the secret to determine whether it has been taken by improper means (rather than reverse engineered) and whether it is being utilized, lawsuits can carry an unacceptably high risk of disclosure.

To avoid these problems, inventors sometimes rely on covenants not to compete. These are contracts between the innovator and those to whom the secret must be told—usually, employees or investors—in which the latter promise not to enter into specified businesses for a specific period of time and within a particular geographic area. Because these contracts spell out overt behavior that must be avoided, they can be enforced without the inventor knowing whether a secret has indeed been stolen and without any need to disclose to the court what the secret is. Covenants not to compete are, of course, limited in that they can be enforced only against people who have entered into agreements with the inventor. However, the typical defendant in a trade secret action is someone who has had contact with the inventor—most often, an ex-employee. Thus, in a high percent of the cases, covenants not to compete mirror the protection offered by trade secrecy, but without the attendant risks.

Should these regimes be deemed preempted by federal intellectual property policy? The Patent Act does not contain a provision equivalent to § 301 of the Copyright Act. To the extent that it touches on trade secrecy law, its effect is practical rather than legal, and its message is ambiguous. As Assignments 17–19 demonstrate, it is unclear whether secret information will defeat a subsequent independent inventor from receiving a patent. Thus, it is difficult to know whether Congress intended to allow creators who could rely on trade secrecy to do so. The federal Economic Espionage Act, which "ups the ante" by criminalizing violations of trade secrecy law, provides a better indication that in Congress's view, these laws should be regarded as important adjuncts to patent protection. For its part, the Supreme Court has vacillated between the extremes, resting for the moment on middle ground.

## 2.  PRINCIPAL PROBLEM

Our client is MAI Systems, a computer "boutique" situated in California. It designs, manufactures, and builds computers to customer specifications. This equipment is sold outright to customers. In addition, MAI designs the programs (operating systems and application programs) that run on its computers. These are not sold—rather, they are licensed to customers and loaded into the computers before they are shipped. Finally, MAI offers its customers service contracts that cover routine maintenance and emergency repairs on all computers and programs. Because virtually all new customers purchase MAI service contracts, MAI routinely loads the diagnostic program it uses for servicing right into the memory of all computers shipped.

In recent years, our client has become concerned by an upstart company, Peak Computers. Organized in 1990, Peak advertises itself as offering maintenance that rivals that of large companies, but at much lower prices. At first, Peak did not do very well. However, in 1991, Eric Francis left his job as customer service manager at MAI and joined Peak. He was rapidly followed by many MAI customers. Indeed, in the years since Francis's departure, Peak has acquired hundreds of customers, over 70% of which bought their equipment from MAI.

MAI suspects that Peak owes its recent success to more than just Eric Francis' business acumen. Rather, it believes that Francis is using MAI-generated information. That is, in MAI's view, the only one in a really good position to diagnose malfunctions in a computer system is its designer. Therefore, the only way that Peak can charge less than MAI and still earn a profit is by utilizing MAI diagnostic equipment—the material that is loaded on the computer at shipment. MAI believes this usage is actionable. The software is not sold, it is only licensed. Although § 117(c) of the Copyright Act permits the owner of a computer to use such a diagnostic program without authorization or payment, MAI required each of its customers to agree not to utilize the diagnostic program or allow anyone to utilize it on its behalf. Thus, in MAI's view, Peak is infringing its trade secrets (and its customers are breaching their licensing agreements with MAI).

MAI further claims that the two most difficult aspects of the service business lie in finding customers and accurately pricing the service contracts sold to them. The latter problem is due to the fact that different customers have different needs and vary in their ability to use computers and programs without messing them up. Since profit margins are low, improperly priced service contracts can spell disaster. MAI suspects that Peak is so successful because when Francis left MAI, he took with him MAI's Customer Database, which lists the names and addresses of all MAI customers and describes each customer's business, computation needs, and repair record. Because MAI has always known the value of the Database, it has long required all employees with access to it to sign confidentiality agreements.

As the computer market becomes saturated, the servicing portion of MAI's business has become more important to its profitability. It has asked us to seek an injunction that will shut Peak down. California has adopted the Uniform Trade Secrets Act, Cal. Civ. Code §§ 3426–3426.10 (West Supp. 1993). Please advise on which aspects of Peak's operations are, indeed, actionable and on the relief you believe MAI can reasonably expect to receive. Do you think it worth our while to turn this case over to the U.S. Attorney's office for criminal prosecution?

## 3.  MATERIALS FOR SOLUTION OF PRINCIPAL PROBLEM

### A.  STATUTORY MATERIAL:

Uniform Trade Secrets Act, Restatement of Unfair Competition §§ 38–45; § 301 of the Copyright Act; Economic Espionage Act, 18 U.S.C. §§ 1831–39.

B:  CASES:

## Dionne v. Southeast Foam Converting & Packaging, Inc.

Supreme Court of Virginia, 1990.
240 Va. 297, 397 S.E.2d 110.

■ POFF, SENIOR JUSTICE.

Robert Dionne, while employed by a corrugated box manufacturer, had developed several new products for use in packaging commodities shipped in commerce. In 1983, Robert created and incorporated Sefco as a family company producing foam products for that purpose. In the company's parking lot one day, he found a board of expanded polystyrene (EPS) which had been crushed beneath the wheels of a truck. Upon examination of the board, brittle in its original form, Robert discovered that the compressed material had become resilient, pliable, and shock-absorbing. Recognizing the potential demand for such a material for packing inside cartons in which furniture and other commodities are transported, he and members of his family began conducting experiments on means and methods of compressing EPS for use in the "inner packaging industry."

Encouraged by what he learned, Robert prepared and forwarded to a patent attorney a description of the process, the product, and its function. A search of the patent records revealed that patents had been issued for 17 foam products made of EPS compressed in different ways for different uses. One of the patents, that for an egg carton, had expired in 1980.

Relying upon the attorney's opinion that Sefco's product did not satisfy the novelty requirement of the patent law, the Dionne family began to focus upon new techniques in the manufacturing process. Two of Robert's sons, Pierre, who had become a full-time Sefco salesman in 1984, and Paul, engaged Mike Harris, a machine shop operator, to build a number of machines designed to facilitate the process and improve the quality of the end product. The brothers required Harris to sign a "non-disclosure" agreement in which he covenanted not to reveal any information about the machines, the manufacturing process, or the product. Employing the new Harris machines and larger hydraulic presses acquired from another source, Sefco made its first sale of compressed EPS to furniture manufacturers in September 1985. The product was sold under the trade name "Durofoam" or "Dur-o-foam."

Robert became terminally ill in 1987, and his wife, Pauline, and their three sons, Paul, Pierre, and Jacques, assumed control and operation of the family business. Robert died in May 1987, and Paul and Pierre renewed their efforts, begun earlier that year, to investigate the possibility of further refinements in the manufacturing process. With the use of a new press designed to create uniform products in mass quantities, they conducted experiments to determine the effects of different levels of pressure applied to blocks of EPS for different periods of time.

Based upon the results of these experiments, Sefco applied for a patent in June 1987. The application identified the product as "Durafoam" and the inventor as Robert Dionne. In a letter she addressed to the patent attorney, Pauline Dionne, who had acquired title to Sefco at Robert's death, asked the attorney "to include Pierre and Paul as co-inventors" because, she wrote, "they discovered a new and improved process of treating EPS for resiliency and enhanced cushioning qualities."

The research conducted by the family prompted an application for another patent. As explained by Paul, "at about the time we were developing Durafoam we were developing the angle packaging material." This product, he said, was "a paper backing material laminated to the Durafoam" and cut into shapes needed to "wrap around corners or . . . edges of tables, dressers, and nightstands." In January 1988, Pierre applied (in his own name as inventor) for a design patent on this product.

Thereafter, a bitter family quarrel developed. In efforts to restore harmony, the parties agreed that Pierre would assign 90% of his interest in the patent pending on the angle-packaging product to Sefco; that Pauline would give each of the three brothers a 10% share of Sefco; and that all Sefco owners would sign a "Confidential Information Agreement" similar to those Sefco consistently had required all its employees, suppliers, customers, contractors, and other plant visitors to execute. In pertinent part, the agreement Pierre signed provided that "[i]n consideration of being employed by SEFCO [the subscriber] shall not during, or at any time after the termination of my employment with the Company, use for myself or others, or disclose or divulge to others any trade secrets, confidential information, or any other data of the Company in violation of this agreement." Consummation of these agreements failed to resolve the family dispute, and Pierre's employment was terminated in June 1988.

Witnesses representing several of Sefco's suppliers and customers testified that Pierre had advised them that he planned to commence a new business manufacturing a foam material for use in the inner packaging industry. The new product, he explained, would be named "Flexfoam", and, while it would be similar in quality to Durafoam, it would be manufactured in a "more cost effective" way.

All these witnesses agreed that Durafoam is a product unique in its market area. Even the witness called by Pierre testified, on cross examination, that he knew of no company other than Sefco that had produced a marketable product with the functional qualities of Durafoam.

When the Dionne family learned of Pierre's plans, Sefco filed its bill of complaint [in a court of equity]. In a letter opinion, the chancellor held that "the manufacture of Durafoam is a trade secret" within the definition of the Uniform Trade Secrets Act, Code § 59.1–336 through–343, and that Pierre's conduct constituted a misappropriation within the meaning of the Act.[a] Applying Code § 59.1–337(A) which provides that "[a]ctual or threat-

---

a The chancellor also ruled that the confidentiality agreement Pierre signed was legally enforceable and that Pierre had breached that agreement. In the view we take of the issues, we need not consider Pierre's attack on those rulings.

ened misappropriation may be enjoined'', the chancellor entered the injunction Pierre challenges on appeal.

Pierre contends that this two-fold holding is twice flawed. First, pointing to the issuance and expiration of the egg-carton patent as an example, he argues that what is involved is merely an "adaptation of previously known technology to a new product line in a different market" and this, he says, is not a trade secret. That term is defined in the Act, adopted by the General Assembly by Acts 1986, c. 210, in the following language:

> "Trade secret" means information, including but not limited to, a formula, pattern, compilation, program, device, method, technique, or process, that:
>
>    (1) Derives independent economic value, actual or potential, from not being generally known to, and not being readily ascertainable by proper means by, other persons who can obtain economic value from its disclosure or use, and
>
>    (2) Is the subject of efforts that are reasonable under the circumstances to maintain its secrecy.

Pierre's first contention misapprehends the nature of a trade secret. The crucial characteristic of a trade secret is secrecy rather than novelty. See generally, Developments in the Law—Competitive Torts, 77 Harv. L.Rev. 888, 949–50 (1964). The secrecy need not be absolute; the owner of a trade secret may, without losing protection, disclose it to a licensee, an employee, or a stranger, if the disclosure is made in confidence, express or implied. Kewanee Oil Co. v. Bicron Corp., 416 U.S. 470, 475, 94 S.Ct. 1879, 1883, 40 L.Ed.2d 315 (1974). Although the subject of a trade secret may be novel in the sense that it is something generally unknown in the trade or business, "[n]ovelty, in the patent law sense, is not required for a trade secret." Id. at 476, 94 S.Ct. at 1883. Indeed, a trade secret "may be a device or process which is clearly anticipated in the prior art or one which is merely a mechanical improvement that a good mechanic can make." Restatement of Torts § 757 comment b (1939).

Summarizing the evidence, the chancellor made a series of factual findings keyed to the several elements of the statutory definition quoted above. Specifically, he found that "the plaintiff has used reasonable security measures designed to maintain the confidentiality of Durafoam"; that "Durafoam has a value and it is generally unknown in the sales area of the plaintiff"; that "[t]he plaintiff has an investment of time, money and effort expended in research and the development of equipment and/or machinery to produce Durafoam"; that "the plaintiff has a competitive advantage in manufacturing and selling Durafoam"; and that "Durafoam is a unique product in said sales area, producing over 80% of the Plaintiff's business."

We hold that the evidence fully supports these findings and that they completely satisfy the statutory definition of the term trade secret. Consequently, we reject Pierre's first contention.

In his second argument, Pierre insists that he cannot be found guilty of misappropriating something which he "personally developed or substantially contributed to developing while employed at SEFCO." We must reject this argument as well.

Pierre relies upon the court's opinion in Structural Dyn. Res. Corp. v. Engineering Mech. R. Corp., 401 F.Supp. 1102 (E.D.Mich.1975). There, the court was asked to decide, among other things, whether employees who had appropriated to their own use trade secrets claimed by their former employer were guilty of an actionable breach of trust. In the course of its opinion, the court weighed competing societal interests. As the court reasoned, the public has an interest in motivating innovation and creativity by placing qualified limits on disclosure of trade secrets, and the public has an interest in preserving the job mobility of workers who have acquired knowledge and skills useful in producing improved consumer products at lower cost. In a common-law analysis, the court struck the balance in favor of the employees on the ground that they personally had created the subjects of the trade secrets.

Pierre's reliance upon this opinion is wholly misplaced. Absent a statute, the weighing process conducted there is a proper judicial function. However, "it is the responsibility of the legislature, not the judiciary, to formulate public policy, to strike the appropriate balance between competing interests, and to devise standards for implementation." Wood v. Board of Supervisors of Halifax Cty., 236 Va. 104, 115, 372 S.E.2d 611, 618 (1988).

By adopting the Uniform Trade Secrets Act, the General Assembly has struck the public-policy balance to be applied by courts in this Commonwealth. In determining whether Pierre is guilty of misappropriation of trade secrets, we look to the words the lawmakers used. Insofar as pertinent here, the act provides: Misappropriation means:

. . . . .

2. Disclosure or use of a trade secret of another without express or implied consent by a person who

. . . . .

   b.  At the time of disclosure or use, knew or had reason to know that his knowledge of the trade secret was

. . . . .

   (2) Acquired under circumstances giving rise to a duty to maintain its secrecy or limit its use. . . .

Code § 59.1–336(2)(b)(2).

Upon consideration of the testimony and other evidence before him, the chancellor had every reason to conclude, as he did, that the Durafoam process was Sefco's trade secret and that Pierre "knew or had reason to know that his knowledge of the trade secret was ... [a]cquired under circumstances giving rise to a duty to maintain its secrecy or limit its use." No member of the Dionne family ever revealed the details of the Durafoam process to anyone except the patent attorney. Unauthorized persons were excluded from the plant. All employees, suppliers, customers, and contractors were required to sign agreements to treat any information they may have acquired as confidential. Each member of the Dionne family, Pierre included, signed such a paper. And it was Pierre himself who prepared and filed an application on behalf of Sefco to convert the trade secret into a patent and then urged Sefco to dispatch "cease and desist" letters to all potential competitors. We agree with the chancellor's conclusions.

Code § 59.1–337(A) provides:

> Actual or threatened misappropriation may be enjoined. Upon application to the court, an injunction shall be terminated when the trade secret has ceased to exist, but the injunction may be continued for an additional reasonable period of time in order to eliminate commercial advantage that otherwise would be derived from the misappropriation.

Referring to this section of the act, Sefco acknowledges on brief that, when the Durafoam process ceases to be a trade secret, "[Pierre] may petition the Court to modify its earlier order and limit the injunction to only such time as would be a reasonable period of time to eliminate the commercial advantage that has been gained as a result of his misappropriation." For such purposes, the decree entered against Pierre expressly provides that the injunction shall continue "until the further order of this Court."

## PepsiCo, Inc. v. Redmond

United States Court of Appeals, Seventh Circuit, 1995.
54 F.3d 1262.

■ Flaum, Circuit Judge.

Plaintiff PepsiCo, Inc., sought a preliminary injunction against defendants William Redmond and the Quaker Oats Company to prevent Redmond, a former PepsiCo employee, from divulging PepsiCo trade secrets and confidential information in his new job with Quaker and from assuming any duties with Quaker relating to beverage pricing, marketing, and distribution. The district court agreed with PepsiCo and granted the injunction. We now affirm that decision.

I

The facts of this case lay against a backdrop of fierce beverage-industry competition between Quaker and PepsiCo, especially in "sports drinks" and "new age drinks." Quaker's sports drink, "Gatorade," is the dominant brand in its market niche. PepsiCo introduced its Gatorade rival, "All Sport," in March and April of 1994, but sales of All Sport lag far behind those of Gatorade. Quaker also has the lead in the new-age-drink category. Although PepsiCo has entered the market through joint ventures with the Thomas J. Lipton Company and Ocean Spray Cranberries, Inc., Quaker purchased Snapple Beverage Corp., a large new-age-drink maker, in late 1994. PepsiCo's products have about half of Snapple's market share. Both companies see 1995 as an important year for their products: PepsiCo has developed extensive plans to increase its market presence, while Quaker is trying to solidify its lead by integrating Gatorade and Snapple distribution. Meanwhile, PepsiCo and Quaker each face strong competition from Coca Cola Co., which has its own sports drink, "PowerAde," and which introduced its own Snapple-rival, "Fruitopia," in 1994, as well as from independent beverage producers.

William Redmond, Jr., worked for PepsiCo in its Pepsi–Cola North America division ("PCNA") from 1984 to 1994. Redmond became the General Manager of the Northern California Business Unit in June, 1993, and was promoted one year later to General Manager of the business unit covering all of California, a unit having annual revenues of more than 500 million dollars and representing twenty percent of PCNA's profit for all of the United States.

Redmond's relatively high-level position at PCNA gave him access to inside information and trade secrets. Redmond, like other PepsiCo management employees, had signed a confidentiality agreement with PepsiCo. That agreement stated in relevant part that he

> w[ould] not disclose at any time, to anyone other than officers or employees of [PepsiCo], or make use of, confidential information relating to the business of [PepsiCo] ... obtained while in the employ of [PepsiCo], which shall not be generally known or available to the public or recognized as standard practices.

Donald Uzzi, who had left PepsiCo in the beginning of 1994 to become the head of Quaker's Gatorade division, began courting Redmond for Quaker in May, 1994. Redmond met in Chicago with Quaker officers in August, 1994, and on October 20, 1994, Quaker, through Uzzi, offered Redmond the position of Vice President—On Premise Sales for Gatorade. Redmond did not then accept the offer but continued to negotiate for more money. Throughout this time, Redmond kept his dealings with Quaker secret from his employers at PCNA.

On November 8, 1994, Uzzi extended Redmond a written offer for the position of Vice President–Field Operations for Gatorade and Redmond accepted. Later that same day, Redmond called William Bensyl, the Senior Vice President of Human Resources for PCNA, and told him that he had an offer from Quaker to become the Chief Operating Officer of the combined Gatorade and Snapple company but had not yet accepted it. Redmond also asked whether he should, in light of the offer, carry out his plans to make calls upon certain PCNA customers. Bensyl told Redmond to make the visits.

Redmond also misstated his situation to a number of his PCNA colleagues, including Craig Weatherup, PCNA's President and Chief Executive Officer, and Brenda Barnes, PCNA's Chief Operating Officer and Redmond's immediate superior. As with Bensyl, Redmond told them that he had been offered the position of Chief Operating Officer at Gatorade and that he was leaning "60/40" in favor of accepting the new position.

On November 10, 1994, Redmond met with Barnes and told her that he had decided to accept the Quaker offer and was resigning from PCNA. Barnes immediately took Redmond to Bensyl, who told Redmond that PepsiCo was considering legal action against him.

True to its word, PepsiCo filed this diversity suit on November 16, 1994, seeking a temporary restraining order to enjoin Redmond from assuming his duties at Quaker and to prevent him from disclosing trade secrets or confidential information to his new employer. From November 23, 1994, to December 1, 1994, the district court conducted a preliminary injunction hearing on the same matter. At the hearing, PepsiCo offered evidence of a number of trade secrets and confidential information it desired protected and to which Redmond was privy. First, it identified PCNA's "Strategic Plan," an annually revised document that contains PCNA's plans to compete, its financial goals, and its strategies for manufacturing, production, marketing, packaging, and distribution for the coming three years. Strategic Plans are developed by Weatherup and his staff with input from PCNA's general managers, including Redmond, and are considered highly confidential. The Strategic Plan derives much of its value from the fact that it is secret and competitors cannot anticipate PCNA's next moves. PCNA managers received the most recent Strategic Plan at a meeting in July, 1994, a meeting Redmond attended. PCNA also presented information at the meeting regarding its plans for Lipton ready-to-drink teas and for All Sport for 1995 and beyond, including new flavors and package sizes.

Second, PepsiCo pointed to PCNA's Annual Operating Plan ("AOP") as a trade secret. The AOP is a national plan for a given year and guides PCNA's financial goals, marketing plans, promotional event calendars, growth expectations, and operational changes in that year. The AOP, which is implemented by PCNA unit General Managers, including Redmond, contains specific information regarding all PCNA initiatives for the forthcoming year. The AOP bears a label that reads "Private and Confidential— Do Not Reproduce" and is considered highly confidential by PCNA managers.

In particular, the AOP contains important and sensitive information about "pricing architecture"—how PCNA prices its products in the marketplace. Pricing architecture covers both a national pricing approach and specific price points for given areas. Pricing architecture also encompasses PCNA's objectives for All Sport and its new age drinks with reference to trade channels, package sizes and other characteristics of both the products and the customers at which the products are aimed. Additionally, PCNA's pricing architecture outlines PCNA's customer development agreements. These agreements between PCNA and retailers provide for the retailer's participation in certain merchandising activities for PCNA products. As with other information contained in the AOP, pricing architecture is highly confidential and would be extremely valuable to a competitor. Knowing PCNA's pricing architecture would allow a competitor to anticipate PCNA's pricing moves and underbid PCNA strategically whenever and wherever the competitor so desired. PepsiCo introduced evidence that Redmond had detailed knowledge of PCNA's pricing architecture and that he was aware of and had been involved in preparing PCNA's customer development agreements with PCNA's California and California-based national customers. Indeed, PepsiCo showed that Redmond, as the General Manager for California, would have been responsible for implementing the pricing architecture guidelines for his business unit.

PepsiCo also showed that Redmond had intimate knowledge of PCNA "attack plans" for specific markets. Pursuant to these plans, PCNA dedicates extra funds to supporting its brands against other brands in selected markets. To use a hypothetical example, PCNA might budget an additional $500,000 to spend in Chicago at a particular time to help All Sport close its market gap with Gatorade. Testimony and documents demonstrated Redmond's awareness of these plans and his participation in drafting some of them.

Finally, PepsiCo offered evidence of PCNA trade secrets regarding innovations in its selling and delivery systems. Under this plan, PCNA is testing a new delivery system that could give PCNA an advantage over its competitors in negotiations with retailers over shelf space and merchandising. Redmond has knowledge of this secret because PCNA, which has invested over a million dollars in developing the system during the past two years, is testing the pilot program in California.

Having shown Redmond's intimate knowledge of PCNA's plans for 1995, PepsiCo argued that Redmond would inevitably disclose that information to Quaker in his new position, at which he would have substantial input as to Gatorade and Snapple pricing, costs, margins, distribution systems, products, packaging and marketing, and could give Quaker an unfair advantage in its upcoming skirmishes with PepsiCo. Redmond and Quaker countered that Redmond's primary initial duties at Quaker as Vice President–Field Operations would be to integrate Gatorade and Snapple distribution and then to manage that distribution as well as the promotion, marketing and sales of these products. Redmond asserted that the integration would be conducted according to a pre-existing plan and that his special knowledge of PCNA strategies would be irrelevant. This irrelevance would derive not only from the fact that Redmond would be implementing pre-existing plans but also from the fact that PCNA and Quaker distribute their products in entirely different ways: PCNA's distribution system is vertically integrated (i.e., PCNA owns the system) and delivers its product directly to retailers, while Quaker ships its product to wholesalers and customer warehouses and relies on independent distributors. The defendants also pointed out that Redmond had signed a confidentiality agreement with Quaker preventing him from disclosing "any confidential information belonging to others," as well as the Quaker Code of Ethics, which prohibits employees from engaging in "illegal or improper acts to acquire a competitor's trade secrets." Redmond additionally promised at the hearing that should he be faced with a situation at Quaker that might involve the use or disclosure of PCNA information, he would seek advice from Quaker's in-house counsel and would refrain from making the decision.

PepsiCo responded to the defendants' representations by pointing out that the evidence did not show that Redmond would simply be implementing a business plan already in place. On the contrary, as of November, 1994, the plan to integrate Gatorade and Snapple distribution consisted of a single distributorship agreement and a two-page "contract terms summary." Such a basic plan would not lend itself to widespread application among the over 300 independent Snapple distributors. Since the integration process would likely face resistance from Snapple distributors and Quaker had no scheme to deal with this probability, Redmond, as the person in charge of the integration, would likely have a great deal of influence on the process. PepsiCo further argued that Snapple's 1995 marketing and promotion plans had not necessarily been completed prior to Redmond's joining Quaker, that Uzzi disagreed with portions of the Snapple plans, and that the plans were open to re-evaluation. Uzzi testified that the plan for integrating Gatorade and Snapple distribution is something that would happen in the future. Redmond would therefore likely have input in remaking these plans, and if he did, he would inevitably be making decisions with PCNA's strategic plans and 1995 AOP in mind. Moreover, PepsiCo continued, diverging testimony made it difficult to know exactly what Redmond would be doing at Quaker. Redmond described his job as "managing the entire sales effort of Gatorade at the field level, possibly including strategic planning," and at least at one point considered his job to be equivalent to that of a Chief Operating Officer. Uzzi, on the other hand, characterized Redmond's position as "primarily and initially to restructure and integrate our—the distribution systems for Snapple and for Gatorade, as per our distribution plan" and then to "execute marketing, promotion and sales plans in the marketplace." Uzzi also denied having given Redmond detailed information about any business plans, while Redmond described such a plan in depth in an affidavit and said that he received the information from Uzzi. Thus, PepsiCo asserted, Redmond would have a high position in the Gatorade hierarchy, and PCNA trade secrets and confidential information would necessarily influence his decisions. Even if Redmond could somehow refrain from relying on this information, as he promised he would, his actions in leaving PCNA, Uzzi's actions in hiring Redmond, and the varying testimony regarding Redmond's new responsibilities, made Redmond's assurances to PepsiCo less than comforting.

On December 15, 1994, the district court issued an order enjoining Redmond from assuming his position at Quaker through May, 1995, and permanently from using or disclosing any PCNA trade secrets or confidential information. The court entered its findings of fact and conclusions of law on January 26, 1995, nunc pro tunc December 15, 1994. The court, which completely adopted PepsiCo's position, found that Redmond's new job posed a clear threat of misappropriation of trade secrets and confidential information that could be enjoined under Illinois statutory and common law. The court also emphasized Redmond's lack of forthrightness both in his activities before accepting his job with Quaker and in his testimony as factors leading the court to believe the threat of misappropriation was real. This appeal followed.

II

A

The Illinois Trade Secrets Act ("ITSA"), which governs the trade secret issues in this case, provides that a court may enjoin the "actual or threatened misappropriation" of a trade secret. 765 ILCS 1065/3(a); George S. May Int'l Co. v. Int'l Profit Associates, 256 Ill.App.3d 779, 195 Ill.Dec. 183, 189, 628 N.E.2d 647, 653 (1st Dist.1993), appeal denied, 156 Ill.2d 557, 202 Ill.Dec. 921, 638 N.E.2d 1115 (1994); see also 2 Melvin F. Jager, Trade Secrets Law § IL.01[7] at IL–7 to 8 (Clark Boardman Callaghan, rev. ed. 1994). A party seeking an injunction must therefore prove both the existence of a trade secret and the misappropriation. The defendants' appeal focuses solely on misappropriation; although the defendants only reluctantly refer to PepsiCo's marketing and distribution plans as trade secrets, they do not seriously contest that this information falls under the ITSA.

The question of threatened or inevitable misappropriation in this case lies at the heart of a basic tension in trade secret law. Trade secret law serves to protect "standards of commercial morality" and "encourage [ ] invention and innovation" while maintaining "the public interest in having free and open competition in the manufacture and sale of unpatented goods." 2 Jager, § IL.03 at IL–12. Yet that same law should not prevent workers from pursuing their livelihoods when they leave their current positions. American Can Co. v. Mansukhani, 742 F.2d 314, 329 (7th Cir.1984).

This tension is particularly exacerbated when a plaintiff sues to prevent not the actual misappropriation of trade secrets but the mere threat that it will occur. While the ITSA plainly permits a court to enjoin the threat of misappropriation of trade secrets, there is little law in Illinois or in this circuit establishing what constitutes threatened or inevitable misappropriation. Indeed, there are only two cases in this circuit that address the issue: Teradyne, Inc. v. Clear Communications Corp., 707 F.Supp. 353 (N.D.Ill.1989), and AMP Inc. v. Fleischhacker, 823 F.2d 1199 (7th Cir. 1987). [These cases and the ITSA] lead to the same conclusion: a plaintiff may prove a claim of trade secret misappropriation by demonstrating that defendant's new employment will inevitably lead him to rely on the plaintiff's trade secrets. See also 1 Jager, § 7.02[2][a] at 7–20 (noting claims where "the allegation is based on the fact that the disclosure of trade secrets in the new employment is inevitable, whether or not the former employee acts consciously or unconsciously"). The defendants are incorrect that Illinois law does not allow a court to enjoin the "inevitable" disclosure of trade secrets. Questions remain, however, as to what constitutes inevitable misappropriation and whether PepsiCo's submissions rise above those of the Teradyne and AMP plaintiffs and meet that standard. We hold that they do.

PepsiCo presented substantial evidence at the preliminary injunction hearing that Redmond possessed extensive and intimate knowledge about PCNA's strategic goals for 1995 in sports drinks and new age drinks. The district court concluded on the basis of that presentation that unless Redmond possessed an uncanny ability to compartmentalize information, he would necessarily be making decisions about Gatorade and Snapple by relying on his knowledge of PCNA trade secrets. It is not the "general skills and knowledge acquired during his tenure with" PepsiCo that Pepsi-Co seeks to keep from falling into Quaker's hands, but rather "the particularized plans or processes developed by [PCNA] and disclosed to him while the employer-employee relationship existed, which are unknown to others in the industry and which give the employer an advantage over his competitors." AMP, 823 F.2d at 1202. The Teradyne and AMP plaintiffs could do nothing more than assert that skilled employees were taking their skills elsewhere; PepsiCo has done much more.

Admittedly, PepsiCo has not brought a traditional trade secret case, in which a former employee has knowledge of a special manufacturing process or customer list and can give a competitor an unfair advantage by transferring the technology or customers to that competitor. See, e.g., Glenayre Electronics, Ltd. v. Sandahl, 830 F.Supp. 1149 (C.D.Ill.1993) (preliminary injunction sought to prevent use of trade secrets regarding pager technology). PepsiCo has not contended that Quaker has stolen the All Sport formula or its list of distributors. Rather PepsiCo has asserted that Redmond cannot help but rely on PCNA trade secrets as he helps plot Gatorade and Snapple's new course, and that these secrets will enable Quaker to achieve a substantial advantage by knowing exactly how PCNA will price, distribute, and market its sports drinks and new age drinks and being able to respond strategically. cf. FMC Corp. v. Varco Int'l, Inc., 677 F.2d 500, 504 (5th Cir.1982) ("Even assuming the best of good faith, Witt will have difficulty preventing his knowledge of FMC's 'Longsweep' manufacturing techniques from infiltrating his work."). This type of trade secret problem may arise less often, but it nevertheless falls within the realm of trade secret protection under the present circumstances.

Quaker and Redmond assert that they have not and do not intend to use whatever confidential information Redmond has by virtue of his former employment. They point out that Redmond has already signed an agreement with Quaker not to disclose any trade secrets or confidential information gleaned from his earlier employment. They also note with regard to distribution systems that even if Quaker wanted to steal information about PCNA's distribution plans, they would be completely useless in attempting to integrate the Gatorade and Snapple beverage lines.

The defendants' arguments fall somewhat short of the mark. Again, the danger of misappropriation in the present case is not that Quaker threatens to use PCNA's secrets to create distribution systems or co-opt PCNA's advertising and marketing ideas. Rather, PepsiCo believes that Quaker, unfairly armed with knowledge of PCNA's plans, will be able to anticipate its distribution, packaging, pricing, and marketing moves. Redmond and Quaker even concede that Redmond might be faced with a decision that could be influenced by certain confidential information that he obtained while at PepsiCo. In other words, PepsiCo finds itself in the position of a coach, one of whose players has left, playbook in hand, to join the opposing team before the big game. Quaker and Redmond's protestations that their distribution systems and plans are entirely different from PCNA's are thus not really responsive.

The district court also concluded from the evidence that Uzzi's actions in hiring Redmond and Redmond's actions in pursuing and accepting his new job demonstrated a lack of candor on their part and proof of their willingness to misuse PCNA trade secrets, findings Quaker and Redmond vigorously challenge. The facts of the case do not ineluctably dictate the district court's conclusion. Redmond's ambiguous behavior toward his PepsiCo superiors might have been nothing more than an attempt to gain leverage in employment negotiations. The discrepancy between Redmond's and Uzzi's comprehension of what Redmond's job would entail may well have been a simple misunderstanding. The court also pointed out that Quaker, through Uzzi, seemed to express an unnatural interest in hiring PCNA employees: all three of the people interviewed for the position Redmond ultimately accepted worked at PCNA. Uzzi may well have focused on recruiting PCNA employees because he knew they were good and not because of their confidential knowledge. Nonetheless, the district court, after listening to the witnesses, determined otherwise. That conclusion was not an abuse of discretion.

Thus, when we couple the demonstrated inevitability that Redmond would rely on PCNA trade secrets in his new job at Quaker with the district court's reluctance to believe that Redmond would refrain from disclosing these secrets in his new position (or that Quaker would ensure Redmond did not disclose them), we conclude that the district court correctly decided that PepsiCo demonstrated a likelihood of success on its statutory claim of trade secret misappropriation.

. . .

## C

For the same reasons we concluded that the district court did not abuse its discretion in granting the preliminary injunction on the issue of trade secret misappropriation, we also agree with its decision on the likelihood of Redmond's breach of his confidentiality agreement should he begin working at Quaker. Because Redmond's position at Quaker would initially cause him to disclose trade secrets, it would necessarily force him to breach his agreement not to disclose confidential information acquired while employed in PCNA. Cf. George S. May Int'l, 195 Ill.Dec. at 189, 628 N.E.2d at 653 ("An employer's trade secrets are considered a protectable interest for a restrictive covenant under Illinois law.").

Quaker and Redmond do not assert that the confidentiality agreement is invalid; such agreements are enforceable when supported by adequate consideration. See, e.g., Corroon & Black of Illinois, Inc. v. Magner, 145 Ill.App.3d 151, 98 Ill.Dec. 663, 669, 494 N.E.2d 785, 791 (1st Dist.1986). Rather, they argue that "inevitable" breaches of these contracts may not be enjoined. The case on which they rely, however, R.R. Donnelley & Sons Co. v. Fagan, 767 F.Supp. 1259 (S.D.N.Y.1991) (applying Illinois law), says nothing of the sort. The R.R. Donnelley court merely found that the plaintiffs had failed to prove the existence of any confidential information or any indication that the defendant would ever use it. *Id.* at 1267. The threat of misappropriation that drives our holding with regard to trade secrets dictates the same result here.

III

For the foregoing reasons, we affirm the district court's order enjoining Redmond from assuming his responsibilities at Quaker through May, 1995, and preventing him forever from disclosing PCNA trade secrets and confidential information.

## The Gillette Company v. Williams

United States District Court for the District of Connecticut, 1973.
360 F.Supp. 1171.

■ Zampano, District Judge.

[Peter Williams was hired by Gillette–England in 1961, having trained as a physicist and worked as a scientist at Imperial Chemical Industries for 13 years. He was hired as group leader in a lab devoted to research in the "wet shave" field (i.e. involving safety razors). Before he began to work, he signed a non-disclosure agreement standard for all Gillette–England employees who are on the monthly payroll. It enjoined him, both during and after his employ, from disclosing or using confidential and secret information. After a few months, he was transferred to a new job that put him in more intimate contact with important confidential wet shave data. At that time, he was required to sign a Special Agreement that provided, in pertinent part, that:

> 3. [Williams] hereby covenants with [Gillette–England] and as separate covenants with [The Gillette Corporation, U.S].:
>
> (a) that for two years following termination of his employment with [Gillette–England] he will not without the consent in writing of [Gillette–England] be employed by or act as officer of or advisor to any firm or Company engaged in the manufacture of safety razors or blades therefor in the United States of America or for sale therein.

In return, Gillette agreed to pay Williams one-half his final Gillette salary for the duration of the two-year period if during that time he wished to accept employment proscribed by the agreement to which Gillette objected.

Williams continued to rise within Gillette and to be exposed to increasingly important data. In 1972, however, he left for a position with Gillette's chief competitor, the Warner–Lambert Company, Schick Safety Razor Division ("Schick"). Within a week, Gillette began sending him letters and notices. One indicated that his employment was terminated, a second reminded him of the covenants he had signed, and the remainder were formal objections to his employment at Schick. When Williams failed to resign, this suit for damages and injunctive relief was filed].

1. Reasonableness of the Covenant

The Court recognizes that the post-employment restrictive covenant is a contract in restraint of trade and, as such, is the subject of special judicial scrutiny. It seems clear that the plaintiff has established the reasonableness of the post-employment restrictive covenant. The highly competitive, specialized and secret nature of Gillette's wet shave business justifies its extraction of such agreements from certain employees to protect its legitimate business interests.

By his own admissions, Williams had access to and acquired knowledge of many trade secrets concerning the wet shave business during certain years of his employment. At the time the parties entered into the contract containing the restrictive covenant, it was reasonable to assume that a key employee, as Williams was, might be familiar with valuable confidential information if he subsequently left Gillette's employment to work for a competitor. Recognizing that it would be virtually impossible to avoid or detect his divulging such information to a competitor, Gillette understandably required Williams to sign the agreement as a condition of employment in order to protect its competitive position in the market.

Williams received an added consideration for signing the restrictive covenant; the two-year limitations period was more than reasonable considering the nature of Gillette's business; the territorial scope of the provision was necessary to protect Gillette's international market position; and there was no financial oppression in the event Williams had to accept a position outside the wet shave field at a lesser salary.

2. Access to and Possession of Confidential Information

The most strongly contested issue between the parties concerns Williams' access to or possession of Gillette's confidential information during the period 1968 to 1972. In lengthy, comprehensive briefs, each party, with remarkable ingenuity, excerpts language from the leading English and American cases to support their respective positions. Fine lines are drawn between "access to" and "possession of" confidential information by Williams at the time he entered Schick's employ.

The primary concern of the Court, however, is the context in which each of the cited cases arose. A careful review of the leading authorities reveals that there is a distinction between actions seeking enforcement of an employee's agreement not to compete, such as the one pending before this Court, and a tort claim for a trade secret misappropriation. It must also be emphasized that the specific contract terms in this case were designed to protect the plaintiff from a former employee's using or divulging "any matter concerning the confidential affairs or secrets of [Gillette–England or the plaintiff] or any confidential information relating thereto.... " and furthermore, from a former employee within the United States working "directly or indirectly . . . in research or development work on or the manufacture of safety razors or blades."

On the present state of the record, the scales balancing the factual presentation of evidence tip slightly in favor of the plaintiff; the defendant certainly may have the opportunity to reverse the balance or bring them into equilibrium.

Accordingly, the defendant's motion to dismiss the plaintiff's application for a preliminary injunction is denied.

## United States v. Lange

United States Court of Appeals for the Seventh Circuit, 2002.
312 F.3d 263.

■ EASTERBROOK, CIRCUIT JUDGE.

Matthew Lange has been convicted of violating 18 U.S.C. § 1832, part of the Economic Espionage Act of 1996. This statute makes it a felony to sell, disseminate, or otherwise deal in trade secrets, or attempt to do so, without the owner's consent. Lange stole computer data from Replacement Aircraft Parts Co. (RAPCO), his former employer, and attempted to sell the data to one of RAPCO's competitors. He allows that his acts violated § 1832, if the data contained "trade secrets," but denies that the data met the statutory definition:

> the term "trade secret" means all forms and types of financial, business, scientific, technical, economic, or engineering information, including patterns, plans, compilations, program devices, formulas, designs, prototypes, methods, techniques, processes, procedures, programs, or codes, whether tangible or intangible, and whether or how stored, compiled, or memorialized physically, electronically, graphically, photographically, or in writing if—(A) the owner thereof has taken reasonable measures to keep such information secret; and (B) the information derives independent economic value, actual or potential, from not being generally known to, and not being readily ascertainable through proper means by, the public[.]

18 U.S.C. § 1839(3). Lange's appeal requires us to apply this definition.

RAPCO is in the business of making aircraft parts for the aftermarket. It buys original equipment parts, then disassembles them to identify (and measure) each component. This initial step of reverse engineering, usually performed by a drafter such as Lange, produces a set of measurements and drawings. See generally Pamela Samuelson & Suzanne Scotchmer, *The Law and Economics of Reverse Engineering,* 111 Yale L.J. 1575, 1582–94 (2002). Because this case involves an effort to sell the intellectual property used to make a brake assembly, we use brakes as an illustration.

Knowing exactly what a brake assembly looks like does not enable RAPCO to make a copy. It must figure out how to make a substitute with the same (or better) technical specifications. Brakes rely on friction to slow the airplane's speed by converting kinetic energy to heat. Surfaces that do this job well are made by sintering—the forming of solid metal, usually from a powder, without melting. Aftermarket manufacturers must experiment with different alloys and compositions until they achieve a process and product that fulfils requirements set by the Federal Aviation Administration for each brake assembly. Completed assemblies must be exhaustively tested to demonstrate, to the FAA's satisfaction, that all requirements have been met; only then does the FAA certify the part for sale. It takes RAPCO a year or two to design, and obtain approval for, a complex part; the dynamometer testing alone can cost $75,000. But the process of experimenting and testing can be avoided if the manufacturer demonstrates that its parts are identical (in composition and manufacturing processes) to parts that have already been certified. What Lange, a disgruntled former employee, offered for sale was all the information required to obtain certification of several components as identical to parts for which RAPCO held certification. Lange included with the package—which he offered via the Internet to anyone willing to pay his price of $100,000—a pirated copy of AutoCAD(R), the computer-assisted drawing software that RAPCO uses to maintain its drawings and specifications data. One person to whom Lange tried to peddle the data informed RAPCO, which turned to the FBI. Lange was arrested following taped negotiations that supply all the evidence necessary for conviction—if the data satisfy the statutory definition of trade secrets.

One ingredient of a trade secret is that "the owner thereof has taken reasonable measures to keep such information secret". Lange contends that the proof fell short, but a sensible trier of fact (in this bench trial, the district judge) could have concluded that RAPCO took "reasonable measures to keep [the] information secret". RAPCO stores all of its drawings and manufacturing data in its CAD room, which is protected by a special lock, an alarm system, and a motion detector. The number of copies of sensitive information is kept to a minimum; surplus copies are shredded. Some information in the plans is coded, and few people know the keys to these codes. Drawings and other manufacturing information contain warnings of RAPCO's intellectual-property rights; every employee receives a notice that the information with which he works is confidential. None of RAPCO's subcontractors receives full copies of the schematics; by dividing the work among vendors, RAPCO ensures that none can replicate the product. This makes it irrelevant that RAPCO does not require vendors to sign confidentiality agreements; it relies on *deeds* (the splitting of tasks) rather than *promises* to maintain confidentiality. Although, as Lange says, engineers and drafters knew where to get the key to the CAD room door, keeping these employees out can't be an ingredient of "reasonable measures to keep [the] information secret"; then no one could do any work. So too with plans sent to subcontractors, which is why dissemination to suppliers does not undermine a claim of trade secret. See *Rockwell Graphic Systems, Inc. v. DEV Industries, Inc.*, 925 F.2d 174, 177 (7th Cir.1991).

The second ingredient is that "the information derives independent economic value, actual or potential, from not being generally known to, and not being readily ascertainable through proper means by, the public[.]"

According to Lange, all data obtained by reverse engineering some other product are "readily ascertainable ... by the public" because everyone can do what RAPCO did: buy an original part, disassemble and measure it, and make a copy. The prosecutor responds to this contention by observing that "the public" is unable to reverse engineer an aircraft brake assembly.

The prosecutor's assumption is that the statutory reference in § 1839(3) to "the public" means the *general* public—the man in the street. Ordinary people don't have AutoCAD and 60–ton flywheels ready to hand. But is the general public the right benchmark? The statute itself does not give an answer: the word "public" could be preceded implicitly by "general" as the prosecutor supposes, but it also could be preceded implicitly by "educated" or "economically important" or any of many other qualifiers. Once we enter the business of adding words to flesh out the statute—and even the addition of "general" to "public" does this—it usually is best to ask what function the law serves. In criminal cases it also is important to inquire whether the unelaborated text is ambiguous, because if it is the language should be read to prevent surprises. That's the function of the Rule of Lenity. See *Staples v. United States,* 511 U.S. 600, 619, 114 S.Ct. 1793, 128 L.Ed.2d 608 (1994). Some elaboration is needed. Although the third circuit assumed in *United States v. Hsu,* 155 F.3d 189, 196 (3d Cir.1998), that "general" belongs in front of "public," it did not explain why (nor was this important to, or a part of, *Hsu*'s holding). Commentators disagree about who "the public" includes. Compare Geraldine Szott Moohr, *The Problematic Role of Criminal Law in Regulating the Use of Information: The Case of the Economic Espionage Act,* 80 N.C. L.Rev. 853, 878–79 (2002), with Arthur J. Schwab & David J. Porter, *Guarding the Crown Jewels: A Guide to Protecting Your Trade Secrets* 85–86 (2002). It is therefore worth a look—though it turns out not to be dispositive here, any more than it was in *Hsu.*

A problem with using the general public as the reference group for identifying a trade secret is that many things unknown to the public at large are well known to engineers, scientists, and others whose intellectual property the Economic Espionage Act was enacted to protect. This makes the general public a poor benchmark for separating commercially valuable *secrets* from obscure (but generally known) information. Suppose that Lange had offered to sell Avogadro's number for $1. Avogadro's number, $6.02 \times 10^{23}$, is the number of molecules per mole of gas. It is an important constant, known to chemists since 1909 but not to the general public (or even to all recent graduates of a chemistry class). We can't believe that Avogadro's number could be called a trade secret. Other principles are known without being comprehended. Most people know that $E = mc^2$, but a pop quiz of the general public would reveal that they do not understand what this *means* or how it can be used productively.

One might respond that the context of the word "public" addresses this concern. The full text of § 1839(3)(B) is: "the information derives independent economic value, actual or potential, from not being generally known to, and not being readily ascertainable through proper means by, the public". Avogadro's number and other obscure knowledge is not "generally known to" the man in the street but might be deemed "readily ascertainable to" this hypothetical person. It appears in any number of scientific handbooks. Similarly one can visit a library and read Einstein's own discussion of his famous equation. See Albert Einstein, *Relativity: The Special and General Theory* (1920). Members of the general public can ascertain even abstruse information, such as Schrodinger's quantum field equation, by consulting people in the know—as high school dropouts can take advantage of obscure legal rules by hiring lawyers. But this approach uses the phrase "readily available" to treat the "general public" *as if* it were more technically competent, which poses the question whether it would be better to use a qualifier other than "general" in the first place.

Section 1839(3) was derived from the definition of a trade secret in the Uniform Trade Secrets Act, which many states have adopted. Section 1(4) of the Uniform Act provides:

> "Trade secret" means information, including a formula, pattern, compilation, program, device, method, technique, or process, that:
>
> (i) derives independent economic value, actual or potential, from not being generally known to, and not being readily ascertainable by proper means by, other persons who can obtain economic value from its disclosure or use, and
>
> (ii) is the subject of efforts that are reasonable under the circumstances to maintain its secrecy.

Section 1839(3)(B) replaces "persons who can obtain economic value from its disclosure or use" with "the public". The prosecutor believes that the substitution supports the conclusion that Congress referred to the *general* public. Yet one could say instead that "the public" is shorthand for the longer phrase, which then would be read as "the *economically relevant* public"—that is, the persons whose ignorance of the information is the source of its economic value. Let us recur to the statutory context of "the public":

> the information derives independent economic value, actual or potential, from not being generally known to, and not being readily ascertainable through proper means by, the public[.]

Section 1839(3)(B) as a whole refers to the source of economic value— that the information is not known to or easily discoverable by persons who could use it productively. To make this work, either the phrase "readily ascertainable" or the phrase "the public" must be understood to concentrate attention on either potential users of the information, or proxies for them (which is to say, persons who have the same ability to "ascertain" the information). And for purposes of this case those people would be engineers and manufacturers of aircraft parts, who have ample means to reverse engineer their competitors' products. It is by keeping secrets from its rivals that RAPCO captures the returns of its design and testing work. Thus it is unnecessary here to decide whether "general" belongs in front of "public"—for even if it does, the economically valuable information is not "readily ascertainable" to the general public, the educated public, the economically relevant public, or any sensible proxy for these groups.

Another line of prosecutorial argument starts with the fact that § 1832(a)(4) makes it a crime to attempt to sell trade secrets without the owner's permission. Even if Lange did not have real trade secrets in his possession, the argument goes, he *thought* he did and therefore may be penalized for an attempted sale. The argument finds support in *Hsu,* which held that in order to avoid graymail—the threat that to obtain a conviction the prosecutor must disclose the secret by putting it in the trial record—a case may be based on § 1832(a)(4) without disclosing all details of the trade secret. Accord, *United States v. Pin Yen Yang,* 281 F.3d 534, 543–44 (6th Cir.2002). We agree with the general approach of these decisions. *Hsu* analogized the attempted sale of information believed to be a trade secret to an attempt such as shooting a corpse, believing it to be alive, or selling sugar, believing it to be cocaine. Events of this sort underlie the maxim that factual impossibility is no defense to a prosecution for attempt. This does not mean, however, that the defendant's belief *alone* can support a conviction. All attempt prosecutions depend on demonstrating that the defendant took a substantial step toward completion of the offense, which could have been carried out unless thwarted. *Braxton v. United States,* 500 U.S. 344, 111 S.Ct. 1854, 114 L.Ed.2d 385 (1991). Although the American Law Institute recommends a definition of attempt linked closely to intent, *Model Penal Code* § 5.01(1)(c), the Supreme Court has not embraced this view and demands in cases under federal law that the prosecutor establish a probability of success. See, e.g., *Spectrum Sports, Inc. v. McQuillan,* 506 U.S. 447, 113 S.Ct. 884, 122 L.Ed.2d 247 (1993) ( "dangerous probability" of success is an ingredient of attempted monopolization).

An attempted murder may be thwarted by substituting a sack of flour for the intended victim; a sale of drugs may be thwarted by substituting sugar for cocaine, or rock candy for crack. These situations present a good chance of success, but for the intervention. So does "the disgruntled former employee who walks out of his former company with a computer diskette full of engineering schematics" (*Hsu,* 155 F.3d at 201)—a fair description of Lange's conduct (though diskettes are obsolete). A sale of trade secrets may be thwarted by substituting a disk with the collected works of Shakespeare for the disk that the defendant believed contained the plans for brake assemblies, or by an inadvertent failure to download the proper file. The attempted sale of the disk is a culpable substantial step. But it is far less clear that sale of information already known to the public could be deemed a substantial step toward the offense, just because the defendant is deluded and does not understand what a trade secret is. Selling a copy of *Zen and the Art of Motorcycle Maintenance* is not attempted economic espionage, even if the defendant thinks that the tips in the book are trade secrets; nor is sticking pins in voodoo dolls attempted murder. Booksellers and practitioners of the occult pose no social dangers, certainly none of the magnitude of those who are tricked into shooting bags of sand that have been substituted for targets of assassination. Lange was more dangerous than our bookseller but much less dangerous than our hypothetical assassin.

Perhaps data purloined from an ex-employer is sufficiently *likely* to contain trade secrets to justify calling the preparation for sale a substantial step toward completion of the offense, and thus a culpable attempt, even if the employee stole the wrong data file and did not get his hands on the commercially valuable information. We need not pursue the subject beyond noting the plausibility of the claim and its sensitivity to the facts—what kind of data did the employee think he stole, and so on. For it is not necessary to announce a definitive rule about how dangerous the completed acts must be in trade secret cases: the judge was entitled to (and did) find that Lange had *real* trade secrets in his possession.

Lange wants us to proceed as if all he tried to sell were measurements that anyone could have taken with calipers after disassembling an original-equipment part. Such measurements could not be called trade secrets if, as Lange asserts, the assemblies in question were easy to take apart and measure. But no one would have paid $100,000 for metes and bounds, while Lange told his customers that the data on offer were worth more than that asking price. Which they were. What Lange had, and tried to sell, were the completed specifications and engineering diagrams that reflected all the work completed *after* the measurements had been taken: the metallurgical data, details of the sintering, the results of the tests, the plans needed to produce the finished goods, everything required to get FAA certification of a part supposedly identical to one that had been approved. Those details "derive[d] independent economic value, actual or potential, from not being generally known to, and not being readily ascertainable through proper means by, the public[.]" Every firm other than the original equipment manufacturer and RAPCO had to pay dearly to devise, test, and win approval of similar parts; the details unknown to the rivals, and not discoverable with tape measures, had considerable "independent economic value . . . from not being generally known". A sensible trier of fact could determine that Lange tried to sell trade secrets. It was his customer's cooperation with the FBI, and not public access to the data, that prevented closing of the sale.

[The portion of the opinion reviewing the sentence is omitted.]

■ RIPPLE, CIRCUIT JUDGE, concurring.

The panel majority notes that the Economic Espionage Act, in defining "trade secret," includes as an ingredient that

> the information derives independent economic value, actual or potential, from not being generally known to, and not being readily ascertainable through proper means by, the public[.] 18 U.S.C. § 1839(3)(B).

This portion of the definition of a trade secret differs markedly from the definition found in the Uniform Trade Secrets Act. The analogous language, found at section 1(4) of the Uniform Act, provides that the information must

> derive[ ] independent economic value, actual or potential, from not being generally known to, and not being readily ascertainable by proper means by, other persons who can obtain economic value from its disclosure or use[.] Unif. Trade Secrets Act, § 1(4) (amended 1985), 14 U.L.A. 438 (1979).

The panel majority declares that this textual difference is of no significance because the phrase "the public" in the federal statute is simply shorthand for the longer phrase of the Uniform Act. Therefore, the panel majority concludes, "the public" ought to be read "the *economically relevant* public." Because Mr. Lange offered information that was unknown to both competitors and to the general public, there is no reason to confront this issue in this case, and, because the correctness of the panel majority's reading of the evidence is not self-evident, we ought not to reject out-of-hand the position of the United States when there is no necessity to do so.

The panel majority bases its reading of the federal statute on its conclusion that "[s]ection 1839(3) was derived from the definition of a trade secret in the Uniform Trade Secrets Act." An examination of the House Report accompanying the statute describes, however, a somewhat more nuanced relationship between the two definitions. Notably, the Report states that the definition of "trade secret" in the federal statute is "based largely" on the definition of that term in the Uniform Trade Secrets Act. H.R.Rep. No. 104–788, at 12 (1996), U.S. Code Cong. & Admin. News 4021, 4030–31. The report goes on to say in the paragraphs immediately following that "information which is generally known to the public, or which the public can readily ascertain through proper means, does not satisfy the definition of trade secret under this section." *Id.* at 13, U.S. Code Cong. & Admin. News at 4031.

Our normal approach to statutory interpretation is to assume that Congress intended what it wrote. Here, the words of the statute are clear on their face. Moreover, the pertinent legislative history supports reliance on the plain wording. Congress used the Uniform Act's definition of "trade secret" as a guide, but it did not adopt it. Instead, Congress made its own choices as to those aspects of the Uniform Act's definition that ought to be adopted and those that needed alteration before incorporation into the federal statute. I see no reason to reject so swiftly and gratuitously the plain wording of the statute, the supportive legislative history, the interpretation of the Court of Appeals for the Third Circuit in *United States v. Hsu,* 155 F.3d 189, 196–97 (3d Cir.1998), and the interpretation of the Executive Branch set forth in the Government's brief.

I would also defer announcing any limitations on the law of attempt as it applies to the Economic Espionage Act in advance of the necessity of doing so. The considered judgment of another circuit to the contrary particularly counsels restraint in this respect. *See Hsu,* 155 F.3d at 198–203. In this case, there is no question that the information Mr. Lange offered for sale was a trade secret. We therefore need not decide whether a defendant can be found guilty of an attempt when no such secret exists.

## Kewanee Oil Co. v. Bicron Corp.

Supreme Court of the United States, 1974.
416 U.S. 470, 94 S.Ct. 1879, 40 L.Ed.2d 315.

■ Mr. Chief Justice Burger delivered the opinion of the Court.

We granted certiorari to resolve a question on which there is a conflict in the courts of appeals: whether state trade secret protection is pre-empted by operation of the federal patent law.

## I

Harshaw Chemical Co., an unincorporated division of petitioner, is a leading manufacturer of a type of synthetic crystal which is useful in the detection of ionizing radiation. In 1949 Harshaw commenced research into the growth of this type crystal and was able to produce one less than two inches in diameter. By 1966, as the result of expenditures in excess of $1 million, Harshaw was able to grow a 17–inch crystal, something no one else had done previously. Harshaw had developed many processes, procedures, and manufacturing techniques in the purification of raw materials and the growth and encapsulation of the crystals which enabled it to accomplish this feat. Some of these processes Harshaw considers to be trade secrets.

The individual respondents former employees of Harshaw who formed or later joined respondent Bicron. While at Harshaw the individual respondents executed, as a condition of employment, at least one agreement each, requiring them not to disclose confidential information or trade secrets obtained as employees of Harshaw. Bicron was formed in August 1969 to compete with Harshaw in the production of the crystals, and by April 1970, had grown a 17–inch crystal.

Petitioner brought this diversity action in United States District Court for the Northern District of Ohio seeking injunctive relief and damages for the misappropriation of trade secrets. The District Court, applying Ohio trade secret law, granted a permanent injunction against the disclosure or use by respondents of 20 of the 40 claimed trade secrets until such time as the trade secrets had been released to the public, had otherwise generally become available to the public, or had been obtained by respondents from sources having the legal right to convey the information. [The Sixth Circuit reversed, finding Ohio's trade secret law to be in conflict with the patent laws of the United States].

## II

Ohio has adopted the widely relied-upon definition of a trade secret found at Restatement of Torts § 757, comment b (1939). According to the Restatement,

> (a) trade secret may consist of any formula, pattern, device or compilation of information which is used in one's business, and which gives him an opportunity to obtain an advantage over competitors who do not know or use it. It may be a formula for a chemical compound, a process of manufacturing, treating or preserving materials, a pattern for a machine or other device, or a list of customers.

The subject of a trade secret must be secret, and must not be of public knowledge or of a general knowledge in the trade or business. This necessary element of secrecy is not lost, however, if the holder of the trade secret reveals the trade secret to another "in confidence, and under an implied obligation not to use or disclose it.'' Cincinnati Bell Foundry Co. v. Dodds, 10 Ohio Dec.Reprint 154, 156, 19 Weekly Law Bull. 84 (Super.Ct.1887).

The protection accorded the trade secret holder is against the disclosure or unauthorized use of the trade secret by those to whom the secret has been confided under the express or implied restriction of nondisclosure or nonuse. The law also protects the holder of a trade secret against disclosure or use when the knowledge is gained, not by the owner's volition, but by some "improper means," Restatement of Torts § 757(a), which may include theft, wiretapping, or even aerial reconnaissance. A trade secret law, however, does not offer protection against discovery by fair and honest means, such as by independent invention, accidental disclosure, or by so-called reverse engineering, that is by starting with the known product and working backward to divine the process which aided in its development or manufacture.

## III

The first issue we deal with is whether the States are forbidden to act at all in the area of protection of the kinds of intellectual property which may make up the subject matter of trade secrets.

Article I, § 8, cl. 8, of the Constitution grants to the Congress the power

> (t)o promote the Progress of Science and useful Arts, by securing for limited Times to Authors and Inventors the exclusive Right to their respective Writings and Discoveries . . .

In the 1972 Term, in Goldstein v. California, 412 U.S. 546, 93 S.Ct. 2303, 37 L.Ed.2d 163 (1973), we held that the cl. 8 grant of power to Congress was not exclusive and that, at least in the case of writings, the States were not prohibited from encouraging and protecting the efforts of those within their borders by appropriate legislation. The States could, therefore, protect against the unauthorized rerecording for sale of performances fixed on records or tapes, even though those performances qualified as "writings" in the constitutional sense and Congress was empowered to legislate regarding such performances and could pre-empt the area if it chose to do so. This determination was premised on the great diversity of interests in our Nation—the essentially non-uniform character of the appreciation of intellectual achievements in the various States. Evidence for this came from patents granted by the States in the 18th century. 412 U.S., at 557, 93 S.Ct., at 2310.

Just as the States may exercise regulatory power over writings so may the States regulate with respect to discoveries. States may hold diverse viewpoints in protecting intellectual property to invention as they do in protecting the intellectual property relating to the subject matter of copyright. The only limitation on the States is that in regulating the area of patents and copyrights they do not conflict with the operation of the laws in this area passed by Congress, and it is to that more difficult question we now turn.

IV

The patent law does not explicitly endorse or forbid the operation of trade secret law. However, as we have noted, if the scheme of protection developed by Ohio respecting trade secrets "clashes with the objectives of the federal patent laws," Sears, Roebuck & Co. v. Stiffel Co., 376 U.S. 225, 231, 84 S.Ct. 784, 789, 11 L.Ed.2d 661 (1964), then the state law must fall. To determine whether the Ohio law "clashes" with the federal law it is helpful to examine the objectives of both the patent and trade secret laws.

The stated objective of the Constitution in granting the power to Congress to legislate in the area of intellectual property is to "promote the Progress of Science and useful Arts." The patent laws promote this progress by offering a right of exclusion for a limited period as an incentive to inventors to risk the often enormous costs in terms of time, research, and development. The productive effort thereby fostered will have a positive effect on society through the introduction of new products and processes of manufacture into the economy, and the emanations by way of increased employment and better lives for our citizens. In return for the right of exclusion—this "reward for inventions," Universal Oil Products Co. v. Globe Oil & Refining Co., 322 U.S. 471, 484, 64 S.Ct. 1110, 1116, 88 L.Ed. 1399 (1944)—the patent laws impose upon the inventor a requirement of disclosure. To insure adequate and full disclosure so that upon the expiration of the 17–year period "the knowledge of the invention enures to the people, who are thus enabled without restriction to practice it and profit by its use," United States v. Dubilier Condenser Corp., 289 U.S. 178, 187, 53 S.Ct. 554, 77 L.Ed. 1114 (1933), the patent laws require that the patent application shall include a full and clear description of the invention and "of the manner and process of making and using it" so that any person skilled in the art may make and use the invention. 35 U.S.C. § 112. When a patent is granted and the information contained in it is circulated to the general public and those especially skilled in the trade, such additions to the general store of knowledge are of such importance to the public weal that the Federal Government is willing to pay the high price of 17 years of exclusive use for its disclosure, which disclosure, it is assumed, will stimulate ideas and the eventual development of further significant advances in the art. The Court has also articulated another policy of the patent law: that which is in the public domain cannot be removed therefrom by action of the States.

The maintenance of standards of commercial ethics and the encouragement of invention are the broadly stated policies behind trade secret law. "The necessity of good faith and honest, fair dealing, is the very life and spirit of the commercial world." National Tube Co. v. Eastern Tube Co., 3 Ohio Cir.Cr.R., N.S. at 462.

In Wexler v. Greenberg, 399 Pa. 569, 578–579, 160 A.2d 430, 434–435 (1960), the Pennsylvania Supreme Court noted the importance of trade secret protection to the subsidization of research and development and to increased economic efficiency within large companies through the dispersion of responsibilities for creative developments.

Having now in mind the objectives of both the patent and trade secret law, we turn to an examination of the interaction of these systems of protection of intellectual property—one established by the Congress and the other by a State—to determine whether and under what circumstances the latter might constitute "too great an encroachment on the federal patent system to be tolerated." Sears, Roebuck & Co. v. Stiffel Co., 376 U.S., at 232, 84 S.Ct., at 789.

As we noted earlier, trade secret law protects items which would not be proper subjects for consideration for patent protection under 35 U.S.C. § 101. As in the case of the recordings in Goldstein v. California, Congress, with respect to nonpatentable subject matter, "has drawn no balance; rather, it has left the area unattended, and no reason exists why the State should not be free to act." Goldstein v. California, 412 U.S., at 570, 93 S.Ct. at 2316 (footnote omitted).

Since no patent is available for a discovery, however useful, novel, and nonobvious, unless it falls within one of the express categories of patentable subject matter of 35 U.S.C. § 101, the holder of such a discovery would have no reason to apply for a patent whether trade secret protection existed or not. Abolition of trade secret protection would, therefore, not result in increased disclosure to the public of discoveries in the area of nonpatentable subject matter. Also, it is hard to see how the public would be benefited by disclosure of customer lists or advertising campaigns; in fact, keeping such items secret encourages businesses to initiate new and individualized plans of operation, and constructive competition results. This, in turn, leads to a greater variety of business methods than would otherwise be the case if privately developed marketing and other data were passed illicitly among firms involved in the same enterprise.

The question remains whether those items which are proper subjects for consideration for a patent may also have available the alternative protection accorded by trade secret law. Certainly the patent policy of encouraging invention is not disturbed by the existence of another form of incentive to invention. In this respect the two systems are not and never would be in conflict. Similarly, the policy that matter once in the public domain must remain in the public domain is not incompatible with the existence of trade secret protection. By definition a trade secret has not been placed in the public domain.

The more difficult objective of the patent law to reconcile with trade secret law is that of disclosure, the quid pro quo of the right to exclude. We are helped in this stage of the analysis by Judge Henry Friendly's opinion in Painton & Co. v. Bourns, Inc., 442 F.2d 216 (C.A.2 1971). There the Court of Appeals thought it useful, in determining whether inventors will refrain because of the existence of trade secret law from applying for patents, thereby depriving the public from learning of the invention, to distinguish between three categories of trade secrets:

> (1) the trade secret believed by its owner to constitute a validly patentable invention; (2) the trade secret known to its owner not to be so patentable; and (3) the trade secret whose valid patentability is considered dubious.

Id., at 224. Trade secret protection in each of these categories would run against breaches of confidence—the employee and licensee situations—and theft and other forms of industrial espionage.

As to the trade secret known not to meet the standards of patentability, very little in the way of disclosure would be accomplished by abolishing trade secret protection. With trade secrets of nonpatentable subject matter, the patent alternative would not reasonably be available to the inventor. "There can be no public interest in stimulating developers of such (unpatentable) knowhow to flood an overburdened Patent Office with applications (for) what they do not consider patentable." Ibid. The mere filing of applications doomed to be turned down by the Patent Office will bring forth no new public knowledge or enlightenment, since under federal statute and regulation patent applications and abandoned patent applications are held by the Patent Office in confidence and are not open to public inspection. 35 U.S.C. § 122; 37 CFR § 1.14(b).

Even as the extension of trade secret protection to patentable subject matter that the owner knows will not meet the standards of patentability will not conflict with the patent policy of disclosure, it will have a decidedly beneficial effect on society. Trade secret law will encourage invention in areas where patent law does not reach, and will prompt the independent innovator to proceed with the discovery and exploitation of his invention. Competition is fostered and the public is not deprived of the use of valuable, if not quite patentable, invention.

Even if trade secret protection against the faithless employee were abolished, inventive and exploitive effort in the area of patentable subject matter that did not meet the standards of patentability would continue, although at a reduced level. Alternatively with the effort that remained, however, would come an increase in the amount of self-help that innovative companies would employ. Knowledge would be widely dispersed among the employees of those still active in research. Security precautions necessarily would be increased, and salaries and fringe benefits of those few officers or employees who had to know the whole of the secret invention would be fixed in an amount thought sufficient to assure their loyalty. Smaller companies would be placed at a distinct economic disadvantage, since the costs of this kind of self-help could be great, and the cost to the public of the use of this invention would be increased. The innovative entrepreneur with limited resources would tend to confine his research efforts to himself and those few he felt he could trust without the ultimate assurance of legal protection against breaches of confidence. As a result, organized scientific and technological research could become fragmented, and society, as a whole, would suffer.

Another problem that would arise if state trade secret protection were precluded is in the area of licensing others to exploit secret processes. The holder of a trade secret would not likely share his secret with a manufacturer who cannot be placed under binding legal obligation to pay a license fee or to protect the secret. The result would be to hoard rather than disseminate knowledge. Instead, then, of licensing others to use his invention and making the most efficient use of existing manufacturing and marketing structures within the industry, the trade secret holder would tend either to limit his utilization of the invention, thereby depriving the public of the maximum benefit of its use, or engage in the time-consuming and economically wasteful enterprise of constructing duplicative manufacturing and marketing mechanisms for the exploitation of the invention. The detrimental misallocation of resources and economic waste that would thus take place if trade secret protection were abolished with respect to employees or licensees cannot be justified by reference to any policy that the federal patent law seeks to advance.

Nothing in the patent law requires that States refrain from action to prevent industrial espionage. In addition to the increased costs for protection from burglary, wire-tapping, bribery, and the other means used to misappropriate trade secrets, there is the inevitable cost to the basic decency of society when one firm steals from another. A most fundamental human right, that of privacy, is threatened when industrial espionage is condoned or is made profitable; the state interest in denying profit to such illegal ventures is unchallengeable.

The next category of patentable subject matter to deal with is the invention whose holder has a legitimate doubt as to its patentability. The risk of eventual patent invalidity by the courts and the costs associated with that risk may well impel some with a good-faith doubt as to patentability not to take the trouble to seek to obtain and defend patent protection for their discoveries, regardless of the existence of trade secret protection. Trade secret protection would assist those inventors in the more efficient exploitation of their discoveries and not conflict with the patent law. In most cases of genuine doubt as to patent validity the potential rewards of patent protection are so far superior to those accruing to holders of trade secrets, that the holders of such inventions will seek patent protection, ignoring the trade secret route. For those inventors "on the line" as to whether to seek patent protection, the abolition of trade secret protection might encourage some to apply for a patent who otherwise would not have done so. Some of the nonpatentable discoveries will be thrown out by the Patent Office, but in the meantime society will have been deprived of use of those discoveries through trade secret-protected licensing. Some of the [nonpatentable discoveries] may not be thrown out. This Court has noted the difference between the standards used by the Patent Office and the courts to determine patentability. Graham v. John Deere Co., 383 U.S. 1, 18, 86 S.Ct. 684, 694, 15 L.Ed.2d 545 (1966). In Lear, Inc. v. Adkins, 395 U.S. 653, 89 S.Ct. 1902, 23 L.Ed.2d 610 (1969), the Court thought that an invalid patent was so serious a threat to the free use of ideas already in the public domain that the Court permitted licensees of the patent holder to challenge the validity of the patent. Better had the invalid patent never issued. More of those patents would likely issue if trade secret law were abolished. Eliminating trade secret law for the doubtfully patentable invention is thus likely to have deleterious effects on society and patent policy which we cannot say are balanced out by the speculative gain which might result from the encouragement of some inventors with doubtfully patentable inventions which deserve patent protection to come forward and apply for patents. There is no conflict, then, between trade secret law and the patent law policy of disclosure, at least insofar as the first two categories of patentable subject matter are concerned.

The final category of patentable subject matter to deal with is the clearly patentable invention, i.e., that invention which the owner believes to meet the standards of patentability. It is here that the federal interest in disclosure is at its peak; these inventions, novel, useful and nonobvious, are "the things which are worth to the public the embarrassment of an exclusive patent." Graham v. John Deere Co., at 9, 86 S.Ct., at 689 (quoting Thomas Jefferson). The interest of the public is that the bargain of 17 years of exclusive use in return for disclosure be accepted. If a State, through a system of protection, were to cause a substantial risk that holders of patentable inventions would not seek patents, but rather would rely on the state protection, we would be compelled to hold that such a system could not constitutionally continue to exist. In the case of trade secret law no reasonable risk of deterrence from patent application by those who can reasonably expect to be granted patents exists.

Trade secret law provides far weaker protection in many respects than the patent law. While trade secret law does not forbid the discovery of the trade secret by fair and honest means, e.g., independent creation or reverse engineering, patent law operates "against the world," forbidding any use of the invention for whatever purpose for a significant length of time. The holder of a trade secret also takes a substantial risk that the secret will be passed on to his competitors, by theft or by breach of a confidential relationship, in a manner not easily susceptible of discovery or proof. Where patent law acts as a barrier, trade secret law functions relatively as a sieve. The possibility that an inventor who believes his invention meets the standards of patentability will sit back, rely on trade secret law, and after one year of use forfeit any right to patent protection, 35 U.S.C. § 102(b), is remote indeed.

Nor does society face much risk that scientific or technological progress will be impeded by the rare inventor with a patentable invention who chooses trade secret protection over patent protection. The ripeness-of-time concept of invention, developed from the study of the many independent multiple discoveries in history, predicts that if a particular individual had not made a particular discovery others would have, and in probably a relatively short period of time. If something is to be discovered at all very likely it will be discovered by more than one person. Singletons and Multiples in Science (1961), in R. Merton, The Sociology of Science 343 (1973). Even were an inventor to keep his discovery completely to himself, something that neither the patent nor trade secret laws forbid, there is a high probability that it will be soon independently developed. If the invention, though still a trade secret, is put into public use, the competition is alerted to the existence of the inventor's solution to the problem and may be encouraged to make an extra effort to independently find the solution thus known to be possible. The inventor faces pressures not only from private industry, but from the skilled scientists who work in our universities and our other great publicly supported centers of learning and research.

Trade secret law and patent law have co-existed in this country for over one hundred years. Each has its particular role to play, and the operation of one does not take away from the need for the other. Trade secret law encourages the development and exploitation of those items of lesser or different invention than might be accorded protection under the patent laws, but which items still have an important part to play in the technological and scientific advancement of the Nation. Trade secret law promotes the sharing of knowledge, and the efficient operation of industry; it permits the individual inventor to reap the rewards of his labor by contracting with a company large enough to develop and exploit it. Congress, by its silence over these many years, has seen the wisdom of allowing the States to enforce trade secret protection. Until Congress takes affirmative action to the contrary, States should be free to grant protection to trade secrets.

■ Mr. Justice Marshall, concurring in the result.

Unlike the Court, I do not believe that the possibility that an inventor with a patentable invention will rely on state trade secret law rather than apply for a patent is "remote indeed." State trade secret law provides substantial protection to the inventor who intends to use or sell the invention himself rather than license it to others, protection which in its unlimited duration is clearly superior to the 17–year monopoly afforded by the patent laws. I have no doubt that the existence of trade secret protection provides in some instances a substantial disincentive to entrance into the patent system, and thus deprives society of the benefits of public disclosure of the invention which it is the policy of the patent laws to encourage. This case may well be such an instance.

But my view of sound policy in this area does not dispose of this case. Rather, the question presented in this case is whether Congress, in enacting the patent laws, intended merely to offer inventors a limited monopoly in exchange for disclosure of their invention, or instead to exert pressure on inventors to enter into this exchange by withdrawing any alternative possibility of legal protection for their inventions. I am persuaded that the former is the case.

■ Mr. Justice Douglas, with whom Mr. Justice Brennan concurs, dissenting [omitted].

## Bonito Boats, Inc. v. Thunder Craft Boats, Inc.

Supreme Court of the United States, 1989.
489 U.S. 141, 109 S.Ct. 971, 103 L.Ed.2d 118.

■ Justice O'Connor delivered the opinion of the Court.

We must decide today what limits the operation of the federal patent system places on the States' ability to offer substantial protection to utilitarian and design ideas which the patent laws leave otherwise unprotected.

I

In September 1976, petitioner Bonito Boats, Inc. (Bonito), a Florida corporation, developed a hull design for a fiberglass recreational boat which it marketed under the trade name Bonito Boat Model 5VBR. App. 5. Designing the boat hull required substantial effort on the part of Bonito. A set of engineering drawings was prepared, from which a hardwood model was created. The hardwood model was then sprayed with fiberglass to create a mold, which then served to produce the finished fiberglass boats for sale. The 5VBR was placed on the market sometime in September 1976. There is no indication in the record that a patent application was ever filed for protection of the utilitarian or design aspects of the hull, or for the process by which the hull was manufactured. The 5VBR was favorably received by the boating public, and "a broad interstate market" developed for its sale. Ibid.

In May 1983, after the Bonito 5VBR had been available to the public for over six years, the Florida Legislature enacted Fla.Stat. § 559.94 (1987). The statute makes "[i]t ... unlawful for any person to use the direct molding process to duplicate for the purpose of sale any manufactured vessel hull or component part of a vessel made by another without the written permission of that other person." § 559.94(2). The statute also makes it unlawful for a person to "knowingly sell a vessel hull or component part of a vessel duplicated in violation of subsection (2)." § 559.94(3). Damages, injunctive relief, and attorney's fees are made available to "[a]ny person who suffers injury or damage as the result of a violation" of the statute. § 559.94(4). The statute was made applicable to vessel hulls or component parts duplicated through the use of direct molding after July 1, 1983. § 559.94(5).

On December 21, 1984, Bonito filed this action in the Circuit Court of Orange County, Florida. [The trial court dismissed the complaint as based on a statute preempted by federal patent law. The Florida Supreme Court affirmed].

II

Article I, § 8, cl. 8, of the Constitution gives Congress the power "[t]o promote the Progress of Science and useful Arts, by securing for limited Times to Authors and Inventors the exclusive Right to their respective Writings and Discoveries." The Patent Clause itself reflects a balance between the need to encourage innovation and the avoidance of monopolies which stifle competition without any concomitant advance in the "Progress of Science and useful Arts." As we have noted in the past, the Clause contains both a grant of power and certain limitations upon the exercise of that power. Congress may not create patent monopolies of unlimited duration, nor may it "authorize the issuance of patents whose effects are to remove existent knowledge from the public domain, or to restrict free access to materials already available." Graham v. John Deere Co. of Kansas City, 383 U.S. 1, 6, 86 S.Ct. 684, 688, 15 L.Ed.2d 545 (1966).

From their inception, the federal patent laws have embodied a careful balance between the need to promote innovation and the recognition that imitation and refinement through imitation are both necessary to invention itself and the very lifeblood of a competitive economy.

[In the next part, the Court reviews the principal requirements for obtaining a patent].

The applicant whose invention satisfies the requirements of novelty, nonobviousness, and utility, and who is willing to reveal to the public the substance of his discovery and "the best mode ... of carrying out his invention," 35 U.S.C. § 112, is granted "the right to exclude others from making, using, or selling the invention throughout the United States," for a period of 17 years. 35 U.S.C. § 154. The federal patent system thus embodies a carefully crafted bargain for encouraging the creation and disclosure of new, useful, and nonobvious advances in technology and design in return for the exclusive right to practice the invention for a period of years.

The attractiveness of such a bargain, and its effectiveness in inducing creative effort and disclosure of the results of that effort, depend almost entirely on a backdrop of free competition in the exploitation of unpatented designs and innovations. The novelty and nonobviousness requirements of patentability embody a congressional understanding, implicit in the Patent Clause itself, that free exploitation of ideas will be the rule, to which the protection of a federal patent is the exception. Moreover, the ultimate goal of the patent system is to bring new designs and technologies into the public domain through disclosure. State law protection for techniques and designs whose disclosure has already been induced by market rewards may conflict with the very purpose of the patent laws by decreasing the range of ideas available as the building blocks of further innovation. The offer of federal protection from competitive exploitation of intellectual property would be rendered meaningless in a world where substantially similar state law protections were readily available. To a limited extent, the federal patent laws must determine not only what is protected, but also what is free for all to use.

Thus our past decisions have made clear that state regulation of intellectual property must yield to the extent that it clashes with the balance struck by Congress in our patent laws. The tension between the desire to freely exploit the full potential of our inventive resources and the need to create an incentive to deploy those resources is constant. Where it is clear how the patent laws strike that balance in a particular circumstance, that is not a judgment the States may second-guess. We have long held that after the expiration of a federal patent, the subject matter of the patent passes to the free use of the public as a matter of federal law.

In our decisions in Sears, Roebuck & Co. v. Stiffel Co., 376 U.S. 225, 84 S.Ct. 784, 11 L.Ed.2d 661 (1964), and Compco Corp. v. Day–Brite Lighting,

Inc., 376 U.S. 234, 84 S.Ct. 779, 11 L.Ed.2d 669 (1964), we found that publicly known design and utilitarian ideas which were unprotected by patent occupied much the same position as the subject matter of an expired patent. The Sears case involved a pole lamp originally designed by the plaintiff Stiffel, who had secured both design and mechanical patents on the lamp. Sears purchased unauthorized copies of the lamps, and was able to sell them at a retail price practically equivalent to the wholesale price of the original manufacturer. Stiffel brought an action against Sears in Federal District Court, alleging infringement of the two federal patents and unfair competition under Illinois law. The District Court found that Stiffel's patents were invalid due to anticipation in the prior art, but nonetheless enjoined Sears from further sales of the duplicate lamps based on a finding of consumer confusion under the Illinois law of unfair competition. The Court of Appeals affirmed, coming to the conclusion that the Illinois law of unfair competition prohibited product simulation even in the absence of evidence that the defendant took some further action to induce confusion as to source.

This Court reversed, finding that the unlimited protection against copying which the Illinois law accorded an unpatentable item whose design had been fully disclosed through public sales conflicted with the federal policy embodied in the patent laws. The Court stated: "In the present case the 'pole lamp' sold by Stiffel has been held not to be entitled to the protection of either a mechanical or a design patent. An unpatentable article, like an article on which the patent has expired, is in the public domain and may be made and sold by whoever chooses to do so. What Sears did was to copy Stiffel's design and sell lamps almost identical to those sold by Stiffel. This it had every right to do under the federal patent laws." 376 U.S., at 231, 84 S.Ct., at 789. [A similar conclusion was reached in Compco].

The pre-emptive sweep of our decisions in Sears and Compco has been the subject of heated scholarly and judicial debate. See, e.g., Symposium, Product Simulation: A Right or a Wrong?, 64 Colum.L.Rev. 1178 (1964). Read at their highest level of generality, the two decisions could be taken to stand for the proposition that the States are completely disabled from offering any form of protection to articles or processes which fall within the broad scope of patentable subject matter. Since the potentially patentable includes "anything under the sun that is made by man," Diamond v. Chakrabarty, 447 U.S. 303, 309, 100 S.Ct. 2204, 2207, 65 L.Ed.2d 144 (1980)(citation omitted), the broadest reading of Sears would prohibit the States from regulating the deceptive simulation of trade dress or the tortious appropriation of private information.

That the extrapolation of such a broad pre-emptive principle from Sears is inappropriate is clear from the balance struck in Sears itself. The Sears Court made it plain that the States "may protect businesses in the use of their trademarks, labels, or distinctive dress in the packaging of goods so as to prevent others, by imitating such markings, from misleading purchasers as to the source of the goods." Sears, 376 U.S., at 232, 84 S.Ct., at 789 (footnote omitted). Trade dress is, of course, potentially the subject matter of design patents. Yet our decision in Sears clearly indicates that the States may place limited regulations on the circumstances in which such designs are used in order to prevent consumer confusion as to source. Thus, while Sears speaks in absolutist terms, its conclusion that the States may place some conditions on the use of trade dress indicates an implicit recognition that all state regulation of potentially patentable but unpatented subject matter is not ipso facto pre-empted by the federal patent laws.

What was implicit in our decision in Sears, we have made explicit in our subsequent decisions concerning the scope of federal pre-emption of state regulation of the subject matter of patent. Thus, in Kewanee Oil Co. v. Bicron Corp., 416 U.S. 470, 94 S.Ct. 1879, 40 L.Ed.2d 315 (1974), we held that state protection of trade secrets did not operate to frustrate the achievement of the congressional objectives served by the patent laws. Despite the fact that state law protection was available for ideas which clearly fell within the subject matter of patent, the Court concluded that the nature and degree of state protection did not conflict with the federal policies of encouragement of patentable invention and the prompt disclosure of such innovations.

Several factors were critical to this conclusion. First, because the public awareness of a trade secret is by definition limited, the Court noted that "the policy that matter once in the public domain must remain in the public domain is not incompatible with the existence of trade secret protection." Id., at 484, 94 S.Ct., at 1887. Second, the Kewanee Court emphasized that "[t]rade secret law provides far weaker protection in many respects than the patent law." Id., at 489–490, 94 S.Ct., at 1889–1890. This point was central to the Court's conclusion that trade secret protection did not conflict with either the encouragement or disclosure policies of the federal patent law. The public at large remained free to discover and exploit the trade secret through reverse engineering of products in the public domain or by independent creation. Thus, the possibility that trade secret protection would divert inventors from the creative effort necessary to satisfy the rigorous demands of patent protection was remote indeed. Finally, certain aspects of trade secret law operated to protect non-economic interests outside the sphere of congressional concern in the patent laws. As the Court noted, "[A] most fundamental human right, that of privacy, is threatened when industrial espionage is condoned or is made profitable." Id., at 487, 94 S.Ct., at 1889 (footnote omitted). There was no indication that Congress had considered this interest in the balance struck by the patent laws, or that state protection for it would interfere with the policies behind the patent system.

At the heart of Sears and Compco is the conclusion that the efficient operation of the federal patent system depends upon substantially free trade in publicly known, unpatented design and utilitarian conceptions. In Sears, the state law offered "the equivalent of a patent monopoly," 376 U.S., at 233, 84 S.Ct., at 789, in the functional aspects of a product which had been placed in public commerce absent the protection of a valid patent.

While, as noted above, our decisions since Sears have taken a decidedly less rigid view of the scope of federal pre-emption under the patent laws, e.g., Kewanee, 416 U.S., at 479–480, 94 S.Ct., at 1885–1886, we believe that the Sears Court correctly concluded that the States may not offer patent-like protection to intellectual creations which would otherwise remain unprotected as a matter of federal law. Both the novelty and the nonobviousness requirements of federal patent law are grounded in the notion that concepts within the public grasp, or those so obvious that they readily could be, are the tools of creation available to all. They provide the baseline of free competition upon which the patent system's incentive to creative effort depends. A state law that substantially interferes with the enjoyment of an unpatented utilitarian or design conception which has been freely disclosed by its author to the public at large impermissibly contravenes the ultimate goal of public disclosure and use which is the centerpiece of federal patent policy. Moreover, through the creation of patent-like rights, the States could essentially redirect inventive efforts away from the careful criteria of patentability developed by Congress over the last 200 years. We understand this to be the reasoning at the core of our decisions in Sears and Compco, and we reaffirm that reasoning today.

## III

We believe that the Florida statute at issue in this case so substantially impedes the public use of the otherwise unprotected design and utilitarian ideas embodied in unpatented boat hulls as to run afoul of the teaching of our decisions in Sears and Compco. It is readily apparent that the Florida statute does not operate to prohibit "unfair competition" in the usual sense that the term is understood. The law of unfair competition has its roots in the common-law tort of deceit: its general concern is with protecting consumers from confusion as to source. While that concern may result in the creation of "quasi-property rights" in communicative symbols, the focus is on the protection of consumers, not the protection of producers as an incentive to product innovation. Judge Hand captured the distinction well in Crescent Tool Co. v. Kilborn & Bishop Co., 247 F. 299, 301 (C.A.2 1917), where he wrote: "[T]he plaintiff has the right not to lose his customers through false representations that those are his wares which in fact are not, but he may not monopolize any design or pattern, however trifling. The defendant, on the other hand, may copy plaintiff's goods slavishly down to the minutest detail: but he may not represent himself as the plaintiff in their sale."

In contrast to the operation of unfair competition law, the Florida statute is aimed directly at preventing the exploitation of the design and utilitarian conceptions embodied in the product itself. The sparse legislative history surrounding its enactment indicates that it was intended to create an inducement for the improvement of boat hull designs. See Tr. of Meeting of Transportation Committee, Florida House of Representatives, May 3, 1983, reprinted at App. 22 ("[T]here is no inducement for [a] quality boat manufacturer to improve these designs and secondly, if he does, it is immediately copied. This would prevent that and allow him recourse in circuit court"). To accomplish this goal, the Florida statute endows the original boat hull manufacturer with rights against the world, similar in scope and operation to the rights accorded a federal patentee. Like the patentee, the beneficiary of the Florida statute may prevent a competitor from "making" the product in what is evidently the most efficient manner available and from "selling" the product when it is produced in that fashion. Compare 35 U.S.C. § 154. The Florida scheme offers this protection for an unlimited number of years to all boat hulls and their component parts, without regard to their ornamental or technological merit. Protection is available for subject matter for which patent protection has been denied or has expired, as well as for designs which have been freely revealed to the consuming public by their creators.

That the Florida statute does not remove all means of reproduction and sale does not eliminate the conflict with the federal scheme. In essence, the Florida law prohibits the entire public from engaging in a form of reverse engineering of a product in the public domain. This is clearly one of the rights vested in the federal patent holder, but has never been a part of state protection under the law of unfair competition or trade secrets. The duplication of boat hulls and their component parts may be an essential part of innovation in the field of hydrodynamic design. Variations as to size and combination of various elements may lead to significant advances in the field. Reverse engineering of chemical and mechanical articles in the public domain often leads to significant advances in technology. If Florida may prohibit this particular method of study and recomposition of an unpatented article, we fail to see the principle that would prohibit a State from banning the use of chromatography in the reconstitution of unpatented chemical compounds, or the use of robotics in the duplication of machinery in the public domain.

Moreover, as we noted in Kewanee, the competitive reality of reverse engineering may act as a spur to the inventor, creating an incentive to develop inventions that meet the rigorous requirements of patentability. The Florida statute substantially reduces this competitive incentive, thus eroding the general rule of free competition upon which the attractiveness of the federal patent bargain depends. The protections of state trade secret law are most effective at the developmental stage, before a product has been marketed and the threat of reverse engineering becomes real. During this period, patentability will often be an uncertain prospect, and to a certain extent, the protection offered by trade secret law may "dovetail" with the incentives created by the federal patent monopoly. In contrast, under the Florida scheme, the would-be inventor is aware from the outset of his efforts that rights against the public are available regardless of his ability to satisfy the rigorous standards of patentability. Indeed, it appears that even the most mundane and obvious changes in the design of a boat hull will trigger the protections of the statute. See Fla.Stat. § 559.94(2)(1987)(protecting "any manufactured vessel hull or component part"). Given the substantial protection offered by the Florida scheme, we cannot dismiss as hypothetical the possibility that it will become a significant competitor to the federal patent laws, offering investors similar protection without the quid pro quo of substantial creative effort required by the federal statute. The prospect of all 50 States establishing similar protections for preferred industries without the rigorous requirements of patentability prescribed by Congress could pose a substantial threat to the patent system's ability to accomplish its mission of promoting progress in the useful arts.

[Finally], one of the fundamental purposes behind the Patent and Copyright Clauses of the Constitution was to promote national uniformity in the realm of intellectual property. Absent such a federal rule, each State could afford patent-like protection to particularly favored home industries, effectively insulating them from competition from outside the State.

Congress has considered extending various forms of limited protection to industrial design either through the copyright laws or by relaxing the restrictions on the availability of design patents. Congress explicitly refused to take this step in the copyright laws, see 17 U.S.C. § 101; H.R.Rep. No. 94–1476, p. 55 (1976), U.S.Code Cong. & Admin.News 1976, pp. 5659, 5668, and despite sustained criticism for a number of years, it has declined to alter the patent protections presently available for industrial design. It is for Congress to determine if the present system of design and utility patents is ineffectual in promoting the useful arts in the context of industrial design. By offering patent-like protection for ideas deemed unprotected under the present federal scheme, the Florida statute conflicts with the "strong federal policy favoring free competition in ideas which do not merit patent protection." Lear, Inc., 395 U.S., at 656, 89 S.Ct., at 1903. We therefore agree with the majority of the Florida Supreme Court that the Florida statute is preempted by the Supremacy Clause, and the judgment of that court is hereby affirmed.

## NOTES

**1.** *Trade Secrets.* The law of trade secrets can be analyzed along lines identical to that of patent law to encompass questions on 1) protectable subject matter, 2) the requirements for protection, 3) the definition of infringing acts, and 4) remedies. There is a large body of state law on these issues and it reflects some minor differences among states (and between the Restatement and the UTSA).[4] The Economic Espionage Act is relatively new (it did not become fully enforceable until 2001), so there is a paucity of decisions construing its provisions. As you can see from *Lange*, it is not even clear whether (and when) federal law incorporates state definitions.[5]

---

[4] The key treatises on trade secrecy law are Roger H. Milgrim, Milgrim on Trade Secrets (1989) and Melvin F. Jager, Trade Secrets Law (1995).

[5] See generally, Rochelle Cooper Dreyfuss, Trade Secrets: How Well Should We Be Allowed to Hide Them? The Economic Espionage Act of 1996, 9 Fordham Intell. Prop. Media & Ent. L.J. 1 (1998). As of this writing, no federal court has considered whether it would look to the state in which it was sitting or the state in which the events constituting the crime took place.

a. *Subject matter.* "Trade secret" is broadly defined under both state and federal law, to cover virtually any kind of innovation, including such things as customer lists, which (even now) would not be regarded as an appropriate subject for patent protection. Prior to the UTSA and the Restatement of Unfair Competition, there was considerable controversy over the protection of ephemeral information, such as marketing plans that are revealed as soon as they are used. However, as you can see from *Pepsico*, even such information can now form the basis for a trade secrecy action.

Should negative information be considered protectable? In Novell Inc. v. Timpanogos Research Group, Inc.,[6] a group of breakaway employees was sued by its former employer, a major software producer. One of the claims was that the group would improperly benefit from Novell because it would not waste resources pursuing projects that it had already learned were dead ends. Knowing information on blind alleys and failed experiments clearly saves time and money, but is it the type of information that derives "independent economic value . . . from not being generally known?"

b. *Requirements.* Both federal and state laws require that the information be secret ("not generally known") and the subject of reasonable measures to maintain secrecy. Do you agree with the way that Judge Easterbrook handled the question whether the relevant community is the public or the industry? Would it make sense to allow an entire industry to keep information it knows away from new entrants?

What sorts of measures should be deemed reasonable? In *Dionne*, the employees understood that information related to Durafoam was to be kept confidential. Pinpointing sensitive information gives employees the knowledge they need to guard it. It also lets them know which aspects of their on-the-job training they can use in the future, and what will be considered off limits. At the same time, however, it identifies the company's crown jewels, alerting the unscrupulous employee to what is worth taking. In most cases, informing employees on a "need to know" basis is enough to meet the test of reasonableness. That way, the number of employees aware of the secret can be minimized. Furthermore, as *Lange* makes clear, confidentiality agreements are usually not necessary; information can be secured by deeds rather than promises.

c. *Infringement.* Under state law, a trade secrecy violation occurs when information 1) is acquired by improper means and 2) is used. As noted in the introduction, reverse engineering and independent invention are not regarded as improper means. In many states, memorizing on-the-job information is also usually not regarded as improper.[7]

What about the Economic Espionage Act? It nowhere indicates what is considered proper means and, in fact, defines what is prohibited quite

---

[6] 46 U.S.P.Q.2d 1197, 1217 (D. Utah 1998).

[7] See, e.g., Inflight Newspapers, Inc. v. Magazines In–Flight, LLC, 990 F.Supp. 119 (E.D.N.Y. 1997)(memorized information is, essentially, training).

broadly: it covers anyone who, without authorization, "copies, duplicates, sketches, draws, photographs, downloads, uploads, alters, destroys, photocopies, replicates, transmits, delivers, sends, mails, communicates, or conveys such information."[8] Given that copying is explicitly mentioned, is it possible that the Act means to criminalize reverse engineering? Under *Bonito Boats*, would it be constitutionally permissible to do so? Is the Act saved by its mens rea requirement, which requires the government to prove "intent to convert a trade secret ... knowing that the offense will injure any owner of that secret?"[9] Note that as with all criminal statutes, the prosecution must prove every element of its case beyond a reasonable doubt.

In state law, there are three aspects to the requirement of use. First, there is a question about *how* the information is being used. Omnitech International Inc. v. The Clorox Co.[10] is an example. In that case, Clorox became interested in the insecticide business. It entered into negotiations with Omnitech, which marketed a product called "Dr. X." The two companies signed an agreement whereby Clorox received permission to use secret information to conduct various laboratory and marketing tests on Dr. X. Based, in part, on information generated in those tests, Clorox decided to buy rights to a different product. Omnitech claimed that using its secret information to make this decision amounted to a trade secret violation. The court held it did not:

> [T]o sustain a trade secrets action under the "use" prong of [the Louisiana Trade Secrets Act], a plaintiff must necessarily demonstrate that the defendant received some sort of unfair trade advantage.... Omnitech has wholly failed to demonstrate that Clorox gained any competitive edge in the insecticide market as a result of any trade secret of Omnitech.

The second prong of the use requirement concerns *what* information is being used. Just as a court in a patent infringement action must determine whether the accused product comes within the scope of the patent claims, a trade secrets court must determine whether the defendant's activity is within the scope of the plaintiff's secret information. As in patent and copyright, complete duplication is not required; obvious variations are also considered actionable.[11]

Third is the issue of *who* is using the information. What if, in the *Dionne* case, Pierre had not started his own company, but instead revealed the Durafoam secrets to Uline, a company that manufactures shipping containers? If Uline used the information, could the Dionne family have sued Uline? Uline, after all, is not bound by the agreement Pierre signed. It is, instead, the recipient of a tip. Federal securities laws sometimes bar those who possess confidential information about firms from using that

---

[8] 18 U.S.C. § 1832(a)(2).

[9] Id.

[10] 11 F.3d 1316 (5th Cir.1994).

[11] See, e.g., Forest Laboratories, Inc. v. Formulations, Inc., 299 F.Supp. 202 (E.D. Wis. 1969), rev'd in part, 452 F.2d 621 (7th Cir.1971).

information to buy and sell stock. Those who receive such "inside information"—"tippees"—are sometimes also barred on the theory that their use of the information inflicts the same injury as the "tipper" creates.[12] Should the recipients of confidential know-how be treated the same as their tippers?[13]

Proof of use is apparently not required under the Economic Espionage Act: the crime is complete when the information is appropriated with the requisite intent. The statute also criminalizes attempts and conspiracies.[14] Note that the Economic Espionage Act also differs from state law (and most other intellectual property laws) in that it is explicitly extraterritorial. It applies whenever the offender is a U.S. citizen, a resident alien, or is organized under the laws of the United States or a state, and also when an activity in furtherance of the offense is committed in the United States.[15]

d.  *Remedies*. Significant difficulties have been encountered in formulating remedies for breach of trade secrecy laws.

(i) Injunctive relief. Because states often conceptualize these laws as property rights, injunctive relief has been the most prevalent remedy. But how long should the injunction endure? In Shellmar Products Co. v. Allen–Qualley Co.,[16] the court permanently enjoined the defendant from using the information it had improperly acquired. This remedy creates the maximum level of deterrence, but to many observers, it seems too long. After all, once others discover the secret, enjoining a single market participant does not help the innovator. It does, however, harm the public in that it removes an important competitor from the marketplace. Accordingly, many courts agree with a position similar to the one taken in *Dionne,* where the injunction was made to last only until the secret became public knowledge. The advantage here is that once the innovator is forced to compete, the defendant can join the market. The downside is that if the defendant is the major competitor, enjoining him may prevent the secret from ever being discovered. Thus, the public is once again the loser. Lamb–Weston, Inc. v. McCain Foods, Ltd.[17] represents a middle ground. In that case, the court attempted to calculate the time it would have taken to acquire the information by proper means—by reverse engineering the plaintiff's product. It then enjoined the defendant for that period of time. This rule, which is endorsed by § 44 of the Restatement of Unfair Competition Law, has the advantage of restoring the innovator to the position she would have been in had the violation not occurred, while—at the same time—freeing the defendant to compete.[18] The main problem with this remedy is that detailed knowledge of a field is required in order to estimate how long it

---

[12] 15 U.S.C.§ 78j; 17 C.F.R. § 240.10b–5

[13] See the Uniform Trade Secrets Act § 1(2)(ii)(B)(III)(yes); Restatement of Unfair Competition § 41 (yes, if the tippee knew of the relationship between the owner of the secret and the tipper).

[14] 18 U.S.C. § 1832(a)(5).

[15] 18 U.S.C. § 1837.

[16] 87 F.2d 104 (7th Cir.1936).

[17] 941 F.2d 970 (9th Cir.1991).

[18] See especially, Rest. 3d Unfair Competition Law § 44, Comment f.

would take to properly acquire the secret. Litigating the question can therefore be protracted and the result may be unsatisfactory to all parties.

Note that although the Economic Espionage Act is mainly aimed at punishing misappropriators, it also permits the government to come to the aid of the trade secret holder by obtaining "appropriate injunctive relief against any violation."[19]

(ii) Monetary damages. Would courts be better off awarding monetary damages rather than injunctive relief? If these damages are considered to be a form of compulsory royalty, the duration problem does not disappear, for the court must still decide how long defendant should be required to pay.[20] However, monetary relief could be thought of as compensating the plaintiff for bearing the full cost of development. If it were possible to calculate the plaintiff's costs (plus a reasonable profit) and require the defendant to share them, then the public would enjoy the benefits of competition, the innovator would enjoy a return on the investment in invention, and all market participants would compete on a level playing field.[21]

(iii) Criminal penalties. In general, intellectual property violations are punished criminally in only the most egregious circumstances, such as trafficking in counterfeit trademarked goods and wholesale piracy of copyrighted works;[22] there are no criminal penalties for patent infringement. Thus, the Economic Espionage Act is somewhat unique. In that legislation, punishment depends on whether the intended beneficiary of the misappropriation is a foreign government or a private party. It includes fines up to $500,000, imprisonment up to 15 years (or both), as well as forfeiture of property used to commit the crime or derived as a result of the crime. The economic proceeds of a conviction go to the government, not to the target of the espionage.[23] The threat of criminal prosecution is generally considered more chilling of behavior than civil liability. Is it appropriate to use it to protect trade secrets?

**2.** *Contractual relationships.* The cases in this Assignment deal with contracts concerning rights over secret information that is not protected by other intellectual property regimes. Is the enforcement of innovation-related agreements limited to that situation? One question is whether the holder of an intellectual property right can ratchet up the terms of protection via contract. For example, reconsider *Husky v. R & D Tool*, the case in Assignment 21 on repair. That case held that in some circumstances, restoring features of a patented invention is not infringement. Should a licensor be allowed to limit the right to repair through contractual agreement? In Mallinckrodt, Inc. v. Medipart, Inc.,[24] the Federal Circuit

---

[19] 18 U.S.C. § 1836.

[20] See Rest. 3d Unfair Competition Law § 45, Comment h.

[21] Cf. J.H. Reichman, Of Green Tulips and Legal Kudzu: Repackaging Rights in Subpatentable Innovation, 53 Vand. L. Rev. 1744 (2000).

[22] See 18 U.S.C. §§ 2320 (trademark) & 2318–19A (copyright).

[23] 18 U.S.C. §§ 1831, 1832, and 1834.

[24] 976 F.2d 700 (Fed.Cir.1992).

indicated that there are circumstances where such limitations are permissible. However, that case involved medical syringes and concerns about safety. Could such a restriction be imposed in other circumstances? Does it make a difference whether the contract provision end-runs a specific public-regarding provision of patent or copyright law or simply adds a prohibition that federal law does not address?[25] Would a perpetual license be enforceable?[26] Are there antitrust concerns that are relevant here? Consider, for example, the Principal Problem, in which rights (possibly copyrights, patents, or trade secrecy rights) over a servicing program are used to prevent independent organizations from competing in the computer servicing market.[27]

Another question is whether trade secrecy law itself can be ratcheted up. For example, we have just seen that trade secrecy rights tend to expire through reverse engineering. What if a product containing nonpublic information is licensed rather than sold, and the licensing agreement prohibits the licensee from reverse engineering? Will the license violate *Bonito Boats*? That case involved a state law that ran against the world. A contract runs only to individuals: is that enough of a difference? Does it matter whether the licensor offers purchasers a choice between a (cheap) contract that bars copying and (an expensive) one that permits it?[28] If licenses can be used to create exclusivity beyond what is permissible under patent law, will anyone pay the costs and endure the disclosure required to obtain a patent?

A final question is whether a license of *public* information is enforceable. Reconsider the question in *Lange* on when information should be considered sufficiently secret to protect. It is not uncommon in the technology sector to license "black art"—that is, information whose status as secret or public is not known. The licensee needs the information, is eager to learn it from the licensor at the price that the licensor is charging, and neither side wants to incur the cost of determining whether the information is "not generally known." Can the licensee invoke *Bonito Boats* to stop paying royalties if it later determines that the information was, in fact, public? Is such an arrangement better characterized as a contract to pay tuition for instruction?[29]

---

[25] Cf. Monsanto Co. v. McFarling, 302 F.3d 1291 (Fed. Cir. 2002)(enforcing a contractual prohibition against using the patented soybeans to produce additional seeds).

[26] Cf. Brulotte v. Thys Co., 379 U.S. 29 (1964).

[27] Cf. In re Independent Service Organizations Antitrust Litigation, 203 F.3d 1322 (Fed. Cir. 2000)(finding there is no antitrust violation when a patentee refuses to sell patented parts to an independent service organization); Image Technical Services, Inc. v. Eastman Kodak Co., 125 F.3d 1195 (9th Cir. 1997)(holding that a refusal to deal with a servicing organization can violate the antitrust laws).

[28] Cf. Lexmark Intern., Inc. v. Static Control Components, Inc., 253 F.Supp.2d 943 (E.D. Ky. 2003)(allowing the Digitial Millennium Copyright Act to be used to require licensees to promise not to reuse nonpatented toner cartridges; alternative arrangements also available).

[29] Similar restrictions are being enforced in the copyright setting, see ProCD, Inc. v. Zeidenberg, 86 F.3d 1447 (7th Cir. 1996)(enforcing a contractual restriction on copying an uncopyrightable fact work).

As explained in Note 10 of Assignment 13, there was a move at one time to promulgate a uniform law, called the Uniform Computer Information Transactions Act (UCITA or Art 2B of the UCC), to facilitate the licensing of intellectual property. Among the reasons the effort was ultimately abandoned was a concern that UCITA would permit parties to license information that was not protected by federal intellectual property laws and that also failed to meet the definition of a trade secret under state law.[30] As noted earlier, UCITA has become the law of Maryland and Virginia; it remains to be seen whether trade secrecy law will be expanded in those jurisdictions and whether an expansive definition of trade secrets under UCITA will survive a preemption challenge.

**3.** *The law of ideas.* Reconsider the facts of the *Dionne* case: what if, instead of setting up his own company to exploit his insight concerning compressed polystyrene, Robert had approached the company producing polystyrene with the idea of compressing it? If the company utilized his idea, could it be forced to compensate him for it? What would be the cause of action? Trade secrecy law would be unavailing. First, as *Clorox* indicates, competition may be a required element, and Robert is not in a position to compete. Moreover, once Robert revealed the idea to the company, it would no longer be a secret, and so there would be no "trade secret" to sell. Of course, he could have asked the company to agree to pay him before he revealed the secret—in which case he could have sued on the contract. But why would the company agree to pay for an idea sight unseen? After all, the idea could turn out to be terrible, or one it was in the process of considering; it could be an idea that was already in the public domain, or claimed by another. (Remember that in the actual case, there were patents on 17 different compressed foam products). This situation, where the innovator is damned if he reveals his insight and equally damned if he doesn't, is called "Arrow's disclosure paradox," after the economist Kenneth Arrow.[31]

Should utilizing an undeveloped idea without authorization be actionable? Great ideas sometimes do occur to people who are not positioned to exploit them. Creating a financial incentive to transmit these ideas to those who can use them is, therefore, in the public interest. However, large companies, particularly movie and television companies, receive so very many ideas, and so very many unoriginal ideas, they would be paralyzed if they were vulnerable to suit by every submitter.

Jurisdictions balance these problems by creating rights of action in favor of idea submitters in only extremely limited circumstances, usually

[30] See, e.g, Mark A. Lemley, Beyond Preemption: The Law and Policy of Intellectual Property Licensing, 87 Cal. L. Rev. 111 (1999); Rochelle Cooper Dreyfuss, Do You Want To Know a Trade Secret? How Article 2B Will Make Licensing Trade Secrets Easier (But Innovation More Difficult), 87 Calif. L. Rev. 193 (1999); David A. Rice, License With Contract and Precedent: Publisher-Licensor Protection Consequences and the Rationale Offered for the Nontransferrability of Licenses Under Article 2B, 13 Berkeley Tech. L.J. 1239 (1998).

[31] See, e.g., Ronald J. Mann, Information Technology and Non-Legal Sanctions in Financing Transactions, 54 Vand. L. Rev. 1627 (2001).

only for the idea that is so novel, concrete, and valuable that it seems unfair to ignore the submitter. In most cases, the law is based on implied contract—either implied-in-fact, from the circumstances of submission, or implied-in-law (quantum meruit), based on the unjust enrichment of the party exploiting the idea. Novelty and concreteness are the touchstones for this cause of action, but the custom of the industry, the track record of the submitter, and the circumstances surrounding the negotiations that led to the submission are all considered as well. For example, in Buchwald v. Paramount Pictures Corp.,[32] the writer Art Buchwald won compensation when Paramount filmed the movie "Coming to America" from a plot idea that he submitted. The idea was spelled out in Buchwald's treatment ("concrete"), it was a new ("novel") idea, and the submitter was someone whom Paramount should have known is usually paid for his writings. Moreover, once Paramount made the movie, the value of the idea plummeted, making it virtually useless to Buchwald.

**4.** *Sui generis legislation. Bonito Boats* considered the validity of Florida's direct molding statute. This legislation recognizes the high cost of creating novel boat hulls and need for a period of time in which the innovator can recoup costs. It also recognizes two gaps. First, the gap between trade secrecy protection and noncompete agreements: the statute protects the innovators of a product that can be easily reverse engineered against parties with whom they cannot contract. Second, it fills a gap between copyright and patent law: boat hulls are not inventive enough to protect by patents but they are too functional to protect via copyright. Interestingly, in an omitted portion of *Bonito Boats,* the Court considered (and rejected) the reasoning in a Federal Circuit decision that upheld a similar direct molding statute from California.[33] That both statutes emanated from coastal states should not be surprising: the importance of the ship-building industry to both states led their legislators to appreciate the deficiencies in other intellectual property laws.

Of course, not all industries that demand special protection are of only local importance. For example, in 1984, the semiconductor chip industry persuaded Congress that it needed special protection on a national scale. Semiconductor chips (sometimes called "mask works") are purely functional products, and so their design does not qualify for copyright protection. And because most semiconductor innovations are too mundane to meet the nonobviousness test of § 103 of the Patent Act, patent protection is also unavailable. The Semiconductor Chip Act creates a 10–year exclusive reproduction, importation, and distribution right for original works that are not staples of the semiconductor industry.[34] The statute contains several features that tailor it to the needs of this industry. One interesting example is § 906. Out of concern for the need to use one chip design as a building block for others, this provision exempts from infringement uses

[32] 13 U.S.P.Q.2d (BNA) 1497 (Cal. Super. 1990).

[33] Interpart Corp. v. Italia, 777 F.2d 678 (Fed.Cir.1985).

[34] 17 U.S.C. §§ 901–914.

that are solely for the purpose of analysis. If the knowledge so obtained is used to design a chip that is original enough to merit its own protection, that chip will not be considered to infringe the design of the chip that was used for inspiration. Similarly, after *Bonito Boats*, Congress enacted federal legislation to protect the boating industry. Paradoxically, this legislation, which (for no discernable reason) is found in the Digital Millennium Copyright Act, see Assignment 8, is actually broader than the law at issue in *Bonito Boats*. The Florida law only prevented one form of copying—duplicating a boat hull by a method similar to the one that dentists use to make an impression of teeth. In contrast, the federal statute protects the design of hulls no matter how copied. It even protects plug molds.[35]

There are two attractive features to sui generis systems. They can adapt bits and pieces of copyright and patent law to conform to the specific needs of particular industries. They can also take better account of public access interests. For example, the emergence of the computer industry highlighted the problem of interoperability. Commentators were worried that the owner of rights in one aspect of a computer system would be able to leverage that position into dominance in other areas. For example the holder of rights in an operating system could refuse to reveal (or, in cases where the programs are patented, license) the Application Program Interfaces (APIs) necessary to write compatible software. A sui generis system of protection for programs could deal with the interoperability problem expressly.[36] Sui generis systems can, however, be difficult to design and put into place at the time when incentives are needed to encourage development in new fields. If a sui generis regime falls outside the main international intellectual property conventions, it will also raise difficult problems of ensuring and coordinating global protection. Finally there is a question of their constitutionality.

**5.** *Preemption: the bottom line.* What is the rule on federal preemption of state law? The two 1964 cases cited in *Bonito Boats,* Sears, Roebuck & Co. v. Stiffel Co.,[37] and Compco Corp. v. Day–Brite Lighting, Inc.,[38] often referred to jointly as *"Sears/Compco,"* had confined states to protecting consumers from confusion. Many observers regard this as too stingy to innovators. Innovators do suffer at the hands of competitors who dress their products up in a way that leads consumers to mistakenly purchase from the wrong vendor (indeed, this is the main thrust of trademark law). However, innovators are also harmed by free riders—those who copy the innovation at low cost and then compete the price down to the point where the innovator cannot recoup the costs of development. When, in 1974, the *Kewanee* Court recognized the free rider problem and approved trade secrecy law, the *Sears/Compco* approach was generally regarded as thor-

---

[35] 17 U.S.C. §§ 1301–1332.

[36] See Pamela Samuelson, Randall Davis, Mitchell Kapor, and J.H. Reichman, A Manifesto Concerning the Legal Protection of Computer Programs, 94 Colum. L. Rev. 2308 (1994). See also Maureen A. O'Rourke, To-ward a Doctrine of Fair Use in Patent Law, 100 Colum. L. Rev. 1177 (2000).

[37] 376 U.S. 225, 231 (1964).

[38] 376 U.S. 234 (1964).

oughly overruled. Thus, *Bonito Boats'* favorable citation of these cases came as something of a surprise.

Does *Bonito Boats* distinguish *Kewanee* persuasively? *Bonito Boats* relies heavily on the notion that trade secrets do not remove knowledge from the public domain whereas the direct molding statute does. *Bonito Boats* does not, however, explain why innovators who cannot hide their innovations from the public are in any less need of protection from free riders than those who can. Some have explained *Bonito Boats* as protecting the public's right to reverse engineer. However, Florida had not prevented the public from reverse engineering. Even under the direct molding statute, anyone could take measurements of desirable boat hulls and build new molds to those measurements. All the statute did was prevent one particular form of copying—a kind that is very inexpensive. The Court derides this distinction, but isn't it precisely the *free* ride that Florida was trying to prevent? Didn't the direct molding statute strike exactly the right balance, giving the public access to the innovative ideas in a new hull without giving it the ability to undercut the innovator?

The Court also gave a kind of Commerce Clause spin to the Copyright Clause, interpreting the provision as promoting national uniformity, that is, as preventing states from insulating their local industries from out-of-state competition. Is this a valid interpretation of the Copyright Clause? Although the legislative history of the Commerce Clause evidences a concern with promoting interstate business, the history of the Copyright Clause does not. Rather, it appears that the Framers were mainly concerned that state-by-state intellectual property protection would be ineffectual.[39] Does *Bonito Boats,* then, overrule the copyright preemption cases that approve state legislative activity in areas of local concern?[40]

Was the Court's real problem that the direct molding statute was enacted after the hull at issue was created, making it clear that no special incentives were needed to motivate its creation? Was it the perpetual nature of the protection that bothered the Court? The federal legislation is explicitly nonretroactive.[41]

Finally, is *Bonito Boats* a constitutional or a statutory case? If it is the Constitution that bars protection of subpatentable inventions, is the Semiconductor Chip Act unconstitutional? Is the Orphan Drug Act discussed in Assignment 22 unconstitutional? Is Congress constitutionally disabled from enacting special legislation for the computer or biotechnology industry?[42] Does the *Feist* case of Assignment 7 add to your analysis?

[39] See Bruce W. Bugbee, Genesis of American Patent and Copyright Law 130 (Public Affairs Press, 1967).

[40] See, e.g., Goldstein v. California, 412 U.S. 546 (1973), discussed in Assignment 13.

[41] 17 U.S.C. § 1332.

[42] See generally, Rochelle Cooper Dreyfuss, A Wiseguy's Approach to Information Products: Muscling Copyright and Patent Into a Unitary Theory of Intellectual Property, 1992 S.Ct. Rev. 195; John J. Flynn, The Orphan Drug Act: An Unconstitutional Exercise of the Patent Power, 1992 Utah L. Rev. 389; John Shepard Wiley, Bonito Boats: Uninformed but Mandatory Innovation Policy, 1989 S.Ct. Rev. 283; Paul Goldstein, Kewan-

**6.** *Federal statutory preemption. Sears/Compco, Kewanee,* and *Bonito Boats* all dealt with the question whether state protection of inventions is inconsistent with federal protection. But there is another sort of preemption argument. It is that the federal regimes are preemptive of each other—that the same innovation cannot be protected by both patent and copyright law, or by both patent and trademark law.

Application of Yardley[43] considered the interaction of copyright and patent law. In that case, the Patent Office refused to grant a design patent on the Spiro Agnew wristwatch on the ground that the picture had been registered in the Copyright Office.[44] The PTO reasoned that the two statutes present creators with a choice. Once one regime is chosen, the creator is estopped from also utilizing the other regime.[45] The CCPA reversed. It saw in neither the Supreme Court's acknowledgment that the "election of protection doctrine" existed, nor in the existence of two separate protective regimes any "intent of Congress to hold that an author-inventor *must* elect between the two available modes of securing exclusive rights."[46] The Court went on to say: "If anything, the concurrent availability of both modes of securing exclusive rights aids in achieving the stated purpose of the constitutional provision."[47]

The germinal case on trademark/patent preemption is Singer Manufacturing Co. v. June Manufacturing Co.[48] Singer controlled the patents on many aspects of the sewing machine. In the years immediately preceding the expiration of its most important patents, it tried to establish the name "Singer" and the shape of its machines as trademarks. However, when the patents expired, competitors entering the field called their machines "Singer" and used similar shapes. Singer sued to enforce its marks and lost, the Supreme Court holding:

> This coincidence between the expiration of the patents and the appearance of the word 'Singer' alone tends to create a strong implication that the company [acted] in order thereby to retain in the possession of the company the real fruits of the monopoly when the monopoly had passed away.[49]

In other words, the Singer Court thought that trademark protection for a formerly patented article would impermissibly extend the term of protec-

---

ee Oil Co. v. Bicron Corp.: Notes on a Closing Circle, 1974 S.Ct.Rev. 92.

[43] 493 F.2d 1389 (C.C.P.A.1974).

[44] Spiro Agnew was a Vice President of the United States who distinguished himself in part by pleading nolo contendere to a criminal charge and resigning from office. The watchface was similar to the more famous Mickey Mouse watch, but showed Mr. Agnew dressed in shorts with the hands of the watch emanating from his belly button.

[45] This estoppel argument is, in fact, also made in connection with state preemption.

An example is Macbeth–Evans Glass Co. v. General Electric Co., 246 Fed. 695 (6th Cir. 1917), which was discussed in Assignment 19. In that case, the court held that Macbeth's decision to practice his invention as a trade secret estopped him from later seeking a patent.

[46] *Yardley,* 493 F.2d at 1394, referring in part, to Mazer v. Stein, 347 U.S. 201 (1954).

[47] *Yardley* at 1396.

[48] 163 U.S. 169 (1896).

[49] Id. at 181.

tion beyond the statutory term of the patent, thereby preventing the public from truly enjoying free access to the invention upon patent expiration.[50]

Is *Singer* still good law? The most recent case on patent/trademark preemption is *TrafFix Devices, Inc. v. Marketing Displays, Inc.*, reproduced in Assignment 2. It stands for the proposition that a patent is evidence that a particular configuration is functional and therefore not protectable as trade dress. While most of the opinion implies that this evidence can be rebutted (in other words, that *Singer* is no longer good law), there are parts *TrafFix* that can also be read consistent with *Singer*, as deeming someone who has enjoyed a patent to have elected patent protection over trade dress protection.

**7.** *Health, safety, and environmental concerns.* Because trade secrets are difficult to monitor, their use can cause environmental damage or risk the health and safety of workers, consumers, and neighbors. These concerns have prompted the enactment of so-called "right to know" laws which compromise trade secrets in order to keep the environment and the workplace safe. For instance, the Occupational Safety and Health Act[51] requires manufacturers to reveal information about secret products in certain circumstances. Several states have similar regulations.[52]

Should these regulations be regarded as unconstitutional takings of property without just compensation? That issue was considered in Ruckelshaus v. Monsanto Co.,[53] which concerned the premarket clearance procedures of the Federal Insecticide, Fungicide, and Rodenticide Act (FIFRA).[54] These procedures require manufacturers to submit to the Environmental Protection Agency data supporting their claims of efficacy and environmental safety. The legislation authorizes the EPA to use the data submitted by one manufacturer in reviewing the applications of other manufacturers who seek to market the same product.[55] Noting that this data can cost millions of dollars to produce, Monsanto claimed that the data was protected by trade secrecy law, and that the legislative authorization to reveal it amounted to a taking. In a profoundly convoluted opinion, the Court held that Monsanto's reasonable expectations of confidentiality were completely determined by the particular statutory scheme in operation when it submitted the data. FIFRA had been changed several times; during periods when the statute failed to explicitly provide that data were submitted in confidence, use of data to review competitors' registrations did not require compensation. However, during periods when FIFRA did provide for confi-

[50] See also Kellogg Co. v. National Biscuit Co., 305 U.S. 111 (1938)(trademark on the words "shredded wheat" was invalid following the expiration of the design patent on pillow-shaped cereal).

[51] 29 U.S.C. §§ 651–678

[52] See, e.g., James T. O'Reilly, Driving a Soft Bargain: Unions, Toxic Materials, and Right to Know Legislation, 9 Harv. L. Rev. 307 (1985). See also Mary L. Lyndon, Secrecy and Innovation in Tort Law and Regulation, 23 N.M. L. Rev. 1, 22–34 (1993); Mary L. Lyndon, Information Economics and Chemical Toxicity: Designing Laws to Produce and Use Data, 87 Mich. L. Rev. 1795, 1855–59 (1989).

[53] 467 U.S. 986 (1984).

[54] 7 U.S.C. §§ 136–136y.

[55] See § 136a(c)(1)(F).

dentiality for trade secrets, the EPA could not reutilize these trade secrets unless the submitter received reasonable compensation.

As a policy matter, what should FIFRA provide? In terms of the competitive picture, are research data any different from other industrial information that is expensive to create and cheap to copy?

**8.** *Employee mobility.* Virtually all states are concerned with the effects of trade secrecy law and the enforcement of covenants not to compete on employment. Employment compensation is, after all, not only monetary: many employees (including graduating law students!) choose their jobs with an eye toward the quality of the training they will receive. If they cannot use the skills acquired in other employment settings, this portion of their compensation has no value. Society also loses because employees cannot put their skills to their most productive use.

Some economists argue that the picture is not so bleak. As in *Pepsico* and *Gillette,* courts enforce agreements of confidentiality and covenants not to compete only when they are supported by adequate consideration. Furthermore, the terms of such agreements are usually scrutinized to determine that the conditions imposed are reasonable in light of the employer's needs; before an agreement is enforced, its terms may be modified to bring them in line with what the court views as appropriate.[56] Because the employer cannot demand too much, and must pay extra for what is demanded, the value of the wage "package" will compensate for employment opportunities that are lost. In pure trade secrecy cases, the "reasonable measures" requirement usually leads to similar results: to adequately protect their secret information, employers must usually tell the employees what must be guarded. As a result, the employees learn which facets of their training will not be portable to other jobs. They can then bargain for hire wages if necessary. Finally, if there is a better—and better paid—use for the employee's talent, the employee can breach the covenant, take the other job, and pay the employer damages.

Despite the theoretical appeal of this analysis, significant concerns nonetheless remain. The employer and employee may not have equal bargaining power (especially in cases like *Gillette,* where the covenant is signed after the employee commits to the job). The employee may not fully understand the implications of the agreement. A court may be persuaded to issue an injunction, and not rely simply on monetary damages. Further, as firms begin to compete on a global basis and companies with divergent innovation programs merge, even very broad employment restraints start to look reasonable. And if *Pepsico's* notion of inevitable disclosure is coupled with the *Novell* theory of protecting negative information, the ability of technology employees to move from one firm in their specialty area to another becomes even more difficult. After all, it is inevitable that a researcher will avoid a project he knows will lead down a blind alley.

[56] See, e.g., McLeod v. Meyer, 237 Ark. 173, 372 S.W.2d 220 (1963); Solari Indus., Inc. v. Malady, 55 N.J. 571, 264 A.2d 53 (1970).

The Economic Espionage Act exacerbates the problem because liability runs not only to the individuals who misappropriate trade secrets, but also to the organizations on whose behalf the information was taken. If the Act had been enforceable at the time of the *Pepsico* case, how would you have advised Quaker on the question whether it should hire Redmond? Quaker had Redmond sign an agreement not to disclose the trade secrets of his earlier job: should that furnish a defense to criminal prosecution? The legislative history expresses concern about chilling employee mobility, but the Act does not create any sort of safe harbor to protect employers or employees. As a result, lawyers are advising clients to adopt rigorous screening requirements and procedures to insulate new employees from projects that would benefit from their prior experience.[57]

Provocatively, California does not enforce noncompete agreements.[58] Is the astounding growth of the computer industry in Silicon Valley a sign that trade secrecy law is counterproductive?[59] Perhaps knowledge grows faster if information within an industry flows readily. For example, in the computer industry, sharing may have produced better hardware, software, and interfaces and thus attracted new customers. Although firms may have lost market share when their innovations were utilized by others, the explosion in demand may have more than compensated for the loss in share. California's position may have other benefits. The freedom to change jobs may attract higher quality employees, and spur students to enter fields that are based in the state. Employers' inability to bind employees through noncompete agreements may force them to find other ways to foster loyalty, such as providing congenial work environments, rapid promotion, or payment in stock or stock options.

**9.** *Employer rights.* Note that in the cases in the Assignment that involve employment situations, the assumption was that any innovation made by the employee belonged to the employer. This is because in each of these cases, the employee's duty was expressly to develop new products. In most such employment relationships, the employer's right to the employee's innovations is secured by contract. In the remainder, the employment contract is read to imply this right. Sometimes, however, an employee who was *not* hired specifically for research and development makes an invention at the place of employment and during working hours: to whom does this invention belong? In most states, the parties split the difference: the employee owns the rights to the invention, but the employer enjoys a "shop right," which is a nonexclusive license to practice the invention in his

[57] See, e.g., James H.A. Pooley, Mark A. Lemley, Peter J. Toren, Understanding the Economic Espionage Act of 1996, 5 Tex. Intell. Prop. L.J. 177, 217–18 (1997); Gerald J. Mossinghoff, J. Derek Mason, David A. Oblon, The Economic Espionage Act: A New Federal Regime of Trade Secret Protection, 79 J. Pat. & Trademark Off. Soc'y 191, 192 (1997).

[58] See, e.g., Cal. Bus. & Prof. Code § 16600 (1993).

[59] Ronald J. Gilson, The Legal Infrastructure of High Technology Industrial Districts: Silicon Valley, Route 128, and Covenants Not to Compete, 74 N.Y.U. L. Rev. 575 (1999). See also Robert G. Bone, A New Look at Trade Secret Law: Doctrine in Search of Justification, 86 Cal. L. Rev. 241(1998).

business. This arrangement is thought to compensate the employer for the use of his time and facilities, while giving the employee the benefits of her ingenuity.[60]

[60] See, e.g., United States v. Dubilier Condenser Corp., 289 U.S. 178 (1933).

\*

# INDEX

References are to pages.

†

1–56662–812–1